Scalable Computing and Communications

WILEY SERIES ON PARALLEL AND DISTRIBUTED COMPUTING

Series Editor: **ALBERT Y. ZOMAYA**

A complete list of the titles in this series appears at the end of this volume.

Scalable Computing and Communications

Theory and Practice

Edited by

Samee U. Khan
North Dakota State University

Albert Y. Zomaya
University of Sydney, Australia

Lizhe Wang
Chinese Academy of the Sciences

A John Wiley & Sons, Inc., Publication

Library of Congress Cataloging-in-Publication Data is available.

ISBN 9781118162651

Printed in the United States of America.

10 9 8 7 6 5 4 3 2 1

To Our Parents

Contents

11. A Framework for Semiautomatic Explicit Parallelization   **209**

Ritu Arora, Purushotham Bangalore, and Marjan Mernik

12. Fault Tolerance and Transmission Reliability in Wireless Networks   **227**

Wolfgang W. Bein and Doina Bein

13. Optimizing and Tuning Scientific Codes   **255**

Qing Yi

Preface

Scalable computing and communications includes environments such as autonomic, cloud, cluster, distributed, energy-aware, parallel, peer-to-peer, green, grid, and utility computing environments. The aforementioned paradigms are necessary to promote collaboration between entities and resources, which are necessary and beneficial to complex scientific, industrial, and business applications, which include weather forecasting, computational biology, telemedicine, drug synthesis, vehicular technology, design and fabrication, finance, and simulations. Therefore, scalable computing is at the heart of all complex applications.

Scalable computing and communications involves the use of computing facilities, which can readily adapt to the demands of more powerful computing and communication capabilities. Scalability is a desirable property for many scientific, industrial, and business applications. Moreover, scalability is also an important feature for hardware, as a computing facility can be scaled as and when there is a need to add computing and communication modules.

There have been great developments and advances in the aforementioned research fields. It is thus a good time to gather current progress in research in a book collection in order to document research achievements and to identify future directions.

To that end, this book on scalable computing and communications presents, discusses, and shares ideas, results, and experiences regarding recent important advances and future challenges. The compiled work ranges from theory to practice, software to hardware, and concepts to prototypes.

We sincerely hope that you will enjoy this compilation, which is hoped to cater to a wide audience.

SAMEE U. KHAN

North Dakota State University, Fargo, ND

ALBERT Y. ZOMAYA

University of Sydney, Sydney, NSW, Australia

LIZHE WANG

Chinese Academy of Sciences, Beijing, China

Contributors

MOHAMMED I. ALGHAMDI, Al-Baha University, Al-Baha City, Kingdom of Saudi Arabia

RITU ARORA, Texas Advanced Computing Center, University of Texas at Austin, Austin, TX

PAVAN BALAJI, Mathematics and Computer Science Division, Argonne National Laboratory, Argonne, IL; Virginia Tech

PURUSHOTHAM BANGALORE, Department of Computer and Information Sciences, University of Alabama at Birmingham, Birmingham, AL

IOANA BANICESCU, Department of Computer Science and Engineering, Mississippi State University, Mississippi State, MS

DOINA BEIN, Applied Research Laboratory, Information Science and Technology Division, Pennsylvania State University, University Park, PA

WOLFGANG W. BEIN, Center for Information Technology and Algorithms, School of Computer Science, University of Nevada, Las Vegas, NV

LADJEL BELLATRECHE, LIAS/ENSMA—Poitiers University, France

SOUMIA BENKRID, LIAS/ENSMA—Poitiers University, France

KASHIF BILAL, Department of Electrical and Computer Engineering, North Dakota State University, Fargo, ND

GEORGE BOSILCA, Innovative Computing Laboratory, The University of Tennessee, Knoxville, TN

KAMEL BOUKHALFA, USTHB University, Algeria

AURELIEN BOUTEILLER, Innovative Computing Laboratory, The University of Tennessee, Knoxville, TN

PASCAL BOUVRY, University of Luxembourg, Luxembourg, Luxembourg

DARIUS BUNTINAS, Mathematics and Computer Science Division, Argonne National Laboratory, Argonne, IL

KIRK W. CAMERON, Virginia Tech, Blacksburg, VA

JIANNONG CAO, The Hong Kong Polytechnic University, Hong Kong

Franck Cappello,   INRIA Saclay-Ile de France, Orsay, France

Harold Castro,   Universidad de los Andes Bogota D.C., Colombia

Harrison Chandler,   Clemson University, Clemson, SC

Hao Che,   The University of Texas at Arlington, Arlington, TX

Jinjun Chen,   School of Systems, Management and Leadership, University of Technology, Sydney, Australia

Kun-Ta Chuang,   National Cheng Kung University, Tainan, Taiwan

Florina M. Ciorba,   Center for Information Services and High Performance Computing, Technische Universit at Dresden, Dresden, Germany

Camille Coti,   LIPN, CNRS-UMR7030, Université Paris 13, Villetaneuse, France

Anthony Danalis,   Innovative Computing Laboratory, The University of Tennessee, Knoxville, TN

Xi Deng,   Stony Brook University, Stony Brook, NY

Cesar O. Diaz,   University of Luxembourg, Luxembourg, Luxembourg

James Dinan,   Mathematics and Computer Science Division, Argonne National Laboratory, Argonne, IL

Matthew Doerksen,   Department of Computer Science, University of Manitoba, Winnipeg, Manitoba, Canada

Jack J. Dongara,   Innovative Computing Laboratory, The University of Tennessee, Knoxville, TN

Wu-Chun Feng,   Department of Computer Science, Virginia Tech, Blacksburg, VA

Nasir Ghani,   University of New Mexico, Albuquerque, NM

Ann Gordon-Ross,   Department of Electrical and Computer Engineering, University of Florida, Gainesville, FL

Jing (Selena) He,   Department of Computer Science, Georgia State University, Atlanta, GA

Thomas Herault,   Innovative Computing Laboratory, The University of Tennessee, Knoxville, TN

Sun-Yuan Hsieh,   National Cheng Kung University, Tainan, Taiwan

Blake Hurd,   Temple University, Philadelphia, PA

Ali R. Hurson,   Missouri University of Science and Technology, Rolla, MO

Shouling Ji,   Department of Computer Science, Georgia State University, Atlanta, GA

Xin Jin,   The University of Hong Kong, Pokfulam, Hong Kong

Miao Ju,   The University of Texas at Arlington, Arlington, TX

Hun Jung,   The University of Texas at Arlington, Arlington, TX

Khaled M. Khan,   Department of Computer Science and Engineering, Qatar University, Qatar

Samee Ullah Khan,   Department of Electrical and Computer Engineering, North Dakota State University, Fargo, ND

Dries Kimpe,   Mathematics and Computer Science Division, Argonne National Laboratory, Argonne, IL

Joanna Kolodziej,   University of Bielsko-Biala, Department of Mathematics and Computer Science, Bielsko-Biala, Poland

Vladik Kreinovich,   Department of Computer Science, University of Texas at El Paso, El Paso, TX

Yu-Kwong Kwok,   The University of Hong Kong, Pokfulam, Hong Kong

Chia-Wei Lee,   National Cheng Kung University, Tainan, Taiwan

DONG LI, Oak Ridge National Laboratory, Small Oak Ridge, TN

KEQIN LI, State University of New York, New Paltz, NY

YINGSHU LI, Department of Computer Science, Georgia State University, Atlanta, GA

ZE LI, Clemson University, Clemson, SC

GUOXIN LIU, Clemson University, Clemson, SC

FENGSHUN LU, College of Computer, National University of Defense Technology, Changsha, China

PIOTR LUSZCZEK, Innovative Computing Laboratory, The University of Tennessee, Knoxville, TN

NAM MA, University of Southern California, Los Angeles, CA

QUTAIBAH MALLUHI, Department of Computer Science and Engineering, Qatar University, Qatar

MARJAN MERNIK, Institute of Computer Science, University of Maribor, Maribor, Slovenia

NASRO MIN-ALLAH, COMSATS Institute of Information Technology, Islamabad, Pakistan

ARSLAN MUNIR, University of Toronto, Toronto, Ontario, Canada

DIMITRIOS S. NIKOLOPOULOS, FORTH-ICS and University of Crete, Heraklion, Crete, Greece

YI PAN, Department of Computer Science, Georgia State University, Atlanta, GA

JOHNATAN PECERO, University of Luxembourg, Luxembourg, Luxembourg

VIKTOR K. PRASANNA, University of Southern California, Los Angeles, CA

FANG QI, Clemson University, Clemson, SC

XIAO QIN, Auburn University, Auburn, AL

SANJAY RANKA, Department of Computer and Information Science and Engineering, University of Florida, Gainesville, FL

KAIJUN REN, College of Computer, National University of Defense Technology, Changsha, China

PASCAL RICHARD, LIAS/ENSMA—Poitiers University, France

XIAOJUN RUAN, West Chester University of Pennsylvania, West Chester, PA

SAHRA SEDIGH, Missouri University of Science and Technology, Rolla, MO

HAIYING SHEN, Clemson University, Clemson, SC

BEHROOZ SHIRAZI, Washington State University, Pullman, WA

JOANNA SIEBERT, The Hong Kong Polytechnic University, Hong Kong

JUNQIANG SONG, College of Computer, National University of Defense Technology, Changsha, China

GERMAN SOTELO, Universidad de los Andes Bogota D.C., Colombia

SRISHTI SRIVASTAVA, Department of Computer Science and Engineering, Mississippi State University, Mississippi State, MS

JAVID TAHERI, School of Information Technologies, University of Sydney, Sydney, Australia

CHIU C. TAN, Temple University, Philadelphia, PA

WEI-GUANG TENG, National Cheng Kung University, Tainan, Taiwan

RUPPA THULASIRAM, Department of Computer Science, University of Manitoba, Winnipeg, Manitoba, Canada

PARIMALA THULASIRAMAN, Department of Computer Science, University of Manitoba, Winnipeg, Manitoba, Canada

Yun Tian,   Auburn University, Auburn, AL

Ioannis E. Venetis,   Department of Computer Engineering and Informatics, University of Patras, Greece

Mario Villamizar,   Universidad de los Andes Bogota D.C., Colombia

C. Shaun Wagner,   Missouri University of Science and Technology, Rolla, MO

Lizhe Wang,   Center for Earth Observation and Digital Earth, Chinese Academy of Sciences, Beijing, China

Yongj Wang,   State Key Laboratory of Computer Science, Institute of Software, Chinese Academy of Sciences, Beijing, China

Jie Wu,   Temple University, Philadelphia, PA

Yanhui Wu,   Center for Earth Observation and Digital Earth, Chinese Academy of Sciences, Beijing, China

Yinglong Xia,   IBM T.J. Watson Research Center Yorktown Heights, NY

Jiong Xie,   Auburn University, Auburn, AL

Yuanyuan Yang,   Stony Brook University, Stony Brook, NY

Qing Yi,   University of Texas at San Antonio, San Antonio, TX

Qian Zhu,   Accenture Technologies, New York, NY; Virginia Tech, Blacksburg, VA

Albert Y. Zomaya,   School of Information Technologies, University of Sydney, Sydney, Australia

1

Scalable Computing and Communications: Past, Present, and Future

Yanhui Wu, Kashif Bilal, Samee U. Khan, Lizhe Wang, and Albert Y. Zomaya

1.1 SCALABLE COMPUTING AND COMMUNICATIONS

Scalability is a paradigm that can adapt to the need of computing requirements of the underlying applications and users. Scalability [1, 2] is also a desirable quality for a network, process, website, or business model. In terms of hardware, a scalable computer system may begin with one node, but more nodes can be added as and when there is a need for more computing capabilities. Scalability, when sold with IT equipment or software, is a feature to convince high-growth businesses that the future needs can be accommodated easily and without recourse to expensive machine replacement or staff retraining. However, a scalable system need not be at one physical address. The ease of availability of high-speed networks and powerful computers has led to the emergence of two computing trends: (1) cluster computing [3, 4] and (2) grid computing [5–9]. Geographically, remote desktop computers, storage systems, data sources, scientific instruments, and clusters can be combined into what are known as computational grids.

Cloud computing [10–17] is an emerging paradigm in which users export data and applications (or computations) to the "cloud" (a remote set of machines) and then access the data or application in a simple and pervasive way. However, the aforementioned is a classic example of central processing. Interestingly, about 50 years ago, a similar situation arose when time-sharing computing servers catered to multiple users. The above-mentioned paradigm took a major shift with the introduction of personal computers (PCs) that allowed data and programs to be stored and processed locally. Most certainly, the evolution of the cloud computing paradigm is not exactly the same as the last cycle (time-sharing to PC) in the computing history, simply due to the fact that computation resources are not scarce anymore. We must understand that the clouds have emerged due to the need to build complex IT infrastructures that demand management of various software installations, configurations, updates, and heterogeneous resources. Computing resources and other hardware are becoming obsolete very rapidly. Therefore, outsourcing computing platforms is the most viable solution for users who would like to handle complex IT infrastructures.

Cloud computing is very rapidly evolving and there seems to be no widely accepted definition. Based on our experience, we proposed an early definition of cloud computing as follows: "A computing cloud is a set of network enabled services, providing scalable, QoS guaranteed, normally personalized, and inexpensive computing infrastructures on demand, which could be accessed in a simple and pervasive way." However, a more rigid and concise definition may be "A cloud computing paradigm is simply put a data center [18–25] that is being accessed by an application programming interface (API)."

Because cloud computing is the state of the art of computing paradigms [26–29], it is imperative to discuss issues related to scalability in the context of clouds. Looking to the future, cloud computing standardization efforts may well mirror what we observed for the standardization efforts toward the Internet.

For clouds, many standards development organizations (SDOs), consortia, and trade associations are busy creating cloud computing standards. As a consequence, there may likely be multiple standards in some areas, while other areas may miss standards entirely. It is this challenge that the IEEE Cloud Computing Initiative aims to address.

The IEEE P2301 [30] is a metastandard, a set of profiles consisting of other standards, publications, and guidelines from many organizations. The metastandard will provide profiles of existing and in-progress cloud computing standards in critical areas, such as applications, portability, management, and interoperability interfaces, file formats, and operation conventions. With capabilities logically grouped so that it addresses different cloud audiences and personalities, the IEEE P2301 metastandard will provide an intuitive roadmap for cloud vendors, service providers, users, developers, and other key stakeholders. When completed, the standard will aid users in procuring, developing, building, and using standards-based cloud computing products and services, enabling better portability, increased commonality, and greater interoperability across the industry. The IEEE P2302 is like any other standards except that it is focuses on inter- and intracloud problems, and there are no other efforts that we know of that are close to such an effort. The IEEE P2302 [31] essentially defines the topology, protocols, functionalities, and the governance required for the reliability of inter- and intracloud interoperability and federation. The standard will help build an economy of scale among cloud product and service providers, which will remain transparent to the users and applications. With a dynamic infrastructure supporting evolving cloud business models, the IEEE P2302 standard is an ideal platform for fostering growth and for improving competitiveness. It will also address fundamental, transparent interoperability and federation, much in the way as SS7/IN did for the global telephony system and as naming and routing protocols did for the Internet.

As the complexity and the size of the underlying systems increase, so does their demand for scalability. Therefore, the issues pertaining to scalability must be addressed head on. It is extremely difficult to come up with the top five problems within the general area of scalable computing. However, based on our experience, expertise, and discussions, the following five problems (in no particular order) seem to be the most critical issues within the realm of scalable computing.

1. *Data-Intensive Scalable Computing.* It is relatively inexpensive to gather digital data compared to a few decades ago. Therefore, more and more applications are emerging that are so-called data guzzlers. Examples of the aforementioned may include medical imaging, surveillance data, inventory data of shopping megastores, and location services [32–34]. The influx of information entails efficient and effective storage, processing, and transportation of such data. This is an uncharted territory for scalable computing. It would be unwise to even cap the scale of such a data influx to exascale computing. The grand solution to the above-mentioned problem will include directions from domains, such as scheduling, data placement, data management, operating systems, databases, programming languages, computer communications, computer architectures, disk storage devices, and middleware.

2. *Scalable Programming Paradigm.* A critical bottleneck in accessing the underlying massive-scale computing devices is the programming interface. Therefore, efficient and effective programming modules, more specifically, parallel programming libraries, must be developed to cater to the massive scales of the new generation of large-scale computing systems [35, 36]. Certain key issues in the aforementioned domain will be (1) reducing bandwidth requirements as much as possible; one methodology could be by introducing the use of mixed precision or storing data in 32-bit arrays wherever possible; and (2) rewriting low-level kernels as stateless functions with large enough granularity to keep a single-instruction multiple-data (SIMD) core busy and small enough that there is a large volume of simultaneous function calls to execute.

3. *High-Dimensional and Highly Dynamic Problem Sets.* More than often, computer algorithms are constructed for a deterministic or a bounded input. However, as the complexity of the underlying system increases, interactions among system components may not be fully captured by a bounded input. Therefore, various methodologies must also be incorporated that can adjust the system resource manager in an autonomic fashion to react to system uncertainties [37]. A plausible solution is to model and simulate the system under various system parametric fluctuations. However, all of the advanced modeling and simulation techniques quickly increase the problem size and parallelism, often by an order of magnitude, and large problems can easily exceed the computing capacity of the currently available computing systems. The simplest of the simulation approaches are "black box" in nature, which does not require a true exascale system (instead requiring a cluster of petascale systems). However, more advanced methods (termed embedded methods)

rely on a tightly coupled aggregation of forward problems and require true exascale systems. The challenge with embedded methods is that they require the transformation of an application into a "subroutine" because embedded methods need to invoke "forward solve" as a function. Most applications are not designed with this mindset, so this transformation will be challenging.

4. *Fault-Resilient Application Environment.* If hardware fault predictions are accurate, exascale systems will have very high fault rates and will, in fact, be in a constant state of restore and recovery. "All of the nodes are up and running," which is our current sense of a well-functioning scalable system, will become infeasible. Instead, we may always have a portion of the system dead, a portion that is dying, a portion continuously producing faulty results, a portion that is coming back to life, and a final, hopefully larger, portion that is computing fast and accurate results. The current hardware and software environments are not well prepared for the above-mentioned "kind of stable" system. In fact, the only reliable, portable resilience mechanism we have is checkpoint–restart. Although there have been many research efforts to achieve fault tolerance, much of this work has been focused on a single layer in the hardware and software stack, without sufficient consideration of the whole set of requirements. One of the biggest needs we have in resilient computing research is an increased effort to include the full vertical scope of the software and hardware stacks into our design discussions. Moreover, we need a full-featured environment to probe the system, to make decisions based on system state, and to recover from system faults, both hardware and software. Without a dramatic improvement in this environment, we are faced with the very real risk that application developers will reject the exascale systems in favor of smaller, more reliable systems that provide a better overall throughput.

5. *Hierarchical Software Engineering.* The software engineering community, by most accounts, has been slow to adopt formal software engineering practices. Although a lot of high-quality software has been developed without formal practices, the demands of collaborative development, multicode environments, and large collective teams require more attention to the benefits that formal practices can provide. Typically, software engineers work in a tightknit team to rapidly produce small software. However, the newer paradigms demand development of complex and multifold larger software, such as Trilinos, which is an example of a "project of projects." The basic idea undertaken when developing Trilinos was (1) cross-fertilization of ideas, techniques, and tools across package teams; (2) adoption of "best practices" from one package across other packages; (3) fostering of trust among disparate groups; (4) software modularity that is naturally enforced by package and team boundaries; and (5) well-defined interfaces between packages for interoperability. The aforementioned may lead to better large-scale software development, but of course, a serious research effort must be undertaken in this direction.

REFERENCES

[1] L. Kuan-Ching, H. Ching-Hsien, and T.Y. Laurence, *Handbook of Research on Scalable Computing Technologies*. Hershey, PA: IGI Global snippet, 2009.

[2] Y.C. Kwong, *Annual Review of Scalable Computing*. Singapore: World Scientific, 2004.

[3] L. Valentini, W. Lassonde, S.U. Khan, N. Min-Allah, S.A. Madani, J. Li, L. Zhang, L. Wang, N. Ghani, J. Kolodziej, H. Li, A.Y. Zomaya, C. Xu, P. Balaji, A. Vishnu, F. Pinel, J.E. Pecero, D. Kliazovich, and P. Bouvry, "An overview of energy efficiency techniques in cluster computing systems," *Cluster Computing*, forthcoming. DOI:10.1007/s10586-011-0171-x.

[4] R. Buyya, *High Performance Cluster Computing: Systems and Architectures*. Prentice Hall, 1999.

[5] J. Joseph and C. Fellenstein, *Grid Computing*. Upper Saddle River, NJ: Prentice Hall, 2005.

[6] L. Wang, W. Jie, and J. Chen, *Grid Computing: Infrastructure, Service, and Applications*. Boca Raton, FL: CRC Press, 2009.

[7] W. Peng, J. Tao, L. Wang, H. Marten, and D. Chen, "Towards providing cloud functionalities for grid users," *IEEE 17th International Conference on Parallel and Distributed Systems (ICPADS)*, December 2011, Tainan, Taiwan.

[8] J. Kolodziej and S.U. Khan, "Data scheduling in data grids and data centers: A short taxonomy of problems and intelligent resolution techniques," *LNCS Transactions on Computational Collective Intelligence*, forthcoming.

[9] P. Lindberg, J. Leingang, D. Lysaker, K. Bilal, S.U. Khan, P. Bouvry, N. Ghani, N. Min-Allah, and J. Li, "Comparison and analysis of greedy energy-efficient scheduling algorithms for computational grids," in *Energy Aware Distributed Computing Systems* (A.Y. Zomaya and Y.C. Lee, eds.), forthcoming.

[10] D. Kliazovich, P. Bouvry, and S.U. Khan, "GreenCloud: A packet-level simulator of energy-aware cloud computing data centers," *Journal of Supercomputing*, forthcoming. DOI: 10.1007/s11227-010-0504-1.

[11] G.L. Valentini, S.U. Khan, and P. Bouvry, "Energy-efficient resource utilization in cloud computing," in *Large Scale Network-centric Computing Systems* (A.Y. Zomaya and A.H. Sarbazi-Azad, eds.), forthcoming.

[12] J. Li, Q. Li, S.U. Khan, and N. Ghani, "Community-based cloud for emergency management," *6th IEEE International Conference on System of Systems Engineering (SoSE)*, June 2011, Albuquerque, NM.

[13] D. Kliazovich, P. Bouvry, Y. Audzevich, and S.U. Khan, "GreenCloud: A packet-level simulator of energy-aware cloud computing data centers," *53rd IEEE Global Communications Conference (Globecom)*, December 2010, Miami, FL.

[14] T. Velte, A.T. Velte, T.J. Velte, and R.C. Elsenpeter, *Cloud Computing, a Practical Approach*. New York: McGraw-Hill, 2009.

[15] N. Antonopoulos and L. Gillam, *Cloud Computing: Principles, Systems and Applications*. London: Springer, 2010.

[16] R. Buyya, J. Broberg, and A.M. Goscinski, *Cloud Computing: Principles and Paradigms*. Hoboken, NJ: Wiley, 2011.

[17] B. Sosinsky, *Cloud Computing Bible*. Hoboken, NJ: Wiley, 2011.

[18] D. Kliazovich, P. Bouvry, and S.U. Khan, "DENS: Data center energy-efficient network-aware scheduling," *Cluster Computing*, forthcoming. DOI: 10.1007/s10586-011-0177-4.

[19] L. Wang and S.U. Khan, "Review of performance metrics for Green data centers: A taxonomy study," *Journal of Supercomputing*, forthcoming. DOI: 10.1007/s11227-011-0704-3.

[20] L. Wang, S.U. Khan, and J. Dayal, "Thermal aware workload placement with task-temperature profiles in a data center," *Journal of Supercomputing*, forthcoming. DOI: 10.1007/s11227-011-0635-z.

[21] S.U. Khan and N. Min-Allah, "A goal programming based energy efficient resource allocation in data centers," *Journal of Supercomputing*, forthcoming. DOI: 10.1007/s11227-011-0611-7.

[22] K. Bilal, S.U. Khan, J. Kolodziej, L. Zhang, K. Hayat, S.A. Madani, N. Min-Allah, L. Wang, and D. Chen, "A comparative study of data center network architectures," *26th European Conference on Modeling and Simulation (ECMS)*, May 2012, Koblenz, Germany.

[23] S.U. Khan and C. Ardil, "A weighted sum technique for the joint optimization of performance and power consumption in data centers," *International Journal of Electrical, Computer, and Systems Engineering*, 3(1):35–40, 2009.

[24] S.U. Khan, "A multi-objective programming approach for resource allocation in data centers," *International Conference on Parallel and Distributed Processing Techniques and Applications (PDPTA)*, July 2009, Las Vegas, NV.

[25] S.U. Khan, "A self-adaptive weighted sum technique for the joint optimization of performance and power consumption in data centers," *22nd International Conference on Parallel and Distributed Computing and Communication Systems (PDCCS)*, September 2009, Louisville, KY.

[26] L. Wang, L. Von, A. Younge, X. He, M. Kunze, J. Tao, and C. Fu, "Cloud computing: A perspective study," *New Generation Computing*, 28(2):137–146, 2010.

[27] L. Wang, R. Ranjan, J. Chen, and B. Benatallah, *Cloud Computing: Methodology, Systems, and Applications*. Boca Raton, FL: Taylor & Francis, 2011.

[28] Q. Zhang, L. Cheng, and R. Boutaba, "Cloud computing: State-of-the-art and research challenges," *Journal of Internet Services and Applications*, 1(1):7–18, 2010.

[29] A. Beloglazov, R. Buyya, Y.L. Choon, and A. Zomaya, "A taxonomy and survey of energy-efficient data centers and cloud computing systems," in *Advances in Computers* (M. Zelkowitz, ed.), San Diego, CA: Elsevier Science, 2011.

[30] IEEE P2301. Available at http://standards.ieee.org/develop/wg/CPWG-2301_WG.html. Accessed April 12, 2012.

[31] IEEE P2302. Available at http://standards.ieee.org/develop/wg/ICWG-2302_WG.html. Accessed Apr 12, 2012.

[32] L. Wang, J. Tao, H. Marten, A. Streit, S.U. Khan, J. Kolodziej, and D. Chen, "MapReduce across distributed clusters for data-intensive applications," *26th IEEE International Parallel and Distributed Processing Symposium (IPDPS)*, May 2012, Shanghai, China.

[33] L. Perkins, P. Andrews, D. Panda, D. Morton, R. Bonica, N. Werstiuk, and R. Kreiser, "Data intensive computing," *Proceedings of the 2006 ACM/IEEE Conference on Supercomputing*, 2006, Tampa, FL.

[34] I. Gorton, P. Greenfield, A. Szalay, and R. Williams, "Data-intensive computing in the 21st century," *Computers*, 44(4):30–32, 2008.

[35] M.D. McCool, "Scalable programming models for massively multicore processors," *Proceedings of the IEEE*, 96(5):816–831, 2008.

[36] K. Hwang and Z. Xu, *Scalable Parallel Computing: Technology, Architecture, Programming*. New York: McGraw-Hill, 1998.

[37] S. Ali, A. Maciejewski, H.J. Siegel, and J. Kim, "Measuring the robustness of a resource allocation," *IEEE Transactions on Parallel and Distributed Systems*, 15(7):630–641, 2004.

2

Reliable Minimum Connected Dominating Sets for Topology Control in Probabilistic Wireless Sensor Networks

Jing (Selena) He, Shouling Ji, Yi Pan, and Yingshu Li

2.1 TOPOLOGY CONTROL IN WIRELESS SENSOR NETWORKS (WSNs)

To ensure sufficient coverage of an area or to protect against node failures, one major characteristic of WSNs is the possibility of deploying many redundant nodes in a small area. These are clear advantages of a dense network deployment; however, there are also disadvantages. To be specific, in a relatively crowded network, many typical wireless networking problems are aggravated by the large number of neighbors, such as many nodes interfering with each other. In order to avoid too many interferences, nodes might use short transmission power to talk to nearby nodes directly; thus, routing protocols might have to recompute routes even if only small node movements have happened [1].

Some of these problems can be overcome by topology-control techniques. Instead of using the possible connectivity of a network to its maximum possible extent, a deliberate choice is made to restrict the topology of the network. The topology of

Scalable Computing and Communications: Theory and Practice, First Edition. Edited by
Samee U. Khan, Albert Y. Zomaya, and Lizhe Wang.
© 2013 John Wiley & Sons, Inc. Published 2013 by John Wiley & Sons, Inc.

a network is determined by the subset of active nodes and the set of active links along which direct communication can occur. Formally speaking, a topology-control algorithm takes a graph $G = (V, E)$ representing the network, where V is the set of all nodes in the network and there is an edge $(v_1, v_2) \in E \subseteq V^2$ if and only if nodes v_1 and v_2 can directly communicate with each other. All active nodes form an induced graph $A = (V_A, E_A)$, such that $V_A \subseteq V$ and $E_A \subseteq E$.

2.1.1   Options for Topology Control

To compute an induced graph A out of a graph G representing the original network G, a topology-control algorithm has a few options [1]:

- The set of active nodes can be reduced ($V_T \subset V$) by periodically switching on/off some nodes in G.
- The set of active links/the set of neighbors for a node can be controlled. Instead of using all links in the network, some links can be disregarded and communication can be restricted to crucial links. When a flat network topology (all nodes are considered equal) is desired, the set of neighbors of a node can be reduced by simply not communicating with some neighbors. One possible approach to choose neighbors for a WSN is to limit a node's transmission range—typically by power control.
- Active links/neighbors can also be rearranged in a hierarchical network topology where some nodes assume special roles.

One example, illustrated in Figure 2.1, is to select some nodes as a *virtual backbone* (VB) for the network and to only use the links within this backbone and direct links from other nodes to the backbone. To do so, the backbone has to form a *dominating set* (DS). Formally speaking, a DS is a subset $D \subset V$ such that all nodes in V

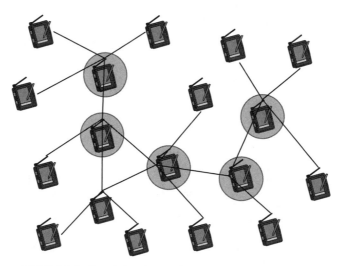

FIGURE 2.1. *Restricting the topology by using dominating sets.*

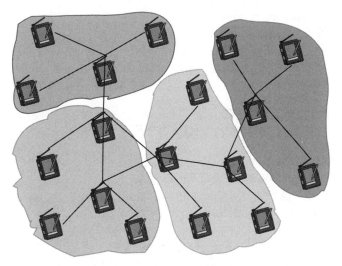

FIGURE 2.2. *Using clusters to partition a graph.*

are either in D itself or are one-hop neighbors of some node $d \in D$ (i.e., $\forall\, v \in V$: $v \in D \vee \exists\, d \in D : (v, d) \in E$). Then, only the links between nodes of the DS or between other nodes and a member of the active set are maintained. For a backbone to be useful, it should be connected. Hence, a *connected dominating set* (CDS) should always be used as a VB in WSNs.

A related but slightly different idea is to partition the network into clusters, illustrated in Figure 2.2. Clusters are subsets of nodes such that, for each cluster, certain conditions hold. The most typical problem formulation is to find clusters with cluster heads, which is a representative of a cluster such that each node is only one hop away from its cluster head.

In summary, there are three main options for topology control: flat networks with a special attention to power control on the one hand, hierarchical networks with backbones or clusters on the other hand.

2.1.2 Measurements of Topology-Control Algorithms

There are a few basic metrics to judge the efficiency and quality of a topology-control algorithm [2]:

- *Connectivity.* Topology control should not disconnect a connected graph G.
- *Stretch Factors.* Removing links from a graph will likely increase the length of a path between any two nodes, u and v. The hop stretch factor is defined as the worst increase in path length for any pair of nodes u and v between the original graph G and the topology-controlled path P. Formally,

$$\text{Hop stretch factor} = \max_{u,v \in V} \frac{|(u, v)_P|}{|(u, v)_G|}, \tag{2.1}$$

where $(u, v)_G$ is the shortest path in graph G and $|(u, v)_G|$ is its length. Similarly, the energy stretch factor can be defined:

$$\text{Energy stretch factor} = \max_{u,v \in V} \frac{E_P(u, v)}{E_G(u, v)}, \qquad (2.2)$$

where $E_G(u, v)$ is the energy consumed along the most energy-efficient path in graph G. Clearly, topology-control algorithms with small stretch factors are desirable.

- *Graph Metrics.* A small number of edges in induced graph A and a low maximum degree for each node in A.
- *Throughput.* The reduced network topology should be able to sustain an amount of traffic comparable to that of the original network.
- *Robustness to Mobility.* When neighborhood relationships are changed in the original graph, other nodes might have to change their topology information.
- *Algorithm Overhead.* Low number of additional messages, low computational overhead. Also, distributed implementation is more practical and more desired.

In the present context of WSNs, connectivity is perhaps the most important characteristic of a topology-control algorithm. In this work, we focus on the CDS-based topology control.

2.2 DS-BASED TOPOLOGY CONTROL

2.2.1 Motivation

Different from wired networks, the topology of a WSN may change from time to time, and the energy of nodes is very limited and irreplaceable. Therefore, designing an energy-efficient communication scheme for WSNs is one of the most important issues that has a significant impact on the network performance. The effectiveness of many communication primitives for WSNs, such as routing [3, 4], multicast/broadcast [5, 6], and service discovery [7], relies heavily on the availability of a VB. A CDS typically serves as a VB of a WSN. A CDS is defined as a subset of nodes in a WSN such that each node in the network is either in the set or adjacent to some node in the set, and the induced graph by the nodes in the set is connected. The nodes in a CDS are called *dominators*, otherwise, *dominatees*. In a WSN with a CDS as its VB, dominatees only forward their data to their connected dominators. In addition to communication schemes, a CDS has many other applications, such as topology control [8], coverage [9, 10], data collection [11–13], data aggregation [14], and query scheduling [15]. Clearly, the benefits of a CDS can be magnified by making its size (the number of the nodes in the CDS) smaller. In general, the smaller the CDS is, the less communication and storage overhead are incurred. Hence, it is desirable to build a minimum-sized connected dominating set (MCDS).

Ever since the idea of employing a CDS for WSNs was introduced [16], a huge amount of effort has been made to find different CDSs for different applications, especially MCDSs. They can be classified into the following four categories based on the network information they use:

- centralized algorithms
- subtraction-based distributed algorithms
- distributed algorithms using a single leader
- distributed algorithms using multiple leaders.

We use n to denote the number of sensors in a WSN, Δ to denote the maximum degree of nodes in the graph representing a WSN, and *opt* to denote the size of any optimal MCDS.

2.2.2 Centralized Algorithms

Guha and Khuller [17] first proposed two centralized greedy algorithms with performance ratios of $2(H(\Delta) + 1)$ and $H(\Delta) + 2$, respectively, where $H(.)$ is a harmonic function. The greedy function is based on the number of white neighbors of each node. At each step, the one with the largest such number becomes a dominator.

Due to the instability of network topology in WSNs, it is necessary to update topology information periodically. Therefore, many distributed algorithms are proposed. These distributed algorithms can be classified into two categories: subtraction-based and addition-based algorithms. The subtraction-based algorithms begin with the set of all the nodes in a network, then remove some nodes according to predefined rules to obtain a CDS. The addition-based CDS algorithms start from a subset of nodes (usually disconnected), then include additional nodes to form a CDS. Depending on the type of the initial subset, the addition-based CDS algorithms can be further divided into single-leader and multiple-leader algorithms.

2.2.3 Subtraction-Based Distributed Algorithms for CDSs

Wu and Li [18] first proposed a completely distributed algorithm to obtain a CDS. The CDS construction procedure consists of two stages. In the first stage, each node collects its neighboring information by exchanging a message with the one-hop neighbors. If a node finds that there is a direct link between any pair of its one-hop neighbors, it removes itself from the CDS. In the second stage, additional heuristic rules are applied to further reduce the size of the CDS. Wu's algorithm [18] uses rule 1 and rule 2, where a node is removed from the CDS, if all its neighbors are covered by its one or two direct neighbors. Later, Dai's work [19] generalizes this as rule k, in which coverage is defined by an arbitrary number of connected neighbors. Dai's algorithm is reduced to Wu's algorithm when k is 1 or 2.

2.2.4 Addition-Based Distributed Algorithms for CDSs

Single-leader distributed algorithms for CDSs use one initiator to initialize the distributed algorithms. Usually, a base station could be the initiator for constructing CDSs in WSNs. In these distributed algorithms, a spanning tree rooted at the initiator is first constructed, and then maximal independent sets (MISs) are identified layer by layer; finally, a set of connectors to connect the MISs is ascertained to form a CDS. Wan et al. [20] presented an ID-based distributed algorithm to construct a CDS using a single initiator. For unit disk graphs (UDGs), Wan et al.'s [20] approach guarantees that the approximation factor on the size of a CDS is at most $8opt + 1$.

The algorithm has $O(n)$ time complexity and $O(n \log n)$ message complexity. Subsequently, the approximation factor on the size of a CDS was improved in another work reported by Cardei et al. [21], in which the authors used the degree-based heuristic and degree-aware optimization to identify Steiner nodes as the connectors in the CDS construction. The approximation factor on the size of a CDS is improved to $8opt$, while this distributed algorithm has $O(n)$ message complexity and $O(\Delta n)$ time complexity. Later, Li et al. [22] reported a better approximation factor of $5.8 + \ln 4$ by constructing a Steiner tree when connecting all the nodes in the MISs.

Distributed algorithms with multiple leaders do not require an initiator to construct a CDS. Alzoubi et al.'s technique [23] first constructs an MIS using a distributed approach without a leader or tree construction and then interconnects these MIS nodes to get a CDS. Li et al. proposed a distributed algorithm r-CDS in Reference 24, whose performance ratio is 172. r-CDS is a completely distributed one-phase algorithm where each node only needs to know the connectivity information within its two-hop-away neighborhood. An MIS is constructed based on each node's r value, which is defined as the number of this node's two-hop-away neighbors minus the degree of this node. The nodes with smaller r values are preferred to serve as MIS nodes. Adjih et al. [25] presented an approach for constructing an MCDS based on multipoint relays (MPRs), but there is no approximation analysis of the algorithm yet. Recently, in Reference 26, another distributed algorithm was proposed whose performance ratio is 147. This algorithm contains three steps. Step 1 constructs a forest in which each tree is rooted at a node with the minimum ID among its one-hop-away neighbors. Step 2 collects the neighborhood information, which is used in step 3 to connect neighboring trees.

2.2.5 Other Algorithms

Because CDSs can benefit a lot from WSNs, a variety of other factors are considered when constructing CDSs. There are more than one CDS that can be found for each WSN. To conserve energy, all CDSs are constructed and each CDS serves as the VB duty cycled in Reference 27. For the sake of fault tolerance, k-connect m-DSs [28] are constructed, where k-connectivity means that between any pair of backbone nodes, there exist at least k independent paths, and m-dominating represents that every dominatee has at least m adjacent dominator neighbors. To minimize delivery delay, a special CDS problem—minimum routing cost connected dominating set (MOC-CDS) [29] is proposed, where each pair of nodes in MOC-CDS has the shortest path. The work [30] considers size, diameter, and average backbone path length (ABPL) of a CDS in order to construct a CDS with better quality. Recently, the authors in References 31–33 take the *load-balance* factor into consideration when constructing an MCDS.

2.3 DETERMINISTIC WSNs AND PROBABILISTIC WSNs

WSNs are usually modeled using the deterministic network model (DNM) in recent literature. Under this model, there is a transmission radius of each node. According to this radius, any specific pair of nodes is always connected to be neighbors if their physical distance is less than this radius, while the rest of the pairs are always disconnected. The UDG model is a special case of the DNM model if all nodes have the same transmission radius. When all nodes are connected to each other, via a single-hop or multihop path, a WSN is said to have full connectivity. In most real applications, however, the DNM model cannot fully characterize the behavior of wireless links. This is mainly due to the transitional region phenomenon, which has been revealed by many empirical studies [34–37]. Beyond the "always connected" region, there is a transitional region where a pair of nodes is probabilistically connected. Such pairs of nodes are not fully connected but are reachable via the so-called lossy links [37]. As reported in Reference [37], there are often many more lossy links than fully connected links in a WSN. Additionally, in a specific setup [38], more than 90% of the network links are lossy links. Therefore, their impact can hardly be neglected.

The employment of lossy links in WSNs is not straightforward since when the lossy links are employed, the WSN may have no guarantee of full network connectivity. When data transmissions are conducted over such topologies, it may degrade the node-to-node delivery ratio. Usually, a WSN has large node density and high data redundancy; thus, this certain degraded performance may be acceptable for many WSN applications. Therefore, as long as an expected percentage of the nodes can be reached, that is, the node-to-node delivery ratio satisfies some preset requirement, lossy links are tolerable in a WSN. In other words, full network connectivity is not always a necessity. Some applications can trade full network connectivity for a higher energy efficiency and larger network capacity [38].

All the above-mentioned existing works either consider to construct an MCDS under the DNM model, to design a routing protocol, or to investigate the topology control under the *probabilistic network model* (PNM). To our best knowledge, however, none of them attempts to construct an MCDS under the PNM model, which is more realistic. This is the major motivation of this research work. Genetic algorithms (GAs) are a family of computational models inspired by evolution, which have been applied in a quite broad range of NP-hard optimization problems [39–42]. Therefore, a GA-based method, namely, reliable minimum-sized connected dominating set genetic algorithm (RMCDS-GA), is proposed in Section 2.5 to construct a reliable minimum-sized connected dominating set (RMCDS) under the PNM model. In RMCDS-GA, each possible CDS in a WSN is represented to be a chromosome (feasible/potential solution), and the fitness function is to evaluate the trade-off between the CDS reliability and the size of the CDS represented by each chromosome.

2.4 RELIABLE MCDS PROBLEM

2.4.1 Motivation Example

In order to well characterize a WSN with lossy links, we propose a new network model called the PNM. Under this model, in addition to the transmission radius, there is a *transmission success ratio* (TSR) associated with each link connecting a pair of nodes, which is used to indicate the probability that one node can successfully directly deliver a package to another. Obviously, the core issue under the PNM

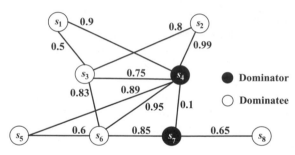

FIGURE 2.3. *A wireless network under the PNM model.*

model is how to guarantee the node-to-node delivery ratio of all possible node pairs satisfying the user requirement, in other words, how to guarantee the transmission quality (TQ). For constructing an MCDS under the PNM model, we propose *CDS reliability* to measure its TQ. Given a PNM model, CDS reliability is defined as the minimum node-to-node delivery ratio between any pair of dominators. Thus, how to find an RMCDS under the PNM model is the major concern of this chapter. The objective is to seek an MCDS whose reliability satisfies a certain application-dependent threshold denoted by σ (e.g., $\sigma = 80\%$). If $\sigma = 100\%$, finding an RMCDS under the PNM model is the same as the traditional MCDS problem under the DNM model. However, a traditional MCDS algorithm may not find an RMCDS under the PNM model. A counterexample is depicted in Figure 2.3. By the latest algorithm proposed in Reference 14, a spanning tree rooted at a specified initiator is first constructed, and then MISs are identified layer by layer. Finally, a set of connectors to connect the MISs is ascertained to form a CDS. According to the topology shown in Figure 2.3, the constructed CDS by Wan et al. [14] using s_4 as the initiator is $D = \{s_4, s_7, s_8\}$, whose reliability is 0.1. If the threshold $\sigma = 0.7$, the CDS D does not satisfy the constraint at all. The objective of our work is to find an MCDS whose reliability is greater than or equal to σ. One example of the satisfied RMCDS is $D' = \{s_3, s_6, s_7\}$ in Figure 2.3.

The key challenge of finding an RMCDS under the PNM model is the computation of the CDS reliability. It is known that given a network topology, the calculation of the node-to-node delivery ratio is NP-hard when network broadcast is used. Indeed, according to the reliability theory [43], the node-to-node delivery ratio is not practically computable unless the network topology is basically series–parallel, namely, the graph representing a WSN can be reduced to a single edge by series and parallel replacements. Nevertheless, most network topologies are not series–parallel structures. Thus, instead of computing the accurate CDS reliability, we design a greedy-based algorithm to approximate the CDS reliability. Another challenge is to find an MCDS, which is also an NP-hard problem [44]. Intuitively, the smaller the CDS is, the lower the reliability of the CDS is. The key issue then becomes how to find a proper trade-off between the MCDS and the CDS reliability while satisfying the optimization constraint (i.e., the CDS reliability is no less than the threshold σ). To address this problem, we explore the GA optimization approach. GAs are numerical search tools that operate according to the procedures that resemble the principles of natural selection and genetics [45]. Because of their flexibility and widespread applicability, GAs have been successfully used in a wide variety of problems in several areas of WSNs [39–42].

2.4.2 Assumptions

We assume a static WSN and all the nodes have the same transmission range. The transmission success ratio (TSR) associated with each link connecting a pair of nodes is available and fixed, which can be obtained by periodic Hello messages or can be predicted using link quality index (LQI) [46]. We also assume that the TSR values are fixed. This assumption is reasonable as many empirical studies have shown that LQI is pretty stable in a static environment [47]. Furthermore, no node failure is considered since it is equivalent to a link failure case. No duty cycle is considered either. We do not consider packet collisions or transmission congestion, which are left to the medium access control (MAC) layer. The degradation of the node-to-node delivery ratio is thus only due to the failure of wireless links.

2.4.3 Network Model

We assume a static WSN and all the nodes have the same transmission range. The transmission success ratio (TSR) associated with each link connecting a pair of nodes is available and fixed. Under the PNM, we model a WSN as an undirected graph $G(V, E, P(E))$, where V is the set of n nodes, denoted by $s_1, s_2, \ldots, s_n$; E is the set of m lossy links, $\forall u, v \in V$; there exists an edge (u, v) in G if and only if (1) u and v are in each other's transmission range and (2) $TSR(e = \{u, v\}) > 0$, for each link $e = \{u, v\} \in E$, where $TSR(e)$ indicates the probability that node u can successfully directly deliver a packet to node v; and $P(E) = \{<e, TSR(e) > | e \in E, 0 \leq TSR(e) \leq 1\}$. We assume edges are undirected (bidirectional), which means two linked nodes are able to transmit and receive information from each other with the same TSR value.

Because of the introduction of $TSR(e)$, the traditional definition of the node neighborhood has changed. Hence, we first give the definition of the one-hop neighborhood and then extend it to the r-hop neighborhood.

Definition 2.1 One-Hop Neighborhood. $\forall u \in V$, the one-hop neighborhood of node u is defined as

$$N_1(u) = \{v \mid v \in V, TSR(e = \{u, v\}) > 0\}.$$

The physical meaning of one-hop neighborhood is the set of the nodes that can be directly reached from node u.

Definition 2.2 r-Hop Neighborhood. $\forall u \in V$, the r-hop neighborhood of node u is defined as

$$N_r(u) = N_{r-1}(u) \cup \left\{ v \mid \exists w \in N_{r-1}(u), v \in N_1(w), v \notin \bigcup_{i=1}^{r-1} N_i(u) \right\}.$$

The physical meaning of the *r*-hop neighborhood is the set of nodes that can be reached from node *u* by passing maximum *r* number of edges.

Definition 2.3 $\Theta_k(i)$. *Given a source node u, its k-hop and (k − 1)-hop neighborhood $N_k(u)$, $N_{k-1}(u)$, for each $i \in N_k(u)$, we denote $\Theta_k(i)$ as a set of edges that gives all the possible ways by which i can be reached from node $i' \in N_{k-1}(u)$:*

$$\Theta_k(i) = \{j \in E \mid j = \{i', i\}, \text{ for } i \in N_k(u) \text{ and } i' \in N_{k-1}(u)\}.$$

Definition 2.4 Node-to-Node Delivery Ratio. *Given a source node u and a destination node v, one path between the node pair can be denoted by the edge permutation $\theta(u, v) = (e_1, e_2, \ldots, e_m)$, and the delivery ratio of the path is denoted by $DR_\theta = \prod_{i=1}^{m} TSR(e_i)$. Furthermore, we use $\Theta(u, v)$ to denote the set of all the possible ways by which node v can be reached from node u. The node-to-node delivery ratio from node u to node v is then defined as*

$$DR^*(u, v) = \max\{DR_\theta, \forall \theta(u, v) \in \Theta(u, v)\}.$$

Clearly, $DR^*(u, v)$ is equivalent to $DR^*(v, u)$.

Definition 2.5 CDS Reliability. *Given a WSN represented by G(V, E, P(E)) under the PNM model, and its CDS denoted by D, the reliability R_D^* of D is the minimum node-to-node delivery ratio between any pair of the nodes in the CDS; that is,*

$$R_D^* = \min\{DR^*(u, v), \forall u, v \in D, u \neq v\}.$$

We use CDS reliability to measure the quality of a CDS constructed under the PNM model. By this definition, when a CDS *D* has a reliability R_D^* satisfying a threshold σ (i.e., $R_D^* \geq \sigma$), we can state that for any pair of the nodes in the CDS, the probability that they are connected is no less than the threshold.

According to the reliability theory [43], we know that the computation of the node-to-node delivery ratio is NP-hard. Therefore, the computation of the CDS reliability is also NP-hard. In summary, we claim that, given a WSN represented by $G(V, E, P(E))$ under the PNM model, a CDS for *G* denoted by *D*, and a predefined threshold $\sigma \in (0, 1]$, it is NP-hard to verify whether $R_D^* \geq \sigma$.

2.4.4 Problem Definition

Definition 2.6 RMCDS. *Given a WSN represented by G(V, E, P(E)) under the PNM model, and a predefined threshold $\sigma \in (0, 1]$, the RMCDS problem is to find a minimum-sized node set $D \subseteq V$, such that*

1. The induced graph $G[D] = (D, E')$, where $E' = \{e|e = (u, v), u \in D, v \in D, (u, v) \in E)\}$, is connected.
2. $\forall u \in V$ and $u \notin D$, $\exists v \in D$, such that $(u, v) \in E$.
3. $R_D^* \geq \sigma$.

We claim that the problem to construct an RMCDS for a WSN under the PNM model is NP-hard. It is easy to see that the traditional MCDS problem under the DNM model is a special case of the RMCDS problem. By setting the TSR values on all edges to 1, we are able to convert the RMCDS problem to the traditional MCDS problem under the DNM model. Thus, the RMCDS problem belongs to NP. The verification of the RMCDS problem needs to calculate the CDS reliability. It is an NP-hard problem, which is mentioned in Section 2.4.3. Therefore, the problem to construct an RMCDS for a WSN under the PNM model is NP-hard.

2.4.5 Remarks

As we already know, computing the node-to-node delivery ratio and the CDS reliability are NP-hard problems. Therefore, instead of computing the accurate node-to-node delivery ratio, we design a greedy-based algorithm to approximate the ratio denoted by $DR(u, v)$. Based on the approximate node-to-node delivery ratio, we then calculate the approximate CDS reliability denoted by R_D. When there is no confusion, $DR^*(u, v)$ and $DR(u, v)$, R_D^* and R_D are interchangeable in the chapter.

Based on Definition 2.6, the key issue of the RMCDS problem is to seek a trade-off between the MCDS and the CDS reliability. GAs are population-based search algorithms that simulate biological evolution processes and have successfully solved a wide range of NP-hard optimization problems [39–42]. In the following, algorithm RMCDS-GA is proposed to solve the RMCDS problem to search the feasible domain more effectively and to reduce the computation time.

2.5 A GA TO CONSTRUCT RMCDS-GA

2.5.1 GA Overview

GAs, first formalized as an optimization method by Holland [48], are search tools modeled after the genetic evolution of natural species. GAs encode a potential solution to a vector of independent variables called chromosomes. The independent variables consisting of chromosomes are called genes. Each gene encodes one component of the target problem. A binary coding is widely used nowadays. GAs differ from most optimization techniques because of their global searching effectuated by one population of solutions rather than from one single solution. Hence, a GA search starts with the creation of the first generation, a random initial population of chromosomes, that is, potential solutions to the problem. Then, these individuals in the first generation are evaluated in terms of their "fitness" values, that is, their corresponding objective function values. Based on their fitness values, a ranking of the individuals in the first generation is dynamically updated. Subsequently, the first generation is allowed to evolve in successive generations through the following steps:

1. *Reproduction.* Selection of a pair of individuals in the current generation as parents. The ranking of individuals in the current generation is used in the selection procedure so that in the long run, the best individuals will have a greater probability of being selected as parents.

2. *Recombination.* Crossover operation and mutation operation:

  (a) Crossover is performed with a crossover probability, P_c, by selecting a random gene along the length of the parent chromosomes and swapping all the genes of the selected parent chromosomes after that point. The operation generates two new children chromosomes.

  (b) Mutation is performed with a mutation probability, P_m, by flipping the value of one gene in the chromosomes (e.g., 0 becomes 1 and 1 becomes 0, if binary coding is used).

3. *Replacement.* Utilization of the fittest individual to replace the worst individual of the current generation to create a new generation, so as to maintain the population number k a constant. Every time new children are generated by a GA, the fitness function is evaluated. And then a ranking of the individuals in the current generation is dynamically updated. The ranking is used in the replacement procedures to decide who among the parents and the children chromosomes should survive in the next population. This is to resemble the natural principles of the "survival of the fittest."

GAs usually stop when a certain number of total generations denoted by G are reached.

Figure 2.4 shows the overview of the RMCDS-GA algorithm.

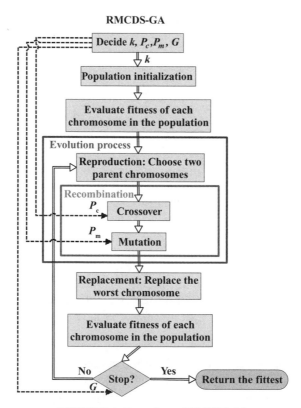

FIGURE 2.4. *Procedure of RMCDS-GA.*

One important feature of GAs that needs to be emphasized here is that the optimization performance of GAs depends mainly on the convergence time of the algorithm. When using GAs, sufficient genetic diversity among solutions in the population should be guaranteed. Lack of such diversity would lead to a reduction of the search space spanned by the GA. Consequently, the GA may prematurely converge to a local minimum because mediocre individuals are selected in the final generation. Alternatively, an excess of genetic diversity, especially at later generations, may lead to a degradation of the optimization performance. In other words, excess genetic diversity may result in very late or even no convergence. In this chapter, genetic diversity is maintained by the crossover, mutation operations and immigrant schemes. In the following part of this section, we will explain RMCDS-GA step by step.

2.5.2 Representation of Chromosomes

In the proposed RMCDS-GA, each node is mapped to a gene in the chromosome. A gene value indicates whether the node represented by this gene is a dominator or not. Hence, a chromosome is denoted as: $C_i = (g_1, g_2, \ldots, g_j, \ldots, g_n)$, where $1 \leq i \leq k$ and k is the number of the chromosomes in the population; $1 \leq j \leq n$ and n is the total number of the nodes in a WSN:

$$\begin{cases} g_j = 1, \text{node } s_j \text{ is a dominator} \\ g_j = 0, \text{node } s_j \text{ is a dominatee.} \end{cases}$$

All the nodes with $g_j = 1$ form a CDS denoted by $D = \{s_j | g_j = 1, 1 \leq j \leq n\}$.

An example WSN under the PNM model is shown in Figure 2.3 to illustrate the encoding scheme. There are eight nodes and the CDS is $D = \{s_4, s_7\}$. Thus, the eight nodes can be encoded using eight genes in a chromosome, for example, $C_1 = (g_1, g_2, \ldots, g_8)$, and then set the values of genes representing the dominators to 1. Finally, the encoded chromosome is $C_1 = (0, 0, 0, 1, 0, 0, 1, 0)$.

2.5.3 Population Initialization

According to the flowchart of the proposed RMCDS-GA shown in Figure 2.4, according to the proposed RMCDS-GA algorithm, after we decide the encoding scheme of the RMCDS problem, the first generation (a population with k chromosomes) should be created. This step is called population initialization in Figure 2.4. A general method to initialize the population is to explore the genetic diversity; that is, for each chromosome, all dominators are randomly generated. However, the dominators must form a CDS. Therefore, we start to create the first chromosome by running an existing MCDS method, for example, Wan's work [14], and then generate the population with k chromosomes by modifying the first chromosome. We call the procedure, generating the whole population by modifying one specific chromosome, inheritance population initialization (IPI).

An example is shown in Figure 2.3 to illustrate the IPI process. In Figure 2.3, the network and its CDS $D_1 = \{s_4, s_7\}$ are given. The values on the edges are TSR values and black nodes are dominators. Furthermore, we assume the CDS is constructed by a traditional MCDS method. According to the encoding scheme mentioned in

Section 2.5.2, $C_1 = (0, 0, 0, 1, 0, 0, 1, 0)$ represents the CDS generated by Wan's work [14] shown in Figure 2.3. Subsequently, we need to generate more chromosomes based on the first chromosome. The IPI algorithm is summarized as follows:

1. Start from the node with the smallest ID; reduce one dominator each time from the original CDS D_1 represented by C_1. If the new obtained node set is still a CDS D_i, then encode it as a chromosome C_i and add it into the initial population. Otherwise, remove the node with the second smallest ID from the original CDS D_1 and make the same checking process as for the node with the smallest ID, repeating the process until no more new chromosomes can be created. The CDS shown in Figure 2.3 is an MCDS; that is, we cannot further reduce its size. Thus, we go to step 2.

2. If the size of the original CDS D_1 cannot be reduced, and the number of the generated chromosomes is less than k, then for all the existing chromosomes $C_1, C_2, \ldots, C_i$ do the following steps until k nonduplicated chromosomes are generated.

   (a) Let $t = 1$.

   (b) In the CDS D_t represented by the chromosome C_t, start from node u with the smallest ID and add one dominatee node in its one-hop neighborhood $N_1(u)$ by the order of its ID into the CDS each time. If the new obtained node sets form CDSs, then encode them as chromosomes and add them into the initial population. In Figure 2.5b, the node with the smallest ID is s_4 in D. Therefore, the chromosomes from C_2 to C_6 are generated by adding one node from set $N_1(s_4) = \{s_1, s_2, s_3, s_5, s_6\}$ each time.

   (c) Move to the node with the second smallest ID in CDS D_t until every node in D_t is checked. In Figure 2.5b, the one-hop neighborhood of the node with the second smallest ID s_7 is $N_1(s_7) = \{s_6, s_8\}$. Since s_6 has already been marked as a dominator, we cannot add it to create a new CDS. By eliminating the duplicates, the chromosome C_7 is created.

   (d) If all the dominators in the current D_t are checked, move to the next CDS by setting $t = t + 1$. Repeat the step from 2b to 2d.

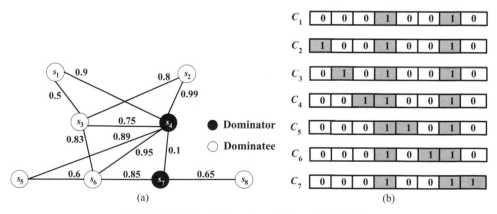

FIGURE 2.5. *Illustration of population of initialization.*

Since each node has two choices, to be a dominator or a dominatee, consequently, there are $2^{n-|D|}$ possible ways to create new chromosomes, where $|D|$ is the size of the CDS denoted by D under the PNM model. Usually, k is much smaller than $2^{n-|D|}$. Hence, the initial population $C_1, C_2, \ldots, C_k$ can be easily generated.

There are several merits that need to be pointed out here when using the above IPI algorithm to generate the initial population. First, we can guarantee every dominator set represented by a chromosome in the first generation is a CDS; that is, each chromosome in the initial population is a feasible solution of the RMCDS problem. Second, the critical nodes (cut nodes) are dominators encoded in each chromosome of the initial population. When performing crossover operations, the critical nodes are still dominators in the new offspring chromosome in the successive generations. Illustration examples will be shown in Section 2.5.6.1. Finally, the IPI stops when k chromosomes are generated. Actually, we can obtain more valid solutions by continuously running the IPI algorithm. As we already know, the population diversity plays an important role in the optimization performance of GAs. Therefore, the extra valid solutions generated by keeping running the IPI algorithm can be used in the replacement process to bring more population diversity in new generations. We will give a more detailed description of the replacement scheme in Section 2.5.6.3.

2.5.4   Fitness Function

Given a solution, its quality should be accurately evaluated by the fitness value, which is determined by the fitness function. In our algorithm, we aim to find an MCDS D whose reliability R_D should be greater than or equal to a preset threshold σ. Therefore, the fitness function of a chromosome C_i in the population is defined as

$$f(C_i) = \frac{R_D^2}{|D|^2}. \tag{2.3}$$

The purpose of raising $|D|$ and R_D to the power of 2 in Equation (2.3) is to enlarge the weight of the size of the CDS D. The denominator in Equation (2.3) needs to be minimized, while the numerator needs to be maximized. As a result, the fitness function value will be maximized.

As mentioned in the previous section, precisely calculating the CDS reliability is an NP-hard problem. According to Definition 2.5, we can easily compute the CDS reliability based on the node-to-node delivery ratio of all possible dominator pairs in the CDS. Therefore, we propose a greedy-based approximate algorithm to calculate the node-to-node delivery ratio. We adopt a greedy-based routing protocol, greedy perimeter stateless routing (GPSR) [49], to find the paths between all dominator pairs. In this work, we modified the greedy criterion to be the largest TSR values in one-hop neighborhoods based on GPSR.

For better understanding, we first illustrate the idea by an example and then summarize the whole process. For the chromosome C_2 shown in Figure 2.5b, the CDS represented by C_2 is $D = \{s_1, s_4, s_7\}$, in which there are three possible dominator pairs, that is, (s_1, s_4), (s_1, s_7), and (s_4, s_7). Assume the reliability threshold is $\sigma = 60\%$. Clearly, the TSRs associated with the edges (s_1, s_4) and (s_4, s_7) are both greater than 60% in Figure 2.5; that is, $TSR(e_1 = \{s_1, s_4\}) = 0.9$ and $TSR(e_2 = \{s_4, s_7\}) = 0.95$.

According to Definition 2.4, we know that $DR(s_1, s_4) = 0.9$ and $DR(s_4, s_7) = 0.95$, respectively. Therefore, the first greedy criterion comes out: The direct edges between sources and destinations with TSR values greater than δ have the highest priority to be chosen as the path between sources and destinations. Obviously, there is no direct edge between dominator pair (s_1, s_7). Thus, we need to find a multihop path between them. The search process starts from the destination s_7. The greedy criterion is based on the TSR values on the edges between s_7 and all its one-hop neighborhood $N_1(s_7) = \{s_4, s_6, s_8\}$. Since $TSR(e_2 = \{s_4, s_7\}) = 0.95 > 0.6$ is the largest TSR value among all the nodes in $N_1(s_7)$, the edge $e_2 = \{s_4, s_7\}$ is chosen. Subsequently, we keep searching from s_4. Apparently, $TSR(e_3 = \{s_2, s_4\}) = 0.99 > 0.6$ is the highest TSR value on the edges from s_4 to all the nodes in $N_1(s_4)$. However, based on the direct edge greedy criterion, that is, there is a direct edge between the source s_1 and the current search node s_4, therefore, $e_1 = \{s_1, s_4\}$ is chosen. According to Definition 2.4, $\theta(s_1, s_7) = \{e_1, e_2\}$, $DR(s_1, s_7) = DR_\theta = \prod_{i=1}^{2} TSR(e_i) = 0.9 \times 0.95 = 0.855$. Finally, based on Definition 2.5, we know $R(D) = \min\{DR(s_1, s_4), DR(s_1, s_7), DR(s_4, s_7)\} = \min\{0.9, 0.855, 0.95\} = 0.855$. The fitness of C_2 can then be calculated using Equation (2.3), $f(C_2) = 0.855^2/3^2 = 0.081225$.

2.5.5 Selection (Reproduction) Scheme

During the evolutionary process, election plays an important role in improving the average quality of the population by passing the high-quality chromosomes to the next generation. The selection operator is carefully formulated to ensure that better chromosomes of the population (with higher fitness values) have a greater probability of being selected for mating but that worse chromosomes of the population still have a small probability of being selected. Having some probability of choosing worse members is important to ensure that the search process is global and does not simply converge to the nearest local optimum. We adopt *roulette wheel selection* (RWS) since it is simple and effective. RWS stochastically selects individuals based on their fitness values $f(C_i)$. A real-valued interval, S, is determined as the sum of the individuals' expected selection probabilities; that is,

$$S = \sum_{i=1}^{k} P_i,$$

where

$$P_i = \frac{f(C_i)}{\sum_{j=1}^{k} f(C_j)}.$$

Individuals are then mapped one to one into contiguous intervals in the range $[0, S]$. The size of each individual interval corresponds to the fitness value of the associated individual. The circumference of the roulette wheel is the sum of all fitness values of the individuals. The fittest chromosome occupies the largest interval, whereas the least fit has a correspondingly smaller interval within the roulette wheel. To select an individual, a random number is generated in the interval $[0, S]$, and the

TABLE 2.1. Fitness of Seven Chromosomes

No.	Chromosome	$f(C_i)$	% of Total
C_1	00010010	$0.95^2/2^2 = 0.226$	35
C_2	10010010	$0.855^2/3^2 = 0.081$	12
C_3	01010010	$0.9405^2/3^2 = 0.098$	15
C_4	00110010	$0.7125^2/3^2 = 0.056$	9
C_5	000110101	$0.8455^2/3^2 = 0.079$	12
C_6	00010110	$0.80725^2/3^2 = 0.072$	11
C_7	00010011	$0.6175^2/3^2 = 0.042$	6
Totals		0.654	100

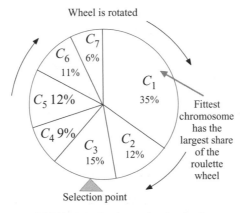

FIGURE 2.6. *Roulette wheel selection.*

individual whose segment spans the random number is selected. This process is repeated until a desired number of individuals have been selected.

We still use the WSN shown in Figure 2.5a to illustrate the RWS scheme. Table 2.1 lists a sample population of seven individuals (shown in Fig. 2.5b). These individuals consist of 8-bit chromosomes. The fitness values are calculated by Equation (2.3). We can see from the table that C_1 is the fittest and C_7 is the weakest. Summing these fitness values, we can apportion a percentage total of fitness. This gives the strongest individual a value of 35% and the weakest 6%. These percentage fitness values can then be used to configure the roulette wheel (shown in Fig. 2.6). The number of times the roulette wheel is spun is equal to size of the population (i.e., k). As can be seen from the way the wheel is now divided, each time the wheel stops, this gives the fitter individuals the greatest chance of being selected for the next generation and subsequent mating pool. According to the survival of the fittest in nature selection, individual $C_1 = (00010010)$ will become more prevalent in the general population because it is the fittest and more apt to the environment we have put it in.

2.5.6 Genetic Operations

The performance of a GA relies heavily on two basic genetic operators: *crossover* and *mutation*. Crossover exchanges parts of the current solutions (the parent chromosomes selected by the RWS scheme) in order to find better ones. Mutation flips the values of genes, which helps a GA keep away from local optimum. The type and implementation of these two operators depend on the encoding scheme and also on the application. In the RMCDS problem, we use the binary coding scheme and all potential solutions must be CDSs. For crossover, we can adopt all classical operations; however, the new obtained solutions may not be *valid* (the dominator set represented by the chromosome is not a CDS) after implementing the crossover operations. Therefore, a correction mechanism needs to be performed to guarantee validity of all the new generated solutions. Similarly, all traditional mutation operations can be adopted to the RMCDS problem, followed by a correction mechanism.

In this section, we introduce three crossover operators and their correction mechanism, followed by a mutation operator and its correction scheme.

2.5.6.1 Crossover In our algorithm, since a chromosome is expressed by binary codes, we adopt three crossover operators called single-point crossover, two-point crossover, and uniform crossover, respectively. With a crossover probability, P_c, each time we use the RWS scheme to select two chromosomes, C_i and C_j, as parents to perform one of the three crossover operators randomly. We use Figure 2.7 to illustrate the three crossover operations.

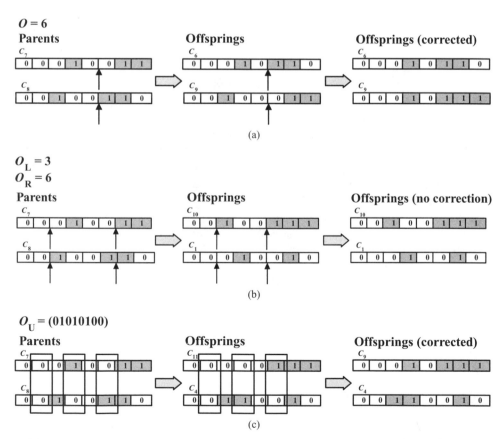

FIGURE 2.7. *Illustration of crossover operations: (a) single-point crossover, (b) two-point crossover, and (c) uniform crossover.*

Suppose that two parent chromosomes, $C_7 = (00010011)$ and $C_8 = (00100110)$, are selected from the population. By the single-point crossover (shown in Fig. 2.7a), the genes from the crossover point to the end of the two chromosomes exchange with each other to get $C_6 = (00010110)$ and $C_9 = (00010111)$. The crossover point denoted by $O = 6$ is generated randomly. After crossing, the first offspring, $C_6 = (00010110)$, is a valid solution. However, the other one, $C_9 = (00100011)$, is not valid; thus, we need to perform the correction mechanism. The correction starts from the gene in the position of the crossover point O, that is, g_6. Since g_6 is 1 in the parent chromosome C_8, it changes to 0 after crossing. We correct it by setting $g_6 = 1$. Then, $C_9 = (00010111)$ is now a valid solution. In general, we can keep correcting the genes until the end of the chromosome. By the two-point crossover (shown in Fig. 2.7b), the two crossover points are randomly generated, which are $O_L = 3$ and $O_R = 6$, and then the genes between O_L and O_R of the two parent chromosomes are exchanged with each other. The two offsprings are $C_{10} = (00100111)$ and $C_1 = (00010010)$, respectively. Since both of the offspring chromosomes are valid, we do not need to do any correction. As we already know, C_1 is the fittest in the population. This is a good illustration; we can obtain a fitter solution during the evolutionary process through genetic operations. For the uniform crossover (shown in Fig. 2.7c), the vector of uniform crossover O_U is randomly generated, which is $O_U = (01010100)$, indicating that g_2, g_4, and g_6 of the two parent chromosomes exchange with each other. Hence, the two offsprings are $C_{11} = (00000111)$ and $C_4 = (00110010)$. Since C_{11} is not a valid solution, we need to perform the correction scheme, and the corrected chromosome becomes $C_{10} = (00110010)$, which is a valid solution.

2.5.6.2 Mutation The population will undergo the mutation operation after the crossover operation is performed. With a mutation probability P_m, we scan each gene g_i on the parent chromosomes. If the mutation operation needs to be implemented, the value of the gene flips; that is, 0 becomes 1 and 1 becomes 0.

An example is shown in Figure 2.8, assume g_3 is mutated in chromosome C_7. The offspring $C_{11} = (00110011)$ is a valid solution; thus, no correction is needed. While g_6 and g_8 are mutated in chromosome C_8, the offspring $C_{12} = (001100011)$ is not a valid solution. Therefore, we perform the similar correction mechanism mentioned in the crossover section to make the offspring C_{12} valid by correcting $g_6 = 1$.

2.5.6.3 Replacement Policy The last step of RMCDS-GA is to create a new population using an appropriate replacement policy. Usually, two chromosomes from the evolution process are utilized to replace the two worst chromosomes in the original population for generating a new population. However, when creating a

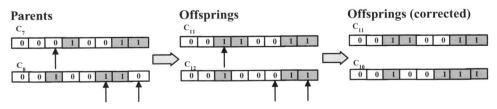

FIGURE 2.8. *Illustration of mutation operation.*

new population by crossover and mutation, we have a big chance to lose the fittest chromosome. Therefore, an elitism strategy, in which the best chromosome (or a few best chromosomes) is retained in the next generation's population, is used to avoid losing the best candidates.

The RMCDS-GA stops and returns the current fittest solution until the number of total generation G is achieved or the best fitness value does not change for continuous 10 generations. In the RMCDS-GA algorithm, we use G to stop the algorithm.

2.6   PERFORMANCE EVALUATION

In the simulations, we implement the RMCDS-GA to solve the RMCDS problem. These algorithms are compared with Wan's work [14] denoted by MIS, which is the latest and best MIS-based CDS construction algorithm.

2.6.1   Simulation Environment

We build our own simulator where all nodes have the same transmission range ($10m$) and all nodes are deployed uniformly in a square area. Moreover, a random value between $[0.9, 0.98]$ is assigned to the TSR value associated with a pair of nodes inside the transmission range; otherwise, a random value between $(0, 0.8]$ is assigned to the TSR value associated with a pair of nodes beyond the transmission range. For a certain n, 100 instances are generated. The results are averaged among 100 instances. Additionally, the particular GA rules and control parameters are listed in Table 2.2.

2.6.2   Simulation Results

In Table 2.3, we show that traditional MCDS construction algorithms cannot solve the RMCDS problem under the PNM model, especially for large-scale WSNs. In Table 2.3, we list the number of times that MIS and RMCDS-GA can find a CDS with a reliability greater than or equal to σ by running 100 simulations separately. σ is decreased from 0.6 to 0.4 by 0.1. From Table 2.3, we find that, with increasing n, the numbers of the times of satisfied CDSs for MIS and RMCDS-GA both decrease. This is because the sizes of CDSs increase, which leads to a lower node-to-node delivery ratio. Moreover, RMCDS-GA can guarantee more satisfied CDSs than MIS, especially when $n \geq 200$. In other words, for large-scale WSNs, it is hard to construct a satisfied CDS for MIS since the MIS algorithm does not consider

TABLE 2.2. GA Parameters and Rules

Population size (k)	20
Number of total generations (G)	100
Selection scheme	Roulette wheel selection
Replacement policy	Elitism
Crossover probability (P_c)	1
Mutation probability (P_m)	0.001

TABLE 2.3. MIS-based CDSs and RMCDS-GA-Generated CDSs

	$\sigma = 0.6$		$\sigma = 0.5$		$\sigma = 0.4$	
n	MIS	GA	MIS	GA	MIS	GA
50	100	100	100	100	100	100
80	94	100	100	100	100	100
120	57	100	98	100	100	100
160	21	100	90	100	100	100
200	5	96	44	100	88	100
250	2	91	12	93	56	100
400	1	90	4	17	10	100

TABLE 2.4. R and $|D|$ Results of MIS and RMCDS-GA Algorithms

Area (m^2)	n	R_{MIS}	R_{GA}	$|D_{MIS}|$	$|D_{GA}|$
40 × 40	50	0.65	0.77	17	18
50 × 50	80	0.59	0.72	24	26
60 × 60	120	0.51	0.68	33	33
70 × 70	160	0.46	0.62	40	44
80 × 80	200	0.44	0.58	51	51
90 × 90	250	0.39	0.53	63	62
100 × 100	400	0.32	0.49	78	78

reliability. Additionally, both MIS and RMCDS-GA can find more satisfied CDSs when σ decreases. In conclusion, traditional MCDS construction algorithms do not take reliability into consideration, while RMCDS-GA can find a satisfied RMCDS, which is more practical in real environments.

In Table 2.4, R_{MIS} and R_{GA} represent the reliability of a CDS generated by MIS and RMCDS-GA, respectively. $|D_{MIS}|$ and $|D_{GA}|$ represent the size of the CDS constructed by MIS and RMCDS-GA, respectively. In Table 2.4, the reliability of CDSs decreases when the area size increases since the number of the dominators increases. RMCDS-GA can guarantee to find a more reliable CDS than MIS; that is, $R_{GA} > R_{MIS}$. More importantly, the sizes of the CDSs obtained by MIS and RMCDS-GA are almost the same. On average, RMCDS-GA can find a CDS with 10% more reliability without increasing the size of a CDS than MIS. In summary, RMCDS-GA does not trade CDS size for CDS reliability.

2.7 CONCLUSIONS

In this chapter, we have investigated the RMCDS problem using a new network model called PNM. The PNM model, based on empirical studies, shows that most wireless links are lossy links, which only probabilistically connect pairs of nodes. Different from the traditional DNM model, which assumes that links are either connected or disconnected, the PNM model enables the employment of lossy links by introducing the TSR value on each lossy link. In this chapter, we focus on constructing an MCDS while its reliability satisfies a preset application-dependent threshold. We claim that RMCDS is an NP-hard problem and propose a GA to address the problem. The simulation results show that compared to the traditional MCDS algorithm, RMCDS-GA can find a more reliable CDS without increasing the size of a CDS.

REFERENCES

[1] H. Karl and A. Willig, *Protocols and Architectures for Wireless Sensor Networks.* Hoboken, NJ: John Wiley & Sons, 2005.

[2] R. Rajaraman, "Topology control and routing in ad hoc networks: A survey," *ACM SIGACT News*, 33(2):60C73, 2002.

[3] W. Di, Q. Yan, and T. Ning, "Connected dominating set based hybrid routing algorithm in ad hoc networks with obstacles," *ICC'06*, Turkey, Istanbul, June 11–15, 2006.

[4] E.H. Wassim, A.F. Ala, G. Mohsen, and H.H. Chen, "On efficient network planning and routing in large-scale MANETs," *IEEE Transactions on Vehicular Technology*, 58(7): 3796–3801, 2009.

[5] L. Ding, Y. Shao, and M. Li, "On reducing broadcast transmission cost and redundancy in ad hoc wireless networks using directional antennas," *WCNC'08*, pp. 2295–2300, 2008.

[6] B.K. Polat, P. Sachdeva, M.H. Ammar, and E.W. Zegura, "Message ferries as generalized dominating sets in intermittently connected mobile networks," *MobiOpp'10*, Pisa, Italy, 2010.

[7] A. Helmy, S. Garg, P. Pamu, and N. Nahata, "CARD: A contact-based architecture for resource discovery in ad hoc networks," *Mobile Networks and Applications*, 10(1):99–113, 2004.

[8] B. Deb, S. Bhatnagar, and B. Nath, "Multi-resolution state retrieval in sensor networks," IWSNPA, 2003.

[9] K.P. Shih, D.J. Deng, R.S. Chang, and H.C. Chen, "On connected target coverage for wireless heterogeneous sensor networks with multiple sensing units," *Sensors*, 9(7):5173–5200, 2009.

[10] H.M. Ammari and J. Giudici, "On the connected k-coverage problem in heterogeneous sensor nets: The curse of randomness and heterogeneity," *ICDCS*, Montreal, Quebec, Canada, 2009.

[11] S. Ji, Y. Li, and X. Jia, "Capacity of dual-radio multi-channel wireless sensor networks for continuous data collection," *INFOCOM*, Shanghai, China, April 10–15, 2011.

[12] S. Ji, Z. Cai, Y. Li, and X. Jia, "Continuous data collection capacity of dual-radio multi-channel wireless sensor networks," *IEEE Transactions on Parallel and Distributed Systems (TPDS)*, 23(10):1844–1855, 2011.

[13] S. Ji and Z. Cai, "Distributed data collection and its capacity in asynchronous wireless sensor networks," Inforcom, Orlando, Florida, March 25–30, 2012.

[14] P.J. Wan, S.C.-H. Huang, L. Wang, Z. Wan, and X. Jia, "Minimum latency aggregation scheduling in multihop wireless networks," *MobiHoc'09*, New Orleans, Louisiana, May 18–21, pp. 185–194, 2009.

[15] M. Yan, J. He, S. Ji, and Y. Li, "Minimum latency scheduling for multi-regional query in wireless sensor networks," *IPCCC*, Orlando, Florida, USA, November 17–19, 2011.

[16] A. Ephremides, J. Wieselthier, and D. Baker, "A design concept for reliable mobile radio networks with frequency hopping signaling," *Proceedings of the IEEE*, 75(1):56–73, 1987.

[17] S. Guha and S. Khuller, "Approximation algorithms for connected dominating sets," *Algorithmica*, 20:374–387, 1998.

[18] J. Wu and H. Li, "On calculating connected dominating set for efficient routing in ad hoc wireless networks," *DIALM*, pp. 7–14, 1999.

[19] F. Dai and J. Wu, "*An extended localized algorithm for connected dominating set formation in ad hoc wireless networks*," *TPDS '04*, 15(10):908–920, 2004.

[20] P. Wan, K. Alzoubi, and O. Frieder, "Distributed construction of connected dominating set in wireless ad hoc networks," *Mobile Networks and Applications*, 9(2):141–149, 2004.

[21] M. Cardei, M. Cheng, X. Cheng, and D. Zhu, "Connected dominating set in ad hoc wireless networks," *Proceedings of the 6th International Confrence on Computer Science and Informatics*, 2002.

[22] Y. Li, M. Thai, F. Wang, C. Yi, P. Wang, and D. Du, "On greedy construction of connected dominating sets in wireless networks," *Wireless Communications and Mobile Computing*, 5(8):927–932, 2005.

[23] K. Alzoubi, P. Wan, and O. Frieder, "Message-optimal connected dominating sets in mobile ad hoc networks," *MobiHoc '02*, pp. 157–164, 2002.

[24] Y. Li, S. Zhu, M. Thai, and D. Du, "Localized construction of connected dominating set in wireless networks," TAWN, Chicago, June, 2004.

[25] C. Adjih, P. Jacquet, and L. Viennot, "Computing connected dominated sets with multipoint relays," *Ad Hoc & Sensor Wireless Networks*, 1(1/2):27–39, 2005.

[26] X. Cheng, M. Ding, D. Du, and X. Jia, "Virtual backbone construction in multihop ad hoc wireless networks," *Wireless Communications and Mobile Computing*, 6(2):183–190, 2006.

[27] R. Misra and C. Mandal, "*Rotation of CDS via connected domatic partition in ad hoc sensor networks*," *TMC*, 8(4), 2009.

[28] D. Kim, W. Wang, X. Li, Z. Zhang, and W. Wu, "A new constant factor approximation for computing 3-connected m-dominating sets in homogeneous wireless networks," *INFOCOM*, 2010.

[29] L. Ding, X. Gao, W. Wu, W. Lee, X. Zhu, and D.Z. Du, "Distributed construction of connected dominating sets with minimum routing cost in wireless networks," *ICDCS*, 2010.

[30] D. Kim, Y. Wu, Y. Li, F. Zou, and D.Z. Du, "Constructing minimum connected dominating sets with bounded diameters in wireless networks," *IEEE Transactions on Parallel and Distributed Systems*, 20(2):147–157, 2009.

[31] J. He, S. Ji, M. Yan, Y. Pan, and Y. Li, "Genetic-algorithm-based construction of load-balanced CDSs in wireless sensor networks," MILCOM 2011, Baltimore, MD, November 7–10, 2011.

[32] J. He, S. Ji, M. Yan, Y. Pan, and Y. Li, "Load-balanced CDS construction in wireless sensor networks via genetic algorithm," *International Journal of Sensor Networks (IJSNET)*, 11(3):166–178, 2011.

[33] J. He, S. Ji, P. Fan, Y. Pan, and Y. Li, "Constructing a load-balanced virtual backbone in wireless sensor networks," International Conference on Computing, Networking and Communications (ICNC), Maui, HI, January 30–February 2, 2012.

[34] M. Zuniga and B. Krishnamachari, "Analyzing the transitional region in low power wireless links," SECON, Santa, Clara, October 4–7, 2004.

[35] G. Zhou, T. He, S. Krishnamurthy, and J. Stankovic, "Impact of radio irregularity on wireless sensor networks," Mobisys, Boston, MA, June 6–9, 2004.

[36] A. Cerpa, J.L. Wong, M. Potkonjak, and D. Estrin, "Temporal properties of low power wireless links: Modeling and implications on multi-hop routing," *MobiHoc,* Urbana-Champaign, IL, May 25–28, 2005.

[37] A. Cerpa, J. Wong, L. Kuang, M. Potkonjak, and D. Estrin, "Statistical model of lossy links in wireless sensor networks," IPSN'05, Los Angeles, CA, 2005.

[38] Y. Liu, Q. Zhang, and L.-M. Ni, *"Opportunity-based topology control in wireless sensor networks,"* TPDS '10, 21(9), 2010.

[39] M. Al-Obaidy, A. Ayesh, and A. Sheta, "Optimizing the communication distance of an ad hoc wireless sensor networks by genetic algorithms," *Artificial Intelligence*, 29:183–194, 2008.

[40] J. Wang, C. Niu, and R. Shen, "Priority-based target coverage in directional sensor networks using a genetic algorithm," *Computers and Mathematics with Applications*, 57:1915–1922, 2009.

[41] A. Bari, S. Wazed, A. Jaekel, and S. Bandyopadhyay, "A genetic algorithm based approach for energy efficient routing in two-tiered sensor networks," *Ad Hoc Networks*, pp. 665–676, 2009.

[42] X. Hu, J. Zhang, Y. Yu, H. Chung, Y. Lim, Y. Shi, and X. Luo, *"Hybrid genetic algorithm using a forward encoding scheme for lifetime maximization of wireless sensor networks,"* ITEC, 14(5):766–781, 2010.

[43] A. Agrawal and R. Barlow, "A survey of network reliability and domination theory," *Operations Research*, 32:298–323, 1984.

[44] M.R. Garey and D.S. Johnson, *Computers and Intractability: A Guide to the Theory of NP-Completeness*. New York: WH Freeman & Co., 1979.

[45] D.E. Goldberg, *Genetic Algorithms in Search, Optimization, and Machine Learning*. Bel Air, CA: Addison-Wesley Publishing Company, 1989.

[46] S. Lin, J. Zhang, G. Zhou, L. Gu, T. He, and J. Stankovic, "Atpc: Adaptive transmission power control for wireless sensor networks," Sensys'06, Boulder, CO, October 31–November 3, 2006.

[47] D. Son, B. Krishnamachari, and J. Heidemann, "Experimental study of concurrent transmission in wireless sensor networks," SenSys'06, Boulder, CO, October 31–November 3, 2006.

[48] J.H. Holland, *Adaptation in Natural and Artificial System*. Ann Arbor, MI: University of Michigan Press, 1975.

[49] B. Karp and H. Kung, "GPSR: Greedy perimeter stateless routing for wireless networks," MobiCom '00, New York, 2000.

3

Peer Selection Schemes in Scalable P2P Video Streaming Systems

Xin Jin and Yu-Kwong Kwok

3.1 INTRODUCTION

With recent advancements in computing and communication technologies, peer-to-peer (P2P) architectures have been successfully deployed and extensively studied in both industry and research communities. In essence, P2P networks are self-organizing and scalable distributed systems to fully exploit computing, streaming, and storage capacities of geographically distributed client users [1–3]. Numerous application scenarios of P2P overlays exist in the market, including both time-insensitive services (e.g., file sharing) [4–6] and instantaneous streaming systems (e.g., live video broadcast) [7–12]. Among them, scalable large-scale P2P multimedia streaming systems have penetrated into our daily lives by supplying real-time dissemination of media, including audio, video, massively multiplayer online games, and interactive social virtual worlds [13–17]. In particular, video streaming has evolved into a killer Internet application [18] and has predominantly occupied the Internet traffic [19].

To attain efficient video streaming, various overlay structures have evolved in the literature: single tree [20], multitree [21, 22], and unstructured meshes [23–25]. Single tree-based structures are vulnerable to peer dynamics, and leaf nodes cannot contribute their streaming capacities. To this end, multiple-tree structures are proposed by dividing the media stream into multiple substreams to decrease the streaming

Scalable Computing and Communications: Theory and Practice, First Edition. Edited by
Samee U. Khan, Albert Y. Zomaya, and Lizhe Wang.
© 2013 John Wiley & Sons, Inc. Published 2013 by John Wiley & Sons, Inc.

dependency on parents and to alleviate the impact of parent failures. Unstructured overlays are most resilient to churn by organizing peers into a randomly connected graph.

In unstructured overlays, each peer will connect to a subset of concurrently online nodes as neighbors. The video content is segmented into constant-size chunks. Swarming dissemination progressively propagates chunks around the neighborhood and further throughout the overlay. Peer selection, dictating the streaming topology, is thus critical to the overlay performance. However, two schools of interpretations to the term *peer selection* coexist in the literature. From the overlay construction perspective, peer selection is used to characterize neighbor discovery for connection [23, 26]. From the chunk scheduling perspective, it means from which to send or request media chunks [27, 28]. To avoid confusion, hereafter, unless otherwise mentioned, the former interpretation is adopted for peer selection. The following: peer selection, neighbor selection, overlay construction, and mesh construction are used interchangeably in this chapter.

The single-tree structure pioneers P2P multimedia streaming by organizing peers into a dissemination tree. Thus, it is important to begin our survey by introducing the basic tree-based structures in Section 3.2, followed by a preliminary description of unstructured meshes. Indeed, even in unstructured networks, if we examine the dissemination path of a single chunk, it still formulates a tree topology. Section 3.3 surveys a plethora of peer selection schemes to accommodate peer dynamics, peer heterogeneity, network friendliness, and cross-channel cooperation. Intriguingly, game theory, as an effective analytical tool, sheds light on incentive mechanism design, efficient overlay construction, and resource allocation in multichannel systems. Section 3.4 provides a game theoretic perspective on peer selection scheme design. We then provide several promising research directions in Section 3.5 and conclude this chapter in Section 3.6.

3.2   OVERLAY STRUCTURES

In this section, we first present an overview of the single-tree structure, followed by an illustration of multiple-tree streaming. Finally, we describe unstructured overlays for resilient and scalable multimedia streaming.

3.2.1   Single-Tree Streaming

As an early implementation to overcome the prohibitive bandwidth demand of servers in the client–server architecture, tree-based overlay streaming seeks for a scalable, reliable, and decentralized design for large-scale application-level distribution of bandwidth-intensive content on the Internet [20]. In tree-based structures, media content is streamed from the source to end peers along the distribution tree. Specifically, media packets are pushed throughout the tree from parents to the corresponding downstream peers. Thus, the tree building protocol determines the streaming performance.

Overcast [20] is an early example of a single-tree multicast. A newly arriving peer joins in the tree overlay by first contacting the root node (i.e., the server). Each peer periodically relocates itself under one of its siblings in the distribution tree if the bandwidth back to the root node via this sibling is not smaller than the bandwidth back to the root via its current parent. Similarly, it can also move up in the tree hierarchy. By maintaining upstream nodes (i.e., ancestors) as backup parents in face of peer dynamics, the tree overlay can mitigate the performance degradation, incurred by peer departures or node failures, by connecting with its ancestors. However, this recovery process invoked after peer dynamics still detrimentally affects the media streaming. Moreover, leaf nodes in the distribution tree cannot contribute their streaming bandwidth to others.

3.2.2 Multiple-Tree Streaming

To solve the problem that leaf nodes in the single-tree structure do not contribute their bandwidth to the streaming process, CoopNet [22, 29] and SplitStream [21] use multiple-tree streaming to further exploit bandwidth resources of leaf nodes. The key idea is to divide the media content into uncorrelated stripes, formulating independent streams. Each stream is distributed in a separate tree. For example, CoopNet [22] encodes the media content utilizing multiple description coding (MDC) to disseminate independent descriptions via separate trees.

Different tree maintenance methods are proposed in CoopNet [22] and in SplitStream [21]. CoopNet [22] minimizes the maximum tree depth via centralized and randomized tree construction, while peers in SplitStream [21] are organized by Pastry [30], a structured P2P overlay network, and Scribe [31], an application-level multicast system built upon Pastry. The main objective of overlay construction for SplitStream [21] is to ensure a peer serves as an interior node in no more than one streaming tree and acts as a leaf node in other trees. Lacked in SplitStream [21], the overlay topology of CoopNet [22] is matched with the underlying network topology by taking node proximity into consideration. This is achieved by deriving node distance information based on the GeoPing technique [32] to select the one closest to the new node among all candidate parents.

In the multiple-tree structure, a leaf node in one tree may be an interior node in another distribution tree. The bandwidth of leaf nodes can be better employed and the distribution load is thus further balanced across different peers. Moreover, it is more resilient to peer dynamics because each node receives streams from multiple parents in different streaming trees. For example, in SplitStream [21], each parent only forwards a single media stream and a parent failure only affects the streaming of the associated stream.

3.2.3 Mesh Overlays

Drawbacks of distribution trees—such as the static mapping of content into a particular distribution tree, the bottleneck of low-bandwidth peers exerted on the streaming tree, and the vulnerability toward peer churns—all contribute to the superiority of the mesh-based swarming content delivery [33].

PRIME [34] is one of the pioneering mesh-based unstructured overlays, inspired by file swarming mechanisms like BitTorrent (BT) [35], to construct a randomly connected mesh and leverage on swarming for multimedia streaming. Specifically, in unstructured meshes [24], media is divided into chunks with the same size for streaming, and each peer maintains a subset of concurrently online nodes as neighbors. The chunk distribution protocol is to progressively disseminate chunks around the neighborhood and further across the overlay topology. For live video streaming [24], each peer only buffers minutes of video chunks within a sliding window, including chunks recently played and to play immediately. In video-on-demand (VoD) systems, due to the unsynchronized nature of peers, each peer contributes a fixed local storage space to store shared video files. Intuitively, video replication to properly utilize such shared disks is crucial to the performance of VoD systems, and various strategies have been proposed to this end [36, 37].

In PPLive [24], trackers are responsible for the maintenance of all concurrently online peers in the system. A newly joining peer joins the overlay network by first retrieving a channel list provided by the bootstrap server. Subsequent to selecting the channel to watch, this peer further registers with the bootstrap server and contacts corresponding trackers to retrieve an initial list of concurrently online peers watching the same video channel. The new peer then communicates with these peers to further update its peer list. Consequently, each peer obtains a list of concurrently online peers watching the same streaming channel. Each peer selects a peer subset as neighbors for streaming cooperation and chunk reciprocation. PRIME [34] adopts a similar method for overlay construction.

CoolStreaming [38], a mesh-pull overlay, adopts random neighbor selection for overlay construction. Each node maintains a membership cache (mCache) with a partial list of concurrently active nodes and a score for each partner. Partners with higher outbound bandwidth and better chunk availability are assigned with higher scores. Peers periodically discover new neighbors by randomly selecting from mCache. After each partner discovery, the one with the lowest score is disconnected to keep a stable number of partners and at the same time to explore nodes of better quality.

Figure 3.1 illustrates the differences among single-tree structure, multiple-tree streaming, and mesh overlays for video streaming, in which only two substreams and two chunks are depicted.

3.3 PEER SELECTION FOR OVERLAY CONSTRUCTION

3.3.1 Overview

To obtain insights into chunk-driven real-deployed commercial P2P TV streaming systems, several measurement studies exist in the literature, providing valuable guidelines for peer selection scheme design [23, 24, 39]:

- *Random Overlay Construction.* The resilience of a random graph in the presence of system perturbation is well known in the scientific community. For example, in PPLive [39], the overlay topology largely resembles a random graph—though larger channels exhibit more clustering as quantified by clustering coefficients [40]—and is thus resilient to massive peer failures. In random peer selection, the goal is to maintain perfectly uniformly distributed local views of other peers. Thus, the crux is a *membership management* protocol to maintain a list of concurrently active and connected nodes, for reliable chunk dissemination especially in the face of network dynamics.

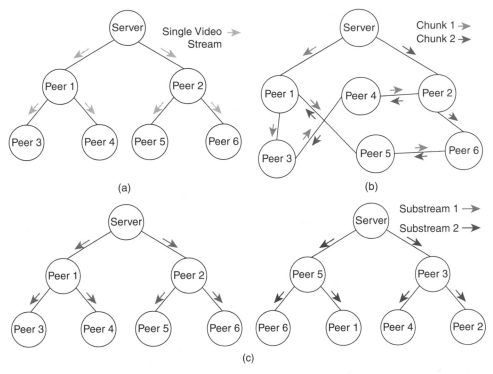

FIGURE 3.1. *Video streaming in three overlay structures: (a) single-tree streaming, (b) mesh overlays, and (c) multiple-tree streaming.*

- *Heterogeneous Overlay Construction.* Peers are endowed with diverse bandwidth accesses, which dictate the reciprocation capacity of peers. In PPLive [24], campus peers with high-bandwidth access are connected with more parters than residential peers with low-bandwidth access. In this fashion, campus peers can maintain a steady number of partners for video traffic exchange. However, residential peers may face difficulty in maintaining enough neighbors for video streaming, especially in unpopular channels. Thus, efficient overlay construction by taking peer heterogeneity into account is indispensable.

- *Network-Aware Overlay Construction.* Peers are geographically distributed across the world and thus may generate long-haul traffic, traveling long distance over the Internet and potentially deteriorating the network performance. Moreover, interautonomous system (AS) traffic is costly to autonomous systems (ASes), escalating the tension between P2P content providers and internet sevice providers (ISPs) [19]. Therefore, it is desirable to embed network awareness into peer selection by taking network proximity into account. Ciullo et al. [23] assessed and gained insights into the level of network awareness in commercial P2P streaming systems: PPLive [7] and TVAnts [11] are slightly biased to peers in the same AS, but SopCast [10] shows little such preference for peer selection. Hence, network friendliness is an essential element of peer selection scheme design.

- *Interoverlay Cooperation.* Diverse coexisting channels in P2P streaming systems experience streaming quality disparity and different peer behaviors. Wu et al.

[41] identified that some channels experience low streaming quality in UUSee, in which the topologies of various channels are largely disjoint. Moreover, Hei et al. [24] showed that in PPLive, peers tend to stay longer in popular programs than in unpopular programs, potentially contributing to the channel performance disparity. Consequently, current designs demand cross-channel cooperation to alleviate the resource imbalance among various channels. We utilize the terms *channel* and *overlay* interchangeably in the discussion of cross-channel design.

3.3.2 Membership Management for Random Overlay Construction

Gossip-based protocols have been widely utilized to decentralize the membership management. The idea of gossip, or rumor mongering, has been around for decades, first developed for replicate database consistency [42]. In a gossip protocol, each peer periodically sends messages to a randomly chosen subset of peers, amortizing the message transmission cost. Each peer gossips the same message for only a limited number of repetitions [43] and/or limited hops [44]. In the following, we first review the work taken by Kermarrec et al. [45] to theoretically demonstrate the system reliability of gossip-based protocols. Then, we present two example gossip protocols for membership management [46, 47].

3.3.2.1 System Reliability Epidemics [48] is usually utilized for analysis purposes by expressing the degree of reliability as a probability [44]. Kermarrec et al. [45] theoretically analyzed gossip-based protocols by relating system reliability, measured by the probability of successful information dissemination, to certain essential system parameters such as system size, failure rates, and gossip target number. They show that reliability, resulting from message forwarding redundancy, can be retained by equipping peers with only a randomized partial view of the global membership.

In the *flat* membership protocol, the partial views are uniformly selected among all participating members [45]. The analysis based on the directed random graph model shows that, in a network with n peers, the fanout (i.e., node partial view size) of a peer is with a sharp threshold at $\log(n)$ to guarantee reliability, not growing rapidly with the increase in node failure rates; that is, the success probability is close to 0 for partial views smaller than $\log(n)$, while close to 1 for local views larger than $\log(n)$. This validates the efficacy and resilience of an overlay topology established by connecting each peer with a small set of peers.

However, the network load can be significantly reduced by organizing members into a *hierarchical* structure reflecting network topology. In this fashion, local views of nodes almost exclusively belong to the same cluster with network proximity, and only a small number of intercluster links are necessary to maintain graph connectivity. The intracluster fanout k represents the connection number with other intracluster nodes. Similarly, the intercluster fanout f denotes the link number that each cluster keeps with nodes from other clusters. In particular, in a network with m clusters, each of which has N peers, a target success probability at least $e^{-\beta}$ yields $f = \log N - \log \beta/2$ and $k = \log mN - \log \beta/2$.

3.3.2.2 Example Gossip Protocols The scalable membership protocol (Scamp) [47], as employed by CoolStreaming [49] for the maintenance of mCache, is a decentralized and self-organizing gossip protocol to provide each peer with a partial view of the system. The partial view sizes scale properly with respect to system size n and naturally converge to the point for reliable communication.

New nodes join the system and distribute a *subscription* request to an arbitrary node, called a contact. The contact is the initial partial view of a new node. Upon receiving a new subscription request, a node forwards the node ID of the corresponding new subscriber to all nodes in its own local view and c additional copies of the new subscription to randomly selected nodes in the local view. Here, c is a design parameter dictating the degree of failure tolerance. Upon the arrival of a forwarded subscription, the subscriber of which is not already in its local view, a node will insert the subscriber into its local view with probability p, depending on the local view size. If the new subscriber has not been kept, the node will further forward the subscription to a randomly chosen node from its local view. Each peer maintains a *PartialView* of nodes for subscription forwarding and an *InView* of nodes to receive subscriptions. In the *unsubscription* mechanism, to preserve the scaling property of view size with system size, an unsubscribing node i informs $c + 1$ members in *InView* to simply remove i from their partial views, while the other members to replace it with a peer in i's partial view.

The system evolves toward an average partial view size $(c + 1)\log(n)$, provided that new nodes participate in the network by initiating the subscription request to a uniformly chosen random member, and unsubscriptions are independent of the local view size. The indirection mechanism is proposed to retain the system scalability even in the scenario that newcomers contact a node selected from a few publicly advertised peers. To prevent a disconnected graph with isolated nodes, a heartbeat mechanism is used to detect and recover from node isolation.

HiScamp [46] is a fully decentralized hierarchical membership management protocol using Scamp [47] at each level in the hierarchy. Each cluster is viewed as an abstract node in the upper level. Figure 3.2 illustrates the difference between the flat protocol and the hierarchical gossip with a two-level hierarchy. HiScamp augments Scamp by taking locality into consideration to support cluster-based gossip, and gossip messages are mainly distributed within clusters. Each node keeps two partial views: *hview* with two levels (i.e., level 1 retaining intracluster nodes to gossip and level 2 with intercluster gossip targets) and the intercluster view *iview* of the residential cluster, common to all nodes within the same cluster. A node i joins the overlay by issuing a subscription request to the closest node s. If i is in s's belonging cluster, the subscription is processed using Scamp in the cluster with level 1 of s's *hview* and $|iview(s)| + c$ additional subscription copies will be sent; otherwise, i creates a new cluster, and the subscription is processed at level 2 utilizing *iview* to initiate Scamp. An analogous unsubscription mechanism Scamp is adopted at each level of i's *InView*, including two levels of nodes gossiping to i: level 1 for all intracluster nodes and level 2 for all intercluster nodes. $|iview|$ and $|hview|$ automatically converge to $(c + 1)\log(M)$ and $(c + 1)\log(n)$, respectively, where M is the number of clusters and n is the total node population.

3.3.3 Heterogeneous Overlay Construction

Although gossip-based protocols can achieve system scalability and reliability, peer bandwidth heterogeneity poses new challenges for peer selection scheme design. Specifically, it is desirable to adapt node degrees to bandwidth capacity, constituting

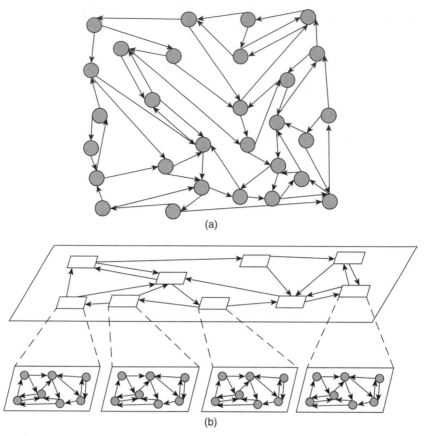

FIGURE 3.2. *The flat and hierarchical membership management [46]. (a) Flat membership protocol. (b) Hierarchical membership protocol.*

a critical step for load balancing. Kwong et al. [50] proposed a scalable and distributed algorithm to construct a capacity-aware topology in a heterogeneous network. The suggested capacity-aware protocol, consisting of two processes: the joining process and the rebuilding process, fully explores high-capacity peers to reduce network diameter.

The joining process is performed to assist newly joining peers to select suitable neighbors by taking node capacity into account. The main idea of the joining process is to connect a newcomer to node i with a probability π_i:

$$\pi_i = \frac{\dfrac{\eta_i}{k_i}}{\sum j \in L(t) \dfrac{\eta_j}{k_j}}, i \in L(t), \tag{3.1}$$

where η_i and k_i, respectively, are the node capacity and node degree of peer i. $L(t)$ is the set of all active nodes in the overlay at time t. Thus, high-capacity peers or low-degree nodes will be connected with higher probabilities.

The rebuilding process is to recover from node departures and henceforth to preclude network breakdown and node isolation. After losing a link, node i rebuilds r_i links to maintain a connected topology. Two rebuilding schemes have been presented: probabilistic-rebuilding scheme and adaptive-rebuilding scheme. In the probabilistic-rebuilding scheme,

$$r_i \triangleq \begin{cases} 1 & k_i^- = 2 \\ r & k_i^- \geq 3 \end{cases}, \tag{3.2}$$

where k_i^- is the node degree of i after a link disconnection. It indicates that each node has to keep at least three links. The adaptive-rebuilding scheme ensures that peers are not overloaded with too many links and, at the same time, maintain connectivity with at least m links. To this end,

$$r_i = \frac{m-1}{k_i^-}. \tag{3.3}$$

Both rebuilding schemes allow a slow growth of the node degree to prevent the overutilization of node resources.

3.3.4 Proximity-Aware Overlay Construction

From the beginning of P2P protocol design, enforcing network proximity by selecting peers with closer physical distance has become an important research direction to improve system performance [30, 51]. It is even more urgent to embed network proximity into system design for scalable video streaming in unstructured overlays, considering its bandwidth-intensive nature. To this end, numerous protocols have been proposed by either building network coordinate systems or not.

3.3.4.1 Network Coordinate Systems
It is difficult and even infeasible to directly measure the distance between any selected peer pair in a large-scale distributed system. Network coordinate systems attempt to embed Internet distances into a virtual geometric space [52–60] in which the distance calculated by the virtual coordinates of two peers is utilized to estimate the end-to-end latency.

Global network positioning (GNP) [55] pioneers and demonstrates the feasibility of Internet latency prediction utilizing network coordinate systems. Nodes in the system adjust their coordinates with respect to a set of landmark nodes $\mathscr{L} = \{L_1, L_2, \ldots, L_{|\mathscr{L}|}\}$. The landmarks' coordinates are calculated by minimizing

$$\sum_{L_i, L_j | i > j} \mathscr{E}\left(d_{L_i L_j}, \hat{d}_{L_i L_j}\right), \tag{3.4}$$

where $\mathscr{E}(\cdot)$ characterizes the measurement errors, and d_{pk} and $\hat{d}_{pk}$, respectively, are the measured and estimated latencies between nodes p and k. A node H can estimate its coordinates by minimizing

$$\sum_{L_i} \mathscr{E}\left(d_{HL_i}, \hat{d}_{HL_i}\right). \tag{3.5}$$

The above minimization problems are approximately solved via the simplex down-hill algorithm [61]. Lighthouses [57], extended from GNP, is more scalable, in which new nodes can relieve the load of landmarks by querying existing nodes instead of landmarks.

Due to the distributed nature of P2P systems, in the following, we review several decentralized virtual coordinate systems. Several challenges exist to design a synthetic coordinate system for large-scale distributed applications [53]: finding a metric space embedding the Internet with little error, scaling to a large node population, decentralized implementation, minimizing probing traffic, and adapting to network dynamics.

PIC [52] is a decentralized network coordinate system. It maps network distances into a d-dimensional Euclidean space. Instead of selecting a fixed landmark set $\mathscr{L}$, PIC maintains a set of peers $\mathscr{N}$, the coordinates of peers in which have already been calculated. Each newly joining peer selects a subset $\mathscr{L}'$ from $\mathscr{N}$, $|\mathscr{L}'| > d$. Similar to GNP, the simplex downhill algorithm is utilized to minimize the error in the predicted distances to all nodes in $\mathscr{L}'$. In this way, it amortizes communication and computation load among distributed nodes. A security test based on triangle inequality is utilized to defend against malicious nodes cheating about their coordinates. Similarly, PCoord [60] also calculates coordinates based on the coordinates of other peers instead of a fixed landmark set. NPS [56] decentralizes the network positioning, similar to PIC and PCoord, but relies on a hierarchical architecture to limit churn and to ensure convergence.

Vivaldi [53] is a decentralized network coordinate system, mimicking a physical mass–spring system and piggybacking probe messages in the application-level traffic. Similar to Vivaldi, big bang simulation [58] also adopts the concept of force field derived from potential energy to embed network distances in Euclidean space. The difference is that it mimics the complicated explosion of particles, in which friction force is introduced to achieve stability. However, how to decentralize it is still unclear [53].

Although low-dimensional virtual spaces can achieve a low-latency prediction error (around 10%), most evaluation studies are based on simulations or small-scale tests on PlanetLab [52, 53, 60]. Prediction errors are inevitable in Euclidean-based embedding due to the violations of triangle inequality. Ledlie et al. [62] tested and experimented the efficacy in the wild by running a million-node network coordinate system in the Azureus file-sharing network [4]. The Azureus data set experiences larger violations than both the MIT King data set [63] and the PlanetLab subset [64], indicating higher errors of Internet-scale network coordinates. However, the Internet can still be embedded into a low-dimensional Euclidean space (e.g., four or five dimensions) due to the flat latency distribution: traffic between Asia and Europe flows through North America.

3.3.4.2 *Proximity Awareness Without Virtual Coordinates*   As noted above, the performance of virtual coordinate systems usually relies on careful parameter selection (e.g., space dimensions d), measurement landmarks, or other supporting mechanisms. Moreover, the estimation errors result in a suboptimal closest node selection. Several proximity-aware overlay construction schemes without network coordinates exist in the literature [65, 66].

Meridian [66], with higher prediction accuracy than both GNP and Vivaldi, utilizes direct probes without the construction of a coordinate space to perform

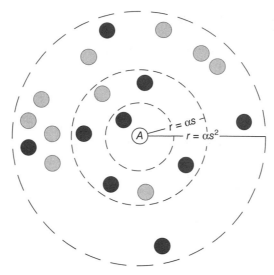

FIGURE 3.3. Each meridian node organizes a fixed number of other nodes into concentric and non-overlapping rings [66].

node selection with network proximity. Each node in Meridian only keeps track of $O(\log n)$ other peers. As shown in Figure 3.3, these peers are organized into a finite number of concentric and nonoverlapping rings of exponentially increasing radii, the ith ring of which is with the inner radius αs^{i-1} and outer radius αs^i, where α is a constant and s is the multiplicative increasing factor. The outermost ring includes all nodes within rings $i > i^*$ with the range $[\alpha s^{i^*}, \infty]$. To propagate a query to a greater region, geographically diverse nodes are maintained within each ring. Meridian utilizes gossip-based node discovery to evenly amortize the maintenance cost among peers.

Meridian [66] can robustly attain the following three goals: closest node discovery, central leader election, and finding nodes within a region bound by multiple latency constraints. Upon receiving a request to discover the closest node to target T, a meridian node with latency d to T will query all ring members within distances $(1 - \beta) \cdot d$ to $(1 + \beta) \cdot d$. The request is propagated to the closest node thus discovered. Smaller acceptance threshold β will result in higher error but with smaller total propagation hops. The process to select the "centrally situated" peers to a target set $\mathcal{T}$ is similar, except that the distance measure is the average latency between the meridian node and all the targets. In node discovery with multiple latency constraints, each constraint is specified by a target node t_i and a latency bound range$_i$, $\forall 0 \le i \le u$. In this manner, the problem is to find nodes satisfying

$$s = \sum_{i=1}^{u} \max(0, d_i - \text{range}_i)^2 = 0, \tag{3.6}$$

where d_i is the latency between the meridian node and t_i. s is the distance measure to meet the latency constraints. Similarly, the meridian node with distance s iteratively queries its peers within the latency range $\max(0, (1 - \beta) \cdot (d_i - \text{range}_i))$ to $(1 + \beta) \cdot (d_i + \text{range}_i)$. It forwards the request to the peer with the closest distance $s_j < \beta \cdot s$, until returning a node satisfying the constraints.

Liu et al. propose a location-aware topology matching (LTM) scheme in References 65 and 67 initially designed to reduce unnecessary query traffic in unstructured P2P file-sharing systems. The basic principle is to detect and disconnect slow overlay links by keeping physically closer nodes measured in terms of network latency as neighbors. Each peer discovers link costs by flooding a TTL2-detector periodically, which can only be propagated for two hops. The source node and all direct neighbors of it will append their own IP addresses and the time stamp to forward the message. The clocks in all peers are synchronized utilizing techniques such as NTP [68]. In this way, the cost of all links between the source node S and the TTL2-detector receiver P can be inferred from the message information.

Following LTM [65], an interoverlay optimization (IOO) scheme is proposed by AnySee [69] to construct an efficient overlay topology by leveraging on interoverlay resources and discovering low-cost source-to-end paths to achieve global network resource optimization and interoverlay load balancing. The mesh overlay manager is based on LTM to optimize the overlay topology by eliminating slow connections. Extensive trace-driven simulation shows that IOO outperforms the CoolStreaming intraoverlay streaming [38] in terms of both resource utilization and streaming QoS. Specifically, with the increase in the overlay number, IOO can achieve better QoS and higher resource utilization.

3.3.5 Locality-Aware Overlay Construction

Several alternatives exist for ISPs to reduce inter-ISP traffic, including bandwidth throttling, gateway peers or cache deployment. Bandwidth throttling limits interdomain traffic or even closes inter-ISP connections (e.g., Comcast [70]) with the sacrifice of user satisfaction. Gateway peers and caches store blocks sent by external peers and redistribute them when requested by internal peers instead of fetching blocks repeatedly from external peers. Obviously, both gateway peers and caches face the problem of scalability.

Bindal et al. [71] propose biased neighbor selection (BNS) to improve traffic locality in BT via topology construction, in which the majority of one's neighbors are from those within the same ISP this peer resides in, while retaining k neighbors from other ISPs. It is assumed that trackers possess perfect locality information of all residing peers in the BT file-sharing networks. In Reference 72, a locality-aware peer selection strategy redirects new joining peers to a selected set of peers, with the assistance of so-called oracle—a centralized service, offered by the ISP and ranking potential neighbors according to preferential metrics. P4P [73] proposes to create an iTracker to recommend peer lists. Ono plugin [74] guides the recommendation of peers in the neighbor set, utilizing the similarity of the redirection ratio of CDN servers without any centralized entity, which is different from the above strategies.

In Reference 75, an approach very similar to BNS is investigated and shows that BT locality enforced with the neighbor set containing almost only local peers enables significant saving on inter-ISP traffic without degrading peer download completion time. As a complementary mechanism to BNS, biased unchoking (BU) [76] divides the neighbor set into two subsets according to locality value and chooses optimistically choked peers from the subset of preferred peers with probability q and with probability $1 - q$ from the other subset. In this literature, the simulation is

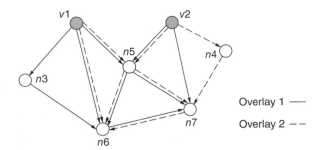

FIGURE 3.4. An example of two concurrent P2P streaming overlays [77].

performed to compare scenarios of regular BT, BT with BNS, BT with BU, and BT with both BNS and BU, with a star AS underlay topology configuration.

Liu et al. [19] go further to construct an AS-level map via on-filed measurements. They evaluate the impact of locality-aware solutions on BT-like P2P applications in terms of both streaming performance and financial cost. The consequent load imbalance points to the necessity of the trade-off between traffic locality and achieving fairness or load balancing among peers.

3.3.6 Interoverlay Cooperation

Wu et al. [77] resolve the bandwidth conflicts among coexisting streaming mesh overlays, in which each peer may participate in multiple overlays, via dynamic bandwidth auction. As shown in Figure 3.4, the example overlay has two streaming servers (i.e., $v1$ and $v2$) and four participating peers. To allocate one's bandwidth among connected peers from multiple overlays, each upstream node i, acting as the auctioneer, independently organizes auction i repeatedly over time. The "goods" for sale is the upload bandwidth of peer i, and downstream peers of i in all its participating overlays are bidders. In each bidding round of auction i, each bidder submits a bid to peer i by indicating the unit price willing to pay and its requested bandwidth share of i's upload capacity. In auction i, upstream peer i allocates its bandwidth by maximizing its revenue. Each bidder j takes the bidding strategy to minimize the incurred cost, including both the latency cost and the bidding cost experienced by peer j streaming from i. In such a fashion, upload bandwidth of both servers and peers in the network is effectively allocated among connected downstream peers from multiple overlays.

Wang et al. [78] propose a bandwidth allocation protocol, named divide and conquer (DAC), for multiview P2P streaming in which each peer may simultaneously watch multiple channel programs. In particular, DAC tackles the cross-channel bandwidth competition problem by first splitting the physically overlapping P2P overlays into logically disjoint overlays and then resolving the utility-based optimal bandwidth allocation. The rationale behind the DAC strategy is to model a single physical peer participating in multiple overlays as multiple independent logical peers. The example shown in Figure 3.5 illustrates three coexisting channels: A, B, and C. For example, user U_2 is split into two independent logical users, U_2^A and U_2^B. The sum of the upload capacity of both logical peers equals the upload capacity of

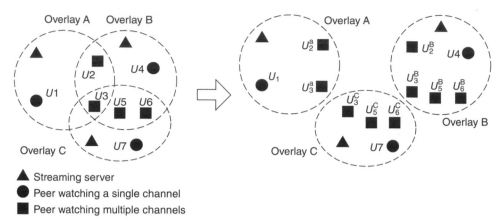

▲ Streaming server
● Peer watching a single channel
■ Peer watching multiple channels

FIGURE 3.5. DAC splits three physically overlapping P2P overlays into three logically disjoint overlays [78].

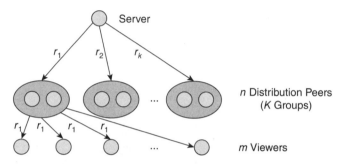

FIGURE 3.6. Substream distribution groups in one channel: The streaming server distributes substreams to each distribution group, which then disseminates the corresponding stream to viewers [80].

U_2. Utility-based global optimization is used to allocate one's bandwidth among its logical peers. Distributed algorithm design is attained via the standard dual decomposition [79]. Simulations show that DAC outperforms the dynamic bandwidth auction scheme as proposed in Reference 77.

To overcome channel churn and channel resource imbalance in multichannel video streaming systems, Wu et al. [80] propose a cross-channel P2P streaming framework, named view-upload decoupling (VUD), via substream swarming. The basic idea of VUD is to decouple the viewing channel from the uploading channel and to achieve cross-channel resource sharing. Inevitable bandwidth overhead, incurred by downloading from an unsubscribed channel, is alleviated via substream swarming. Similar to multiple-tree streaming, each channel is divided into K substreams and each substream r_k is assigned with every Kth constant-size chunk starting with chunk r_k, $0 \leq r_k \leq K - 1$. Peers in each substream swarming establish a substream distribution group and disseminate chunks in the corresponding substream in a P2P manner. The streaming source only distributes each substream to one single peer in the substream distribution group, and each viewer downloads all substreams from all distribution groups as shown in Figure 3.6. Peer assignment to substream distribution groups is achieved by recursively moving low-bandwidth utilization peers from substreams with high-bandwidth provision to others with low-bandwidth availability. VUD substreaming can achieve higher streaming quality compared with the isolated channel design (ISO), in which peers in the same channel cooperate with each other for chunk dissemination.

Wu et al. [81] apply infinite-server Jackson queuing network models to both the ISO and the VUD design to study their asymptotic behaviors for P2P live streaming with both channel churn and peer dynamics. Specifically, it theoretically validates the strength of VUD compared with ISO, and a refined VUD is proposed to further enhance the streaming performance.

3.4 A GAME THEORETIC PERSPECTIVE ON PEER SELECTION

Recently, game theory [82] has been widely utilized as a tool for incentive provision, selfish behavior analysis, and efficient overlay construction [26, 83–88]. The dynamic bandwidth auction [77] as discussed in Section 3.3.6 is an application of game theory to interoverlay bandwidth allocation.

3.4.1 Game Theoretic Incentive Scheme Design

In PPLive [24], three classes of peers coexist: *amplifiers* distributing chunks at rates greatly exceeding the streaming rate, *forwarders* disseminating chunks at roughly the video rate, and *sinks* forwarding very few chunks during the lifetime. Despite their contribution variations, diverse peers almost enjoy the same video streaming rate in PPLive. This shows the necessity of incentive provision for fairness promotion.

Buragohain et al. [83] pioneer game theoretic incentive mechanism design in P2P systems by modeling interactions among rational and strategic peers as a noncooperative game [82]. Peers are rational to maximize their own utility and strategic with the capacity to adjust their own actions (e.g., the level of resource contribution). Contribution of one peer incurs cost to itself while rewarding some other peers. Incentives are provided via differentiated service. The basic idea is to reward peers proportional to their contribution. Nash equilibrium (NE) is adopted for strategic behavior analysis, in which no peer can gain by unilaterally changing its strategy.

However, incentive provision for multimedia streaming exhibits particular characteristics. Measurement studies [24, 89] on both PPLive and UUSee have demonstrated a significant reciprocal relationship for chunk exchange among peers in the mesh-based overlays. This may explain the efficacy of a tit for tat [35] like strategy combining with MDC as proposed in Reference 90 to provide redistribution incentives via service differentiation in heterogeneous networks. The main idea is to exploit the direct chunk exchange relationships between connected peers by rewarding high-contributing neighbors more.

Parallel to this line of thought, Yeung and Kwok [88] propose the repeated packet exchange game (PEG) to motivate cooperation between two neighboring peers and packet distribution game (PDG) to promote immediate neighbors (i.e., peers receiving streaming packets directly from the server) to contribute more bandwidth to further packet routing. In PEG, the punish-k strategy is adopted by contributing less for k periods as punishments if the counterpart deviates from an initial high contribution. PDG is a strategic game between the server s and immediate peers. The basic principle is that the server s's bandwidth assignment to immediate peer p is proportional to p's bandwidth contribution to others.

Lin et al. [86] propose cheat-proof and attack-resistant cooperation strategies for P2P live streaming. A two-player P2P live streaming game model is first studied. The cost of sending a chunk is the chunk size over its total data sending capacity during each time period, by taking peer heterogeneity into account from a practical point of view. To attain cheat prevention, each peer only sends no more chunks than it receives from its counterpart. However, in real-deployed networks, a peer maximizes its utility by optimally requesting from multiple user neighbors and the repeated game model is no longer applicable because mutual benefits cannot be simultaneously guaranteed. To this end, they propose a multiuser cooperation strategy in which peer i requests chunks from peer j with the highest successful chunk reception probability. Attack resistance is achieved via a credit mechanism in which the number of extra chunks that i successfully sends to j compared with the number that it successfully receives from j by time t is upper bound by the credit line.

Recently, several adaptive learning models [85, 91] are proposed in the literature. Zhao et al. [91] provide a general analytical framework by stochastically investigating the evolution of incentive policies. In particular, peers will learn from the environment and adapt to strategies with higher expected gain. Two learning models are discussed to this end: Each peer switches to the strategy currently with the highest expected gain with certain probability in the *current-best learning* model, while it randomly selects a teacher in the *opportunistic learning* model and adapts to its strategy if it can achieve higher gain. The current-best learning requires an entity with certain centralized authority to find the current-best strategy. Yet, the opportunistic learning can be attained in a distributed fashion.

A reinforcement learning-based mechanism by modeling interactions among peers as a repeated game is proposed in Reference 85 to improve fairness and to discourage free riding in BT systems. The basic idea is to learn from partial interaction histories between peers and to determine repeatedly peer selection policies seeking for utility maximization measured by the discounted average of forecasted upload rates obtained from neighboring peers.

3.4.2 Selfish Overlay Construction

In Reference 87, Moscibroda et al. investigate the impact of selfish neighbor selection from a game theoretic perspective. Specifically, they assume that egoistic peers exploit network proximity and avoid to maintain too many neighbors. The Price of Anarchy, the worst NE social cost over the optimal topology social cost, is used to bound the performance degradation incurred by selfish peers. In particular, for any metric space in which peers are arbitrarily located, higher link maintenance cost results in more deteriorated topologies. Intriguingly, even a static P2P network with such selfish peers may never achieve a stable topology due to consistent strategy changes. It is NP-hard to decide the existence of NE for a given P2P network.

Chen et al. [84] investigate interactions among geographically neighboring peers to serve as agents to download chunks from peers outside the neighboring group. Efforts are exerted to act as agents due to the low-speed intergroup links, while streaming quality suffers, if without enough agents in a neighboring group. An evolutionary game is established to analyze one's willingness to serve as an agent, and an evolutionarily stable strategy is approached by learning from one's own payoff history.

3.4.3 Game Theoretic Efficient Overlay Construction

In structured P2P media streaming, peers judiciously select its upstream and downstream peers. Yeung and Kwok [26] model such peer selection as a cooperative game [82] by taking node bandwidth capacity into account, in which the players are parent p and its children $c_1, c_2, \ldots, c_n$. In the cooperative game, a coalition G includes a subset of peers with the aggregate value (i.e., total payoff):

$$V(G) = \sum_{x \in G} v(x), \tag{3.7}$$

from which player x receives the share of value $v(x)$. The design objective is to establish a stable coalition in which each peer possesses no incentive to leave the current one either unilaterally or as a group with some other peers.

In the proposed peer selection protocol, upon receiving a connection request from a candidate child x with $v(x) \geq e$, parent y will reply with a normalized bandwidth allocation with respect to the streaming rate

$$b(x, y) = \alpha \times v(x), \tag{3.8}$$

where $v(x) = V(G \cup x) - V(G) - e$ and e is the contribution effort of a child in the coalition. Peer x joins the streaming overlay by first obtaining a list of candidate parents, to which it sends connection requests. Based on the received bandwidth allocation, it iteratively contacts and accepts the parent with the highest bandwidth allocation until the total bandwidth allocation from all its parents is no smaller than the streaming rate.

To equip higher bandwidth peers with more resilience to peer dynamics, they are assigned with more upstream peers. To attain this, a specific value function is well crafted:

$$V(G) = \begin{cases} \log\left(1 + \sum_{\forall i \neq p} \dfrac{1}{b_i}\right) & p \in G \\ 0 & \text{otherwise,} \end{cases} \tag{3.9}$$

where b_x represents the total outbound bandwidth contribution of x. Therefore, $v(x)$ decreases with respect to b_x, resulting in more connected parents for nodes with higher outbound bandwidths. Simulations demonstrate the strength of the proposed protocol to improve streaming quality in the presence of peer dynamics.

3.5 DISCUSSION AND FUTURE WORK

Despite the large body of literature on peer selection for scalable video streaming, several promising research arenas deserve deeper investigation. First, current studies on traffic locality to confine chunk dissemination within the same ISP or AS still rely on the complete information. Obviously, this deviates from the scalable principle of P2P system design. It is still unclear how to decentralize locality-aware peer selection. The conflict between traffic locality and load imbalance implies another future research direction to strike a trade-off between traffic locality and load balancing so that moderate network friendliness can be retained, provided that system performance is not deteriorated at the same time. Moreover, current cross-channel cooperation schemes perform a thorough study on bandwidth allocation among coexisting overlays. However, peers, including multichannel participating nodes, are selfish, and incentive provision is thus critical to promoting interoverlay cooperation, which is still a hitherto uncharted research avenue. Interoverlay bandwidth allocation is only an essential building block of cross-channel cooperation. However, how to schedule chunks by efficiently exploiting the allocated bandwidth and how to actively match bandwidth-deficient peers with bandwidth-rich nodes in a distributed manner are still largely unexplored. Finally, existing works on incentive provision prohibitively focus on resource sharing (i.e., chunk reciprocation) relationships among connected peers. However, if we look into the big picture of the entire overlay topology, peers are selfish even if they are willing to contribute local resources. In particular, peers may favor others with high-bandwidth access or in the proximity for connection. In a more idealistic fashion, peers are able to adaptively explore topological features of the streaming overlay on behalf of its own long-term interest. Therefore, an in-depth investigation into the evolutionary dynamics from such a perspective is promising. Specifically, it is intriguing to study the coexistence of multiple peer types or various features as exhibited by rational peers in diverse overlay topologies.

3.6 SUMMARY

P2P video streaming overlays are inherently constructed via the neighboring relationships among distributed peers. To guarantee high streaming performance, in the presence of system dynamics, judicious peer selection is inevitable to attain efficient overlay construction. In this chapter, we first systematically scrutinize diverse state-of-the-art peer selection schemes, seeking for random, heterogeneous, network-aware, or cross-channel overlay construction. Then, we provide a survey on game theoretic peer selection, considering that game theory has recently been widely adopted in the research community for both modeling endeavors and efficient scheme design.

Gossip-based protocols effectively decentralize the membership management. Yet, peers are endowed with heterogeneous bandwidth capacity. Therefore, heterogeneous peer selection is a crucial step to attain load balancing by adapting node degree to bandwidth capacity. Topology matching effectively localizes streaming traffic in the Internet. Cross-channel cooperation sheds light on solutions to channel resource imbalance in multichannel streaming systems by reallocating node bandwidth among multiple overlays. We expect bandwidth allocation schemes, in which peers can *actively* help the streaming of unsubscribed channels.

Game theoretic studies are most widely used for incentive provision to preclude free-riding behaviors in P2P streaming systems. Until recently, the impact of peer rationality on overlay construction is investigated in a few studies. For example, peers may favor peers with certain network proximity. However, the topological dynamics in P2P overlays indicates the problem complexity, going beyond the single metric of network distance. Peer rationality to exploit network characteristics thus constitutes a research arena in prospect.

REFERENCES

[1] S. Androutsellis-Theotokis and D. Spinellis, "A survey of peer-to-peer content distribution technologies," *ACM Computing Surveys*, 36(4):335–371, 2004.

[2] Y.-K. Kwok, "Autonomic peer-to-peer systems: Incentive and security issues," in *Autonomic Computing and Networking*, Chapter 9 (M.K. Denko, L.T. Yang, and Y. Zhang, eds.), pp. 205–238. Bloomingdale, IL: Springer, 2009.

[3] Y. Liu, Y. Guo, and C. Liang, "A survey on peer-to-peer video streaming systems," *Peer-to-Peer Networking and Applications*, 1(1):18–28, 2008.

[4] Azureus. 2011. Available at http://azureus.sourceforge.net.

[5] BitTorrent. 2011. Available at http://www.bittorrent.com.

[6] eDonkey. 2011. Available at http://www.emule.com.

[7] PPLive. 2011. Available at http://www.pptv.com.

[8] PPStream. 2011. Available at http://www.pps.tv/.

[9] Skype. 2011. Available at http://www.skype.com.

[10] SopCast. 2011. Available at http://www.sopcast.org.

[11] TVAnts. 2011. Available at http://tvants.en.softonic.com.

[12] UUSee. 2011. Available at http://www.uusee.com.

[13] S. Douglas, E. Tanin, A. Harwood, and S. Karunasekera, "Enabling massively multiplayer online gaming applications on a P2P architecture," in *Proceedings of the International Conference on Information and Automation*, December 2005.

[14] L. Fan, H. Taylor, and P. Trinder, "Mediator: A design framework for P2P MMOGs," in *Proceedings of NetGames*, September 2007.

[15] S.-Y. Hu, T.-H. Huang, S.-C. Chang, W.-L. Sung, J.-R. Jiang, and B.-Y. Chen, "FLoD: A framework for peer-to-peer 3D streaming," in *Proceedings of IEEE INFOCOM*, April 2008.

[16] M. Varvello, C. Diot, and E. Biersack, "A walkable kademlia network for virtual worlds," in *Proceedings of IPTPS*, April 2009.

[17] M. Varvello, C. Diot, and E. Biersack, "P2P second life: Experimental validation using Kad," in *Proceedings of IEEE INFOCOM*, April 2009.

[18] K. Xu, H. Li, J. Liu, W. Zhu, and W. Wang, "PPVA: A universal and transparent peer-to-peer accelerator for interactive online video sharing," in *Proceedings of IEEE IWQoS*, June 2010.

[19] B. Liu, Y. Cui, Y. Lu, and Y. Xue, "Locality-awareness in BitTorrent-Like P2P applications," *IEEE Transactions on Multimedia*, 11(3):361–371, 2009.

[20] J. Jannotti, D.K. Gifford, and K.L. Johnson, "Overcast: Reliable multicasting with an overlay network," in *Proceedings of Operating Systems Design And Implementation*, October 2000.

[21] M. Castro, P. Druschel, A.-M. Kermarrec, and A. Nandi, "SplitStream: High-bandwidth multicast in cooperative environments," in *Proceedings of ACM SOSP*, October 2003.

[22] V.N. Padmanabhan, H.J. Wang, and P.A. Chou, "Resilient peer-to-peer streaming," in *Proceedings of IEEE ICNP*, November 2003.

[23] D. Ciullo, M.A. Garcia, A. Horvath, E. Leonardi, M. Mellia, D. Rossi, M. Telek, and P. Veglia, "Network awareness of P2P live streaming applications: A measurement study," *IEEE Transactions on Multimedia*, 12(1):54–63, 2010.

[24] X. Hei, C. Liang, J. Liang, Y. Liu, and K.W. Ross, "A measurement study of a large-scale P2P IPTV system," *IEEE Transactions on Multimedia*, 9(8):1672–1687, 2007.

[25] L. Vu, I. Gupta, J. Liang, and K. Nahrstedt, "Measurement and modeling of a large-scale overlay for multimedia streaming," in *Proceedings of QShine*, August 2007.

[26] M.K.H. Yeung and Y.-K. Kwok, "On game theoretic peer selection for resilient peer-to-peer media streaming," *IEEE Transactions on Parallel and Distributed Systems*, 20(10):1512–1525, 2009.

[27] A.P.C. da Silva, E. Leonardi, M. Mellia, and M. Meo, "A bandwidth-aware scheduling strategy for P2P-TV systems," in *Proceedings of IEEE P2P*, September 2008.

[28] C. Liang, Y. Guo, and Y. Liu, "Investigating the scheduling sensitivity of P2P video streaming: An experimental study," *IEEE Transactions on Multimedia*, 11(3):348–360, 2009.

[29] V.N. Padmanabhan, H.J. Wan, P.A. Chou, and K. Sripanidkulchai, "Distributing streaming media content using cooperative networking," in *Proceedings of the 12th International Workshop on Network and Operating Systems Support for Digital Audio and Video*, May 2002.

[30] A. Rowstron and P. Druschel, "Pastry: Scalable, decentralized object location and routing for large-scale peer-to-peer systems," in *Proceedings of the 18th IFIP/ACM International Conference on Distributed Systems Platforms (Middleware 2001)*, November 2001.

[31] M. Castro, P. Druschel, A.-M. Kermarrec, and A.I.T. Rowstron, "Scribe: A large-scale and decentralized application-level multicast infrastructure," *IEEE Journal on Selected Areas in Communications*, 20(8):1489–1499, 2002.

[32] V.N. Padamanabban and L. Subramanian, "Determining the geographic location of internet hosts," in *Proceedings of ACM SIGMETRICS*, June 2001.

[33] N. Magharei, R. Rejaie, and Y. Guo, "Mesh or multiple-tree: A comparative study of live P2P streaming approaches," in *Proceedings of IEEE INFOCOM*, May 2007.

[34] N. Magharei and R. Rejaie, "PRIME: Peer-to-peer receiver-driven mesh-based streaming," *IEEE/ACM Transactions on Networking*, 17(4):1052–1065, 2009.

[35] B. Cohen, "Incentives build robustness in BitTorrent," in *Proceedings of the Second Workshop on the Economics of Peer-to-Peer Systems*, June 2003.

[36] H. Li, X. Ke, and J. Seng, "Towards health of replication in large-scale P2P-VoD systems," in *Proceedings of IEEE IPCCC*, December 2009.

[37] W. Wu and J.C.S. Lui, "Exploring the optimal replication strategy in P2P-VoD systems: Characterization and evaluation," in *Proceedings of IEEE INFOCOM*, April 2011.

[38] X. Zhang, J. Liut, B. Lis, and T.-S.P. Yum, "CoolStreamingDONet: A data-driven overlay network for peer-to-peer live media streaming," in *Proceedings of IEEE INFOCOM*, March 2005.

[39] L. Vu, I. Gupta, K. Nahrstedt, and J. Liang, "Understanding overlay characteristics of a large-scale peer-to-peer IPTV system," *ACM Transactions on Multimedia Computing, Communications, and Applications*, 6(4):31.1–31.24, 2010.

[40] D.J. Watts and S.H. Strogatz, "Collective dynamics of 'Small-World' networks," *Nature*, 393(6684):440–442, 1998.

[41] C. Wu, B. Li, and S. Zhao, "Diagnosing network-wide P2P live streaming inefficiencies," in *Proceedings of IEEE INFOCOM*, April 2009.

[42] A. Demers, D. Greene, C. Hauser, W. Irish, J. Larson, S. Shenker, H. Sturgis, D. Swinehart, and D. Terry, "Epidemic algorithms for replicated database maintenance," in *Proceedings of ACM PODC*, August 1987.

[43] K.P. Birman, M. Hayden, O. Ozkasap, Z. Xiao, M. Budiu, and Y. Minsky, "Bimodal multicast," *ACM Transactions on Computer Systems*, 17(2):41–88, 1999.

[44] P.T. Eugster, R. Guerraoui, S.B. Handurukande, P. Kouznetsov, and A.-M. Kermarre, "Lightweight probabilistic broadcast," *ACM Transactions on Computer Systems*, 21(4): 341–374, 2003.

[45] A.-M. Kermarrec, L. Massoulie, and A.J. Ganesh, "Probabilistic reliable dissemination in large-scale systems," *IEEE Transactions on Parallel and Distributed Systems*, 14(3): 248–258, 2003.

[46] A.-M. Kermarrec, A.J. Ganesh, and L. Massoulie, "HiScamp: Self-organizing hierarchical membership protocol," in *Proceedings of ACM SIGOPS European workshop*, July 2002.

[47] A.-M. Kermarrec, A.J. Ganesh, and L. Massoulie, "Peer-to-peer membership management for gossip-based protocols," *IEEE Transactions on Computers*, 52(2):139–149, 2003.

[48] N.T.J. Bailey, *The Mathematical Theory of Infectious Diseases and Its Applications*. New York: Hafner Press, 1975.

[49] M. Zhang, J.-G. Luo, L. Zhao, and S.-Q. Yang, "A peer-to-peer network for live media streaming—Using a push-pull approach," in *Proceedings of ACM Multimedia*, November 2005.

[50] K.-W. Kwong and D.H.K. Tsang, "Building heterogeneous peer-to-peer networks: Protocol and analysis," *IEEE/ACM Transactions on Networking*, 16(2):281–292, 2008.

[51] F. Dabek, J. Li, E. Sit, J. Robertson, M.F. Kaashoek, and R. Morris, "Designing a DHT for low latency and high throughput," in *Proceedings of USENIX NSDI*, March 2004.

[52] M. Costa, M. Castro, A. Rowstron, and P. Key, "PIC: Practical internet coordinates for distance estimation," in *Proceedings of ICDCS*, March 2004.

[53] F. Dabek, R. Cox, F. Kaashoek, and R. Morris, "Vivaldi: A decentralized network coordinate system," in *Proceedings of ACM SIGCOMM*, August 2004.

[54] H. Lim, J.C. Hou, and C.-H. Choi, "Constructing internet coordinate system based on delay measurement," in *Proceedings of Internet Measurement Conference*, Octobor 2003.

[55] T.S.E. Ng and H. Zhang, "Predicting internet network distance with coordinates-based approaches," in *Proceedings of IEEE INFOCOM*, June 2002.

[56] T.S.E. Ng and H. Zhang, "A network positioning system for the internet," in *Proceedings of USENIX*, June 2004.

[57] M. Pias, J. Crowcroft, S. Wilbur, T. Harris, and S. Bhatti, "Lighthouses for scalable distributed location," in *Proceedings of IPTPS*, February 2003.

[58] Y. Shavitt and T. Tankel, "Big-bang simulation for embedding network distances in euclidean space," in *Proceedings of IEEE INFOCOM*, April 2003.

[59] L. Tang and M. Crovella, "Virtual landmarks for the internet," in *Proceedings of Internet Measurement Conference*, Octobor 2003.

[60] L. Lehman and S. Lerman, "PCoord: Network position estimation using peer-to-peer measurements," in *Proceedings of IEEE NCA*, August 2004.

[61] J.A. Nelder and R. Mead, "A simplex method for function minimization," *The Computer Journal*, 7(4):308–313, 1965.

[62] J. Ledlie, P. Gardner, and M. Seltzer, "Network coordinates in the wild," in *Proceedings of NSDI*, April 2007.

[63] K.P. Gummadi, S. Saroiu, and S.D. Gribble, "King: Estimating latency between arbitrary internet end hosts," in *Proceedings of SIGCOMM IMW*, November 2002.

[64] J. Stribling, All-pairs-ping trace of PlanetLab, 2011. Available at http://pdos.csail.mit.edu/~strib/.

[65] Y. Liu, L. Xiao, X. Liu, L.M. Ni, and X. Zhang, "Location awareness in unstructured peer-to-peer systems," *IEEE Transactions on Parallel and Distributed Systems*, 16(2):163–174, 2005.

[66] B. Wong, A. Slivkins, and E.G. Sirer, "Meridian: A lightweight network location service without virtual coordinates," in *Proceedings of ACM SIGCOMM*, August 2005.

[67] Y. Liu, L. Xiao, X. Liu, L.M. Ni, and X. Zhang, "A two-hop solution to solving topology mismatch," *IEEE Transactions on Parallel and Distributed Systems*, 19(11):1591–1600, 2008.

[68] NTP: The Network Time Protocol. 2011. Available at http://www.ntp.org.

[69] X. Liao, H. Jin, Y. Liu, and L.M. Ni, "Scalable live streaming service based on interoverlay optimization," *IEEE Transactions on Parallel and Distributed Systems*, 18(12):1663–1674, 2007.

[70] Comcast Throttles BitTorrent Traffic. 2007. Available at http://torrentfreak.com/comcast-throttles-bittorrent-traffic-seeding-impossible.

[71] R. Bindal, P. Cao, and W. Chan, "Improving traffic locality in BitTorrent via biased neighbor selection," in *Proceedings of IEEE ICDCS*, July 2006.

[72] V. Aggarwal, A. Feldmann, and C. Scheideler, "Can ISPs and P2P users cooperate for improved performance? *ACM SIGCOMM Computer Communication Review*, 37(3):29–40, 2007.

[73] H. Xie, Y.R. Yang, A. Krishnamurthy, Y. Liu, and A. Silberschatz, "P4P: Provider portal for applications," in *Proceedings of ACM SIGCOMM*, August 2008.

[74] D.R. Choffnes and F.E. Bustamante, "Taming the torrent: A practical approach to reducing cross-ISP traffic in P2P systems," in *Proceedings of ACM SIGCOMM*, August 2008.

[75] S. Le Blond, A. Legout, and W. Dabbous, "Pushing BitTorrent locality to the limit," *Computer Networks*, 55(3):541–557, 2011.

[76] S. Oechsner, F. Lehrieder, T. Hoßfeld, F. Metzger, D. Staehle, and K. Pussep, "Pushing the performance of biased neighbor selection through biased unchoking," in *Proceedings of IEEE P2P*, September 2009.

[77] C. Wu, B. Li, and Z. Li, "Dynamic bandwidth auctions in multi-overlay P2P streaming with network coding," *IEEE Transactions on Parallel and Distributed Systems*, 19(6):806–820, 2008.

[78] M. Wang, L. Xu, and B. Ramamurthy, "A flexible divide-and-conquer protocol for multi-view peer-to-peer live streaming," in *Proceedings of IEEE P2P*, September 2009.

[79] D.P. Palomar and M. Chiang, "Alternative distributed algorithms for network utility maximization: Framework and applications," *IEEE Transactions on Automatic Control*, 52(12):2254–2269, 2007.

[80] D. Wu, C. Liang, Y. Liu, and K. Ross, "View-upload decoupling: A redesign of multi-channel P2P video systems," in *Proceedings of IEEE INFOCOM Mini-Conference*, April 2009.

[81] D. Wu, Y. Liu, and K.W. Ross, "Queueing network models for multi-channel P2P live streaming systems," in *Proceedings of IEEE INFOCOM*, April 2009.

[82] M.J. Osborne, *An Introduction to Game Theory*. New York: Oxford University Press, 2004.

[83] C. Buragohain, D. Agrawal, and S. Suri, "A robust protocol for building superpeer overlay topologies," in *Proceedings of IEEE P2P*, August 2004.

[84] Y. Chen, B. Wang, W.S. Lin, Y. Wu, and K.J.R. Liu, "Cooperative peer-to-peer streaming: An evolutionary game-theoretic approach," *IEEE Transactions on Circuits and Systems for Video Technology*, 20(10):1346–1357, 2010.

[85] R. Izhak-Ratzin, H. Park, and M. van der Schaar, "Reinforcement learning in BitTorrent systems," in *Proceedings of IEEE INFOCOM*, April 2011.

[86] W.S. Lin, H.V. Zhao, and K.J.R. Liu, "Incentive cooperation strategies for peer-to-peer live multimedia streaming social networks," *IEEE Transactions on Multimedia*, 11(3):396–412, 2009.

[87] T. Moscibroda, S. Schmid, and R. Wattenhofer, "On the topologies formed by selfish peers," in *Proceedings of ACM PODC*, July 2006.

[88] M.K.H. Yeung and Y.-K. Kwok, "Game-theoretic scalable peer-to-peer media streaming," in *Proceedings of IEEE IPDPS*, April 2008.

[89] C. Wu and B. Li, "Exploring large-scale peer-to-peer live streaming topologies," *ACM Transactions on Multimedia Computing, Communications, and Applications*, 4(3):19.1–19.23, 2008.

[90] Z. Liu, Y. Shen, S.S. Panwar, K.W. Ross, and Y. Wan, "P2P video live streaming with MDC: Providing incentives for redistribution," in *Proceedings of IEEE ICME*, July 2007.

[91] B.Q. Zhao, J.C.S. Lui, and D.-M. Chi, "Analysis of adaptive incentive protocols for P2P networks," in *Proceedings of IEEE INFOCOM*, April 2009.

4

Multicore and Many-Core Computing

Ioannis E. Venetis

Multicore and future many-core processors (which are generally considered to be processors that include over 100 cores) have brought a great deal of changes in the way that programmers and users view computer systems. Concepts previously known to a relatively small and specialized community, like parallelism and synchronization, have now forcefully entered the everyday life of many more people. A common question is why we moved to this new technology. Uniprocessor systems have served us well for the last few decades. A vast number of tools have been developed over the years, which made programming and use of these systems easy and intuitive. Improvements in execution speed have made it possible to implement and use applications that were previously impossible to use. In this chapter, we will try to understand why this well-established development model of processors and applications had to be changed. We will analyze the main obstacles that appeared in the development of uniprocessor systems and how they led to the development of multicore systems. Furthermore, we will discuss current trends in the architecture of multicore systems and the obstacles that have to be overcome and will lead to many-core systems. Finally, we will cover the impact that changes made in the hardware have in the development of software and how this leads to the introduction of programming models that are tailored toward multicore systems.

4.1 INTRODUCTION

The first ever microprocessor was introduced from Intel in 1971. The 4004 was a simple 4-bit, in-order microprocessor clocked at 740 kHz, primarily intended for

Scalable Computing and Communications: Theory and Practice, First Edition. Edited by
Samee U. Khan, Albert Y. Zomaya, and Lizhe Wang.
© 2013 John Wiley & Sons, Inc. Published 2013 by John Wiley & Sons, Inc.

calculators and for other calculator-like products like cash registers and banking teller equipment. Its 2300 transistors seem nowadays like a very small number, but at that time, it was a huge achievement that allowed a great innovation. For the first time, a complete CPU had been put on a single chip. About a year later, Intel introduced the 8008 microprocessor, which included 3500 transistors, and some implementations were clocked at 800 kHz. The additional transistors were used to extend the microprocessor to an 8-bit design. Continuing improvements in technology allowed Intel to introduce the 8080 in 1974, another 8-bit microprocessor that consisted of 6000 transistors and was clocked up to 2 MHz. In 1977, it introduced the 8085 with 6500 transistors and a clock rate of up to 6 MHz. The first 16-bit microprocessor from Intel was introduced in 1978. The 8086 included 29,000 transistors and was running at a clock speed of up to 10 MHz. This processor was the basis for the well-known series of "x86" processors from Intel. The list continues with many more processors, up to the latest single-core processor, the Core 2 Solo SU3500, with 410 million transistors running at 1.4 GHz.

Other lines of microprocessors followed a similar trend. The Alpha developed by Digital Equipment Corporation (DEC) started with the EV4 in 1992. It contained 1.68 million transistors and was initially clocked at 100 MHz. The last processor of this line was produced in 2004 containing 130 million transistors and was running at 1.3 GHz. Similarly, the first processor of the MIPS architecture was introduced in 1985. The R2000 contained 110,000 transistors and was clocked at 8 MHz. The R16000 introduced in 2002 was the last single-core processor of the series. It contained 7.2 million transistors and was clocked up to 1 GHz.

From the above, it is obvious that the main improvement that led to faster uniprocessor systems over the past decades was the increase in the number of transistors that could be integrated into a single chip and the increase in clock speed. Software development companies started to rely on this fact. They were continuously identifying application areas for which older hardware was not powerful enough, but current hardware would achieve the lowest acceptable limits of execution time. Hence, more demanding applications pushed the existing hardware components to their limits. Games, financial applications, databases, and simulations are a few examples of such applications. Computer architects tried to respond to the increasing demands of applications and improved their designs, building on top of the advancements in integrated circuit technology. Naturally, software developers improved or added more functionality to their existing applications but also further expanded their application areas to take advantage of the improved performance of the new systems. This led to a cycle of hardware and software improvements that served the computing industry well for decades.

Alongside with the above developments, new fields in computer science emerged. Data structures to efficiently represent data that are required in different situations and improved algorithms that perform fewer operations to complete the same calculations are typical examples. In addition, improvements in tools to create applications were also impressive. Compilers, integrated development environments (IDEs), programming languages, debuggers, and profilers helped programmers to create software faster, with fewer errors, and with better user interfaces. Naturally, all these tools targeted serial computing systems since this was the dominating architecture. Although parallel systems were available, they were targeted toward specific applications with extremely large computations. Hence, their development and improvements in ease of programming were quite slower. As we will see, however, this has now started to change.

Ironically, the two main pillars on which the hardware–software cycle rested for so many years, the increase of the number of transistors in a chip and the increase in clock speed, are the reasons for which this model seems currently to fade out, giving its place to multicore architectures. This has profound implications at many levels of the hardware and software industry. On one hand, a larger area of the hardware design space is currently being explored in order to pinpoint the best choices for the emerging multicore architectures. On the other hand, programming these new systems is not as straightforward as uniprocessor systems, and programmers have to familiarize themselves with new concepts. Despite these difficulties, it seems that currently, this is a one-way path that we have to walk in order to continue to improve our computing systems.

4.1.1 Implications of Moore's Law

In 1965, Intel cofounder Gordon E. Moore described a trend about the number of transistors that can be placed on an integrated circuit [1]. The observation, now known as Moore's law, states that the number of transistors that can fit on a given area of a chip doubles approximately every 2 years. The law has since been used in the semiconductor industry to guide long-term planning and to set targets for research and development. Figure 4.1 shows the number of transistors for different architectures throughout time.

In the early stages of integrated circuits and single chip processors, Moore's law has been an invaluable tool. It was now possible to predict the number of transistors that a future implementation of a processor could include and to start designing it far ahead, including features that would be possible to implement with the predicted numbers. Over the years, there have been many interesting ideas that could increase

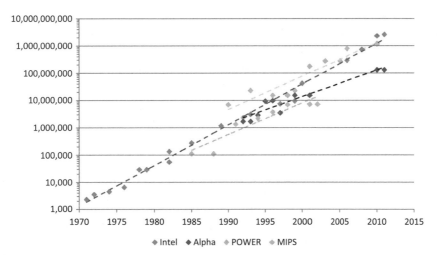

FIGURE 4.1. *Number of transistors over time for four different architectures. The graph illustrates that the number of transistors increases more or less exponentially over time. The rate of increase is not dependent on the specific architecture of the processor.*

the performance of a processor but could not be implemented due to the limited number of available transistors. Moore's law and the advancements in technology behind it allowed these ideas to evolve and to be included one after the other in processors.

An example of such an advancement was the use of a cache memory hierarchy, which dates back to the early 1960s. Due to scarcity and the high cost of semiconductor memories, computers of the time used several types of memory to fetch data and instructions into the fastest available memory type, before the processor actually needed the data. These techniques were further developed, and in 1968, the first documented use of a data cache appeared in the IBM System/360 Model 85 [2]. Later on, the first level of cache was integrated into the same chip with the processor, and soon, the second level followed. Moore's law allowed the expansion of caches into larger and larger sizes. This improved the execution speed of applications since it was possible for them to store more of their frequently used data in a fast memory. Recently, however, the size of the cache has not increased as rapidly as in the past. The reason for this change was the realization that every application has a maximum working set, that is, data that have to be accessed over a period of time in order to complete a calculation [3]. If all data of the working set reside in the cache, then there is no meaning to add larger caches to a system since applications will not be able to exploit it. As a result, even though larger caches could be integrated into current processor architectures due to increasing numbers of available transistors, the benefit would be minimal.

A second example in this category is the exploitation of instruction-level parallelism (ILP). A multitude of techniques have been developed to execute multiple instructions of a program at the same time. The first and probably best known is the introduction of the pipeline in processors. Instructions are divided into smaller basic operations. Each operation is handled at one level of the pipeline and the results are handed over to the next level. When this happens, the previous level can start executing the corresponding operation of the next instruction in the program. As a result, multiple instructions are executing concurrently, although they are at different stages of their execution. Naturally, the introduction of the pipeline required the addition of more logic into the chip, which was possible by the increased number of transistors. Some processors reached up to more than 20 stages in their pipelines. Obviously handling the logic of such large pipelines requires a large amount of transistors. Eventually, however, it became clear that increasing the size of the pipeline did not contribute to better performance of the processor. In the same way that caches reached their point of diminishing returns, pipelines also eventually reached it.

In the same category of exposing more ILP fits also branch prediction. The idea behind branch prediction is to record the history of branches and to determine when they are taken and when not. Using this statistical analysis, processors try to predict whether the next branch will be taken or not. In order to keep the history of already executed branches, branch-prediction buffers are required. A considerable amount of bits has to be used for this purpose. Again, the increase in the number of transistors made this technique applicable. But again, adding more and more entries to the buffer had, after some point, no more effect in the performance of applications.

Another important idea that is worth mentioning is multiple issue of instructions. Instead of reading one after another instruction from memory and feeding it into the pipeline of the processor for execution, it is possible to fetch more instructions at once. If these instructions are of a different kind (e.g., an instruction that operates on integer numbers, another one that operates on floating-point numbers, and another one that accesses memory), then these could potentially be executed simultaneously. In order to achieve this, there have to be separate functional units that can execute all of these instructions at the same time. Moreover, since the mix of instructions might not always be the same as in the example, there should be more replicas of the same functional units to handle this case. Not surprisingly, all this adds again to the logic required for the processor to operate correctly and to output the results in the order that is expected by the program. As you might already have guessed, again there is a limit in this method. It is not by chance that most processors issue two, three, or four instructions at most at any point in time. There are a few exceptions, like the Intel Itanium processor that issues up to six instructions, but this is due to the fact that it belongs to another category of processors.

The list could continue with more techniques that improve performance of processors [4, 5]. However, the discussions about these techniques would all end with the same observation. Adding transistors to enhance each one of them leads to a point where more transistors do not improve performance anymore. But this observation creates a question that is essential for the computer industry. Moore's law still holds and more transistors will be available, at least for the near future. What should we do with these transistors, if all techniques that we have incorporated into our processors have reached their limit? I assume from the discussion up to this point that the answer is already in the mind of the reader. Since we have twice as many transistors every 2 years, why do we not simply put two identical processors on the same chip? This would double the computing power of a processor and would allow applications to run faster. And this is exactly the path that most, if not all, hardware vendors currently follow. And until some radical changes happen, it is foreseen that more and more cores will be added to processors.

4.1.2 Implications of Frequency Scaling

The use of a signal that synchronizes execution of operations across all functional units within a processor, the clock as it is commonly known, prevailed as a method to operate processors. Synchronizing all functional units makes their design much easier and also simplifies the interaction among them. Now every unit can propagate its results to the next unit only at specific points in time. However, since all units are bound through the clock in order to propagate their results, this has to be done at the speed of the slowest unit. As a result, the slowest unit determines the clock speed, which in order determines the overall speed of a processor. It comes as no surprise that a significant effort has been invested in increasing the speed of the clock. However, this is not as straightforward as it sounds. First, the clock signal requires time to travel from one point to another and requires more time to get to the farthest parts of the chip. Although the differences in time of the signal arriving at different parts of the chip are small, they have important effects. Second, after the signal arrives, transistors require some time to change their state. In the meantime no further signal from the clock should arrive. Despite these problems, improvements were steadily made and the clock frequency increased orders of magnitude compared to the first processors.

Recently, the increase in clock speed has been substantially slower on each new generation of processors. Some could think that we have hit some physical limit and that it is not possible anymore to go faster. This is not the case, however. Several companies assure us that they could easily build processors clocked at 10 GHz. But why are they not producing them? The answer lies in the way that transistors operate. Although simplified, the main idea is as follows. Whenever a transistor has to change its state, some power has to be consumed. If we start increasing the rate at which these changes happen, that is, we increase the clock rate, then we must do it more forcefully in order to make electrons move faster, that is, we need higher voltage. The power required to change the state of a transistor depends on the square of the voltage and the frequency. As a result, power consumption increases drastically as we move toward higher frequencies, making processors inefficient power-wise. Moreover, the power consumed is transformed into heat, which must be dissipated to the environment; otherwise processors would melt from their own temperature. Hence, cooling systems are required to be attached to processors, which also require power to operate.

Let us have a look at the Teraflops Research Chip, a research prototype multicore processor from Intel. It contains 80 cores and is actually very power efficient. However, it is interesting to see how power consumption changes when it runs at different frequencies. At 3.16 GHz, the processor requires 0.95 V to operate, consumes 62 W, and achieves a performance of 1.01 Tflops. At 5.7 GHz it requires 1.35 V, consumes 265 W and achieves 1.81 Tflops. As we can see, a 1.8 times increase in the clock speed results in a more than four times increase in power consumption. Let us now assume that we are given the low-frequency version of the processor and we are asked to propose a method to double its performance. One way would be to make a few more improvements and actually double the frequency at which the processor operates. From the teraflops achieved at each frequency, we would expect that this would also double the performance. Although this seems to hold in our case, be aware that this is not a general conclusion as many factors hinder doubling the performance when doubling the clock speed. As we have seen, this would now more than quadruple power consumption. If we were asked to double the performance again and would double the clock speed, this would lead to an exponential growth in power consumption over generations of processors of this architecture. This would make our processors extremely unattractive. But is there another way to double performance? Assume that, instead of doubling the clock speed, we take advantage of Moore's law and incorporate double the cores into the same chip. Now, instead of quadrupling power consumption, we would only double it. As a result, we would have less severe problems cooling our system. However, doubling the number of cores requires now applications to be written in a way that exploits all available cores and doubles their performance. The difficulty has now moved to programmers of applications.

4.2   ARCHITECTURAL OPTIONS FOR MULTICORE SYSTEMS

Multicore systems are a relatively new technology. As with every new technology, it is not certain what the best options and design decisions are to create the fastest and most easily programmable processor of this kind. As a result, researchers and development companies are proposing and exploring a number of different options for several architectural aspects of multicore processors. In this section, we will discuss the architectural features of processors that are affected most in this aspect. But first, we will try to clarify a common misunderstanding, which is the difference between a multicore processor and a processor that supports simultaneous multithreading (SMT). The misunderstanding stems from the fact that both technologies advertise that they support execution of multiple threads simultaneously. As we will see, not only are these two technologies not the same but they also differ in a fundamental way.

4.2.1 SMT and Multicore

As we have seen earlier, issuing multiple instructions and dynamically scheduling them for execution is currently a typical way to improve performance on a uniprocessor system. In this case, however, the exploitation of multiple functional units that are possibly available in the processor is subject to the dependencies among the instructions that have been issued. Furthermore, a cache miss might completely stall the execution of the application until the required data or instruction has been fetched from the main memory. The left part of Figure 4.2 illustrates the exploitation of resources for such a case. As can be seen, several issue slots are unused during each clock cycle.

In order to overcome the underutilization of the available functional units of a single processor, SMT [6] has been introduced. Under this scheme, the processor is able to issue instructions from more applications at the same time. This reduces the number of unused issue slots and improves the throughput of the processor. The important point is that the instructions issued from different applications share in this case the functional units of a single processor. Obviously, there is no meaning

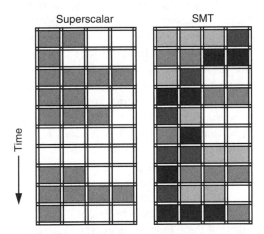

FIGURE 4.2. *Issuing instructions in a typical superscalar architecture and an architecture that supports simultaneous multithreading. The vertical dimension represents a sequence of clock cycles. The horizontal dimension represents the instruction issue capability in each clock cycle. A white box indicates that the corresponding issue slot is unused in a clock cycle. The shades of gray correspond to four different threads in the simultaneous multithreading processor.*

in issuing instructions from an arbitrary number of applications since there is a limit in the number of functional units that are available.

In contrast, in a multicore processor, each core is in itself a complete processor and does not share its functional units with the rest of the cores. As a result, each core might be issuing and executing instructions from a different application without implications from other cores (with some exceptions as we will see next). Obviously, it is possible to apply SMT on each core of a multicore system, which is actually what most vendors of multicore processors do. The reader might be familiar with the Hyper-Threading Technology of Intel processors, which is an example of an implementation of SMT. We will see more examples later on in this chapter.

4.2.2 Shared Cache or Not?

Typically, a single-core processor contains two levels of cache memory, which are both smaller in size but faster to access than main memory. The first level of the cache, known as level 1 or L1 cache, is small but extremely fast. The second level, known as level 2 or L2 cache, is larger in size but slower than L1. The operation of the cache hierarchy is quite straightforward. Data required to perform calculations are first looked up in the L1 cache. If it is not found in L1, then it is looked up in L2. If it is not found there either, then the data are fetched from the main memory. In the last case, data are also transferred into the cache memory, so that they can be accessed faster next time they are required. Depending on the design of the cache, data residing in adjacent memory locations will also be transferred into the cache. This is done in order to exploit locality of references, that is, a property of most programs that, after accessing a specific location in memory, then it is highly possible that they will soon require data that reside in adjacent memory locations. A typical example is the calculation of values in an array. Using a loop, programs calculate elements of the array one after the other, which means that these programs access continuous locations in memory. Having next elements of the array in a level of the cache allows faster access and hence fewer stalls in the processor.

The advent of multicore processors generated an important question with respect to cache memory. Should each core have its own hierarchy of the cache, or should cores share some or all levels of the cache? A more radical question is whether there should be any cache at all. We will discuss this option in more detail in Section 4.5. The answers to these questions are not straightforward since a number of parameters have to be taken into account. Assume, for example, that an application has been parallelized and is executing alone on a multicore system using all available cores. Some could argue that if each core has its own L1 and L2 data cache, then the portion of the application that is running on a core will exploit optimally its cache and achieve the highest possible performance since it will not interfere with other cores and no data it still needs will accidentally be evicted from the cache by another core. On the other hand, if some level of the cache is shared, data (and its adjacent locations) brought into this level by one core could potentially be used by another core that needs that data. Furthermore, the shared level of the cache is now larger in size since it is the combination of the caches of all cores. As a result, if a core requires at some point in time a small amount of cache, the other cores can use a larger portion and can achieve better performance. This could also be the case when multiple, diverse applications are executing on different cores. It is highly possible that their requirements differ significantly and sharing a level of the cache could benefit some of them. But again, interference among such applications could overall hurt the performance of most of them.

Obviously, there is no easy way to determine whether and which levels of cache should be local to a core and which ones should be shared. It depends largely on the applications that will run on the system. Therefore, different processor architectures provide different solutions, starting from the number of levels in the cache, the size of each level, and whether each level is shared or not among cores. It would be ideal to know which data in the cache correspond to which application. In this case, a level of the cache that is shared at the hardware could be handled dynamically by changing the size that is assigned to each core, depending on the current needs of each application. Some proposals for implementing this idea in hardware already exist [7–10]. However, no architecture implements these proposals yet. Therefore, other proposals that handle the situation at the software level have also been proposed [11]. As we will examine contemporary multicore architectures later in this chapter, we will highlight the different parameters of the cache hierarchy.

4.2.3 Identical Cores or Not?

Applications from one area of science obviously do not behave in the same manner as applications from another area. For example, image processing applications heavily depend on specific algorithms like fast Fourier transform (FFT), whereas simulations of physical processes rely on algorithms that have completely different requirements. Even within a given application some computations might have different requirements than others. General-purpose processors try to strike a balance among all these different requirements and to execute all types of computations with an acceptable performance. Nowadays, special-purpose hardware accelerators are available for a large range of domains. Their purpose is to execute faster specific computations and thus to reduce the overall execution time of an application. Digital signal processing (DSP) units are designed to perform frequently used algorithms like FFT faster than general-purpose processors. Physics simulation engines implemented in hardware are also available. Such accelerators are usually connected to the processor through the supported interconnection network of the system. If a program needs to calculate one of the functions that the accelerator supports, it off-loads the calculation to it. When the latter finishes, the result is returned to the processor. A disadvantage of this method is that applications have to be written so that they explicitly use the accelerator.

Since the number of cores in a processor is anticipated to increase drastically in the next few years, the idea to incorporate different types of special-purpose accelerators into a single chip has emerged. Instead of integrating an ever-increasing number of the same core on a chip, it would be possible to use some of the available space for a few hardware accelerators. The number of general-purpose cores in the chip would be still large enough to handle the majority of applications, but for the applications that require it, the appropriate accelerator would be available. DSP units, physics emulation engines, cryptography hardware, and others could be included in a small percentage of the area of a chip. Even the graphics unit could be integrated into the same chip. Currently, exchanging data to process it on the graphics unit requires a good fraction of the total execution time of the calculation since the data have to be sent over the interconnection network to the graphics unit and back. Integrating the graphics unit into the same chip with all other cores could eliminate this time and provide faster graphics.

4.2.4 On-Chip Interconnection Networks

The role of the interconnection network is to connect the functional units of a parallel system and allow them to communicate and exchange information. For example, all cores of a processor must be able to communicate with the main memory to store and retrieve data. The architecture of the interconnection network has always been a significant decision in the design of a parallel system. Several factors play an important role and define its properties. For example, network latency is defined as the time that elapses from the moment the sender initiates a communication until the moment the receiver receives the first bit of information. Obviously, low latency is a desired property of a network. Bandwidth refers to the rate that data can be sent over the network, which makes a high value of this property very important for a network. Some other factors that are taken into account are the behavior under contention, scalability, speed of elements that are connected, and, of course, the cost to implement the network.

With respect to multicore architectures, three types of connections seem to concentrate a lot of attention: how a core is connected to the cache or its local storage (see Section 4.5), how a core is connected to the main memory, and how a core is connected with other cores. A crossbar switch is a possible solution to connect cores to the cache. The Oracle SPARC T3 processor uses such a network for this purpose. The Sony/IBM/Toshiba Cell BE processor (see Section 4.3.5) uses a more specialized network. A ring, the element interconnect bus (EIB), connects all cores. Through this ring, data can be sent from one core to another. In order to connect cores to the main memory, typically a memory controller is provided inside the chip, which is responsible to receive requests for communication with the memory and serve them. The controller can be connected with the memory modules in several ways. The Intel QuickPath Interconnect (QPI) provides point-to-point links, which are also used to connect the internal cores, the I/O hub, and other processors in the system. The Oracle SPARC T3 uses serial links from the memory controller to the memory modules. In Cell, requests to the main memory have to move through the EIB to the memory interface controller (MIC) and from there they are forwarded to the memory. There is still a great deal of dispersion in the field of interconnection networks for multicore systems and designs that concentrate on a specific architecture. As previously mentioned, this is a phenomenon to be expected in technologies that have not completely matured yet.

4.3 MULTICORE ARCHITECTURE EXAMPLES

In the following paragraphs, we will mention a few contemporary multicore processors and their main characteristics. It is worth to mention that, with the exception of the Sony/IBM/Toshiba Cell BE processor, the cores contained in these processors are based on typical single-core processors that are simply put together on a chip. The main difference is that now cores share some level of the cache hierarchy. As we will see later (Section 4.5), a new trend is to use simpler and smaller cores, allowing for a larger number of them to be integrated on each chip. However, such changes are accompanied with more architectural changes that have other implications.

4.3.1 The Intel Core i7 Processor

The Core i7 processor from Intel is the first processor we will examine. It is composed of four cores, each one supporting two-way SMT or Hyper-Threading as it is called by Intel. As a result, a total of eight threads can execute concurrently on this processor. Many of the design decisions for this architecture were driven by the desire to reduce power consumption and to retain more or less the same amount of performance. A notable example is the dismissal of the 2-bit branch predictor used in previous Intel processors with a simpler 1-bit predictor. Halving the number of bits used in this functional unit also halved its power consumption. Of course, the use of SMT itself is also a factor that reduces power consumption since functional units of the processor are better exploited. This is just one example of how significant power consumption has become in modern processors.

The Core i7 includes a three-level cache hierarchy. Each core of the processor has a local L1 cache of 32 kB and a local L2 cache of 256 kB. The L3 cache is shared among cores and is 8 MB in size. Each core can fetch up to four instructions per clock cycle. In order to interconnect all functional units of the processor, the crossbar switch used in previous architectures has been replaced with a ring bus. The bus provides faster transfer rates but also reduced power consumption.

Most desktop systems equipped with multicore processors from Intel take advantage of the additional cores by running multiple, different applications on separate cores. Only a small fraction of applications used every day is parallelized to take advantage of the multiple cores and SMT. As more cores will be integrated into chips, this is expected to change. A typical user does not execute concurrently a sufficient number of applications to use the number of cores that will be available in the future. Applications will have to be parallelized in order to take full advantage of future processors.

4.3.2 The AMD Phenom II Processor

The AMD Phenom II processor consists of six cores. In contrast to most other architectures, it does not include support for SMT. As the Intel Core i7, it includes a three-level cache memory hierarchy. Each core of the processor has a local L1 cache of 64 kB and a local L2 cache of 512 kB. The larger L1 and L2 caches provide more space to each core to keep its working set and to experience less stalls. This enables functional units to get used more efficiently and compensates for the absence of SMT. The L3 cache is shared among cores and is 6 MB in size. Another example of the importance of power consumption in modern processors is the fact that this processor includes three distinct technologies to consume less power. The PowerNow technology allows for enhanced power management features, which automatically adjusts performance states and features based on processor performance requirements. CoolCore technology reduces processor energy consumption by turning off unused parts of the processor. Finally, Dual Dynamic Power

Management enables more granular power management capabilities to reduce processor energy consumption.

4.3.3 The IBM POWER7 Processor

The IBM POWER7 processor contains eight cores, each one of them supporting four-way SMT. This leads to a total of 32 threads that can be concurrently active on this processor. Performance of each core is further improved through an aggressive and deeper out-of-order execution design, better branch prediction, and reduced latencies to various resources, such as the caches and translation look-aside buffers. During each cycle, up to eight instructions can be fetched from memory. There are a total of 12 execution units within each core: 2 fixed-point units, 2 load-store units, 4 double-precision floating-point unit pipelines, 1 vector, 1 branch execution unit, 1 condition register logic unit, and 1 decimal floating-point unit pipeline. This is an example where more functional units of the same type reside in each core, allowing multiple threads running on that core to execute instructions of the same type simultaneously.

The POWER7 has a three-level cache hierarchy, with the first two levels being local to each core. More specifically, the L1 cache is 32 kB and the L2 cache is 256 kB, both the same size as in the Intel i7. Finally, the shared L3 cache is 32 MB, significantly larger compared to all other architectures. The large size and the fact that the L3 cache is shared among cores have a great, positive impact on the performance of each thread. The L3 cache is divided into eight 4-MB local regions, which serve a dual role. Their primary operation is to act as a victim cache for its associated L2 cache and, secondarily, as a victim cache for the other seven 4-MB regions. A set of heuristics achieves a balance between these roles by monitoring and managing capacity and bandwidth allocation according to workload dynamics.

4.3.4 The Oracle SPARC T3 Processor

The Oracle SPARC T3 processor is composed of 16 cores. Each core supports eight-way SMT, which results in a total of 128 threads that can run concurrently on this processor. The T3 is an interesting example of a multicore architecture as it focuses strongly on exploiting thread-level parallelism (TLP) rather than ILP. Combining multiple cores with SMT allows this processor to significantly increase throughput. Only two instructions are issued at each cycle. This is the same as its immediate predecessor, the UltraSPARC T2, but the UltraSPARC T1, the first processor of the line, was a single-issue processor. The two instructions issued per cycle are less than the instructions issued by most contemporary multicore processors, like the Intel i7, which issues four instructions per cycle.

Each core consists of two relatively small pipelines, one 8-stage integer pipeline and a 12-stage floating-point pipeline. The T3 uses fine-grained multithreading, switching to a new thread on each clock cycle. As a result, the processor's execution pipeline remains active doing useful work, even as memory operations for stalled threads continue in parallel. Threads that are idle because they are waiting due to a pipeline delay or cache miss are bypassed during scheduling. Hence, a core is idle only when all eight threads are idle or stalled. Each core of the T3 has access to its local 16-kB instruction cache and its own 8-kB L1 data cache. All cores are connected through a crossbar switch to the 6 MB of shared L2 data cache, which is composed of 16 banks. A cache coherency protocol ensures that the latest value of data is found in the memory hierarchy. Interestingly, the T3 includes six cache coherency links that allow it to connect to three more processors on the same system without any additional logic and to retain the cache coherence protocol among all processors.

4.3.5 The Sony/IBM/Toshiba Cell BE Processor

The Cell BE processor was designed cooperatively by Sony, IBM, and Toshiba. In contrast to the previous processors, which simply integrated multiple copies of existing or slightly modified processors on a single chip, this processor is based on a radically different design. First, it is composed of two different types of cores. There is a single copy of the first type of core, which is known as the Power Processor Element (PPE). The PPE is based on the 64-bit PowerPC general-purpose processor. It supports two-way SMT and includes 32 kB of L1 cache and 512 kB of L2 cache. The PPE is used to execute code but, most importantly, to control and distribute work and data to the eight Synergistic Processing Elements (SPEs). An SPE is a self-contained vector processor clocked at 4 GHz, which can execute code independently. An SPE contains 128 registers, each one 128 bits wide. It also includes four single-precision floating-point units and four integer units. A distinct feature of SPEs is the fact that they do not include any cache memory. Instead, they are supported by a small 256-kB local store, which is a fast memory that is local to each SPE. This is the only memory that an SPE can directly access. In contrast to the cache, which is manipulated in hardware and is transparent to the programmer, the local store is handled by the application itself. The programmer has to decide when the PPE will send data to the local store. Furthermore, the code to be executed by an SPE must also be transferred to the local store. Although this makes programming more complicated (or unconventional, if you like), it allows simplification of the design of the memory subsystem and thus increases its performance. Another important difference is that the PPE and the SPEs are in-order processors without any out-of-order capabilities. This means that the optimizations performed by the compiler are extremely important to achieve good performance. Thankfully, the 128 registers of each SPE provide the compiler with the required space to apply optimizations like loop unrolling and overcome the need for out-of-order execution.

Although a quite different design, compared to the processors that most of us are familiar with, it seems that most future multicore and many-core architectures will incorporate the characteristics of the Cell BE processor. In particular, the use of local store instead of a hardware-managed cache seems to be an alternative that is examined for several future designs.

4.4 PROGRAMMING MULTICORE ARCHITECTURES

In this section, we will shortly analyze programming models that can be used to program applications for multicore systems. The first three are models that have been extensively used to program more traditional shared-memory and distributed-memory architectures. Naturally, they can be used to program multicore systems too. The rest of the programming models are more or less inspired from the advent of multicore systems and are designed to better exploit them. However, they also support other types of parallel architectures. It is possible to find more information about these models in the references that accompany them. The reader is also encouraged to look for other similar projects like CellSs, SMPSs, Fresh Breeze [12], and Concurrent Collections [13].

4.4.1 Message-Passing Interface (MPI)

MPI [14] is probably one of the most successful programming models used in parallel computing. It has been designed for distributed-memory architectures, which are composed of computing nodes connected through a network. A process is employed on every node to execute the part of the computation that corresponds to it. If a node consists of multiple processors or cores, more processes can be spawned to take advantage of the additional computing power. If data residing in one process are required from another process, a message has to be sent from the first process to the second one.

MPI can also be used on multicore systems, which are typically shared-memory systems, by spawning multiple processes that will run on different cores. In this case, performance might not be as high as using a programming model that targets shared-memory systems. Normally, MPI uses communication primitives of the network to exchange data, even when processes reside on the same node. Naturally, this introduces some overhead. Some implementations of MPI optimize this shortcoming by exchanging data through memory. Again, however, communication has to be performed between processes, which do not share the same address space. Overall, although it is possible to use MPI to program multicore systems, it is not something that is seen very frequently.

4.4.2 Threads

The most typical way to program shared-memory architectures, including current multicore systems, is to employ some threading library. Threads are used as execution vehicles that run on top of the available processors or cores of the system. Computation is partitioned among threads using a multitude of scheduling techniques, ranging from the simple static scheduling to more advanced techniques like dynamic creation of tasks and distribution to threads through a queueing system.

POSIX Threads [15] are the best-known representative of this class of programming models. Their behavior is completely described in an international standard and implementations exist for almost all available architectures. Many applications and benchmarks are implemented using POSIX Threads. However, there is a multitude of other available threading libraries. This diversity stems from the fact that these libraries focus more on other aspects, for example, supporting a specific higher-level programming model or a dataflow-like execution of threads.

In contrast to MPI, where synchronization among processes is implicit through the exchange of messages, special primitives of the used threading library have to be exploited to ensure correct synchronization among threads. Ensuring that data modified by multiple threads will always contain consistent values is typically a task of the programmer. Identifying that correct synchronization is achieved in all possible execution scenarios is already a difficult task, let alone when high-performance implementations of algorithms are exploited to reduce the overhead of synchronization. As the number of cores on processors will raise, the overhead of synchronization will become an even more important factor in the development of applications. Therefore, improvements of basic synchronization primitives have started being incorporated into hardware. Barriers [16], context switching, and faster implementations of mutual exclusion in hardware [6] are some examples.

An important distinction between threading libraries is whether they implement kernel-level or user-level threads. Kernel-level threads are primitives provided and scheduled by the operating system. For every thread being created in an application, the threading library creates a kernel-level thread and assigns to it the computations that have to be performed. This is also known as a 1-to-1 model. Execution of these threads is the responsibility of the operating system. An implementation using kernel-level threads is quite straightforward. However, this type of thread is quite heavyweight, as entering and returning from the kernel of the operating system is required for several operations of the library. In contrast, user-level threads are implemented completely in user space, which makes them very lightweight. The application creates several threads that run on top of the single kernel-level thread of the application, a model known as 1-to-N. This, however, has a significant drawback. Since the operating system is not aware of the user-level threads, it cannot schedule them to all available processors and cores. In order to overcome this limitation the M-to-N model is typically employed. This model is a combination of the previous two models. It is the most difficult to implement but provides the best way to exploit parallelism on multiprocessor systems. Typically, a number of kernel-level threads are created, which equal the number of processors that the application requests. The user-level runtime system then creates user-level threads, which are scheduled from the user-level scheduler on top of the kernel-level threads. This allows the creation of hundreds or even thousands of threads with a relatively low overhead. The question that follows is which of these models is best for multicore architectures. The answer is not obvious and the fact that more cores per processor are expected in the future makes the selection even more difficult. It seems, however, that the M-to-N model is the one preferred by most implementers of threading runtime systems.

Although all of the following programming models do not directly expose threads to the programmer, they use threads internally to represent and schedule parallel tasks to available processors and cores. Hence, features of the underlying threading library are important for the performance that can be achieved and how easily a programming model can be mapped to the available primitives of the threading library. As the number of cores available on processors is expected to increase significantly in the next few years, choices made at this level are certain to have a great impact.

4.4.3 Directive Based (OpenMP)

It soon became obvious that manually creating threads and distributing work among them is a procedure that follows patterns in most applications, especially for loop-level parallelism. In order to simplify this procedure, directive-based programming models were introduced. In these models the programmer specifies through special directives where and how parallelism should be created. The compiler is then in charge of creating the parallelism and distributing work among threads according to the directives. Although a number of such models has been proposed, only few of them were successful. The main reason for this was the fact that most of them were specific to a system. As a result, source code written in one of these models could not be easily ported to another system. This increased the cost of developing a parallel application and made these models unattractive.

OpenMP [17] is a directive-based model that was supported by a large number of organizations and companies from its design stages. The large number of implementations on a diverse range of systems has made it quite successful. One of its main features, allowing parallelization of an application in stages, made it attractive for large codes where parallelization using other models is much more difficult. Since it targets shared-memory systems, its use in current multicore architectures is straightforward. It is also quite common to combine the use of OpenMP and MPI, when the architecture under consideration is composed of multiple nodes with distributed memory, but each node is a smaller shared-memory system. In such cases, OpenMP is used to parallelize code inside a node and MPI to distribute work among nodes.

4.4.4 Intel Array Building Blocks

Intel Array Building Blocks provide a data-parallel programming environment designed to effectively utilize the power of existing and upcoming throughput-oriented features on modern processor architectures. This includes current and future multicore and many-core systems. The programming environment provides a C++ template library that allows programmers to continue writing code using the standard C++ language with some extensions. The programming model was created by merging the data-parallel programming models proposed by RapidMind [18], a company acquired by Intel before the merge, and Ct [19], a model also proposed by Intel.

The programming model adds new types and operators to the C++ language through header files and a runtime library, using only standard C++ capabilities. This separation allows code using these features to coexist with C++ code and requires only specific portions of an application to be rewritten to utilize parallel features of the underlying hardware system. These new features give the developer an expressive and safer parallel programming environment by isolating its data objects from the rest of the application and by restricting conflicting concurrent accesses to shared objects through structured primitives. This eliminates the need for low-level constructs like locks and avoids data races.

4.4.5 Intel Threading Building Blocks

Intel Threading Building Blocks is another C++ template-based library. In contrast to Intel Array Building Blocks, it focuses on loop-level parallelism. Instead of creating explicitly threads to distribute work, the programmer defines tasks that are then scheduled and executed automatically on top of the threads that the library creates. The components of Intel Threading Building Blocks include generic parallel algorithms, concurrent containers, low-level synchronization primitives, and a task scheduler.

Programmers using Intel Threading Building Blocks can parallelize the execution of loop iterations by treating chunks of iterations as tasks and allowing the Intel Threading Building Blocks task scheduler to determine the task sizes, the number of threads to use, the assignment of tasks to those threads, and how those threads are scheduled for execution. The task scheduler will give precedence to tasks that have been most recently in a core of the processor. The purpose of this strategy is to better exploit the cache. Running a task on such a core increases the likelihood of required data being found on the core's cache. The task scheduler utilizes a task-stealing mechanism to balance the load during execution. If a thread has no tasks assigned to it, but another thread has more tasks, then the first thread will steal tasks to help the progress of execution.

4.4.6 Sequoia

Sequoia is a programming paradigm that extends C++ and pays special attention to movement and placement of data in different levels of the memory hierarchy [20]. For this purpose, it provides first-class language mechanisms to provide the programmer with explicit control over data. Sequoia includes the notion of hierarchical memory directly into the programming model to gain both portability and performance. To accomplish this, the memory hierarchy of a system is abstracted as a tree of distinct memory modules, and the program describes how data are moved and where they reside in a machine's memory hierarchy. Since the organization of memory in a multicore system plays an important role in performance, Sequoia can be thought of as an interesting approach to programming such systems. The second abstraction used in this programming model is tasks. These are defined as self-contained units of computation that include descriptions of key information such as communication and working sets. An important property of tasks is that they isolate each computation in its own local address space. In other words, a task can only access data from the address space in which it is defined.

In order to run Sequoia programs, a description of the memory hierarchy of the system to be used has to be created. This description includes information about the size of data that can reside at each level of the memory hierarchy for the specific problem that is being solved. For example, if the system under consideration is a Symmetric MultiProcessing (SMP) system, the description would include the size of the problem that fits into the shared main memory and the size of the problem that fits into the local L2 and local L1 cache of each processor. In addition, a number of task variants have to be created. Typically, the actual computation will be performed on the data that reside in the last level of the memory hierarchy. Hence, a task that handles this case is required. For the previous levels of the memory hierarchy, another task will have to be created. Its purpose is to divide the problem size that it receives from the previous level into smaller pieces that fit into the memory of the current level. In the previous example, the total problem size that fits into the shared main memory would be divided into smaller tasks that fit into the L2 cache of each processor. Each of these tasks would be divided further into smaller tasks that fit into the L1 cache. The actual computation would be performed from the task that corresponds to this level.

4.4.7 X10

X10 [21] is a class-based object-oriented programming language designed for high-performance, high-productivity computing on high-end computers supporting tens of thousands of hardware threads. It is a member of the partitioned global address space (PGAS) family of languages. These languages allow us to think of a computation as running across multiple processors on a common shared address space. Data are distributed and reside at some processor. Each processor can operate directly on the data it contains but must use some indirect mechanism to access or update data at other processors.

X10 is based on state-of-the-art object-oriented programming ideas primarily to take advantage of their proven flexibility and ease of use for a wide range of programming problems. However, it has been adapted to the context of high-performance numerical computing. The sequential core of X10 is a container-based object-oriented language similar to Java and C++. Additional features of X10 have been added to address concurrency. An X10 program is intended to run on a wide range of computers, from uniprocessors to large clusters of parallel processors supporting millions of concurrent operations. To support this scale, X10 introduces the central concept of a place. A place can be thought of as a virtual shared-memory multiprocessor: a computational unit with a finite (though perhaps changing) number of hardware threads and a bounded amount of shared memory, uniformly accessible by all threads. In other words, a place is a repository for data and activities, corresponding loosely to a process or a processor. An X10 computation typically runs over a large collection of places. Each place hosts some data and runs one or more activities, which are extremely lightweight threads of execution. Places induce a concept of "local." The activities running in a place may access data items located at that place with the efficiency of on-chip access. Accesses to remote places may take orders of magnitude longer.

Instead of traditional semaphores or mutexes provided by most threading libraries to synchronize access to shared data, X10 provides the concept of atomic blocks. Atomic blocks are a high-level construct for coordinating the access to shared data. They can be used to guarantee that invariants of shared data structures are maintained even as they are being accessed simultaneously by multiple activities running in the same place. Finally, several other high-level constructs are provided that facilitate the programming of concurrent applications. Clocks allow ordering of computations, distributed arrays spread data across many places, and it is possible to start asynchronous activities.

4.4.8 Chapel

Chapel [22] is another programming language with a target of improving productivity of parallel programming. The language is built around four principles. First, Chapel is designed to support general parallel programming through the use of high-level language abstractions. For this purpose, it supports a global-view programming model that pays attention in how data and control flow are abstracted. The first concept used to achieve this goal are locales. A locale is an abstraction of a unit of uniform memory access on a target architecture; that is, within a locale, all threads exhibit similar access times to any specific memory address. For example, a locale in a commodity cluster could be defined to be a single core of a processor, a multicore processor, or an SMP node of multiple processors. On top of this, global-view data structures are defined, which are arrays and other data aggregates whose sizes and indices are expressed globally, but their implementation in the supporting runtime system may distribute them across locales. Furthermore, Chapel supports the concept of a global view of control, which means that a user's program commences execution with a single logical thread of control and then introduces additional parallelism through the use of certain language concepts.

The second important concept in Chapel is locality-aware programming, which allows the user to optionally and incrementally specify where data and computation should be placed on the physical machine. Such control over program locality is essential to achieve scalable performance on distributed-memory architectures. The third concept of Chapel is the use of object-oriented programming, which has been of great importance in raising productivity in the mainstream programming community. This is achieved through encapsulation of related data and functions within a single software component, its support for specialization and reuse, and its use as a clean mechanism for defining and implementing interfaces. Chapel supports objects in order to make these benefits available to parallel programming. Finally, the last principle governing Chapel is support for generic programming and polymorphism. These features allow code to be written in a style that is generic across types. In other words, code is produced that is independent of the type of variables, and the compiler takes the responsibility to produce the correct instructions according to the type of the variables that are used to call the code. The main advantage of such an approach is that it allows algorithms to be expressed without explicitly replicating them for each possible type.

4.4.9 Habanero

Habanero [23] is a collection of research projects that try to address multicore programmability issues. Research is performed in numerous areas of parallel software. Overall, Habanero covers almost every aspect of parallel programming, introduces interesting new ideas, but also uses extensively ideas that have proven to be efficient and easy to grasp by most programmers. On the programming language front, new portable constructs are introduced to support explicit parallelism for homogeneous and heterogeneous multicore systems, implicit deterministic parallelism through support of array views [24] and single-assignment constructs, and finally, implicit nondeterministic parallelism through unordered iterators [25] and partially ordered statement blocks. In order to compile these constructs and to produce efficient code, a new parallel intermediate representation has been introduced into compilers, and several transformations and optimizations are applied to it. Several more optimizations have been implemented in order to handle parallelism more efficiently and make it possible to exploit larger numbers of cores. These include optimizations of high-level arrays [26], iterators, synchronization, data transfer, and transactional memory operations [27].

Certainly, an important aspect of any proposed programming model is the runtime system that will implement it. Habanero has put a great effort into extending work-stealing [28] task scheduling algorithms and into supporting fine-grained producer–consumer synchronization through the idea of phasers [29]. Finally, research is performed on parallel program analysis tools that spot common parallel software errors and extract both statically and dynamically information about the percentage of execution time that is contributed by several constructs of applications.

4.5 MANY-CORE ARCHITECTURES

As more and more cores are expected to be integrated into a single chip, computer architects have already started experimenting with architectural options that are quite different from what we have been accustomed to, especially in general-purpose processors. Although there has been no consensus yet about which of the alternative possibilities should be used in future processors, it seems that some of them have an edge over others and are used in more designs. The large number of cores puts a lot of attention to power consumption. Hence, most of these proposals have a direct connection with this issue. In general, architectures seem to move to simpler designs, discarding methods that increase single-core throughput and instead freeing space to integrate even more cores in a chip. For example, out-of-order execution, which has been perfected over many generations of processors, is being abandoned in many cases. Instead, simple in-order cores are employed, which require less logic and consume less power. In addition, lower clock speeds are used, again to save power. Instead, good performance is achieved through better cooperation of more cores. Special attention is also paid toward programmability issues. The architecture of the memory subsystem plays a key role in this aspect. Do cores share memory or not? Is there a hardware-managed cache or only fast local storage? Are the levels of memory coherent? Design decisions here determine the possible programming models that can extract most of the performance of these systems.

A lot of effort is being concentrated toward answering the question whether a hardware-managed cache or a software-managed local storage should be employed in such architectures. In most current systems, hardware-managed caches are coherent among cores and other processors of a multiprocessor system. In other words, the system is always able to determine where the last value of a variable can be found, whether it is in the cache of the requesting core, the main memory, or the cache of another core or processor. In any case, this last value will always be used. However, the protocols used to ensure coherence are relatively slow, require a significant portion of the die area of a multicore processor, and increase exponentially in size and time with the number of cache memories that have to be kept coherent. It is expected that around half of the die area of a chip will be required simply to implement the coherency protocol, when integration levels reach around 100 cores per processor. As a result, several many-core architectures have started moving toward local storage. A second reason for this move is the fact that cache memories tend to consume more power than local storage. Although simpler to implement, local storage has an important drawback. The memory subsystem is not anymore a direct extension of the memory subsystem of a single-core processor. Programmers were not required to do anything special in their applications in order to find the last value of a variable. On a system with local storage, this is not true anymore. It is the explicit responsibility of the programmer to ensure when data are moved into and out of local storage. Again, there is no agreement yet which programming model is the best to achieve this. Therefore, many such programming models are actually tied to specific architectures.

4.6 MANY-CORE ARCHITECTURE EXAMPLES

Although the computer industry seems currently to prepare for the arrival of many-core architectures, the number of such processors that is currently available is quite limited. Furthermore, most of them seem to be more special-purpose processors that are designed for specific domain areas. Nonetheless, it is worthwhile to see a few examples and their characteristics. Some of the architectures mentioned here have less than 100 cores, which would typically put them in the multicore category. They are mentioned in this section because most of their other architectural features are closer to the many-core architectures we expect to see in the future.

4.6.1 Cisco 188-Core Metro Chip

In 2004 Cisco Systems introduced its CRS-1 high-end router. An interesting feature of the system is the fact that it uses the Metro processor, a specialized and massively parallel network processor that contains 188 cores. Four additional cores are provided for redundancy. Cisco designed and implemented the processor in cooperation with IBM and Tensilica. Each core is a simple 32-bit RISC processor clocked at 250 MHz. A traditional five-stage RISC pipeline is used to improve the throughput of the processor. There is a small cache available for instructions, but data are kept in a local memory. The complete chip requires only 35 W to operate, and its main purpose is to handle network traffic. A simple software programming model has been employed. Every packet received from the network is processed in a run-to-completion manner. This reduces overhead of switching among different tasks. The large number of available cores allows for such an approach. This methodology is also being explored for other architectures since it allows easier programming, and the large number of cores expected in future processors provides the resources to handle at the same time multiple applications or threads.

Each core of the Metro chip, also named a packet processing element (PPE), is only 0.5 mm^2 in size. It is worth noticing that the chip is implemented using a 130-nm technology. However, a 32-nm technology is already available to build processors, which means that more than 1000 cores could easily be put into the same die area of the chip. Although this currently holds for a special-purpose many-core processor, it is not difficult to foresee that such numbers of cores will be soon integrated into general-purpose processors.

4.6.2 ClearSpeed 192-Core CSX700 Chip

The ClearSpeed CSX700 is built from two multithreaded array processors, each one containing 96 processing elements. This amounts to a total of 192 processing elements. Eight more processing elements are provided for redundancy. The clock speed is 250 MHz and only 15 W is required in a typical workload to operate the chip. This puts the CSX700 into the group of processors with an excellent performance per watt consumed. Each processing element contains a 32/64-bit floating-point multiplier, a 32/64-bit floating-point adder, an integer arithmetic logic unit, a 16-bit integer multiply-accumulate unit, and 6 kB of local SRAM memory. It is worth mentioning that the technology used to implement the processor is 90 nm. Hence, using the current 32-nm approach would allow for a much larger number of cores on the chip.

4.6.3 Tilera TILEPro64 64-Core Chip

The TILEPro64 is a many-core processor chip comprising 64 power-efficient general-purpose cores connected by six 8×8 mesh networks. The clock frequency is 866 MHz and power consumption is at 23 W. Cache coherence across the cores, the memory, and I/O allows for standard shared-memory programming. Each processing core comprises a 32-bit five-stage very long instruction word (VLIW) pipeline with 64 registers, 16-kB L1 instruction and data caches, and 64-kB L2 combined data and instruction cache. The L2 caches from each of the cores form a distributed L3 cache accessible by any core and I/O device. The short pipeline depth reduces power consumption and the penalty for a branch-prediction miss to two cycles. Each core is an in-order processor that can issue up to three instructions every cycle. Static branch prediction and in-order execution further reduce the area and power required. Translation look-aside buffers support virtual memory and allow full memory protection. As with the CSX700 chip, this processor is implemented using a 90-nm technology.

4.6.4 Intel 48-Core Single-Chip Cloud Computer (SCC)

The SCC is a research processor from Intel. It is composed of 48 cores, which are arranged in a 6×4 grid of tiles. Each tile contains two cores. Each core is a slightly altered P54C Pentium processor and includes a private 16-kB L1 cache and a private 256-kB L2 cache. The clock is at 1 GHz and power consumption is 125 W. The distinct feature of SCC is the fact that it has two levels of memory coherence management. Each core has a coherent L1 and L2 cache. However, these are not coherent with the cache memories of all other cores. Furthermore, although the main memory is shared among cores, it is not coherent with the caches. This means that the programmer has to pay special attention when data are distributed among cores and to maintain coherency in software whenever necessary. For this purpose, Intel developed a special message-passing architecture.

4.6.5 Intel 80-Core Teraflops Research Processor

The Teraflops Research Chip is a research processor from Intel containing 80 cores. The cores are arranged in a 10×8 mesh and they operate at up to 5.7 GHz. We discussed earlier power consumption issues for this processor (Section 4.1.2). Each core contains two independent fully pipelined single-precision floating-point multiply-accumulator units, 3-kB single-cycle instruction memory, and 3 kB of local data memory. The purpose of the chip is to explore the possibilities of many-core architectures and to experiment with various forms of networking and communication within the next generation of processors. One of the purposes of developing the Ct programming language [19] (Section 4.4.4) was the introduction of this processor.

4.7 SUMMARY

The continuing validity of Moore's law and the desire to keep power consumption of processors from an exponential explosion has led to the design and development of multicore systems. Almost, if not all, vendors that produce processors move currently toward this direction. The additional transistors that can be put onto a single chip due to the improvements in integration technology have been used in the past to improve the performance of uniprocessor systems. This has been achieved by extending and/or replicating functional units of these processors. However, it recently became clear that these well-studied and perfected techniques have all reached their point of diminishing returns. The alternative currently in use is to add more cores onto each chip.

The advent of multicore processors has brought new challenges. Hardware designers are currently exploring alternatives for the architectural features of processors at several levels, such as caches, numbers of cores, hardware accelerators, and interconnection networks. For all of these subsystems, new approaches are being considered or previous approaches are adapted to the new era. This process is still active and the impact of each of these changes will soon be clear. Furthermore, the expectation that even thousands of cores will be available on a single chip in a few years leads processor architects to introduce even more radical ideas, like abandoning well-established features used in current processors. Some ideas that gain acceptance right now are the replacement of hardware-managed cache hierarchies with software-managed local memory hierarchies and the use of simple in-order cores that require less power to operate and fewer transistors to be implemented.

All these changes in hardware have naturally an impact in the software area. Programming models used to program parallel architectures of the recent past are being adapted to the current multicore architectures. But the expectation that many more cores will be available soon with quite different architectural features drives the introduction of new programming models that are targeted toward these future hardware architectures. As in the case of the hardware, it is not certain yet which of the proposed features will be easily exploitable by the majority of programmers. In any case, it is certain that right now, the multicore era and, soon, the many-core era will impose changes in the way that programmers have been thinking about programming until now, and it will require them to become familiar with new concepts.

REFERENCES

[1] G.E. Moore, "*Cramming more components onto integrated circuits*," *Electronics Magazine*, 38(8):13, 1965.

[2] IBM Systems Development Division, IBM System/360 Model 85 Functional Characteristics, June 1968.

[3] S.C. Woo, M. Ohara, E. Torrie, J.P. Singh, and A. Gupta, "The SPLASH-2 programs: Characterization and methodological considerations," in *Proceedings of the 22nd*

International Symposium on Computer Architecture (ISCA '95), Santa Margherita Ligure, Italy, pp. 24–36, June 1995.

[4] J.L. Hennessy and D.A. Patterson, *Computer Architecture: A Quantitative Approach.* Amsterdam: Elsevier Science & Technology, 2011.

[5] D.A. Patterson and J.L. Hennessy, *Computer Organization and Design: The Hardware/ Software Interface.* Amsterdam: Elsevier Science & Technology, 2008.

[6] D. Tullsen, S.J. Eggers, and H. Levy, "Simultaneous multithreading: Maximizing on-chip parallelism," in *Proceedings of the 22nd Annual International Symposium on Computer Architecture*, Santa Margherita Ligure, Italy, pp. 392–403, 1995.

[7] D. Chandra, F. Guo, S. Kim, and Y. Solihin, "Predicting inter-thread cache contention on a chip multi-processor architecture," in *Proceedings of the 11th International Symposium on High-Performance Computer Architecture (HPCA '05)*, San Francisco, CA, pp. 340–351, February 2005.

[8] R. Iyer, "CQoS: A framework for enabling QoS in shared caches of CMP platforms," in *Proceedings of the 18th International Conference on Supercomputing (ICS '04)*, Malo, France, pp. 257–266, June 2004.

[9] M.K. Qureshi and Y.N. Patt, "Utility-based cache partitioning: A low-overhead, high-performance, runtime mechanism to partition shared caches," in *Proceedings of the 39th Annual IEEE/ACM International Symposium on Microarchitecture (MICRO '06)*, Orlando, FL, pp. 423–432, December 2006.

[10] E.G. Suh, L. Rudolph, and S. Devadas, "Dynamic partitioning of shared cache memory," *Journal of Supercomputing*, 28:7–26, 2004.

[11] D. Tam, R. Azimi, L. Soares, and M. Stumm, "Managing shared L2 caches on multicore systems in software," in *Workshop on the Interaction between Operating Systems and Computer Architecture*, June 2007.

[12] J.B. Dennis, "A parallel program execution model supporting modular software construction," in *Proceedings of the 1997 Conference on Massively Parallel Programming Models*, Washington, DC, pp. 50–60, 1997.

[13] Z. Budimlic, A. Chandramowlishwaran, K. Knobe, G. Lowney, V. Sarkar, and L. Treggiari, "Multi-core implementations of the Concurrent Collections programming model," in *Proceedings of the 14th Workshop on Compilers for Parallel Computing (CPC '09)*, Zurich, Switzerland, January 2009.

[14] Message Passing Interface Forum, MPI: A Message-Passing Interface Standard, Version 2.2, September 2009.

[15] IEEE, IEEE Std. 1003.1c-1995 Thread Extensions, 1995.

[16] J. del Cuvillo, W. Zhu, Z. Hu, and G.R. Gao, "TiNy threads: A thread virtual machine for the Cyclops64 cellular architecture," in *Proceedings of the 5th Workshop on Massively Parallel Processing*, Denver, CO, April 2005.

[17] OpenMP Architecture Review Board, OpenMP Application Program Interface, Version 3.1, June 2011.

[18] M.D. McCool, "Data-parallel programming on the cell BE and the GPU using the RapidMind development platform," in *Proceedings of the GSPx Multicore Applications Conference*, Santa Clara, CA, October 2006.

[19] A. Ghuloum, E. Sprangle, J. Fang, G. Wu, and X. Zhou, Ct: A Flexible Parallel Programming Model for Tera-scale Architectures, 2007.

[20] K. Fatahalian, D.R. Horn, T.J. Knight, L. Leem, M. Houston, J.Y. Park, M. Erez, M. Ren, A. Aiken, W.J. Dally, and P. Hanrahan, "Sequoia: Programming the memory hierarchy," in *Proceedings of the 2006 ACM/IEEE Conference on Supercomputing (SC '06)*, Tampa, FL, November 2006.

[21] K. Ebcioglu, V. Saraswa, and V. Sarkar, "X10: Programming for hierarchical parallelism and non-uniform data access," in *Proceedings of the 3rd International Workshop on Language Runtimes*, Vancouver, British Columbia, Canada, October 2004.

[22] B.L. Chamberlain, D. Callahan, and H.P. Zima, "Parallel programmability and the Chapel language," *International Journal of High Performance Computing Applications*, 21:291–312, 2007.

[23] Habanero multicore software research project web page. 2008. Available at http://habanero.rice.edu.

[24] J. Shirako, H. Kasahara, and V. Sarkar, *Languages and Compilers for Parallel Computing*. Chapter Language Extensions in Support of Compiler Parallelization, pp. 78–94. Berlin, Heidelberg: Springer-Verlag, 2007.

[25] M. Kulkarni, K. Pingali, B. Walter, G. Ramanarayanan, K. Bala, and L.P. Chew, "Optimistic parallelism requires abstractions," in *Proceedings of the 2007 ACM SIGPLAN Conference on Programming Language Design and Implementation (PLDI '07)*, San Diego, CA, pp. 211–222, 2007.

[26] K.E. Iverson, *A Programming Language*. New York: Wiley, 1962.

[27] M. Herlihy and J.E.B. Moss, "Transactional memory: Architectural support for lock-free data structures," in *Proceedings of the 20th International Symposium on Computer Architecture (ISCA '93)*, San Diego, CA, pp. 289–300, 1993.

[28] F.W. Burton and M.R. Sleep, "Executing functional programs on a virtual tree of processors," in *Proceedings of the 1981 Conference on Functional Programming Languages and Computer Architecture (FPCA '81)*, Portsmouth, NH, pp. 187–194, 1981.

[29] J. Shirako, D.M. Peixotto, V. Sarkar, and W.N. Scherer, "Phasers: A unified deadlock-free construct for collective and point-to-point synchronization," in *Proceedings of the 2008 International Conference on Supercomputing (ICS '08)*, Isloand of Kos, Greece, June 2008.

5

Scalable Computing on Large Heterogeneous CPU/GPU Supercomputers

Fengshun Lu, Kaijun Ren, Junqiang Song, and Jinjun Chen

5.1 INTRODUCTION

Recent advances in the graphics processing unit (GPU) technology have brought enormous benefits to the high-performance computing (HPC) community. Many scientific and engineering applications have achieved order-of-magnitude speedups on energy-efficient CPU/GPU clusters, such as TianHe-1A (TH-1A) [1], Nebulae [2], Lincoln [3] and TSUBAME [4]. Besides the heterogeneity in their processing units, these HPC systems also have complex memory hierarchy: distributed memory across different compute nodes, shared memory within each node, and device memory on GPUs. Consequently, scientific researchers and domain scientists are confronted with great challenges to perform efficient and scalable computing on these heterogeneous HPC infrastructures.

Although most issues of scalable computing on traditional CPU-based HPC systems have been extensively addressed in the past decades [5–9], the scalability issue for newly acknowledged heterogeneous CPU/GPU systems has not been well addressed. We herein give an overview of the recent work on the scalability issue of GPU applications. Goddeke et al. [10] investigated the weak scalability of finite element method (FEM) calculations on a 160-node GPU cluster and observed that the performance of the FEM applications scaled favorably with the number of

Scalable Computing and Communications: Theory and Practice, First Edition. Edited by
Samee U. Khan, Albert Y. Zomaya, and Lizhe Wang.
© 2013 John Wiley & Sons, Inc. Published 2013 by John Wiley & Sons, Inc.

nodes. Ltaief et al. [11] addressed the challenges in developing scalable algorithms for CPU/GPU platforms and demonstrated that the hybrid Cholesky factorization scaled well with the increasing CPU/GPU couples. Lashuk et al. [12] implemented the fast-multipole method and achieved good weak scalability with the workload of 256 million points on 256 GPUs, which was attributed to the scalable reduction algorithm for the evaluation phase and the data structure transformation tailored for GPU architecture. Jetley et al. [3] scaled the hierarchical *N*-body simulations on GPU clusters and found that the scalability of applications could be improved by utilizing optimization techniques, such as optimal kernel organization, removal of serial bottlenecks, and workload balance between CPUs and GPUs. Shimokawabe et al. [4] efficiently ported their production weather code to the 528-GPU TSUBAME supercomputer and achieved 80-fold performance over that on a single CPU core. They optimized the boundary-exchange operation by overlapping its communication with the computation to achieve better scalability.

Among the large-scale scientific and engineering applications, there are many legacy programs (such as IFS [13] and WRF [14]) that cannot directly benefit from the immense computational capabilities of heterogeneous HPC systems. It is also impractical to implement them from scratch with other languages like OpenCL [15] or programming paradigms like MapReduce [16]. As such, the ideal approaches are expected not only to preserve most of the legacy code but also to accelerate the computation-intensive kernels on GPUs with vendor-provided programming models. In this chapter, we endeavor to find scalable approaches to make the legacy code benefit from large heterogeneous CPU/GPU systems.

With our approaches, we adopt the existing programming models to construct viable programming patterns targeting large-scale CPU/GPU clusters. We take advantage of the NAS Parallel Benchmarks (NPBs) [17] and a production code for radiation physics in the WRF model to illustrate the strategy of making the legacy code benefited from heterogeneous systems. The remainder of the chapter is organized as follows. Section 5.2 gives a simple overview of the heterogeneous computing environments that include the TH-1A supercomputer and the relevant parallel programming models. Section 5.3 presents our proposed scalable programming patterns for large GPU clusters, which is followed by the detailed hybrid implementations for NPB kernels and RRTM–LW radiation process in Section 5.4. The experimental results and performance analysis are given in Section 5.5. Finally, Section 5.6 concludes this chapter.

5.2 HETEROGENEOUS COMPUTING ENVIRONMENTS

In this section, we give a short overview of the TH-1A supercomputer and the existing programming models based on which we construct scalable parallel programming patterns for large GPU clusters.

5.2.1 TianHe-1A Supercomputer

The TH-1A supercomputer is built by the National University of Defense Technology and deployed in the National Supercomputing Center in Tianjin. It ranked number 1 in the 36th TOP500 List [18] with maximal Linpack performance of 2.566 PFlops.

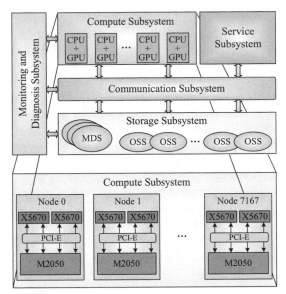

FIGURE 5.1. *TH-1A system architecture and the detailed compute subsystem. Adapted from literature [1].*

As depicted in Figure 5.1, TH-1A consists of five subsystems: compute subsystem, service subsystem, storage subsystem, communication subsystem, and the monitoring and diagnosis subsystem. We herein give an emphasis on the compute subsystem and refer the interested readers to References 1 and 19 for more information.

The compute subsystem is constructed with 7168 compute nodes, each of which is configured with two Intel CPUs and one NVIDIA GPU. The CPU is six-core Xeon X5670 (2.93 GHz) and the GPU is Tesla M2050 (1.15 GHz). The peak double-precision performance of each compute node is 655.64 Gflops (i.e., CPU has 140.64 Gflops and GPU has 515 Gflops). The CPUs in compute node fulfill various functionalities, such as running operating systems, managing system resources, and performing general-purpose computation. The GPU mainly executes the computation with abundant data parallelisms in the single-instruction multiple-data (SIMD) scheme. Note that nearly 20% (i.e., 140.64 out of 655.64 Gflops) of the peak performance for each compute node is attributed to the two CPUs. Therefore, efficiently exploiting the computational capacities of both CPUs and GPUs is quite important for HPC on heterogeneous clusters.

5.2.2 Programming Models

Message-passing interface (MPI) [20] provides a standard set of subprogram definitions for implementing parallel programs with a distributed-memory programming model. In the MPI programming model, users manage the communication operations between different MPI processes by calling routines to send and receive messages. In addition, users completely control the workload distribution, which permits the optimization of data locality and workflow. Since it has the advantages of excellent scalability and portability, MPI is an appropriate programming model to accomplish the communication functionality between different compute nodes of large GPU clusters.

OpenMP [21] is an open specification for shared-memory programming. It consists of compiler directives, environment variables, and runtime library routines. Programmers explicitly specify the actions to be taken by the compiler and the runtime system for executing the program in parallel. All OpenMP programs follow the fork-and-join execution model and utilize the work-sharing directives to distribute the workload among the spawned threads. The issues of data dependencies, data conflicts, race conditions, and deadlocks should be addressed by programmers. OpenMP is often used to exploit the fine-grained parallelism of applications on shared-memory architecture.

CUDA [22] is the programming model developed by NVIDIA to harness its powerful GPUs. It has provided support for high-level languages like C/C++ and Fortran, which maintains a low learning curve for programmers. The scientists throughout the industry and academia have already achieved dramatic speedups on production and research applications by utilizing CUDA. In this model, GPU programs are organized into kernels that are performed with abundant threads in the form of thread-blocks. Each thread-block must be scheduled onto one particular streaming multiprocessor (SM), and several thread-blocks may reside on the same SM to hide various latencies. For the devices with compute capability 2.x or higher, programmers can exploit three levels of parallelism within applications, namely, the *thread*-level, the *block*-level, and the *grid*-level parallelism.

5.3 SCALABLE PROGRAMMING PATTERNS FOR LARGE GPU CLUSTERS

Scalable hybrid programming patterns should enable the exploitation of all the computational resources in state-of-the-art GPU clusters, namely, the multicore CPUs and many-core GPUs. CPUs and GPUs can cooperate in the following three ways: (1) CPU accounts for the task of preparing and transferring data and GPU performs arithmetic operations [23]; (2) they perform arithmetic operations from different workloads [24]; and (3) they cooperatively compute the same workload. In this section, we present two hybrid programming patterns and a workload distribution scheme used in the later pattern to ensure the load balance between the CPUs and GPUs.

5.3.1 MPI+CUDA (MC) Hybrid Pattern

The MC pattern depicted in Figure 5.2 has been widely utilized on large clusters based on NVIDIA GPUs [10]. In this hybrid pattern, MPI performs the communication between different nodes of HPC systems and CUDA drives the powerful GPUs. Programs coded under the MC pattern are executed with one MPI process launched on each CPU core, all of which jointly drive the GPU device with CUDA application programming interfaces (APIs).

The latest GPUs support simultaneous execution of kernels from different MPI processes and maintain a separate context for each of these processes. The one-context-per-process scheme inhibits the MPI processes from sharing the objects that

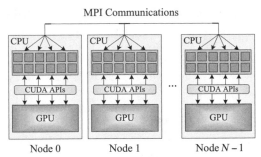

FIGURE 5.2. Schematic diagram for MPI+CUDA parallel programming pattern.

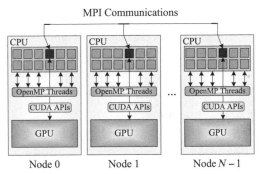

FIGURE 5.3. Schematic diagram for MPI+OpenMP/CUDA parallel programming pattern.

reside in the same GPU device. For example, much common data of "state-heavy" geosciences applications can be shared by different MPI processes in the CPU code; however, GPU needs to create data instances for all the MPI processes, resulting in redundant allocations of device memory. Therefore, the problem scale may be bounded by the device memory constraint. Besides, all the MPI processes have to upload data to and download results from GPUs, which inevitably results in many data transfers and exacerbates the memory bandwidth pressure. To address these issues, the MC pattern can be amended by allowing only part of these MPI processes to interact with GPUs and by employing a complicated strategy to ensure the load balance between them.

5.3.2 MPI+OpenMP/CUDA (MOC) Hybrid Pattern

We try to address the aforementioned issues by amending the MC pattern with the introduction of OpenMP threads to exploit the parallelism within multicore CPUs.

Figure 5.3 presents another parallel programming model called MOC for large GPU clusters. In this model, only one MPI process is launched on each compute node, which brings two aspects of benefits to state-heavy geosciences applications like WRF. On the one hand, only one context for the MPI process is maintained by GPU and the underutilization of device memory is eliminated. On the other hand, compared with the MC scenario, many fewer data transfers are performed and each one has larger volume, which is favored by GPU devices and can alleviate the memory bandwidth pressure. The MPI process spawns as many OpenMP threads as the amount of CPU cores within each compute node. Only the *master* thread cooperates with GPU and the others perform relevant arithmetic operations in parallel. Hence, domain experts can exploit the coarse-grained parallelism within applications through MPI and the fine-grained parallelism with OpenMP and CUDA.

Note that the MOC pattern requires a thread-compliant MPI implementation. It should support four thread levels. We mainly focus on the *MPI_Thread_Funneled* and *MPI_Thread_Multiple* of them. On the former level, only the *master* thread can make MPI calls, and all the threads are idle except the master one during the communication process. However, no restrictions exist for the latter level, and multiple threads can call MPI subroutines. When one thread is fulfilling the communication task, other threads can perform computational operations if the task-scheduling scheme is efficiently adjusted [25]. For the sake of simplicity, the MOC pattern only requires the MPI_Thread_Funneled thread-support; otherwise, a complex task-scheduling scheme must be introduced to each application for fully taking advantage of the MPI_Thread_Multiple level.

5.3.3 Workload Distribution Scheme

Assuming that there are M n-core CPUs corresponding to each GPU within a single compute node, the workload assigned to CPUs is accomplished with $Mn - 1$ CPU cores, leaving one CPU core to interact with GPU. Since CPUs and GPUs have different arithmetic capacities, the key issue for hybrid computing is how to efficiently distribute the workload between these two computing resources. The best workload distribution can be directly obtained by enumerating all the possible distributions and executing the application with each of them. However, that method is rather time-consuming and an efficient workload distribution scheme is highly demanded. In this section, we present an efficient workload distribution scheme for the embarrassingly parallel (EP) applications, which have independent workload and negligible I/O operations.

Let P_{CPU} denote the computing power of each CPU core, then the effective computational capacity of M CPUs and one GPU can be approximated with $(Mn - 1)P_{CPU}$ and P_{GPU}, respectively. Given the workload W, the wall-clock time T for the workload can be shown in Equation (5.1):

$$\begin{cases} T = \max\{T_{CPU}, T_{GPU}\} \\ T_{GPU} = W\alpha/P_{GPU} \\ T_{CPU} = W(1-\alpha)/(P_{CPU} \times (Mn-1)), \end{cases} \tag{5.1}$$

where $T_{CPU}(T_{GPU})$ denotes the wall-clock time for CPU (GPU) to accomplish the relevant workload, and α represents the workload distribution ratio for GPU. T reaches its minimum at the workload distribution ratio:

$$\alpha = \cfrac{1}{1 + (Mn - 1)\cfrac{P_{CPU}}{P_{GPU}}}, \tag{5.2}$$

when T_{CPU} is equal to T_{GPU}. Hence, if the relative computing power of CPU over GPU is accurately evaluated, the best workload distribution ratio α can be determined.

Given the GPU implementation of some particular application, we can obtain its speedup S over the single CPU core counterpart. We substitute P_{CPU}/P_{GPU} of Equation (5.2) with $1/S$ and get the best workload distribution scheme as

$$\alpha = \frac{1}{1 + \dfrac{Mn - 1}{S}}. \tag{5.3}$$

5.4 HYBRID IMPLEMENTATIONS

5.4.1 NAS Parallel Benchmarks

The NPBs [17] are well-known applications for evaluating parallel systems and tools. Its components are all abstracted from a large-scale computational fluid dynamics legacy code. In this section, we extend the EP and computational grid (CG) of MPI-NPB 3.3 with the MOC model targeting large GPU clusters like TH-1A. Note that the terminologies *device* and *host* comply with the convention in CUDA.

5.4.1.1 EP The EP benchmark is typical of many Monte Carlo simulation applications. Each MPI process can independently generate pseudorandom numbers and uses them to compute pairs of normally distributed numbers. No communication is needed until at the very end when all MPI processes are combined to verify the results.

The skeleton of EP–MOC is given in Algorithm 5.1. The *MPI_Init_Thread* is called (line 1) to enable the multithreaded MPI environment. The number of OpenMP threads spawned by the MPI process depends on the environment variable *OMP_NUM_THREADS*. We enable the nested parallelism (line 5) so that one OpenMP thread drives GPU while the other $Mn - 1$ threads simultaneously perform *ep_cpu*. Based on the relative computational capacity of CPUs and GPUs, the workload distribution (line 4) is performed with the scheme presented in Section 5.3.3.

Subroutines *vranlc* and *gpairs* compose the main body of EP benchmark. We implement them on GPUs with three CUDA kernels: (1) *vranlc_ker*, which generates uniform pseudorandom numbers and stores them into device memory d_x; (2) *gpairs_ker*, whose threads load elements from d_x to assign x_1 (x_2) and keep the temporary Gaussian deviate sum S_x (S_y) in device memory d_sx (d_sy); and (3) *reduce_ker*, which performs a sum reduction of data in d_sx (d_sy) to obtain the total Gaussian deviate.

Algorithm 5.1
EP–MOC: **call** MPI_Init_Thread; **do** some initialization; **call** warm_gpu; **assign** CPU and GPU the workload; **call** omp_set_nested(true); !\$ **omp parallel num_threads**(2) **if** tid=0 **then call** ep_gpu; **else call** ep_cpu; **endif** !\$ **omp end parallel do** the verification. **subroutine** ep_cpu {!\$ **omp parallel num_threads** ($Mn - 1$) **call** vranlc;

call gpairs. !$ **omp end parallel** } **subroutine** ep_gpu { **do** memory allocation; **call** vranlc_ker<<<conf>>>(d_x); **call** gpairs_ker<<<conf>>>(d_sx,d_sy,d_x); **call** reduce_ker<<<conf>>>(sx,sy,d_sx,d_sy); **copy** sx(sy) to $S_x(S_y)$; **free** memories.}

5.4.1.2 CG The CG benchmark employs the conjugate gradient method to approximately compute the smallest eigenvalue of a large sparse symmetric positive definite matrix. Each iteration of CG consists of two dot product operations, three vector updates, and one sparse matrix–vector multiplication (SpMV) that is by far the most expensive operation. In our GPU implementation of CG, only the SpMV operation is ported onto GPUs and others are executed on multicore CPUs.

CG uses the compressed sparse row (CSR) format to store the sparse matrix A. The array a contains all nonzero elements of A; array *colidx* contains column indices of these nonzero elements; and entries of array *rowstr* point to the first elements of subsequent rows of A in the previous arrays a and *colidx*. The SpMV operation can be accomplished by assigning each thread the workload of one row. However, this straightforward GPU implementation performs badly and sometimes can even be outperformed by the optimized CPU counterpart. The primary reason is that threads within a warp cannot access arrays a and *rowstr* in a coalesced manner. Hence, we assign one warp of threads to each matrix row [26] so as to reduce the memory bandwidth pressure.

The detailed CG–MOC implementation is presented in Algorithm 5.2. In the subroutine *cg_hybrid*, the arrays a, *colidx*, and *rowstr* are copied to device memory only once (line 8), while the array p is transferred between the host and device memory back and forth (lines 11, 14, and 17). Since the iterations of the CG algorithm are dependent from each other, there are no parallelisms within the outer *it*-loop and inner *i*-loop. We can only exploit the parallelism among the most expensive SpMV operation. Note that the detailed OpenMP parallelization of other operations is not shown in Algorithm 5.2, and we include the date-transfer overhead introduced by operations relevant to lines 11, 14, and 17.

Algorithm 5.2
CG–MOC: **call** MPI_Init_Thread; **do** some initialization; **call** warm_gpu; **call** cg_hybrid; **do** the verification. **subroutine** cg_hybrid {**do** memory allocation; **copy** a,colidx,rowstr to device memory; **for** $it = 1{\rightarrow}niter$ **do** $z = 0$; $r = x$; $\rho = r^T r$; $p = r$; **copy** p to device memory; **for** $i = 1{\rightarrow}25$ **do call** Ap_ker<<<conf>>>(d_w); **copy** d_w to host memory; $\alpha = \rho/(p^T q)$; $z = z + p\alpha$; $\rho_0 = \rho$; $r = r - q\alpha$; $\rho = r^T r$; $\beta = \rho/\rho_0$; $p = r + p\beta$; **copy** p to device memory; **endfor endfor free** memories.}

5.4.2 RRTM–LW: Longwave Radiation Process

The radiation process is one of the most important atmospheric physics processes in operational numerical weather prediction or climate models. Specially, the RRTM–LW [27] scheme can calculate fluxes and cooling rates for the longwave region (10–3000 cm^{-1}) in arbitrary atmosphere. The RRTM–LW scheme represents the atmosphere using a collection of three-dimensional cells, whose two horizontal dimensions are over an equally spaced Cartesian coordinate system and the third one over vertical levels of the atmosphere in pressure-based terrain-following coordinates. It belongs to the "column physics," [28] and its code structure is shown in

```
1    do j = jts to jte
2       do i = its to ite
3          call INIRAD;
4          call MM5ATM;
5          call SETCOEF;
6          call GASABS;
7          call RTRN.
8       enddo
9    enddo
```

FIGURE 5.4. Code structure of RRTM–LW scheme.

TABLE 5.1. Three Different Decomposition Methods and Their Corresponding Data Parallelisms (#DP)

Method	#DP	Kernel	Description
1	4380	Inirad, mm5atm, setcoef, gasabs	Thread per column
2	122640	rtrn_pre	Thread-per-column layer
3	613200	rtrn_dn1, rtrn_dn2, rtrn_up	Thread-per-column g-point

Figure 5.4. The subroutine *INIRAD* performs the initialization; *MM5ATM* inputs atmospheric profiles, such as the temperature, pressure, and molecular amounts for various absorption species; *SETCOEF* computes indices and fractions used for interpolating the temperature and pressure of a given atmosphere; *GASABS* consists of 16 subroutines, each of which calculates gaseous optical depth for the corresponding longwave spectral band; and *RTRN* obtains the fluxes and cooling rates for arbitrary atmosphere.

Each of these subroutines is implemented with a separate kernel except the last two ones that are too large to run efficiently as single kernels. *GASABS* is split into 16 kernels corresponding to the 16 longwave spectral bands, and *RTRN* is divided into 6 kernels. For most kernels, we assign each CUDA thread the workload of one "column." In order to further exploit the fine-grained data parallelism, we even divide the workload of some kernels based on the layer or g-point dimension. Therefore, three decomposition strategies exist in our GPU implementation of RRTM–LW and they result in three different data parallelisms as listed in Table 5.1.

Let N_x and N_y denote the latitudinal and longitudinal grid dimensions, respectively. The computations for the $N_x \times N_y$ "columns" are independent from each other, and we distribute the workload between CPUs and GPUs with the scheme presented in Section 5.3.3. The RRTM–LW belongs to the EP problems and the skeleton of its MOC version is similar to Algorithm 5.1. Hence, the detailed algorithm for MOC-RRTM is not shown here.

5.5 EXPERIMENTAL RESULTS

In this section, we first validate the workload distribution scheme with RRTM_LW, then perform NPB and RRTM–LW on the TH-1A supercomputer and analyze their strong scalabilities.

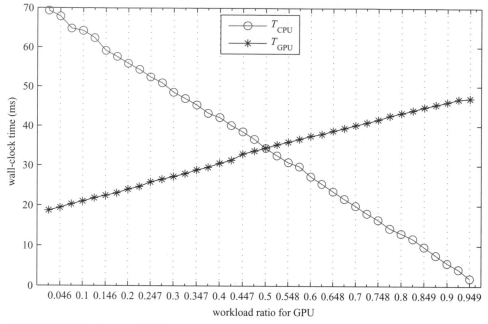

FIGURE 5.5. Results for RRTM–LW with 73×60 horizontal grid points and 27 vertical levels. T_{CPU} and T_{GPU} is the wall-clock time for performing the workload assigned to CPUs and GPUs, respectively.

5.5.1 Validation of Workload Distribution Scheme

There are 12 CPU cores in each compute node of TH-1A supercomputer; hence, 12 OpenMP threads are spawned by each MPI process and Mn in Equation (5.3) is equal to 12. The workload of RRTM–LW is distributed to CPU and GPU by splitting both the i and j loops depicted in Figure 5.4. We gradually decrease the GPU workload by $10 \times PT$ ij-loops, where PT (i.e., 11 for TH-1A) denotes the number of OpenMP threads performing arithmetic operations in each compute node.

Figure 5.5 presents the results for RRTM–LW (medium workload) with 73×60 horizontal grid points and 27 vertical levels. The predicted workload distribution ratio α relevant to the medium workload is 0.597 obtained by substituting S in Equation (5.3) with 16.3. However, Figure 5.5 shows that RRTM–LW performs best when α reaches 0.5. We owe the deviation of 0.097 in workload distribution ratio to the start overhead T_O of CUDA runtime environments. When only 4.6% workload is assigned to GPU, T_{GPU} is still about 20 ms, most of which is contributed by T_O. Consequently, T_{GPU} is not proportional to workload distribution ratio α, which is different from T_{CPU}.

To further validate our workload distribution scheme, we scale the workload downward and upward and present the results in Figure 5.6 (small workload) and Figure 5.7 (large workload), respectively. For RRTM–LW with small workload, the relevant S is 10.37 and hence the predicted α is 0.485. Figure 5.6 portrays that T_{CPU} equals T_{GPU} when α reaches 0.376, which results in a deviation of 0.109 in the workload distribution ratio α. Similarly, the predicted α for RRTM–LW with large

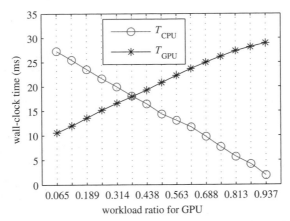

FIGURE 5.6. *Results for RRTM–LW with 42 × 42 horizontal grid points and 27 vertical levels.*

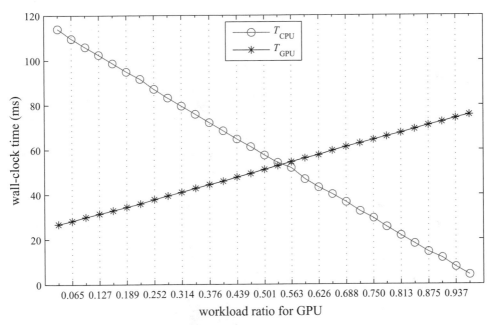

FIGURE 5.7. *Results for RRTM–LW with 84 × 84 horizontal grid points and 27 vertical levels.*

workload is 0.601 obtained with the speedup S of 16.58. Note that RRTM–LW achieves its best performance when α is about 0.532, and a deviation of 0.068 can also be observed.

We observe that the actual workload distribution ratio α is always smaller than the predicated one for various workloads because of T_O. In practical run, we can calculate the workload distribution ratio α based on Equation (5.3) and then amend it with an empirical value corresponding to T_O of different workload scales.

5.5.2 Strong Scalability of EP and CG

There are many EP applications in the HPC community, such as Monte Carlo simulations, dense linear algebra applications (like DGEMM). EP is representative of applications in this category, and its relevant performance under different programming paradigms is portrayed in Figure 5.8. Note that the *y*-axis is in *log* scale and the execution configuration $m \times n$ denotes m compute nodes, each of which is launched with n MPI processes.

We observe that EP–MPI achieves a speedup of 7.96× at execution configuration 2048×1 over at 256×1, which demonstrates that EP–MPI has a good strong scalability. For the EP–MOC implementation, a maximal speedup of 55.8× is obtained at the execution configuration 256×1. When the number of MPI processes reach up to 2048, the performance speedup decreases to 33.7×, which mainly owes to the reduced workload for each MPI process.

Although GPUs are adept in dealing with computation-intensive applications, Figure 5.9 illustrates that memory-bounded applications like CG benchmark can

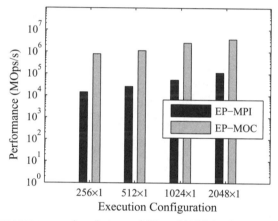

FIGURE 5.8. *Performance comparison between MPI and MOC implementations of EP at class E.*

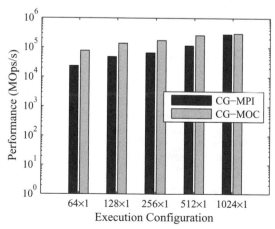

FIGURE 5.9. *Performance comparison between MPI and MOC implementations of CG at class D.*

still achieve great performance improvement through GPU acceleration. Compared with the CG–MPI implementation, the CG–MOC counterpart gains about 3.3× performance at the execution configuration 64 × 1. When the number of compute nodes gradually increases up to 1024, the speedup decreases to 1.06, which is attributed to the relatively large overhead of data transferring between host and device memory against the decreasing workload for each GPU device.

It can be noticed that the 2× or 3× speedup is relatively small compared with that of the EP implementations. The reasons for this are as follows: (1) We maintain the CSR format of CG benchmark to storage the sparse matrix, which is not the best choice for the GPU hardware; (2) the launched threads are underutilized in our implementation. We utilize one 32-thread warp to compute the elements within each matrix row. However, the matrices in all the available workload scales of CG have fewer than 32 nonzero elements per row. For example, matrices in class D have 21 nonzero elements and in class E 26 nonzero entries. The matrix FEM/accelerator used in literature [26] has an average of 21.6 nonzero elements per row and a performance speedup of 2× is reported, which is analogous to our results.

5.5.3 Strong Scalability of RRTM–LW

We integrate RRTM–MOC implementation of RRTM–LW into the WRF parallel benchmark (WPB) [29] and perform WPB on the 2.5-km case with up to 1024 compute nodes. The default WRF configuration is used. All the 12 CPU cores of each compute node are utilized: (1) 12 MPI processes are launched on these CPU cores for RRTM–MPI, and (2) only 1 MPI process is launched on each compute node for RRTM–MOC and 12 OpenMP threads are spawned by the MPI process. Figure 5.10 presents the wall-clock times for RRTM–MPI and RRTM–MOC on various processor scales.

It is observed that the wall-clock times for both RRTM–MPI and RRTM–MOC implementations drop linearly when the processor scale is gradually increased. Besides, the speedup fluctuates about 2.1 when the number of compute nodes increases from 256 to 1024, which demonstrates a good strong scalability. Note that

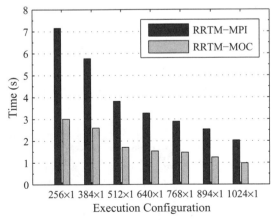

FIGURE 5.10. *Performance comparison between MPI and MOC implementations of RRTM–LW.*

the speedup decreases from 2.375 at 256 compute nodes to 2.077 at 1024 ones. We owe this to the shrinking computational workload for the relatively powerful GPUs.

5.6   CONCLUSIONS

Scalability is a key concept for parallel computing on large-scale distributed systems. Many scalability metrics and models have been proposed for homogeneous and heterogeneous systems with traditional CPUs. However, the scalability for newly acknowledged heterogeneous CPU/GPU systems has not been well addressed. In this chapter, we have constructed a scalable hybrid programming pattern for large GPU clusters. Based on the TH-1A supercomputer, we have performed extensive experiments with several benchmarks and production codes to find the factors affecting the scalability for large-scale scientific and engineering applications. Experimental results show that the scalability of GPU applications is jointly determined by several factors, such as starting overhead of GPU computing environments, data-transfer cost between the host and the device memories, load imbalance, and MPI communication cost.

Although some factors for scalability of GPU applications have been identified, we have not reduced a comprehensive function on these factors, based on which we can further conduct a quantitative analysis. In the future, we will research more applications on GPU clusters and endeavor to obtain such scalability function after doing more experiments.

ACKNOWLEDGMENTS

This work was partially supported by the National Nature Science Foundation of China under Grant Nos. 60903042, 60736013, and 60872152, and by National 863 Plans Projects under Grant No. 863-2010AA012404.

REFERENCES

[1] X.J. Yang, X.K. Liao, K. Lu, Q.F. Hu, J.Q. Song, and J.S. Su, "The TianHe-1A supercomputer: Its hardware and software," *Journal of Computer Science and Technology*, 26(3):344–351, 2011.

[2] N.H. Sun, J. Xing, Z.G. Huo, G.M. Tan, J. Xiong, B. Li, and C. Ma, "Dawning Nebulae: A petaFLOPS supercomputer with a heterogeneous structure," *Journal of Computer Science and Technology*, 26(3):352–362, 2011.

[3] P. Jetley, L. Wesolowski, F. Gioachin, L.V. Kale, and T.R. Quinn, "Scaling hierarchical N-body simulations on GPU clusters," in *Proceedings of the 2010 ACM/IEEE Conference on Supercomputing*, New Orleans, LA, pp. 1–11, IEEE, 2010.

[4] T. Shimokawabe, T. Aoki, C. Muroi, J. Ishida, K. Kawano, T. Endo, A. Nukada, N. Maruyama, and K. Matsuoka, "An 80-fold speedup, 15.0 TFlops full GPU acceleration of non-hydrostatic weather model ASUCA production code," in *Proceedings of the 2010 ACM/IEEE Conference on Supercomputing*, New Orleans, LA, pp. 1–11, IEEE, 2010.

[5] D. Macri, "The scalability problem," *ACM Queue*, 10(1):66–73, 2004.

[6] Y. Cui, K.B. Olsen, T.H. Jordan, K. Lee, J. Zhou, P. Small, D. Roten, G. Ely, D.K. Panda, A. Chourasia, J. Levesque, S.M. Day, and P. Maechling, "Scalable earthquake simulations on petascale supercomputers," in *Proceedings of the 2010 ACM/IEEE Conference on Supercomputing*, New Orleans, LA, pp. 1–20, IEEE, 2010.

[7] X.H. Sun, "Scalability versus execution time in scalable systems," *Journal of Parallel and Distributed Computing*, 62:173–192, 2002.

[8] D. Muller-Wichards and W. Ronsch, "Scalability of algorithms: An analytic approach," *Parallel Computing*, 21:937–952, 1995.

[9] P. Jogalekar and M. Woodside, "Evaluating the scalability of distributed systems," *IEEE Transactions on Parallel and Distributed Systems*, 11(6):589–603, 2000.

[10] D. Goddeke, R. Strzodka, J. Mohd-Yusof, P. McCormick, S.H.M. Buijssen, M. Grajewski, and S. Turek, "Exploring weak scalability for FEM calculations on a GPU-enhanced cluster," *Parallel Computing*, 33:685–699, 2007.

[11] H. Ltaief, S. Tomov, R. Nath, P. Du, and J. Dongarra, "A scalable high performant Cholesky factorization for multicore with GPU accelerators," in *High Performance Computing for Computational Science-VECPAR 2010*, pp. 93–101, Springer-Verlag, 2010.

[12] I. Lashuk, A. Chandramowlishwaran, H. Langston, T.-A. Nguyen, R. Sampath, A. Shringarpure, R. Vuduc, L. Ying, D. Zorin, and G. Biros, "A massively parallel adaptive fast-multipole method on heterogeneous architectures," in *Proceedings of the 2009 ACM/IEEE Conference on Supercomputing*, Portland, OR, pp. 1–12, IEEE, 2009.

[13] S.R.M. Barros, D. Dent, L. Isaksen, G. Robinson, G. Mozdzynski, and F. Wollenweber, "The IFS model: A parallel production weather code," *Parallel Computing*, 21(10):1621–1638, 1995.

[14] J. Michalakes, J. Dudhia, D. Gill, T. Henderson, J. Klemp, W. Skamarock, and W. Wang, "The weather research and forecast model: Software architecture and performance," in *Proceedings of the 11th ECMWF Workshop on the Use of High Performance Computing In Meteorology*, Reading, UK, pp. 156–168, 2004.

[15] J.E. Stone, D. Gohara, and G.C. Shi, "OpenCL: A parallel programming standard for heterogeneous computing systems," *Computing in Science and Engineering*, 12(3):66–73, 2010.

[16] J. Dean and S. Ghemawat, "MapReduce: Simplified data processing on large clusters," *Communications of the ACM*, 51(1):107–113, 2008.

[17] NPB homepage. Available at http://www.nas.nasa.gov/Resources/Software/npb.html. Accessed May 15, 2011.

[18] 36th TOP500 list. Available at http://www.top500.org/lists/2010/11. Accessed May 15, 2011.

[19] X.J. Yang, X.K. Liao, W.X. Xu, J.Q. Song, Q.F. Hu, J.S. Su, L.Q. Xiao, K. Lu, Q. Dou, J.P. Jiang, and C.Q. Yang, "TH-1: China's first petaflop supercomputer," *Frontiers of Computer Science in China*, 4(4):445–455, 2010.

[20] MPI homepage. Available at http://www.mpi-forum.org/. Accessed May 15, 2011.

[21] OpenMP homepage. Available at http://openmp.org/wp/. Accessed May 15, 2011.

[22] J. Nickolls, I. Buck, M. Garland, and K. Skadron, "Scalable parallel programming with CUDA," *ACM Queue*, 6(2):40–53, 2008.

[23] K. Spafford, J. Meredith, J. Vetter, J. Chen, R. Grout, and R. Sankaran, "Accelerating S3D: A GPGPU case study," in *Euro-Par 2009 Workshops, LNCS 6043* (H.X. Lin, et al., eds.), pp. 122–131, 2009.

[24] S.J. Park, J.A. Ross, D.R. Shires, D.A. Richie, B.J. Henz, and L.H. Nguyen, "Hybrid core acceleration of UWB SIRE radar signal processing," *IEEE Transactions on Parallel and Distributed Systems*, 22(1):46–57, 2011.

[25] T. Yoshinaga and T.Q. Viet, "Optimization for hybrid MPI-OpenMP programs on a cluster of SMP PCs," in *Proceedings of Joint Japan-Tunisia Workshop on Computer Systems and Information Technology*, Tokyo, Japan, pp. 1–8, 2004.

[26] N. Bell and M. Garland, "Efficient sparse matrix-vector multiplication on CUDA," Technical Report NVR-2008-004, NVIDIA Corporation, 2008.

[27] M.J. Iacono, E.J. Mlawer, S.A. Clough, and J.-J. Morcrette, "Impact of an improved long-wave radiation model, RRTM, on the energy budget and thermodynamic properties of the NCAR community climate mode, CCM3," *Journal of Geophysical Research*, 105: 14873–14890, 2000.

[28] J. Michalakes and M. Vachharajani, "GPU acceleration of numerical weather prediction," *Parallel Processing Letters*, 18(4):531–548, 2008.

[29] WPB homepage. Available at http://www.mmm.ucar.edu/WG2bench/. Accessed May 15, 2011.

6

Diagnosability of Multiprocessor Systems

Chia-Wei Lee and Sun-Yuan Hsieh

6.1 INTRODUCTION

The rapid advances in very-large-scale integration (VLSI) technology and wafer-scale integration (WSI) technology have made it possible to design and produce a multiprocessor system containing hundreds or even thousands of processors (nodes) on a single chip. As the number of nodes in a multiprocessor system increases, node fault identification in such systems becomes more crucial for reliable computing. The process of discriminating between faulty nodes and fault-free nodes in a system is called *fault diagnosis*. When a faulty node is identified, it is replaced by a fault-free node to maintain the system's reliability. The *diagnosability* of a system is the maximum number of faulty nodes that the system can identify.

Determining the diagnosability of multiprocessor systems based on various strategies and models has been the focus of a great deal of research in recent years (e.g., see References 1–25). Among the proposed models, two of which, namely, the *PMC model* (after Preparata, Metze, and Chien [19]) and the *MM model* (after Maeng and Malek [18]), are well known and widely used. In the PMC model, every node u is capable of testing whether another node v is faulty if there exists a communication link between them. The PMC model assumes that the tests of faulty nodes performed by fault-free ones always return one and that the tests performed by faulty nodes return arbitrary results. The PMC model was also adopted in References 2, 4, 9, 15, and 16. In an attempt to have a more realistic representation of systems

Scalable Computing and Communications: Theory and Practice, First Edition. Edited by
Samee U. Khan, Albert Y. Zomaya, and Lizhe Wang.
© 2013 John Wiley & Sons, Inc. Published 2013 by John Wiley & Sons, Inc.

whose nodes have a rather complex structure, Barsi et al. [26] introduced a modification of the PMC model, namely, the *BGM model* (after Barsi, Grandoni, and Maestrini). The BGM model uses the same testing strategy as the PMC model, but it assumes that a faulty node is always tested as faulty regardless of the state of the tester. The BGM model was adopted in Reference 27.

In the MM model, on the other hand, a comparison is performed such that a node, chosen to be a comparator, monitors a pair of its neighboring nodes executing the same test input and compares their responses. We use $(u, v)_w$ to represent a *comparison* (or *test*) in which nodes u and v are compared by w. For this reason, the MM model is also called the *comparison diagnosis model*. The method of the MM model takes advantage of the homogeneity of multiprocessor systems in which comparisons can be made easily. This approach seems attractive because no additional hardware is required and transient and permanent faults may be detected before completing the comparison program. There is no faulty voter problem because the comparator can also be tested. Moreover, the MM model can be considered to be a generalization of the PMC model because if for each comparison edge $(u, v)_w$, either $w = u$ or $w = v$, then the comparison model corresponds directly to the PMC model [20]. Sengupta and Dahbura [20] further suggested a modification of the MM model, called the MM* model, in which any node has to test another two nodes if the former is adjacent to the latter two. The MM* model might be leading the way toward a polynomial-time diagnosis algorithm for the more general MM self-diagnosable systems, and complexity results on determining the level of diagnosability of systems. The MM* model was also adopted in References 4, 11, 13, 14, and 24.

6.2   FUNDAMENTAL CONCEPTS

An *undirected graph* (*graph*) $G = (V, E)$ is composed of a *node set V* and an *edge set E*, where V is a finite set and E is a subset of $\{(u, v)|(u, v)$ is an unordered pair of $V\}$. We also use $V(G)$ and $E(G)$ to denote the node set and edge set of G, respectively. For an edge (u, v), we call u and v the *end nodes* of the edge. A *subgraph* of $G = (V, E)$ is a graph (V', E') such that $V' \subseteq V$ and $E' \subseteq E$. Given $U \subseteq V(G)$, the *subgraph of G induced by U* is defined as $G[U] = (U, \{(u, v) \in E(G)|u, v \in U\})$. A *multigraph* is similar to an undirected graph, but there may exist multiple edges as well as self-loops between its nodes. A *multiprocessor system* can be modeled as a undirected graph G in which the nodes represent processors and the edges represent communication links.

The *node connectivity* (*connectivity* for short) of a graph G, denoted by $\kappa(G)$, is the minimum size of a node set S such that $G - S$ is disconnected or contains only one node.[1] A graph G is *t-connected* if $\kappa(G) \geq t$. If (u, v) is an edge in a graph G, we say that u is *adjacent* to v. A *neighbor* of a node u in $G = (V, E)$ is any node that is adjacent to u. Let V' be a nonempty subset of $V(G)$. The *neighborhood set of node u in V'* is defined as $N_G(u, V') = \{v \in V'|(u, v) \in E(G)\}$. When $V' = V(G) - u$, $N_G(u, V')$ is reduced to $N_G(u)$. We also call each node in $N_G(u)$ a *neighbor* of u. The *degree*

---

[1]The notation $G–S$ represents the graph obtained by deleting all the nodes in S from G.

of a node u in a simple graph G, denoted by $\deg_G(u)$, is the number of edges incident to u, that is, $\deg_G(u) = |N_G(u)|$. The *minimum degree* of a graph $G = (V, E)$, denoted by $\delta(G)$, is $\min_{u \in V}\{\deg(u)\}$. For convenience, the subscript G can be deleted from the above notations if no ambiguity occurs. The relation between the minimum degree and the connectivity of a graph is formulated as follows:

Lemma 6.1 [28] $\kappa(G) \le \delta(G)$.
The *symmetric difference* of two distinct sets, F_1 and F_2, is defined as the set $F_1 \Delta F_2 = (F_1 - F_2) \cup (F_2 - F_1)$.

6.2.1 The (1,2)-Matching Composition Networks ((1,2)-MCN)

A *matching* in a graph G is a set of nonloop edges with no shared end nodes. The nodes incident to the edges of a matching M are *saturated* by M; the others are *unsaturated*. Two matchings are *distinct* if they have no common edge. A *perfect matching* in a graph is a matching that saturates every node. The class of *(1,2)-MCNs* is defined as follows.

Definition 6.1 *Suppose that G_1 and G_2 are two graphs with the same number of nodes. Then, the resulting graph G, constructed from G_1 and G_2 by connecting $V(G_1)$ and $V(G_2)$ via an arbitrary perfect matching between $V(G_1)$ and $V(G_2)$ or via two arbitrary distinct perfect matchings between $V(G_1)$ and $V(G_2)$, is called a (1,2)-MCN.*

Figure 6.1 illustrates (1,2)-MCNs in which the bold lines and dotted lines represent two distinct perfect matchings. Note that each node $v \in V(G_1)$ has exactly one neighbor (respectively, two neighbors) in $V(G_2)$ if G is constructed from G_1 and G_2 by connecting $V(G_1)$ and $V(G_2)$ via a perfect matching (respectively, two distinct perfect matchings) between $V(G_1)$ and $V(G_2)$. For a (1,2)-MCN G, we use the notation $G(G_1, G_2; PM_1)$ (respectively, $G(G_1, G_2; PM_2)$) to represent that G is constructed from G_1 and G_2 by connecting $V(G_1)$ and $V(G_2)$ via a perfect matching PM_1 (respectively, two distinct perfect matchings PM_2) between $V(G_1)$ and $V(G_2)$. Note that $V(G(G_1, G_2; PM_k)) = V(G_1) \cup V(G_2)$ and $E(G(G_1, G_2; PM_k)) = E(G_1) \cup E(G_2) \cup PM_k$ for $k \in \{1, 2\}$.

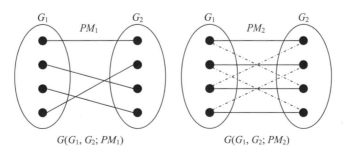

$G(G_1, G_2; PM_1)$ $G(G_1, G_2; PM_2)$

FIGURE 6.1. *Examples of (1,2)-MCNs.*

6.2.2 The Diagnosis Model

A system G is said to be *t-diagnosable* if all faulty nodes can be identified without replacement, provided that the number of occurring faults does not exceed t. The diagnosability of G, denoted by $d(G)$, refers to the maximum number of faulty nodes that can be identified by the system. In other words, a system is t-diagnosable if and only if each pair of distinct sets $S_1, S_2 \subseteq V(G)$ with $|S_1|, |S_2| \leq t$ are distinguishable, and the diagnosability of G is $\max\{t|G$ is *t-diagnosable*$\}$.

6.2.2.1 The PMC Model   The PMC model diagnoses whether or not a node is faulty by sending a task from a node u to its neighbor v, and then checks the response. We use the notation $\overrightarrow{uv}$ to represent the test performed by u on v. The *outcome* of $\overrightarrow{uv}$ is 0 (respectively, 1) if u determines that v is fault free (respectively, faulty).

The *test assignment* of a system G can be modeled as a directed multigraph $T = (V(G), L)$, where $\overrightarrow{uv} \in L$ implies that u and v are adjacent in G. The result of all tests in $T = (V(G), L)$ is called a *syndrome* of the diagnosis. Given a syndrome σ, a set $F \subseteq V(G)$ is said to be consistent with σ if and only if the following conditions hold:

1. If $u \in V(G) - F$ and $v \in F$, then $\sigma(\overrightarrow{uv}) = 1$.
2. If $u \in V(G) - F$ and $v \in V(G) - F$, then $\sigma(\overrightarrow{uv}) = 0$.

Formally, a syndrome is a function $\sigma: L \rightarrow \{0, 1\}$ such that F is consistent with σ.

Lemma 6.2 [29]   *A system $G = (V, E)$ is t-diagnosable if and only if, for any two distinct sets $F_1, F_2 \subset V$ with $|F_1| \leq t$, $|F_2| \leq t$, and $F_1 \neq F_2$, there exists at least one test performed by a node u in $V - (F_1 \cup F_2)$ on a node v in $F_1 \Delta F_2$ (see Fig. 6.2).*

The following two results related to t-diagnosable systems were reported by Hakimi and Amin [12] and Preparata et al. [19], respectively.

Lemma 6.3 [12]   *The following two conditions are sufficient for a system G containing n processors to be t-diagnosable:*

1. $n \geq 2t + 1$.
2. $\kappa(G) \geq t$.

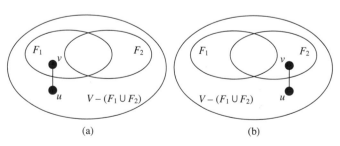

(a)   (b)

FIGURE 6.2. *Illustration of Lemma 6.2.*

Lemma 6.4 [19] *Let $G = (V, E)$ be a graph representation of a system, where V represents the processors and E represents the interconnections among the processors. Then, the following two conditions are necessary for G to be t-diagnosable:*

1. $n \geq 2t + 1$.
2. $\delta(G) \geq t$.

6.2.2.2 The MM* Model The MM model deals with the fault diagnosis by sending the same task from a node w to a pair of distinct neighbors, u and v, and then comparing their responses. In order to be consistent with the MM model, the following assumptions are made:

1. All faults are permanent.
2. A faulty processor produces incorrect output for each of its given tasks.
3. The outcome of a comparison performed by a faulty processor is unreliable.
4. Two faulty processors, when given the same inputs and task, do not produce the same output.

The *comparison scheme* of a system G can be modeled as a multigraph without self-loops, denoted by $M(V(G), L)$, where L is the labeled-edge set. If nodes u and v can be compared by another node w, then there is an edge (u, v) associated with a label w, denoted by $(u, v)_w$, which represents a *comparison* (or *test*) in which nodes u and v are compared by w. An edge (u, v) may have multiple labels $w_1, w_2, \ldots, w_k$, which means that u and v can be compared by each w_i for $1 \leq i \leq k$. The result of all comparisons in $M(V(G), L)$ is called the *syndrome* of the diagnosis. Briefly, a syndrome σ is a function from L to $\{0, 1\}$, and we use $\sigma((u, v)_w)$ to represent the result of the comparison $(u, v)_w$ in σ. In the special case of the MM model, called the MM* model, if $u, v, w \in V(G)$ and $(u, w), (v, w) \in E(G)$, then $(u, v)_w$ must be in L. In other words, all possible comparisons of G must be in the comparison scheme of G. Hereafter, the results reported in this chapter are for systems under the MM* model. Figure 6.3 illustrates a system with its comparison schemes under the MM and MM* models.

Let G be a system with its comparison scheme $M(V(G), L)$. Given a node $u \in V(G)$, we define the *order graph* of u, denoted by $G^u = (X^u, Y^u)$, as follows:

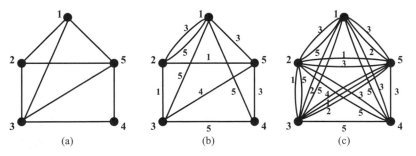

(a)   (b)   (c)

FIGURE 6.3. *(a) A system* G, *(b) a comparison scheme of* G *under the MM model, and (c) a comparison scheme of* G *under the MM* model.*

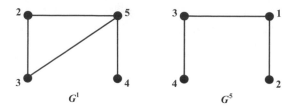

FIGURE 6.4. *The order graphs* G¹ *and* G⁵ *for graph* G *illustrated in Figure 6.3.*

1. $X^u = \{v|(u, v) \in E(G) \text{ or } (u, v)_w \in L\}$; that is, X^u consists of all the nodes that are adjacent to u or can be compared with u by any node w.
2. $Y^u = \{(v, w)|v, w \in X^u \text{ and } (u, v)_w \in L\}$; that is, edge (v, w) is in Y^u if u can be compared with v by node w.

The *order* of u, denoted by $\text{order}_G(u)$, is defined as the cardinality of a minimum node cover of G^u. Given $V' \subseteq V(G)$, we define the *probing set* of V', denoted by $P(G, V')$, to be the set $\{u \in V'|(u, v)_w \in L \text{ and } v, w \in V(G) - V'\}$. It means that all nodes in V' can be compared with some node in $V(G) - V'$ by another node in $V(G) - V'$ (Fig. 6.4).

For a given syndrome σ, $S \subseteq V(G)$ is said to be *a consistent fault set* with σ if and only if the following conditions hold:

1. If $u \in S$ and $v, w \in V(G) - S$, $\sigma((u, v)_w) = 1$.
2. If $u, v \in S$ and $w \in V(G) - S$, $\sigma((u, v)_w) = 1$.
3. If $u, v, w \in V(G) - S$, $\sigma((u, v)_w) = 0$.

The syndrome σ can be produced from the situation where all nodes in S are faulty and all nodes in $V(G) - S$ are fault-free. Because a faulty comparator w can lead to an unreliable result, the result by a faulty comparator may be 1 or 0 every time, and thus a given faulty set S may produce different syndromes. Let $\sigma(S)$ denote all syndromes which S is consistent with.

Two distinct subsets $S_1, S_2 \subseteq V(G)$ are said to be *indistinguishable* if $\sigma(S_1) \cap \sigma(S_2) \neq \varnothing$; otherwise, S_1 and S_2 are said to be *distinguishable*. (S_1, S_2) is said to be an *indistinguishable* (respectively, a distinguishable) *pair* if S_1 and S_2 are indistinguishable (respectively, distinguishable).

Sengupta and Dahbura [20] proposed necessary and sufficient conditions for two distinct sets being distinguishable:

Lemma 6.5   [20] *For any $S_1, S_2 \subset V(G)$ and $S_1 \neq S_2$, (S_1, S_2) is a distinguishable pair if and only if at least one of the following conditions is satisfied (see Fig. 6.5):*

1. $\exists u, w \in V(G) - S_1 - S_2$ and $\exists v \in (S_1 - S_2) \cup (S_2 - S_1)$ such that $(u, v)_w \in L$.
2. $\exists u, v \in S_1 - S_2$ and $\exists w \in V(G) - S_1 - S_2$ such that $(u, v)_w \in L$.
3. $\exists u, v \in S_2 - S_1$ and $\exists w \in V(G) - S_1 - S_2$ such that $(u, v)_w \in L$.

Lemma 6.6   [20] *A system G is t-diagnosable if and only if for each pair of sets S_1, $S_2 \subset V(G)$ such that $S_1 \neq S_2$ and $|S_1|, |S_2| \leq t$, at least one of the conditions of Lemma 6.5 is satisfied.*

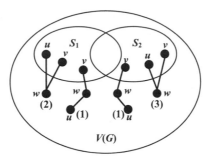

FIGURE 6.5. *Illustration of Lemma 6.5.*

Lemma 6.7 *Let G be a system with N nodes and S_1, $S_2 \subset V(G)$ be two distinct sets with $|S_1|$, $|S_2| \leq t$ and $|S_1 \cap S_2| = p$, where $0 \leq p \leq t - 1$. If $|P(G, S_1 \cup S_2)| > p$, then (S_1, S_2) is a distinguishable pair.*

Proof: Let $M(V(G), L)$ be the comparison scheme of G. If $|P(G, S_1 \cup S_2)| > p$, then there must exist a node $u \in P(G, S_1 \cup S_2)$ such that $u \notin S_1 \cap S_2$. This implies that $u \in (S_1 - S_2) \cup (S_2 - S_1)$. By the definition of the probing set, there exist two nodes $v, w \in V(G) - (S_1 \cup S_2)$ such that $(u, v)_w \in L$, which satisfies condition 1 of Lemma 6.5. Therefore, (S_1, S_2) is a distinguishable pair.   ∎

Lemma 6.8 *Suppose that $G = (V, E)$ is a connected graph with $order_G(v) \geq t$ for each node v in G, where $t \geq 0$. If $U \subset V$ with $|U| \leq t$, then $P(G, U) = U$.*

Proof: Let u be a node in U. Since $order_G(u) \geq t$, the cardinality of the minimum node cover in the order graph $G^u = (X^u, Y^u)$ is also at least t. Clearly, $U - \{u\}$ is not a node cover of G^u because $|U - \{u\}| < t$. This implies that there exists an edge (v, w) in Y^u such that v and w are both in $\bar{U}$. Moreover, by the definition of the order graph, (v, w) in Y^u if the comparison $(u, v)_w$ exists. Therefore, $u \in P(G, U)$ and $P(G, U) = U$.   ∎

6.3 DIAGNOSABILITY OF (1,2)-MCNs UNDER PMC MODEL

In this section, we consider the diagnosability of (1,2)-MCNs under the PMC model. The following properties are useful for our analysis.

Lemma 6.9 *Let $G = (V, E)$ be a graph representation of a system, where V represents the processors and E represents their interconnections. Then, $d(G) \leq \delta(G)$ under the PMC model.*

Proof: Let u be a node in G with $\deg(u) = \delta(G)$. Suppose, by contradiction, that $d(G) = \delta(G) + 1 > \delta(G)$. We then consider the following two distinct sets $F_1 = \{u\} \cup N(u)$ and $F_2 = N(u)$. Clearly, $F_1 \neq F_2$, $|F_1|$, $|F_2| \leq \delta(G) + 1$. However, there is no edge between $V(G) - (F_1 \cup F_2)$ and $F_1 \Delta F_2$. According to Lemma 6.2, this contradicts the fact that G is $(\delta(G) + 1)$-diagnosable. Therefore, the result holds.   ∎

Lemma 6.10 *Let G_1 and G_2 be two graphs with the same number of nodes N, and let $t \geq 2$ be a positive integer. If both G_1 and G_2 are t-connected and $N \geq t + k$, then $G(G_1, G_2; PM_k)$ is $(t + k)$-connected for $k \in \{1, 2\}$.*

Proof: Let $G = G(G_1, G_2; PM_k)$. Suppose, by contradiction, that $\kappa(G) \leq t + k - 1$. Then, there exists a set $U \subset V(G)$ with $|U| \leq t + k - 1$ such that $G - U$ is disconnected. Let $U_1 = U \cap V(G_1)$, $U_2 = U \cup V(G_2)$, $n_1 = |U_1|$, and $n_2 = |U_2|$. Without loss of generality, we assume that $n_1 \geq n_2$ and consider the following cases. ■

Case 1: $n_1 < t$ and $n_2 < t$. Since $\kappa(G_i) \geq t > n_1 \geq n_2$ for $i \in \{1, 2\}$, both $G_1 - U_1$ and $G_2 - U_2$ are connected. Since $G - U$ is disconnected, each edge $(u, v) \in PM_k$ must have $u \in U$ or $v \in U$. Otherwise, if there is an edge $(u, v) \in PM_k$ with $u \notin U$ and $v \notin U$, then $G - U$ could be connected by connecting the connected components of $G_1 - U_1$ and $G_2 - U_2$ via (u, v), which would be a contradiction. Moreover, because each node in G_i for $i \in \{1, 2\}$ is incident to exactly k edges in PM_k, $|U| \geq N \geq t + k$, but this contradicts the assumption that $|U| \leq t + k - 1$.

Case 2: $n_1 = t$ and $n_2 \leq k - 1 \leq 1$. Since $n_2 \leq k - 1$ and each node in G is incident to exactly k edges in PM_k, each node u in $G_1 - U_1$ has at least one neighbor in $G_2 - U_2$. Moreover, since G_2 is t-connected and $n_2 = k - 1 \leq 1 < 2 \leq t$, $G_2 - U_2$ is also connected. Therefore, $G - U$ is connected, but this is a contradiction.

Case 3: $n_1 = t + 1$ and $n_2 \leq k - 2$. Since $n_2 \geq 0$ and $k \in \{1, 2\}$, we have $k = 2$. Hence, G is constructed from G_1 and G_2 by connecting $V(G_1)$ and $V(G_2)$ via two distinct perfect matchings PM_2 between $V(G_1)$ and $V(G_2)$. As each node u in $G_1 - U_1$ has two neighbors in G_2 and $n_2 = 0$, $G - U$ is connected. This is also a contradiction.

By combining the above cases, we complete the proof. ■

Next, we demonstrate the diagnosability of (1,2)-MCNs under the PMC model.

Lemma 6.11 *Let $t \geq 2$ be a positive integer and let G_1 and G_2 be two graphs with the same number of nodes N, where $N \geq t + 3$. If G_1 and G_2 are t-connected, then $G(G_1, G_2; PM_k)$ is $(t + k)$-diagnosable for $k \in \{1, 2\}$.*

Proof: We prove this lemma by showing that the condition of Lemma 6.2 holds. Let $F_1, F_2 \subset V(G)$ be two distinct sets with $|F_1|, |F_2| \leq t + k$ for $k \in \{1, 2\}$; and let $|F_1 \cap F_2| = p$, where $0 \leq p \leq t + k - 1$.

Since $|F_1 \cup F_2| = |F_1| + |F_2| - |F_1| \cup |F_2|$, $|F_1 \cup F_2| \leq 2(t + k) - p$; hence, we have $|F_1 \cup F_2| \leq 2(t + k)$. Moreover, because $|V(G_1)| = |V(G_2)| = N \geq t + 3$, $|V(G) - (F_1 \cup F_2)| \geq 2(t + 3) - 2(t + k) = 6 - 2k \in \{2, 4\}$ for $k \in \{1, 2\}$, so at least two nodes must be in $G - (F_1 \cup F_2)$. Furthermore, $|F_1 \Delta F_2| \neq 0$ because F_1 and F_2 are two distinct sets. On the other hand, since G_1 and G_2 are t-connected, then by Lemma 6.10, $G(G_1, G_2; PM_k)$ is $(t + k)$-connected for $k \in \{1, 2\}$. This means $G - (F_1 \cap F_2)$ is also connected because $0 \leq p \leq t + k - 1$. Therefore, there must exist a path in $G - (F_1 \cap F_2)$ that joins a node in $V(G) - (F_1 \cup F_2)$ to a node in $F_1 \Delta F_2$, which implies that an edge (u, v) exists, where $u \in V(G) - (F_1 \cup F_2)$ and $v \in F_1 \Delta F_2$. By Lemma 6.2, G is $(t + k)$-diagnosable. ■

Lemma 6.12 *Let $t \geq 2$ be a positive integer and let G_1 and G_2 be two graphs with the same number of nodes N. If G_1 and G_2 are t-diagnosable and t-connected, then a (1,2)-MCN $G(G_1, G_2; PM_k)$ is $(t + k)$-diagnosable for $k \in \{1, 2\}$.*

Proof: We prove this lemma by showing that the two conditions of Lemma 6.3 hold. Since G_1 and G_2 are t-diagnosable, then by condition 1 of Lemma 6.4, we have $N \geq 2t + 1$. Moreover, the number of nodes in G is equal to $2N \geq 2(2t + 1) > 2(t + k) + 1$ for $k \in \{1, 2\}$ and $t \geq 2$. Therefore, condition 1 of Lemma 6.3 holds.

On the other hand, since G_1 and G_2 are both t-connected, then by Lemma 6.10, $G(G_1, G_2; PM_k)$ is $(t + k)$-connected for $k \in \{1, 2\}$; that is, $\kappa(G(G_1, G_2; PM_k)) \geq t + k$. Therefore, condition 2 of Lemma 6.3 holds. Because both conditions of Lemma 6.3 hold, $G(G_1, G_2; PM_k)$ is $(t + k)$-diagnosable for $k \in \{1, 2\}$.   ∎

6.4 DIAGNOSABILITY OF 2-MCNs UNDER MM* MODEL

In this section, we study the diagnosability of 2-MCNs under the MM* model. Some useful properties are shown as follows.

Lemma 6.13 *Let $G = (V, E)$ be a graph representation of a system, where V represents the processors and E represents their interconnections. Then, $d(G) \leq \delta(G)$ under the MM* model.*

Proof: Suppose, by contradiction, that G is $(\delta(G) + 1)$-diagnosable. Let u be an arbitrary node in G, and let $F_1 = \{u\} \cup N(u)$ and $F_2 = N(u)$. Clearly, $F_1 \neq F_2$, $N(u) = F_1 \cap F_2$, and $|F_1|, |F_2| \leq \delta(G) + 1$. However, node u cannot be compared by any other node in $V(G) - F_1 - F_2$, which implies that none of the conditions in Lemma 6.5 is satisfied. This is contrary to that G is $(\delta(G) + 1)$-diagnosable, which leads to that $d(G) \leq \delta(G)$, the result holds.   ∎

Lemma 6.14 *Let G_1 and G_2 be two networks with the same number of nodes N, and let $t \geq 2$ be a positive integer. If $\text{order}_{G_i}(v) \geq t$ for each node v in G_i, where $i = 1, 2$, then $\text{order}_G(v) \geq t + 2$ for each node v in $G(G_1, G_2; PM_2)$.*

Proof: For convenience, let $G = G(G_1, G_2; PM_2)$. Let v be an arbitrary node of G. Without loss of generality, we assume that $v \in V(G_1)$, and let u and w be two v's neighbors in G_2, where $(v, u), (v, w) \in PM_2$. Recall that G_1^v and G^v denote the order graphs of v for G_1 and G, respectively. Because G_1^v is a subgraph of G^v, every node cover of G^v contains a node cover of G_1^v. Moreover, since each node in G_2 has the order $t \geq 2$, the cardinality of a minimum node cover of G_2^u (respectively, G_2^w) is at least 2, which implies that $|N_{G_2}(u)| \geq 2$ (respectively, $|N_{G_2}(w)| \geq 2$) because $N_{G_2}(u)$ (respectively, $N_{G_2}(w)$) forms a node cover of G_2^u (respectively, G_2^w). Let $u', u'' \in N_{G_2}(u)$ and $w', w'' \in N_{G_2}(w)$. Then, we have the following possible cases: (1) $|\{u', u''\} \cap \{w', w''\}| = 2$, that is, u' and u'' (w' and w'') are both common neighbors of u and w (see Fig. 6.6a); (2) $|\{u', u''\} \cap \{w', w''\}| = 1$, that is, u and w have exactly one common neighbor (see Fig. 6.6b); (3) $|\{u', u''\} \cap \{w', w''\}| = 0$, that is, u and w have no common neighbor (see Fig. 6.6c). In each of the above cases, at least two nodes must be included into a node cover to cover edges (u, u'), (u, u''), (w, w'), and (w, w'').

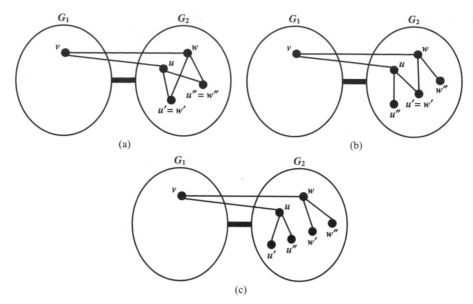

FIGURE 6.6. *Illustration of the proof of Lemma 6.14.*

Since edges $(u, u'), (u, u''), (w, w'),$ and (w, w'') belong to $E(G^v) - E(G_1^v)$ and every node cover of G^v contains a node cover of G_1^v, $\text{order}_G(v) \geq \text{order}_{G_1}(v) + 2 \geq t + 2$. ∎

Now, we are ready to state and prove the following theorem about the diagnosability of 2-MCNs under the MM* model.

Theorem 6.1 *Let $t \geq 2$ be a positive integer and let G_1 and G_2 be two graphs with the same number of nodes N, where $N \geq t + 3$. If $\text{order}_{G_i}(v) \geq t$, $\kappa(G_i) \geq t$, and $|N_{G_i}(v)| \geq 3$ for each node $v \in V(G_i)$, where $i = 1, 2,$ then $G(G_1, G_2; PM_2)$ is $(t + 2)$-diagnosable.*

Proof: For convenience, let $G = G(G_1, G_2; PM_2)$. Let $S_1, S_2 \subset V(G)$ be two distinct sets with $|S_1|, |S_2| \leq t + 2$ and let $|S_1 \cap S_2| = p$, where $0 \leq p \leq t + 1$. Also, let $S_{G_i} = V(G_i) \cap (S_1 \cup S_2)$ for $i = 1, 2$ with $|S_{G_1}| = n_1$ and $|S_{G_2}| = n_2$. Clearly, $n_1 + n_2 \leq 2(t + 2) - p$. Without loss of generality, we assume that $n_1 \leq n_2$. Since

$$0 \leq n_1 \leq \frac{2(t+2) - p}{2},$$

the maximum value of n_1 is equal to $t + 2$ when $p = 0$ and $n_1 = t + 2$. We divide the proof into two cases, according to the combined values of $n_1, n_2,$ and t. The first case is $n_2 \leq t$, which implies $n_1 \leq t$. The second case is $n_2 > t$, and this case is further divided into three subcases: $n_1 < t$, $n_1 = t$, and $n_1 > t$. For simplicity, we say that a comparison $(u, v)_w$ is *good* if it satisfies condition 1 of Lemma 6.5.

    Case 1: $n_2 \leq t$, and this implies $n_1 \leq t$. By Lemma 6.8, $P(G_1, S_{G_1}) = S_{G_1}$ and $P(G_2, S_{G_2}) = S_{G_2}$. Then, $|P(G, S_1 \cup S_2)| \geq |P(G_1, S_{G_1})| + |P(G_2, S_{G_2})| = |S_{G_1}| + |S_{G_2}| = |S_1 \cup S_2| > |S_1 \cap S_2| = p$. Therefore, by Lemma 6.7, (S_1, S_2) is a distinguishable pair.

Case 2: $n_2 > t$. We have the following scenarios.

Case 2.1: $n_1 < t$. This implies $n_2 > n_1$.

Case 2.1.1: $n_2 > p$. By Lemma 6.8, $|P(G_1, S_{G_1})| = |S_{G_1}| = n_1$. Moreover, since each node in S_{G_2} is adjacent to exactly two nodes in G_1 (via PM_2) and $n_2 > n_1$, S_{G_2} contains a set R with $|R| \geq n_2 - n_1$ such that each node in R is adjacent to some node in $V(G_1) - S_{G_1}$. Let $u \in R$ be an arbitrary node and let w be a node in $V(G_1) - S_{G_1}$ adjacent to u. Since $\kappa(G_1) \geq t$ and $|S_{G_1}| = n_1 < t$, $G[V(G_1) - S_{G_1}]$ is connected, which implies that there is another node $v \in V(G_1) - S_{G_1}$ adjacent to w. Clearly, $(u, v)_w$ is a comparison. By combining the above arguments, we have $|P(G, S_1 \cup S_2)| \geq |P(G_1, S_{G_1})| + (n_2 - n_1) = |S_{G_1}| + (n_2 - n_1) = n_2 > p$. Therefore, by Lemma 6.7, (S_1, S_2) is a distinguishable pair.

Case 2.1.2: $n_2 = p$. In this case, from $n_2 \geq t + 1$ and $p \leq t + 1$, this implies $n_2 = p = t + 1$; from $n_1 + n_2 \leq 2(t + 2) - p$, it follows $n_1 \leq 2$; and also, $n_1 > 0$ from $n_2 = p$ and S_1, S_2 are distinct. Thus, $0 < |(S_{G_1} \cup S_{G_2}) - (S_1 \cap S_2)| \leq 2$. We have the following scenarios.

Case 2.1.2.1: $|S_{G_1} - (S_1 \cap S_2)| \geq 1$. Let u be such a node in $S_{G_1} - (S_1 \cap S_2)$. Since $n_1 \leq 2$ and $|N_{G_1}(u)| \geq 3$ by the hypothesis, there exists a node $w \in V(G_1) - S_{G_1}$ adjacent to u. Moreover, because $n_1 < t$ and $\kappa(G_1) \geq t$, $G[V(G_1) - S_{G_1}]$ is connected, which implies that there is another node $v \in V(G_1) - S_{G_1}$ adjacent to w (see Fig. 6.7a). Then, comparison $(u, v)_w$ is good. Therefore, (S_1, S_2) is a distinguishable pair.

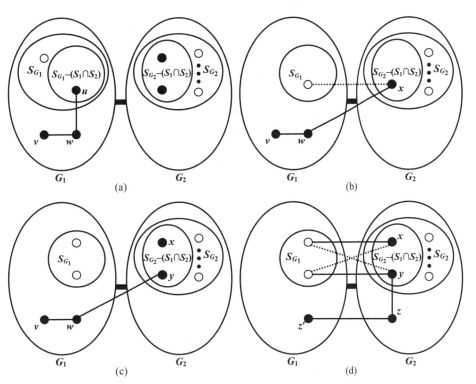

FIGURE 6.7. Illustration of Case 2.1.2 in the proof of Theorem 6.1.

Case 2.1.2.2: $|S_{G_1} - (S_1 \cap S_2)| = 0$. This implies $|S_{G_2} - (S_1 \cap S_2)| = n_2 - (p - n_1)$ $= n_1$, as $p = n_2$ and $S_{G_1} \cap S_{G_2} = \varnothing$.

Case 2.1.2.2.1: $n_1 = 1$, which implies that there is exactly one node in $S_{G_2} - (S_1 \cap S_2)$. Let x be the node in $S_{G_2} - (S_1 \cap S_2)$. Since $n_1 = 1$, there exists at least one node $w \in V(G_1) - S_{G_1}$ adjacent to x via PM_2 (see Fig. 6.7b). Then, the result that (S_1, S_2) is a distinguishable pair can be shown using a similar argument to that presented in Case 2.1.2.1.

Case 2.1.2.2.2: $n_1 = 2$; that is, $|S_{G_2} - (S_1 \cap S_2)| = 2$ (note that this case does not occur when $t = 2$, as $n_1 < t$). Let $\{x, y\} = S_{G_2} - (S_1 \cap S_2)$. If at least one node in $\{x, y\}$ is adjacent to some node $w \in V(G_1) - S_{G_1}$ (see Fig. 6.7c), then the result that (S_1, S_2) is a distinguishable pair can be shown using a similar argument to that presented in Case 2.1.2.1.

Otherwise, edges in PM_2 that are incident to the nodes in $\{x, y\}$ are also incident to the node in S_{G_1} and vice versa (recall that $n_1 = |S_{G_1}| = 2$) (see Fig. 6.7d). This implies that the nodes in $V_{G_2} - S_2$ cannot be adjacent to nodes in S_{G_1} via PM_2. Thus, every node $z \in V(G_2) - S_{G_2}$ must be adjacent to some node $z' \in V(G_1) - S_{G_1}$ via PM_2. Since $n_2 = |S_{G_2}| = t + 1$ and G_2 is t-connected, $G[V(G_2) - (S_{G_2} - \{x, y\})]$ is connected. Hence, at least one node in $\{x, y\}$, say, y, must be adjacent to some node $z \in V(G_2) - S_{G_2}$ and, in turn, z must be adjacent to some node $z' \in V(G_1) - S_{G_1}$. Thus, comparison $(y, z')_z$ is good, and (S_1, S_2) is a distinguishable pair.

Case 2.2: $n_1 = t$. Since $n_2 \geq t + 1$ and $n_1 + n_2 \leq 2(t + 2) - p$, we have $p \leq 3$. We have the following scenarios.

Case 2.2.1: $p \leq t$.

Case 2.2.1.1: $|(S_1 \cap S_2) \cap S_{G_1}| < p$. By the assumption of this case and $n_1 = t \geq p$, $S_{G_1} - (S_1 \cap S_2)$ contains at least one node. Then, by an argument similar to the one used in Case 2.1.2.1, we can show that (S_1, S_2) is a distinguishable pair.

Case 2.2.1.2: $|(S_1 \cap S_2) \cap S_{G_1}| = p$. This implies $S_1 \cap S_2 \subseteq S_{G_1}$, and sets $V(G_2) \cap S_1$ and $V(G_2) \cap S_2$ are disjoint. If there exists at least one isolated node in $G[V(G_2) - S_{G_2}]$, let w be one such node. Since $|N_{G_2}(w)| \geq 3$, w is adjacent to three nodes in S_{G_2} and to at least two nodes in either $(S_1 - S_2)$ or $(S_2 - S_1)$, which implies that condition 2 or 3 of Lemma 6.5 holds (see Fig. 6.8a). Therefore, (S_1, S_2) is a distinguishable pair.

Otherwise, given that G_2 is connected, there exists a node u in either $V(G_2) \cap S_1$ or $V(G_2) \cap S_2$, which is adjacent to some node w in $V(G_2) - S_{G_2}$. Since w is not an isolated node in $G[V(G_2) - S_{G_2}]$, w must be adjacent to some node v also in $V(G_2) - S_{G_2}$, which implies that $(u, v)_w$ is good (see Fig. 6.8b). Therefore, (S_1, S_2) is a distinguishable pair.

Case 2.2.2: $p > t$. Note that this case occurs only when $t = 2$, as $p \leq 3$. Thus, $n_1 = 2$, $p = 3$, and $n_2 = 3$.

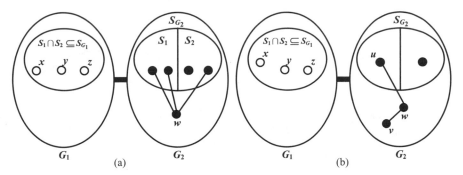

FIGURE 6.8. *Illustration of Case 2.2.1.2 in the proof of Theorem 6.1.*

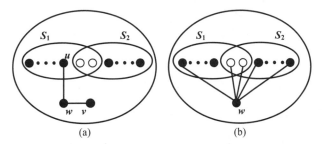

FIGURE 6.9. *Illustration of Case 2.3.2 in the proof of Theorem 6.1.*

Case 2.2.2.1: $|S_{G_1} - (S_1 \cap S_2)| \geq 1$; that is, $S_{G_1} - (S_1 \cap S_2)$ contains at least one node. Then, the result that (S_1, S_2) is a distinguishable pair can be shown using an argument similar to that presented in Case 2.1.2.1.

Case 2.2.2.2: $|S_{G_1} - (S_1 \cap S_2)| = 0$; this implies that there are exactly two nodes in $S_{G_2} - (S_1 \cap S_2)$. Then, the result that (S_1, S_2) is a distinguishable pair can be shown using an argument similar to that presented in Case 2.1.2.2.2.

Case 2.3: $n_1 > t$; thus, $n_2 \geq n_1 > t$. Moreover, since $n_1 + n_2 \leq 2(t + 2) - p$, we have $p \leq 2$. There are the following scenarios.

Case 2.3.1: $p = 0$; this implies $S_1 \cup S_2 = (S_1 - S_2) \cup (S_1 - S_2)$. By using an argument similar to that presented in Case 2.2.1.2, we can show that (S_1, S_2) is a distinguishable pair.

Case 2.3.2: $p > 0$. We first consider the situation where every connected component in $G[V(G) - S_1 - S_2]$ contains at least two nodes. Since $p = |S_1 \cap S_2| \leq 2$ and $\kappa(G) \geq t + 2 \geq 4$ for $t \geq 2$ (according to Lemma 6.10), $G - (S_1 \cap S_2)$ is connected. Hence, there exists a node $u \in (S_1 - S_2) \cup (S_2 - S_1)$ adjacent to some node w, which belongs to a component C in $G[V(G) - S_1 - S_2]$. Since $|V(C)| \geq 2$, there is a node $v \in C$ adjacent to w. Then, $(u, v)_w$ is good, and thus, (S_1, S_2) is a distinguishable pair (see Fig. 6.9a).

Otherwise, every connected component $G[V(G) - S_1 - S_2]$ is an isolated node. Let w be an arbitrary isolated node in $G[V(G) - S_1 - S_2]$. Since $|N_{G_i}(v)| \geq 3$ for every node $v \in V(G_i)$, we have $|N_G(w)| \geq 5$. Moreover, because $p \leq 2$, v is adjacent to at least two nodes in $S_1 - S_2$ or $S_2 - S_1$,

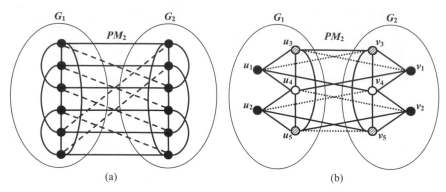

FIGURE 6.10. *Two 2-MCNs for illustrating the usage of Theorem 6.1: (a) a 5-diagnosable 2-MCN, and (b) a non-4-diagnosable 2-MCN, where the white, gray, and black nodes belong to $S_1 \cap S_2$, $(S_1 - S_2) \cup (S_2 - S_1)$, and $V(G) - (S_1 \cup S_2)$, respectively.*

which implies that condition 2 or 3 of Lemma 6.5 holds (see Fig. 6.9b). Therefore, (S_1, S_2) is a distinguishable pair.

By combining the above cases, we complete the proof. ■

Figure 6.10a illustrates a 2-MCN $G = G(G_1, G_2; PM_2)$ with $order_{G_i}(v) = 3$, $\kappa(G_i) = 3$, and $|N_{G_i}(v)| \geq 3$ for each node v in G_i, where $i = 1, 2$. By Theorem 6.1, G is 5-diagnosable 2-MCN. Figure 6.10b illustrates a 2-MCN $G = G(G_1, G_2; PM_2)$ with $order_{G_i}(v) = 2$, $\kappa(G_i) = 2$, and $|N_{G_i}(v)| \geq 2$ for each node v in G_i, where $i = 1, 2$. Since G does not satisfy the condition where $|N_{G_i}(v)| \geq 3$ in Theorem 6.1, it is not 4-diagnosable. Let $S_1 = \{u_3, u_4, u_5, v_4\}$ and $S_2 = \{u_4, v_3, v_4, v_5\}$ with $S_1 \cap S_2 = \{u_4, v_4\}$. Clearly, none of the nodes in $(S_1 - S_2) \cup (S_2 - S_1) = \{u_3, v_3, u_5, v_5\}$ can be compared by another two nodes in $V(G) - (S_1 \cup S_2) = \{u_1, v_1, u_2, v_2\}$. By Lemmas 6.5 and 6.6, G is not 4-diagnosable.

Corollary 6.1 *Let $t \geq 3$ be a positive integer and let G_1 and G_2 be two graphs with the same number of nodes N, where $N \geq t + 3$. If $order_{G_i}(v) \geq t$ and $\kappa(G_i) \geq t$ for $i = 1$, 2, then $G(G_1, G_2; PM_2)$ is $(t + 2)$-diagnosable.*

6.5 APPLICATION TO MULTIPROCESSOR SYSTEMS

In this section, we apply the lemmas derived in Sections 6.3 and 6.4 to several popular multiprocessor systems. Of course, they can also be applied to many other potentially useful systems.

6.5.1 The Diagnosability of Hypercubes

An *n-dimensional hypercube* Q_n has 2^n nodes and can be defined recursively as follows. Q_1 is a complete graph with two nodes labeled 0 and 1, respectively. For $n \geq 2$, Q_n consists of two Q_{n-1}s, denoted by Q_{n-1}^0 and Q_{n-1}^1, respectively. In addition, there exists a perfect matching PM_1 between $V(Q_{n-1}^0) = \{0u_{n-2}u_{n-3} \ldots u_0 \mid u_i \in \{0, 1\}\}$ and $V(Q_{n-1}^1) = \{1v_{n-2}v_{n-3} \ldots v_0 \mid v_i \in \{0, 1\}\}$ so that node $u = 0u_{n-2}u_{n-3} \ldots u_0 \in V(Q_{n-1}^0)$ is connected to node $v = 1v_{n-2}v_{n-3} \ldots v_0 \in V(Q_{n-1}^1)$ if and only if $u_i = v_i$ for $0 \leq i \leq n - 2$. Figure 6.11 illustrates Q_3 and Q_4.

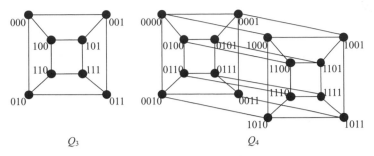

FIGURE 6.11. Q₃ and Q₄.

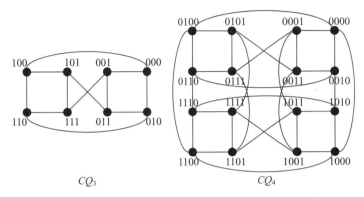

FIGURE 6.12. CQ₃ and CQ₄.

Lemma 6.15 Q_n *is n-diagnosable for $n \geq 5$ under the PMC model.*

Proof: By the definition of hypercubes, $Q_n = G(Q_{n-1}^0, Q_{n-1}^1; PM_1)$. Since Q_n is n-connected for $n \geq 3$ [30] and $|V(Q_{n-1}^0)| = |V(Q_{n-1}^1)| = 2^{n-1} \geq (n-1) + 3 = n + 2$ for $n \geq 4$, then by Lemma 6.11, Q_n is n-diagnosable for $n \geq 5$. ∎

Theorem 6.2 $d(Q_n) = n$ *for $n \geq 5$ under the PMC model.*

Proof: By Lemma 6.15, $d(Q_n) \geq n$ for $n \geq 5$. Moreover, since Q_n for $n \geq 1$ is a regular graph with a common degree n, that is, $\delta(Q_n) = n$, then by Lemma 6.9, $d(Q_n) \leq \delta(Q_n) = n$. Hence, $d(Q_n) = n$ for $n \geq 5$. ∎

6.5.2   The Diagnosability of Crossed Cubes

An *n-dimensional crossed cube* CQ_n [31] has 2^n nodes and can be defined recursively as follows. CQ_1 is a complete graph with two nodes labeled 0 and 1, respectively. For cases where $n \geq 2$, CQ_n consists of two CQ_{n-1}s, denoted by CQ_{n-1}^0 and CQ_{n-1}^1, respectively. In addition, there exists a perfect matching PM_1 between $V(CQ_{n-1}^0) = \{0u_{n-2}u_{n-3}\ldots u_0 \mid u_i \in \{0,1\}\}$ and $V(CQ_{n-1}^1) = \{1v_{n-2}v_{n-3}\ldots v_0 \mid v_i \in \{0,1\}\}$ so that $u = 0u_{n-2}u_{n-3}\ldots u_0 \in V(CQ_{n-1}^0)$ is connected to node $v = 1v_{n-2}v_{n-3}\ldots v_0 \in V(CQ_{n-1}^1)$ if and only if (1) $u_{n-2} = v_{n-2}$ if n is even; and (2) $(u_{2i+1}u_{2i}, v_{2i+1}v_{2i}) \in \{(00,00), (10,10), (01,11), (11,01)\}$ for

$$0 \leq i < \left\lfloor \frac{n-1}{2} \right\rfloor.$$

Figure 6.12 illustrates CQ_3 and CQ_4.

Lemma 6.16 CQ_n is n-diagnosable for $n \geq 5$ under the PMC model.

Proof: By the definition of crossed cubes, $CQ_n = G(CQ_{n-1}^0, CQ_{n-1}^1; PM_1)$. Moreover, since a CQ_n is n-connected for $n \geq 3$ [32], and $|V(CQ_{n-1}^0)| = |V(CQ_{n-1}^1)| = 2^{n-1} \geq (n-1) + 3 = n + 2$ for $n \geq 4$, therefore, by Lemma 6.11, CQ_n is n-diagnosable for $n \geq 5$. ∎

Theorem 6.3 $d(CQ_n) = n$ for $n \geq 5$ under the PMC model.

Proof: By Lemma 6.16, $d(CQ_n) \geq n$ for $n \geq 5$. Since CQ_n for $n \geq 1$ is a regular graph with a common degree n, that is, $\delta(CQ_n) = n$, then, by Lemma 6.9, $d(CQ_n) \leq \delta(CQ_n) = n$. Hence, $d(CQ_n) = n$ for $n \geq 5$. ∎

6.5.3 The Diagnosability of Möbius Cubes

For a binary bit x, let $\bar{x}$ be one's complement of x, that is, $\bar{x} = 1$ iff $x = 0$, and $\bar{x} = 0$ iff $x = 1$. An *n-dimensional 0-Möbius cube* 0-MQ_n (respectively, *1-Möbius cube* 1-MQ_n) [33] has 2^n nodes, and can be recursively defined as follows. 0-MQ_1 (respectively, 1-MQ_1) is a complete graph with two nodes labeled 0 and 1, respectively. 0-MQ_2 is a graph with $V(0\text{-}MQ_2) = \{00, 01, 10, 11\}$ and $E(0\text{-}MQ_2) = \{(00, 01), (00, 10), (01, 11), (10, 11)\}$. 1-$MQ_2$ is a graph with $V(1\text{-}MQ_2) = \{00, 01, 10, 11\}$ and $E(1\text{-}MQ_2) = \{(00, 01), (00, 11), (01, 10)\}, (10, 11)\}$. For $n \geq 3$, 0-MQ_n (respectively, 1-MQ_n) consists of 0-MQ_{n-1} and 1-MQ_{n-1}, and there is a perfect matching PM_1 between $V(0\text{-}MQ_{n-1}) = \{0u_{n-2}u_{n-3} \ldots u_0 | u_i \in \{0, 1\}\}$ and $V(1\text{-}MQ_{n-1}) = \{1v_{n-2}v_{n-3} \ldots v_0 | v_i \in \{0, 1\}\}$ so that node $u = 0u_{n-2}u_{n-3} \ldots u_0 \in V(0\text{-}MQ_{n-1})$ is connected to node $v = 1v_{n-2}v_{n-3} \ldots v_0 \in V(1\text{-}MQ_{n-1})$ in 0-MQ_n (respectively, 1-MQ_n) if and only if $u_i = v_i$ (respectively, $u_i = \bar{v}_i$) for all $0 \leq i \leq n - 2$. Figure 6.13 illustrates MQ_3 and MQ_4.

Lemma 6.17 MQ_n is n-diagnosable for $n \geq 5$ under the PMC model.

Proof: By the definition of Möbius cubes, $MQ_n = G(0\text{-}MQ_{n-1}, 1\text{-}MQ_{n-1}; PM_1)$. Moreover, an MQ_n is n-connected for $n \geq 3$ [9], and $|V(0\text{-}MQ_{n-1})| = |V(1\text{-}MQ_{n-1})| = 2^{n-1} \geq (n - 1) + 3 = n + 2$ for $n \geq 4$; therefore, by Lemma 6.11, MQ_n is n-diagnosable for $n \geq 5$. ∎

Theorem 6.4 $d(MQ_n) = n$ for $n \geq 5$ under the PMC model.

Proof: By Lemma 17, $d(MQ_n) \geq n$ for $n \geq 5$. Since MQ_n for $n \geq 1$ is a regular graph with a common degree n, that is, $\delta(MQ_n) = n$, then by Lemma 6.9, $d(MQ_n) \leq \delta(MQ_n) = n$. Hence, $d(MQ_n) = n$ for $n \geq 5$. ∎

6.5.4 The Diagnosability of Twisted Cubes

An *isomorphism* from a simple graph G to a simple graph H is a one to one and onto function $\pi: V(G) \rightarrow V(H)$ such that $(u, v) \in E(G)$ if and only if $(\pi(u), \pi(v)) \in E(H)$. We say "$G$, written as $G \cong H$, is *isomorphic to H*" if there is an isomorphism from G to H. Given a binary string $u = u_{n-1}u_{n-2} \ldots u_0$ for $u_i \in \{0, 1\}$,

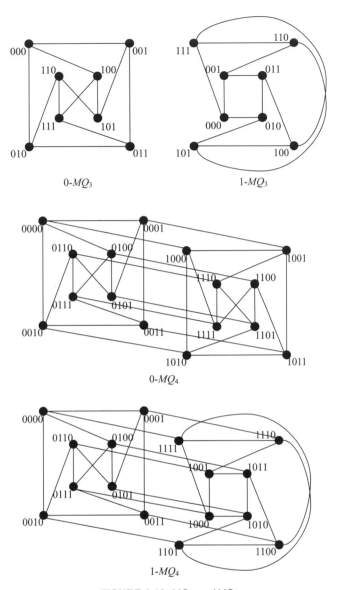

FIGURE 6.13. MQ$_3$ and MQ$_4$.

let $P_i(u) = u_i \cdot u_{i-1} \cdot \ldots \cdot u_0$, where $\cdot$ represents an *exclusive-or* operation. An *n-dimensional twisted cube* TQ_n [34] for an odd integer n has 2^n nodes, and can be defined recursively as follows. TQ_1 is a complete graph with two nodes labeled 0 and 1, respectively. For an odd integer $n \geq 3$, TQ_n is decomposed into four sets: $TQ_{n-2}^{0,0}, TQ_{n-2}^{0,1}, TQ_{n-2}^{1,0}$, and $TQ_{n-2}^{1,1}$, where $TQ_{n-2}^{i,j} = \{u_{n-1}u_{n-2}\ldots u_0 \mid u_{n-1} = i, u_{n-2} = j$ for $(i, j) \in \{(0, 0), (0, 1), (1, 0), (1, 1)\}\}$. Note that the subgraph induced by $TQ_{n-2}^{i,j}$ in TQ_n is isomorphic to TQ_{n-2}. Moreover, node $u_{n-1}u_{n-2}u_{n-3}\ldots u_0$ is connected to nodes $\bar{u}_{n-1}\bar{u}_{n-2}u_{n-3}\ldots u_0$ and $\bar{u}_{n-1}u_{n-2}u_{n-3}\ldots u_0$ ($u_{n-1}\bar{u}_{n-2}u_{n-3}\ldots u_0$ and $\bar{u}_{n-1}u_{n-2}u_{n-3}\ldots u_0$, respectively) if and only if $P_{n-3}(u) = 0$ (respectively, $P_{n-3}(u) = 1$). Figure 6.14 illustrates TQ_3 and TQ_5.

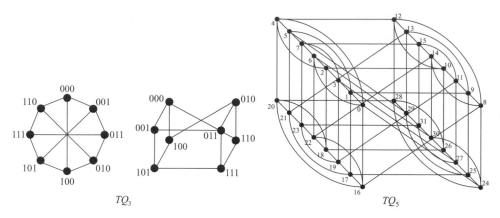

FIGURE 6.14. TQ$_3$ and TQ$_5$.

Based on the above definition, TQ_n is composed of four TQ_{n-2}'s, which are subgraphs induced, respectively, by $V(TQ_{n-2}^{0,0})$, $V(TQ_{n-2}^{0,1})$, $V(TQ_{n-2}^{1,0})$, and $V(TQ_{n-2}^{1,1})$, where $n \geq 3$ is an odd integer. Let S_0 and S_1 be two subgraphs of TQ_n induced by $V(TQ_{n-2}^{0,0}) \cup V(TQ_{n-2}^{1,0})$ and $V(TQ_{n-2}^{0,1}) \cup V(TQ_{n-2}^{1,1})$, respectively. In fact, $S_0 = G(TQ_{n-2}^{0,0}, TQ_{n-2}^{1,0}; PM_1))$ and $S_1 = G(TQ_{n-2}^{0,1}, TQ_{n-2}^{1,1}; PM_1)$. Moreover, each node $u = u_{n-1}u_{n-2}u_{n-3} \ldots u_1u_0 \in S_0$ is connected to $\bar{u}_{n-1}\bar{u}_{n-2}u_{n-3} \ldots u_1u_0 \in S_1$ if $P_{n-3}(u) = 0$, and to $u_{n-1}\bar{u}_{n-2}u_{n-3} \ldots u_1u_0 \in S_1$ if $P_{n-3}(u) = 1$. It is not difficult to see that each node $u \in S_0$ has exactly one neighbor v in S_1. Therefore, the edges between S_1 and S_2 in TQ_n form a perfect matching; that is, $TQ_n = G(S_0, S_1; PM_1)$.

Lemma 6.18   Let $S_j = G(TQ_{n-2}^{0,j}, TQ_{n-2}^{1,j}; PM_1)$ for $j = 0, 1$. Then, S_j is $(n-1)$-connected for $n \geq 4$.

Proof: Since TQ_n is n-connected for $n \geq 3$ [35], then by Lemma 6.10, S_j is $(n-1)$-connected for $n \geq 4$.   ∎

Lemma 6.19 TQ_n is n-diagnosable for $n \geq 5$ under the PMC model.

Proof: By the definition of twisted cubes, $TQ_n = G(S_0, S_1; PM_1)$. Moreover, by Lemma 6.18, $S_j = G(TQ_{n-2}^{0,j}, TQ_{n-2}^{1,j}; PM_1)$ for $j = 0, 1$ is $(n-1)$-connected for $n \geq 4$, and $|V(S_0)| = |V(S_1)| = 2^{n-1} \geq (n-1) + 3 = n + 2$ for $n \geq 4$; therefore, by Lemma 6.11, TQ_n is n-diagnosable for $n \geq 5$.   ∎

Theorem 6.5 $d(TQ_n) = n$ for $n \geq 5$ under the PMC model.

Proof: By Lemma 6.19, $d(TQ_n) \geq n$ for $n \geq 5$. Since TQ_n for $n \geq 1$ is a regular graph with a common degree n, that is, $\delta(TQ_n) = n$, then by Lemma 6.9, $d(TQ_n) \leq \delta(TQ_n) = n$. Hence, $d(TQ_n) = n$ for $n \geq 5$.   ∎

6.5.5   The Diagnosability of Locally Twisted Cubes

An *n-dimensional locally twisted cube* LTQ_n [36] has 2^n nodes and can be defined recursively as follows. LTQ_1 is a complete graph with two nodes labeled 0 and 1, respectively. LTQ_2 is a graph with $V(LTQ_2) = \{00, 01, 10, 11\}$ and $E(LTQ_2) = \{(00, 01), (01, 11)\}, (11, 10), (10, 00)\}$. For $n \geq 3$, LTQ_n consists of two LTQ_{n-1}, denoted by LTQ_{n-1}^0 and LTQ_{n-1}^1, respectively. In addition, there is a perfect matching PM_1 between $V(LTQ_{n-1}^0) = \{0v_{n-2}v_{n-3} \ldots v_0 \,|\, v_i \in \{0, 1\}\}$ and $V(LTQ_{n-1}^1) = \{1v_{n-2}v_{n-3} \ldots v_0 \,|\, v_i \in \{0, 1\}\}$ such that node $0v_{n-2}v_{n-3} \ldots v_0 \in V(LTQ_{n-1}^0)$ is connected to node $1(v_{n-2} \star v_0)v_{n-3} \ldots v_0 \in LTQ_{n-1}^1$, where "$\star$" denotes a "mod 2" operation. Figure 6.15 illustrates LTQ_3 and LTQ_4.

Lemma 6.20 *LTQ_n is n-diagnosable for $n \geq 5$ under the PMC model.*

Proof: By the definition of locally twisted cubes, $LTQ_n = G(LTQ_{n-1}^0, LTQ_{n-1}^1; PM_1)$. Moreover, since an LTQ_n is n-connected for $n \geq 3$ [36] and $|V(LTQ_{n-1}^0)| = |V(LTQ_{n-1}^1)| = 2^{n-1} \geq (n-1) + 3 = n + 2$ for $n \geq 4$, then, by Lemma 6.11, LTQ_n is n-diagnosable for $n \geq 5$. ∎

Theorem 6.6 *$d(LTQ_n) = n$ for $n \geq 5$ under the PMC model.*

Proof: By Lemma 6.20, $d(LTQ_n) \geq n$ for $n \geq 5$. Since LTQ_n for $n \geq 1$ is a regular graph with a common degree n, that is, $\delta(LTQ_n) = n$, then, by Lemma 6.9, $d(LTQ_n) \leq \delta(LTQ_n) = n$. Hence, $d(LTQ_n) = n$ for $n \geq 5$. ∎

6.5.6 The Diagnosability of Generalized Cubes

Two edges in a graph G are said to be *independent* if they do not share a common node. Given two independent edges, (x, y) and (u, v) in $E(G)$, an *X-change* operation on (x, y) and (u, v), denoted by $X[(x, y), (u, v)]$, would replace the two edges (x, y) and (u, v) with two new edges, (x, v) and (y, u), as shown in Figure 6.16. Note that an X-change operation preserves the degree of the graph.

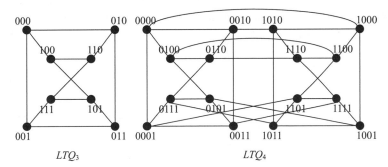

LTQ_3 LTQ_4

FIGURE 6.15. LTQ_3 and LTQ_4.

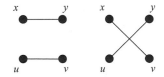

FIGURE 6.16. An X-change operation.

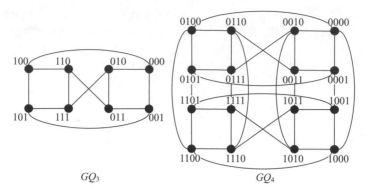

FIGURE 6.17. GQ$_3$ and GQ$_4$.

An *n-dimensional generalized twisted cube* GQ_n [37] has 2^n nodes and can be defined as follows. GQ_0 is a single node. GQ_1 is a complete graph with two nodes labeled 0 and 1, respectively. GQ_2 is a graph with $V(GQ_2) = \{00, 01, 10, 11\}$ and $E(GQ_2) = \{(00, 01), (01, 11), (11, 10), (10, 00)\}$. For $n \geq 3$, $GQ_n = TQ_3 \times GQ_{n-3}$, where $\times$ is the Cartesian product of two graphs. Alternatively, GQ_n can be represented by $K_2 \times GQ_{n-1}$ if mod$(n, 3) = 1$ or 2, and $K_2 \odot GQ_{n-1}$ if mod$(n, 3) = 0$, where $\odot$ indicates that the Cartesian product operation is followed by the X-change operations $X[010b_{n-4}b_{n-5} \ldots b_0, 110b_{n-4}b_{n-5} \ldots b_0), (011b_{n-4}b_{n-5} \ldots b_0, 111b_{n-4}b_{n-5} \ldots b_0)]$, where $b_{n-4}b_{n-5} \ldots b_0 \in \{0, 1\}^{n-3}$ [37]. Based on the above definition, GQ_n belongs to the class of (1,2)-MCNs and is isomorphic to $G(GQ_{n-1}, GQ_{n-1}; PM)$. Figure 6.17 illustrates GQ_3 and GQ_4.

Lemma 6.21 GQ_n *is n-diagnosable for $n \geq 5$ under the PMC model.*

Proof: By the definition of generalized twisted cubes, $GQ_n \cong G(GQ_{n-1}, GQ_{n-1}; PM_1)$. Moreover, a GQ_n is *n*-connected for $n \geq 3$ [38], and $|V(GQ_{n-1})| = |V(GQ_{n-1})| = 2^{n-1} \geq (n-1) + 3 = n + 2$ for $n \geq 4$; therefore, by Lemma 6.11, GQ_n is *n*-diagnosable for $n \geq 5$. ∎

Theorem 6.7 $d(GQ_n) = n$ *for $n \geq 5$ under the PMC model.*

Proof: By Lemma 6.21, $d(GQ_n) \geq n$ for $n \geq 5$. Since GQ_n for $n \geq 1$ is a regular graph with a common degree n, that is, $\delta(GQ_n) = n$, then, by Lemma 6.9, $d(GQ_n) \leq \delta(GQ_n) = n$. Hence, $d(GQ_n) = n$ for $n \geq 5$. ∎

6.5.7   The Diagnosability of a Recursive Circulant

A *recursive circulant* [39, 40] $G(N, d)$ for $d \geq 2$ is defined as follows: The node set $V = \{v_0, v_1, v_2, \ldots, v_{N-1}\}$ and the edge set $E = \{(v_i, v_j)|$ there exists k for $0 \leq k \leq \lceil \log_d N \rceil - 1$ such that $i + d^k \equiv j \pmod{N}\}$. In fact, $G(N, d)$ is a *circulant graph* [41] with N nodes and jumps to the power of d, that is, $d^0, d^1, d^2, \ldots, d^{\lceil \log_d N \rceil - 1}$. Recursive circulant $G(N, d)$ has a recursive structure when $N = cd^n$ for $1 \leq c < d$. $G(cd^n, d)$ for $n \geq 1$ can be constructed recursively on d copies of $G(cd^{n-1}, d)$ as

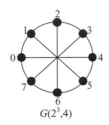

$$G(2^3, 4)$$

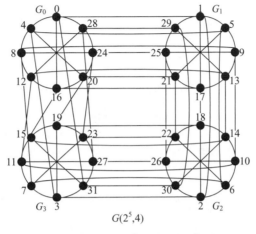

$$G(2^5, 4)$$

FIGURE 6.18. G$(2^3, 4)$ and G$(2^5, 4)$.

follows: Let $G_i = (V_i, E_i)$ for $0 \le i \le d - 1$ be a copy of $G(cd^{n-1}, d)$ with $V_i = \{v_0^i, v_1^i, \cdots, v_{cd^{n-1}-1}^i\}$, where G_i is isomorphic to $G(cd^{n-1}, d)$ by the isomorphism mapping v_j^i to v_j. We can relabel v_j^i as v_{jd+i}. The node set V of $G(cd^n, d)$ is $\bigcup_{0 \le i \le d-1} V_i$, and the edge set E is $\bigcup_{0 \le i \le d-1} E_i \cup X$, where $X = \{(v_j, v_{j'}) | j + 1 \equiv j' \pmod{cd^n}\}$. In this chapter, we focus $G(N, d)$ with $N = 2^n$ and $d = 4$. In the recursive structure, $G(2^n, 4)$ consists of four components: G_0, G_1, G_2, and G_3, each of which is isomorphic to $G(2^{n-2}, 4)$. Figure 6.18 illustrates $G(2^3, 4)$ and $G(2^5, 4)$.

Let H_0 and H_1 be two subgraphs of $G(2^n, 4)$ induced by $V(G_0) \cup V(G_1)$ and $V(G_2) \cup V(G_3)$, respectively, where $G_i \in G(2^{n-2}, 4)$ for $i \in \{0, 1, 2, 3\}$. In fact, $H_0 = (G_0, G_1; PM_1)$ and $H_1 = (G_2, G_3; PM_1)$. Moreover, it is not difficult to see that each node $u \in H_0$ has exactly one neighbor v in H_1. Therefore, the edges between S_1 and S_2 in $G(2^n, 4)$ form a perfect matching; that is, $G(2^n, 4) = (H_0, H_1; PM_1)$.

Lemma 6.22 *Let H_0 and H_1 be two subgraphs of $(G_0, G_1; PM_1)$ and $(G_2, G_3; PM_1)$, respectively, where $G_i \in G(2^{n-2}, 4)$ for $i \in \{0, 1, 2, 3\}$. Then, H_0 and H_1 are $(n-1)$-connected for $n \ge 4$.*

Proof: Since $G(2^n, 4)$ is n-connected for $n \ge 3$ [42], then, by Lemma 6.10, H_0 and H_1 are $(n-1)$-connected for $n \ge 4$.   ∎

Lemma 6.23 *$G(2^n, 4)$ is n-diagnosable for $n \ge 5$ under the PMC model.*

Proof: By the definition of recursive circulants $G(2^n, 4)$, $G(2^n, 4) = G(H_0, H_1; PM_1)$. Moreover, by Lemma 6.22, $H_0 = (G_0, G_1; PM_1)$ and $H_1 = (G_2, G_3; PM_1)$ are $(n-1)$-connected for $n \geq 4$, and $|V(H_0)| = |V(H_1)| = 2^{n-1} \geq (n-1) + 3 = n + 2$ for $n \geq 4$; therefore, by Lemma 6.11, $G(2^n, 4)$ is n-diagnosable for $n \geq 5$. ∎

Theorem 6.8 $d(G(2^n, 4)) = n$ *for* $n \geq 5$ *under the PMC model.*

Proof: By Lemma 6.23, $d(G(2^n, 4)) \geq n$ for $n \geq 5$. Since $G(2^n, 4)$ for $n \geq 3$ is a regular graph with a common degree n, that is, $\delta(G(2^n, 4)) = n$, then, by Lemma 6.9, $d(G(2^n, 4)) \leq \delta(G(2^n, 4)) = n$. Hence, $d(G(2^n, 4)) = n$ for $n \geq 5$. ∎

6.5.8 The Diagnosability of Hyper-Petersen Networks

The *Petersen graph P* is a simple graph in which the nodes are two-element subsets of a five-element set and the edges are pairs of disjoint two-element subsets. An *n-dimensional hyper-Petersen network* [43], denoted by HP_n for $n \geq 3$, has $HP_n \cong Q_{n-3} \times P$. Alternatively, $HP_n \cong HP_{n-1} \times K_2$, where $n \geq 4$; that is, $HP_n \cong G(HP_{n-1}, HP_{n-1}; PM_1)$. Figure 6.19 illustrates HP_3 and HP_4. Note that HP_n is a regular graph with $1.25(2^n)$ nodes that have a common degree n.

Lemma 6.24 HP_n *is n-diagnosable for* $n \geq 4$ *under the PMC model.*

Proof: By the definition of hyper-Petersen networks, $HP_n \cong G(HP_{n-1}, HP_{n-1}; PM_1)$. Moreover, HP_n is n-connected for $n \geq 3$ [44], and $|V(HP_{n-1})| = |V(HP_{n-1})| = 1.25$

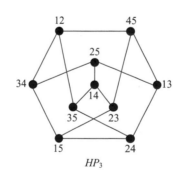

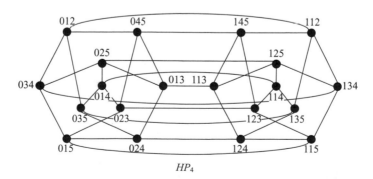

FIGURE 6.19. HP_3 and HP_4.

$(2^{n-1}) \geq (n-1) + 3 = n + 2$ for $n \geq 3$; therefore, by Lemma 6.11, HP_n is n-diagnosable for $n \geq 4$. ∎

Theorem 6.9 $d(HP_n) = n$ for $n \geq 4$ under the PMC model.

Proof: By Lemma 6.24, $d(HP_n) \geq n$ for $n \geq 4$. Since HP_n for $n \geq 3$ is a regular graph with a common degree n, that is, $\delta(HP_n) = n$, then, by Lemma 6.9, $d(HP_n) \leq \delta(HP_n) = n$. Hence, $d(HP_n) = n$ for $n \geq 4$. ∎

6.5.9 The Diagnosability of Folded Hypercubes

An *n-dimensional folded hypercube* [45], denoted by FQ_n, is a regular n-dimensional hypercube augmented by adding more edges between its nodes. More specifically, FQ_n has 2^n nodes and can be defined as follows. FQ_1 is a complete graph with two nodes labeled 0 and 1, respectively. For $n \geq 2$, there exists a PM_2 between $V(Q_{n-1}^0) = \{0u_{n-2}u_{n-3}\ldots u_0 \mid u_i \in 0,1\}$ and $V(Q_{n-1}^1) = \{1v_{n-2}v_{n-3}\ldots v_0 \mid v_i \in 0,1\}$ in such a way that node $u = 0u_{n-2}u_{n-3}\ldots u_0 \in V(Q_{n-1}^0)$ is connected to node $v = 1v_{n-2}v_{n-3}\ldots v_0 \in V(Q_{n-1}^1)$ if and only if one of the following conditions hold: (1) $u_i = v_i$ for $0 \leq i \leq n-2$ (called a *hypercube edge*), or (2) $u_i = \bar{v}_i$ for $0 \leq i \leq n-2$ (called a *complementary edge*) (Fig. 6.20).

Lemma 6.25 FQ_n is $(n+1)$-diagnosable for $n \geq 5$ under the PMC model.

Proof: By the definition of folded hypercubes, $FQ_n = G(Q_{n-1}^0, Q_{n-1}^1; PM_2)$. Moreover, a Q_n is n-connected for $n \geq 3$ [30], and $|V(Q_{n-1}^0)| = |V(Q_{n-1}^1)| = 2^{n-1} \geq (n-1) + 3 = n + 2$ for $n \geq 4$; therefore, by Lemma 6.11, FQ_n is $(n+1)$-diagnosable for $n \geq 5$. ∎

Theorem 6.10 $d(FQ_n) = n+1$ for $n \geq 5$ under the PMC model.

Proof: By Lemma 6.25, $d(FQ_n) \geq n$ for $n \geq 5$. Since FQ_n for $n \geq 1$ is a regular graph with a common degree $n+1$, that is, $\delta(FQ_n) = n+1$, then, by Lemma 6.9, $d(FQ_n) \leq \delta(FQ_n) = n+1$. Hence, $d(FQ_n) = n+1$ for $n \geq 5$. ∎

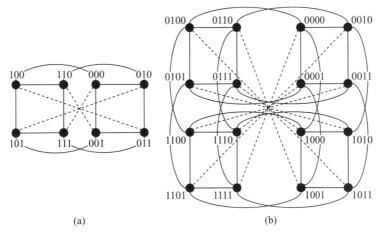

(a)   (b)

FIGURE 6.20. (a) A three-dimensional folded hypercube FQ₃, and (b) a four-dimensional folded hypercube FQ₄. The dotted lines represent the complementary edges.

Lemma 6.26   *FQ_n is $(n + 1)$-diagnosable for $n \geq 4$ under the MM* model.*

Proof: By the definition, FQ_n is obtained by connecting two $(n - 1)$-dimensional hypercubes via PM_2; that is, $FQ_n = G(Q_{n-1}^0, Q_{n-1}^1; PM_2)$. Since an n-dimensional hypercube is n-connected and the order of each node equals n [24] for $n \geq 3$, then, by Corollary 6.1, FQ_n is $(n - 1) + 2 = (n + 1)$-diagnosable for $n \geq 4$.   ∎

Theorem 6.11   *$d(FQ_n) = n + 1$ for $n \geq 4$ under the MM* model.*

Proof: By Lemma 6.26, $d(FQ_n) \geq n + 1$ for $n \geq 4$. Next, we show that $d(FQ_n) \leq n + 1$. Since FQ_n for $n \geq 1$ is a regular graph with a common degree $n + 1$, that is, $\delta(FQ_n) = n + 1$, then, by Lemma 6.13, $d(FQ_n) \leq \delta(FQ_n) \leq n + 1$. Hence, $d(FQ_n) = n + 1$ for $n \geq 4$.   ∎

6.5.10   The Diagnosability of Augmented Cubes

The *n-dimensional augmented cube AQ_n* [46] has 2^n nodes and can be recursively defined as follows. AQ_1 is a complete graph with two nodes labeled 0 and 1, respectively. For $n \geq 2$, AQ_n consists of two AQ_{n-1}'s, denoted by AQ_{n-1}^0 and AQ_{n-1}^1, respectively. In addition, there exists a PM_2 between $V(AQ_{n-1}^0) = \{0u_{n-2}u_{n-3} \dots u_0 \mid u_i \in 0, 1\}$ and $V(AQ_{n-1}^1) = \{1v_{n-2}v_{n-3} \dots v_0 \mid v_i \in 0, 1\}$ in such a way that node $u = 0u_{n-2}u_{n-3} \dots u_0 \in V(AQ_{n-1}^0)$ is connected to node $v = 1v_{n-2}v_{n-3} \dots v_0 \in V(AQ_{n-1}^1)$ if and only if one of the following conditions hold: (1) $u_i = v_i$ for $0 \leq i \leq n - 2$ (called a *hypercube edge*), or (2) $u_i = \bar{v}_i$ (called a *complementary edge*) for $0 \leq i \leq n - 2$ (Fig. 6.21).

Lemma 6.27   *AQ_n is $(2n - 1)$-diagnosable for $n \geq 5$ under the PMC model.*

Proof: By the definition of augmented cubes, $AQ_n = G(AQ_{n-1}^0, AQ_{n-1}^1; PM_2)$. Moreover, an AQ_n is $(2n - 1)$-connected for $n \geq 4$ [46] and $|V(AQ_{n-1}^0)| = |V(AQ_{n-1}^1)| =$

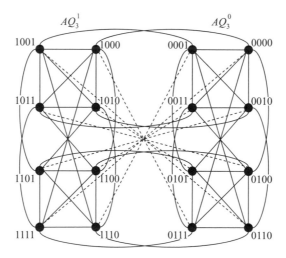

FIGURE 6.21. *A four-dimensional augmented cube AQ_4; the dotted lines represent the complementary edges.*

$2^{n-1} \geq (n-1)+3 = n+2$ for $n \geq 4$; therefore, by Lemma 6.11, AQ_n is $(2n-1)$-diag-nosable for $n \geq 5$. ■

Theorem 6.12 $d(AQ_n) = 2n - 1$ for $n \geq 5$ under the PMC model.

Proof: By Lemma 6.27, $d(AQ_n) \geq 2n - 1$ for $n \geq 5$. Since an AQ_n for $n \geq 1$ is a regular graph with a common degree $2n - 1$, that is, $\delta(AQ_n) = 2n - 1$, then, by Lemma 6.9, $d(AQ_n) \leq \delta(AQ_n) = 2n - 1$. Hence, $d(AQ_n) = 2n - 1$ for $n \geq 5$. ■

Lemma 6.28   *The order of each node v in AQ_n is at least $2n - 1$ for $n \geq 4$.*

Proof: We prove this lemma by induction on n. Since AQ_n is node symmetric [46], we only need to consider the order graph G^{0000} for node 0000 in AQ_4. Figure 6.22b illustrates the order graph G^{0000} for AQ_4. It is not difficult to verify that the

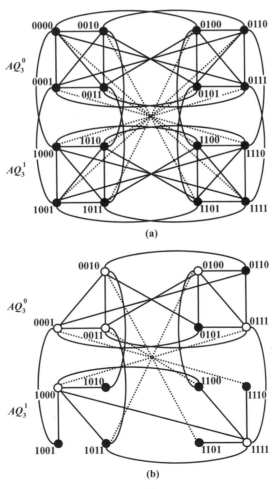

FIGURE 6.22. *(a) AQ_4 and (b) the order graph G^{0000}, where the white nodes form a minimum node cover.*

cardinality of a minimum node cover equals $7(=2 \times 4 - 1)$ using an exhaustive search. Thus, the base case holds. Assume that the lemma holds for dimension $n - 1$ for $n \geq 5$. Now, we consider AQ_n, which is constructed from two AQ_{n-1}s via PM_2. By the induction hypothesis, the order of each node in AQ_{n-1} is at least $2(n - 1) - 1 = 2n - 3$. Therefore, by Lemma 6.14, the order of AQ_n is at least $(2n - 3) + 2 = 2n - 1$. ∎

Lemma 6.29 AQ_n is $(2n - 1)$-diagnosable for $n \geq 5$ under the MM* model.

Proof: By the definition, AQ_n is obtained by connecting two $(n - 1)$-dimensional augmented cubes via PM_2; that is, $AQ_n = G(AQ_{n-1}^0, AQ_{n-1}^1; PM_2)$. By Lemma 6.28, Corollary 6.1, and AQ_n is $(2n - 1)$-connected [46], AQ_n is $(2(n - 1) - 1) + 2) = (2n - 1))$-diagnosable. ∎

Theorem 6.13 $d(AQ_n) = 2n - 1$ for $n \geq 5$ under the MM* model.

Proof: By Lemma 6.29, $d(AQ_n) \geq 2n - 1$ for $n \geq 5$. We next show that $d(AQ_n) \leq 2n - 1$. Since AQ_n for $n \geq 1$ is a regular graph with a common degree $2n - 1$, that is, $\delta(AQ_n) = 2n - 1$, then, by Lemma 6.13, $d(AQ_n) \leq \delta(AQ_n) = 2n - 1$. Hence, $d(AQ_n) = 2n - 1$ for $n \geq 5$. ∎

6.6 CONCLUDING REMARKS

Fault diagnosis in multiprocessor systems has received a great deal of attention since Preparata et al. [19] proposed the concept of system-level diagnosis. In this chapter, we have established sufficient conditions that can be utilized to determine the diagnosability of (1,2)-MCNs under the PMC model, and the diagnosability of 2-MCNs under the MM* model. By using the established lemmas, we can successfully compute the diagnosability of hypercubes, crossed cubes, Möbius cubes, twisted cubes, locally twisted cubes, generalized twisted cubes, recursive circulants for odd n, hyper-Petersen networks, folded hypercubes, and augmented cubes under the PMC model. Furthermore, we can also successfully compute the diagnosability of folded hypercubes and augmented cubes under the MM* model. In the future work, we will apply our strategy to some other classes of networks.

REFERENCES

[1] T. Araki and Y. Shibata, "(t,k)-Diagnosable system: A generalization of the PMC models," *IEEE Transactions on Computers*, 52(7):971–975, 2003.

[2] J.R. Armstrong and F.G. Gray, "Fault diagnosis in a Boolean n cube array of multiprocessors," *IEEE Transactions on Computers*, 30(8):587–590, 1981.

[3] G.Y. Chang and G.H. Chen, "(t,k)-Diagnosability of multiprocessor systems with applications to grids and tori," *SIAM Journal on Computing*, 37(4):1280–1298, 2007.

[4] G.Y. Chang, G.J. Chang, and G.H. Chen, "Diagnosabilites of regular networks," *IEEE Transactions on Parallel and Distributed Systems*, 16(4):314–323, 2005.

[5] G.Y. Chang, G.H. Chen, and G.J. Chang, "(t,k)-Diagnosis for matching composition networks," *IEEE Transactions on Computers*, 55(1):88–92, 2006.

[6] G.Y. Chang, G.H. Chen, and G.J. Chang, "(t,k)-Diagnosis for matching composition networks under the MM* model," *IEEE Transactions on Computers*, 56(1):73–79, 2007.

[7] K.Y. Chwa and S.L. Hakimi, "On fault identification in diagnosable systems," *IEEE Transactions on Computers*, 30(6):414–422, 1981.

[8] A. Das, K. Thulasiraman, and V.K. Agarwal, "Diagnosis of $t/(t + 1)$-diagnosable systems," *SIAM Journal on Computing*, 23(5):895–905, 1994.

[9] J. Fan, "Diagnosability of the Möbius cubes," *IEEE Transactions on Parallel and Distributed Systems*, 9(9):923–928, 1998.

[10] J. Fan, "Diagnosability of crossed cubes under the two strategies," *Chinese Journal of Computers*, 21(5):456–462, 1998.

[11] J. Fan, "Diagnosability of crossed cubes under the comparison diagnosis model," *IEEE Transactions on Parallel and Distributed Systems*, 13(7):687–692, 2002.

[12] S.L. Hakimi and A.T. Amin, "Characterization of connection assignment of diagnosable systems," *IEEE Transactions on Computers*, 23(1):86–88, 1974.

[13] S.Y. Hsieh and Y.S. Chen, "Strongly diagnosable systems under the comparison diagnosis model," *IEEE Transactions on Computers*, 57(12):1720–1725, 2008.

[14] S.Y. Hsieh and Y.S. Chen, "Strongly diagnosable product networks under the comparison diagnosis model," *IEEE Transactions on Computers*, 57(6):721–732, 2008.

[15] S.Y. Hsieh and T.Y. Chuang, "The strong diagnosability of regular networks and product networks under the PMC model," *IEEE Transactions on Parallel and Distributed Systems*, 20(3):367–378, 2009.

[16] A. Kavianpour and K.H. Kim, "Diagnosability of hypercubes under the pessimistic one-step diagnosis strategy," *IEEE Transactions on Computers*, 40(2):232–237, 1991.

[17] J.K. Lee and J.T. Butler, "A characterization of t/s-diagnosability and sequential t-diagnosability in designs," *IEEE Transactions on Computers*, 39(10):1298–1304, 1990.

[18] J. Maeng and M. Malek, "A comparison connection assignment for self-diagnosis of multiprocessor systems," in *Proceedings of the 11th International Symposium on Fault-Tolerant Computing*, pp. 173–175, 1981.

[19] F.P. Preparata, G. Metze, and R.T. Chien, "On the connection assignment problem of diagnosable systems," *IEEE Transactions on Computers*, EC-16:448–454, 1967.

[20] A. Sengupta and A. Dahbura, "On self-diagnosable multiprocessor system: Diagnosis by the comparison approach," *IEEE Transactions on Computers*, 41(11):1386–1396, 1992.

[21] A.K. Somani, "Sequential fault occurrence and reconfiguration in system level diagnosis," *IEEE Transactions on Computers*, 39(12):1472–1475, 1990.

[22] A.K. Somani, V.K. Agarwal, and D. Avis, "A generalized theory for system level diagnosis," *IEEE Transactions on Computers*, 36(5):538–546, 1987.

[23] A.K. Somani and O. Peleg, "On diagnosability of large fault sets in regular topology-based computer systems," *IEEE Transactions on Computers*, 45(8):892–903, 1996.

[24] D. Wang, "Diagnosability of hypercubes and enhanced hypercubes under the comparison diagnosis model," *IEEE Transactions on Computers*, 48(12):1369–1374, 1999.

[25] C.L. Yang, G.M. Masson, and R.A. Leonetti, "On fault isolation and identification in t_1/t_1-diagnosable systems," *IEEE Transactions on Computers*, 35(7):639–643, 1986.

[26] F. Barsi, F. Grandoni, and P. Maestrini, "A theory of diagnosability of digital systems," *IEEE Transactions on Computers*, C-25(6):585–593, 1976.

[27] L.C. Albini, S. Chessa, and P. Maestrini, "Diagnosis of symmetric graphs under the BGM model," *The Computer Journal*, 47(1):85–92, 2004.

[28] D.B. West, *Introduction to Graph Theory*, 2nd ed. Upper Saddle River, NJ: Prentice Hall, 2001.

[29] A.T. Dahbura and G.M. Masson, "An $O(n^{2.5})$ fault identification algorithm for diagnosable systems," *IEEE Transactions on Computers*, 33(6):486–492, 1984.

[30] Y. Saad and M.H. Schultz, "Topological properties of hypercubes," *IEEE Transactions on Computers*, 37(7):867–872, 1988.

[31] K. Efe, "The crossed cube architecture for parallel computation," *IEEE Transactions on Parallel and Distributed Systems*, 3(5):513–524, 1992.

[32] P. Kulasinghe, "Connectivity of the crossed cube," *Information Processing Letters*, 61(4):221–226, 1997.

[33] P. Cull and S.M. Larson, "The Möbius cubes," *IEEE Transactions on Computers*, 44(5):647–659, 1995.

[34] P.A.J. Hilbers, M.R.J. Koopman, and J.L.A. van de Snepscheut, "The twisted cube," in *Proceedings of the Conference on Parallel Architectures and Languages Europe, Volume I: Parallel Architectures*, pp. 152–159, 1987.

[35] C. Chang, J.N. Wang, and L.H. Hsu, "Topological properties of twisted cube," *Information Science*, 113:147–167, 1999.

[36] X. Yang, D.J. Evans, and G.M. Megson, "The locally twisted cubes," *International Journal of Computer Mathematics*, 82(4):401–413, 2005.

[37] F.B. Chedid, "On the generalized twisted cube," *Information Processing Letters*, 55(1): 49–52, 1995.

[38] F.B. Chedid and R.B. Chedid, "A new variation on hypercubes with smaller diameter," *Information Processing Letters*, 46(6):275–280, 1993.

[39] J.H. Park, "Panconnectivity and edge-pancyclicity of faulty recursive circulant $G(2^m,4)$," *Theoretical Computer Science*, 390(1):70–80, 2008.

[40] J.H. Park and K.Y. Chwa, "Recursive circulants and their embeddings among hypercubes," *Theoretical Computer Science*, 244:35–62, 2000.

[41] F.T. Boesch and R. Tindell, "Circulants and their connectivities," *Journal of Graph Theory*, 8:129–138, 1984.

[42] S.W. Jung, S.Y. Kim, J.H. Park, and K.Y. Chwa, "Connectivities of recursive circulant graphs," in *Proceedings of the 19th KISS Spring Conference*, pp. 591–594, 1992.

[43] S.K. Das and A.K. Banerjee, "Hyper Petersen network: Yet another hypercube-like topology," in *Proceedings of the 4th Symposium on the Frontiers of Massively Parallel Computation (Froniters '92)*, McLean, VA, pp. 270–277, IEEE Computer Society, 1992.

[44] S.K. Das, S. Öhring, and A.K. Banerjee, "Embeddings into hyper Petersen networks: Yet another hypercube-like interconnection topology," *VLSI Design*, 2(4):335–351, 1995.

[45] A.E.I. Awawy and S. Latifi, "Properties and performance of folded hypercubes," *IEEE Transactions on Parallel and Distributed Systems*, 2(1):31–42, 1991.

[46] S.A. Choudum and V. Sunitha, "Augmented cubes," *Networks*, 40(2):71–84, 2002.

A Performance Analysis Methodology for MultiCore, Multithreaded Processors

Miao Ju, Hun Jung, and Hao Che

7.1 INTRODUCTION

As chip multiprocessors (CMPs) become the mainstream processor technology, challenges arise as to how to design and program CMPs to achieve the desired performance for applications of diverse nature. There are two scalability barriers that the existing CMP analysis approaches (e.g., simulation and benchmark testing) find difficult to overcome. The first barrier is the difficulty for the existing approaches to effectively analyze CMP performance as the number of cores and threads of execution becomes large. The second barrier is the difficulty for the existing approaches to perform comprehensive comparative studies of different architectures as CMPs proliferate. In addition to these barriers, how to analyze the performance of various possible design/programming choices during the initial CMP design/programming phase is particularly challenging, when the actual instruction-level program is not available.

To overcome the above scalability barriers, approaches that work at much coarser granularities (e.g., overlooking microarchitectural details) than the existing ones must be sought to keep up with the ever-growing design space. Such an approach

Scalable Computing and Communications: Theory and Practice, First Edition. Edited by Samee U. Khan, Albert Y. Zomaya, and Lizhe Wang.
© 2013 John Wiley & Sons, Inc. Published 2013 by John Wiley & Sons, Inc.

should be able to characterize the general performance properties for a wide variety of CMP architectures and a large workload space at coarse granularity. Moreover, such an approach cannot assume the availability of the instruction-level programs as input for performance analysis. The aim is to narrow down the design space of interest at coarse granularity in the initial design/programming phase, in which an existing approach can work efficiently to further pin down the optimal points at finer granularities in a later design/programming phase. To this end, we believe that an overarching new approach, encompassing both existing and future design and workload spaces, should be sought. In this chapter, we discuss a new methodology in an attempt to achieve such a design objective.

The proposed methodology aims at exploring a large design space at coarse granularity. More specifically, it works at the thread level, overlooking instruction-level and microarchitectural details, except those having significant impact on thread-level performance, such as an instruction for memory access or instructions that cause serialization effects. The methodology works in a large design space, covering various processor organizations, pipelined/parallel core configurations, thread-scheduling disciplines, and memory access mechanisms. This methodology leads to the successful development of a queuing network modeling technique with closed-form solutions, making it possible to study the general performance properties of CMPs over a large design space. Moreover, it also leads to the development of a lightweight simulation tool (ST) with extremely low time and space complexities, also viable for large design space exploration. In this chapter, we introduce the methodology, the ST, and the modeling technique focusing on the following performance measures: throughput, delay, and loss. Other performance measures, such as power and memory consumptions, will be incorporated in the future. The results in this chapter are partially presented in References 1 and 2.

The rest of this chapter is organized as follows. Section 7.2 describes the methodology. Sections 7.3 and 7.4 present the ST and the analytic modeling technique developed based on this methodology, respectively. Section 7.5 provides test results for the queuing modeling technique against the simulated ones. Section 7.6 discusses the related work. Finally, Section 7.7 presents the conclusions and future work.

7.2 METHODOLOGY

The main idea of our methodology is to capture only activities that have a major impact on the thread-level performance. In other words, the instruction level and microarchitectual details are overlooked unless they trigger events that may have significant effects at the thread level, such as an instruction for memory access that causes the thread to stall or instructions corresponding to a critical region that cause serialization effect at the thread level. Correspondingly, all the components including CPU, cache/memory, and interconnection network are modeled at a highly abstract level, overlooking microarchitectual details, just enough to capture the thread-level activities. For example, for a CPU running a coarse-grained thread-scheduling discipline and a memory with a FIFO queue, they are modeled simply as queuing servers running a coarse-grained thread-scheduling algorithm and FIFO discipline, respectively. The following sections describe, at the thread level, the modeling of the CMP organization, the workload, and the design space, separately.

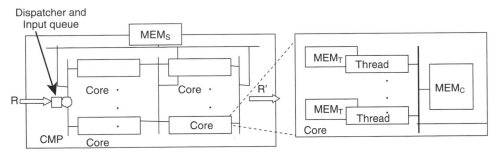

FIGURE 7.1. *CMP organization.*

Since in the CMP family communication processors (CPs) are particularly difficult to model due to their workload dependence on packet arrival processes, which are stochastic in nature, in the rest of this chapter and without loss of generality, we discuss CMP in the context of CP. All we need to note is that, for a CP, program tasks mapped to a thread in a core, which determine the workload characteristics, come from packets, rather than a program or program tasks loaded in that core.

7.2.1 CMP Organization

We consider a generic CP organization depicted in Figure. 7.1. This organization focuses on the characterization of multicore and multithread features common to most of the CMP architectures, leaving all other components being summarized in highly abstract forms. More specifically, in this organization, a CP is viewed generically as composed of a set of cores and a set of on-chip and/or off-chip supporting components, such as I/O interfaces, memory, level one and level two caches, special processing units, scratch pads, embedded general-purpose CPUs, and coprocessors. These supporting components may appear at three different levels, that is, the thread, core, and system (including core cluster) levels, collectively denoted as MEM_T, MEM_C, and MEM_S, respectively. Each core may run more than one thread and the threads are scheduled based on a given thread-scheduling discipline.

Cores may be configured in parallel and/or multistage pipelining (a two-stage configuration is shown in Fig. 7.1), and there is a packet stream coming in from one side and going out through the other side. Packet processing tasks may be partitioned and mapped to different cores at different pipeline stages or different cores at a given stage. A dispatcher distributes the incoming packets to different core pipelines based on any given policies. Backlogged packets are temporarily stored in an input buffer. A small buffer may also present between any two consecutive pipeline stages to hold backlogged packets temporarily. Packet loss may occur when any of these buffers overflow.

Clearly, the above organization also applies to non-CP-based CMPs. The only difference is that, in this case, there is no packet arrival, or departure processes and tasks mapped to different cores are generated by one or multiple applications mapped to those cores. This chapter is concerned with the CP throughput, latency, and loss performance only, and the power and memory resource constraints are assumed to be met. This implies that we do not have to keep track of memory or program store resource availabilities or power budget.

7.2.2 Workload

At the core of our methodology is the modeling of the workload, defined as a mapping of program tasks to threads in different cores, known as code paths. For tasks mapped to a given thread, a piece of pseudocode for those tasks can be written. Then a unique branch from the root to a given leaf in the pseudocode is defined as a code path associated with that thread. A specific packet processing or instantiation of program execution is associated with a specific code path, or a sequence of events that the thread needs to execute to fulfill the tasks. For a CP, the program tasks mapped to a thread may be on and off, which is a function of the packet arrival process. Moreover, what code path a thread may need to handle in a given time period is dependent on the actual mixture of packets of different types arriving in that time period, each being associated with some distinct program tasks to be fulfilled, known as a mixture of code paths. For example, while an IP packet may be subject to the entire cycle of both layer 2 and layer 3 processing, resulting in a long code path, a packet carrying IS–IS routing information is forwarded to the control plane immediately after it is identified at layer 2, which leads to a very short code path.

In this chapter, a code path is defined at the thread level, which is composed of a sequence of segments corresponding to different events that have a significant impact on the thread-level performance. For each segment, we are only concerned with the segment length in terms of the number of core cycles. It can be formally defined as follows:

$T_k(M_k; m_{1,k}, t_{1,k}, \tau_{1,k}, \cdots, m_{M_k,k}, t_{M_k,k}\tau_{M_k,k})$: Code path k with event $m_{i,k}$ occurred at the $t_{i,k}$-th core clock cycle and with event duration $\tau_{i,k}$, where $k = 1, \ldots, K$ and $i = 1, 2, \ldots, M_k$; K is the total number of code paths in the pseudocode; and M_k is the total number of events in the code path k.

A graphic representation of such a code path is given in Figure 7.2.

We note that a code path thus defined is simply a sequence of events with event interarrival times $t_{i+1,k} - t_{i,k} = \tau_{i,k}$ for $i = 1, 2, \ldots, M_k - 1$. The events $m_{i,k} \in$ CPU are represented by the white segments, and the corresponding $\tau_{i,k}$ is the number of core cycles the CPU spends on this thread in this segment. All other events are separated by the CPU events. For an event $m_{i,k} \in \text{MEM}_T$, MEM_C, or MEM_S, $\tau_{i,k}$ represents the unloaded resource-access latency. An event can be introduced to account for the serialization effect caused by, for example, a critical region. Hence, the length of the code path T_k, denoted as $|T_k|$, is the total duration of code path k handled by a thread in the absence of resource contention, that is, without waiting times due to contention with other threads for CPU, memory, and any other resource accesses. An event is defined as one that is expected to have a significant impact on the thread-level activities. Currently, we have defined the following four types of events:

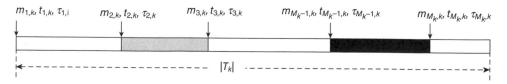

FIGURE 7.2. $T_k(M_k; m_{1,k}, t_{1,k}, \tau_{1,k}, \cdots, m_{M_k,k}, t_{M_k,k}, \tau_{M_k,k})$.

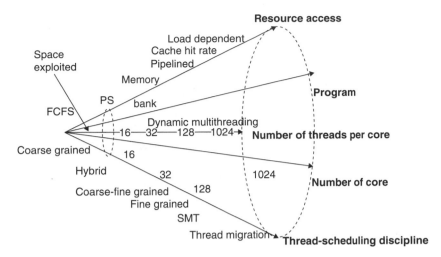

FIGURE 7.3. *Design space.*

(1) CPU events; (2) resource-access events, which may cause significant delay and thread-level interactions (i.e., context switching), that is, $m_{i,k} \in \mathrm{MEM_T}$, $\mathrm{MEM_C}$, or $\mathrm{MEM_S}$; and (3) events that cause serialization effects, for example, a critical region. More types of events can be incorporated if they are expected to contribute significantly to the thread-level activities.

7.2.3 Design Space

We want the design space to be as large as possible to encompass as many CMP architectures and workloads as possible. Figure. 7.3 depicts such a design space. It is a five-dimensional space, including resource-access dimension, thread scheduling-discipline dimension, program dimension, number-of-thread-per-core dimension, and number-of-core dimension. Figure 7.3 also shows the part (i.e., the small cone on the left) that has been (incompletely) explored by the existing work using queuing network modeling techniques (see Section 7.6 for more details). Clearly, the existing work only covers a tiny part of the entire design space.

The thread scheduling-discipline dimension determines what CPU or core type is in use. The existing commercial processors use fine-grained, coarse-grained, simultaneous multithreading (SMT), and hybrid coarse-and-fine-grained thread-scheduling disciplines. Some systems may also allow a thread to be migrated from one core to another.

The resource-access dimension determines the thread access mechanisms to CMP resources other than CPU. It may include memory, cache, interconnection network, and even a critical region. The typical resource-access mechanisms include first come, first served (FCFS), process sharing (parallel access), parallel resources (e.g., memory bank), and pipelined access. For cache access, a cache hit model may have to be incorporated, which may be load dependent. The program dimension includes all possible programs. This dimension is mapped to a workload space, involving all possible code path mixtures, for a given type of processor organization. The number-of-core and number-of-thread-per-core dimensions determine the size of the CMP in terms of the numbers of cores and threads. The number-of-thread-per-core dimension also needs to deal with dynamic multithreading, where the number of threads used for a program task may change over time due to on-and-off packet arrivals or the variation of the level of parallelism in a program.

In summary, this section described a methodology that provides a coarse-granular, thread-level view of a CMP in general and a CP in particular in terms of its organization and design space. Based on this methodology, the following two sections demonstrate how an analytic modeling technique and a framework for fast program-task-to-core mapping can be developed to allow much of the design space in Figure 7.3 to be explored.

7.3   SIMULATION TOOL (ST)

7.3.1   Basic Idea

Our ST [2] focuses on three performance measures: throughput, delay, and loss. All three measures can be obtained at runtime as long as the latency L_k for a packet with code path k in each core can be simulated, which can be expressed as

$$L_k = |T_k| + \sum_{j=1}^{M_k} \left(\tau_{j,k}^q + \tau_{j,k}^w \right), \tag{7.1}$$

where $\tau_{j,k}^q$ is the thread queuing time for the event $m_{j,k}$ and $\tau_{j,k}^w$ is the waiting time in the ready state after the event $m_{j,k}$ finishes. For an event $m_{j,k} \in$ MEM$_T$, MEM$_C$, or MEM$_S$, $\tau_{i,k}$, which contributes to $|T_k|$ (see Fig. 7.4), is dependent on the nature of $m_{j,k}$ access (number of memory reads or writes) and the access speed (bus speed and memory speed), which is assumed to be provided by the user as a plug-in. $\tau_{j,k}^q$ and $\tau_{j,k}^w$ are dominated by multithreading effects, dependent on the thread scheduling and queuing mechanism for resource $m_{j,k}$ access, which is the core parameter to be simulated at runtime.

Hence, for throughput, delay, and loss performance analysis, all that is needed from the user is a set of plug-ins that estimate $\tau_{j,k}$ for $m_{j,k} \in$ MEM$_T$, MEM$_C$, or MEM$_S$ (note that $\tau_{j,k}$ for an event corresponding to a critical region can be estimated

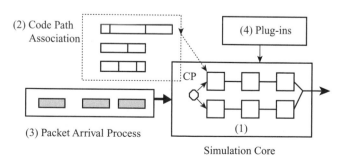

FIGURE 7.4. *Proposed simulation model.*

from the pseudocode itself). Note that, although modeling CMP-specific features in general is a nontrivial task, it should not be difficult to come up with empirical memory access latency models, for example, in the form of charts or tables for a given CMP. For example, by loading a given memory with different types of requests and measuring the corresponding unloaded latencies using a cycle-accurate simulator or test board, one can build empirical charts or tables offline to be used to quickly estimate $\tau_{j,k}$ at runtime. There is no need to emulate the microscopic process for memory access at runtime, saving significant amounts of simulation time. As demonstrated in Reference 2, with the unloaded memory access latencies provided by Intel, as well as a memory access waiting time estimated based on a simple FIFO queuing model (QM), our ST accurately characterizes IXP1200/2400 performance without further information about IXP1200/2400-specific features.

7.3.2 Simulation Model

With the above preparation, we now describe our simulation model, which focuses on emulating common features pertaining to all CMP architectures, including core topology, multithreading, code path, code path mixtures, and packet arrival processes, with a limited number of plug-ins to account for CMP-specific features. The plug-ins are predeveloped and plugged into the simulation model. Figure 7.4 gives a logic diagram for the proposed simulation model, which is composed of four major components: (1) a simulation core based on the generic CP organization described in Figure 7.1, (2) code path association with a packet in a core, (3) a packet arrival process, and (4) a set of plug-ins to the simulation core.

Based on the generic CP architecture in Figure 7.1, the simulation model focuses on emulating multithreaded cores, which can be configured in any pipeline/parallel topology. Each core is modeled at a highly abstract level, running any number of threads based on a given thread-scheduling discipline. No further details of the core are modeled. A thread in a core that receives a packet will be assigned a code path. The way to assign code paths to threads in a core determines the mixture of code paths in that core. The packet arrival process can be generated from real traces (which also determine the code path mixture in each core), stochastic models, or deterministic models. Traditionally, the code path assignment and packet arrival process generation are not part of the ST design but are user-provided inputs. Since all four components can be designed independent of one another, the design of components (1) and (4) combined constitutes a fast performance analysis tool in the traditional sense. In other words, as in traditional approaches, our tool allows any user-provided packet arrival processes and/or mixtures of code paths to be simulated. In Reference 2, we also designed components (2) and (3) such that for any given program-task-to-core mapping, the tool can quickly return the maximal line rate a CP can sustain. However, due to the page limitation, here we shall not discuss the design of these two components. The ST is event driven, and it processes a linked list of events corresponding to the segment boundaries in the execution sequence rather than instruction by instruction. A code path generally involves only a few to a few dozen events, which makes the tool extremely fast (see Section 7.5 for case studies). Moreover, since the next event is generally triggered by the execution of a current event, the linked list can be kept extremely small, consuming a negligible amount of memory resource. As a result, the ST is lightweight and fast.

7.4 ANALYTIC MODELING TECHNIQUE

7.4.1 General Model

As explained in detail in Reference 3, based on the proposed methodology, any types of CMPs with M_l active threads in the lth core (for $l = 1, \ldots, N_c$), N_c^l components associated with the lth core (including shared resources), and any long-run workloads can be generally modeled as a closed queuing network with N_c job classes and M_l jobs in the lth class, N_c^l queuing servers of various service types in terms of queue scheduling disciplines, and a workload space (μ_i^l, p_{ij}^l) for job class l, spanned by various possible combinations of service time distributions μ_i^l and routing probabilities p_{ij}^l (note that the subscripts i and j are indices of the components associated with the lth core). The central task is then to develop mathematical techniques to analytically solve this closed queuing network model. The solution should be able to account for as many service types and as large a workload space as possible, aiming at covering a wide range of CMP architectures.

7.4.2 Design Space Coverage

The queuing network modeling techniques at our disposal limit the size of the design space to one that must be mathematically tractable. This makes the coverage of the design space in Figure 7.3 a challenge. In this section, we discuss our solutions in meeting the challenge.

7.4.2.1 Memory/Interconnect Network and Thread Scheduling-Discipline Dimensions
Without resorting to any approximation techniques, the existing queuing network modeling techniques will allow both of these dimensions to be largely explored analytically. Any instance in either of these two dimensions can be approximately modeled using a queuing server model that has local balance equations (i.e., it leads to queuing network solutions of product form or closed form). More specifically, Table 7.1 shows how individual instances in these two dimensions can be modeled by three QMs with local balance equations (according to the BCMP theorem [4]), including $M/G/\infty$, $M/M/mFCFS$ (including $M/M/1$), and $M/G/1PS$ (processor sharing). Note that memory banks should be modeled as separate queuing servers and, hence, are not listed in this table. Also note that for all the multi-thread-scheduling disciplines except the hybrid-fine-and-coarse-grained one (to be explained below) in Table 7.1, the service time distribution of a QM models the time distribution for a thread to be serviced at the corresponding queuing server. With these in mind, the following explains the rationales behind the mappings in Table 7.1:

- *SMT.* It allows multiple issues in one clock cycle from independent threads, creating multiple virtual CPUs. If the number of threads in use is no greater than the number of issues in one clock cycle, the CPU can be approximately modeled as an $M/G/\infty$ queue, mimicking multiple CPUs handling all the threads in parallel; otherwise, it can be approximately modeled as an $M/M/m$ queue, that is, not enough virtual CPUs to handle all the threads, and some may have to be queued.

TABLE 7.1. Component Modeling Using Queuing Models with Local Balance Equations

Queue Model Component	$M/G/\infty$	$M/M/m$FCFS	$M/G/1$PS	$M/M/1$
SMT	√	√		
Fine-grained thread scheduling			√	
Coarse-grained thread scheduling				√
Hybrid-fine-and-coarse-grained thread scheduling		√		
Resources dedicated to individual threads	√			
FCFS shared memory, cache, interconnection network, or critical region				√
FCFS memory with pipelined access		√		

- *Fine-Grained Thread-Scheduling Discipline.* All the threads that access the CPU resource will share the CPU resource at the finest granularity, that is, one instruction per thread in a round-robin fashion. This discipline can be approximately modeled as an $M/G/1$PS queue; that is, all the threads share equal amounts of the total CPU resource in parallel.

- *Coarse-Grained Thread-Scheduling Discipline.* All the threads that access the CPU resource will be serviced in a round-robin fashion and the context is switched only when the thread is stalled, waiting for the return of other resource accesses. This can be approximately modeled as an FCFS queue, for example, an $M/M/1$ queue.

- *Hybrid-Fine-and-Coarse-Grained Thread-Scheduling Discipline.* It allows up to a given number of threads, say, m, to be processed in a fine-grained fashion and the rest to be queued in an FCFS queue. This can be modeled as an $M/M/m$ FCFS queue. In this QM, the average service time for each thread being serviced is m times longer than the service time if only one thread were being serviced, mimicking fine-grained PS effect.

- *Resources Dedicated to Individual Threads.* Such resources can be collectively modeled as a single $M/G/\infty$ queue; that is, there is no contention among different threads accessing these resources.

- *FCFS Shared Memory, Cache, Interconnect Network, or Critical Region.* This kind of resource can be modeled as an $M/M/1$ queue.

- *FCFS Memory with Parallel Access.* Memory banks can be accessed in parallel. It can be modeled as an $M/M/m$ FCFS queue, with up to the number-of-bank worth of memory accesses serviced in parallel and the rest queued in an FCFS queue.

- *FCFS Memory with Pipelined Access.* Same as above. The pipeline depth determines how many threads can be serviced simultaneous in the $M/M/m$ FCFS queue.

We note that the memory/interconnection-network dimension also includes load-dependent cache hit rate. The cache hit probability (i.e., the routing probability to move back to the CPU) is generally load dependent in the sense that it may either be positively or negatively correlated with the number of threads in use due to temporal locality and cache resource contention. These effects can be accounted for in our framework without approximation by means of the existing load-dependent routing techniques (e.g., see Reference 5). We also note that the thread scheduling-discipline dimension includes thread migration. The thread migration allows a thread to be migrated from one core to another for, for example, load balancing purpose. This effect can be accounted for without approximation by allowing jobs to have nonzero probabilities to switch from one class to another [6, 7]. More capabilities may be identified and included in these two dimensions as long as they are mathematically tractable.

7.4.2.2 *Program Dimension*

In principle, this dimension can be fully explored through a thorough study of the workload space, characterized by the service time distributions and routing probabilities, that is, a collection of $(\{\mu_i\}, \{p_{ij}\})$'s. However, for the solvable queuing server models in Table 7.1, such as $M/M/m$ and $M/M/1$ queues, the service time distribution μ_i is a given, that is, exponential distribution. Since the exponential distribution is characterized by only a single parameter, that is, the mean service time t_i, it can only capture the first-order statistics of the code path segments corresponding to that server, hence providing *a first-order approximation of the program dimension or workload space*. Although our future research will explore more sophisticated QMs in an attempt to overcome this limitation, we expect that the first-order approximation could actually provide good performance data due to the well-known robustness property [6], which states that for closed queuing networks, the system performance is insensitive to the service time distributions. To calculate $(\{\mu_i\}, \{p_{ij}\})$, we first define p^k, the probability that an incoming packet is associated with code path k (for $k = 1, 2, \ldots, K$). In other words, p^k defines a code path mixture. We further define τ_i^k, f_i^k, and q_{ij}^k as the average service time at queuing server i, the frequency to access queuing server i, and the probability to access queuing server j upon exiting queuing server i, respectively, for a thread handling code path k. These statistic parameters are collectable from the pseudocode. Then, the average service rates and routing probabilities for a given job class can be written as

$$\mu_i^l = \frac{\sum_{k=1}^{K} p^k f_i^k}{\sum_{k=1}^{K} p^k f_i^k \tau_i^k}, \quad i = 1, \cdots, N_c^l \tag{7.2}$$

and

$$P_{ij}^l = \sum_{k=1}^{K} p^k q_{ij}^k, \quad i = 1, \cdots, N_c^l. \tag{7.3}$$

Here, a job class is defined as threads that follow these same statistics. In general, all the threads that belong to the same core form a job class.

7.4.2.3 *Number-of-Core and Number-of-Thread Dimensions*

First, we note that the number-of-thread dimension should allow dynamic multithreading, meaning that at different program execution stages, the number of active threads may vary. In Section 7.5, we propose a possible solution, which will be further studied in the future. Second, we need to address the scalability issues in calculating the generation functions as the numbers of cores and threads increase. We consider a general closed queuing network modeling an N-core (or core cluster) system with P shared resources. We want to be able to get closed-form generation function G for such closed queuing networks, from which any performance measures can be derived. As long as all the queuing servers in the system have local balance equations (e.g., following the queuing server models in Table 7.1), the generation function or normalization function can be generally written as

$$G = \sum_{\sum_{i=1}^{N+P} m_{il}=M_l} \cdots \sum_{\sum_{i=1}^{N+P} m_{iN}=M_N} f_l(m_{ll}) \cdots f_N(m_{NN}) \prod_{j=1}^{P} f_i(m_{jl}, \cdots, m_{jN}), \qquad (7.4)$$

where $f_i(m_{ik})$ is a function corresponding to the probability that there are m_{ik} threads currently in core i (for $i = 1, \ldots, N$, where N is the number of cores) for thread class k (for $k = 1, \ldots, N$; i.e., the threads from each core form a class), $f_i(m_{j1}, \ldots, m_{jN})$ is a function corresponding to the probability that there are m_{j1} threads of class one, m_{j2} threads of class two, and so on, in queuing server j (for $j = 1, \ldots, P$), and M_i is the total number of threads belonging to core i (for $i = 1, \ldots, N$). $f_i(x)$'s take different forms for different core organizations, in terms of, for example, CPU, cache, and local memory of different types from the resource-access dimension and thread scheduling-discipline dimension of the design space. On one hand, we note that G is defined on the entire design space (with the first-order approximation of the program dimension or workload space). Understanding the general properties of G over this space will allow the properties of individual points in the design space to be understood. On the other hand, we also note that the number-of-core and number-of-thread-per-core dimensions create scalability barriers that prevent us from being able to effectively calculate G. This is because the computational complexity for G is $O(N_S M^{N+P})$, where M is the average number of threads per core and N_S is the average number of queuing servers per core. Our experiments on an Intel Core Duo, T2400, 1.83-GHz processor showed that for $N_S = M = 2$ and $P = 1$, it takes about 24 hours to compute the generation function for a 20-core system. Clearly, it is computationally too expensive to cover the entire number-of-core and number-of-thread dimensions. In the following, we develop an iterative procedure to overcome this scalability barrier.

7.4.2.4 An Iterative Procedure
The difficulty to calculate $G(x)$ lies in the fact that different cores interact with one another through shared resources. A key intuition is that *the effect on each core due to resource sharing with other cores would become more and more dependent on the first-order statistics (i.e., mean values) and less sensitive to the higher-order statistics (e.g., variances) or the actual distributions as the number of cores sharing the resources increases* (reminiscent of the law of large numbers and the central limit theorem in statistics and the mean field theory in physics, although actual formal analysis could be difficult). With this observation in mind, we were able to design an iterative procedure to decouple the interactions among cores so that the performance of each core can be evaluated quickly as if it were a stand-alone core.

Assume there are N cores sharing a common FIFO memory. Initially, we calculate the sojourn time $T_i(0)$ and throughput $\lambda_i(0)$ for single-core system i consisting of

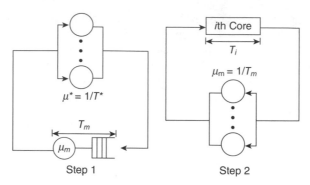

FIGURE 7.5. Iterative procedure.

a core and the common memory (for $i = 1, \ldots, N$). Then, the initial mean sojourn time for all the cores, $T^*(1)$, is calculated based on the following formula:

$$T^*(n) = \sum_{i=1}^{N} \frac{\lambda_i(n)}{\sum_{j=1}^{N} \lambda_j(n)} T_i(n). \tag{7.5}$$

Then, we enter an iteration loop as shown in Figure 7.5. At the nth iteration, first the average sojourn time for the common memory, $T_m(n)$, is calculated based on a two-server queuing network (on the left of Fig. 7.5), including a queuing server for the common memory and an $M/M/\infty$ queuing server characterized by the mean service time $T^*(n)$. There are a total of $M = \sum_{i=1}^{N} m_i$ threads circulating in this network, where m_i is the number of active threads in core i. In other words, we approximate the aggregate effect of all the threads from all the cores on the common memory using a single $M/M/\infty$ queuing server with the mean service time $T^*(n)$. Then, we test if $|T_m(n) - T_M(n-1)| \leq \varepsilon$ holds, for a predefined small value ε. If it does, exit the loop and finish; otherwise, do the following. The sojourn time $T_i(n)$ and throughput $\lambda_i(n)$ for core i (for $i = 1, \ldots, N$) are updated based on the closed queuing network on the right of Figure 7.5. This time, the effects of other cores on core i are accounted for using a single $M/M/\infty$ server with the mean service time $T_m(n)$. There are m_i threads circulating in this network. Finally, $T^*(n)$ is updated before entering the next iteration. Note that both steps involve only queuing network models that have closed-form solutions, which make each iteration loop extremely fast.

7.5 TESTING

The testing results for the ST against the cycle-accurate simulation were presented in Reference 2. The performance data for the ST were shown to be within 5% of the cycle-accurate simulation data for applications run on IXP1200 and IXP2400 network processors. In this section, we test the accuracy of the queuing modeling technique for CMPs with 1000 cores and up to several thousands of threads. The

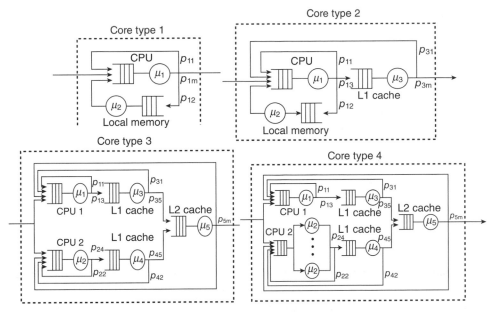

FIGURE 7.6. *Algorithm.*

results are compared against those obtained by our ST. Note that our ST is the only existing tool that can scale to CMPs in a large design space involving thousands of cores and threads, and various component models.

We consider a CMP with 1000 cores and core clusters sharing a common FIFO memory. There are two types of cores (i.e., core type 1 with 6 active threads and core type 2 with 9 active threads) and two core clusters (i.e., core type 3 with 8 active threads and core type 4 with 10 active threads), 250 each, as given in Figure 7.6. Core type 1 may model a CPU with a cache (with hit probability p_{11}, overlooking queuing effects), a local memory (with routing probability p_{12}), and routing probability p_{1m} to access the common memory. Core type 2 involves an additional server, modeling, for example, an L2 cache. Core type 3 models a two-core cluster with dedicated L1 and L2 caches and local shared memory or L3 cache. Core type 4 differs from core type 3 just in one of its cores, which runs SMT CPU instead of a coarse-grained one (i.e., an $M/M/m$ queue and all the rest are $M/M/1$ queues).

The parameter settings for each type of core are given as follows:

- Type 1-group1 (single class):
  $(\mu_1, \mu_2) = (0.05, 0.03)$
  $(p_{11}, p_{12}, p_{1m}) = (0.25, 0.7, 0.05)$
  $m_1 = 6$
- Type 2-group2 (single class):
  $(\mu_1, \mu_2, \mu_3) = (0.2, 0.1, 0.1)$
  $(p_{11}, p_{12}, p_{13}, p_{31}, p_{3m}) = (0.3, 0.6, 0.1, 0.95, 0.05)$
  $m_1 = 9$

- Type 3-group3 (multiclass):
  $(\mu_1, \mu_2, \mu_3, \mu_4, \mu_4) = (0.2, 0.2, 0.2, 0.2, 0.1)$
  $(p_{11}, p_{13}, p_{22}, p_{23}, p_{31}, p_{35} \ (p_{42}, p_{45}, p_{5m})$
      $=(0.2, 0.8, 0.2, 0.8, 0.9, 0.1, 0.9, 0.1, 0.02)$
  $(m_1, m_2) = (8,8)$
- Type 4-group4 (multiclass):
  $(\mu_1, \mu_2, \mu_3, \mu_4, \mu_4) = (0.2, 0.1, 0.15, 0.15, 0.1)$
  $(p_{11}, p_{13}, p_{22}, p_{23}, p_{31}, p_{35} \ (p_{42}, p_{45}, p_{5m})$
      $=(0.2, 0.8, 0.2, 0.8, 0.9, 0.1, 0.9, 0.1, 0.02)$
  $(m_1, m_2) = (10,10)$

For the ST, simulation stops when all nodes in all cores execute at least 10^6 events. For the iteration procedure, ε is set at 0.1% of $T_m(n)$. The test results for the proposed QM and ST at three different common memory service rates are listed in Tables 7.2–7.4. Both QM and ST are done on an Intel Pentium 4 computer. The computation and simulation times are also listed.

In each table, there are three columns with different common memory service rates representing three distinctive cases. In the first case, the memory capacity is larger than the aggregate capacity of all the cores (i.e., the memory in underloaded condition). In the second case, their capacities are almost the same. In the last case, the aggregate capacity of all the cores is larger than the memory capacity (i.e., the

TABLE 7.2. All and Each Type's Throughputs with Various Common Memory Service Times

	1.0			0.95			0.90		
μ_∞	QM	ST	Error (%)	QM	ST	Error (%)	QM	ST	Error (%)
λ_∞	9.7924E-1	9.6386E-1	1.6	9.4971E-1	9.4595E-1	0.39	9.0000E-1	9.0217E-1	0.24
λ_{type1}	1.9259E-3	1.8654-3	3.2	1.8132E-3	1.8023E-3	0.60	1.6220E-3	1.6523E-3	1.8
λ_{type2}	7.9755E-4	7.9075E-4	0.86	7.9211E-4	7.8340E-4	1.1	7.8448E-4	7.8112E-4	0.43
λ_{type3}	6.1341E-4	6.1010E-4	0.54	6.1341E-4	6.0860E-4	0.79	6.1341E-4	6.0652E-4	1.1
λ_{type4}	5.8007E-4	5.7904E-4	0.18	5.8007E-4	5.7836E-4	0.30	5.8007E-4	5.7768E-4	0.41
Runtime	0.2 second (four loops)	3h47m40s		0.5 second (nine loops)	3h46m06s		0.4 second (eight loops)	3h47m23s	

TABLE 7.3. Changes in All Cores in Group 1 ($\mu = 0.05 \to 0.03$, $m_1 = 6 \to 8$)

	0.90			0.85			0.80		
μ_∞	QM	ST	Error (%)	QM	ST	Error (%)	QM	ST	Error (%)
λ_∞	8.6503E-1	8.5914E-1	0.68	8.4999E-1	8.4440E-1	0.66	8.0000E-1	8.0362E-1	0.45
λ_{type1}	1.4686E-3	1.4542-3	0.99	1.4199E-3	1.4178E-3	0.15	1.2458E-3	1.2685E-3	1.8
λ_{type2}	7.9806E-4	7.9302E-4	0.64	7.8660E-4	7.8537E-4	0.16	7.6069E-4	7.5950E-4	0.16
λ_{type3}	6.1341E-4	6.0855E-4	0.80	6.1341E-4	6.0870E-4	0.77	6.1341E-4	6.0281E-4	1.7
λ_{type4}	5.8007E-4	5.7997E-4	0.02	5.8007E-4	5.7857E-4	0.26	5.8007E-4	5.7778E-4	0.40
Runtime	0.3 second (6 loops)	3h46m55s		1.3 seconds (26 loops)	3h47m34s		0.6 second (12 loops)	3h45m10s	

TABLE 7.4. A Change in One Target Core in Group 4 (L2 Hit Rate 98% → 90%)

	1.0			0.90			0.80		
μ_∞	QM	ST	Error (%)	QM	ST	Error (%)	QM	ST	Error (%)
λ_∞	8.8917E-1	8.8405E-1	0.58	8.8693E-1	8.7861E-1	0.95	8.0000E-1	8.0179E-1	0.22
λ_{type1}	1.4714E-3	1.4595-3	0.82	1.4646E-3	1.4529E-3	0.81	1.1658E-3	1.2157E-3	4.1
λ_{type2}	7.9904E-4	7.9179E-4	0.91	7.9680E-4	7.8993E-4	0.87	7.4787E-4	7.4614E-4	0.23
λ_{type3}	6.1341E-4	6.1068E-4	0.45	6.1341E-4	6.0946E-4	0.64	6.1341E-4	5.9980E-4	2.3
λ_{type4}	5.8007E-4	5.7801E-4	0.36	5.8007E-4	5.7906E-4	0.17	5.8007E-4	5.7644E-4	0.63
Runtime	0.2 second (3 loops)	3h46m53s		0.5 second (10 loops)	3h47m11s		0.6 second (12 loops)	3h48m03s	

shared memory is a potential bottleneck resource). Each column has three subcolumns, with the first subcolumn showing the results from QM and the second from ST and the last the difference between them. Table 7.2 gives the results for the above parameter settings. Tables 7.3 and 7.4 give the results with some parameter changes (see the parameter changes at the top of each table).

It turns out that our iterative procedure is highly accurate and fast. For the cases in Table 7.2 and 7.4, it takes less than 12 iterations to get the results. For the case in Table 7.3, the number of iterations increases up to 26. For all the cases studied, the technique is three orders of magnitude faster than ST, finishing within a few seconds. This allows a large design space (or parameter space) to be scanned numerically. Moreover, for all the cases, the results are consistently within 5% of the simulation results.

One can further reduce the time complexity by running the iterative procedure only once for a given set of parameters to get effective T_m. Then, study the performance for any target core in a workload parameter range based on the closed queuing network in Figure 7.5 (the one on the right) with T_m fixed. One can expect that changing parameters for just one core out of 1000 cores should not significantly affect T_m as is the case in Table 7.4 compared to Table 7.3. This approximation further reduces the time complexity by another two orders of magnitude.

As one can see, with the proposed analytic modeling technique, the closed queuing network models can now be effectively used to explore the design space in Figure 7.3. A user of our technique may start with a coarse-grained scan of the space first, which will allow the user to identify areas of further interests in the space. Then, perform a finer-grained scan of the areas of interest.

7.6 RELATED WORK

Since this chapter is concerned with both analytical queuing network modeling and simulation, we review the existing results on both separately.

In terms of queuing network modeling, since Jackson's seminal work [8] in 1963 on queuing networks of product form, a wealth of results on the extension of his work has been obtained for both closed and open queuing networks. Notable results include the extensions from $M/M/1$ FCFS to last come, first served (LCFS) preemptive resume, PS, and IS queuing disciplines, multiple job classes (or chains) and class migrations, load-dependent routing and service times, and exact solution techniques such as convolution and mean value analysis (MVA), and approximate solution techniques for queuing networks with or without product form. Sophisticated queuing network modeling tools were also developed, making queuing modeling and analysis much easier. These results are well documented in standard textbooks, tutorials, and research papers (e.g., see References 6, 7, 9, and 10). As a result, in the past few decades, queuing networks were widely adopted in modeling computer systems and networks (e.g., see References 1 and 11–14). However, very few analytical results are available for multicore processor analysis. In Reference 15, an MVA of a multithreaded multicore processor is performed. The performance results reveal that there is a performance valley to be avoided as the number of threads increases, a phenomenon also found earlier in multiprocessor systems studied based on queuing network models [3]. Markovian models are employed in Reference 16 to model a cache memory subsystem with multithreading. However, to the best of our knowledge, the only work that attempts to model multithreaded multicore using the queuing network model is given in Reference 17. But since only one job class (or chain) is used, the threads belonging to different cores cannot be explicitly identified and separated in the model, and hence multicore effects are not fully accounted for.

Most relevant to our work is the work in Reference 13. In this work, a multiprocessor system with distributed shared memory is modeled using a closed queuing network model. Each computing subsystem is modeled as composed of three $M/M/1$ servers and a finite number of jobs of a given class. The three servers represent a multithreaded CPU with coarse-grained thread-scheduling discipline, an FCFS memory, and an FCFS entry point to a crossbar network connecting to other computing subsystems. The jobs belonging to the same class or subsystem represent the threads in that subsystem. The jobs of a given class have given probabilities to access local and remote memory resources. This closed queuing network model has a product-form solution.

The above existing application of queuing results to the multithreaded multicore and multiprocessor systems is preliminary (i.e., within the small cone on the left in Fig. 7.3). The only queuing discipline studied is the FCFS queue, which characterizes the coarse-grained thread-scheduling discipline at a CPU and FCFS queuing discipline for memory or interconnection network. No framework has ever been proposed that can cover the design space in Figure 7.3 and that allows system classes to be analyzed over the entire space. In terms of simulation, there are a vast number of processor STs available [18–33] (e.g., cycle accurate, allowing detailed timing analysis, and providing primitives for flexible component modeling). Particularly relevant to our work are the CP analysis tools (e.g., see References 18, 22, 24–26, 28, and 30–33).

Most CP simulation software (e.g., see References 18, 24, 25, and 31) aims at providing rich features to allow detailed statistical or per-packet analysis, which is useful for program fine tuning, rather than fast CP performance testing. Even for the most lightweight NP simulator described in Reference 31, it is reported that to simulate 1 second of hardware execution, it takes 1 hour on a Pentium III 733 PC. Moreover, it assumes the availability of the executable program or microcode as input for the simulation. On the other hand, the algorithms for data path functions to CP core topology mapping (e.g., see References 30 and 32–34) are generally fast, but at the expense of having to overlook many essential processing details that may have an impact on the overall system performance. To make the problem tractable, a common technique used in these approaches is to partition the data path functions into tasks, and each task is then associated with one or multiple known resource demand metrics, for example, the core latency and program size. Then an optimization problem under the demand constraints is formulated and solved to find a feasible/optimal mapping of those tasks to a pipelined/parallel core topology. Since the actual resource demand metrics for each task are, in general, complex functions of mapping itself and are a strong function of the number of threads and thread-scheduling discipline in use at each core, these approaches cannot provide mappings with high accuracy. Although the approach in Reference 30 accounts for certain multithreading effects, it only works for a single memory access and under a coarse-grained scheduling discipline.

7.7 CONCLUSIONS AND FUTURE WORK

In this chapter, we proposed a methodology for performance analysis of many-core systems in a large design space. The novelty of the methodology lies in the fact that it works at the thread level and it studies the general properties of system classes over the entire space. Hence, it is free of scalability issues.

The framework can cover the entire design space in Figure 7.3 except the dynamics of multithreading. In the future, we plan to explore the following possible solution. We plan to use a set of ancillary thread classes with different delay loops to join and leave the queuing network modeling a core. It can be easily shown that with n thread classes and 2^{i-1} threads in the ith class for $i = 1, \ldots, n$, any number of threads in the range $[1, 2^n + 1 - 1]$ can be generated in the core. For example, with $n = 4$, any number of threads in the range of $[1, 31]$ can be generated. The first thread class has only one thread in it. This thread class runs in the queuing network modeling the core. The rest $n-1$ thread classes run in the delay loops. It can also be shown that by properly setting the delay value for each delay loop, the proposed model can match any distribution of parallelism (i.e., with probability P_k that k threads are presented in the core). The queuing network with these delay loops has a closed-form solution.

REFERENCES

[1] D. Ghosal and L. Bhuyan, "Performance evaluation of a dataflow architecture," *IEEE Transactions on Computers*, 39(5):615–627, 1990.

[2] H. Jung, M. Ju, H. Che, and Z. Wang, *A Fast Performance Analysis Tool for Multicore, Multithreaded Communication Processors*. December 2008.

[3] A. Agarwal, "Performance tradeoffs in multithreaded processors," *IEEE Transactions on Parallel and Distributed Systems*, 3(5):525–539, 1992.

[4] F. Baskett, K.M. Chandy, R.R. Muntz, and F. Palacios, "Open, closed, and mixed networks of queues with different classes of customers," *Journal of the ACM*, 22(2):248–260, 1975.

[5] D. Towsley, "Queuing network models with state-dependent routing," *Journal of the ACM*, 27(2):323–337, 1980.

[6] G. Bolch, S. Greiner, H. de Meer, and K.S. Trivedi, *Queueing Networks and Markov Chains*, 2nd ed. John Wiley, 2006.

[7] ITU-D Study Group 2, *Teletraffic Engineering*, 2002.

[8] J.R. Jackson, "Jobshop-like queuing systems," *Management Science*, 10:131–142, 1963.

[9] I.F. Akyildiz and A. Sieber, "Approximate analysis of load dependent general queuing networks," *IEEE Transactions on Software Engineering*, 14(11):1537–1545, 1988.

[10] A. Thomasian and P.F. Bay, "Integrated performance models for distributed processing in computer communication networks," *IEEE Transactions on Software Engineering*, SE-11(10):1203–1216, 1985.

[11] P.P. Chen, "Queuing network model of interactive computing systems," in *Proc. of the IEEE*, June 1975.

[12] N. Lopez-Benitez and K.S. Trivedi, "Multiprocessor performability analysis," *IEEE Transactions on Reliability*, 42(4):579–587, 1993.

[13] S.S. Nemawarkar, R. Govindarajan, G.R. Gao, and V.K. Agarwal, "Analysis of multi-threaded multiprocessors with distributed shared memory," in *Proceedings of the 5th IEEE Symposium on Parallel and Distributed Processing*, December 1993.

[14] B. Smilauer, "General model for memory interference in multiprocessors and mean value analysis," *IEEE Transactions on Computer*, 34(8):744–751, 1985.

[15] Z. Guz, E. Bolotin, I. Keidar, A. Kolodny, A. Mendelson, and U.C. Weiser, "Many-core vs. many-tthread machines," *IEEE Computer Architecture Letter*, 8(1):25–28, 2009.

[16] X.E. Chen and T.M. Aamodt, "A first-order fine-grained multithreaded throughput model," in *Proceedings of the 15th IEEE International Symposium on High-Performance Computer Architecture (HPCA)*, February 2009.

[17] V. Bhaskar, "A closed queuing network model with multiple servers for multithreaded architecture," *Journal of Computer Communications*, 31(14):3078–3089, 2008.

[18] *Advanced Software Development Tools for Intel IXP2xxx Network Processors*, 2003. Intel White Paper.

[19] T. Austin, E. Larson, and D. Ernst, "SimpleScalar: An infrastructure for computer system modeling," *IEEE Computer*, 35(2):59–67, 2002.

[20] J. Emer, "Asim: A performance model framework," *IEEE Computer*, 35(2):68–72, 2002.

[21] Z. Huang, J.P.M. Voeten, and B.D. Theelen, "Modeling and simulation of a packet switch system using POOSL," in *Proceedings of the PROGRESS Workshop*, October 2002.

[22] E. Johnson and A. Kunze, *IXP 1200 Programming*. Intel Press, 2002.

[23] E. Kohler, R. Morris, B. Chen, J. Janotti, and M.F. Kaashoek, "The click modular router," *ACM Transactions on Computer Systems*, 18(3):263–297, 2000.

[24] Y. Luo, J. Yang, L.N. Bhuyan, and L. Zhao, "NePSim: A network processor simulator with a power evaluation framework," *IEEE Micro, Special Issue on Network Processors for Future High-End Systems and Applications*, 24(5):34–44, Sep 2004.

[25] P. Paulin, C. Pilkington, and E. Bensoudane, "StepNP: A system-level exploration platform for network processors," *IEEE Design and Test of Computers*, 19(6):17–26, 2002.

[26] R. Ramaswamy, N. Weng, and T. Wolf, "Analysis of network processing workloads," in *Proceedings of the IEEE International Symposium on Performance Analysis of Systems and Software (ISPASS)*, Mar 2005.

[27] M. Rosenblum, E. Bugnion, S. Devine, and S.A. Herrod, "Using the SimOS machine simulator to study complex computer systems," *Modeling and Computer Simulations*, 7(1):78–103, 1997.

[28] L. Thiele, S. Chakraborty, M. Gries, and S. Kiinzli, "Design space exploration of network processor architectures," in *Network Processor Design: Issues and Practices* (P. Crowley,

M. Franklin, H. Hadimioglu, and P. Onufryk, eds.), p. 1. Burlington, MA: Morgan Kaufmann Publishers, 2002.

[29] M. Vachharajani, N. Vachharajani, D. Penry, J. Blome, and D. August, "The Liberty Simulation Environment, version 1.0," *Performance Evaluation Review: Special Issue on Tools for Architecture Research*, 31, 2004.

[30] N. Weng and T. Wolf, "Pipelining vs multiprocessors? Choosing the right network processor system topology," in *Proceedings of the Advanced Networking and Communications Hardware Workshop (ANCHOR 2004) in conjunction with ISCA 2004*, June 2004.

[31] W. Xu and L. Peterson, "Support for software performance tuning on network processors," *IEEE Network*, 17(4):40–45, 2003.

[32] L. Yang, T. Gohad, P. Ghosh, D. Sinha, A. Sen, and A. Richa, "Resource mapping and scheduling for heterogeneous network processor systems," in *Proceedings of the Symposium on Architecture for Networking and Communications Systems*, 2005.

[33] J. Yao, Y. Luo, L. Bhuyan, and R. Iyer, "Optimal network processor topologies for efficient packet processing," in *Proceedings of IEEE GLOBECOM*, November 2005.

[34] H. Che, C. Kumar, and B. Menasinahal, "Fundamental network processor performance bounds," in *Proceedings of IEEE NCA*, July 2005.

8

The Future in Mobile Multicore Computing

Blake Hurd, Chiu C. Tan, and Jie Wu

8.1 INTRODUCTION

Mobile computers are with us everywhere, allowing us to work and entertain ourselves at any venue. Due to this, mobile computers are replacing desktops as our personal computers. Already, we see signs of smartphones becoming more popular than traditional desktop computers [1]. A recent survey of users reveals that e-mail, Internet access, and a digital camera are the three most desirable features in a mobile phone, and the consumers wanted these features to be as fast as possible [2]. The increasing sales of more powerful phones also indicate consumer demand for more powerful phones [1, 3].

There are two ways to improve mobile computing. The first way is to execute the computation *remotely*, where the mobile phone transfers the processing to a remote platform, such as a cloud computing environment, to perform the computation and then retrieves the output. The alternative is for the mobile device to execute the computation *locally* using its own hardware. The following three factors make remote computation less ideal than local computation:

1. *Security.* Remote computation requires outsourcing data to a third party, which increases the security risks since the third party may not be trustworthy. For instance, the third party may utilize the data to violate the user's privacy. Local computation, on the other hand, does not have this problem.

Scalable Computing and Communications: Theory and Practice, First Edition. Edited by Samee U. Khan, Albert Y. Zomaya, and Lizhe Wang.

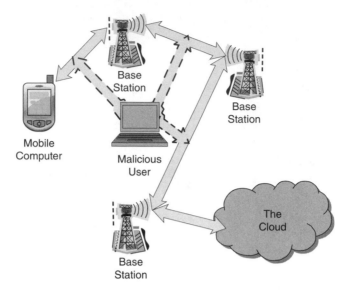

FIGURE 8.1. *Remote computation requires greater security, energy, and latency consideration than local computation.*

2. *Efficiency.* Transmitting data to a remote server may incur a higher energy cost [4] due to the large communication overhead of the wireless transmission. Furthermore, remote computation requires utilizing more bandwidth, which can be more expensive in environments where bandwidth is metered. Local computation can avoid the high-bandwidth charges and, as we will show in subsequent sections, may be more power efficient.

3. *Timeliness.* It is difficult to guarantee timeliness when using remote computation due to the unpredictability of wireless communications under different environmental conditions, such as traveling on a subway. Local computation is not affected by this issue (Fig. 8.1).

In this chapter, we are concerned with scenarios where local computation is better than remote computation. Local computation has its own set of challenges, specifically to increase its energy efficiency while improving its timeliness. The two requirements are somewhat contradictory since reducing the processor speed is an important component of improving the energy efficiency; however, this will result in a longer computation time and will decrease timeliness. This is the case in a single-core architecture. In this chapter, we will show that multicore architectures do not have this limitation.

8.2   BACKGROUND

The adoption of general-purpose graphics processing units (GPGPUs) and multi-core CPUs into mobile devices allows these devices to perform powerful local computations. GPGPUs allow parallelized programs to run on the graphics processing unit (GPU). These programs run on both the CPU and GPU as needed, and this level of hardware flexibility allows software to present a better user experience. We define mobile multicore computing (MMC) as a mobile computer computing with a GPGPU and/or multicore CPU. MMC is quickly becoming a reality: Tablets are available, and smartphones will be available during the first quarter 2011. Projections suggest that by 2013, most mobile platforms, 88%, will have MMC architecture [5].

We explore three technical issues related to MMC: implementation of GPGPUs, intelligent power scaling, and multitasking applications. There are more issues, but we expect these three to be the most important currently and in the future. For each issue, we will examine its importance to MMC as well as the challenges. We divide our discussion into hardware and software components. We analyze why each is difficult to solve and why each is beneficial. We discuss hardware and software support and the impact of this support on these issues.

GPGPU, power scaling, and multitasking, enabled by MMC hardware and software support, will allow for increased performance and increased energy efficiency to be possible. For example, there are advantages in using a multicore CPU. Single-core CPUs increase performance linearly at the expense of an exponential increase in power; multicore CPUs can increase performance linearly for a linear increase in power. In other words, if we get similar throughput from two 400-MHz cores versus one 800-MHz core, we save power by using the two 400-MHz cores. NVIDIA tests this concept and demonstrates a 40% power improvement to achieve the same performance benchmark on their latest mobile chipset [6].

8.2.1 GPGPU Implementation

GPGPU uses the GPU's synchronized group of cores to process small, parallelized, nongraphic tasks in parallel to run certain tasks faster and more efficiently than CPUs. GPGPU processing is suitable for tasks that can be split into parallel data, such as matrices or arrays of data where each sector needs the same instruction executed. These highly parallel tasks are best run on the GPGPU instead of the CPU. For example, video encoding and decoding is more efficient when run via the GPGPU.

The GPGPU cannot be widely implemented until an agreed standard between hardware and software is achieved. Each chipset needs to incorporate a GPGPU that supports a language for sending tasks to the GPU and for retrieving results. The language supported must be a determined standard; otherwise, programs must be redeveloped based on what device the programs are running on.

Mobile computers have to calculate a multitude of massively parallel problems like video processing, wireless baseband processing, fast Fourier transform (FFT), and packet routing. If these calculations are run via the GPGPU rather than the CPU, the performance gained and power efficiency are highly beneficial.

8.2.2 Intelligent Power Scaling Implementation

All current chipsets allow dynamic voltage frequency scaling (DVFS) and static power domains. This allows complex, robust implementations for intelligently scaling chipset power consumption. Static power domains allow the CPU to move between frequency boundaries, and DVFS allows dynamic voltage and CPU frequency tweaking. A sufficiently intelligent power scaling implementation wields these features optimally.

When all applications are running on one core, finding the optimal frequency is simple, and thus, a power scaling implementation is simple. However, in a multicore environment, cores manage different workloads, and some environments require each core to run at the same frequency. Overall, this problem, optimal power management for DVFS-enabled multicore processing, is proven to be NP-hard [7].

If each processor core runs at a frequency that meets the user's requirements and no faster, then the mobile device may conserve power. The benefits are substantial: With hundreds of millions of smartphones (there are supposedly 170 million [8] sold every year), improving phone power consumption efficiency by 5% will save the amount of energy equivalent of 8.5 million smartphones.

8.2.3 Multitasking Implementation

Multitasking refers to running as many tasks at the same time as possible. The goal is to give the user the perception of complete parallelization—that one can run as many applications as one wants to without any limitations. Multitasking is essentially multithreading; each application is separated into *threads*, or *tasks*, and then each thread/task is scheduled in proper balance to multitask.

The difficulty is developing an intelligent scheduler that balances as many processes/threads as possible while providing a satisfactory experience. Mobile multitasking is more challenging due to limited memory and power. Limited memory requires applications to be small. In addition, code reuse is also necessary if multiple applications are kept in memory at the same time. If the foreground application needs memory that other applications are using, it will slow down and more power is spent. Background applications also drain the battery when the ongoing workload causes a measurable task switching overhead. Users may launch applications without ending any running applications and inadvertently drain the limited power. Finally, because most mobile phones use ARM-designed CPUs, the scheduler must consider the design's slower task/process switching.

If multithreading is enabled, the operating system (OS) may redesign their scheduler to share independent threads across multiple cores once available. Non-multitasking OSs only maintain the thread(s) allocated to the application in-use with the thread(s) used by the OS itself. Such OSs can only schedule the OS thread(s) on a different core, and there would be trouble with scheduling the thread(s) allocated to the application in use; the application may require an order to commence thread execution and may lock up the cores, or the application may have a single thread.

8.3 HARDWARE INITIATIVES

Hardware initiatives create a new hardware architecture foundation for solving our three technical issues. *Chipsets* are the main hardware initiative; a new chipset allows software to utlize more capabilities and to present a stronger device. The latest chipsets mostly rely on the latest ARM designs, which are licensed to most companies releasing chipsets. The chipsets are created by combining a CPU, a GPU, specialized processing units, and memory.

8.3.1 Chipset Support

We discuss the progress of multicore CPUs and the progress of GPGPUs; then, we discuss the state of current and future generation smartphone architectures in utilizing these MMC components.

Most mobile CPUs are based on ARM's design licenses. There are four relevant generations of mobile ARM CPU designs: the ARM11 MPCore, the ARM Cortex-A8, the ARM Cortex-A9, and the ARM Cortex-A15. The ARM11 MPCore is the oldest and the least energy-efficient, but it is the cheapest to produce. The Cortex-A8 only allows a single core. Otherwise, the other three generations allow multicore, up to four cores, at improved energy efficiency and performance between generations.

Various mobile GPUs are available to pair with these CPUs. PowerVR's SGX series is the most popular, and a GPGPU was released that is available for the future generation of smartphones. The early 2011 generation added dual-core CPUs, but later 2011 models should include GPGPUs, starting with Apple's newest smartphone.

Every CPU in the 2010 generation smartphone architectures is single-core (see Table 8.1). All current phones support DVFS for power scaling, and almost all current phones have multicore sequels in development. There is a popular mobile GPU that introduces GPGPU support [9]; most future generation mobile phones should use this GPU and thus should implement GPGPU.

Multicore chipsets (see Table 8.2) were available in smartphones and other mobile computers in early 2011, and multicore is common in future smartphone architecture. The ARM Cortex-A9 CPU supports shared DVFS and four static

TABLE 8.1. Current Smartphone Architectures

Phone	CPU	GPU	GPGPU	Power Scaling	Multitasking
Apple iPhone 3G	ARM11 MPCore	PowerVR MBX Lite	No	Yes	No
Apple iPhone 3GS	ARM Cortex-A8	PowerVR SGX535	No	Yes	Partial
Apple iPhone 4	ARM Cortex-A8	PowerVR SGX535	No	Yes	Partial
HTC Nexus One	Qualcomm Scorpion	Qualcomm Adreno 200	No	Yes	Partial
HP-Palm Pre	ARM Cortex-A8	PowerVR SGX530	No	Yes	Partial
HP-Palm Pixi	ARM11 MPCore	Qualcomm Adreno 200	No	Yes	Partial
HP-Palm Pre 2	ARM Cortex-A8	PowerVR SGX530	No	Yes	Partial
HTC Evo 4G	Qualcomm Scorpion	Qualcomm Adreno 200	No	Yes	Partial
Microsoft Kin One and Two	ARM11 MPCore	NVIDIA ULP GeForce	No	Yes	Partial
Motorola Droid	ARM Cortex-A8	PowerVR SGX530	No	Yes	Partial
Samsung Galaxy S	ARM Cortex-A8	PowerVR SGX540	No	Yes	Partial

TABLE 8.2. Upcoming Chipsets

Chipset	CPU	GPU	GPGPU	Power Scaling	Multitasking
Apple A5 ARM	Cortex-A9	PowerVR SGX543MP2	Yes	Shared	Yes
Qualcomm Snapdragon QSD8x50A	Qualcomm Scorpion	Qualcomm Adreno 205	No	Per-core	Partial
Qualcomm Snapdragon MSM8x60	Qualcomm Scorpion	Qualcomm Adreno 220	No	Per-core	Yes
Qualcomm Snapdragon QSD8x72	Qualcomm Scorpion	Qualcomm Adreno 220	No	Per-core	Yes
NVIDIA Tegra 2 T20	ARM Cortex-A9	NVIDIA ULP GeForce	No	Shared	Yes
NVIDIA Tegra 2 AP20H	ARM Cortex-A9	NVIDIA ULP GeForce	No	Shared	Yes
NVIDIA Tegra 2 3D T25/AP25	ARM Cortex-A9	NVIDIA ULP GeForce	No	Shared	Yes
TI OMAP4430	ARM Cortex-A9	PowerVR SGX540	No	Shared	Yes
TI OMAP4440	ARM Cortex-A9	PowerVR SGX540	No	Shared	Yes
Samsung Orion	ARM Cortex-A9	ARM Mali-400	No	Shared	Yes
ST-Ericsson U8500	ARM Cortex-A9	ARM Mali-400	No	Shared	Yes

power domains, whereas the Qualcomm Scorpion CPU supports a per-core DVFS. Shared DVFS means that each core in the same power domain must run at the same frequency, and each power domain provides an upper and lower bound for modifying the frequency. In per-core, each core can always run at a frequency independent of other cores. Per-core DVFS thus allows more flexible power scaling solutions.

8.3.2 Impact

As discussed in chipset support, all chipsets in the current generation do not implement GPGPU. Chipsets in future generations will. Incorporating the GPGPU into the chipset allows software initiatives to be designed to take advantage of the GPGPU.

Power scaling has hardware support in the previous generation but is more important in this next generation. With two CPU cores to manage, either with shared or per-core DVFS, algorithms must handle more conditions, but the potential energy efficiency achieved is more beneficial. The industry is counting on implementations of intelligent power scaling algorithms to take advantage of parallelism to lower the system's power consumption.

Multitasking was limited in the previous generation. With one CPU core to run on and no GPGPU support, multitasking was largely about swapping running tasks fast enough to give the user the perception of multitasking. With two CPU cores available for general-purpose programming and with GPGPU support upcoming, tasks can be distributed across the available hardware and can be executed at virtually the same time. This requires additional research to better perform load balancing of the various requirements. Load-balanced multitasking is also related to power scaling; if CPU cores are multitasking the workload at the best balance possible, we can measure the minimum frequency needed to maintain that balance and set the CPU to that frequency.

8.4 SOFTWARE INITIATIVES

Software initiatives use the foundation laid by the hardware initiatives to solve the issues that MMC presents. Languages are the main software initiative, specifically streaming languages. Streaming languages provide the software side of implementing GPGPU on a mobile computer and also assist power scaling algorithms. Streaming languages allow for better parallelization of each application. A higher degree of parallization will allow power scaling algorithms to better balance the energy and thus lower the overall power consumption. The streaming languages may also support load balancing algorithms for multitasking and balancing programs over CPUs and the GPGPU.

8.4.1 Language Support

Streaming languages allow fine-grained parallelization to weave into serial programming. A set of data, called a *stream*, is presented with a list of operations, called *kernel functions*, which are then applied to every element in the data stream. These streams can illustrate a graph and allow the stream language compiler to parallelize the program. The most popular languages are OpenCL and CUDA. OpenCL is the future standard, but CUDA remains available due to the limited hardware and software support for OpenCL. In addition to these, we briefly discuss Brook and StreamIt, which are popular in academia.

OpenCL is an open-source project that is supported by the mobile industry as the future of parallel programming. AMD and NVIDIA support OpenCL on their GPUs, so OpenCL will be supported on most, if not all, GPUs in the future. OpenCL provides a framework for managing CPUs and other processing units through a sublanguage that is used beside higher level languages like C++ or Java. Serial programming is still allowed by programming in C++ and Java without the bindings and weaves into parallel programming through OpenCL bindings. OpenCL will be available to mobile chipsets before CUDA, as the first mobile GPGPU supports OpenCL [9].

GPGPU is possible if executing on an NVIDIA GPU that supports CUDA. However, the latest mobile NVIDIA chipsets do not support CUDA, so a mobile GPGPU through CUDA is currently not possible. Furthermore, CUDA only controls GPGPUs; CUDA does not affect the programming framework of different types of processing units and multicore CPU management. NVIDIA continues to support CUDA but also supports OpenCL, releasing application programming interfaces (APIs) for converting code from CUDA to the OpenCL framework.

Brook and StreamIt are two academic languages for parallel programming. Brook is similar to OpenCL and CUDA, predating both languages. StreamIt, alternatively, is unique and remains popular in research, presenting a high-level language for designing highly parallel programs. StreamIt depends on its own compiler, and its syntax restricts its capacity for handling serial code. However, StreamIt remains popular and papers continue to be published, as it is effective for creating highly parallel programs.

8.4.2   Impact

GPGPUs need a streaming language; otherwise, programs cannot communicate to them. Every major GPU developer has chosen to support OpenCL, releasing an OpenCL driver to support OpenCL on their GPU. Writing OpenCL then allows programs to execute in parallel on the GPU, thus completing GPGPU implementation.

Power scaling may be addressed by software support. Application developers can parallelize their programs by using the tools available to develop more power-efficient and scalable algorithms. Power scaling algorithms can also account for the differences of a CPU execution versus a GPGPU execution.

Multitasking solutions can be created with the help of streaming languages. Streaming languages allow programs to be designed as parallel as possible. These parallel components can be run on the MMC hardware to multitask.

8.5   ADDITIONAL DISCUSSION

Now, we discuss new advances in industry and related academic research that are relevant to MMC.

8.5.1   Company-Specific Initiatives

There are many different initiatives geared toward MMC among companies, and some are collaborative projects between them. We mention leading companies in the mobile marketplace and how they approach the technical issues of MMC.

- *Google.* Google's Android platform does not support GPGPUs yet and has not taken direct steps to improve power scaling. However, Google licensed the WebM codec, also known as the VP8 codec, which is designed as a complex encoding process with a simple, low-power decoding process. Both the encoder and decoder algorithms are parallelizable for MMC. When fully implemented, the codec may provide a multimedia experience that is more power efficient than current methods. Google's Android platform continues to develop its scheduler algorithm to multitask better. When multicore becomes the standard, multitasking will be further pursued on the platform.
- *Texas Instruments.* Texas Instruments also does not support GPGPUs yet. Texas Instruments' latest platform supports power scaling like other platforms but requires more intelligent algorithms due to multicore availability. Texas Instruments is also supporting symmetric multiprocessing (SMP) on their latest platform; SMP means that each processor core shares memory and can run any task presented by the OS, given that the task is not being run on another core, allowing for multitasking.
- *ST-Ericsson/ARM/Google.* ST-Ericsson does not support GPGPUs. However, ST-Ericsson and ARM are working on a joint development on the Android OS to take advantage of SMP when executing their latest platform, which contains a multicore CPU. Like Texas Instruments' SMP support, this can lead to power scaling and multitasking improvements.

- *Apple.* Apple is prioritizing support for GPGPUs; their OS introduced support for GPGPU [9]. Their latest smartphone will contain a dual-core OpenCL-enabled GPGPU [10], and better power scaling and multitasking efforts may be attainable.

- *Microsoft.* Microsoft does not discuss implementing GPGPUs or power scaling on its mobile platform. However, on multitasking, Microsoft's Barrelfish research project considers a distributed multikernel OS where each application is assigned to a set of cores, is completely independent of other applications, and can asynchronously communicate with other applications.

- *Nokia.* Nokia contributes to OpenCL and further develops GPGPU implementations. Nokia's Research Center also works on power scaling under the Nokia Research High Performance Mobile Platforms Project, but no publications in this topic have been released yet. Nokia has not announced any initiatives toward improving multitasking on mobile computers.

- *HP-Palm.* HP-Palm does not discuss GPGPU for Pre/WebOS. An implementation of intelligent power scaling was added via patching WebOS. WebOS partially supports multitasking, but it does not run on non-MMC hardware; applications run in parallel from the user's perspective, but the OS schedules intelligently on a single core. With new funding from HP, the Pre/WebOS may improve solutions to all three issues.

8.5.2 Embedded Computing Research Initiatives

Embedded computing research is tied to MMC as mobile computers and smartphones are a subset of embedded computing.

There is research on using GPGPUs on mobile/embedded computers, but presently, most GPGPU research is about running applications on desktops where the applications are potentially useful in a mobile environment, such as wireless processing, packet routing, and network coding.

In recent years, research focused on developing an intelligent power scaling scheduling algorithm that load balances and unbalances intelligently, maintaining the same performance while saving power via controlled usage of DVFS. There are many contributions in this area [11–14], and we expect that more will follow, as scheduling for optimal power management on multicore is an NP-hard problem [7]. Some papers propose strategies that are alternative approaches and do not compare to previous strategies. We expect that combinations of these methods will be a future research topic as a more robust implementation, capable of handling more workload scenarios optimally, may be possible. These scheduling algorithms must create even load balancing to save power; thus, such algorithms also contribute to the topic of improving multitasking.

8.6 FUTURE TRENDS

As MMC research progresses, there are several trends we observe.

Trend 1. *Software Driven Energy Efficiency.* More advanced software solutions will be designed given the upcoming influx of MMC hardware that makes

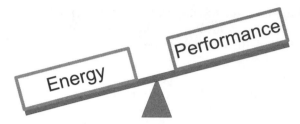

FIGURE 8.2. Future trend 1: Software in MMC will push energy efficiency; the energy versus performance trade-off.

MMC possible. Current software solutions must be redeveloped to balance the energy efficiency and the performance while taking advantage of multiple cores, balancing GPGPU execution versus CPU execution (Fig. 8.2).

Trend 2. *Adding Cores.* Hardware development will add cores for both CPUs and GPUs. For CPUs, dual core is available, and quad core is not far behind. The first mobile GPGPU supports 2 to 16 GPU cores, allowing future generations to scale as necessary. Adding cores adds valuable granularity and flexibility for improved energy efficiency and improved performance. Research is unclear on when adding cores will no longer offer any advantages in a mobile environment; that will be more important in the future.

Trend 3. *GPGPU Implementation and Its Future in MMC.* GPGPUs will be implemented on every mobile computer with a GPU, and we expect GPGPUs to be widespread within the next few years. All MMC smartphones are slated to release in the first half of 2011 with a non-GPGPU. However, the latest of these GPUs in their respective families have GPGPU support through OpenCL support. When GPGPUs are fully implemented, increasingly many algorithms will adopt OpenCL, allowing for easy parallelization across CPUs and GPUs. We expect the implications of using a GPGPU on a mobile device to be a burgeoning topic of research.

8.7 CONCLUSION

In conclusion, we observed the progress of mobile computing, its trend toward MMC, and three important technical issues: GPGPUs are not yet being implemented; intelligent power scaling algorithms are needed; and multitasking algorithms are needed. We discussed hardware and software support for solutions to these issues. We additionally discussed some leading companies in the mobile marketplace, and their solutions, and different research initiatives to these issues. We discussed the field of embedded computing research, its relation to MMC, and its contributions toward these issues, specifically its contributions to an intelligent power scaling algorithm. Discussing these issues and initiatives reveals three future trends of the MMC industry that we discussed briefly: Software will be developed to use the hardware more effectively to provide more energy efficiency; hardware will add more cores, allowing for more flexibility and granularity to software solutions for improved energy efficiency; GPGPUs will take the forefront as a valuable tool for improving both energy efficiency and performance for solutions to many types of problems in mobile computing.

REFERENCES

[1] D. McGrath, "IDC: Smartphones out shipped PCs in Q4," in *EE Times*, 2011.

[2] O. R. C. News, "Consumers want smarter, faster phones." 2010.

[3] E. Woyke, "The Most Powerful Smart Phones," in *Forbes.com*, 2009.

[4] J. Baliga, R. Ayre, K. Hinton, and R. Tucker, "Green cloud computing: Balancing energy in processing, storage, and transport," 2011.

[5] Softpedia, "In-stat research predicts multi-core CPUs in 88% of mobile platforms by 2013." 2009.

[6] NVIDIA, "The benefits of multiple CPU cores in mobile devices." 2010.

[7] C.-Y. Yang, J.-J. Chen, and T.-W. Kuo, "An approximation algorithm for energy-efficient scheduling on a chip multiprocessor, in *IEEE Design, Automation and Test in Europe (DATE)*, 2005.

[8] Gartner, "Gartner says worldwide mobile phone sales to end users grew 8 per cent in fourth quarter 2009; market remained flat in 2009." 2010.

[9] Imagination Technologies, Imagination Technologies extends graphics IP Core family with POWERVR SGX543." 2009.

[10] AppleInsider.com, "Apple to pack ultrafast, dual core SGX543 graphics into iPad 2, iPhone 5." 2011.

[11] X. Huang, K. Li, and R. Li, "A energy efficient scheduling base on dynamic voltage and frequency scaling for multi-core embedded real-time system," in *International Conference on Algorithms and Architectures for Parallel Processing (ICA3PP)*, 2009.

[12] X. Wu, Y. Lin, J.-J. Han, and J.-L. Gaudiot, "Energy-efficient scheduling of real-time periodic tasks in multicore systems," in *IFIP International Conference on Network and Parallel Computing (NPS)*, 2010.

[13] D. Bautista, J. Sahuquillo, H. Hassan, S. Petit, and J. Duato, "A simple power-aware scheduling for multicore systems when running real-time applications," in *IEEE International Parallel and Distributed Processing Symposium*, 2008.

[14] E. Seo, J. Jeong, S. Park, and J. Lee, "Energy efficient scheduling of real-time tasks on multicore processors," in *IEEE Transactions of Parallel Distributed Systems*, 2008.

9

Modeling and Algorithms for Scalable and Energy-Efficient Execution on Multicore Systems

Dong Li, Dimitrios S. Nikolopoulos, and Kirk W. Cameron

9.1 INTRODUCTION

Traditional single microprocessor designs have exerted great effort to increase processor frequency and exploit instruction-level parallelism (ILP) to improve performance. However, they have arrived at a bottleneck wherein doubling the number of transistors in a serial CPU results in only a modest increase in performance with a significant increase in energy. This bottleneck has motivated us into the multicore era. With multicore, we can achieve higher throughput with acceptable power, although the core-level frequency of a multicore processor may be lower than that of a serial CPU. The switch to multicore processors implies widespread in-depth changes to software design and implementation. The popularity of multicore architectures calls for new design considerations for high-performance applications, parallel programming models, operating systems, compiler designs, and so on.

In this chapter, we discuss two topics that are important for high-performance execution on multicore platforms: scalability and power awareness. They are two of the major challenges on multicores [1]. Scalable execution requires efficient resource management. Resource management includes determining the configuration of

Scalable Computing and Communications: Theory and Practice, First Edition. Edited by
Samee U. Khan, Albert Y. Zomaya, and Lizhe Wang.
© 2013 John Wiley & Sons, Inc. Published 2013 by John Wiley & Sons, Inc.

applications and systems at a given concurrency level, for example, how many tasks should be placed within the same multicore node and how to distribute tasks scheduled into the same node between idle cores. Resource management may also indicate adjusting adaptable frequencies of processors by voltage and frequency settings. Along with an increasing number of nodes and number of processors/cores in high-end computing systems, resource management becomes more challenging because the exploration space available for choosing configurations increases explosively. We predict that this resource management problem will be further exacerbated for future exascale systems equipped with many-core chips. The explosively increased exploration space requires scalable resource management. To determine the appropriate configurations, we must pinpoint the optimal points in the exploration space without testing every possible configuration. We also must avoid introducing a negative performance impact during the process of configuration determination.

Power-aware execution is the other challenge posed by multicore. Growth in the number of cores of large-scale systems causes continual growth in power. Today, several of the most powerful supercomputers equipped with multicore nodes on the TOP500 List require up to 10 MW of peak power—enough to sustain a city of 40,000 people [2]. The best supercomputer power efficiency is about 0.5–0.7 Gflops/W [3]. As far as the future exascale systems are concerned, they will require at least 40 Gflops/W to maintain the total cost of ownership, which means two orders of magnitude improvement is needed [3]. With the present trend in power increase, the cost of supplying electrical power will quickly become as large as the initial purchase price of the computing system. High power consumption leads to high utility costs and causes many facilities to reach full capacity sooner than expected. It can even limit performance due to thermal stress on hardware [2].

In this chapter, we study how to create efficient and scalable software control methodologies to improve the performance of high-performance computing (HPC) applications in terms of both execution time and energy. Our work is an attempt to adapt software stacks to emerging multicore systems.

9.2 MODEL-BASED HYBRID MESSAGE-PASSING INTERFACE (MPI)/OpenMP POWER-AWARE COMPUTING

To exploit many cores available on a single chip or a single node with shared memory, programmers tend to use programming models with efficient implementations on cache-coherent shared-memory architectures, such as OpenMP. At the same time, programmers tend to use programming models based on message passing, such as MPI, to execute parallel applications efficiently on clusters of compute nodes with disjoint memories. We expect that hybrid programming models, such as MPI/OpenMP, will become more popular because the current high-end computing systems are scaled to a large amount of nodes, each of which is equipped with processors packing more cores. The hybrid programming models can utilize both shared memory and distributed memory of high-end computing systems.

In this section, we particularly consider hybrid programs that use the common THREAD_MASTERONLY model [4]. Its hierarchical decomposition closely matches most large-scale HPC systems. In this model, a single master thread invokes all MPI communication outside of parallel regions and OpenMP directives

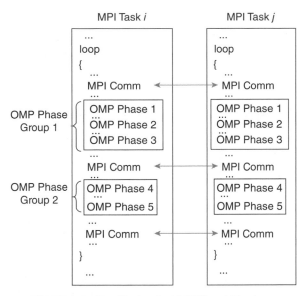

FIGURE 9.1. *Simplified typical MPI/OpenMP scheme.*

parallelize the sequential code of the MPI tasks. Almost all MPI programming environments support the THREAD_MASTERONLY model. This model exploits fast intratask data communication through shared memory via loop-level parallelism. While other mechanisms (e.g., POSIX threads) could add multithreading to MPI tasks, OpenMP supports incremental parallelization and, thus, is widely adopted by hybrid applications. Figure 9.1 depicts a typical iterative hybrid MPI/OpenMP computation, which partitions the computational space into subdomains, with each subdomain handled by one MPI task. The communication phase (MPI operations) exchanges subdomain boundary data or computation results between tasks. Computation phases that are parallelized with OpenMP constructs follow the communication phase. We use the term *OpenMP phases* for the computation phases delineated by OpenMP parallelization constructs.

Collections of OpenMP phases delineated by MPI operations form *OpenMP phase groups*, as shown in Figure 9.1. Typically, MPI collective operations (e.g., MPI_Allreduce and MPI_Barrier) or grouped point-to-point completions (e.g., MPI_Waitall) delineate OpenMP phase groups. No MPI primitives occur within an OpenMP phase group. MPI operations may include slack since the wait times of different tasks can vary due to load imbalance. Based on notions derived from critical path analysis, the *critical task* is the task upon which all other tasks wait.

Our goal is to adjust *configurations* of OpenMP phases of hybrid MPI/OpenMP applications by dynamic concurrency throttling (DCT) and dynamic voltage and frequency scaling (DVFS). A *configuration* includes concurrency configurations and CPU frequency settings. The *concurrency configuration* specifies how many OpenMP threads to use for a given OpenMP phase and how to map these threads to processors and cores. This can be done by OpenMP mechanisms for controlling the number of threads and by setting the CPU affinity of threads using system calls. We use DCT and DVFS to adjust configurations so as to avoid performance loss while saving as

TABLE 9.1. Power-Aware MPI/OpenMP Model Notation

M	Number of OpenMP phases in an OpenMP phase group
$\Delta E_{ij}^{\text{dct}}$	Energy saving by DCT during OpenMP phase j of task i
x_{ij}, y_{ij}	Number of processors (x_{ij}) and number of cores per processor (y_{ij}) used by OpenMP phase j of task i
X, Y	Maximum available number of processors (X) and number of cores (Y) per processor on a node
T_{ij}	Time spent in OpenMP phase j of task i under a configuration using X processors and Y cores per processor
t_{ij}	Time spent in OpenMP phase j of task i after DCT
t_i	Total OpenMP phases time in task i after DCT
$t_{ij,thr}$	Time spent in OpenMP phase j of task i using a configuration *thr* with thread count $|thr|$
N	Number of MPI tasks
f_0	Default frequency setting (highest CPU frequency)
Δt_{ijk}	Time change after we set frequency f_k during phase j of task i

much energy as possible. Also, configuration selection should have negligible overhead. For this selection process, we sample selected hardware events during several iterations in the computation loop for each OpenMP phase and collect timing information for MPI operations. From this data, we build a power-aware performance prediction model that determines configurations that, according to predictions, can improve application-wide energy efficiency.

9.2.1 Power-Aware MPI/OpenMP Model

Our power-aware performance prediction model estimates the energy savings that DCT and DVFS can provide for hybrid MPI/OpenMP applications. Table 9.1 summarizes the notation of our model. We apply the model at the granularity of OpenMP phase groups. OpenMP phase groups exhibit different energy-saving potential since each group typically encapsulates a different major computational kernel with a specific pattern of parallelism and data accesses. Thus, OpenMP phase groups are an appropriate granularity at which to adjust configurations to improve energy efficiency.

DCT attempts to discover a concurrency configuration for an OpenMP phase group that minimizes overall energy consumption without losing performance. Thus, we prefer configurations that deactivate complete processors in order to maximize the potential energy savings. The energy saving achieved by DCT for task i is

$$\Delta E_i^{\text{dct}} = \sum_{1 \leq j \leq M} \Delta E_{ij}^{\text{dct}}, \qquad (9.1)$$

where $\Delta E_{ij}^{\text{dct}}$ is the energy savings for phase j relative to using all cores, when we use $x_{ij} \leq X$ processors and $y_{ij} \leq Y$ cores per processor. If the time for phase j, t_{ij}, is no longer than the time using all cores T_{ij}, as we try to enforce, then $\Delta E_{ij}^{\text{dct}} \geq 0$ and DCT saves energy without losing performance.

Ideally, DCT selects a configuration for each OpenMP phase that minimizes execution time and, thus, the total computation time in any MPI task. We model this total execution time of OpenMP phases in MPI task i as

$$t_i = \sum_{j=1}^{M} \min_{1 \leq |thr| \leq X \cdot Y} t_{i,j,thr}. \tag{9.2}$$

The subscript *thr* in Equation (9.2) represents a configuration with thread count $|thr|$.

The critical task has the longest execution time, the *critical time*, which we model as

$$t_c = \max_{1 \leq i \leq N} \sum_{j=1}^{M} \min_{1 \leq |thr| \leq X \cdot Y} t_{i,j,thr}. \tag{9.3}$$

The time difference between the critical task and other (noncritical) tasks in an OpenMP phase group is slack that we can exploit to save energy with DVFS. Specifically, we can use a lower CPU frequency during the OpenMP phases of noncritical tasks. These frequency adjustments do not incur any performance loss if the noncritical task, executed at the adjusted frequencies, does not spend more time inside the OpenMP phase group than the critical time. The *slack time* that we can disperse to the OpenMP phase group of a noncritical task i by DVFS is

$$\Delta t_i^{\text{slack}} = t_c - t_i - t_i^{\text{comm\_send}} - t_{\text{dvfs}}. \tag{9.4}$$

Equation (9.4) reduces the available slack by the DVFS overhead (t_{dvfs}) and the communication time ($t_i^{\text{comm\_send}}$) for sending data from task i in order to avoid reducing the frequency too much. We depict two slack scenarios for MPI collective operations and MPI_Waitall in. In each scenario, task 0 is the critical task and task 1 disperses its slack to its OpenMP phases.

We select a CPU frequency setting for each OpenMP phase based on the noncritical task's slack ($\Delta t_i^{\text{slack}}$). We discuss how we select the frequency in Section 9.2.3. We ensure that the selected frequency satisfies the following two conditions:

$$\sum_{1 \leq j \leq M} \Delta t_{ijk} \leq \Delta t_i^{\text{slack}} \tag{9.5}$$

$$\sum_{1 \leq j \leq M} t_{ijk} f_k \leq t_i f_0. \tag{9.6}$$

Equation (9.5) sets a time constraint: Δt_{ijk} refers to the time change after we set the frequency of the core or processor executing task i in phase j to f_k. Equation (9.5) requires that the total time changes of all OpenMP phases at the selected frequencies do not exceed the available slack we want to disperse. Equation (9.6) sets an energy constraint: t_{ijk} refers to the time taken by phase j of task i running at frequency f_k. We approximate the energy consumption of the phase as the product of time and frequency. Equation (9.6) requires that the energy consumption with the selected frequencies does not exceed the energy consumption at the highest frequency.

Intuitively, energy consumption is related to both time and CPU frequency. Longer time and higher frequency lead to more energy consumption. By computing the product of time and frequency, we capture the effect of both. Empirical observations [5] found average *system power* is approximately linear in frequency under a certain CPU utilization range. These observations support our estimate since HPC applications usually have very high CPU utilization under different CPU frequencies (e.g., all of our tests have utilization beyond 82.4%, well within the range of a near-linear relationship between frequency and system power).

9.2.2 Time Prediction for OpenMP Phases

Our DVFS and DCT control algorithms rely on accurate execution time prediction of OpenMP phases in response to changing either the concurrency configuration or voltage and frequency. Changes in concurrency configuration should satisfy Equation (9.2). Changes in voltage and frequency should satisfy Equations (9.5) and (9.6).

We design a time predictor that extends previous work that only predicted instructions per cycle (*IPC*) since intranode DCT only requires a rank ordering of configurations [6, 7]. We require time predictions in order to estimate the slack to disperse. We also require time predictions to estimate energy consumption. We use execution samples collected at runtime on specific configurations to predict the time on other untested configurations. From these samples, our predictor learns about each OpenMP phase's execution properties that impact the time under alternative configurations. The input from the sample configurations consists of elapsed CPU clock cycles and a set of n hardware event rates $(e_{(1\cdots n,s)})$ observed for the particular phase on the sample configuration s, where the event rate $e_{(i,s)}$ is the number of occurrences of event i divided by the number of elapsed cycles during the execution of configuration s. The event rates capture the utilization of particular hardware resources that represent scalability bottlenecks, thus providing insight into the likely impact of hardware utilization and contention on scalability. The model predicts time on a given target configuration t, which we call Time$_t$. This time includes the time spent within OpenMP phases plus the parallelization overhead of those phases.

For an arbitrary collection of samples, S, of size $|S|$, we model Time$_t$ as a linear function:

$$\text{Time}_t = \sum_{i=1}^{|S|} \left(\text{Time}_i \cdot \alpha_{(t,i)}(e_{(1\cdots n,i)}) \right) + \lambda_t(e_{(1\cdots n,S)}) + \sigma_t. \tag{9.7}$$

The term λ_t is defined as

$$\lambda_t(e_{(1\cdots n,S)}) = \sum_{i=1}^{n} \left(\sum_{j=1}^{|S|-1} \left(\sum_{k=j+1}^{|S|} \left(\mu_{(t,i,j,k)} \cdot e_{(i,j)} \cdot e_{(i,k)} \right) \right) \right)$$
$$+ \sum_{j=1}^{|S|-1} \left(\sum_{k=j+1}^{|S|} \left(\mu_{(t,j,k,\text{time})} \cdot \text{Time}_j \cdot \text{Time}_k \right) \right) + l_t. \tag{9.8}$$

Equation (9.7) illustrates the dependency of terms $\alpha_{(t,i)}$, λ_t, and σ_t on the target configuration. We model each target configuration t through coefficients that capture the varying effects of hardware utilization at different degrees of concurrency, different mappings of threads to cores, and different frequency levels. The term $\alpha_{(t,i)}$ scales the observed Time$_i$ on the sample configurations up or down based on the observed values of the event rates in that configuration. The constant term σ_t is an event rate-independent term. It includes the overhead time for parallelization or synchronization. The term λ_t combines the products of each event across configurations and of Time$_{jlk}$ to model interaction effects. Finally, μ is the target configuration-specific coefficient for each event pair and l is the event rate-independent term in the model.

We use multivariate linear regression (MLR) to obtain the model coefficients (α, μ, and constant terms) from a set of training benchmarks. We select the training benchmarks empirically to vary properties such as scalability and memory boundedness. The observed time $Time_i$, the product of the observed time $Time_i$, and each event rate and the interaction terms on the sample configurations are independent variables for the regression, while $Time_t$ on each target configuration is the dependent variable. We derive sets of coefficients and model each target configuration separately.

We use the event rates for model training and time prediction that best correlate with execution time. We use three sample configurations: One uses the maximum concurrency and frequency, while the other two use configurations with half the concurrency—with different mappings of threads to cores—and the second highest frequency. Thus, we gain insight into utilization of shared caches and memory bandwidth while limiting the number of samples.

We verify the accuracy of our models on systems with three different node architectures. One has four AMD Opteron 8350 quad-core processors. The second has two AMD Opteron 265 dual-core processors. The third has two Intel Xeon E5462 quad-core processors. We present experiments with seven OpenMP benchmarks from the NAS Parallel Benchmarks Suite (v3.1) with CLASS B input. We collect event rates from three sample configurations and make time predictions for OpenMP phase samples in the benchmarks. We then compare the measured time for the OpenMP phases to our predictions. Figure 9.2 shows the cumulative distribution of our prediction accuracy, that is, the total percentage of OpenMP phases with error under the threshold indicated on the x-axis. The results demonstrate the high accuracy of the model in all cases: More than 75% of the samples have less than 10% error.

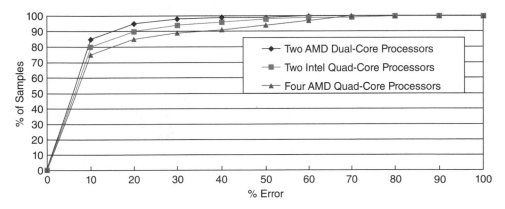

FIGURE 9.2. Cumulative distribution of prediction accuracy.

9.2.3 DCT

With input from samples of hardware event counters collected at runtime, we predict performance for each OpenMP phase under all feasible concurrency configurations based on Section 9.2.2. Intuitively, using the best concurrency configuration for each OpenMP phase should minimize the computation time of each MPI task. We call this DCT strategy the *profile-driven static mapping*. To explore how well this strategy works in practice, we applied it to the AMG benchmark from the ASC Sequoia Benchmark suite. AMG has four OpenMP phases in the computation loop of its solve phase. Phases 1 and 2 are in phase group 1; phases 3 and 4 are in phase group 2; and the phase groups are separated by MPI_Waitall. We describe AMG in detail in Section 9.2.5. We run these experiments on two nodes, each with four AMD Opteron 8350 quad-core processors.

We first run the benchmark with input parameters $P = [2\ 1\ 1]$, $n = [512\ 512\ 512]$ under a fixed configuration throughout the execution of all OpenMP phases in all tasks for the entire duration of the run. We then manually select the best concurrency configuration based on these static observations, thus avoiding any prediction errors. The configuration of four processors and two threads per processor, shown as the first bar in each group of bars in Figure 9.3, has the lowest total time in the solve phase and, thus, is the best static mapping that we use as our baseline in the following discussion.

Under this whole-program configuration, each individual OpenMP phase may not use its best concurrency configuration. We select the best configuration for each OpenMP phase and rerun the benchmark, as the second bar in each group of bars in Figure 9.3 shows. We profile each OpenMP phase with this profile-driven static mapping, which we compare with the best static mapping to explore the source of the performance loss. The profiling reveals that three of the four OpenMP phases incur more misses with the profile-driven static mapping, leading to lower overall

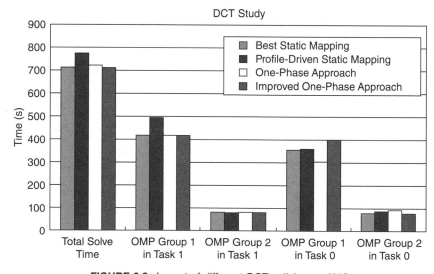

FIGURE 9.3. *Impact of different DCT policies on AMG.*

performance despite using the best configuration based on the fixed configuration runs. This increase arises from frequent configuration changes from one OpenMP phase to another under the profile-driven static mapping.

Previous work [6] showed that the profile-driven static mapping can outperform the best static mapping. These results combine with ours to demonstrate that the profile-driven static mapping has no performance guarantees: It benefits from improved concurrency configurations while often suffering additional cache misses. We would have to extend our time prediction model to consider the configuration of the previous OpenMP phase in order to capture the impact on cache hit rates. We would also need to train our model under various thread mappings instead of a unique thread mapping throughout the run, which would significantly increase the overhead of our approach.

A simple solution to avoid cache misses caused by changing configurations is to use the same concurrency configuration for all OpenMP phases in each task in isolation. We can predict time for this combined phase and select the configuration that minimizes the time of the combined phase in future iterations under this *one-phase approach*. Figure 9.3 shows that this strategy greatly reduces the performance loss for AMG compared to the profile-driven static mapping. However, we still incur significant performance loss compared to the best static mapping. Further analysis reveals that the one-phase approach can change the critical task for specific phases despite minimizing the time across all OpenMP phases.

This problem arises because configurations are selected without coordination between tasks. Instead, each task greedily chooses the best configuration for each combined phase regardless of the global impact. To solve this problem, we propose an *improved one-phase approach*: Each task considers the time at the critical task when making its DCT decision. Each task selects a configuration that does not make its OpenMP phase groups longer than the corresponding ones in the critical task. Although this strategy may result in a configuration where performance for a task is worse than the one achieved with the best static mapping, it maintains performance as long as the OpenMP phase group time is shorter than the corresponding one in the critical task. Unlike the profile-driven static mapping, this strategy has a performance guarantee: It selects configurations that yield overall performance no worse than the best static mapping, as Figure 9.3 shows.

9.2.4 DVFS Control for Energy Saving

Different MPI tasks in a parallel application can have different execution times because of the following: (1) The workload may not be evenly divisible between them; (2) the workload may scale differently in different tasks; (3) heterogeneity of the computing environment; and (4) other system events that may distort execution, such as overheads for the management of parallelism in the runtime system and operating system noise. Any of these events leads to load imbalance, which, in turn, causes slack in one or more MPI tasks. We use DVFS to reduce slack by extending the execution times of OpenMP phases of noncritical tasks, which, in turn, reduces overall energy consumption. More specifically, we use DVFS to select frequencies for the cores that execute each OpenMP phase. We assume for simplicity and to avoid introducing more load imbalance that all cores that execute an OpenMP phase within an MPI task use the same frequency.

We formulate frequency selection as a variant of the 0-1 knapsack problem [8], which is NP-complete. We define the time of each OpenMP phase under a particular core frequency f_k as an *item*. With each item, we associate a weight, w, which is the time change under frequency f_k compared to using the peak frequency, and a value, p, which is the energy consumption under frequency f_k. The optimization objective is to keep the total weight of all phases under a given limit, which corresponds to the slack time Δt^{slack}, and to minimize the total value of all phases. Our formulation is a variant of the basic problem since we require that some items cannot be selected together since we assume that we cannot select more than one frequency for each OpenMP phase.

Dynamic programming can solve the knapsack problem in pseudopolynomial time. If each item has a distinct value per unit of weight ($v = p/w$), the empirical complexity is $O((\log(n))^2)$, where n is the number of items. For convenience in the description of the dynamic programming solution of our variant, we replace p with $-p$ so that we maximize the total value. Let L be the number of CPU frequency levels available and, for OpenMP phase i ($0 \leq i < N$, where N is the number of OpenMP phases), let $w_{i,j}$ ($1 \leq j \leq L$) be the available weights associated with CPU frequencies from the lowest to the highest. Let $p_{i,j}$ ($1 \leq j \leq L$) be the available values. The total number of items is $n = N \times L$. The total weight limit is W (i.e., the available slack time). The maximum attainable value with weight less than or equal to Y using items up to j is $A(j, Y)$, which we define recursively as

$$A(0, Y) = -\infty, \quad A(j, 0) = -\infty. \tag{9.9}$$

For the OpenMP phase i,
if $\forall\, 1 \leq j < L\colon w_{i,j} > Y$, then

$$A(iL, Y) = A((i-1)L, Y) + p_{i,L}; \tag{9.10}$$

else,

$$A(iL, Y) = \max(A((i-1)L, Y) + p_{i,L}, \max_j(p_{i,j} + A((i-1)L, Y - w_{i,j}))). \tag{9.11}$$

We choose frequencies by calculating $A(n, \Delta t_i^{\text{slack}})$ for task i. For a given total weight limit W, the empirical complexity is still $O((\log(n))^2)$.

9.2.5 Performance Evaluation

We implemented our power-aware MPI/OpenMP system as a runtime library that performs online adaptation of DVFS and DCT. The runtime system predicts execution times of OpenMP phases based on collected hardware event rates and controls the execution of each OpenMP phase in terms of the number of threads, their placement on cores, and the DVFS level. To use our library, we instrument applications with function calls around each adaptable OpenMP phase and selected MPI operations (collectives and MPI_Waitall). This instrumentation is straightforward and could easily be automated using a source code instrumentation tool in combination with a PMPI wrapper library.

In this section, we evaluate our model with two real applications (IRS and AMG) from the ASC Sequoia Benchmark suite. IRS uses a preconditioned conjugate gradient method for inverting a matrix equation. We group its OpenMP phases into four groups. Some OpenMP phase groups include serial code. We regard serial code as a special OpenMP phase with the number of threads fixed to 1. Although DCT is not applicable to serial code, it could be imbalanced between MPI tasks and hence provide opportunities for saving energy through DVFS. We use input parameters NDOMS=8 and NZONES_PER_DOM_SIDE=90. The IRS benchmark has load imbalance between the OpenMP phase groups of different tasks. AMG [9] is a parallel algebraic multigrid solver for linear systems on unstructured grids. Its driver builds linear systems for various three-dimensional problems; we choose a Laplace-type problem (problem parameter set to 2). The driver generates a problem that is well balanced between tasks. We modified the driver to generate a problem with imbalanced load. The load distribution ratio between pairs of MPI tasks in this new version is 0.45 : 0.55. Figures 9.4 and 9.5 show simplified computational kernels for IRS and AMG.

We deploy our tests in large scales in order to investigate how our model reacts as the number of nodes changes. The following experiments consider the power-awareness scalability of HPC applications, which we call the *scalability of energy-saving opportunities*. We present results from experiments on the System G supercomputer at Virginia Tech. System G is a unique research platform for Green HPC, with thousands of power and thermal sensors. System G has 320 nodes powered by Mac Pro computers, each with two quad-core Xeon processors. Each processor has two frequency settings for DVFS. The nodes are connected by Infiniband (40 Gb/s). We vary the number of nodes and study how our power-aware model performs under strong and weak scaling. We use the execution under the

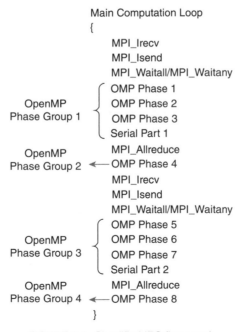

FIGURE 9.4. *Simplified IRS flow graph.*

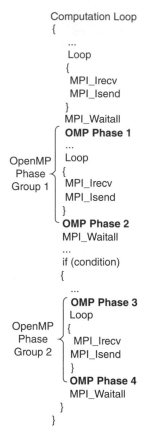

FIGURE 9.5. *Simplified AMG flow graph.*

configuration using two processors and four cores per processor and running at the highest processor frequency, which we refer to as $(2, 4)$, as the baseline by which we normalize reported times and energy.

Figure 9.6 displays the results of AMG and IRS under strong scaling input (i.e., maintaining the same total problem size across all scales). Actual execution time is shown above normalized execution time bars to illustrate how the benchmark scales with the number of nodes. On our cluster, the OpenMP phases in AMG scale well, and hence DCT does not find energy-saving opportunities in almost all cases, although with 64 nodes or more, DCT leads to concurrency throttling on some nodes. However, due to the small length of OpenMP phases at this scale, DCT does not lead to significant energy savings. When the number of nodes reaches 128, the per-node workload in OpenMP phases is further reduced to a point where some phases become shorter than our DCT minimum phase granularity threshold, and DCT simply ignores them. On the other hand, our DVFS strategy saves significant energy in most cases. However, as the number of nodes increases, the ratio of energy saving decreases from 3.72% (4 nodes) to 0.121% (64 nodes) because the load difference between tasks becomes smaller as the number of nodes increases. With 128 nodes, load imbalance is actually less than DVFS overhead, so DVFS becomes

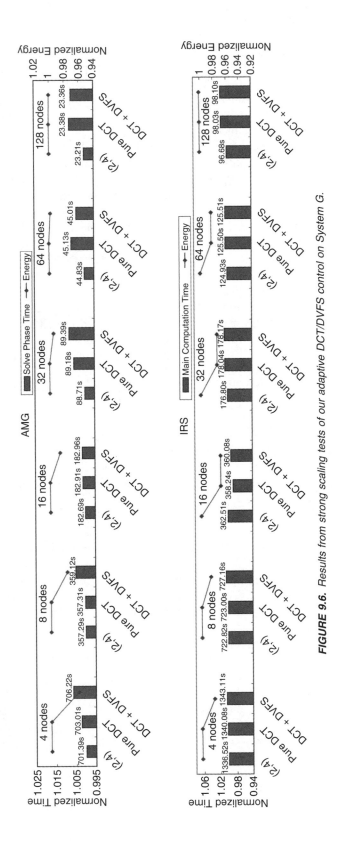

FIGURE 9.6. Results from strong scaling tests of our adaptive DCT/DVFS control on System G.

ineffective. In IRS, our DCT strategy leads to significant energy saving when the number of nodes is more than eight. We even observe performance gains by DCT when the number of nodes reaches 16. However, DCT does not lead to energy saving in the case of 128 nodes for similar reasons to AMG. DVFS leads to energy saving with less than 16 nodes but does not provide benefits as the number of nodes becomes large and the imbalance becomes small.

Figures 9.7 displays the weak scaling results. We adjust the input parameters (AMG and IRS) or change the input problem definition (BT-MZ) as we vary the number of nodes so that the problem size per node remains constant (or close to it). For IRS and BT-MZ, the energy-saving ratio grows slightly as we increase the number of nodes (from 1.9% to 2.5% for IRS and from 5.21% to 6.8% for BT-MZ). Slightly increased imbalance, as we increase the problem size, allows additional energy savings. For AMG, we observe that the ratio of energy saving stays almost constant (2.17~2.22%), which is consistent with AMG having good weak scaling. Since the workload per node is stable, energy-saving opportunities are also stable as we vary the number of nodes.

In general, energy-saving opportunities vary with workload characteristics. They become smaller as the number of nodes increases under a fixed total problem size because the subdomain allocated to a single node becomes so small that the energy-saving potential that DVFS or DCT can leverage falls below the threshold that we can exploit. An interesting observation is that, when the number of nodes is below the threshold, some benchmarks (e.g., IRS with less than 16 nodes) present good scalability of energy-saving opportunities for DCT because of the changes in their workload characteristics (e.g., scalability and working data sets) as the allocated subdomain changes. With weak scaling, energy-saving opportunities are usually stable or increasing, and actual energy saving from our model tends to be higher than with strong scaling. Most importantly, under any case, our model can leverage any energy-saving opportunity without significant performance loss as the number of nodes changes.

9.3 POWER-AWARE MPI TASK AGGREGATION PREDICTION

Modern high-end computing systems have many nodes with several processors per node and multiple cores per processor. The distribution of tasks across the cores of multiple nodes impacts both execution time and energy. Current job management systems, which typically rely on a count of available cores for assigning jobs to cores, simply treat parallel job submissions as a two-dimensional (2-D) chart with time along one axis and number of cores along the other [10, 11]. They regard each job as a rectangle with width equal to the number of cores requested by the job and height equal to the estimated job execution time. Most scheduling strategies are based on this model, which has been extensively studied [12, 13]. Unfortunately, these job schedulers ignore the power-performance implications of the layouts of cores available in compute nodes to execute tasks from parallel jobs.

In the previous section, we assume one MPI task per node without consideration of task distribution. In this section, we remove this assumption and consider the effects of task distribution. In particular, we propose power-aware task aggregation.

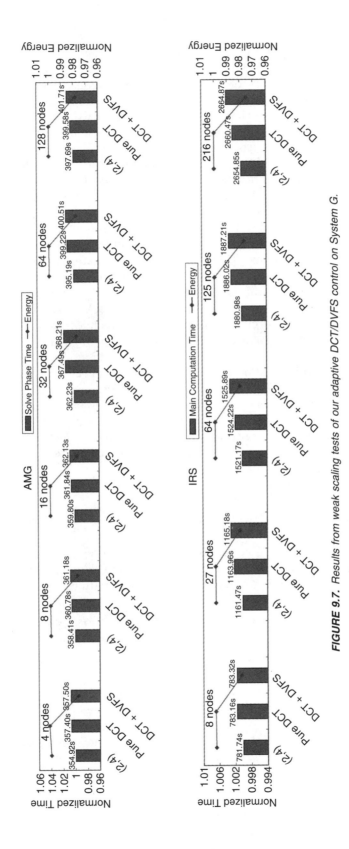

FIGURE 9.7. Results from weak scaling tests of our adaptive DCT/DVFS control on System G.

Task aggregation refers to aggregating multiple tasks within a node with shared memory. A fixed number of tasks can be distributed across a variable number of nodes using different degrees of task aggregation per node. Aggregated tasks share system resources, such as the memory hierarchy and network interface, which has an impact on performance. This impact may be destructive because of contention for resources. However, it may also be constructive. For example, an application can benefit from the low latency and high bandwidth of intranode communication through shared memory. Although earlier work has studied the performance implications of communication through shared memory in MPI programs [14, 15], the problem of selecting the best distribution and aggregation of a fixed number of tasks has been left largely to ad hoc solutions.

Task aggregation significantly impacts energy consumption. A job uses fewer nodes with a higher degree of task aggregation. Unused nodes can be set to a deep low-power state while idling. At the same time, aggregating more tasks per node implies that more cores will be active running tasks on the node, while memory occupancy and link traffic will also increase. Therefore, aggregation tends to increase the power consumption of active nodes. In summary, task aggregation has complex implications on both performance and energy. Job schedulers should consider these implications in order to optimize energy-related metrics while meeting performance constraints.

We target the problem of how to distribute MPI tasks between and within nodes in order to minimize execution time, or minimize energy, under a given performance constraint. The solution must make two decisions: how many tasks to aggregate per node; and how to assign the tasks scheduled on the same node to cores, which determines how these tasks will share hardware components such as caches, network resources, and memory bandwidth. In all cases, we select a task aggregation pattern based on performance predictions.

We assume the following:

- The number of MPI tasks is given and fixed throughout the execution of the application.
- The number of nodes used to execute the application and the number of tasks per node is decided at job submission time, and this decision depends on a prediction of the impact of different aggregation patterns on performance and energy.
- Any aggregation must assign the same number of tasks to each node.
- Jobs are single-program, multiple-data (SPMD) programs.
- MPI communication patterns—including message size and communication target—can vary across tasks.
- Aggregation patterns must not result in total DRAM requirements that exceed a node's physical memory.

Allowing aggregation patterns that place more tasks on some nodes than others may be more efficient in imbalanced applications; however, the resulting load imbalance would hurt performance and waste energy in well-balanced SPMD applications. In these cases, the system could leverage slack to save energy. We studied energy-saving opportunities due to slack in the previous section.

We decompose the aggregation problem into three subproblems: predicting the impact of task count per node on computation, predicting the communication cost of all aggregation patterns, and combining the computation and communication predictions. We study the impact of aggregation on computation and communication separately since the same aggregation pattern can impact computation and communication differently. Our test platform is a cluster with 16 nodes, each of which has two quad-core processors. The possible aggregation patterns on our platform are shown in Figure 9.8. These aggregation patterns are used throughout this section.

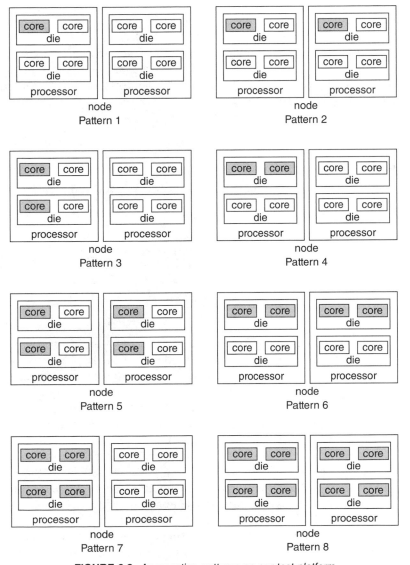

FIGURE 9.8. *Aggregation patterns on our test platform.*

9.3.1   Predicting Computation Performance

We predict performance during computation phases by predicting *IPC*. We derive an empirical model based on previous work [6, 7], which predicts the *IPC* of computation phases in OpenMP applications. We use iteration samples collected at runtime on specific aggregation patterns to predict the *IPC* for each task on other untested aggregation patterns. The *IPC* for each aggregation pattern is the average value of the *IPC* of all tasks. The model methodology is similar to the one in Section 9.2.2. The model derivation is shown in Equation (9.12):

$$IPC_t = \sum_{i=1}^{|S|} \left(IPC_i \cdot \alpha_{(t,i)}(e_{(1\cdots n,i)}) \right) + \lambda_t (e_{(1\cdots n,S)}) + \sigma_t. \tag{9.12}$$

The model predicts the *IPC* of a specific aggregation pattern t based on information collected in S samples. We collect n hardware event rates $e_{(1\cdots n,i)}$ and IPC_i in each sample i. The function $\alpha_{(t,i)}()$ scales the observed IPC_i in sample i up or down based on the observed values of event rates, while λ_t is a function that accounts for the interaction between events and σ_t is a constant term for the aggregation pattern t. For a specific sample s, we define α_t as

$$\alpha_t(e_{(1\cdots n,s)}) = \sum_{j=1}^{n} \left(x_{(t,j)} \cdot e_{(j,s)} + y_{(t,j)} \right) + z_t, \tag{9.13}$$

where $e_{(j,s)}$ is a hardware event in sample s, and $x_{(t,j)}$, $y_{(t,j)}$ and z_t are coefficients. λ_t is defined as

$$\lambda_t(e_{(1\cdots n,S)}) = \sum_{i=1}^{n} \left(\sum_{j=1}^{|S|-1} \left(\sum_{k=j+1}^{|S|} \left(\mu_{(t,i,j,k)} \cdot e_{(i,j)} \cdot e_{(i,k)} \right) \right) \right)$$
$$+ \sum_{j=1}^{|S|-1} \left(\sum_{k=j+1}^{|S|} \left(\mu_{(t,j,k,IPC)} \cdot IPC_j \cdot IPC_k \right) \right) + l_t, \tag{9.14}$$

where $e_{(i,j)}$ is the ith event of the jth sample. $\mu_{(t,i,j,k)}$, $\mu_{(t,j,k,IPC)}$ and l_t are coefficients.

We approximate the coefficients in our model with MLR. *IPC*, the product of *IPC* and each event rate, and the interaction terms in the sample aggregation patterns serve as independent variables, while the *IPC* on each target aggregation pattern serves as the dependent variable. We record *IPC* and a predefined collection of event rates while executing the computation phases of each training benchmark with all aggregation patterns. We use the hardware event rates that most strongly correlate with the target *IPC* in the sample aggregation patterns. We develop a model separately for each aggregation pattern and derive sets of coefficients independently. We use the 12 SPEC MPI 2007 benchmarks under different problem sets as training benchmarks. These benchmarks demonstrate wide variation in execution properties such as scalability and memory boundedness.

We classify computation phases into four categories based on their observed *IPC* during the execution of the sample aggregation patterns and use separate models for different categories in order to improve prediction accuracy. Specifically, we classify phases into four categories with *IPC* $[0, 1)$, $[1, 1.5)$, $[1.5, 2.0)$, and $[2.0, +\infty)$. Thus, our model is a piecewise linear regression that attempts to describe the relationship between dependent and independent variables more accurately by separately handling phases with low and high scalability characteristics.

We test our model by comparing our predicted *IPC* with the measured *IPC* of the computation phases of six NAS MPI parallel benchmarks. Our model is highly accurate with a worst-case absolute error of 2.109%. The average error in all predictions is 1.079% and the standard deviation is 0.7916.

9.3.2 Task Grouping

An aggregation pattern determines how many tasks to place on each node and processor; we must also determine which tasks to collocate. If an aggregation groups k tasks per node and a program uses n tasks, there are $\binom{n}{k}$ ways to group the tasks to achieve the aggregation. For nodes with $p \geq k$ processors, we then can place the k tasks on one node in $\binom{p}{k} k! = p!/(p-k)!$ ways on the available cores. The grouping of tasks on nodes and their placement on processors has an impact on the performance of MPI point-to-point communication. Computation phases are only sensitive to how tasks are laid out in each node and not to which subset of tasks is aggregated in each node since we assume SPMD applications with balanced workloads between processors. The impact of task placement for MPI collective operations depends on the characteristics of the network; they are relatively insensitive to task placement with flat networks such as fat trees. Thus, we focus on point-to-point operations as we decide which specific MPI ranks to locate on the same node or processor.

Intranode communication has low latency for small messages, while internode high-bandwidth communication is more efficient for large messages because sharing the node's memory bandwidth between communicating tasks while they exchange large messages incurs sufficient overhead to make it less efficient than internode communication [16]. In addition, the performance of intranode communication is sensitive to how the tasks are laid out within a node: Intranode communication can benefit from cache sharing due to processor die sharing or whole processor sharing. Based on this analysis, we prefer aggregations that group tasks based on whether their communication performance is the best. However, we cannot decide whether to colocate a given pair of tasks based only on individual point-to-point communications between them. Instead, we must consider all communications performed between those tasks and all communications between all tasks. Overall performance may be best even though some (or all) point-to-point communication between two specific tasks is not optimized.

This task grouping problem is an NP-complete problem [17]. We formalize the problem as a graph partitioning problem and use an efficient heuristic algorithm [18] to solve it. We briefly review this algorithm in the following section.

9.3.2.1 Algorithm Review
The algorithm partitions a graph G of kn nodes with associated edge costs into k subpartitions, such that the total cost of the edge cut, the edges connecting subpartitions, is minimized. The algorithm starts with an

arbitrary partitioning into k sets of size n and then tries to bring the partitioning as close as possible to being pairwise optimal by the repeated application of a two-way partitioning procedure.

The two-way partitioning procedure starts with an arbitrary partitioning $\{A, B\}$ of a graph G and tries to decrease the initial external cost T (i.e., the total cost of the edge cut) by a series of interchanges of subsets of A and B. The algorithm stops when it cannot find further pairwise improvements. To choose the subsets of A and B, the algorithm first selects two graph nodes a_1, b_1 such that the gain g_1 after interchanging a_1 with b_1 is maximal. The algorithm temporarily sets aside a_1 and b_1 and chooses the pair a_2, b_2 from $A - \{a_1\}$ and $B - \{b_1\}$ that maximizes the gain g_2. The algorithm continues until it has exhausted the graph nodes. Then, the algorithm chooses m to maximize the partial sum $\sum_{i=1}^{m} g_i$. The corresponding nodes $a_1, a_2, \ldots,$ a_m and $b_1, b_2, \ldots, b_m$ are exchanged.

9.3.2.2 *Applying the Algorithm*

Task aggregation must group T tasks into n partitions, where n is the number of nodes of a specific aggregation pattern. We regard each MPI task as a graph node and communication between tasks as edges. Aggregating tasks into the same node is equivalent to placing graph nodes into the same partition. We now define an edge cost based on the communication between task pairs.

The original algorithm tries to minimize the total cost of the edge cut. In other words, it tries to place graph nodes with a small edge cost into different partitions. Thus, we must assign a small (large) cost value on an edge that favors internode (intranode) communication. We observe two further edge cost requirements:

- The difference between the small cost value (for internode communication) and the large cost value (for intranode communication) should be large.
- The edge values should form a range that reflects the relative benefit of intranode communication.

A large difference between edge costs reduces the probability of the heuristic algorithm selecting a poor partitioning. The range of values reflects that colocation benefits some task pairs that communicate frequently more than others.

To assign edge costs, we measure the size of every message between each task pair during execution to obtain a communication table. We then estimate the communication time for each pair of communicating tasks i and j if we place them in the same partition (t_{ij}^{intra}) and if we place them in different partitions (t_{ij}^{inter}). We estimate these communication times a priori, using a communication benchmark such as MPPtest. Our intranode communication time prediction is conservative since we use the worst-case intranode communication (i.e., two tasks with no processor or die sharing). Finally, we compare t_{ij}^{intra} and t_{ij}^{inter} to decide whether the tasks i and j benefit from colocation. If $t_{ij}^{\text{intra}} > t_{ij}^{\text{inter}}$, then we set the edge cost to $c_{ij} = 1.0/(t_{ij}^{\text{intra}} - t_{ij}^{\text{inter}})$. Alternatively, if $t_{ij}^{\text{intra}} \leq t_{ij}^{\text{inter}}$, we set $c_{ij} = C + (t_{ij}^{\text{inter}} - t_{ij}^{\text{intra}})$. These edge costs provide a range of values that reflect the relative benefit of intranode communication as needed.

C is a parameter that ensures the difference of edge costs for pairs of tasks that favor intranode communication and pairs of tasks that favor internode communication is large. We define C as

$$C = k^2 \Delta t, \tag{9.15}$$

where k is the number of tasks per node; k^2 is the maximum number of edge cuts between the two partitions; and Δt is defined as $\max\{1.0/(t_{ij}^{intra} - t_{ij}^{inter})\}$ between all task pairs (i, j) that benefit from internode communication.

Overall, our edge costs reflect whether the communication between a task pair is in the intranode or internode communication regime. We apply the graph partitioning algorithm based on these edge costs to group tasks into n nodes. We then use the same algorithm to determine the placement of tasks on processors within a node. Thus, this algorithm calculates a task placement for each aggregation pattern.

9.3.3 Predicting Communication Performance

Modeling and predicting communication time is challenging due to the following reasons:

- computation/communication overlap
- overlap and interference of concurrent communication operations
- even in the absence of overlap, many factors, including task placement (i.e., how MPI tasks are distributed between processors, sockets, and dies in the node), task intensity (i.e., the number of tasks assigned to the node), communication type (i.e., intranode or internode), and communication volume and intensity impact communication interference.

We propose an empirical method to predict a reasonable upper bound for MPI point-to-point communication time.

We trace MPI point-to-point operations to gather the end points of communication operations. We also estimate potential interference based on the proximity of the calls. We use this information to estimate parameters for task placement and task intensity that interfere with each communication operation for each aggregation pattern. Since we predict an upper bound, we assume that the entire MPI latency overlaps with noise from other concurrent communication operations. This assumption is reasonable for well-balanced SPMD applications because of their bulk-synchronous execution pattern.

We construct a prediction table based on our extracted parameters, namely, type of communication (intranode/internode), task intensity, task placement for both communicating and interfering tasks, and message size. We populate the table by running MPI point-to-point communication tests under various combinations of input parameters. We reduce the space that we must consider for the table by considering groups of task placements with small performance difference as symmetric. The symmetric task placements have identical hardware sharing characteristics with respect to observed communication and noise communication.

We use a similar empirical scheme for MPI collectives. However, the problem is simplified since collectives on MPI_COMM_WORLD involve all tasks; we leave extending our framework to handle collective operations on derived communicators as future work. Thus, we only need to test the possible task placements for specific task counts per node for the observed communication.

9.3.4   Choosing an Aggregation Pattern

Our prediction framework allows us to predict the aggregation pattern that either optimizes performance or optimizes energy under a given performance constraint.

We predict the best aggregation pattern based on our computation and communication performance predictions. Since our goal is to minimize energy under a performance constraint, we pick candidates based on their predicted performance and then rank them considering a ranking of their energy consumption.

We predict performance in terms of *IPC* (Section 9.3.1). To predict performance in terms of time, we measure the number of instructions executed with one aggregation pattern and assume that this number remains constant across aggregation patterns. We verify this assumption by counting the number of instructions under different aggregation patterns for 10 iterations of all NAS MPI parallel benchmarks on a node of our cluster. The maximum variance in the number of instructions executed between different aggregation patterns is negligible (8.5E-05%).

We compare aggregation patterns by measuring their difference to a reference pattern, where there is no aggregation of tasks in a node. We compute the difference as

$$\Delta t = t_1^{\text{comp}} + t_1^{\text{comm}} - t_0^{\text{comp}} - t_0^{\text{comm}}, \tag{9.16}$$

where t_1^{comp}, t_1^{comm} are our estimated computation time and communication time upper bound for the given aggregation pattern, respectively, and t_0^{comp}, t_0^{comm} are the computation and communication times for the reference pattern, respectively. Comparing patterns in terms of the difference with a reference pattern partially compensates for the effect of overlap and other errors of time prediction, such as the gap between the actual and predicted communication time. Our analysis in Sections 9.3.1 and 9.3.3 estimates performance for each task. For a specific aggregation pattern, Equation (9.16) uses the average computation time of all tasks and the longest communication time.

We choose candidate patterns for aggregation using a threshold of 5% for the performance penalty that any aggregation pattern may introduce when compared to the reference pattern. We discard any aggregation pattern with a higher-performance penalty, which ensures that we select aggregations that minimally impact user experience. An aggregation may actually *improve* performance; obviously, we consider any such aggregations.

We choose the best aggregation candidate by considering energy consumption. Instead of estimating actual energy consumption, we rank aggregation patterns based on how many nodes, processors, sockets, and dies they use. We rank aggregation patterns that use fewer nodes (more tasks per node) higher. Among aggregation patterns that use the same number of nodes, we prefer aggregation patterns that use fewer processors. Finally, among aggregation patterns that use the same number of nodes and processors per node, we rank aggregation patterns that use fewer dies per processor higher. In the event of a tie, we prefer the aggregation pattern with the better predicted performance. According to this ranking method, the energy ranking of the eight aggregation patterns for our platform in Figure 9.8 from most energy-friendly to least energy-friendly corresponds with their pattern IDs.

9.3.5 Performance

We implemented a tool suite for task aggregation in MPI programs. The suite consists of a PMPI wrapper library that collects communication metadata, an implementation of the graph partitioning algorithm, and a tool to predict computation and communication performance and to choose aggregation patterns. To facilitate collection of hardware event rates for computation phases, we instrument applications with calls to a hardware performance monitoring and sampling library.

We evaluate our framework with the NAS 3.2 MPI Parallel Benchmark suite, using OpenMPI-1.3.2 as the MPI communication library. We present experiments from the System G supercomputer at Virginia Tech.

We set the threshold of performance loss to 5% and use one task per node as the reference aggregation pattern. The choice of the reference aggregation pattern is intuitive since our goal is to demonstrate the potential energy and performance advantages of aggregation, and our reference performs no task aggregation. More specifically, energy consumption is intuitively greatest with one task per node since it uses the maximum number of nodes for a given run. Task aggregation attempts to reduce energy consumption through reduction of the node count. Given that each node consumes a few hundred watts, we will save energy if we can reduce the node count without sacrificing performance. Using one task per node will often improve performance since that choice eliminates destructive interference during computation or communication phases between tasks running on the same node. However, using more than one task per node can improve performance, for example, if tasks exchange data through a shared cache. Since the overall performance impact of aggregation varies with the application, our choice of the reference aggregation pattern enables exploration of the energy-saving potential of various aggregation patterns.

Figure 9.9 shows that our prediction selects the best observed aggregation pattern, namely, the pattern that minimizes energy while not violating the performance constraint, in all cases. We indicate the best observed and predicted task aggregations with stripes. The performance loss threshold is shown with a dotted line. We achieve the maximum energy savings with sp.D.16 (70.03%) and average energy savings of 64.87%. Our prediction of the time difference between aggregation patterns for both computation and communication follows the variance of actual measured time. For FT and BT, we measure performance gains from some aggregation patterns in computation phases and our predictions correctly capture these gains.

The applications exhibit widely varied computation-to-communication ratios, ranging from communication intensive (FT) to computation intensive (LU). The communication time difference across the different aggregation patterns depends on message size and communication frequency. Small messages or less frequent communication result in a smaller communication time difference. For example, 99.98% of the MPI communication operations in lu.D.16 transfer small messages of a size close to 4 kB. The communication time differences in patterns 2–6 are all less than 10.0%; the communication time differences in patterns 7 and 8 (the most intensive aggregation patterns) are less than 22.7%.

The FT benchmark runs with an input of size $1024 \times 512 \times 1024$ and has MPI_ Alltoall operations, in which each task sends 134-MB data to other tasks and receives 134-MB data from other tasks. The communication time differences in

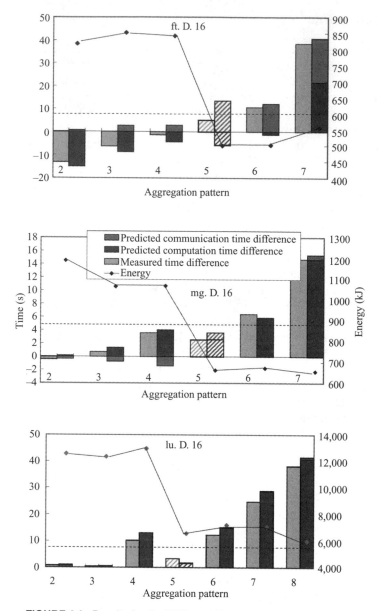

FIGURE 9.9. Results for the NAS 3.2 MPI Parallel Benchmark suite.

patterns 2–6 range between 28.96% and 144.1%. The communication time difference in pattern 7 (the most intensive aggregation pattern) is as much as 209.7%.

We also observe that CG is very sensitive to the aggregation pattern: Different
patterns can have significant performance differences due to CG's memory intensity.
Colocating tasks saturate the available memory bandwidth, resulting in significant
performance penalties. Finally, we observe MG communication can benefit from
task aggregation due to the low latency of communicating through shared memory.

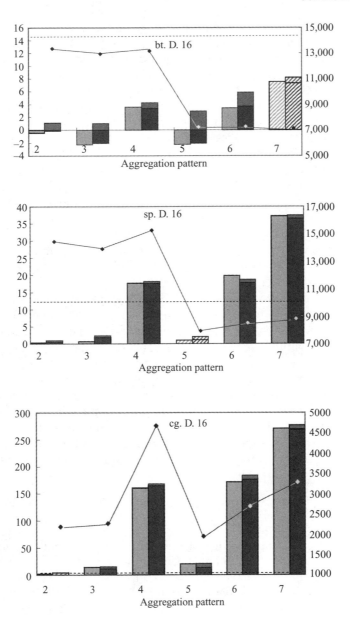

FIGURE 9.9. (Continued)

In particular, communication time at patterns 2, 3, and 4 reduce by 12.08%, 25.68%, and 48.81%, respectively.

9.4 CONCLUSIONS

The popularity of multicore architectures demands reconsideration of high-performance application and system designs. Scalable and power-aware execution of parallel applications are two major challenges on multicores. This chapter presents a series of methods and techniques to solve the problems of scalability and energy efficiency for high-end computing systems. We start with research into a power-aware hybrid MPI/OpenMP programming model based on the observation that the hybrid MPI/OpenMP model is gaining popularity. Then, we study power-aware MPI task aggregation, with the goal to improve energy efficiency further. Our power-aware hybrid MPI/OpenMP programming model solves the problem of performance optimization and energy efficiency in a 2-D plane (i.e., DCT + DVFS). We found performance loss when applying DCT at a fine granularity and propose a novel approach to avoid performance loss. To develop a power-aware parallel programming model, we found that the effects of power-saving techniques on local nodes should be considered, as well as the effects on other nodes (i.e., global effects). We introduce task coordination to account for these global effects. We also extend the previous *IPC*-based DCT performance model to predict execution time based on the requirements of energy estimation and slack time computing. Our scaling study demonstrates that power saving opportunities continue or increase under weak scaling but diminish under strong scaling.

We further research power-aware MPI task aggregation. To predict the impact of task aggregation, we propose a series of methods and techniques. We first predict computation performance. We base our prediction on the information collected from sample aggregation patterns. From this information, we learn execution properties and predict the performance of untested aggregation patterns. We then identify a task grouping problem on which communication performance relies. We formalize the task grouping problem and map it to a classic graph partitioning problem. Given the task grouping, we propose a prediction method based on our analysis of the effects of concurrent intertask communication. We evaluate our methods across different aggregation patterns. Our methods lead to substantial energy saving through aggregation (64.87% on average and up to 70.03%) with tolerable performance loss (under 5%).

REFERENCES

[1] M.F. Curtis-Maury, "Improving the efficiency of parallel applications on multithreaded and multicore systems." PhD Thesis, Virginia Tech, 2008.

[2] W. Feng and K. Cameron, "The Green500 List: Encouraging sustainable supercomputing," *IEEE Transactions on Computer*, 40:50–55, 2007.

[3] C. Stunkel, Exascale: Parallelism gone wild! IPDPS Key Note, 2010. Available at http://www.ipdps.org/ipdps2010/ipdps2010-slides/keynote/2010%2004%20TCPP%20 Exascale%20FINAL%20clean.pdf.

[4] R. Rabenseifner and G. Wellein, "Communication and optimization aspects of parallel programming models on hybrid architectures," *International Journal of High Performance Computing Applications*, 17:49–62, 2002.

[5] T. Horvath and K. Skadron, "Multi-mode energy management for multi-tier server clusters," in *Proceedings of the 17th International Conference on Parallel Architectures and Compilation Techniques (PACT)*, 2008.

[6] M. Curtis-Maury, F. Blagojevic, C.D. Antonopoulos, and D.S. Nikolopoulos, "Prediction-based power-performance adaptation of multithreaded scientific codes," *IEEE Transactions on Parallel and Distributed Systems (TPDS)*, 2008.

[7] M. Curtis-Maury, A. Shah, F. Blagojevic, D.S. Nikolopoulos, B.R. de Supinski, and M. Schulz, "Prediction models for multi-dimensional power-performance optimization on many cores," in *Proceedings of the 17th International Conference on Parallel Architectures and Compilation Techniques (PACT)*, 2008.

[8] M. Silvano and P. Toth, *Knapsack Problems: Algorithms and Computer Implementations*. New York: John Wiley & Sons, 1990.

[9] H. Van Emden and U.M. Yang, "BoomerAMG: A parallel algebraic multigrid solver and preconditioner," *Applied Numerical Mathematics*, 41:155–177, 2000.

[10] D. G., Feitelson, L. Rudolph, and U. Schwiegelshohn. "Parallel job schueduling—A status report," *Lecture Notes in Computer Science*, 3277:1–16, 2005.

[11] S. Srinivasan, R. Keetimuthu, V. Subramani, and P. Sadayappan, "Characterization of backfilling strategies for parallel job scheduling," in *Proceedings of the 2002 International Workshops on Parallel Processing*, 2002.

[12] L. Barsanti and A. Sodan, "Adaptive job scheduling via predictive job resource allocation," *Lecture Notes in Computer Science*, 4376:115–140, 2007.

[13] C.B. Lee and A.E. Snavely, "Precise and realistic utility functions for user-centric performance analysis of schedulers," in *Proceedings of the 16th International Symposium on High Performance Distributed Computing*, 2007.

[14] L. Chai, Q. Gao, and D.K. Panda, "Understanding the impact of multi-core architecture in cluster computing: A case study with intel dual-core system," in *The 7th IEEE International Symposium on Cluster Computing and the Grid (CCGrid)*, 2007.

[15] T. Leng, R. Ali, J. Hsieh, V. Mashayekhi, and R. Rooholamini, "Performance impact of process mapping on small-scale SMP clusters—A case study using high performance linpack," in *Proceedings of the International Parallel and Distributed Processing Symposium (IPDPS)*, 2002.

[16] D. Li, D.S. Nikolopoulos, K.W. Cameron, B.R. de Supinski, and M. Schulz, "Power-aware MPI task aggregation prediction for high-end computing systems," in *Proceedings of the IEEE Parallel and Distributed Processing Symposium (IPDPS)*, 2010.

[17] J.M. Orduna, F. Silla, and J. Duato, "On the development of a communication-aware task mapping technique," *Journal of Systems Architecture*, 50(4):207–220, 2004.

[18] B.W. Kernighan and S. Lin, "An efficient heuristic procedure for partitioning graphs," *Bell System Technical Journal*, 49:291–308, 1970.

10

Cost Optimization for Scalable Communication in Wireless Networks with Movement-Based Location Management

Keqin Li

10.1 INTRODUCTION

To effectively and efficiently deliver network services to mobile users in a wireless communication network, a key component of the network, that is, a dynamic location management scheme, should be carefully designed, and its cost should be thoroughly analyzed. There are two essential tasks in location management, namely, location update (location registration) and terminal paging (call delivery). Location update is the process for a mobile terminal to periodically notify its current location to a network so that the network can revise the mobile terminal's location profile in a location database. Terminal paging is the process for a network to search a mobile terminal by sending polling signals based on the information of its last reported location so that an incoming phone call can be routed to the mobile terminal.

Both location update and terminal paging consume significant communication bandwidth of a wireless network, battery power of mobile terminals, memory space

Scalable Computing and Communications: Theory and Practice, First Edition. Edited by
Samee U. Khan, Albert Y. Zomaya, and Lizhe Wang.
© 2013 John Wiley & Sons, Inc. Published 2013 by John Wiley & Sons, Inc.

in location registers and databases, and computing time at base stations. Therefore, both location update cost and terminal paging cost should be minimized. However, there is a trade-off between the cost of location update and the cost of terminal paging. More location updates reduce the cost of terminal paging, while insufficient location update increases the cost of terminal paging. A dynamic location management scheme has the capability to adjust its location update and terminal paging strategies based on the mobility pattern and incoming call characteristics of a mobile terminal, such that the combined cost of location update and terminal paging is minimized.

Analysis and minimization of the total location management cost for a single mobile terminal has been studied extensively by many researchers. However, there are two problems in existing research. First, cost of location update (measured by the number of location updates and related to resource consumption in base stations) and cost of terminal paging (measured by the number of cells in a paging area (PA) and related to communication bandwidth) are different in nature and difficult to be unified. Second, cost minimization should be carried out at the network level for multiple heterogeneous mobile terminals which simultaneously exist in a network and share network resources, not just for a single mobile terminal, so that network-wide performance optimization and network scalability can be considered. Hence, the traditional way of finding the best movement threshold that minimizes the total location management cost for a single mobile terminal might not be interesting and might not make much sense.

In this chapter, we consider the problem of cost optimization in wireless communication networks with movement-based location management. Our approach is to minimize the total cost of terminal paging of all mobile terminals with a constraint on the total cost of location update of all mobile terminals and to minimize the total cost of location update with a constraint on the total cost of terminal paging. These problems are formulated as multivariable optimization problems and are solved numerically. This approach allows network administration to freely control one of the total cost of location update and the total cost of terminal paging of all mobile terminals in a wireless network and to minimize the other. (This is not the case for a single mobile terminal, for which the determination of one cost also determines the other.) This is an effective way to handle cost trade-off, as in many other computing and communication systems. Such network-wide cost control and optimization is extremely important for scalable communication in a wireless network when the number of mobile terminals increases. Our approach also eliminates the issue of cost unification of location update and terminal paging since the two kinds of cost are separated. To the best of our knowledge, such cost optimization in an entire wireless communication network with heterogeneous mobile terminals has not been considered before.

The rest of the chapter is organized as follows. In Section 10.2, we provide necessary background information on dynamic location management in wireless communication networks. In Section 10.3, we discuss cost measure and optimization for a single mobile terminal. In Section 10.4, we define and solve the terminal paging cost minimization problem subject to constraint on location update cost. In Section 10.5, we define and solve the location update cost minimization problem subject to constraint on terminal paging cost. In Section 10.6, we present a numerical example. In Section 10.7, we summarize the chapter.

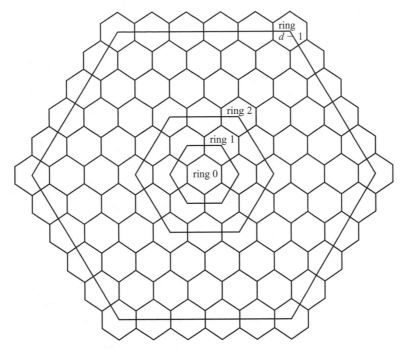

FIGURE 10.1. *The hexagonal cell configuration.*

10.2 BACKGROUND INFORMATION

Our model of a wireless communication network follows that in Reference 1. A wireless communication network has the common hexagonal cell configuration or mesh cell configuration. In the *hexagonal cell structure* (see Fig. 10.1), cells are hexagons of identical size and each cell has six neighbors. In the *mesh cell structure* (see Fig. 10.2), cells are squares of identical size and each cell has eight neighbors. Throughout the chapter, we let q be a constant such that $q = 3$ for the hexagonal cell configuration and $q = 4$ for the mesh cell configuration. By using the constant q, the hexagonal cell configuration and the mesh cell configuration can be treated in a unified way. For instance, we can say that each cell has $2q$ neighbors without mentioning the particular cell structure. The network is homogeneous in the sense that the behavior of a mobile terminal is statistically the same in all the cells.

Let s be the cell registered by a mobile terminal in the last location update. The cells in a wireless network can be divided into rings, where s is the center of the network and is called ring 0. The $2q$ neighbors of s constitute ring 1. In general, the neighbors of all the cells in ring r, except those neighbors in rings $r - 1$ and r, constitute ring $r + 1$. For all $r \geq 0$, the cells in ring r have distance r to s. For all $r \geq 1$, the number of cells in ring r is $2qr$. Notice that the rings are defined with respect to s. When a mobile terminal updates its location to another cell s', s' becomes the center of the network, and ring r consists of the $2qr$ cells whose distance to s' is r.

A mobile terminal u constantly moves from cell to cell. Such movement also results in movement from ring to ring. Let the sequence of cells visited by u before

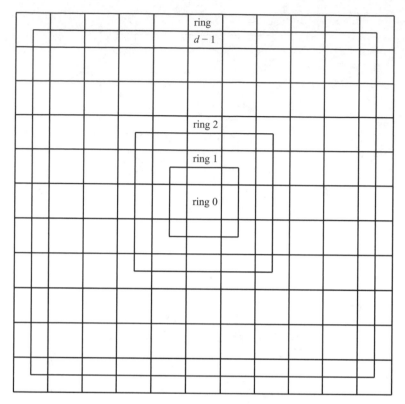

FIGURE 10.2. *The mesh cell configuration.*

the next phone call be denoted as $s_0, s_1, s_2, \ldots, s_d, \ldots$, where $s_0 = s$ is u's last registered cell (not the cell in which u received the previous phone call) and considered as u's current location. There are three location update methods proposed in the current literature, namely, the distance-based method, the movement-based method, and the time-based method.

- In the *distance-based location update method*, location update is performed as soon as u moves into a cell s_j in ring d, where d is a distance threshold; that is, the distance of u from the last registered cell s is d, such that s_j is registered as u's current location. It is clear that $j \geq d$, that is, it takes at least d steps for u to reach ring d.
- In the *movement-based location update method*, location update is performed as soon as u has crossed cell boundaries for d times since the last location update, where d is a movement threshold. It is clear that the sequence of registered cells for u is $s_d, s_{2d}, s_{3d}, \ldots$.
- In the *time-based location update method*, location update is performed every τ units of time, where τ is a time threshold, regardless of the current location of u.

In all dynamic location management schemes, a current PA consists of rings $0, 1, 2, \ldots, d - 1$, where d is some value appropriately chosen. We say that such a PA has radius d. Since the number of cells in ring r is $2qr$, for all $r \geq 1$, the total number of cells in a PA is $qd^2 - qd + 1$. It should be noticed that a PA is defined with respect to the current location of a mobile terminal and is changed whenever a mobile terminal updates its location. The radius d of a PA can be adjusted in accordance with various cost and performance considerations. On the other hand, the location and size of a cell are fixed in a wireless network.

We will consider two different call handling models:

- In the *call plus location update* (CPLU) model, the location of a mobile terminal is updated each time a phone call arrives; that is, in addition to distance-based or movement-based or time-based location updates, the arrival of a phone call also initiates location update and defines a new PA. This causes the original location update cycle of a mobile terminal being interrupted.

- In the *call without location update* (CWLU) model, the arrival of a phone call has nothing to do with location update; that is, a mobile terminal still keeps its original location update cycles.

Our cost analysis and optimization will be conducted for both models.

For a random variable T, we use $E(T)$ to represent the expectation of T and $\lambda_T = E(T)^{-1}$. The probability density function (pdf) of T is $f_T(t)$. There are two important random variables in the study of dynamic location management. The *intercall time* T_c is defined as the length of the time interval between two consecutive phone calls. The *cell residence time* T_s is defined as the time a mobile terminal stays in a cell before it moves into a neighboring cell. The quantity $\rho = \lambda_{T_c} / \lambda_{T_s}$ is the *call-to-mobility ratio*.

The cost of dynamic location management contains two components, that is, the cost of location update and the cost of terminal paging. The cost of location update is proportional to the number of location updates. If there are X_u location updates between two consecutive phone calls, the cost of location update is $\Delta_u X_u$, where Δ_u is a constant. Since X_u is a random variable, the location update cost is actually calculated as $\Delta_u(EX_u)$. The cost of terminal paging is proportional to the number of cells paged. If a PA has radius d, the cost of paging is $\Delta_p(qd^2 - qd + 1)$, where Δ_p is a constant.

Dynamic location management is per-terminal based. A mobile terminal is specified by $f_{T_c}(t)$ and $f_{T_s}(t)$, where $f_{T_c(t)}$ is the call pattern and $f_{T_s(t)}$ is the mobility pattern. Since a location update method determines the location update cost and a terminal paging method determines the terminal paging cost, for given a mobile terminal, we need to find a balanced combination of a location update method and a terminal paging method, such that the total location management cost for the mobile terminal is minimized.

Dynamic location management has been studied extensively by many researchers. The performance of movement-based location management schemes has been investigated in References 2–9. The performance of distance-based location management schemes has been studied in References 3 and 10–14. The performance of time-based location management schemes has been considered in References 3 and 15–17. Terminal paging methods with low cost and time delay have been studied by several researchers [2, 12, 18–22]. Others studied were reported in References 23–32. Dynamic location management in a wireless communication network with a finite number of cells has been treated as an optimization problem that is solved by using bioinspired methods such as simulated annealing, neural networks, and genetic algorithms [33–38]. The reader is also referred to the surveys in References 39–42 (Chapter 15) and 43 (Chapter 11).

10.3   COST MEASURE AND OPTIMIZATION FOR A SINGLE USER

Minimization of total location management cost for a single mobile terminal has been studied extensively. Traditionally, the performance measure for a single mobile user is the cost of location management (including the cost of location update and the cost of terminal paging) between two consecutive phone calls. However, different mobile terminals have different intercall times. Our performance measure in this chapter is the cost of location management per unit of time so that the cost of different users can be added.

In this chapter, we will focus on the movement-based location update method. Our investigation in this chapter is based on our recent work in Reference 1, where we successfully developed closed-form expressions of location update cost for a mobile terminal under both CPLU and CWLU models.

The following theorem gives the cost of location management per unit of time for a single mobile user under the CPLU model.

Theorem 10.1   *If $f_{T_s(t)}$ has an Erlang distribution, the total cost of location management per unit of time under the CPLU model is*

$$M_{CPLU}(d) = \lambda_{T_s} \Delta_u \left(\left(\frac{(\rho)}{2} + 1 \right) \frac{1}{d} + \frac{\rho}{2} \right) + \lambda_{T_c} \Delta_p (qd^2 - qd + 1),$$

where $\rho = \lambda_{T_c}/\lambda_{T_s}$, for any probability distribution $f_{T_c(t)}$.

Proof: It was proven in Reference 1 that if $f_{T_s(t)}$ has an Erlang distribution, the total cost of location management between two consecutive phone calls under the CPLU model is

$$\Delta_u \left(\frac{1}{\rho d} + \frac{d+1}{2d} \right) + \Delta_p (qd^2 - qd + 1),$$

for any probability distribution $f_{T_c(t)}$. Since there are λ_{T_c} phone calls per unit of time, we get the theorem.   ∎

The following theorem gives the cost of location management per unit of time for a single mobile user under the CWLU model.

Theorem 10.2   *The total cost of location management per unit of time under the CWLU model is*

$$M_{CWLU}(d) = \lambda_{T_s} \frac{\Delta_u}{d} + \lambda_{T_c} \Delta_p (qd^2 - qd + 1)$$

for any probability distributions $f_{T_c(t)}$ and $f_{T_s(t)}$.

Proof: It was proven in Reference 1 that for any probability distributions $f_{T_c(t)}$ and $f_{T_s(t)}$, the total cost of location management between two consecutive phone calls under the CWLU model is

$$\frac{\Delta_u}{\rho d} + \Delta_p(qd^2 - qd + 1).$$

Since there are λ_{T_c} phone calls per unit of time, we get the theorem. ∎

Let us consider the derivative of $M_{\mathrm{CPLU}}(d)$ in Theorem 10.1 for the CPLU model:

$$\frac{\partial M_{\mathrm{CPLU}}(d)}{\partial d} = -\lambda_{T_s}\Delta_u\left(\frac{\rho}{2}+1\right)\frac{1}{d^2} + \lambda_{T_c}\Delta_p q(2d-1) = 0;$$

that is,

$$-\Delta_u\left(\frac{\rho+2}{2\rho}\right)1d^2 + \Delta_p q(2d-1) = 0,$$

which yields

$$2d^3 - d^2 - y_{\mathrm{CPLU}} = 0,$$

where

$$y_{\mathrm{CPLU}} = \left(\frac{\rho+2}{2\rho q}\right)\left(\frac{\Delta_u}{\Delta_p}\right).$$

It can be verified that $2d^3-d^2 \geq 0$ if $d \geq 1/2$, and $2d^3 - d^2$ is an increasing function in the range $[1/2, \infty)$. Thus, for $y \geq 0$, there is a unique solution: $d \in [1/2, \infty)$, which satisfies $2d^3-d^2 = y$. Furthermore, $d \geq 1$ if and only if $y \geq 1$. To ensure that there is a solution of $d \geq 1$, we assume that $y_{\mathrm{CPLU}} \geq 1$. The above equation of d can be solved using basic algebra, and the solution is given below. We define a function $g(y)$ as

$$g(y) = \sqrt[3]{\frac{1}{4}\left(y+\left(\frac{1}{54}\right)+\sqrt{y^2+\frac{y}{27}}\right)} + \sqrt[3]{\frac{1}{4}\left(\left(y+\frac{1}{54}\right)-\sqrt{y^2+\frac{y}{27}}\right)} + \frac{1}{6}.$$

We have the following theorem.

Theorem 10.3 *The optimal value of the movement threshold which minimizes $M_{CPLU}(d)$ is either $\lfloor d \rfloor$ or $\lceil d \rceil$, where $d = g(y_{CPLU})$, whichever minimizes $M_{CPLU}(d)$.*

Let us consider the derivative of $M_{\mathrm{CWLU}}(d)$ in Theorem 10.2 for the CWLU model:

$$\frac{\partial M_{\mathrm{CWLU}}(d)}{\partial d} = -\lambda_{T_s}\frac{\Delta_u}{d^2} + \lambda_{T_c}\Delta_p q(2d-1) = 0;$$

that is,

$$-\frac{\Delta_u}{\rho d^2} + \Delta_p q(2d-1) = 0,$$

which yields

$$2d^3 - d^2 - y_{\text{CWLU}} = 0,$$

where

$$y_{\text{CWLU}} = \frac{1}{\rho q}\left(\frac{\Delta_u}{\Delta_p}\right).$$

Again, we assume that $y_{\text{CWLU}} \geq 1$. The above equation of d can be solved using basic algebra, and the solution is given below.

Theorem 10.4   *The optimal value of the movement threshold which minimizes $M_{CWLU}(d)$ is either $\lfloor d \rfloor$ or $\lceil d \rceil$, where where $d = g(y_{CWLU})$, whichever minimizes $M_{CWLU}(d)$.*

10.4   COST OPTIMIZATION WITH LOCATION UPDATE CONSTRAINT

In this section, we consider the terminal paging cost minimization problem with constraint on location update cost.

10.4.1   The CPLU Model

Assume that there are n heterogeneous mobile terminals $u_1, u_2, \ldots, u_n$ in a wireless communication network. Each u_i has $\lambda_{T_c,i}$, $\lambda_{T_s,i}$, $\rho_i = \lambda_{T_c,i}/\lambda_{T_s,i}$, and

$$y_i = \left(\frac{\rho_i + 22}{\rho_i q}\right)\left(\frac{\Delta_u}{\Delta_p}\right),$$

where $1 \leq i \leq n$. We are going to minimize the total cost of terminal paging of all mobile terminals per unit of time, which is defined as a function of $d_1, d_2, \ldots, d_n$; that is,

$$P_{\text{CPLU}}(d_1, d_2, \ldots, d_n) = \Delta_p \sum_{i=1}^{n} \lambda_{T_c,i}(qd_i^2 - qd_i + 1),$$

with a constraint on the total cost of location update of all mobile terminals per unit of time; that is,

$$U_{\text{CPLU}}(d_1, d_2, \ldots, d_n) = \Delta_u \sum_{i=1}^{n} \lambda_{T_s,i}\left(\left(\frac{\rho_i}{2}+1\right)\frac{1}{d_i}+\frac{\rho_i}{2}\right) = \tilde{U},$$

where

$$\frac{1}{2}\Delta_u \sum_{i=1}^{n} \lambda_{T_c,i} = U_1 < \tilde{U} \leq U_2 = \Delta_u \sum_{i=1}^{n} \lambda_{T_s,i}(\rho_i + 1).$$

Notice that the lower bound U_1 for $\tilde{U}$ is the total cost of location update of the n mobile terminals per unit of time when all the d_i's are infinity. The upper bound U_2 for $\tilde{U}$ is the total cost of location update of the n mobile terminals per unit of time when all the d_i's are 1. For mathematical convenience, we treat the d_i's as continuous variables in the range $[1/2, \infty)$.

To minimize $P_{\text{CPLU}}(d_1, d_2, \ldots, d_n)$, we establish a Lagrange multiplier system:

$$\nabla P_{\text{CPLU}}(d_1, d_2, \ldots, d_n) = \alpha \nabla U_{\text{CPLU}}(d_1, d_2, \ldots, d_n),$$

where α is a Lagrange multiplier. The above equation implies that

$$\frac{\partial P_{\text{CPLU}}(d_1, d_2, \ldots, d_n)}{\partial d_i} = \frac{\alpha \partial U_{\text{CPLU}}(d_1, d_2, \ldots, d_n)}{\partial d_i};$$

that is,

$$\Delta_p \lambda_{T_c,i} q(2d_i - 1) = -\alpha \Delta_u \lambda_{T_s,i} \left(\frac{\rho_i}{2} + 1 \right) \frac{1}{d_i^2},$$

for all $1 \le i \le n$. From the last equation, we get

$$2d_i^3 - d_i^2 - Y_i = 0,$$

where

$$Y_i = -\alpha y_i = -\alpha \left(\frac{\rho_i + 2}{2\rho_i q} \right) \left(\frac{\Delta_u}{\Delta_p} \right),$$

which implies that

$$d_i = g(Y_i).$$

Substituting $d_1, d_2, \ldots, d_n$ into the constraint

$$U_{\text{CPLU}}(d_1, d_2, \ldots, d_n) = \tilde{U},$$

we obtain

$$\Delta_u \sum_{i=1}^{n} \lambda_{T_s,i} \left(\left(\frac{\rho_i}{2} + 1 \right) \frac{1}{g(Y_i)} + \frac{\rho_i}{2} \right) = \tilde{U}.$$

What remains to be done is to solve the above equation of α.

It is easy to see that the left-hand side of the last equation is an increasing function of α in the range $(-\infty, 0]$. To find α, we need to find α_1 and α_2, such that α is guaranteed in the range $[\alpha_1, \alpha_2]$. We notice that

$$g(y) > \sqrt[3]{\frac{y}{2}}.$$

Therefore, we have

$$\Delta_u \sum_{i=1}^{n} \lambda_{T_s,i} \left(\left(\frac{\rho_i}{2+1}\right) \frac{1}{g(Y_i)} + \frac{\rho_i}{2} \right) < \Delta_u \sum_{i=1}^{n} \lambda_{T_s,i} \left(\left(\frac{\rho_i}{2}\right) + 1 \sqrt[3]{\frac{2}{Y_i}} + \frac{\rho_i}{2} \right).$$

We further let

$$\Delta_u \sum_{i=1}^{n} \lambda_{T_s,i} \left(\left(\frac{\rho_i}{2+1}\right) \sqrt[3]{\frac{2}{Y_i}} + \frac{\rho_i}{2} \right) = \tilde{U};$$

that is,

$$\Delta_u \sum_{i=1}^{n} \lambda_{T_s,i} \left(\left(\frac{\rho_i}{2+1}\right) \sqrt[3]{-\frac{2}{\alpha} \cdot \frac{2\rho_i q}{\rho_i+2} \cdot \frac{\Delta_p}{\Delta_u}} + \frac{\rho_i}{2} \right) = \tilde{U},$$

or

$$\frac{1}{\sqrt[3]{-\alpha}} \sum_{i=1}^{n} \lambda_{T_s,i} \left(\frac{\rho_i}{2} + 1 \right) \sqrt[3]{\frac{4\rho_i q}{\rho_i+2} \cdot \frac{\Delta_p}{\Delta_u}} = \frac{\tilde{U} - U_1}{\Delta_u}.$$

The last equation implies that if

$$\alpha = \alpha_1 = - \left(\left(\sum_{i=1}^{n} \lambda_{T_s,i} \left(\frac{\rho_i}{2} + 1 \right) \sqrt[3]{4 \frac{\rho_i q}{\rho_i+2} \cdot \frac{\Delta_p}{\Delta_u}} \right) \middle/ \left(\frac{\tilde{U} - U_1}{\Delta_u} \right) \right)^3,$$

we have

$$\Delta_u \sum_{i=1}^{n} \lambda_{T_s,i} \left(\left(\frac{\rho_i}{2} + 1\right) \frac{1}{g(Y_i)} + \frac{\rho_i}{2} \right) < \tilde{U}.$$

We also notice that $g(0) = 1/2 < 1$. Hence, if $\alpha = \alpha_2 = 0$, we have

$$\Delta_u \sum_{i=1}^{n} \lambda_{T_s,i} \left(\left(\frac{\rho_i}{2} + 1\right) \frac{1}{g(Y_i)} + \frac{\rho_i}{2} \right) > U_2 \geq \tilde{U}.$$

The classical bisection method can be employed to search for a numerical solution to α in the range $[\alpha_1, \alpha_2]$.

10.4.2 The CWLU Model

The terminal paging cost minimization problem with constraint on location update cost for the CWLU model is described and solved in a way similar to that for the CPLU model. Each u_i has $\lambda_{T_c,i}$, $\lambda_{T_s,i}$, and $\rho_i = \lambda_{T_c,i}/\lambda_{T_s,i}$. Let

$$y_i = \frac{1}{\rho_i q} \left(\frac{\Delta_u}{\Delta_p} \right).$$

We are going to optimize the total cost of terminal paging of all mobile terminals per unit of time; that is,

$$P_{\text{CWLU}}(d_1, d_2, \ldots, d_n) = \Delta_p \sum_{i=1}^{n} \lambda_{T_c,i}(qd_i^2 - qd_i + 1),$$

subject to the constraint

$$U_{\text{CWLU}}(d_1, d_2, \ldots, d_n) = \Delta_u \sum_{i=1}^{n} \frac{\lambda_{T_s,i}}{d_i} = \tilde{U},$$

where

$$0 = U_1 < \tilde{U} \leq U_2 = \Delta_u \sum_{i=1}^{n} \lambda_{T_s,i}.$$

Notice that the lower bound U_1 is the total cost of location update of the n mobile terminals per unit of time when all the d_i's are infinity. The upper bound U_2 is the total cost of location update of the n mobile terminals per unit of time when all the d_i's are 1.

To minimize $P_{\text{CWLU}}(d_1, d_2, \ldots, d_n)$, we establish a Lagrange multiplier system,

$$\nabla P_{\text{CWLU}}(d_1, d_2, \ldots, d_n) = \alpha \nabla U_{\text{CWLU}}(d_1, d_2, \ldots, d_n),$$

where α is a Lagrange multiplier. The above equation implies that

$$\frac{\partial P_{\text{CWLU}}(d_1, d_2, \ldots, d_n)}{\partial d_i} = \alpha \frac{\partial U_{\text{CWLU}}(d_1, d_2, \ldots, d_n)}{\partial d_i};$$

that is,

$$\Delta_p \lambda_{T_c,i} q(2d_i - 1) = -\alpha \Delta_u \lambda_{T_s,i} \frac{1}{d_i^2},$$

for all $1 \leq i \leq n$. From the last equation, we get

$$2d_i^3 - d_i^2 - Y_i = 0,$$

where

$$Y_i = -\alpha y_i = -\frac{\alpha}{\rho_i q}\left(\frac{\Delta_u}{\Delta_p}\right),$$

which implies that

$$d_i = g(Y_i).$$

Substituting $d_1, d_2, \ldots, d_n$ into the constraint

$$U_{\text{CWLU}}(d_1, d_2, \ldots, d_n) = \tilde{U},$$

we obtain

$$\Delta_u \sum_{i=1}^{n} \frac{\lambda_{T_s,i}}{g(Y_i)} = \tilde{U},$$

which gives an equation of α.

To solve the above equation of α, we need to find α_1 and α_2, such that α is guaranteed in the range $[\alpha_1, \alpha_2]$. By using the fact that $g(y) > \sqrt[3]{y/2}$, we obtain

$$\Delta_u \sum_{i=1}^{n} \frac{\lambda_{T_s,i}}{g(Y_i)} < \Delta_u \sum_{i=1}^{n} \lambda_{T_s,i} \sqrt[3]{\frac{2}{Y_i}}.$$

Let

$$\Delta_u \sum_{i=1}^{n} \lambda_{T_s,i} \sqrt[3]{\frac{2}{Y_i}} = \tilde{U};$$

that is,

$$\Delta_u \sum_{i=1}^{n} \lambda_{T_s,i} \sqrt[3]{-\frac{2\rho_i q}{\alpha} \cdot \frac{\Delta_p}{\Delta_u}} = \tilde{U}.$$

The last equation implies that if

$$\alpha = \alpha_1 = -\left(\Delta_u \tilde{U} \sum_{i=1}^{n} \lambda_{T_s,i} \sqrt[3]{2\rho_i q \cdot \frac{\Delta_p}{\Delta_u}} \right)^3,$$

we have

$$\Delta_u \sum_{i=1}^{n} \frac{\lambda_{T_s,i}}{g(Y_i)} < \tilde{U}.$$

It is clear that if $\alpha = \alpha_2 = 0$, we have

$$\Delta_u \sum_{i=1}^{n} \frac{\lambda_{T_s,i}}{g(Y_i)} > U_2 \geq \tilde{U}.$$

Again, we can use the classical bisection method to search for a numerical solution to α in the range $[\alpha_1, \alpha_2]$.

10.5   COST OPTIMIZATION WITH TERMINAL PAGING CONSTRAINT

We now consider the location update cost minimization problem with constraint on terminal paging cost.

10.5.1 The CPLU Model

Assume that there are n heterogeneous mobile terminals $u_1, u_2, \ldots, u_n$ in a wireless communication network. Each u_i has $\lambda_{T_c,i}$, $\lambda_{T_s,i}$, $\rho_i = \lambda_{T_c,i}/\lambda_{T_s,i}$, and

$$y_i = \left(\frac{\rho_i + 2}{2\rho_i q}\right)\left(\frac{\Delta_u}{\Delta_p}\right),$$

here $1 \le i \le n$. We are going to minimize the total cost of location update of all mobile terminals per unit of time, which is defined as a function of $d_1, d_2, \ldots, d_n$; that is,

$$U_{\mathrm{CPLU}}(d_1, d_2, \ldots, d_n) = \Delta_u \sum_{i=1}^{n} \lambda_{T_s,i}\left(\left(\frac{\rho_i}{2}+1\right)\frac{1}{d_i} + \frac{\rho_i}{2}\right),$$

with a constraint on the total cost of terminal paging of all mobile terminals per unit of time; that is,

$$P_{\mathrm{CPLU}}(d_1, d_2, \ldots, d_n) = \Delta_p \sum_{i=1}^{n} \lambda_{T_c,i}(qd_i^2 - qd_i + 1) = \tilde{P},$$

where

$$\Delta_p \sum_{i=1}^{n} \lambda_{T_c,i} = P_1 \le \tilde{P} < P_2 = \infty.$$

Notice that the lower bound P_1 for $\tilde{P}$ is the total cost of terminal paging of the n mobile terminals per unit of time when all the d_i's are 1. The upper bound P_2 for $\tilde{P}$ is the total cost of terminal paging of the n mobile terminals per unit of time when all the d_i's are infinity.

To minimize $U_{\mathrm{CPLU}}(d_1, d_2, \ldots, d_n)$, we establish a Lagrange multiplier system:

$$\nabla U_{\mathrm{CPLU}}(d_1, d_2, \ldots, d_n) = \beta \nabla P_{\mathrm{CPLU}}(d_1, d_2, \ldots, d_n),$$

where β is a Lagrange multiplier. The above equation implies that

$$\frac{\partial U_{\mathrm{CPLU}}(d_1, d_2, \ldots, d_n)}{\partial d_i} = \beta \frac{\partial P_{\mathrm{CPLU}}(d_1, d_2, \ldots, d_n)}{\partial d_i};$$

that is,

$$-\Delta_u \lambda_{T_s,i}\left(\frac{\rho_i}{2}+1\right)\frac{1}{d_i^2} = \beta \Delta_p \lambda_{T_c,i} q(2d_i - 1),$$

for all $1 \le i \le n$. From the last equation, we get

$$2d_i^3 - d_i^2 - Y_i = 0,$$

where

$$Y_i = -\frac{y_i}{\beta} = -\frac{1}{\beta}\left(\frac{\rho_i+2}{2\rho_i q}\right)\left(\frac{\Delta_u}{\Delta_p}\right),$$

which implies that

$$d_i = g(Y_i).$$

Substituting $d_1, d_2, \ldots, d_n$ into the constraint

$$P_{\text{CPLU}}(d_1, d_2, \ldots, d_n) = \tilde{P},$$

we obtain

$$\Delta_p \sum_{i=1}^{n} \lambda_{T_c,i}\left(q(g(Y_i))^2 - qg(Y_i) + 1\right) = \tilde{P}.$$

What remains to be done is to solve the above equation of β.

It is easy to see that the left-hand side of the last equation is an increasing function of β in the range $(-\infty, 0)$. To find β, we need to find β_1 and β_2, such that β is guaranteed in the range $[\beta_1, \beta_2]$. We notice that

$$g(y) \le \sqrt[3]{y}$$

if $y \ge 1$. Therefore, we have

$$\Delta_p \sum_{i=1}^{n} \lambda_{T_c,i}\left(q(g(Y_i))^2 - qg(Y_i) + 1\right) < \Delta_p \sum_{i=1}^{n} \lambda_{T_c,i}\left(q\sqrt[3]{Y_i^2} + 1\right).$$

We further let

$$\Delta_p \sum_{i=1}^{n} \lambda_{T_c,i}\left(q\sqrt[3]{Y_i^2} + 1\right) = \tilde{P};$$

that is,

$$\Delta_p \sum_{i=1}^{n} \lambda_{T_c,i}\left(q\sqrt[3]{\left(-\frac{1}{\beta}\cdot\frac{\rho_i+2}{2\rho_i q}\cdot\frac{\Delta_u}{\Delta_p}\right)^2} + 1\right) = \tilde{P},$$

or

$$\frac{1}{\sqrt[3]{(-\beta)^2}}\sum_{i=1}^{n} \lambda_{T_c,i}\sqrt[3]{\left(\frac{\rho_i+2}{2\rho_i q}\cdot\frac{\Delta_u}{\Delta_p}\right)^2} = \frac{\tilde{P}-P_1}{q\Delta_p}.$$

The last equation implies that if

$$\beta = \beta_1 = -\left(\left(\sum_{i=1}^{n} \lambda_{T_c,i} \sqrt[3]{\left(\frac{\rho_i + 2}{2\rho_i q} \cdot \frac{\Delta_u}{\Delta_p}\right)^2}\right) \middle/ \left(\frac{\tilde{P} - P_1 q}{\Delta_p}\right)\right)^{3/2},$$

we have

$$\Delta_p \sum_{i=1}^{n} \lambda_{T_c,i} \left(q(g(Y_i))^2 - qg(Y_i) + 1\right) < \tilde{P}.$$

As for β_2, we need to choose β_2, which is sufficiently close to 0, such that

$$\Delta_p \sum_{i=1}^{n} \lambda_{T_c,i} \left(q(g(Y_i))^2 - qg(Y_i) + 1\right) \geq \tilde{P}.$$

Thus, we must have $\beta \in [\beta_1, \beta_2]$, which can be found by using the bisection method.

10.5.2 The CWLU Model

The location update cost minimization problem with constraint on terminal paging cost for the CWLU model is formulated and solved in a way similar to that for the CPLU model. Each u_i has $\lambda_{T_c,i}$, $\lambda_{T_s,i}$, and $\rho_i = \lambda_{T_c,i}/\lambda_{T_s,i}$. Let

$$y_i = \frac{1}{\rho_i q}\left(\frac{\Delta_u}{\Delta_p}\right).$$

We are going to optimize the total cost of location update of all mobile terminals per unit of time; that is,

$$U_{\text{CWLU}}(d_1, d_2, \ldots, d_n) = \Delta_u \sum_{i=1}^{n} \frac{\lambda_{T_s,i}}{d_i},$$

subject to the constraint

$$P_{\text{CWLU}}(d_1, d_2, \ldots, d_n) = \Delta_p \sum_{i=1}^{n} \lambda_{T_c,i}(qd_i^2 - qd_i + 1) = \tilde{P},$$

where

$$\Delta_p \sum_{i=1}^{n} \lambda_{T_c,i} = P_1 \leq \tilde{P} < P_2 = \infty.$$

Notice that the lower bound P_1 is the total cost of terminal paging of the n mobile terminals per unit of time when all the d_i's are 1. The upper bound P_2 is the total cost of terminal paging of the n mobile terminals per unit of time when all the d_i's are infinity.

To minimize $U_{\mathrm{CWLU}}(d_1, d_2, \ldots, d_n)$, we establish a Lagrange multiplier system:

$$\nabla U_{\mathrm{CWLU}}(d_1, d_2, \ldots, d_n) = \beta \nabla P_{\mathrm{CWLU}}(d_1, d_2, \ldots, d_n),$$

where β is a Lagrange multiplier. The above equation implies that

$$\frac{\partial U_{\mathrm{CWLU}}(d_1, d_2, \ldots, d_n)}{\partial d_i} = \beta \frac{\partial P_{\mathrm{CWLU}}(d_1, d_2, \ldots, d_n)}{\partial d_i};$$

that is,

$$-\Delta_u \lambda_{T_s,i} \frac{1}{d_i^2} = \beta \Delta_p \lambda_{T_c,i} q (2d_i - 1),$$

for all $1 \le i \le n$. From the last equation, we get

$$2d_i^3 - d_i^2 - Y_i = 0,$$

where

$$Y_i = -\frac{y_i}{\beta} = -\frac{1}{\beta}\left(\frac{1}{\rho_i q}\right)\left(\frac{\Delta_u}{\Delta_p}\right),$$

which implies that

$$d_i = g(Y_i).$$

Substituting $d_1, d_2, \ldots, d_n$ into the constraint

$$P_{\mathrm{CWLU}}(d_1, d_2, \ldots, d_n) = \tilde{P},$$

we obtain

$$\Delta_p \sum_{i=1}^{n} \lambda_{T_c,i} \left(q(g(Y_i))^2 - q g(Y_i) + 1\right) = \tilde{P},$$

which gives an equation of β.

To solve the above equation of β, we need to find β_1 and β_2, such that β is guaranteed in the range $[\beta_1, \beta_2]$. By using the fact that $g(y) \le \sqrt[3]{y}$, we obtain

$$\Delta_p \sum_{i=1}^{n} \lambda_{T_c,i} \left(q(g(Y_i))^2 - q g(Y_i) + 1\right) < \Delta_p \sum_{i=1}^{n} \lambda_{T_c,i} \left(q\sqrt[3]{Y_i^2} + 1\right).$$

Let

$$\Delta_p \sum_{i=1}^{n} \lambda_{T_c,i} \left(q\sqrt[3]{Y_i^2} + 1\right) = \tilde{P};$$

that is,

$$\Delta_p \sum_{i=1}^{n} \lambda_{T_c,i} \left(q \sqrt[3]{\left(-\frac{1}{\beta} \cdot \frac{1}{\rho_i q} \cdot \frac{\Delta_u}{\Delta_p} \right)^2} + 1 \right) = \tilde{P}.$$

The last equation implies that if

$$\beta = \beta_1 = -\left(\left(\sum_{i=1}^{n} \lambda_{T_c,i} \sqrt[3]{\left(\frac{1}{\rho_i q} \cdot \frac{\Delta_u}{\Delta_p} \right)^2} \right) \middle/ \left(\frac{\tilde{P} - P_1}{q \Delta_p} \right) \right)^{3/2},$$

we have

$$\Delta_p \sum_{i=1}^{n} \lambda_{T_c,i} \left(q (g(Y_i))^2 - q g(Y_i) + 1 \right) < \tilde{P}.$$

As for β_2, we need to choose β_2, which is sufficiently close to 0, such that

$$\Delta_p \sum_{i=1}^{n} \lambda_{T_c,i} \left(q (g(Y_i))^2 - q g(Y_i) + 1 \right) \geq \tilde{P}.$$

A numerical solution to β can be found by using the bisection method.

10.6 NUMERICAL DATA

In this section, we demonstrate numerical data.

We consider $n = 9m$ mobile terminals classified into nine categories:

- few calls with low mobility: $\lambda_{T_c,i} = 1$, $\lambda_{T_s,i} = 10$, $\rho = 0.1$.
- few calls with moderate mobility: $\lambda_{T_c,i} = 1$, $\lambda_{T_s,i} = 30$, $\rho = 0.03$.
- few calls with high mobility: $\lambda_{T_c,i} = 1$, $\lambda_{T_s,i} = 100$, $\rho = 0.01$.
- moderate calls with low mobility: $\lambda_{T_c,i} = 5$, $\lambda_{T_s,i} = 10$, $\rho = 0.5$.
- moderate calls with moderate mobility: $\lambda_{T_c,i} = 5$, $\lambda_{T_s,i} = 30$, $\rho = 0.17$.
- moderate calls with high mobility: $\lambda_{T_c,i} = 5$, $\lambda_{T_s,i} = 100$, $\rho = 0.05$.
- many calls with low mobility: $\lambda_{T_c,i} = 20$, $\lambda_{T_s,i} = 10$, $\rho = 2$.
- many calls with moderate mobility: $\lambda_{T_c,i} = 20$, $\lambda_{T_s,i} = 30$, $\rho = 0.67$.
- many calls with high mobility: $\lambda_{T_c,i} = 20$, $\lambda_{T_s,i} = 100$, $\rho = 0.2$.

The number of mobile terminals in each category is $m = 10$.

We set the parameters Δ_p and Δ_u as $\Delta_p = 1$ and $\Delta_u = 10, 20, 30, 40$.

In Figures 10.3–10.6, we display the impact of location update constraint on terminal paging cost optimization for the CPLU model with $q = 3$ in Figure 10.3, the CWLU model with $q = 3$ in Figure 10.4, the CPLU model with $q = 4$ in Figure 10.5, and the CWLU model with $q = 4$ in Figure 10.6. Each curve shows the terminal paging cost $P_{\text{CPLU}}(d_1, d_2, \ldots, d_n)$ or $P_{\text{CWLU}}(d_1, d_2, \ldots, d_n)$ (divided by 10^4) versus $\tilde{U}$

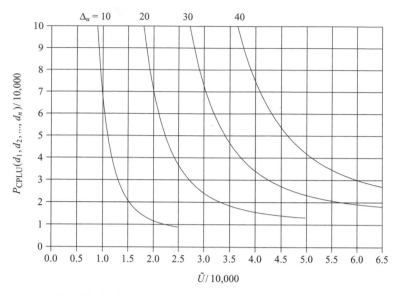

FIGURE 10.3. *Optimization with location update constraint (CPLU, q = 3).*

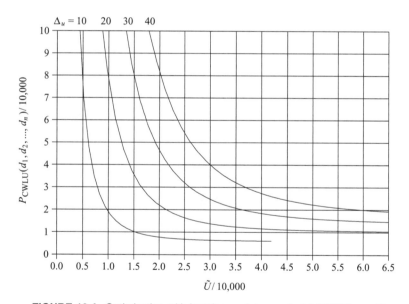

FIGURE 10.4. *Optimization with location update constraint (CWLU, q = 3).*

(divided by 10^4). The interval $[U_1, U_2]$ shifts to the right on the $\tilde{U}$-axis and the length of the interval increases as Δ_u increases. It is observed that in the range $[U_1 + (U_2 - U_1)/3, U_2]$, $P_{\text{CPLU}}(d_1, d_2, \ldots, d_n)$ or $P_{\text{CWLU}}(d_1, d_2, \ldots, d_n)$. increases smoothly as $\tilde{U}$ decreases. However, further reduction of $\tilde{U}$, that is, more location update constraint, causes dramatic increase in $P_{\text{CPLU}}(d_1, d_2, \ldots, d_n)$ or $P_{\text{CWLU}}(d_1, d_2, \ldots, d_n)$ due to the quadratic terminal paging cost.

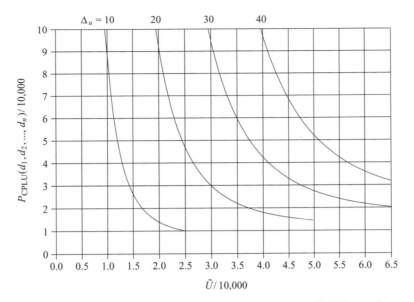

FIGURE 10.5. *Optimization with location update constraint (CPLU, q = 4).*

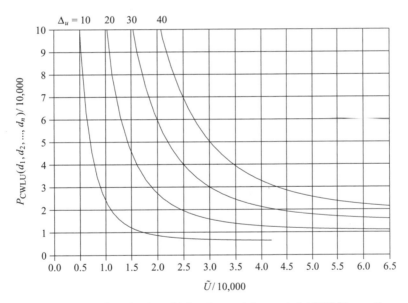

FIGURE 10.6. *Optimization with location update constraint (CWLU, q = 4).*

In Figures 10.7–10.10, we display the impact of terminal paging constraint on location update cost optimization for the CPLU model with $q = 3$ in Figure 10.7, the CWLU model with $q = 3$ in Figure 10.8, the CPLU model with $q = 4$ in Figure 10.9, and the CWLU model with $q = 4$ in Figure 10.10. Each curve shows the location update cost $U_{CPLU}(d_1, d_2, \ldots, d_n)$ or $U_{CWLU}(d_1, d_2, \ldots, d_n)$ (divided by 10^4) versus $\tilde{P}$ (divided by 10^4). It is observed that as \ increases, $U_{CPLU}(d_1, d_2, \ldots, d_n)$ or $U_{CWLU}(d_1, d_2, \ldots, d_n)$ decreases smoothly.

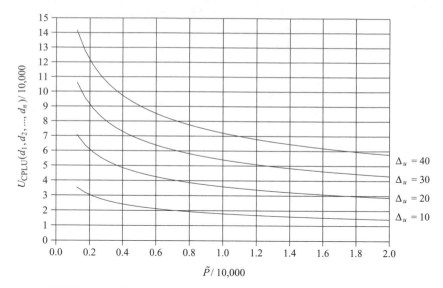

FIGURE 10.7. Optimization with terminal paging constraint (CPLU, $q = 3$).

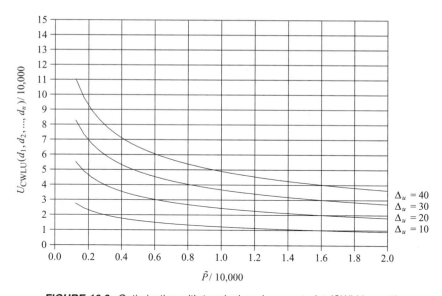

FIGURE 10.8. Optimization with terminal paging constraint (CWLU, $q = 3$).

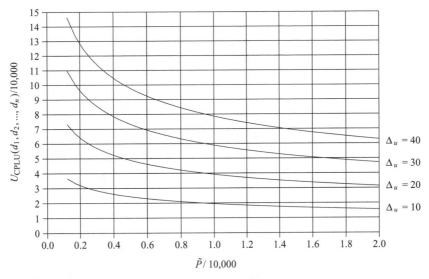

FIGURE 10.9. Optimization with terminal paging constraint (CPLU, q = 4).

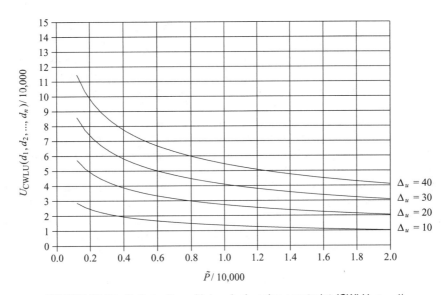

FIGURE 10.10. Optimization with terminal paging constraint (CWLU, q = 4).

10.7   CONCLUDING REMARKS

We have emphasized the motivation and significance of network-wide cost control and optimization for scalable communication in a wireless network with heterogeneous mobile terminals. Our approach is to minimize one of the total cost of location update and the total cost of terminal paging of all mobile terminals in a wireless network by fixing the other. Our cost minimization problems are formulated as multivariable optimization problems and are solved numerically for the CPLU model and the CWLU model. Our approach eliminates the issue of cost unification of location update and terminal paging since the two kinds of cost are separated. The model and method developed in this chapter provide an effective way to handle cost trade-off in large-scale wireless communication networks.

REFERENCES

[1] K. Li, "Cost analysis and minimization of movement-based location management schemes in wireless communication networks: A renewal process approach," *Wireless Networks*, 17(4):1031–1053, 2011.

[2] I.F. Akyildiz, J.S.M. Ho, and Y.-B. Lin, "Movement-based location update and selective paging for PCS networks," *IEEE/ACM Transactions on Networking*, 4:629–638, 1996.

[3] A. Bar-Noy, I. Kessler, and M. Sidi, "Mobile users: To update or not update? " *Wireless Networks*, 1:175–185, 1995.

[4] Y. Fang, "Movement-based mobility management and trade off analysis for wireless mobile networks," *IEEE Transactions on Computers*, 52(6):791–803, 2003.

[5] J. Li, H. Kameda, and K. Li, "Optimal dynamic mobility management for PCS networks," *IEEE/ACM Transactions on Networking*, 8(3):319–327, 2000.

[6] J. Li, Y. Pan, and X. Jia, "Analysis of dynamic location management for PCS networks," *IEEE Transactions on Vehicular Technology*, 51(5):1109–1119, 2002.

[7] Y.-B. Lin, "Reducing location update cost in a PCS network," *IEEE/ACM Transactions on Networking*, 5(1):25–33, 1997.

[8] R.M. Rodríguez-Dagnino and H. Takagi, "Movement-based location management for general cell residence times in wireless networks," *IEEE Transactions on Vehicular Technology*, 56(5):2713–2722, 2007.

[9] Y. Zhang, J. Zheng, L. Zhang, Y. Chen, and M. Ma, "Modeling location management in wireless networks with generally distributed parameters," *Computer Communications*, 29(12):2386–2395, 2006.

[10] A. Abutaleb and V.O.K. Li, "Location update optimization in personal communication systems," *Wireless Networks*, 3(3):205–216, 1997.

[11] V. Casares-Giner and J. Mataix-Oltra, "Global versus distance-based local mobility tracking strategies: A unified approach," *IEEE Transactions on Vehicular Technology*, 51(3):472–485, 2002.

[12] J.S.M. Ho and I.F. Akyildiz, "Mobile user location update and paging under delay constraints," *Wireless Networks*, 1:413–425, 1995.

[13] U. Madhow, M.L. Honig, and K. Steiglitz, "Optimization of wireless resources for personal communications mobility tracking," *IEEE/ACM Transactions on Networking*, 3(12):698–707, 1995.

[14] C.K. Ng and H.W. Chan, "Enhanced distance-based location management of mobile communication systems using a cell coordinates approach," *IEEE Transactions on Mobile Computing*, 4(1):41–55, 2005.

[15] I.F. Akyildiz and J.S.M. Ho, "Dynamic mobile user location update for wireless PCS networks," *Wireless Networks*, 1:187–196, 1995.

[16] F.V. Baumann and I.G. Niemegeers, "An evaluation of location management procedures," in *Proceedings of IEEE International Conference on Universal Personal Communications*, pp. 359–364, 1994.

[17] C. Rose, "Minimizing the average cost of paging and registration: A timer-based method," *Wireless Networks*, 2(2):109–116, 1996.

[18] A. Abutaleb and V.O.K. Li, "Paging strategy optimization in personal communication systems," *Wireless Networks*, 3(3):195–204, 1997.

[19] A. Bar-Noy, Y. Feng, and M.J. Golin, "Paging mobile users efficiently and optimally," in *Proceedings of the 26th IEEE International Conference on Computer Communications*, pp. 1910–1918, 2007.

[20] C. Rose and R. Yates, "Minimizing the average cost of paging under delay constraints," *Wireless Networks*, 1:211–219, 1995.

[21] M. Verkama, "Optimal paging—A search theory approach," in *Proceedings of IEEE International Conference on Universal Personal Communications*, pp. 956–960, 1996.

[22] W. Wang, I.F. Akyildiz, G.L. Stüber, and B.-Y. Chung, "Effective paging schemes with delay bounds as QoS constraints in wireless systems," *Wireless Networks*, 7:455–466, 2001.

[23] I.F. Akyildiz and W. Wang, "A dynamic location management scheme for next-generation multitier PCS systems," *IEEE Transactions on Wireless Communications*, 1(1):178–189, 2002.

[24] T.X. Brown and S. Mohan, "Mobility management for personal communications systems," *IEEE Transactions on Vehicular Technology*, 46(2):269–278, 1997.

[25] E. Cayirci and I.F. Akyildiz, "User mobility pattern scheme for location update and paging in wireless systems," *IEEE Transactions on Mobile Computing*, 1(3):236–247, 2002.

[26] P.G. Escalle, V.C. Giner, and J.M. Oltra, "Reducing location update and paging costs in a PCS network," *IEEE Transactions on Wireless Communications*, 1(1):200–209, 2002.

[27] Y. Fang, "General modeling and performance analysis for location management in wireless mobile networks," *IEEE Transactions on Computers*, 51(10):1169–1181, 2002.

[28] Y. Fang, I. Chlamtac, and Y.-B. Lin, "Potable movement modeling for PCS networks," *IEEE Transactions on Vehicular Technology*, 49(4):1356–1363, 2000.

[29] C. Rose, "State-based paging/registration: A greedy technique," *IEEE Transactions on Vehicular Technology*, 48(1):166–173, 1999.

[30] C.U. Saraydar, O.E. Kelly, and C. Rose, "One-dimensional location area design," *IEEE Transactions on Vehicular Technology*, 49(5):1626–1632, 2000.

[31] G. Wan and E. Lin, "Cost reduction in location management using semi-realtime movement information," *Wireless Networks*, 5:245–256, 1999.

[32] A. Yener and C. Rose, "Highly mobile users and paging: Optimal polling strategies," *IEEE Transactions on Vehicular Technology*, 47(4):1251–1257, 1998.

[33] E. Alba, J. García-Nieto, J. Taheri, and A. Zomaya, "New research in nature inspired algorithms for mobility management in GSM networks," *Lecture Notes in Computer Science*, 4974:1–10, 2008.

[34] R. Subratal and A.Y. Zomaya, "Dynamic location management for mobile computing," *Telecommunication Systems*, 22(1–4):169–187, 2003.

[35] J. Taheri and A.Y. Zomaya, "A simulated annealing approach for mobile location management," *Computer Communications*, 30(4):714–730, 2007.

[36] J. Taheri and A.Y. Zomaya, "A combined genetic-neural algorithm for mobility management," *Journal of Mathematical Modelling and Algorithms*, 6(3):481–507, 2007.

[37] J. Taheri and A.Y. Zomaya, "Clustering techniques for dynamic location management in mobile computing," *Journal of Parallel and Distributed Computing*, 67(4):430–447, 2007.

[38] J. Taheri and A.Y. Zomaya, "Bio-inspired algorithms for mobility management," in *Proceedings of the International Symposium on Parallel Architectures, Algorithms, and Networks*, pp. 216–223, 2008.

[39] I.F. Akyildiz, J. McNair, J.S.M. Ho, H. Uzunalioğlu, and W. Wang, "Mobility management in next-generation wireless systems," *Proceedings of the IEEE*, 87(8):1347–1384, 1999.

[40] N.E. Kruijt, D. Sparreboom, F.C. Schoute, and R. Prasad, "Location management strategies for cellular mobile networks," *IEE Electronics & Communication Engineering Journal*, 10(2):64–72, 1998.

[41] S. Tabbane, "Location management methods for third-generation mobile systems," *IEEE Communications Magazine*, vol. 35, pp. 72–84, 1997.

[42] B. Furht and M. Ilyas, eds., *Wireless Internet Handbook—Technologies, Standards, and Applications*. Boca Raton, FL: CRC Press, 2003.

[43] S.G. Glisic, *Advanced Wireless Networks—4G Technologies*. Chichester, England: John Wiley & Sons, 2006.

11

A Framework for Semiautomatic Explicit Parallelization

Ritu Arora, Purushotham Bangalore, and Marjan Mernik

11.1 INTRODUCTION

With advancement in science and technology, computational problems are growing in size and complexity, thereby resulting in higher demand for high-performance computing (HPC) resources. To keep up with competitive pressure, the demand for reduced time to solution is also increasing, and simulations on high-performance computers are being preferred over physical prototype development and testing. Recent studies have shown that though HPC is gradually becoming indispensable for stakeholders' growth, the programming challenges associated with the development of HPC applications (e.g., lack of HPC experts, learning curve, and system manageability) are key deterrents to adoption of HPC on a massive scale [1, 2]. Therefore, a majority of organizations (in science, technology, and business domains) are stalled at the desktop-computing level. Some of the programming challenges associated with HPC application development are the following:

1. There are multiple parallel programming platforms and hence multiple parallel programming paradigms, each best suited for a particular platform. For example, message-passing interface (MPI) [3] is best suited for developing parallel programs for distributed-memory architectures, whereas OpenMP [4] is widely used for developing applications for shared-memory architectures.

Scalable Computing and Communications: Theory and Practice, First Edition. Edited by Samee U. Khan, Albert Y. Zomaya, and Lizhe Wang.
© 2013 John Wiley & Sons, Inc. Published 2013 by John Wiley & Sons, Inc.

2. It is increasingly difficult to harness the peak performance provided by modern HPC platforms due to the slow rate of advancement in the area of parallel programming environments.

3. Adapting the applications to new architectures is a time-consuming activity because it might require manual retuning, reoptimization, or reimplementation of the application [5].

In light of the aforementioned challenges related to fast-changing, increasingly complex, and diverse computing platforms, key questions that arise are the following:

1. Can we bring scalability and performance to domain experts in the form of parallel computing without any need to learn low-level parallel programming?

2. Can computers automatically generate efficient parallel programs from specifications provided by domain experts?

There is no single silver bullet [6] to alleviate all the complexities associated with the HPC application development process. In our opinion, only through an effective combination of multiple modern software engineering techniques can one attack the challenges associated with the development of HPC applications. Frameworks that enable domain experts to do rapid application development and testing are needed. Such frameworks should not force the domain experts to rewrite their applications and should support code reuse by isolating the commonly occurring computation and communication patterns in parallel applications in the form of abstractions. For example, in all MPI applications, it is required to include the MPI library file, to set up the MPI execution environment, and to terminate the MPI execution environment. All these common steps can be abstracted so that there is no need to write them manually while writing any MPI application. In fact, more involved steps like data distribution and data collection can also be abstracted from the domain experts; this is explained in the rest of the chapter.

11.2 EXPLICIT PARALLELIZATION USING MPI

HPC applications for distributed-memory architectures can be developed using methods of either implicit parallelization or explicit parallelization. Implicit parallelization is achieved by using implicitly parallel languages like X10 [7] and Fortress [8]. Because the parallelism is characteristic of the language itself, the language compiler or interpreter is able to automatically parallelize the computations on the basis of the language constructs used. This method of parallelization allows the programmer to focus on the problem to be solved instead of worrying about the low-level details of how the parallelization is achieved. This method, however, does not leverage from existing legacy applications and entails rewriting of the entire code.

Explicit parallelization is achieved by using specialized libraries for parallelization in conjunction with the programming language of the programmer's choice. With this approach, the programmer inserts the library calls in the existing application at the points where parallelization is desired. Thus, this approach helps the programmer to leverage their existing sequential applications. Though it gives the desired control, flexibility, and performance to the programmers, it also puts the burden on them in terms of time and effort required to parallelize their applications. MPI [3] and OpenMP [4] are the two widely used standards for developing applications for distributed- and shared-memory architectures using the explicit mode of parallelization.

The main focus of our research was to simplify the process of explicit parallelization that is based on MPI [5]. It has been observed that the typical process of developing parallel applications using MPI begins with a working sequential application. The programmers identify concurrency in the existing sequential application and express the same in terms of data or task distribution among the available processes by including MPI routines and making other structural changes to the existing code. The programmers have to explicitly map the tasks to the processors, manually orchestrate the exchange of messages, and be responsible for load balancing and synchronization. The parallel version generated by inserting the MPI routines in the sequential application is further optimized, as per the machine architecture, to obtain maximum efficiency or speedup. The manual optimization of the code might involve several iterations of code changes. Thus, the process of developing, debugging, optimizing, and maintaining MPI-based parallel applications is a challenging task that involves manual, invasive reengineering and handling of low-level message-passing details.

The software development process using MPI involves ad hoc design decisions [5]. There are multiple options available for setting the communication between the processes and each option has certain trade-offs (e.g., synchronous vs. asynchronous), but there are no clear guidelines that can help the programmer choose one option over the other.

There are some mechanical steps for setting up the MPI environment that can be found in every MPI program. Analyses of code samples from diverse domains also shows replicated code constructs for tasks other than setting up the MPI environment [5]. Such commonalities (replicated code constructs) indicate that there is a scope for reducing the effort involved in developing HPC applications by promoting code reuse through frameworks.

A framework called Framework for Synthesizing Parallel Applications (FraSPA) has been developed to mitigate the aforementioned challenges—those associated with using MPI in particular and HPC in general. FraSPA is useful for developing parallel applications without burdening the end user (or domain expert) to learn or use MPI. However, the end users of FraSPA are still required to identify concurrency in their applications and to express the same in a very succinct manner. Therefore, FraSPA employs a user-guided approach to synthesize optimized parallel programs from existing sequential programs. It has been developed using the generative programming [9] approach and can synthesize parallel programs for a wide range of application domains.

11.3 BUILDING BLOCKS OF FRASPA

Besides achieving the immediate goal of supporting the synthesis of parallel applications based on the MPI paradigm, it was required to build the capability to cater to a wide variety of parallel programming paradigms and languages in the future. The ability to add new features or concepts to FraSPA, without having to modify the existing code, was also required. Therefore, FraSPA was designed to have extensibility and flexibility. These two main properties of FraSPA are further explained below:

- *Extensibility.* The property of the framework that allows the user to add extra functionality at a later stage is called extensibility. In context of FraSPA, extensibility is desired so that the support for multiple programming models (e.g., OpenMP and OpenCL) and languages (e.g., Fortran) can be provided in future.
- *Flexibility.* The property of the framework that allows users to compose their own design patterns from the existing components by assembling them in any order is called flexibility. In the context of FraSPA, this means that there is no restriction in the order of specifying the Application Programming Interface (API) for different parallel operations. Also, there is no restriction imposed by FraSPA on the combination of various parallel operations.

A domain-specific language (DSL) [10] was developed so that end users can provide specifications related to parallelization at a high level. DSLs or "little languages" are high-level languages that have limited capability in terms of what they can be used for, but they are highly expressive for the domain for which they are developed. FraSPA converts a sequential application into a parallel one through a powerful combination of a source-to-source compiler (SSC) [9, 11], which is also referred to as a program transformation engine, and concurrency specifications provided by the end user via the DSL developed in this research. This high-level, declarative, and platform-independent DSL is called High-Level Parallelization Language (Hi-PAL) [5].

As shown in Figure 11.1, the Hi-PaL (or *DSL*) code is parsed by the *rule generator* to generate intermediate code. The intermediate code is a set of rules (*generated rules* in Fig. 11.1) that the SSC can comprehend. These rules contain the precise information about the modifications desired by the end user (with respect to parallelization), and the place in the *existing code* where these modifications should take effect. By applying the generated rules and other code components, for example,

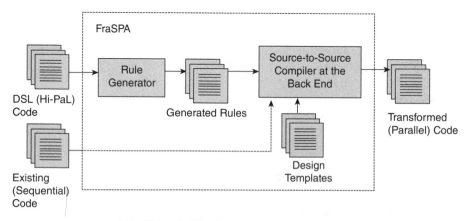

FIGURE 11.1. *High-level architecture of FraSPA.*

design templates, the SSC transforms the existing code into *transformed code*. In this research, both the existing code and the transformed code have the same base language (C/C++). The SSC used in this research is also capable of transforming code written in one language to another (e.g., C to Fortran) [11, 12].

The complete workflow—from parsing of the input Hi-PaL code to generating the transformed code—is part of FraSPA. Hi-PaL serves as the interface between the end user and FraSPA. The end users are only responsible for analyzing their existing applications and for expressing the transformations that they desire (data distribution, data collection, etc.) by the means of Hi-PaL. The other steps responsible for transformations are like a "black box" to them. Thus, the end user is freed from the burden of learning low-level parallel programming.

FraSPA has a three-layered architecture composed of front end, middle layer, and back end. All the layers are decoupled from each other and a description of each of them is as follows:

1. *Front End (Hi-PaL)*. This is the primary interface between the end user and FraSPA. It comprises the abstractions for expressing the specifications for explicit parallelization.
2. *Middle Layer (Rule Generator)*. This layer is not visible to the end user and is used for translating the high-level abstractions obtained from the front end into the intermediate code to be used by the back end.
3. *Back End (SSC)*. This layer is also hidden from the end user and is required for code instrumentation—that is, for inserting the code for parallelization into the existing sequential application on the basis of the intermediate code generated by the middle layer.

The rule generator consists of templates written in Atlas Transformation Language [13] and Ant scripts [14]. The generated rules are specific to the application that the end user wants to parallelize and have the required C/C++/MPI code constructs for parallelization. The code in the rules is in the form of the nodes of abstract syntax tree so that the SSC, without any manual intervention, can analyze and transform the sequential application into a parallel one. The glue code, also written as Ant scripts, is responsible for invoking the SSC and for making the generated (transformed) code available to the end user. A detailed discussion of the middle layer and back end can be found in Reference 12.

The design templates that are a part of FraSPA are codified design patterns for interprocess communication, data distribution, and synchronization. FraSPA automatically selects the best design template during the parallelization process on the basis of the Hi-PaL specifications. The parallel application thus generated can be compiled and run like any manually written parallel application.

The Hi-PaL syntax is influenced by the syntax of aspect-oriented programming (AOP) languages [15]. Similar to AOP languages, even with Hi-PaL, the end user should specify the places in the sequential application, known as hooks, where the changes in the structure or behavior of the code is desired. The definition of the hook should include the specification of hook type and hook element. There are three types of hooks—*before*, *after*, and *around*—and there are three types of hook elements—*statement*, *function call*, and *function execution*. Along with a hook, a search pattern (a statement in the sequential application) is also required. Every syntactically correct statement in a sequential application can qualify as a search pattern in Hi-PaL. The hooks are nothing but anchors in existing sequential applications before, after, or around (implies instead of), which the code for parallelization should be woven. For example, if in a hook definition the hook element is a statement in a program and hook type is *around*, then the program statement serving as a hook will get replaced with code for parallelization.

In addition to the hook, the end user is also required to provide the specifications related to the data mapping in the parallel version of the existing application. The mapping of data arrays to the memories of the processors is known as data mapping. The choice of data mapping can impact the performance of an application [5]. Some examples of the data distribution schemes are block (or linear) and cyclic [16]. In block distribution, each processor gets a contiguous block of data, whereas in cyclic distribution, the assignments are done in a round-robin fashion. For example, if there are two processors (p0, p1), and one has to divide 100 iterations of a for-loop among them using block distribution, then one processor (p0) works on iterations 0–50, and the other processor (p1) works on iterations 51–100. In cyclic distribution, one process (p0) could be working on all even-numbered iterations, whereas the second processor (p1) could be working on all odd-numbered iterations.

In order to succinctly obtain the end-user specifications regarding parallel operations, a set of Hi-PaL API was developed [5, 17]. An excerpt of the Hi-PaL API is shown in Figure 11.2. Also shown in the figure is a brief description associated with each API, that is, the type of MPI routine or the code for parallelization that is

Hi-PaL API	Description
ReduceSumInt(<variable name>)	MPI_Reduce with sum operation
ReduceMinValInt(<variable name>)	MPI_Reduce with min operation
ReduceMaxValInt(<variable name>)	MPI_Reduce with max operation
AllReduceSumInt(<variable name>)	MPI_Allreduce with sum operation
ParDistributeVectorInt(<vector name>, <num of rows>)	MPI_Scatterv to distribute the vector
ParGather2DArrayInt(<array name>, <num of rows>,<num of columns>)	MPI_Gatherv to collect the data
ParBroadCast2DArrayInt(<array name>, <num of rows>, <num of columns>)	MPI_Bcast to broadcast the data
ParExchange2DArrayInt(<array name>,<num of rows>, <num of columns>)	Exchange neighboring values in stencil-based computations
Parallelize_For_Loop where (<for_init_stmt>;<condition>;<stride>)	Parallelize for-loop with matching initialization statement, condition, and stride

FIGURE 11.2. *Excerpt of the Hi-PaL API.* Reprinted with kind permission from Springer Science+ Business Media: R. Arora, P. Bangalore, and M. Mernik, Raising the level of abstraction for developing message passing applications, *The Journal of Supercomputing,* 59(2):1079–1100, 2012.

Parallel section begins after ("t1=gettime();")

   mapping is Linear {

     ParBroadCast2DArrayDouble(popCurrent, M, N)

     after statement ("popCurrent = mutation(popCurrent,..);")

     && in function("main")

   }

FIGURE 11.3. *Sample Hi-PaL code showing the broadcast operation specification.*

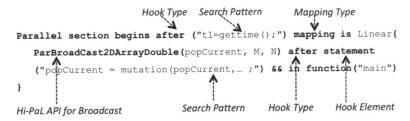

FIGURE 11.4. *Mapping of Hi-PaL code into structural elements.*

associated with the API. The API names are descriptive enough so that the end user can get an idea about their purpose by reading the name. For example, the API, `AllReduceSumInt(<variable name>)`, means that the value of the variable specified by <variable name> is of type integer and it should be collected (or reduced) from all processes, and the global sum of the collected values (MPI_SUM operation) should be returned to all processes.

Figure 11.3 shows a sample program written in Hi-PaL. This sample code demonstrates the method of specifying the broadcast operation on a matrix of type double and named popCurrent in function main. The standard structural elements shown in boldface (e.g., "`Parallel section begins after`") are going to remain the same in all the Hi-PaL programs. By default, the hook element for specifying the beginning of a parallel section is a statement and, therefore, it is not required in the specification. Mapping of the Hi-PaL code in Figure 11.3 to the structural elements of Hi-PaL is shown in Figure 11.4. More examples of the usage of Hi-PaL are presented in Section 11.4.

11.4 EVALUATION OF FRASPA THROUGH CASE STUDIES

The applications generated through FraSPA were evaluated for performance, accuracy, and scalability by comparing them to their manually written counterparts. The framework itself was evaluated for the amount of effort involved in generating applications belonging to various domains. Two test cases (circuit satisfiability and Mandelbrot set) and the experimental setup for evaluating FraSPA are described in this section. The selected test cases had existing sequential and parallel implementations that were written manually in C/C++/MPI. The existing sequential applications were used to embed the code for parallelization such that the generated parallel versions had communication patterns similar to their manually written counterparts. The selected test cases demonstrated that FraSPA is application

TABLE 11.1. Parallel Operations Applied on the Test Cases

Test Case	Parallel Operation	Communication Pattern
Circuit satisfiability	For-loop, reduce sum	Parallel loop
Mandelbrot set	Distribute, gather	Manager–worker

domain neutral, reduces the programmer effort through code reuse, and reduces the application development time by reducing the number of lines of code (LoC) that the programmer has to write.

For parallelizing the applications through FraSPA, the programmers should be familiar with the logic of the corresponding applications, must be aware of the hot spots for parallelization, and must express the specifications for the desired parallelization through Hi-PaL code. The programmer must then specify the places in the sequential application where code insertions need to be performed. A summary of parallel operations applied on the two test cases and the associated communication patterns are presented in Table 11.1. The classification of test cases as per the communication pattern they exhibit is done according to the guidelines provided in Reference 18.

A brief description of some of the patterns codified in FraSPA are as follows:

- *Embarrassingly Parallel.* This pattern describes the concurrent execution of a collection of independent tasks (having no data dependencies). Implementation techniques include parallel loops and manager–worker.
  - *Parallel Loop.* If the computation fits the simplest form of the pattern such that all tasks are of the same size and are known a priori, then they can be computed by using a parallel loop that divides them as equally as possible among the available processors.
  - *Manager–Worker.* Also known as task queue, this pattern involves two sets of processors—manager and worker. There is only one manager that creates and manages a collection of tasks (task queue) by distributing it among the available workers and collecting the results back from them.
- *Mesh.* Also known as "stencil-based computations," this pattern involves a grid of points in which new values are computed for each point in the grid on the basis of the data from the neighboring points in the grid.
- *Pipeline.* This pattern involves the decomposition of the problem into an ordered group of data-dependent tasks. The ordering of tasks does not change during the computation.
- *Replicable.* This pattern involves multiple sets of operations that need to be performed using a global data structure and hence having dependency. The global data are replicated for each set of operations, and after the completion of operations, the results are reduced.

11.4.1 Circuit Satisfiability

This is an embarrassingly parallel application adapted from Michael Quinn's book on parallel programming [19]. The application determines whether a combination of inputs to the circuit of logical gates produces an output of 1 by performing an

```
1.   //other code
2.   low = 0;
3.   high = pow(2, n);
4.   solution_num = 0;
5.   t1 = gettime();
6.   for ( i=low; i<high; i++ ){
7.      //other code
8.      value = circuit_value ( n, bvec );
9.      if ( value == 1 ) {
10.         solution_num = solution_num + 1;
11.         //other code
12.      }
13.   }
14.   t2 = gettime();
```

FIGURE 11.5. *Code snippet from the sequential circuit satisfiability application.*

```
1. Parallel section begins after ("high=pow(2,n);")
   mapping is Linear {
2.   Parallelize_For_Loop where (i=low; i<high; i++)
   after statement ("high=pow(2,n);") && in function ("main");
3.   ReduceSumInt(solution_num) before statement
   ("t2=gettime();") && in function ("main")
4. }
```

FIGURE 11.6. *Hi-PaL code for parallelizing the circuit satisfiability application.*

exhaustive search of all the possible combinations of the specified number of bits in the input. For example, for a circuit having N bits of input, the search space would involve 2^N combinations of the bits or 2^N possibilities. A code snippet from the sequential version of the application is shown in Figure 11.5.

The for-loop on lines 6–13 of Figure 11.5 has computations that can be done in parallel such that the individual results of the computation done on multiple processes can be combined by means of a reduce operation. The programmer expresses the intention of parallelizing the computation in the for-loop beginning at line 6 of Figure 11.5, and collects the results with a reduce operation before line 14 of Figure 11.5 via the Hi-PaL code shown in Figure 11.6. As can be noticed from the code in Figure 11.6, the programmer also specifies the region in the sequential code from where the parallel section should begin, which is after the statement on line 3 of Figure 11.5. In Hi-PaL, the && operator is used to create powerful match expressions that can constrain the code transformation process (see Figure 11.6). If the programmer had not included the constraints on for-loop parallelization (see line 2 of Figure 11.6, after statement (`"high=pow(2,n);"`) && in function (`"main"`)), then every for-loop in the program with matching conditions and stride (`i=low; i<high; i++`) will get parallelized. The code snippet of the generated parallel code is shown in Figure 11.7. Though not shown in the snippet, the code for all the

```
1. //other code. Files included & Variable declaration
   //section extended.
2. low = 0;
3. high = pow(2, n);
4. MPI_Init(NULL, NULL);
5. MPI_Comm_size(MPI_COMM_WORLD, &size_Fraspa);
6. MPI_Comm_rank(MPI_COMM_WORLD, &rank_Fraspa);
7. lower_limit_Fraspa = rank_Fraspa *((high - low).....;
8. upper_limit_Fraspa=((rank_Fraspa==(size_Fraspa - 1))?...;
9. solution_num = 0;
10. t1 = MPI_Wtime();
11. for (i=lower_limit_Fraspa; i<=upper_limit_Fraspa;i++){
12.     value = circuit_value ( n, bvec );
13.     if ( value == 1 ) {
14.         solution_num = solution_num + 1;
15.         //other code
16.     }
17. }
18. MPI_Reduce(&solution_num,&solution_num_Fraspa,...)
19. solution_num = solution_num_Fraspa;
20. t2 = MPI_Wtime();
```

FIGURE 11.7. Code snippet from the generated parallel circuit satisfiability application.

required variables, API, and files to include (e.g., mpi.h and design templates) will be automatically inserted in the generated parallel code.

11.4.2 Mandelbrot Set

The Mandelbrot set is a commonly used example from the domain of complex dynamics and it involves fractals [20]. Generation of this set involves iteratively solving an equation of complex numbers. Any number belonging to the Mandelbrot set is depicted in colors, whereas the numbers that do not belong to the set are colored as white. The code snippet of the sequential version of the Mandelbrot set generation application is shown in Figure 11.8; the Hi-PaL code for parallelizing the same is shown in Figure 11.9; and the generated parallel code is shown on Figure 11.10. This test case involves the distribution and gathering of data in a two-dimensional array, and as can be noticed in Figure 11.10, the generated code has calls to function templates for splitting and gathering the data in the two-dimensional array (lines 35 and 46, respectively).

11.4.3 Evaluation and Experimental Setup

All the experiments for this research were run on a 128-node dual-processor Xeon cluster. Each node in this cluster has 4 GB of RAM and a low-latency InfiniBand network. FraSPA was evaluated according to the following criteria:

```
1.  //other code
2.  N= 1000;
3.  //other code
4.  bigmat = allocarray(bigmat, M+2, N+2);
5.  for(y=0; y < M+2; y++) {
6.    for(x=0; x < N+2; x++) {
7.      bigmat[y][x] = 55;
8.    }
9.  }
10. t1 = gettime();
11. for(y=0; y < M+2; y++) {
12.   for(x=0; x < N+2; x++) {
13.     c.real = ((float) x - 500.0)/250.0;
14.     c.imag = ((float) y - 500.0)/250.0;
15.     color = compute(c, maxiter);
16.     bigmat[y][x]=color;
17.   }
18. }
19. t2=gettime();
```

FIGURE 11.8. *Code snippet of the sequential Mandelbrot set application.*

```
1. Parallel section begins after ("N= 1000;") mapping is
   Linear{
2.  ParDistribute2DArrayInt(bigmat, M, N) before statement
          ("t1=gettime();") && in function ("main");
3.  ParGather2DArrayInt(bigmat, M, N) after statement
          ("t2=gettime();") && in function ("main")
4. }
```

FIGURE 11.9. *Hi-PaL code for parallelizing the Mandelbrot set.*

1. performance and accuracy of the generated versions of the parallel code versus their manually written counterparts
2. the number of LoC that the programmer has to write in C/C++/MPI in order to parallelize an application versus the number of lines of Hi-PaL code the programmer has to write for parallelizing the application
3. the number of LoC that were generated by the framework in order to parallelize the applications.

11.4.4   Results and Analysis

The runtime and speedup of the manually written parallel code was compared with the runtime and speedup of the code generated through the framework. The results

```
1. //other code
2. N= 1000;
3. MPI_Init(NULL, NULL);
4. MPI_Comm_size(MPI_COMM_WORLD, &size_Fraspa);
5. MPI_Comm_rank(MPI_COMM_WORLD, &rank_Fraspa);
6. create_2dgrid(MPI_COMM_WORLD, &comm2d_Fraspa,....);
7. create_diagcomm(MPI_COMM_WORLD, size_Fraspa,...);
8. rowmap_Fraspa.init(M, P_Fraspa, p_Fraspa);
9. colmap_Fraspa.init(N, Q_Fraspa, q_Fraspa);
10. myrows_Fraspa = rowmap_Fraspa.getMyCount();
11. mycols_Fraspa = colmap_Fraspa.getMyCount();
12. M_Fraspa = M;
13. N_Fraspa = N;
14. M = myrows_Fraspa;
15. N = mycols_Fraspa;
16. if (argc != 2) {
17.   printf("Usage: %s <outputfile>\n", argv[0]);
18.   exit(-1);
19. }
20. if ((fp = fopen(argv[1],"w")) == NULL) {
21.   printf("Unable to open file %s for write\n", argv[1]);
22.   exit(-1);
23. }
24. bigmat = allocarray(bigmat, M+2, N+2);
25. for(y=0; y < M+2; y++) {
26.   for(x=0; x < N+2; x++) {
27.     bigmat[y][x] = 55;
28.   }
29. }
30. if (rank_Fraspa == 0)
31. {
32.   bigmat_Fraspa = allocMatrix<int>(bigmat_Fraspa,...);
33.   initMatrix<int>(bigmat_Fraspa,M_Fraspa,N_Fraspa,value);
34. }
35. bigmat = split<int>(bigmat_Fraspa, bigmat, M_Fraspa,...);
36. t1 = MPI_Wtime();
37. for(y=0; y < M+2; y++) {
38.   for(x=0; x < N+2; x++) {
39.     c.real = ((float) x - 500.0)/250.0;
40.     c.imag = ((float) y - 500.0)/250.0;
41.     color = compute(c, maxiter);
42.     bigmat[y][x]=color;
43.   }
44. }
45. t2= MPI_Wtime();
46. bigmat_Fraspa = collect<int>(bigmat, bigmat_Fraspa,....);
47. //other code
```

FIGURE 11.10. Code snippet of the generated parallel Mandelbrot set.

TABLE 11.2. Runtime and Speedup for Circuit Satisfiability Application

	Runtime (s)		Speedup	
Processes	Manual	Generated	Manual	Generated
30	7.706	7.718	27.097	27.055
40	6.073	6.075	34.383	34.372
50	5.077	5.097	41.129	40.967

TABLE 11.3. Runtime and Speedup for Mandelbrot Set Application

	Runtime (s)		Speedup	
Processes	Manual	Generated	Manual	Generated
2	1.8413	1.8437	1.7705	1.7682
5	0.8528	0.8515	3.8227	3.8285
10	0.5207	0.5207	6.2692	6.2692

TABLE 11.4. Performance Comparison of Various Test Cases

Application	Problem Size	Processors	Serial (s)	Parallel Manual (s)	Parallel Generated (s)
Circuit satisfiability	30 input bits	30	208.81	7.70	7.19
Mandelbrot set	10,000 × 10,000	10	3.26	0.52	0.52

TABLE 11.5. Comparing the LoC for Various Test Cases

Application	Serial	Parallel Manual	Hi-PaL	Parallel Generated
Circuit satisfiability	86	102	4	104
Mandelbrot set	93	494	3	515

are shown in Tables 11.2 and 11.3. A summary of the problem size and the execution time for different versions (sequential, manually written parallel, and generated parallel) of all the test cases is presented in Table 11.4. Each application was run on different numbers of processors to test if they are scalable. No significant loss in performance was observed in any test case and the results from the generated version were almost identical to that of the manually written version. A comparison of the number of LoC that the end user has to write when using FraSPA and when developing the parallel application manually is presented in Table 11.5. For all the test cases that we have considered to date, the performance of the generated application is within 5% of that of the manually written application.

11.5 LESSONS LEARNED

FraSPA has helped us find affirmative answers to the questions that were raised in the introduction section. We were able to generate parallel programs that looked similar to their handwritten versions. The performance of the generated parallel programs was impressive and commensurate to the effort spent. The general lessons learnt during the process of developing FraSPA could be useful for building high-level abstractions in future undertakings. We summarize them as follows:

- The end-user interface should be kept intuitive and high level so that the learning curve is not steep. For example, choose API names that are descriptive and closer to the jargon of the problem domain.
- The solution space is constantly evolving. Therefore, the framework should be designed such that new features can be added to it without modifying the existing features/code.
- A framework should not force its end users to modify their applications to conform to any generic interfaces.
- The end user should be able to comprehend the code generated by the framework so that they are able to map their specifications to the generated code and to modify their specifications, if need be, to get improved results.

11.6 RELATED WORK

On the basis of the literature review, a comparison of some of the high-level approaches for raising the level of abstraction of parallel programming is presented in this section. The comparisons are based on the following criteria: approaches that are language based, design pattern based, and those that support separation of sequential and parallelization concerns [5, 15].

Charm++ [21] is an explicit parallel language and adaptive runtime system that is based upon the object-oriented programming paradigm having its roots in C++. The execution model of Charm++ is asynchronous and message-driven (or event-driven). The programmer must decompose the computation into small virtual message-driven processes called chares. The data mapping to processors, fault tolerance, and load balancing is done by the system. The programmer must also write an interface file to provide the methods of the chare object that can be invoked by other chare objects. The language can be used for writing multiple-instruction multiple-data (MIMD) parallel programs for both shared-memory and distributed-memory applications and handles the portability issues really well. This approach provides separation of sequential and parallel concerns and is best suited for applications meant to be written from scratch. A steep learning curve is associated with the usage of Charm++.

Design Patterns and Distributed Process (DPnDP) [22] is a pattern-based system for developing parallel applications. It is extensible, flexible, and demonstrates the advantages of keeping the sequential and parallel concerns separate in an application (and thereby reducing code complexity) while promoting code reuse and correctness. The DPnDP system generates the code skeleton depending upon the parameters (e.g., master–slave pattern and the number of processors) specified by the programmer. The programmer is then required to edit the generated files that contain code skeletons to insert the sequential entry procedures into the skeleton.

The MAP$_3$S system [23] is also an extensible, flexible, and pattern-based system that demonstrates that generative pattern systems can be successfully implemented using the combination of MPI and C. The system uses customization and tuning parameters provided by the programmer to develop efficient parallel code templates. The programmer is also required to provide macros for packing the processing elements into MPI packets. However, low-level specifications, like the maximum size of packet that can be transmitted between the processors or the timing for synchronization, place the burden on the programmer to understand the limitations of the MPI.

SPIRAL [24] is a domain-specific library generation system that generates HPC code for selected domains (such as digital signal processing) using high-level specifications. In SPIRAL, an algorithm is captured at a high level and the executable is generated using rewrite systems. To select an optimal solution for a particular platform, SPIRAL uses a feedback mechanism to explore the solution space (set of candidate solutions).

Catanzaro et al. [25] are developing a set of DSLs for different application domains to simplify the process of developing applications for heterogeneous architectures. Their set of DSLs captures the domain-specific computations (for mesh-based partial differential equation (PDE), physics library PhysBAM, and machine learning), promises to deliver optimized parallel solutions, and seems to be suitable for applications that are to be written from scratch.

MapReduce [26] is a programming model developed at Google that is used for processing and generating large data sets. Programs written using MapReduce are automatically parallelized and executed on distributed-memory machines. The partitioning of the input data, scheduling the program's execution, handling machine failures, and managing the required intermachine communication are all done automatically. MapReduce, therefore, helps the programmers in utilizing the resources of a large distributed system without learning parallel programming.

Out of all the approaches discussed in this chapter, FraSPA is best suited for the scenarios in which the legacy applications already exist and the end users intend to transform these applications to parallelize them. Charm++, DPnDP, MAP$_3$S, and MapReduce are suitable for the scenarios in which the applications are being written from scratch. While FraSPA, Charm++, and many other approaches are application domain neutral, MapReduce has limited functionality because all types of applications cannot be solved by the MapReduce algorithm. MapReduce is best suited for data-parallel applications that process vast amounts of data. Apart from MapReduce, SPIRAL and Catanzaro et al.'s work can also be classified as application domain specific. The approaches that support separation of sequential and parallel concerns to make code maintenance and code reuse easy are Charm++, DPnDP, MAP$_3$S, and FraSPA.

The approaches that are design pattern based are DPnDP, MAP$_3$S, and FraSPA. Compared to DPnDP and MAP$_3$S, FraSPA does not involve any intrusive reengineering of the existing code and the programmer is not required to specify any low-level parameters. Unlike SPIRAL, which generates optimized libraries, FraSPA generates complete parallel applications from existing sequential applications. However, in contrast to SPIRAL, currently, FraSPA does not support architecture-specific optimizations for any particular domain.

Unlike the approach of Catanzaro et al., FraSPA is useful for synthesizing optimized parallel applications in a noninvasive and domain-neutral manner; that is, it can parallelize sequential applications from diverse domains. A single DSL is used to capture the specifications of parallel tasks per se (e.g., reduce data, gather data, and distribute data), and the end users are not required to specify their core computations in conformance to any standard interface.

11.7 SUMMARY

FraSPA brings performance and scalability to domain experts in the form of parallel computing without the need to learn low-level parallel programming or to do intrusive reengineering. FraSPA, therefore, raises the level of abstraction of the scientific application development process. It generates the desired code for parallelization for a wide range of applications using reusable code components, design templates, SSC, DSLs, and glue code. Design templates that are a part of FraSPA promote code reuse and code correctness. It increases programmer productivity in terms of the decrease in the number of LoC written manually. It also reduces the time to solution due to the reusable nature of its code components. FraSPA can be extended to provide support for additional functionality and helps in the incremental development of applications with multiple alternatives.

REFERENCES

[1] E. Joseph, C.G. Willard, D. Shaffer, A. Snell, S. Tichenor, and S. Conway, "Council on competitiveness study of ISVs serving the high performance computing market. Part A—Current market dynamics," 2005. Available at http://www.compete.org.

[2] High Performance Computing Reveal, "Council on Competitiveness and USC-ISI Broad Study of Desktop Technical Computing End Users and HPC," 2008. Available at http://www.compete.org.

[3] MPI Forum, The Message Passing Interface Standard. Available at http://mpi-forum.org.

[4] OpenMP Forum, The OpenMP API specification for parallel programming. Available at http://openmp.org/wp/.

[5] R. Arora, P. Bangalore, and M. Mernik, "Raising the level of abstraction for developing message passing applications," *The Journal of Supercomputing*, 59(2):1079–1100, 2012.

[6] F.P. Brooks, Jr., "No silver bullet essence and accidents of software engineering," *Computer*, 20(4):10–19, 1987.

[7] P. Charles, C. Grothoff, V.A. Saraswat, C. Donawa, A. Kielstra, K. Ebcioglu, C. von Praun, and V. Sarkar, "X10: An object-oriented approach to non-uniform cluster computing," OOPSLA 2005, pp. 519–538.

[8] G. Steele, "Parallel programming and parallel abstractions in fortress," *Functional and Logic Programming, 8th International Symposium, LNCS 3945*, p. 1, 2006.

[9] K. Czarnecki and U. Eisenecker, *Generative Programming: Methods, Tools, and Applications*. New York: Addison-Wesley, 2000. pp. 1–832.

[10] M. Mernik, J. Heering, and A.M. Sloane, "When and how to develop domain-specific languages," *ACM Computing Surveys*, 37(4):316–344, 2005.

[11] I. Baxter, "Design maintenance systems," *Communications of the ACM*, 35(4):73–89, 1992.

[12] S. Roychoudhury, F. Jouault, and J. Gray, "Model-based aspect weaver construction," International Workshop on Language Engineering, 2007, pp. 117–126.

[13] F. Jouault and I. Kurtev, "Transforming Models with ATL," Model Transformations in Practice Workshop at MoDELS, 2005.

[14] Apache Ant. Available at http://ant.apache.org/.

[15] G. Kiczales, J. Lamping, A. Mendhekar, C. Maeda, C. Lopes, J.-M. Loingtier, and J. Irwin, "Aspect-oriented programming," *European Conference on Object-Oriented Programming, Springer-Verlag LNCS 1241*, 1997, pp. 220–242.

[16] C. Koelbel, D. Loveman, R. Schreiber, G. Steele, and M. Zosel, *The High Performance Fortran Handbook*. Cambridge, MA: MIT Press, 1993.

[17] Hi-PaL API. Available at http://www.cis.uab.edu/ccl/index.php/Hi-PaL.

[18] T.G. Mattson, B.A. Sanders, and B.L. Massingill, *A Pattern Language for Parallel Programming*, Addison Wesley Software Patterns Series, 2004.

[19] M. Quinn, *Parallel programming in C with MPI and OpenMP*. New York: McGraw-Hill, 2004.

[20] B. Wilkinson and M. Allen, *Parallel Programming: Techniques and Applications Using Networked Workstations*. Upper Saddle River, NJ: Prentice Hall, 1998.

[21] L.V. Kale and S. Krishnan, "CHARM++: A portable concurrent object oriented system based on C++," *ACM SIGPLAN Notices*, 28(10):91–108, 1993.

[22] D. Goswami, A. Singh, and B.R. Preiss, "Building parallel applications using design patterns," in *Advances in Software Engineering: Topics in Comprehension, Evolution and Evaluation*, pp. 243–265. New York: Springer-Verlag, 2002.

[23] P. Mehta, J.N. Amaral, and D. Szafron, "Is MPI suitable for a generative design-pattern system?" *Parallel Computing*, 32(7-8):616–626, 2006.

[24] M. Puschel, J.M.F. Moura, J. Johnson, D. Padua, M. Veloso, B. Singer, J. Xiong, F. Franchetti, Y.V. Aca Gacic, K. Chen, R.W. Johnson, and N. Rizzolo, "SPIRAL: Code generation for DSP transforms," *IEEE, Special issue on Program Generation, Optimization, and Adaptation*, 93(2):232–275, 2005.

[25] B. Catanzaro, A. Fox, K. Keutzer, D. Patterson, B.-Y. Su, M. Snir, K. Olukotun, P. Hanrahan, and H. Chafi, "Ubiquitous parallel computing from Berkeley, Illinois, and Stanford," *IEEE Micro*, 30(2):41–55, 2010.

[26] J. Dean and S. Ghemawat, "MapReduce: Simplifed data processing on large clusters," *Communications of the ACM*, 51(1):107–113, 2008.

12

Fault Tolerance and Transmission Reliability in Wireless Networks

Wolfgang W. Bein and Doina Bein

12.1 INTRODUCTION: RELIABILITY ISSUES IN WIRELESS AND SENSOR NETWORKS

With the rapid proliferation of networks, be they wired or wireless, a large number of interconnected devices have been deployed unattended to perform various tasks, ranging from monitoring the nation's critical infrastructure to facilitating civilian applications and business collaborations, to providing intelligence for tactical operations. In the military arena, modern warfare practices mandate the rapid deployment of energy-limited units that stay in constant communication with each other, command centers, and supporting systems such as sensor networks, satellites, and unmanned vehicles. Sensors coupled with integrated circuits, known as "smart sensors," provide high sensing from their relationship with each other and with higher-level processing layers. Smart sensors find their applications in a wide variety of fields such as military, civilian, biomedical, and control systems. In military applications, sensors can track troop movements and help decide deployment of troops. In civilian applications, sensors can typically be applied to detect pollution, burglary, fire hazards, and the like. Wireless body sensors (called "biosensors") implanted in the body must be energy-efficient, robust, lightweight, and fault-tolerant, as they are not easily replaceable, repairable, or rechargeable. Biosensors need a dynamic, fault-tolerant network with high reliability. To deliver robust sensor fusion performance,

Scalable Computing and Communications: Theory and Practice, First Edition. Edited by Samee U. Khan, Albert Y. Zomaya, and Lizhe Wang.
© 2013 John Wiley & Sons, Inc. Published 2013 by John Wiley & Sons, Inc.

it is important to dynamically control and optimize the available resources. Network resources that are affected by intermittent or permanent disruptions are the sensors and the network capacity. In this chapter, we thus focus on the following: (1) reliable and fault-tolerant placement algorithms, (2) fault-tolerant backbone construction for communication, and (3) minimization of interference by selective adjustment of the transmission range of nodes.

The nodes in a wireless environment are greatly dependent on battery life and power. But if all sensors deployed within a small area are active simultaneously, an excessive amount of energy is used, redundancy is generated, and packet collision can occur. At the same time, if areas are not covered, events can occur without being observed. A density control function is required to ensure that a subset of nodes is active in such a way that coverage and connectivity are maintained. The term "coverage" refers to the total area currently monitored by active sensors; this must include the area required to be covered by the sensor networks. The term "connectivity" refers to the connectivity of the sensor network modeled as a graph. Minimizing the energy usage of the network while keeping its functionality is a major objective in designing a reliable network. But sensors are prone to failures and disconnection. Only minimal coverage of a given region without redundancy would make such a network unattractive from a practical point of view. Therefore, not only is it necessary to design for minimal coverage but also fault-tolerance features must be viewed in light of the additional sensors and energy used. Fault tolerance is a critical issue for sensors deployed in places where they are not easily replaceable, repairable, or rechargeable. Furthermore, the failure of one node should not incapacitate the entire network. As sensor networks have become commonplace, their reliability and fault tolerance, as well as redundancy and energy efficiency, are increasingly important.

Network communication (wired or wireless) is frequently affected by link or node crashes, temporary failure, congestion (wired), and bandwidth. In an ad hoc environment, the set of immediate or nearer neighbors can change at arbitrary moments of time. In sensor networks, the battery determines the lifetime of a node; a node failure can occur frequently as the node becomes older. Thus, in order to increase the throughput on routing the packets, nodes should use fewer routes (a so-called communication backbone of a network). At the same time, since in an ad hoc or sensor network a node can fail or move somewhere else with high frequency, the selected nodes must be provided with enough redundancy for communication. This is done by them acting as alternative routers, and alternative routes have to be available before crashes affect the communication backbone. Wireless communication is less stable than wired since it depends on the nodes' power levels (which affect the transmission range of individual nodes), though it is more flexible and has lower cost. In a wireless environment, every node u in the transmission range of another node v can receive messages from v and send them to other nodes outside the range of v. Unlike in the wired environment, bidirectional communication is not guaranteed between any pairs of nodes since their communication range is not fixed and can vary also based on node power.

Started as a Defense Advanced Research Projects Agency (DARPA) project, the Sensor Information Technology (SensIT) program focused on decentralized, highly redundant networks to be used in various aspects of daily life. The nodes in sensor networks are usually deployed for specific tasks: surveillance, reconnaissance, disaster relief operations, medical assistance, and the like. Increasing computing and wireless communication capabilities will expand the role of the sensors from mere information dissemination to more demanding tasks such as sensor fusion, classification, and collaborative target tracking. The sensor nodes are generally densely scattered in a sensor field, and there are one or more nodes called sinks (or also initiators), capable of communicating with higher-level networks (Internet, satellites, etc.) or applications. By a dense deployment of sensor nodes, we mean that the nearest neighbor is at a distance much smaller than the transmission range of the node.

In general, a spatial distribution of the sensors is a two-dimensional (2-D) Poisson process. The nodes must coordinate to exploit the redundancy provided when they are densely deployed, to minimize the total energy consumption—thus extending the lifetime of the system overall—and to avoid collisions. Selecting fewer nodes saves energy, but the distance between neighboring active nodes could be too large; thus, the packet loss rate could be so large that the energy required for transmission becomes prohibitive. Energy can be wasted by selecting more nodes, and shared channels will be congested with redundant messages; thus, collision and, subsequently, loss of packets can occur. Therefore, minimizing communication cost incurred in answering a query in a sensor network will result in longer-lasting sensor networks. Communication-efficient execution of queries in a sensor network is of significant interest. Wireless sensor networks provide target sensing, data collection, information manipulation, and dissemination in a single integrated framework. Due to the geographical distribution of sensors in a sensor network, each piece of data generated in a sensor network has a geographic location associated with it in addition to a time stamp. Hence, to specify the data of interest over which query should be answered, each query in a sensor network has a time window and a geographical region associated with it. Given a query in a sensor network, we wish to select a small number of sensors that are sufficient to answer the query accurately and satisfy the conditions of coverage as well as connectivity. Constructing an optimal connected sensor cover for a query enables execution of the query in a very energy-efficient manner as we need to involve only the sensors in the connected sensor cover for processing the query without compromising on its accuracy. When data are sent from one node to the next in a multihop network, there is a chance that a particular packet may be lost, and the odds grow worse as the size of the network increases. When a node sends a packet to a neighboring node and the neighbor has to forward it, the receiving and forwarding processes use energy. The bigger the network, the more nodes that must forward data and the more energy is consumed. The end result is that the network performance degrades. Energy-efficient approaches try to limit the redundancy such that minimum amount of energy is required for fulfilling a certain task. At the same time, redundancy is needed for providing fault tolerance since sensors might be faulty, malfunctioning, or even malicious.

The chapter is organized as follows: Section 12.2 discusses the coverage problem for sensor networks from the fault-tolerance and reliability point of view. We describe two 1-fault-tolerant models, the square and hexagonal, and we compare them with one other, as well as with the minimal coverage model proposed by Zhang and Hou [1]. We describe Markov models for various schemes and give their reliability. Section 12.3 describes schemes to choose a set of nodes called "pivots," from all the nodes in a network, to reduce routing overhead and excessive broadcast redundancy. Section 12.4 focuses on the energy optimization based on the incremental exploration of the network. We perform one-hop neighborhood exploration, but the work can be generalized to two-hop, three-hop, . . . up to the diameter of the network (the *diameter* of a network is the minimum number of hops between any two nodes in the network). We describe various distributed algorithms for self-adjusting the transmission range of nodes in a wireless sensor network. We list a number of open problems and we conclude in Section 12.5.

12.2   RELIABILITY AND FAULT TOLERANCE OF COVERAGE MODELS FOR SENSOR NETWORKS

In this section, we focus on the coverage problem for wireless sensor networks from the fault-tolerance and reliability point of view. We describe two 1-fault-tolerant models, the square and hexagonal. We compare these models with each other and with the minimal coverage model proposed by Zhang and Hou [1], and we give the Markov models for their reliability assuming an exponential time-dependent failure rate.

The section is organized as follows. In Section 12.2.1, we present existing work addressing the coverage problem. In Section 12.2.2, we present the two 1-fault coverage models; we compare them among each other and the minimal coverage model in terms of the model efficiency (the area covered versus the portion of the sensors area used for coverage) and the probability for the model to function. In Section 12.2.3, we design the Markov models for the reliability of each coverage scheme assuming an exponential time-dependent failure rate.

12.2.1   Background

Finding a minimum number of sensors needed to cover a certain area and thus finding patterns for wireless sensor networks that are optimal in the sense of coverage are difficult problems, and few results are available in the literature. In the case where both coverage and connectivity are desired, Zhang and Hou [1] have shown that a regular triangular lattice pattern (also known as "uniform sensing range model") is optimal when the ratio between the communication range and the sensing range, denoted as r_{cs}, is not greater than $\sqrt{3}$. This result can be also found in the work of Kershner [2]. Zhang and Hou [1] also have shown that if the ratio $r_{cs} \geq 2$, then coverage implies connectivity.

For certain fixed values of connectivity, several patterns for coverage have been considered. When a network is sought to have the connectivity of 1, then the strip pattern proposed by Wang et al. [3] was shown by Bai et al. [4] to be asymptotically optimal for any ratio r_{cs}. For the connectivity of 2, a variant of this strip pattern was shown by Bai et al. [4] to be asymptotically optimal. For such a strip pattern, consider two sensors, *a* and *b*, relatively close to each other; that is, the distance between them is larger than the communication range but smaller than twice the communication range. Now if *a* and *b* belong to two consecutive strips, say strips 1 and 2, they can have a long communication path, which may be as large as the number of sensors on a strip. Sensors *a* and *b* communicate using sensors that are at the left or right end of strip 1 and strip 2. Sensor *a* sends the packet toward one end (say, the right end) of strip 1, which is forwarded by each sensor on strip 1 in that direction. The sensor placed at the end of strip 1 then sends the packet to another sensor placed between the ends of the two strips. This sensor, in turn, sends it to end of strip 2, and then finally, it is forwarded from right to left toward sensor b. To shorten such a communication path and to achieve 4-connectivity, Bai et al. [5] have used Voronoi polygons and have proposed a diamond pattern that is asymptotically optimal when the ratio $r_{cs} > \sqrt{2}$. If the ratio $r_{cs} \geq \sqrt{2}$, the diamond pattern is the minimal coverage model. If the ratio $r_{cs} < \sqrt{2}$, the diamond pattern is our proposed square model.

Hunag and Tseng [6] have focused on determining whether each point of a target area is covered by at least k sensors. Zhou et al. [7] have extended the problem further and have considered the selection of a minimum size set of sensor nodes that are connected in such a way that each point inside the target area is covered by at least k sensors. Starting from the minimal coverage model, Wu and Yang [8] have proposed two models in which sensors have different sensing ranges. Variable sensing ranges are novel, and in some cases, the proposed models achieve lower energy when energy consumed by the sensor is proportional to the quadratic power of its transmission range. However, both models are worse than the minimal coverage model in terms of achieving better coverage: The ratios of the two proposed models between the area covered and the sum of areas covered by each sensor—we call this ratio the *efficiency*—are lower than the ratio for the minimal coverage model. Also, the second model proposed in Reference 8 requires (for some sensors) the communication range to be almost four times larger than the sensing range; otherwise, connectivity is not achieved. More precisely, the ratio of the communication range and the coverage range has to be at least $2/\sqrt{2-\sqrt{3}} \approx 3.86$.

Delaunay triangulations have been used extensively for wireless networks, especially for topology control of ad hoc networks (see the work of Hu [9]). As well, Voronoi polygons have been used in ad hoc networks for routing boundary coverage and distributed hashing (see the work of Stojmenovic et al. [10–12]). We also mention that a relay node, also called *gateway* (Gupta and Younis [13]) or *application* node (Pan et al. [14]), acts as cluster head in the corresponding cluster. Hao et al. [15] have proposed a fault-tolerant relay node placement scheme for wireless sensor networks and a polynomial time approximation algorithm that selects a set of active nodes, given the set of all the nodes.

Placing the sensors in a network that provides connectivity, coverage, and fault tolerance is of interest in biomedicine. Schwiebert et al. [16] have described how to build a theoretical artificial retina made up of smart sensors, used for reception and transmission in a feedback system. The sensors produce electrical signals that are subsequently converted by the underlying tissue into chemical signals to be sent to the brain. The fault-tolerance aspect of such a network ensures that, in case a sensor fails, there is no immediate need in replacing the sensor or the entire network for the artificial retina to continue its functionality.

12.2.2 Proposed Fault-Tolerant Models

Two parameters are important for a sensor node: the wireless communication range of a sensor, r_C, and the sensing range, r_S. They generally differ in values, and a common assumption is that $r_C \geq r_S$. Obviously, two nodes, u and v, whose wireless communication ranges are r_{C_u} and r_{C_v}, respectively, can communicate directly if $\text{dist}(u, v) \leq \min(r_{C_u}, r_{C_v})$. Zhang and Hou [1] proved that if all the active sensor nodes have the same radio range r_C and the same sensing range r_S, and the radio range is at least twice of the sensing range $r_C \geq 2 \times r_S$, complete coverage of an area implies connectivity among the nodes. Under this assumption, the connectivity problem reduces to the coverage problem.

There is a trade-off between minimal coverage and fault tolerance. For the same set of sensors, a fault-tolerant model will have a smaller area to cover. Or, given an area to be covered, more sensors will be required, or the same number of sensors but with a higher transmission range. A network is k-fault-tolerant if, by removal of any k nodes, the network preserves its functionality. A k-fault-tolerant network that covers a given region will be able to withstand k removals: By removing any k nodes, the region remains covered. A 0-tolerant network will not function in case some node is removed. To transform a 0-fault-tolerant network into a 1-fault-tolerant network, straightforward approaches are to either double the number of sensors at each point or to double the transmission range of each sensor. Similar actions can be taken to transform a 1-fault-tolerant network into a 2-fault-tolerant one, and so forth.

We present first the square 1-fault-tolerant model. The basic structure for this model is composed of four sensors arranged in a square-like shape of side r and is shown in Figure 12.1. A 2-D region of dimension $(rN) \times (rM)$, with N and M strictly positive integers, requires $(N + 1) \times (M + 1)$ sensors arranged in this pattern.

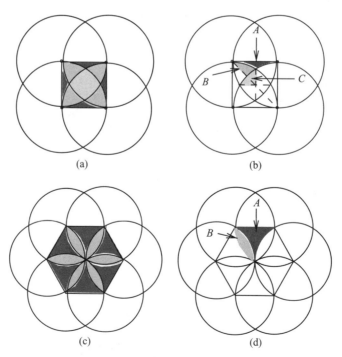

FIGURE 12.1. *The square (a,b) and the hexagonal model (c,d).*

We partitioned the square surface $S_4 = r^2$ into three areas: one area covered by exactly two sensors (S_{2s}^{square}), one area covered by exactly three sensors (S_{3s}^{square}), and one area covered by exactly four sensors (S_{4s}^{square}). To analyze the fault tolerance of such placement, we compute the surface of each such areas. (See Bein et al. [17] for a discussion of methods.) Let A, B, and C be the disjoint areas as drawn in Figure 12.1. We observe that $S_{2s}^{square} = 4S_A$, $S_{3s}^{square} = 8S_B$, and $S_{4s}^{square} = 4S_C$, and we obtain that

$$
\begin{cases}
S_{2s}^{square} = 4r^2 - r^2\sqrt{3} - \dfrac{2\Pi r^2}{3} \\[2mm]
S_{3s}^{square} = -4r^2 + 2r^2\sqrt{3} + \dfrac{\Pi r^2}{3} \\[2mm]
S_{4s}^{square} = r^2 - r^2\sqrt{3} + \dfrac{\Pi r^2}{3}.
\end{cases}
$$

Therefore, given a 2-D region of dimension $(rN) \times (rM)$, the ratio between the sensor area used and the area covered is

$$
\frac{(N+1)(M+1)\Pi r^2}{NMr^2} = \frac{(N+1)(M+1)\Pi}{NM}.
$$

The area covered by two sensors is

$$
NMS_{2s}^{square} = NM\left(4r^2 - r^2\sqrt{3} - \frac{2\Pi r^2}{3} \right).
$$

The area covered by three sensors is

$$
NMS_{3s}^{square} = NM\left(-4r^2 + 2r^2\sqrt{3} + \frac{\Pi r^2}{3} \right).
$$

The area covered by four sensors is

$$
NMS_{4s}^{square} = NM\left(r^2 - r^2\sqrt{3} + \frac{\Pi r^2}{3} \right).
$$

A similar analysis can be done for the hexagonal 1-fault-tolerant model. The basic structure for this model is composed of six sensors arranged in a regular hexagon-like shape of side r and is shown in Figure 12.1. A 2-D region of dimension $(rN) \times (rM)$, with N and M strictly positive integers, requires $2 + 4\lfloor N/2 \rfloor \lfloor 4M/\sqrt{3} \rfloor$ sensors arranged in this pattern.

The hexagonal surface $S_6 = 3\sqrt{3}/2$ is partitioned into two areas: one area covered by exactly two sensors ($S_{2s}^{hexagon}$) and one area covered by exactly three sensors $S_{3s}^{hexagon}$. To analyze the fault tolerance of such placement, we compute the surface of each such areas. (See also Bein et al. [17].) Let A and B be the disjoint areas as drawn in Figure 12.1. We observe that $S_{2s}^{hexagon} = 6S_A$ and $S_{3s}^{hexagon} = 6S_B$, and we obtain that

$$
\begin{cases}
S_{2s}^{hexagon} = \dfrac{9r^2\sqrt{3}}{2} - 2\Pi r^2 \\[2mm]
S_{3s}^{hexagon} = -3r^2\sqrt{3} + 2\Pi r^2.
\end{cases}
$$

TABLE 12.1. Comparisons among the Models

Model	Area	Used	Efficiency	Prob. to Function
Square	r^2	Πr^2	$1/\Pi \approx 0.318$	$(1-p)^2(1+2p-p^2)$
Hexagonal	$3r^2\sqrt{3}/2$	$2\Pi r^2$	$3\sqrt{3}/4\Pi \approx 0.413$	$(1-p)^3(1+3p-2p^3)$
Minimum coverage	$9\sqrt{3}r^2/2$	$3\Pi r^2$	$3\sqrt{3}/2\Pi \approx 0.827$	$(1-p)^7$

Given a 2-D region of dimension $(rN) \times (rM)$, the ratio between the sensor area used and the area covered is

$$\frac{\left(2+4\left\lfloor \frac{N}{2} \right\rfloor \left\lfloor \frac{4M}{\sqrt{3}} \right\rfloor\right)\Pi r^2}{NMr^2} = \frac{\Pi\left(2+4\left\lfloor \frac{N}{2} \right\rfloor \left\lfloor \frac{4M}{\sqrt{3}} \right\rfloor\right)}{NM}.$$

We compare next the minimal coverage model of Zhang and Hou [1] with the two proposed models in terms of the model efficiency (the area covered versus the portion of the sensors area used for coverage) and the probability for the model to function.

Table 12.1 contains comparative results. We use the following notations. The term *area* denotes the area covered by the polygonal line formed by the sensors. The term *used* denotes the portion of the sensor areas used for covering that area. (This value aids in calculating the energy used for covering the region.) This value is obtained by adding for each sensor the portion of its sensor area that covers it. The term *efficiency* denotes the efficiency of using a particular model and is defined as the ratio between the covered area and the portion used. The term *prob. to function* denotes the probability for the model to be functional. Assume that all the sensors, independent of their sensing range, have the probability p to fail, $0 \leq p \leq 1$; thus, the probability to function for the sensor is $1 - p$. Also, we assume that any two failures are independent of one another.

The probabilities to function are obtained as follows. In the case of the minimum coverage model, this network functions only if all sensors are functional; the probability in this case is $(1-p)^7$. Thus, the probability to function is

$$P_{\text{min.cov.}} = (1-p)^7.$$

In the case of the square model, this basic network functions if either all sensors are functional (the probability in this case is $(1-p)^4$) or three sensors are functional and one is not (the probability in this case is $p(1-p)^3$ and is multiplied by the number of such combinations, which is 4), or two diagonally opposed sensors are functional and the other two are not (the probability in this case is $p^2(1-p)^2$ and is multiplied by the number of such combinations, which is 2). The probability to function is

$$P_{\text{square}} = (1-p)^4 + 4p(1-p)^3 + 2p^2(1-p)^2$$
$$= (1-p)^2(1+2p-p^2).$$

In case of the hexagonal model, this basic network functions if either all sensors are functional (the probability in this case is $(1-p)^6$) or five sensors are functional and one is not (the probability in this case is $p(1-p)^5$ and is multiplied by the number of such combinations, which is 6), or two nonconsecutive sensors are not functional and the others are (the probability in this case is $p^2(1-p)^4$ and is multiplied by the number of such combinations, which is 15), or three nonconsecutive sensors are not functional and the others are (the probability in this case is $p^3(1-p)^3$ and is multiplied by the number of such combinations, which is 2). The probability to function is

$$P_{\text{hexa}} = (1-p)^6 + 6p(1-p)^5 + 15p^2(1-p)^4 + 2p^3(1-p)^3$$
$$= (1-p)^2(1+3p+6p^2-8p^3).$$

From Table 12.1 we note that the minimal coverage model has the best efficiency, followed by the hexagonal and square model.

As far as the probability to function, the minimal coverage model has the lowest value. For any value of $p \in [0, 1]$, the square model is better than the hexagonal.

12.2.3 Reliability Function of the Proposed Models

Reliability is one of the most important attributes of a system. Markov modeling is a widely used analytical technique for complex systems [18–20]. It uses system state and state transitions. The state of the system comprises all it needs to be known to fully describe it at any given instant of time [18]. Each state of the Markov model is a unique combination of faulty and nonfaulty modules. There is one state called *F*, which is the failed state (the system does not function anymore). A state transition occurs when one or more modules had failed or had recovered (if possible), and is characterized by probabilities (to fail or to recover).

The *exponential failure law* states that the reliability of a system varies exponentially as a function of time, for a constant failure rate function. The reliability of the system at time *t*, *R(t)*, is an exponential function of the failure rate, λ, which is a constant:

$$R(t) = e^{-\lambda t},$$

where λ is the constant failure rate.

If we assume that each module (in our case, each sensor) in the models we have proposed obeys the exponential failure law and has a constant failure rate of λ, the probability of each module (sensor) being failed at some time $t + \Delta t$, given that the module (sensor) was operational at time *t*, is given by $1 - e^{-\lambda \Delta t}$. For small values of Δt, the expression reduces to $1 - e^{-\lambda \Delta t} \approx \lambda \Delta t$. In other words, the probability that a sensor will fail within the time period Δt is approximately $\lambda \Delta t$.

We make three assumptions that are commonly made in reliability:

1. The system starts with no failures (a perfect state).
2. A failure is permanent: Once a module has failed, it does not recover.
3. There is one failure at a time: Two or more simultaneous failures are seen as sequential ones.

For a generic system state *S*, let $P_S(t)$ be the probability that the system is in state *S* at the moment time *t*. For each state *S*, the probability of the system being in that

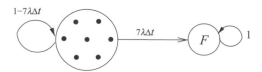

FIGURE 12.2. *Markov model of the min. cov. model.*

state at some time $t + \Delta t$ depends on the probability that the system was in that state S at time t and on any probability that the system was in another state S', and it has transitioned from S' to S.

The minimum coverage model is 0-tolerant: The failure of a single node makes the network nonfunctional. The Markov model is shown in Figure 12.2. The single state in which all seven sensors are operational is named "7." The failed state is named F and is reached when any of the sensors fails. The probability of a sensor to fail within the time interval Δt is $\lambda\Delta t$. Thus, the probability of the system to go from state 7 to state F is the probability of any sensor to fail multiplied by the number of such cases, which is 7. The probability of the system to remain in state 7 is 1 minus the probability of the system to go into any other state. Since state F is the only other state reachable from state 7, the probability of the system to remain in state 7 is $1 - 7\lambda\Delta t$.

The equations of the Markov model of the minimum coverage model can be written from the state diagram shown in Figure 12.2 as follows.

The reliability of the system is the probability of the system to be in any of the nonfailed states $R_{\text{min.cov.}}(t) = 1 - P_F(t) = P_7(t)$. We obtain the system of equations below, with the initial values for $P_7(0) = 1$ and $P_F(0) = 0$. Taking the limit as Δt approaches 0 results in a set of differential equations to which Laplace transformation can be applied. Then, we applied the reverse Laplace transformation:

$$\begin{cases} P_7(t+\Delta t) = (1 - 7\lambda\Delta t)P_7(t) \\ P_F(t+\Delta t) = P_F(t) + 7\lambda\Delta t)P_7(t) \end{cases}$$

$$\Rightarrow \begin{cases} P_7(t) = e^{-7\lambda t} \\ P_F(t) = 1 - 7e^{-7\lambda t} \end{cases}.$$

We obtain the reliability of the system to be $R_{\text{min.cov.}}(t) = e^{-7\lambda t}$.

Now for the square fault-tolerant model. The square fault-tolerant model is 1-fault-tolerant: The system is still functional if a single node fails. If two adjacent nodes fail, the system becomes nonfunctional, but if two diagonally opposite nodes fail, the system remains functional. The Markov model of the square fault-tolerant model is shown in Figure 12.3a. It can be reduced further as follows. The single state in which all four sensors are operational is named "4." The four states in which a single sensor has failed can be reduced to one state named "3." The two states in which two diagonally opposite sensors have failed can be reduced to one state named "2." The reduced Markov model is shown in Figure 12.3b.

The reliability of the system is the probability of the system to be in any of the nonfailed states: $R_{\text{square}}(t) = 1 - P_F(t) = P_4(t) + P_3(t) + P_2(t)$.

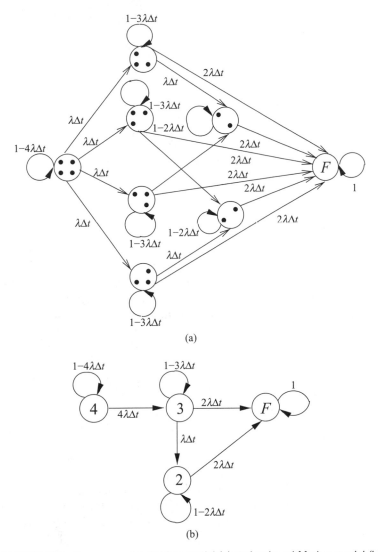

FIGURE 12.3. *Square model: Markov model (a) and reduced Markov model (b).*

The equations of the Markov model of the square fault-tolerant model can be written from the reduced state diagram shown in Figure 12.3b. Taking the limit as Δt approaches 0 results in a set of differential equations to which Laplace transformation can be applied. Then, we applied the reverse Laplace transformation. We obtain the reliability of the system to be $R_{\text{square}}(t) = 2e^{-2\lambda t} - e^{-4\lambda t}$. (See Reference 17 for more details.)

A similar approach for the hexagonal fault-tolerant model gives a Markov model with more than 30 states. We obtain the reliability of the system to be $R_{\text{hexagon}}(t) = 2e^{-3\lambda t} + 3e^{-4\lambda t} - 6e^{-5\lambda t} + 2e^{-6\lambda t}$. (See also Bein et al. [17].)

12.3 FAULT-TOLERANT κ-FOLD PIVOT ROUTING IN WIRELESS SENSOR NETWORKS

In this section, we describe two schemes to choose a set of nodes called pivots, from all the nodes in a network, in order to reduce the routing overhead and excessive broadcast redundancy.

The section is organized as follows. In Section 12.3.1, we present the problem of backbone construction for a given network and present related work in the literature. In Section 12.3.2, we describe an ordering of nodes based on distance values, the notion of k-fold cover t-set, and the two approximation algorithms for constructing covers.

12.3.1 Background

Current research in wireless networks focuses on networks where nodes themselves are responsible for building and maintaining proper routing (self-configure, self-managing). For all the above reasons, hierarchical structures as dominating sets or a link-cluster architecture are not able to provide sufficiently fast redundancy or fault tolerance for high-speed or real-time networks, where the latency in every node should be very short. The time spent at every node to decide how to route messages should be comparable to the time of the propagation delay between neighboring nodes.

Finding the *k-fold* dominating set for an arbitrary graph was suggested for the first time by Kratochvil [21]; the problem is $\mathcal{NP}$-complete (Kratochvil et al. [22]). Liao and Change [23] showed that it is $\mathcal{NP}$-complete for split graphs (a subclass of chordal graphs) and for bipartite graphs. The particular case $k = 1$ is, in fact, the minimum dominating set (MDS) problem, and it is $\mathcal{NP}$-complete for any type of graphs. Approximation algorithms for finding the k-fold dominating set in general graphs were given by Vazirani [24] and Kuhn et al. [25]. The first algorithm for an arbitrary graph of n nodes and the maximum degree of a node Δ by Kuhn et al. [25] runs in $O(t^2)$ and gives an approximation ratio of $O(t\Delta^{2/t} \log \Delta)$ for some parameter t. The second algorithm, for a unit disk graph, is probabilistic and runs in $O(\log \log n)$ time, with an $O(1)$ expected approximation. The k-fold dominating set is related to the k-dominating set [26–28] and to the k-connected k-dominating set [29, 30]. The k-dominating set $D \subseteq V$ has the property that every node in G is not further than $k - 1$ hops from a node in D. Finding the minimum k-dominating set is $\mathcal{NP}$-hard, and a number of approximation algorithms are proposed in References 26 and 27. The k-connected k-dominating set has the property that it is k-connected (i.e., by removing at most $k - 1$ nodes, the graph remains connected, and every node is either in the set or has k immediate neighbors in the set).

The dominating set problem (DS for short) is defined as follows. Given a weighted graph $G = (V, E)$, where each node $v \in V$ has associated a weight w_v, and a positive integer m, $0 < m \leq |V|$, find a subset D of size at most m of nodes in V such that every $v \in V$ is either in D or has at least one immediate neighbor in D, and the sum $\sum_{v \in D} w_v$ is minimized. The corresponding minimization problem is to find the MDS; that is, the size of D is to be minimized. It is approximable within a factor of $1 + \log|V|$ but is not approximable within c for any constant $c > 0$. Generally, the graph G is considered unweighted ($w_v = 1$, for all $v \in V$). DS is a particular case of the k-fold dominating set problem defined formally as follows. Given a weighted graph $G = (V, E)$, where each node $v \in V$ has associated a weight w_v, and two positive integers k and m, $0 < k \leq |V|$ and $0 < m \leq |V|$, find a subset C of size at most m of nodes in V such that every node $v \in V \backslash C$ has at least k immediate neighbors in C, every node in C has at least $k - 1$ immediate neighbors in C, and the sum $\sum_{v \in C} w_v$ is minimized. We refer to the minimization version of the k-fold dominating set problem as k-fold MDS. Note that MDS is thus a particular case of k-fold MDS, where $k = 1$. Not every graph has a k-fold dominating set for some arbitrary k; in that case, it is called *unfolding*.

Obviously, a minimum requirement for a network to have a k-fold dominating set is that $k \leq c$, where c is the network connectivity. A graph has *connectivity* of c if by removing any $1, 2, \ldots, c - 1$ nodes, the graph remains connected. A natural way to minimize the number of nodes in the k-fold dominating set is to select not only nodes from the immediate neighborhood but also nodes located at two or more hops. In this way, we do not only have the nodes in the k-fold cover set D act as a backbone for the communication in the network but they can also take on the role of alternative routers for the entire network. Thus, the network can tolerate up to k node failures without losing the routing infrastructure. A *k-fold cover t-set* (for short, k-fold cover) can be defined as a natural extension of the k-fold dominating set by replacing the term "immediate neighbors" with the term of "nearer neighbors." Given a fixed parameter t, every node v gathers information about its t nearest neighbors (in terms of distance)—the set called the t-ball of v, B_v (Eilam et al. [31]). A set $D \subseteq V$ is a k-fold cover t-set if, for any node v, $|D \cap B_v| \geq k$ (D contains at least k nodes from any t-ball in the network). The elements of D are called *pivots*.

There is a trade-off between selecting a smaller set of nodes and the power consumption of the selected nodes. Maintaining the routing infrastructure to only a subset of nodes reduces the routing overhead and excessive broadcast redundancy. At the same time, to save energy, unused nonbackbone nodes can go into a sleeping mode and wake up only when they have to forward data or have selected themselves in the k-fold cover set due to failure or movement of nodes. Selecting fewer nodes to act as routers has a power consumption disadvantage: The routers will deplete their power faster than the nonrouter nodes. Thus, once the power level of these nodes falls below a certain threshold, those nodes can be excluded as routers, and some other nodes have to replace them.

Two particular cases of the DS problem are the connected dominating set and the weakly connected dominating set. The *connected dominating set* problem requires the set of nodes selected as the dominating set to form a connected subgraph of the original graph. The *weakly connected dominating set* problem, defined by Dunbar et al. [32], requires the subgraph induced by the nodes in the set and their immediate neighbors to form a connected subgraph of the original graph.

12.3.2 Distributed *k*-Fold Pivot *t*-Set

A wireless network, which is a point-to-point communication network, is modeled as a connected, weighted, finite digraph $G = (V, E, w)$ that does not contain multi-arcs or self-loops. The set of processors in the network have unique identification

(ID) and they are represented by a set of nodes V, $|V| = n$. We assume that the unique IDs are a contiguous set $\{1, \ldots, n\}$. Note that the unique ID of nodes induces a total order; thus, for every pair of nodes $u, v \in V$, either $u < v$ or $v < u$. An arc $e = (u, v) \in E$ is a unidirectional communication link that exists if the transmission range of u is large enough for any message sent by u to reach v. Every arc in the network $e = (u, v) \in E$ has associated a weight $w(e)$ that represents the cost (energy) spent by u to transmit a message that will reach v. Because of the nonlinear attenuation property for radio signals, the energy consumption for sending is proportional to at least the square of the power of the transmission range. For simplicity, we extend the domain of w to include all pairs of nodes in the network such that, if node v is not within the transmission range of node u, then $w(u, v) = \infty$.

The wireless channel has a *broadcast* advantage that distinguishes it from the wired channel. When a node p uses an omnidirectional antenna, every transmission by p can be received by all nodes located within its communication range. This notion is called *wireless multicast advantage (WMA)*. Thus, a single transmission from a node u suffices to reach all neighbors of u. Note that for any pair of nodes u and v, $w(u, v)$ is not necessarily equal to $w(v, u)$. Given a simple directed path P in the graph, the length of $|P|$ is the sum of the weights of the arcs of P. The distance $\text{dist}(u, v)$ in G is the length of the shortest path. For every node v, we can order the rest of the nodes in the digraph G with respect to their distance from v, breaking ties by increasing node ID (Eilam et al. [31]): Formally, $x <_v y$ if and only if $\text{dist}(x, v) < \text{dist}(y, v)$ or $\text{dist}(x, v) = \text{dist}(y, v)$ and $x < y$. The *t-ball* of node v, $B_v(t)$, is the ordered set of the first t nodes according to the total order $<_v$. We have (Fact 2.1 from Eilam et al. [31]): If $u \in B_v(t)$, then for every node x on the shortest path from v to u, $u \in B_x(t)$.

Definition 12.1   *Consider a collection $\mathscr{C}$ of subsets of size t of elements from the node set V. Each subset represents the t closest neighbors (in terms of distance) for some node v in V.*

Given a parameter k, $k > 0$, a set D is a k-fold cover t-set for the collection $\mathscr{C}$, or k-fold cover for short, if for every $B \in \mathscr{C}$, D contains at least k elements from B, we write $|B \cap D| \geq k$.

The problem of finding the minimum size k-fold cover set can be modeled as a linear program. Let $y_i \in \{0, 1\}$ be a binary variable associated with some node $i \in \{1, \ldots, n\}$ such that $y_i = 1$ iff node i is in the k-fold cover. The goal is to minimize the sum of all y variables such that in every t-ball of some node i, there are at least k nodes from the k-fold cover, including node i if i is in the cover. In other words, nodes not in the k-fold dominating set have to be covered at least k times, and nodes in the k-fold dominating set have to be covered at least $k - 1$ times. The linear program follows:

$$\min \sum_{i=1}^{n} y_i$$

$$\text{such that} \sum_{j \in B_i(t) \cup \{i\}} y_j \geq k$$

$$y_i = 0 \vee y_i = 1.$$

Next, we present two techniques to approximate a solution for the minimum k-fold cover; one uses a greedy method to select these nodes (so-called pivots), while the second one uses randomization to select them.

Computing the minimum size k-fold cover for any $k \geq 1$ is $\mathcal{NP}$-complete. We extend the two techniques from Awerbuch et al. [33] to generate relatively small k-fold covers for a given collection of sets of a given fixed size t. The first technique (Algorithm *Cover*1) uses a greedy approach to select the nodes. The second technique (Algorithm *Cover*2) selects each node with a certain probability.

Algorithm *Cover*1 starts with the set D to be initially $\varnothing$ and iteratively adds to D an element in V occurring in the most uncovered sets. A set is *covered* if it contains at least k elements, which are also in D. The set D is then called a *greedy k-fold cover* for C. As in Reference 25, the algorithm to be described uses a coloring mechanism (variable c_i of some node i) to distinguish between two types of nodes: (1) *gray* color for nodes that are not in the cover and are covered by at least k nodes in the cover, or nodes that are in the cover and are covered by at least $k - 1$ nodes in the cover, and (2) *white* color for the nodes that are not in the cover and are not covered by k nodes in the cover, and nodes that are in the cover and are not covered by at least $k - 1$ nodes in the cover.

Each node in the graph knows the value of n, the total number of nodes in the graph. Besides c_i, a node i uses a variable x_i, which takes discrete values in the set $\{1/(n-1), 2/(n-1), \ldots, (n-1)/(n-1)\}$. Initially, all the nodes are white, $D = \varnothing$, and all x-values are 0. Each node i sends a value $1/(n-1)$ to all the nodes in its t-ball $B_i(T)$, and the value 0 to the nodes outside its t-ball, excluding itself. There are at most $n + 1$ rounds (where $n = |V|$). In round 0, nodes will collect the values received from all the other nodes, and the sum of all the received values is stored in x_i. For some node i, variable x_i has a discrete value from the set $\{1/(n-1), 2/(n-1), \ldots, (n-1)/(n-1)\}$. The larger the value x_i, the higher is the chance for node i to be selected in set D. In round 1, all nodes with $x_i = (n-1)/(n-1) = 1$ announce themselves as pivots and they add themselves to D. Their x-value is already 1. Some white node i receives these messages and stores the IDs of the pivots that are also in its t-ball $B_i(t)$ in variable D_i. If $|D_i| \geq k$, then node i changes its color to gray. If, at the end of round 1, there are any white nodes, then the algorithm continues with round 2. In round 2, all nodes with $x_i = (n-2)/(n-1)$ announce themselves as pivots, they add themselves to D, and set their x-value to 1. Some white node i receives these messages and adds the IDs of the pivots that are also in its t-ball $B_i(t)$ to variable D_i. If $|D_i| \geq k$, then node i changes its color to gray. At the end of round 2, if there are any white nodes, then the algorithm continues with round 3, and so on. If, at the end of round k, $1 \leq k \leq n - 1$, all nodes are gray, then the algorithm executes the last round, called *terminate*. In round terminate, all nodes not selected in the k-fold cover ($x_i \neq 1$) reset their x-variable to 0.

Lemma 12.1 *Let D be a greedy k-fold cover for $\mathscr{C}$. Then, $|D| < |V| \cdot k \cdot (ln|C| + 1)/t$.*

Algorithm 12.1 Algorithm for *Cover*1
Actions executed at node i
Initialization (Round 0):
    $x_i = 0$
    $c_i = white$

$D_i = \varnothing$
$D = \varnothing$
send the value $1/(n-1)$ to each node in $B_i(t)$ and
the value 0 to each node in $(V\setminus\{i\})\setminus B_i(t)$

$$x_i = \sum_{\text{all } j \neq i} \text{values sent by node } j$$

Round k, $1 \leq k \leq n-1$:
  if $x_i = (n-k)/(n-1)$ then
  $x_i = 1$
  broadcast the message $msg(pivot, i)$ that node i is a pivot
  on receiving $msg(pivot, j)$
  $D \leftarrow D \cup \{j\}$
  if $(j \in B_i(t))$ then $D_i \leftarrow D_i \cup \{j\}$
  if $(|D_i| \geq k) \wedge (x_i = 1 \wedge |D_i| \geq k-1)$ then $c_i = gray$
  if all nodes are gray, then terminate
Round terminate
  if $x_i \neq 1$ then $x_i = 0$

Proof: If D_1 is a simple, greedy cover for $\mathscr{C}$, then $|D_1| < |V|(\ln|\mathscr{C}| + 1)/t$ (Lovasz [34]).
  Selecting an element for a simple cover of $\mathscr{C}$ corresponds to selecting at most k elements for a k-fold cover. Thus, if D is a greedy k-fold cover for $\mathscr{C}$, then $|D| < |V| \cdot k \cdot (\ln|\mathscr{C}| + 1)/t$. ∎

Corollary 12.1 *If D is a k-fold cover constructed by Algorithm Cover1 for G, then $|D| < n \cdot k \cdot (\ln n + 1)/t$.*

Proof: For our collection $\mathscr{C}$, $|\mathscr{C}| = |V| = n$ (one t-set for each node). Thus, a greedy k-fold cover for G will have at most $n \cdot k \cdot (\ln n + 1)/t$ elements. ∎

Given that $|D| \leq n$, one can derive some relationships between k and t from Lemma 12.1 and Corollary 12.1. If k is a constant and given that $t < n$, it follows that $t > k(\ln n + 1)$. Conversely, if t is fixed, that is, there is an upper bound on how many other nodes a node can keep track of, then it follows that $k < t/(\ln n + 1)$. Furthermore, if $D \ll n$, it follows that $t \gg k(\ln n + 1)$ (when k is fixed) and $k \ll t/(\ln n + 1)$ (when t is fixed), respectively.
  For example, consider the network in Figure 12.4 ($n = 10$). Each node has associated a pair (ID_i, r_i), where ID_i is the unique ID of the node taken from the set $\{1, \ldots, n\}$, and r_i is the transmission radius of node i. As a result, the weight of any outgoing arc of i has the same value, which is proportional with r_i^2. Let $t = \lfloor \sqrt{n \cdot ln(n)} \rfloor = 4$ and $k = 3$. Note that the minimum threefold cover is $D_{opt} = \{2, 5, 8, 10\}$. While selecting the t-balls of size 4, ties are broken by node ID. We enumerate the nodes in a t-ball of some node i in nonascending order of its distance with respect to node i. The t-balls for the nodes in the network are $B_1(4) = \{9, 2, 5, 10\}$, $B_2(4) = \{3, 4, 8, 5\}$, $B_3(4) = \{2, 4, 8, 5\}$, $B_4(4) = \{2, 3, 8, 5\}$, $B_5(4) = \{6, 8, 10, 2\}$, $B_6(4) = \{5, 7, 8, 2\}$, $B_7(4) = \{6, 8, 2, 5\}$, $B_8(4) = \{2, 5, 6, 7\}$, $B_9(4) = \{1, 2, 5, 10\}$, $B_{10}(4) = \{2, 5, 8, 9\}$.
  At the end of round 0, all nodes are white (see Fig. 12.5a) and the x-values are $x_1 = 1/9$, $x_2 = 9/9$, $x_3 = x_4 = 2/9$, $x_5 = 9/9$, $x_6 = 3/9$, $x_7 = 2/9$, $x_8 = 7/9$, $x_9 = 2/9$, and $x_{10} = 3/9$. In round 1, nodes 2 and 5 are selected in the threefold cover (marked with

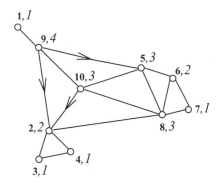

FIGURE 12.4. *Network of* n = 10 *nodes.*

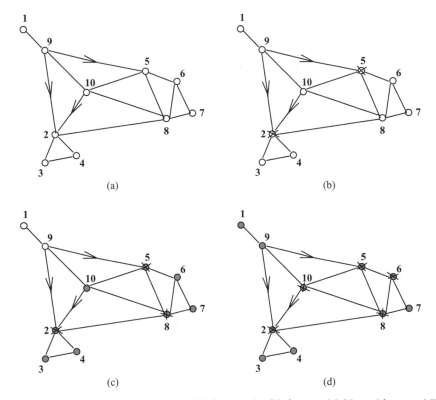

FIGURE 12.5. *End of rounds: for round 0 (a), for round 1 (b), for round 3 (c), and for round 7 (d).*

a cross), and no node becomes gray (see Fig. 12.5b). In round 2, no node is selected. In round 3, node 8 is selected in the threefold cover, and all nodes except 1 and 9 become gray (see Fig. 12.5c). In rounds 4–6, no node is selected. In round 7, nodes 6 and 10 are selected, and all the nodes are gray (see Fig. 12.5d). After round *terminate* executes, the greedy *k*-fold cover is $D = \{2, 5, 6, 8, 10\}$, which has only one extra node (node 6) compared to the optimum threefold cover $D_{\text{opt}} = \{2, 5, 8, 10\}$.

Randomization provides yet another method for building the cover. Algorithm *Cover2* simply selects into D each element of V with the probability $c \cdot k \cdot \ln|\mathcal{C}|$, for some constant $c > 1$. D is called a *randomized k-fold cover* for $\mathcal{C}$.

Algorithm 12.2   Algorithm for *Cover2*
Actions executed at node i
   With the probability $c \cdot k \cdot \ln|\mathscr{C}|$ set $x_i = 1$ else set $x_i = 0$
   If $x_i = 1$ then broadcast *msg(pivot, i)* (node i is a pivot)

Lemma 12.2   *Assuming* $|V| > 2t$ *and* $\ln|\mathscr{C}| = o(t)$, *let D be a randomized k-fold cover for* $\mathscr{C}$. *Then with probability of at least* $1 - 1/|\mathscr{C}|^{c-1}$, *D is a k-fold cover for* $\mathscr{C}$ *and* $|D| < 2c \cdot |V| \cdot k \cdot \ln|\mathscr{C}|/t$, *for some constant* $c > 1$.

Proof: With probability of at least $1 - 1/|\mathscr{C}|^{c-1}$, a randomized, simple cover set D_1 can be constructed for $\mathscr{C}$, and the expected size of the constructed cover is $|D_1| < 2c \cdot |V| \cdot \ln|\mathscr{C}|/t$, for some constant $c > 1$ (Awerbuch et al. [33]).

   Selecting an element for a simple cover of $\mathscr{C}$ corresponds to selecting, at most, k elements for a k-fold cover. Thus, with probability of at least $1 - 1/|\mathscr{C}|^{c-1}$, a randomized k-fold cover D can be constructed for $\mathscr{C}$, and the expected size of D is $|D| < 2c \cdot |V| \cdot k \cdot \ln|\mathscr{C}|/t$.   ∎

Corollary 12.2   *If D is a k-fold cover constructed by Algorithm Cover2 for G, then the expected size of D is* $|D| < 2 \cdot c \cdot n \cdot k \cdot \ln n/t$, *with probability of at least* $1 - 1/|C|^{c-1}$, *for some constant* $c > 1$.

Proof: For our collection $\mathscr{C}$, we have $|\mathscr{C}| = |V| = n$ (one t-set for each node). Thus, the expected size of D is $|D| < 2 \cdot c \cdot n \cdot k \cdot \ln n/t$, with probability of at least $1 - 1/n^{c-1}$.   ∎

From the definition of k-fold cover set, it can simply be observed that if the degree of some node is smaller than k, the k-fold dominating set has no solution. Thus, the degree of one node can compromise the existence of a k-fold cover set.

   But then the k-fold cover set depends less on k and more on t, the number of nodes some node keeps track of. The value of t can vary; it is generally assumed to be more than k. Thus, the k-fold cover set has the advantage that it can be defined for graphs in which the k-fold dominating set cannot be defined. The graph in Figure 12.4 has no threefold dominating set since the degrees of nodes 1, 2, 3, 4, and 7 are less than 3.

   On the other hand, if D is a k-fold dominating set for G, then D is also a k-fold cover t-set for G, provided that $t \geq k$.

12.4   IMPACT OF VARIABLE TRANSMISSION RANGE IN ALL-WIRELESS NETWORKS

In this section, we focus on developing a communication system optimized for sensor networks that require low power consumption and cost. While the sensor itself requires power, we can design the communication system to use as little power as possible so that the system power will be limited by sensors and not by communication.

   The section is organized as follows. In Section 12.4.1, we present work related to reliable communication in wireless sensor networks and the WMA in transmission. In Section 12.4.2, we present the proposed algorithms for adjusting the transmission range (increase or decrease) of selected nodes in the network.

12.4.1 Background

Sankarasubramanian et al. [35] have described wireless sensor networks as event-based systems that rely on the collective effort of several microsensor nodes. Reliable event detection at the sink is based on collective information provided by source nodes and not by any individual report. Conventional end-to-end reliability definitions and solutions are inapplicable in wireless sensor networks. Event-to-sink reliable transport (ESRT) is a novel transport solution developed to achieve reliable event detection in wireless sensor networks with minimum energy expenditure. It includes a congestion control component that serves the dual purpose of achieving reliability and conserving energy. The self-configuring nature of ESRT makes it a robust to random, dynamic topology in wireless sensor networks. It can also accommodate multiple concurrent event occurrences in a wireless sensor field.

Wan et al. [36] have discussed event-driven sensor networks that operate under an idle or light load and then suddenly become active in response to a detected or monitored event. The transport of event pulses is likely to lead to varying degrees of congestion in the network depending on the sensing application. To address this challenge, they proposed an energy-efficient congestion control scheme for sensor networks called congestion detection and avoidance (CODA). *Bursty convergecast* is proposed by Zhang et al. [37] for multihop wireless networks where a large burst of packets from different locations needs to be transported reliably and in real time to a base station.

A sensor network is a collection of sensor nodes equipped with sensing, communication (short-range radio) and processing capabilities. Each node in a sensor network is equipped with a radio transceiver or other wireless communication device, and a small microcontroller. The power for each sensor node is derived from a battery. The energy budget for communication is many times more than computation with the available technology. Figure 12.6 depicts a wireless sensor network.

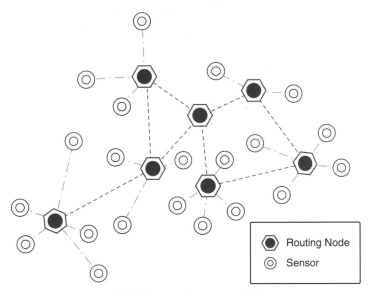

FIGURE 12.6. *Routing in WSN.*

A sensor will be able to communicate with its neighbors over the shared wireless medium but does not have global knowledge of the entire network. The communication is wireless: for example, radio, infrared, or optical media. Due to the large number of nodes and thus the amount of overhead, the sensor nodes may not have any global ID. In some cases, they may carry a global positioning system (GPS). For most of the wireless sensor networks, nodes are not addressed by their IP addresses but by the data they generate. In order to be able to distinguish between neighbors, nodes may have local unique IDs. Examples of such identifiers are 802.11 MAC addresses [38] and Bluetooth cluster addresses [39].

The neighbors of a sensor are defined as all the sensors within its transmission range. The whole network can be viewed as a dynamic graph with time-varying topology and connectivity. Sensor networks have frequently changing topology: Individual nodes are susceptible to sensor failures. The communications between nodes must be performed in a distributed manner.

Let P_{ij} be the minimum power necessary for some node i to transmit one message that will reach some other node j in a single hop. The transmission range of node i is the maximum distance to which another node j can be placed such that a single transmission of node i will reach node j. All nodes within the communication range of a transmitting node can receive its transmission (see Fig. 12.7). A transmission of power $P_1 = P_{ij}$ will reach only node j. A transmission of power $P_2 = \max(P_{ij}, P_{ik})$ will reach both nodes j and k.

The ability to exploit this property of wireless communication is referred to as *WMA*. A crucial issue in wireless networks is the trade-off between the "reach" of wireless transmission and the resulting interference by that transmission.

12.4.2 Algorithms

The sensor nodes start arbitrarily with different transmission ranges. The nodes positions are fixed and can adjust the transmission power. However, increasing the transmission power to reach more nodes may consume more energy. Thus, the goal is to reduce the transmission power (i.e., save energy) of a node without disconnecting the node from the rest of the network. By decreasing the transmission range,

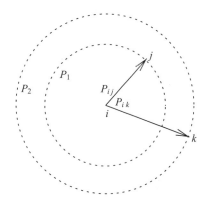

FIGURE 12.7. *The wireless multicast advantage.*

the distance between various sensors may increase; thus, the diameter of the network may increase. A larger diameter implies a higher chance of interference between the neighboring nodes, while a lower diameter implies a higher chance of message duplication (i.e., the same message will be received twice). When two nodes are not in the communication range of each other, there is a chance that both nodes may send the packets to each other at the same time using the same channel. The nodes will not be able to decide by themselves; hence, a collision will occur. This is known as the *hidden terminal problem*.

Let r_i be the transmission range of node i, N_i^1 the one-hop neighborhood of node i, and N_i^2 the set of nodes situated at no more than two hops. The variables N_i^1 and N_i^2 are maintained by an underlying local topology maintenance protocol that adjusts its value in case of topological changes in the network due to failures of nodes or links. There are two objectives:

- *Objective 1.* Reaching more nodes with less increase in power. In the algorithm *Adjust_Range*, each node will virtually increase its transmission range to reach the current two-hop neighbors. In the algorithm *Increase_Range*, each node will virtually double its transmission range. For both algorithms, within each neighborhood (i.e., the node and its one-hop neighbors), the node that reaches the most new nodes will be selected to permanently increase its transmission range.
- *Objective 2.* Reducing the transmission power without losing connectivity in order to save energy. In the algorithm *Decrease_Range*, within each neighborhood, the node that "loses" the least number of nodes when its transmission range is halved and will not become isolated will be selected.

We are now ready to describe the algorithms. If node i decides to extend its transmission range to reach its two-hop neighbors, node i will be able to acquire more nodes in its new one-hop neighborhood. The cost of this increase is measured in terms of how many new nodes can be reached in one hop by this increase in the transmission range. Assume that every node performs this δ increase. Let $N_{i,\delta}^1$ be the one-hop neighborhood of node i obtained by increasing its transmission range from r_i to $r_i + \delta$. The number of new nodes node i reaches is $|N_{i,\delta}^1 \setminus N_i^1|$.

Now we describe the algorithm *Adjust_Range*.

Algorithm 12.3 *Adjust_Range*
For each node i::

Step 1: Calculate N_i^1.

Step 2: Calculate N_i^2.

Step 3: Calculate the transmission range r_i' necessary such that node i will reach its two-hop neighbors.

Calculate the increase in transmission range

$$\Delta r_i = r_i' - r_i.$$

Step 4: Calculate the new set of one-hop neighbors NN_i^1 that are obtained by i increasing its transmission range as specified above.

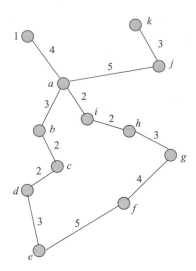

FIGURE 12.8. *A wireless network.*

Step 5: Calculate the ratio

$$NR_i = \frac{\text{increase in transmission range}}{\text{increase in number of nodes}} = \frac{\Delta r_i}{\left| NN_i^1 \backslash N_i^1 \right|}$$

For all $v \in N_i^1$:: Select v_i^* that has the highest NR-value.

The one-hop neighbors are $N_a^1 = \{b, i, j, l\}$, $N_b^1 = \{a, c\}$, $N_c^1 = \{b, d\}$, $N_d^1 = \{c, e\}$, $N_e^1 = \{d, f\}$, $N_f^1 = \{e, g\}$, $N_g^1 = \{f, h\}$, $N_h^1 = \{g, i\}$, $N_i^1 = \{a, h\}$, $N_j^1 = \{a, k\}$, $N_k^1 = \{j\}$, and $N_l^1 = \{a\}$. The two-hop neighbors are $N_a^2 = \{c, h, k\}$, $N_b^2 = \{d, i, j, l\}$, $N_c^2 = \{a\}$, $N_d^2 = \{b, f\}$, $N_e^2 = \{c, g\}$, $N_f^2 = \{h\}$, $N_g^2 = \{e, i\}$, $N_h^2 = \{a, f\}$, $N_i^2 = \{b, g, j, l\}$, $N_j^2 = \{b, i, l\}$, $N_k^2 = \{a\}$, and $N_l^2 = \{b, i, j\}$. Consider the network in Figure 12.8 where the numbers are Euclidean distances between pairs of nodes. Nodes have the following transmission ranges: $r_a = 5, r_b = 3, r_c = 2, r_d = 2, r_e = 5, r_f = 5, r_g = 4, r_h = 3, r_i = 2, r_j = 5, r_k = 3$, and $r_l = 4$.

To reach all its two-hop neighbors, a node will alter its transmission range to r', presented in Table 12.2a. The increase in transmission range Δr and the ratio of increase NR are also presented. In *Adjust_Range*, the node with the smallest NR-value will be selected to increase its transmission range. For the given example, it is node a. If a node increases its transmission range to reach all its two-hop neighbors, there are cases when other nodes that were at three-hop distance or more will become also reachable. For example, when node a increases its transmission range to reach in one hop its two-hop neighbors, the nodes $\{d, g\}$ will be now in one-hop range to node a.

The algorithm *Increase_Range* is described next.

TABLE 12.2. Increasing Transmission Range

(a) Adjusting Range to Reach N^2

	a	b	c	d	e	f	g	h	i	j	k	l
r'	8	8	5	8	9	8	9	7	7	9	8	9
Δr	3	5	3	6	4	3	5	4	5	4	5	5
NR	$\frac{3}{5}$	$\frac{5}{6}$	$\frac{3}{1}$	$\frac{6}{3}$	$\frac{4}{3}$	$\frac{3}{1}$	$\frac{5}{3}$	$\frac{4}{3}$	$\frac{5}{5}$	$\frac{4}{4}$	$\frac{5}{1}$	$\frac{5}{5}$

(b) Doubling Transmission Range

	a	b	c	d	e	f	g	h	i	j	k	l
r'	10	6	4	4	10	10	8	6	4	10	6	8
DR	$\frac{5}{6}$	$\frac{3}{1}$	$\frac{2}{0.1}$	$\frac{2}{1}$	$\frac{5}{4}$	$\frac{5}{4}$	$\frac{4}{2}$	$\frac{3}{1}$	$\frac{2}{0.1}$	$\frac{5}{5}$	$\frac{3}{0.1}$	$\frac{4}{3}$

Algorithm 12.4 *Increase_Range*
For each node i::

Step 1: Calculate N_i^1.

Step 2: Double the transmission range r_i' and calculate the new set of one-hop neighbors DN_i^1 that are obtained by i doubling its transmission range.

Step 3: Calculate the ratio

$$DR_i = \frac{\text{increase in transmission range}}{\text{increase in number of nodes}} = \frac{\Delta r_i}{\left| DN_i^1 \backslash N_i^1 \right|}$$

For all $v \in N_i^1$ :: Select v_i^* that has the highest DR-value.

In Figure 12.8, by doubling the transmission ranges, the ratios of increase are presented in Table 12.2b; the ratio of increase DR is also presented. Node a has the smallest DR-value and will be selected to increase its transmission range.

The algorithm *Decrease_Range* is presented next.

Algorithm 12.5 *Decrease_Range*
For each node i::

Step 1: Calculate N_i^1.

Step 2: Halve the transmission range and calculate the new set of one-hop neighbors HN_i^1 that are obtained by i halving its transmission range.

Step 3: Calculate the ratio

$$HR_i = \frac{\text{decrease in transmission range}}{\text{decrease in the number of nodes}} = \frac{\Delta r_i}{\left| N_i^1 \backslash HN_i^1 \right|}$$

For all $v \in N_i^1$:: Select v^* that has the highest HR-value and does not become isolated, $HN_i^1 \neq \varnothing$.

12.5 CONCLUSIONS AND OPEN PROBLEMS

We have proposed two 1-fault-tolerant models, and we have compared them with one another, and with the minimal coverage model expanded to seven nodes instead of three nodes. We note that the minimal coverage model has the best efficiency followed by the hexagonal and the square model. As far as the probability to function, the minimal coverage model has the lowest value. For any value of $p \in [0, 1]$, the square model is better than the hexagonal model. The most unreliable model among these models is the minimum coverage model; the square model is more reliable than the hexagonal model. Currently, work is on algorithms to move sensors in order to preserve the network functionality when more than one fault occurs. If the network layout is composed of hundreds of patterns (as proposed here), in some cases, sensors need to be moved to cover areas left uncovered by faulty or moving sensors.

Selecting a small set of nodes among all the nodes in a network, and maintaining the routing infrastructure to only a subset of nodes reduces the routing overhead and excessive broadcast redundancy. Since nodes can maintain shortest paths to a small number of other nodes with limited memory, a simple cover set guarantees coverage but not fault tolerance. (A simple cover set guarantees that every node is "covered" by at least one pivot, the nearest one in terms of distance or weight.) By imposing that every node should be covered by at least k pivots, we guarantee an f-fault-tolerant communication, where $f = \min(k, c)$, c being the network connectivity. An important difference between the k-fold MDS and the k-fold cover is that we can extend the range of searching for a pivot. Pivots are not necessarily selected among the immediate neighbors but from a larger neighborhood further away, thus allowing smaller subsets and a better chance of stability when an event affects an entire region of nodes. The relationship between the size of the k-fold cover set and the k-fold dominating set is still open. We conjecture that the size of the k-fold cover set is no greater than the size of the k-fold dominating set.

We name the principles used in the energy optimization method described here on the *incremental exploration of the network*. We perform one-hop neighborhood exploration, but the principle can be easily generalized to two-hop, three-hop, . . . up to the diameter of the network. The three algorithms proposed vary the transmission radii of selective sensor nodes to lower the energy spent in broadcasting or the diameter. So, the goal is to reduce the transmission power (i.e., save energy) without reducing the reachability (in terms of the number of nodes). We have proposed algorithms that increase or decrease the transmission range of nodes. Increasing the transmission range of selective nodes will lower the diameter but will increase the total energy. The ratio of the increase in the transmission range to the increase in the number of nodes is calculated for every sensor node, and the node with the smallest ratio will be selected to increase its transmission range. Decreasing the transmission range will lower the total energy but will increase the diameter of the network. Also, a larger diameter implies a higher chance of interference between the neighboring nodes. The ratio of the decrease in the transmission range to the decrease in the number of nodes is calculated for every node, and the node with the highest ratio is selected to decrease its transmission range. Details on variable transmission range beyond the presentation of this book chapter can be found in Reference 40. When two nodes are in not in the communication range of each other, there is a probability that both the nodes send the packets to each other at the same time using the same channel. The nodes will not be able to decide by themselves; hence, a collision will occur (hidden terminal problem). A lower diameter also implies a higher chance of message duplication; that is, the same message will be received twice. Though in our experiments we have modified the transmission range of a single node in the network, we have described our algorithms in terms of selecting nodes from individual neighborhoods. A *neighborhood* is a node together with its neighbors. Also, experiments were conducted in 2-D Euclidean space. The three algorithms can be applied to graphs using three-dimensional Euclidean metrics. In fact, our algorithms can be applied to general graphs in which the distance between two nodes is an arbitrary positive value.

A venue to be explored in adjusting the transmission range of selective nodes is to apply a load balancing algorithm to either the entire network or to the neighborhood surrounding these selective nodes. It will be interesting to find out whether the structure of the network (e.g., a specific pattern) has influence on the algorithmic procedure of adjusting the transmission range.

REFERENCES

[1] H. Zhang and J.C. Hou, "Maintaining sensing coverage and connectivity in large sensor networks," in *Proceedings of NSF International Workshop on Theoretical and Algorithmic Aspects of Sensor, Ad Hoc Wireless, and Peer-to-Peer Networks*, 2004.

[2] R. Kershner, "The number of circles covering a set," *American Journal of Mathematics*, 61:665–671, 1939.

[3] Y. Wang, C. Hu, and Y. Tseng, "Efficient deployment algorithms for ensuring coverage and connectivity of wireless sensor networks," in *Proceedings of IEEE WICON*, pp. 114–121, 2005.

[4] X. Bai, S. Kumer, D. Xuan, Z. Yun, and T.H. Lai, "Deploying wireless sensors to achieve both coverage and connectivity," in *Proceedings of ACM MOBIHOC*, pp. 131–141, 2006.

[5] X. Bai, Z. Yun, D. Xuan, T.H. Lai, and W. Jia, "Deploying four-connectivity and full coverage wireless sensor networks," in *Proceedings of INFOCOM*, pp. 296–300, 2008.

[6] C.F. Huang and Y.C. Tseng, "The coverage problem in a wireless sensor network," in *ACM International Workshop on Wireless Sensor Networks and Applications (WSNA)*, pp. 115–121, 2003.

[7] Z. Zhou, S. Das, and H. Gupta, "Connected k-coverage problem in sensor networks," in *International Conference on Computer Communications and Networks (ICCCN)*, pp. 373–378, 2004.

[8] J. Wu and S. Yang, "Coverage issue in sensor networks with ajustable ranges," in *International Conference on Parallel Processing (ICPP)*, pp. 61–68, 2004.

[9] L. Hu, "Topology control for multihop packet radio networks," *IEEE Transactions on Communications*, 41:1474–1481, 1993.

[10] I. Stojmenovic, "Voronoi diagram and convex hull based geocasting and routing in wireless networks," Technical Report TR-99-11, University of Ottawa, 1995.

[11] I. Stojmenovic, A. Ruhil, and D.K. Lobiyal, "Voronoi diagram and convex hull based geocasting and routing in wireless networks," in *Proceedings of IEEE ISCC*, pp. 51–56, 2003.

[12] I. Stojmenovic, A. Ruhil, and D.K. Lobiyal, "Voronoi diagram and convex hull based geocasting and routing in wireless networks," *Wireless Communications and Mobile Computing*, 6(2):247–258, 2006.

[13] G. Gupta and M. Younis, "Fault-tolerant clustering of wireless sensor networks," in *Proceedings of IEEE Wireless Communications and Networking Conference (WCNC)*, pp. 1579–1584, 2003.

[14] J. Pan, Y.T. Hou, L. Cai, Y. Shi, and S.X. Shen, "Topology control for wireless sensor networks," in *Proceedings of ACM MOBICOM*, pp. 286–299, 2003.

[15] B. Hao, J. Tang, and G. Xue, "Fault-tolerant relay node placement in wireless sensor networks: Formulation and approximation," in *IEEE Workshop on High Performance Switching and Routing (HPSR)*, pp. 246–250, 2004.

[16] L. Schwiebert, S.K.S. Gupta, and J. Weinmann, "Research challenges in wireless networks of biomedical sensors," in *ACM Sigmobile Conference*, pp. 151–165, 2001.

[17] W. Bein, D. Bein, and S. Malladi, "Fault tolerant coverage models for sensor networks," *International Journal of Sensor Networks*, 5(4):199–209, 2009.

[18] B.W. Johnson, *Design and Analysis of Fault-Tolerant Digital Systems*. Reading, MA: Addison-Wesley Publishing Company, Inc., 1989.

[19] M.L. Shooman, *Probabilistic Reliability: An Engineering Approach*. New York: McGraw-Hill, 1968.

[20] K.S. Trivedi, *Probability and Statistics with Reliability, Queuing, and Computer Science Applications*. Englewood Cliffs, NJ: Prentice-Hall, 1982.

[21] J. Kratochvil, Problems discussed at the workshop on cycles and colourings, 1995. Personal communication.

[22] J. Kratochvil, P. Manuel, M. Miller, and A. Proskurowski, "Disjoint and fold domination in graphs," *Australasian Journal of Combinatorics*, 18:277–292, 1998.

[23] C.S. Liao and G.J. Change, "k-tuple domination in graphs," *Information Processing Letters*, 87:45–50, 2003.

[24] V. Vazirani, *Approximation Algorithms*. Springer: Morgan Kaufmann Publishers, 2001.

[25] F. Kuhn, T. Moscibroda, and R. Wattendorf, "Fault-tolerant clustering in ad hoc and sensor networks," in *Proceedings of the 26th IEEE International Conference on Distributed Computing Systems (ICDCS 06)*, page 68, 2006.

[26] S. Kutten and D. Peleg, "Fast distributed construction of small k-dominating sets and applications," *Journal of Algorithms*, 28:40–66, 1998.

[27] L.D. Penso and V.C. Barbosa, "A distributed algorithm to find k-dominating sets," *Discrete Applied Mathematics*, 141(1-3):243–253, 2004.

[28] F.H. Wang, J.M. Chang, Y.L. Wang, and S.J. Huang, "Distributed algorithms for finding the unique minimum distance dominating set in split-stars," *Journal of Parallel and Distributed Computing*, 63:481–487, 2003.

[29] F. Dai and J. Wu, "On constructing k-connected k-dominating set in wireless networks," in *Proceedings of IEEE International Parallel & Distributed Processing Symposium (IPDPS)*, April 2005.

[30] F. Dai and J. Wu, "On constructing k-connected k-dominating set in wireless ad hoc and sensor networks," *Journal of Parallel and Distributed Computing*, 66(7):947–958, 2006.

[31] T. Eilam, C. Gavoille, and D. Peleg, "Compact routing schemes with low stretch factor," in *PODC*, pp. 11–20, 1998.

[32] J.E. Dunbar, J.W. Grossman, J.H. Hattingh, S.T. Hedetniemi, and A.A. McRae, "On weakly-connected domination in graphs," *Discrete Mathematics*, 168/169:261–269, 1997.

[33] B. Awerbuch, A. Bar-Noy, N. Linial, and D. Peleg, "Compact distributed data structures for adaptive routing," in *Symposium on Theory of Computing (STOC)*, Vol. 2, pp. 230–240, 1989.

[34] L. Lovasz, "On the ratio of optimal integral and fractional covers," *Discrete Mathematics*, 13:383–390, 1975.

[35] I. Akyildiz, W. Su, Y. Sankarasubramanian, and E. Cayirci, "A survey on sensor networks," *IEEE Communication Magazine*, 42(5):102–114, August 2002.

[36] C.Y. Wan, S.B. Eisenman, and A.T. Campbell, "CODA: Congestion detection and avoidance in sensor networks," in *Proceedings of ACM SenSys*, pp. 266–279, 2003.

[37] H. Zhang, A. Arora, Y. Choi, and M. Gouda, "Reliable bursty convergecast in wireless sensor networks," in *Proceedings of ACM MobiHoc*, 2005.

[38] IEEE Computer Society LAN MAN Standards Committee, "Wireless lan medium access control (mac) and physical layer (phy) specifications," Technical Report Tech Report 802.11-1997, Institute of Electrical and Electronics Engineering, New York, 1997.

[39] The Bluetooth Special Interest Group, Bluetooth v1.0b specification, 1999. Available at http://www.bluetooth.com.

[40] D. Bein, A.K. Datta, P. Sajja, and S.Q. Zheng, "Impact of variable transmission range in all-wireless networks," *42nd Hawaii International Conference in System Sciences (HICSS 2009)*, 10 pages, 2009.

13

Optimizing and Tuning Scientific Codes

Qing Yi

13.1 INTRODUCTION

Scientific computing categorizes an important class of software applications that utilize the power of high-end computers to solve important problems in applied disciplines such as physics, chemistry, and engineering. These applications are typically characterized by their extensive use of loops that operate on large data sets stored in multidimensional arrays such as matrices and grids. Applications that can predict the structure of their input data and access these data through array subscripts analyzable by compilers are typically referred to as *regular* computations, and applications that operate on unstructured data (e.g., graphs of arbitrary shapes) via indirect array references or pointers are referred to as *irregular* computations.

This chapter focuses on enhancing the performance of regular scientific computations through source-level program transformations, examples of which include loop optimizations such as automatic parallelization, blocking, interchange, and fusion/fission, redundancy elimination optimizations such as strength reduction of array address calculations, and data layout optimizations such as array copying and scalar replacement. In addition, we introduce POET [1], a scripting language designed for parameterizing architecture-sensitive optimizations so that their configurations can be empirically tuned, and use the POET optimization library to demonstrate how to effectively apply these optimizations on modern multicore architectures.

Scalable Computing and Communications: Theory and Practice, First Edition. Edited by Samee U. Khan, Albert Y. Zomaya, and Lizhe Wang.
© 2013 John Wiley & Sons, Inc. Published 2013 by John Wiley & Sons, Inc.

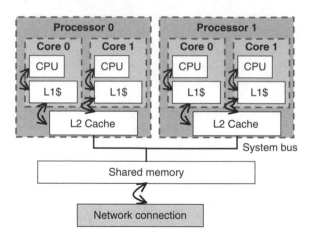

FIGURE 13.1. *Intel Core2Duo architecture [37].*

13.2 AN ABSTRACT VIEW OF THE MACHINE ARCHITECTURE

Figure 13.1 shows an abstract view of the Intel Core2Duo architecture, which includes two processors (processors 0 and 1), each with a private L2 cache while sharing a common system memory with the other via the system bus. Each processor, in turn, contains two CPU cores (cores 0–1 and 2–3), each core with a private CPU and L1 cache while sharing a common L2 cache with another core on the same processor. Most multicore computers today have an architecture similar to the one shown in Figure 13.1, although much larger numbers of processors and cores may be included. To achieve high performance on such machines, software must effectively utilize the following resources:

- Concurrent CPU cores, which require applications to be partitioned into multiple threads of computations so that different threads can be evaluated in parallel on different cores. Multithreading can be implemented using OpenMP [2] or various threading libraries such as Pthreads [3] and the Intel TBB [4] library.
- Shared memory, which requires that concurrent accesses to data shared by multiple threads be synchronized if the data could be modified by any of the threads. A variety of mechanisms, for example, locks and mutexes, can be used to coordinate global data accesses to shared memory. However, frequent synchronizations are expensive and should be avoided when possible.
- The cache hierarchy, which requires that data accessed by CPU cores be reused in their private caches to reduce traffic to the main memory. The affinity of each thread with its data is critical to the overall performance of applications, as the cost of accessing data from shared memory or remote caches can be orders of magnitude slower than accessing data from a private L1 cache.

13.3 OPTIMIZING SCIENTIFIC CODES

The concept of *performance optimization* here refers to all program transformations that change the implementation details of a software application without affecting its higher-level algorithms or data structures so that the implementation details, for example, looping structures and data layout, can be more efficiently mapped to an underlying machine for execution. Such optimizations can be separated into two general categories: those targeting removing redundancies in the input code, for example, moving repetitive computations outside of loops, and those targeting reordering of operations and data to more efficiently utilize architectural components, for example, by evaluating operations in parallel on different CPUs. *Redundancy elimination* can improve performance irrespective of what machine is used to run the applications. In contrast, *reordering optimizations* are usually extremely sensitive to the underlying architecture and could result in severe performance degradation if misconfigured. This section summarizes important optimizations in both categories.

13.3.1 Computation Reordering Optimizations

Most scientific codes are written using loops, so the most important way to reorder their computation is through restructuring of loops. Here, each loop iteration is viewed as a unit of computation, and evaluation order of these units is reordered so that they collectively utilize the resources offered by modern architectures more efficiently. Among the mostly commonly used loop optimizations are loop interchange, fusion, blocking, parallelization, unrolling, and unroll&jam, illustrated in Figure 13.2 and summarized in the following. To ensure program correctness, none of these optimizations should violate any inherit dependences within the original computation [5].

13.3.1.1 Loop Interchange   As illustrated in Figure 13.2b, where the outermost k loop at line 7 of Figure 13.2a is moved to the innermost position at line 9 in Figure 13.2b, loop interchange rearranges the order of nesting loops inside one another. After interchange, each iteration (k_x, j_x, i_x) of the original loop nest in Figure 13.2a is now evaluated at iteration (j_x, i_x, k_x) in Figure 13.2b. The transformation is safe if each iteration (k_x, j_x, i_x) in Figure 13.2a depends on only those iterations (k_y, j_y, i_y) that satisfy $k_y \le k_x, j_y \le j_x, i_y \le i_x$, so that after interchange, iteration (j_y, i_y, k_y) is still evaluated before (j_x, i_x, k_x) in Figure 13.2b. Loop interchange is typically applied early as proper loop nesting order is required for the effectiveness of many other optimizations.

13.3.1.2 Loop Fusion   As illustrated in Figure 13.2c, which fuses the two loop nests at lines 4 and 7 of Figure 13.2b into a single loop, *loop fusion* merges disjoint looping structures so that iterations from different loops are now interleaved. It is typically applied to loops that share a significant amount of common data so that related iterations are brought closer and are evaluated together, thereby promoting better cache and register reuse. After fusion, each iteration (j_x, i_x) of the second loop nest at line 7 of Figure 13.2b is now evaluated before all iterations $\{(j_y, i_y) : j_y > j_x$ or $(j_y = j_x$ and $i_y > i_x)\}$ of the first loop nest at line 4. Therefore, the transformation is safe if each iteration (j_x, i_x) of the second loop nest does not depend on iterations (j_y, i_y) of the first loop nest that satisfy the condition. Similar to loop interchange, loop fusion is applied early so that the merged loops can be collectively optimized further.

```
1: void dgemm(double *a,
       double *b, double *c,
       double beta, int n)
2: {
3:  int i,j,k;
4:  for (j = 0; j < n; j ++)
5:  for (i = 0; i < n; i ++)
6:   c[j*n+i] = beta*c[j*n+i];
7:  for (k = 0; k < n; k ++)
8:  for (j = 0; j < n; j ++)
9:  for (i = 0; i < n; i ++)
10:  c[j*n+i] +=
         a[k*n+i] * b[j*n+k];
11:}
```

(a)

```
1: void dgemm(double *a,
       double *b, double *c,
       double beta, int n)
2: {
3:  int i,j,k;
4:  for (j = 0; j < n; j ++)
5:  for (i = 0; i < n; i ++)
6:   c[j*n+i] = beta*c[j*n+i];
7:  for (j = 0; j < n; j ++)
8:  for (i = 0; i < n; i ++)
9:  for (k = 0; k < n; k ++)
10:  c[j*n+i] +=
         a[k*n+i] * b[j*n+k];
11:}
```

(b)

```
1: void dgemm(double *a,
       double *b, double *c,
       double beta, int n)
2: {
3:  int i,j,k;
4:  for (j = 0; j < n; j ++)
5:  for (i = 0; i < n; i ++) {
6:   c[j*n+i] = beta*c[j*n+i];
7:   for (k = 0; k < n; k ++) {
8:    c[j*n+i] +=
         a[k*n+i] * b[j*n+k];
9:   }
10:}
11:}
```

(c)

```
1: void dgemm(double *a,double *b,
       double *c, double beta, int n)
2: {
3:  int i,j,k,i1,j1,k1;
4:#pragma omp for private(j1,i1,k1,j,i,k)
5:  for (j1=0; j1<n; j1+=32)
6:  for (i1=0; i1<n; i1+=32)
7:  for (k1=0; k1<n; k1+=32)
8:  for (j=0; j<min(32,n-j1); j++)
9:  for (i=0; i<min(32,n-i1); i++) {
10:  if (k1 == 0)
11:   c[(j1+j)*n+(i1+i)] =
         beta*c[(j1+j)*n+(i1+i)];
12:  for (k = k1; k<min(k1+32,n); k++)
13:   c[(j1+j)*n+(i1+i)] += a[(k1+k)*n
         +(i1+i)] * b[(j1+j)*n+(k1+k)];
14:  }
15: }
```

(d)

```
1: void dgemm(double *a,double *b,
       double *c, double beta, int n)
2: {
3:  int i,j,k;
4:  for (j = 0; j < n; j++)
5:  for (i = 0; i < n ; i+=2) {
6:   c[j*n+i] = beta*c[j*n+i];
7:   c[j*n+i+1] = beta*c[j*n+i+1];
8:   for (k = 0; k<n; k +=4) {
9:    c[j*n+i] += a[k*n+i] * b[j*n+k];
10:   c[j*n+i] += a[(k+1)*n+i] * b[j*n+(k+1)];
11:   c[j*n+i] += a[(k+2)*n+i] * b[j*n+(k+2)];
12:   c[j*n+i] += a[(k+3)*n+i] * b[j*n+(k+3)];
13:   c[j*n+i+1] += a[k*n+i+1] * b[j*n+k];
14:   c[j*n+i+1] += a[(k+1)*n+i+1] * b[j*n+(k+1)];
15:   c[j*n+i+1] += a[(k+2)*n+i+1] * b[j*n+(k+2)];
16:   c[j*n+i+1] += a[(k+3)*n+i+1] * b[j*n+(k+3)];
17:  }
18: }
19:}
```

(e)

FIGURE 13.2. Applying loop optimizations to a matrix multiplication routine. (a) Original code. (b) Apply loop interchange to (a). (c) Apply loop fusion to (b). (d) Apply loop blocking + parallelization to (c). (e) Apply loop unrolling + unroll&jam to (c).

13.3.1.3 Loop Blocking

Figure 13.2d shows an example of applying *loop blocking* to Figure 13.2c, where each of the three loops at lines 4, 5, and 7 of Figure 13.2c is now split into two loops: an outer loop, which increments its index variable each time by a stride of 32, and an inner loop, which enumerates only the 32 iterations skipped by the outer loop. Then, all the outer loops are placed outside at lines 5–7 of Figure 13.2d so that the inner loops at lines 8, 9, and 12 comprise a small computation block of 32 * 32 * 32 iterations, where 32 is called the *blocking factor* for each of the original loops.

Loop blocking is the most commonly applied technique to promote cache reuse, where a loop-based computation is partitioned into smaller blocks so that the data accessed by each computation block can fit in some level of cache and thus can be reused throughout the entire duration of evaluating the block. The transformation is safe if all the participating loops can be freely interchanged.

13.3.1.4 Loop Parallelization

When there are no dependences between different iterations of a loop, these iterations can be arbitrarily reordered and therefore can be evaluated simultaneously on different processing cores (CPUs). On a symmetric multiprocessor (SMP) architecture such as that in Figure 13.1, the parallelization can be expressed using OpenMP [2]. For example, the OpenMP pragma at line 4 of Figure 13.2d specifies that different iterations of the outermost $j1$ loop at line 5 can be assigned to different threads and evaluated in parallel, with each thread treating $j1, i1, k1, j, i,$ and k as private local variables and treating all the other data as shared. At the end of the $j1$ loop, all threads are terminated and the evaluation goes back to sequential mode. To reduce the cost of thread creation and synchronization, it is economic to try to parallelize the outermost loop when possible for typical scientific computations.

13.3.1.5 *Loop Unrolling and Unroll&Jam*   When the body of a loop nest contains only a small number of statements, for example, the loops in Figure 13.2a–d, iterations of the innermost loop can be *unrolled* to create a bigger loop body, thus providing the compiler with a larger scope to apply back-end optimizations (e.g., instruction scheduling and register allocation). For example, the k loop at line 7 of Figure 13.2c is unrolled in Figure 13.2e at line 8, where the stride of the k loop in Figure 13.2c is increased from 1 to 4 in Figure 13.2e, and the skipped iterations are then explicitly enumerated inside the loop body at lines 9–12 of Figure 13.2e. The number of iterations being unrolled inside the loop body is called the *unrolling factor*. *Loop unrolling* is typically applied only to the innermost loops so that after unrolling, the new loop body contains a long sequence of straight-line code.

A similar optimization called *unroll&jam* can be applied to unroll outer loops and then jam the unrolled outer iterations inside the innermost loop so that iterations of the outer loops are now interleaved with the inner loop to form an even bigger loop body. For example, the i loop at line 5 of Figure 13.2c is unrolled with a factor of 2 at line 5 of Figure 13.2e, and the unrolled iterations are jammed inside the k loop body at lines 13–16. Loop unrolling is always safe. Loop unroll&jam, on the other hand, can be safely applied only when *loop interchange* is safe between the outer loop being unrolled and the inner loop being *jammed*. Loop unrolling is typically applied solely to increase the size of the loop body, while loop unroll&jam is applied to additionally enhance reuse of data within the innermost loop body.

13.3.2 Data Layout Reordering Optimizations

On a modern multicore architecture such as that illustrated in Figure 13.1, data structures need to be laid out in memory in a way where items being accessed close together in time have affinity in memory as well so that they can be brought to caches together in a group and would not evict each other from the caches. Since different regions of a program may access a common data structure (e.g., an array) in dramatically different orders, we consider an optimization called *array copying*, which dynamically rearranges the layout of array elements by copying them into a separate buffer. Allocating registers for selective array elements can be considered a special case of array copying [6] and is accomplished through an optimization called *scalar replacement*. Figure 13.3 illustrates the application of both optimizations.

13.3.2.1 *Array Copying*   When a small group of consecutively evaluated statements access elements that are far away from each other in a array, the efficiency

```
1: void dgemm(double *a,double *b,          1: void dgemm(double *a,double *b,
      double *c, double beta, int n)              double *c, double beta, int n)
2: {                                        2: {
3:   int i,j,k,i1,j1,k1,cds, cbs;           3:   int i,j,k;
4:   double* a_cp;                          4:   double c0,c1,b0,b1,b2,b3;
5:   cds = 32 * (31+n)/32; cbs=32*32;       5:   for (j = 0; j < n; j++)
6:   a_cp=(double*)malloc(cds*cds*sizeof(double));   6:   for (i = 0; i < n ; i+=2) {
7:   /* copy data from a to a_cp*/          7:     c0 = beta*c[j*n+i];
8:   for (i1=0; i1< n; i1+=32)              8:     c1 = beta*c[j*n+i+1];
9:   for (k1=0; k1< n; k1+=32)              9:     for (k = 0; k<n; k +=4) {
10:  for (i=0; i< min(32,n-i1); i ++)       10:      b0=b[j*n+k];
11:  for (k=0; k<min(32,n-k1); k ++)        11:      b1=b[j*n+(k+1)];
12:  a_cp[i1*cds+k1*cbs+i*32+k]=a[(k1+k)*n+(i1+i)];   12:      b2=b[j*n+(k+2)];
13:  /* Use a_cp instead of a in computation*/    13:      b3=b[j*n+(k+3)];
14:  for (j1=0; j1<n; j1+=32)               14:      c0 += a[k*n+i] * b0;
15:  for (i1=0; i1<n; i1+=32)               15:      c0 += a[(k+1)*n+i] * b1;
16:  for (k1=0; k1<n; k1+=32)               16:      c0 += a[(k+2)*n+i] * b2;
17:  for (j=0; j<min(32,n-j1); j++)         17:      c0 += a[(k+3)*n+i] * b3;
18:  for (i=0; i<min(32,n-i1); i++) {       18:      c1 += a[k*n+i+1] * b0;
19:    if (k1 == 0)                         19:      c1 += a[(k+1)*n+i+1] * b1;
20:      c[(j1+j)*n+(i1+i)] =               20:      c1 += a[(k+2)*n+i+1] * b2;
          beta*c[(j1+j)*n+(i1+i)];          21:      c1 += a[(k+3)*n+i+1] * b3;
21:    for (k = k1; k<min(k1+32,n); k ++) {  22:    }
22:      c[(j1+j)*n+(i1+i)] += a_cp[i1*cds+k1*cbs+   23:    c[j*n+i] = c0;
          i*32+k] * b[(j1+j)*n+(k1+k)];     24:    c[j*n+i+1] = c1;
23:    }                                    25:  }
24:  }                                      26: }
26: free(a_cp);
26:}
```

(a)   (b)

FIGURE 13.3. Applying data layout optimizations to Figure 13.2. (a) Apply array copy to Figure 13.2d. (b) Apply scalar replacement to Figure 13.2e.

of memory accesses can be improved by copying these elements into a contiguous buffer. Figure 13.2d illustrates such a situation, where each iteration of the innermost k loop at line 12 accesses an array a element that is n elements apart from the one accessed in the previous iteration. Figure 13.3a shows the result of applying the copying optimization to array a. Here, a new temporary array a_cp allocated at line 6 of Figure 13.3a is used to group all the array a elements accessed by iterations of the inner j, i, k loops at lines 8–15 of Figure 13.2d into contiguous memory. Note that the size of a_cp is allocated to be a multiple of 32 * 32, the number of array a elements accessed by each of the computation blocks. The statements at lines 7–12 of Figure 13.3a then copy all the elements from the original a array to a different location in a_cp. Finally, lines 13–24 contain the modified computation which accesses data from a_cp instead from the original array a. It is obvious that the array copying operations at lines 7–12 will incur a significant runtime overhead. However, it is anticipated that the savings in repetitively accessing a_cp instead of a at lines 14–24 will more than compensate the copying overhead. The assumption is not true for all architectures and input matrix sizes. Therefore, array copying need to be applied with caution to avoid slowdown of the original code.

13.3.2.2 Scalar Replacement While copying a large amount of data can be expensive, copying repetitively accessed array elements to registers is essentially free and can produce immense performance gains. Since register allocation is typically handled by back-end compilers that do not keep arrays in registers, array elements need to be first copied to scalar variables to be considered later for register promotion. The optimization is called scalar replacement, and Figure 13.3b illustrates the result of using scalars to replace the elements of arrays C and B accessed by loops j and k in Figure 13.2e. Here, lines 7–8 of Figure 13.3b use $c0$ and $c1$ to save the values of $c[j * n + i]$ and $c[j * n + i + 1]$, respectively, and lines 10–13 use $b0 - b3$ to save the values of $b[j * n + k]$ through $b[j * n + (k + 3)]$, respectively. Lines 14–21 then use the new scalars instead of the original array elements to perform relevant computation. Finally, the values of $c0$ and $c1$ are saved back to array c at lines 23–24. Although scalar replacement presumably has no runtime overhead, when overly applied, it could create too many scalar variables and could overwhelm the back-end compiler register allocation algorithm into generating inefficient code. Therefore, it needs to be applied cautiously and preferably based on empirical feedbacks.

13.3.3 Redundancy Elimination

Most of the optimized codes in Figures 13.2 and 13.3 contain long expressions used as subscripts to access array elements. Repetitive evaluation of these expressions can be prohibitive if not properly managed. The key insight of redundancy elimination optimizations is that if an operation has already been evaluated, do not evaluate it again, especially if the operation is inside multiple nested loops. The optimizations are typically applied only to integer expressions that do not access data from arrays, by completely eliminating redundant evaluations, moving repetitive evaluations outside of loops, and replacing expensive evaluations with cheaper ones, illustrated in Figure 13.4 and summarized in the following.

```
void initialize(float* A,
    float *B, int N, int M)
{
  for (int i=0; i<N; ++i)
    for (int j=0; j<M; ++j)
      *(A+i*M+j) = *(B+i*M+j);
}
```

(a)

```
void initialize(float* A,
    float *B, int N, int M)
{
  for (int i=0; i<N; ++i)
    for (int j=0; j<M; ++j) {
      int index = i*M+j;
      *(A+index) = *(B+index);
    }
}
```

(b)

```
void initialize(float* A,
    float *B, int N, int M)
{
  for (int i = 0; i < N; ++i) {
    int i1 = i * M;
    for (int j = 0; j < M; ++j) {
      int index = i1 + j;
      *(A+index) = *(B+index);
    }
  }
}
```

(c)

```
void initialize(float* A,
    float *B, int N, int M)
{
  for (int i = 0; i < N; ++i) {
    for (int j = 0; j < M; ++j) {
      *(A+j) = *(B+j);
    }
    A = A + M; B = B + M;
  }
}
```

(d)

```
void initialize(float* A,
    float *B, int N, int M)
{
  for (int i = 0; i < N; ++i) {
    for (int j = 0; j < M; ++j) {
      *(A++) = *(B++);
    }
  }
}
```

(e)

FIGURE 13.4. Examples of applying redundancy elimination optimizations. (a) Original code. (b) Redundant evaluation elimination. (c) Loop-invariant code motion. (d) Strength reduction for A + i*M and B + i*M. (e) Strength reduction for A + i*M + j and B + i*M + j.

13.3.3.1 Eliminating Redundant Evaluations If an expression e has already been evaluated on every control-flow path leading to e from the program entry, the evaluation can be removed entirely by saving and reusing the result of the previous identical evaluations. As an example, Figure 13.4a shows a simple C routine where the expression $i * M + j$ is evaluated twice at every iteration of the surrounding i and j loops. The second evaluation of $i * M + j$ can be eliminated entirely by saving the result of the first evaluation, as shown in Figure 13.4b.

13.3.3.2 Loop-Invariant Code Motion In Figure 13.4b, the result of evaluating $i * M$ never changes at different iterations of the j loop. Therefore, this loop-invariant evaluation can be moved outside of the j loop, as shown in Figure 13.4c. In general, if an expression e is evaluated at every iteration of a loop, and its evaluation result never changes, e should be moved outside of the surrounding loop so that it is evaluated only once. The underlying assumption is that, at runtime, the loop will be evaluated more than once. Since the assumption is true for the majority of loops in software applications, loop-invariant code motion is automatically applied extensively by most compilers.

13.3.3.3 Strength Reduction Many expressions inside loops are expressed in terms of the surrounding loop index variables, similar to the expressions $A + i * M + j$ and $B + i * M + j$ in Figure 13.4a. When the surrounding loops increment their index variables each time by a known integer constant, the cost of evaluating these expressions can be reduced via an optimization called *strength reduction*. Figure 13.4d shows an example of applying strength reduction to optimize the evaluation of $A + i * M + j$ and $B + i * M + j$ in Figure 13.4a. Here, the two array pointers, A and B, are incrementally updated at every iteration of the i loop instead of reevaluating $A + i * M$ at every iteration, shown in Figure 13.4b. Similarly, instead of evaluating $A + j$ at every iteration of the j loop, we can perform another strength reduction optimization by incrementing A with 1 at every iteration of the j loop. The result of this optimization is shown in Figure 13.4e. Strength reduction is a highly effective technique and is frequently used by compilers to reduce the cost of evaluating subscripted addresses of array references, such as those in Figures 13.2 and 13.3.

13.4 EMPIRICAL TUNING OF OPTIMIZATIONS

Many of the loop and data layout optimizations in Sections 13.3.1 and 13.3.2 are extremely sensitive to the underlying architectures. As the result, it is difficult to predict how to properly configure these optimizations a priori.

A better approach is to parameterize their configurations and to try to evaluate the efficiency of differently optimized code using a set of representative input data. Proper optimization configurations can then be determined based on the experimental data collected. This approach is referred to as *empirical tuning* of optimization configurations.

POET [1] is an open-source interpreted program transformation language designed to support flexible parameterization and empirical tuning of architecture-sensitive optimizations to achieve portable high performance on varying architectures [1]. Figure 13.5 shows its targeting optimization environment, where an

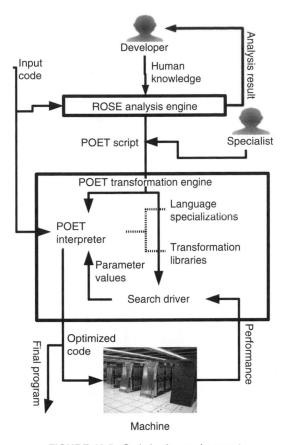

FIGURE 13.5. *Optimization environment.*

optimizing compiler named *ROSE analysis engine* [7] or a computational specialist (i.e., an experienced developer) performs advanced optimization analysis to identify profitable program transformations and then uses POET to extensively parameterize architecture-sensitive optimizations to the input code. This POET output can then be ported to different machines together with the user application, where local POET transformation engines empirically reconfigure the parameterized optimizations until satisfactory performance is achieved.

13.4.1   The POET Language

Table 13.1 provides an overview of the POET language, which includes a collection of atomic and compound values to accurately represent the internal structure of arbitrary input codes, systematic variable management and control flow to build arbitrary program transformations, and special-purpose concepts to support dynamic parsing of arbitrary programming languages, effective tracing of optimized codes, and flexible composition of parameterized transformations. Figure 13.6 shows an example of using these components in a typical POET script.

TABLE 13.1. Overview of the POET Language [1]

	Types of Values	
1	`atomic types`	int (e.g., 1, 20, −3), string (e.g., "abc," "132")
2	$e_1\ e_2\ \cdots\ e_n$	A list of n elements $e_1, e_2, \ldots, e_n$
3	$e_1,\ e_2,\ \ldots,\ e_n$	A tuple of n elements $e_1, e_2, \ldots, e_n$
4	`MAP{`f_1`=>`t_1`, . . . , `f_n`=>`t_n`}`	An associative map of n entries
5	`c#(`p_1`, . . . , `p_n`)`	An object of code template c with $p_1, \ldots, p_n$ as values
6	$f[v_1$`=`p_1`; . . . ; `v_n`=`$p_n]$	A xform handle f with optional parameters
	Operating on Different Types of Values	
7	`+, −, *, /, %, <, <=, > ,>=`	Integer arithmetics and comparison
8	`==, !=, !, &&, ||`	Equality and Boolean operators
9	`==, !=`	Equality comparison between arbitrary types of values
10	$a{\wedge}b$	Concatenate two values a and b into a single string.
11	`SPLIT(p,a)`	Split string a with p as separator or at index p if p is int.
12	`a :: b`	Prepend a in front of list b s.t. a is head of the new list.
13	`HEAD(l), car(l)`	The first element of a list l
14	`TAIL(l), cdr(l)`	The tail behind the first element of a list l
15	`a[b] where `a` is a tuple`	The bth element of a tuple a
16	`a[b] where `a` is a map`	The value mapped to entry b in an associative map a
17	`a[c.d] where `c` is a type`	The value of c code template parameter d in object a
18	`LEN(a) where `a` is a string`	The number of characters in string a
19	`LEN(a) where `$a \neq$` string`	The number of entries in a list, tuple, or map
	VariableAssignment and Control Flow	
20	`a = b`	Modify a variable a to have value b; return b as result.
21	`a[i] = b`	Modify map a so that i is mapped to b; return b as result.
22	`(a1, . . . , am) =` `(b1, . . . , bm)`	Modify $a1, \ldots, am$ with $b1, \ldots, bm$, respectively.
23	`a1; a2; . . . ; am`	Evaluate expressions $a1\ a2\ldots am$ in order; return am
24	`RETURN `a	Return a as result of the current $xform$ invocation.
25	`if (`a`) {`b`} [ else {`c`} ]`	Return b or c as result if a is TRUE or FALSE.
26	`for (e1; e2; e3) {`b`}`	Equivalent to the for loop in C
27	`BREAK, CONTINUE`	Equivalent to $break$ and $continue$ in C
	Pattern Matching and Transformation Operators	
28	`a:b`	Return whether value a matches the pattern specifier b.
29	`switch(`a`){case `b_1`:`c_1` . . . }`	Match a against b_i ($i = 1, \ldots$) in turn; return matching c_i.
30	`foreach(a:b:c) {d}`	Evaluate $d;c$ for each object in a that matches pattern b.
	`foreach_r(a:b:c) {d}`	Same as $foreach$ but traverse values in a in reverse order
31	`REPLACE(c1, c2, e)`	Replace all occurrences of $c1$ with $c2$ in e.
32	`REPLACE(((`o_1`, `r_1`)...), e)`	Traverse e in preorder, replacing each o_i ($i = 1, \ldots$) with r_i.

TABLE 13.1. (*Continued*)

33	`REBUILD(e)`	Rebuild each code template object inside *e*.
34	`DUPLICATE(c1, c2, e)`	Replicate *e*, each time replacing *c*1 by a new value in *c*2.
35	`PERMUTE ((`i_1`, . . . , `i_m`), e)`	Reorder *e* s.t. the *j*th (*j* = 1, . . . , *m*) value is at i_j in return.
	Global Type/Variable Declarations and Commands	
36	`<define a b/>`	Declare a global macro variable *a* with *b* as its value.
37	`<trace a1, ..., am/>`	Declare a list of tracing handles *a*1, . . . , *am*.
38	`<parameter p type=t default=v parse=r message=d/>`	Declare a global parameter *p* with type *t*, default value *v*, meaning *d*, and value parsed from command-line using *r*.
39	`<input cond=c from=f syntax=s to=t/>`	If *c* is true, parse the input code from file *f* using syntax defined in file *s*, then save the parsing result to variable *t*.
40	`<eval s1, ..., sm />`	Evaluate the group of expressions/statements *s*1, . . . , *sm*.
41	`<output from=t to=f syntax=s cond=c/>`	If *c* is true, unparse result of evaluating *t* to file *f* using syntax descriptions defined in file *s*.

```
1: include utils.incl

2: <*The code template type for all loops supported by the POET optimization library *>
3: <code Loop pars=(i:ID, start:EXP, stop:EXP, step:EXP) >
4: for (@i@=@start@; @i@<@stop@; @i@+=@step@)
5: </code>
6: <xform ReverseList pars=(list) prepend=""> <<* a xform routine which reverses the input list
7:   result = HEAD(list) :: prepend;
8:   for (p_list = TAIL(list); p_list != ""; p_list = TAIL(p_list))
9:   {
10:     result = HEAD(p_list) :: result;
11:  }
12:  result
13: </xform>

14:<define OPT_STMT CODE.Loop />
15:<parameter inputFile message="input file name"/>
16:<parameter inputLang default="" message="file name for input language syntax" />
17:<parameter outputFile  default="" message="file name for output" />
18:<trace inputCode/>

19:<input cond=(inputLang!="") from=(inputFile) syntax=(inputLang) to=inputCode/>
20:<eval  backward = ReverseList[prepend="Reversed\n"](inputCode);
       succ = XFORM.AnalzeOrTransformCode(inputCode); />
21:<output cond=(succ) to=(outputFile) syntax=(inputLang) from=inputCode/>
```

FIGURE 13.6. *An example illustrating the overall structure of a POET file.*

13.4.1.1 The Type System

POET supports two types of atomic values: integers and strings. Two Boolean values, *TRUE* and *FALSE*, are provided but are equal to integers 1 and 0, respectively. Additionally, it supports the following compound types:

- *Lists.* A POET list is a singly linked list of arbitrary values and can be constructed by simply enumerating all the elements. For example, (*a* "<=" *b*) produces a list with three elements, *a*, "<=," and *b*. Lists can be dynamically extended using the :: operator at line 12 of Table 13.1.

- *Tuples.* A POET tuple contains a finite sequence of values separated by commas. For example, $(i, 0, m, 1)$ constructs a tuple with four values, i, 0, m, and 1. A tuple cannot be dynamically extended and is typically used to group multiple parameters of a function call.

- *Associative Maps.* A POET *map* associates pairs of arbitrary values and is constructed by invoking the *MAP* operator at line 4 of Table 13.1. For example, *MAP{3=>"abc"}* builds a map that associates 3 with *abc*. Associative maps can be dynamically modified using assignments, shown at line 21 of Table 13.1.

- *Code Templates.* A POET code template is a distinct user-defined data type and needs to be explicitly declared with a type name and a tuple of template parameters, shown at lines 2–5 of Figure 13.6, before being used. It is similar to the *struct* type in C, where template parameters can be viewed as data fields of the C struct. A code template object is constructed using the # operator at line 5 of Table 13.1. For example, $Loop\#(i, 0, N, 1)$ builds an object of the code template *Loop* with $(i, 0, N, 1)$ as values for the template parameters.

- *Xform Handles.* Each POET xform handle refers to a global *xform* routine, which is equivalent to a global function in C. It is constructed by following the name of the *routine* with an optional list of configurations to set up future invocations of the routine, shown at line 6 of Table 13.1. Each *xform* handle can be invoked with actual parameters just like a function pointer in C.

13.4.1.2 *Variables and Control Flow* POET variables can hold arbitrary types of values, and their types are dynamically checked during evaluation to ensure type safety. These variables can be separated into the following three categories:

- *Local variables*, whose scopes are restricted within the bodies of individual code templates or *xform* routines. For example, at lines 2–13 of Figure 13.6, i, *start*, *stop*, *step* are local variables of the code template *Loop*, and *list*, *result*, and *p_list* are local variables of the *xform* routine *ReverseList*. Local variables are introduced by declaring them as parameters or by simply using them in the body of a code template or xform routine.

- *Static variables*, whose scopes are restricted within an individual POET file and can be used freely within the file without explicit declaration. For example, at line 20 of Figure 13.6, both *backward* and *succ* are file-static variables, which are used to store temporary results across different components of the same file.

- *Global variables*, whose scopes span across all POET files being interpreted. Each global variable must be explicitly declared as a *macro* (e.g., the *OPT_STMT* variable declared at line 14 of Fig. 13.6), a *command-line parameter* (e.g., *inputFile*, *inputLang*, and *outputFile* declared at lines 15–17), or a *tracing handle* (e.g., *inputCode* declared at line 18).

In summary, only global variables need to be explicitly declared. All other identifiers are treated as local or static variables based on the scopes of their appearances unless an explicit prefix, for example, *GLOBAL*, *CODE*, or *XFORM*, is used to qualify the name as a global macro, a code template, or a xform routine, respectively. An example of such qualified names is shown at line 14 of Figure 13.6.

POET variables can be freely modified within their scopes using assignments, shown at line 20 of Table 13.1. Additionally, global *macros* can be modified through the *define* command illustrated at line 14 of Figure 13.6; *command-line parameters* can be modified through command-line options; and *tracing handles* can be modified implicitly by POET special-purpose operators and thus can be used by POET library routines to directly modify their input data structures (for more details, see Section 13.4.2.2).

As summarized in lines 20–35 of Table 13.1 and illustrated in lines 6–13 of Figure 13.6, POET program transformations are defined as *xform routines*, which can use arbitrary control flow such as conditionals, loops, and recursive function calls; can build compound data structures such as lists, tuples, hash tables, and code templates; and can invoke many built-in operations (e.g., pattern matching, replacement, and replication) to modify the input code. The full programming support for defining arbitrary customizable transformations distinguishes POET from most other existing special-purpose transformation languages, which rely on template- or pattern-based rewrite rules to support definition of new transformations.

13.4.1.3 The Overall Structure of a POET Script Figure 13.6 shows the typical structure of a POET script, which includes a sequence of *include* directives (line 1), type declarations (lines 2–13), global variable declarations (lines 14–18), and executable commands (lines 19–21). The *include* directives specify the names of other POET files that should be evaluated before the current one and thus must appear at the beginning of a POET script. All the other POET declarations and commands can appear in arbitrary order and are evaluated in their order of appearance. *Comments* (see lines 2 and 6 of Fig. 13.6) can appear anywhere.

POET supports three global commands, *input*, *eval*, and *output*, summarized in Table 13.1 at lines 39–41 and illustrated in Figure 13.6 at lines 19–21. The *input command* at line 19 of Figure 13.6 parses a given file named by *inputFile* using the language syntax file *inputLang* and then stores the parsed internal representation of the input code to variable *inputCode*. The *eval command* at line 20 specifies a sequence of expressions and statements to evaluate. Finally, the *output Command* at line 21 writes the transformed *inputCode* to an external file named by *outputFile*.

Most POET expressions and statements are embedded inside the global *eval* commands or the bodies of individual code templates or *xform* routines. Most POET expressions are *pure* in that unless tracing handles are involved, they compute new values instead of modifying existing ones. POET statements, as shown at lines 20–27 of Table 13.1, are used to support variable assignment and program control flow. Except for loops, which always have an empty value, all the other POET statements have values just like expressions. When multiple statements are composed in a sequence, only the value of the last statement is returned.

13.4.2 Using POET to Support Optimization Tuning

POET provides a library of routines to support many well-known source-level optimizations to achieve high performance for scientific codes on modern architectures. A subset of these routines is shown in Table 13.2, which can be invoked by an arbitrary POET script with command-line parameters so that their configurations

TABLE 13.2. Selected Optimization Routines Supported by the POET Opt Library

Interface	Semantics	Configuration Parameters
PermuteLoops[order=o](n,x) FuseLoops(n, x)	Permute loops between n and x Fuse loops in n to replace x	o: loop nesting order
BlockLoops[factor=f](n,x)	Block loops in between n and x	f: blocking factors

ParallelizeLoop[threads=t;
  private=p; reduction=r]
  (x)
	Parallelize loop x using
	  OpenMP pragma
		p/r: private vars; r:
		  reduction vars; t:
		  number of threads to
		  run x

UnrollLoop[factor=u](x)	Unroll loop x	u: unrolling factor

UnrollJam[factor=u](n,x)	Unroll loops in between n and
	  x; jam the unrolled loops
	  inside n
		u: unrolling factors

CleanupBlockedNests(x)	Cleanup loops in x after
	  blocking/unrolling has been
	  applied	

CopyRepl[init_loc=i;
  save_loc=s; delete_
  loc=d; permute=p](a, n,
  x)
	Copy data referenced by a via
	  surrounding loops n; replace
	  references inside x with
	  copied data
		i/s/d: where to initialize/
		  save/delete buffer; p:
		  permute loops in n
		  during copy

ScalarRepl[[init_loc=i;
  save_loc=s](a, n, x)
	Replace data referenced by a
	  via loops n with scalars in x
		i/s: where to initialize/
		  save scalar vars

FiniteDiff[exp_type=t]
  (e,d,x)
	Reduce the cost of evaluating
	  $e + d$ in input code x
		t: expression type

TraceNestedLoops(h,x)	Modify tracing handles in h to contain nested loops in x	

```
1: void dgemm_test(const int M, const int N, const int K, const double alpha, const double *A,
   const int lda, const double *B, const int ldb, const double beta, double *C, const int ldc)
2: {
3:   int i,j,l;                              //@=>gemmDecl=Stmt
4:   for (j = 0; j < N; j += 1)              //@ BEGIN(nest1=Nest)
5:     for (i = 0; i < M; i += 1)            //@ BEGIN(nest3=Nest)
6:     {
7:        C[j*ldc+i] = beta * C[j*ldc+i];
8:        for (l = 0; l < K; l +=1)          //@ BEGIN(nest2=Nest)
9:          C[j*ldc+i] += alpha * A[l*lda+i]*B[j*ldb+l];
10:    }
11: }
```

FIGURE 13.7. *An example POET input code with embedded annotations.*

can be empirically tuned based on the runtime performance of differently optimized codes. Figure 13.9 illustrates such an example, which optimizes the matrix–matrix multiplication kernel in Figure 13.7 through the following steps.

- Include the POET opt library (line 1); declare command-line parameters (lines 2–10) and tracing handles (lines 11–12); specify input code to optimize (line 13).
- Declare macros to configure the library (lines 14–19); invoke library routines to optimize the input code (lines 20–29); specify where to output result (line 30).

The following sections explain these components in more detail.

13.4.2.1 Tagging Input Code for Optimization POET is language neutral and uses syntax specifications defined in external files to dynamically process different input and output languages. For example, the input command at line 13 of Figure 13.9 specifies that the input code should be read from a file named "dgemm_test.C" and then parsed using C syntax defined in file "Cfront.code."

POET supports automatic tracing of various fragments of the input code as they go through different transformations by tagging these fragments with tracing handles inside *comments* of the input code. As illustrated in Figure 13.7, each POET tag either starts with "//@" and lasts until the line break, or starts with "/*@" and ends with "@*/." A single-line tag applies to a single line of program source and has the format $\Rightarrow x = T$, where T specifies the type of the tagged code fragment and x specifies the name of the tracing handle used to keep track of the fragment. A multiline tag applies to more than one lines of program source and has the format $BEGIN(x = T)$. For example, line 4 of Figure 13.7 indicates that the tracing handles nest1 should be used to trace the fragment starting from the *for* loop and lasting until the code template *Nest* (i.e., the whole loop nest) has been fully parsed (i.e., until line 10).

13.4.2.2 Tracing Optimizations of the Input Code Each POET script may apply a long sequence of different optimizations to an input code and can specify a large number of command-line parameters to dynamically reconfigure its behavior, as illustrated in lines 2–10 of Figure 13.9. POET provides dedicated language support to automatically trace the modification of various code fragments to support extremely flexible composition of parameterized optimizations so that their configurations can be easily adjusted [1].

In order to trace transformations to an input code, a POET script needs to explicitly declare a group of special global variables as tracing handles, as illustrated in lines 11–12 of Figure 13.9. These tracing handles can be used to tag the input code, illustrated in Figure 13.7, so that after successfully parsing the input file, they are embedded inside the internal representation, named abstract syntax tree (AST), of the input code. Figure 13.8 illustrates such an AST representation of the input code

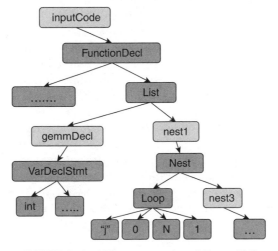

FIGURE 13.8. *AST representation of Figure 13.7.*

```
1:  include opt.pi
2:
3:  <parameter outputFile default="" message="Output file name"/>
4:  <parameter par parse=INT default=2 message="# of threads to run nest1"/>
5:  <parameter par_bk parse=INT default=256 message="# of iterations to run on each thread"/>
6:  <parameter cache_bk parse=LIST(INT," ") default=1 message="blocking factor for nest1"/>
7:  <parameter cp parse=INT default=0 message="whether to copy array A"/>
8:  <parameter uj parse=LIST(INT," ") default=(2 2) message="Unroll&jam factor for nest1"/>
9:  <parameter ur parse=INT default=2 message="Unroll factor for nest2"/>
10: <parameter scalar parse=INT default=1 message="whether to scalar repl A"/>

11: <trace inputCode,decl,nest1,nest3,nest2/>
12: <trace nest1_private = ("j" "i" "l")  A_ref =(ArrayAccess#("A","l"*"lda"+"i"))/>
13: <input from="dgemm_test.C" syntax="Cfront.code" to=inputCode/>
14: <define TRACE_DECL decl/>
15: <define TRACE_INCL inputCode/>
16: <define TRACE_VARS nest1_private/>
17: <define TRACE_TARGET inputCode />
18: <define TRACE_EXP A_ref/>
19: <define ARRAY_ELEM_TYPE "double"/>
20: <eval BlockLoops[factor=par_bk](nest1[Nest.body], nest1);
21:   ParallelizeLoop[threads=par;private=nest1_private](nest1);
22:   if (par > 1) TraceNestedLoops(nest1, nest1[Nest.body]);
23:   BlockLoops[factor=cache_bk](nest2, nest1);
24:   if (cp) CopyRepl[init_loc=nest1;delete_loc=nest1;permute=(2 1)]
                 (A_ref, (nest3 nest2), nest1);
25:   if (cache_bk != 1) TraceNestedLoops((nest1 nest3 nest2),nest2[Nest.body]);
26:   UnrollJam[factor=uj](nest2,nest1);
27:   UnrollLoop[factor=ur](nest2);
28:   if (scalar) ScalarRepl[init_loc=nest2[Nest.body]](A_ref,(nest3 nest2),nest2[Nest.body]);
29:   CleanupBlockedNests(inputCode);/>
30: <output to=outputFile syntax="Cfront.code" from=(inputCode)/>
```

FIGURE 13.9. *A POET script for optimizing Figure 13.7.*

in Figure 13.7 with embedded tracing handles. Here, since tracing handles are contained as an integral component of the input code, they can be automatically modified by routines of the POET optimization library even when the optimization routines cannot directly access them through their names.

13.4.2.3 *Composing Parameterized Optimizations* In Figure 13.9, lines 14–29 illustrate how to apply six heavily parameterized optimizations: OpenMP parallelization (lines 20–21), cache blocking (line 23), copying of array *A* (line 24), loop unroll&jam (line 26), loop unrolling (line 27), and scalar replacement (line 28), to the matrix multiplication code in Figure 13.7. Each optimization is implemented via simple invocations of POET opt library routines defined in Table 13.2, with tuning parameters of each routine controlled command-line parameters. Finally, line 29 explicitly invokes the *CleanupBlockedNexts* routine in Table 13.2 to clean up any inefficiencies produced by the previous optimizations.

In Figure 13.9, in spite of the heavy parameterization, each optimization is specified independently of others with minimal configuration, although any of the previous optimizations could be turned on or off via command-line parameters. This flexibility is supported by the declaration of several tracing handles at lines 11–12. In particular, the tracing handles *inputCode*, *decl*, *nest*1, *nest*3, and *nest*2 are used to track various fragments of the input code and have been used to tag the input code in Figure 13.7; *nest*1_*private* is used to track thread-local variables when parallelizing *nest*1; and *A_ref* is used to track the expression used to access array *A*. At lines

TABLE 13.3. Macro Configurations Supported by the POET Opt Library

TRACE_DECL	Tracing handle for inserting all variable declarations
TRACE_INCL	Tracing handle for inserting all header file inclusions
TRACE_VARS	Tracing handle for inserting all the new variables created
TRACE_TARGET	Tracing handle for tracking all modifications to the input code
TRACE_EXP	Tracing handle for tracking expressions used in optimizations
ARRAY_ELEM_TYPE	The element type of all arrays being optimized

14–19, these handles are set as values of various configuration macros of the POET opt library so that they are automatically modified by all the opt library routines to reflect changes to the input code. The semantics of these configuration macros are defined in Table 13.3. Through these macros, although each optimization is identified independently based on the original source code in Figure 13.7, the transformation remains correct irrespective of how many other optimizations have been applied, as long as each optimization uses these tracing handles as input and configuration parameters and then modifies them accordingly afterward. A POET script can also directly modify tracing handles as it transitions from one optimization to another. For example, in Figure 13.9, line 22 modifies *nest*1 so that if OpenMP parallelization has been applied, later optimizations are applied to the sequential computation block within each thread. Similarly, if cache blocking has been applied, line 25 modifies *nest*1, *nest*3, and *nest*2 so that later register-level optimizations are applied to the inner computation block.

13.4.2.4 Correctness and Efficiency of Optimized Code   When using POET to optimize the source code of an input program, the correctness of optimization depends on two factors: whether the POET optimization library is correctly implemented and whether the library routines are invoked correctly in the user-specified POET script. If either the library or the optimization script has errors, the optimized code may be incorrect. An optimizing compiler, for example, the ROSE analysis engine in Figure 13.5, can ensure the correctness of its auto-generated POET scripts via conservative program analysis. For user supplied POET scripts, additional testing can be used to verify that the optimized code is working properly. Therefore, each optimized code should be tested for correctness before its performance is measured and used to guide the empirical tuning of optimization configurations.

13.4.3 Empirical Tuning and Experimental Results

When used to support auto-tuning of performance optimizations, POET relies on an empirical search driver [8], shown in Figure 13.5, to automatically explore the optimization configuration space for varying architectures. Our previous work has developed POET scripts both manually [9, 10] and automatically through the ROSE loop optimizer [11]. For several linear algebra kernels, our manually written POET scripts have achieved similar performance as that achieved by manually written assembly in the widely used ATLAS library [12]. A sample of the performance comparison is shown in Table 13.4. More details of the experimental results can be found in Reference 10.

To illustrate the need for empirical tuning of optimization configurations, Figure 13.10 shows the performance variations of a 27-point *Jacobi* kernel when optimized

TABLE 13.4. Performance in Megaflops of Differently Optimized Matrix Multiplication Codes [10]

| Kernel name | 2.66-Ghz Core2Duo | | | | | 2.2-Ghz Athlon-64 X2 | | | | |
| | gcc + ref | icc + ref | ATLAS | | PT + spec | gcc + ref | ATLAS | | PT + spec |
			gen	full			gen	full	
sgemmK	571	6226	4730	13972	15048	1009	4093	7651	6918
dgemmK	649	3808	4418	8216	7758	939	3737	4009	3754

sgemmK/dgemmK: single-precision/double-precision matrix–matrix multiplication kernel; gcc + ref/icc + ref: naive implementation compiled with gcc/icc; ATLAS gen/full: ATLAS implementation using source-generator/full search; PT + spec: implementation produced by POET transformation engine.

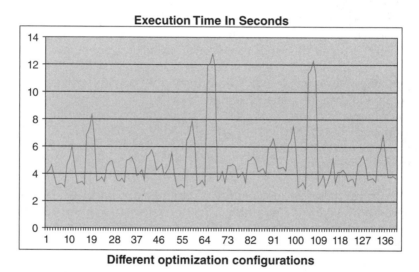

FIGURE 13.10. *Performance of a 27-point Jacobi kernel when optimized with different blocking factors on an Intel Nehalem eight-core machine [9].*

with different blocking factors [9]. Here, the execution time ranges from 2.9 to over 12.0 seconds as the stencil kernel parallelized with a pipelining strategy utilizes machine resources with a variety of different efficiencies. It is typical for different optimization configurations, especially different blocking factors, to make an order of magnitude difference in performance with little predictability. Consequently, empirical tuning is necessary to automatically achieve portable high performance on varying architectures.

13.5 RELATED WORK

The optimization techniques discussed in Section 13.3 are well-known compiler techniques for improving the performance of scientific applications [13–19] and can be fully automated by compilers based on loop-level dependence analysis [5] or more sophisticated integer programming frameworks such as the polyhedral framework [20]. Our ROSE analysis engine in Figure 13.5 is based on an optimization technique called *dependence hoisting* [21], which does not use integer programming.

While we built our analysis engine within the ROSE compiler [22], other source-to-source optimizing compilers, for example, the Paralax infrastructure [23], the Cetus compiler [24], and the Open64 compiler [25], can be similarly extended to serve as our analysis engine.

POET is a scripting language that can be used by developers to directly invoke advanced optimizations to improve the performance of their codes [1, 10]. POET is designed with a focus to support flexible composition of parameterized optimizations so that their configurations can be experimented on the fly and empirically tuned. POET supports existing iterative compilation frameworks [26–31] by providing a transformation engine that enables collective parameterization of advanced compiler optimizations. The POET transformation engine can be easily extended to work with various search and modeling techniques [30, 32–34] in auto-tuning.

Besides POET, various annotation languages such as OpenMP [2] and the X language [35] also provide programmable control of compiler optimizations. The work by Hall et al. [36] allows developers to provide a sequence of *loop transformation recipes* to guide transformations performed by an optimizing compiler. These languages serve as a programming interface for developers to provide additional inputs to an optimizing compiler. In contrast, POET allows developers to directly control the optimization of their codes without relying on an existing optimizing compiler.

13.6 SUMMARY AND FUTURE WORK

As modern computer architectures evolve toward increasingly large numbers of power-efficient parallel processing cores, achieving high performance on such machines entails a large collection of advanced optimizations including partitioning of computation for parallel execution, enhancing data reuse within multiple levels of caches, reducing the synchronization or communication cost of accessing shared data, and carefully balancing the utilization of different functional units in each CPU. This chapter focuses on a number of critical optimization techniques for enhancing the performance of scientific codes on multicore architectures and introduces how to use the POET language to flexibly parameterize the composition of these optimizations so that their configurations can be empirically tuned. A survey of optimization techniques for high-performance computing on other modern architectures such as graphics processing units (GPUs), many-cores, and clusters is left to future work.

ACKNOWLEDGMENTS

This research is funded by National Science Foundation grants CCF0747357 and CCF-0833203, and Department of Energy grant DE-SC0001770.

REFERENCES

[1] Q. Yi, "POET: A scripting language for applying parameterized source-to-source program transformations," in *Software: Practice & Experience*, 2011.

[2] L. Dagum and R. Menon, "OpenMP: An industry standard API for shared-memory programming," *Computational Science & Engineering, IEEE*, 5(1):46–55, 1998.

[3] B. Nichols, D. Buttlar, and J.P. Farrell, *Pthreads Programming*. Sebastopol, CA: O'Reilly Media, Inc., 1996.

[4] J. Reinders, *Intel Threading Building Blocks*, 1st ed. Sebastopol, CA: O'Reilly & Associates, Inc., 2007.

[5] R. Allen and K. Kennedy, *Optimizing Compilers for Modern Architectures*. Burlington, MA: Morgan Kaufmann, 2001.

[6] Q. Yi, "Applying data copy to improve memory performance of general array computations," in *LCPC '05: The 18th International Workshop on Languages and Compilers for Parallel Computing*, Hawthorne, New York, October 2005.

[7] D. Quinlan, M. Schordan, Q. Yi, and S. Bronis, "Semantic-driven parallelization of loops operating on user-defined containers," in *LCPC '03: 16th Annual Workshop on Languages and Compilers for Parallel Computing*, Lecture Notes in Computer Science, October 2003.

[8] S.F. Rahman, J. Guo, and Q. Yi, "Automated empirical tuning of scientific codes for performance and power consumption," in *HIPEAC '11: High-Performance and Embedded Architectures and Compilers*, Heraklion, Greece, January 2011.

[9] S.F. Rahman, Q. Yi, and A. Qasem, "Understanding stencil code performance on multicore architectures," in *CF '11: ACM International Conference on Computing Frontiers*, Ischia, Italy, May 2011.

[10] Q. Yi and C. Whaley, "Automated transformation for performance-critical kernels," in *LCSD '07: ACM SIGPLAN Symposium on Library-Centric Software Design*, Montreal, Canada, October 2007.

[11] Q. Yi, "Automated programmable control and parameterization of compiler optimizations," in *CGO '11: ACM/IEEE International Symposium on Code Generation and Optimization*, April 2011.

[12] R.C. Whaley, A. Petitet, and J. Dongarra, "Automated empirical optimizations of software and the ATLAS project," *Parallel Computing*, 27(1):3–25, 2001.

[13] S. Carr and K. Kennedy, "Improving the ratio of memory operations to floating-point operations in loops," *ACM Transactions on Programming Languages and Systems*, 16(6):1768–1810, 1994.

[14] A. Cohen, M. Sigler, S. Girbal, O. Temam, D. Parello, and N. Vasilache, "Facilitating the search for compositions of program transformations," in *ICS '05: Proceedings of the 19th Annual International Conference on Supercomputing*, pp. 151–160, New York: ACM, 2005.

[15] M. Lam, E. Rothberg, and M.E. Wolf, "The cache performance and optimizations of blocked algorithms," in *Proceedings of the Fourth International Conference on Architectural Support for Programming Languages and Operating Systems (ASPLOS-IV)*, Santa Clara, April 1991.

[16] K. McKinley, S. Carr, and C. Tseng, "Improving data locality with loop transformations," *ACM Transactions on Programming Languages and Systems*, 18(4):424–453, 1996.

[17] L.-N. Pouchet, C. Bastoul, A. Cohen, and N. Vasilache, "Iterative optimization in the polyhedral model: Part I, one-dimensional time," in *Proceedings of the International Symposium on Code Generation and Optimization, CGO '07*, pp. 144–156, Washington, DC, 2007. IEEE Computer Society.

[18] A. Tiwari, C. Chen, J. Chame, M. Hall, and J.K. Hollingsworth, "A scalable auto-tuning framework for compiler optimization," in *IPDPS '09: Proceedings of the 2009 IEEE International Symposium on Parallel & Distributed Processing*, pp. 1–12, Washington, DC, 2009. IEEE Computer Society.

[19] M.J. Wolfe, "More iteration space tiling," in *Proceedings of Supercomputing*, Reno, November 1989.

[20] U. Bondhugula, A. Hartono, J. Ramanujam, and P. Sadayappan, "A practical automatic polyhedral parallelizer and locality optimizer," in *Proceedings of the 2008 ACM SIGPLAN Conference on Programming Language Design and Implementation, PLDI '08*, pp. 101–113, New York: ACM, 2008.

[21] Q. Yi, K. Kennedy, and V. Adve, "Transforming complex loop nests for locality," *The Journal of Supercomputing*, 27:219–264, 2004.

[22] M. Schordan and D. Quinlan, "A source-to-source architecture for user-defined optimizations," in *Joint Modular Languages Conference Held in Conjunction with EuroPar '03*, Austria, August 2003.

[23] H. Vandierendonck, S. Rul, and K. De Bosschere, "The Paralax infrastructure: Automatic parallelization with a helping hand," in *Proceedings of the 19th International Conference on Parallel Architectures and Compilation Techniques, PACT '10*, pp. 389–400, New York: ACM, 2010.

[24] C. Dave, H. Bae, S.-J. Min, S. Lee, R. Eigenmann, and S. Midkiff, "Cetus: A source-to-source compiler infrastructure for multicores," *IEEE Computer*, 42:36–42, 2009.

[25] J.N. Amaral, C. Barton, A.C. Macdonell, and M. Mcnaughton, Using the sgi pro64 open source compiler infra-structure for teaching and research, 2001.

[26] G. Fursin, A. Cohen, M. O'Boyle, and O. Temam, "A pratical method for quickly evaluating program optimizations," in *HiPEAC*, November 2005.

[27] T. Kisuki, P. Knijnenburg, M. O'Boyle, and H. Wijsho, "Iterative compilation in program optimization," in *Compilers for Parallel Computers*, pp. 35–44, 2000.

[28] Z. Pan and R. Eigenmann, "Fast automatic procedure-level performance tuning," in *Proceedings of Parallel Architectures and Compilation Techniques*, 2006.

[29] G. Pike and P. Hilfinger, "Better tiling and array contraction for compiling scientific programs," in *SC*, Baltimore, MD, November 2002.

[30] A. Qasem and K. Kennedy, "Profitable loop fusion and tiling using model-driven empirical search," in *Proceedings of the 20th ACM International Conference on Supercomputing (ICS06)*, June 2006.

[31] M. Stephenson and S. Amarasinghe, "Predicting unroll factors using supervised classification," in *CGO*, San Jose, CA, March 2005.

[32] C. Chen, J. Chame, and M. Hall, "Combining models and guided empirical search to optimize for multiple levels of the memory hierarchy," in *International Symposium on Code Generation and Optimization*, March 2005.

[33] R. Vuduc, J. Demmel, and J. Bilmes, "Statistical models for automatic performance tuning," *International Journal of High Performance Computing Applications*, 18(1):65–94, 2004.

[34] K. Yotov, X. Li, G. Ren, M. Garzaran, D. Padua, K. Pingali, and P. Stodghill, "A comparison of empirical and model-driven optimization," in *IEEE Special Issue on Program Generation, Optimization, and Adaptation*, 2005.

[35] S. Donadio, J. Brodman, T. Roeder, K. Yotov, D. Barthou, A. Cohen, M.J. Garzarán, D. Padua, and K. Pingali, "A language for the compact representation of multiple program versions," in *LCPC*, October 2005.

[36] M. Hall, J. Chame, C. Chen, J. Shin, G. Rudy, and M.M. Khan. "Loop transformation recipes for code generation and auto-tuning," in *LCPC*, October 2009.

[37] T. Tian, "Effective use of the shared cache in multi-core architectures," *Dr. Dobb's*, January 2007.

14

Privacy and Confidentiality in Cloud Computing

Khaled M. Khan and Qutaibah Malluhi

14.1 INTRODUCTION

Cloud computing is an emerging computation model in which applications, data, computational processes, computing resources, and operating platforms are offered to consumers as services. This model provides the opportunity for utility-like virtually unlimited computational power and capacity at a lower cost with greater flexibility as well as elasticity. This new paradigm promotes and facilitates cost-effective outsourcing of computations and data in a shared infrastructure, enabling enterprises to cut information technology costs while focusing on their core business functionalities. Therefore, enterprises are increasingly becoming interested in running their business applications on the cloud.

In spite of the obvious benefits offered by this open computing environment, privacy and confidentiality of consumers' data and processes are the paramount concerns for propelling cloud computing adoption in a wider scale. Cloud computing poses several privacy and confidentiality challenges that can be the major stumbling blocks for moving applications into the cloud. These concerns include the risk of data breaches, malicious corruption of computed results, uncertainty about data privacy, and lack of consumer control on their data assets residing on third-party infrastructure. Consumers' data processed by cloud computing are often sensitive, such as containing commercial secrets, information of national security importance, legal requirements related to privacy laws that pertain to medical records, financial records, or educational records.

Scalable Computing and Communications: Theory and Practice, First Edition. Edited by Samee U. Khan, Albert Y. Zomaya, and Lizhe Wang.
© 2013 John Wiley & Sons, Inc. Published 2013 by John Wiley & Sons, Inc.

Consumers of cloud computing often do not want their data as well as computed output to be seen by the server. This is an issue of data confidentiality. For example, Alice likes to have the computational services of cloud computing but does not want the cloud computing server to "see," "know," or "derive" anything about her input data, processing model, and output data. In other words, cloud servers are supposed to process consumers' data without "seeing" and "comprehending" the actual input and output.

In the database context, there must be assurances that the cloud data center is provably unable to identify individuals with sensitive information. This is an issue of privacy because privacy laws are usually applicable to individually identifiable data. In such privacy and confidentiality requirements, pooling storage resources with consumers' data and their manipulation on the providers' servers raise serious concerns regarding data privacy and confidentiality. These issues force security experts to rethink and reconsider the existing practices in light of this new frontier of privacy and confidentiality problems previously unaccounted for [1]. In cloud environments, flexible and dynamic resource allocation must occur in real time based on events and security policy on a scale that no provider has yet materialized [2]. The challenges are to ensure that appropriate technologies are in place to prevent cloud providers from seeing consumer queries, identifying individuals with sensitive data, and seeing and using consumers' data in a way not agreed upon.

The privacy concern is often addressed with contractual agreements such as service level agreements (SLAs). Interestingly, SLAs might not work for consumers because these are more related to providing compensation to consumers when a violation occurs rather than prevention of privacy and confidentiality violation. Consumers are usually more concerned about the loss of data privacy and not about compensation after the data breach because, for most enterprises, privacy breaches of enterprise data are often irreparable and priceless [3]. In contrast, this chapter focuses more on the concept of prevention rather than on being compensated after privacy and confidentiality breaches. We discuss technological solutions that could enhance consumers' confidence in cloud computing by enabling them to outsource their computational needs with privacy and confidence on the cloud. We are interested in solutions that minimize or even eliminate the utilization of expensive encryption in order to make them more practical.

14.2 CLOUD STAKEHOLDERS AND COMPUTATIONAL ASSETS

Cloud computing is still an evolving paradigm. To understand the entire spectrum of privacy and confidentiality issues of this paradigm, we need to recognize its landscape such as its stakeholders and their computational assets. In this context, computational assets refer to data and processes such as algorithms or specific computing models. Privacy and confidentiality issues are closely related to customers of cloud computing and their computational assets. Figure 14.1 depicts various stakeholders of cloud computing and their computational assets.

14.2.1 Stakeholders

Cloud computing can have two major stakeholders at different levels of its abstraction: *provider* and *consumer*.

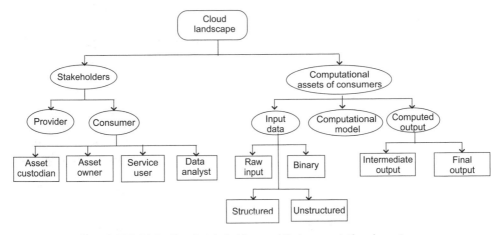

FIGURE 14.1. *Cloud stakeholders and their computational assets.*

14.2.1.1 *Provider* Cloud providers typically own and manage cloud computing resources such as hardware, networks, and systems software. They serve cloud consumers by offering services such as on-demand utility computing, storage, data processing, software services, infrastructure, and operating platform.

14.2.1.2 *Consumer* Cloud consumers are the entities that consume cloud services offered by providers (such as software as a service and database as a service) by outsourcing their computational needs. We can classify cloud consumers into four broader groups: asset custodian, asset owner, service user, and data analyst:

- *Asset Custodian.* This is the entity that produces, manipulates, and stores data on behalf of someone else but does not own them, such as a hospital, which is the custodian of patients' data. A data custodian usually manages data of multiple owners who might have access to their data consigned to the cloud.
- *Asset Owner.* This entity is described by data or to whom the data belong. For example, a patient is the owner of his or her own medical records. Any disclosure of data may affect the privacy of the owner. It is also not uncommon that the data owner and the data custodian are the same entity. Owners could have either direct or indirect access to their data stored in the cloud through their asset custodian.
- *Service User.* Service users only consume the services provided by the cloud without providing input data or computational models. They are the passive consumers of the cloud without owning any data.
- *Data Analyst.* Data analysts periodically use data available on cloud for their own purposes. They usually perform various data mining operations such as analyzing patterns, finding trends, and computing forecasts on data stored on the cloud. Typically, various government agencies fall in this category of the stakeholder. Data analysts analyze populated data on the cloud for various purposes. They can also make available their analysis results on the cloud so that service users could use the results.

14.2.2 Computational Assets of Consumers

The outsourcing of consumers' computational assets involves three types of entities that, in most cases, are considered sensitive and should be kept private and/or confidential:

- *Input Data.* The input data submitted to cloud by consumers often represent information that are sensitive such as business secrets, private information about individuals, national security information, and strategic information. Input data submitted to cloud computing for processing or storage can be classified into four major groups:
  - raw data (e.g., scientific data, matrices, series of numbers, and stream of characters)
  - structured (e.g., relational database and complex data structures)
  - unstructured (e.g., narrative texts)
  - binary (e.g., multimedia objects and images).
- *Computational Models.* Consumers may also use their own customized computational models that embody consumer-specific algorithms, simulations, analyses, processes, and so on. These are often private and confidential in a sense that a disclosure of such models may make consumers lose their competitive advantage or may put them in disadvantageous situations financially and/or legally.
- *Computed Output Data.* Results produced by cloud servers can be classified into two broad categories:
  - intermediate output
  - final output.

These are also considered confidential. The cloud server should not be able to deduce any knowledge out of the computed intermediate or final output.

14.3 DATA PRIVACY AND TRUST

Consumers' computational assets can be sensitive, such as containing commercial secrets involving national security-related information, or subject to legal requirements and regulatory compliances such as the Health Insurance Portability and Accountability Act (HIPAA) legislation for health records, Gramm–Leach–Bliley Act for financial records, or Family Education Rights and Privacy Act (FERPA) for student records. For example, consumers in the European Union (EU) having contract with cloud providers located outside the EU/European Economic Area (EEA) are subject to the EU regulations on export of personal data [4]. Cloud computing is being criticized by privacy advocates for greater control by the companies hosting the cloud services (i.e., cloud providers), and, thus, they can monitor at will, lawfully or unlawfully, the consumers' communication and data.

Cloud consumers have many reasons to be concerned regarding their data and computational models consigned on the cloud:

- *Loss of Control.* Consumers' loss of control on their data and processes once they are on the cloud, and fear of overdependence on third party for manipulating their data stored on remote machines are serious concerns.
- *Leakage of Information.* The possibility of leakage of consumers' proprietary information to competitors such as revealing business secrets, corporate strategy, and data owners' private information may drive the consumers' decision to use the cloud.
- *Regulatory Compliance.* The potential of transborder data movement among cooperating service providers may not be supportive to regulatory compliance such as HIPAA because data located in different countries may be governed by different jurisdictions.
- *Legal Liability.* Compromising private information caused by cloud providers may lead to embarrassments and lawsuits against the consumers and/or providers. Compliance with privacy laws may make it illegal to share data with others such as third-party cloud providers.

Therefore, an important requirement on cloud environments is that the cloud servers learn nothing about the customer's input data, the computational models, and the computed results. The servers of the cloud provider process consumers' data without seeing it, as well as without comprehending the meaning of the computed products. The consumer needs to query the database from time to time but without revealing to the remote server either the queries or the results. Another requirement is that private data are not compromised by preventing linking sensitive information to individuals.

14.4 A CLOUD COMPUTING EXAMPLE

Let us consider an example in order to flesh out the roles of different stakeholders of cloud computing and the privacy and confidentiality issues in relation to outsourcing of scientific computing and relational databases. Figure 14.2 illustrates the scenario of cloud computing with

- different types of stakeholders and their roles
- their outsourcing needs
- their privacy and/or confidentiality requirements.

In this scenario, we can find different stakeholders with their role and security requirements: *CloudLab* (the provider), *MatrixCom* (consumer and asset owner), *ImageGE* (consumer and asset owner), *Penrith Hospital* (consumer but not asset owner), *Medi Insurance* (data analyst), *a medicine manufacturer* (service user), and *patients* (asset owner, but not cloud consumer).

14.4.1 Scientific Computing: Matrix Multiplication

Imagine a company called MatrixCom that handles expensive algebraic computations such as convolution and deconvolution involving multiplications of large

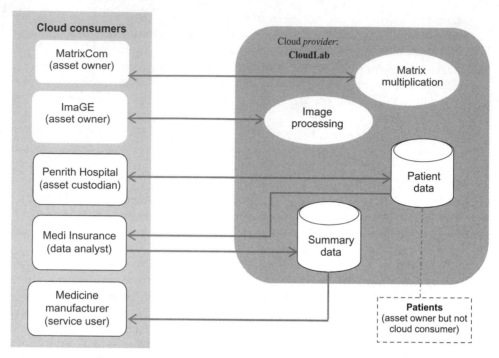

FIGURE 14.2. *A cloud computing scenario with stakeholders and their computational assets.*

matrices. For MatrixCom, the input values of the matrices as well as output are sensitive, and should remain confidential. MatrixCom, an asset owner in this case, is considering to outsource all computationally expensive matrix multiplication tasks to CloudLab (a cloud provider) in a manner that ensures its following data confidentiality and integrity requirements:

1. *Confidentiality.* The servers of the provider CloudLab learn nothing about the input matrices, intermediate output, and the computed output matrix. For example, CloudLab is required to multiply two $n \times n$ matrices A and B sent by MatrixCom. CloudLab should not be allowed to learn any of A, B, or the output matrix C. MatrixCom should be able to hide A and B by doing no more than linear work in terms of the size of matrices A and B.

2. *Integrity of Output.* The cloud consumer MatrixCom requires the computation to be done in such a way that it is able to detect with high probability if the servers of CloudLab did carry out the computations correctly and without cheating. The cloud server may cheat by not carrying out the full expensive computation to save resources; that is, MatrixCom should also be able to validate with high probability that the generated output matrix C is equal to $A \times B$.

3. *Efficiency.* To hide its data and to validate the integrity of the output, MatrixCom should not be required to perform expensive operations that will negate the benefits of outsourcing. Therefore, MatrixCom should only do $O(n^2)$ operations. Otherwise, outsourcing would not make sense because

hiding the input and output data will be as expensive as (or will have similar complexity to) performing the computation itself. In addition, hiding the input and output should not require the server to do operations that have higher complexity than the intended matrix multiplication operation (e.g., the server should not take more than $O(n^3)$ if the brute force matrix multiplication algorithm is used).

14.4.1.1 *Current Practices* Several techniques for secure outsourcing of matrix multiplications exist in the literature [5, 6]. In Reference 5, simple protocols for matrix multiplications that satisfy the above requirements have been presented. These protocols disguise the input/output matrices by shuffling the matrix elements and by adding or multiplying them by random values. These protocols are efficient. However, they suffer from very weak protection as they can easily be attacked.

Relevant and much more secure techniques in the literature include homomorphic encryption and server-aided secret computation [7], which are considered to be expensive. Other relevant work includes protocols for secure multiparty computation and secure function evaluation [8]. However, these protocols do not satisfy the requirements of asymmetric load distribution between the consumer and the server, and the ability to validate the produced output. Researchers have also addressed similar solutions for other types of scientific computations (e.g., DNA analysis [9] and linear programming [10]).

The technique proposed in Reference 11 uses a scheme that requires more than one server. Servers need to perform expensive homomorphic encryptions. The approach is vulnerable to collusion by the participating servers to learn the input. In the classical homomorphism approach [12], the server can perform certain selected operations on data while it remains encrypted; the data owner needs only to decrypt the data received from the server to get the real data. The homomorphic encryption used in Reference 13 requires communication between two participating servers, which may lead to learning the data. The approach also suffers from the need for expensive computation.

14.4.1.2 *Proposed Approach* We envision a framework without any expensive encryption where consumers could only do work that is linear (or close to linear) in the size of their inputs, and the cloud servers do all of the superlinear computational burden. We need techniques that are more efficient and practical than the current state of the art.

In this section, we present a simple protocol as an example for a matrix multiplication that satisfies all the MatrixCom requirements. This protocol is based on the concept of orthogonal matrices. An orthogonal matrix is a matrix whose inverse is its transpose. Therefore, if matrix X is an orthogonal matrix, we have $X^{-1} = X^T$. Let

$$P = \begin{bmatrix} P^1 & & & \\ & P^2 & & 0 \\ & & P^3 & \\ & & & \ddots \\ 0 & & & & P^k \end{bmatrix}, \tag{14.1}$$

where $P^1, P^2, \ldots, P^k$ are 2×2 orthogonal matrices. Each P^i is generated from a random value θ_i as computed in Equation (14.2):

$$P^i = \begin{bmatrix} \sin\theta_i & \cos\theta_i \\ \cos\theta_i & -\sin\theta_i \end{bmatrix}. \tag{14.2}$$

It can easily be verified that P^i is orthogonal and, subsequently, P is also orthogonal. In other words, we have it as shown in Equation (14.3):

$$P^T = \begin{bmatrix} (p^1)^T & & & & \\ & (p^2)^T & & 0 & \\ & & (p^3)^T & & \\ 0 & & & \ddots & \\ & & & & (p^k)^T \end{bmatrix} = P^{-1}. \tag{14.3}$$

Based on the above basic equations, we can outline the following protocol for secure matrix multiplication on the cloud.

14.4.1.3 *Protocol Description*   A consumer wants to compute $C = A \times B$.

1. The consumer generates
   - P, Q, and R, which are random orthogonal matrices generated as indicated in the above equations
   - T and U, which are matrices generated by random shuffling of the rows of the identity matrix I.
2. The consumer computes A', B' as follows:
   - $A' = (T \times Q) \times A \times R$
   - $B' = R^T \times B \times (U \times P)$.
3. The consumer sends A', B' to the provider.
4. The provider calculates $C' = A' \times B'$ and returns the result C' to the consumer.
5. The consumer can find the values of $A \times B$ as follows:
   - $A \times B = (T \times Q)^T \times C' \times (U \times P)^T$.

Notice that the consumer computes:

$$(T \times Q)^T \times C' \times (U \times P)^T = (T \times Q)^T \times (A' \times B') \times (U \times P)^T$$
$$= (T \times Q)^T \times (T \times Q) \times A \times R \times R^T \times B \times (U \times P) \times (U \times P)^T = A \times B.$$

Also, notice that the consumer does not need more than $O(n^2)$ because of the following:

- Multiplication by T and U has the effect of shuffling the rows of the matrix and is done in $O(n^2)$.
- Multiplication by P, Q, and R is $O(n^2)$ because every column or row of these matrices has at most two nonzero elements.

- Cheating detection can be done in $O(n^2)$ in the same way as presented in Reference 11.

14.4.2 Scientific Computing: Image Processing

An image processing company ImaGE deals with various image-related operations ranging from image template matching, sharpening the edges of objects, reducing random noise, correcting the unequal illumination in large digital images, and so on. In image matching, the template represented as a kernel or filter is a description of the object to be matched in the image. ImaGE requires mathematical computations such as convolving the original image with an appropriate filter kernel, producing the filtered image, and correlating the template with the image. Correlation and convolution are basic operations that the company ImaGE needs to extract from or to match particular information in images. Correlation is usually used to find locations in an image. These operations have two main features: shift invariant and linear. In shift-invariant operation, the same operation is performed at every point in the image, whereas in linear operation, every pixel is replaced with a linear combination of its neighbors. The output values of the convolution are simple linear combinations of certain input pixel values.

However, the image convolution requires ImaGE computers to perform an enormous amount of calculations. For example, when a 1024×1024 pixel image is convolved with a 64×64 pixel filter, more than a billion multiplications and additions are needed (i.e., $64 \times 64 \times 1024 \times 1024$). ImaGE considers outsourcing its image processing to CloudLab because operations tend to be computationally intensive and their data are often captured by computationally weak hardware. The confidentiality requirements of ImaGE are the following:

1. The server of CloudLab will not know the values of the original image and the filter.
2. The server will also not know the values of the output convolved image.

14.4.2.1 *Current Approaches*

In current approaches, encryption of images is usually used to make the images secure during the communication process. However, the research on hiding the actual pixel values of images from the server is still in the infancy stage. In one approach, the random splitting of the image into several pieces is used to hide the pixel; however, this approach is not very effective in securing the pixel values.

14.4.2.2 *Proposed Approach*

In our vision, we believe that a template matching operation requires computing a difference measure between the template and all possible portions of the image that could match the template. Various difference measures have different mathematical as well as computational properties. More precisely, let Q be an $m \times m$ matrix (the image) and P an $n \times n$ matrix (the template represented as in a filter), $n \le m$. The entries of both Q and P come from some s-element alphabet $A = a_1, a_2, \ldots, a_s$, where the a_i's are typically positive integer values. The goal is then to compute an $(m - n + 1) \times (m - n + 1)$ matrix C, where $C(i, j)$ is of the form $C(i, j) = \sum_{k=0}^{n-1} \sum_{k'=0}^{n-1} f(Q(i+k, j+k'), P(k, k'))$, for some function f, $0 \le i, j \le m - n$.

A method similar to matrix multiplications can be used for the *Euclidean* distance metric that corresponds to $f(x, y) = (x - y)^2$.

In order to hide the actual values of the original image and the filter from the server without encryptions, we adopt the similar approach as proposed for matrix multiplications in the previous section. According to our approach, the pixel values of the rows and columns of images are randomly shuffled, scaled, and additively split. These could be augmented with an efficient image splitting technique in which the images are randomly split into several pieces and sent to the server piece by piece. When CloudLab returns the processed pieces of images to ImaGE, it needs to reconstruct the image by computing the pieces together, which should not require ImaGE heavy computing efforts.

14.4.3 Database Outsourcing: Query Processing on Relational Databases

Consider a database-as-a-service model offered by CloudLab. Penrith Hospital likes to use this service in order to outsource its patients' clinical data for storage and query processing. The clinical data include patients' illnesses, prescribed medications to patients, doctor's name, patients' personal information, treatment dates, and so on. In this case, Penrith Hospital is the consumer of CloudLab, whereas patients are the owners of data processed by CloudLab (but not the consumers of this CloudLab service). Penrith Hospital is also the custodian of the patients' clinical data, which are considered sensitive and private, and patients should not be identified with their clinical data to any entities without their consent. Penrith Hospital is liable to patients for data privacy; therefore, it requires the following in order to preserve confidentiality and privacy of its patients' data:

1. CloudLab should be prevented from seeing clinical information of any patients and from linking their identity with sensitive information such as their illness and drugs prescribed.
2. CloudLab should enable third-party data users or data analysts such as government agencies to access parts of the patients' data without violating privacy restrictions. Data analysts could perform, for example, statistical operations on patients' clinical databases without knowing clinical information about individuals or the identity of the patients.
3. Penrith Hospital should be able to fully query its database. The database queries should substantially be processed by the CloudLab servers. Penrith Hospital should perform small amounts of computing to get the final answers of queries that are partially (but substantially) processed by the servers.

14.4.3.1 Current Practices Known techniques to prevent a third party from seeing confidential information in outsourced data include using encryption, or information hiding techniques on data such as perturbation, generalization, and swapping [14]. Databases can be stored on cloud servers in encrypted form. However, encrypted databases do not allow query processing on the server. Data anonymization models like *k*-anonymity [15] and *l*-diversity [16, 17] have been developed to provide guarantees of privacy protection [14]. Some anonymization techniques such as order-preserving partial encryption, anatomy, and generalization enable partial

TABLE 14.1. Original Table with Identifying and Sensitive Data

Name	Age	Zip Code	Illness
David	44	75,000	Cancer
Ali	63	36,100	Influenza
Alice	70	61,230	Cancer
Bob	35	45,000	Diabetics

Encrypted Link

Name	Age	Zip Code	GroupID	Seq
David	44	75000	1	1
Ali	63	36100	2	2
Alice	70	61230	2	3
Bob	35	45000	1	4

(a)

H(Seq)	GroupID	Illness
H(1)	1	Cancer
H(2)	2	Influenza
H(3)	2	Cancer
H(4)	1	Diabetics

(b)

FIGURE 14.3. *Partitioned tables into identifying and sensitive information. (a) Identifying information. (b) Sensitive information.*

query processing on the server but with data loss. In Reference 18, a bucketization technique has been proposed to enable a third party to partially execute data owners' queries on the encrypted database to get the actual result of the queries.

14.4.3.2 Proposed Approach Most of the above techniques usually lead to information loss (e.g., information is lost when an address is generalized to/replaced by a zip code). In contrast, we are aiming for using an advanced anonymization technique such as proposed in Reference 19 that would enable private database outsourcing without or with minimum loss of information while enabling query processing on the server. Advanced anonymization techniques should ensure no data loss in order to provide regular full query processing on the database while preserving data privacy. Let us consider an example. Table 14.1 depicts a database of patients that Penrith Hospital stores on CloudLab. The illness of the individual patient is considered sensitive as well as private to the patient. The table contains identifying information such as name, age, and zip code of the patient, and sensitive information such as illness.

Applying the anatomy model [15] and anonymization technique [19] to the table, the consumer, Penrith Hospital, separates sensitive data (illness) from the identifying information of the patient (name, age, zip code), divides the tuples into groups, and stores them on CloudLab, as shown in Figure 14.3.

In the basic anatomy model, the consumer, Penrith Hospital, loses the information linking individuals to their illness. Therefore, we propose an approach in which Penrith Hospital maintains an encrypted link between these two tables by using a unique key enabling join of the tables. The efficient symmetric encryption techniques can be used for encrypting this link. The symmetric encryption key is only known to Penrith Hospital; servers of CloudLab have no knowledge about the key. In this case, the data are minimally encrypted. The identifying and sensitive information in isolation, such as the two tables (Figure 14.3a,b, respectively) in Figure 14.3, do not violate the privacy constraints. An example of a privacy constraint is k-anonymity, which requires that any tuple in the table cannot be linked with less than k individuals. It is clear that, in Figure 14.3, the records satisfy the 2-anonymity constraint. However, only the authorized consumer (i.e., Penrith Hospital) with the key will have full access to the database and can have queries that link these two tables (i.e., links corresponding tuples from the two tables). The service provider (or the third-party user) can only have anonymized (e.g., 2-anonymous) information from these partitioned data. This approach enables the server to partially execute queries of the consumer, who has the key to link the partitioned tables [19]. The consumer gets partial results that can be used to easily extract the intended result through decrypting the hidden link between the partial results. Since the server would not have access to identifiable data, it would not be protected from being subject to violation of privacy laws.

14.5 CONCLUSION

The privacy and confidentiality model of cloud computing should focus more on the prefailure rather than the postfailure of cloud services. Therefore, it is quite vital that clouds should provide technological guarantees in addition to contractual agreements to consumers that their data as well as processing always remain private and confidential on the cloud. This chapter has provided some efficient techniques for private and confidential manipulation of consumer data on the cloud without expensive cryptographic processing. It also shows that much of the controlling power remains in the hand of cloud consumers whose data should be protected. With the proposed technologies, the consumer is able to decide which part of its data could be revealed to the servers. The proposed approaches advocate for improving the efficiency by minimizing the use of expensive encryption to preserve privacy and confidentiality and by shipping the expensive data processing operations to the more powerful cloud servers (rather than performing them on the weak consumer machines). These methods will promote the consumers' trust in the cloud and will allow cloud providers to ensure secure and trustworthy services.

ACKNOWLEDGMENTS

This publication was made possible by the support of a National Priorities Research Program grant from the Qatar National Research Fund (QNRF). The statements made herein are solely the responsibility of the authors.

REFERENCES

[1] A. Ghosh and I. Arce, "In cloud computing we trust but should we? " IEEE Security and Privacy, November/December 2010, pp. 14–16.

[2] P. Banarjee, et al., "Everything as a service: Powering the new information economy," *IEEE Computer*, 44(3):36–43, 2011.

[3] K. Khan and Q. Malluhi, "Establishing trust in cloud computing," *IEEE IT Pro*, September/October 2010.

[4] T. Helbing, "How the new EU rules on data export affect companies in and outside the EU." Available at http://www.thomashelbing.com/en.

[5] M. Atallah, K. Pantazopoulos, J. Rice, and E. Spafford, "Secure outsourcing of scientific computations," *Advances in Computers*, 54(6):215–272, 2001.

[6] K. Frikken and M. Atallah, "Securely outsourcing linear algebra computations," *Proceedings of the 5th ACM Symposium on Information, Computer and Communications Security (AsiaCCS 2010)*, Beijing, China, April 2010.

[7] P. Beguin and J. Quisquater, "Fast server-aided RSA signatures secure against active attacks," in *CRYPT0 95*, pp. 57–69, 1995.

[8] A. Yao, "Protocols for secure computation," *Proceedings of the 23rd Annual IEEE Symposium on Foundations of Computer Science*, pp. 160–164, 1982.

[9] M. Blanton and M. Aliasgari, "Secure outsourcing of DNA searching via finite automata," in *Annual IFIP Conference on Data and Applications Security (DBSec '10)*, pp. 49–64, June 2010.

[10] C. Wang, K. Ren, and J. Wang, "Secure and practical outsourcing of linear programming in cloud computing," *30th IEEE International Conference on Computer Comm. (INFOCOM '11)*, Shanghai, China, April 2011.

[11] D. Benjamin and M. Atallah, "Private and cheating-free outsourcing of algebraic computations," in *6th Annual Conference on Privacy, Security, and Trust (PST 2008)*, pp. 240–245. Fredericton, New Brunswick, Canada, 2008.

[12] R. Rivest, L. Adleman, and M. Dertouzos, "On data banks and privacy homomorphisms," in *Foundations of Secure Computation* (R. DeMillo, D. Dobkin, A. Jones, and R. Lipton, eds.), New York: Academic Press, pp. 169–180, 1978.

[13] M. Atallah and J. Li, "Secure outsourcing of sequence comparisons," *International Journal of Information Security*, 4(4):277–286, 2005.

[14] B. Hore, S. Mehrotra, and H. Hacigumus, Managing and querying encrypted data in *Handbook of Database Security: Applications and Trends*, pp. 163–190, 2007. Available at http://dx.doi.org/10.1007/978-0-387-48533-17.

[15] X. Xiao and Y. Tao, "Anatomy: Simple and effective privacy preservation," *Proceedings of the 32nd International Conference on Very Large Databases (VLDB 2006)*, Seoul, Korea, September 2006.

[16] M. Machanavajjhala, et al., "l-Diversity: Privacy beyond k-anonymity," *ACM Transactions on Knowledge Discovery from Data (TKDD)*, 1(1):1–52, 2007.

[17] L. Sweeney, "k-Anonymity: A model for protecting privacy," *International Journal on Uncertainty, Fuzziness and Knowledge-Based Systems*, 10(5):557–570, 2002.

[18] H. Hacigumus, B. Iyer, and S. Mehrotra, "Executing SQL over encrypted data in the database-service-provider model," in *Proceedings of the 2002 ACM SIGMOD International Conference on Management of Data*, Madison, WI, June 4–6, pp. 216–227, 2002. Available at http://doi.acm.org/10.1145/564691.564717.

[19] A. Nergiz and C. Clifton, "Query processing in private data outsourcing using anonymization," *Proceedings of the Conference on Database Security (DBSec 2011), Lecture Notes in Computer Science*, pp. 138–153.2011.

15

Reputation Management Systems for Peer-to-Peer Networks

Fang Qi, Haiying Shen, Harrison Chandler, Guoxin Liu, and Ze Li

15.1 INTRODUCTION

In recent years, peer-to-peer (P2P) networks have gained popularity in many large-scale, distributed Internet applications. P2P networks enable the sharing of globally scattered computer resources, allowing them to be collectively used in a cooperative manner for different applications such as file sharing [1–4], instant messaging [5], audio conferencing [6], and distributed computing [7]. Node cooperation is critical to achieving reliable P2P performance but proves challenging since networks feature autonomous nodes without preexisting trust relationships. Additionally, some internal nodes may be compromised, misbehaving, selfish, or even malicious. Then, a critical problem arises: How can a resource requester choose a resource provider that is trustworthy and provides high quality of service (QoS) from among many resource providers?

The main way to address this problem is with reputation management systems. Like the reputation systems in the eBay [8], Amazon [9] and Overstock [10] e-commerce platforms, reputation systems employed in P2P networks compute and publish global reputation values for each node based on a collection of local ratings from others in order to provide guidance in selecting trustworthy nodes. They thwart the intentions of uncooperative and dishonest nodes and provide incentives for high QoS.

Scalable Computing and Communications: Theory and Practice, First Edition. Edited by
Samee U. Khan, Albert Y. Zomaya, and Lizhe Wang.
© 2013 John Wiley & Sons, Inc. Published 2013 by John Wiley & Sons, Inc.

For example, in a P2P file-sharing system, a file requester needs to choose a single file provider from many file providers. The requester can refer to the reputation management system to obtain the reputations of the file providers and to choose the highest-reputed file provider for high QoS file provision.

Substantial research has been conducted on reputation management systems. These works can be classified into two categories: scalability/accuracy and security. The works on scalability/accuracy describe methods to efficiently collect feedback on past node behaviors, provide node reputation values, and accurately evaluate a node's trustworthiness. The works on security describe methods to avoid malicious behaviors in order to ensure the correct operation and dependability of reputation systems in guiding trustworthy node selection. One particularly bothersome behavior is collusion. A colluding collective is a group of malicious peers who know each other, give each other high ratings, and give all other peers low ratings in an attempt to subvert the system and to gain high global reputation values [11]. Reputation systems are generally vulnerable to node collusion [12, 13], and works on collusion resilience describe methods to deter collusion or to reduce the adverse effects of collusion on reputation systems. In this chapter, we will focus on discussing these two categories of works.

The rest of this chapter is structured as follows. Section 15.2 introduces works in the above two categories. Section 15.3 presents case studies on three reputation management systems. Section 15.4 discusses open problems with reputation management systems in P2Ps. Finally, Section 15.5 summarizes the chapter.

15.2 REPUTATION MANAGEMENT SYSTEMS

15.2.1 Approaches for Scalability and Accuracy

In a P2P network, millions of nodes are scattered across geographically distributed areas and enter or leave the system continuously and unpredictably. The large-scale, wide geographic distribution and dynamism of these networks pose a challenge to achieving high scalability in reputation management. Also, the accuracy of calculated global node reputation values determines the effectiveness of a reputation system in discouraging uncooperative and dishonest behaviors and encouraging cooperative behaviors. This section presents the techniques that enable a reputation system to scale to serve a large number of nodes in terms of feedback collection efficiency and overhead, and to achieve high accuracy in node trustworthiness reflection.

15.2.1.1 EigenTrust EigenTrust [11] can minimize the impact of malicious peers on the performance of a P2P network. In this system, the global reputation of a peer is calculated by its received local trust values from other peers and is weighted by the global reputations of the peers. Specifically, the system computes a global trust value for a peer by calculating the left principal eigenvector of a matrix of normalized local trust values, thus taking into consideration the entire system's history with each single peer. EigenTrust carries out these computations in a scalable and distributed manner; all peers in the network participate in computing global reputation values node symmetrically, with minimal overhead on the network.

Furthermore, EigenTrust ensures the security of the computations and minimizes the probability that malicious peers in the system lie for their own benefit. Peers that provide material deemed inappropriate by the users of a P2P network are accurately identified by EigenTrust and effectively isolated from the network. This system is highly effective in decreasing the number of unsatisfactory downloads, even when up to 70% of the peers in the network form a malicious collective in an attempt to subvert the system. In P2P simulations, using reputation values to bias peers against certain providers has shown to reduce the number of inauthentic files in the network under a variety of threat scenarios. Furthermore, rewarding highly reputable peers with better QoS induces nonmalicious peers to share more files and to self-police their own file repository for inauthentic files.

15.2.1.2 *PeerTrust*

PeerTrust [14] is a dynamic P2P trust model for quantifying and assessing the trustworthiness of peers in P2P e-commerce communities. A unique characteristic of the trust model is the identification of five important factors for evaluating the trustworthiness of a peer in an evolving P2P e-commerce community, as listed below:

1. the feedback a peer receives from other peers
2. the feedback scope, such as the total number of transactions that a peer has conducted with other peers
3. the credibility of the feedback sources
4. the transaction context factor for distinguishing mission-critical transactions from less critical or noncritical ones
5. the community context factor for addressing community-related characteristics and vulnerabilities.

PeerTrust defines a general trust metric that combines the parameters of the above factors and implements the trust model in a decentralized P2P environment. It can significantly reduce common security threats in P2P environments, such as man-in-the-middle attacks, compromised peers, and the distribution of tampered-with information.

15.2.1.3 *TrustGuard*

TrustGuard [15] is a highly dependable reputation-based trust-building framework with a storage service built on top of PeerTrust. The TrustGuard framework is equipped with several safeguards that are critical for minimizing the potential threats and vulnerabilities in the reputation system itself. It guards against strategic oscillations, detects fake transactions, and filters out dishonest feedback. First, TrustGuard incorporates the historical reputations and behavioral fluctuations of a node into the estimation of its trustworthiness, guaranteeing that reputation is built gradually but drops quickly if a node starts to behave maliciously. Second, TrustGuard has a feedback admission control mechanism to ensure that only transactions with secure proofs can be used to file feedback; this prevents malicious nodes from misusing the system by flooding feedback. Third, TrustGuard has an effective mechanism to rate the feedback credibility of nodes and to discount dishonest feedback in order to filter out dishonest feedback when computing the reputation-based trust of a node (including the feedback filed by malicious nodes through collusion). TrustGuard's approach can efficiently and effectively secure a large-scale distributed reputation system, making it more dependable than other existing reputation-based trust systems.

15.2.1.4   *FuzzyTrust*   FuzzyTrust [16] is a prototype P2P reputation system that helps establish mutual trust among strangers in P2P transaction applications. The authors first analyzed auction-based transaction trace data from eBay to sort out client behavioral characteristics and then proposed FuzzyTrust based on the data analysis. The system uses fuzzy logic inference rules to calculate local trust scores and to aggregate global reputation. It benefits from the distinct advantages of fuzzy inferences, which can effectively handle imprecise or uncertain linguistic terms collected from peers. Furthermore, the system uses a distributed hash table (DHT) overlay network to perform fast and secure reputation dissemination among peers. Experimental results show that FuzzyTrust identifies malicious peers effectively and has a low message overhead in the global reputation aggregation process.

15.2.1.5   *Reputation Systems for Pollution Avoidance*   In content pollution in P2P file-sharing systems, polluters camouflage polluted files and share them with other users; unsuspecting users then download these files, wasting bandwidth and CPU resources. Furthermore, polluted files are often left in the shared folders of normal users, thus rapidly spreading the files through the system. Credence [17] and Scrubber [18] are reputation systems that fight content pollution.

Credence is a decentralized distributed object reputation system in which users assign reputations to the objects they download with regard to their authenticity. It is based on a distributed vote gathering protocol for disseminating object reputations in the network and on a correlation scheme that more heavily weights votes from like-minded peers. Credence also periodically runs a gossip protocol where each peer randomly selects another peer to retrieve its correlation coefficients. Transitive correlations are computed by multiplying retrieved correlation coefficients by the local weights given to the contacted peers.

Scrubber is a distributed and decentralized peer reputation system that quickly identifies and severely punishes active polluters but also includes inherent incentives for peer rehabilitation by giving passive polluters (i.e., peers that share polluted content by negligence) an incentive to remove polluted content they have downloaded. Scrubber has a distributed and decentralized architecture, thus simplifying deployment. Compared with Credence, Scrubber converges much faster to a competitive maximum efficiency, quickly reducing the fraction of daily downloads that are polluted objects to less than 8%, as long as at least 25% of the peers react to punishment by deleting their polluted objects. Otherwise, Credence somewhat outperforms Scrubber in the long run.

Costa and Almeida proposed a hybrid reputation system [19] that is a hybrid peer and object reputation system combining the benefits of both Scrubber and Credence. Despite a quick convergence, Scrubber is not always able to clean polluted objects shared by peers that only occasionally upload them. Credence, on the other hand, converges much more slowly but is eventually able to isolate all polluted objects. The hybrid system combines the benefits of both Scrubber and Credence by building a mechanism for peers to vote on the authenticity of objects into Scrubber. The hybrid system has two key components: the object reputation and the peer reputation. The peer and object reputations are evaluated based on the assumption that a peer well reputed as a content provider (or voter) is an honest reputation reporter. Like Scrubber, the hybrid system must take the network opinion into account by applying quick punishments to polluters to be a viable solution for large-scale P2P systems, where the frequency of interaction between the same pair of peers is typically low. Memory requirements are roughly equal for all three systems, and most memory is used for the storage of local and remote opinions of peers. The main benefits are the following: (1) The hybrid system converges to a maximum efficiency much faster than Credence and Scrubber, even under collusion and Sybil attacks [20]; (2) the hybrid system is less sensitive to parameter settings than Scrubber, providing cost-effectiveness for various configurations; and (3) the hybrid system is able to restrain pollution dissemination even in very uncooperative and unreliable communities, despite depending greatly on user cooperation and reliable feedback.

15.2.1.6 *GossipTrust*

GossipTrust GossipTrust [21] is a scalable, robust, and secure reputation management system specifically designed for unstructured P2P networks. This system leverages a gossip-based protocol to aggregate global reputation scores; specifically, each peer randomly contacts others and exchanges reputation data periodically. Gossip-based protocols do not require any error recovery mechanism and thus enjoy simplicity and moderate overhead when compared with optimal deterministic protocols [22] such as the construction of data dissemination trees. GossipTrust is built around a fast reputation aggregation module with enhanced security support that strengthens the robustness of the gossip protocol under disturbances from malicious peers. The system has a novel data management scheme to answer reputation queries and to store reputation data with low overhead. Identity-based cryptography is applied to ensure the confidentiality, integrity, and authenticity of the exchanged reputation data without using certified public keys or preshared secret keys.

GossipTrust was improved [23] with higher speed and accuracy in aggregating local trust scores into global reputation ranks. The improved GossipTrust enables peers to compute global reputation scores in a fully distributed, secure, scalable, and robust fashion. Simulation results show that the system scales well with increasing network size. The system can also tolerate link failures and peer collusion. The technical innovations of this improved reputation system are summarized in four aspects:

1. *Fast Gossip-Based Reputation Aggregation Algorithms with Small Aggregation Error.* The $O(\log_2 n)$ time complexity, where n is the number of nodes in the network, makes the gossip search as attractive as a DHT-based table lookup.
2. *Efficient Reputation Storage Using Bloom Filters with Low False-Positive Error.* Even for a network of one million nodes, the memory required to rank nodes by reputation is just 512 kB per node, and the false-positive error is at most 15%.
3. *Limited Network Traffic Overhead in Gossip Message Spreading.* The total network traffic increase of $O(n \log_2 n)$ is low compared to multicast or broadcast approaches.

4. *Combating Peer Collusion by Using Power Nodes Dynamically.* GossipTrust leverages the rank of all nodes in terms of their relative standing in the global reputation vector. The effects of peer collusion are minimized due to each colluding peer's low rank.

15.2.1.7 Personalized Trust (PET)

PET [24] is a personalized trust model in the context of economic-based solutions for P2P resource sharing. The trust model consists of two parts: reputation evaluation and risk evaluation. Reputation evaluation is the accumulative assessment of a long-term behavior, while risk evaluation is the assessment of a short-term behavior. Risk is employed to deal with dramatic behavior changes in peers. PET novelly models risk as an opinion of short-term trustworthiness and combines this with a traditional reputation evaluation to derive trustworthiness. In this model, recommendations play a moderate role as one of the many factors from which local trustworthiness values are derived. PET only takes into account a peer's behavior within an employed risk window; as the window shifts forward, the risk value reflects the fresh statistics of the peer's recent behaviors. The risk model is very important in PET since risk evaluation can combat malicious recommendations. The authors' observations are summarized below:

1. Giving risk a high weight more effectively improves the performance of the model in such measures as sensitivity, effectiveness, hit ratio, and applicability when more peers in the community are malicious or uncooperative.
2. A small risk window size is helpful in improving the sensitivity of the model when the weight of the risk is high.
3. Giving recommendations a low weight improves the performance of the model while maintaining resistance to malicious recommendations.

The PET model is promising for resource sharing in P2P networks with large numbers of dynamic peers, uncooperative peers, and malicious recommenders.

15.2.1.8 H-Trust

Peer-to-peer desktop grid (P2PDG) has emerged as a pervasive cyberinfrastructure tackling many large-scale applications with high impact, such as SETI@Home and DNA@Home. In a P2PDG environment, users run large-scale and cooperative computational applications, and most computing jobs are accomplished by workgroups. However, nearly all existing reputation systems do not consider issues with group reputation for collaborative services and resource sharing. In addition, most of the current reputation schemes must decide between low network overhead or high accuracy in reputation aggregation. To address these issues, a robust and lightweight group trust management system was proposed, called H-Trust [25], which was inspired by the H-index aggregation approach [26]. Leveraging the robustness of the H-index algorithm under incomplete and uncertain circumstances, H-Trust offers a robust reputation evaluation mechanism for both individual and group trusts with minimal communication and computation overhead. Users in this system only store information they can explicitly use for their own benefit. H-Trust further considers spatial and temporal information to update and adapt trust scores for individuals and groups. The H-Trust reputation aggregation scheme is implemented in five phases:

1. The trust recording phase records past service information in a trust history table, which is maintained in the DHT-based overlay network.

2. In the local trust evaluation phase, a local trust score is calculated by a local trust manager using a weighted reputation aggregation algorithm.

3. The trust query phase is required when trust information is not available locally. The credibility of the responses and the H-index aggregation are proposed in this phase to yield an individual's reputation.

4. The spatial-temporal update phase is activated periodically to renew local trust scores and credibility factors.

5. The group reputation evaluation phase aggregates a group reputation using the H-Trust algorithm.

15.2.1.9 A Trust Inference System Lee et al. [27] proposed a distributed scheme for trust inference in the context of the NICE system, which is a platform for implementing cooperative applications over the Internet. The inferred trust values represent how likely a user considers other users to be cooperative and are used to price resources in the NICE system.

The trust inference system aims to classify all users as either cooperative or uncooperative with no errors. In this scheme, for each transaction in the system, each involved user produces a signed statement (called a cookie) about the quality of the transaction. The scheme infers trust using a directed graph called a trust graph. The vertices in the graph correspond exactly to the users in the system. There is an edge directed from user A to user B if and only if user B holds a cookie from user A. The value of the $A—B$ edge denotes how much user A trusts user B and depends on the set of user A's cookies held by user B.

Given a path $A_0 \rightarrow A_1 \rightarrow A_k$ in the trust graph, A_0 could infer a number of plausible trust values for A_k, including the minimum value of any edge on the path or the product of the trust values along the path; these inferred trust values are called the strength of the $A_0 \rightarrow A_k$ path. Assume node A has access to the trust graph and wants to infer a trust value for node B. Node A can use (1) the strongest path, which takes the minimum trust value on the path as the trust value for B, or (2) a weighted sum of the strongest disjoint paths. Users locate trust information about other users in a distributed manner. Each user stores a set of signed cookies that it receives as a result of previous transactions. Suppose node A wants to use some resources at node B. There are two possibilities: Either A already has cookies from B or nodes A and B have not had any transactions yet. For the case in which A already has cookies from B, A presents these to B. Node B can verify that these are indeed its cookies since it has signed them. From the cookies, node B can compute a trust value for A. When A has no cookies from B, A initiates a search for B's cookies at nodes from whom A holds cookies. After the search is over, A presents B with a union of directed paths, which all start at B and end at A, which correspond exactly to the union of directed edges on the trust graph used for the previously described centralized trust inference. Thus, B can infer a trust value for A.

Through the above scheme, the trust inference system lets benign nodes find each other quickly and efficiently and prevents malicious nodes and cliques from breaking up cooperating groups by spreading misinformation to benign nodes; thus, the system achieves its goal of classifying all users as either cooperative or uncooperative.

15.2.1.10 A Reputation-Based Trust Management System In the reputation-based trust management system proposed in Reference 28, each peer maintains a trust vector for every other peer it has dealt with in the past. Trust vectors are of constant length and are binary. A 1 bit represents an honest transaction, and a 0 bit represents a dishonest one. Based on the trust vector, a peer calculates trust and distrust ratings for other peers. The trust query process is similar to the file query process except that the subject of the query is a peer about whom trust information is desired. The responses are sorted and weighted by the credibility ratings of the responders. Credibility ratings are derived from the credibility vectors maintained by the local peer, which are similar to the trust vectors: A 0 in a credibility vector shows a failed judgment from that peer in the past, and a 1 shows a successful judgment. The threshold specifies the number of responses to be evaluated for each trust query. The queried trust/distrust rating is the average of the evaluated trust ratings weighted by the credibility of their senders. This trust management system features the following:

1. *The Separate Treatment of Distrust Ratings.* Handling distrust ratings separately means that a dishonest dealing cannot be easily erased by a few honest transactions, thus closely modeling real-life trust relationships in which a single dishonest transaction in someone's history is a more significant indicator than several honest transactions.

2. *Temporal Adaptivity Consideration, That Is, the Ability to Respond Rapidly to Changing Behavioral Patterns.* The trust rating design utilizing binary vectors is an efficient exponential aging scheme with an aging factor of 0.5. Moreover, implementing the aging scheme by fixed-length registers rather than floating-point arithmetic has the desirable feature of enabling peers to cleanse their history by doing a reasonable amount of community service after a bad deed.

3. *The Use of a Credibility Rating System Separate from Trust Ratings.* The main risk of using trust ratings for credibility evaluation comes from coordinated attacks where some malicious peers do as much faithful public service as they can to build a strong reputation and then use their credibility for supporting others who spread malicious content. Having separate trust and credibility rating systems precludes such attacks.

15.2.2 Approaches for Security

An important challenge in managing trust relationships is designing a protocol to secure the placement and access of trust ratings. Specifically, a reputation system should ensure the following [29]:

1. *Security.* Due to decentralized management of trust relationships, the trust rating of a peer is stored at other peers in the network; it is critical that these trust hosting peers are protected from targeted attacks.

2. *Reliability.* It is important that anybody querying for a trust value gets the true trust value despite the presence of various malicious users.

3. *Accountability.* In peer review-based trust systems, it is important that peers are accountable for the feedback they provide about other peers. Any malicious peer trying to manipulate trust ratings should be identifiable.

In this section, we present the methods proposed to achieve some of the above properties.

15.2.2.1 *Maze P2P File-Sharing System*

Of particular concern in reputation and trust systems is collusion, that is, multiple nodes working together to game the system. Collusion subverts any strategy in which everyone in the system agrees on the reputation of a player (objective reputation). The effect of collusion is magnified in systems with zero-cost identities, where users can create fake identities that report false statements [30].

Maze [12] is a popular Napster-like P2P network designed, implemented, and deployed by an academic research team at Peking University, Beijing, China. The authors searched for the existence of a colluding behavior by examining the complete user logs of the entire system and used a set of collusion detectors to identify several major collusion patterns:

1. *Detector 1 (Repetition Detector).* Large amounts of upload traffic with repeated content.
2. *Detector 2 (Pairwise Detector).* Large amounts of mutual upload traffic between a pair of nodes compared to total uploads.
3. *Detector 3 (Spam Account Detector).* High peer to machine ratios indicating spam account collusion.
4. *Detector 4 (Traffic Concentration Detector).* Exceptionally high traffic concentration degrees, which is the ratio of a peer's highest upload traffic to a single machine to his total upload traffic.

15.2.2.2 *Stamp Trading Protocol*

Reputation and payment protocols are two methods of introducing cooperation incentives to nodes in P2P networks. In reputation protocols, nodes with low reputations will find it difficult to obtain service in the network. A reputation protocol can ensure that nodes need to successfully contribute to the network in order to have a high reputation. In payment protocols, nodes receive credits only by successfully providing service to other nodes. Those that do not provide services cannot gain the credits that they need to buy services. The stamp trading protocol [31] is a natural generalization of both reputation and payment protocols. In the protocol, nodes issue or trade personalized stamps with their neighbors, which can later be redeemed for services at the issuing nodes. In order to obtain service from node i, nodes need to present stamps originally issued by node i. A node can trade either its own stamps or those it has received from other nodes. By relating the exchange rate of stamps to their issuers' behavior, it is in a node's interest to get into a position where it is able to obtain sufficient stamps to do what it wants. The exact nature of the incentives arises in the method used to determine the stamp exchange rates.

A stamp trading scheme is a stamp trading protocol along with a method for valuing the stamps. The stamps that a node has in circulation represent the amount of service to which it has committed itself. A node's credit is the total value of stamps it has on hand (stamps not issued by itself plus the total value of stamps that it has yet to issue). Because nodes can give stamps away to neighboring nodes, the total credit in the network equals the total value of stamps in circulation (stamps issued by a node are held on hand by others in the network). A stamp trading scheme is token compatible if the total credit (value of stamps in circulation) in the network is bounded. This fits the notion of a payment protocol, where tokens cannot be forged or minted so that the economy is bounded. Additionally, a scheme is trust compatible if failure by a node to successfully redeem a stamp never increases its credit; that is, stamp value is monotonically decreasing with an increasing number of failures. This fits the notion of a reputation protocol where nodes cannot gain trust by misbehaving.

15.2.2.3 *Reciprocative Decision Function*   Feldman et al. [30] modeled the P2P network using the generalized prisoner's dilemma (GPD) and proposed the reciprocative decision function as the basis of a family of incentive techniques including discriminating server selection, maxflow-based subjective reputation, and adaptive stranger policies. Specifically, the authors used GPD to capture the essential tension between individual and overall network utility, asymmetric payoff matrices to allow asymmetric transactions between peers, and a learning-based [32] population dynamic model to specify the behavior of individual peers, which can be changed continuously. The proposed family of scalable and robust incentive techniques includes the following:

1. *Discriminating Server Selection.* Cooperation requires familiarity between entities either directly or indirectly. However, the large population and high turnover of P2P systems make it less likely that repeat interactions will occur with a familiar entity. If each peer keeps a private history of the actions of other peers toward itself and uses discriminating server selection, the reciprocative decision function can scale to large populations and moderate levels of turnover.

2. *Shared History.* Scaling to higher turnover and mitigating asymmetry of interest requires shared history. For example, take three nodes: *A*, *B*, and *C*, where *C* has been served by *A* and has served *B*. With shared history, *B* can be familiar with *A*'s service to *C* and would thus be willing to serve *A*. With only private history, *B* would not know that *A* has served *C*, so *B* would not be willing to serve *A*. Shared history results in a higher level of cooperation than private history. The cost of shared history is a distributed infrastructure (e.g., DHT-based storage) to store the history.

3. *Maxflow-Based Subjective Reputation.* Shared history creates the possibility of collusion. For example, *C* can falsely claim that *A* served him, thus deceiving *B* into providing service. A maxflow-based algorithm that computes reputation subjectively promotes cooperation despite collusion; using this algorithm in the previous example, *B* would only believe *C* if *C* had already provided service to *B*.

4. *Adaptive Stranger Policy.* Zero-cost identities allow noncooperating peers to escape the consequences of their behaviors by switching to a new identity. If reciprocative peers treat strangers (peers with no history) using a policy that adapts to the behaviors of previous strangers, peers have little incentive to switch to new identities.

5. *Short-Term History.* History also creates the possibility that a previously well-behaved peer with a good reputation will turn malicious and use its good reputation to exploit other peers. The peer could be making a strategic

decision or someone may have hijacked its identity (e.g., by compromising its host). Long-term history exacerbates this problem by allowing peers with many previous transactions to exploit that history for many new transactions; short-term history prevents malicious nodes from disrupting cooperation.

15.2.2.4 *XRep and X²Rep*

XRep [33] is a reputation-based trust management system designed to reduce the number of malicious or low-quality resources distributed in a Gnutella file-sharing network. Associating reputations with servents becomes a difficult problem for an anonymous P2P environment, where resource providers are identified by a pseudonym and an IP address. To overcome the limitations of servent-only-based methods, the XRep protocol uses the combined reputations of servents and resources. Servent reputations are associated with a tamper-resistant servent identifier. Resource reputations are tightly coupled to the resources' content via their digest, thus preventing their forging on the part of malicious peers. Reputations are cooperatively managed via a distributed polling algorithm in order to reflect the community's view of the potential risk involved with the download and use of a resource. Each servent maintains information on its own experiences with resources and other servents, and can share such experiences with others upon request. The XRep protocol also improves the global security and quality of content distribution within P2P networks. It protects P2P networks against most known attacks such as self-replication, man in the middle, pseudospoofing, ID stealth, and shilling.

Trust semantics specify the model for the evaluation of trust through the computation of gathered reputation information. X^2Rep [34] enhances the trust semantics of the XRep protocol. X^2Rep gives peers more expressive power to express their opinion about resources that they have downloaded and resource providers.

Ensuring the reliability of gathered reputation information is a major challenge to the development of a reputation system. In particular, it is vital that any "vote spoofing" activity is as difficult or expensive as possible for malicious agents. The XRep protocol uses a complex process of challenge and response messages to ensure that a vote is supplied by a real peer. X^2Rep eliminates this complexity by employing an extensive vote generation and evaluation system that makes use of voter credibility information to help an evaluating peer determine the trustworthiness of a vote through the evaluation of the voter's previous voting activity. The X^2Rep reputation system provides safeguards against threats posed by the collusion of malicious peers, achieving its security goal while reducing communication overhead.

15.2.2.5 *Sorcery*

Sorcery [35] aims to detect the deceptive behavior of peers in P2P networks. It is a challenge–response mechanism based on the notion that the participant with dominant information in an interaction can detect whether the other participant is telling a lie. Here, challenge denotes a query about votes for some content, and response denotes the response messages to answer the challenge. Sorcery encompasses three key techniques to detect and punish the deceivers in P2P content-sharing systems:

1. *Social Network Mechanism.* So that each client has dominant information, Sorcery introduces a social network into the P2P content-sharing system; thus, each client can establish his own friend relationships. These friends share their

own information (e.g., content and votes) with the client, and the friend information of the client is confidential to other peers in the system.

2. *Challenge–Response Mechanism.* Sorcery clients utilize the voting histories of their friends to test the voting history of the content provider and to judge whether the content provider is a deceiver or not based on the correctness of his response.

3. *Punishment Mechanism.* Sorcery clients rank each search result based on the honesty of the content providers; therefore, the probability of impact brought by deceivers is reduced.

Sorcery can effectively address the problem of deceptive behavior based on the confidential information extracted from social networks. However, some other types of attacks can also be mounted against Sorcery, such as man-in-the-middle attacks, Sybil attacks, and denial-of-service (DoS) attacks.

15.2.2.6   *P2PRep*   In P2PRep [36], servents can keep track of and share the reputations of their peers. Reputation sharing is based on a distributed polling algorithm by which resource requesters can access the reliability of prospective providers before initiating a download in the P2P network. P2PRep allows a servent *p* to inquire about the reputation of providers by polling its peers before deciding from where to download a file. After receiving the responses, *p* selects a servent (or a set of servents) based on the quality of the provider and its own past experience. Then, *p* polls its peers by broadcasting a message requesting their opinion about the selected servents. All peers can respond to the poll with their opinions about the reputation of each servent. The poller *p* can use the opinions expressed by these voters to make its decision. There are two variations of this approach. In the first variation, called basic polling, the servents responding to the poll do not provide their *servent_id*. In the second variation, called enhanced polling, voters provide their *servent_id*, which *p* can use to weight the votes received (*p* can judge some voters as being more credible than others).

This approach is complicated by the need to prevent exposure of polling to security violations by malicious peers. In particular, both the authenticity of servents and the quality of the poll needs to be ensured. Ensuring the quality of the poll means ensuring the integrity of each single vote (e.g., detecting modifications to votes in transit) and ruling out the possibility of dummy votes expressed by servents acting as a clique under the control of a single malicious party. To this end, P2PRep has a suspect identification procedure that tries to reduce the impact of forged votes. This procedure relies on computing clusters of voters whose common characteristics suggest that they may have been created by a single, possibly malicious user.

15.2.2.7   *Honest Players*   In general, existing trust schemes are only effective when applied to honest players who act with consistency, as opposed to adversaries who can behave arbitrarily. The work in Reference 37 investigated the modeling of honest entities in decentralized systems and built a statistical model for the transaction histories of honest players. This statistical model serves as a profiling tool to identify suspicious entities. It is combined with existing trust schemes to ensure that the schemes are applied to entities whose transaction records are consistent with the statistical model. A two-phase approach is used to integrate the modeling of honest players with trust functions. In the first phase, the transaction history of an entity is examined. If the entity follows the model of honest players, then trust functions will be applied to further determine trustworthiness. Those who do not pass the first phase may either be discarded as untrustworthy (as they appear to manipulate the reputation system) or selected for further examination. This approach limits the manipulation capability of adversaries and thus can improve the quality of reputation-based trust assessment. The contributions of this work are detailed as below:

1. A statistical model of the behavior of honest players. Specifically, the number of good transactions (those offering satisfactory services and receiving positive feedback accordingly) of an honest player is considered to be a random variable x. The work shows that if an entity's behavior is consistent and is not affected by other factors, then x follows a binomial distribution $B(n, p)$, where n is the number of transactions a party conducted during a period of time and p is the percentage of good transactions among these n transactions.

2. An algorithm that determines with high confidence whether a party follows the behavior of honest players given the transaction history of a party.

3. An extended statistical model of behavior resistant to collusion and false feedback.

15.2.2.8 SFTrust Most of the trust models use a single trust metric, which cannot reflect the practical trust values of peers effectively. SFTrust [38] is a decentralized and dependable trust model in unstructured P2P networks using service trust and feedback trust. In SFTrust, each peer has two trust values: service trust and feedback trust. Service trust represents whether the peer can supply high-quality service, while feedback trust denotes whether the peer can give equitable recommendations to other peers. The two trust metrics are independent. For example, a peer with a high service trust and a low feedback trust is able to supply high-quality service but lies when giving feedback so as to indirectly improve its trust values by debasing other peers.

SFTrust has three major building modules: a trust storage module, a trust computing module, and a trust update module. Specifically, when peer i requests services from peer j, it calculates the service trust of j to decide whether peer j is a trustable provider. First, i checks its service trust table to find the direct trust of j, that is, the trust value based on the direct experiences of i. Second, i aggregates the weighted trust values about j from its neighbor peers with the recommendation management module. Third, i uses the trust computing module to compute j's service trust by integrating direct trust and recommending trust. Last but not least, i decides whether to obtain services from j while simultaneously updating the feedback trust of recommending peers in its feedback trust record module.

In unstructured P2P trust models, the topology is not strictly defined, and there is no relationship between trust storage and topology. Each peer has a set of neighbors that are chosen upon joining the system. Thus, malicious peers can form a spiteful group to destroy the system to some extent, where they besmirch the reputations of good peers or help malicious peers obtain high reputations. Because of the large quantity of peers, general punishment mechanisms cannot accurately identify collusive peers. In SFTrust, the topology adaption protocol establishes neighborships in such a way that malicious nodes are prevented from easily forming collusive groups. SFTrust also includes counter measures to resist other attacks such as on–off attacks [39], free riding [14], Sybil attacks, and newcomer attacks [40].

15.2.2.9 TrustMe   TrustMe [29] is an anonymous and secure protocol for maintaining and accessing trust rating information. TrustMe uses public key cryptography schemes to provide security and is resistant to various attacks. It is characterized by its support for mutual anonymity in managing peer trust relationships; both the peers who access the trust ratings and the peers who store the trust ratings remain anonymous. This protects the peers who store trust ratings from targeted attacks. TrustMe mainly addresses two problems: (1) Where should the trust value of a peer be stored? and (2) how can other peers' trust values be securely accessed? TrustMe broadly functions in the following manner. Each peer is equipped with several public–private key pairs. The trust values of a peer, say peer B, are randomly assigned to another peer (trust-holding agent [THA] peer) in the network. This assignment is done by the bootstrap server in such a way that the trust-holding responsibilities are equally distributed among the participating peers. This assignment is unknown to all peers, including peer B. All communication with the THA peer is carried out using a special key that indicates its knowledge of the trust value of peer B. One peer interested in querying for the trust value of peer B, say, peer A, can broadcast a trust query for peer B. The THA peer replies with the trust value along with some other information. Depending upon the trust value, peer A can decide to interact with peer B or not. Also, after an interaction, peer A can securely file a report (after giving adequate proof of the interaction) on peer B indicating peer A's new trust value for peer B. Then, the THA peer can modify the trust rating of peer B. To provide security, reliability, and accountability, TrustMe uses tested, effective public key cryptography mechanisms.

15.2.2.10 Pseudo Trust (PT)   Most trust models in P2P networks are identity based, which means that, in order for one peer to trust another, it needs to know the other peer's identity. Hence, there exists an inherent trade-off between trust and anonymity. Since currently no P2P protocol provides complete mutual anonymity as well as authentication and trust management, the PT protocol [41] was proposed. It is a zero-knowledge authentication scheme in which each peer generates an unforgeable and verifiable pseudonym using a one-way hash function so that peers can be authenticated without leaking sensitive information. Peers construct anonymous onion paths and find tail nodes based on the APFS protocol [42]. PT has five key components, including (1) pseudoidentity generation and issuance, (2) new peer initialization, (3) authentication and session key exchange, (4) file delivery, and (5) trust and reputation management. PT can effectively defend against impersonation, replay attacks, man-in-the-middle attacks, collaborated attacks, and DoS attacks. With the help of PT, most existing identity-based trust management schemes become applicable in mutually anonymous P2P systems. The design strengths of PT include (1) no need for a centralized trusted party, (2) high scalability and security, (3) low traffic and cryptography processing overhead, and (4) man-in-the-middle attack resistance.

15.2.2.11 ***Reliable Rating Aggregation System*** The reliability of online rating systems largely depends on whether unfair ratings and dishonest raters can be detected and removed. Dealing with unfair and dishonest ratings in online feedback-based rating systems has been recognized as an important problem. The lack of realistic attack behavior models and unfair rating data from real human users has become an obstacle toward developing reliable rating systems. To solve this problem, Feng et al. [43] designed and launched a rating challenge to collect unfair rating data from real human users. In order to broaden the scope of the data collection, they also developed a reliable rating aggregation system [43], a signal-based unfair rating detection system [43]. The detection system not only outperforms existing schemes but also encourages creative attacks from the participants in the rating challenge. The process of the reliable rating aggregation system contains four steps:

1. Raw ratings are analyzed. Four analysis methods (arrival rate detection, model change detection, histogram detection, and mean change detection) are applied independently.
2. The outcomes of the four detectors are combined to detect the time intervals in which unfair ratings are highly likely. Additionally, the suspicious rating detection module can mark some specific ratings as suspicious.
3. A trust manager, which is a simplification of the generic framework of trust establishment proposed in Reference 44, determines how much individual raters can be trusted.
4. Highly suspicious ratings are removed from the raw ratings by a ratings filter. Then, the ratings are combined by the rating aggregation algorithm.

15.2.2.12 ***Reputation-Based Fines in Electronic Markets*** The effectiveness of online feedback mechanisms for rating the performance of providers in electronic markets can be hurt by the submission of dishonest ratings. Papaioannou et al. [45] dealt with ways to elicit honest ratings in a competitive electronic market where each participant can occasionally act as both provider and client. The authors assumed that each service provision is rated by both parties involved; only when the ratings agree are they included in the calculation of reputation for the provider's performance. The authors first studied the effectiveness of an incentive mechanism as a single-shot game; that is, upon evidence of lying (i.e., disagreement between submitted feedback), there are fixed fines to both parties that differ for the provider and the client. The authors proved that the submission of honest feedback can be a stable equilibrium for the whole market under certain initial system conditions. Then, the authors refined the game model for repeated transactions and calculated proper reputation-based fines for lying. These fines make the submission of honest feedback a stable Nash equilibrium of the repeated game and reduce social losses due to unfair punishments.

15.2.2.13 ***Decentralized Recommendation Chains*** The absence of a central authority in P2P networks poses unique challenges for reputation management in the network, the most important of which is availability of reputation data. Dewan and Dasgupta [46] presented a cryptographic protocol for ensuring the secure and timely availability of a peer's reputation data to other peers at low cost. The cryptographic protocol is coupled with self-certification and cryptographic mechanisms for identity management and Sybil attack resistance.

All peers in the P2P network are identified by identity certificates (aka identities). The reputation of a given peer is attached to its identity. The identity certificates are generated using self-certification, and all peers maintain their own (and hence trusted) certificate authority, which issues the identity certificate(s) to the peer. Each peer owns the reputation information pertaining to its past transactions with other peers in the network and stores the information locally. The main contributions of this work include the following:

1. A self-certification-based identity system protected by cryptographically blind identity mechanisms. This reduces the threat of Sybil attacks by binding the network identity of a peer to his or her real-life identity while still providing anonymity.

2. A lightweight and simple reputation model. This reduces the number of malicious transactions and consumes less bandwidth per transaction.

3. An attack-resistant cryptographic protocol for the generation of authentic global reputation information. The global reputation data are protected against any malicious modification by a third-party peer and are immune to any malicious modifications by their owner.

15.2.2.14 A Robust Reputation System Buchegger and Boudec [47] proposed a robust reputation system to cope with the spread of false reputation ratings (i.e., false accusations or false praise). In the proposed system, everyone maintains a reputation rating and a trust rating about everyone else who they care about. For example, node i maintains two ratings about node j. The reputation rating represents the opinion formed by node i about node j's behavior as an actor in the base system (e.g., whether node j provides the correct files in a P2P file-sharing system). The trust rating represents node i's opinion about how honest node j is as an actor in the reputation system (i.e., whether the reported first-hand information summaries published by node j are likely to be true). From time to time, first-hand reputation information is exchanged with others; using a modified Bayesian approach, only second-hand reputation information that is not incompatible with the current reputation rating is accepted. Thus, reputation ratings are slightly modified by accepted information. Trust ratings are updated based on the compatibility of second-hand reputation information with prior reputation ratings. Data are entirely distributed; a node's reputation and trust is the collection of ratings maintained by others. Every node uses its rating to periodically classify other nodes according to two criteria: (1) normal/misbehaving and (2) trustworthy/untrustworthy. Both classifications are performed using the Bayesian approach. Reevaluation and reputation fading are further employed to enable redemption and to prevent the sudden exploitation of good reputations built over time.

15.2.2.15 A Fine-Grained Reputation System Zhang and Fang [48] found three problems in previous reputation systems: (1) a binary QoS differentiation method that classifies a service as either good or bad without any interim state, thus limiting the potential for use by P2P applications in which servers have diverse capabilities and clients have various QoS demands; (2) no strong incentives designed to stimulate honest participation in the reputation system; and (3) failure to protect the privacy of references, which is important for obtaining honest feedback. To address these problems, the authors proposed a fine-grained reputation system to support reliable service selection in P2P networks with the following properties:

1. *QoS Aware.* The authors proposed a Dirichlet reputation engine based on multivariate Bayesian inference [49]. Firmly rooted in statistics, the reputation engine can satisfy the diverse QoS requirements of individual nodes by means of a fine-grained QoS differentiation method.

2. *Incentive Aware.* Honest participation in the reputation system is motivated by charging users who inquire about others' reputations and rewarding those who provide honest feedback.

3. *Socially Aware.* The concept of social groups is incorporated into the reputation system design as a reliable means of soliciting honest feedback and alleviating the cold-start problem. This design is motivated by the sociological fact that people tend to contribute to their associated social groups.

4. *Application Independent.* Unlike many previous solutions that were designed for a concrete P2P application, this reputation system can simultaneously serve unlimited P2P applications of different types. It can greatly amortize the design and development costs of the reputation system.

5. *Semidistributed.* This system features a central server that maintains user accounts and answers reputation inquiries. All application-related QoS information, however, is stored across system users either in a random fashion or through a DHT.

6. *Secure.* This system can protect the privacy of references and can withstand various misbehavior, such as defamation and flattery, using lightweight techniques like multivariate outlier detection [50] and symmetric-key cryptographic functions.

15.3 CASE STUDY OF REPUTATION SYSTEMS

15.3.1 PowerTrust

PowerTrust [51] is a robust and scalable P2P reputation system that uses a trust overlay network (TON) to model the trust relationships among peers. The authors of PowerTrust, Zhou and Hwang, first examined eBay transaction data from over 10,000 users and discovered a power-law distribution in user feedback. Their mathematical analysis justifies that a power-law distribution effectively models any dynamically growing P2P feedback systems, whether structured or unstructured. The authors then developed the PowerTrust system to leverage the power-law feedback characteristics of P2P systems. The PowerTrust system dynamically selects a small number of the most reputable nodes as determined by a distributed ranking mechanism; these nodes are termed power nodes. Using a look-ahead random walk (LRW) strategy and leveraging power nodes, PowerTrust significantly improves on previous systems with respect to global reputation accuracy and aggregation speed. PowerTrust is adaptable to highly dynamic networks and robust to disturbances by malicious peers.

As one of the major building blocks in a PowerTrust system, a TON is built on top of all peers in a P2P system. It is a virtual network represented by a directed graph on top of a P2P system. The graph nodes correspond to the peers. The directed edges or links are labeled with the feedback scores between two interacting peers. Whenever a transaction takes place between a peer pair, each peer in the pair evaluates the other. Therefore, all peers frequently send local trust scores among themselves. These scores are considered the raw data input to the PowerTrust system. The system aggregates the local scores to calculate the global reputation score of each participating peer. All global scores form a reputation vector, $V = (v_1, v_2, v_3, \ldots, v_n)$, which is the output of the PowerTrust system. All global scores are normalized with $\sum_i v_i = 1$, where $i = 1, 2, \ldots, n$ and n is the TON network size.

The system is built with five functional modules. The regular random walk module supports the initial reputation aggregation. The LRW module is used to periodically update reputation scores. To this end, the LRW also works with a distributed ranking module to identify power nodes, which are leveraged to update global reputation scores.

In PowerTrust, feedback scores are generated by Bayesian learning [47] or by an average rating based on peer satisfaction. Each node normalizes all issued feedback scores and stores them in a trust matrix. Consider the trust matrix $R = (r_{ij})$ defined over an n-node TON, where r_{ij} is the normalized local trust score defined by $r_{ij} = s_{ij}/\sum_j s_{ij}$ and s_{ij} is the most recent feedback score about node j from node i. If there is no link from node i to node j, s_{ij} is set to 0. Therefore, for all $1 \le i, j \le n$, $0 \le r_{ij} \le 1$, and $\forall i \sum_{j=1}^{n} r_{ij} = 1$. In other words, matrix R is a stochastic matrix, in which all entries are fractions and each row sum equals 1. This demands that the scores issued by the same node to other peers are normalized.

All global reputation scores v_i for n nodes form a normalized reputation column vector $V = (v_i)$, where $\sum_i v_i = 1$. The reputation vector V is computed by Equation (15.1) and is given an arbitrary initial reputation vector $V_{(0)}$ and small error threshold ε. For a system of n nodes, the authors initialized $v_i = 1/n$. For all $t = 1, 2, \ldots, k$, while $|V_{(i)} - V_{(i-1)}| > \varepsilon$, the successive reputation vectors are computed recursively by

$$V_{(t+1)} = R^T \times V_{(t)}. \tag{15.1}$$

After a sufficient number of k iterations, the global reputation vector converges to the eigenvector of the trust matrix R [11].

The LRW strategy efficiently aggregates global reputations. Each node in the TON not only holds its own local trust scores but also aggregates its neighbors' first-hand trust scores. The enhanced trust matrix S is computed by $S = R^2$. The extra aggregation overhead grows linearly in sparse power-law graphs [52]. PowerTrust uses a DHT to implement its distributed ranking mechanism. Every node has a score manager that accumulates its global reputation. When a new node i joins the system, the successor node of k_i is assigned to be the score manager of node i, where k_i is the hash of node i's unique identifier by a predefined hash function. All other nodes can access the global reputation of node i by issuing a lookup request with the key equal to k_i. Several different hash functions can be used to enable multiple score managers for each node in case a malicious score manager reports false global reputation scores.

Each node i sends all local trust scores to the score managers of its out-degree neighbors for the initial global reputation aggregation. After the first round of aggregation, the score managers collaborate with each other to find power nodes. Triplet (i, v_i, j) means that node i has global reputation score v_i and node j is node i's score manager. If node x stores the triplet (i, v_i, j) and finds i to be a power node, node x will notify node i's score manager, j. Because the trust matrix R is dynamically changing as new peers join and new transactions occur, the global reputation scores should be updated periodically, especially for power nodes. These global reputation updates leverage the capabilities of power nodes.

PowerTrust is distinguished by its fast reputation aggregation, ranking, updating, system scalability and wide applicability, and system robustness and operational efficiency. Experimental results have confirmed PowerTrust's effectiveness and robustness for use in a wide variety of P2P applications.

15.3.2 SocialTrust

SocialTrust [53] leverages social networks to enhance the effectiveness of current reputation systems in combating collusion. A social network is a social structure consisting of individuals (nodes) that are linked by one or more specific types of relationships, such as common interests, friendship, or kinship [54].

To investigate the impact of a social network on user purchasing and rating patterns, the authors of SocialTrust analyzed a real trace of 450,000 transaction ratings during 2008–2010 crawled from Overstock Auctions (abbreviated to Overstock). Overstock is an online auction platform similar to eBay, but it distinguishes itself by integrating a social network into the market community. The authors found that social closeness and interest similarity impact user purchasing and rating patterns. First, users tend to buy products from high-reputed users. Second, users tend to buy products from socially close (three hops or less) users and give socially close users high ratings. Third, 88% of a user's purchases are within 20% of the user's product interest categories on average, and 60% of transactions are conducted between users sharing >30% interest similarity. Based on these observations, suspicious collusion behavior patterns were identified from the distance and interest relationships between peers in a social network:

1. (B1) Socially distant users frequently and highly rate each other.
2. (B2) Users frequently and highly rate low-reputed socially close users.
3. (B3) Users with few common interests frequently and highly rate each other.
4. (B4) Users frequently give common-interest users low ratings.

SocialTrust derives social closeness (denoted by Ω_d) from the social network graph and node interactions, and interest similarity (denoted by Ω_c) from node profiles or activities between a pair of nodes. SocialTrust detects action patterns of suspicious collusion behaviors and then reduces the weight of the ratings from suspected colluders based on the two coefficients.

The authors first introduced a method to calculate the social closeness between two adjacent nodes in a social network and then introduced a method for nonadjacent nodes having no direct social relationship. The closeness of a pair of nodes, n_i

and n_j, is determined by two factors: the number of social relationships and the interaction frequency. Therefore, the social closeness, $\Omega_{d(i,j)}$, between two adjacent nodes, n_i and n_j, is calculated by

$$\Omega_{d(i,j)} = \frac{m_{(i,j)} f_{(i,j)}}{\sum_{k=0}^{|S_i|} f_{(i,k)}}, \tag{15.2}$$

where $m_{i,j} \geq 1$ denotes the number of social relationships between n_i and n_j, $f_{i,j}$ denotes the interaction frequency from n_i to n_j, S_i denotes a set of neighbors of node i, and $|S_i|$ denotes the number of neighbors in the set of S_i. Using S_i and S_j to denote the set of friends of two nonadjacent nodes n_i and n_j, respectively, the social closeness between n_i and n_j is defined as

$$\Omega_{d(i,j)} = \sum_{k \in |S_i \cap S_j|} \frac{\Omega_{d(i,k)} + \Omega_{d(k,j)}}{2}; \tag{15.3}$$

that is, the authors found all the common friends n_k between n_i and n_j. The social closeness between n_i and n_j through n_k is calculated by averaging the closeness of $\Omega_{(i,k)}$ and $\Omega_{(k,j)}$.

According to B3 and B4, when n_i gives n_j high ratings with high frequency, if $\Omega_{d(i,j)}$ is very low or very high and n_j's reputation is low, n_i is potentially a colluder. Then, SocialTrust reduces the weight of the ratings from n_i to n_j based on $\Omega_{d_{i,j}}$.

As shown in Figure 15.1, SocialTrust uses the Gaussian function to adjust the ratings from n_i to n_j, denoted by $r_{(i,j)}$:

$$r_{(i,j)} = r_{(i,j)} \cdot \alpha \cdot e^{-\frac{(\Omega_{d(i,j)} - \bar{\Omega}_{d_i})^2}{2|\max \Omega_{d_i} - \min \Omega_{d_i}|^2}}, \tag{15.4}$$

where α is the function parameter and $\max \Omega_{d_i}$, $\min \Omega_{d_i}$, and $\bar{\Omega}_{d_i}$ denote the maximum, minimum, and average social closenesses of n_i to other nodes that n_i has rated.

The exponent in Equation (15.4) is the deviation of the social closeness of n_i and n_j from the normal social closeness of n_i to other nodes it has rated. As Figure 15.1 shows, the Gaussian function significantly reduces the weights of the ratings from nodes with very high or very low social closeness to the rated nodes and mildly reduces the weights of those from the nodes with high or low social closeness to the rated nodes, while nearly maintaining the ratings from the nodes with normal closeness to the rated nodes. As a result, the weights of the ratings from suspected colluders are reduced.

In SocialTrust, each node has an interest vector $V = <v_1, v_2, v_3, \ldots, v_k>$ indicating its interests. The social interest similarity of n_i to n_j is calculated by

$$\Omega_{c(i,j)} = \frac{|V_i \cap V_j|}{\min(|V_i|, |V_j|)}. \tag{15.5}$$

According to B3 and B4, SocialTrust reduces the weights of the ratings from suspected colluders that have very high or low $\Omega_{c(i,j)}$ with the rated node using the Gaussian function:

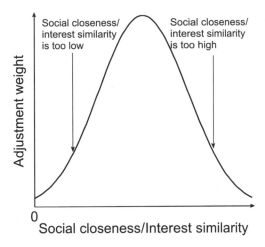

FIGURE 15.1. *One-dimensional reputation adjustment.*

$$r_{(i,j)} = r_{(i,j)} \cdot \alpha \cdot e^{-\frac{(\Omega_{c(i,j)} - \bar{\Omega}_{c_i})^2}{2|\max \Omega_{c_i} - \min \Omega_{c_i}|^2}}, \tag{15.6}$$

where $\max \Omega_{c_i}$, $\min \Omega_{c_i}$, and $\bar{\Omega}_{c_i}$ denote the maximum, minimum, and average interest similarity of node n_i with the nodes it has rated, respectively. The rating from n_i to n_j is adjusted according to Equation (15.6) when n_i frequently rates n_j with high ratings and $(\Omega_{c(i,j)} - \bar{\Omega}_{c_i})^2 < 0$, which implies that n_i and n_j share few interests, or when n_i frequently rates n_j with low ratings and $(\Omega_{c(i,j)} - \bar{\Omega}_{c_i})^2 > 0$, which implies that n_i and n_j share many interests. Combining Equations (15.4) and (15.6), with simultaneous consideration of social closeness and interest similarity, the reputation can be adjusted by

$$r_{(i,j)}(\Omega_d, \Omega_c) = r_{(i,j)} \cdot \alpha \cdot e^{-\left(\frac{(\Omega_{d(i,j)} - \bar{\Omega}_{d_i})^2}{2|\max \Omega_{d_i} - \min \Omega_{d_i}|^2} + \frac{(\Omega_{c(i,j)} - \bar{\Omega}_{c_i})^2}{2|\max \Omega_{c_i} - \min \Omega_{c_i}|^2} \right)}. \tag{15.7}$$

Let H_d and L_d denote very high and low social closeness, and let H_c and L_c denote very high and low interest similarity. Then, the rating values between the nodes that have (H_d, H_c), (H_d, L_c), (L_d, H_c), and (L_d, L_c) are greatly reduced. Therefore, based on Equation (15.7), the influences of the collusion listed in B1–B4 are reduced.

In reputation systems, each resource manager is responsible for collecting the ratings and for calculating the global reputation of certain nodes. Thus, each resource manager can keep track of the rating frequencies and values of the nodes it manages, which helps them to detect collusion in SocialTrust. A manager adjusts the ratings from suspected colluders when calculating global node reputation periodically.

Experiment results show SocialTrust greatly enhances the capability of eBay's reputation system and EigenTrust in countering collusion. SocialTrust can even detect colluders when compromised pretrusted and high-reputed nodes are involved in collusion.

15.3.3 Accurate Trust Reflection

Shen and Zhao [55] claimed that existing reputation systems fall short in accurately reflecting node trust and providing the right guidance for server selection for two main reasons. First, they directly regard node reputation as trust, which is not appropriate in general. Reputation represents the opinion formed by other nodes about a node's QoS behavior, while trust is an assessment of a node's honesty and willingness to be cooperative. Because the additional factors other than trust (e.g., capacity and longevity) that contribute to reputation are heterogeneous and time-varying attributes, a node's reputation does not reflect its trust and its current QoS. Benign but overloaded nodes may get low reputations due to insufficient capacity or overwhelming service requests. Benign but low-longevity nodes may also have low reputation values due to their short longevity. Second, they guide a node to select the server with the highest reputation, which may not actually select a high-QoS server and would overload the highest-reputed nodes.

The authors used an experiment to study the relationship reputation has with capacity and longevity. In this experiment, all nodes are trustworthy with a 100% probability of serving requests, and they each receive approximately the same number of requests. A node's available capacity equals $c_a = c - w$, where c is its capacity, represented by the number of service requests it can handle during a time unit, and w is its workload, represented by the number of its received requests during a time unit. Based on the observation, the authors developed an optimal server selection algorithm that separately considers node trust and the current values of additional factors to ensure high QoS (Fig. 15.2).

First, the authors tested the relationship between node reputation and capacity with the assumption that each server's longevity is high enough to complete the requested services. In this case, since a higher available capacity enables a server to offer higher QoS, a node gives its server a reputation value of r_c, which equals the server's available capacity, c_a. Figure 15.3 shows the reputation of each node versus its capacity. It demonstrates that node capacity positively influences a node's reputation.

Second, the authors tested the relationship between node reputation and node longevity with the assumption that each server's available capacity is high enough to complete the services requested from it. In this case, a server's reputation should

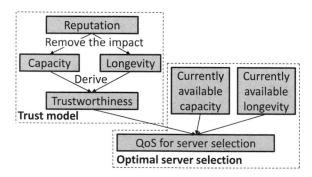

FIGURE 15.2. *The proposed trust system.*

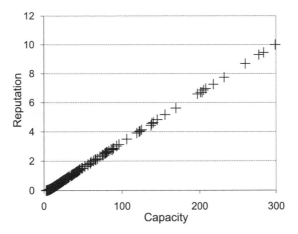

FIGURE 15.3. *Reputation versus capacity.*

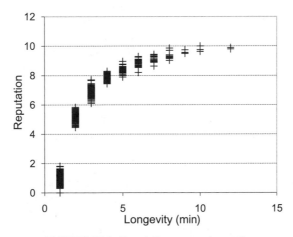

FIGURE 15.4. *Reputation versus longevity.*

be evaluated according to the percent of the requested services it has completed. Thus, the reputation value r_l equals

$$r_l = \begin{cases} l_a/l_r & \text{if } l_a/l_r < 1 \\ 1 & \text{otherwise,} \end{cases} \tag{15.8}$$

where l_a is the available longevity of a server and l_r is the time requirement of a requested service. Figure 15.4 shows the reputation of each node versus its longevity. It demonstrates that the relationship between reputation and longevity exhibits a logarithmic trend, and higher-longevity nodes have higher reputations.

The experiment results confirm that a reputation value itself cannot directly reflect node trust since trust is also affected by capacity and longevity. Thus, reputation cannot be directly used for optimal server selection. The effect of a node's previous capacity and longevity on the reputation should be removed when evaluating a node's trustworthiness, and the currently available capacity and longevity should be considered with trust in choosing a service provider.

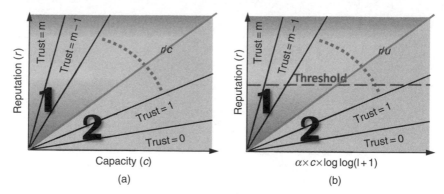

FIGURE 15.5. *(a) Capacity-based trust. (b) Capacity and longevity-based trust.*

The proposed trust models can be built on any reputation system. The resource managers build the trust models, which need information on additional factors when evaluating node trust. Thus, each node i periodically sends its resource manager a vector including its current values for the additional factors that affect reputation, denoted $V_i = <c_a, l_a, \ldots>$ using Insert(ID_i, V_i), where c_a and l_a are the node's current available capacity and available longevity, respectively. After the resource manager computes the global reputation value of node i, it uses V_i to derive its trustworthiness using the proposed trust models.

The authors introduced two trust models: manual and automatic. These models help to remove the influence of node capacity and longevity on reputation when determining node trust.

Since the reputation has a linear relationship with capacity, if there are no other factors that influence reputation except capacity, the ratio of a node's reputation over its capacity can be used to measure its trust; that is, $t_c = r/c$, where r and c denote the node's reputation and capacity, respectively. t_c represents the reputation earned by a node for each unit of capacity it has contributed to providing service. The authors assumed there are m levels of trust in the system. The normalized t_c determines a node's trust level. Figure 15.5a shows a coordinate graph with the x-axis representing capacity and the y-axis representing reputation. The space is divided into different sections, each representing a trust level. A higher trust level means a node's reputation is high relative to its capacity. The authors mapped a node's normalized t_c to the graph according to its capacity. Based on its coordinate location, the node's trust level is determined. Figure 15.5b shows that the reputation has a logarithmic relationship with longevity. Using MATLAB, the logarithmic curve is transformed to a line by changing longevity l to $\log\log(l+1)$. Hence, reputation has a linear relationship to $\log\log(l+1)$. As with capacity, the authors used $r/\log\log(l+1)$ to measure a node's trust level when there are no other additional factors except longevity. By considering both capacity and longevity, the authors introduced spatial/temporal values. By viewing node capacity in a spatial domain and node longevity in a temporal domain, the spatial/temporal value u is defined as

$$u = \alpha \times (c \cdot \log\log(l+1)),$$

where α is a constant factor. Based on the above analysis, the relationship between reputation r and u can be approximately regarded as a linear relationship. A node

Input units (*p*)   Hidden units (*h*)   Output unit (*y*)

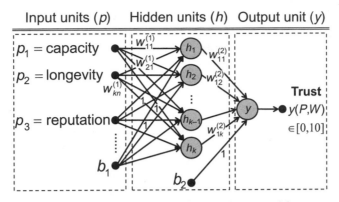

FIGURE 15.6. *Neural network-based trust model.*

with a higher *u* should have a higher reputation and vice versa. Thus, each resource manager builds a manual trust model as shown in Figure 15.5b. The model is a two-dimensional space where spatial/temporal value and reputation are coordinates. A node's trust value is calculated by $t_v = r/u$. Locality-preserving hashing [56] is used to normalize the trust value in order to obtain trust level t_l; that is, $t_l = m \cdot t_v/(\max(t_v) - \min(t_v))$, where *m* is the number of trust levels in the system, and $\max(t_v)$ and $\min(t_v)$ are the maximum and minimum values of t_v in the system, respectively. The authors mapped a node's normalized t_l to the graph according to its *u*. Based on its coordinate location, the node's trust level is determined.

The automatic trust model uses a neural network technique [57] for node trust evaluation by catching the nonlinear relationship between reputation, trust, and additional factors including capacity and longevity. The authors built a neural network with one layer of hidden units [58] as shown in Figure 15.6.

It is a nonlinear function from a set of input variables $P = \{p_1, p_2, \dots\}$ to output variable $y \in [0, 10]$ controlled by a set of vectors of adjustable weight parameters $W(w_{ji} : 1 \le i \le n, 1 \le j \le k)$. The input units are a node's attribute variables including reputation, longevity, capacity, and other additional factors, and the output is the node's trust level. The activation of a hidden unit is a function F_i of the weighted inputs plus a bias as given in the following equation:

$$y(P, W) = F_j\left(\sum_{j=1}^{k} w_{1j}^{(2)} F_i\left(\sum_{i=1}^{n} w_{ji}^{(1)} p_i + b_1 \right) + b_2 \right),$$

where

$$F(x) = \frac{1}{1 + e^{-x}}.$$

After training, a resource manager can directly use the trained neural network for trust evaluation of its responsible nodes.

The proposed optimal server selection algorithm considers the trust derived by the trust model and the current available capacity and longevity. When choosing a server, a client first identifies all servers with sufficient capacity and longevity to meet its needs. It then chooses the nodes from these options that have the highest trust. These selected servers can reliably satisfy the client's request. Then, in order to distribute the load among nodes according to their available capacity without overloading a server, lottery scheduling [59] is adopted in the final server selection so that servers with higher available capacity receive more requests and vice versa.

15.4 OPEN PROBLEMS

Though significant research has been conducted in reputation management systems, there still exists a number of open problems in this area that need to be resolved.

The first problem is handling intelligent adversaries. An intelligent adversary can manipulate the policies of the reputation system, adjusting the degree of his misbehavior such that he can evade the misbehavior detection system. For example, several nodes may collude to boost their reputation values. Malicious nodes control a large pool of subnodes in order to dominate a large portion of the identity space so as to increase their power in voting, leaving other nodes vulnerable to DoS attacks. Although a number of research works have been conducted to detect collusion or Sybil attacks based on their interaction graphs or social relationships, this interaction and social information can still be manipulated by intelligent adversaries.

The second problem is estimating node reputation quickly. In most reputation systems, it takes a while to build reputation and trust among nodes in a network. Minimizing this startup period is still an open issue. Most reputation systems investigate a system at a stable stage where the reputation value of nodes is already calculated based on their historical interaction behaviors. Since it takes a long time to accumulate reputation values of nodes in order to identify malicious nodes, during this time, a malicious node may cause serious damage to the system. Therefore, ways to identify malicious nodes in a short time, predict the trustworthiness of a newly joined node, and design an effective access control mechanism are also very important.

The third problem is truly reflecting node trustworthiness in reputation systems. Most reputation systems calculate the reputation values of peers based on their previous behaviors. A good behavior leads to an increased reputation, while a bad behavior leads to a decreased reputation. However, sometimes, the misbehavior of users is not the result of malicious intentions but, rather, of system errors such as network congestion or I/O errors. A method to distinguish between causes of misbehavior is an interesting problem to be investigated in the future.

The fourth problem is reputation evaluation in a social network environment. Considering social trustworthiness between users, the ratings of common-interest nodes or friends should be considered more trustable. Qualitatively estimating the influence of social closeness on the trust between users and on server selection is also an interesting problem.

15.5 CONCLUSION

P2P networks play an important role nowadays, especially for data sharing and digital media distribution like video on demand. In order to enhance the robustness, availability, and security of P2P networks, reputation management systems are used as a tool to detect malicious peers and to provide cooperation incentives in P2P networks. Numerous technologies based on reputation systems have been proposed. These advances were designed to solve practical and challenging problems, including collusion, content pollution, free riding, and P2P network attacks.

In this chapter, we have classified the main works on reputation systems into two categories, scalability/accuracy and security, and presented a comprehensive review of research works in each category. In the case studies, we have presented three representative reputation systems that enable high scalability, collusion avoidance, and accurate trust reflection. Finally, we have briefly discussed open problems in the research area of reputation systems. These open problems, as well as the difficulty in implementing complex reputation systems, introduce many challenges in P2P network design. Solutions to these problems will accelerate the maturation of P2P networks, creating a new generation of secure, trustworthy P2P applications.

ACKNOWLEDGMENTS

This research was supported in part by U.S. National Science Foundation (NSF) grants NSF-CSR 1025649, OCI-1064230, CNS-1049947, CNS-1156875, CNS-0917056 and CNS-1057530, CNS-1025652, and CNS-0938189; Microsoft Research Faculty Fellowship 8300751; and Sandia National Laboratories grant 10002282.

REFERENCES

[1] Kazaa Lite. Available at http://www.kazaalite.pl/.

[2] BitTorrent. Available at http://www.bittorrent.com/.

[3] I. Stoica, R. Morris, D. Liben-Nowell, D. Karger, M. Frans Kaashoek, F. Dabek, and H. Balakrishnan, "Chord: A scalable peer-to-peer lookup protocol for Internet applications," *IEEE/ACM Transactions on Networking*, 11(1):17–32, 2003.

[4] A. Rowstron and P. Druschel, "Pastry: Scalable, decentralized object location and routing for large-scale peer-to-peer systems," in *Proceedings of Middleware*, 2001.

[5] Skype. Available at http://www.skype.com/.

[6] X. Wang, Z. Yao, Y. Zhang, and D. Loguinov, "Enhancing application-layer multicast for P2P conferencing," in *Proceedings of the IEEE Consumer Communications and Networking Conference*, 2007.

[7] H. Shen, Z. Li, T. Li, and Y. Zhu, "PIRD: P2P-based intelligent resource discovery in Internet-based distributed systems," in *Proceedings of the International Conference on Distributed Computing Systems*, 2008.

[8] eBay. Available at http://www.ebay.com/.

[9] Amazon. Available at http://www.amazon.com/.

[10] Overstock. Available at http://www.overstock.com/.

[11] S. Kamvar, M. Schlosser, and H. Garcia-Molina, "The eigentrust algorithm for reputation management in P2P networks," in *Proceedings of the 12th International World Wide Web Conference*, 2003.

[12] Q. Lian, Z. Zhang, M. Yang, B. Zhao, Y. Dai, and X. Li, "An empirical study of collusion behavior in the Maze P2P file-sharing system," in *Proceedings of the International Conference on Distributed Computing Systems*, 2007.

[13] S. Zhao and V. Lo, "Result verification and trust-based Scheduling in open peer-to-peer cycle sharing systems," in *Proceedings of Peer-to-Peer Computing*, 2005.

[14] L. Xiong and L. Liu, "PeerTrust: Supporting reputation-based trust for peer-to-peer electronic communities," *IEEE Transactions on Knowledge and Data Engineering*, 16(7):843–857, 2004.

[15] M. Srivatsa, L. Xiong, and L. Liu, "TrustGuard: Countering vulnerabilities in reputation management for decentralized overlay networks," in *Proceedings of the International World Wide Web Conference*, 2005.

[16] S. Song, K. Hwang, R. Zhou, and Y. Kwok, "Trusted P2P transactions with Fuzzy reputation aggregation," *IEEE Internet Computing*, 9(6):24–34, 2005.

[17] K. Walsh and E. Sirer, "Fighting peer-to-peer SPAM and decoys with object reputation," in *Proceedings of Economics of P2P Systems*, 2005.

[18] C. Costa, V. Soares, J. Almeida, and V. Almeida, "Fighting pollution dissemination in peer-to-peer networks," in *Proceedings of the Symposium on Applied Computing*, 2005.

[19] C. Costa and J. Almeida, "Reputation systems for fighting pollution in peer-to-peer file sharing systems," in *Proceedings of Peer-to-Peer Computing*, 2007.

[20] J. Douceur, "The Sybil attack," in *Proceedings of the 1st International Workshop on Peer-to-Peer Systems*, 2002.

[21] R. Zhou and K. Hwang, "Gossip-based reputation aggregation for unstructured peer-to-peer networks," in *Proceedings of IEEE International Parallel and Distributed Processing Symposium*, 2007.

[22] D. Kempe, A. Dobra, and J. Gehrke, "Gossip-based computation of aggregate information," in *Proceedings of the IEEE Symposium on Foundations of Computer Science*, 2003.

[23] R. Zhou, K. Hwang, and M. Cai, "GossipTrust for fast reputation aggregation in peer-to-peer networks," *IEEE Transactions on Knowledge and Data Engineering*, 20(9):1282–1295, 2008.

[24] Z. Liang and W. Shi, "PET: A personalized trust model with reputation and risk evaluation for P2P resource sharing," in *Proceedings of Hawaii International Conference on System Sciences*, 2005.

[25] H. Zhao and X. Li, "H-Trust: A robust and lightweight group reputation system for peer-to-peer desktop grid," in *Proceedings of the International Conference on Distributed Computing Systems Workshops*, 2008.

[26] J. Hirsch, "An index to quantify an individual's scientific research output," in *Proceedings of the National Academy of Sciences*, 2005.

[27] S. Lee, R. Sherwood, and B. Bhattacharjee, "Cooperative peer groups in NICE," in *Proceedings of the IEEE International Conference on Computer Communications*, 2003.

[28] A. Selcuk, E. Uzun, and M. Pariente, "A reputation-based trust management system for P2P networks," in *Proceedings of the IEEE/ACM International Symposium on Cluster, Cloud, and Grid Computing*, 2004.

[29] A. Singh and L. Liu, "TrustMe: Anonymous management of trust relationships in decentralized P2P systems," in *Proceedings of Peer-to-Peer Computing*, 2003.

[30] M. Feldman, K. Lai, I. Stoica, and J. Chuang, "Robust incentive techniques for peer-to-peer networks," in *Proceedings of the ACM Conference on Electronic Commerce*, 2004.

[31] T. Moreton and A. Twigg, "Trading in trust, tokens, and stamps," in *Proceedings of the 1st Workshop on Economics of Peer-to-Peer Systems*, 2003.

[32] D. Fudenberg and D. Levine, *The Theory of Learning in Games*. Cambridge, MA: MIT Press, 1999.

[33] E. Damiani, S. di Vimercati, S. Paraboschi, P. Samarati, F. Violante, and A. Reputation-Based, "Approach for choosing reliable resources in peer-to-peer networks," in *Proceedings of the 9th ACM Conference on Computer and Communications Security*, 2002.

[34] N. Curtis, R. Safavi-Naini, and W. Susilo, "X^2Rep: enhanced trust semantics for the XRep protocol," in *Proceedings of the International Conference on Applied Cryptography and Network Security*, 2004.

[35] E. Zhai, R. Chen, Z. Cai, L. Zhang, E. Lua, H. Sun, S. Qing, L. Tang, and Z. Chen, "Sorcery: Could we make P2P content sharing systems robust to deceivers? in *Proceedings of Peer-to-Peer Computing*, 2009.

[36] F. Cornelli, E. Damiani, S. di Vimercati, S. Paraboschi, and P. Samarati, "Choosing reputable servents in a P2P network," in *Proceedings of the 11th World Wide Web Conference*, 2002.

[37] Q. Zhang, W. Wei, and T. Yu, "On the modeling of honest players in reputation systems," *Computer Science and Technology*, 24(5):808–819, 2009.

[38] Y. Zhang, S. Chen, and G. Yang, "SFTrust: A double trust metric based trust model in unstructured P2P system," in *Proceedings of the IEEE International Parallel and Distributed Processing Symposium*, 2009.

[39] Y. Sun, Z. Han, and K.J.R. Liu, "Defense of trust management vulnerabilities in distributed networks," *IEEE Communications Magazine*, 46(2):112–119, 2008.

[40] H. Yu, M. Kaminsky, P. Gibbons, and A. Flaxman, "Sybilguard: Defending against sybil attacks via social networks," in *Proceedings of the ACM Special Interest Group on Data Communication*, 2006.

[41] L. Lu, J. Han, Y. Liu, L. Hu, J. Huai, L. Ni, and J. Ma, "Pseudo Trust: Zero-knowledge authentication in anonymous P2Ps," *IEEE Transactions on Parallel and Distributed Systems*, 19(10):1325–1337, 2008.

[42] V. Scarlata, B. Neil Levine, and C. Shields, "Responder anonymity and anonymous peer-to-peer file sharing," in *Proceedings of the IEEE International Conference on Network Protocols*, 2001.

[43] Q. Feng, Y. Yang, Y. Sun, and Y. Dai, "Modeling attack behaviors in rating systems," in *Proceedings of the International Conference on Distributed Computing Systems Workshops*, 2008.

[44] Y. Sun and Y. Yang, "Trust establishment in distributed networks: Analysis and modeling," in *Proceedings of the IEEE International Conference on Communications*, 2007.

[45] T. Papaioannou, G. Stamoulis, and A. Honest, "Ratings with reputation-based fines in electronic markets," in *Proceedings of the IEEE International Conference on Computer Communications*, 2008.

[46] P. Dewan and P. Dasgupta, "P2P reputation management using distributed identities and decentralized recommendation chains," *IEEE Transactions on Knowledge and Data Engineering*, 22(7):1000–1013, 2010.

[47] S. Buchegger and J. Boudec, "A robust reputation system for P2P and mobile ad-hoc networks," in *Proceedings of Economics of Peer-to-Peer Systems*, 2004.

[48] Y. Zhang and Y. Fang, "A fine-grained reputation system for reliable service selection in peer-to-peer networks," *IEEE Transactions on Parallel and Distributed Systems*, 18(8): 1134–1145, 2007.

[49] A. Gelman, J. Carlin, H. Stern, and D. Rubin, *Bayesian Data Analysis*. Boca Raton, FL: Chapman & Hall, 1995.

[50] S. Bay and M. Schwabacher, "Mining distance-based outliers in near linear time with randomization and a simple pruning rule," in *Proceedings of the International Conference on Knowledge Discovery and Data Mining*, 2003.

[51] R. Zhou and K. Hwang, "PowerTrust: A robust and scalable reputation system for trusted peer-to-peer computing," *IEEE Transactions on Parallel and Distributed Systems*, 18(4):460–473, 2007.

[52] M. Mihail, A. Saberi, and P. Tetali, "Random walks with lookahead in power law random graphs," in *Proceedings of the International World Wide Web Conference*, 2004.

[53] Z. Li, H. Shen, and K. Sapra, "Leveraging social networks to combat collusion in reputation systems for peer-to-peer networks," in *Proceedings of the IEEE International Parallel and Distributed Processing Symposium*, 2011.

[54] M. Mcpherson, "Birds of a feather: Homophily in social networks," *Annual Review of Sociology*, 27(1):415–444, 2001.

[55] H. Shen and L. Zhao, "Refining reputation to truly select high-QoS servers in peer-to-peer networks," in *Proceedings of the IEEE 20th International Conference on Computer Communications and Networks*, 2011.

[56] M. Cai, M. Frank, J. Chen, and P. Szekely, "MAAN: A multi-attribute addressable network for grid information services," *Journal of Grid Computing*, 2(1):3–14, 2004.

[57] C. Bishop, *Pattern Recognition and Machine Learning*. New York: Springer, 2006.

[58] K. Hornik, M. Stinchcombe, and H. White, "Multilayer feed-forward networks are universal approximators," *Neural Networks*, 2(5):359–366, 1989.

[59] C. Waldspurger and W. Weihl, "Lottery scheduling: flexible proportional-share resource management," in *Proceedings of the USENIX Symposium on Operating Systems Design and Implementation*, 1994.

16

Toward a Secure Fragment Allocation of Files in Heterogeneous Distributed Systems

Yun Tian, Mohammed I. Alghamdi, Xiaojun Ruan, Jiong Xie, and Xiao Qin

16.1 INTRODUCTION

16.1.1 Security Problems in Distributed Systems

An increasing number of scientific and business files need to be stored in large-scale distributed storage systems. The confidentiality of security-sensitive files must be preserved in modern distributed storage systems because such systems are exposed to an increasing number of attacks from malicious users [1].

Although there exist many security techniques and mechanisms (e.g., see References 2 and 3), it is quite challenging to secure data stored in distributed systems. In general, security mechanisms need to be built for each component in a distributed system, then a secure method of integrating all the components in the system can be implemented. It is critical and important to maintain the confidentiality of files stored in a distributed storage system when malicious programs and users compromise some storage nodes in the system.

In addition to cryptographic systems, secret sharing is an approach to providing data confidentiality by distributing a file among a group of n storage nodes, to each of which a fragment of the file is allocated. The file can be reconstructed only when

Scalable Computing and Communications: Theory and Practice, First Edition. Edited by
Samee U. Khan, Albert Y. Zomaya, and Lizhe Wang.

a sufficient number (e.g., more than k) of the fragments are available to legitimate users. Attackers are unable to reconstruct a file using the compromised fragments when a group of servers are compromised if fewer than k fragments are disclosed.

16.1.2 Heterogeneous Vulnerabilities

In a large-scale distributed system, different storage sites use a variety of methods to protect data. The same security policy may be implemented in various mechanisms. Data encryption schemes may vary; even with the same encryption scheme, key lengths may vary across the distributed system. The above-mentioned factors can contribute to different vulnerabilities among storage sites. Although security mechanisms deployed in multiple storage sites can be implemented in a homogeneous way, different vulnerabilities may exist due to heterogeneities in computational units.

We started to address security heterogeneity issues by categorizing storage servers into different server-type groups. Each server type represents a level of security vulnerability. In a server-type group, storage servers with the same vulnerabilities share the same weaknesses that allow attackers to reduce the servers' information assurance. Although it may be difficult to categorize all servers in a system into a large number of groups, a practical way of identifying server types is to organize those with similar vulnerabilities into one group.

In light of server types and heterogeneous vulnerabilities, we investigated in this study a fragment allocation scheme called S-FAS to improve the security of a distributed system where storage sites have a wide variety of vulnerabilities.

16.1.3 File Fragmentation and Allocation

The file fragmentation technique is often used in distributed and parallel systems to improve availability and performance. Several file fragmentation schemes have been proposed to achieve high assurance and availability in large distributed systems [4, 5]. In real-world distributed systems, the fragmentation technique is usually combined with replication to achieve better performance at the cost of increased security risk to data stored in the systems. A practical distributed system normally contains multiple heterogeneous servers providing services with various vulnerabilities. Unfortunately, the existing fragmentation algorithms do not take the heterogeneity issues into account.

To address the aforementioned limitations, we focused on the development of a file fragmentation and allocation approach to improving the assurance and scalability of a heterogeneous distributed system. If one or more fragments of a file have been compromised, it is still very difficult and time-consuming for a malicious user to reconstruct the file from the compromised fragments. Our solution is different from those previously explored because it utilizes heterogeneous features regarding vulnerabilities among servers.

To evaluate our method for fragment allocations, we developed static and dynamic assurance models to quantify the assurance of a heterogeneous distributed storage system handling data fragments.

16.1.4 Main Contributions

The following are the main contributions of this study: We addressed the heterogeneous vulnerability issue by categorizing storage nodes of a distributed system into different server-type groups based on their vulnerabilities. Each server-type group represents a group of storage nodes with the same group of security vulnerabilities. We proposed a secure fragmentation allocation scheme called S-FAS to improve the security of a distributed system where storage nodes have a wide variety of vulnerabilities. We developed storage assurance and dynamic assurance models to quantify information assurance and to evaluate the proposed S-FAS scheme. We developed a secure allocation processing (SAP) algorithm to improve security and system performance by considering the heterogeneous feature of a large distributed system. We discovered principles to improve assurance levels of heterogeneous distributed storage systems. The principles are general guidelines to help designers achieve a secure fragment allocation solution for distributed systems. In order to conduct the performance analysis for the S-FAS scheme and SAP allocation algorithm, we developed a prototype for our S-FAS scheme.

16.1.5 The Organization of This Chapter

The rest of this chapter is organized as follows. In Section 16.2, we review related work. Section 16.3 presents the system and threat models of this study. Section 16.4 describes S-FAS—a secure fragmentation allocation scheme. In Section 16.5, we describe static and dynamic assurance models for distributed storage systems. In Section 16.6, the SAP allocation algorithm principles are presented, and the architecture and design of our prototype is illustrated. In Section 16.7, we quantitatively evaluate the assurance and do some performance analysis of the proposed S-FAS scheme combined with our proposed SAP algorithm in the context of distributed systems. Section 16.8 summarizes this chapter.

16.2 RELATED WORK

16.2.1 Security Techniques for Distributed Systems

Much research has been performed concerning the improvement of the security of distributed and high-performance computing systems such as grids. For example, Pourzandi et al. proposed a structured security approach that incorporates both distributed authentication and distributed access control mechanisms [1].

Intrusion detection techniques have been widely used to provide basic assurance of security in distributed systems; however, most intrusion detection techniques are inadequate to protect data stored in distributed systems [6]. One of the most effective approaches to improving information assurance in distributed systems is intrusion tolerance [5, 7]. To enhance security assurance, researchers have developed a range of intrusion-tolerant tools and mechanisms. The fragmentation technique summarized below is one of the intrusion tolerance methods that can be used in combination with intrusion detection techniques.

16.2.2   Fragmentation Techniques

A fragmentation technique partitions a security-sensitive file into multiple fragments that are distributed across different nodes in a distributed system. A lot of fragmentation schemes have proven to be valuable tools in the improvement of the security of data stored in distributed systems (e.g., see References 4 and 8–12).

Many fragmentation approaches aim to improve the availability and performance of distributed systems by applying data replication methods. For example, Dabek et al. developed a wide-area cooperative storage system in which they implemented a fragmentation scheme to improve availability and to facilitate load balancing [13].

Although a scheme combining fragmentation and replication can enhance performance and availability, data replications may impose security risks due to an increasing number of file fragments handled by distributed storage servers. A file is more likely to be compromised when more replications of the file are stored in a distributed storage system.

All existing file fragmentation technologies are inadequate to address the issue of heterogeneous vulnerabilities in large-scale distributed systems. Our preliminary results show that security can be improved in a distributed storage system when a fragmentation scheme incorporates the heterogeneous vulnerability feature.

16.2.3   Secret Sharing

Secret sharing is a method of distributing a secret among a group of participants by allocating each a share of the secret. The secret can be successfully reconstructed only when a sufficient number of shares are combined together [11, 14]. Shamir proposed the (k, n) secret sharing scheme that divides data D into n pieces in such a way that D can be easily reconstructed from any k pieces. If fewer than k pieces are disclosed, the data cannot be reconstructed from the revealed pieces. The secret sharing scheme has been extended and employed in different application domains [15]. For example, Bigrigg et al. proposed an architecture called PASIS for secure storage systems. The PASIS architecture integrates the secret sharing scheme with information dispersal to improve security, integrity, and availability [16, 17]. In a storage system with PASIS, the confidentiality of stored data in the system is still preserved even if an attacker compromises a limited (i.e., fewer than the threshold) subset of storage nodes. The aforementioned secret sharing solutions designed for distributed storage systems ignore the issue of heterogeneous vulnerabilities. This fact motivated us to extend the secret sharing scheme by considering heterogeneity in vulnerabilities in the context of distributed storage systems.

16.2.4   Comparison of Our Work with Existing Solutions

The fragment allocation solution we describe in this chapter is entirely different from the existing fragment allocation schemes found in the literature. Our approach incorporates the vulnerability heterogeneity feature of distributed storage systems into file fragment allocation. Our solution captures heterogeneous features regarding vulnerabilities of the nodes in order to improve the security level of the data stored in a distributed system. In this study, the data replication technique is not considered because fragment allocation and data replication are independent of each other. Thus, the availability and performance of fragment allocation schemes can be improved when data replication modules are integrated.

16.3 SYSTEM AND THREAT MODELS

In this section, we will outline the system and threat models that capture main characteristics of distributed storage systems. The system model is used as a basis to design the S-FAS fragmentation allocation scheme, whereas the threat model helps us identify vulnerabilities and certain potential attacks in distributed storage systems.

16.3.1 System Model

The S-FAS fragmentation allocation scheme was designed for a distributed storage system (see Fig. 16.1) where each storage site is a cluster storage subsystem. Different cluster storage subsystems may be connected within some subnetworks to form a larger-scale distributed storage sysytem. A cluster storage subsystem consists of a number of storage nodes and a gateway. Considering heterogeneous vulnerability in large-scale storage systems, we categorize storage nodes into different server-type groups.

Before presenting details on the system model, let us summarize all notations used throughout this chapter in Table 16.1.

In this study, we will consider a distributed storage system containing L cluster storage subsystems (i.e., $R_1, R_2, \ldots, R_L$). Cluster storage subsystem R_i consists of H_i storage nodes (i.e., $R_i = \{r_{i1}, r_{i2}, \ldots, r_{iH_i}\}$). All the storage nodes connected in cluster R_i have heterogeneous vulnerabilities.

Since all the nodes, including a master node, are fully connected in a cluster storage subsystem, we model the topology of a cluster storage system as a general

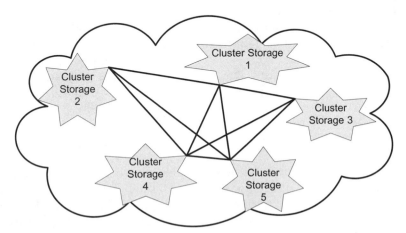

FIGURE 16.1. *A distributed storage system is composed of a set of cluster storage subsystems. Multiple fragments of a file can be stored either in storage nodes within a single cluster storage subsystem or in nodes across multiple cluster storage subsystems.*

TABLE 16.1. Notations

Items	Meaning	Items	Meaning
U	The whole system considered	N	Total number of storage nodes
F	A file stored in the system	F_i	Fragment i of file F
K	Total number of storage node types	m	Threshold of secret sharing scheme
T_j	Server type j in the system	$P(X)$	Probability of event X occurring
R_i	Cluster storage subsystem	$P(Y)$	Probability of event Y occurring
r_{ij}	Node j in subsystem i	$P(Z)$	Probability of event Z occurring
α	An allocation mapping of file F	$P(V)$	Probability of event V occurring
L	Number of subsystems in the whole system	H_i	Number of server nodes in the subsystem i
Y	An event if X occurs, at least m fragments can be compromised using the same attack method	n	Total number of fragments of each file in the secret sharing scheme
X	The event by which a set of storage nodes is chosen to be attacked	Z	The event of a successful attack to a certain fragment of a file
S_j	The size of a certain server type j in a cluster	P_N	The probability of a successful attack on a node
P_f	The probability of successfully compromising a fragment in a compromised node	$SA(\alpha)$	The storage assurance of an allocation mapping α of file F
q	Number of fragments needed to reconstruct a file transmitted from outside of the subsystem	g	Number of fragments compromised out of the q fragments transmitted across subsystems
P_L	The probability that a fragment is intercepted during its transmission	P_D	The probability that a file F is intercepted because of the compromised transmitted fragments
V	The event file F is compromised under one attack method	$DA(\alpha)$	The dynamic assurance of an allocation mapping α of file F
I_{ij}	Decreasing sorted list of fragments to be allocated	LoadB	Workload that a fragment brings to the node where it is stored

graph. Cluster storage subsystem R_i has a gateway, which hides the cluster's internal architecture from users by forwarding file requests to storage nodes.

Data in cluster storage subsystem R_i can be accessed through its master node. When a read request is submitted to cluster R_i, the master node is responsible for reconstructing file fragments and for returning the file to users. When a write request of a file is issued, the master node updates all fragments of the file.

Legitimate users access cluster storage subsystems through master nodes; malicious users may bypass the master nodes to access storage nodes without being authorized. See Section 16.3.2 for details on the threat model.

16.3.2 Threat Model

It is not reasonable to assume that if a malicious user breaks into a storage node, fragments of a file stored on the node are thereby compromised. Normally, a malicious user requires two steps to compromise fragments of a file stored on a server. First, the malicious user must successfully compromise the server. Second, fragments are retrieved by the malicious user.

Let P_N be the probability that a storage server is successfully attacked; let P_f be the probability that authorized users retrieve fragments stored on the server, provided that the server has been compromised. We define event Z as a successful attack on a fragment (i.e., unauthorized disclosure of the fragment). Since the above two consecutive attack steps are independent, the probability that event Z occurs is a product of probability P_N and probability P_f. Thus, the probability that a fragment is disclosed to an unauthorized attacker can be expressed as

$$P(Z) = P_N \times P_f. \tag{16.1}$$

Given two storage nodes with different vulnerabilities, successful attacks of the nodes are not correlated. This statement is true for many potential threats, because compromising one storage node does not necessarily lead to the successful attack of another.

16.4 S-FAS: A SECURE FRAGMENT ALLOCATION SCHEME

In this section, we first outline the motivation for addressing the heterogeneity issues in the vulnerability of distributed storage systems. Next, we describe a security problem addressed in this study. Last, we present a secure fragment allocation scheme called S-FAS for distributed storage systems.

16.4.1 Heterogeneity in the Vulnerability of Data Storage

Since the existing security techniques (see Section 16.2) developed for distributed systems are inadequate for distributed systems with heterogeneity in vulnerabilities, the focus of this study is heterogeneous vulnerabilities in large-scale distributed storage systems. Vulnerabilities of storage nodes in a distributed system are heterogeneous in nature due to the following four main reasons. First, storage nodes have different ways to protect data. Second, a security policy can be implemented in a variety of mechanisms. Third, the key length of an encryption scheme may vary across multiple storage nodes. Fourth, heterogeneities exist in computational units of storage sites. We believe that future security mechanisms for distributed systems must be aware of vulnerability heterogeneities.

16.4.2 A Motivational Example

If the above heterogeneous vulnerability features are not incorporated into fragment allocation schemes for distributed storage systems, a seemingly secure fragment allocation decision can lead to a breach of data confidentiality. The following motivational example illustrates a security problem caused by ignoring vulnerability heterogeneities.

Let us consider a file F with three partitioned fragments: f_a, f_b, and f_c, and a distributed storage system (see Fig. 16.2a) that contains 16 storage nodes categorized into four server-type groups (or server groups for short), that is, T_1, T_2, T_3, and T_4. Storage nodes in each server group offer similar services with the same vulnerabilities. In this example, server group T_1 consists of nodes r_1, r_5, r_9, r_{13}; that is, $T_1 = \{r_1, r_5, r_9, r_{13}\}$. Similarly, we define the other three server groups as $T_2 = \{r_2, r_6, r_{10}, r_{14}\}$, $T_3 = \{r_3, r_7, r_{11}, r_{15}\}$, and $T_4 = \{r_4, r_8, r_{12}, r_{16}\}$.

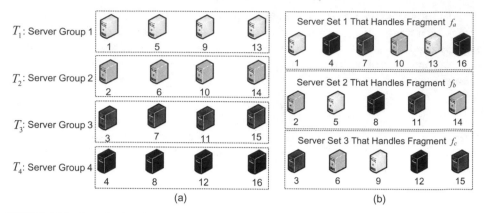

FIGURE 16.2. *A motivational example: (a) A distributed storage system contains 16 storage nodes, which are divided into four server-type groups, that is, T_1, T_2, T_3, and T_4; (b) possible insecure file fragment allocation decision made using a hashing function (see equation 11 in Reference 4).*

Figure 16.2b shows that it is possible to make insecure fragment allocation decisions when vulnerability heterogeneity is not taken into account. The decision made using a hashing function (see equation 11 in Reference 4) randomly allocates the three fragments of file F to three different nodes, each of which belongs to one of the three server sets illustrated in Figure 16.2b. For example, the three fragments, f_a, f_b, and f_c, are stored on nodes r_1, r_6, and r_8, respectively. This fragment allocation happens to be a good solution because r_1, r_6, and r_8 have different vulnerabilities as the three nodes belong to different server groups (i.e., T_1, T_2, and T_4). A malicious user must launch at least three successful attacks (one for each server group) in order to compromise all three fragments.

The above fragment allocation scheme fails to address the threat described in Section 16.3. This is because an attacker can first retrieve one fragment of F by compromising a single node and then wait for the other two fragments to be passed through the compromised node. To solve this security problem, Zanin et al. developed a static algorithm to decide whether a particular storage node is authorized to handle a file fragment of F [17]. Zanin's algorithm can generate an insecure fragment allocation because heterogeneous vulnerabilities are not considered. For example, if the three fragments are respectively stored on nodes r_4, r_8, and r_{12}, which share the same vulnerability in server group T_4 (see Fig. 16.2b), rather than three attacks, one successful attack against server group T_4 allows unauthorized users to access the three fragments of file F. Two other insecure fragment allocations are (1) allocating f_a, f_b, f_c to nodes r_1, r_5, and r_9, respectively, and (2) allocating f_a, f_b, f_c to nodes r_7, r_{11}, and r_{15}, respectively. These three fragment allocation decisions are unacceptable because the fragments are assigned to a group of storage nodes with the same vulnerability, meaning that an attacker who comprised one node within a group can easily compromise the other nodes in the group. The attacker can reconstruct F from f_a, f_b, and f_c stored on the comprised server group.

16.4.3 Design of the S-FAS Scheme

To solve the above security problem, we must incorporate vulnerability heterogeneities into fragment allocation schemes. Specifically, we designed a simple yet efficient approach to allocating fragments of a file to storage nodes with various vulnerabilities. Since allocating fragments of a file into different storage subsystems can degrade performance, our S-FAS scheme attempts to allocate fragments to storage nodes in as few clusters as possible. To improve the assurance of a distributed storage system while maintaining high I/O performance, each cluster storage subsystem must be built with high vulnerability heterogeneity. This causes the fragments of a file to be less likely distributed across multiple storage clusters.

Because of the following two reasons, the S-FAS scheme can significantly improve data security when fragments are stored in a large-scale distributed storage system. First, S-FAS integrates the fragmentation technique with secret sharing. Second, S-FAS addresses the issue of heterogeneous vulnerabilities when file fragments are allocated to a distributed storage system.

The S-FAS scheme makes fragment allocation decisions by following the four policies below:

- *Policy 1.* All the storage nodes in a distributed storage system are classified into multiple server-type groups based on their various vulnerabilities. Each server group consists of storage nodes with the same vulnerabilities.
- *Policy 2.* To improve the security of a distributed storage system, S-FAS allocates fragments of a file to storage nodes belonging to as many different server groups as possible. In doing so, it is impossible to compromise the file's fragments using a single successful attack method.
- *Policy 3.* The fragments of a file try to be allocated to nodes within a wide range of vulnerabilities all within the fewest cluster storage subsystems which are close to clients. The goal of this policy is to improve the performance of the storage system by making the fragments less likely to be distributed across too many distant clusters.
- *Policy 4.* The (m, n) secret sharing scheme is integrated with the S-FAS allocation mechanism.

If a file's fragment allocation decisions are guided by the above four policies, successful attacks against less than m server groups have little chance of gaining unauthorized accesses to files stored in a distributed system. In other words, if the number of compromised fragments of a file is less than m, attackers are unable to reconstruct the file from the fragments that are accessed by the unauthorized attackers. The S-FAS scheme can improve information assurance of files stored in a distributed storage system without enhancing confidentiality services deployed in cluster storage subsystems of the distributed system because S-FAS is orthogonal to security mechanisms that provide confidentiality for each server group in a distributed storage system. Thus, S-FAS can be seamlessly integrated with any confidentiality service employed in distributed storage systems in order to offer enhanced security services.

16.5 ASSURANCE MODELS

We developed assurance models to quantitatively evaluate the security of a heterogeneous distributed storage system in which S-FAS handles fragment allocations.

16.5.1 Storage Assurance Model

For encrypted files, their encryption keys are partitioned and allocated using the same strategy that handles file fragments. Once a storage node in set U is compromised, file fragments and encryption key fragments stored on the node are both breached. If a malicious user wants to crack a file, at least m nodes within U must be successfully hacked.

We first investigate the probability that a file is compromised using one attack method. Let X be the event that a set of storage nodes is chosen to be attacked. Let Y be the event that if X occurs, at least m fragments can be compromised using the same attack method. As we have already defined in Section 16.3, event Z represents a successful attack to a certain fragment of a file. Applying the multiplication principle, we calculate the probability that V—an event that file F is compromised under one attack—occurs as

$$P(V) = \sum_{j=1}^{k} P(X)P(Y)P(Z), \qquad (16.2)$$

where $P(X)$, $P(Y)$, and $P(Z)$ are probabilities that events X, Y, and Z occur when the total number of different server-type groups (server group for short) is K. The probability $P(V)$ is proportional to probability $P(Z)$, which largely depends on the quality of security mechanisms deployed in the storage system, as well as the attacking skills of hackers.

Note that when k equals 1, there is no vulnerability difference among storage nodes. Supposing that all the fragments of a file can be compromised using one successful attack method, the probability that Y occurs becomes 1. Then, we can express $P(V)$ as

$$P(V) = \sum_{j=1}^{k} P(X)P(Z). \qquad (16.3)$$

Let S_j be the number of storage nodes in *server type T_j* set and N be the total number of nodes in a distributed system. The probability that nodes in set T_j are randomly attacked can be derived as $P(X) = S_j/N$.

Probability $P(Y)$ in Equation (16.2) can be calculated as follows:

$$P(Y) = \sum_{i=m}^{n} \frac{C_{S_j}^{i} C_{N-S_j}^{n-i}}{C_N^n}, (j = 2, \dots K), \qquad (16.4)$$

where C_N^n is the total number of possibilities of allocating fragments of a file, and the product of $C_{S_j}^{i}$ and $C_{N-S_j}^{n-i}$ is the number of possibilities that a file is compromised using a successful attack method, which means at least m (it may be $m + 1, m + 2, \dots$, n) fragments of the file are compromised.

To simplify the model, one may assume that security mechanisms and attacking skills have no significant impacts on information assurance of the entire distributed storage system. This assumption is reasonable because of two factors. First, S-FAS is independent of security mechanisms that provide confidentiality for server groups in a distributed storage system. Second, if empirical studies can provide values for probability $P(Z)$, the probability $P(V)$ can be derived from $P(Z)$ and the model (see Equation 16.4) that calculates $P(Y)$. Since the study of the distribution of $P(Z)$ is not within the range of this work, in Section 16.7, the impact of probability $P(Z)$ on $P(V)$ is ignored by setting the value of $P(Z)$ to 1. Now we can derive Equation (16.5) from Equation (16.4) as

$$P(V) = \sum_{j=1}^{K} \left(\frac{S_j}{N} P(Z) \sum_{i=m}^{n} \frac{C_{S_j}^i C_{N-S_j}^{n-i}}{C_N^n} \right). \tag{16.5}$$

The confidentiality of file F is assured if F is not compromised. Thus, we can derive the assurance $SA(\alpha)$ of the storage system from Equation (16.5) as

$$SA(\alpha) = 1 - P(V) = 1 - \sum_{j=1}^{K} \left(\frac{S_j}{N} P(Z) \sum_{i=m}^{n} \frac{C_{S_j}^i C_{N-S_j}^{n-i}}{C_N^n} \right). \tag{16.6}$$

16.5.2 Dynamic Assurance Model

During read and write operations, some fragments of a file may be transmitted among different storage clusters or subnetworks. We assume that data transmissions within a cluster are secure, while connections among clusters and subnetworks may be insecure. Let P_L be the probability that a fragment is intercepted during its transmission on an insecure link. We consider a common case in which some fragments of file F are allocated outside a cluster. The probability P_D that a fragment of F is intercepted during its transmission can be expressed as

$$P_D = \mu_1 \mu_2 P_L + \mu_3 [1 - P_L] P_L, \tag{16.7}$$

where $\mu_1 = 1$ indicates that connections among storage clusters are insecure and $\mu_1 = 0$ means the connections are secure. $\mu_2 = 1$ indicates that fragments are transferred among different clusters; otherwise, $\mu_2 = 0$. Similarly, $\mu_3 = 1$ means that fragments are transmitted across different subnetworks. When μ_1, μ_2, and μ_3 equal 0, there is no fragment transmission risk. If q fragments need to be collected outside a cluster processing read/write operations, then probability $P_q(g)$ that g out of q fragments are intercepted can be expressed as

$$P_q(g) = C_q^g P_D^g (1 - P_D)^{q-g}. \tag{16.8}$$

Now we model the dynamic assurance of an allocation mapping α of file F. For simplicity, let us focus on a time period during which there is only one attempt to attack storage nodes where F is stored. During this time period, we assume that only one read or write operation is issued to access F. There are two cases in which file F can be compromised. First, a malicious user can reconstruct F from m compromised fragments using the same attack method. Second, although less than m fragments are compromised, other g fragments are intercepted during their transmissions. Hence, we can derive the dynamic assurance $DA(\alpha)$ (Equation 16.9) from the storage risk (see Equation 16.5) and the transmission risk (see Equation 16.8), as shown here:

$$DA(\alpha) = 1 - \left(P(V) + \left(\sum_{g=(m-i)}^{q} P_q(g) \right) \sum_{j=1}^{K} \left(\frac{S_j}{N} \sum_{i=0}^{m-1} \frac{C_{S_j}^i C_{N-S_j}^{n-i}}{C_N^n} \right) \right). \tag{16.9}$$

16.6   SAP ALLOCATION PRINCIPLES AND PROTOTYPE

We developed a prototype using the multithreading technique for the SAP algorithm to guide the file allocation. We then conducted some experiments to evaluate the performance of SAP integrated in the S-FAS scheme. Results show that the proposed solution can not only improve the storage security level but can also enhance the throughput of the distributed storage system with heterogeneous vulnerabilities.

16.6.1   Allocation Principles

The design of our S-FAS scheme is mainly focused on the improvement of system security. Considering the heterogeneity of the system can also be used to improve system performance, we developed a SAP algorithm for the S-FAS scheme to improve the security level and considered its performance using the heterogeneous feature of a large distributed system. The SAP allocation algorithm, a key component, addresses the issues of load balancing, delayed effects caused by the workload variance of many consecutive requests [18, 19], and the heterogeneous feature of distributed storage systems.

There are three main factors affecting the processing delay of a request from a client, namely, workload, network traffic, and I/O latency at storage nodes. In our algorithm design, we consider load balacing among storage nodes and network interconnects to improve the system performance. Initially, all nodes are logically categorized into different types based on the similarities of their vulnerabilities. The basic principles of the SAP allocation algorithm are described below:

1. to sort the two-dimensional list I_{ij} of file (i) fragments (j) in a decreasing order based on the burdens of the input files
2. to sort all storage nodes in a two-dimensional list in a decreasing order based on their vulnerability type and processing speed
3. to allocate each fragment in list I_{ij} to storage nodes.

There are two constraints used when deciding whether a fragment should be allocated to a node: (1) There is enough space to store the fragment; and (2) the available LoadB is higher than 80% (the upper bound of the storage load can be adjusted to a different level to control the storage space efficiency on a server) of the LoadB of the current fragment.

It is possible that fragments of a file can be allocated in the same type of nodes. Nevertheless, the chances of allocating multiple fragments of a file to nodes of the same type is much less than those in the random allocation scheme.

16.6.2 Prototype Architecture and Design

In order to evaluate the S-FAS scheme along with the SAP algorithm, we designed and implemented a prototype to test system throughput on a distributed storage testbed. We applied the multithreading technique, allowing one thread to process one request of fragment read/write to enhance processing performance.

In the implimentation of the prototype, system nodes are divided into three main groups—computing nodes (clients), storage nodes, and a storage server. The storage server is responsible for handling file allocation using the SAP algorithm, managing the metadata and dealing with the incoming read or write requests from the clients. The storage nodes are categorized into a few groups based on their heterogeneous vulnerability features. The client nodes can directly access storage servers through the network interconnect.

16.7 EVALUATION OF SYSTEM ASSURANCE AND PERFORMANCE

The assurance models described in Section 16.5 indicate that system assurance is affected by the K number of storage types, the N number of storage nodes in the system, and the S_j number of nodes of the jth storage type. In addition, threshold m and the n number of fragments of a file also have an impact on system assurance.

In this section, we will first evaluate the impact of these factors (K, N, S_j, n, and m) on storage assurance (see Sections 16.7.1–16.7.5). We will compare our approach with a traditional fragment allocation scheme that does not consider vulnerability heterogeneities. Then, we will measure dynamic assurance of S-FAS to analyze the impact of P_L and q on system dynamic assurance (see Sections 16.7.6 and 16.7.7). We will evaluate a distributed storage system with the threshold value m. The default n number of fragments of a file is set to 12 (the value can vary according to system sizes) and $S_j = N/K$ for all j from 1 to K.

In the last part of this section, we will discuss experimental results for the SAP algorithm and the prototype. To explore the affecting factors that influence the system performance, we will evaluate the impact of the file size and fragment number on system throughput(see Section 16.7.8).

16.7.1 Impact of Heterogeneity on Storage Assurance

If all storage nodes in the evaluated distributed system are identical in terms of vulnerability, the probability that fragments of a file can be compromised using one successful attack method is 1. Figure 16.3 shows the impact of the K number of storage types on system assurance. The results plotted in Figure 16.3 suggest that, for a distributed system with homogeneous vulnerability, threshold m has no impact on system assurance. For a distributed system with heterogeneous vulnerabilities, the system assurance increases significantly with increasing values of K and threshold m (see Figure 16.3). Such a trend implies that a high heterogeneity level of vulnerability gives rise to high confidentiality assurance.

16.7.2 Impact of System Size on Storage Assurance

To quantify the impact of system size N on the assurance of a file stored in the system, we gradually increase the system size from 45 to 70 by increments of 5. We

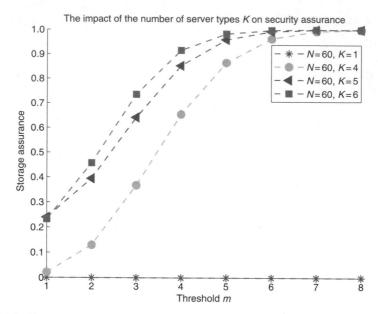

FIGURE 16.3. *Heterogeneous system and homogeneous system using the secret sharing scheme.*

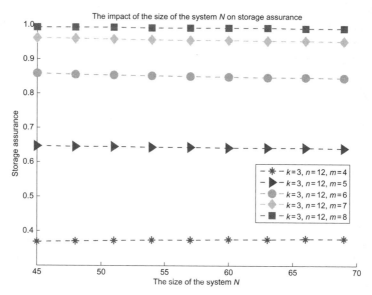

FIGURE 16.4. *The impact of the system size* N *on storage assurance.*

keep k at 3 and also vary m from 4 to 8. Figure 16.4 reveals that the storage assurance of the system is not very sensitive to the system size, indicating that storage assurance largely depends on the vulnerability heterogeneity level rather than on system size. Thus, large-scale distributed storage systems with low levels of vulnerability heterogeneities may have lower assurance than small-scale distributed systems. These results suggest that one way to improve system assurance is to

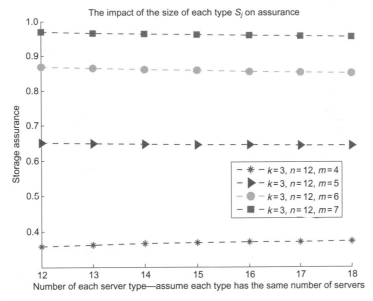

FIGURE 16.5. *The impact of server-group size on data storage assurance. The server-group size means the number of storage nodes in a server-type group.*

increase vulnerability heterogeneity while increasing the scale of a distributed storage system. A high heterogeneity level in vulnerability helps in increasing threshold m, making it difficult for attackers to compromise multiple server groups and to reconstruct files.

16.7.3 Impact of Size of Server Groups on Storage Assurance

Figure 16.5 illustrates the impact of server-group size on data storage assurance. Note that the server-group size is the number of storage nodes in a server-type group, in which all the storage nodes share the same group of vulnerabilities. We vary the server-group size from 12 to 18 by increments of 1. We observe from Figure 16.5 that, when threshold m is small (e.g, $m = 4$), the assurance of systems with large server-group sizes is slightly higher than that of systems with small server-group sizes. Interestingly, the opposite is true when the threshold m is large (e.g, $m > 4$). Given a fixed number of storage nodes in a distributed storage system, increasing the server-group size can decrease the number of server groups, which in turn tends to reduce vulnerability heterogeneity. The results shown in Figure 16.5 match the results in the previous experiments in which a low level of vulnerability heterogeneity results in degraded storage assurance.

16.7.4 Impact of *n* Number of File Fragments on Storage Assurance

Figure 16.6 illustrates the impact of the n number of fragments of a file on storage assurance. In this experiment, we increased the n number of fragments from 11 to 20 and measured data storage assurance using our model. The parameters k and N

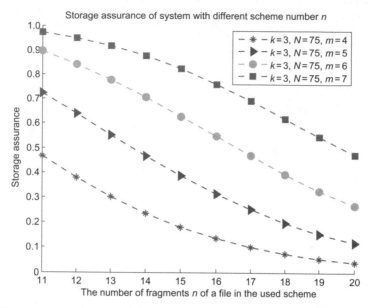

FIGURE 16.6. *The impact of the number* n *of fragments of a file on storage assurance.*

were set to 3 and 75, respectively. We also varied threshold m from 4 to 7. Results depicted in Figure 16.6 confirm that the system assurance is reduced with the increasing value of fragment number n. The results indicate that a large number of file fragments leads to low data storage assurance of the file. This assurance trend is reasonable because more fragments are likely to be allocated to storage nodes with the same vulnerability. If one storage node is compromised by an attacker, fragments stored on nodes with the same vulnerabilities can also be obtained by the attacker, who is therefore more likely to be able to reconstruct the file from the disclosed fragments.

In addition, Figure 16.6 shows that increasing the value of threshold m can improve storage assurance. This pattern is consistent with the results obtained in the previous experiments.

16.7.5   Impact of Threshold m on Storage Assurance

Figures 16.3–16.6 clearly show the impact of threshold m on the storage assurance of a distributed system. More specifically, regardless of other system parameters, the storage assurance always goes up with the increasing threshold value m. The results indicate that the more fragments an attacker needs in order to reconstruct a file, the higher data storage assurance can be preserved for the file in distributed storage systems. These results suggest that to improve the data storage assurance of a file, one needs to partition the file and to allocate fragments in such a way that an attacker must compromise more server groups (the best case is m server groups when all fragments of the file are allocated to nodes of different server types) in order to reconstruct the file.

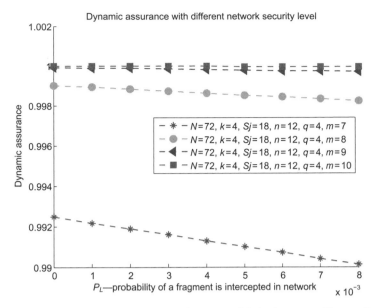

FIGURE 16.7. Impact of P_L (the probability that a fragment might be intercepted by an attacker during the fragment's transmission).

16.7.6   Impact of P_L on Dynamic Assurance

Now we are in a position to evaluate the dynamic assurance of distributed storage systems. The three parameters μ_1, μ_2, and μ_3 in Equation (16.7) have an important impact on dynamic assurance because they indicate whether there is risk during fragment transmission. Please refer to Sections 16.7.1–16.7.5 for details on the impacts of a set of parameters on data storage assurance. P_L—the probability that a fragment might be intercepted by an attacker during the fragment's transmission through an insecure link—has a noticeable impact on the dynamic assurance of a distributed storage system provided that threshold m is small (e.g., smaller than 9). Figure 16.7 shows the dynamic assurance of a distributed system when P_L is varied from 0 to 8×10^{-3} by increments of 1×10^{-3}. We also vary threshold m (i.e., m is varied from 7 to 10) to evaluate the sensitivity of dynamic assurance on parameter P_L under different threshold m.

Figure 16.7 demonstratively confirms that when threshold m is equal to or smaller than 8, a large value of P_L results in low dynamic assurance of the system. These results are expected since a high value of P_L means that the transmitted fragments are likely to be intercepted by an attacker. Once the attacker has collected enough fragments of a security-sensitive file, the file can be reconstructed. When threshold m is larger than 8, the dynamic assurance is not noticeably sensitive to the probability P_L that a fragment is compromised during its network transfer.

16.7.7   Impact of q on Dynamic Assurance

Like parameter P_L, the q number of fragments transmitted to and from a storage cluster also has an impact on the dynamic assurance of a distributed storage system.

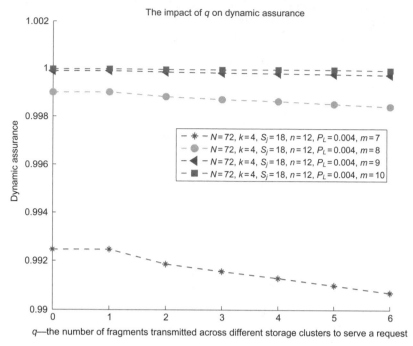

FIGURE 16.8. *Impact of* q *(q fragments transmitted across storage clusters.)*

Intuitively, Figure 16.8 shows that, when the number of fragments of a file that must be transmitted through insecure links is increasing, the dynamic assurance of the file drops. Interestingly, when threshold m is larger than 8, the dynamic assurance becomes very insensitive to the number q of fragments. This observation suggests that, when the threshold is small, the S-FAS fragment allocation scheme must specifically attempt to lower the value of q in order to maintain a high dynamic assurance level.

In addition, we observe from Figure 16.8 that dynamic assurance is always lower than the corresponding storage assurance (where $q = 0$ in Fig. 16.8). This trend is always true because in a dynamic environment, file fragments have to be transmitted through insecure network links where malicious users may intercept the fragments in order to reconstruct files.

16.7.8 Performance Evaluation of S-FAS

We made use of the prototype to evaluate the performance of S-FAS. We conducted some experiments by varying two parameters that noticeably affect both security and performance. We conducted an experiment to test the file allocation process by varying the workload and fragment number of the S-FAS scheme as described in the following:

- *File Size.* In our experiments, the test file size is varied from 950 MB (996,147,200 bytes) to 2300 MB(2,411,724,800 bytes). The details can be seen in the corresponding figures.

• *Fragment Number of a File.* We varied the fragment number from 3 to 15. We set the upper bound to less than 16 since we have 16 storage nodes in our test bed, and the S-FAS performs better when one storage node stores one fragment of a file at most.

Figure 16.9a plots the impact of the allocating file size on the throughput of S-FAS. From Figure 16.9a, we observe that the S-FAS scheme improves the throughput compared to the traditional nonfragmented storage method. Because we use the multithreading method to deal with the fragments of a file in the S-FAS scheme, the system performance is significantly improved in our scheme. The other trend we can observe from Figure 16.9a is that, with the increasing of file sizes, the system throughput first increases and then decreases after the file size is larger than 1.2 GB. This trend applies to S-FAS and the non-S-FAS schemes. When file size is relatively small, the throughput increases with the increasing of the file size. The reason is that the load is still below the upper bound of the system peak performance. This experiment for high-performance distributed storage systems suggests that implementing the S-FAS scheme using the multithreading method is very important.

Figure 16.9b shows the impact of the fragment number on the throughput. Figure 16.9b shows that the throughput goes up when the fragment number is increased in the S-FAS scheme. Because we use one thread to deal with one fragment of a file in the S-FAS scheme, the performance is improved with the increasing number of the fragments. The throughput does not noticeably change when the number of fragments is anywhere between 7 and 11 because we set the thread number equal to 8. When a file has more than eight fragments, the first eight fragments are concurrently processed by the multithreads, while the other fragments are waiting to be served. We can conclude from Figure 16.9a,b that using the multithreading method can improve the throughput compared with the traditional scheme.

16.8 CONCLUSION

It is critical to maintain the confidentiality of files stored in a distributed storage system, even when some storage nodes in the system are compromised by attackers. In recognizing that storage nodes in a distributed system have heterogeneous vulnerabilities, we investigated a secure fragment allocation scheme by incorporating secret sharing and heterogeneous vulnerability to improve the security of distributed storage systems.

We addressed the security heterogeneity issue by categorizing storage servers into different server-type groups (or server group for short), each of which represents a level of security vulnerability. With heterogeneous vulnerabilities in place, we developed a fragment allocation scheme called S-FAS to improve the security of a heterogeneous distributed system. S-FAS allocates fragments of a file in such a way that even if attackers compromised a number of server groups but fewer than k fragments are disclosed, the file cannot be reconstructed from the compromised fragments.

To evaluate the S-FAS scheme, we built the static and dynamic assurance models in order to quantify the assurance of a heterogeneous distributed storage system processing file fragments. We developed a SAP file allocation algorithm based on

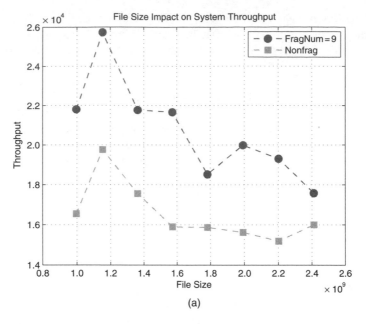

(a)

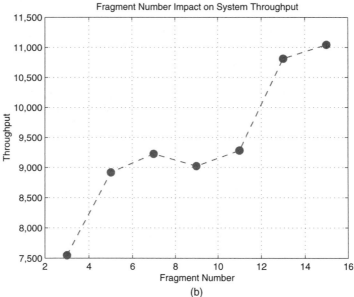

(b)

FIGURE 16.9. *File size and fragment number impact on system throughput: (a) impact of file size(file size:byte; throughput: byte per millisecond) and (b) impact of fragment number(fragment number: 3, 5, 7, . . . , 15; throughput: byte per millisecond.*

the analysis of the assurance model as well as the proposed S-FAS scheme. In order to measure the performance of the S-FAS scheme and the algorithm, we built a prototype in a real-world distributed storage system.

We demonstrated how S-FAS incorporates the vulnerability heterogeneity feature into file fragment allocation for distributed storage systems. Experimental results show that increasing heterogeneity levels can improve file assurance in a distributed storage system. The experimental results of our prototype implementation offer us inspiration on how to use S-FAS to efficiently improve security and performance in distributed storage systems with heterogeneous vulnerabilities.

ACKNOWLEDGMENTS

This research was supported by the U.S. National Science Foundation under grants CCF-0845257 (CAREER), CNS-0917137 (CSR), CNS-0757778 (CSR), CCF-0742187 (CPA), CNS-0831502 (CyberTrust), CNS-0855251 (CRI), OCI-0753305 (CI-TEAM), DUE-0837341 (CCLI), and DUE-0830831 (SFS), as well as Auburn University under a startup grant, and a gift (No. 2005-04-070) from the Intel Corporation.

REFERENCES

[1] M. Pourzandi, D. Gordon, W. Yurcik, and G.A. Koenig, "Clusters and security: Distributed security for distributed systems," in *IEEE International Symposium on Cluster Computing and the Grid, 2005. CCGrid 2005*, Vol. 1, pp. 96–104, May 2005.

[2] H. Mantel, "On the composition of secure systems," in *2002 IEEE Symposium on Security and Privacy*, 2002.

[3] W. Yurcik, G.A. Koenig, X. Meng, and J. Greenseid, "Cluster security as a unique problem with emergent properties: Issues and techniques," in *The 5th LCI International Conference on Linux Clusters: The HPC Revolution 2004*, pp. 18–20, 2004.

[4] S. Jajodia, A. Mei, and L.V. Mancini, "Secure dynamic fragment and replica allocation in large-scale distributed file systems," *IEEE Transactions on Parallel and Distributed Systems*, 14(9):885–896, 2003.

[5] T. Wu, M. Malkin, and D. Boneh, "Building intrusion tolerant applications," in *SSYM '99: Proceedings of the 8th Conference on USENIX Security Symposium*, pp. 7–7. Berkeley, CA: USENIX Association, 1999.

[6] J.F. Bouchard and D.L. Kewley, "Darpa information assurance program dynamic defense experiment summary," *IEEE Transactions on Systems, Man and Cybernetics, Part A: Systems and Humans*, 31(4):331–336, 2001.

[7] B.M. Thuraisingham and J.A. Maurer, "Information survivability for evolvable and adaptable real-time command and control systems," *IEEE Transactions on Knowledge and Data Engineering*, 11(1):228–238, 1999.

[8] J. Kubiatowicz, D. Bindel, Y. Chen, S. Czerwinski, P. Eaton, D. Geels, R. Gummadi, S. Rhea, H. Weatherspoon, W. Weimer, C. Wells, and B. Zhao, "Oceanstore: An architecture for global-scale persistent storage," *SIGPLAN Notices*, 35:190–201, 2000.

[9] S. Lakshmanan, M. Ahamad, and H. Venkateswaran, "Responsive security for stored data," *IEEE Transactions on Parallel and Distributed Systems*, 14(9):818–828, 2003.

[10] M.O. Rabin, "Efficient dispersal of information for security, load balancing, and fault tolerance," *Journal of the ACM*, 36:335–348, 1989.

[11] A. Shamir, "How to share a secret," *Communications of the ACM*, 22(11):612–613, 1979.

[12] M. Tu, P. Li, I.-L. Yen, B.M. Thuraisingham, and L. Khan, "Secure data objects replication in data grid," *IEEE Transactions on Dependable and Secure Computing*, 7(1):50–64, 2010.

[13] F. Dabek, M.F. Kaashoek, D. Karger, R. Morris, and I. Stoica, "Wide-area cooperative storage with cfs," in *SOSP '01: Proceedings of the 18th ACM Symposium on Operating Systems Principles*, pp. 202–215, New York, 2001. ACM.

[14] T. Pedersen, "Non-interactive and information-theoretic secure verifiable secret sharing," in *Proceedings of the 11th Annual International Cryptology Conference on Advances in Cryptology, CRYPTO '91*, pp. 129–140. London, UK: Springer-Verlag, 1992.

[15] G.J. Simmons, "How to (really) share a secret," in *CRYPTO '88: Proceedings of the 8th Annual International Cryptology Conference on Advances in Cryptology*, pp. 390–448. London, UK: Springer-Verlag, 1990.

[16] J.D. Strunk, G.R. Ganger, H. Kiliccote, P.K. Khosla, J.J. Wylie, and M.W. Bigrigg, "Survivable information storage systems," *Computer*, 33(8):61–68, 2000.

[17] G. Zanin, A. Mei, and L.V. Mancini, "Towards a secure dynamic allocation of files in large scale distributed file systems," in *HOT-P2P '04: Proceedings of the 2004 International Workshop on Hot Topics in Peer-to-Peer Systems*, pp. 102–107. Washington, DC: IEEE Computer Society, 2004.

[18] L.W. Lee, P. Scheuermann, and R. Vingralek, "File assignment in parallel i/o systems with minimal variance of service time," *IEEE Transactions on Computers*, 49(2):127–140, 2000.

[19] P. Scheuermann, G. Weikum, and P. Zabback, "Data partitioning and load balancing in parallel disk systems," *The VLDB Journal*, 7(1):48–66, 1998.

17

Adopting Compression in Wireless Sensor Networks

Xi Deng and Yuanyuan Yang

17.1   INTRODUCTION

Recent years have witnessed the development and proliferation of wireless sensor networks (WSNs), attributed to the technological advances of microelectromechanical systems (MEMS) and wireless communications. A WSN is composed of a number of sensor nodes, which are distributed in a specific area to perform certain sensing tasks. A typical sensor node is a low-cost battery-powered device equipped with one or more sensors, a processor, memory, and a short-range wireless transceiver. A variety of sensors, including thermal, optical, magnetic, acoustic, and visual sensors, are used to monitor different properties of the environment. The processor and memory enable the sensor node to perform simple data processing and storing operations. The transceiver makes the sensor node capable of wireless communications, which is critical for WSNs. With many WSNs located in difficult-to-access areas, users usually cannot collect the data in sensor nodes directly. In this case, sensors nodes can transmit the data through the wireless channel to the user or the data sink either directly or by relaying through multiple sensor nodes. Due to the same geographical difficulty, the batteries, as the power supply of the sensor nodes, are difficult to recharge or replace, restricting nodes' energy budget. Therefore, energy efficiency is the primary design concern in many WSNs.

Delay-sensitive WSNs are a special type of WSNs that require real-time delivery of sensing data to the data sink. Such networks are widely adopted in various

Scalable Computing and Communications: Theory and Practice, First Edition. Edited by Samee U. Khan, Albert Y. Zomaya, and Lizhe Wang.

real-time applications including traffic monitoring, hazard detection, and battlefield surveillance, where decisions should be made promptly once the emergent events occur. Thus, delay-sensitive WSNs are more focused on minimizing the communication delay during data delivery rather than the energy efficiency. Recent study in this area has mainly focused on the algorithm design of efficient routing strategies and data aggregation to reduce such delay and to provide real-time delivery guarantees [1–4]. In this chapter, we approach this problem from a different and orthogonal angle by considering the effect of data compression. Compression was initially adopted as an effective approach to save energy in WSNs. In fact, it can also be used to reduce the communication delay in delay-sensitive WSNs.

In WSNs, compression reduces the data amount by exploiting the redundancy resided in sensing data. The reduction can be measured by the *compression ratio*, defined as the original data size divided by the compressed data size. A higher compression ratio indicates larger reduction on the data amount and results in shorter communication delay. Thus, much work in the literature has been endeavored to achieve better compression ratio for sensing data. However, from the implementation perspective, most of the compression algorithms are complex and time-consuming procedures running on sensor nodes which are very resource constrained. As the processing time of compression could not be simply neglected in such nodes, the effect of compression on the total delay during data delivery becomes a trade-off between the reduced communication delay and the increased processing time. As a result, compression may increase rather than decrease the total delay when the processing time is relatively long.

We first analyze the compression effect in a typical data gathering scheme in WSNs where each sensor collects data continuously and delivers all the packets to a data sink. To do so, we need to first obtain the processing time of compression, which depends on several factors, including the compression algorithm, processor architecture, CPU frequency, and the compression data. Among numerous compression algorithms, we use the Lempel–Ziv–Welch (LZW) [5] as an example, which is a lossless compression algorithm suitable for sensor nodes. We implement the algorithm on a TI MSP430F5418 microcontroller (MCU) [6], which is used in the current generation of sensor nodes. Experiments reveal that the compression time in such a system is comparable to the transmission time of packets and thus cannot be simply ignored. To support the study in large-scale WSNs, we utilize a software estimation approach to providing runtime measurement of the algorithm execution time in the network simulation. The simulation results show that compression may lead to several times longer overall delay under light traffic loads, while it can significantly reduce the delay under heavy traffic loads and increase maximum throughput.

Since the effect of compression varies heavily with network traffic and hardware configurations, we give an online adaptive algorithm that dynamically makes compression decisions to accommodate the changing state of WSNs. In the algorithm, we adopt a queueing model to estimate the queueing behavior of sensors with the assistance of only local information of each sensor node. Based on the queueing model, the algorithm predicts the compression effect on the average packet delay and performs compression only when it can reduce packet delay. The simulation results show that the adaptive algorithm can make decisions properly and yield near-optimal performance under various network configurations.

17.2   COMPRESSION IN SENSOR NODES

Due to the limited energy budget in sensor networks, compression is considered as an effective method to reduce energy consumption on communications and has been extensively studied. In the meanwhile, the spatial-temporal correlation in the sensing data makes it suitable for compression. Akyildiz et al. proposed a theoretical framework to model the correlation and its utilization in several possible ways [7]. Scaglione and Servetto proved that the optimal compression efficiency can be achieved by source coding with proper routing algorithms [8]. The relationship between compression and hierarchical routing was also discussed in Reference 9. Pattem et al. analyzed the bound on the compression ratio achieved by lossless compression and showed that a simple, static cluster-based system design can perform as well as sophisticated adaptive schemes for joint routing and compression [10]. In Reference 11, a framework of distributed source coding (DSC) was given to compress correlated data without explicit communications. However, the implementation of DSC in practice could be difficult as it requires the global knowledge of the sensor data correlation structure.

Compression algorithms for sensor nodes can be classified into lossy compression and lossless compression. Lossy compression is defined in the sense that the compressed data may not be fully recovered by decompression. A series of algorithms utilized the data correlation to reduce the amount of data to be gathered while keeping the data within an affordable level of distortion. The approaches include data aggregation [12, 13], where only summarized data are required, approximate data representation using polynomial regression [14], line segment approximation [15], and low-complexity video compression [16].

Lossless compression can reconstruct the original data from the compressed data. Coding by ordering [17] is a compression strategy that utilizes the order of packets to represent the values in the suppressed packets. PINCO [18] was proposed to compress the sensing data by sharing the common suffix for the data. This approach is more useful for data with sufficiently long common suffices, such as node ID and time stamp. In Reference 19, the implementation of the LZW compression algorithm in sensor nodes was extensively studied and showed to have a good compression ratio for different types of sensing data. Another compression algorithm, Squeeze.KOM [20], uses a stream-oriented approach that transmits the difference, rather than the data itself, to shorten the transmission. Interested readers can also find a survey on compression algorithms in Reference 21.

Here we use the LZW algorithm as an example to evaluate its compression effects. Compared to other compression algorithms, LZW is relatively simple but yields a good compression ratio for sensor data as shown in Reference 19. Next, we briefly introduce the LZW algorithm and the approach to obtain its execution time at the software level instead of running the algorithm on hardware.

17.2.1   LZW Algorithm

LZW compression is a dictionary-based algorithm that replaces strings of characters with single codes in the dictionary. The first 256 codes in the dictionary by default correspond to the standard character set. As shown in Table 17.1, the algorithm sequentially reads in characters and finds the longest string s that can be recognized

TABLE 17.1. LZW Compression Algorithm

```
STRING = first character
while there are still input characters
        C = next character
        look up STRING+C in the dictionary
        if STRING+C is in the dictionary
                STRING = STRING+C
        else
                output the code for STRING
                add STRING+C to the dictionary
                STRING = C
        end if
end while
output the code for STRING
```

by the dictionary. Then, it encodes s using the corresponding code word in the dictionary and adds string $s + c$ in the dictionary, where c is the character following string s. This process continues until all characters are encoded. A more detailed description of the LZW algorithm can be found in Reference 5.

We consider only the compression process but not the decompression process because the latter can be finished in a relatively short time when it is performed at the sink node with more powerful computation capability. To adapt the LZW compression to sensor nodes, we set the dictionary size to 512, which has been shown to yield good compression ratios in real-world deployments [19].

To achieve a good compression ratio, which is the ratio of the original data size to the compressed data size, the string should be long enough to provide sufficient redundancies. Thus, the LZW algorithm is more suitable for WSNs that collect heavier load data, such as images and audio clips. Even in the compression algorithms specifically designed for this type of data, the processing in the algorithms could be complex and time-consuming. Hence, the evaluation result on the LZW algorithm can provide guidance for adopting these algorithms. In addition, in large-scale WSNs, distant nodes require multiple hops of transmissions to reach the sink, and the nodes closer to the sink may endure unaffordable traffic. In this case, aggregation is often used (e.g., in cluster-based networks) to reduce the traffic, and such aggregated packets consisting of several lighter load packets are also suitable for compression.

17.2.2 Compression Delay in Sensor Nodes

We examine the compression process on a TI MSP430F5418 MCU, which is used in the current generation of sensor nodes. It is a 16-bit ultra-low-power MCU with 128-kB flash and 16-kB RAM. The CPU has a peak working frequency of 18 MHz, a very high frequency among the current generation of sensor nodes.

To facilitate the evaluation of the compression effect in large-scale WSNs, we adopt a software estimation approach to simulate the compression processing time.

TABLE 17.2. A Mapping Example for a Function in the LZW Algorithm

void put(long key, int element){

put:

006190	153B	pushm.w	#4,R11
006192	4C0A	mov.w	R12,R10
006194	4D0B	mov.w	R13,R11
006196	4E08	mov.w	R14,R8

int b = hash_code(key);

006198	13B0 5FDC	calla	#hash_code

if(table[b].key == NOT_USED){

00619C	5C0C	rla.w	R12
00619E	4C0F	mov.w	R12,R15
0061A0	5C0C	rla.w	R12
0061A2	5F0C	add.w	R15,R12
0061A4	93BC 1C00	cmp.w	#0xFFFF,0x1C00(R12)
0061A8	2009	jne	0x61BC
0061AA	93BC 1C02	cmp.w	#0xFFFF,0x1C02(R12)
0061AE	2006	jne	0x61BC

table[b].key = key;

0061B0	4A8C 1C00	mov.w	R10,0x1C00(R12)
0061B4	4B8C 1C02	mov.w	R11,0x1C02(R12)

table[b].element = element;

0061B8	488C 1C04	mov.w	R8,0x1C04(R12)

return;

0061BC	1738	popm.w	#4,R11
0061BE	0110	reta	

C statements in source code are highlighted. The statement block after each C statement is the corresponding assembly code of that C statement.

Since instructions are sequentially executed in the CPU of this MCU, the processing time can be calculated as the total number of instruction cycles divided by the CPU frequency. Thus, obtaining the precise cycle counts becomes the main task, which we describe below.

The source code of the LZW algorithm written in C language is first compiled to assembly code using the instruction set of the MSP430X CPU series. A mapping is performed between the source code and the corresponding assembly code, with an example shown in Table 17.2. As each instruction in assembly code has a fixed number of execution cycles, the number of cycles of each C statement can be counted by summing up the numbers of cycles of the corresponding assembly instructions. The numbers for all C statements are then recorded in the source code by code instrumentation so that the execution cycles can be obtained at runtime. For the efficiency consideration, the instrumentation codes only appear at the end of each basic block, in which statements are sequentially executed without conditional branches. This way, the total count of cycles can be obtained at the completion of the LZW algorithm, then the processing time is obtained by dividing the total execution cycles by the working frequency.

17.3   COMPRESSION EFFECT ON PACKET DELAY

In this section, we study the compression effect on packet delay for data gathering in WSNs. We consider the all-to-one data gathering scenario where all sensors continuously generate packets and deliver them to a single sink. The performance metric used is the end-to-end packet delay, which is the interval from the time a packet is generated at the source to the time the packet is delivered to the sink. To evaluate the compression effect, we compare the end-to-end packet delay with compression and without compression. In the rest of this chapter, we refer to these two schemes as *compression scheme* and *no-compression scheme*, respectively.

17.3.1   Experiment Setup

The experiments are conducted in the NS-2 simulator, a widely used network simulator. To simplify the evaluation, we examine the performance on a two-dimensional (2-D) grid wireless network. Two networks of a 5×5 grid and a 7×7 grid with the sink at the center of the grids are considered. In the simulation, the transmission range is set to 16 m and the distance between neighboring nodes is 10 and 15 m, respectively, to create different network topologies. The packet generation on each sensor node follows an i.i.d. Poisson process, and we assume an identical packet length for all the packets generated in a single experiment. Two different packet lengths (256 and 512 B) are used to create different compression ratios and processing delays.

At the network layer, we adopt a multipath routing strategy [22]. Specifically, each sensor is assigned a level number, which indicates the minimum number of hops required to deliver a packet from this sensor to the sink. Such information can be obtained at the initial setup in the sensor deployment. A sensor with a level number i is called a level i node. A level i node only forwards the packets to its level $i - 1$ neighbors. Such a routing strategy is easy to implement but may not necessarily yield the best real-time performance. However, since the compression strategy adopted does not consider interpacket compression, the choice of the routing strategy will not substantially affect the performance evaluation that targets at the compression algorithm.

As we aim at delay-sensitive networks where packet delay rather than energy efficiency is the primary concern, we adopt the commonly used 802.11 protocol as the medium access control (MAC) layer protocol, and the wireless bandwidth is set to 1 Mb/s. The data set is automatically generated by the tool described in Reference 23, which provides a good approximation on the real sensing data in the evaluation of several representative network applications. We use such synthetic data so that the simulation can be performed sufficiently long to capture the steady-state behavior without exhausting the simulation data.

Compression is performed on each packet when it is generated at the source node. Since each sensor is equipped with a sequential processor, multiple packets are served in the first-come-first-served order and a sufficiently large buffer is assumed so that no packets are dropped at the compression stage. The compression process is simulated according to the estimation approach described in Section 17.2. The CPU frequency is 18 MHz. With these settings, we obtain that the average compression ratio is 1.25 and 1.6 when the packet length is 256 and 512 B, respectively. The average processing delay is 0.016 second for 256-B packets and 0.045 second for 512-B packets. The delays are further compared with the measurements on the real hardware, and the simulation accuracy is over 95%. Besides, the processing delay could be increased if lower CPU frequencies or more complex compression algorithms are adopted. For example, it is suggested that the Burrows–Wheeler transform (BWT) [24] can be performed on the sensor data to assist the subsequent LZW compression to obtain better compression ratio. Such processing delay can greatly affect the performance of high-resolution mission-critical applications, including real-time multimedia surveillance and other applications with timeliness requirement, where the extra delay could be critical for some packets to meet their deadlines.

17.3.2 Experimental Results

Based on the routing strategy, a packet generated at a level i node requires i-hop transmissions to reach the sink, resulting in different packet delays for nodes at different levels. In this section, we examine the average packet delay for all the nodes at the same level. Figure 17.1 shows the average delays of different levels in the 5×5 network with the neighboring distance set to 15 m and the packet length set to 512 B.

The primary observation drawn from the figure is that compression has a two-sided effect on the real-time performance depending on the packet generation rate. When the rate is low, compression clearly increases the average delay at each level. For example, when the rate is 2, the average delay of level 1 is increased by about 2.7 times from 13.6 to 51.5 ms when compression is adopted. Such increase is also observed for other levels, the least of which is 75% for level 4. Note that under such light traffic load, the delay is almost the packet transmission time due to little contention for the wireless channel. Since the packet transmission time reduced by compression is much less than the increase caused by the compression processing time, the overall delay increases, indicating a negative effect of compression. We

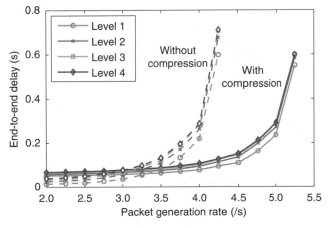

FIGURE 17.1. *Average packet delays for packets generated at different levels.*

also notice that such increase is smaller for nodes at higher levels, which can be explained by the fact that nodes at higher levels require more hops of transmissions to reach the sink, while each transmission is shortened due to the compression. Hence, their delay increase caused by compression processing becomes a smaller portion in the total packet delay.

On the other hand, when the packet generation rate becomes higher, the average delays in both schemes increase and the increase in the no-compression scheme grows much faster than that in the compression scheme. When the rate is higher than 3.5, the compression effect becomes positive and yields significant reduction on average delay. In this case, the traffic in the no-compression scheme becomes heavy and the wireless channel is approaching saturation. Consequently, the packet transmission time and the waiting delay grow rapidly due to channel contentions. On the other hand, compression shortens the packet length and the transmission time, thus effectively reducing the channel utilization and the packet delay, which explains the much slower growth of the packet delay with compression.

Another observation we can draw is that the delays of different levels are quite similar. It implies that the main effect of compression is on the transmissions from level 1 nodes to the sink. This is due to the fact that level 1 nodes undergo the heaviest traffic and hence the longest transmission delay. In this case, compression can achieve much more benefit for the transmissions of level 1 nodes than those nodes at higher levels. Thus, based on this observation, it is reasonable to use the average delay among all the nodes in the network to approximate the delays of nodes at different levels. Figure 17.2 thus shows the average end-to-end delay with different network configurations. We can see that the results reveal a similar trend on the end-to-end delay for different network configurations.

To further examine the details of compression effect, we define two rates: *maximum packet generation rate* and *threshold rate*. The maximum packet generation rate is the rate at which the wireless channel approaches saturation. Technically, we define it as the maximum rate at which the packet delay is smaller than 1 second. The threshold rate is the generation rate at which the packet delay remains unchanged in both no-compression and compression schemes. When the packet generation rate is between the threshold rate and the maximum generation rate, compression reduces the end-to-end delay, showing a positive effect. Otherwise, it increases the packet delay, showing a negative effect. Figure 17.3 shows the relationship between the threshold rates and the maximum generation rates in the compression scheme under different network configurations. We can see that the maximum generation rate and the threshold rate vary a lot with different network configurations. Intuitively, compression should be performed only when the packet generation rate is higher than the threshold rate. However, as shown in the figure, the threshold rate cannot be obtained in advance. Therefore, it is necessary to design an online adaptive algorithm to determine when to perform compression on incoming packets at each node.

17.4 ONLINE ADAPTIVE COMPRESSION ALGORITHM

In this section, we introduce an online adaptive compression algorithm that can be easily implemented in sensor nodes to assist the original LZW compression

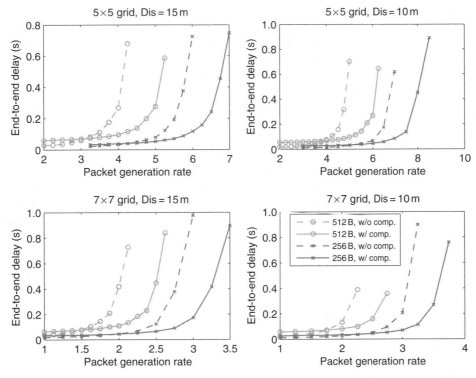

FIGURE 17.2. *Average packet delays under various configurations, where* d *represents the neighboring distance.*

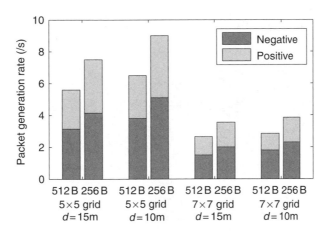

FIGURE 17.3. *Different threshold rates under various configurations, where* d *represents the neighboring distance. The compression effect at the threshold rate is neither positive nor negative.*

algorithm. The goal is to accurately predict the difference of average end-to-end delay with and without compression by analyzing the local information at a sensor node and to make right decisions on whether to perform packet compression at the node. The adaptive algorithm is implemented on each sensor node as *adaptive compression service (ACS)* in an individual layer created in the network stack to minimize the modification of existing network layers. Next, we first introduce the architecture of ACS and then describe the algorithm in detail.

17.4.1 Architecture of ACS

The architecture of ACS is described in Figure 17.4. Located between the MAC layer and its upper layer, ACS consists of four functional units: a controller, an LZW compressor, an information collector, and a packet buffer. The controller manages the traffic flow and makes compression decisions on each incoming packet in this layer. The LZW compressor is the functional unit that performs the actual packet compression by the LZW algorithm. The information collector is responsible for collecting local statistics information about the current network and hardware conditions. The packet buffer is used to temporarily store the packets to be compressed.

With ACS, the traffic between the MAC layer and the upper layer is now intervened by the controller in ACS. All outgoing packets coming down from the upper layer are received by the controller, which maintains two states. In the no-compression state, all packets are directed to the MAC layer without further processing; in the compression state, only compressed packets, which are received from other nodes, will be directly sent down to the MAC layer, and other packets are sent to the packet buffer for compression. On the other hand, for incoming packets from the MAC layer, only the arrival time is recorded by the collector and the packets themselves are sent to the network layer without delays.

Since compression is managed by the node state, the function of the adaptive algorithm is to determine the node state according to the network and hardware

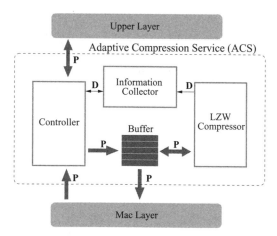

FIGURE 17.4. *Architecture of ACS, which resides in a created layer between the MAC layer and its upper layer. **P**, packet; **D**, statistics data.*

conditions. In the adaptive algorithm, we utilize a queueing model to estimate current conditions based on only local information of sensor nodes. In the next section, we introduce the queueing model.

17.4.2 Queueing Model for a WSN

The queueing model for a WSN includes both the network model and the MAC model, which defines the network topology, traffic model, and MAC layer protocol. For a clear presentation, we list the notations that will be used in the model in Table 17.3.

17.4.2.1 Network Model: Topology and Traffic
We consider a WSN where N sensor nodes are randomly distributed in a finite 2-D region. For calculation convenience, we consider a region of a circular shape with radius R. (As will be seen in the experimental results, when the region shape changes, it will not substantially affect the performance of the algorithm.) Every node has an equal transmission range r. A data sink is located at the center of the circular region, and all sensor nodes send the collected data to the sink via the aforementioned multipath routing strategy.

If the node density is sufficiently high, we can assume that each node can always find a neighbor whose distance to the sink is shorter than its own distance to the sink by r. Thus, nodes between two circles with radius $(i - 1) \cdot r$ and $i \cdot r$ can deliver packets to the sink with i transmissions. According to the routing strategy, these

TABLE 17.3. Notations

N	Number of sensor nodes in the WSN
R	Radius of the circular region, also the number of levels
n_i	Number of nodes in level i
λ_g	Packet generation rate
λ_e	Arrival rate of external packets from neighbors
p_{kj}	Transition probability, the probability that a packet is served by node k and transferred to node j
λ^i	Mean arrival rate for nodes in level i
T_{tran}	The minimum time of a successful transmission
L_{data}	Length of the data packet
T_{ctl}	Sum of length of all control packets in a transmission
n_{sus}	Number of suspensions in the backoff stage
T_{mac}	MAC layer service time
c_{mac}	Coefficient of variance (COV) of the MAC layer service time
$\bar{T}$	Average packet waiting time of the queue
λ	Arrival rate of the queue
P	Utilization of the queue
c_A	COV of the interarrival time
c_B	COV of the service time
r_c	Average compression ratio
T_p	Average compression processing time
c_p	COV of the processing time
p_c	Ratio of compressed packets in all packets
T_{com}	Average packet waiting time at the compression queue
$\Delta T_{mac}(i)$	Delay reduction in level i
ΔT_{min}	Lower bound of total delay reduction

nodes are considered level i nodes. Without loss of generality, we assume $r = 1$, and there are a total of R levels of nodes. Denote the number of nodes at level i as n_i. Then, the average number of nodes at level i can be calculated by

$$E[n_i] = \frac{\pi i^2 - \pi(i-1)^2}{\pi R^2} N = \frac{(2i-1)N}{R^2}. \qquad (17.1)$$

Such a network can then be represented by an open queueing network where each sensor node is modeled as a queue with an external arrival rate λ_g, which corresponds to the packet generation rate. Denote λ_j^i as the arrival rate of node j at level i. When $i < R$, by queueing theory, we have

$$\lambda_j^i = \lambda_g + \sum_{k=1}^{n_{i+1}} \lambda_k^{i+1} p_{kj}, \qquad (17.2)$$

where p_{kj} is the transition probability from node k at level $i + 1$ to node j at level i.

As all λ_j^i's have the same expected value, we denote it as λ^i. Summing λ_j^i and taking expectation on both sides of the equation lead to

$$E[n_i]\lambda^i = E[n_i]\lambda_g + \lambda^{i+1} E\left[\sum_{j=1}^{n_i}\sum_{k=1}^{n_{i+1}} p_{kj}\right]. \qquad (17.3)$$

Since $\sum_{j=1}^{n_i}\sum_{k=1}^{n_{i+1}} p_{kj} = n_{i+1}$, the above equation can be written as

$$\lambda^i = \lambda_g + \frac{E[n_{i+1}]}{E[n_i]}\lambda^{i+1} = \lambda_g + \frac{2i+1}{2i-1}\lambda^{i+1}. \qquad (17.4)$$

Thus, each node can estimate the arrival rates of nodes at other levels based on its own arrival rate. To evaluate the performance of the queueing system, we also need another important parameter, the average packet service time, which includes the possible packet compression time and the MAC layer service time. While the compression time can be obtained directly from the LZW algorithm, the calculation of the MAC layer service time requires an understanding of the MAC model.

17.4.2.2 MAC Model   The MAC layer packet service time is measured from the time when the packet enters the MAC layer to the time when the packet is successfully transmitted or discarded due to transmission failure. To analyze the packet service time, we first briefly describe the distributed coordination function (DCF) of IEEE 802.11 [25] used as the MAC layer protocol.

DCF employs a backoff mechanism to avoid potential contentions for the wireless channel. To transmit a packet, a node must conduct a backoff procedure by starting the backoff timer with a count-down time interval, which is randomly selected between $[0, CW)$ where CW is the contention window size. The timer is decremented by 1 in each time slot when the channel is idle and is suspended upon the sensing of an ongoing transmission. The suspension will continue until the channel becomes idle again. When the timer reaches zero, the node completes the backoff procedure and starts transmission. The entire procedure is completed if the transmission is successfully acknowledged by the receiver. Otherwise, the transmission is considered failed, which invokes a retransmission by restarting the backoff timer. In each retransmission, the contention window size *CW* will be doubled until it reaches the upper bound defined in DCF. Finally, the packet will be discarded if the number of retransmissions reaches the predefined limit.

In the MAC layer, we also adopt the request to send (RTS)/clear to send (CTS) mechanism to reduce transmission collisions. Thus, it requires at least four transmissions to successfully transmit a data packet: the transmissions of RTS, CTS, data, and acknowledgment (ACK) packets. Let T_{tran} denote the minimum packet transmission time, which can be calculated as the sum of all packet lengths divided by network bandwidth *Bw*

$$T_{\text{tran}} = \frac{L_{\text{data}} + L_{\text{ctl}}}{Bw}, \tag{17.5}$$

where $L_{\text{ctl}} = L_{\text{RTS}} + L_{\text{CTS}} + L_{\text{hdr}} + L_{\text{ACK}}$ and L_{hdr} is the header size of the data packet. Let T_{sus} denote the average duration of the timer suspension in the backoff stage and T_{col} denote the average time spent in transmission collisions. The suspension duration is actually the time waiting for other nodes to complete a packet transmission. Under the assumption of the constant packet length, we can approximately have $T_{\text{sus}} = T_{\text{tran}}$. On the other hand, with the RTS/CTS mechanism, the collision mainly occurs during the transmission of RTS and continues until the timeout for CTS. Hence,

$$T_{\text{col}} \approx \frac{L_{\text{RTS}} + L_{\text{CTS}}}{Bw}.$$

The overall MAC layer packet service time can then be calculated as

$$\begin{aligned} T_{\text{mac}} &= n_{\text{sus}}T_{\text{sus}} + n_{\text{col}}T_{\text{col}} + T_{\text{tran}} \\ &= (n_{\text{sus}} + 1)T_{\text{tran}} + n_{\text{col}}T_{\text{col}} \\ &\approx (n_{\text{sus}} + 1)T_{\text{tran}}, \end{aligned} \tag{17.6}$$

where n_{sus} represents the number of suspensions and n_{col} is the number of transmission collisions. The last step approximation in Equation (17.6) is due to the relatively small value of both n_{col} and T_{col}. We also exclude the backoff time and some interframe spaces in the above equation due to the same reason.

17.4.2.3 Queueing Analysis for a Sensor Node
The queueing model of a sensor node is different in different node states. In the no-compression state, each node is considered as a single queue. Its arrival process is a combination of the local packet generation process and the departure processes of its neighbors that send packets to the node. As the simulation results in Reference 26 showed, the departure process of nodes adopting IEEE 802.11 MAC protocol can be approximated as a Poisson process. Thus, we assume that the arrival process of each node is a Poisson process and each node is an *M/G/1* (i.e., exponential interarrival time distribution/general service time distribution/a single server) queue. In the compression state, the queueing model of each node can be modified as a system of two queues as

shown in Figure 17.5 with the compression queue and the transmission queue corresponding to ACS and the MAC layer, respectively. The compression queue can be modeled as an $M/G/1$ queue because its arrival process, as a split of the arrival process of the sensor node, can also be considered as a Poisson process. On the other hand, since its departure process, a part of the arrival process of the transmission queue, is not a Poissonian, we model the transmission queue as a GI/G/1 queue where GI represents the general independent interarrival time distribution.

For the $M/G/1$ queue, according to the well-known Pollaczek–Khinchin formula, the average number of packets $\bar{N}$ in an $M/G/1$ queue can be calculated as

$$\bar{N}_{M/G/1} = \rho + \frac{\rho^2}{1-\rho} \cdot \frac{1+c_B^2}{2}, \tag{17.7}$$

where ρ is the utilization of the queue and c_B is the coefficient of variance (COV) of the service time. By Little's law, given the arrival rate λ, the average packet waiting time, which is the packet delay in the node, can be derived as

$$\bar{T}_{M/G/1} = \frac{\bar{N}}{\lambda} = \frac{2\rho - \rho^2(1-c_B^2)}{2\lambda(1-\rho)}. \tag{17.8}$$

To derive the average packet waiting time for the transmission queue, we use the diffusion approximation method [27], which is briefly introduced here. Consider an open GI/G/1 queueing network with n nodes. Given the arrival rate λ_k for node k, $k \in [1, n]$, the COV of the interarrival time at node j, c_{Aj}, can be approximated as

$$c_{Aj}^2 = 1 + \sum_{k=0}^{n} (c_{Bk}^2 - 1) \cdot p_{kj}^2 \cdot \lambda_k \cdot \lambda_j^{-1}, \tag{17.9}$$

where c_{Bk} represents the COV of the service time at node k and c_{B0} represents the COV of the external interarrival time. In Figure 17.5, we assume the COV of the service time at the compression queue is c_p and the portion of compressed packets in all packets is p_c. Then, we obtain the COV of the service time at the transmission queue as

$$c_A^2 = 1 + (c_p^2 - 1)(1 - p_c). \tag{17.10}$$

The average packet waiting time can then be approximated by

$$\bar{T}_{GI/G/1} = \frac{\rho}{\lambda(1-\hat{\rho})}, \tag{17.11}$$

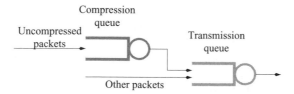

FIGURE 17.5. *Queueing model of a sensor node with compression.*

where

$$\hat{\rho} = \exp\left(-\frac{2(1-\rho)}{c_A^2 \cdot \rho + c_B^2}\right). \tag{17.12}$$

17.4.3 Adaptive Compression Algorithm

We are now in the position to describe the adaptive compression algorithm, which can be divided into two stages: information collection and node state determination.

17.4.3.1 Information Collection In ACS, the information collector is responsible for collecting three types of statistics information:

1. Compression statistics, including the average compression ratio r_c, the average compression processing time T_p, and the COV of the processing time c_p. Upon each packet compression, the compression ratio, the processing time, and its square are recorded. The statistics is updated after every m packet is compressed. In the experiments, we set $m = 100$. Since the compression statistics can only be collected when nodes perform compression, the network should include an initial phase when all nodes perform compression to obtain the initial values. We assume the sensing data has a stable distribution so that the collecting method above is sufficient to provide proper statistics.

2. Packet arrival rates, which include the arrival rate of external packets from neighbors λ_e and the packet generation rate λ_g. The calculations follow a time-slotted fashion. In each time slot, the total number of packets arrived is counted and the arrival rates are calculated by dividing the total counts by time. Noting that not all external packets are compressed in the adaptive algorithm, we also record the ratio of compressed packets in the external packets as p_c.

3. MAC layer service time. Since the MAC layer service is considered as an arbitrary process in the queueing model, its mean T_{mac} and COV c_{mac} are calculated and recorded for the subsequent analysis. The calculation is done along with the calculation of arrival rates in the same time slot to reduce the implementation complexity.

17.4.3.2 State Determination In ACS, the controller determines the appropriate node state according to the statistics information collected. Since most of the information is collected in a time-slotted manner, the decision on the node state is made at the end of each time slot. Depending on the current node state, the decision process is slightly different. Thus, we first consider the case when the node is currently in the no-compression state. Then, the task of the controller is to decide whether performing compression on this node can reduce packet delays. From the experimental results in Section 17.3, we know that compression introduces an extra delay due to compression processing and reduces the packet delay from the current node to the sink. We now discuss these two delays separately.

The incoming packets of the compression queue are the uncompressed portion of the arrival packets at the node. With the information provided by the collector, the arrival rate can be calculated by $\lambda_c = \lambda_e(1 - p_c) + \lambda_g$, while the service rate is $1/T_p$, and the utilization equals $\lambda_c T_p$. By Equation (17.8), the increased compression time for a packet can be derived as

$$T_{com} = \frac{1}{2} \cdot \frac{2T_p - \lambda_c T_p^2 (1 - c_p^2)}{1 - \lambda_c T_p}. \tag{17.13}$$

As the ultimate goal of compression is to reduce the average delay, which is equivalent to reducing the sum of delays of all packets, we define *normalized delay* as the total delay for all packets in a unit time. Thus, for a time interval t, the total increased delay due to compression is $\lambda_c t T_{com}$, and the normalized delay increase is $\lambda_c T_{com}$.

Now let us look at the delay reduction in packet delivery after compression. While it is difficult to accurately calculate this reduction, we can easily obtain a lower bound. Given the compression ratio r_c and the length of the original packet L, the packet length is shortened by $L - L/r_c$ after compression and its transmission time is reduced by at least

$$\frac{L(r_c - 1)}{r_c \cdot Bw}.$$

For a level i node, there are i transmissions for this packet after compression. Thus, the total reduction is at least

$$\Delta T_{min} = \frac{i \cdot L(r_c - 1)}{r_c \cdot Bw}.$$

We compare this lower bound with the increased compression time T_{com}. If $T_{com} \leq \Delta T_{min}$, the node is switched to the compression state.

When $T_{com} > \Delta T_{min}$, we need to calculate the normalized delay reduction. In fact, if only one node performs compression, there will be no extra reduction other than the reduced transmission time because the surrounding traffic will not change. However, according to the network model, nodes at the same level should share very similar traffic conditions; thus, although made independently, their state determination is likely to coincide. Therefore, when we consider the delay reduction due to compression on a node, it is reasonable to assume that other nodes at the same level will also perform compression. In this sense, compression actually affects the transmissions of all packets in the node rather than only the uncompressed packets. Furthermore, such effect not only resides in the local node but also in the downstream nodes on the routing path when they receive those compressed packets. Thus, we need to examine the delay reduction level by level.

We first examine the delay reduction in the local node. Without loss of generality, we assume the node is at level i. The packet delay before compression can be obtained by Equation (17.8), where $\lambda = \lambda_g + \lambda_e$, $\rho = \lambda \cdot T_{mac}$, and $c_B = c_{mac}$. When compression is performed, the transmission queue is modeled as a GI/G/1 queue and the packet delay is calculated by Equations (17.11) and (17.12). According to Figure 17.5, the arrival rate of the transmission queue does not change after the compression. c_A can be calculated by Equation (17.10) and c_B is approximated to be c_{mac}. Next, we derive the average service time after compression from T_{mac}. Based on the analysis in Section 17.4.2, the service time T_{mac} is approximately proportional to the packet transmission time T_{tran} and hence $L_{data} + L_{ctl}$. We assume the original packet length is L and the compressed packet length is then L/r_c, where r_c is the compression ratio obtained in the collector. Thus, L_{data} is reduced from $L - p_c(L - L/r_c)$ to L/r_c by compression, while L_{ctl} keeps unchanged. The average service time after compression can then be calculated as

$$
\begin{aligned}
T'_{mac} &= T_{mac} \cdot \frac{L/r_c + L_{ctl}}{L - p_c(L - L/r_c) + L_{ctl}} \\
&= \frac{T_{mac}(L + L_{ctl} \cdot r_c)}{L(r_c + p_c - r_c \cdot p_c) + L_{ctl} \cdot r_c}.
\end{aligned}
\tag{17.14}
$$

With all these parameters known, the packet delay after compression can be obtained and so is the delay reduction, denoted as $\Delta T_{mac}(i)$.

Now we estimate the delay reduction at a level k node ($k < i$) on the routing path. According to the analysis in Section 17.3, higher-level nodes enjoy more compression benefit through the transmissions on longer routes, indicating that they tend to perform compression more aggressively. Given the local node in the no-compression state, it is reasonable to assume that the nodes with the same packet generation rates at level k are also in the no-compression state. Then, the packet delay at this node is calculated with Equation (17.8). By Equation (17.4), we can derive the arrival rate by λ_g and λ_e. The calculation of the service time T_{mac} mainly depends on the value of n_{sus} and T_{tran}. While T_{tran} can be calculated in a similar way as for the local node, n_{sus} cannot be derived intuitively. In Reference 28, it was shown that n_{sus} is proportional to the utilization ρ if ρ is shared by all nodes in its interfering range. For the network under consideration, we approximately assume that nodes in the interfering range of a level k node are all in level k. Then, we have

$$
\begin{aligned}
\frac{n_{sus}^k}{n_{sus}^i} &= \frac{\rho^k}{\rho^i} = \frac{\lambda^k}{\lambda^i} \cdot \frac{T_{mac}^k}{T_{mac}^i} = \frac{\lambda^k}{\lambda^i} \cdot \frac{(n_{sus}^k + 1)T_{tran}^k}{(n_{sus}^i + 1)T_{tran}^i}, \\
n_{sus}^k &= \frac{c \cdot n_{sus}^i}{n_{sus}^i - c \cdot n_{sus}^i + 1}, \quad c = \frac{\lambda^k T_{tran}^k}{\lambda^i T_{tran}^i},
\end{aligned}
\tag{17.15}
$$

where parameters for the level i and k nodes are labeled with the superscript i and k, respectively. With n_{sus} and T_{tran} obtained, the service time can be obtained and so is the reduction, which we denote as $\Delta T_{mac}(k)$.

The normalized delay reduction can be calculated as

$$
\Delta T_{mac} = \sum_{j=1}^{i} \lambda^j \Delta T_{mac}(j).
\tag{17.16}
$$

The decision on the state of the node is then made by comparing ΔT_{mac} with $\lambda_c T_{com}$. The procedure of the state determination in pseudocode is given Table 17.4.

When the node is currently in the compression state, all the calculations will also be performed. The only difference is that we compare the reduced processing time with the increased transmission time due to compression cancellation.

TABLE 17.4. State Determination Procedure, Performed at the End of Each Time Slot for a Node in the No-Compression State

For each node at level i:
if state = No-Compression **then**
    read statistics from the information collector
    compute T_{com} and ΔT_{min}
    if $T_{com} \leq \Delta T_{min}$ **then**
        set state to Compression
    else
        set i to the node's level number
        set ΔT_{mac} to zero
        while $i > 0$
            Calculate λ^i
            compute reduction $\Delta T_{mac}(i)$
            add $\lambda^i \Delta T_{mac}(i)$ to ΔT_{mac}
            decrease i by one
    end while
    if $\lambda_c T_{com} \leq \Delta T_{mac}$ **then**
        set state to Compression
    end if
    end if
end if

17.5 PERFORMANCE EVALUATIONS

With the online adaptive compression algorithm, each node can dynamically decide whether a packet is compressed or not, adapting to the current network and hardware environment. In this section, we present the performance evaluation results for the adaptive compression algorithm. We compare the performance of the adaptive scheme with other two schemes: the no-compression scheme, in which no packets are compressed at all, and the compression scheme, where all packets are compressed in data gathering.

The experiments are conducted in three networks: a 7×7 grid, a 9×9 grid, and a 11×11 grid. The sink is located at the center of the grid. The transmission range is 1.5 times of the neighboring distance. The original packet length is set to 512 B. Other parameters are similar to the configuration in the previous experiments in Section 17.3.

In the simulation, the packet generation rate starts at a rate lower than the threshold rate and then increases linearly every 300 seconds. Such increase continues until the maximum rate is reached, at which time the simulation also ends. The time slot length used in the information collector is 30 seconds. Figure 17.6 shows the average end-to-end delays for three schemes in different networks. We can see that the delay for the adaptive scheme is always close to the lower one of the no-compression and compression schemes, indicating overall good adaptiveness of the algorithm on the network traffic. In particular, when the generation rate is lower than the threshold rate, the adaptive scheme chooses not to compress packets and thus yields nearly the same results as the no-compression scheme. When the generation rate is slightly higher than the threshold, the adaptive scheme yields similar results as the compression scheme except some points with slightly longer delays

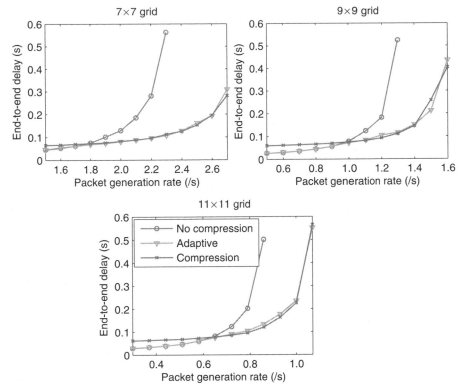

FIGURE 17.6. *The overall average packet delays under three schemes in three different networks.*

in the 9×9 grid and the 11×11 grid. The largest increase in delay is only 10% when the generation rate is 0.9 in the 11×11 grid. Such consistently good performance in different networks indicates a good scalability of the algorithm on the network size.

We further examine the delays for different levels to provide a comprehensive illustration. Figure 17.7 depicts the average delays for different levels in the 9×9 grid network. It can be noticed that, for nodes at level 1, the adaptive scheme outperforms other two schemes when the generation rate exceeds the threshold rate. For nodes at levels 3 and 4 at the same generation rate, however, the average delays under the adaptive scheme are slightly longer than that under the compression scheme. This can be explained by the observation that the threshold rates for higher-level nodes are lower than the thresholds for lower-level nodes. When the generation rate is between two different threshold rates, higher-level nodes perform compression, while the lower-level nodes do not. Therefore, without suffering from the compression processing delay, lower-level nodes can still enjoy the benefit of the reduced average packet length as they receive packets from higher-level nodes, resulting in shorter delays than that under the compression scheme. On the other hand, since lower-level nodes do not perform compression, the average packet length and the subsequent transmission delay become longer, increasing the end-to-end delay for other nodes. Such increase is also more evident for higher-level

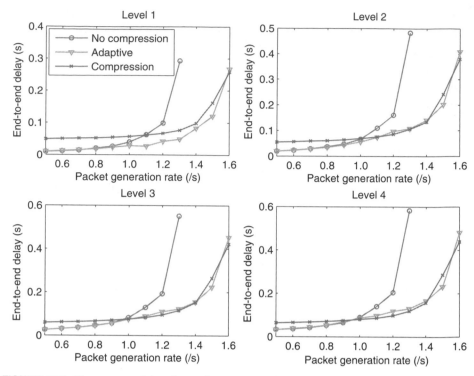

FIGURE 17.7. *The average delays for packets generated at different levels under three schemes in 9 × 9 grid network.*

nodes as the generated packets in these nodes endure more hops of prolonged transmissions during the delivery to the sink.

17.6 SUMMARY

In this chapter, we have discussed the effect of the compression on end-to-end packet delay in data gathering in WSNs. To accurately examine the effect of compression, we incorporate the hardware processing time of compression in the experiments by utilizing a software estimation approach to measuring the execution time of a lossless compression algorithm, LZW, on TI MSP430F5418 MCU. Through simulations, we have found that compression has a two-sided effect on packet delay in data gathering. While compression increases the maximum achievable throughput, it tends to increase the packet delay under light traffic loads and to reduce the packet delay under heavy traffic loads. We also evaluate the impact of different network settings on the effect of compression, providing a guideline for choosing appropriate compression parameters.

We then describe an online adaptive compression algorithm to make compression decisions based on the current network and hardware conditions. The adaptive algorithm runs in a completely distributed manner. Based on a queueing model, the algorithm utilizes local information to estimate the overall network condition and switches the node state between compression and no-compression according to the potential benefit of compression. The experimental results show that the adaptive algorithm can fully exploit the benefit of compression while avoiding the potential hazard of compression. Finally, it should be pointed out that this adaptive algorithm is not restricted to the LZW compression algorithm, and in fact, it can be applied to any practical compression algorithms by simply replacing the compressor in ACS.

REFERENCES

[1] T. He, J.A. Stankovic, C. Lu, and T. Abdelzaher, "SPEED: A stateless protocol for real-time communication in sensor networks," in *Proceedings of the IEEE ICDCS*, 2003.

[2] E. Felemban, C. Lee, and E. Ekici, "MMSPEED: Multipath multi-SPEED protocol for qos guarantee of reliability and timeliness in wireless sensor networks," *IEEE Transactions on Mobile Computing*, 5(6):738–754, 2006.

[3] T. He, B.M. Blum, J.A. Stankovic, and T. Abdelzaher, "AIDA: Adaptive application independent data aggregation in wireless sensor networks," *ACM Transactions on Embedded Computing Systems*, 3(2): 426–457, 2004.

[4] S. Zhu, W. Wang, and C.V. Ravishankar, "PERT: A new power-efficient real-time packet delivery scheme for sensor networks," *International Journal of Sensor Networks*, 3(4): 237–251, 2008.

[5] T.A. Welch, "A technique for high-performance data compression," *IEEE Computer*, 17(6):8–19, 1984.

[6] TI MSP430F5418. Available at http://focus.ti.com/docs/prod/folders/print/ msp430f5418. html.

[7] I.F. Akyildiz, M.C. Vuran, and O.B. Akan, "On exploiting spatial and temporal correlation in wireless sensor networks," in *Proceedings of WiOpt: Modelling and Optimization in Mobile, Ad hoc and Wireless Networks*, 2004.

[8] A. Scaglione and S. Servetto, "On the interdependence of routing and data compression in multi-hop sensor networks," *Wireless Networks*, 11:149–160, 2005.

[9] S.J. Baek, G. de Veciana, and X. Su, "Minimizing energy consumption in large-scale sensor networks through distributed data compression and hierarchical aggregation," *IEEE Journal on Selected Areas in Communications*, 22(6):1130–1140, 2004.

[10] S. Pattem, B. Krishnamachari, and R. Govindan, "The impact of spatial correlation on routing with compression in wireless sensor networks," *ACM Transactions on Sensor Networks*, 4(4):1–33, 2008.

[11] S.S. Pradhan, J. Kusuma, and K. Ramchandran, "Distributed compression in a dense microsensor network," *IEEE Signal Processing Magazine*, 19(2):51–60, 2002.

[12] M.A. Sharaf, J. Beaver, A. Labrinidis, and P.K. Chrysanthis, "TiNA: A scheme for temporal coherency-aware in-network aggregation," in *Proceedings of the 3rd ACM international Workshop on Data Engineering for Wireless and Mobile Access*, 2003.

[13] S. Yoon and C. Shahabi, "An energy conserving clustered aggregation technique leveraging spatial correlation," in *Proceedings of SECON*, 2004.

[14] T. Banerjee, K. Chowdhury, and D. Agrawal, "Tree based data aggregation in sensor networks using polynomial regression," in *Proceedings of the International Conference on Information Fusion*, 2005.

[15] T. Schoellhammer, B. Greenstein, B. Osterwiel, M. Wimbrow, and D. Estrin, "Lightweight temporal compression of microclimate datasets wireless sensor networks," in *Proceedings of the IEEE International Conference on Local Computer Networks*, 2004.

[16] E. Magli, M. Mancin, and L. Merello, "Low-complexity video compression for wireless sensor networks," in *Proceedings of the International Conference on Multimedia and Expo*, 2003.

[17] D. Petrovic, R.C. Shah, K. Ramchandran, and J. Rabaey, "Data funneling: Routing with aggregation and compression for wireless sensor networks," in *Proceedings of the 1st IEEE International Workshop on Sensor Network Protocols and Applications*, 2003.

[18] T. Arici, B. Gedik, Y. Altunbasak, and L. Liu, "PINCO: A pipelined in-network compression scheme for data collection in wireless sensor networks," in *Proceedings of ICCCN*, 2003.

[19] C.M. Sadler and M. Martonosi, "Data compression algorithms for energy-constrained devices in delay tolerant networks," in *Proceedings of SenSys*, 2006.

[20] A. Reinhardt, M. Hollick, and R. Steinmetz, "Stream-oriented lossless packet compression in wireless sensor networks," in *Proceedings of SECON*, 2009.

[21] N. Kimura and S. Latifi, "A survey on data compression in wireless sensor networks," in *Proceedings of ITCC*, 2005.

[22] X. Hong, M. Gerla, H. Wang, and L. Clare, "Load balanced, energy-aware communications for mars sensor networks," in *Proceedings of the Aerospace Conference*, Vol. 3, 2002.

[23] A. Jindal and K. Psounis, "Modeling spatially correlated data in sensor networks," *ACM Transactions on Sensor Networks*, 2(4):466–499, 2006.

[24] M. Burrows and D.J. Wheeler, "A block-sorting lossless data compression algorithm," *Digital Systems Research Center Research Report*, 1994.

[25] IEEE Computer Society LAN MAN Standards Committee et al., Wireless LAN Medium Access Control (MAC) and Physical Layer (PHY) Specifications, *ISO/IEC 8802-11: 1999(E)*, 1999.

[26] H. Zhai, Y. Kwon, and Y. Fang, "Performance analysis of IEEE 802.11 MAC protocols in wireless LANs," *Wireless Communications and Mobile Computing*, 4(8): 917–931, 2004.

[27] G. Bolch, S. Greiner, H. de Meer, and K.S. Trivedi, *Queuing Networks and Markov Chains*, Chapter 10, John Wiley and Sons, 1998.

[28] N. Bisnik and A.A. Abouzeid, "Queueing network models for delay analysis of multihop wireless ad hoc networks," *Ad Hoc Networks*, 7(1):79–97, 2009.

18

GFOG: Green and Flexible Opportunistic Grids

Harold Castro, Mario Villamizar, German Sotelo, Cesar O. Diaz, Johnatan Pecero, Pascal Bouvry, and Samee U. Khan

18.1 INTRODUCTION

Large-scale computing platforms and current networking technologies enable sharing, selection, and aggregation of highly heterogeneous resources for solving complex real problems. Opportunistic grids are distributed platforms built out of the available resources (volunteers or donors) of an existing hardware platform that harvest the computing power of nondedicated resources when they are idle. Internet opportunistic grids are designed to take advantage of the capabilities of thousands or millions of desktop computers distributed through the Internet. On the other hand, institutional opportunistic grids involve the use of hundreds or thousands of computers available in a single organization or institution. In both opportunistic grid types, on the volunteer or donor desktops, an agent is executed to control, manage, and monitor the execution of grid tasks. Two main approaches are used to execute the agent:

- A desktop client runs an executable program to provide access to a set of resources of the desktop in a limited manner.
- A client executes a virtual machine, which is used to isolate and limit the execution environment required to execute the grid tasks.

In this last approach, isolation of both environments is critical; therefore, the use of virtualization is a promising approach.

Scalable Computing and Communications: Theory and Practice, First Edition. Edited by
Samee U. Khan, Albert Y. Zomaya, and Lizhe Wang.
© 2013 John Wiley & Sons, Inc. Published 2013 by John Wiley & Sons, Inc.

According to the TOP500 Supercomputer Sites [1], Latin American countries do not provide sufficient dedicated clustering infrastructures compared with the United States or Europe. Dedicated clusters are expensive. Therefore, for these countries to provide a certain level of high-performance computing (HPC), they may use existing resources available at universities or companies. For universities, computer labs are underused resources to take advantage of. In the case of Universidad de los Andes, dedicated clusters are composed of less than 200 cores. If we take into account that all of the available computer labs can provide more than 2000 cores, an opportunistic grid infrastructure could be a good approach. To implement this approach, some issues need to be studied beforehand, such as the impact of energy consumption, isolation of the owner-user (e.g., the human user currently using the hardware) and grid service (i.e., the grid task) environments, and the division of resources between these two environments, keeping in mind that owner-users have priority over any grid computing environment. Moreover, energy consumption is another important concern; it is essential nowadays to provide a mechanism that is also energy-efficient [2–7]. Virtual machines are a natural solution to provide complete isolation between both environments, namely, grid computing and owner-user ones. Virtualization provides mechanisms that guarantee the properties mentioned above; however, hardware resources must be shared between these two environments in such a way that both kinds of users have sufficient resources required to perform their tasks, and the energy efficiency of using virtualization to provide HPC environments executed on commodity desktops is still in doubt.

In this work, we exploit a virtualization technique used and tested on an existing opportunistic grid infrastructure, termed UnaGrid, to share resources between desktop computers and grid computing environments. We show that using this technique leads to a reduction of energy consumption with regard to using a *dedicated* computing architecture and, furthermore, improves its scalable performance.

18.2   RELATED WORK

Over the years, desktop grid systems have been working as a particular kind of volunteer computing system, where the computing resources are provided by individuals and have become among the largest distributed systems in the world [8]. Nowadays, there are several approaches to classify desktop grid systems, moreover to visualize them in an energy-efficient opportunistic grid environment. Therefore, we must take into account three factors: scalable opportunistic grids, virtualization technologies, and energy consumption in opportunistic grids.

18.2.1   Scalable Opportunistic Grids

Scalability is one of the most important goals that must be met to make building a desktop grid worth the effort. In other words, scalability refers to the capability of the system to adapt to any change in infrastructure, location, or management. Therefore, the scalability in one system can be identified by at least three components:

1. numerically or with respect to its size; that is, the feasibility to add more users and resources to the system [9]

2. geographically scalable; that is, the distance between the farthest nodes within the system

3. administrative scalability; that is, the ability to manage even if it encompasses many independent administrative organizations [10].

Opportunistic grids or desktop grid and volunteer computing systems (DGVCSs) have allowed the aggregation of millions of partially computing resources for different scientific projects. Initial projects such as Worm [11] and Condor [12] focused on taking advantage of the idle resources available in an organization. With the massive growth of the Internet, projects such as GIMPSs [13] and SETI@home [14] have begun to use the capabilities of volunteers around the world for executing single-purpose applications. The Distributed.net [15] and BOINC [16] projects were designed to support the execution of multiple-purpose applications over an Internet infrastructure whose resources are managed or controlled by a central organization. When grid computing emerged as a large and scalable computing solution that allowed the integration of resources of different organizations, projects such as Bayanihan.NET [17], Condor-G [18], and InteGrade [19] began to use grid middleware to allow the aggregation of idle or dedicated resources available in different administrative domains.

All of the aforementioned projects execute grid tasks directly on the physical resources using a desktop client installed on each desktop computer, so they have some problems to support new or existing applications, such as application portability to different architectures or operating systems, isolation of environment used by the owner-user and grid user (security, intrusion, and checkpoint issues), and modification of legacy or new applications. When virtualization technologies appear, projects such as XtremWeb [20], OurGrid [21], ShareGrid [22], CernVM [23], BOINC-CernVM [24], SUCSI [25], UnaGrid [26], and Cloud@home [27] began to use virtual machines to execute the grid tasks. In these projects, a virtual machine is executed on each desktop computer and used to execute the grid tasks in a sandbox environment. The use of virtualization imposes some performance degradation issues; however, virtualization facilitates the portability of the application to different architectures and operating systems, the isolation of environments, and the incorporation of the legacy application without requiring recompilations or modifications. With recent virtualization advances, the performance is increasingly better. UnaGrid [26] is an opportunistic grid solution developed to allow different research groups to take advantage of the idle processing capabilities available in the computer labs at a university campus, when they need computational capabilities using an on-demand approach. Unlike OurGrid, ShareGrid, CernVM, and BOIN-CernVM, UnaGrid was designed to be a large and shared institutional opportunistic grid (not an Internet DGVCS). The SUCSI project uses a virtualization strategy similar to that used by UnaGrid; however, SUSCI changes the way researchers execute the applications because it does not allow grid users to customize and execute the application in its native environment (command-line, operating systems, grid middleware, libraries, etc.). Due to the use of customized virtual clusters (CVCs), in UnaGrid, researchers can continue executing their application in the native environment and can deploy the CVCs when they need to execute grid tasks; these features guarantee the high usability and the efficient use of the infrastructure. Cloud@home is a proposal to define a desktop cloud computing solution that takes advantage of the benefits of the cloud computing paradigm and the opportunistic grid systems; although it is a design proposal, it is similar to UnaGrid in that it also uses an on-demand approach to request resources (or services in the cloud computing world) when they are needed. However, Cloud@home is designed to integrate different commercial and open cloud computing service providers, and heterogeneous and independent nodes such as those found in DGVCSs.

18.2.2 Virtualization Technologies

Virtualization is a mechanism used to offer a certain kind of virtual machine environment, which is possible only given the right combination of hardware and software elements [28,29]. A virtual machine is a software implementation of a computer that performs applications and programs like a real-life computer. Virtual machines are divided into two major categories, based on their use and degree of association to any real computer: (1) A system virtual machine grants an entire system platform, which carries out the execution of a complete operating system, and (2) on the contrary, a process virtual machine is intended to support a single process execution [28]. An essential characteristic of a virtual machine is that the software running inside is limited to the resources and abstractions provided by the configuration of the virtual machine, meaning it cannot use more than the values it has configured as part of its virtual world. System virtual machines allow sharing the underlying physical machine resources between different environments, each one running its own operating system [30, 31]. The software layer controlling the virtualization is called a hypervisor. The main advantage of this kind of virtual machine is that several operating system platforms can coexist on the same physical machine in total isolation from each other. This way, some quality of service is provided because a virtual machine configured with limits can use only the amount of resources it has set as its virtual world or has been enforced to set. There are many types of virtual machine software that provide the aforementioned characteristics, the most popular being Virtual Box, VMware, and Xen. UnaGrid uses VMware Workstation [32] to manage each virtual machine (e.g., operations such as start, resume, and power-off) and VMware Player as the system virtual machine. UnaGrid also uses the hardware-assisted virtualization (or native virtualization) features available in desktops with physical processors that support this technology, such as AMD-V [33] and Intel-VT [34]. The use of this technology improves the performance when grid applications are executed in virtual machines.

18.2.3 Energy Consumption on Opportunistic Grids

Virtualization technologies have been used in data centers for different purposes, one of which is energy consumption saving. Different analyses have shown than virtualization technologies allow reduction of the energy consumption by more than 30% [35]; depending on the energy optimization techniques, the virtualization technologies, and the application and operating systems executed on virtual machines, this percentage may vary [36]. In conventional computing clusters, the energy consumption is based mainly on the consumption of servers and cooling systems. In desktop grids, the energy consumption is based on the consumption of the desktop machines used to execute the grid tasks. Cooling consumption is not taken into account due to desktop machines being regularly available in large open spaces. Few efforts have been developed to analyze the energy consumption in opportunistic grids. From the energy consumption point of view, most desktop grids select the resources to execute grid tasks using an algorithm that takes into account only the best physical resource to execute the jobs without having in mind the energy consumption used to execute the tasks. Regarding the Condor project, an effort [37] has been made to analyze the energy consumption of a Condor cluster and to optimize the energy consumption when desktops used to execute the grid tasks are selected. A more detailed and general project, termed DEGISCO, has been proposed [38]. This DEGISCO proposal examines several aspects of energy consumption and computational performance of different desktop grids around the world; however, at the time of this publication, the project is in its initial phase. In the current UnaGrid implementation, when a user requires the execution of virtual machines, these virtual machines are deployed on turned-on desktops using a random algorithm, without taking into account the current state of the desktop (turned off, hibernating, idle, or busy), and we consider that the energy consumption used to execute a grid task on a virtual machine depends on the state of the desktop used to execute it.

18.3   UNAGRID INFRASTRUCTURE

18.3.1   UnaGrid Architecture

UnaGrid is a virtual opportunistic grid infrastructure that takes advantage of the idle processing capabilities available in the computer labs of Universidad de los Andes. UnaGrid was designed to meet four main goals:

1. to allow the aggregation of the idle processing capabilities available in heterogeneous computer labs
2. to allow different research groups to use those capabilities when they require HPC, using an on-demand approach
3. to allow researchers to continue executing applications in the native environment and using the cluster or grid middleware they have been using
4. to operate without being intrusive to the owner-users of the desktops.

To achieve these goals, virtualization technologies are used. Virtualization allows the deployment, on-demand, of several scalable CVCs capable of providing the amount of HPC required for the development of different projects. A CVC is a set of interconnected desktops executing virtual machines through virtualization tools. A virtual cluster can be set up on a large number of desktop computers in which a virtual machine image performs as a slave of the cluster, and a dedicated machine performs as the master of the virtual cluster. Virtual machines use the idle capabilities permanently while owner-users carry out their daily activities. To operate in a nonintrusive manner, virtual machines are executed as low-priority background processes, guaranteeing that the owner-users have available all of the computational resources (if such are required), while the virtual machine consumes only the resources that the owner-users are not using (or all of these in the case of unused computers). To facilitate different research groups deploying several CVCs on the same physical infrastructure, an image of each one of the possible CVCs that may be executed is stored on each physical computer. The UnaGrid architecture is shown in Figure 18.1.

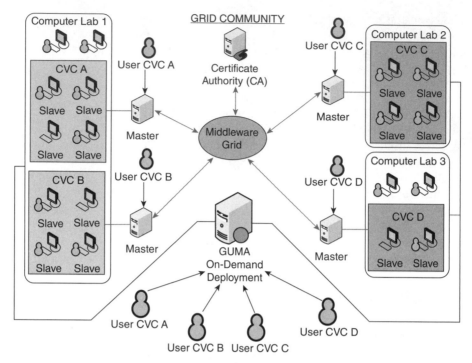

FIGURE 18.1. UnaGrid architecture.

Another aspect to take into account when implementing a CVC is handling the data corresponding to each application, so a distributed file system would seem to be a good approach. For UnaGrid, a network file system server is used for the complete infrastructure. The final users of the UnaGrid infrastructure can customize a virtual cluster and deploy it over different desktops. The deployment of a virtual machine requires a specific configuration concerning grid users, applications, and cluster and grid middleware, such as Condor, Globus, Sun Grid Engine, gLite, and PBS. The solution implemented is focused on the execution of a single virtual machine per physical computer in order to avoid competition of resources among virtual machines. For using the infrastructure, researchers use a web portal, termed Grid Uniandes Management Application (GUMA) [26]. GUMA allows for users from different research groups to deploy, on-demand, CVCs on desktops available in different computer labs, for specific time periods. GUMA communicates with the Java agents installed on each desktop to deploy the CVCs required by grid users. GUMA uses a client/server model with authentication, authorization, and privacy mechanisms, providing many services to manage the UnaGrid infrastructure from thin clients (only a Web browser is required), hiding the complexities associated with the location, distribution, and heterogeneity of computing resources and providing an intuitive graphical user interface (GUI). Management services include selection, shutdown, and monitoring of physical and virtual machines. Grid users can also manage their own virtual machines. GUMA is the main contribution of UnaGrid to DGVCSs because it gives high usability to an opportunistic system, using an on-demand deployment approach.

18.3.2 UnaGrid Implementation

UnaGrid has been tested executing applications from several scientific domains, all of them bag-of-tasks applications, including biology, chemical, and industrial engineering applications. In the biology domain, the HAMMER application was utilized in the analysis of genetic sequencing of the *Phytophthora infestans* genome [39]. In the chemical domain, the BSGrid application was used for the simulation of the *Bacillus thuringiensis* bacterium [40], and in the industrial engineering domain, the JG2A framework was used to solve an optimization problem in the routing of vehicles and design of routes [41]. When grid users require large processing capabilities, the addition of CVCs becomes handy. There are three options to make this feasible: (1) Configure and deploy more virtual cluster images; (2) take advantage of the aggregate capabilities of computer resources offered by some schedulers; and (3) install a grid middleware on master nodes allowing the execution of applications on different virtual clusters. To manage this situation, Globus Toolkit 4.2 is used, so the installation of a certificate authority becomes essential. The UnaGrid implementation is shown in Figure 18.2.

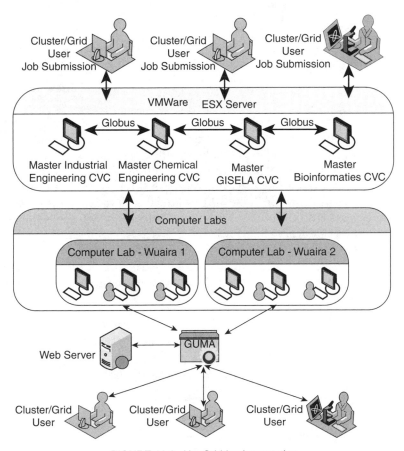

FIGURE 18.2. *UnaGrid implementation.*

18.4 ENERGY CONSUMPTION MODEL

Currently, all of the desktops that may execute as virtual machines are always turned on during business hours (6 AM–9 PM). As mentioned above, UnaGrid currently selects the physical machine to execute virtual machines using a random algorithm; however, the physical machines may be in four possible states (idle, busy, hibernating, turned off) and those states are not taken into account by UnaGrid where new virtual machines are going to be executed. Our hypothesis is focused in that UnaGrid should select physical machines where there are users doing daily tasks. Although this can be contradictory with the idea of getting the maximum resources for our CVCs, we advocate that the gain in energy savings is greater than the loss in computing power available for the scientific applications running on UnaGrid.

18.4.1 Energy Consumption for a Physical Machine

Let us suppose there is a real function f that returns the energy consumption rate of a physical computer given its CPU usage percentage. Let assume that f is crescent, so

$$\frac{\delta f}{\delta x} > 0, \quad \text{for} \quad 0 \le x \le 100. \tag{18.1}$$

When a computer is being used (busy state), its monitor is power up, so the function that describes the energy consumption rate (ECR) of a computer with a user is

$$f_{user} = f(x) + \text{MEC}, \tag{18.2}$$

where monitor energy consumption (MEC) is the energy consumed by the monitor when there is a user using a physical machine. In idle state, the monitor is turned off automatically, so in any other state, the monitor is turned off.

When there are no virtual machines in execution on a physical desktop, the energy consumption rates and CPU usage of a desktop according to the possible desktop states are as shown in Table 18.1, where P_{user} is the mean processor usage when there is a user using a physical machine (state 2) and E_{user} is the energy consumption rate of a physical machine when there is a user using it. E_{hib} is the energy consumption rate when a physical machine is hibernated (state 3).

When a virtual machine of the UnaGrid infrastructure is being executed on a physical machine, we assume the physical machines increase the processor usage to

TABLE 18.1. Energy Consumption Rate and Processor Usage for Desktop Computers

Computer State	Energy Consumption Rate without Virtual Machine	Mean Processor Usage
1 (idle)	$f(0)$	0
2 (busy)	E_{user}	P_{user}
3 (hibernation)	E_{hib}	0
4 (turned off)	0	0

TABLE 18.2. Energy Consumption Rate and Processor Usage for Desktop Computers Running Virtual Machines

Computer State	Energy Consumption Rate with Virtual Machine
1 (idle)	$f(100)$
2 (busy)	$f(100)$ + MEC
3 (hibernation)	$f(100)$
4 (turned off)	$f(100)$

TABLE 18.3. ECR Used by UnaGrid Intensive-Computing Task

		(ECR with VM – ECR without VM)
1 (idle)	T_i	$f(100) - f(0)$
2 (busy)	$\dfrac{100}{P_{\text{free}}} T_i$	$f(100)$ + MEC $- E_{\text{user}}$
3 (hibernation)	T_i	$f(100) - E_{\text{hib}}$
4 (turned off)	T_i	$f(100)$

VM, virtual machine.

100%. So, in Table 18.2, we present the energy consumption rate, for each state, of a desktop computer running virtual machines executing CPU-intensive tasks.

If we suppose that the execution time of a CPU-intensive task is linearly proportional to the amount of free processor used of the machine that is running it, we have the following execution time for a grid task:

$$T_i(P_{\text{free}}) = \frac{100}{P_{\text{free}}} T_i, \qquad (18.3)$$

where T is the amount of time needed to run the task when the physical machine has all its free CPU, and T_i is the time required to execute a grid task in a busy desktop with a free CPU capacity of P_{free}. The amount of energy and time needed to run a CPU-intensive task is shown in Table 18.3 (obtained from Tables 18.1 and 18.2 and Equation 18.3).

To define which is the best state to execute virtual machines, we executed different experimental tests, as shown in the next section.

18.4.2 Energy Consumption for a Computer Lab

To scale the energy consumption of a computer lab, we use three consumption energy values for a desktop machine: (1) a minimum (min) when the machine is idle, (2) an average (avg) when an owner-user is making use of a physical machine, and (3) a maximum (max) when a physical machine has both environments running or just the HPC environment. To simplify the model during the calculation of a complete lab, the hibernation and turned-off states were grouped into the idle state due to the fact that in the current UnaGrid implementation, the machines are always turned on during business hours. With these assumptions, if during a time period there exist n physical machines available, m of which are vacant for HPC tasks, u has an owner-user working, and a virtual cluster of l virtual machines needs to be initiated, a dedicated cluster will have an expected energy consumption of $E\_HPC = l \times f(\mathrm{max}) + (m - 1) \times f(\mathrm{min})$. Moreover, a computer lab environment will have an expected energy consumption of $E_u = u \times f(\mathrm{avg}) + (n - u) \times f(\mathrm{min})$ during the time the HPC environment is running. In a computer lab environment, with n physical machines available, u of which have an owner-user working, and a virtual cluster of l virtual machines needs to be initiated, there are two ways to choose the physical machines where GUMA will start the virtual machines: (1) randomly or (2) where there are users working. The first approach can be modeled using hypergeometric distribution causing the expected number of machines to launch where the owner-user is $\mu = (u \times 1/n)$. Thus, the energy consumption expected during the job execution is

$$E_r = l \times f(\mathrm{max}) + (u - \mu) \times f(\mathrm{avg}) + [n - u - (l - \mu)] \times f(\mathrm{min}). \qquad (18.4)$$

On the other hand, for the second approach, as it will first choose the machines where there are users working, the energy consumption expected is

$$
\begin{aligned}
E_s &= l \times f(\mathrm{max}) + (u - l) \times f(\mathrm{avg}) + (n - u) \times f(\mathrm{min}) \quad l \le u \\
E_s &= l \times f(\mathrm{max}) + (n - l) \times f(\mathrm{min}) \quad l > u.
\end{aligned}
\qquad (18.5)
$$

Let us say that the current energy consumption rate of a dedicated cluster and a computer lab while UnaGrid is not in execution can be expressed as $E_T = E\_HPC + E_u$. When UnaGrid is in execution, it is easy to see that $E_s \le E_r$. Moreover, $E_r \le E_T$, which implies that opportunistic grids are energy-savers. The percentage gained by randomly chosen physical machines is $G_r = (E_T - E_r)/E_r$ and by selectively chosen physical machines is $G_s = (E_T - E_s)/E_s$. So, the approach used by GUMA aims to minimize the energy consumption.

18.5   EXPERIMENTAL RESULTS

We execute tests to evaluate the UnaGrid intrusion level over owner-user, to calculate the energy consumption rate of a single desktop machine and a complete computer lab, and to analyze the performance of the UnaGrid infrastructure to execute grid tasks.

Two computer labs were used to deploy the UnaGrid infrastructure described here. The experimental grid task for each scenario was a multiple multiplication of double-precision matrices. The virtualization technology used was VMware Workstation, with four cores for each virtual machine, and currently, our desktop computers have the following configuration:

- Hardware configuration of physical machines: processor, Intel Core™ i5, 3.33 GHz; disk space, 250 GB; memory, 8 GB; operating system, Windows 7 Professional; network interface card, 1.
- Hardware configuration of virtual machines: processors, four virtual cores; disk space, 20 GB; memory, 2 GB; operating system, Debian 5.0; virtual network interface card, 1.

TABLE 18.4. Results for Disk Usage

Scenario	File Size (GB)	Zip Completion Time(s)
Without running VM	1	521.16
Running VM with one core	1	526.63
Running VM with two cores	1	527.06

The grid tasks used to measure the profit of the opportunistic infrastructure consist of executing 100×100 matrix (A) multiplication tasks to compute $A^{40,000}$.

18.5.1 Intrusion Level

The tests wc performed aimed at measuring the impact of executing an HPC virtual machine on a desktop computer. We wanted to know how owner-users are perturbed because of the execution of jobs in the virtual machine as well as how efficient a virtual cluster is as a tool for HPC is. Three different variables determine the overall performance of an application: I/O, CPU, and memory consumption. As we are proposing a virtual environment for execution of CPU-intensive applications, we will not consider the I/O requests from the computing environment. Also, as memory consumption is limited by the virtual machine configuration, we do not have to study its impact on the owner-user experience. The only impact we have to analyze is the one caused by the use of the CPU. We then simulated different kinds of owner-users sharing their physical machines with CPU-intensive grid environments.

18.5.1.1 I/O Performance To measure the impact of the HPC virtual machine on the I/O performance for the owner-user, a file was zipped in this environment and the completion time is taken, first, without running a virtual machine and then, running a virtual machine with one and two cores, respectively. The results for this test are presented in Table 18.4. The performances of the I/O operations are not greatly impacted by the addition of a running virtual machine with two cores (less than 3%). The reason for this is that the grid tasks running in the virtual machines do not require a large amount of I/O resources in order to be executed. Thus, the additional time required to complete the file zipping is not noticeable by the owner-user.

18.5.1.2 CPU Performance The goal of this experiment is to measure the amount of CPU processing lost by the owner-user when his or her host is used for an HPC virtual machine. A Java application that requires a large amount of CPU resources as the owner-user is executing a task and the completion time of the task was taken, first, without running a virtual machine and, second, running a virtual machine with one and two cores. The tasks consisted of a simple test using a naive algorithm. The results for this test are presented in Table 18.5. For this scenario, the CPU usage perception is not affected by the use of a running virtual machine with one and two cores (less than 1%).

One observation is that both environments (owner-user and HPC virtual machine) share the two cores of the underlying physical machine (i.e., as the owner-user process does not require the whole computing power); one core is used by this

TABLE 18.5. Results for CPU Usage

Scenario	File Size (MB)	Task Completion Time(s)
Without running VM	524,287	98.01
Running VM with one core	524,287	98.42
Running VM with two cores	524,287	99.46

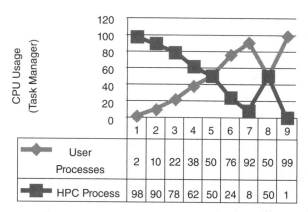

	1	2	3	4	5	6	7	8	9
User Processes	2	10	22	38	50	76	92	50	99
HPC Process	98	90	78	62	50	24	8	50	1

FIGURE 18.3. CPU usage for HPC and owner-user processes.

process and the other one is used by the HPC environment. To explore this subject, it is necessary to look at another scenario, one where the user process demands the whole computing power. We analyzed the CPU usage of the owner-user and the HPC virtual machine when both environments are in execution; the results are shown in Figure 18.3.

An HPC virtual machine and an owner-user virtual machine were initiated. Both virtual machines were configured with two cores and two CPU-intensive tasks, setting the priority for the HPC computing process to idle. In Figure 18.3, point (1) represents the situation when the HPC process is consuming all computing power because the owner-user is not processing CPU-intensive tasks. In points (2) and (3), the owner-user processes starts demanding more computing power. In points (4)–(7), the owner-user initiates a virtual machine and starts demanding computing power to complete the process. Then, when the owner-user virtual machine is completely initiated, the operating system yields 50% CPU usage for each environment (point 8). Finally, in point (9), when a CPU-intensive task is sent by the owner-user, all CPU resources are completely granted to the owner-user processes. Here, it is clear that the operating system yields the computing power to the owner-user processes because they have higher priority than the HPC virtual machine. As a result, the tasks in the HPC environment are not progressing to achieve their goal, and they will take longer to completely finish. Here, we see one of the costs of maintaining both environments in a single desktop computer and permitting the isolation of them. In the next section we explore this subject in more detail.

18.5.2 Energy Consumption Rate for a Single Desktop Machine

Several tests were made to measure the energy consumption function of a single machine. To measure the consumed energy, we used a HAMEG HM8115-2

TABLE 18.6. Energy Consumption versus CPU Usage

CPU Usage	Mean energy Consumption Rate	Standard Deviation
1	47.089	2601
5	55.175	3.773
10	67.979	1.359
15	74.579	1.078
20	72.356	0.565
26	73.637	2.230
30	77.581	2.682
35	81.247	2.691
40	86.493	1.862
45	85.597	2.095
50	85.272	0.930
55	86.866	1.735
61	88.014	1.196
65	91.668	1.106
70	91.510	1.240
75	92.881	0.384
81	95.052	0.816
85	96.108	1.120
90	96.600	0.791
100	96.752	0.115

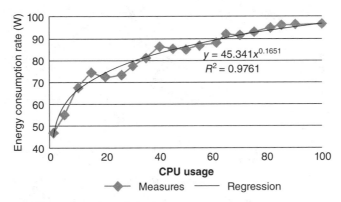

FIGURE 18.4. *Energy consumption rate versus CPU usage.*

wattmeter connected to a computer. We used a computer lab desktop machine and ran a CPU-intensive application that allowed us to obtain a stable CPU usage for our tests. For each test case, we measured the energy consumption rate of the computer each second on a lapse of 47 seconds. With these data, we obtained an energy consumption rate profile for a physical machine executing CPU-intensive applications. The results are shown in Table 18.6.

To define a function $f(x)$ that returns the energy consumption rate (ECR) of a desktop given its CPU usage, we calculate a regression with the data of Table 18.6. Figure 18.4 shows the regression and data used to predict the energy consumption rate of a machine based on CPU usage.

Taking into account the above results, each computer state of a physical machine without executing a virtual machine has the energy consumption rates and processor

TABLE 18.7. Experimental Results of ECR Used by a Physical Machine without a VM

Computer State	Energy Consumption Rate (W) without VM	Mean Processor Usage (%)
1 (idle)	47	0
2 (busy)	87	10
3 (hibernation)	3	0
4 (turned off)	0	0

TABLE 18.8. Experimental Results of ECR Used by a Physical Machine Running a VM

Computer State	Mean Energy Consumption Rate with VM (W)	Mean Processor Usage (%)
1 (idle)	96	100
2 (busy)	116	100
3 (hibernation)	93	100
4 (turned off)	96	100

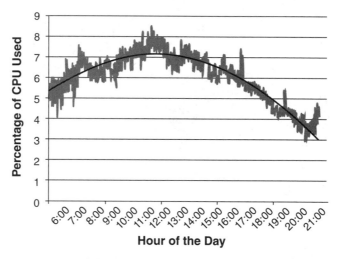

FIGURE 18.5. CPU usage per hour.

usage presented in Table 18.7. The mean percentage usage when there is a user using a desktop machine (P_{user}) was calculated analyzing the CPU consumption of a computer lab (70 computers) during 1 month; Figure 18.5 shows the average CPU usage during daylight working hours where the computer laboratories are open to students. On the average, CPU utilization does not exceed 10%; this value is consistent with different works on this same subject [42, 43].

In Table 18.8, we present the ECR of a desktop machine after submitting an HPC virtual machine for every possible state.

Taking into account the results of Tables 18.3, 18.7, and 18.8, the amount of energy and the time needed to run a CPU-intensive task (which takes a time T to be executed in a dedicated computer) in a UnaGrid virtual machine executed on a desktop computer that can be in four possible states are shown in Table 18.9.

TABLE 18.9. Experimental Results of ECR Used by a Physical Machine Running a VM

Computer State	Execution Time with VM (W)	Mean ECR (W)	Energy Consumption
1 (idle)	T	49	49 W $\times$ T
2 (busy)	$\frac{10}{9}T$	29	32 W $\times$ T
3 (hibernation)	T	93	93 W $\times$ T
4 (turned off)	T	96	96 W $\times$ T

TABLE 18.10. Energy Consumption Rate When Several Virtual Machines (VMs) Are Executed per Physical Machine

VM	CPUs per VM	Total Running Jobs	CPU Usage	Mean ECR (W)
1	4	0	1	48.93
1	4	2	50	84.03
1	4	4	100	90.01
2	2	0	1	49.38
2	2	2	50	84.68
2	2	4	100	90.86
4	1	0	1	49.62
4	1	2	50	85.07
4	1	4	100	89.67

Results of Table 18.9 show that from the energy consumption point of view, the best desktop machines to deploy UnaGrid virtual machines are those being used (state 2), followed by the machines that are in idle state (state 1), hibernation (state 3), and turned off (state 4).

Because the desktop machines in the future will have more processing cores, we also executed tests to measure the energy consumption rate for a physical machine running one, two, and four virtual machines executing grid tasks. In Table 18.10, we can see, for each test, the number of running virtual machines, the number of cores assigned per virtual machine, and the number of total running jobs.

Results in Table 18.10 show that if multiple virtual machines are executed on a desktop computer, the ECR used by the grid tasks is very close to that used when a single virtual machine is executed.

18.5.3 Energy Consumption Tests for a Complete Computer Lab

These tests were executed to evaluate the energy consumption of a complete computer lab used to execute grid tasks. As a first step, we calculated the energy consumption rate of a computer lab on a typical day and compared it with the energy consumption rate when executing HPC virtual machines. Figure 18.6 shows the ECR of a computer lab with 70 physical machines in each case. As can be seen, the ECR is increased when executing HPC tasks (as expected). The baseline under the 5 kW corresponds to the actual consumption of the computer lab with no students or virtual machines using it. A global energy saving, only for using UnaGrid to support HPC tasks (independent of the desktop computers state used to execute virtual machines), is close to 55% considering that, currently, this ECR

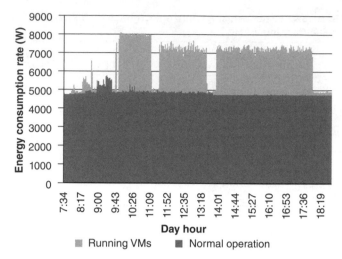

FIGURE 18.6. Computer lab energy consumption.

TABLE 18.11. Energy Consumption per Environment

Cluster Size (Cores)	Dedicated Cluster (kW)	User Lab (kW)	Opportunistic Grid	
			Energy	Gain
20	0.55	0.33	0.54	61
40	1.1	0.61	1.08	62
60	1.65	1.0	1.63	64
80	2.2	1.35	2.20	61
100	2.75	1.68	2.77	60
200	5.5	3.39	5.47	62
268	7.37	4.55	7.29	62

is used permanently during business hours. As we mentioned before, the grid tasks used to measure the profit of the opportunistic infrastructure consists in executing 100×100 matrix (A) multiplication tasks to compute $A_{40,000}$.

To measure all costs generated by the maintenance of an opportunistic grid, another scenario was established. The intention is to measure and compare the number of finished jobs and the amount of energy consumed to complete grid jobs. The experimental task for the scenario was the same multiple multiplication of double-precision matrices.

For this scenario, we used a computer lab with up to 268 cores. For the whole lab, we measured the average ECR when exclusively owner-users use the computers (user lab), when there are HPC virtual machines exclusively executing (dedicated cluster), and when both environments are in execution (opportunistic grid). Table 18.11 shows the detailed results. To avoid the need to reserve all computers to make dedicated tests, we reserved 10 computers and then we extrapolated the data for each cluster size. We show measures to different cluster sizes.

Based on the observations of the UnaGrid infrastructure, at least 60% of the physical machines are being used at any moment. As Table 18.11 shows, the average gain by using machines on an opportunistic model is about 61% for each test, a very significant value in terms of energy saving.

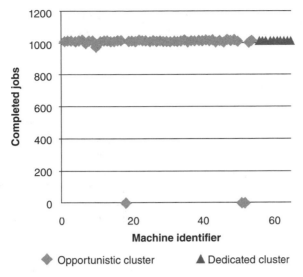

FIGURE 18.7. *Completed jobs per machine.*

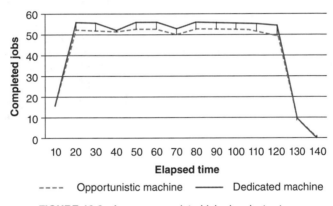

FIGURE 18.8. *Average completed jobs by cluster type.*

18.5.4   Performance Degradation Perceived by Grid Users

To test the performance degradation when grid users executed tasks on a CVC, a comparison of computational power between both environments was made by starting 40,000 jobs on 67 computers and varying the number of machines needed to perform HPC tasks during 6.2 hours. Ten of these computers had been reserved so no owner-users could use them. Figure 18.7 shows the number of completed jobs for each machine after 140 minutes of execution. As can be seen, the behavior of machines is approximately the same when they are reserved compared with when they are not. This shows that computer labs' potential is being underutilized by owner-users.

As the behavior of machines in both opportunistic and dedicated clusters is fairly equal, we calculated the average behavior of each environment using a smaller scale. Figure 18.8 shows in a detailed way the behavior of each environment under the test. The figure shows the number of completed jobs on lapses of 10 minutes. From this figure, we see that a dedicated machine can complete on average 6% more jobs than an opportunistic one, validating our original hypothesis.

18.6   CONCLUSIONS AND FUTURE WORK

Opportunistic grids are a good alternative to develop HPC. In this work, we presented an opportunistic grid infrastructure that uses virtualization technologies to provide complete isolation between both environments: grid computing and owner-user ones. The results showed that giving low priority to the CVCs does not disturb the owner-users, who were targeted to reap the profits of the technology investments originally. Another important aspect showed in this work is that virtualization allows not only an efficient computational environment but also an energy-efficient and scalable opportunistic environment [44]. Using existing resources, industries can reduce technology investments, and the isolation of both environments allows reduction of the energy costs. When a CVC needs to be initiated, two approaches are possible: (1) Choose the idle physical machines and (2) choose physical machines where there are users working [45]. No matter which strategy is used, experimental results show that opportunistic environments offer better gains in terms of energy consumption. Comparing the two approaches presented, the gain percentage of energy saving using busy desktop computers was always greater than the other approaches. It is important to show some observations regarding the number of people using the computer labs on a daily basis. Almost 60% of the physical machines are being used at any moment, which gives a considerable saving percentage in energy consumption. Owner-users use a maximum of 10% of the CPU, so the UnaGrid infrastructure can take advantage permanently of most of the CPU capabilities available in computer labs.

REFERENCES

[1] TOP500, "TOP500 Supercomputer Series," Available at http://www.top500.org/list/2009/06/100. [Online] June 2009.

[2] J. Kolodziej, S.U. Khan, and F. Xhafa, "Genetic algorithms for energy-aware scheduling in computational grids," 6th IEEE International Conference on P2P, Parallel, Grid, Cloud, and Internet Computing (3PGCIC), Barcelona, Spain, October 2011.

[3] S.U. Khan and I. Ahmad, "A cooperative game theoretical technique for joint optimization of energy consumption and response time in computational grids," *IEEE Transactions on Parallel and Distributed Systems*, 20(3):346–360, 2009.

[4] S.U. Khan, "A goal programming approach for the joint optimization of energy consumption and response time in computational grids," in *28th IEEE International Performance Computing and Communications Conference (IPCCC)*, pp. 410–417, Phoenix, AZ, December 2009.

[5] L. Wang and S.U. Khan, "Review of performance metrics for green data centers: A taxonomy study," *Journal of Supercomputing*, forthcoming.

[6] S. Zeadally, S.U. Khan, and N. Chilamkurti, "Energy-efficient networking: Past, present, and future," *Journal of Supercomputing*, forthcoming.

[7] M.A. Aziz, S.U. Khan, T. Loukopoulos, P. Bouvry, H. Li, and J. Li, "An overview of achieving energy efficiency in on-chip networks," *International Journal of Communication Networks and Distributed Systems*, 5(4):444–458, 2010.

[8] F. Gilles, *Recent Advances and Research Challenges in Desktop Grid and Volunteer Computing.* [book auth.] Core GRID. "Grids, P2p and Services Computing." London: Springer, 2010.

[9] A.S. Tanenbaum and M.V. Steen, *Distributed Systems: Principles and Paradigms*, 1st ed. Upper Saddle River, NJ: Prentice Hall PTR, 2001.

[10] B.C. Neuman, "Scale in distributed systems," in *Readings in Distributed Computing Systems* (T.L. Casavant and M. Singhal, eds.), Los Alamitos, CA: IEEE Computer Society Press, pp. 50–62, 1994.

[11] J.F. Shoch and J.A. Hupp, "The 'Worm' programs early experience with a distributed computation," *Communications of the ACM*, 25(3):172–188, 1982.

[12] M. Litzkow, M. Livny, and M. Mutka, "Condor—A hunter of idle workstations" in *8th IEEE International Conference on Distributed Computing Systems*, pp. 104–111, San Jose, CA, 1988.

[13] Mersenne Research, Inc., "GIMPS: 'Great Internet Mersenne Prime'." Available at http://www.mersenne.org/. [Online] January 2010. Accessed June 15, 2009.

[14] D.P. Anderson, J. Cobb, E. Korpela, M. Lebofsky, and D. Werthimer, "SETI@home an experiment in public-resource computing," *Communications of the ACM*, 45:56–61, 2002.

[15] Distributed.Net, "Distributed.net FAQ-O-Matic," Available at http://www.distributed.net. [Online] July 2011. Accessed June 17, 2009.

[16] D. Anderson, "BOINC: A system for public-resource computing and storage," in *5th IEEE/ACM International Workshop on Grid*, pp. 4–10, Pittsburgh: ACM, 2004.

[17] L.F.G. Sarmenta, S.J.V. Chua, R.J.V. Chua, P. Echevarria, J.M. Mendoza, R.-R. Santos, A. de Manila, S. Tan, and R.P. Lozada, "Bayanihan computing. NET: Grid computing with XML web services," in *2nd IEEE/ACM International Symposium on Cluster Computing and the Grid*, p. 434, 10.1109/CCGRID.2002.1017182. Berlin: IEEE/ACM, 2002.

[18] J. Frey, T. Tannenbaum, M. Livny, I. Foster, and S. Tuecke, "Condor-G: A computation management agent for multi-institutional grids," in *10th IEEE International Symposium on High Performance Distributed Computing*, pp. 55–63, San Francisco: IEEE, August 2001.

[19] A. Goldchleger, F. Kon, A. Goldman, M. Finger, and G.C. Bezerra, "InteGrade: Object-oriented grid middleware leveraging the idle computing power of desktop machines," *Concurrency and Computation: Practice and Experience*, 16:449–459, 2004.

[20] C. Germain, V. Nri, G. Fedak, and F. Cappello, "XtremWeb: Building an experimental platform for global computing," *Lecture Notes in Computer Science*, 1971/2000:107–129, 2000.

[21] N. Andrade, W. Cirne, F. Brasileiro, and P. Roisenberg, "OurGrid: An approach to easily assemble grids with equitable resource sharing," *Lecture Notes in Computer Science*, 2862/2003:61–86, 2003.

[22] C. Anglano, M. Canonico, and M. Guazzone, "The ShareGrid peer-to-peer desktop grid: Infrastructure, applications, and performance evaluation," *Journal of Grid Computing*, 8:543–570, 2010.

[23] P. Buncic, C. Aguado Sanchez, J. Blomer, L. Franco, A. Harutyunian, P. Mato, and Y. Yao, "CernVM a virtual software appliance for LHC applications. Buncic," *Journal of Physics*, 219, 2010. DOI:10.1088/1742-6596/219/4/042003.

[24] J.G. Pedersen and C.U. Sttrup, *"Developing Distributed Computing Solutions Combining Grid Computing and Public Computing,"* FatBat Software. Available at http://www. fatbat.dk/?content=thesis.new. Accessed January 12, 2010.

[25] D. Wang and G. Bin, "SUCSI: A light-weight desktop grid system using virtualization for application sandboxing," in *International Conference on Network Computing and Information Security (NCIS)*, pp. 352–356, IEEE, 2011.

[26] H. Castro, E. Rosales, M. Villamizar, and A. Miller, "UnaGrid—On demand opportunistic desktop grid," in *10th IEEE/ACM International Conference on Cluster, Cloud and Grid Computing*, pp. 661–666, Melbourne: IEEE, June 2010.

[27] R. Aversa, M. Avvenuti, A. Cuomo, B. Di Martino, G. Di Modica, S. Distefano, A. Puliafito, M. Rak, O. Tomarchio, A. Vecchio, S. Venticinque, U. Villano, M. Guarracino, F. Vivien, J. Trff, M. Cannataro, M. Danelutto, A. Hast, F. Perla, A. Knpfer, and M. Alexander, "The Cloud@Home project: Towards a new enhanced computing paradigm," in *Euro-Par 2010 Parallel Processing Workshops*, Vol. 6586, pp. 555–562, Springer, 2010.

[28] J. Sahoo, S. Mohapatra, R.B. Lath, "Virtualization: A survey on concepts, taxonomy and associated security issues," in *Second International Conference on Computer and Network Technology (ICCNT)*, pp. 222–226, IEEE, 2010.

[29] D. Kliazovich, P. Bouvry, Y. Audzevich, and S.U. Khan, "GreenCloud: A packet-level simulator of energy-aware cloud computing data centers," 53rd IEEE Global Communications Conference (Globecom), Miami, FL, December 2010.

[30] J.P. Walters, V. Chaudhary, M. Cha, S. Guercio, Jr., and G. Steve, "A comparison of virtualization technologies for HPC," in *22nd International Conference on Advanced Information Networking and Applications*, pp. 861–868, New York: IEEE Press, 2008.

[31] G.L. Valentini, W. Lassonde, S.U. Khan, N. Min-Allah, S.A. Madani, J. Li, L. Zhang, L. Wang, N. Ghani, J. Kolodziej, H. Li, A.Y. Zomaya, C.-Z. Xu, P. Balaji, A. Vishnu, F. Pinel, J.E. Pecero, D. Kliazovich, and P. Bouvry, "An overview of energy efficiency techniques in cluster computing systems," *Cluster Computing*, forthcoming.

[32] VMware, Inc., *VMware Workstation*. Available at http://www.vmware.com/products/ workstation/, 2011. Accessed July 31, 2011.

[33] AMD, "AMD Virtualization (AMD-V) Technology." Available at http://sites.amd.com/ us/business/it-solutions/virtualization/Pages/amd-v.aspx. [Online] July 2011.

[34] R. Uhlig, G. Neiger, D. Rodgers, A.L. Santoni, F.C.M. Martins, A.V. Anderson, S.M. Bennett, A. Kagi, F.H. Leung, and L. Smith, "Intel virtualization technology," *Computer*, 38:48–56, 2005.

[35] M. Pretorius, M. Ghassemian, and C. Ierotheou, "An Investigation into energy efficiency of data centre virtualisation," in *International Conference on P2P, Parallel, Grid, Cloud and Internet Computing (3PGCIC)*, pp. 157–163, IEEE, 2010.

[36] X. Liao, H. Liting, and H. Jin, "Energy optimization schemes in cluster with virtual machines," *Cluster Computing*, 13:116–126, 2010.

[37] University of Liverpool, "Condor High Throughput Computing." Available at http:// www.liv.ac.uk/csd/escience/condor/power_save.pdf. [Online] April 2010.

[38] B. Schott and A. Emmen, "Green methodologies in desktop-grid," in *International Multiconference on Computer Science and Information Technology (IMCSIT)*, pp. 671–676, IEEE, 2010.

[39] A.M. Vargas, L.M. Quesada Ocampo, M.C. Cspedes, N. Carreo, A. Gonzlez, A. Rojas, A.P. Zuluaga, K. Myers, W.E. Fry, P. Jimenz, A.J. Bernal, and S. Restrepo, "Characterization of *Phytophthora infestans* Populations in Colombia," First Report of the A2 Mating Type." pp. 82–88. DOI:10.1094/PHYTO-99-1-0082. Bogot: s.n., 2009.

[40] A. Gonzalez, H. Castro, M. Villamizar, N. Cuervo, G. Lozano, S. Restrepo, and S. Orduz, "Mesoscale modeling of the *Bacillus thuringiensis* sporulation network based on stochastic kinetics and its application for in silico scale-down," in *International Workshop on igh Performance Computational Systems Biology*," pp. 3–12, IEEE, HIBI '09, 2009.

[41] A. Bernal, M.A. Ramirez, H. Castro, J.L. Walteros, and A.L. Medaglia, "JG2A: A grid-enabled object-oriented framework for developing genetic algorithms," in *IEEE Systems and Information Engineering Design Symposium SIEDS'09*," pp. 67–72, Virginia: IEEE, 2009.

[42] D. Kondo, G. Fedak, F. Cappello, A.A. Chien, and H. Casanova, "Characterizing resource availability in enterprise desktop grids," *Future Generation Computer Systems—FGCS*, 23:888–903, 2007.

[43] P. Domingues, P. Marques, and L. Silva, "Resource usage of Windows computer laboratories," in *International Conference Workshops on Parallel Processing (ICPP)*, pp. 469–476, IEEE, 2005.

[44] F. Pinel, J.E. Pecero, P. Bouvry, and S.U. Khan, "A two-phase heuristic for the scheduling of independent tasks on computational grids," ACM/IEEE/IFIP International Conference on High Performance Computing and Simulation (HPCS), Istanbul, Turkey, July 2011.

[45] S.U. Khan and I. Ahmad, "Non-cooperative, semi-cooperative, and cooperative games-based grid resource allocation," 20th IEEE International Parallel and Distributed Processing Symposium (IPDPS), Rhodes Island, Greece, April 2006.

Maximizing Real-Time System Utilization by Adjusting Task Computation Times

Nasro Min-Allah, Samee Ullah Khan, Yongji Wang, Joanna Kolodziej, and Nasir Ghani

19.1 INTRODUCTION

A real-time system is any information processing system that has to respond to externally generated input stimuli within a finite and specified period: the correctness depends not only on the logical result but also on the time it was delivered; the failure to respond is as bad as the wrong response [1]. Real-time systems can be constructed out of sequential programs but are typically built from concurrent programs called tasks. A real-time task is an executable entity of work that, at a minimum, is characterized by the worst-case execution time (*WCET*) [2] and time constraints [3]. The *WCET* is estimated as the maximal time required by the processor to execute the task. A typical timing constraint of a real-time task is the deadline, which is defined as the maximal completion time of a task without causing any damage to the system [4–6].

There are two main classes of real-time systems: (1) hard and (2) soft real-time systems. The hard real-time must meet its deadlines. In case of failure, its operation is without value and the system for which it is a component is of no use. Embedded systems are often hard real-time systems. Such systems have practical applications

Scalable Computing and Communications: Theory and Practice, First Edition. Edited by Samee U. Khan, Albert Y. Zomaya, and Lizhe Wang.

in tasks or events where strict deadlines are to be followed. In the case where system failure results in a damage or loss of life, the deadlines must be kept [7]. In soft real-time systems, however, there is some room for lateness. A delayed process may not cause the entire system failure. Instead, it may affect the quality of the process or system.

With emergence of many mature scheduling techniques, today the designers of the real-time systems have the freedom to adapt any suitable existing scheduling algorithm that will drive the system efficiently when operational. Therefore, running the time-critical applications with such a scheduling algorithm requires predictable behaviors under all possible circumstances and, hence, mature scheduling techniques need to be adapted. These algorithms are based on system utilization; that is, systems with utilization less than 70% are always schedulable. Developing applications, when the intended workload is fixed, are generally required to fully exhaust the processor capacity when the workload is high or to reduce the energy consumption of the system when the workload is low by reducing operating frequency.

In real-time systems, running the time-critical applications with a scheduling algorithm requires predictable behaviors under all possible circumstances; that is, if a deadline must be missed, it is better to miss the deadline of a less important task than missing the deadline of an important task. Currently, the most commonly used approach to scheduling real-time tasks is priority driven, which falls into two types: fixed priority and dynamic priority [7]. A fixed-priority algorithm assigns the fixed/same priority to all jobs (instances of a task) in each task, which should be different from the priorities assigned to jobs generated by other tasks in the system. In contrast, dynamic-priority scheduling algorithms place no restrictions upon the manner in which priorities are assigned to individual jobs. Although dynamic algorithms are considered better theoretically over fixed-priority techniques, they are difficult to implement in commercial kernels that do not provide explicit support for timing constraints, such as periods and deadlines [8].

Assuming unlimited priority levels, the problem of scheduling periodic tasks under the fixed-priority scheme was first addressed by Liu and Layland [9] in 1973; they derived the optimal static priority scheduling algorithm for an implicit-deadline model (when deadlines coincide with respective periods) called rate monotonic (RM) algorithm. RM assigns static priorities on task activation rates (periods) such that for any two tasks, τ_i and τ_j, priority $(\tau_i) >$ priority $(\tau_j) \Rightarrow$ period $(\tau_i) <$ period (τ_j), while ties are broken arbitrarily. For a task set with relative deadlines less than or equal to periods (constrained deadline systems), an optimal priority ordering has been shown in Reference 10 to be deadline monotonic (DM), where the priority assigned is inversely proportional to relative deadlines. RM and DM become identical in behaviors when task deadlines and periods are equal. In the last four decades that have followed (since 1973), many of these assumptions are relaxed, and the effects of such changes are highlighted on the monotonic scheduling policy and the corresponding feasibility conditions are provided.

In real-time systems, the system utilization is based on the three basic task parameters, namely, execution time, deadline, and period. Since task periods are usually set by the system requirement as a real-time task has its own periodicity, task deadlines and execution times are the only choices that can be modified in order to improve system utilization. Results are available for modifying the task deadline [11]. Similarly, authors in Reference 12 recently presented a generalized bound for adjusting the task execution times in the context of preemptive RM scheduling policy over uniprocessor systems. In this chapter, we highlight the work of Min-Allah et al. [12] and explain its effectiveness to real-time systems, especially, dynamic voltage scaling (DVS)-enabled systems.

Let $\Gamma = \{\tau_1, \tau_2, \ldots, \tau_n\}$ represent a nonconcrete periodic task system having periodic tasks. A nonconcrete periodic task τ_i recurs and is represented by a tuple (c_i, d_i, p_i), where c_i, d_i, p_i represent the WCET, relative deadline, and task period, respectively. Determine whether Γ is RM feasible. There are two possible outcomes: Yes or No. If Γ is feasible, then how much freedom do we have to increase the value of the parameter c_i in order to have a higher system utilization while still satisfying schedulability constraints? If the answer is No (Γ is infeasible), then how is the parameter c_i to be adjusted so that the new task set becomes schedulable?

The application of the aforementioned formulations is enormous, ranging from enhancing quality of service (QoS) to higher system utilization, and so on. A readily available reference is its applicability in a battery-operated embedded system, where DVS is applied to scale down the processor frequency when the processor is not fully loaded [13] for reducing the system energy consumption or increasing system speed for better QoS. The above formulation can be converted into a typical optimization problem concerning the minimization or maximization of a function subject to different types of constraints (equality or inequality) in operation research, which can be solved by any mature algorithm for an efficient solution.

19.2 EXPRESSING TASK SCHEDULABILITY IN POLYLINEAR SURFACES

To find schedulability of a task τ_i, the concept of workload was introduced by the authors of Reference 14. The workload constituted by τ_i at time t consists of its execution demand, c_i, as well as the interference it encounters due to higher-priority tasks from τ_{i-1} to τ_1 and can be expressed mathematically as

$$w_i(t) = c_i + \sum_{j=1}^{i-1} \left\lceil \frac{t}{p_j} \right\rceil c_j. \tag{19.1}$$

A periodic task τ_i is feasible if we find some $t \in [0, p_i]$ satisfying

$$L_i = \min_{0 < t \leq p_i} (w_i(t) \leq t). \tag{19.2}$$

To check that such a t exists, Equation (19.1) is tested at all points in S_i:

$$S_i = \{ap_b \mid b = 1, \ldots, i; a = 1, \ldots, \lfloor p_i/p_b \rfloor\}. \tag{19.3}$$

We have the following fundamental theorems to determine whether an individual task and a task set is feasible.

Theorem 19.1 [14]   *Given a set of n periodic tasks $\tau_1, \ldots, \tau_n, \tau_i$ can be feasibly scheduled for all task phasings using RM iff*

$$L_i = \min_{t \in S_i} \frac{w_i(t)}{t} \leq 1. \tag{19.4}$$

Theorem 19.2 [14]   *The entire task set Γ is feasible iff*

$$L = \max_{1 \leq i \leq n} L_i \leq 1. \tag{19.5}$$

With Equation (19.3), L_i is needed to be analyzed only at a finite number of points.

Definition 19.1 F_i **[12].** *The schedulability region $\mathbf{F_i}$ is defined as*

$$F_i(c_1, c_2, \dots, c_i) = \{(c_1, c_2, \dots, c_i) \mid \tau_i \text{ is schedulable by RMA},$$
$$c_j \geq 0; j = 1, 2, \dots, i\}. \tag{19.6}$$

Definition 19.2   Generalized Bound (P-Bound) [12]. *The generalized bound (P-bound) of task τ_i is an inequality $g_i(c_1, c_2, \dots, c_i) \leq 0$ such that*

- *Any point in the region F_i satisfies $g_i(c_1, c_2, \dots, c_i) \leq 0$.*
- *Any point that violates $g_i(c_1, c_2, \dots, c_i) > 0$ is not in the region F_i.*

Definition 19.3   Schedulability Region. *According to Definition 19.1, scheduling region F_i that guarantees the schedulability of τ_i is obtained with*

Theorem 19.3 [15]   *The schedulability region F_i is given by*

$$F_i(c_1, c_2, \dots, c_i) = \{(c_1, c_2, \dots, c_i) \underset{t \in S_i}{\vee} \sum_{j=1}^{i} \left\lceil \frac{t}{p_j} \right\rceil c_j - t \leq 0;$$
$$c_j \geq 0; j = 1, 2, \dots, i\}. \tag{19.7}$$

where "$\vee$" denotes logic OR and $S_i = \{rp_j | j = 1, \dots i; r = 1, \dots, \lfloor p_i/p_j \rfloor\}$.

It is observed that Equation (19.7) consists of a set of inequalities with logic OR relations. In the following, a mathematical transformation is proposed to remove logic OR relationships among the inequalities, which enables us to derive the generalized bound.

19.2.1   Generalized Bound/P-Bound

Lemma 19.1 [16]   *Let $g_i \leq 0$ be a constraint on the schedulability of task τ_i. Suppose $g_1 \leq 0, g_2 \leq 0, \dots, g_m \leq 0$ are constraints with logic OR relationships, then $\forall j = 1, \dots, m$, $g_1 \leq 0 \vee g_2 \leq 0 \vee \dots \vee g_m \leq 0$ can be determined by $\left(\Delta v - \sum_{j=1}^{m} \left(\sqrt{g_j^2} - g_j \right) \right) \leq 0$ as a small positive value $\Delta v \to 0$.*

By Lemma 19.1, the constraints with logic OR relationships are turned into one general inequality.

■ EXAMPLE 19.1

Inequalities $x \leq 4 \vee x \geq 6$ can be determined by

$$\Delta v - \left(\left(\sqrt{(x-4)^2} - (x-4) \right) + \left(\sqrt{(6-x)^2} - (6-x) \right) \right) \leq 0.$$

Note that in Lemma 19.1, $g_1 = 0 \vee g_2 = 0 \vee \ldots \vee g_m = 0$ is just barely determined by $\left(\Delta v - \sum_{j=1}^{m} \left(\sqrt{g_j^2} - g_j \right) \right) \leq 0$ because when $\Delta v \to 0^+$, we have that $\exists j, g_j \to 0^-$.

From Lemma 19.1, we have

Theorem 19.4 [12]   *The schedulability region F_i can be determined by*

$$
F_i(c_1, c_2, \ldots, c_i) = \{(c_1, c_2, \ldots, c_i) \mid
$$

$$
\Delta v - \sum_{j=1}^{k_i} \left(\sqrt{\left(\sum_{m=1}^{i} \left\lceil \frac{S_{ij}}{p_m} \right\rceil c_m - S_{ij} \right)^2} - \left(\sum_{m=1}^{i} \left\lceil \frac{S_{ij}}{p_m} \right\rceil c_m - S_{ij} \right) \right) \tag{19.8}
$$

$$
\leq 0; c_m \geq 0; m = 1, 2, \ldots, i\},
$$

where S_{ij} is the jth element of S_i, $S_i = \{rp_j \mid j = 1, \ldots i; r = 1, \ldots, \lfloor p_i/p_j \rfloor\}$ and k_i is the number of elements in S_i.

19.3   TASK EXECUTION TIME ADJUSTMENT BASED ON THE P-BOUND

The task execution times adjustment problem can be integrated with the P-bound. Say, task periods are fixed and the tasks execution times are kept flexible to improve the system performance. In a very general framework, c_i is the design variable to represent the possible choices of the designer at the stage of the system design; the P-bound is the constraint to ensure the task schedulability; and the objective function is designed as a measure of the overall system performance. Consequently, the problem can be formulated as nonlinear programming optimization problems, which determine the optimum c_i by applying the classical nonlinear optimization approaches.

To make things worse, the time needed to execute these instructions depends on the machine architectures, which is again a complicated activity (the interested reader is referred to References 9, 12, 17, and 18). The point is that, even an estimate on *WCET* for this simple code is tedious; using loops makes it worst. Assuming a good estimate is made of the source code, there is still uncertainty involved at runtime due to data cache and so on. Another extreme case would be the best-case execution time (*BCET*). The difference between *BCET* and *WCET* can be as large as 80% [19]. The G-bound can be used in this situation by first putting $c_i = BCET$ and then, if the task τ_i is schedulable, the value of c_i can be increased such that $c_i = WCET$. In case the task is infeasible, the code for τ_i can be readjusted, making *WCET* lower accordingly. Sometimes, two replicas of the same task can be considered, namely, a primary task and an alternate version of the same task. The primary version has a higher *WCET* than the alternative one. In such situations, completing either version results in the task being completed. Though the primary version having high quality is desired, the alternative version of the task with acceptable quality may be executed when overload occurs.

The above condition is extended to a more general one by assuming that the execution times $c_i(i = 1, 2, \ldots, n)$ vary within a range; that is, they are described by $c_i^{\min} \leq c_i \leq c_i^{\max}$. When feasibility is determined with c_is, there are two possible outcomes: a Yes or a No. The Yes or No answers can be combined into a single optimization problem, which can be formulated formally as follows: Given a set of n periodic tasks $\Gamma = \{\tau_1, \tau_2, \ldots, \tau_n\}$, where the task execution time c_i varies in a range with a lower bound $c_i^{\min}$ and an upper bound $c_i^{\max}$, and p_i is known a priori, find a set of the execution times c_i under the RM schedulability constraints such that a system performance index is maximized.

Suppose the task system is optimal in the sense that the total processor utilization is maximized. The extended problem can be expressed as a maximization problem:

$$\text{maximize } f(c_1, c_2, \ldots, c_n) \tag{19.9}$$

subject to Equation (19.10), $\forall i = 1, \ldots, n,$

$$\Delta v - \sum_{j=1}^{k_i} \left(\sqrt{\left(\sum_{m=1}^{i} \left\lceil \frac{S_{ij}}{p_m} \right\rceil \alpha c_m - S_{ij} \right)^2} - \left(\sum_{m=1}^{i} \left\lceil \frac{S_{ij}}{p_m} \right\rceil \alpha c_m - S_{ij} \right) \right) \leq 0 \tag{19.10}$$

$$c_i^{\min} \leq c_i \leq c_i^{\max}. \tag{19.11}$$

For a given schedulable set, the above maximization problem can be interpreted as computing the minimum processor speed, denoted by α, such that the task set is still schedulable at that speed. Real-time systems are usually battery powered, and the battery is required to be replenished regularly to keep the system operational. These systems generally remain underutilized, and it is recommended to adjust the system speed subject to the workload so that the CPU energy consumption is minimized and the battery life is extended. The speed reduction is considered as scaling the execution times c_i by a factor α. The P-bound for τ_i becomes

$$\delta v - \sum_{j=1}^{k_i} \left(\sqrt{\left(\sum_{m=1}^{i} \lceil s_{ij} p_m \rceil \alpha c_m - s_{ij} \right)^2} - \left(\sum_{m=1}^{i} \lceil s_{ij} p_m \rceil \alpha c_m - s_{ij} \right) \right) \leq 0. \tag{19.12}$$

The minimum speed $\alpha_{\min}$, is given by

$$\text{maximize } \alpha \tag{19.13}$$

subject to inequality (Equation 19.12), $\forall i = 1, \ldots, n.$ \hfill (19.14)

The constraints ensure that all the tasks are schedulable. The above maximization problem also is applicable to the cases when an unschedulable task set needs to be converted into a feasible one with the minimum processor speed α, such that the task set becomes schedulable at that speed.

The above maximization formulation allows the systems designer to find the optimal value for the task computation times c_i of a task τ_i within a flexible range, that is, $c_i^{\min} \leq c_i \leq c_i^{\max}$. Any other lower value can result in making the system underutilized, while a higher value can make the system infeasible. Adding α into the feasibility problem determines the lowest possible speed for the system to make it run at the lowest possible feasible speed, hence reducing the overall energy consumption of the system.

19.4 CONCLUSIONS

Real-time applications should remain predictable under all possible circumstances; they should always respect the timing constraints. In this chapter, sensitivity analysis is made for real-time systems and results are applied to sample task sets. It is shown how to use one inequality to express the single task schedulability constraint. The problem of determining the tasks execution times in the space of RM schedulability is solved using optimization techniques. It is concluded that, while designing real-time systems, the P-bound can be directly applied for higher system utilization.

ACKNOWLEDGMENTS

This work is supported by the grand project of the Institute of Software, Chinese Academy of Sciences no. yocx285056, and Higher Education Commission (HEC) of Pakistan under PPCR scheme.

REFERENCES

[1] A. Burns and A. Wellings, *Real-Time Systems and Programming Languages. Ada 95, Real-Time Java and Real-Time POSIX*, 3rd ed. Boston: Addison Wesley Longman, 2001.

[2] P. Puschner and C. Koza, "Calculating the maximum execution time of real-time programs," *Real-Time Systems*, 1(2):159–176, 1989.

[3] K. Ramamritham, "Where do time constraints come from and where do they go?" *International Journal of Database Management*, 7(2):4–10, 1996.

[4] S. Baruah, "Efficient computation of response time bounds for preemptive uniprocessor deadline monotonic scheduling," *Real-Time Systems*, 47(6):517–533, 2011.

[5] P.M. Colom, "Analysis and design of real-time control systems with varying control timing constraints." PhD Thesis, Automática e Informática Industrial, Barcelona, 2002.

[6] S.U. Khan, S. Zeadally, P. Bouvry, and N. Chilamkurti, "Green networks," *The Journal of Supercomputing*, forthcoming.

[7] J.W.S. Liu, *Real Time Systems*, 1st ed. Upper Saddle River, NJ: Prentice Hall, 2000.

[8] G.C. Buttazzo, "Rate monotonic vs. edf: Judgment day," *Real-Time Systems*, 29(1):5–26, 2005.

[9] H. Aydin, R.G. Melhem, D. Moss, and P. Meja-Alvarez, "Optimal reward-based scheduling for periodic real-time tasks," *IEEE Transactions on Computers*, 50(2):111–130, 2001.

[10] J. Leung and J. Whitehead, "On the complexity of fixed-priority scheduling of periodic," *Performance Evaluation*, 2:237–250, 1982.

[11] N. Min-Allah, X. Jiansheng, and Y. Wang, "Utilization bound for periodic task set with composite-deadline," *Journal of Computers and Electrical Engineering*, 36(6):1101–1109, 2010.

[12] N. Min-Allah, S.U. Khan, and Y. Wang, "Optimal task execution times for periodic tasks using nonlinear constrained optimization," *The Journal of Supercomputing*, 59(3):1120–1138, 2012.

[13] K. Seth, A. Anantaraman, F. Mueller, and E. Rotenberg, "Fast: Frequency-aware static timing analysis," *Proceedings of the 24th IEEE Real-Time Systems Symposium*, pp. 40–51, 2003.

[14] J. Lehoczky, L. Sha, and Y. Ding, "The rate monotonic scheduling algorithm: Exact characterization and average case behavior," in *Proceedings of the IEEE Real-Time System Symposium*, pp. 166–171, 1989.

[15] E. Bini and G.C. Buttazzo, "Schedulability analysis of periodic fixed priority systems," *IEEE Transactions on Computers*, 53(11):1462–1473, 2004.

[16] Y. Wang and D.M. Lane, "Solving a generalized constrained optimization problem with both logic and and or relationships by a mathematical transformation and its application to robot path planning," *IEEE Transactions on Systems, Man and Cybernetics, Part C: Application and Reviews*, 30(4):525–536, 2002.

[17] C.M. Krishna and K.G. Shin, *Real Time Systems*. New York: McGraw-Hill, 1997.

[18] W.K. Shih, J.W.S. Liu, and J.Y. Chung, "Algorithm for scheduing tasks to minimize total error," *SIAM Journal on Computing*, 20:537–552, 1991.

[19] J. Wegener and F. Mueller, "A comparison of static analysis and evolutionary testing for the verification of timing constraints," *Real-Time Systems*, 21(3):241–268, 2001.

20

Multilevel Exploration of the Optimization Landscape through Dynamical Fitness for Grid Scheduling

Joanna Kolodziej

20.1 INTRODUCTION

Highly parameterized modern computational grids (CGs) are composed of large numbers of virtually connected various devices such as computers and databases. These systems must provide a wide range of services and should not be limited to high-performance computing platforms [1]. Typical grid users in one node or network cluster might not be able to have control over other parts of the system. Various types of information and data processed in the large-scale dynamic environment may be incomplete, imprecise, fragmentary, or overloading. All of those aspects make the scheduling and resource management problems in CGs challenging issues. Depending on the restrictions imposed by the grid application, different access policies in different network clusters, and different users' requirements, the complexity of those problems can be determined by the number of objectives to be optimized (single vs. multiobjective), the type of the environment (static vs. dynamic), the

Scalable Computing and Communications: Theory and Practice, First Edition. Edited by
Samee U. Khan, Albert Y. Zomaya, and Lizhe Wang.
© 2013 John Wiley & Sons, Inc. Published 2013 by John Wiley & Sons, Inc.

processing mode (immediate vs. batch), task interrelations (independence vs. dependency), and so on.

Theoretical analysis of the optimization landscapes for many classical combinatorial problems, such as the *traveling salesman problem*, *graph bipartitioning*, and *flowshop* scheduling [2], may be defined as a background of formal models of the wider *NK* family of the optimization landscapes and may be used to better describe the distribution of solutions. The characteristics of the global search space depend on the resolution methods used for solving the problem. On the other hand, it allows the tuning of the configuration of the optimizers for a fair adaptation of their search mechanisms to the particular instance of the problem. However, in grid scheduling, such modeling is much more complicated, mainly because of different local scheduling policies and the system dynamics [3]. Simple optimization models and methods usually fail in the case of dynamic large-scale systems.

Most of the available metaheuristic algorithms attempt to find an optimal solution with respect to a specific fixed fitness measure [4]. In the case of evolutionary algorithms (EAs) a great deal of effort has gone into designing efficient representation schemes and genetic operators so as to produce rapid convergence to a good solution [5]. The rapid decrease in diversity of the population results in a highly fit but homogeneous population. Such algorithms cannot perform well in most of the dynamic environments. Two major challenges to the use of evolutionary-based techniques for solving dynamic optimization problems are (1) to generate and maintain sufficiently high diversity levels in the population and (2) to evolve robust solutions that track the optimal solutions identified during the process. Ideally, we want an adaptive algorithm that responds in an appropriate way every time a change in the environment occurs.

This chapter presents a comprehensive empirical analysis of the efficiency of three different methods of exploration of the fitness landscape for the independent batch scheduling problem in CG, namely, single-population genetic algorithm (GA), multipopulation hierarchic genetic scheduler (HGS-Sched), and a two-level hybrid of the genetic algorithm and tabu search (GA + TS) method. The general characteristics of the scheduling landscape with makespan and flowtime as two main scheduling criteria are followed by the empirical evaluation of the proposed schedulers in large-scale static and dynamic grid scenarios.

The implementation of the GA + TS hybrid grid scheduler presented in this chapter is based on the method proposed by Xhafa et al. [6]. In this model, GA plays the role of a steering module of the whole strategy and the tabu search (TS) algorithm is activated to replace the mutation operation. This hybridization method is a simple extension of the conventional hybridization technique for grid schedulers presented in Reference 7.

The HGS-Sched grid scheduler has been proposed by Kołodziej and Xhafa [8, 9] as an efficient alternative to single-population GA schedulers and island models. The general concept is based on the hierarchic genetic strategy (HGS) model [10] used for the combinatorial optimization. The main goal of this method is an effective hierarchical multilevel exploration of the search space by using the family of dependent genetic processes. The HGS method has been successfully applied in solving continuous global optimization problems with multimodal and weakly convex objective functions [11]. It was also used as an efficient method for permutation flowshop scheduling [12] as well as for solving some practical engineering problems [13].

The chapter presents the following three fundamental contributions:

- simple formal characteristics of the fitness landscape for the independent job scheduling problem in CG
- design of a few variants of GAs for combinatorial optimization and their implementation as evolutionary mechanisms in multilevel metaheuristic grid schedulers, namely, the HGS-Sched and a hybridization of the GA technique with tabu search metaheuristics (GA + TS), for effective exploration of the optimization landscape
- comprehensive empirical analysis of the schedulers' performance in static and dynamic four-grid scenarios by using the grid simulator.

The rest of the chapter is organized as follows. Section 20.2 defines an independent batch scheduling problem and briefly characterizes the hierarchical grid model. General characteristics of the fitness optimization landscape for a considered problem instance are presented in Section 20.3. Two multilevel grid schedulers are defined in Section 20.4. Section 20.5 presents a comprehensive empirical study of the single-population genetic scheduler, HGS-Sched, and GA + TS techniques are evaluated under the heterogeneity, the large-scale, and dynamic conditions using a HyperSim-G grid simulator. The chapter concludes with Section 20.6.

20.2 STATEMENT OF THE PROBLEM

The main aim of efficient scheduling in modern distributed computational environments is an efficient mapping of tasks to the set of available resources. The tasks and resources could be dynamically added to and dropped into and from the system. Scheduling in CG remains a challenging NP-complete global optimization problem due to the large-scale heterogeneous structure of the system and the coexistence of local geographically dispersed job managers and resource owners who usually work in different autonomous administrative domains.

A CG is usually modeled as a hierarchical multilevel and multilayer system [14]. The hierarchy usually consists of two or three levels, depending on the system knowledge, access to data and resources, and the organization of the scheduling process. The general concept of the multilevel hierarchical architecture of the grid cluster with intrasite, intersite, and global levels is presented in Figure 20.1.

It is assumed in this chapter that CGs' clusters are defined as three-level hierarchical systems. The architectural model of a cluster can be viewed as a compromise between centralized and decentralized task and resource management systems. There is a central metascheduler in each cluster, which interacts with local task dispatchers in order to define optimal schedules. The local brokers have limited knowledge of grid resources and cannot monitor the whole system. Their main duty is to collect information about the "execution capability" of the resource supplied by the resource owners. They moderate this information and send it to the scheduler. The tasks–machine planning results are sent back from the metascheduler to the brokers for the resource allocation. The metaschedulers in different clusters can communicate with each other through the Internet or other wired or wireless wide

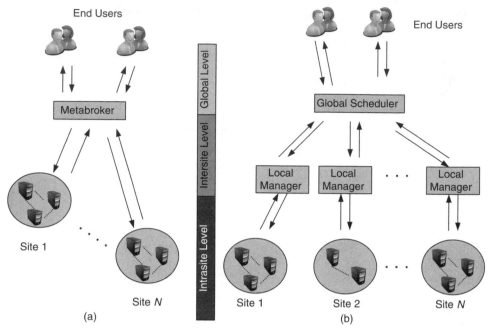

FIGURE 20.1. *Two-level (a) and three-level (b) hierarchical architectures of the cluster in a computational grid.*

area networks. The hierarchical grid model is well suited to capture the realistic administrative features of the grids, in which many complex scheduling criteria may be considered.

Different types of scheduling problems in grids are generated by the various configurations of the main scheduling attributes, where the system architecture, task processing policy, and interrelations among tasks in the users' applications are the major characteristics [7, 9]. This chapter addresses an independent grid job scheduling, where tasks are executed independently of each other and are processed in the batch mode. This means that the whole batch is scheduled as a group of tasks. The problem is formalized by using an expected time to compute (ETC) matrix model [15]. Let us denote by n a number of tasks in the batch and by m a number of machines available in the system. An instance of the problem in this model is defined by the following set of the input data:

- a *workload vector* for tasks in the batch, $W = [w_1, \ldots, w_n]$, where w_j denotes the computational load of the task j expressed as a number of computational cycles needed for completion of this task
- a vector of *speed parameters* for the machines, $S = [s_1, \ldots, s_m]$, in which s_i denotes the frequency of machine i defined as the number of computational cycles per time unit (second)
- a *ready times* vector, ready times = $[\text{ready}_1, \ldots, \text{ready}_m]$, where ready_i is the time needed for reloading the machine m_i after finishing the last assigned task to make this machine ready for the further assignments

- an *expected time to compute (ETC)* matrix, ETC = $[ETC[j][i]]_{n \times m}$, of expected (estimated) times of the tasks on machines calculated for all possible *task–machine* pairs.

In the simplest case, the elements of the ETC matrix can be computed by dividing the workload by computational load for each task–machine pair, that is, $ETC[j][i] = w_j/s_i$.

Tasks in this model may be considered as monolithic applications or metatasks with no dependencies among the components. The workloads of tasks can be estimated based on specifications provided by the users or on historical data, or can be obtained from system predictions [16]. The term "machine" refers to a single or multiprocessor computing unit or even to a local small-area network.

20.3 GENERAL CHARACTERISTICS OF THE OPTIMIZATION LANDSCAPE

The theory of global optimization landscapes is needed for better understanding of the problems and the improvement of the performance of the search algorithms [2]. A *fitness landscape* can be formally defined as the following triplet:

$$(X, N, f), \tag{20.1}$$

where X represents the search space, N denotes a neighborhood operator, and f is a fitness function. It can be represented by a labeled graph, in which the vertices correspond to genotype solutions and edges connecting a pair of vertices indicate that each vertex is reachable from another with one application of the operator N. In the simplest case, the neighborhood of a given solution is generated based on an *adjacency* matrix defined for the landscape graph.

In grid scheduling, the search space is determined by the permutations of tasks or machine labels, but the lengths of these permutation strings may vary because the numbers of tasks and/or machines in the system can change over time. Therefore, additional probability distributions should be specified for an estimation of actual states of the system. The following two sections define basic components of two variants of the scheduling landscapes for CG, namely, large-scale static and dynamic grid landscapes.

20.3.1 Schedule Representation

The search space in the grid scheduling optimization landscape is determined by the set of all possible schedules generated for a given batch of tasks and the set of machines available in the system. Let us denote by $N_l = \{1, \ldots, n\}$ and $M_l = \{1, \ldots, m\}$ the sets of task and machine labels, respectively. Let *Schedules* denote the set of all *permutations with repetitions* of the length n over the set of machine labels M_l.

A *schedule* $S \in Schedules$ is encoded by the following vector:

$$S = [i_1, \ldots, i_n]^T, \tag{20.2}$$

where $i_j \in M_l$ is the number of machines to which the task labeled by j is assigned. This encoding method is called a *direct representation* of the schedule S.

The lengths of the scheduling vectors are constant in the case of the static scheduling and can vary in the dynamic scenario. In the dynamic case, some additional probability distributions for modeling the changes of the system states (the changes in the numbers of tasks and machines) are needed. Therefore, the task labels $\tilde{N}_l$ in the dynamic scheduling are represented by the following set of parameters:

$$\tilde{N}_l = [\text{init}_t, \max_t, E(\text{inter}_t)], \tag{20.3}$$

where init_t is the initial number of tasks in the system, $\max_t$ is the maximal number of tasks in the system, and $E(\text{inter}_t)$ is the exponential probability distribution of the new tasks arrived to the system.

The machine labels $\tilde{M}_l$ in the dynamic scheduling are represented by the following parameters:

$$\tilde{M}_l = [\text{init}_m; \min_m; \max_m \, G(\text{add}_m)G(\text{del}_m)], \tag{20.4}$$

where init_m stands for the initial number of machines, $\min_m$ denotes the minimal number of machines, $\max_m$ denotes the maximal number of machines, $G(\text{add}_m)$ is the Gaussian probability distribution [17] of adding (arriving) the machines to the system, and $G(\text{del}_m)$ is the Gaussian probability distribution of removing machines from the system.

20.3.2 Scheduling Criteria

The grid scheduling problem is usually considered as the multiobjective optimization problem with numerous scheduling criteria and the scheduling objective functions [18]. The are two basic models used in grid multiobjective optimization: hierarchical and simultaneous modes. In the *simultaneous mode*, all scheduling criteria are optimized simultaneously. In the *hierarchical* case, different scheduling criteria are sorted a priori according to their importance in the model. The process starts by optimizing the most important objective function. When further improvements are not possible, the second objective function is optimized and the values of the first objective function are kept at the optimal level. The method proceeds until all criteria are optimized. It is very hard in grid scheduling to define or efficiently approximate the Pareto front, especially in dynamic scheduling.[1] This set of Pareto optimal solutions may extend very fast together with the scale of the grid and the number of the submitted tasks. The specification of the structure of the Pareto front is also an open problem in grid scheduling. Due to the sheer size of the grid itself and the huge number of possible schedulers even for a small amount of tasks, an effective and fast exploration of the search space for the problem is very difficult.

In this chapter, grid scheduling is defined as a bi-objective optimization problem with makespan and flowtime as the main criteria.

20.3.2.1 Calculation of the Makespan
Makespan is expressed as a finishing time of the latest task. It can be formally defined as follows:

---

[1]A solution is Pareto optimal if it is not possible to improve a given objective function without deteriorating at least another one [18].

$$\text{Makespan} = \max_{j \in N} F_j, \tag{20.5}$$

where F_j denotes the time when task j is finalized.

Using the ETC matrix model, the makespan can be defined in terms of the completion times of the machines as the maximal completion time of the machines available for the batch of tasks. Let us denote by *completion* a vector of size m. The ith coordinate in this vector is denoted by completion[i] and indicates the total time needed for reloading the machine i after finalizing the previously assigned tasks and for completing the tasks actually scheduled to the machine. The completion[i] parameters can be calculated in the following way:

$$\text{completion}[i] = \text{ready}_i + \sum_{j \in T(i)} \text{ETC}[j][i], \tag{20.6}$$

where $T(i)$ is the set of tasks assigned to the machine i.

The makespan can be now expressed as follows:

$$\text{Makespan} = \max_{i \in M} \text{completion}[i]. \tag{20.7}$$

20.3.2.2 Calculation of the Flowtime The flowtime is expressed as the sum of finalization times of all the tasks. It can be defined in the following way:

$$\text{Flowtime} = \sum_{j \in N} F_j. \tag{20.8}$$

Flowtime is usually considered as a *quality of service (QoS)* criterion. In terms of the ETC matrix model, the flowtime objective function can be calculated as a workflow of the sequence of tasks on a given machine i, that is to say,

$$\text{Flowtime}[i] = \text{ready}_i + \sum_{j \in \text{sorted}[i]} \text{ETC}[j][i], \tag{20.9}$$

where sorted[i] denotes the set of tasks assigned to the machine i sorted in ascending order by the corresponding ETC values.

The cumulative flowtime in the whole system is defined as the sum of $F[i]$ parameters; that is,

$$\text{Flowtime} = \sum_{i \in M} F[i]. \tag{20.10}$$

Both makespan and flowtime are expressed in arbitrary time units. In fact, their values are in incomparable ranges: Flowtime has a higher magnitude order over makespan, and its values increase as more tasks and machines are considered. Therefore, in this approach, the mean_flowtime = flowtime/m function is implemented for the evaluation of the flowtime criterion.

20.3.2.3 Cumulative Objective Function The bi-objective scheduling problem is transformed into the mono-objective problem by aggregating the makespan and mean_flowtime functions into the following cumulative weight function:

$$\text{Fitness} = \lambda \cdot \text{makespan} + (1 - \lambda) \cdot \text{mean\_flowtime}. \tag{20.11}$$

The weight coordinate $\lambda \in (0, 1)$ is used, in fact, for the specification of the priorities of the considered scheduling criteria. It is assumed that $\lambda \neq 0$ and $\lambda \neq 1$. Based on the experimental tuning results presented in Reference 19, the following three values of the λ coefficient are considered in the empirical analysis presented in Section 20.5: (1) $\lambda = 0.25$, (2) $\lambda = 0.50$, and (3) $\lambda = 0.75$.

20.4   MULTILEVEL METAHEURISTIC SCHEDULERS

The general characteristics of a grid scheduling fitness landscape usually depend on the features of the resolution method defined for the considered scheduling model. This section presents the characteristics of a generic model of a single-population genetic scheduler, which can be used independently as the scheduling algorithm or can be integrated with the general frameworks of hierarchical or hybrid genetic strategies. The general concepts of two multilevel grid schedulers, namely, HGS-Sched and a combination of genetic algorithm and tabu search (GA + TS) metaheuristics, are presented in Sections 20.4.2 and 20.4.3.

20.4.1   Single-Population Genetic Schedulers

The general model of a single-population genetic scheduler is based on the framework of the GAs used in the combinatorial optimization [20]. This model is also used as a basic genetic engine in numerous multipopulation and multilevel genetic schedulers. The general framework of this engine is defined in Figure 20.2. This method was adapted to the grid scheduling problem through an implementation of specialized encoding methods and genetic operators.

Beyond the direct representation of the schedules, defined in Section 20.3.1, another encoding method, namely, the *permutation-based encoding* method, is needed for the implementation of the specialized genetic operators. In this method, each schedule is represented by the following pair of vectors:

Generate the initial population P^0 of size μ; $t=0$
Evaluate P^0;
   while {not termination-condition} **do**
       Select the parental pool T^t of size λ; $T^t := Select(P^t)$;
       Perform crossover procedure on pars of individuals in T^t with probability p_c;
                                      $P_c^t := Cross(T^t)$;
       Mutate the individuals in P_c^t with probability p_m
                                      $P_m^t := Mutate(P_c^t)$;
       Evaluate P_m^t;
       Create a new population P^{t+1} of size μ from individuals in P^t and P_m^t
                               $P^{t+1} := Replace(P^t; P_m^t)$;
       $t:=t+1$;
   end while
 return Best found individual as solution;

FIGURE 20.2. *The general framework of the single-population genetic grid schedulers.*

$$x = (u; v), u = [u_i, \ldots, u_n]^T, v = [v_1, \ldots, v_m]^T, \qquad (20.12)$$

where $u_i \in N_l$, $v_j = 1, \ldots, n$.

Vector u defines a permutation of task labels. It can be interpreted as a concatenation of the sequences of tasks assigned to particular machines. The tasks in these sequences are increasingly sorted with respect to their completion times. Information about the number of tasks mapped to each machine is encoded by vector v.

An initial population in GA defined in Figure 20.2 is generated by using the MCT + LJFR-SJFR method, in which all but two individuals are generated randomly. Those two individuals are created by using the *longest job to fastest resource–shortest job to fastest resource (LJFR-SJFR)* and *minimum completion time (MCT)* heuristics [21]. In the LJFR-SJFR method, initially the number of m tasks with the highest workload is assigned to the available m machines sorted under the computing capacity criterion. Then, the remaining unassigned tasks are allocated in the fastest available machines. In the MCT heuristics, a given task is assigned to the machine yielding the earliest completion time.

The following genetic operators have been implemented in the main loop of the GA presented in Figure 20.2:

- *Selection Operators.* Linear ranking
- *Crossover Operators.* Partially mapped crossover (PMX), cycle crossover (CX)
- *Mutation Operators.* Move, swap
- *Replacement Operators.* Steady state, elitist generational.

All the above-mentioned operators are commonly used in the genetic metaheuristics dedicated to solving combinatorial optimization problems [22].

In the *linear ranking* method, a selection probability for each individual in a population is proportional to the rank of the individual. The rank of the worst individual is defined as zero, while the best rank is defined as pop_size − 1, where pop_size is the size of the population.

In *partially mapped crossover (PMX)*, a segment of one parent chromosome is mapped to a segment of the other parent chromosome (corresponding positions) and the remaining genes are exchanged according to the mapping relationship. The main idea of the *CX* is that each task in a chromosome must occupy the same position so that only interchanges between alleles (positions) can be made. First, a cycle of alleles is identified. The crossover operator leaves the cycles unchanged, while the remaining segments of the parental strings are exchanged.

In the *move* mutation, a task is moved from one machine to another one. Although the task can be appropriately chosen, this mutation strategy tends to unbalance the number of jobs per machine. In the *swap* mutation, the number of tasks assigned to the given machine remains unchanged, but two tasks are swapped in two different machines.

The base population for a new GA loop may be defined by using the *elitist generational* replacement method, where a new population contains two best solutions from the old base population and the rest are the newly generated offsprings. A *steady-state strategy* is implemented as an alternate replacement technique. In this method, the set of the best offsprings replaces the worst solutions in the old base population.

20.4.2   Hybridization of the GA Scheduler with TS

One important feature of genetic-based metaheuristics is that they can be easily hybridized with another optimization method. There are two main aspects that should be taken into account in designing the effective hybrid models: (1) a selection criterion for hybrid components and (2) a hybridization level. The first issue refers to two different types of the optimization techniques that are hybridized, namely,

- *metaheuristic + metaheuristic*, where both combined methodologies are metaheuristics, and
- *metaheuristic + local search method*, where a metaheuristic is hybridized with a low-cost, deterministic, or stochastic local search algorithm.

The hybridization level issue refers to the methods of the implementation of the hybrid structure and the cooperation of the hybridized modules. The components in the combined algorithms may be *strongly coupled*, which means that the hybridized metaheuristics interchange their inner procedures. In the case of *loosely coupled* combination, the flow of each algorithm remains unchanged and both methods are executed one after another. One component in the hybrid structure can be selected as a *control strategy* and can play the role of the main unit in the system. The second method in such a system supports the main algorithm. Finally, all hybrid components can be executed sequentially or simultaneously.

In this work, the classical GA-based scheduler presented in the previous section has been combined with the TS method. TS is a metastrategy for guiding known heuristics to overcome local optimality (premature convergence) in global optimization [23]. It can be viewed as an iterative technique that explores the set of problem solutions by periodical "modification" of the set of solutions by using the neighbor solutions (located in the neighborhoods of the solutions from a given set) in order to improve the quality of the search procedure. The GA presented in Figure 20.2 is defined as the control metaheuristic, and the TS algorithm is implemented as a supporting metaheuristic to replace the mutation operation; that is, selection, crossover, and mutation in GA is replaced by selection, crossover, and TS procedures. Figure 20.3 depicts a general flow of the proposed GA + TS hybrid scheduler.

A generic pseudocode of the TS module is defined in Figure 20.4 [6].

The TS algorithm is activated for a population generated by the application of the crossover procedure in GA. The structure of this population is modified by the TS algorithm by replacing the current schedules by their better neighbor solutions if this replacement improves the fitness values of the solutions.

The important component of the TS method is a *historical memory* module, which consists of a *short-term memory* list with information on recently visited solutions and a *long-term memory* list for collecting the information gathered during the whole exploration process. The "movements" in these two lists cannot be activated, which means that their status is "tabu." Therefore, some *aspiration criteria* are needed for eliminating the tabu movements from the memory component. Additionally, some *local search* inner heuristics are needed for an exploration of a

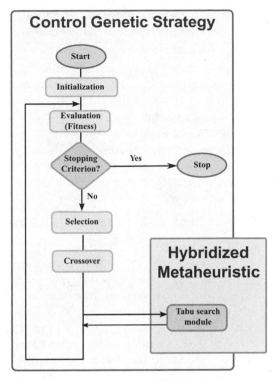

FIGURE 20.3. *Model of a hierarchic GA + TS grid scheduler.*

Read an initial solution **S** for TS generated as a result of crossover in GA ;
$\hat{S} \leftarrow S;$
Reset the ***tabu*** and ***aspiration*** conditions;
    while {not termination-condition} **do**
        Generate a subset of solutions ***N*(S)*** that do not violate the
        tabu conditions or hold the ***aspiration*** criteria;
        Choose the best ***S'***   ***N*(S)*** with respect to the GA-fitness function;
        S ← S';
        if improvement(S', Ŝ) then Ŝ ← S';
        if (intensification condition) then Perform intensification procedure;
        if (diversification condition) then Perform diversification procedures;
        end while
    return $\hat{S}$;

FIGURE 20.4. *A template of tabu search module in hybrid genetic grid schedulers.*

neighborhood of a given solution. The *intensification and diversification procedures* can be activated for the management of the exploration/exploitation trade-off in the global search.

In this chapter, the following configuration of the TS algorithm is specified:

- *Historical Memory.* Both short- and long-term memories are used. For the *recency* memory, a tabu list matrix $TL_{(n \times m)}$ is generated to maintain the tabu status. In addition, a tabu hash table (TH) is used in order to further filter the tabu solutions.

- *Neighborhood Exploration.* Steepest descent/mildest ascent method with *swap* moving strategy, which exchanges two tasks assigned to different machines [24].
- *Aspiration Criterium.* GA fitness function.
- *Intensification.* This procedure is executed for the detailed exploration of promising regions in the optimization landscape by rewarding (attributes of) the current solution. The structure of the neighborhood of a given solution is modified by performing all possible swap movements between two machines and just one transfer from one machine to the other [23].
- *Diversification.* A *soft* diversification method is realized by using a *penalization of ETC values* technique, and a *strong* diversification method is realized by random modifications in the assignments of a sufficient number of tasks.

20.4.3 Hierarchic Genetic Strategy Scheduler (HGS-Sched)

HGS-Sched [11] is a multilevel genetic-based global optimization technique that enables a concurrent search in the grid environment by the simultaneous execution of many dependent evolutionary processes. This dependency relation is modeled as the multilevel decision tree with a restricted number of levels. Figure 20.5 depicts a simple graphical representation of three levels of HGS-Sched.

Each active evolutionary process is interpreted as a branch in this structure. The root of the tree is created by the algorithm of the lowest accuracy, which governs the search process and is responsible for the detection of promising regions in the optimization domain. Thereafter, more accurate processes are activated in those

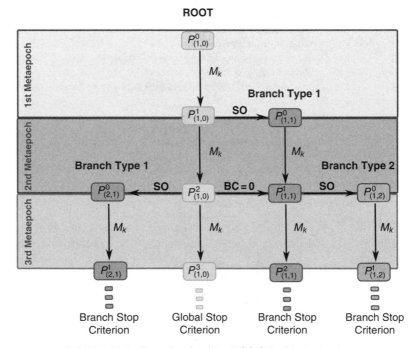

FIGURE 20.5. *Three levels of the HGS-Sched tree structure.*

regions. The accuracy of search in HGS-Sched branches is defined by a *degree* parameter with the lowest value, for example, 0, set for the root of the system.[2]

The hierarchical structure of the scheduler is updated periodically after the execution of *k*-generation evolutionary processes in each active branch. Such a process is called a *k-periodic metaepoch* M_k, $(k \in \mathbb{N})$ and is defined in the following way:

$$M_k(P^e_{(r,t)}) = (P^{e+1}_{(r,t)}, \hat{s}), \qquad (20.13)$$

where $\hat{s}$ is the best adapted individual in the metaepoch, $P^e_{(r,t)}$, $(t \in \{1, \dots, M\}, M \in \mathbb{N})$ denotes a population evolving in the branch of degree t, e is the global metaepoch counter, M is the maximal degree of a branch, and r is the number of branches of the same degree.

New branches of the higher degree are created by using a *sprouting operation* (SO) defined as follows:

$$SO(P^e_{(r,t)}) = (P^e_{(r,t)}, P^0_{(r',t+1)}), \qquad (20.14)$$

where $P^e_{(r,t)}$ is a parental branch and $P^0_{(r+1,t+1)}$ denotes an initial population for a new branch of degree $(t + 1)$. Individuals to this population are selected from an s_t-neighborhood $(1 \le s_t \le n)$ of the best adapted individual $\hat{s}$ in the parental population $P^e_{(r,t)}$. This neighborhood is created by all possible permutations or reassignments of tasks in $(n - s_t)$-length suffix of $\hat{s}$. The values of s_t parameters may be different in branches of the different degrees. In this work, the lengths of suffixes are calculated in the following way:

$$s_t = (\text{suf})^t \cdot n, \qquad (20.15)$$

where suf $\in [0, 1]$ is a global strategy parameter called a *neighborhood parameter* and t is the branch degree.

The sprouting operation is conditionally activated depending on the outcome of a *branch comparison* (BC) binary operator applied for parental and its all directly sprouted branches. It is used for the detection of "similarity" of the resulting populations in each parental-sprouted pair of branches. The outcome of the BC operator is 1 if the parental branch and its "descendant" (sprouted) branch operate in a similar region in the optimization landscape. In such a case, another metaepoch is executed in the parental branch without creating any new process. This technique is crucial in an effective management of the algorithm structure by preventing the activation of many similar processes in the same local region, which usually increase significantly the complexity of the whole strategy.

Similarity of populations can be estimated by using the hash technique to reduce the execution time of the BC procedure. The main procedure in the hash method is a hash table with the *task–resource allocation* key denoted by K. The value of this key is calculated as the sum of the absolute values of the subtraction of each position and its precedent in the s_t-length suffix in direct representation of the schedule

---

[2]The HGS-Sched framework may be used for the implementation of the single-population genetic algorithms and evolutionary strategies. In such a case, the tree is created by just one branch (root).

vector (reading the suffix in a circular way). The hash function f_{hash} is defined as follows:

$$f_{hash}(K) = \begin{cases} 0, & K < K_{min} \\ \left\lfloor N \cdot \left(\dfrac{K - K_{min}}{K_{max} - K_{min}} \right) \right\rfloor & K_{min} \leq K < K_{max}, \\ N-1, & K \geq K_{max} \end{cases} \qquad (20.16)$$

where K_{min} and K_{max}, respectively, correspond to the smallest and the largest value of K in the population and N is the population size.

In the case of the conditional sprouting of the new branches of the degree $(t + 1)$ from the parental branch of the degree t, the keys are calculated for the best individual in the parental branch and individuals in all populations in all active branches of the degree $(t + 1)$. If there is any individual in the higher-degree branches, for which the key matches the key of the best adapted individual in the parental branch, then the value of BC is 1 and no branch of the degree $(t + 1)$ is sprouted.

In the case of the comparison of the branches of the same degree t, all branches, in which there exists the individuals with the identical keys, have to be reduced and a single joint branch is created (the value of BC is 1). The individuals in this branch are selected from the "youngest" (in the sense of the population evolution) populations in all reduced branches.

20.5 EMPIRICAL ANALYSIS

All considered metaheuristics have been integrated with a discrete event-based HyperSim-G [25] grid simulator for the purpose of the empirical comparative evaluation of the performance of single- and multilevel genetic schedulers. Based on the idea of the ETC matrix model presented in Section 20.2, the simulator creates an instance of the scheduling problem by using the following input data: (1) workload vector of tasks, (2) computing capacity of machines, (3) prior load of machines, and (4) the ETC matrix. The defined instance is passed on to the scheduler's module, which computes or estimates the optimal solutions of the scheduling problem. Finally, the scheduler sends back the information about planned assignment of tasks to the simulator, which provides the resource allocation.

The instances generated by the simulator are divided into static and dynamic grid scheduling benchmarks. In the static case, the number of tasks and the number of machines remain constant during the simulation, while in the dynamic case, both parameters may vary over time. In both static and dynamic cases, four grid size scenarios are considered: (1) "small" (32 hosts/512 tasks), (2) "medium" (64 hosts/1024 tasks), (3) "large" (128 hosts/2048 tasks), and (4) "very large" (256 hosts/4096 tasks).

The simulator is highly parameterized in order to reflect the realistic grid scenarios. The main parameters are defined as follows:

- *Number of Hosts.* Number of resources in the environment
- *Cycles.* Normal distribution modeling computing capacity of resources

TABLE 20.1. Values of Key Parameters of the Grid Simulator in Static and Dynamic Cases

	Small	Medium	Large	Very Large
Static case				
Number of hosts	32	64	128	256
Resource cap. (in MHz CPU)	N (5,000, 875)			
Total number of tasks	512	1,024	2,048	4,096
Workload of tasks	N (250,000,000, 43,750,000)			
Dynamic case				
$init_m$	32	64	128	256
max_m	37	70	135	264
min_m	27	58	121	248
Resource cap. (in MHz CPU)	N (5,000, 875)			
G (add_m)	N (625,000, 93,750)	N (562,500, 84,375)	N (500,000, 75,000)	N (437,500, 65,625)
G (del_m)	N (625,000, 9,375)			
max_t	512	1,024	2,048	4,096
$init_t$	384	768	1,536	3,072
Workload	N (250,000,000, 43,750,000)			
E ($inter_t$)	E (7,812.5)	E (3,906.25)	E (1,953.125)	E (976.5625)

- *Total Tasks.* Number of tasks to be scheduled
- *Workload.* Normal distribution modeling the workload of tasks
- *Host Selection.* Selection policy of resources (*all* means that all resources of the system are selected for scheduling purposes)
- *Task Selection.* Selection policy of tasks (*all* means that all tasks in the system must be scheduled)
- *Number of Runs.* Number of simulations done with the same parameters. Reported results are then averaged over this number.

Table 20.1 presents the key input parameters of the simulator in static and dynamic cases.[3]

All experiments in this section are scheduled as follows. In the first part of the analysis are eight possible variants of the standard GA-based schedulers defined in Section 20.4.1 with different crossover, mutation, and replacement operators in order to compose an optimal combination of genetic operations. This tuning of the main operators in GA is necessary for the design of the efficient genetic engine in both proposed multilevel schedulers—HGS-Sched and GA + TS hybrid algorithms. The experimental comparative evaluation of these methods and simple statistical analysis of the results are performed as the main part of the multilevel exploration of the grid scheduling landscape.

20.5.1 Tuning of the GA Engine

The analysis starts with tuning the genetic operations in single-population GAs and the weight coordinates in the fitness function defined in Equation (20.11). The

---

[3]See Section 20.3.1. The notations N (a, b) and E (c, d) are used for Gaussian and exponential probability distributions.

TABLE 20.2. Eight Variants of GA-Based Grid Schedulers

Scheduler	Crossover Method	Mutation Method	Replacement Method
GA-PMX-M-SS	Partially mapped (PMX)	Move	Steady state
GA-PMX-M-EG	Partially mapped (PMX)	Move	Elitist generational
GA-PMX-S-SS	Partially mapped (PMX)	Swap	Steady state
GA-PMX-S-EG	Partially mapped (PMX)	Swap	Elitist generational
GA-CX-M-SS	Cycle (CX)	Move	Steady state
GA-CX-M-EG	Cycle (CX)	Move	Elitist generational
GA-CX-S-SS	Cycle (CX)	Swap	Steady state
GA-CX-S-EG	Cycle (CX)	Swap	Elitist generational

TABLE 20.3. GA Setting for Large Static and Dynamic Benchmarks

Parameter	Elitist Generational	Steady State
Evolution steps	$5 \times n$	$20 \times n$
Population size (pop_size)	$\lceil (\log_2 n^2) - \log_2 n \rfloor$	$4 \times \log_2 n - 1$
Intermediate population	pop_size $- 2$	(pop_size)/3
Cross probability	0.8	1.0
Mutation probability	0.2	
Initialization	LJFR-SJFR + MCT + random	
max_time_to_spend	25 seconds (static)/40 seconds (dynamic)	

configurations of the genetic operators for eight variants of single-population GAs are presented in Table 20.2.

The values of key parameters for each scheduler are presented in Table 20.3.

Eight GA metaheuristics were evaluated in static and dynamic grid environments. Each experiment was repeated 30 times under the same configuration of operators and parameters. Tables 20.4–20.6 present the average fitness values achieved by all schedulers for the following weight parameters (see Equation 20.11): $\lambda = 0.25$, $\lambda = 0.50$, and $\lambda = 0.75$. All results are expressed in arbitrary time units (not necessary milliseconds or seconds).

The best results in the fitness minimization achieved by all considered metaheuristics are observed in the case of $\lambda = 0.75$. It means that makespan is defined as the dominant scheduling criteria. The fitness function is defined as follows (see Equation 20.11):

$$\text{Fitness} = 0.75 \times \text{makespan} + 0.25 \times \text{flowtime}. \qquad (20.17)$$

The weight coordinate in the fitness function is three times higher for makespan than for flowtime.

It follows from the results presented in Table 20.6 that the algorithms with the *steady-state* replacement mechanism are three times more effective in the makespan minimization than the other schedulers. Particularly in the dynamic case, the combination of steady-state replacement with CX crossover and swap mutation seems to be an optimal configuration for a genetic makespan optimizer.

In the case of the flowtime optimization, the GA-CX-S-SS algorithm outperforms the other techniques in dynamic scheduling, which is the most realistic scenario in grid computing.

TABLE 20.4. Average Fitness Values for $\lambda = 0.25$, [±SD]

Strategy	Small	Medium	Large	Very Large
Static instances				
GA-PMX-M-SS	5,154,060.347	5,308,229.558	5,416,429.379	5,485,311.493
	[±979,375.185]	[±504,243.294]	[±340,018.388]	[±459,027.474]
GA-PMX-M-EG	5,348,542.621	5,344,447.165	5,516,015.978	5,553,430.445
	[±585,654.925]	[±966,332.379]	[±695,133.702]	[±466,800.814]
GA-PMX-S-SS	5,125,732.310	5,269,785.619	537,932.151	5,347,571.524
	[±774,027.402]	[±573,973.508]	[±796,644.646]	[±505,652.631]
GA-PMX-S-EG	5,121,314.617	5,251,962.018	5,330,732.431	5,583,922.019
	[±409,787.452]	[±573,439.547]	[±702,880.553]	[±796,885.939]
GA-CX-M-SS	517,697.716	5,246,603.051	5,322,601.221	5,403,400.886
	[±593,094.022]	[±749,699.472]	[±285,542.708]	[±488,100.246]
GA-CX-M-EG	5,123,932.003	5,217,076.642	5,227,897.326	5,253,444.811
	[±535,413.928]	[±825,496.556]	[±648,283.928]	[±665,857.645]
GA-CX-S-SS	**5,092,261.426**	5,198,054.817	5,206,808.308	**5,219,877.832**
	[±622,042.407]	[±885,930.555]	[±772,579.871]	**[±794,577.409]**
GA-CX-S-EG	5,174,765.888	**5,168,779.460**	**5,185,522.431**	528,113.559
	[±800,173.505]	**[±501,796.002]**	**[±818,986.790]**	[±490,065.458]
Dynamic instances				
GA-PMX-M-SS	5,297,585.495	5,353,319.453	5,465,324.682	5,482,288.731
	[±570,835.666]	[±427,463.984]	[±741,772.927]	[±834,299.621]
GA-PMX-M-EG	5,224,706.894	5,289,996.755	5,354,293.111	5,429,089.884
	[±686,317.207]	[±738,507.021]	[±614,051.452]	[±532,269.350]
GA-PMX-S-SS	5,223,908.150	5,251,685.728	5,317,259.530	5,381,923.449
	[±817,573.231]	[±992,063.052]	[±653,862.043]	[±555,347.563]
GA-PMX-S-EG	5,257,442.590	5,264,926.162	5,302,456.945	5,349,500.682
	[±614,152.634]	[±537,188.614]	[±982,161.014]	[±735,170.095]
GA-CX-M-SS	5,142,025.087	5,231,500.041	5,316,620.416	5,363,494.607
	[±844,860.522]	[±416,003.564]	[±900,112.544]	[±798,094.918]
GA-CX-M-EG	51,066,958.016	5,146,163.005	51,714,227.396	5,273,338.541
	[±840,447.516]	[±958,141.791]	[±481,418.062]	[±773,181.436]
GA-CX-S-SS	5,049,312.388	**5,066,443.604**	**5,150,740.901**	**5,205,488.874**
	[±770,060.925]	**[±473,368.574]**	**[±707,608.136]**	**[±559,398.723]**
GA-CX-S-EG	**5,014,086.668**	5,113,140.731	5,218,301.251	5,242,843.678
	[±424,884.351]	[±699,161.584]	[±957,789.303]	[±618,250.154]

SD, standard deviation.

Based on the fitness results, the GA-CX-S-SS algorithm is selected as the most effective single-population scheduler, and it is implemented as the genetic engine for the empirical analysis of multilevel grid scheduling presented in the following section.

20.5.2 Empirical Evaluation of Single-Population Scheduler, HGS-Sched, and GA + TS Hybrid Metaheuristic in Static and Dynamic Grid Environments

The objective of the study presented in this section is to verify and compare the efficiency of the best single-population genetic scheduler generated in the previous section, namely, GA-CX-S-SS, HGS-Sched, and GA + TS algorithms in the exploration of the complex grid scheduling landscape. The GA-CX-S-SS algorithm has also

TABLE 20.5. Average Fitness Values for $\lambda = 0.50$ [±SD]

Strategy	Small	Medium	Large	Very Large
Static instances				
GA-PMX-M-SS	4,706.275.554	4,724,224.238	5,066,931.489	5,070,970.902
	[±767,028.616]	[±510,414.940]	[±858,838.569]	[±467,570.399]
GA-PMX-M-EG	4,563,591.933	4,831,766.317	4,983,024.688	5,053,748.216
	[±564,325.786]	[±809,341.827]	[±167,929.710]	[±201,841.545]
GA-PMX-S-SS	4,554,005.283	4,989,861.536	5,006,590.001	5,119,415.784
	[±451,823.722]	[±850,971.742]	[±960,641.531]	[±852,622.759]
GA-PMX-S-EG	4,510,814.823	4,927,869.118	4,997,453.728	5,078,419.792
	[±507,254.100]	[±517,898.586]	[±448,687.862]	[±786,058.958]
GA-CX-M-SS	4,499,965.044	4,661,810.366	4,694,202.862	4,737,662.444
	[±447,489,290]	[±766,372.698]	[±599,093.553]	[±930,932.647]
GA-CX-M-EG	4,430,124.465	453,318.590	4,836,633.782	4,910,668.019
	[±751,391.220]	[±258,467.909]	[±842,763.449]	[±614,756.165]
GA-CX-S-SS	**4,355,170.118**	**4,436,603.728**	**4,460,115.540**	4,681,919.035
	[±369,091.033]	**[±728,998.709]**	**[±551,199.151]**	[±944,578.947]
GA-CX-S-EG	4,358,903.160	4,478,221.567	4,534,292.778	**4,561,206.249**
	[±994,943.055]	[±777,353.688]	[±767,253.226]	**[±137,925.791]**
Dynamic instances				
GA-PMX-M-SS	4,796,926.963	4,802,112.844	5,106,759.203	5,161,769.975
	[±366,158.095]	[±794,906.206]	[±542,190.516]	[±535,363.348]
GA-PMX-M-EG	4,688,478.187	4,805,932.271	4,997,421.335	5,015,052.743
	[±847,670.666]	[±677,829.836]	[±522,007.108]	[±862,139.403]
GA-PMX-S-SS	4,771,581.749	4,747,776.689	4,929,758.195	4,937,424.772
	[±615,321.008]	[±809,463.665]	[±852,771.647]	[±920,649.002]
GA-PMX-S-EG	4,677,453.469	4,823,078.416	4,931,940.900	5,022,202.409
	[±458,942.335]	[±567,979.680]	[±906,896.109]	[±863,034.530]
GA-CX-M-SS	4,571,787.503	4,760,677.987	4,838,578.667	4,880,468.046
	[±807,537.211]	[±867,918.725]	[±895,375.784]	[±674,284.274]
GA-CX-M-EG	4,413,368.225	4,595,047.783	4,918,451.116	4,920,265.074
	[±665,937.347]	[±988,515.979]	[±409,346.261]	[±693,110.648]
GA-CX-S-SS	4,274,848.934	**4,380,138.059**	**4,401,326.465**	4,686,204.418
	[±620,059.371]	**[±465.982.596]**	**[±875,794.740]**	[±952,478.455]
GA-CX-S-EG	**4,218,035.680**	4,434,272.607	4,510,008.945	**4,547,479.723**
	[±616,622.123]	[±246,334.660]	[±523,088.387]	**[±486,541.257]**

SD, standard deviation.

been implemented as the basic genetic mechanism in the multilevel metaheuristics. Tables 20.7 and 20.8 present the key parameters of HGS-Sched and GA + TS.

It is assumed that HGS-Sched tree is composed of the branches of degrees 0 and 1, and the search process in the sprouted branches is approximately two times slower than in the core (the mutation rate in the sprouted branches is just a half of the mutation rate in the core). Also, the populations in the sprouted branches are much smaller than a global population in the core of the tree, which is crucial in the efficient local exploration of the genetic optimization landscape. In the case of elitist-like replacement mechanisms, small populations can escape much faster from the basin of attractions of a local solution compared with the big sets of individuals.

In the TS algorithm, the size of the tabu hash table (TH) is set to 918,133, as it is recommended by Srivastava [26]. The maximum number of iterations a solution remains tabu (max_tabu_status) is generated uniformly from the interval $[m, 2 \cdot m]$

TABLE 20.6. Average Fitness Values for $\lambda = 0.75$ [±SD]

Strategy	Small	Medium	Large	Very Large
Static instances				
GA-PMX-M-SS	4,102,673.327	4,172,014.024	4,234,782.436	4,284,900.721
	[±758,130.079]	[±562,277.970]	[±546,155.847]	[±864,118.226]
GA-PMX-M-EG	4,108,242.873	4,200,135.827	4,216,981.012	4,286,359.298
	[±630,680.041]	[±473,615.448]	[±896,931.120]	[±361,796.005]
GA-PMX-S-SS	**3,983,722.422**	4,089,834.534	**4,082,903.467**	4,222,736.028
	[±647,076.091]	[±834,055.986]	[±736,168.357]	[±830,365.418]
GA-PMX-S-EG	4,071,018.744	4,197,551.633	4,201,359.893	4,245,643.075
	[±922,695.531]	[±562,246.868]	[±761,807.895]	[±462,697.755]
GA-CX-M-SS	4,007,867.000	4,155,408.001	4,194,538.827	4,334,402.774
	[±680,442.770]	[±933,354.640]	[±781,975.723]	[±993,902.120]
GA-CX-M-EG	4,067,320.903	4,164,339.982	4,210,330.342	4,193,769.532
	[±582,153.618]	[±949,208.701]	[±805,732.750]	[±680,531.412]
GA-CX-S-SS	3,983,847.672	**4,053,438.673**	4,099,672.240	**4,182,951.283**
	[±639,338.706]	**[±807,048.780]**	[±286,575.579]	**[±546,146.594]**
GA-CX-S-EG	3,992,183.019	4,125,293.387	4,103,277.276	4,197,426.188
	[±563,534.984]	[±773,176.641]	[±810,231.900]	[±473,879.361]
Dynamic instances				
GA-PMX-M-SS	4,183,064.389	4,326,544.500	4,342,342.027	4,511,579.014
	[±365,842.665]	[±920,352.622]	[±734,941.015]	[±409,339.539]
GA-PMX-M-EG	4,101,660.637	4,307,559.346	4,350,769.729	4,428,943.912
	[±750,403.950]	[±652,006.458]	[±856,329.110]	[±917,168.563]
GA-PMX-S-SS	4,196,676.780	4,338,808.678	4,344,756.208	4,402,796.820
	[±624,253.283]	[±587,156.508]	[±402,928.895]	[±675,273.683]
GA-PMX-S-EG	4,129,602.691	4,279,778.902	4,322,790.083	4,310,973.780
	[±449,942.230]	[±795,087.562]	[±440,732.887]	[±58,447.627]
GA-CX-M-SS	4,096,232.073	4,253,218.110	4,284,422.323	4,298,744.263
	[±416,890.727]	[±591,763.854]	[±766,418.443]	[±697,776.280]
GA-CX-M-EG	4,109,712.181	4,193,788.995	4,201,965.814	42,099,289.242
	[±471,475.653]	[±553,998.536]	[±627,325.354]	[±712,393.274]
GA-CX-S-SS	**3,986,872.198**	**4,072,483.354**	**4,174,651.986**	**4,169,893.365**
	[±801,362.797]	**[±570,158.644]**	**[±247,617.560]**	**[±660,815.632]**
GA-CX-S-EG	4,098,111.691	4,202,987.983	4,239,790.044	4,291,857.920
	[±272,055.161]	[±516,848.578]	[±739,747.307]	[±987,970.195]

SD, standard deviation.

TABLE 20.7. HGS-Sched Settings for Static and Dynamic Benchmarks

Parameter	
period_of_metaepoch	$20 \times n$
nb_of_metaepochs	10
Degrees of branches (t)	0 and 1
Population size in the root	$3 \times (\lceil 4 \times (\log_2 n - 1)/(11.8) \rceil)$
Population size in the sprouted branches (b_pop_size)	$(\lceil 4 \times (\log_2 n - 1)/(11.8) \rceil)$
Intermediate population in the root	$abs((r\_pop\_size)/3)$
Intermediate population in the sprouted branch	$abs((b\_pop\_size)/3)$
Cross probability	0.9
Mutation probability in the root	0.4
Mutation probability in the sprouted branches	0.2
max_time_to_spend	40 seconds (static)/70 seconds (dynamic)

TABLE 20.8. Parameterization of TS Algorithm

Parameter	
start_choice	Min-Min method
tabu_size	918,133
max_tabu_status	32
max_repetitions	69
nb_diversifications	8
nb_intensifications	8
nb_iterations	8,192
elite_size	30
aspiration_value	20
max_time_to_spend	100 seconds

(m—number of machines), and the maximum number of successive iterations without improvements of the current solution implying the activation of the intensification is fixed to $4\ln(n) \cdot \ln(n)$. The number of iterations of the diversification and the intensification procedures are set to $\log_2(n)$. Finally, 30 elite solutions are kept in each iteration, and the parameter (max_tabu_status/2) $- \log_2$(max_tabu_status) defines the minimum number of iterations after which the tabu movement can aspire. The algorithm runs for 100 seconds (a realistic runtime for scheduling tasks in grids).

Each experiment has been repeated 30 times under the same configuration of operators and parameters. The weight coordinate in the fitness function is $\lambda = 0.75$. The average makespan and flowtime values achieved by three genetic schedulers are presented in Figure 20.6.

It can be observed that the effectiveness of both schedulers in flowtime optimization is in the same range; the differences in the results are very minor. The analysis of the makespan reduction is much more interesting. The GA + TS hybrid scheduler is more efficient in the static case. It may stem from the fact that TS technique may be an appropriate methodology for an accurate exploration of the highly parametrized local static neighborhoods of the temporary solutions found by the genetic steering module. However, this technique may be sensitive on any modifications of the system state. The TS metaheuristic cannot guarantee a fast escape from a basin of attraction of already detected local optima in the case of appearance of new promising solutions. Therefore, in the dynamic scenario, the HGS-Sched algorithm seems to be better adapted for an exploration of new regions in the optimization landscape. Finally, we observed that both multilevel schedulers outperform the single-population GA-CX-S-SS scheduler in all considered instances.

20.5.2.1 Statistical Analysis of the Results The results presented in Figure 20.6 give us just a general information about the schedulers' performances. In order to make our comparison analysis more reliable, we calculated a *coefficient of variation* and performed *Student's t-test* for means for the verification of the statistical significance of the results.

20.5.2.2 Coefficient of Variation The coefficient of variation (CV) [17] is defined as the statistical measure of the dispersion of data around the average value.

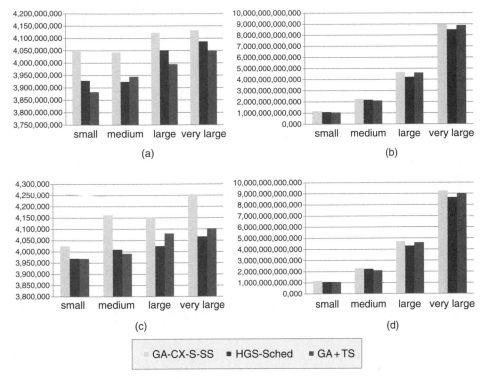

FIGURE 20.6. *Experimental results achieved by GA-CX-S-SS, HGS-Sched and GA + TS schedulers: in static case—(a) average makespan, (b) average flowtime; in dynamic case—(c) average makespan, (d) average flowtime.*

It expresses the variation of the data as a percentage of its mean value and is calculated as follows:

$$CV(x) = \frac{SD}{mean(x)} \cdot 100\%. \tag{20.18}$$

CVs calculated for stable heuristic methods should not be greater than 5%. Table 20.9 presents the coefficients of variation calculated for all makespan and flowtime results achieved by GA-CX-S-SS, HGS-Sched, and GA + TS schedulers.

It can be observed that, in all instances, the values of CVs for HGS-Sched and GA + TS algorithms are in the range 0–3.2%, which confirms the stability of those metaheuristics. The values of CVs calculated for GA-CX-S-SS algorithms are in [5.87; 13.08], which shows the low stability of this scheduler.

20.5.2.3 *Student's* t-*Test for Means*   A simple comparison of the averaged values of the scheduling objective functions and the standard deviations is usually insufficient to measure the relative performance of the schedulers. Therefore, the standard Student's t-test for the comparison of two means [17] was used for the verification of statistical significance of all empirical results of minimization of makespan and flowtime. The result of this test is the acceptance or rejection of the

TABLE 20.9. Comparison of the Coefficients of Variation (CV) for Makespan and Flowtime Values in the Large Size Static and Dynamic Instances (All Values in %)

	Makespan				Flowtime			
Strategy	Small	Medium	Large	Very Large	Small	Medium	Large	Very Large
Static instances								
GA-CX-S-SS	5.98	7.16	6.03	5.87	8.75	7.33	8.08	7.94
HGS-Sched	1.95	1.25	2.04	1.98	1.86	1.25	1.02	0.65
GA + TS	1.80	1.44	1.62	1.49	1.87	1.24	1.02	0.64
Dynamic instances								
GA-CX-S-SS	11.10	12.93	12.60	11.99	12.77	13.08	12.55	12.16
HGS-Sched	2.16	2.03	1.60	0.47	1.86	1.28	1.23	0.68
GA + TS	2.13	2.31	1.92	1.19	1.87	0.98	1.23	0.66

TABLE 20.10. Comparison of the Two-Tailed p-Values for Makespan and Flowtime Results in the Large Size Static and Dynamic Instances

	Makespan				Flowtime			
Strategy	Small	Medium	Large	Very Large	Small	Medium	Large	Very Large
Static instances								
GA-CX-S-SS	0.194	0.099	0.143	0.225	0.202	0.115	0.074	0.228
HGS-Sched	0.069	1.0	0.126	0.178	0.016	0.028	1.0	1.0
GA + TS	1.0	0.101	1.0	1.0	1.0	1.0	0.199	0.215
Dynamic instances								
GA-CX-S-SS	0.094	0.139	0.147	0.211	0.210	0.194	0.195	0.212
HGS-Sched	1.0	0.065	1.0	1.0	0.0005	0.097	1.0	1.0
GA + TS	<0.001	1.0	0.357	0.185	1	1.0	0.198	1.03

null hypothesis ($H0$), which states that any differences in results are purely random. An erroneous rejection of the null hypothesis defines a *type 1* error.

The best achieved makespan and flowtime values in each problem instance have been defined as the reference values in the verification of the "null" hypothesis, and the confidence level was 95% in each instance of the t-test.

Table 20.10 shows the probabilities of type 1 errors (p-values) [17]. The difference in results is not statistically significant if the p-value is not greater than 0.05 (p-value is 1 for the base (best) results to which the remaining results are referred).

In the static instances, HGS-Sched is better than GA + TS hybrid in the case of medium grid size for makespan, and large and very large grids for flowtime. The differences in results achieved by two multilevel metaheuristics in all instances but large and very large grids for flowtime are statistically significant, which means that in the static scenario, HGS-Sched is more effective in flowtime reduction, while GA + TS outperforms the hierarchical algorithm in the makespan minimization. The situation is different in the dynamic scenario, where the higher effectiveness of HGS-Sched is demonstrated in all but the medium grid case. In all cases, the results achieved by the single-population algorithm are significantly worse than the results generated by the two multilevel schedulers.

20.6 CONCLUSIONS

This chapter presents the empirical analysis of three different techniques of exploration of the bi-objective fitness landscape for independent grid scheduling. The first methodology is based on the hybrid two-level search of GA and TS algorithms. GA plays a role in the control strategy, while TS in the subordinated module is responsible for the accurate exploration of the neighborhoods of suboptimal schedulers detected by GA. The results of experiments show the high effectiveness of this metaheuristic in static scheduling. Indeed, the TS component is successful in the fast reduction of the main objective (makespan). It can also distinguish the similar (optimal) solutions distributed in the small narrow regions of the search space. On the other hand, the major drawback of this method may be the low resistance to the system dynamics. In such cases, the hierarchical genetic strategy outperforms the other similar approaches. Both multilevel metaheuristics achieved better results that single-population schedulers. It seems that local search in some promising regions in the optimization landscape or concurrent exploration of this landscape by many dependent genetic processes with various accuracy of search is more effective in the large-scale dynamic combinatorial optimization than conventional genetic methodologies.

Similar to the classical combinatorial optimization, even a simple theoretical analysis of the scheduling landscapes in CGs may be a strong support to the design of the scalable grid schedulers that can be easily adapted to actual system states. This research area is still very superficially explored, and each progress in the landscape characteristics may be the hottest research issue in future generation grid and cloud computing.

REFERENCES

[1] E.-G. Talbi and A.Y. Zomaya, *Grids for Bioinformatics and Computational Biology*. Hoboken, NJ: John Wiley & Sons, 2007.

[2] P. Stadler, Towards a theory of landscapes in *Complex Systems and Binary Networks* (R. Lopéz-Peña et al., ed.), *Lecture Notes in Physics*, Berlin: Springer Verlag, pp. 77–163, 1995.

[3] M. Maheswaran, S. Ali, H.J. Siegel, D. Hensgen, and R.F. Freund, "Dynamic mapping of a class of independent tasks onto heterogeneous computing systems," *Journal of Parallel and Distributed Computing*, 59:107–131, 1999.

[4] C.R. Reeves, "Landscapes, operators and heuristic search," *Annals of Operations Research*, 86:473–490, 1999.

[5] D. Whitley and S., Rana and R.B. Heckendorn"The island model genetic algorithm: On separability, population size and convergence," *Journal of Computing and Information Technology*, 7:33–47, 1998.

[6] F. Xhafa, J. Carretero, E. Alba, and B. Dorronsoro, "Tabu search algorithm for scheduling independent jobs in computational grids," *Computer and Informatics*, Special Issue on Intelligent Computational Methods, J. Burguillo-Rial, J. Kołodziej and L. Nolle, eds., 28(2):237–249, 2009.

[7] A. Abraham, R. Buyya, and B. Nath, "Nature's heuristics for scheduling jobs on computational grids," in *Proceedings of the 8th IEEE International Conference on Advanced Computing and Communications, India*, pp. 45–52, 2000.

[8] J. Kołodziej and F. Xhafa, "Meeting security and user behaviour requirements in grid scheduling," *Simulation Modelling Practice and Theory*, 19(1):213–226, 2011.

[9] J. Kołodziej and F. Xhafa, "Enhancing the genetic-based scheduling in computational grids by a structured hierarchical population," *Future Generation Computer Systems*, 27:1035–1046, 2011.

[10] J. Kołodziej, R. Gwizdała, and J. Wojtusiak, "Hierarchical genetic strategy as a method of improving search efficiency," in *Advances in Multi-Agent Systems* (R. Schaefer and S. Sedziwy, eds.), Cracow: UJ Press, pp. 149–161, 2001.

[11] R. Schaefer and J. Kołodziej, "Genetic search reinforced by the population hierarchy," in *FOGA VII, Morgan Kaufmann*, pp. 383–401, 2003.

[12] J. Kołodziej and M. Rybarski, An application of hierarchical genetic strategy in sequential scheduling of permutated independent jobs. in *Evolutionary Computation and Global Optimization* (J. Arabas ed.), Vol. 1. Warsaw: Warsaw University of Technology, Lectures on Eletronics, pp. 95–103, 2009.

[13] J. Kołodziej, W. Jakubiec, M. Starczak, and R. Schaefer, "Hierarchical genetic strategy applied to the problem of the coordinate measuring machine geometrical errors," in *Proceedings of the IUTAM '02 Symposium on Evolutionary Methods in Mechanics*, pp. 22–30, Cracow, Poland, Kluver Ac. Press, September 24–27, 2002, 2004.

[14] R. Buyya and K. Bubendorfer eds., *Market Oriented Grid and Utility Computing.* Hoboken, NJ: Wiley, 2009.

[15] S. Ali, H.J. Siegel, M. Maheswaran, S. Ali, and D. Hensgen, "Task execution time modeling for heterogeneous computing systems," in *Proceedings of the Workshop on Heterogeneous Computing*, pp. 185–199, 2000.

[16] S. Hotovy, "Workload evolution on the cornell theory center IBM SP2," in *Proceedings of the Workshop on Job Scheduling Strategies for Parallel, IPPS '96*, pp. 27–40, 1996.

[17] P.S. Mann, *Introductory Statistics*, 7th ed. Hoboken, NJ: Wiley, 2010.

[18] E.-G. Talbi, *Metaheuristics: From Design to Implementation.* Hoboken, NJ: John Wiley & Sons, 2009.

[19] F. Xhafa, E. Alba, B. Dorronsoro, and B. Duran, "Efficient batch job scheduling in grids using cellular memetic algorithms," *Journal of Mathematical Modelling and Algorithms*, 7(2):217–236, 2008.

[20] Z. Michalewicz, *Genetic Algorithms + Data Structures = Evolution Programs.* Berlin: Springer Verlag, 1992.

[21] F. Xhafa, J. Carretero, and A. Abraham, "Genetic algorithm based schedulers for grid computing systems," *International Journal of Innovative Computing, Information and Control*, 3(5):1053–1071, 2007.

[22] L. Davis, ed., *Handbook of Genetic Algoriithms.* New York: Van Nostrand Reinhold, 1991.

[23] F. Glover and M. Laguna, *Tabu Search.* Norwell, MA: Kluwer Academic Publishers, 1997.

[24] A. Thesen, "Design and evaluation of tabu search algorithms for multiprocessor scheduling," *Journal of Heuristics*, 4(2):141–160, 1998.

[25] F. Xhafa, J. Carretero, L. Barolli, and A. Durresi, "Requirements for an event-based simulation package for grid systems," *Journal of Interconnection Networks*, 8(2):163–178, 2007.

[26] B. Srivastava, "An affective heuristic for minimising makespan on unrelated parallel machines," *Journal of the Operational Research Society*, 49(8):886–894, 1998.

21

Implementing Pointer Jumping for Exact Inference on Many-Core Systems

Yinglong Xia, Nam Ma, and Viktor K. Prasanna

21.1 INTRODUCTION

Many recent parallel computing platforms install many-core processors or multiple multicore processors to deliver high performance. Such platforms are known as many-core systems, for example, the 24-core AMD Magny-Cours system, 32-core Intel Nehalem-EX system, 64-hardware-thread UltraSPARC T2 (Niagara 2) Sun Fire T2000 [1], and 80-core IBM Cyclops64 [2]. To accelerate the execution of applications in a many-core system, we must keep the cores busy. However, as the number of cores increases, a fundamental challenge in parallel computing is how to keep many cores busy, especially for applications with inherently sequential computation.

Pointer jumping is a parallel computing technique for exploring parallel activities from applications [3]. In this chapter, we especially consider applications offering limited parallelism. Such applications typically consist of a few long chains in their structures, where the computation along a chain must be performed sequentially. However, we can leverage pointer jumping to find more parallelism so that we can keep more cores busy simultaneously and therefore improve the overall performance.

Scalable Computing and Communications: Theory and Practice, First Edition. Edited by Samee U. Khan, Albert Y. Zomaya, and Lizhe Wang.
© 2013 John Wiley & Sons, Inc. Published 2013 by John Wiley & Sons, Inc.

We use a sample application called *exact inference* in junction trees to discuss the implementation of pointer jumping in many-core systems [4]. A *junction tree* is a probabilistic graphical model that can be used to model many real-world systems [5]. Each node in a junction tree is called a *clique*, consisting of a set of random variables. Each edge represents the shared variables between two adjacent cliques. *Inference* is the computation of the conditional probability of a set of random variables, given knowledge of another set of random variables. Existing parallel techniques for exact inference explore data parallelism and structural parallelism [6]. However, if a junction tree consists of only a few long chains, it is not straightforward to find enough parallelism for keeping all the cores busy in a many-core system.

In this chapter, we have the following contributions: (1) We adapt the pointer jumping for exact inference in junction trees. The proposed method is suitable for junction trees offering limited data parallelism and structural parallelism. (2) We analyze the impact of the number of cores on the speedup of the proposed method with respect to a serial algorithm. (3) We implement the proposed method using Pthreads on two state-of-the-art many-core systems. (4) We evaluate our implementation and compare it with our baseline method exploiting structural parallelism.

The rest of the chapter is organized as follows: In Section 21.2, we review pointer jumping and exact inference in junction trees. Section 21.3 discusses related work. Sections 21.4 and 21.5 present our proposed algorithm and its performance analysis. Section 21.6 discusses how to generalize the proposed work. We describe our implementation and experiments in Section 21.7 and then conclude the chapter in Section 21.8.

21.2   BACKGROUND

21.2.1   Pointer Jumping

Pointer jumping is a parallel technique used in computations with inherently sequential operations, such as finding the prefix sum for a list of data [3, 7]. Given a list of N elements, pointer jumping allows data transfer from each node to all of its successors in $\log N$ iterations, whereas the serial transfer takes $O(N)$ iterations. Figure 21.1 illustrates the iterations of pointer jumping on a list of N elements. Initially, only $\mathscr{A}_0$ has the updated data. Let $pa(\mathscr{A}_i)$ denote the parent of $\mathscr{A}_i$, that is, $\mathscr{A}_{i-1}$,

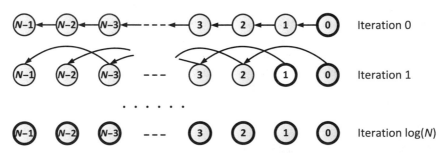

FIGURE 21.1. *Pointer jumping on a list.*

$0 < i \leq N - 1$. We propagate the data from $\mathscr{A}_0$ to the rest of the nodes as follows: In the first iteration, we transfer data from $pa(\mathscr{A}_i)$ to $\mathscr{A}_i$ for each $i \in \{1 \dots N\}$ in parallel. Then, for each node, we let the pointer to its parent jump to its grandparent, that is, letting $pa^2(\mathscr{A}_i) = pa(pa(\mathscr{A}_i))$. After log N iterations, all the elements complete transferring their data to their successors, as shown in Figure 21.1.

On the concurrent-read exclusive-write parallel random access machine (CREW-PRAM) [3] with P processors, $1 \leq P \leq N$, each element of the list is assigned to a processor. Note that the update operations are implicitly synchronized at the end of each pointer jumping iteration. Each iteration takes $O(N/P)$ time to complete $O(N)$ update operations. Thus, the pointer jumping-based algorithm runs in $O((N \cdot \log N)/P)$ time using a total number of $O(N \log N)$ update operations.

21.2.2 Exact Inference

A *Bayesian network* is a probabilistic graphical model that exploits conditional independence to compactly represent a joint distribution. Figure 21.2a shows a sample Bayesian network, where each node represents a random variable. Each edge indicates the probabilistic dependence between two random variables. The *evidence* in a Bayesian network is the set of instantiated variables. Exact inference in a Bayesian network is the computation of updating the conditional distribution of the random variables given the evidence.

Exact inference using Bayes' theorem fails for networks with undirected cycles [6]. Most methods convert a Bayesian network to a cycle-free hypergraph called a junction tree. We illustrate a junction tree converted from the Bayesian network in Figure 21.2. Each vertex in Figure 21.2b is called a clique, which contains multiple random variables from the Bayesian network. We use the following notations in this chapter. A junction tree is represented as $J = (\mathbb{T}, \hat{\mathbb{P}})$, where $\mathbb{T}$ represents a tree and $\hat{\mathbb{P}}$ denotes the parameters in the tree. Given adjacent cliques $\mathscr{C}_i$ and $\mathscr{C}_j$, the *separator* is defined as $\mathscr{C}_i \cap \mathscr{C}_j$. $\hat{\mathbb{P}}$ is a set of *potential tables*. The potential table of $\mathscr{C}_i$, denoted $\psi_{\mathscr{C}_i}$, can be viewed as the joint distribution of the random variables in $\mathscr{C}_i$. For a clique with w variables, each having r states, the number of entries in $\mathscr{C}_i$ is r^w [4].

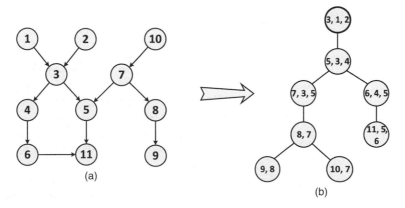

(a)

(b)

FIGURE 21.2. (a) A sample Bayesian network and (b) the corresponding junction tree.

In a junction tree, exact inference is performed as follows: Assuming evidence is $E = \{A_i = a\}$ and $A_i \in \mathscr{C}_\mathscr{Y}$, E is *absorbed* at $\mathscr{C}_\mathscr{Y}$ by instantiating the variable A_i and renormalizing the remaining variables of the clique. The evidence is then propagated from $\mathscr{C}_\mathscr{Y}$ to any adjacent cliques $\mathscr{C}_\mathscr{X}$. Let $\psi^*_\mathscr{Y}$ denote the potential table of $\mathscr{C}_\mathscr{Y}$ after E is absorbed, and $\psi_\mathscr{X}$ the potential table of $\mathscr{C}_\mathscr{X}$. Mathematically, *evidence propagation* is represented as [6]

$$\psi^*_\mathscr{S} = \sum_{\mathscr{Y} \backslash \mathscr{S}} \psi^*_\mathscr{Y}, \psi^*_\mathscr{X} = \psi_\mathscr{X} \cdot \frac{\psi^*_\mathscr{S}}{\psi_\mathscr{S}}, \tag{21.1}$$

where $\mathscr{S}$ is a separator between cliques $\mathscr{X}$ and $\mathscr{Y}$; $\psi_\mathscr{S} (\psi^*_\mathscr{S})$ denotes the original (updated) potential table of $\mathscr{S}$, $\psi^*_\mathscr{S}$ is the updated potential table of $\mathscr{C}_\mathscr{X}$. A junction tree is updated using the above evidence propagation in two phases, that is, *evidence collection* and *evidence distribution*. In evidence collection, evidence is propagated from the leaves to the root. A clique $\mathscr{C}$ is ready to propagate evidence to its parent when $\mathscr{C}$ has already been updated, that is, when all of the children of $\mathscr{C}$ have finished propagating evidence to $\mathscr{C}$. Evidence distribution is the same as collection, except that the evidence propagation direction is from the root to the leaves. The two phases ensure that evidence at any cliques can be propagated to all the other cliques [6].

21.3 RELATED WORK

There are several works on parallel exact inference. In Reference 8, the authors explore *structural parallelism* in exact inference by assigning independent cliques to separate processors for concurrent processing. In Reference 9, structural parallelism is explored by a dynamic task scheduling method, where the evidence propagation in each clique is viewed as a task. Unlike the above techniques, *data parallelism* in exact inference is explored in References 8, 10 and 11. Since these solutions partition potential tables and update each part in parallel, they are suitable for junction trees with large potential tables. If the input junction tree offers limited structural and data parallelism, the performance of the above solutions are adversely affected.

Pointer jumping has been used in many algorithms, such as list ranking, parallel prefix [3]. In Reference 12, the authors use pointer jumping to develop a new spanning tree algorithm for symmetric multiprocessors that achieves parallel speedups on arbitrary graphs. In Reference 5, the authors propose a pointer jumping-based method for exact inference in Bayesian networks. The method achieves logarithmic execution time regardless of structural or data parallelism in the networks. However, the method proposed in Reference 5 exhibits limited performance for multiple evidence inputs. In addition, no experimental study has been provided Reference 5. Our proposed algorithm combines the pointer jumping technique with Lauritzen and Spiegelhalter's two-phase algorithm, which is efficient for multiple evidence inputs.

21.4 POINTER JUMPING-BASED ALGORITHMS FOR SCHEDULING EXACT INFERENCE

21.4.1 Evidence Propagation in Chains

We formulate evidence propagation in a chain of N cliques as follows. Let clique $\mathscr{C}_i = \{S_{i+1,i}, V_i, S_{i-1,i}\}$, where separator $S_{i+1,i} = \mathscr{C}_{i+1} \cap \mathscr{C}_i$, $S_{i,i-1} = \mathscr{C}_i \cap \mathscr{C}_{i-1}$, and $V_i = \mathscr{C}_i \backslash \{S_{i+1,i} \cup S_{i,i-1}\}$, $0 < i < N$. For the sake of simplicity, we let $S_{0,-1} = S_{N,N-1} = \emptyset$ and joint probability $P(\mathscr{C}_i) = P(S_{i+1,i}, V_i, S_{i,i-1}) = \psi_{\mathscr{C}}$. We rewrite $P(\mathscr{C}_i)$ as a conditional distribution:

$$
\begin{aligned}
P(S_{i+1,i}, V_i | S_{i,i-1}) &= \frac{P(S_{i+1,i}, V_i, S_{i,i-1})}{P(S_{i,i-1})} \\
&= \frac{P(\mathscr{C}_i)}{\displaystyle\sum_{S_{i+1,i} \cup V_i} P(\mathscr{C}_i)}
\end{aligned}
\tag{21.2}
$$

$$
\begin{aligned}
P(S_{i+1,i} | S_{i,i-1}) &= \frac{\displaystyle\sum_{V_i} P(S_{i+1,i}, V_i, S_{i,i-1})}{P(S_{i,i-1})} \\
&= \sum_{V_i} \frac{P(\mathscr{C}_i)}{\displaystyle\sum_{S_{i+1,i} \cup V_i} P(\mathscr{C}_i)}.
\end{aligned}
\tag{21.3}
$$

Using Equations (21.2) and (21.3), in iteration 0, we propagate the evidence from $pa(\mathscr{C}_i)$ to $\mathscr{C}_i$ by

$$
P(S_{i+1,i}, V_i | S_{i-1,i-2}) = \sum_{S_{i,i-1}} P(S_{i+1,i}, V_i | S_{i,i-1}) P(S_{i,i-1} | S_{i-1,i-2})
\tag{21.4}
$$

$$
P(S_{i+1,i} | S_{i-1,i-2}) = \sum_{V_i} P(S_{i+1,i}, V_i | S_{i-1,i-2}).
\tag{21.5}
$$

In iteration k, we propagate evidence from $pa^{2^k}(\mathscr{C}_i)$ to $\mathscr{C}_i$ by

$$
\begin{aligned}
&P(S_{i+1,i}, V_i | S_{i-2^k, i-2^k-1}) \\
&= \sum_{S_{i-2^{k-1}, i-2^{k-1}-1}} P(S_{i+1,i}, V_i | S_{i-2^{k-1}, i-2^{k-1}-1}) P(S_{i-2^{k-1}, i-2^{k-1}-1} | S_{i-2^k, i-2^k-1})
\end{aligned}
\tag{21.6}
$$

$$
P(S_{i+1,i} | S_{i-2^k, i-2^k-1}) = \sum_{V_i} P(S_{i+1,i}, V_i | S_{i-2^k, i-2^k-1}).
\tag{21.7}
$$

Performing Equations (21.6) and (21.7) for each $k, 0 \le k \le \log N - 1$, we propagate the evidence from $\mathscr{C}_0$ to all the cliques in a chain of N cliques.

Input: Junction tree J with a height of H
Output: J with updated potential tables
  {evidence collection}

1: for $k = 0,1,\ldots, (\log H) - 1$ do
2:   for $C_i \in J$ pardo
3:     for all $\mathcal{C}_j \in ch^{2^k}(\mathcal{C}_i)$ do
4:       Propagate evidence from C_j to C_i according to Eqs. 1.6 and 1.7
5:     end for
6:   end for
7: end for
  {evidence distribution}
8: for $k = 0,1,\ldots, (\log H) - 1$ do
9:   for $C_i \in J$ pardo
10:     $\mathcal{C}_j \in pa^{2^k}(\mathcal{C}_i)$
11:     Propagate evidence from C_j to C_i according to Eqs. 1.6 and 1.7
12:   end for
13: end for

Algorithm 21.1   Pointer jumping based exact inference in a junction tree.

21.4.2 Pointer Jumping-Based Algorithm

Algorithm 21.1 shows exact inference in a junction tree using pointer jumping. Given a junction tree J, let $ch(\mathcal{C}_i)$ denote the *set* of children of $\mathcal{C}_i \in J$; that is, $ch(\mathcal{C}_i) = \{\mathcal{C}_j | pa(\mathcal{C}_j) = \mathcal{C}_i\}$. We define $ch^d(\mathcal{C}_i) = \{\mathcal{C}_j | pa^d(\mathcal{C}_j) = \mathcal{C}_i\}$ and $pa^d(\mathcal{C}_j) = pa(pa^{d-1}(\mathcal{C}_j)) = pa(\cdots(pa(\mathcal{C}_j)))$, where $d \geq 1$. We denote H as the height of J.

In Algorithm 21.1, lines 1–7 and 8–13 correspond to evidence collection and distribution, respectively. Lines 3 and 10 show how the pointer jumping technique is used in the algorithm. In each iteration, all the cliques can be updated independently. In evidence collection, a clique $\mathcal{C}_i$ in J is updated by performing evidence propagation from cliques in $ch^{2^k}(\mathcal{C}_i)$ at the kth iteration, $k = 0, \cdots, \log H - 1$. Similarly, in evidence distribution, a clique $\mathcal{C}_i$ is updated by performing evidence propagation from clique $pa^{2^k}(\mathcal{C}_i)$ at the kth iteration.

21.5 ANALYSIS WITH RESPECT TO MANY-CORE PROCESSORS

21.5.1 Complexity Analysis

We analyze Algorithm 21.1 using the CREW-PRAM model. Assume that P processors, $1 \leq P \leq N$, are employed. Let $W = \max_i\{W_i\}$, where W_i is the number of cliques at level i of the junction tree, $0 \leq i < H$. Assuming each evidence propagation takes unit time, updating a clique takes $O(W)$ time during evidence collection since the clique must be updated by sequentially performing $O(W)$ evidence propagations from its children. In contrast, updating a clique takes $O(1)$ time during evidence distribution since only one evidence propagation from its parent is needed. In each iteration, there are at most $O(N)$ clique updates performed by P processors. The algorithm performs $\log(H + 1)$ iterations for each evidence collection and distribution. Thus, the complexity of the algorithm is $O((W \cdot N \cdot \log(H + 1))/P)$ for evidence collection and $O((N \cdot \log(H + 1))/P)$ for evidence distribution. The overall complexity is $O((W \cdot N \cdot \log(H + 1))/P)$. The algorithm is attractive if the input junction tree offers limited structural parallelism. For example, for a chain of N cliques, we have $W = 1, H = N—1$; the complexity of the algorithm is $O((N \cdot \log N)/P)$.

Lemma 21.1 *Consider pointer jumping in a tree consisting of N nodes. If the height of the tree is H, then the number of cliques at any level is no more than $(N - H)$.*

Proof: We prove the lemma by contradiction. Assume there is a level denoted L has $(N - H + 1)$ cliques. Since the height of the tree is H, there are $(H + 1)$ cliques on the longest root–leaf path R. Since R must cross level L, one and only one clique at L belongs to R. Thus, the number of cliques in L and R is $(N - H + 1) + (H + 1) - 1 = N + 1 > N$. This contradicts with the fact that the tree consists of only N nodes. Therefore, the number of cliques at *any* level is less or equal to $(N - H)$.   ■

According to Lemma 21.1, we have $W \le N - H$. Thus, the complexity of Algorithm 21.1 is

$$O((N - H) \cdot N \cdot (\log(H + 1))/P). \qquad (21.8)$$

The complexity in Equation (21.8) implies that, whether Algorithm 21.1 is superior to the serial exact inference of complexity $O(N)$, it depends on the relationship between H, N, and P. We explain this observation by two cases:

Case 1: If the junction tree is a *chain*, that is, $H = N - 1$, according to Equation (21.8), we have $O((N - (N - 1)) \cdot N \cdot (\log((N - 1) + 1))/P) = O(N \cdot (\log N)/P)$. This is superior to the complexity of serial exact inference when $P > \log N$.

Case 2: If the junction trees is a star graph, that is, $D = 1$, according to Equation (21.8), we have $O((N - 1) \cdot N \cdot (\log(1 + 1))/P) = O(N^2/P)$. Since $1 \le P \le N$, Algorithm 21.1 is *not* superior to serial exact inference.

Thus, the effectiveness of Algorithm 21.1 is impacted by H, N, and P. We discuss the impact of H, N, and P on the speedup of Algorithm 21.1 with respect to serial exact inference in the following section.   ■

21.5.2 Speedup Discussion

Given the height H of a junction tree, we divide the tree into $(H + 1)$ levels L_0, $L_1, \ldots, L_H$, where L_0 are the leaves of the tree; L_{i+1} consists of the cliques with all children at level L_i or lower, and L_H consists of the root. If we view each level as a supernode, then we have a chain of supernodes. Performing Algorithm 21.1 on the junction tree is exactly *equivalent* to performing pointer jumping on the chain. Thus, without loss of generality, we discuss the speedup of Algorithm 21.1 with respect to a serial exact inference in a chain of cliques.

For the sake of simplicity, we let t denote the execution time for updating a clique. Thus, the sequential execution time for updating the chain, denoted t_s, is given by

$$t_s = (N-1) \cdot t. \tag{21.9}$$

Using pointer jumping, we update the chain in $\log N$ iterations. In the first iteration, each clique except $\mathscr{C}_0$ is updated in parallel. Thus, if we have P processors (we assume $P \leq N$), the parallel execution time is $(N-1) \cdot t/P$. In the second iteration, since both $\mathscr{C}_0$ and $\mathscr{C}_1$ have been updated, the parallel execution time is $(N-2) \cdot t/P$. Similarly, the parallel execution time for the jth iteration is $t_p^j = (N-2^{j-1}) \cdot t/P$. Therefore, the overall parallel execution time is given by

$$t_p = \sum_{j=1}^{\log N} t_p^j = \sum_{j=1}^{\log N} (N - 2^{j-1}) \cdot t/P$$
$$= (N \cdot \log N - N + 1) \cdot t/P. \tag{21.10}$$

According to Equations (21.9) and (21.10), the speedup is

$$Sp(N,P) = t_s/t_p = \frac{(N-1) \cdot P}{N \log N - N + 1} = \frac{(1 - 1/N) \cdot P}{\log N - 1 + 1/N}. \tag{21.11}$$

Lemma 21.2   *Given a platform of P cores and a chain of length N, Algorithm 21.1 leads to lower execution time than the serial exact inference if N is less than a threshold (i.e., 2^{P+1} for a chain of equal-size cliques); otherwise, the serial inference results in lower execution time.*

Proof: When $N \leq P$, we can only use N processors. Thus, we have $Sp(N,P) = (N^2 - N)/(N \log N - N + 1) \approx N/\log N$, which increases as N increases. When $N \geq P$, we have the following partial derivative less than 0:

$$\frac{\partial Sp(N,P)}{\partial N} = \frac{P \cdot (N \log N - N + 1) - P(N-1) \cdot \log N}{(N \log N - N + 1)^2}$$
$$= \frac{(\log N + 1) - N}{(N \log N - N + 1)^2/P} < 0. \tag{21.12}$$

Thus, $Sp(N, P)$ decreases monotonically as N increases when $N \geq P$. By letting Equation (21.11) equal to 1, we have $N \approx 2^{P+1}$. Thus, when $N > 2^{P+1}$, Algorithm 21.1 cannot outperform a serial exact inference. When $N \gg 2^{P+1}$, we have $\lim_{N \to \infty} Sp(N,P) = 0$. Thus, Algorithm 21.1 leads to lower execution time than the serial exact inference only when $1 \leq N \leq 2^{P+1}$. ∎

Therefore, we conclude that the number of cores in a many-core processor implies a range for the number of cliques, where the proposed method shows superior performance compared with the serial exact inference. Note that the range for the number of cliques can decrease if workload is not balanced across the processors.

21.6 FROM EXACT INFERENCE TO GENERIC DIRECTED ACYCLIC GRAPH (DAG)-STRUCTURED COMPUTATIONS

We can generalize the proposed technique to some applications other than exact inference as long as the application satisfies the following constraints: (1) The application can be modeled by a DAG, where each node represents a task and the edges indicate the precedence constraints among these tasks. This is called a DAG structured computation. (2) For any adjacent tasks in the DAG, say, $A \rightarrow B \rightarrow C$, the application allows us to first partially execute task C using B that has not been updated by A, and then fully update C using A. For example, in exact inference, we can first update the potential table of clique C using the potential table of B. As a result, the separator between B and A is brought into C to form a separator between C and A. Thus, in the next jump, C can be fully updated by A.

We generalize the proposed technique for DAG structured computations satisfying the above constraint in two steps. We first represent a given problem by a DAG. Each node in the DAG represents a set of computations on the data associated with the node. For example, in exact inference, the data associated with a node are the potential tables of the corresponding clique and the adjacent separators. The computation is to update the potential tables using node level primitives (see Section 21.2).

Second, if the DAG is not a tree or chain, we must convert it into a tree so that the proposed technique for junction trees can be used in a straightforward way. We convert a DAG into a tree as follows. We create a virtual root and connect it to all nodes without preceding nodes. There is no computation on the virtual root. Then, we identify the maximum *undirected* cycle in the DAG iteratively and represent each cycle as a new node. When executing a task corresponding to such a new node, we execute all the tasks in the cycle according to their original precedence constraints. Note that there is at most one preceding node for a maximum undirected cycle. This node becomes the parent of the new node. All successors of the nodes in the cycle become the children of the new node.

The above two steps convert a DAG into a tree. Due to the particular structure of a DAG, the resulting tree may or may not be suitable for pointer jumping. For example, if the undirected version of a DAG is a complete graph, the resulting tree degrades into a single node, which is not suitable for pointer jumping. The suitability of a tree for pointer jumping on parallel platforms is discussed in Section 21.5.

After we convert a DAG into a tree, we can follow Algorithm 21.1 in Section 21.4 but replace evidence propagation in lines 4 and 11 by computations associated with the corresponding nodes in the DAG. Note that Algorithm 21.1 includes two processes, bottom-up update (evidence collection) and top-down update (evidence distribution). Up on the specific application, we may only need one of the two processes. In this way, we generalize the proposed technique to some other DAG structured computations.

21.7 EXPERIMENTS

21.7.1 Platforms

We conducted experiments on two state-of-the-art many-core platforms:

- A 32-core Intel Nehalem-EX-based system consisting of four Intel Xeon X7560 processors fully connected through 6.4-GT/s QPI links. Each processor has 24-MB L3 cache and eight cores running at 2.26 GHz. All the cores share a 512-GB DDR3 memory. The operating system on this system is Red Hat Enterprise Linux Server release 5.4.
- A 24-core AMD Magny-Cours-based system consisting of two AMD Opteron 6164 HE processors. Each processor has 12-MB L3 cache and 12 cores running at 1.70 GHz. All the cores share a 64-GB DDR3 memory. The operating system on the system is CentOS Release 5.3.

21.7.2 Data Set

We evaluated the performance of our proposed algorithm using three families of junction trees: chains, balanced binary trees, and slim trees. Define junction tree width $W = \max_i\{W_i\}$ for a junction tree, where W_i is the number of cliques at level i of the junction tree. We call a junction tree a *slim tree* if it satisfies $W < H$, where H is the height of the tree. Note that W is an upper bound on the number of sequential evidence propagations required for updating a clique. H determines the number of pointer jumping iterations. Using slim trees, we can observe the performance of the proposed algorithm, even though there exists some amount of structural parallelism in such junction trees. The clique size, that is, the number of variables in the clique, was $W_d = 12$ in our experiments. This offered a limited amount of data parallelism. The random variables were set as binary, that is, $r = 2$, in our experiments. We utilized a junction tree of $N = 6,425,610,244,096$. The three different types of slim trees used in our experiments are shown in Figure 21.3. For a given N, we varied b to change slim tree topology:

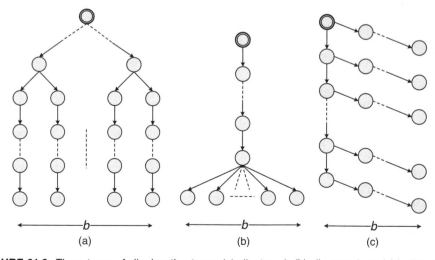

FIGURE 21.3. *Three types of slim junction trees: (a) slim tree 1, (b) slim tree 2, and (c) slim tree 3.*

- *Slim tree 1* was formed by first creating a balanced binary tree with b leaf nodes. Then each of the leaf nodes was connected to a chain consisting of $\lceil N - (2b - 1)/b \rceil$ nodes. The height of the tree is $(\lceil \log b \rceil + \lceil N - (2b - 1)/b \rceil)$. Increasing b increases the amount of structural parallelism.

- *Slim tree 2* was formed by connecting b cliques to the head of a chain consisting of $(N - b)$ nodes. The height of the tree is $(N - b + 1)$. Increasing b increases the amount of structural parallelism. A larger b also results in more sequential operations to update a clique during evidence collection.

- *Slim tree 3* was formed by first creating a chain of length $\lceil N/b \rceil$. Then, each clique in the chain was connected to another chain consisting of $(b - 1)$ cliques, except that the last chain connected to the root may have less than $(b - 1)$ cliques. The height of the tree is $(\lceil N/b \rceil + b - 1)$. Increasing b reduces the amount of structural parallelism.

21.7.3 Baseline Implementation

We use a parallel implementation as the baseline to evaluate our proposed method. The parallel implementation explores structural parallelism offered by junction trees. A collaborative scheduler proposed in Reference 13 was employed to schedule tasks to threads, where each thread was bound to a separate core. We call this baseline implementation as the scheduling-based exact inference (SEI). In this implementation, we represented a junction tree as an adjacency array, each element representing a clique and the links to the children of the clique. Each task had an attribute called the dependency degree, which was initially set as the in-degree of the corresponding clique. The scheduling activities were distributed across the threads. The adjacency array was shared by all the threads. In addition to the shared adjacency array, each clique had a ready task list to store the assigned tasks that are ready to be executed. Each core fetched a task from its ready task list and executed it locally. After the task was completed, the core reduced the dependency degree of the children of the clique. If the dependency degree of a child became 0, the child clique was assigned to the ready task list hosted by the core with the lightest workload.

21.7.4 Implementation Details

We implemented our proposed algorithm using Pthreads on many-core systems. We initiated as many threads as the number of hardware cores in the target platform. Each thread was bound to a separate core. These threads persisted over the entire program execution and communicated with each other using the shared memory.

The input junction tree was stored as an adjacency array in the memory. Similar to the SEI, the adjacency array consists of a list of nodes, each corresponding to a clique in the given junction tree. Each node has links to its children and a link to its parent. Note that the links were dynamically updated due to the nature of pointer jumping.

We define a *task* as the computation for updating a clique in an iteration of pointer jumping. The input to a task includes the clique to be updated and the set of cliques propagating evidence to this clique. The output of a task is the input clique after being updated. In iteration k of pointer jumping in evidence collection, a task corresponds to lines 3–5 in Algorithm 21.1, which updates clique $\mathscr{C}_i$ by sequentially performing multiple evidence propagations using cliques in $ch^{2^k}(\mathscr{C}_i)$. In iteration k of pointer jumping in evidence distribution, a task corresponds to lines 10–11 in Algorithm 21.1, which updates clique $\mathscr{C}_i$ by performing a single evidence propagation using clique $pa^{2^k}(\mathscr{C}_i)$.

In each iteration of pointer jumping (in both evidence collection and evidence distribution), all of the tasks can be executed in parallel. These tasks were statically distributed to the threads by a straightforward scheme: The task corresponding to clique $\mathscr{C}_i$, $O \le i < N$, is distributed to thread (i mod P), where P is the number of threads. Hence, a clique is always updated by the same thread, although the cliques propagating evidence to it vary from iteration to iteration. Note that, in an iteration, the execution time of the tasks can vary due to the different number of evidence propagations performed.

We explicitly synchronized the update operations across the threads at the end of each iteration of pointer jumping using a barrier.

21.7.5 Results

Figures 21.4–21.6 illustrate the performance of the proposed algorithm and the SEI for various junction trees. We consider the execution time and the scalability with respect to the number of processors for each algorithm.

For chains, as shown in Figure 21.4, SEI showed limited scalability; in contrast, the proposed algorithm scaled very well with the number of cores. This is because SEI had no structural parallelism to exploit for chains. For a chain of 4096 cliques, on a single core, the proposed algorithm ran much slower than SEI; however, when the number of cores exceeded 16, the proposed algorithm ran faster than SEI.

For balanced trees, as shown in Figure 21.5, both methods scaled well due to available structural parallelism. The scalability of SEI was even better than that of the proposed algorithm. This is because for balanced trees, some cliques are updated by sequentially performing a large number of evidence propagations from its children during evidence collection in the proposed algorithm. Load imbalance can occur due to the straightforward scheduling scheme that we employed. By employing the work-sharing scheduler, SEI had better load balance. Note that SEI ran much faster than the proposed algorithm.

To better understand the impact of junction tree topology on scalability, we used slim trees for the experiments. The results are shown in Figure 21.6. The number of cliques (N) was 4096. We varied the amount of structural parallelism offered by the junction trees by changing the parameter b for each type of slim tree.

For slim tree 1, we observed that SEI did not scale when the number of cores P exceeded b. However, the proposed algorithm still scaled well since the scalability of the proposed algorithm is not significantly affected by b. Thus, when b was small and P was large, for example, $b = 4$ and $P = 32$, the proposed algorithm ran faster than SEI.

For slim tree 2, increasing b made SEI scale better. In contrast, the proposed algorithm did not scale well when b increased because of the load imbalance. Load imbalance occurs because in each iteration of pointer jumping in evidence collec-

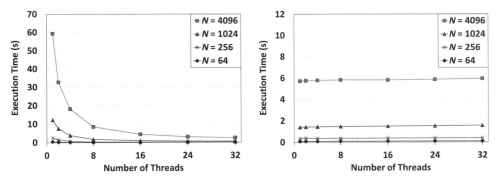

FIGURE 21.4. *Comparison between the proposed algorithm (left) and SEI (right) using chains on the 32-core Intel Nehalem-EX-based system.*

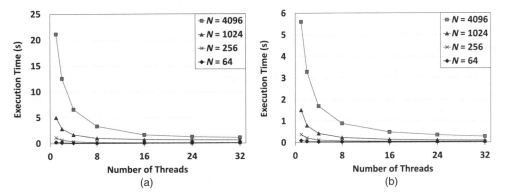

FIGURE 21.5. *Comparison between the proposed algorithm (left) and SEI (right) using balanced trees on the 32-core Intel Nehalem-EX-based system.*

tion, some cliques are updated by sequentially performing b evidence propagations, while the other cliques perform only one evidence propagation. Thus, when b was large, for example, 256 or 1024, for the number of cores used in the experiments, SEI ran faster than the proposed algorithm. When b was small and P was large, for example, $b = 16$ and $P = 32$, the proposed algorithm ran faster than SEI.

For slim tree 3, although increasing b reduces the amount of structural parallelism, it also reduces the length of the sequential path (chains consisting of $\lceil N/b \rceil$ cliques). Hence, as long as N/b is greater than the number of cores P, increasing b makes SEI scale better. If N/b is less than P, then all the processors are not fully utilized by SEI. We observed that, for $N = 4096$ and $b = 256$, SEI no longer scaled when the number of cores P exceeded 16. The proposed algorithm scaled best when $b = 4$. When $b = 4$ and $P = 32$, the proposed algorithm ran faster than SEI.

Examining the execution time of the proposed algorithm and SEI in all the cases, we can conclude that when SEI does not scale with the number of cores due to lack of structural parallelism, the proposed algorithm can offer superior performance compared with SEI by using a large number of cores.

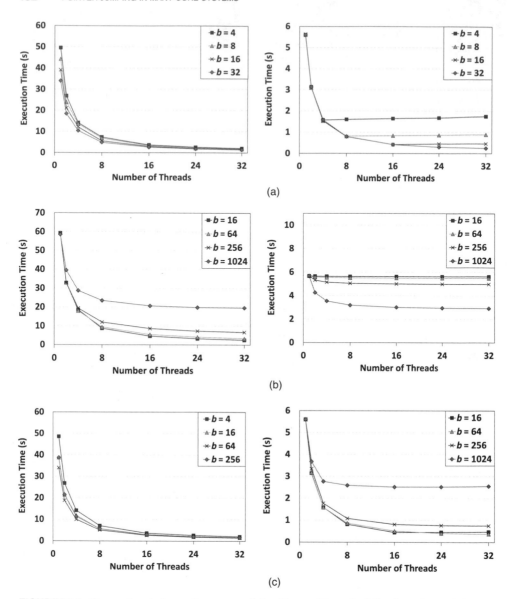

FIGURE 21.6. *Comparison between the proposed algorithm and the scheduling-based exact inference (SEI) using slim trees with N = 4096 cliques on a 32-core Intel Nehalem-EX-based system. (a) The proposed algorithm (left) and SEI (right) for slim tree 1. (b) The proposed algorithm (left) and SEI (right) for slim tree 2. (c) The proposed algorithm (left) and SEI (right) for slim tree 3.*

In Figures 21.7–21.9, we illustrate the scalability of pointer jumping-based exact inference, compared with the SEI using various junction trees on a 24-core AMD Magny-Cours-based system. They correspond to the results from a 32-core Intel Nehalem-EX-based system shown in Figures 21.4–21.6. In Figure 21.7, SEI shows no scalability since there is no structural parallelism available. However, the pointer jumping-based method worked very well. Note that, when a single core is used, the

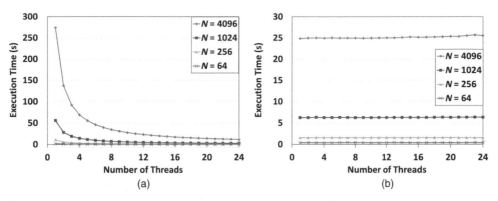

FIGURE 21.7. *Comparison between the proposed method (a) and SEI (b) using chains on a 24-core AMD Magny-Cours-based system. (a) Pointer jumping-based exact inference. (b) Scheduling-based exact inference.*

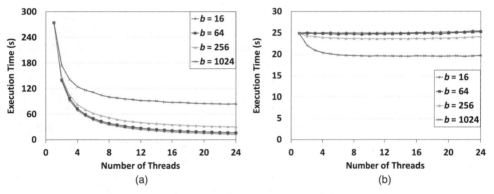

FIGURE 21.8. *Comparison between the proposed method (a) and SEI (b) using slim tree 2 on a 24-core AMD Magny-Cours based system. (a) Pointer jumping-based exact inference. (b) Scheduling-based exact inference.*

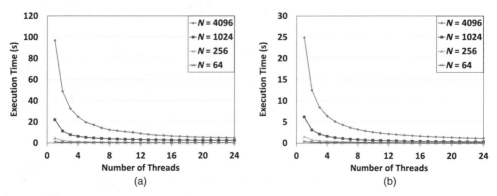

FIGURE 21.9. *Comparison between the proposed method (a) and SEI (b) using balanced trees on a 24-core AMD Magny-Cours based system. (a) Pointer jumping-based exact inference. (b) Scheduling-based exact inference.*

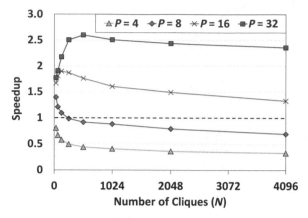

FIGURE 21.10. Speedup of pointer jumping-based exact inference with respect to serial implementation on a 32-core Intel Nehalem-EX-based system.

pointer jumping-based method took much more time due to the additional workload caused by pointer jumping. In Figure 21.8, the scalability of the scheduling-based method improved slightly as b increases since a large b results in higher structural parallelism at the bottom level (see Fig. 21.3b). However, since a larger b results in shorter chains, it leads to poor scalability for pointer jumping. Both methods showed scalability when using balanced trees in Figure 21.9. However, the execution time was different due to the additional workload in the pointer jumping-based method. As we can see, the results on the 24-core AMD Magny-Cours-based system are consistent to those from the 32-core Intel Nehalem-EX-based system.

In Figure 21.10, we show the speedup of pointer jumping-based exact inference with respect to a serial implementation, given various numbers of cores. Since pointer jumping-based exact inference involves additional work, it may not always outperform the scheduling-based method. We can see from Figure 21.10 that the speedup increased quickly when N was smaller than P, but then the speedup gradually decreases. When P is small, we observed that the speedup is lower than 1. This observation is consistent with our analysis in Section 21.5: Speedup can be achieved when the number of cliques in a chain (or the height of a tree) is within a range given by $[1, 2^{P+1})$; otherwise, the performance of pointer jumping can be adversely affected. Note that the real range can be much smaller than the above estimate due to the imbalanced workload across the levels of a tree, especially when P is small and N is large. Thus, in Figure 21.6, we can barely observe the range for $P \leq 8$.

21.8 CONCLUSIONS

In this chapter, we adapted a pointer jumping-based method to explore exact inference in junction trees with limited data and structural parallelism on many-core systems. The proposed method parallelizes both evidence collection and distribution. Due to the sequential update for each clique with respect to its children, the performance of the pointer jumping-based evidence collection depends on the topology of the input junction tree. Our experimental results show that for junction trees with limited structural parallelism, the proposed algorithm is well suited for many-core platforms. In the future, we plan to improve the load balance across threads within each iteration of pointer jumping. In addition, we are considering extending the algorithm by integrating the methods exploring structural parallelism and data parallelism, so that the algorithm can automatically choose the best method for a given junction tree. We also plan to investigate the parallelization of clique update with respect to its children during evidence collection.

REFERENCES

[1] D. Sheahan, "Developing and tuning applications on UltraSPARC T1 chip multithreading systems," Technical Report, 2007.

[2] G. Tan, V.C. Sreedhar, and G.R. Gao, "Analysis and performance results of computing betwenness centrality on IBM Cyclops64," *Journal of Supercomputing*, 2009.

[3] J. JáJá, *An Introduction to Parallel Algorithms*. Reading, MA: Addison-Wesley, 1992.

[4] Y. Xia and V.K. Prasanna, "Parallel exact inference," in *Parallel Computing: Architectures, Algorithms and Applications*, Vol. 38, Amsterdam: IOS Press, pp. 185–192, 2007.

[5] D. Pennock, "Logarithmic time parallel Bayesian inference," in *Proceedings of the 14th Annual Conference on Uncertainty in Artificial Intelligence*, pp. 431–438, 1998.

[6] S.L. Lauritzen and D.J. Spiegelhalter, "Local computation with probabilities and graphical structures and their application to expert systems," *J. R. Stat. Soc. Ser. B*, 50:157–224, 1988.

[7] T.H. Cormen, C.E. Leiserson, and R.L. Rivest. *Introduction to Algorithms*. MIT Press and McGraw-Hill, 1990.

[8] A.V. Kozlov and J.P. Singh, "A parallel Lauritzen-Spiegelhalter algorithm for probabilistic inference," in *Proceedings of Supercomputing*, pp. 320–329, 1994.

[9] Y. Xia, X. Feng, and V.K. Prasanna, "Parallel evidence propagation on multicore processors," in *The 10th International Conference on Parallel Computing Technologies*, pp. 377–391, 2009.

[10] B. D'Ambrosio, T. Fountain, and Z. Li, "Parallelizing probabilistic inference: Some early explorations," in *UAI*, pp. 59–66, 1992.

[11] Y. Xia and V.K. Prasanna, "Node level primitives for parallel exact inference," in *Proceedings of the 19th International Symposium on Computer Architecture and High Performance Computing*, pp. 221–228, 2007.

[12] D.A. Bader and G. Cong, "A fast, parallel spanning tree algorithm for symmetric multiprocessors (SMPs)," *Parallel and Distributed Computing*, 65(9):994–1006, 2005.

[13] Y. Xia and V.K. Prasanna, "Collaborative scheduling of dag structured computations on multicore processors," in *CF '10: Proceedings of the 7th ACM International Conference on Computing Frontiers*, pp. 63–72, 2010.

22

Performance Optimization of Scientific Applications Using an Autonomic Computing Approach

Ioana Banicescu, Florina M. Ciorba, and Srishti Srivastava

22.1 INTRODUCTION

In most scientific applications, the presence of parallel loops is the main source of parallelism. To obtain high performance and to take advantage of parallelism in such applications, which are in general large, computationally intensive, and data parallel, these parallel loops are executed on multiple processors. Simplistically allocating an equal number of loop iterations to the constituent processors almost always delivers unsatisfactory application performance. Performance degradation is mostly due to factors such as interprocessor communication overhead, unequal processor capabilities, processor load differences, and processor synchronization, among others. The overhead related to the differences in processor loads, or the *load imbalance*, is in many cases the dominant factor causing the processors to finish executing their loop iterations at widely different times, with some processors remaining idle, while others remain heavily loaded. Load imbalance is caused by the interactive effects of irregularities in problem, algorithmic, and systemic characteristics ([1], Chapter 4). Problem irregularities are mainly brought about by a nonuniform distribution of application data among processors, while algorithmic

Scalable Computing and Communications: Theory and Practice, First Edition. Edited by
Samee U. Khan, Albert Y. Zomaya, and Lizhe Wang.
© 2013 John Wiley & Sons, Inc. Published 2013 by John Wiley & Sons, Inc.

irregularities are often due to different conditional execution paths within loops. The systemic irregularities may be due to factors such as nonuniform memory access times, cache misses, and interrupts. Distribution of input data and variations of algorithmic nature cause intrinsic imbalance, while variations of systemic nature cause extrinsic imbalance [2].

To address the load imbalance problem, various scheduling algorithms have been developed. Such algorithms perform load balancing via loop scheduling since the parallel loops embody the majority of the application computational load. The interested reader is referred to the background work in factoring (FAC) [3], fractiling (FRAC) [4], weighted factoring (WF) [5], adaptive factoring (AF) [6, 7], adaptive weighted factoring (AWF) [8, 9], and variants of adaptive weighted factoring (AWF-B, AWF-C) [10]. These dynamic loop scheduling (DLS) algorithms have been shown to be the most effective for scheduling loop iterations to provide load balancing in unpredictable environments. These techniques are based on probabilistic analyses, rendering them inherently capable of addressing uncertainties coming from problem, algorithmic, and systemic characteristics. For a comprehensive review of these techniques, refer to References 11 and 12.

Selecting an effective and efficient scheduling algorithm from the currently available options to achieve load balancing for applications executing in an unpredictable environment is a difficult task. The difficulty is due to the complex nature of application characteristics, which may change during runtime, combined with the dynamic nature and unpredictability of the computing environment. Load balancing may be necessary in several parts of an application, and each part may require different scheduling algorithms for optimal performance. Furthermore, certain scientific applications require the execution of their computations repeatedly over the computational domain. The repetitive calculations are usually performed over a series of time steps. Such applications are referred to as time-stepping applications, and examples include heat solvers, solving time-dependent Euler equations, N-body simulations, and simulation of wavepacket dynamics. In applications requiring a large number of time steps, the load imbalance characteristics of each part may vary as the application execution progresses through the time steps. A scheduling algorithm selected *offline*, which performs well early in the application's lifetime, may later become inappropriate. Therefore, in this scenario, the selection of a scheduling algorithm for such a dynamic environment is a very difficult task, and a relatively more intelligent entity is needed to dynamically select during runtime the best scheduling algorithm for (possibly each part of) an application. The problematic issues associated with the offline selection of the appropriate DLS algorithm mandate the need for an *autonomic* selection mechanism. In general, autonomic computing (AC) systems are self-managing systems that can sense their operating environment, model their behavior in that environment, and take action either to change the environment or their behavior. An automatic self-managing system has the properties of self-configuration, self-healing, self-optimization, and self-protection. In this work, the AC aspect of the execution of an application is focused on the application's self-management attributes with respect to performance optimization. Therefore, the dynamic selection of the DLS algorithms must be based on the application performance during its execution. An intelligent agent is, therefore, needed to make informed decisions about which DLS algorithm to select in every particular case.

Over the past few years, intelligent systems have been developed and implemented in real-world problem domains, such as game playing [13, 14] and robotics [15–17]. A more related example is one of program selection [18]. In these applications, the system achieves its perceived intelligence through learning via the use of a computational technique called *reinforcement learning* (RL). RL is an active area of research in artificial intelligence, specifically in machine learning. Its objective is general, and therefore, it has potentially widespread applicability in different scientific contexts. RL uses a goal-oriented approach to solve problems by interacting with a complex and unpredictably changing environment. It solves the problems via learning, planning, and decision making.

Extensive research has been conducted in recent years to use RL strategies for addressing load balancing problems [19–22]. Specifically, RL techniques have been used for the dynamic load balancing of coarse-grain data-intensive applications, solving real-time systems management problems, and adaptively scheduling tasks in heterogeneous multiprocessor systems. These approaches make various assumptions that are described later in Section 22.4.2. An RL agent implementing two RL techniques, *Q-learning* and *state–action–reward–state–action* (SARSA) [23], has been integrated with a scientific parallel application characterized by a large number of time steps (a time-stepping application) [24, 25]. This RL agent provides a generic framework for the autonomic selection of the best suited DLS algorithm for load balancing time-stepping scientific applications in a dynamic environment using RL. Employing this framework improved the performance of a scientific application as compared to the traditional offline selection methods. The large number of time steps in the application gives the RL agent the opportunity to learn and to make informed decisions about the DLS algorithm selection.

In this chapter, the application of RL to realize an *autonomic mechanism* for the selection of DLS techniques is proposed. The benefits, significance, and usefulness of a DLS-*with*-RL approach are demonstrated for the performance improvement of time-stepping scientific applications containing computationally intensive parallel loops. The simulation of wave packets using the quantum trajectory method (QTM) is considered as a case study.

22.2 SCIENTIFIC APPLICATIONS AND THEIR PERFORMANCE

Scientific applications are typically data parallel, irregular, and often, computationally intensive. They contain loops with large number of iterations and are easily amenable for parallelization. In applications such as partial differential equations (PDEs), Monte Carlo simulations, N-body simulations, sparse matrix computations, and unstructured grid solvers, iteration execution times could vary due to the *algorithm*, such as, for instance, conditional statements, or the *problem*, for instance, nonuniform data distribution. Even in applications where there are no variances in iteration lengths due to algorithmic or problem characteristics, loop iteration execution times may vary due to interferences from other iterations, other applications, or *systemic* variances, such as, for instance, the operating system or network latency. The cumulative effect of variances in loop iteration execution times could, ultimately, lead to processor load imbalance and, therefore, to severe performance degradation of parallel applications. A fundamental performance trade-off in scheduling parallel loop iterations is that of balancing processor loads while minimizing communication and scheduling overhead. In addition to problems encountered in load balancing on homogeneous systems, the different speeds of processors together with their different architectures and memory capacities can significantly impact performance. Moreover, in case of heterogeneous networks of workstations, loads and availability of the workstations are unpredictable, and thus, it is difficult to know in advance the effective speed of each machine.

Depending on the number of time steps required by the algorithm to find the solution to a problem, scientific applications can be broadly classified as *noniterative* and *iterative* simulations. The iterative applications often contain a large number of time steps, whereby with each time step, the solution to the problem converges to the overall solution that is reached at the end of the computation. Examples of such applications include N-body simulations, wavepacket simulations, and computational fluid dynamics (CFD) simulations. An application in this class evolves over N time steps and is therefore referred to as *time stepping* (Fig. 22.1). Within a single time step, L computationally intensive parallel loops are executed, possibly with different lengths and nonuniform iteration execution times. Typically, there are also other statements between the loops, and the results of the computations from the earlier executed loops might be needed by other, later executed loops. Since the loops are parallel, DLS will be utilized for load balancing to minimize the loop completion times. General-purpose loop scheduling routines have already been developed and can be integrated into compilers, or even as load balancing tools into such applications [26–30].

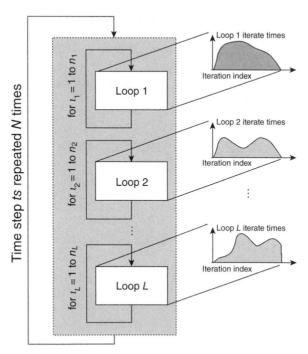

FIGURE 22.1. *High-level structure of a time-stepping application with* L *parallel loops executed over* N *time steps.*

22.3 LOAD BALANCING VIA DLS

The problem of load imbalance in scientific applications on parallel and distributed environments has often been addressed by loop scheduling algorithms. Extensive research has been dedicated to developing these algorithms, integrating them in runtime systems, and implementing them in applications. Over the years, there has been significant advancement in the development of loop scheduling algorithms that address load imbalance problems with increasing levels of complexity. The development of loop scheduling algorithms includes a wide range of algorithms from *static scheduling* (STATIC) to *self-scheduling* (SS). Among them, the DLS algorithms represent a prominent class of loop scheduling algorithms and include *fixed-size chunking* (FSC), *guided self-scheduling* (GSS), FAC, WF, FRAC, AF, AWF, and its variants (AWF-B, AWF-C) [3, 4, 6, 7, 9, 31–35].

All the DLS techniques are based on probabilistic analyses and schedule loop iterations in chunks with variable sizes. The chunk sizes are dynamically chosen at runtime as a function of the number of iterations, n, and the number of processors, p, and have a high probability of being completed within the optimal time. The techniques also accommodate changes present in the heterogeneous system and handle most of the performance degradation factors caused by predictable phenomena (e.g., irregular data) and unpredictable phenomena (e.g., data access latency and operating system interference). The DLS algorithms are broadly classified as *nonadaptive* and *adaptive* algorithms. The nonadaptive algorithms include SS, FSC, GSS, FAC, and WF [3, 5, 32, 34, 35], and determine the chunk size based on the assumptions or information available before starting the loop execution. The adaptive algorithms include AWF, AWF-B, AWF-C, and AF [6–10, 12], and determine the information of the workloads during the loop execution or from the previous execution of the loop iterations. The modeling of the adaptive techniques is more complex, allowing them to address a larger number of load imbalance factors than the nonadaptive techniques. These scheduling techniques have been incorporated into load balancing libraries and underwent extensive testing on a wide variety of applications (e.g., CFD, quantum physics, automatic quadrature routines, and *N*-body simulations) on both distributed-memory and shared-memory environments [27, 36]. For a comprehensive review of the DLS techniques and their effectiveness in improving the performance of scientific applications, the reader is referred to Reference 11.

22.4 THE USE OF MACHINE LEARNING IN IMPROVING THE PERFORMANCE OF SCIENTIFIC APPLICATIONS

In this section, an introduction is given on machine learning and its various techniques used for solving load balancing problems in scientific applications on parallel and distributed environments. Extensive research has been conducted over the years in the area of machine learning, and many of its techniques are being used either for solving scientific problems or for improving their performance.

22.4.1 Machine Learning Basics

The main research objective of machine learning is the study and development of learning algorithms that induce intelligent programs through experience. The main idea is based on the interaction between an intelligent system called the agent (or learner) and the environment in which it operates. Machine learning can be categorized into *supervised learning* (SL), *unsupervised learning* (UL), and RL.

22.4.1.1 Supervised Learning In SL, the training data consist of examples of both inputs and desired outputs, thus enabling learning a function. Knowledge is gained from a supervisor (or teacher) that uses a sample of input–output pairs, while the SL agent is instructed what actions to perform. The agent should then be able to generalize from the presented data to unseen examples. In situations where data labeling comes at a cost, a method known as *active learning* may be used, where the agent chooses which data to label. Learning is conducted *offline*, and obtaining the input–output pairs for real-time applications under all possible environmental conditions is often impossible because an exhaustive representation of all possible situations is not feasible, especially in a dynamically changing computing environment. Examples of SL algorithms include *logistic regression* and *naive Bayes classifier*.

22.4.1.2 Unsupervised Learning The training set of vectors does not have associated function values in UL. The problem is typically that of partitioning the training set into subsets, in some appropriate way. In this case, UL can be regarded as a problem of learning a function, in which the value of the function is the name of the subset to which an input vector belongs. A UL agent may learn to reduce the problem size, while it is possible that it may not learn the correct outputs. The agent helps in finding the relationships and extracting regularities from the learning process, rather than in finding the correct solution. The procedures in UL learning attempt to find natural partitions of patterns. UL methods have application in problems involving taxonomies, where there is a need to invent ways to classify data into meaningful categories. Examples of UL methods include *clustering* and *dimensionality reduction*.

22.4.1.3 Reinforcement Learning RL is an intermediate technique between the two extremes, SL and UL, using an approach that involves solving the problems via learning, planning, and decision making. Unlike SL, the RL agent is not told what to do, and also, it is not left on its own to learn to correct the outputs, as in UL. An RL system learns about the environment *online*, during its operation, through a *trial-and-error* process [37]. The agent receives an immediate reinforcement, or "reward," for taking a particular action, and observes the effect of the action on the "state" of the environment. The RL agent is thus enabled to learn the optimal path to the goal by learning through experience that comes from the feedback it gains about the states, actions, and rewards in unpredictably changing environments. Learning does not require any input–output pairs, being done online, such that the problem is concurrently solved while learning [37]. The trial-and-error learning mechanism and the concept of reward makes RL distinct from other learning techniques. A challenging problem and a key aspect in RL is the trade-off between exploration and exploitation. To *exploit* is to use the best experienced action, while to *explore* requires the agent to try new actions to discover better action selections for the future. Different strategies have been designed to address this trade-off problem, including ideas from optimal control theory and stochastic approximation [37].

RL approaches can be *model based* and *model free*. In a model-based approach, the agent uses a *model M*, and a *utility function* U_M, such that M executes a control

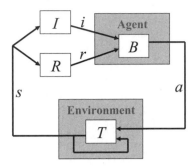

FIGURE 22.2. *Components of an RL system, where* I *is the set of inputs (*i*),* R *is the set of rewards (*r*),* B *is the set of policies for action selection,* a *is an action,* T *is the transition function, and* s *is a state.*

policy for the purpose of learning about the environment. Conversely, in the model-free approach, the agent uses an action-value *function Q* to learn the policy directly by interacting with the environment, without storing experience states, actions, and rewards, or learning a model. Examples of model-based learning are Dyna [17], prioritized sweeping [38], Queue-Dyna [39], and real-time dynamic programming [40]. Model-based learning, however, is *not* applicable to autonomic selection of algorithms because the model of the environment *M* is unknown, and building the model of the environment for real-time applications is a time-consuming process. Therefore, a model-free learning approach is herein proposed and used. An example of a model-free approach is temporal difference (TD). The TD updates the estimates from the learned estimates and learns *without* a model. The TD class of RL algorithms include Q-learning and SARSA [23].

22.4.2 RL and Its Use in Scientific Applications

22.4.2.1 An RL System In a standard RL model, an agent is connected to its environment via perception and action (Fig. 22.2). The environment can be in any *state s* from a set of distinct states. The *transition function T* drives the change in the state of the environment and depends on the *action a* performed by the agent on the current state of the environment. The selection of *a* depends on the *reward r* the agent receives and also on the observation of the current state *s* of the environment. The reward is a scalar reinforcement signal from a *set R*, which communicates the changes in the states of the environment to the agent and helps in deciding whether a state is desirable or not. The reward is used to guide the learning process, to specify the wide range of planning goals, and maximizes the benefits achieved in the long run. The states and, therefore, the rewards in RL are well defined by the *Markov decision process* (MDP). This implies that the decisions made by the RL agent do not depend on previous states or actions but are considered to be functions of the current state of the environment. At a specific time instance, the agent is guided in the selection of actions by a *policy B*. A policy maps the states of the environment and the actions taken when the agent is in a particular known state [41].

The general learning scenario in an RL system is as follows. The agent receives an *input i* from the *set* of inputs *I* when it is in a current state and takes an action.

The action is chosen from a state guided by a policy B to produce new output. The value of the transition changing the state of the environment is given as a reward. This reward reinforces the signal, allowing the agent to choose actions that tend to maximize the agent's goal function, that is, increasing the long-run sum of values of the reinforcement signal. The agent can learn to do this over time via systematic trial and error, guided by a wide variety of algorithms.

SARSA and Q-learning are RL algorithms that use a TD-based model-free approach to learning. SARSA (Fig. 22.3a) learns the transitions from a state–action pair to another state–action pair and finds the policy by using a greedy approach. To update the value function, it needs to know the next action to be taken. Q-learning (Fig. 22.3b) uses a delayed reinforcement and chooses an action that maximizes the policy via a Q function, directly approximating the optimal value Q^* independent of the policy being followed. Both techniques use a pair of learning parameters, namely, the learning rate (α) and the discount factor (γ).

22.4.2.2 *RL in Scientific Applications*

In recent years, extensive research has been conducted to employ machine learning strategies for load balancing problems. RL techniques have been used for dynamic load balancing of coarse-grain data-intensive applications [19]. Each processor used an independent RL agent learning to request an optimal chunk size of data from the master. The goal was to minimize the blocking time for other processors. The experiments have only been conducted using synthetic applications, which were not iterative. The improvements were reported against a static load balancer. With an increasing number of slaves, the task of reducing the blocking time becomes harder. The prospects for applying RL within AC systems have been studied and several recent case studies have been described to demonstrate interesting challenges in applying various RL approaches to real-time systems management problems [20]. One such case study showed that combining the strengths of both RL and queuing models in a hybrid RL approach supports an autonomic resource allocation in a given computing system for a set of applications [21]. The use of a model-based RL approach to adaptively schedule tasks in heterogeneous multiprocessor systems has also been investigated, and a number reinforcement-based schedulers have been proposed [22]. The schedules are assumed to be created before runtime, considering the communication times known a priori and the processor speeds remaining constant. These assumptions pose certain limitations to the applicability of the schedulers to specific problems and systems.

In general, the techniques described above have addressed integration of RL strategies at a coarser granularity and not at a finer granularity level *within* an application. A time-stepping scientific application requiring dynamic load balancing provides an excellent environment for the use of RL. Irregularities in the application and in the underlying computing system may evolve unpredictably. Hence, a load balancing algorithm performing well in earlier time steps may prove to be inefficient in later time steps. However, a large number of time steps provide the agents with ample opportunities to learn. An RL agent following the model-free learning approach becomes very useful for *autonomically* selecting the appropriate load balancing algorithm during the lifetime of an application.

In Reference 24, an RL agent incorporating Q-learning and SARSA was embedded into a parallel scientific application, namely, simulation of wavepacket dynamics using the QTM. To our best knowledge, Reference 24 is the first work that has attempted to integrate an RL agent with a parallel scientific application for autonomic DLS algorithm selection. Subsequent works investigated and reported on a performance comparison of the QTM application in terms of T_p *with* and *without* the RL agent, with varying learning rates (α) and discount factors (γ), and the influence of a particular RL technique for a particular set of learning parameters (α, γ) [25, 42].

In the approach described in detail later in Section 22.5, the number of RL agents is equal to the number of computationally intensive parallel loops, which is smaller than in the case of each processor using an RL agent, as considered in Reference 19. In the approach proposed herein, RL agents are embedded *within* an application to optimize its performance, which is simultaneously improved via DLS. This is in contrast to the approach where application load imbalance is mitigated only via the use of RL agents alone [19]. The approach presented herein uses model-free RL techniques (Q-learning and SARSA), given that it is impossible to train the model of the environment for all possible conditions, as required by model-based RL techniques. This is in contrast to the case of a specific RL framework for solving scheduling problems as mentioned in Reference 22.

22.5 DESIGN STRATEGIES AND AN INTEGRATED FRAMEWORK

In this section, a framework is described for integrating RL into a class of scientific applications for an autonomic selection of DLS algorithms to improve applications' performance in parallel and distributed environments. The work presented herein is focused on one of the self-management aspects of AC systems, which is directed toward performance optimization.

The adaptive and nonadaptive DLS described in Section 22.3 have been incorporated into scientific applications, and their performance has been analyzed by the use of load balancing tools [27, 36]. However, for time-stepping scientific applications with large numbers of time steps executing in an unpredictable environment, and given several DLS algorithms, it is difficult to dynamically find the optimal one. One has to test all the scheduling algorithms in order to find the best strategy to balance the parallel loops. The current implementation of the scheduling algorithms does not explore the possibilities of choosing at runtime, among all the DLS algorithms, the optimal one, for a particular computing environment on which the application is executing and at a specific time at which it is executed. This limitation raises a compelling need for designing an autonomic agent that can use *machine learning* (ML) techniques to dynamically determine an optimal scheduling algorithm through learning, by simultaneously interacting with the environment and the scheduling algorithms.

22.5.1 Integrated Framework for Algorithm Selection

The foundations of the design layout for an integrated framework are described herein, with a focus on the autonomic selection of scheduling algorithms for performance optimization of large-scale scientific applications using RL strategies. The design goals for the proposed selection framework are the following: (1) automatic runtime selection of an optimal DLS in an unpredictably changing environment; (2) provision of a generic design framework for addressing application, architectural,

```
Initialize Q(s,a) arbitrarily
Repeat for each episode (time step)
  Initialize s
  Choose a from s using policy derived from Q
  Repeat for each episode
    Take action a, observe r, s'
    Choose a' from s' using policy derived from Q
    Q(s,a) = Q(s,a) + α[r + γ(Q(s',a') − Q(s,a))]
    a = a'; s = s'
  until s is terminal
```
(a)

```
Initialize Q(s,a) arbitrarily
Repeat for each episode (time step)
  Initialize s
  Choose a from s using policy derived from Q
  Repeat for each episode
    Take action a, observe r, s'
    Choose a' from s' using policy derived from Q
    Q(s,a) = Q(s,a) + α[r + γ(Q(s',a') − Q(s,a))]
    a = a'; s = s'
  until s is terminal
```
(b)

FIGURE 22.3. *(a) SARSA (b) Q-learning.*

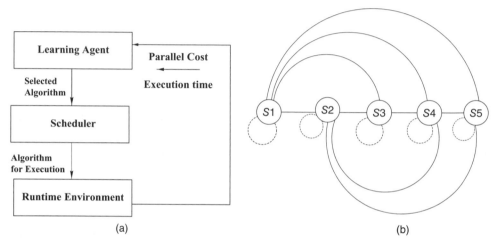

(a)

(b)

FIGURE 22.4. *(a) Interaction between the learning agent, scheduler, and the runtime environment. (b) State–action transition diagram.*

and computing environment irregularities; (3) portability across different computing platforms; (4) cost minimization and efficient utilization of computing resources; and (5) provision for incorporating new DLS algorithms and RL techniques for future enhancements to solve a wide variety of scientific problems.

22.5.1.1 Integrated Framework Design

The process of selecting the best scheduling algorithm depending on the dynamic environmental conditions can be considered as an MDP (Fig. 22.4) with states, actions, parallel costs, transition functions, and a "value minimization function" or the "objective function." Therefore, RL techniques are suitable for solving the problem. A high-level description of the proposed selection framework, illustrating the interaction between the learning agent, the scheduler, and the runtime environment, is depicted in Figure 22.4a.

The states are represented by the various scheduling algorithms, including information about the execution of a particular algorithm during the previous time steps. The scheduling algorithms are equivalent in terms of the problem they solve, and address the dynamic nature of the runtime environment at different complexity levels. The actions constitute the selection of a particular scheduling algorithm based on the a priori performance of all algorithms and of the recently executed algorithm.

The state–action transitions (Fig. 22.4a) are provided from the state–action transition matrix, updated after every execution of the chosen algorithm and used in the action selection process during the next time step (iteration or episode). The Q-learning and SARSA reinforcement techniques are used for obtaining the optimal value selection and for finding the optimal policy. The "cost" represented by the execution time of the current time step (iteration) is used in the decision of selecting the scheduling algorithm for execution during the next time step. The goal of the selection process is to reduce the overall computation time by making effective use of the parallel execution on processors.

The state–action transition diagram, illustrated in Figure 22.4b, is described next. Each node of the graph represents a state s_i. The arcs from one node to another represent actions. The dotted lines represent transitions when the previous state and the next state are same. After receiving feedback, the scheduling algorithm may remain in the same state or move to a different state. In the scenario of the problem being considered, the states are defined by various DLS algorithms. The feedback value and Q-values are obtained after the execution of a particular algorithm and are used for learning the best scheduling algorithm during the next time step. Here, an algorithm is considered as defined by a state, while the reward is defined by the execution time obtained from the runtime environment (Fig. 22.4a). The action is defined by the decision to execute or not to execute an algorithm. The multiple state transitions are exhibited by the change in state during runtime.

The integrated framework for algorithm selection, illustrated in Figure 22.5, is designed to consist of three components: (1) *application*, (2) *scheduling*, and (3) *RL*.

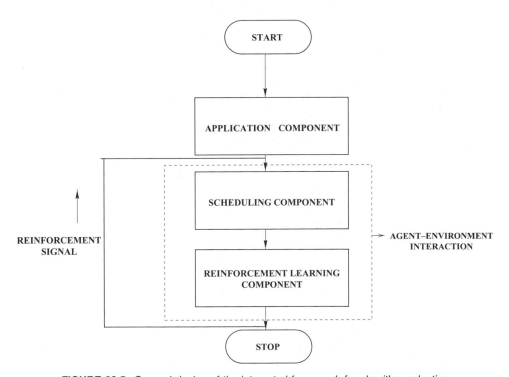

FIGURE 22.5. General design of the integrated framework for algorithm selection.

(i) The *application component* contains the information and computations specific to a time-stepping application, which consists of multiple parallel loops with a large number of iterations. As described earlier in Section 22.2, the performance of the application is affected by predictable and unpredictable factors. The data distribution may be irregular or may dynamically change during runtime. The problem characteristics may also change for different architectures, workloads, and processors. These factors are very difficult to accurately be determined. There may be several loops with different execution patterns, requiring different algorithms to efficiently address the load imbalance problem. This component contains such applications to which scheduling strategies are applied to address the load imbalance problem dynamically at runtime. The selection of the appropriate scheduling algorithm is provided by RL techniques.

(ii) The *scheduling component* provides DLS algorithms for performance improvement of executing parallel loops in scientific applications that are subject to load imbalance due to problem, algorithmic, or systemic characteristics. The DLS algorithms are based on a master–worker strategy, and their description has been provided in Section 22.3. At the beginning of the scheduling process, one processor acts as a *master processor* or a "scheduler" and assigns the partitions of the iteration domain to be executed by the workers. These partitions may be either "replicated" or "distributed" on the processors, and a detailed discussion on various implementations has been provided in Reference 11. All other processors act as *worker processors*, and each processor initially works on chunks from its own partition. When there is severe imbalance in the workloads, a fast processor may be involved in work on partitions initially assigned to slower processors. After completing the execution of all loop iterations, the computed results are sent to all processors to synchronize the data that may be required for further computations. The scheduler coordinates with the worker processors in assigning chunk sizes of loop iterations, receiving computed results, and sending termination signals to the processors when there is no pending work and they have completed their assigned work. The scheduler broadcasts the results of the computation to all the processors after the termination of the loop execution. The interaction between the scheduler and the worker processors is facilitated by transfer of messages for specific functions.

(iii) The *RL component* contains algorithms for the autonomic selection of the DLS algorithms during application runtime, depending on the performance characteristics of the parallel loop under consideration. This component is an interface between the runtime environment and the scheduling layer, providing control and optimization to the scheduling component. It addresses the problem of *adaptive learning* of an autonomous agent through its interaction with the dynamic environment by using a combination of exploration and exploitation techniques.

The RL component consists of the states, actions, rewards, and the environment. It monitors the performance of the selected DLS algorithms and specifies the optimal DLS algorithm by interacting with the runtime environment. For the problem of algorithm selection for scientific applications, the *states* are the "DLS algorithms," while an *action* is a "decision to select the optimal DLS algorithm." A *reward* is an "evaluative feedback" reflecting the performance of the selected scheduling algorithms. The application is provided with a set of scheduling algorithms. The RL system learns to select (using an RL method, such as, for instance, Q-learning or SARSA) the best scheduling algorithm through its interaction with the set of scheduling routines and the assessment of the algorithm's performance. This leads to the selection and application of a particular DLS algorithm in unpredictable environmental conditions, selection that otherwise cannot optimally be accomplished.

All these components coordinate among themselves to improve the overall performance of the scientific application. The functionality of each component is kept modular, such that the optimization and the software development in one component can take place independent of the ones in other components. One advantage of using this approach is that no a priori information is required regarding the problem characteristics or regarding the runtime environment before starting the execution of an application.

22.5.1.2 *An RL System for Time-Stepping Applications*   A high-level general description of a time-stepping application with a number of L computationally intensive sections expressed as parallel loops is given in Figure 22.1 and has been presented in detail in Section 22.2. As these loops execute in parallel, appropriate DLS techniques are selected and applied for load balancing, such that the overall parallel execution time is minimized, while the overall performance is maximized.

A common practice for the selection of an appropriate DLS technique is to use application profiling employing iteratively all available DLS algorithms and to choose the algorithm that gives the optimal performance for a particular application run. This is feasible only if the application has a single parallel loop section that does not significantly change its characteristics at every time step. This approach also requires that the parallel execution environment be dedicated to the current application. The difficulty of the selection problem increases even more when the application contains several parallel loops, each having unique load balancing requirements that vary with every time step. Moreover, the dynamic nature of a parallel and distributed system, represented by events such as unpredictable network latencies or operating system interferences, further complicates the selection problem. The cumulative performance degradation resulting from these uncertainties justifies the need for employing at runtime an intelligent agent for the selection of the best DLS algorithm for executing each parallel loop section.

The algorithm selection problem is addressed by providing a generic design of an RL system to *autonomically* determine at runtime the optimal scheduling algorithm for a time-stepping application using RL techniques. Figure 22.6 illustrates the design of the proposed RL system, derived by adding the loop scheduling context to the environment of the generic RL system in Figure 22.2.

The goal of the proposed RL system for time-stepping applications is to minimize the total time spent by the application executing the parallel loops. This implies minimizing the completion time of each loop invocation. During the first few invocations of the loop, the agent simply specifies each algorithm in the library in a *round-robin* fashion, in the absence of prior knowledge about the characteristics of the loop. When sufficient knowledge is obtained during this initial learning period, the agent applies an adaptive learning policy B (Q-learning or SARSA) on the

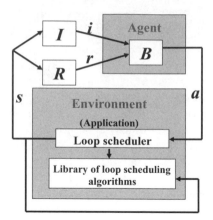

FIGURE 22.6. *RL system for* autonomic *selection of DLS methods, where* I *is the set of inputs* i *(set of methods, current time step, set of loop IDs);* R *is the set of rewards* r *(loop execution time);* B *is the set of policies for action selection (Q-learning, SARSA);* a *is an action (using a particular DLS* method*); and* s *is a state (application is using DLS* method*).*

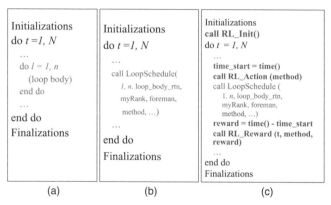

FIGURE 22.7. *Integrating an RL system in time-stepping applications with parallel loops. (a) Serial form. (b) Parallel form. (c) With RL system.*

accumulated information to select an algorithm (action *a*—select a particular DLS method) from the library of DLS algorithms, and the environment moves to another state *s* (application is using the particular selected DLS method).

The loop completion time using the selected DLS algorithm determines a performance level, which is the basis of the reward *r* for the action *a* taken by the RL agent. The application communicates information *i* about the changed state *s* and the reward *r* to the RL agent, for continuous learning by the policy *B*. If the agent takes action only after a specified number of loop invocations, the application simply reuses the algorithm associated with the current state *s*, denoted by the loopback arrow from the environment to the library (Fig. 22.6).

To better illustrate the use of the proposed strategy, its application for improving the performance of a time-stepping application with a single parallel loop is shown in Figure 22.7. The *left* part outlines the serial form of the time-stepping application. The *middle* part illustrates the parallel form in which a DLS algorithm is integrated.

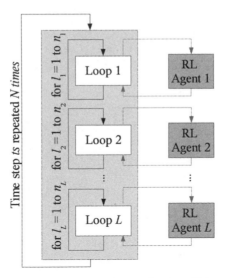

FIGURE 22.8. *High-level structure of a time-stepping application with* L *parallel loops integrated with a number of* L *RL agents.*

The part on the *right* shows the integration of RL, complementing the parallel form. Even though the above proposed system is described for a single loop, the strategy is suitable for a wide variety of scientific applications with one or several parallel loops. This can be seen in Figure 22.8, where RL is integrated into a time-stepping application with L parallel loops.

The components of the above system (Figs. 22.5 and 22.6) work independently. The application can execute the loop without the use of the loop scheduling library. The library can be linked to any other time-stepping application with parallel loops. The RL agent can also be used by other time-stepping applications. However, the integration of these components yields a highly flexible design and allows upgrades to be incorporated into any component without affecting the others, such as additional scheduling algorithms for the library, new learning policies into the agent, and more accurate formulas into the application.

22.5.2 Implementation and Evaluation of the Integrated Framework

22.5.2.1 *Integrating RL in a QTM with DLS*
The integrated framework is tested on a computationally intensive scientific application, namely, the wavepacket simulation using the QTM [43, 44]. This is a time-stepping application with five parallel loops. The generic serial code of the QTM application is illustrated in Figure 22.9. In this scientific application code, a set of pseudoparticles is used to represent a physical particle. Each pseudoparticle executes a quantum trajectory governed by the Lagrangian *quantum fluid dynamics–equation of motion* (QFD-EOM) and the quantum potential. The pseudoparticles form a wave packet, which collectively represents the physical particle. The arrays containing values of the positions, velocities, and probability densities of the n pseudoparticles representing the wave packet are denoted by $r[.]$, $v[.]$, and $\rho[.]$, respectively. These arrays are initialized with appropriate values at the beginning of the simulation. During each time step, values

```
Initialize  t, r[.], v[.], ρ[.]
for  t = 1, N  do  ! Time loop
 for  l₁ = 1, n  do  ! Loop 1
  Call MWLS(l₁, r[.], ρ[.], n_{p₁}, n_b)
  Compute  Q[l₁]
 end for

 for  l₂ = 1, n  do  ! Loop 2
  Call MWLS(l₂, r[.], Q[.], n_{p₂}, n_b)
  Compute  f_q[l₁]
 end for

 for  l₃ = 1, n  do  ! Loop 3
  Call MWLS(l₃, r[.], v[.], n_{p₃}, n_b)
  Compute  dv[l₁]
 end for

 for  l₄ = 1, n  do  ! Loop 4
  Compute  V[l₄],  f_c[l₄]
 end for

 Output  t,  r[.],  v[.],  ρ[.],  V[.],
         f_c[.],  Q[.],  f_q[.],  dv[.]

 for  l₅ = 1, n  do  ! Loop 5
  Update  ρ[l₅],  r[l₅],  v[l₅]
 end for
end for
```

FIGURE 22.9. *Serial QTM.*

for the classical potential $V[.]$, classical force $f_c[.]$, quantum potential $Q[.]$, quantum force $f_q[.]$, and derivative of velocity $dv[.]$ are derived from $r[.]$, $v[.]$, and $\rho[.]$ of the previous time step. The moving weighted least squares (MWLS) algorithm is used for $Q[.]$, $f_q[.]$, and $dv[.]$ for curve fitting, and the resulting curve is differentiated to obtain the required derivatives. For each pseudoparticle, the algorithm solves an overdetermined linear system of size $n_p \times n_b$. A detailed description of the MWLS algorithm is given in Reference 44. The values of $r[.]$, $v[.]$, $\rho[.]$ are then updated for use in the next time step. In the algorithm, loops 2–4 can be combined into a single loop; however, these are separated to be suitable for loop scheduling with DLS algorithms.

The execution profile of a straightforward serial implementation of the QTM indicates that the bulk of the total execution time is spent in the MWLS routine called by loop 1 (quantum potential), loop 2 (quantum force), and loop 3 (derivative of velocity). Thus, a significant decrease in the overall simulation time can be achieved by distributing the iterations of these loops. Each of these loops is a *parallel loop*, for which the iterations can be executed in any order without affecting the correctness of the algorithm. Therefore, the DLS algorithms may appropriately be applied. (Loops 4 and 5 are also parallel loops, but the scheduling overhead will be

```
Initialize t,r[.],v[.],ρ[.]
Call DLS_Setup(MPI_COMM_WORLD,Info)
DLS_Method=5 ! e.g., FAC
for t = 1, N do !Time loop
  ...
  call DLS_StartLoop(Info,1,n,DLS_Method)
  while ( !DLS_Terminated(Info) ) do
   call DLS_StartChunk(Info,Start,Size)
   for l₁=Start,Start+Size-1 do !Loop 1
     Call MWLS(l₁,r[.],ρ[.],n_{p1},n_b)
     Compute Q[l₁]
   end for
   call DLS_EndChunk(Info)
  end while
  ... ! Integrate DLS for
  ... ! Loops 2 & 3 as above

  for l₄ = 1, n do ! Loop 4
   Compute V[l₄], f_c[l₄]
  end for

  Output t, r[.], v[.], ρ[.], V[.],
         f_c[.], Q[.], f_q[.], dv[.]

  for l₅ = 1, n do ! Loop 5
   Update ρ[l₅], r[l₅], v[l₅]
  end for
end for
```

FIGURE 22.10. *QTM with DLS.*

more expensive than the computations as they contain only simple formulae and are computationally less intensive.)

In previous studies, one specific DLS algorithm was used for all the three loops, with no concern regarding their specific computational requirements (Fig. 22.10). The algorithm was specified statically during the initiation of the computation process and did not change throughout the application execution. To cater to the specific characteristics of these different computational loops, RL techniques are employed in selecting the optimal DLS algorithm for each of the three individual loops in the QTM application (Fig. 22.11).

Considering the computation of the quantum trajectory problem using wave-packet simulations, the performance degradation due to load imbalance during its execution in a distributed environment has effectively been addressed by novel DLS algorithms [43]. The RL problem is mapped to the QTM application as follows. The design framework shown in Figure 22.6 is replicated for each of the three parallel loop sections of the QTM application, resulting in one RL agent for each of these sections (Fig. 22.8). Each RL agent is an autonomic element and acts independently, working only with the parallel loop section for which it is employed. There is no

```
Initialize t,r[.],v[.],ρ[.]
Call DLS_Setup(MPI_COMM_WORLD,Info)
Select one DLS_Method from library
call RL_Init(...)
for t = 1, N do !Time loop
  ...
  if(I_am_the_scheduler) then
   time_start=time()
   call RL_Action(t,Loop1,DLS_Method)
  end if
  {execute Loop 1 using DLS_Method}
  if(I_am_the_scheduler) then
   reward=time()-time_start
   call RL_Reward(t,Loop1,
        DLS_Method,reward)
  end if
  ... ! Integrate RL+DLS for
  ... ! Loops 2 & 3 as above
  for l4 = 1, n do ! Loop 4
   Compute V[l4], fc[l4]
  end for

  Output t, r[.], v[.], ρ[.], V[.],
         fc[.], Q[.], fq[.], dv[.]
  for l5 = 1, n do ! Loop 5
   Update ρ[l5], r[l5], v[l5]
  end for
end for
```

FIGURE 22.11. QTM with DLS and RL.

interagent communication. The scheduling algorithms for achieving load balancing are modeled as different states, dynamically selected depending on the variability of the environment. The actions determine the particular choice of an algorithm from one state to another. The transition from one state to another takes place as shown in Figure 22.4b, the arcs representing transitions from one state to another. The environment is a dynamic system of clusters on which the application is executed. The reinforcement signal or reward is modeled using the parallel execution cost, which is the product of the number of processors and the loop execution time, and is given as feedback to the reinforcement learner. Each of the three loops (loops 1, 2, and 3) has an individual reinforcement learner capable to select the best algorithm suited for that loop, thereby reducing the overall computing time when compared to the traditional approach of exhaustive selection and execution. The total number of time steps in the application is modeled as episodes.

22.5.2.2   *Implementation of QTM with DLS and RL*   The QTM application is coded in Fortran 90. The library of loop scheduling algorithms contains implementations of the nine loop scheduling methods described earlier in Section 22.3. The loop scheduling methods contained in the library can be classified into three distinct categories: *equal-size chunks* (STATIC, FSC, and MFSC), *decreasing-size chunks* (GSS, FAC, AWF, AWF-B, and AWF-C), and *variable-size chunks* (AF). MFSC is modified FSC, where the number of chunks is the same as in FAC (i.e., the MFSC technique has the same overhead cost as FAC). In AWF-B, the processor weights are updated after every batch, and chunks are assigned in batches (as in FAC), while AWF-C is similar to AWF-B, with the difference that weights are updated after each chunk rather than after each batch.

The loop scheduling algorithms are based on a master–worker strategy. The distribution of data to worker processors can be implemented as follows: (1) The processors receive the data from the master together with the size of the chunk they are assigned to execute; (2) the data are initially replicated on all worker processors, and each processor works only on the data required by the chunk size it was assigned by the master; or (3) initially, the data are distributed among the participating worker processors, and each processor is assigned a specific portion of the iterations, to later work in chunk sizes determined by the master at runtime. For the experiments reported in this work, the data are replicated on all processors.

The loop scheduling algorithms contain utility functions in Fortran 90 and use the MPI message-passing paradigm for the execution of the QTM application in a distributed-memory environment. The RL component, coded in C, is called from the Fortran 90 application [24]. The architecture is generic for any operating system on which it is built. The design is independent of the underlying architecture and chooses the appropriate functions during the execution. The interface between the RL agent and the QTM simulation code requires only two additional statements for each of the three parallel loops (as illustrated in Figs. 22.7b and 22.11). Before a loop starts execution, the agent is called to compute the index of the scheduling algorithm, and after the loop ends execution, the agent is supplied with the algorithm index and the loop completion time.

22.6 EXPERIMENTAL RESULTS, ANALYSIS, AND EVALUATION

The verification and validation of this novel approach is discussed through experiments and their analysis in this section.

22.6.1 Experimental Setup and Results

To evaluate and analyze the significance and usefulness of the proposed RL system, two sets of experiments have been designed and conducted.

Experiment #1 Test the hypothesis that on a given number of processors, the QTM application using different load balancing methods selected by the RL agent during time stepping (LEARN) will perform better than the application using a single load balancing method determined before runtime (NOLEARN).

LEARN has two levels representing the learning methods used: Q-learning and SARSA. NOLEARN has eight levels representing the loop scheduling algorithms contained in the load balancing library: STATIC, FSC, MFSC, GSS, FAC, AF, AWF, and AWF-B. LEARN and NOLEARN are groups of load balancing techniques, m, which is hypothesized to affect the performance of the application. The QTM

```
1 α = 0.5; γ = 0.1;
2 NOLEARN={STATIC,FSC,MFSC,GSS,FAC,AF,AWF,AWF-B};
3 LEARN={Q-learning,SARSA};
4 for m in NOLEARN ∪ LEARN
5   for p in {2, 4, 8, 12, 16, 20, 24}
6     repeat the following 5 times:
7       ◇ execute QTM application using <m,p,α,γ>;
8       ◇ record Tₚ;
9   next p
10 next m
```

FIGURE 22.12. *Algorithm used for running the two-factorial <m × p> Experiment #1.*

```
1  for RL in {Q-learning,SARSA}
2    for p in {4, 8, 12}
3      for α, γ in {0.1,0.2,...,0.9}
4        repeat the following 5 times:
5          ◇ execute QTM application using <RL,p,α,γ>;
6          (a) record Tₚ;
7          (b) record frequency a DLS algorithm is
               selected for each loop in QTM;
8        next α, γ
9    next p
10 next RL
```

FIGURE 22.13. *Algorithm used for running the quad-factorial <RL × p × α, γ> Experiment #2.*

application was run on different numbers of processors, as illustrated in Figure 22.12, line 5. The experiment is, thus, a two-factor factorial experiment with m as the first factor and p as the second factor. A free particle represented as a wave packet of $n=501$ pseudoparticles was simulated for $N=10{,}000$ time steps.

Experiment #2 (a) Study of the effects of the learning parameters α and γ on the parallel runtime T_p of the QTM application, and (b) identify the number of times a DLS method was chosen by the RL agent.

This experiment is described by the algorithm shown in Figure 22.13. The aim of this experiment is to investigate, for the two learning techniques of the RL agent, the effects of the α and γ parameters' combinations on the completion time T_p of the QTM application. An additional objective is to compare the DLS selection results obtained when the two RL techniques (Q-learning and SARSA) are used. In line 5 of Figure 22.13, the QTM application is executed using <RL, p, α, γ>, and a particular DLS algorithm is selected by the RL agent. Given that Experiment #1 indicates that, in particular, the amount of concurrency present in the selected QTM application for the chosen simulation settings is not suitable for a number of processors larger than 12, no more than 12 processors have been considered in this experiment. A free particle represented as a wave packet of $n=1001$ pseudoparticles was simulated for $N=500$ time steps.

The testbed for performing both experiments was a general-purpose Linux cluster of 1038 Pentium III (1.0 and 1.266 GHz) processors with the Red Hat Linux operating system. Two processors reside in one node; 32 nodes are connected via fast Ethernet switch to comprise a rack; and the racks are connected via gigabit Ethernet uplinks. On this cluster, the queuing system (PBS) attempts to assign homogeneous computing nodes to a job, but this is not guaranteed. Network traffic volume is also not predictable because the cluster is general purpose. Other jobs were running along with the simulations.

22.6.2 Performance Analysis and Evaluation

Experiment #1   To model the variability of the performance measurements induced by the underlying computing architecture, the application was run with five replicates (as indicated in Fig. 22.12, line 6). The parallel execution time T_p for each $<m \times p>$ factor combination was measured and averaged across the five replicates. The mean T_p values are graphed in Figure 22.14 and annotated with letters. The letters, ranging from "a" through "v," represent the statistical groupings from the means least squares method. Mean values annotated with the same letter belong to one statistical group. The differences of the mean values in the same statistical group are not significantly different from zero according to the t-statistics at 0.05 significance. Following an analysis of the results in Figure 22.14, the following observations can be made:

Obs. 1   For each p, the T_p of the application with either RL technique (from the LEARN set) is significantly lower than the T_p of the application without learning (i.e., a DLS method from the NOLEARN set).

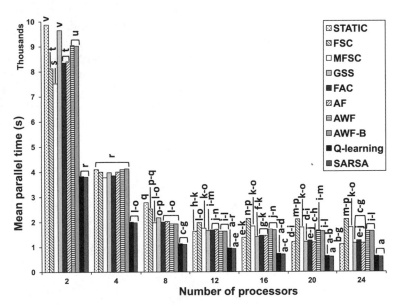

FIGURE 22.14. *Mean parallel time (T_p) for wavepacket simulation using QTM with 501 pseudoparticles using different load balancing methods and RL techniques at increasing the number of processors. Mean values with the same letter are not significantly different at 0.05 significance level via t-statistics using the means least squares method.*

Obs. 2 For each p, there is no significant difference between the T_p obtained using Q-learning or SARSA.

Obs. 3 For the LEARN set, there is a significant drop in the T_p when p is increased from $p=2$ to $p=8$. T_p does not significantly change, however, as p is further increased from $p=12$ to $p=24$. When using RL, the optimum p for the application with 501 pseudoparticles is $p^*=12$.

Obs. 4 For the NOLEARN set, STATIC has the worst T_p from $p=2$ to $p=8$, but has better T_p than most other techniques in NOLEARN from $p=16$ to $p=24$. The explanation is that, with a fixed problem size, the performance of a dynamic scheduling method degrades with additional processors due to the increase in scheduling overhead. It is well known that STATIC has no scheduling overhead; therefore, it is not penalized as the dynamic techniques when using more processors.

Obs. 5 The T_p for the LEARN set at $p=2$ is not significantly different from the T_p for the NOLEARN set at $p=4$. Similarly, the T_p for LEARN at $p=4$ is statistically comparable to the T_p for NOLEARN at $p=8$, with the exception of STATIC and FSC. For $p\leq8$, the QTM application using RL on p processors has statistically the same T_p as the application without RL on the next higher p. The T_p for the LEARN set at $p=12$ is even significantly better than the T_p for the NOLEARN set at $p=16$.

These results validate the suitability of RL as a viable procedure for online selection of DLS algorithms from a library to improve the performance of a class of large, time-stepping scientific applications with computationally intensive parallel loops.

Experiment #2(a) Figure 22.15 shows the mean T_p values for all (α, γ) values combinations, for 12 processors using Q-learning and SARSA techniques. Each of the values in charts is a mean of the completion times of five runs of the QTM application, as indicated in Figure 22.13, line 4.

A close inspection of the plots for each case indicates negligible variations in the T_p when the learning rate α and the discount factor γ-values are varied between 0.1 and 0.9. Similar charts were obtained also for four and eight processors, and also showed the same trends, except that T_p for the two cases is bound by 8000 and 4500 seconds, respectively. Figure 22.15 indicates that, for a given number of processors (i.e., $p=4, 8$, or 12) and a given RL technique (i.e., Q-learning or SARSA), the values of α and γ do not affect the completion time T_p of the QTM application.

This observation is also supported by the data in Figure 22.16. In the figure, the number of the processors is denoted by p; RL technique Q-learning is denoted by "RL 0," while the RL technique SARSA is denoted by "RL 1." The extremely small standard deviation values relative to the mean T_p values indicate negligible variations in T_p for all six cases.

Hypothesis Test 1: The following steps were performed to statistically support the above claims:

Step 1 Arbitrarily select an α-value for a particular p, and for a particular RL technique.

Step 2 Vary the γ-value from 0.1 to 0.9.

Step 3 Perform a *hypothesis test* between the differences in the respective mean values.

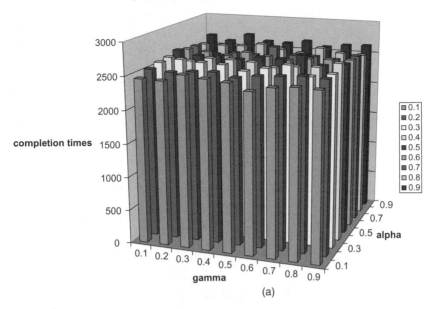

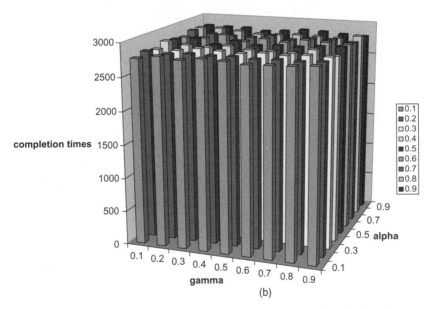

FIGURE 22.15. *Mean parallel completion time* (T_p) *for 12 processors with varying learning rate* α *and discount factor* γ. *(a) Q-learning. (b) SARSA.*

The α-values selected for Q-learning are 0.6, 0.3, and 0.2 for 4, 8, and 12 processors, respectively. The corresponding *t*-scores for a 95% confidence interval (CI) were calculated. Most of the *t*-scores are bounded by ±2.776 (the critical points for a 95% CI). Similarly, the α-values selected for SARSA are 0.4, 0.7, and 0.5 for 4, 8, and 12 processors, respectively. Again, the corresponding *t*-scores for a 95% CI were calculated and identical results were obtained for SARSA as were obtained for

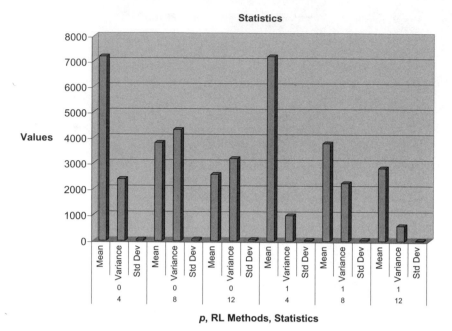

FIGURE 22.16. T_p *statistics graph showing the mean, variance, and standard deviation for the different experiment scenarios. The numbers 0 and 1 indicate Q-learning and SARSA, respectively. The numbers 4, 8, and 12 are the number of processors used.*

Q-learning, indicating that most of the *t*-scores are bounded by the 95% CI critical values, ±2.776 in this case as well.

The calculations were repeated with a fixed γ and varying α under identical constraints. Essentially, the same quantities are assigned to fixed γ-values as were assigned for α-values in the previous calculation. In this case, however, the α-values were then varied. The *t*-scores obtained for 95% CI give similar indication as was obtained previously. In other words, most of the *t*-scores are bounded by ±2.776. There is no significant difference in the T_p for a given RL technique and processor combination when α and γ are varied. As a result, it can be stated with 95% confidence level that the T_p of the QTM application is *not sensitive* to the α and γ variations for a given RL technique and for a given number of processors.

In both scenarios, however, a small number of outlier *t*-scores are attributed to the fact that the cluster used for our experiments was a nondedicated, shared, and general-purpose system. It was, therefore, subject to interferences, such as unpredictability in application scheduling and unpredictability in processor rack assignments of the cluster nodes.

Hypothesis Test 2: The next set of calculations are carried out to verify whether there are significant differences in T_p when different RL techniques are used. To this end, the following steps were followed:

Step 1   Arbitrarily fix a set of nine α- and γ-values as (0.1, 0.3), (0.2, 0.7), (0.3, 0.2), (0.4, 0.6), (0.5, 0.1), (0.6, 0.9), (0.7, 0.4), (0.8, 0.5), and (0.9, 0.8).

Step 2   For a particular p, perform the hypothesis test on the differences in the T_p mean values for RL techniques Q-learning and SARSA.

Once again, the analysis indicated that the *t*-scores are bounded by ±2.776 critical values, and no significant difference in the T_p for a given α, γ, and p combination was found when the RL techniques were varied. Therefore, it can be stated with 95% confidence level that, for a given p, the completion time T_p is also *not sensitive* to the type of RL technique used.

Experiment #2(b) Figure 22.17 presents the diagrams representing the number of times each of the DLS algorithms were selected for a given p and RL technique. In the figure, the numbers 4, 8, and 12 are the numbers of processors used, while

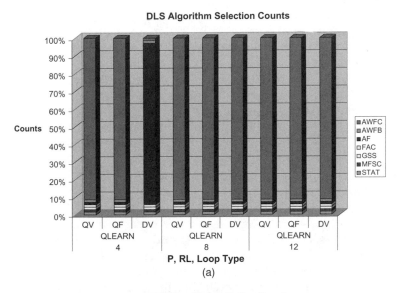

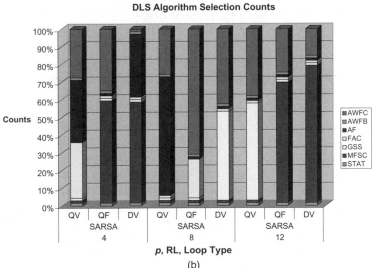

FIGURE 22.17. *DLS algorithm selection pattern for various* p *and the two RL techniques. (a) Q-learning. (b) SARSA.*

"QV," "QF," and "DV" represent loop 1, loop 2, and loop 3 of the QTM application, respectively (Figs. 22.9–22.11). As can be seen, there are significant differences in the selection pattern indicating the number of times each of the DLS algorithms was selected for each of the two RL techniques. This indicates that different RL techniques will select a different DLS algorithm at a different rate in order to succeed, even though their overall performance is similar.

22.6.2.1 Summary of Experiments Each computationally intensive parallel loop is assigned an RL agent, which automatically selects a DLS algorithm from a library to minimize the loop completion time. Two RL techniques (Q-learning and SARSA) are applied and both use a pair of learning parameters (α, γ). Investigations and comparisons on the parallel performance of the QTM application with and without the RL agent are conducted by means of pairwise comparisons via t-statistics using the means least squares method. The analysis of the results indicates that, for any number of processors, p, the simulation performs statistically better with the RL agent than without it. There is no significant difference in the performance of the simulation for any p using either of the two RL techniques. The analysis also identifies the optimal number of processors p^* for the wavepacket size tested. For $p < p^*$, the performance of the simulation *with* the RL agent is comparable or even superior to that when a higher number of processors are used *without* the RL agent. Further, investigations and comparisons about the influence of the learning parameters α and γ on the performance of the QTM application are also conducted, in conjunction with investigations on the influence of using a particular RL technique on the application performance for certain values of α and γ. Moreover, a study was conducted on investigating the differences in the number of times each of the DLS algorithms was selected by the RL techniques. The analysis of the results shows that for a fixed p, the simulation completion time is *insensitive* to the values of α and γ used in the experiments. In addition, there is no advantage of choosing one RL technique over the other, even though these RL techniques significantly differ in the number of times each of them selects various DLS algorithms. These claims are statistically validated by the experimental results.

22.7 CONCLUSIONS, FUTURE WORK, AND OPEN PROBLEMS

In this chapter, an AC *mechanism* is presented focused on performance self-optimization of scientific applications. The mechanism uses RL for the selection of DLS techniques. The benefits, significance, and usefulness of a DLS-with-RL approach are demonstrated for the performance improvement of a time-stepping scientific application (simulation of wavepacket dynamics using the QTM), which contains computationally intensive parallel loops with nonuniform iteration execution times. The optimal number of processors is also identified for a fixed problem size. The DLS-with-RL approach uses two model-free RL techniques (Q-learning and SARSA) for online DLS algorithm selection while solving the scientific problem. The results show that the DLS-with-RL approach performs statistically better than the DLS-*only* approach regardless of the RL technique used (and the number of times each of the DLS algorithms is selected) or the values chosen for the learning parameters.

In conclusion, these results validate the suitability of RL as a viable AC approach for improving the performance of a class of large, time-stepping scientific applications with computationally intensive parallel loops. This has been accomplished via an online selection of algorithms from a DLS library. The approach has numerous advantages, including improved performance and adaptability, and the capacity to learn a load balancing policy for a particular computing environment and application, without extensive programming and analysis. One important advantage of this approach is that the RL techniques used in this chapter consider only *one* state variable, namely, the loop execution time at a given time-step iteration, which results in fast execution. However, there is no loss of generality because the DLS techniques are based on probabilistic analyses and *already* implicitly address simultaneously all, at both algorithm and system levels, the causes of irregularity that would result in load imbalance during the execution of a time-stepping application. Furthermore, the proposed approach is portable and generic, facilitating the continuous and successive integration of new DLS or RL techniques.

Future work plans include the integration of other types of RL techniques in the present framework and evaluation with other time-stepping applications. One open question regards the scalability of RL-based approaches for performance optimization of scientific applications. The large size of computing systems today and the even larger expected size of future systems mandate the need to study the *scalability* of the proposed RL approach in terms of increased number of processors and increased number of RL agents.

ACKNOWLEDGMENTS

The authors would like to thank the National Science Foundation for its support of this work through the following grants: CAREER #9984465, ITR #0081303, and IIP #1034897. This work was partially also supported by the German Research Foundation (DFG) in the Collaborative Research Center 912 "Highly Adaptive Energy-Efficient Computing." Special thanks go to Ricolindo L. Cariño, Sumithra Dhandayuthapani, Jaderick P. Pabico, and Mahbubur Rashid for their prior contribution leading to the current work.

REFERENCES

[1] N.R. Satish, "Compile time task and resource allocation of concurrent applications to multiprocessor systems." PhD Thesis, EECS Department, University of California, Berkeley, January, 2009.

[2] C. Boneti, R. Gioiosa, F.J. Cazorla, and M. Valero, "Using hardware resource allocation to balance HPC applications," in *Parallel and Distributed Computing* (A. Ros, ed.), Chapter 7. Rijeka, Croatia: InTech, 2010.

[3] S.F. Hummel, E. Schonberg, and L.E. Flynn, "Factoring: A method for scheduling parallel loops," *Communications of the ACM*, 35(8):90–101, 1992.

[4] I. Banicescu and S.F. Hummel, "Balancing processor loads and exploiting data locality in *N*-body simulations," ACM/IEEE Conference on Supercomputing (SC 1995) (on CDROM), 1995.

[5] S.F. Hummel, J. Schmidt, R.N. Uma, and J. Wein, "Load-sharing in heterogeneous systems via weighted factoring," in *8th Annual ACM Symposium on Parallel Algorithms and Architectures (SPAA 1996)*, pp. 318–328, 1996.

[6] I. Banicescu and Z. Liu, "Adaptive factoring: A dynamic scheduling method tuned to the rate of weight changes," in *High Performance Computing Symposium (HPC 2000)*, pp. 122–129, 2000.

[7] I. Banicescu and V. Velusamy, "Load balancing highly irregular computations with the adaptive factoring," in *16th IEEE International Parallel and Distributed Processing Symposium (IPDPS-HCW 2002) (on CDROM)*, 2002.

[8] I. Banicescu and V. Velusamy, "Performance of scheduling scientific applications with adapative weighted factoring," in *15th IEEE International Parallel and Distributed Processing Symposium (IPDPS-HCW 2001) (on CDROM)*, 2001.

[9] I. Banicescu, V. Velusamy, and J. Devaprasad, "On the scalability of dynamic scheduling scientific applications with adaptive weighted factoring," *Cluster Computing*, 6(3):213–226, 2003.

[10] R.L. Cariño and I. Banicescu, "Dynamic scheduling parallel loops with variable iterate execution times," in *16th IEEE International Parallel and Distributed Processing Symposium (IPDPS-PDSECA 2002) (on CDROM)*, 2002.

[11] I. Banicescu and R.L. Cariño, "Addressing the stochastic nature of scientific computations via dynamic loop scheduling," *Electronic Transactions on Numerical Analysis, Special Issue on Combinatorial Scientific Computing*, 21:66–80, 2005.

[12] R.L. Cariño and I. Banicescu, "Dynamic load balancing with adaptive factoring methods in scientific applications," *The Journal of Supercomputing*, 44(1):41–63, 2008.

[13] M.L. Littman, "Markov games as a framework for multi-agent reinforcement learning," *11th International Conference on Machine Learning (ICML 1994)*, pp. 157–163, 1994.

[14] G. Tesauro, "Temporal difference learning and TD-Gammon," *Communications of the ACM*, 38(3):58–68, 1995.

[15] S. Mahadevan and J. Connell, "Automatic programming of behavior-based robots using reinforcement learning," *9th National Conference on Artificial Intelligence (NCAI 1991)*, 1991.

[16] M.J. Mataric, "Reward functions for accelerated learning," *11th International Conference on Machine Learning (ICML 1994)*, 1994.

[17] S. Schaal and C.G. Atkeson, "Robot juggling: An implementation of memory-based learning," *Control Systems Magazine*, 14(1):57–71, 1994.

[18] M.G. Lagoudakis and M.L. Littman, "Algorithm selection using reinforcement learning," *17th International Conference on Machine Learning (ICML 2000)*, pp. 511–518, 2000.

[19] J. Parent, K. Verbeeck, J. Lemeire, A. Nowe, K. Steenhaut, and E. Dirkx, "Adaptive load balancing of parallel applications with multi-agent reinforcement learning on heterogeneous systems," *Scientific Programming, Distributed Computing and Applications*, 12:71–79, 2004.

[20] G. Tesauro, "Reinforcement learning in autonomic computing: A manifesto and case studies," *IEEE Internet Computing*, 11(1):22–30, 2007.

[21] G. Tesauro, N.K. Jong, R. Das, and M.N. Bennani, "On the use of hybrid reinforcement learning for autonomic resource allocation," *Cluster Computing*, 10:287–299, 2007.

[22] A.Y. Zomaya, M. Clements, and S. Olariu, "A framework for reinforcement-based scheduling in parallel processor systems," *IEEE Transactions on Parallel and Distributed Systems*, 9(3):249–260, 1998.

[23] C.J.C.H. Watkins and P. Dyan, "Q-learning," *Machine Learning*, 8(3–4):279–292, 1992.

[24] S. Dhandayuthapani, "Automatic selection of dynamic loop scheduling algorithms for load balancing using reinforcement learning." Master's Thesis, Mississippi State University, 2004.

[25] S. Dhandayuthapani, I. Banicescu, R.L. Cariño, E. Hansen, J.P. Pabico, and M. Rashid, "Automatic selection of loop scheduling algorithms using reinforcement learning," in *Challenges of Large Applications in Distributed Environments (CLADE 2005)*, pp. 87–94, 2005.

[26] M. Balasubramaniam, K. Barker, I. Banicescu, N. Chrisochoides, J.P. Pabico, and R.L. Cariño, "A novel dynamic load balancing library for cluster computing," in *3rd IEEE International Symposium on Parallel and Distributed Computing, International Workshop on Algorithms, Models and Tools for Parallel Computing on Heterogeneous Networks (ISPDC/HeteroPar '04)*, pp. 346–352, 2004.

[27] I. Banicescu, R.L. Cariño, J.P. Pabico, and M. Balasubramaniam, "Design and implementation of a novel dynamic load balancing library for cluster computing," *Parallel Computing*, 31:736–756, 2005.

[28] R.L. Cariño and I. Banicescu, "A load balancing tool for distributed parallel loops," in *International Workshop on Challenges of Large Applications in Distributed Environments (CLADE 2003)*, pp. 39–46, 2003.

[29] R.L. Cariño and I. Banicescu, "A load balancing tool for distributed parallel loops," *Cluster Computing*, 8:313–321, 2005.

[30] R.L. Cariño and I. Banicescu, "A tool for a two-level dynamic load balancing strategy in scientific applications," *Scalable Computing: Practice and Experience, Special Issue on Practical Aspects of Large-Scale Distributed Computing*, 8(3):249–261, 2007.

[31] I. Banicescu, S. Ghafoor, V. Velusamy, S. Russ, and M. Bilderback, "Experiences from integrating algorithmic and systemic load balancing strategies," *Concurrency and Computation: Practice and Experience*, 13(2):121–139, 2001.

[32] Z. Fang, P. Tang, P.-C. Yew, and C.-Q. Zhu, "Dynamic processor self-scheduling for general parallel nested loops," *IEEE Transactions on Computers*, 39:919–929, 1990.

[33] S.F. Hummel, I. Banicescu, C. Wang, and J. Wein, "Load balancing and data locality via fractiling: An experimental study," in *Languages, Compilers and Run-Time Systems for Scalable Computers* (B.K. Szymanski and B. Sinharoy, eds.), Chapter 7, pp. 85–98. Boston: Kluwer Academic Publishers, 1996.

[34] C.P. Kruskal and A. Weiss, "Allocating independent subtasks on parallel processors," *IEEE Transactions on Software Engineering*, 11(10):1001–1016, 1985.

[35] C.D. Polychronopoulos and D.J. Kuck, "Guided self-scheduling: A practical scheduling scheme for parallel supercomputers," *IEEE Transactions on Computers*, 36(12):1425–1439, 1987.

[36] K. Govindaswamy, An API for adaptive loop scheduling in shared address space architectures. Master's Thesis, Mississippi State University, July, 2003.

[37] R.S. Sutton and A.G. Barto, *Reinforcement Learning: An Introduction*. Cambridge, MA: The MIT Press, 1998.

[38] A.W. Moore and C.G. Atkeson, "Prioritized sweeping: Reinforcement learning with less data and less real time," *Machine Learning*, 13:103–130, 1993.

[39] J. Peng and R.J. Williams, "Efficient learning and planning with the Dyna framework," *Adaptive Behavior*, 1(4):437–454, 1993.

[40] A.G. Barto, S.J. Bradtke, and S.P. Singh, "Learning to act using real-time dynamic programming," *Artificial Intelligence*, 72(1):81–138, 1995.

[41] L.P. Kaelbling, M.L. Littman, and A.P. Moore, "Reinforcement learning: A survey," *Journal of Artificial Intelligence Research*, 4:237–285, 1996.

[42] M. Rashid, I. Banicescu, and R.L. Cariño, "Investigating a dynamic loop scheduling with reinforcement learning approach to load balancing scientific applications," in *7th IEEE International Symposium on Parallel and Distributed Computing (ISPDC 2008)*, pp. 123–130, 2008.

[43] R.L. Cariño, I. Banicescu, R.K. Vadapalli, C.A. Weatherford, and J. Zhu, "Parallel adaptive quantum trajectory method for wavepacket simulation," in *17th IEEE International Parallel and Distributed Processing Symposium (IPDPS-PDSECA 2003), (on CDROM)*, 2003.

[44] R.L. Cariño, I. Banicescu, R.K. Vadapalli, C.A. Weatherford, and J. Zhu, "Message passing parallel adaptive quantum trajectory method," in *High Performance Scientific and Engineering Computing* (L.T. Yang and Y. Pan, eds.), Chapter 9, pp. 127–139. Norwell, MA: Kluwer Academic Publishers, 2004.

23

A Survey of Techniques for Improving Search Engine Scalability through Profiling, Prediction, and Prefetching of Query Results

C. Shaun Wagner, Sahra Sedigh, Ali R. Hurson, and Behrooz Shirazi

23.1 INTRODUCTION

Search engines are vital tools for handling large repositories of electronic data. As the availability of electronic data continues to grow, search engine scalability gains importance [1]. As noted in the literature, researchers have measured search engine performance in terms of response time and relevance [2–5], both of which suffer as the number of potential search results increases. Response (or search) time is the time elapsed between initiation of a query and when the desired data item is available to the user. Relevance quantifies the relevance of the results returned. Search engines typically exhibit a trade-off between response time and relevance [6]. However, irrelevant search results (even when delivered quickly) require that the

Scalable Computing and Communications: Theory and Practice, First Edition. Edited by
Samee U. Khan, Albert Y. Zomaya, and Lizhe Wang.
© 2013 John Wiley & Sons, Inc. Published 2013 by John Wiley & Sons, Inc.

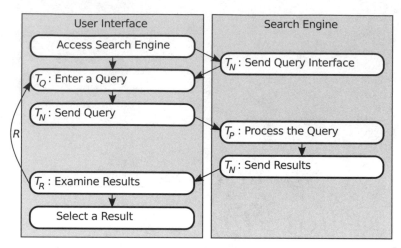

FIGURE 23.1. *Operational flow of a standard query–response search engine.*

query be refined and repeated, increasing the overall search time [2]. This chapter presents a survey of techniques that can be used to increase the relevance and to reduce the response time of search engines by predicting user queries and prefetching the results.

When a user is querying for a specific item, such as a book title, searching an information repository is a trivial task of carrying out an equality search on an index, that is, metadata. There is little room for improvement in response time or relevance. In practice, users often carry out searches with only a vague description of a topic or concept. In this case, the user attempts to form a descriptive query of what he or she is looking for, and it is up to the search engine to determine the semantics of the request and to generate query results that best match the semantic concept of the query. If this determination is made incorrectly, the search results returned will be irrelevant, necessitating that the user refine and repeat the query. This query–response system, depicted in Figure 23.1, is the basis of all popular search engines [3, 4].

Equation (23.1) expresses the total search time (T_T) as a sum of the time spent on each independent step of the search process: query entry time (T_Q), query processing time (T_P), and search result examination time (T_R). If the search results are not acceptable, the entire process is repeated R times:

$$T_T = T_N + (T_O + T_N + T_P + T_N + T_R)R. \qquad (23.1)$$

Network access time, for example, network latency (T_N), is repeated in Equation (23.1): to represent a need to access the search engine interface, to send the query to the search engine, and to send the results back to the user. Normally, when a server sends a result list to the user, it also displays the query interface. Therefore, the initial network access time is not repeated on successive queries. Very little data are communicated between the client and servers throughout the query processing time, limiting the benefit of reducing T_N to increase scalability. Furthermore, reduction of T_N is primarily related to hardware, not software. As such, we will omit network access time from the total search time for the remainder of this chapter.

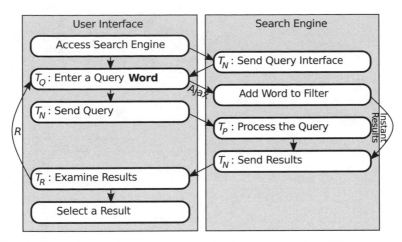

FIGURE 23.2. *Google Instant displays search results after each word typed. The user may select a result at any time.*

Traditionally, search engine improvement was primarily due to improved index-ing techniques, which by default decreased the time spent processing the query and displaying relevant search results (T_P) [4]. Recent advances in search engine improvement are focused on query caching and methods designed to create an overlap between T_Q and T_P [7, 8]. The literature abounds with techniques and solu-tions for data caching in general, and web caching in particular, as a means to improve web searching. The speedup gain due to web caching is based on the fact that the results of popular search topics are often cached (see Appendix A.2). Caching the top searches and their results decreases the query processing time of similar future searches to a significant extent [3, 9].

Google visibly attempted to speed up the query process through Google Instant—a more interactive query entry process (depicted in Fig. 23.2) [10]. Normally, search engine users are required to enter a complete query and to submit it to the server. This entry and submission time (T_Q) takes 9 seconds on average [4, 10]. With Google Instant, Ajax is used to overlap the user's query entry time with the server's query processing time. Each time the user presses the space bar, demarcating one word from the next, the query that has been entered so far is sent to the search engine for processing. Word by word, a result filter is produced and a running list of search results is displayed while the user continues to enter his or her query. By the time the user submits the complete query, most of the processing is complete. Google Instant is designed to avoid complete query entry. It is expected that the user will obtain a relevant result after only a portion of the query has been entered, eliminating the need for the remainder of the query entry process. In other words, network access (of duration T_N) + and query processing (of duration T_P) are per-formed *during* T_Q, for an average time reduction of 2–5 seconds per search [10].

A further improvement in total search time would be to bypass the query entry and processing time ($T_Q + T_N + T_P$) and have immediate search results available to the user (see Fig. 23.3). In this case, the user accesses the search engine. The search engine recognizes the user and while displaying a standard query interface, also displays a list of predicted search results. The user has the option to use the search

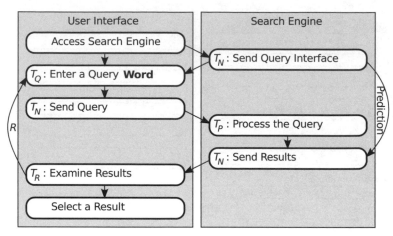

FIGURE 23.3. *A predictive search engine sends predicted results along with the query interface.*

interface to enter a query or can immediately select one of the predicted search results, saving about 10 seconds per query [10].

While this predictive search engine would save time, a method of guiding users to information assumed relevant would redefine the way search engines are used [11]. Instead of having a complete idea and searching for information on the idea, a search engine can begin with the start of an idea and provide a list of results from other users' search histories, guiding the user through the search process that others have followed.

From the user's point of view, prediction not only saves time but it also takes search engines beyond a simple search for information to a search for information from a sequence of related queries. The benefit of providing a sequence of search results can be shown in two scenarios. In the first example, a user sees an error message on a digital camera and wants to know what is wrong and how to fix it. In the second, an instructor is composing a sequence of topics for a course lesson plan.

In the first scenario, assume the user searches for a fix for an "E:61:10" error on a Sony DSC camera. Using both Google and Bing, the search results consist primarily of forum threads discussing the problem. It is possible that one of the threads will contain a solution to the problem, but searching through the threads is likely to be very time-consuming. Taking advice from forums may even result in damage to the camera because the solutions suggested include hitting the camera, smacking the camera on a desk, and soaking the camera in a bath of rubbing alcohol and bleach. However, E:61:10 is a common error for the Sony DSC camera, and as such, the search engine will have multiple records of other users searching for solutions to the very same error message. Instead of requiring the user to type the exact query needed to find a search result containing the solution, a predictive search engine will utilize these records to identify commonly selected destinations from other users' search histories—based on the assumption that useful solutions will be selected most often from among the search results returned. The user of the predictive search engine begins with a search for a solution to the camera's error. The search results returned by the search engine will include a predicted path directly to the common destinations that contain a solution to the problem that led to initiation of the search.

In the second scenario, the instructor begins by searching for information about the initial topics for a course that he or she will teach. For example, the instructor first searches for information on vector algebra and selects a search result that appears promising. Then, the instructor searches for a dot product and selects another promising search result. The predictive search engine identifies the two previously selected search results and compares those to other user's histories. Before the instructor begins another query, search results pertaining to cross product (the logical successor to the previous two topics) are shown. After selecting a destination from among the cross product results and returning to the search engine, search results pertaining to lines and planes are shown—before the instructor types a query. In this fashion, the search engine will present the instructor with a sequence of topics, that is, results from consecutive searches, that many others have utilized. This order is the logical order of topics for a majority of users. In this case, the instructor knows the destination for the course should be vector-valued functions, but is looking for the common sequence of topics, from beginning to end. In both scenarios, the power of the search engine is in prediction of user behavior based on the behavior of other users.

In the implementation of prediction, a search engine could either predict the query that the user will enter or predict the search result that the user will select. Prediction of search queries is less scalable than predicting selected search results. Many query terms are indexed for each search result, making the search space for queries exponentially larger than the search space for results [3, 11]. Consider the query "hedgehog information." It yields search results for a small spiny mammal, a chocolate desert, and a spiked antisubmarine weapon—three very unrelated data items. Furthermore, if the search query is predicted, only the physical time spent typing the query will be saved. For example, the search engine will predict that the user will type "homes for sale in Albuquerque." If the prediction is correct, the user submits the predicted query and gets the search results, just as if he or she had typed the query.

Unlike a query, a specific search result refers to a specific data item, for example, a URL for a web search engine or an image for an image search engine. By selecting a search result, the user is selecting a specific data item. Where prediction of a search query yields a vague prediction of multiple data items, prediction of a search result yields a specific data item. Therefore, the user's selection from among search results is what should be predicted, as opposed to the search query itself.

Prediction is typically based on a model of user behavior, which is in turn based on profile information from multiple users. User behavior, within the realm of a search engine, is an ordered set of search results selected by him or her. With each user contributing a history of queries and (selected) search results, a vast collection of user histories is available for use in modeling and prediction of user behavior—in the context of this chapter, selection from among results returned in response to a query.

This chapter examines current methods of modeling and predicting user behavior. These methods use the behavior of multiple people to develop a model of user behavior. Then, the model (or models) is (are) used for prediction. Common methods are defined with examples as necessary. The rest of the chapter is organized as follows. Section 23.2 defines behavior modeling with examples. Often, a single model is incapable of accurately capturing the behavior of a population. In such cases, the population is divided into groups or neighborhoods, and the behavior of each is modeled separately. In Section 23.3, we discuss and analyze several grouping techniques, for example, k-nearest neighbor (KNN), a vector-based similarity method, and singular value decomposition (SVD). Algorithms for calculating a similarity value are used in both grouping and modeling. With rare exception, these algorithms fall under either vector- or string-based methods. Both techniques are examined in detail in Section 23.4. Vector methods generally require less processing time but lack accuracy. On the other hand, string-based methods are processing intensive but offer increased accuracy. Sections 23.4.1 and 23.4.2 further analyze different vector-based and string-based methods, respectively. With user profiles grouped into neighborhoods of similarity, the next step in prediction is to develop a behavior model for each neighborhood. Given a target user, the neighborhood with users most similar to the target user is identified, and its behavior model is used in predicting the behavior of the target user. Section 23.5 is dedicated to this issue and serves to conclude the chapter and discuss future research directions.

23.2   MODELING USER BEHAVIOR

Both modeling and prediction of human behavior are established fields that gained popularity as psychology developed alongside early computers [12]. While the possibilities of human behavior appear to be infinite, the actual behavior of humans is limited by task goals and environment. Therefore, it is possible to describe human behavior as a sequence of dynamic states that can be captured by a state-space model. One such model is a Markov chain, which represents user behavior with a set of interconnected nodes [4]. Each node is a time-ordered action or observation. The weight of the directed link connecting two nodes represents the probability of transitioning from the first to the second, that is, that the action denoted by the destination node will immediately follow that of the source node. What differentiates Markov models from other state-space models is their memoryless feature: The next state only depends on the current state; that is, the current state subsumes the entire history of transitions.

Figure 23.4 is a model of user behavior at a vending machine. Many of the actions and observations are omitted, leaving only the most common actions and observations. User actions are in circles. User observations are in squares. Weighted arrows designate a transition from one state (be it an action or observation) to another by means of a user action. The weights (percentages) are the important part of the behavior model as they determine the likelihood of the transition. For example, 5% of the time, a person would press the coin return directly after inserting change. After pressing a product button, the user will observe, 100% of the time, either that an item is received or that nothing happens. The relative frequency of these two outcomes characterizes the behavior of the vending machine and, as such, does not appear in the user behavior model.

Given such a model, a computer can monitor user behavior and predict what the user's upcoming actions and observations will be. If a user inserts change, there is a 95% chance that the user will press a button to select an item. More complex

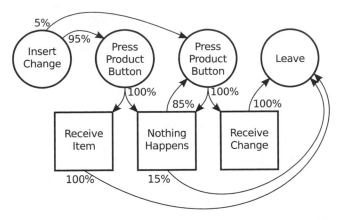

FIGURE 23.4. *A model of typical user behavior at a vending machine.*

predictions can be made, such as estimation of the probability that a user will press the coin return. After inserting change, there is a 5% chance that a user will press the coin return. If the user presses a button to select an item, there is still a chance that the user will press the coin return, which is based on the chance that "nothing happens" will be observed by the user. Because "nothing happens" is an observation and not a decision for the user, the computer can monitor the vending machine to determine the probability of nothing happening. Assume that it is 10%, and that the vending machine behavior is independent of that of the user—a reasonable assumption. Users who select an item will observe nothing happening 10% of the time, and 85% of those users will press the coin return. Therefore, 8.5% of users who select an item will eventually press the coin return. The overall chance of the coin return being pressed is 13.5%. Further, there is a possibility that those who press the coin return will observe that nothing happens. In this case, there is an 85% chance that the user will press the coin return a second time.

This form of Markov modeling has been successfully tested for observation and prediction of complex human behavior. Toledo and Katz used a similar model to represent and accurately predict lane change behavior by automobile drivers [13]. While it is rare for drivers to change lanes in the exact same order or at the exact same location, the overall behavior was predicted by observing a specific driver's actions and utilizing the Markov model that was developed by observing many other drivers.

Similarly, Pentland and Liu used Markov models to define general actions performed by automobile drivers [14]. They increased the accuracy of predictions by producing multiple Markov models. Drivers that exhibited similar behavior were clustered into similarity groups. A separate model was developed for each group. The models contained many common attributes but were different enough to clearly identify differences in behavior among the various similarity groups. New drivers were observed to produce a short history of their respective driving behaviors. That history was used to place each new driver in one of the similarity groups. Then, the model for that group was used to predict the driver's behavior. The resulting predictions proved to be 95% accurate.

23.3   GROUPING USERS INTO NEIGHBORHOODS OF SIMILARITY

When discussing prediction of user behavior, a common example is Amazon's product recommendation algorithm. Customers recognize it as the "Customers Who Bought This Item Also Bought" feature. It is a popular and somewhat effective neighborhood model for collaborative filtering [15]. The goal is to identify objects by specific attributes and then use those attributes to cluster or group the objects by similarity. Each cluster is commonly referred to as a neighborhood. For Amazon, the customer's attributes are the set of products purchased by the customer. Regardless of the similarity among the products purchased by a particular customer, customers whose respective search histories have considerable overlap are considered similar.

Metrics for search engine usage are abundant. As an example, Google has patented many of its measurements of search result relationships, such as keyword identification, hand ranking, geospatial relationships [16], and number of inbound links. Following Amazon's model, search engine users who have selected a large number of the same search results are considered similar and should be grouped into a neighborhood of similarity in developing a predictive search engine.

23.3.1   Neighborhood Model

The KNN is commonly used to group objects into neighborhoods of similarity [17–19]. Objects are characterized by a predefined set of simple attributes, often a small fraction of the attributes that could potentially characterize an object. The choice of attributes to include in this set greatly affects the usefulness of the resulting neighborhood model. Objects with similar attributes are grouped together. Once grouped, it is assumed that objects within the same neighborhood will share all attributes, including those not used in developing the neighborhood model.

As an example, the Piggly Wiggly grocery store may create neighborhoods of similarity based on the time of day a customer is most likely to make a purchase, the average cost of each purchase, and the specific store at which the purchase was made. From there, a neighborhood of morning shoppers who make purchases over $200 per trip to a beachside store may be identified as a neighborhood. With three simple attributes in common, Piggly Wiggly assumes that other attributes are shared. If a portion of customers in that neighborhood suddenly purchase a specific product, Piggly Wiggly can target marketing for the product to everyone in that specific group, instead of the general population. Obviously, Piggly Wiggly can use a more complex algorithm for grouping customers into neighborhoods, but the concept remains the same [20].

Regardless of application, the KNN algorithm can be broken into three simple steps. In these steps, a concept of distance is often used instead of similarity. Distance is a measure based on the attributes of two objects. The distance between two identical objects is zero. The larger the distance between two objects, the less similar the objects are. The term "distance" is derived from vector distance. Assuming that the attributes for an object are treated as a vector, the distance between the attribute vectors of two objects is the distance between the objects themselves. Common methods for determining distance are discussed in Section 23.4.

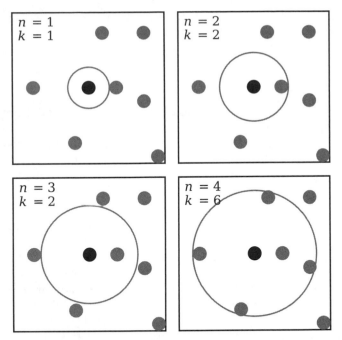

FIGURE 23.5. *Effect of increasing the neighborhood radius (n) on the neighborhood cardinality (k).*

To create a single neighborhood based on a target object within a large set of objects, the following steps are necessary:

1. Compute the distance from the target object to all other objects using predefined attributes.
2. Order the objects from least distant (similar) to most distant (different).
3. Select an optimal number (k) of nearest neighbors to include in the neighborhood of the target object. The value of k may be chosen beforehand or calculated based on an optimal neighborhood radius size [21]. See Figure 23.5 for examples of how the choice of neighborhood radius, n, affects the neighborhood size, k. Increasing n may or may not increase k.

An "object" may be any entity that will be modeled. For the purpose of collaborative filtering in a user–product environment, some models cluster the users together, while others cluster the products. Amazon.com is an example of a successful collaborative filtering environment in which the users are compared to one another based on their respective purchasing histories, as in the "Customers Who Bought This Item Also Bought" feature [15]. Pandora.com is an example of a successful collaborative filtering environment in which the products, songs in this case, are matched by similarity across many metrics identified by the Music Genome Project [22]. Users who like one song are offered songs within the same neighborhood of similarity. Each approach (clustering users instead of products) has its own merits [23]. Users with similar attributes are likely to behave in a similar manner. Products with similar attributes are likely to be purchased (or perused) in a similar manner. It is also possible to have a complex grouping scheme that compares both users and products in determining neighborhoods of similarity.

23.3.2 SVD Model

It is often necessary to define a relationship between two sets of objects, such as customers and products. One method of doing so is to group each set of objects into neighborhoods of similarity, respectively, and then compare and contrast the various neighborhoods. The KNN algorithm is used to create a single neighborhood for a single object, not a set of neighborhoods for all objects. Further, the KNN algorithm is not capable of handling missing attributes—a common problem in real-world data.

Grouping and comparing objects is subject to several challenges—beyond missing attributes. These challenges include synonymy and polysemy. *Synonymy* occurs when two identical attributes have different names. *Polysemy* occurs when a single name refers to multiple attributes. To correct for missing data, synonymy, and polysemy, SVD has been widely used as a part of latent semantic indexing (LSI) [24] (see Section 23.4.1.2). Decreasing missing data, synonymy, and polysemy with SVD in turn increases the accuracy of grouping by similarity [25].

The purpose of SVD is to decompose a matrix M into three matrices that represent its rows, columns, and the relationship between the rows and columns, respectively. Specifically, SVD will convert an $m \times n$ matrix M into a collection of three matrices: an $m \times m$ unitary matrix U that describes the rows of M, an $n \times n$ unitary matrix V that describes the columns of M, and an $m \times n$ diagonal matrix Σ that describes the relationship between the rows and columns of M [26]. In practice, a thin form of SVD is implemented because it produces the same estimation with fewer calculations and values to store [27]. A thin SVD calculates only n columns of U and n rows of Σ. When compared to a full SVD, producing m columns of U and m rows of Σ does not provide a significantly more accurate result. The following example uses a thin SVD. With V^T denoting the conjugate transpose of V, the SVD of matrix M is defined as in Equation (23.2):

$$M \approx U\Sigma V^T. \tag{23.2}$$

Relating this to users, assume each of three users, X, Y, and Z, is characterized by four attributes, a, b, c, and d. Matrix M, in Table 23.1, contains the attribute values for each user. Averaging the values of a single attribute over all three users produces

TABLE 23.1. An Attribute Matrix Estimated by the Product of Two Matrices Containing Mean Average Values

	M				U		V^T		
	X	Y	Z		Attr Avg		User Avg		
							X	Y	Z
a	0.41	0.40	0.32		0.38				
b	1.0	−1.0	1.0	≈	0.33	×	0.64	0.04	0.55
c	0.21	0.24	0.13		0.19				
d	0.95	0.50	0.75		0.73				

TABLE 23.2. An Attribute Matrix Approximated by the Product of Two Matrices Containing Normalized Mean Values and a Scaling Factor

	M			U	Σ		V^T		
	X	Y	Z	Attr Avg			X	Y	Z
a	0.41	0.40	0.32	0.41	Scale		0.76	0.04	0.65
b	1.0	−1.0	1.0	0.37	0.77				
c	0.21	0.24	0.13	0.21					
d	0.95	0.50	0.75	0.81					

Values: a row $\approx$ Attr Avg $\times$ Scale $\times$ User Avg

TABLE 23.3. Estimating the Original Matrix *M*

U	Σ	V^T				M′		
Attr Avg		User Avg				X	Y	Z
0.41	Scale	X	Y	Z	a	0.24	0.01	0.21
0.37	0.77	0.76	0.04	0.65	b	0.22	0.01	0.19
0.21					c	0.12	0.01	0.11
0.81					d	0.47	0.02	0.41

the attribute average column U. The user average row V^T is produced by taking the average of the four attributes for each user.

After calculating the average for all attributes and users (matrices U and V^T, respectively), the averages are normalized to place them on the same scale. The standard for doing so is to divide each value in a set by the square root of the sum of the square of each value in the set. Equations (23.3) and (23.4) show the calculation of the base for normalization of U and V^T, respectively.

$$\sqrt{0.38^2 + 0.33^2 + 0.19^2 + 0.73^2} = 0.91 \tag{23.3}$$

$$\sqrt{0.64^2 + 0.04^2 + 0.55^2} = 0.85. \tag{23.4}$$

Each value in U is divided by 0.91. Each value in V^T is divided by 0.85. The product of the two scaling factors, 0.77, forms the single-value matrix, Σ. As shown in Table 23.2, the original matrix, M, is estimated by the product of the three matrices, that is, $U\Sigma V^T$. Thus, the attribute and user matrices are normalized while the product of the two matrices, U and V^T normalized, and the scaling factor, Σ, is the same as the product of the original U and V^T matrices.

At this point, it is important to note that the information originally represented as 12 separate values is now summarized in only eight separate values. By multiplying the average and scale matrices, an estimate of the original matrix can be produced as shown in Table 23.3.

The estimated matrix, M', is radically different from the original matrix, M. This discrepancy arises from the inaccuracy resulting from the use of the mean as the averaging function. The sets of user or attribute values are vectors. The similarity between vector objects is dependent on vector angles, not magnitudes. Taking the mean values of the vectors of a matrix will usually change the angle of the norm of the matrix. Taking the eigenvalues of the vectors of a matrix will change the magnitude but not the angle of the norm of the vector. Therefore, using the eigenvalue

TABLE 23.4. Producing U and V^T with Eigenvalues

| | M | | | U | | V^T | | | | M' | | |
	X	Y	Z	Attr Avg	Σ	User Avg				X	Y	Z
a	0.41	0.40	0.32	−0.21	Scale	X	Y	Z	a	0.30	−0.09	0.27
b	1.0	−1.0	1.0	≈ −0.81 ×	1.98	× −0.72	0.22	−0.66	= b	1.15	−0.35	1.06
c	0.21	0.24	0.13	−0.09					c	0.13	−0.04	0.12
d	0.95	0.50	0.75	−0.54					d	0.77	−0.24	0.71

TABLE 23.5. A New U', Σ, and $V^{T'}$ Produced from the Difference between M and M'

| | M − M' | | | U' | | V^T' | | |
	X	Y	Z	Attr Avg	Σ'	User Avg		
a	0.11	0.49	0.05	0.43	Scale	X	Y	Z
b	−0.15	−0.65	−0.06	≈ −0.58 ×	1.17	× 0.23	0.97	0.07
c	0.08	0.28	0.01	0.25				
d	0.18	0.74	0.04	0.65				

TABLE 23.6. M'' Produced from a More Complete U, Σ, and V^T

| U | | Σ | | V^T | | | M'' | | | |
Attr Avg		Σ		User Avg				X	Y	Z
−0.21	0.43	Scale		X	Y	Z	a	0.42	0.39	0.31
−0.81	−0.58 ×	1.98	0	× −0.72	0.22	−0.66	= b	1.00	−1.01	1.01
−0.09	0.25	0	1.17	0.23	0.97	0.07	c	0.20	0.24	0.14
−0.54	0.65						d	0.95	0.50	0.76

as the averaging function maintains the similarity between the objects being compared. Repeating the above operations with eigenvalues produces the entries in Table 23.4.

While the estimated matrix, M', in Table 23.4 is not identical to the original matrix, M, the relationships between the objects are maintained. X and Y are negatively related. X and Z are positively related. To correct for the error in the estimated matrix, the residual difference between the original and estimated matrices is used to calculate a new set of averages (U and V^T) and another scaling factor (Σ). The new matrices are shown in Table 23.5.

The original and new matrices (from Tables 23.4 and 23.5, respectively) are concatenated to produce two columns as U and two rows as V^T. The new scaling factor is placed diagonally in a new Σ. Repeating the multiplication, a new matrix M'' is produced. Comparing Table 23.6 with Table 23.5 illustrates that M'' is significantly better than M' as an estimate of M.

The difference between this estimated matrix M'' and the original matrix M is used to create another matrix of residual values, which in turn are used to create another column of attribute averages in U, another scaling factor in Σ, and another row of user averages in V^T. The result is shown in Table 23.7.

TABLE 23.7. *U*, *Σ*, and *V^T* are Completed by Repeating the Decomposition Method on *M – M'*

	M – M'			U				Σ			V^T		
	X	Y	Z		Attr Avg							User Avg	
											X	Y	Z
a	−0.01	0.02	0.01		−0.21	0.43	0.69	Scale					
b	0	0.01	−0.01	≈	−0.81	−0.58	0.02	× 1.98	0	0	× −0.72	0.22	−0.66
c	0.01	0	−0.01		−0.09	0.25	−0.70	0	1.17	0	0.23	0.97	0.07
d	0	0	−0.01		−0.54	0.65	−0.17	0	0	0.02	−0.65	0.10	0.75

TABLE 23.8. Using *Σ* to Estimate *d* for a New User *T*

d				Σ				T		T.d
−0.54	0.65	−0.17	×	1.98	0	0	×	0.27	=	0.26
				0	1.17	0		0.72		
				0	0	0.02		0.19		

Table 23.7 depicts the SVD for the original matrix M. Attribute averages are represented by the U matrix. User averages are represented by the V^T matrix. The scale is represented by the $Σ$ matrix. Multiplied together, $UΣV^T = M$. Further, the U and V^T matrices are not required to identify the relationships between the users and attributes. The $Σ$ matrix reflects composite information about the relationships between users and attributes. The U and V^T matrices contain information about specific attributes and users, not about relationships across the two sets. Since SVD is intended to store relationship information, only the diagonal values of the $Σ$ matrix are required. For this example, from Table 23.7, the user attribute relationship of M is represented by the vector {1.98, 1.17, 0.02}.

Once the SVD for existing data is calculated, it is possible to predict missing attributes for users. Assume a new user, T, is introduced. Only the first three attributes, a, b, and c, are known for this user. Using these three attributes, the user average column for T is calculated to be {0.27, 0.72, 0.19}. The value of the missing attribute, d, for T is estimated in Table 23.8.

By estimating missing attributes for users, it is possible to maintain accurate similarity measures among all users. Further, SVD is not affected by synonymy or polysemy. The KNN algorithm compares each attribute separately. Synonymy and polysemy artificially alter the weight of attributes. SVD produces a relationship value, $Σ$, from all attributes for all users at the same time. Having a value repeated or two values combined in the attributes will result in U, $Σ$, and V^T matrices that produce the original matrix M with the same repeated or combined attributes.

23.3.3 Data Sparsity

Even with SVD, clustering is often difficult due to the sparsity of data [28]. The ability of a clustering algorithm to handle slight changes or omissions in data is often referred to as *numerical stability*. Without numerical stability, the overfitting of estimated or rounded values will likely be magnified in the final result [23]. Impuning missing values in sparse data without skewing the overall data set is important in many areas of statistical analysis [29].

Netflix has offered rewards for assistance in developing numerically stable algorithms for recommending movies to their customers. Due to the fact that most customers have relatively few movie selections (as compared to the number of movies available in the Netflix library), the Netflix data set is extremely sparse [30]. Calculating the SVD and then using it to accurately estimate missing data can be a time-consuming task.

The Lanczos algorithm was designed specifically as a method for calculating SVD [31]. It is an effective iterative algorithm for handling large but sparse data sets. Being iterative, the Lanczos algorithm will result in round-off error. Depending on implementation, it is possible to lose numerical stability. Three techniques to combat numerical instability when implementing the Lanczos algorithm are (1) preventing the loss of orthogonality, (2) recovering orthogonality after the basis is generated, and (3) removal of spurious eigenvalues after all eigenvalues have been identified [32].

The Lanczos algorithm is a simplified form of the Arnoldi algorithm [31]. As such, existing methods of implementing the Arnoldi algorithm are often used in place of the Lanczos algorithm. Due to computations that benefit from SVD in fluid dynamics, electrical engineering, and materials science, research continues to find methods of accelerating both the Lanczos and Arnoldi algorithms [33].

The overall issue of data sparsity is important for a predictive search engine. Consider the user-to-item ratio for Google. Google stores over one trillion (10^{12}) unique URLs in their database [34]. With fewer than seven billion people in the world, each person could view 140 URLs, without any two people viewing the same URL. Further, even an avid web user will not have visited a significant percentage of the available URLs. As a result, Google users cannot be expected to have much user history in common. To compare and predict usage, most of the user data must be estimated.

In search engine usage, the user-to-item relationship is either "visited" or "not visited." As such, search engine usage data are binary and estimation of user data is less complex than other estimation tasks, such as estimating how users might rate a movie or song. Many statistical techniques have been developed that successfully analyze sparse binary matrices using SVD [35]. These methods have been proven so effective that nonbinary data sets have been converted to binary data sets for quick estimation and analysis [30]. Therefore, binary SVD analysis will increase information and decrease sparsity by estimating what other items the user would likely select.

23.3.4 Grouping with SVD

As demonstrated previously, SVD is commonly used for handling data synonymy, polysemy, and scarcity. Less commonly cited is another benefit of SVD, the ability to perform efficient and reliable similarity clustering [23, 36]. If the original matrix M is a mapping of customers to products, the matrices U and V^T, respectively, describe the customers and products with normalized values. Consider the example eight-customer matrix V (transposed from V^T) depicted in Table 23.9. First, each positive value is replaced with a "1." Each negative value is replaced with a "0." To make the result easier to read, the elements of each row are collectively read as a single binary number, which is then represented in decimal. As an example, the

TABLE 23.9. Producing Groups of Similarity for Eight Customers Using SVD

S	0.52	0.19	0.78	S	1	1	1	S	7
T	0.14	0.25	−0.32	T	1	1	0	T	6
U	0.48	−0.34	0.19	U	1	0	1	U	5
V	0.49	0.37	0.88	V	1	1	1	V	7
W	0.95	0.18	−0.18	W	1	1	0	W	6
X	0.11	−0.38	0.48	X	1	0	1	X	5
Y	0.56	−0.65	0.84	Y	1	0	1	Y	5
Z	0.78	0.74	0.54	Z	1	1	1	Z	7

elements of row 1 of the middle matrix in Table 23.9, all three of which are binary "1," are read as the binary number "111," which is then represented as the decimal number "10." The result of carrying out this operation on the customer matrix is a vector that represents each customer with one number. Customers with the same decimal number are in the same group. Customers S, V, and Z are in the same neighborhood of similarity. Customers U, X, and Y are in another neighborhood. If desired, the U matrix (produced from the original customer–product matrix M) (see Table 23.1) could be used to easily group the products into neighborhoods of similarity.

The benefit of using the same function to group all objects into neighborhoods of similarity is obvious, but it comes at a cost. SVD is a complex and time-consuming function. It does not allow for limiting the size of neighborhoods. Within a neighborhood, it does not indicate the relative similarity among objects. When speed, the ability to constrain the size of neighborhoods, or relative similarity are important, the KNN algorithm is preferred. Further, the SVD does not define what it means to be similar as it places customers into neighborhoods of similarity.

23.4 SIMILARITY METRICS

Accurate identification of similar (or different) objects is entirely contingent upon definition of a meaningful metric for similarity. There is no standard for a perfect measure of similarity. Consistency is one important consideration; given the same two objects, a similarity metric should always yield the same result. With rare exception, similarity metrics can be classified as either vector- or string based. Vector-based metrics treat data as a vector defined on a multidimensional space and compare the angle between vectors to determine similarity. String-based metrics treat data as ordered arrays of values and compare the elements of the arrays. Both categories of similarity metrics are examined in this section.

23.4.1 Vector-Based Similarity Metrics

Vector-based similarity metrics are common due to their simplicity of implementation and speed of calculation. The comparison between two vectors can be performed in linear time; that is, two objects with n attributes can be compared in $O(n)$ time, compared with the $O(n^2)$ complexity of most string comparisons of n attributes. Consequently, vector-based similarity metrics are appropriate for objects with large attribute sets. For example, vector similarity is the standard method used in

TABLE 23.10. Genre of the Top Ten Movies of 2009, on a Scale of 0–9

Movie	Comedy	Romance	Action	Drama
Alvin and the Chipmunks 2	9	2	3	0
Avatar	1	7	5	6
The Blind Side	2	0	4	9
The Hangover	9	1	5	3
Harry Potter 6	2	4	7	8
Sherlock Holmes	1	3	6	3
Star Trek	2	1	8	6
Transformers 2	1	2	9	6
Twilight 2	1	9	3	8
Up	7	3	5	7

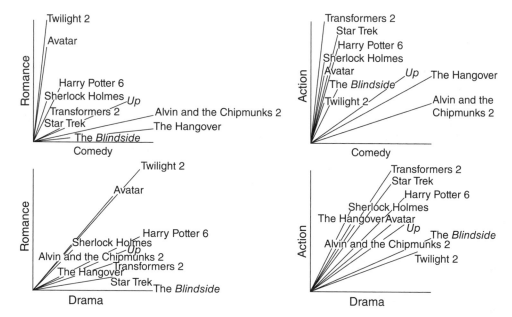

FIGURE 23.6. Attributes of the top 10 movies of 2009, plotted in four vector graphs.

data mining to compare large volumes of text [37]; vectors represent frequencies of words found in the text. The result of a vector-based comparison will be "0" for completely dissimilar texts and "1" for identical texts.

The drawback to vector-based algorithms is the limitation of vector-based attributes. Given a large set of items, all items must be characterized using the same set of attributes. Each attribute becomes a dimension in the vector comparison. Table 23.10 is an example of using the attributes of comedy, romance, action, and drama to describe and compare the top 10 movies of 2009. Each attribute ranks the movie's relevance to the particular genre from 0 to 9.

The purpose of vector-based similarity metrics is to calculate the angle between two vectors. The attribute vectors for each movie are plotted in Figure 23.6, with two attributes per graph. The angle between each pair of vectors is a measure of similarity. The smaller the angle between the two vectors, the more similar the corresponding movies.

Based on Figure 23.6, *Alvin and the Chipmunks 2* appears to be similar to *The Hangover*; however, one is a children's movie and the other is intended for adults. What is missing is a dimension that differentiates movies aimed at children from movies aimed at adults. The missing attribute leads to inaccurate vector similarity. Adding more attributes will increase the accuracy of vector similarity, at the cost of complexity in calculating the angles between all dimensions of the vectors. While some implementations, such as Amazon's technique [15], aim for low dimensionality, others tolerate higher dimensionality, such as the Music Genome Project, which processes approximately 400 dimensions [22].

Examining Figure 23.6, it can be seen that the angles between *Transformers 2* and *Star Trek* are relatively small. In the romance/comedy graph, *Transformers 2* is at $(1, 2)$ and *Star Trek* is at $(2, 1)$. The angle between the vectors is 36.86°, as shown in the first line of the equation set (Equation 23.5). The average of all four angles is 14.73°, which is relatively small compared to the maximum possible, 90°:

$$
\begin{aligned}
\left|\arctan\left(\frac{2}{1}\right) - \arctan\left(\frac{1}{2}\right)\right| &= |63.43° - 26.57°| = 36.86° \\[2mm]
\left|\arctan\left(\frac{9}{1}\right) - \arctan\left(\frac{8}{2}\right)\right| &= |83.66° - 75.96°| = 7.70° \\[2mm]
\left|\arctan\left(\frac{2}{6}\right) - \arctan\left(\frac{1}{6}\right)\right| &= |18.43° - 9.46°| = 8.97° \\[2mm]
\left|\arctan\left(\frac{9}{2}\right) - \arctan\left(\frac{8}{1}\right)\right| &= |77.47° - 82.87°| = 5.40°.
\end{aligned}
\tag{23.5}
$$

23.4.1.1 *Vector Cosine*

Many common recommendation algorithms, such as the one implemented by Amazon, use vector cosine as a measure of similarity [15]. While maintaining reasonable accuracy, vector cosine is extremely fast compared to the trigonometric method (and the string-based methods of Section 23.4.2). Given two object attribute vectors, A and B, similarity is defined as the cosine of the angle between them. It is calculated with Equation (23.6), based on the "dot product" and "magnitude" vector operations. The dot product of two vectors is obtained by multiplying their corresponding elements, then adding the products to yield a scalar. The magnitude of a vector is the square root of the sum of the square of each element of the vector:

$$
S(A, B) = \cos(\theta) = \frac{A \cdot B}{\|A\|\|B\|}.
\tag{23.6}
$$

In the context of customer similarity, the attribute vectors A and B are usually a list of products purchased by customers A and B, respectively. For product similarity, the attribute vectors are usually a list of products purchased together. The resulting similarity is between −1, indicating polar opposition, to 1, indicating identity. A similarity value of 0 is commonly understood to be a sign of independence, indicating that the two objects have no relationship.

As an example, consider matrix M, in Table 23.11, where each object is represented by four attributes: a, b, c, and d, and attribute values are normalized between −1 and 1.

TABLE 23.11. Example of Normalized Attributes (a, b, c, and d) for Three Objects (X, Y, and Z)

	X	Y	Z
a	0.41	0.40	0.32
b	1	−1	1
c	0.21	0.24	0.13
d	0.95	0.50	0.75

Using Equation (23.6), the similarity between X and Y is calculated in Equation (23.7):

$$S(X,Y) = \frac{[0.41 \quad 1 \quad 0.21 \quad 0.95]\cdot[0.40 \quad -1 \quad 0.24 \quad 0.50]}{\|[0.41 \quad 1 \quad 0.21 \quad 0.94]\|\|[0.40 \quad -1 \quad 0.24 \quad 0.50]\|}$$

$$= \frac{0.41\times0.40+1\times(-1)+0.21\times0.24+0.95\times0.50}{\sqrt{0.41^2+1^2+0.21^2+0.95^2}\times\sqrt{0.40^2+(-1)^2+0.24^2+0.50^2}}$$

$$= \frac{-0.31}{1.45\times1.21} = -0.18. \tag{23.7}$$

Likewise, the similarity between X and Z is 0.99, and the similarity between Y and Z is −0.3. It is not necessary to compare Y to X as the result will be the same as comparing X to Y due to the commutative property of the similarity function. Once all three vector cosines have been calculated, it can be stated that X and Z are most similar while X and Y are least similar.

With only three objects and four attributes, it is difficult to identify which object is most similar to X. Objects X and Y are most similar with respect to the a and b attributes. However, objects X and Z are most similar in the b and d attributes. Simply scanning data is not an effective means of comparing similarity. Vector cosine provides a method for producing a repeatable measurement of similarity. Increasing the number of attributes increases the computational complexity of determining similarity. In Equation (23.6), adding another attribute will increase the calculation by one multiplication and one addition in the numerator, and two squares and two additions in the denominator. In total, there will be an increase of three multiplications and three additions. With the addition of each attribute, the number of operations increases linearly—growing at a constant rate of three multiplications and three additions per attribute. Therefore, the complexity for vector cosine is bounded by $O(n)$.

23.4.1.2 Vector Divergence   Vector cosine is a symmetric similarity metric, such that $S(A, B) = S(B, A)$ for two vectors, A and B. Not all similarity metrics are symmetric. For example, if consumers tend to claim that Coke is similar to Pepsi, they should also make the symmetric claim that Pepsi is similar to Coke. In practice, the asymmetric claim that Pepsi is not similar to Coke persists [38]. A common asymmetric similarity metric is the Kullback–Leibler (KL) divergence. KL divergence is often used as a metric of difference, not similarity. More precisely, it is a measure of the difficulty of translating from one set of values (set A) to another (set B). The resulting value represents how many changes must be made to the original set (A) to attain the derived set (B). The greater the number of changes required, the more difficult the translation will be, indicating greater difference between sets A and B.

KL divergence is formally defined as in Equation (23.8), where each value $A_i \in A$ is considered a measured value, and each value $B_i \in B$ is considered an estimated value:

$$\text{KL}(A, B) = \sum_i A_i \log \frac{A_i}{B_i}. \qquad (23.8)$$

Comparing X and Z in matrix M (see Table 23.11), we can let the attributes of X be the reference set A. Then, the attributes of Z are the estimated set B. KL divergence produces a measure of difference between two sets of attributes (the greater the value, the greater the difference). As calculated in Equation (23.9), the difference between X and Z is 0.186. To make this value useful, it must be compared to a measurement between two other objects:

$$\begin{aligned}
\text{KL}(A, B) &= \sum_i A_i \log \frac{A_i}{B_i} \\
&= \left(0.41 \log \frac{0.41}{0.32}\right) + \left(1 \log \frac{1}{1}\right) + \left(0.21 \log \frac{0.21}{0.13}\right) + \left(0.95 \log \frac{0.95}{0.75}\right) \qquad (23.9) \\
&= .044 + 0 + .044 + 0.098 = 0.186.
\end{aligned}$$

Of note, KL divergence could not be used to measure the difference between X and Y because attribute b would produce $\log(-1)$. This is a limitation of KL divergence. A_i and B_i must have the same sign. Taking the absolute value of A_i or B_i to make both positive would consider opposite values to be the same, creating an invalid comparision between A and B. Further, B_i cannot be zero. When A_i is zero, $0 \log(0)$ is interpreted as zero [39]. If attribute b of X and Y is ignored (as doing so will not alter the KL divergence value for X and Z), the KL divergence value of X and Y would be 0.245. In other words, X and Y are more different from X and Z when attribute b is ignored, allowing KL divergence to be an alternative to vector cosine for data sets that meet the KL divergence constraints.

KL divergence is commonly used within LSI, a method that identifies patterns in relationships between sets of terms and sets of concepts in unstructured text [40, 41]. LSI has proven capable of overcoming two common hurdles in recommender system development. First, LSI easily handles synonymy. If two (or more) items in a data set are actually the same product, the items will be translated as identical vectors for analysis, making the synonymy obvious and easy to ignore. Second, LSI easily handles polysemy. If an item in a data set is actually more than one product, the item will be translated as a special vector for analysis that has the properties of each product that the item represents [42].

With recommender systems, LSI uses SVD to quickly calculate the KL divergence between a set of items and a set of customers. A problem in real-world implementations of LSI is that the divergence is calculated once. Over time, the divergence between items and customers may drift. A simple solution is to repeat the SVD/KL divergence calculation on a regular basis. Another solution is to approximate the drift in divergence as new information is gathered. This approximation is often referred to as ensemble learning, with variational divergence as a common form of ensemble learning [41]. With KL divergence, variational divergence is easy to estimate [40].

Given the standard KL divergence in Equation (23.8), the difference between the estimated relationship between A and B for a data set D is defined in Equation (23.10). Because this equation requires only an examination of the new data and the previously calculated SVD for A and B, it requires less time than a complete recalculation of the SVD:

$$D_{KL}(A, B) = \sum_i A_i \log \frac{A_i}{B_i \mid D_i}. \qquad (23.10)$$

Since the only bound on KL divergence is a lower bound of zero (no upper bound), repeatedly adjusting for new data may cause an incremental upward drift [40]. To avoid this possibility, it is helpful to calculate an upper bound that specifies a maximum level of difference. It is obvious that A is identical to itself and has a KL divergence of zero when compared to itself. Anything else that may be compared to A will have a difference greater than zero. When viewing the universe of possible sets, set A will be the origin. All other sets of information will be placed at varying distances away from the origin. At some point, there is a distance (or radius) away from the origin at which the information is deemed to be so different that further distinction between how different the information may be is meaningless. This information radius becomes the upper limit for KL divergence. Any values beyond the information radius are arbitrarily placed at the information radius.

Jensen–Shannon (JS) divergence may be used to calculate the aforementioned information radius [43]. Based on KL divergence, JS divergence has the useful addition of a finite result. In general, JS divergence, defined in Equation (23.11), is a symmetrized and smoothed version of KL divergence. Note that the equation for JS divergence makes two references to the equation for KL divergence. Therefore, the information radius comes at a cost of doubling the computation requirements:

$$JS(A, B) = \frac{1}{2} KL\left(A, \frac{1}{2}(A + B)\right) + \frac{1}{2} KL\left(B, \frac{1}{2}(A + B)\right). \qquad (23.11)$$

23.4.1.3 *Variations on Vector Cosine* When attributes for an object have binary values, vector cosine may be simplified to the Jaccard similarity coefficient [44]. Given two sets of attributes, A and B, the Jaccard similarity coefficient is defined with the intersection and union operators (Equation 23.12). This results in a much faster operation than vector cosine (Equation 23.6). With n attributes, vector cosine will require about $3n$ multiplications and additions, along with two square root calculations. The Jaccard similarity coefficient is a counting function that can be performed with $2n$ additions and a division: First, count how many elements are in one of the sets by adding 1 to the count n times. (Because n is likely known beforehand, this count may not be necessary.) Then, count how many elements in each set are equal for the second set of addition. Divide the equal count by the size count to produce a Jaccard similarity:

$$J(A, B) = \frac{|A \cap B|}{|A \cup B|}. \tag{23.12}$$

The speed advantage of the Jaccard similarity coefficient comes with a slight loss of accuracy if vector cosine is considered a more correct metric of similarity. Consider two binary vectors, $\{1, 1, 0, 1\}$ and $\{1, 0, 1, 1\}$. The vector cosine of the two vectors is 0.67. The Jaccard similarity coefficient of the two vectors is 0.50. It is difficult to see how Jaccard similarity coefficient and vector cosine relate to one another directly. However, the mathematical difference between the two is obvious when examining the Tanimoto coefficient [45].

If we limit all attribute values to binary 0 or 1, the Jaccard similarity and Tanimoto coefficients yield the same result [45]. The formula for the Tanimoto coefficient is defined in Equation (23.13):

$$T(A, B) = \frac{A \cdot B}{\|A\|^2 + \|B\|^2 - A \cdot B}. \tag{23.13}$$

With the previous vectors $\{1, 1, 0, 1\}$ and $\{1, 0, 1, 1\}$, the Jaccard similarity coefficient was 0.50. The Tanimoto coefficient is also 0.50. So, the Tanimoto coefficient shows how the Jaccard similarity coefficient may be written as a dot product and vector magnitude function, similar to vector cosine. The numerator is $A \cdot B$ in both functions, but the denominator of the Tanimoto coefficient is distinctly different from the denominator of the vector cosine. That produces a difference between the vector cosine and the Tanimoto coefficient (or Jaccard similarity). However, as with the vector cosine, the measure of similarity with either Jaccard or Tanimoto coefficients is simple and precise, allowing the Jaccard similarity coefficient to be a good option over vector cosine.

23.4.1.4 Similarity Indices

Vector cosines, along with Jaccard and Tanimoto, are often referred to as *similarity coefficients*, which are considered to be multiplicative factors of similarity. A coefficient of 0.50 implies similarity twice that of a coefficient of 0.25. Many other measures of similarity are referred to as indices. They are used for indexing items into clusters or groups of similarity. As such, a value of 0.50 does not necessarily reflect twice as much similarity as an index of 0.25. Unfortunately, the two terms are often used interchangeably, losing their meaning.

Many similarity indices come from the need to classify items, such as flowers, by similarity. Biological sciences have produced the most commonly used similarity indices, such as the Jaccard similarity coefficient and the Sørensen index. Given two binary sets, the Sørensen index (which also happens to be the definition of Dice's coefficient) is identical to twice the Jaccard similarity coefficient. The common equation for both the Sørensen index and the Dice coefficient is shown in Equation (23.14) [46, 47]:

$$D(A, B) = \frac{2|A \cap B|}{|A| + |B|}. \tag{23.14}$$

The only issue in calculating Equation (23.14) is interpretation of $|A \cup B|$ and $|A| + |B|$. For binary sets, some interpretations opt to omit zeros from $|A \cup B|$. If zeros are maintained, the number of items in the union of A and B is the same as the number of items in A added to the number of items in B. However, a purely mathematical view of $|A| + |B|$ would consider it equal to $|A \cup B| + |A \cap B|$. If that is the case, Dice's coefficient is related to the Jaccard similarity coefficient by Equation (23.15):

$$
\begin{aligned}
D(A, B) &= \frac{2|A \cup B|}{|A| + |B|} \\
&= \frac{2|A \cup B|}{|A \cup B| + |A \cap B|} \\
&= \frac{2\dfrac{|A \cap B|}{|A \cup B|}}{\dfrac{|A \cup B|}{|A \cup B|} + \dfrac{|A \cap B|}{|A \cup B|}} \\
&= \frac{2J(A, B)}{1 + J(A, B)}.
\end{aligned}
\tag{23.15}
$$

Within the scope of comparing the expansive search history of multiple users, similarity metrics that are based solely on union and intersection operators will require fewer operations on a computer than vector cosine. Further, because set operations are dependent on counting, specialized incrementers may be used in place of standard adders. Both up and down counters can be implemented to run much faster than an adder [48].

23.4.1.5 *Limitation of Similarity* As mentioned in Section 23.3, a common experience that most users have with similarity measures is Amazon's recommendation system. Each customer is categorized by the products that he or she has purchased. SVD and vector cosine are used to place customers into similarity neighborhoods. Amazon then recommends products to each customer based on the products purchased by others in the same similarity neighborhood [15].

This is effective in defining which products, collectively, groups of customers are purchasing. It also helps identify products that tend to be purchased together. However, this method is greatly limited by the loss of order. Amazon does not suggest which products be purchased next. The sequence in which purchases were made is not considered in making a recommendation.

Consider a book series, such as the *Harry Potter* series. After purchasing Book 5 in the series, Amazon will suggest purchasing Books 1, 2, 3, and 4. However, it is highly unlikely that many people purchase book 5 in a series without having already read the previous four books. If order was taken into account, Amazon may suggest purchasing Books 6 and 7 and ignore the previous books.

Vector-based comparisons consider all attributes as dimensions. Without any priority order among attributes, no dimension comes before another dimension. Values within a dimension are not time ordered. The lack of order leads to a very fast calculation of similarity, but a loss of time-ordered relevance. A comparison that keeps events, such as books ordered by customers, in order would be preferable for a recommendation system, especially a search engine recommendation system.

Users are interested in seeing which search results come next, not search results that may have been visited in the past.

23.4.1.6 *Summary of Vector Comparison Algorithms*   Vector comparison algorithms are based on the observation that when objects are represented as vectors originating at the origin, the angle between the vectors is smaller when the objects are similar and larger when the objects are different. The angle is commonly measured with the vector cosine equation. With many multiplications and square root functions, the vector cosine equation can be considered complex. Simpler functions exist that produce equivalent results when the attributes are represented as binary values. Because much of the data used in real-world applications are binary, it is common to find the Jaccard similarity coefficient or the Sørensen index used in place of the vector cosine. Both of the former are based on union and intersection functions, which are implemented as simple counting functions. By using the Tanimoto coefficient as a reference, it is possible to see how the union and intersection functions may be rewritten as dot product and vector magnitude functions, similar to vector cosine, which demonstrates the validity of using the simpler coefficients in place of vector cosine.

23.4.2 String-Based Comparison Algorithms

If events are time ordered and can be represented symbolically, it is possible to treat a sequence of events as an ordered set or a string. There are many order-preserving algorithms for comparing two strings [19, 49]. For the most part, these algorithms descend from Hamming distance, which directly relates to vector-based similarity.

Hamming distance is a measure of the number of positions in which two strings have different symbols [50]. The two binary strings, "1011001" and "1001101," have a Hamming distance of two because they differ in two positions (bits three and five). This type of measurement is nearly identical to the Jaccard coefficient (and the related Tanimoto, Sørensen, and Dice measurements).

If each position is considered as an attribute, the first string is the set {1, 0, 1, 1, 0, 0, 1} and the second string is the set {1, 0, 0, 1, 1, 0, 1}. The two sets share five of the seven attributes considered. The Jaccard coefficient is calculated as in Equation (23.16):

$$
\begin{aligned}
J(A, B) &= \frac{[1 \ \ 0 \ \ 1 \ \ 1 \ \ 0 \ \ 0 \ \ 1] \cap [1 \ \ 0 \ \ 0 \ \ 1 \ \ 1 \ \ 0 \ \ 1]}{[1 \ \ 0 \ \ 1 \ \ 1 \ \ 0 \ \ 0 \ \ 1] \cup [1 \ \ 0 \ \ 0 \ \ 1 \ \ 1 \ \ 0 \ \ 1]} \\
&= \frac{5}{7}.
\end{aligned}
\tag{23.16}
$$

Note that the application of Hamming distance is limited to strings of equal length. Therefore, the denominator used to account for sets of different lengths in the Jaccard coefficient would be the same value for all comparisons when all strings have equal length. Being redundant, the denominator is not needed in the Hamming distance. If the denominator of the Jaccard coefficient is removed, the Hamming distance is the length of either string minus the Jaccard coefficient. In other words, the Jaccard coefficient is a measure of similarity and the Hamming distance is a measure of difference.

23.4.2.1 *Converting Difference to Similarity*

String-based comparison algorithms tend to measure the distance (or difference) between two strings. They do not measure similarity. Two identical strings will have absolutely no difference. From there, the difference grows as a distance from being identical. Because there is no universal measure of absolute difference, distance from being identical is a reasonable measure.

To convert difference to similarity, the maximum difference must be known. A distance of zero indicates identical strings. If the maximum difference between two strings is M, the range between being identical and being completely different is known. Similarity may be calculated as shown in Equation (23.17):

$$\text{Sim}(A, B) = \frac{M - d}{M}. \tag{23.17}$$

If the distance is 0, similarity will be 100%. If the distance is M, similarity will be 0%. While this is an effective method for converting difference to similarity, it has limitations dependent on the algorithms used to measure difference.

Consider an application that attempts to match unknown words to a dictionary of known words. Using a string difference algorithm (the specific algorithm is not important in this example), the word "busnes" is compared to "busses" and "business." The algorithm calculates the difference for both comparisons to be 2. For this algorithm, assume that the maximum possible difference is the length of the longest string among the strings being compared. Converting to similarity, busnes is $(6 - 2)/6 = 0.67$ similar to busses and $(8 - 2)/8 = 0.75$ similar to business. While the difference is the same for both strings, the conversion to similarity clearly gives precedence to longer strings when making comparisons.

23.4.2.2 *Levenshtein Distance*

Most string-based distance measurements are based on Levenshtein distance, an extension of Hamming distance [51]. It removes the limitation of a binary alphabet, allowing for an alphabet of any arbitrary size. It also removes the limitation that the two strings must be of equal length. In doing so, Levenshtein distance measures three differences between the two strings being compared:

- *Insertion.* The difference between "cat" and "coat" is an insertion of "o."
- *Deletion.* The difference between "link" and "ink" is a deletion of "l."
- *Substitution.* The difference between "lunch" and "lurch" is the substitution of "r" for "n."

Each difference is counted. The total number of differences is the Levenshtein distance between the two strings. For example, the Levenshtein distance between "Sunday" and "Saturday" is three: an insertion of "a," an insertion of "t," and a substitution of "r" for "n."

23.4.2.3 *Calculating Levenshtein Distance*

As an optimization problem over two arbitrary length strings, calculating Levenshtein distance is a common example used in dynamic programming [52, 53]. The Wagner–Fischer algorithm is a dynamic programming method for calculating Levenshtein distance. Given two strings of

TABLE 23.12. Initializing a Matrix for the Wagner–Fischer Algorithm

		S	A	T	U	R	D	A	Y
	0	1	2	3	4	5	6	7	8
S	1								
U	2								
N	3								
D	4								
A	5								
Y	6								

TABLE 23.13. Completed Matrix for the Wagner–Fischer Algorithm

		S	A	T	U	R	D	A	Y
	0	1	2	3	4	5	6	7	8
S	1	0	1	2	3	4	5	6	7
U	2	1	1	2	2	3	4	5	6
N	3	2	2	2	3	3	4	5	6
D	4	3	3	3	3	4	3	4	5
A	5	4	3	4	4	4	4	3	4
Y	6	5	4	4	5	5	5	4	3

length m and n, respectively, the runtime of the Wagner–Fischer algorithm is $O(mn)$ [54]. A typical recursive solution requires $O(mn^2)$.

The Wagner–Fischer algorithm is a matrix solution for two strings, A and B. For strings A and B of length m and n, respectively, an $(m + 1) \times (n + 1)$ matrix is created. The top row of the matrix is filled with increasing integers $0, 1, 2, 3 \ldots$ from left to right. Similarly, the leftmost column is populated with increasing integers from top to bottom. For comparing "SUNDAY" (string A) to "SATURDAY" (string B), the initial matrix is shown in Table 23.12.

With the initial matrix setup, each of its elements is filled in, from top to bottom and left to right, according to Equation (23.18):

$$
M_{ij} = \begin{cases} M_{(i-1)(j-1)}, \textit{if } A_i = B_j \\ \min \begin{pmatrix} M_{(i-1)(j-1)} \\ M_{(i-1)j} \\ M_{i(j-1)} \end{pmatrix} + 1, \textit{if } A_i \neq B_j \end{cases}. \tag{23.18}
$$

For example, as "S" equals "S" in the first element to fill in, $M_{1,1}$ is set to zero. S in SUNDAY does not match "A" in SATURDAY; hence, $M_{1,2}$ gets the value $\min(1, 2, 0)$ + 1, which is 1. After completing all elements, the matrix will contain the values shown in Table 23.13.

When completed, the value in the bottom right corner is the Levenshtein distance between the two strings. For SUNDAY and SATURDAY, the distance is three. Because the maximum Levenshtein distance is the length of the longest string (8 in this example), the similarity would be $(8 - 3)/8$ or 62.5%. This value is comparable to that of vector-based measures of similarity: Jaccard coefficient = 5/8 = 62.5%; Dice's coefficient = $2 \times 5/(6 + 7)$ = 76.9%.

Consider changing the order of the characters in the strings. Doing so does not change the vector-based measures. Each character is an attribute without order. From a string-based comparison, "DAYSUN" and "SATURDAY" have a difference of 7, which is a similarity of $(8 - 7)/8 = 12.5\%$.

For comparison of search engine usage, Levenshtein distance accurately indicates the ordered difference between users because the order in which the search results are selected is maintained. A user with a history of $\{A, B, C, D\}$ will be considered very different from a user with a history of $\{D, C, B, A\}$ with a string-based comparison, while a vector-based comparison will show that the two users selected the same results.

As noted previously, converting difference to similarity can produce undesirable results due to the varying length of strings being compared. Levenshtein distance is unreliable at comparing short strings to extremely long strings. What if one user has a history of $\{A, B, C\}$, and another user with a search history containing over 100 items also has visited A, B, and C, in the same order? Further, what if many users have visited A, B, D, C, in that specific order? Identifying this common behavior is important to predicting overall search engine use. A method of finding out if a short string is nearly a substring of a long string is necessary.

23.4.2.4 String Alignment
Given two strings, A and B, a common task that is related to testing for similarity is the task of alignment. Assuming that A is shorter in length than B, the goal is to alter A in order to maximize similarity (minimize difference) of A compared to B. There are two forms of string alignment: global and local.

Global alignment will add gaps (a special null symbol) to A, increasing the length of A to the same length as B. While doing so, the difference between A and B is minimized.

Local alignment not only alters A but it also identifies a substring of B for which the substring and the altered A have the minimum distance. This is technically a global alignment between A and a substring of B.

For global alignment and local alignment, the Needleman–Wunsch algorithm [55] and the Smith–Waterman algorithm [51] are commonly used, respectively. Both are slight adaptations of the Wagner–Fischer algorithm.

23.4.2.5 Global Alignment: Needleman–Wunsch Algorithm
The Needleman–Wunsch algorithm is a matrix solution [55]. Given two strings, A and B, of length m and n, respectively, an $(m + 1) \times (n + 1)$ matrix M is created. Traditionally, the shorter string is placed from top to bottom along the left side of the matrix. The longer string is placed from left to right along the top of the matrix.

Similar to the Wagner–Fischer algorithm, each cell of the matrix is filled according to Equation (23.19). The Needleman–Wunsch algorithm adds a gap penalty, g, which helps place gaps in A such that the difference between A and B is minimized. The value of the gap penalty depends on the application and the desired result. Also, it is popular to use a similarity matrix to weight different comparisons between a and b (elements of A and B, respectively). This is indicated in Equation (23.19) as the function Sim. An example similarity matrix is shown in Table 23.14. Using this similarity matrix, if $a = $ G and $b = $ C, the similarity is -5. It is possible to replace the similarity matrix with a similarity function that performs a mathematical calculation

TABLE 23.14. An Example Similarity Matrix for Comparing DNA Sequences

	A	G	C	T
A	10	−1	−3	−4
G	−1	7	−5	−3
C	−3	−5	9	0
T	−4	−3	0	8

TABLE 23.15. Initializing a Table for the Needleman–Wunsch Algorithm

		A	R	T	I	C	L	E
	0	−1	−2	−3	−4	−5	−6	−7
R	−1							
A	−2							
C	−3							
E	−4							

TABLE 23.16. A Completed Table for the Needleman–Wunsch Algorithm

		A	R	T	I	C	L	E
	0	−1	−2	−3	−4	−5	−6	−7
R	−1	−1	0	−1	−2	−3	−4	−5
A	−2	0	−1	−1	−2	−3	−4	−5
C	−3	−1	−1	−2	−2	−1	−2	−3
E	−4	−2	−2	−2	−3	−2	−2	−1

on the values of a and b. In the case of Levenshtein distance, the similarity function produces 0 when $a = b$ and 1 otherwise:

$$M_{ij} = \max \begin{pmatrix} M_{(i-1)(j-1)} + \mathrm{Sim}(a,b) \\ M_{(i-1)j} + g \\ M_{i(j-1)} + g \end{pmatrix}. \tag{23.19}$$

Before filling in the cells of M, the top row and left column are initialized with values based on the gap penalty. For rows $i = 0$ to m, $M_{(i,0)}$ is filled with $g \times i$, where g is the gap penalty. For columns $j = 0$ to n, $M_{(0,j)}$ is filled with $g \times j$. Using a gap penalty of −1 to compare "RACE" to "ARTICLE," the initialized matrix is shown in Table 23.15.

For columns $j = 1$ to n in row $i = 1$, each cell $M_{i,j}$ is filled by comparing a to b with Equation (23.19). Unlike the Wagner–Fischer algorithm, the Needleman–Wunsch algorithm lowers values for a mismatch. Table 23.16 is a completed matrix where $\mathrm{Sim}(a,b)$ is set to "1" on equality and "−1" on inequality. The gap penalty g, is "−1."

After completing the matrix, global alignment is discovered by backtracking from the lower right corner to the upper left corner. For each cell, the direction to the neighbor with the largest value is indicated. Only three neighboring cells are compared: the cells above, above to the left, and to the left. When more than one cell

TABLE 23.17. A Completed Needleman–Wunsch Table with Backtracking Arrows

		A	R	T	I	C	L	E
	0	←−1	←−2	←−3	←−4	←−5	←−6	←−7
R	↑−1	↖−1	↖0	←−1	←−2	←−3	←−4	←−5
A	↑−2	↖0	↑−1	↖−1	↖−2	↖−3	↖−4	↖−5
C	↑−3	↑−1	↖−1	↖−2	↖−2	↖−1	←−2	←−3
E	↑−4	↑−2	↖−2	↖−2	↖−3	↑−2	↖−2	↖−1

contains the greatest value, the indicator can point to either. Table 23.17 includes arrows indicating the neighbor with the greatest value.

The best global alignment is calculated by following the arrows from the lower right corner of Table 23.17 to the upper left corner. When in a cell in which the symbol of A matches the symbol of B for the cell, write down the symbol. If the symbol of A does not match the symbol of B, write a gap symbol. When complete, the aligned A will be "–R– –C–E": a string that is the same length as B with minimum distance.

With this example, it may be shown that global alignment is also useful for identifying a common path. Assume that ARTICLE is a set of seven ordered locations, such as websites or street intersections, each identified by a letter. Then, assume that RACE is another set of four ordered locations. After creating a global alignment, –R– –C–E is produced. The common path between ARTICLE and RACE is "RCE," in that specific order. Even though both sets contain the location "A," it is not part of the global alignment and, therefore, not part of the common path.

23.4.2.6 Local Alignment: Smith–Waterman Algorithm The Smith–Waterman algorithm is yet another adaptation of the same matrix solution used in the algorithms previously discussed in Sections 23.4.2.3 and 23.4.2.5. With strings A and B, of lengths m and n, respectively, a matrix M of size $(m + 1) \times (n + 1)$ is created. All cells in the top row and left column of M are initialized to zero. The similarity function is similar to the Needleman–Wunsch algorithm. In this example, the similarity function is given in Equation (23.20):

$$\text{Sim}(a, b) = \begin{cases} 2, \text{if } a = b \\ -1, \text{if } a \neq b \end{cases}. \tag{23.20}$$

Whereas the Needleman–Wunsch algorithm had a single gap penalty, the Smith–Waterman algorithm has both a deletion (p_d) and an insertion (p_i) penalty. If $p_d = p_i$, it is essentially equivalent to a single gap penalty. Separating the gap penalty into two penalties allows the implementation to add extra weight to either deletions or insertions. For simplicity, the following example will use −1 for both p_d and p_i.

After the top row and left column are initialized to zero, the rest of the matrix is populated. Similar to the Wagner–Fischer and Needleman–Wunsch algorithms, the cells are filled in from the top left to the bottom right, using Equation (23.21):

TABLE 23.18. A Completed Smith–Waterman Matrix

	U	M	B	R	E	L	L	A
	0	0	0	0	0	0	0	0
B	0	0	0	S	1	0	0	0
E	0	0	0	1	1	3	2	1	0
L	0	0	0	0	0	2	5	4	3
L	0	0	0	0	0	1	4	7	6

$$M_{ij} = \max \begin{pmatrix} 0 \\ M_{(i-1)(j-1)} + \mathrm{Sim}(a, b) \\ M_{(i-1)j} + p_{\mathrm{d}} \\ M_{i(j-1)} + p_{\mathrm{i}} \end{pmatrix}. \qquad (23.21)$$

It is important to note that including the zero in values compared by the max function eliminates the possibility of a negative value in any cell of the matrix. Therefore, the cells that contain nonzero values will be those cells in which a match has generated an increase in value from the neighboring cells. An example that compares "BELL" to "UMBRELLA" is shown in Table 23.18.

To locate the local alignment of a completed Smith–Waterman matrix, the cell with the greatest value is located (the cell with a value of 7 in the example in Table 23.18). From the current cell, the neighboring cell (up, up/left, or left) that contains the greatest value is located. This continues until all neighboring cells contain a zero. In this example, the best alignment begins at the cell containing a 7, continues up/left to a 5, up/left to a 3, then either left or up/left to a 1, and finally to the cell containing a 2. When the symbols in both strings match, write the symbol. A gap symbol is used otherwise. The local alignment of BELL to UMBRELLA is "B-ELL."

Local alignment is a useful tool for identifying the part of a long sequence that is a good match for a short sequence. For example, assume that a customer's last four purchases are known, each item identified by a letter to be BELL. To locate trends, the complete purchase history of other customers will be searched for the same sequence of items. Instead of limiting the search specifically to BELL, local alignment allows for a search of subsequences that are very similar, such as "BRELL." As such, the number of matching search histories will likely be larger than the number that contains BELL without alteration.

23.4.2.7 *Wagner–Fischer Complexity Improvements*
The primary reason that the Wagner–Fischer and related algorithms are not commonly used is their high complexity. For strings of length m and n, the complexity is bounded by $O(mn)$. Methods of addressing the complexity challenge of the Wagner–Fischer algorithm include the following:

- By maintaining the values of only two rows at a time, the space required in memory is reduced from mn to $2m$. This decreases memory requirement. In the case of large values of m and n, reducing memory requirement may reduce memory swapping, which in turn may reduce total execution time.

- If the only interest is in detecting a difference that exceeds a threshold k, then it is only necessary to calculate a diagonal stripe of width $2k + 1$. The complexity becomes $O(kn)$, which is faster whenever $k < m$ [49, 56].
- Using lazy evaluation on the diagonals instead of rows, the complexity becomes $O(m(1 + d))$, where d is the calculated Levenshtein distance. When the distance is small, this is a significant improvement [57].

Estimation is a popular method applied to calculating global and local alignments in DNA sequences. Two algorithms have been developed: BLAST and FASTA. BLAST greatly reduces the execution time of the Smith–Waterman algorithm by first estimating a match against a subset of a DNA database and then comparing groups of positions, usually three at a time [58]. FASTA operates in the same manner, using a different heuristic for estimating the initial match against a subset of a DNA database [56].

To apply either of these approaches to comparing search engine results, a database of common sequences of results must be created. When there are many users over a relatively small set of possible results, it will be expected that specific sequences of three or four search results will occur frequently. However, many search engines have very few users compared to the set of possible results. Consequently, the odds of having a high number of repeated sequences of search results drop significantly. Further, calculating the longest and most common sequences of results in a data set is time-consuming. Such calculations are very similar to the task of identifying common sequences of bytes in a file when executing common file compression algorithms, such as bzip2 or LZMA. Assume that the search results to be checked will not be presorted by frequency of occurrence or selection. The expected complexity of most common compression algorithms will be $O(n \log n)$, where n is the total number of search result selections across all users being compared [59].

Assuming that a compression method is implemented, a new problem arises. If the sequence of results ("A," "B," "C") is encoded with "1" and the sequence ("A," "C") is encoded with "2," it is no longer possible to compare 1 to 2 and detect matching characters. Instead, a similarity matrix must be created that compares all encodings to one another. In this case, 1 is 2/3 similar to 2. The complexity of generating the similarity matrix will be at least $O(n^2)$ for n encodings.

An alternative that nearly matches the benefits of BLAST is to create a simple k-length dictionary from string B when comparing the two strings A and B. The dictionary is simply a list of all k-length substrings in B. For the string UMBRELLA and $k = 3$, the dictionary contains "UMB," "MBR," "BRE," and so on. Instead of searching A for sequences in a database, each substring in the dictionary is compared to A. If A is BELL, the only matching substring is "ELL." Then, an attempt is made to expand the match. Because both UMBRELLA and BELL contain a "B" before "ELL," the match is expanded to include "B" with a gap. The resulting local alignment is "B-ELL." Increasing the value of k will decrease the execution time by decreasing the number of substrings in the dictionary. However, higher values of k decrease sensitivity in locating small local alignment. For example, with $k = 4$, there is no match between BELL and UMBRELLA.

A similar method of comparing two strings in smaller sections was proposed by Monge and Elkan [60]. If the strings of data to be compared can be logically reduced to distinct substrings, such as dividing full names into first, middle, and last names, then each substring pair is compared in place of the overall comparison. For example, comparing "John Paul Jones" to "Jones, John P." directly would require $15 \times 14 = 210$ steps. The string "John Paul Jones" is obviously a concatenation of the substrings "John," "Paul," and "Jones." Sorted, they become the set ("Paul," "John," "Jones"). The string "Jones, John P." becomes the sorted set ("P.," "John," "Jones"). (The punctuation could be omitted but is retained in this example for a worst-case scenario.) In the Monge–Elkan algorithm, "Paul" is compared to "P." in $4 \times 2 = 8$ steps, "John" is compared to "John" in $4 \times 4 = 16$ steps, and "Jones" is compared to "Jones," in $5 \times 6 = 30$ steps. The total number of steps is $8 + 16 + 30 = 54$, an improvement of 74%. Unfortunately, the requirement of logical and sortable substrings greatly limits the benefit of the Monge–Elkan algorithm.

23.4.2.8 *Summary of String Comparison Algorithms*   The strong relationship between the Jaccard similarity coefficient and Hamming distance makes it evident that vector-based and string-based comparison algorithms are similar. The difference between the two is order. Given three attributes, such as A, B, and C, vector-based algorithms will consider only the value of each attribute. String-based algorithms will consider the order in which an object implements each of the attributes, along with the attribute's value.

Three very common forms of string-based algorithms are Levenshtein distance, Needleman–Wunsch distance, and Smith–Waterman distance. All are commonly implemented through adaptations of the Wagner–Fischer matrix-based dynamic programming solution. Levenshtein distance is used to identify the distance between two strings of data. Needleman–Wunsch distance is used to identify distance while adding gaps to the shorter string to produce two strings that are of the same length and have minimal distance. This is referred to as global alignment. Local alignment, by contrast, aligns the shorter string with a substring of the longer string of data. Smith–Waterman distance provides local alignment.

Because of the complexity involved in calculating string-based comparisons, many shortcuts have been developed. Within the realm of DNA comparison and sequencing, BLAST and FASTA have been used to estimate alignment with a dictionary of common sequence comparisons. It is difficult to produce a similar dictionary for data where the range of values vastly exceed the four DNA values of a, g, t, and c. One solution is to divide strings of data into logical substrings and then to compare the substrings with one another, as in the Monge–Elkan algorithm. When this division is feasible, the resulting improvement in complexity is significant. However, it is often difficult to define logical substrings in real data. Therefore, string-based comparison algorithms tend to be used only when order is vital to the overall task. Otherwise, vector-based algorithms are implemented.

23.5 CONCLUSION AND FUTURE WORK

The goal of this research is to use historical data for all users of a search engine to predict which search results a specific user will likely select in the future. This can be accomplished by developing a behavior model to predict user behavior. To improve the accuracy of the predictions, the users should be separated into neighborhoods of similarity based primarily on previous search engine usage. Other user information, such as locale or gender, may be used for similarity comparisons. A behavior model is then generated for each neighborhood.

Grouping users into neighborhoods is a general concept, with many options. Each user's history, as well as any known information about the users, must be normalized into a distinct set of user attributes. Given a matrix of users and attributes, it is possible to compare users for similarity. However, it is expected that the matrix will suffer from sparsity, synonymy, and polysemy. Data correction through the use of SVD should limit all three issues. SVD can be implemented quickly with either Lanczos or Arnoldi iterative algorithms. If limited to binary data, binary SVD algorithms have been noted for accurate estimation in sparse binary data sets.

Once data correction is complete, comparison of users could be a simple vector comparison or a complex string comparison. Within the realm of vector comparisons, vector cosine is an efficient method of identifying similarity between two users. Within the realm of string comparisons, Levenshtein distance is a more accurate measure of differences in the history of each user. Vector cosine executes within a bound of $O(n)$. Levenshtein has complexity of $O(n^2)$.

In choosing between a vector or string comparison, computational complexity is not the only issue to consider. A vector comparison will identify users who have selected similar search results in the past, regardless of the order in which those results were selected. A string-based comparison considers the order and, depending on the algorithm used, aligns users such that similarity of history is considered while ignoring divergence of history.

Grouping users into neighborhoods and identifying behavior models are two distinctly different steps in the process of designing a predictive search engine. As such, it is reasonable to implement both vector-based comparisons and string-based comparisons as needed. Vector-based comparisons will be significantly faster when grouping users into neighborhoods of similarity. Once grouped, string-based comparisons will be useful in aligning user search histories and in developing a user behavior model for the group.

The success of this predictive method can be tested by gathering usage logs from multiple search engines. Grouping the users into neighborhoods of similarity should be validated first. A user behavior model should then be developed for each group. The goal is to have a usage model that, given the sequence of search items previously selected, has a very high probability of successfully predicting the search items that the users within the neighborhood will select next. If successfully and correctly implemented, this predictive search method can considerably reduce total search time. As an additional benefit, the method can direct a user to a sequence of resources that are popular within the user's similarity neighborhood.

Appendix A
Comparative Analysis of Comparison Algorithms

Table A.1 is a comparison of the popular comparison algorithms described in this chapter. For all algorithms, the sets being compared are referred to as A and B. Each set consists of independent data items, m items in A and n items in B. Limitations on the types of data items allowed are indicated for each algorithm. For example, Hamming distance is limited to binary data. Complexity is directly related to estimated execution time. Complexity is shown with trivial cases here for comparison. For example, (mn) is slightly less complex than $(mn + n)$, though both are $O(mn)$.

TABLE A.1. A Comparison of Comparison Algorithms

Algorithm	Complexity Notes	Min	Max
Vector Cosine	(n)	−1.0	1.0
m = n. Numerical values. Cannot all be zero.			
Jaccard coefficient	$(m + n)$	0	1.0
Dice's coefficient	$(m + n)$	1.0	0.2
Tanimoto coefficient	(n)	−0.33	1.0
m = n. Numerical values.			
Hamming distance	(n)	0	m
m = n. Binary values.			
Levenshtein distance	(mn)	abs($m − n$)	max(m, n)
Wagner–Fisher implementation			
Needleman–Wunsch distance	$(mn + n)$	abs($m − n$)	max(m, n)
Smith–Waterman distance	$(mn + n)$	abs($m − n$)	min(m, n)
FASTA	$(cn + n)$	abs($m − n$)	max(m, n)
BLAST	$(m(n − c) + n)$	abs($m − n$)	min(m, n)
Monge–Elkan distance	$(mn)/c^2$	abs($m − n$)	max(m, n)
Sets must be divided into sortable subsets.			

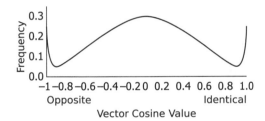

FIGURE A.1. *Distribution of vector cosine values for 1,000,000 random sets.*

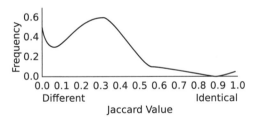

FIGURE A.2. *Distribution of Jaccard coefficient values for 1,000,000 random sets.*

Some algorithms work with elements in groups. In such cases, the group size is represented as *c*. The minimum, maximum, and distribution of values are shown.

Most comparison metrics do not produce a linear distribution of results from the minimum to maximum value. To plot an expected distribution, each metric was calculated for 1,000,000 random set pairs *A* and *B*. The results were plotted by frequency (normalized by dividing each frequency count by the square root of the square of all frequency counts). When using real-world data, the distribution will likely be different due to the expected bias of the real-world data compared to purely random data (Figs. A.1–A.8).

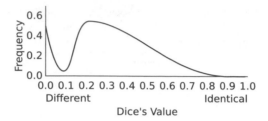

FIGURE A.3. *Distribution of Dice's coefficient values for 1,000,000 random sets.*

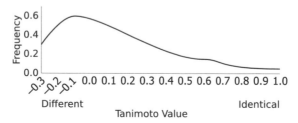

FIGURE A.4. *Distribution of Tanimoto coefficient values for 1,000,000 random sets.*

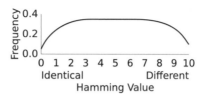

FIGURE A.5. *Distribution of Hamming distance values for 1,000,000 random sets.*

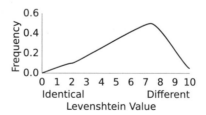

FIGURE A.6. *Distribution of Levenshtein distance values for 1,000,000 random sets.*

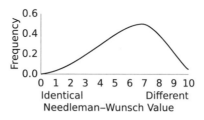

FIGURE A.7. *Distribution of Needleman–Wunsch distance values for 1,000,000 random sets.*

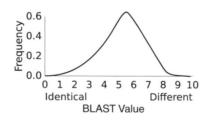

FIGURE A.8. *Distribution of BLAST distance values for 1,000,000 random sets.*

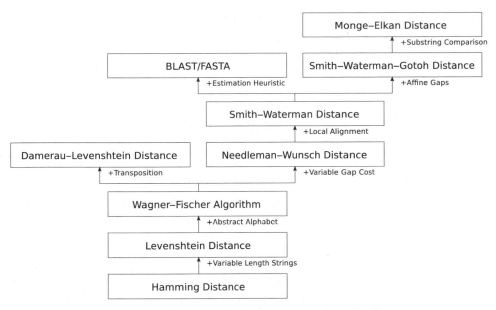

FIGURE A.9. *Evolution of string-based comparison algorithms.*

A.1 VECTOR-BASED COMPARISONS

For two sets A and B, the common vector-based comparison metrics are listed in Equations A.1–A.4:

$$\text{Vector cosine} \quad S(A, B) = \frac{A \cdot B}{\|A\|\|B\|} \tag{A.1}$$

$$\text{Jaccard coefficient} \quad J(A, B) = \frac{|A \cap B|}{|A \cup B|} \tag{A.2}$$

$$\text{Dice coefficient} \quad D(A, B) = \frac{2|A/capB|}{|A| + |B|} \tag{A.3}$$

$$\text{Tanimoto coefficient} \quad T(A, B) = \frac{A \cdot B}{\|A\|^2 + \|B\|^2 - A \cdot B}. \tag{A.4}$$

A.2 STRING-BASED COMPARISONS

The evolution of common string-based comparison metrics, from Hamming distance to modern algorithms, is shown in Figure A.9.

Appendix B
Most Popular Searches

Search engine traffic usage is tracked by Experian Hitwise (http://hitwise.com). Based on 4 weeks of usage (shown in Table B.1), the top five keyword searches comprise approximately 5% of all searches.

TABLE B.1. Top Search Terms for Four Weeks Ending March 27, 2010

	Google		Yahoo		Bing	
Rank	Search Terms	Pct (%)	Search Terms	Pct (%)	Search Terms	Pct (%)
1	Facebook	1.17	Facebook	1.70	Facebook	2.60
2	YouTube	0.66	Myspace	0.99	Google	1.12
3	Facebook login	0.58	Facebook login	0.93	Facebook.com	1.00
4	Craigslist	0.54	Craigslist	0.84	Facebook login	0.85
5	Myspace	0.51	YouTube	0.78	Myspace	0.74
Total		3.46		5.24		6.31

Source: Experian Hitwise.

Based on this knowledge, if a search engine designer wished to decrease the load on the query processor by 5%, he or she should simply cache the top five queries. As a result, if a user were to perform a query for Facebook or Myspace, the search engine would not process the query in a normal manner. It would recognize the query as one of the popular queries and would simply pull the results from cache.

Keeping a running list of which searches are most popular is not difficult. Many algorithms exist for keeping track of most popular events over time without allowing for past popular events to overshadow new events [61].

REFERENCES

[1] A. Rangaswamy, C.L. Giles, and S. Seres, "A strategic perspective on search engines: Thought candies for practitioners and researchers," *Journal of Interactive Marketing*, 23(1):49–60, 2009.

[2] D. Hawking, N. Craswell, P. Brailey, and K. Griffihs, "Measuring search engine quality," *Information Retrieval*, 4(1):33–59, 2001.

[3] M. Levene, *An Introduction to Search Engines and Web Navigation*. Hoboken, NJ: John Wiley & Sons, 2010. 2 ed.

[4] D. Lewandowski, "Search engine user behaviour: How can users be guided to quality content?" *Information Services and Use*, 28(3–4):261–268, 2008.

[5] D. Tumer, M.A. Shah, and Y. Bitirim, "An empirical evaluation on semantic search performance of keyword-based and semantic search engines: Google, Yahoo, msn and Hakia," in *Proceedings of the 2009 4th International Conference on Internet Monitoring and Protection*, pp. 51–55, IEEE Computer Society, 2009.

[6] W.A. Wickelgren, "Speed-accuracy trade-off and information processing dynamics," *Acta Psychologica*, 41(1):67–85, 1977.

[7] Q. Gan and T. Suel, "Improved techniques for result caching in web search engines," in *Proceedings of the 18th International Conference on World Wide Web*, WWW '09, pp. 431–440, ACM, 2009.

[8] R. Ozcan, I.S. Altingovde, B.B. Cambazoglu, F.P. Junqueira, and Õ. Ulusoy, "A five-level static cache architecture for web search engines," *Information Processing & Management*, 47(2):147–308, 2011.

[9] L.A. Adamic, "The small world web," in *Proceedings of the 3rd European Conference on Research and Advanced Technology for Digital Libraries*, ECDL '99, pp. 443–452, Springer-Verlag, 1999.

[10] About google instant. Available at http://www.google.com/instant/, November 2010.

[11] N.Y. Yen, T.K. Shih, L.R. Chao, and Q. Jin, "Ranking metrics and search guidance for learning object repository," *IEEE Transactions on Learning Technologies*, 3(3):250–264, 2010.

[12] B.F. Skinner, *The Behavior of Organisms*. Acton, MA: Copley Publishing Group, 1938.

[13] T. Toledo and R. Katz, "State dependence in lane-changing models," *Transportation Research Record: Journal of the Transportation Research Board*, 2124:81–88, 2009.

[14] A. Pentland and A. Liu, "Modeling and prediction of human behavior," *Neural Computation*, 11(1):229–242, 1999.

[15] G. Linden, B. Smith, and J. York, "Amazon.com recommendations: Item-to-item collaborative filtering," *IEEE Internet Computing*, 7(1):76–80, 2003.

[16] M.T. Jones, B. McClendon, A.P. Charaniya, and M. Ashbridge, "Entity display priority in a distributed geographic information system." Available at http://www.google.com/patents/about?id=ZVepAAAAEBAJ&dq=patent:7278103, June 2007.

[17] S. Cleger-Tamayo, J.M. Fernández-Luna, J.F. Huete, R. Pérez-Vázquez, and J.C. Rodríguez Cano, "A proposal for news recommendation based on clustering techniques," in *Trends in Applied Intelligent Systems* (N. García-Pedrajas, F. Herrera, C. Fyfe, J. Manuel Benítez, and M. Ali, eds.), Vol. 6098 of *Lecture Notes in Computer Science*, pp. 478–487. Berlin/Heidelberg: Springer, 2010.

[18] T.M. Cover and P.E. Hart, "Nearest neighbor pattern classification," *IEEE Transactions on Information Theory*, 13(1):21–27, 1967.

[19] R. Xu and D.C. Wunsch II, "Survey of clustering algorithms," *IEEE Transactions on Neural Networks*, 16(3):645–678, 2005.

[20] M. Mukiibi and J.O. Bukenya, "Segmentation analysis of grocery shoppers in alabama," in *The Southern Agricultural Economics Association Annual Meeting*, February 2008.

[21] D. Bremner, E. Demaine, J. Erickson, J. Iacono, S. Langeman, P. Morin, and G. Toussaint, "Output-sensitive algorithms for computing nearest-neighbour decision boundaries," *Discrete & Computational Geometry*, 33(4):593–604, 2005.

[22] J. John, "Pandora and the Music Genome Project," *Scientific Computing*, 23(10):40–41, 2006.

[23] Y. Koren, R. Bell, and C. Volinsky, "Matrix factorization techniques for recommender systems," *Computer*, 42:30–37, 2009.

[24] S. Deerwester, S.T. Dumais, G.W. Fumas, T.K. Landauer, and R. Harshman, "Indexing by latent semantic analysis," *Journal of the American Society for Information Science*, 41(6):391–407, 1990.

[25] D. Billsus and M.J. Pazzani, "Learning collaborative information filters," in *Proceedings of the 15th International Conference on Machine Learning*, ICML '98, pp. 46–54, 1998.

[26] G.H. Golub and W. Kahan, "Calculating the singular values and pseudo-inverse of a matrix," *Journal of the Society for Industrial and Applied Mathematics*, 2(2):205–224, 1965.

[27] M. Brand, "Fast online svd revisions for lightweight recommender systems," *Proceedings of the 3rd SIAM International Conference on Data Mining*, pages 37–46, 2003.

[28] A.-M. Kermarrec, V. Leroy, A. Moin, and C. Thraves, "Application of random walks to decentralized recommender systems," in *Principles of Distributed Systems* (C. Lu, T. Masuzawa, and M. Mosbah, eds.), Vol. 6490 of *Lecture Notes in Computer Science*, pp. 48–63. Berlin/Heidelberg: Springer, 2010.

[29] T. Marwala, *Computational Intelligence for Missing Data Imputation, Estimation, and Management: Knowledge Optimization Techniques*, 1st ed. Boston: Pearson Addison-Wesley, 2009.

[30] R.M. Bell and Y. Koren, "Lessons from the netflix prize challenge," *ACM SIGKDD Explorations Newsletter*, 9:75–79, 2007.

[31] J.K. Cullum and R.A. Willoughby, *Lanczos Algorithms for Large Symmetric Eigenvalue Computations*. Würzburg, Germany: Birkhauser Boston, 1984.

[32] H.D. Simon, "The Lanczos algorithm with parial reorthogonalization," *Mathematics of Computation*, 42(165):115–142, 1984.

[33] K. Dookhitram, R. Boojhawon, and M. Bhuruth, "A new method for accelerating Arnoldi algorithms for large scale eigenproblems," *Mathematics and Computers in Simulation*, 80(2):387–401, 2009.

[34] J. Alpert and N. Hajaj, "We knew the web was big . . . ." Available at http://googleblog. blogspot.com/2008/07/we-knew-web-was-big.html, July 2008.

[35] J. de Leeuw, "Principal component analysis of binary data by iterated singular value decomposition," *Computational Statistics and Data Analysis*, 50(1):21–39, 2006.

[36] M. Vozalis and K.G. Margaritis, "Using svd and demographic data for the enhancement of generalized collaborative filtering," *Journal of Information Sciences: An International Journal*, 177(15):3017–3037, 2007.

[37] P.-N. Tan, M. Steinbach, and V. Kumar, *Introduction to Data Mining*. Boston: Pearson Addison-Wesley, 2005. 1 ed.

[38] M.D. Johnson, "Consumer similarity judgements: A test of the contrast model," *Psychology and Marketing*, 3(1):47–60, 1986.

[39] S. Kullback, "Letter to the editor: The Kullback–Leibler distance," *The American Statistician*, 41(4):340–341, 1987.

[40] J.R. Hershey, P.A. Olsen, and S.J. Rennie, "Variational Kullback–Leibler divergence for hidden markov models," *Automatic Speech Recognition & Understanding*, pp. 323–328, December 2007.

[41] Y. Koren, "Collaborative filtering with temporal dynamics," *Communications of the ACM*, 53(4):89–97, 2010.

[42] G.W. Fumas, T.K. Landauer, L.M. Gomez, and S.T. Dumais, "The vocabulary problem in human-system communication: An analysis and a solution," *Communications of the ACM*, 30(11):964–971, 1987.

[43] C.D. Manning and H. Schutze, *Foundations of Statistical Natural Language Processing*. Cambridge, MA: MIT Press, 1999.

[44] P. Jaccard, "Étude comparative de la distribution florale dans une portion des alpes et des jura," *Bulletin del la Société Vaudoise des Sciences Naturelles*, 37:547–579, 1901.

[45] T.T. Tanimoto, "An elementary mathematical theory of classification and prediction." IBM Internal Report, 1957.

[46] L.R. Dice, "Measures of the amount of ecologic association between species," *Ecology*, 26(3):297–302, 1945.

[47] T. Sørensen, "A method of establishing groups of equal amplitude in plant sociology based on similarity of species content and its application to analysis of the vegetation on danish commons," *Biologiske Skrifter*, 5:1–34, 1948.

[48] M.R. Stan, A.F. Tenca, and M.D. Ercegovac, "Long and fast up/down counters," *IEEE Transactions on Computers*, 47:722–735, 1998.

[49] D. Gusfield, *Algorithms on Strings, Trees and Sequences: Computer Science and Computational Biology*, 1st ed. Cambridge, UK: Cambridge University Press, 1999.

[50] R.W. Hamming, "Error detecting and error correcting codes," *Bell System Technical Journal*, 29(2):147–160, 1950.

[51] M.S. Waterman and T.F. Smith, "Identification of common molecular subsequences," *Journal of Molecular Biology*, 147:195–197, 1981.

[52] D.P. Bertsekas, *Dynamic Programming and Optimal Control*, 3rd ed. Nashua, NH: Athena Scientific, 2007.

[53] T.H. Cormen, C.E. Leiserson, R.L. Rivest, and C. Stein, *Introduction to Algorithms*, 3rd ed. Cambridge, MA: The MIT Press, 2009.

[54] R.A. Wagner and M.J. Fischer, "The string-to-string correction problem," *Journal of the ACM*, 21(1):168–173, 1974.

[55] S.B. Needleman and C.D. Wunsch, "A general method applicable to the search for similarities in the amino acid sequence of two proteins," *Journal of Molecular Biology*, 48(3):443–453, 1970.

[56] D.J. Lipman and W.R. Pearson, "Rapid and sensitive protein similarity searches," *Science*, 227(4693):1435–1441, 1985.

[57] L. Allison, "Lazy dynamic-programming can be eager," *Information Processing Letters*, 43(4):207–212, 1992.

[58] S.F. Altschul, W. Gish, W. Miller, E.W. Myers, and D.J. Lipman, "Bastic local alignment search tool," *Journal of Molecular Biology*, 215(3):403–410, 1990.

[59] D.A. Huffman, "A method for the construction of minimum-redundancy codes," *Institute of Radio Engineers*, 40(9):1098–1101, 1952.

[60] A. Monge and C. Elkan, "The field matching problem: Algorithms and applications," in *Proceedings of the 2nd International Conference on Knowledge Discovery and Data Mining*, pp. 267–270, 1996.

[61] C.-H. Chang, M. Kayed, M.R. Girgis, and K. Shaalan, "A survey of web information extraction systems," *IEEE Transactions on Knowledge and Data Engineering*, 18(10): 1411–1428, 2006.

24

KNN Queries in Mobile Sensor Networks

Wei-Guang Teng and Kun-Ta Chuang

24.1 INTRODUCTION

Mobile sensor networks have received a significant amount of research attention in recent years because they can support a wide range of applications, for example, intelligent transportation systems (ITS) [1], wildlife conservation systems [2], and battlefield surveillance systems [3]. In most applications for sensor networks, it is expected that data on sensor nodes can be periodically queried by an external source. Important statistical information about the underlying physical processes can thus be collected for further use.

Recently, query processing techniques, including range queries, k-nearest neighbor (KNN) queries, and snapshot queries, have been widely utilized in different applications. Among the various query types for aggregating sensor information, the KNN query, which aims at finding the KNNs around a query point, q, has been recognized as one of the key spatial queries in mobile sensor networks [4–7]. Applications of KNN queries include vehicle navigation, wildlife social discovery, and squad/platoon searching on the battlefields. KNN queries can also be applied to emergency situations such as tracing the insurgents of a traffic accident, discovering the impact of a forest fire, and seeking our nearby survivors around a battlefield stronghold.

The problem of developing an efficient algorithm for a KNN search in a spatial or multidimensional database is a major research topic for various applications [8–12]. Traditional KNN query processing techniques usually assume that location

Scalable Computing and Communications: Theory and Practice, First Edition. Edited by Samee U. Khan, Albert Y. Zomaya, and Lizhe Wang.
© 2013 John Wiley & Sons, Inc. Published 2013 by John Wiley & Sons, Inc.

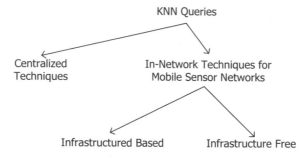

FIGURE 24.1. *Categorization of KNN query processing mechanisms.*

data are available in a centralized database and focus on improving the index performance [5, 13–15]. However, in new applications where data sources are geographically spread (e.g., sensor networks [2, 16], wireless ad hoc networks [17], or ITS [1]), pulling data from a large number of data sources (e.g., sensor nodes, laptops, or vehicles) is usually infeasible because of high energy consumption, high communication costs, or long latencies [18, 19]. Thus, for applications in mobile sensor networks, a number of studies have recently explored the so-called in-network KNN query processing techniques [9–12, 20–22]. These techniques rely on certain in-network infrastructure—index or data structures (e.g., clustered indices or spanning trees) that are distributed among the sensor nodes—to select KNN candidates, to propagate queries, and to aggregate the result.

As shown in Figure 24.1, current techniques for KNN or range query processing can be classified into two categories, that is, the *centralized* and the *in-network* approaches. Note that, in the mobile sensor network environment, the locations of the nodes may change frequently. Also, when the nodes move, the direct wireless link between the nodes and the centralized index may no longer exist. Using centralized indices may lead to substantial message routing/relay overhead. In addition, it is prohibitively expensive to maintain the up-to-date locations of moving sensors in centralized solutions. In contrast, the in-network approach does not rely on a centralized index; instead, it propagates the query directly among the sensor nodes in the network and collects relevant data to form the final result [9–12, 20–23]. This approach is favored in mobile sensor networks to prevent high energy consumption and high maintenance overhead for a centralized database.

We thus focus on the recent development of in-network KNN approaches for mobile sensor networks. Specifically, the in-network approach can be further divided into two subcategories: those relying on a certain sort of in-network infrastructure and those that are infrastructure free. The term "infrastructure" refers to a data structure distributed among the sensor nodes that is created, either once on the fly or to be updated constantly, to support the query processing. Nevertheless, the maintenance of the in-network data structure could become prohibitively costly when the sensor nodes become mobile. To eliminate this problem, infrastructure-free methods are thus proposed. The infrastructure-free methods do not rely on any precomputed network index to process queries but instead propagate a KNN query along some well-designed itineraries to collect the data [19, 21]. Recently, a number of studies have addressed continuous queries using in-network techniques [5, 15, 23]. These methods are appropriate for the constant monitoring of queries of long-standing interest but are orthogonal to the on-demand queries (one time only) that we focus on in this chapter.

24.2 PRELIMINARIES AND INFRASTRUCTURE-BASED KNN QUERIES

24.2.1 Preliminaries

We give the review of the peer-tree [20], distributed spatial index (DSI) [9], KNN perimeter tree (KPT) [11, 12], density-aware itinerary-based KNN (DIKNN) [21], and parallel concentric-circle itinerary-based (PCIKNN) [22] because they are the most notable in-network frameworks for KNN queries in mobile sensor networks.

Before discussing the details of each work, we first give the formal definition of the KNN problem for sensor networks. The query that we discussed is a type of snapshot query, which is expected to obtain the query result only once during its lifetime. The KNN problem is defined as follows.

Definition 24.1 (KNN Query)   *Given a set of sensor nodes S, a geographic location q (i.e., the query point), and a valid time T, find a subset S′ of S with k nodes (i.e., $S′ \subseteq S, |S1| = k$) such that at time T, $\forall n1 \in S′, n2 \in (S - S′): DIST(n1, q) \leq DIST(n2, q)$, where DIST denotes a distance function (usually the Euclidean distance is used).*

Ideally, we expect to obtain the exact result set $S′$ comprising the KNNs of q at a given time T. However, because of node mobility and efficiency considerations [18, 19], we may obtain an approximate result set instead. Query result accuracy is measured by the percentage ratio of the correct KNNs (at a valid time T) that is returned. Depending on different application needs, the valid time T can be defined either as the time the query is issued or the time the result set is received.

Note that Definition 24.1 does not specify the types of information that are returned with $S′$. If the node order in $S′$ is desired, then each node may return its geolocation, and the user receiving $S′$ can simply determine the order of nodes by comparing their distances to the query point.

In general, the network is in the ad hoc mode, so nodes far away from their mutual coverage communicate with each other through multihops. It is expected that all of the sensor nodes are capable of storing data locally and answering the queries individually. In addition, the moving speed and directions of sensor nodes are arbitrary. Each sensor node is aware of its geolocation. Beacons with locations and identities (IDs) are periodically broadcasted. Every sensor node also maintains a table that includes IDs and locations of neighbor nodes that fall within its radio range r. Note that this network scenario complies with IEEE Standard 802.15.4 [16], in the low-rate wireless personal area network (LR-WPAN), to achieve maximum compatibility.

24.2.2 Infrastructure-Based KNN Queries

24.2.2.1 Peer-to-Peer Indexing Structure (Peer-Tree)   The peer-tree [20] is devised with a decentralized R-tree [13]. As shown in Figure 24.2, a network is partitioned into a hierarchy of minimum bounding rectangles (MBRs). Each MBR covers a geographic region that includes all of the sensor nodes that are located

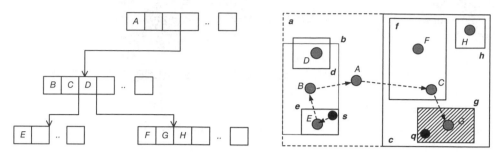

FIGURE 24.2. *An example of peer-tree.*

inside. An MBR in the higher hierarchy (say, region a in Fig. 24.2) covers all of the regions of the sub-MBRs in the child hierarchy (regions $b, c,$ and d in Fig. 24.2). One specific node is designated as a cluster head (i.e., distributed index) in each MBR. A cluster head knows the locations and IDs of all of the other nodes within the same MBR. The cluster head also knows the locations and IDs of its parent and child cluster heads. While a 1NN (i.e., $k = 1$) query is issued, the source node s routes the query message to its cluster head (node E in Fig. 24.2). Upon receiving the message, the cluster head forwards the message upward in the hierarchy until the query point q is covered by the MBR of a cluster head (in this case, node A in Fig. 24.2). The cluster head then forwards the message downward in the hierarchy, looking for a child cluster head (node G in Fig. 24.2) that contains q with a minimal MBR. After that, the location of the nearest neighbor (NN) of q can be determined and the NN is informed of the query message by a unicast. Supporting the KNN queries is more complicated because it requires multiple cluster heads to find and to propagate the query message in different MBRs. Because every query message goes through the cluster heads, the major problem of these approaches is that cluster heads easily become the system bottleneck.

Peer-tree is the first work to utilize in-network hierarchies to maintain locations of sensor nodes. However, the solution may be vulnerable to any index failure. It is clear that there are many unnecessary hops from s to the KNN nodes because each query message is routed along the hierarchy of cluster heads, as depicted by the arrows in Figure 24.2.

24.2.2.2 DSI Similar to peer-tree, the DSI [9] also utilizes the concept of index decentralization to maintain location information in distributed environments. DSI refers to the Hilbert curve to determine the order of objects (sensors). The basic idea is to divide all of the objects into a set of disjoint frames and to associate each frame with an index table. While linearly looking at the index table, the sensor distribution around the query point can be obtained. The major issue for the KNN search in DSI is to quickly determine a precise search space that contains k neighbors. Initially, the search space is the whole spatial area when a new KNN query is issued. The search space incrementally shrinks when a new index table is received.

Similar to peer-tree, DSI is also vulnerable to any index change. The maintenance overhead that results from the sensors moving reduces the algorithm's performance. Such overhead may become significant in the large-scale sensor networks where the distance between cluster heads is large.

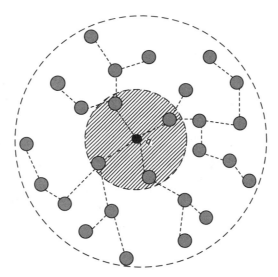

FIGURE 24.3. *An example of KPT.*

24.2.2.3 KNN Perimeter Tree (KPT) To resolve the overhead in the peer-tree and DSI algorithms, the KPT algorithm [11, 12] is proposed to handle the KNN query without fixed indexing. This work assumes that each sensor node is location aware. After a query is issued from s, it is routed to the sensor node, named the *home node*, which is closest to q. To avoid flooding the entire network, a conservative boundary that contains at least k candidates is estimated by the home node. Multiple trees rooted at the home node are then constructed to propagate queries and to aggregate data, as shown in Figure 24.3. Upon aggregating data at the home node, the node determines the correct KNNs (by sorting locations) and transmits their query responses back to the source s.

KPT assumes an optimal network condition when each node is stationary. It encounters two serious drawbacks in the presence of mobility. First, constructing or maintaining the trees while the sensor nodes are moving incurs considerable overhead. Partially collected data may be forwarded again and again between new and old tree nodes. Second, the conservative (large) boundary grows quadratically as k increases, which leads to high energy consumption and a long latency. Although such a boundary is expected to cover at least k nodes in the worst case, sensor nodes may either move in or move out of the boundary during tree construction and data aggregation. As such, KPT is likely to return poor query results.

24.3 INFRASTRUCTURE-FREE KNN QUERIES

24.3.1 Overview of Infrastructure-Free KNN Queries

Because the maintenance overhead of infrastructure-based solutions is a critical concern when the sensor nodes are mobile, the state-of-the-art algorithms of KNN queries in mobile sensor networks thus turn to use the infrastructure-free concept when processing KNN queries [21, 22]. Currently, infrastructure-free KNN

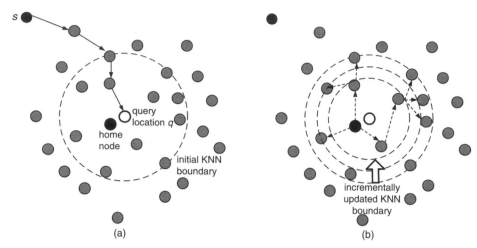

FIGURE 24.4. *An illustrative example of itinerary-based KNN query processing. (a) Routing and boundary KNN estimation phases. (b) Query dissemination and data collection phase.*

algorithms are all devised based on the *itinerary-based concept*. In fact, the concept of itinerary traversal is inspired by a number of research efforts in unicast routing [24], data fusion [25], network surveillance [26], and window query processing [19]. The DIKNN algorithm [21] is the first work to exploit the idea of itineraries in KNN queries for sensor networks. In general, the itinerary-based query consists of three phases: (1) the routing phase, (2) the KNN boundary estimation phase, and (3) the query dissemination and data collection phase.

We show an illustrative example of an itinerary-based KNN query in Figure 24.4. Initially, a source node issues a KNN query. At the routing phase, the query is routed to the sensor node that is nearest to the query location q (such a node is referred to as the home node) by a georouting protocol such as the greedy perimeter stateless routing (GPSR) algorithm [27]. The next step, that is, the KNN boundary estimation phase, is to estimate an initial radius that can conservatively cover all of the KNN sensors. The boundary can be dynamically updated during the third step of the query dissemination. The message is propagated from the home node to each node that is located within the incrementally updated KNN boundary. Finally, the query results are aggregated from the data that are collected along the itinerary of the query dissemination.

Compared to infrastructure-based algorithms, which inevitably pay for the maintenance overhead for a stable infrastructure, the itinerary-based KNN query is more feasible in a dynamic sensor network with scarce resources. Clearly, the performance, including the query latency and the energy consumption, is highly dependent on the design of the itineraries. A long itinerary traversal may lead to long query latency and high energy consumption. How to plan a good itinerary executed in the query dissemination phase is deemed as the key to the success of the itinerary-based KNN processing.

To better capture the execution of the main phase of itinerary-based KNN processing, that is, the query dissemination phase, we assume that the KNN boundary is given beforehand. Specifically, suppose that the radius of the KNN boundary is

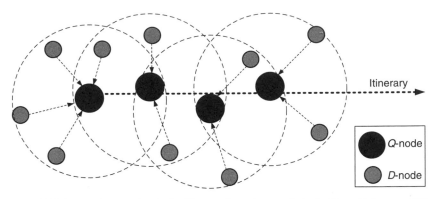

FIGURE 24.5. *Various nodes in the itinerary-based query (adapted from Reference 21).*

R. The home node n_p enters the query dissemination phase, aiming to inform all of the sensor nodes inside the boundary of the query message Q and to collect their responses. One naive infrastructure-tree solution is to flood the query within the boundary. Each node inside the boundary, upon receiving Q, routes its response back to s end to end and then broadcasts Q again. This approach, however, is extremely resource consuming and has poor scalability because of the excessive number of independent routing paths from sensor nodes to s [19, 21].

The itinerary-based dissemination technique is proposed to resolve such issues. The execution of the itinerary query dissemination can be best understood by the illustration in Figure 24.5. A set of *query nodes* (Q-nodes) in the KNN boundary is selected for the query dissemination. Upon receiving a query, a Q-node broadcasts a probe message that includes information about Q, R, and the itinerary (e.g., the itinerary width). When hearing the probe message, the neighbor nodes that are qualified to reply to the query, called *data nodes* (D-nodes), report their query response back to the Q-node. After obtaining the data from all of the D-nodes as well as the partial result that was received from the previous Q-node, the current Q-node selects the next Q-node based on the itinerary information and forwards this new partial query result to the selected next Q-node. This procedure repeats until the query traverses the entire KNN boundary along a predefined (say, spiral) itinerary structure, as shown in Figure 24.6. Responses of all nodes that are held by the last Q-node are then returned back to the sink node s in a single message.

24.3.1.1 Correctness of the Itinerary-Based Solution

The correctness of the itinerary execution has been proven in previous works [19, 21]. Formally, the itinerary width w, as shown in Figure 24.6, specifies the minimum distance between different segments of an itinerary. Obviously, a small w results in denser itinerary traversal, which ensures the KNN boundary to be fully covered by the traversal. On the other hand, the small w incurs unnecessary transmission and long latency because of the increased itinerary length. The following theorem is quoted from Reference 21.

Theorem 24.1 *Let r denote the transmission range of the sensor nodes. To guarantee full coverage of a KNN boundary, the itinerary width w must be less than $\sqrt{3}r/2$.*

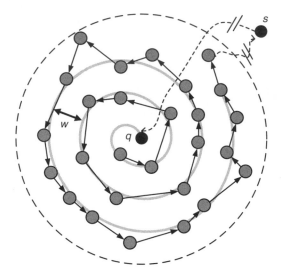

FIGURE 24.6. Itinerary-based query dissemination (adapted from Reference 21).

It can be shown [19] that letting $w = \sqrt{3}r/2$ yields full coverage while ensuring the minimal itinerary length, thus producing a good balance between query accuracy and energy efficiency. Second, data collection from multiple D-nodes must be better scheduled to avoid collisions and delays. The *contention-based data collection scheme* (the data collection scheme can combine both the *token ring-based* and the *contention-based* schemes to achieve higher performance [21]) can be utilized to prevent serious contention and to sustain network dynamics. In this scheme, a reference line emanating from the current Q-node is included in the probe message. The probe message also contains a precedence list indicating the reply order of D-nodes. Upon receipt of the probe message, each D-node sets a timer with timer $= (\alpha/2\pi)im$, where α is the angle formed by the specified reference line and the line connecting the current Q-node and the current D-node, i is the received precedence, and m is a time unit for the Q-node waiting for each D-node to report its data. A D-node does not respond to the Q-node until its timer expires. Discussions on the other issues such as fault tolerance and traveling in low-connectivity areas with itinerary voids (i.e., situations when a Q-node cannot find the next Q-node for query forwarding) can be found in References 19 and 27.

In the mobile sensor network, when the Q-node moves outside the current segment during the data collection phase, it may immediately forward the partial collected results to the node nearby its original location. The data collection can be resumed on the new Q-node with a new probe message targeting only those D-nodes that did not report yet. To avoid duplicated data, each D-node can report its own ID along with the sensed data to the Q-node. By keeping the IDs of the nodes (including Q-nodes and D-nodes) collected so far in the partial query result, each Q-node is able to determine whether the coming data are duplicated or not. Note that because k is usually small, the maintenance of these IDs may not result in too much overhead.

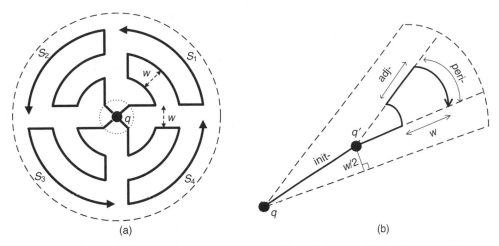

FIGURE 24.7. *Concurrent query dissemination (adapted from Reference 21). (a) Concurrent itineraries. (b) Various itinerary segments.*

24.3.1.2 *Concurrent Itinerary Structures*   Generally, the performance of dissemination solely depends on the itinerary design. Query latency can be significantly improved by considering the *parallel dissemination*. Nevertheless, concurrent itineraries may increase the likelihood of channel contention and collision at the data link and physical layers, causing the degradation of network throughput. Parallelization should be exercised cautiously to avoid the overhead and should satisfy the following criteria. First, the number of routing paths leading back to the sink s, after dissemination, should be controllably small to prevent high energy consumption in large-scale sensor networks. Second, as concurrent itinerary traversals may incur channel interference in wireless transmission, the chance that they meet should be as small as possible [21].

To fulfill the above criteria, a KNN boundary could be partitioned into multiple sectors, as shown in Figure 24.7a. Such a cone-shaped itinerary is the itinerary design used in Reference 21. In each sector, the query is propagated along a subitinerary. The distance between subitineraries in adjacent sectors is w, to ensure full coverage of the KNN boundary when $w \le \sqrt{3}r/2$. Each subitinerary consists of three segments: the init-, adj-, and peri-segments, as illustrated in Figure 24.7b. The init-segment is a portion of a subitinerary that has a distance that is less than $w/2$ on either side of a sector's border. This segment is formed by a straight line to reduce the interference as soon as possible.

Ideally, two subitineraries in adjacent sectors interfere with each other only at their init-segments. An important observation discussed in Reference 21 shows that even if these two subitineraries are traversed at different speeds, extra interference can only occur at adj-segments, which are relatively short as compared to peri-segments. Therefore, such a cone-shaped itinerary structure is highly adaptive to various degrees of parallelism. Note that the shape of a subitinerary degenerates into a straight line if the number of sectors is large enough. This allows for the best efficiency when no interference occurs in the sensor network (e.g., when a *contention-free period* [CFP] is exercised in LR-WPAN).

The concurrent itinerary traversal is a powerful functionality for the scalability issue, which has been utilized in all of the proposed itinerary-based solutions. The difference between two state-of-the-art itinerary-based algorithms lies in their design of itineraries and the corresponding KNN boundary estimation. In the following, we describe the distinguished points of two representative approaches, that is, DIKNN and PCIKNN.

24.3.2 DIKNN

24.3.2.1 KNN Boundary Estimation in DIKNN The DIKNN algorithm [21] is the first study that employs the concept of itineraries in the KNN query processing for sensor networks. In addition to the design of itineraries, this type of algorithm also incurs a challenging issue when precisely estimating the KNN boundary. The decision of the KNN boundary must be made with very limited knowledge, which can only be obtained from query propagation. To resolve this issue, DIKNN adopts a simple and effective algorithm, named the KNN boundary (KNNB), which is tailored for sensor nodes with a limited ability.

The basic idea behind KNNB is to collect necessary information during the routing phase. In the routing phase, a query Q is routed from sink node s to the nearest neighbor n_p (i.e., the home node) around the query point q. By utilizing the geographic face routing protocol [27, 28], information collection is performed between hops. An additional list L is sent along with Q. On the ith ($1 \le i < p$) hop to the destination where p denotes the number of hops along the routing path, the corresponding node (i.e., the sensor node triggering the ith hop) appends its own location loc_i and the number of newly encountered neighbors enc_i to L. To avoid duplicate information, enc_i can simply be counted by checking the number of neighbors that have a distance larger than r from the corresponding node of the $(i-1)$th hop. Note that such an information gathering technique consumes very few extra resources because only nodes around the route are involved.

Upon receipt of the query message and the list L from the previous phase, it starts estimating the KNN boundary by determining its radius length r. As described previously, too large a boundary incurs high energy consumption and a long latency. In contrast, a small boundary loses the query accuracy. The determination of r must balance two conflicting factors: (1) increasing r to enclose correct KNN points, as many as possible, and (2) decreasing r to reduce the energy consumption.

KNNB has an essential assumption: The sensor nodes are uniformly distributed *within the optimal KNN boundary* (i.e., the boundary containing exactly KNNs). Clearly, this assumption is easily violated when k is large. A solution to reduce the bias of estimation is also proposed. Readers can refer to the details in Reference 21.

24.3.2.2 Issues of Spatial Irregularity in DIKNN Note that DIKNN assumes that sensor nodes are uniformly distributed around the query point q. As such, DIKNN may suffer from the issue of spatial irregularity in large-scale networks, resulting in communicacion voids and the loss of the query accuracy [29]. To handle this problem, Q-nodes in different sectors can adjust their own r during dissemination. Note that DIKNN inverses the direction of peri-segments in every interseptal

sector. In such a configuration, the face-to-face adj-segments of different subitineraries together form *rendezvous segments*, in which two Q-nodes from adjacent subitineraries can, with little cost of latency, meet with each other and exchange the latest statistics. By repeating this procedure, the jth rendezvous segment in a subitinerary can obtain information from $2, 4, \ldots, \min\{2j, S\}$ nearby sectors at the jth, $(j - 1)$th, $\ldots$, first level of the peri-segments, respectively. Each sector can thus infer how many nodes around q are explored so far (totally) and can dynamically adjust r to stop or to continue the dissemination.

24.3.2.3 Issues of Mobility Concern in DIKNN

The mobility of the sensor nodes degrades the query accuracy because the nodes may move in or move out of the KNN boundary during dissemination. For applications for which discovering correct KNNs is the most important concern, the support of flexible expansion of r to include more candidates is critical. One naive approach is to modify the KNNB algorithm so that $r' = cr$ is returned, where r' denotes the adjusted radius of the KNN boundary and c, $c > 1$, denotes a constant. Obviously, for larger c, we may guarantee more correct KNNs with r'; however, more energy is consumed as well. This arrangement makes it very difficult for an application to determine a satisfactory value of c.

In DIKNN, this issue is considered in the query dissemination phase, where the last Q-node is obligated to determine how much farther a subitinerary will continue. Specifically, each application is allowed to specify an attribute, named the *assurance gain* g, $0 \leq g \leq 1$, at the time when a KNN query is issued. By acquiring the moving speed of each sensor node along with its data collection, each subitinerary can maintain a record μ that specifies the fastest moving speed that was traced so far. Upon receiving this record, the last Q-node is able to measure the maximum shift of the sensor nodes by $(t_s - t_e)\mu$, where t_s and t_e denote the time stamps of the moment the home node n_p receives the query and the query dissemination ends, respectively. Thus, an appropriate expansion of r can be obtained by $r' = r + g(t_s - t_e)\mu$.

To address the interaction between the mobility and spatial irregularity, it is reasonable to first adjust the KNN boundary according to the updated density information during the itinerary traversal. Afterward, a final expansion is decided (to guarantee the worst case performance) by considering the uncertainty introduced by the node mobility.

24.3.2.4 Fault Tolerance in DIKNN

Wireless sensor networks encompass various types of packet losses, which may occur because of the mobility of the sensor nodes, environmental interference, low signal-to-noise ratios (SNR), and contentions in channel access. In DIKNN, a fault-tolerant data collection scheme is proposed. Benefiting from location awareness, a D-node receiving a probe message knows the relative reply precedence with its neighbor D-nodes. A D-node monitors (i.e., caches) its own precedence. If no acknowledgment (from the Q-node to monitored D-node) is received, then the monitoring D-node sends cached data together with its own response. This construct helps to overcome the loss of D-node responses. On the other hand, when sending the response, each D-node piggybacks the probe message upon its response so that the nearby D-nodes will have a chance to hear the probe again if the original probe from the Q-node is lost.

24.3.3 PCIKNN

Recently, a new solution, called the PCIKNN algorithm [22], has been proposed to resolve several issues found from the execution of the DIKNN algorithm. PCIKNN argues that the method for dynamic adjustment of the KNN boundary estimation in DIKNN is not always feasible in different sensor network models. In addition, determining the number of optimized KNN query threads is left unresolved for users in DIKNN.

Generally, PCIKNN also has three phases, that is, the routing phase, the KNN boundary estimation phase, and the query dissemination phase. In PCIKNN, the estimated KNN boundary can be dynamically refined while the query is propagated within the KNN boundary. Explicitly, the home node needs to collect partial results to dynamically adjust the KNN boundary. The partial data collection in the home node can also be used to guarantee that the final query result contains k-nearest nodes.

The most distinguished contribution in PCIKNN is the novel design of parallel concentric-circle itineraries, as shown in the example in Figure 24.8. The idea of parallel itineraries is first utilized in the itinerary-based query processing. Each itinerary will fork parallel threads for aggregating data in different directions. Unlike the DIKNN algorithm, which uses a single itinerary in each segment, parallel threads can help to reduce duplicated data transmissions when traversing in the inverse direction, thus leading to better power savings and improving the query latency. Furthermore, comprehensive analysis is provided to prove the model validation and to show how the PCIKNN can resist impact from spatial irregularity and mobility issues [22].

In terms of the KNN boundary estimation, DIKNN needs to record collected local information in each hop that is visited during the routing phase, which inevitably incurs extra energy overhead. To avoid energy consumption, the PCIKNN uses a linear regression technique to estimate the area that is covered by sensor nodes.

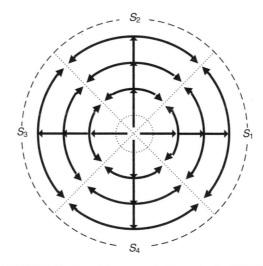

FIGURE 24.8. *Parallel concentric itineraries in PCIKNN.*

As reported in corresponding experimental studies [22], the regression-based solution can achieve a better boundary estimation with a relatively small energy cost.

Generally speaking, the PCIKNN algorithm uses a similar idea to handle network issues such as the mobility concern and the link failure issue. Readers can refer to the article for the discussion of such impacts on using parallel itinerary threads [22].

24.4 FUTURE RESEARCH DIRECTIONS

Query processing in mobile sensor networks remains a challenging issue. It is especially difficult to resolve the KNN issue with minimum energy consumption. Using infrastructure-based solutions will lead to prohibitively expensive maintenance overhead for index structures. On the other hand, using the infrastructure-free solution will face another critical issue when attempting to decide the KNN boundary precisely.

Currently, common research directions focus on infrastructure-free solutions because they are expected to have relatively small energy overhead (the energy issue is the most important concern in the sensor network [30]). However, we still could find some studies that demand further research, which can be summarized in the following directions.

24.4.1 Can KNN Results be Approximate?

The current KNN query processing focuses on finding precise KNN results. However, an approximate result is satisfactory in quite many applications [27]. The approximate answer is even more feasible because it is likely to be achieved at the cost of light energy consumption. Consequently, this concept would be an excellent start for further research.

24.4.2 In Addition to Itinerary-Based Solutions, Can We Have Another Way with the Infrastructure-Free Concept?

Clearly, the infrastructure-free solutions can alleviate energy concerns in mobile sensor networks. However, current solutions are all devised using itinerary traversal. Itinerary traversal inevitably faces the issues of network reliability. Even worse, duplicate data transmission cannot be completely prevented because of the node mobility. Another innovative algorithm to prevent such weaknesses under various network conditions will be a possible direction.

24.5 CONCLUSIONS

In this chapter, we have presented the status of KNN queries in mobile sensor networks. Because of its various applications, the KNN query has become one of the most important spatial queries in mobile sensor networks. We have discussed the comparison between infrastructure-based solutions and infrastructure-free solutions. To date, the itinerary-based KNN traversal, which requires no infrastructures and is able to sustain rapid changes in network topology, has been deemed as the better solution with minimum maintenance overhead and energy consumption. We have summarized possible research directions for improving current KNN queries, for example, to propose new solutions that can effectively return approximate KNN results. Finally, as technologies of sensor networks evolve, we believe that the KNN issue still requires further research effort to achieve both high precision and low power consumption.

REFERENCES

[1] U.S. Department of Transportation, "Intelligent Transportation System Joint Program Office." Available at http://www.its.dot.gov/.

[2] P. Juang, H. Oki, Y. Wang, M. Martonosi, L.S. Peh, and D. Rubenstein, "Energy-efficient computing for wildlife tracking: Design tradeoffs and early experiences with zebranet," in *Proceedings of the 10th International Conference on Architectural Support for Programming Languages and Operating Systems*, pp. 96–107, 2002.

[3] Federation of American Scientists, "Remote Battlefield Sensor System (REMBASS)," 2000. Available at http://www.fas.org/man/dod-101/sys/land/rembass.htm.

[4] H. Ferhatosmanoglu, E. Tuncel, D. Agrawal, and A.E. Abbadi, "Approximate nearest neighbor searching in multimedia databases," in *Proceedings of the 17th International Conference on Data Engineering*, pp. 503–511, 2001.

[5] H.D. Chon, D. Agrawal, and A.E. Abbadi, "Range and KNN query processing for moving objects in grid model," *Mobile Networks and Applications*, 8(4):401–412, 2003.

[6] N. Roussopoulos, S. Kelley, and F. Vincent, "Nearest neighbor queries," in *Proceedings of the 1995 ACM SIGMOD International Conference on Management of Data*, pp. 71–79, 1995.

[7] Z. Song and N. Roussopoulos, "*K*-nearest neighbor search for moving query point," *Proceedings of the 7th International Symposium on Advances in Spatial and Temporal Databases*, pp. 79–96, 2001.

[8] M.-S. Chen, K.-L. Wu, and P.S. Yu, "Optimizing index allocation for sequential data broadcasting in wireless mobile computing," *IEEE Transactions on Knowledge and Data Engineering*, 15(1):161–173, 2003.

[9] W.-C. Lee and B. Zheng, "DSI: A fully distributed spatial index for location-based wireless broadcast services," in *Proceedings of the 25th IEEE International Conference on Distributed Computing Systems*, pp. 349–358, 2005.

[10] B. Liu, W. Lee, and D. Lee, "Distributed caching of multi-dimensional data in mobile environments," in *Proceedings of the 6th International Conference on Mobile Data Management*, pp. 229–233, 2005.

[11] J. Winter and W.-C. Lee, "KPT: A dynamic KNN query processing algorithm for location-aware sensor networks," in *Proceedings of the 1st International Workshop on Data Management for Sensor Networks*, pp. 119–124, 2004.

[12] J. Winter, Y. Xu, and W.-C. Lee, "Energy efficient processing of *K* nearest neighbor queries in location-aware sensor networks," in *Proceedings of the 2nd Annual International Conference on Mobile and Ubiquitous Systems: Networking and Services*, pp. 281–292, 2005.

[13] A. Guttman, "R-Trees: A dynamic index structure for spatial searching," in *Proceedings of the 1984 ACM SIGMOD International Conference on Management of Data*, pp. 47–57, 1984.

[14] G.R. Hjaltason and H. Samet, "Distance browsing in spatial databases," *ACM Transactions on Database Systems*, 24(2):265–318, 1999.

[15] M. Mokbel, X. Xiong, and W. Aref, "SINA: Scalable incremental processing of continuous queries in spatio-temporal databases," in *Proceedings of the 2004 ACM SIGMOD International Conference on Management of Data*, pp. 623–634, 2004.

[16] IEEE Standard Association, IEEE-SA 802.15.4-2003, *Wireless Medium Access Control (MAC) and Physical Layer (PHY) Specifications for Low Rate Wireless Personal Area Networks*. 2003.

[17] IEEE Standard Association, IEEE-SA 802.11-1997, *IEEE Standard for Wireless LAN Medium Access Control (MAC) and Physical Layer (PHY) Specifications*. 1997.

[18] M. Bawa, A. Gionis, H. Garcia-Molina, and R. Motwani, "The price of validity in dynamic networks," *Journal of Computer and System Sciences*, 73(3):245–264, 2007.

[19] Y. Xu, W.-C. Lee, J. Xu, and G. Mitchell, "Processing window queries in wireless sensor networks," in *Proceedings of the 22nd International Conference on Data Engineering*, p. 70, 2006.

[20] M. Demirbas and H. Ferhatosmanoglu, "Peer-to-peer spatial queries in sensor networks," in *Proceedings of the 3rd International Conference on Peer-to-Peer Computing*, p. 32, 2003.

[21] S.-H. Wu, K.-T. Chuang, C.-M. Chen, and M.-S. Chen, "Toward the optimal itinerary-based KNN query processing in mobile sensor networks," *IEEE Transactions on Knowledge and Data Engineering*, 20(12):1655–1668, 2008.

[22] T.-Y. Fu, W.-C. Peng, and W.-C. Lee, "Parallelizing itinerary-based KNN query processing in wireless sensor networks," *IEEE Transactions on Knowledge and Data Engineering*, 22(5):711–729, 2010.

[23] R. Cheng, B. Kao, S. Prabhakar, A. Kwan, and Y. Tu, "Adaptive stream filters for entity-based queries with non-value tolerance," in *Proceedings of the 31st International Conference on Very Large Data Bases*, pp. 37–48, 2005.

[24] D. Niculescu and B. Nath, "Trajectory based forwarding and its applications," in *Proceedings of the 9th Annual International Conference on Mobile Computing and Networking*, pp. 260–272, 2003.

[25] S. Patil, S.R. Das, and A. Nasipuri, "Serial data fusion using space-filling curves in wireless sensor networks," in *Proceedings of the 1st IEEE Communications Society Conference on Sensor and Ad Hoc Communications and Networks*, pp. 182–190, 2004.

[26] C. Gui and P. Mohapatra, "Virtual patrol: A new power conservation design for surveillance using sensor networks," in *Proceedings of the 4th International Symposium on Information Processing in Sensor Networks*, pp. 246–253, 2005.

[27] B. Karp and H. Kung, "GPSR: Greedy perimeter stateless routing for wireless networks," in *Proceedings of the 6th Annual International Conference on Mobile Computing and Networking*, pp. 243–254, 2000.

[28] F. Kuhn, R. Wattenhofer, Y. Zhang, and A. Zollinger, "Geometric ad-hoc routing: Of theory and practice," in *Proceedings of the 22nd Annual Symposium on Principles of Distributed Computing*, pp. 63–72, 2003.

[29] D. Ganesan, S. Ratnasamy, H. Wang, and D. Estrin, "Coping with irregular spatio-temporal sampling in sensor networks," *ACM SIGCOMM Computer Communication Review*, 34(1):125–130, 2004.

[30] I.F. Akyildiz, W. Su, Y. Sankarasubramaniam, and E. Cayirci, "A survey on sensor networks," *IEEE Communications Magazine*, 40(8):102–114, 2002.

25

Data Partitioning for Designing and Simulating Efficient Huge Databases

Ladjel Bellatreche, Kamel Boukhalfa, Pascal Richard, and Soumia Benkrid

25.1 INTRODUCTION

Data warehousing is becoming more complex in terms of applications, data size, and queries, including joins and aggregations. Data warehouse projects always stress performance and scalability because of the data volumes and the query complexity. For instance, eBay's data warehouse includes 2 petabytes of user data and millions of queries per day.[1] Data distribution for ensuring high parallelism becomes a crucial issue for the research community.

Most of the major commercial database systems support data distribution and parallelism (Teradata, Oracle, IBM, Microsoft SQL Server 2008 R2 Parallel Data Warehouse, Sybase, etc.). Data warehouses store large volumes of data mainly in relational models such as star or snowflake schemas. A star schema contains a large fact table and various dimension tables. A star schema is usually queried in various combinations involving many tables. The most used operations are joins, aggregations, and selections [1]. Joins are well known to be expensive operations, especially when the involved relations are substantially larger than the size of the main memory [2], which is usually the case in business intelligence applications. The typical queries defined on the star schema are commonly referred to as star join queries and exhibit the following two characteristics: (1) There is a multitable join

---

[1]http://www.dbms2.com/2009/04/30/ebays-two-enormous-data-warehouses/.

Scalable Computing and Communications: Theory and Practice, First Edition. Edited by
Samee U. Khan, Albert Y. Zomaya, and Lizhe Wang.

among the large fact table and multiple smaller dimension tables, and (2) each of the dimension tables involved in the join operation has multiple selection predicates on its descriptive attributes. To speed up star join queries, many optimization techniques were proposed. In Reference 3, we classified them into two main categories: redundant techniques such as materialized views, advanced index schemes, vertical partitioning, and parallel processing with replication, and nonredundant techniques like ad hoc joins, where joins are performed without additional data structures like indexes (hash join, nested loop, sort merge, etc.), horizontal partitioning (HP), and parallel processing without replication. In this chapter, we concentrate only on horizontal partitioning since it is more adapted to reduce the cost of star join queries.

HP has been mainly used in logical distributed and parallel database design in the last decades [4, 5]. Recently, has become a crucial part of physical database design [1, 6–9], where most of today's commercial DBMS offer native data definition language (DDL) support for defining horizontal partitions (fragments) of a table [8]. In the context of relational warehouses, HP allows tables, indexes, and materialized views to be partitioned into disjoint sets of rows that are physically stored and accessed separately. Contrary to materialized views and indexes, horizontal data partitioning does not replicate data, thereby reducing space requirements and minimizing the update overhead. The main characteristic of data partitioning is its ability to be combined with some redundant optimization techniques such as indexes and materialized views [10]. It also affects positively query performance, database manageability, and availability. Query performance is guaranteed by performing partition elimination. If a query includes a partition key as a predicate in the WHERE clause, the query optimizer will automatically route the query to only relevant partitions. Partitioning can also improve the performance of multitable joins by using a technique known as partition-wise joins. It can be applied when two tables are being joined together, and at least one of these tables is partitioned on the join key. Partition-wise joins break a large join into smaller joins. With partitioning, maintenance operations can be focused on particular portions of tables. For maintenance operations across an entire database object, it is possible to perform these operations on a per-partition basis, thus dividing the maintenance process into more manageable chunks. The administrator can also allocate partitions in different machines [6, 11]. Another advantage of using partitioning is that when it is time to remove data, an entire partition can be dropped, which is very efficient and fast, compared to deleting each row individually. Partitioned database objects provide partition independence. This characteristic of partition independence can be an important part of a high-availability strategy. For example, if one partition of a partitioned table is unavailable, all of the other partitions of the table remain online and available. The application can continue to execute queries and transactions against this partitioned table, and these database operations will run successfully if they do not need to access the unavailable partition.

Two versions of HP exist [12, 13]: primary and derived (known as referential partitioning in Oracle 11g [7]). Primary HP of a table is performed using attributes defined on that table. Derived HP, on the other hand, is the fragmentation of a table using attributes defined on another table. In other words, the derived HP of a table is based on the fragmentation schema of another table (the fragmentation schema is the result of the partitioning process of a given table). The derived partitioning of a table R according to a fragmentation schema of S is feasible if and only if there is a join link between R and S (R contains a foreigner key of S). It has been used to optimize data transfer when executing queries in the distributed database environment.

In traditional databases (relational and object oriented), tables/classes are horizontally partitioned in isolation. Consequently, the problem of selecting horizontal fragments of a given table T of a database may be formulated as follows:

Given a representative workload W defined on the table T, find a partitioning schema FS of T, such that the overall query processing cost ($\Sigma_{Q \in W} f_Q \times \text{Cost}(Q, FS)$, where f_Q represents the access frequency of the query Q) is minimized. According to this formalization, the database administrator (DBA) does not have any control on the generated fragments of table T. Since each table is fragmented in an isolated way, it is difficult to measure the impact of generated fragments on the rest of the tables of database schema.

In relational data warehouses, HP is more challenging compared to that in traditional databases. This challenge is due to the different choices to partition a star schema:

1. Partition only the dimension tables using simple predicates defined on these tables (a simple predicate p is defined by $p: A_i \, \theta \, \text{Value}$, where A_i is an attribute of a dimension table, $\theta \in \{=, <, >, \leq, \geq\}$, and Value $\in \text{Dom}(A_i)$). This scenario is not suitable for online analytical processing (OLAP) queries because the size of the dimension tables is generally smaller than the size of the fact table, and any star query accesses the fact table. Therefore, any HP that does not take into account the fact table is *discarded*.

2. Partition only the fact table using simple predicates defined on this table if they exist, since it is very large. Usually, restriction (selection) predicates are defined on dimension tables and not on fact tables. The raw data of the fact table usually never contain descriptive (textual) attributes because the fact relation is designed to perform arithmetic operations such as summarization, aggregation, and average on such data. Recall that star join queries access dimension tables first and, after that, the fact tables. This choice is also *discarded*.

3. Partition some/all dimension tables using their predicates, and then partition the fact table based on the fragmentation schemas of dimension tables using referential partitioning mode. This approach is more adapted to partition relational data warehouses since it takes into consideration the star join query requirements and the relationship between the fact table and dimension tables. In our study, we adopt this scenario. To illustrate it, we consider the following example.

■ EXAMPLE 25.1

Let us consider a star schema with three dimension tables (*Customer, Time, and Product*) and one fact table, *Sales*. Suppose that the dimension table Customer is partitioned into two fragments, *CustFemale* and *CustMale*, using the *Gender* attribute, and table Time into two fragments, *TimeHalf$_1$* and *TimeHalf$_2$*, using the *Month* attribute, as follows:

- CustFemale = $\sigma_{(Gender="F")}$(Customer)
- CustMale = $\sigma_{(Gender="M")}$(Customer)
- TimeHalf$_1$ = $\sigma_{(Month\leq6)}$(Time)
- TimeHalf$_2$ = $\sigma_{(Month>6)}$(Time)

Following the third scenario, the fact table Sales is then fragmented based on the partitioning schema of Customer and Time into four fragments Sales$_1$, Sales$_2$, Sales$_3$, and Sales$_4$ such as

- Sales$_1$ = Sales $\ltimes$ CustFemale $\ltimes$ TimeHalf$_1$
- Sales$_2$ = Sales $\ltimes$ CustFemale $\ltimes$ TimeHalf$_2$
- Sales$_3$ = Sales $\ltimes$ CustMale $\ltimes$ TimeHalf$_1$
- Sales$_4$ = Sales $\ltimes$ CustMale $\ltimes$ TimeHalf$_2$.

The initial star schema (Sales, Customer, Product, Time) may be represented as the juxtaposition of four substar schemas S_1, S_2, S_3, and S_4 such as S_1: (Sales$_1$, CustFemale, TimeHalf$_1$, Product) (sales activities for only female customers during the first half); S_2: (Sales$_2$, CustFemale, TimeHalf$_2$, Product) (sales activities for only female customers during the second half); S_3:(Sales$_3$, CustMale, TimeHalf$_1$, Product) (sales activities for only male customers during the first half); and S_4: (Sales$_4$, CustMale, TimeHalf$_2$, Product) (sales activities for only male customers during the second half).

The generated number of fragments (N) of the fact table is given by $N = \prod_{i=1}^{g} m_i$, where m_i and g represent the number of fragments of the dimension table D_i and the number of dimension tables participating in the fragmentation process, respectively. This number may be very large. For example, suppose we have the Customer table partitioned into 50 fragments using the State attribute (case of 50 states in the United States), Time into 36 fragments using the Month attribute (if the sale analysis is done based on the last 3 years), and Product into 80 fragments using the Package_type attribute. Therefore, the fact table is decomposed into 144,000 fragments ($50 \times 36 \times 80$) using the referential partitioning mode. Consequently, instead of managing one star schema, the DBA will manage 144,000 substar schemas. It will be very hard for her or him to maintain all these substar schemas [14]. To avoid the explosion of the number of fact table fragments, we formalize the problem of selecting a HP schema as an optimization problem:

Given a representative workload W defined on a relational data warehouse schema with n dimension tables $\{D_1, \ldots, D_n\}$ and one fact table F and a constraint (called maintenance bound B) representing the number of fact fragments, identify dimension tables that could be used for derived partitioning of the fact table F, such that ($\Sigma_{Q \in W} f_Q \times Cost(Q, FS)$) is minimized and maintenance constraint is satisfied ($N \leq B$). The number B may be given by the DBA.

We present in this chapter a comprehensive study of the HP problem including primary and referential modes based on six aspects: (1) proposition of a methodology for HP in relational data warehouses guided by the total number of fragments, (2) study of complexity of referential data HP problem, (3) proposition of two selection algorithms ensuring simultaneously primary and referential partitioning, (4) proposition of combined selection approach of HP and bitmap join indexes (BJI), (5) experimental study to show the benefit and limitations of HP, and (6) proposition of simulator tool assisting data warehouse administrators (DWAs) to perform the physical design (partitioning and/or indexing).

The rest of the chapter is organized as follows: Section 25.2 presents the state of the art and related work. Section 25.3 is devoted to the presentation of our HP approach. In Section 25.4, we study the complexity of the HP selection problem and we show its hardness. Section 25.5 presents two selection algorithms, simulated annealing and hill climbing, to select near-optimal fragmentation schemes. Section 25.6 presents our combined selection approach of HP and BJI. In Section 25.7, we present the experiments that we conducted using the most popular benchmark APB1. Section 25.8 describes in detail our simulator tool, baptized SimulPh.D, to assist the administrator during his or her tasks. Section 25.9 concludes the chapter by summarizing the main results and discussing future works.

25.2 BACKGROUND AND RELATED WORK

HP has been largely studied in the literature, where several algorithms were proposed that we propose to classify into two main categories: *unconstrained approaches* and *threshold-based approaches* (Fig. 25.1). Early work on horizontal fragmentation can be found in the first category. They select a partitioning schema for a database without worrying about the number of generated fragments. We have shown that this number may be very important, which greatly complicates their manageability. We can find two classes in this category of approaches: *minterm generation-based approaches* and *affinity-based approaches*.

The minterm generation-based [4] approach starts with a table T and a set of predicates $p_1, \cdots, p_n$ of the most frequently asked queries defined on relation T and outputs a set of horizontal fragments of the table T. The main steps of the

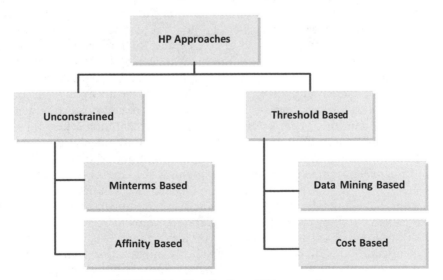

FIGURE 25.1. *Classification of HP approaches.*

minterm generation-based approach are (1) generation of minterm predicates $M = \{m \mid m = \wedge(1 \leq k \leq n)P_k^*\}$, where P_k^* is either p_k or $\neg p_k$, (2) simplification minterms in M and elimination of useless ones, and (3) generation of fragments: Each minterm m generates a fragment defined as $\sigma_m(R)$ (σ is a selection operation). This approach is simple, but it has a high complexity. For n simple predicates, this algorithm generates 2^n minterms. It can be used for a reasonable number of simple predicates. In order to reduce this complexity, another approach was proposed, which adapts the vertical partitioning algorithm [15]. Predicates having a high affinity are grouped together. An affinity between two predicates, p_i and p_j, is computed as the sum of frequencies of queries accessing simultaneously these two predicates. Each group gives a horizontal fragment defined as a conjunction of its predicates. This algorithm has a low complexity [16], but it takes into account only access frequencies to generate horizontal fragments and ignores parameters like size of tables and selectivity factors of predicates.

Given the need to have a reasonable and controlled number of fragments, new threshold-based approaches are proposed. This threshold represents the maximum number of fragments that the administrator wants to have. The main objective of threshold-based approaches is to partition a table into B fragments such that B is less than or equal to the threshold (constraint bound). Thus, in addition to the set of selection predicates, these approaches require that the administrator sets the threshold value. Two major classes of works exist in this category: *data mining-based approaches* and *cost-based approaches*.

The data mining-based approach was proposed in the context of XML data warehouses [17]. It uses the K-means clustering algorithm to group selection predicates that can fragment the data warehouse. The threshold B (number of fragments) is given as the input parameter for the K-means algorithm. K-means is used to group the predicates in B groups. The proposed approach consists in three main steps: (1) coding of selection predicates, (2) classification of predicates, and (3) generating fragments. The coding of a predicate is to assign each predicate to the query in which it is referenced to build the extraction context. The classification of predicates uses the clustering algorithm K-means [18] to create B classes of predicates. The construction of fragments is based on classes of predicates identified in the classification stage. Each class of predicates is used to generate a horizontal partition. The approach proposes to partition the dimension document by horizontal primary partitioning and the facts document by horizontal derived fragmentation. To ensure complete fragmentation, a fragment ELSE is added. It is the negation of all conjunctions of predicates. This approach controls the number of generated fragments but does not guarantee performance of the generated fragmentation schema.

The cost-based approach starts with a set of potential fragmentation schemes of relation R and using a cost model measuring the number of inputs and outputs required for executing a set of queries; it computes the goodness of each schema [19]. The schema with a low cost is considered as the final solution. The DBA may quantify the benefit obtained by this solution. Its main drawback is that the DBA does not have control of the number of generated fragments.

All the work we cited has proposed approaches for HP of isolated selection. Several works proposed to combine HP with other optimization techniques. Sanjay et al. [8] proposed an integration of horizontal and vertical fragmentation in the physical design of databases. Stöhr et al. [11] proposed the combination of HP with parallel processing in parallel data warehouses. The approach exploits hierarchies of dimensions to fragment data warehouses modeled by a star schema. The approach exploits parallelism within and between queries to reduce the cost of query execution. The approach also proposes the use of BJI defined on attributes not used to partition the data warehouse. In Reference 20, we proposed the HP&BJI approach, which combines HP and BJI in the physical design of relational data warehouses. HP&BJI starts with selecting a HP schema and then identifying the set of nonprofitable queries after partitioning and the set of attributes not used to partition the data warehouse. In the second step, HP&BJI select a configuration of join indexes based on the two sets of attributes and queries identified in the last stage. The main particularity of this approach is that it prunes the search space of an optimization technique (indexes) using another optimization technique (HP). Recently, Bellatreche et al. [6] proposed a combination design approach of parallel data warehouses using HP. Unlike existing works that consider the problems of fragmentation and allocation independently, the proposed approach considers a combined problem of fragmentation and allocation. Actually, horizontal fragmentation is an integral part of the physical design of most important DBMS editors: Oracle [13], DB2 [21], SQL Server [22], PostgreSQL [23], and MySQL [24]. To show this interest, we consider an example of one of the most popular DBMSs, which is Oracle.

Figure 25.2 shows the main partitioning modes in Oracle. The first HP mode supported by Oracle was *range partitioning* (in Oracle 8). It is defined by a tuple (c,

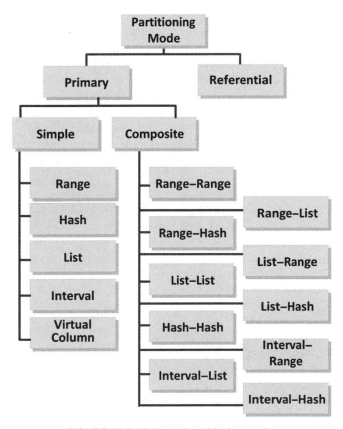

FIGURE 25.2. Horizontal partitioning modes.

V), where *c* is a column type and *V* is an ordered sequence of values from the domain of *c*. In this partitioning, an access path (table, materialized view, and index) is split according to a range of values of a given set of columns. Oracle 9 and 9i added other modes like *Hash* and *List* and *Composite* (Range–Hash, Range–List). The Hash mode decomposes the data according to a hash function (provided by the system) applied to the values of the partitioning columns. *List partitioning* splits a table according to the list values of a column. *Composite partitioning* is supposed by using PARTITION–SUBPARTITION statement. Note that these modes are also supported by other commercial databases like SQL Server, Sybase, and DB2. These partitioning modes are considered as basic modes of any partitioning tool supported by commercial DBMS. Oracle 11g proposes several fragmentation modes. The composite partitioning method has been enriched to include all possible combinations of basic methods (except those that begin with the hash mode): List–List, Range–Range, List–Range, and List–Hash. Recently, a new composite mode, Hash–Hash, is supported by Oracle 11g Release 2 [13]. Another interesting mode called *virtual column partitioning* is proposed, which allows a table to be decomposed using a virtual attribute defined by an expression, using one or more existing columns of a table, and storing this expression as metadata only. Oracle supports another partitioning mode, *interval partitioning*. This mode extends the capabilities of the range mode to define equipartitioned ranges using an interval definition. Rather than specifying individual ranges explicitly, Oracle will create any partition automatically as needed whenever data for a partition is inserted for the very first time. Recently, in Oracle 11g Release 2, the *interval composite mode* is introduced. Three interval composites are supported: interval–range, interval–list and interval–hash. Note that all these modes concern only the primary HP, where a table is partitioned using its attribute(s). The *referential partitioning mode* allows partitioning a table by leveraging an existing parent–child relationship. This partitioning is similar to derived HP [12]. Unfortunately, a table may be partitioned based only on one table.

Oracle and several commercial DBMSs provide DDL for managing partitions. Two main functions are provided: *merge partitions* and *split partition*. The first function consists in merging two partitions into one. The second function splits a partition into two partitions. The syntax of the use of these functions is given below:

```
ALTER TABLE <table_name>
MERGE PARTITIONS <first_partition>,<second_partition>
INTO PARTITION <partition_name>
TABLESPACE <tablespace_name>;
ALTER TABLE <table_name>
SPLIT PARTITION <partition_name>
AT <range_definition>
INTO (PARTITION <first_partition>, PARTITION
<second_partition>)
```

Note that other functions are available, such as deleting a partition, adding a new partition, moving a partition, and renaming a partition.

Oracle also allows index fragmentation. An index created on a table is either coupled or uncoupled with the underlying partitioning mode of this table. Two kinds of partitioned indexes are supported in Oracle: local and global partitioned indexes.

A local index is created on a partitioned table that is coupled with the partitioning strategy of this table (attributes, mode, and number of fragments). Consequently, each partition of a local index corresponds to one and only one partition of the underlying table. A local index enables optimized performance and partition maintenance. When a query references one partition, only its local index is loaded instead of the entire index. When a partition is dropped/updated, only its local index will be removed/updated. Local indexes are very suitable for OLAP applications. A global partitioned index is defined on a partitioned or nonpartitioned table. It is partitioned using a different partitioning strategy than the indexed table. For example, table Customer could be range partitioned by attribute Age, while a global index is range partitioned by attribute Salary. This kind of index is suitable for online transactional processing (OLTP) applications.

By exploring most academic and industrial works, we figure out that most of the approaches in selecting a HP schema suppose a decomposition of domain values of attributes participating in the fragmentation process. We can classify these approaches into two main categories (see Fig. 25.3): (1) *user-driven approaches* and (2) *query-driven approaches*. In the first category, the DBA decomposes the domain values of each partitioning attribute based on her or his knowledge of database applications and imposes a priori the number of generated horizontal fragments. For example, the following statement allows partitioning the table Customer using State attribute using the list mode into four fragments:

```
CREATE TABLE Customer (CID NUMBER(5), Name VARCHAR2(30),
State VARCHAR2(20), City Varchar2(20))
```

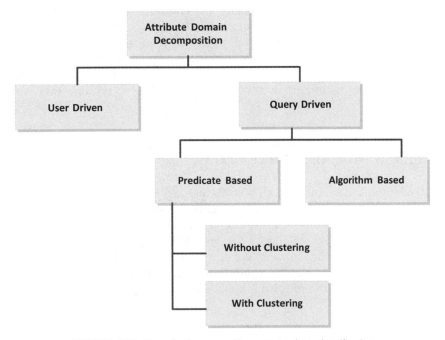

FIGURE 25.3. Domain decomposition approaches classification.

```
PARTITION BY LIST(State) (
PARTITION Customer _west VALUES('California', 'Hawaii'),
PARTITION Customer _east VALUES ('New York', 'Virginia',
'Florida'),
PARTITION Customer _central VALUES('Texas', 'Illinois'),
PARTITION Customer _other VALUES(DEFAULT));
```

The main characteristic of this category is that the DBA controls the number of generated fragments. She or he sets this number based on her or his knowledge and experience on database applications. Its main drawbacks are (1) the absence of a metric measuring the quality of the generated partitioning schema, (2) the difficulty on choosing attributes that will participate on fragmenting a table, and (3) an efficient decomposition of domains of fragmentation attributes is not ensured.

In *query-driven partitioning approaches*, the domain values of fragmentation attributes are explicitly decomposed based on simple selection predicates of the most frequently asked queries defined on relation *T*. We can classify these approaches into two categories: those that use predicates to generate the final decomposition of domains and those that use algorithms to do so. We can distinguish two trends in the first category: *approaches without predicates clustering* and *approaches with predicates clustering*. The first trend uses directly selection predicates for generating minterms [4]. Minterms are used to generate the domain decomposition. The *predicate clustering approach* begins with a step of grouping predicates into multiple partitions. These partitions are used to generate domain decomposition. Clustering is based on either the affinities [16] or clustering algorithm like *K*-means [17]. All the approaches we have presented do not guarantee the quality of the final domain decomposition. To overcome this problem, greedy approaches have been proposed. Their idea is to start by initial decomposition (random or issued from a different approach we have cited), then to iteratively improve decomposition by merging or splitting subdomains. Improving the initial decomposition is guided by a cost model, which estimates the execution cost of frequently asked queries on a partitioned schema generated by domain decomposition. We present in the next section our fragmentation methodology and the two selection algorithms that we have proposed.

25.3 FRAGMENTATION METHODOLOGY

As for redundant technique (materialized views, indexes) selection problems, horizontal selection schema selection is done based on a set of the most frequently asked queries ($\{Q_1, \ldots, Q_w\}$), where each query Q_j has an access frequency f_{Q_j}. Note that each star join query Q_j is defined by a set of selection predicates and a set of join predicates. The selection predicates are essential for the partitioning process. Note that each selection predicate has a selectivity factor. To partition a relational data warehouse, we present the following methodology:

1. Extraction of all selection predicates used by the queries.
2. Assignment to each dimension table D_i ($1 \leq i \leq n$) its set of selection predicates, denoted by $SSPD_i$.

3. Ignorance of dimension tables having an empty SSPD (i.e., they will not participate in fragmenting the fact table). Let $D^{candidate}$ be the set of all dimension tables having a nonempty SSPD. Let g be the cardinality of $D^{candidate}$ ($g \leq n$).

4. Identification of the set fragmentation attributes SFAC candidate. A fragmentation attribute is an attribute of dimension tables participating in the partitioning process.

5. A decomposition of domain values of each fragmentation attribute into subdomains. This decomposition may be done either intuitively by the DBA using her or his knowledge of warehouse applications or guided by simple predicates defined on each fragmentation attribute. Each subdomain may be represented by a simple predicate and it has a selectivity factor defined on the fact table.

6. Selection of a final fragmentation schema using an algorithm that exploits the decomposition of all domains of fragmentation attributes. Such algorithm shall reduce query processing cost and satisfy the maintenance constraint. In order to illustrate this methodology, let us consider the following example.

■ EXAMPLE 25.2

Suppose that SFAC contains three attributes (*Age*, *Gender*, *Season*), where Age and Gender belong to the Customer dimension table, whereas Season belongs to Time ($D^{candidate}$ = {Customer, Time}). The domains of these attributes are Dom(Age) = [0, 120], Dom(Gender) = {"M," "F"}, and Dom(Season) = {"Summer," "Spring," "Autumn," "Winter"}. We assume that DBA splits domains of these attributes into subdomains as follows: Dom(Age) = $d_{11} \cup d_{12} \cup d_{13}$, with d_{11} = [0, 18], d_{12} = [18, 60], d_{13} = [60, 120]. Dom(Gender) = $d_{21} \cup d_{22}$, with d_{21} = {"M"}, d_{22} = {"F"}. Dom (Season) = $d_{31} \cup d_{32} \cup d_{33} \cup d_{34}$, where d_{31} = {"Summer"}, d_{32} = {"Spring"}, d_{33} = {"Autumn"}, and d_{34} = {"Winter"}. The subdomains of all three fragmentation attributes are represented in Figure 25.4a.

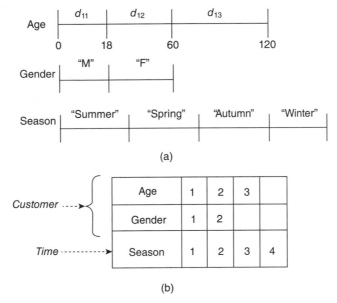

FIGURE 25.4. An example of decomposition of domains in subdomains.

TABLE 25.1. An Example of Partitioning Schema

Age	1	1	2	
Gender	1	2		
Season	1	1	1	1

Domain partitioning of different fragmentation attributes may be represented by *multidimensional arrays*, where each array represents the domain partitioning of a fragmentation attribute. The value of each cell of a given array representing an attribute A_i^k belongs to $(1..n_i)$, where n_i represents the number of subdomain of the attribute A_i^k (see Fig. 25.4b). Based on this representation, the fragmentation schema of each dimension table D_j is generated as follows:

1. All cells of a fragmentation attribute of D_j have different values: this means that all subdomains will be used to partition D_j. For instance, the cells of each fragmentation attribute in Figure 25.4b are different. Therefore, they all participate in fragmenting their corresponding tables (Customer and Time). The final fragmentation schema will generate 24 fragments of the fact table.

2. All cells of a fragmentation attribute have the same value: This means that it will not participate in the fragmentation process. Table 25.1 gives an example of a fragmentation schema, where all subdomains of Season (of dimension table Time) have the same value; consequently, it will not participate in fragmenting the warehouse schema.

3. Some cells have the same value: Their corresponding subdomains will be merged into one. In Table 25.1, the first ([0, 18]) and the second ([18, 60]) subdomains of Age will be merged to form only one subdomain, which is the union of the merged subdomains ([0, 60]). The final fragmentation attributes are Gender and Age of dimension table Customer.

The above coding (in Table 25.1) may be used by DBA to partition the dimension table Customer and the fact table Sales using the primary partitioning (*Range* on Age and *List* on Gender) and referential partitioning modes, respectively:

```
CREATE TABLE Customer
(CID NUMBER, Name Varchar2(20), Gender CHAR, Age Number)
PARTITION BY RANGE (Age)
SUBPARTITION BY LIST (Gender)
SUBPARTITION TEMPLATE (SUBPARTITION Female VALUES ('F'),
SUBPARTITION Male VALUES ('M'))
(PARTITION Cust_0_60 VALUES LESS THAN (61),
PARTITION Cust_60_120 VALUES LESS THAN (MAXVALUE));
```

Since the Customer was partitioned into four fragments, the fact table is also partitioned into four partitions as follows:

```
CREATE TABLE Sales (customer_id NUMBER NOT NULL, product_
id NUMBER NOT NULL, time_id Number NOT NULL, price NUMBER,
quantity NUMBER,
```

TABLE 25.2. Two Ways to Represent the Same Individual

Subdomain	d_1	d_2	d_3
Array 1	0	1	0
Array 2	1	0	1

```
constraint Sales_customer_fk foreign key(customer_id)
references Customer(CID))

PARTITION BY REFERENCE (Sales_customer_fk);
```

25.3.1 Multi-instantiation of Our Coding

Our coding may suffer from multi-instantiation. To illustrate this problem, we consider a set $D = \{d_1, d_2, d_3\}$, then every subset in the partition of D, for instance, $\{\{d_1, d_3\}, \{d_2\}\}$, can be represented by an array of integers. Nevertheless, a given partition can be represented by different arrays of integers (see Table 25.2).

Clearly, arrays 1 and 2 only differ by integers used for representing these subsets: In both solutions, d_1 and d_3 belong to the same subset, and d_2 is in the other subset. Such a problem can be solved by using restricted growth functions:

Let $[n]$ be a set $\{1, \ldots, n\}$; a restricted growth function is a function f such as $F: [n] \rightarrow [n]$ such that

$$f(1) = 0.$$

$f(i + 1) \leq \max f(1), \ldots, f(i) + 1$, where $f(i)$ defines the subset index where the item i belongs to. For instance, the partition $\{\{1, 3, 5\}, \{2, 6\}, \{4\}\}$ is represented by the restricted growth function $[0, 0, 0, 1, 1, 2]$, where 0 is the index of the first subset. There is a one-to-one equivalence between set partitions and restricted growth functions. In our previous example, only array 1 respects the lexicographic order induced by restricted growth functions, while array 2 will never be considered during the set partitioning.

Theorem 25.1 *There is a one-to-one correspondence between the set of [n] and the set of restricted growth functions.*

Several algorithms are known for generating all partitions of a set D in lexicographic order (see Reference 25, for instance).

■ EXAMPLE 25.3

To show the contribution of the restricted growth function in eliminating multi-instantiation, let us consider the following example. The two top codings of Figure 25.5 represent the same fragmentation schema. The application of the restricted growth function gives only one schema (the bottom one).

25.4 HARDNESS STUDY

We consider the HP of the data warehouse through a simplified decision problem that considers the derived HP of the fact table based on the partitioning schema of

Gender	1	2		
Season	1	3	2	2
Age	2	2	1	

Gender	2	1		
Season	2	1	3	3
Age	3	3	1	

Gender	1	2		
Season	1	2	3	3
Age	1	1	2	

FIGURE 25.5. *An example of using the restricted growth function.*

one dimension table using only one attribute. The corresponding optimization problem consists in computing a partition of the fact table so that the number of partitions is bounded by a constant B and the maximum number of input/output (I/O) operations is minimized. We state the decision problem as follows:

Problem: One-Domain HP

Instance:

- A set D of disjoint subdomains $\{d_1, \cdots, d_n\}$ of the fragmentation attribute of the partitioned dimension table and the number of I/O operations in order to read data corresponding to the subdomain d_i in the fact table, denoted $l(d_i), 1 \leq i \leq n$
- A set of queries $\{q_1, \cdots, q_m\}$, where each query q_j has a list $f(q_j) \subseteq D$ of used subdomains until the query completion: $\{d_{j1}, \cdots, d_{jn_j}\}$, where n_j is the number of subdomains used in the fact table to run q_j
- Two positive integers, K and L, representing, respectively, the maximum number of partitions that can be created and the maximum number of I/O operations allowed for each query, $L \geq \Sigma_{d \in f(q_j)} l(d)$

Question: Can D be partitioned in at most K subsets, $D_1, \cdots, D_K$ such that every query requires at most L I/O operations?

The optimal number of I/O operations required by a query q_j is $\Sigma_{d \in f(q_j)} l(d)$. It assumes that only required data are loaded in memory to run q_j. According to a given partition, the number of I/O operations increases since all data of a partition are loaded when used by a given query, even if that query does not require all data of the partition (i.e., a subset of domains in the partition). Thus, the number of I/O operations required by a query after partitioning does not depend on the used subdomains but only on used partitions. The number of I/O operations while loading a partition D is defined by $l(D) \geq \Sigma_{d \in D} l(d)$. As a consequence, the number of I/O operations required by running a query can be defined as $l(q_j) = \Sigma_{D \in F(q_j)} l(D)$, where $F(q_j)$ is the list of partitions used by a query q_j.

The objective is to perform a derived HP of the fact table such that the number of partitions is limited to K and the number of I/O operations is bounded by L for every query. Obviously, if $K \leq n$, the optimal HP is achieved by defining exactly one partition to every d_i ($d_i \in D$). In that way, every query only loads required data during its execution. We shall see that our simplified decision problem becomes hard when $K < n$. We also assume $L \geq \Sigma_{d \in f(q_j)} l(d)$ since, otherwise, the answer of the one-domain HP is always false.

Theorem 25.2   *One-domain HP is NP-complete in the strong sense.*

Proof: One-domain HP clearly belongs to NP since, if one guesses a partition of D, then a polynomial time algorithm can check that, at most, K partitions are used and that every query requires, at most, L I/O operations. We now prove that one-domain HP is NP-complete in the strong sense. We shall use 3-partition that is strongly NP-complete [26].   ■

Problem: 3-Partition
Instance: Set A of $3m$ elements, a bound $B \in Z^+$, and a size $s(a) \in Z^+$, for each $a \in A$ such that $B/4 < s(a) < B/2$ and such that $\Sigma_{\alpha \in A} S(\alpha) = mB$
    Question: Can A be partitioned into m disjoint sets $A_1, \cdots, A_m$ such that, for $1 \leq i \leq m$, $\sum_{a \in A_i} S(a) = B$ (note that each A_i must therefore contain exactly three elements from A)?
    To prove the NP-completeness of one-domain HP, we reduce from 3-partition. To every 3-partition instance, an instance of one-domain HP is defined as follows:

- To every $a_i \in A$, a subdomain d_i is created so that $l(d_i) = s(a_i)$, $1 \leq i \leq 3m$.
- $3m$ queries are created such that every query uses exactly one subdomain: $f(q_i) = \{d_i\}$, $1 \leq i \leq 3m$.
- $K = L = B$.

Clearly, the transformation is performed in polynomial time since it consists in a one-to-one mapping of 3-partition elements into subdomains and queries. We now prove that we have a solution to the 3-partition instance if and only if we have a solution to the one-domain HP instance.

25.4.1 Necessary Condition

Assume that we have a solution of the one-domain HP, and then it satisfies the following conditions:

- Since $B/4 < l(d) < B/2$, every subset of D will be defined with exactly three subdomains (as in every 3-partition instance).
- Since we have a feasible solution of the one-domain HP, then no query requires more than I/O operations. By construction we verify that $\Sigma_{d \in D} l(d) = mB$. As a consequence, every query requires exactly B I/O in the fact tables (otherwise, it is not a solution). Using a one-to-one mapping of subdomains into elements of a 3-partition, a feasible solution of the 3-partition instance is obtained.

25.4.2 Sufficient Condition

Assume that we have a solution to the 3-partition instance. Then, every subset A_i is a total size of B and is composed of exactly three elements of A. Starting from A_1, we define a subdomain partition using subdomains with the same indexes of elements belonging to A_1. Since every query is associated with exactly one subdomain and three subdomains are grouped in every partition, then exactly three queries use a given partition. As a consequence, the number of I/O associated with these three corresponding queries is exactly B. Repeat this process for every remaining subset A_i, and then a feasible solution of the *one-dimension HP problem* is obtained.

Every subdomain can be used to define a HP of the fact table. As a consequence, the number of solutions (i.e., the number of ways to partition the fact table) is defined by the number of partitions of the set D. For a set of size k, this number is defined by the Bell number. Even if the number of solutions is limited when k is small, it vastly becomes intractable (e.g., if $k = 10$, then the number of different partitions is 115,975).

25.5 PROPOSED SELECTION ALGORITHMS

Due to the high complexity of the HP selection problem, development of heuristics selecting near-optimal solutions is recommended. In this section, we present the hill climbing and simulated annealing (SA) algorithms [27] with several variants.

25.5.1 Hill Climbing Algorithm

The hill climbing heuristic consists of the following two steps:

1. Find an initial solution.
2. Iteratively improve the initial schema solution by using the hill climbing operations until no further reduction in total query processing time can be achieved and the maintenance bound B is satisfied. Since there is a finite number of fragmentation schemes, the heuristic algorithm will complete its execution.

25.5.1.1 Choices of the Initial Solution Theoretically, the choice of the initial solution of hill climbing has an impact on the quality of the final solution. We propose three initial solutions: (1) a uniform distribution, (2) a Zipf distribution, and (3) a random distribution. Let C be the cardinal of set of fragmentation attributes SFAC, where each attribute A_k has n_k subdomains.

Uniform Distribution. In this solution, each cell i of fragmentation attribute (A_k) is filled using the following formula: $\text{Array}[i]_k = \lfloor i/n \rfloor$, where n is an integer $(1 \leq n \leq \max_{(1 \leq j \leq C)}(n_j))$. To illustrate this distribution, let us consider three fragmentation attributes: Gender, Season and Age, where $n_{\text{Gender}} = 2$, $n_{\text{Season}} = 4$, and $n_{\text{Age}} = 3$ (see Example 25.2). The coding in Figure 25.6 represents uniform distribution with $n = 2(n_{\text{Gender}})$, $n = 3(n_{\text{Age}})$, and $n = 4(n_{\text{Season}})$. The generated fragments of partitioning schema corresponding to $n = 2$, $n = 3$, and $n = 4$ are 12, 4, and 2, respectively. If a DBA wants an initial fragmentation schema with a large number of fragments, she

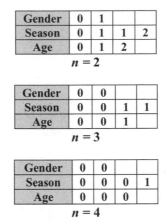

Gender	0	1		
Season	0	1	1	2
Age	0	1	2	

$n = 2$

Gender	0	0		
Season	0	0	1	1
Age	0	0	1	

$n = 3$

Gender	0	0		
Season	0	0	0	1
Age	0	0	0	

$n = 4$

FIGURE 25.6. *An example of generation of initial solution with uniform distribution.*

Gender	1	2		
Season	1	1	2	3
Age	1	1	2	

$p = 0$

Gender	1	1		
Season	1	1	1	2
Age	1	1	1	

$p = 1$

FIGURE 25.7. *An example of generation of initial solution with direct Zipf distribution.*

or he considers n with a low value. In this case, all initial subdomains (proposed by the DBA) have the same probability to participate on the fragmentation process.

Zipf Distribution. This distribution is largely used in database physical design [28] and Web access documents [29], where it is used as follows: The relative probability of a request for a document is inversely proportional to its popularity rank I ($1 \leq i \leq N$). The probability $P(i)$ of a request for the ith popular document is proportional to $1/i^{\alpha}$ ($0 < \alpha \leq 1$).

In our context, we claim that it is appropriate to model the subdomain access using this Zipf-like distribution. Let N_1 be the number of subdomains of the first partition of domain of fragmentation attribute A_k. Each cell of A_k is filled as follows: $\text{Array}[i]_k = \lfloor N_l/i \rfloor$, where N_l is obtained by dividing the number total of subdomains of A_k per 2 and incrementing the result per p (p is an integer $1 \leq p \leq \max_{1 \leq j \leq C}(n_j)$).

This distribution is called *direct (simple) Zipf* (see Fig. 25.7). We can imagine two other distributions: *random Zipf* and *inverse Zipf*. In the random Zipf distribution, cells of each fragmentation attribute are filled randomly following the direct Zipf law. The final coding is reorganized by applying the restricted growth function. An example of this coding is given in Figure 25.8.

Inverse Zipf distribution is similar to the simple Zipf distribution; the only difference is that the first partition of each domain has a smaller number of subdomains. An example of this coding is illustrated in Figure 25.9.

Gender	1	2		
Season	1	2	3	1
Age	1	2	1	

$$p = 0$$

Gender	1	1		
Season	1	2	1	1
Age	1	1	1	

$$p = 1$$

FIGURE 25.8. An example of generation of initial solution with random Zipf distribution.

Gender	1	2		
Season	1	2	3	3
Age	1	2	2	

$$p = 0$$

Gender	1	1		
Season	1	2	2	2
Age	1	1	1	

$$p = 1$$

FIGURE 25.9. An example of generation of initial solution with inverse Zipf distribution.

We notice that all Zipf variants generate the same number of fragments.

Random Distribution. In this distribution, multidimensional arrays representing fragmentation is filled randomly. Two variants of this distribution are considered: random with renumbering using restricted growth functions and random without renumbering.

Improvement of the Initial Solution   In order to improve the initial solution, two operations, namely, *merge* and *split*, are applied to reduce the total query processing cost. They have the same semantic of those used by commercial DBMS (see Section 25.2).

MERGE   This function has the following signature: Merge(P_i^k, P_j^k, A^k, SF) → SF'. It takes two partitions, P_i^k and P_j^k, of the fragmentation attribute A^k of fragmentation schema SF and gives another schema, SF', where P_i^k and P_j^k are merged. The merging process consists in assigning the same number of their respective cells. This operation reduces the number of fragments. This operation is used when the number of generated fragments is greater than the maintenance constraint B.

SPLIT   This function has the following signature: Split(P_i^k, A^k, SF) → SF'. It takes one partition P_i^k of the fragmentation attribute A^k of fragmentation schema SF and gives another schema SF', where P_i^k is split into two partitions. This operation increases the number of fragments.

■ EXAMPLE 25.4

Figure 25.10 presents a coding of a fragmentation schema SF generating 12 fragments of the fact table: 2 (fragments generated by Age) × 2 (fragments generated

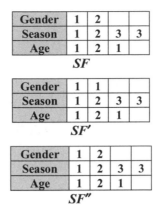

Gender	1	2		
Season	1	2	3	3
Age	1	2	1	

SF

Gender	1	1		
Season	1	2	3	3
Age	1	2	1	

SF′

Gender	1	2		
Season	1	2	3	3
Age	1	2	1	

SF″

FIGURE 25.10. *Applying merge and split operations.*

by Gender) × 3 (fragments generated by Season). On this schema, we first apply the merge function on attribute Gender, where subdomains 1 and 2 are merged. We obtain another fragmentation schema *SF′* generating six fragments since the attribute Gender will not participate on fragmenting the Customer table. We can apply the split function (which is a dual operation of merge) on the fragmentation schema *SF′* on the Gender attribute, where we get the fragmentation schema *SF″*, which is identical to *SF*.

25.5.1.2 *Problems When Using Merge and Split Operations*   When applying these two functions, we have identified three main problems: (1) the order of applying merge and split functions, (2) the choice of starting attributes for merge and split functions, and (3) the choice of subdomains.

1. *The Order of Applying Merge and Split Functions.* To solve this problem, we have used a feasibility criterion for each solution. A fragmentation schema is *feasible* if it does not violate the maintenance constraint (the generated fragments should satisfy the maintenance bound *B*). Therefore, if a solution is feasible, the split function is first applied in order to generate a solution with more fragments than the current one. Otherwise, if the current solution is not feasible, then the merge function is applied in order to reduce the number of generated fragments.

2. *Choice of Starting Attributes.* Recall that each fragmentation schema solution is coded using multidimensional arrays, where each row represents a fragmentation attribute. In order to apply merge and split, fragmentation attributes are sorted using their access frequencies. The frequency of each attribute is calculated as the sum of query frequencies using that attribute. The merge function is applied on least frequently used attributes in order to reduce their use on the fragmentation process, whereas the split function is used on most frequently used attributes in order to increase their participation on fragmenting the data warehouse schema.

3. *Choice of Subdomains Participating on Merge and Split Operations.* If an attribute is chosen, all its cells are candidate for merge and split functions. Our choices are realized as follows:

- *Merge Function.* To apply the *merge* function on attribute A^k, we do all pairwise subdomain merges. The quality of each merge operation is evaluated using a cost model. If attribute A^k has m_k subdomains, $m_k \times (m_k - 1)/2$ merge operations are possible. In order to select the best merge, we define a function, called BestMerge, with the following signature: BestMerge$(A^k, SF) \rightarrow SF$. It takes an attribute A^k and a fragmentation schema SF and gives the best merge among all possible merges.
- *Split Function.* Generating all possible splits is more complicated compared to merges. In our study, we propose to split subdomains having a high selectivity factor. This choice reduces the size of generated fragments. In order to select the best split, we define a function, called BestSplit, with the following signature: BestSplit$(A^k, SF) \rightarrow SF$.

Evaluation of the Quality of Generated Solution   The application of these operations is controlled by a cost model computing the number of inputs and outputs required for executing a set of queries on the selected HP schema. A particularity of this model is that it considers buffer size when executing a query. For lack of space, it cannot be presented in this chapter. Now we have all ingredients to present our hill climbing algorithm (see Fig. 25.11)

```
Hill climbing algorithm
Inputs:
        Set of most frequently asked queries W, B
Output:
        Fragmentation schema SF
Variables:
N: number of fragmentation attributes
        Use[]: array containing N attributes sorted using their access frequencies
Begin
        FS← intial_solution() ;
        If ((¬IsFeasible(FS)) Or (NS = W)) Then i ← 0 ;
        While ( ¬IsFeasible(FS) AND (I < N)) Do Attrib ← USE[i] ;
            If (¬SF.CanMerge(attrib)) Then  i ←i+1;
            End If
            If ((SF.CanMerge(attrib))  And  (¬SF.IsFeasible())) Then SF.BestMerge(attrib);
            End If
        End While
        Else  j ←N-1;
          While ((SF.IsFeasible()) And (j ≥0))  Do  attrib1 ← USE[j];
            If  (¬SF.CanSplit(attrib1)) Then  j ←j-1;
            Endif
            If ((SF.CanSplit(attrib1)) And (SF.IsFeasible()))  Then
                SF.BestSplit(attrib1);
                j ←j-1;
            End If
          End While
        End If
        Return (SF);
End.
```

FIGURE 25.11. *Hill climbing algorithm description.*

25.5.2 Simulated Annealing Algorithm

It is well known that one of the main weaknesses of the hill climbing approach is that it suffers from the problem of local optima. To overcome such a problem, a simulating annealing approach can be applied instead. It is a randomized technique for finding a near-optimal solution of difficult combinatorial optimization problems [30]. It starts with a randomized candidate solution, then it repeatedly attempts to find a better solution by moving to a neighbor with higher fitness until it finds a solution where none of its neighbors has a higher fitness. To avoid getting trapped in poor local optima, simulated annealing allows occasionally uphill moves to solutions with lower fitness by using a temperature parameter to control the acceptance of the moves but also uphill moves with some probability that depends on a number of parameters.

In our context, simulated annealing has an input an initial fragmentation schema as for hill climbing algorithm (*random*, *uniform*, and *Zipf*). It uses a function called *RandomTransform* which takes a fragmentation schema *FS* and returns a schema *FS'* with better quality. This function applies random changes on the initial schema using the two functions, merge and split (see hill climbing algorithm), but the choice of attributes and subdomains is done randomly. The main structure of this algorithm is described in Figure 25.12.

```
Simulated Annealing Algorithm
Inputs: Set of most frequently asked queries W, B
Output: Fragmentation schema SF
Variables:
Fragmentation schema SFinitial, SFfinal, tempo
TEMPR: initial temperature which will be decreased during execution of algorithm
STOP: stopping condition of algorithm
Equilibrium: number of iterations to each value of temperature
coefDecr: temperature decrease's coefficient
Begin
    SFinitial ← initial_solution();
    Temperature ← TEMPR;
    J ← 1;
    While (j < STOP) Do i  ← 1;
        While (i < Equilibrium) Do
            tempo ← RandomTransform(SFinitial);
            If (tempo.Score() > SFinitial.Score()) Then SFinitial ← tempo;
                If (SFinitial.Cost() < SFfinal.Cost()) Then SFfinal ← SFinitial;
                End If
            Else
            delta ← (tempo.Score() – SFinitial.Score());
            Deterioration ← exp((delta) / Temperature));
            If (deterioration > RandomFunction()) Then SFinitial ← tempo;
                If (SFinitial.Cost()<SFfinal.Cost()) Then SFfinal ← SFinitial;
                End If
            End If
            i ← i + 1;
        End While
        Temperature ← (Temperature * coefDecr);
        j ← j + 1;
    End While
    Return (SFfinal);
End
```

FIGURE 25.12. Simulated annealing algorithm description.

25.6 IMPACT OF HP ON DATA WAREHOUSE PHYSICAL DESIGN

We have shown that HP is constrained by a threshold representing the number of fragments that the DWA wants to have for her or his application. As a consequence, HP cannot optimize all queries especially those containing selection predicates defined on attributes not used to partition the data warehouse. Therefore, DWA needs to use another optimization technique from the existing ones: materialized views, indexing, compression, and so on. By studying different optimization techniques, we identify a strong similarity between HP and BJI. BJI are multitable indexes proposed to precompute joins between the fact and dimension tables. They are defined on the fact table using one or more dimension attributes. BJI are more suitable for low cardinality attributes since its size strictly depends on the number of distinct values of columns on which it is built [31]. In the next section, we show the similarity between HP and BJI.

25.6.1 Similarity between HP and BJI

To show the similarity between HP and BJI, we consider the following example. Suppose we have a data warehouse represented by three dimension tables (Time, Customer, and Product) and one fact table (Sales). The population of this schema is given in Figure 25.13. Assume that the DWA wants to have *the number of sales for customers living in Poitiers for beauty products during June.* The query to meet this need is

```
SELECT COUNT(*)
FROM Sales S, Customer C, Product P, Time T
WHERE S.CID = C.CID AND S.TID = T.TID AND S.PID = P.PID
AND C.City = 'Poitiers' AND T.Month = 'June' AND P.
Range = 'Beauty'
```

This query has three selection predicates defined on dimension table attributes *City*, *Range*, and *Month* and three join operations. To optimize this query, DWA can use HP or BJI.

a. *Optimization Using HP.* DWA can partition the dimension tables Customer, Time and Product on attributes City, Month, and Range, respectively:
   - Customer is partitioned into three fragments, each corresponding to a city (*Poitiers*, *Paris*, and *Nantes*).
   - Product is partitioned into five fragments each corresponding to a range (*Beauty*, *Multimedia*, *Toys*, *Gardening*, and *Fitness*).
   - Time is partitioned into six fragments each corresponding to one month (*January*, *February*, *March*, *April*, *May*, and *June*).

The fact table Sales can be derived partitioned using the partitioning schema of the previous three dimension tables on 90 partitions ($3 \times 5 \times 6$). Each fragment of the table Sales is defined as follows:

$$\text{Sales}_i = \text{Sales} \ltimes \text{Customer}_j \ltimes \text{Time}_k \ltimes \text{Product}_p \ (1 \le i \le 90, 1 \le j \le 3, 1 \le k \le 6, 1 \le p \le 5).$$

Customer

C_RID	CID	Name	City	Gender	Age
6	616	Gilles	Poitiers	M	43
5	515	Yves	Paris	M	22
4	414	Patrick	Nantes	M	17
3	313	Didier	Nantes	M	36
2	212	Eric	Poitiers	M	26
1	111	Pascal	Poitiers	M	61

Product

P_RID	PID	Name	Range
6	106	Sonoflore	Beauty
5	105	Clarins	Beauty
4	104	WebCam	Multimedia
3	103	Barbie	Toys
2	102	Manure	Gardening
1	101	SlimForm	Fitness

Time

T_RID	TID	Month	Season
6	11	January	Winter
5	22	February	Winter
4	33	March	Spring
3	44	April	Spring
2	55	May	Spring
1	66	June	Summer

Sales

S_RID	CID	PID	TID	Amount
1	616	106	11	25
2	616	106	66	28
3	616	104	33	50
4	515	104	11	10
5	414	105	66	14
6	212	106	55	14
7	111	101	44	20
8	111	101	33	27
9	212	101	11	100
10	313	102	11	200
11	414	102	11	102
12	414	102	55	103
13	515	102	66	100
14	515	103	55	17
15	212	103	44	45
16	111	105	66	44
17	212	104	66	40
18	515	104	22	20
19	616	104	22	20
20	616	104	55	20
21	212	105	11	10
22	212	105	44	10
23	212	105	55	18
24	212	106	11	18
25	313	105	66	19
26	313	105	22	17
27	313	106	11	15

FIGURE 25.13. A sample of a data warehouse population.

Note that the initial star schema is partitioned on 90 substar schemas. Figure 25.14c shows the substar schema containing the fact fragment Sales_PJB corresponding to *sales of beauty products realized by customers living at Poitiers during June.* To execute the above query, the optimizer shall rewrite it. Therefore, it loads only the fact fragment Sales_PJB and only counts the number of lines found in this fragment (there are two). The above query is then rewritten as follows:

SELECT Count(*) FROM Sales_PJB

By partitioning the data warehouse, the DWA may have two types of improvements: (1) A single partition of the fact table was loaded instead of 90 partitions and (2) no join operation was calculated.

   b. *Optimization Using BJI.* The DWA creates a BJI on three dimension attributes: City, Month, and Range as follows:

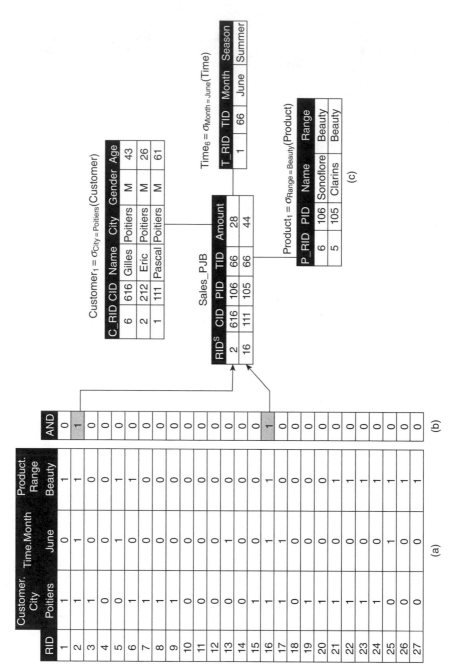

FIGURE 25.14. (a) The bitmap join index. (b) The result of AND operation. (c) The substar schema.

```
CREATE
BITMAP INDEX sales_cust_city_prod_range_time_month_bjix
ON Sales(Customer.City, Product.Range, Time.Month)
FROM Sales S, Customer C, Time T, Produit P
WHERE S.CID = C.CID AND S.PID = P.PID AND S.TID = T.TID
```

Figure 25.14a shows the generated BJI. To execute the above query, the optimizer just accesses the bitmaps corresponding to the columns representing June, Beauty, and Poitiers and performs an AND operation. It then calculates the number of 1 in the result vector; there are also two (see Fig. 25.14b). By creating the BJI, the DWA may have two types of improvements: (1) Only the BJI was loaded (no tables have been loaded) and (2) any join operation was performed.

This example shows the similarity between HP and BJIs: (1) They reduce the queries' execution cost by reducing the amount of loaded data; (2) they precompute join operations between the fact table and dimension tables; and (3) they share the same resource that is the set of selection attributes. Based on this similarity, we propose a new approach for selecting simultaneously HP and BJIs. To summarize our finding in similarities between HP and BJI, we can say that both BJI and HP are fundamentally similar: Both are structures that speed up query execution, precompute join operations, and are defined on selection attributes of dimension tables. Furthermore, BJIs and HP can interact with one another; that is, the presence of an index can make a partitioned schema more attractive and vice versa. Unfortunately, the identified similarities are not considered during the joint selection of HP and BJI since both selection problems are done in an isolated way. Note that several studies have shown the hardness of BJI selection [32]. In the next section, we propose to exploit these similarities to select BJI schemes and HP schemas [20, 33]. This selection prunes the research space of the BJI problem.

25.6.2 Our Selection Approach of HP and BJI

Our selection approach of HP and BJI (HP&BJI) exploits the similarities between these two techniques, in particular, the sharing of selection attributes [34]. The approach begins by fragmenting the data warehouse using a fragmentation algorithm, then selecting a set of BJI on a fragmented data warehouse using nonprofitable queries and attributes not used by HP. Note that partitioning the data warehouse before selecting BJI reduces the complexity of the BJI selection problem because the number of candidate attributes decreased. Therefore, our approach prunes the search space of BJI using HP. This increases the importance of HP in the physical design of data warehouses. Figure 25.15 shows the architecture of our approach. It is composed of four steps: (1) fragmentation of the data warehouse, (2) identifying no profitable queries, (3) identification of indexable attributes, and (4) selection of a BJI configuration:

1. The selection of a partitioning schema is performed using an algorithm that we proposed (genetic algorithm, simulated annealing, or hill climbing). The algorithm takes as input a workload of queries $Q = \{Q_1, Q_2, \ldots, Q_m\}$, the set of selection attributes (*SASET*), and the threshold B and generates a

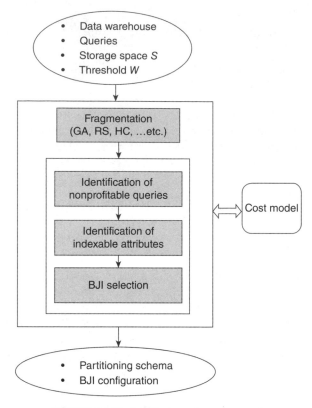

FIGURE 25.15. *Architecture of our approach.*

partitioning schema (*PS*). *PS* is defined on a set of fragmentation attributes (*FASET*).

2. Among all *m* queries, some benefit from the fragmentation and others do not. A query gets benefit from the fragmentation if its execution cost is significantly reduced. To identify the set of profitable queries, we use a rate defined for each query as $\text{Rate}(Q_j) = \text{Cost}(Q_j, PS)/\text{Cost}(Q_j, \phi)$, where $\text{Cost}(Q_j, \phi)$ and $\text{Cost}(Q_j, PS)$ represent the execution cost of the query Q_j on unpartitioned data warehouse and partitioned with *PS*, respectively. The DWA has the right to set up this rate using a threshold λ: If $\text{rate}(Qj) \leq \lambda$, then Q_j is a profitable query, otherwise, no profitable query. The set of no profitable queries is denoted by $Q' = \{Q'_1, Q'_2, \ldots, Q'_n\}(Q' \subseteq Q)$.

3. Indexable attributes are identified among selection attributes (*SASET*) with low cardinality and which are not used to fragment the data warehouse. The set of these attributes is denoted by *BJISET*.

4. The selection of BJI configuration is done using a greedy algorithm under storage constraint. This algorithm takes as input the set of no profitable queries Q', the set of indexable attributes (*BJISET*), and the constraint storage *S* and generates a configuration of BJI reducing the execution cost of Q'. This algorithm uses a cost model that estimates the execution cost of queries using BJI [32].

25.7 EXPERIMENTAL STUDIES

We have conducted many experimental studies in order to evaluate and to compare the proposed algorithms: hill climbing and simulated annealing with their variants. We first evaluate each algorithm and then we jointly study them. We have conducted also experiments to evaluate our combined selection approach (HP&BJI).

Data Set: We use the data set from the APB1 benchmark [35]. The star schema of this benchmark has one fact table *Actvars* (33,324,000 tuples) and four dimension tables: *Prodlevel* (99,000 tuples), *Custlevel* (990 tuples), *Timelevel* (24 tuples), and *Chanlevel* (10 tuples). This schema is implemented using Oracle 11g.

Workload: We have considered a workload of 55 single block queries (i.e., no nested subqueries) with 40 selection predicates defined on 10 different attributes: *Class_Level, Group_Level, Family_Level, Line_Level, Division_Level, Year_Level, Month_Level, Quarter_Level, Retailer_Level, All_Level.* The domains of these attributes are split into 4, 2, 5, 2, 4, 2, 12, 4, 4, and 5 subdomains, respectively. We did not consider update and delete queries. Note that each selection predicate has a selectivity factor computed using SQL query executed on the data set of APB1 benchmark. In our coding, cells representing subdomains are arranged in ascended sorted order based on their selectivity factors. Our algorithms have been implemented using Visual C++ performed under Intel Pentium Centrino with a memory of 3 Go.

25.7.1 Evaluation of Hill Climbing Algorithm

Figure 25.16 compares the performance in terms of number of inputs and outputs of our hill climbing algorithm and its variants by varying the threshold. This variation is given in Table 25.3.

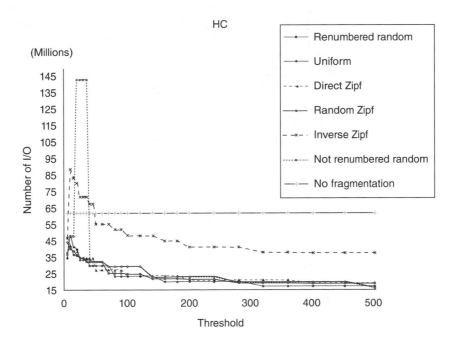

FIGURE 25.16. *Evaluation of variants of the hill climbing algorithm.*

TABLE 25.3. Variation of the Threshold

5	10	15	20	25	30	35	40	45
50	60	70	80	90	100	120	140	160
180	200	240	280	320	360	400	450	500

Six variants of hill climbing heuristic are evaluated: *uniform, direct Zipf, inverse Zipf, random Zipf, not renumbered random,* and *renumbered random (using restricted growth function)*. Each variant is executed in order to generate the fragmentation schema of the APB1 data warehouse by varying the threshold. All variants are tested against the nonfragmentation case (where the data warehouse is not partitioned). The cost of the 55 queries is estimated using our cost model that uses the size of dimension and fact tables, selectivity factors, buffer size, and so on, over each fragmentation schema generated by each variant. The first observation is that the fragmentation schema obtained by all variants of hill climbing algorithm outperforms the nonfragmentation case, especially when the threshold becomes large. The second observation concerns the maintenance constraint (threshold) on its effect on performance of queries. When the threshold increases, hill climbing gives better results compared with the nonfragmented case. From a threshold varying from 280 and 500, we get fragmentation schemas with the same quality. This result is very interesting since it allows the DBA to choose his or her maintenance constraint from this range to ensure a high performance of his or her queries. Another observation concerns the impact of the initial solution on the quality of generated solution by the hill climbing algorithm. The uniform distribution is the best choice for the hill climbing solution. In our experiments, the uniform distribution is used with $n = 4$ ($\text{Array}[i]_k = \lfloor i/n \rfloor$). In this case, all initial subdomains have the same probability to participate on fragmenting tables. *Zipf inverse* distribution has less performance compared to the other variants; since subdomains of each fragmentation attribute are sorted, merge operations are usually done on subdomains with high selectivity. This generates fragments with a large population.

In Figure 25.17, we study the effect of buffer size on performance of queries. To do so, we vary the buffer size from 0 to 1500 pages and we execute the hill climbing with the uniform variant (since it is the best variant) and we compute the cost of execution all queries. The threshold is fixed at 50. This experiment shows the impact of buffer on query performance, especially when we increase its size. When buffer size is around 900 pages, the behavior of the hill climbing algorithm is stable.

25.7.2   Evaluation of Simulated Annealing Algorithm

Figure 25.18 shows the performance of simulated annealing and its variants (*random renumbered, random Zipf, uniform, random not renumbered,* and *simple Zipf*). We conducted the same experiments as for hill climbing. All variants of simulated annealing outperformed largely the nonfragmentation case, contrary to the hill climbing algorithm. We found that uniform distribution outperforms the other variants for all variations of the threshold. We note a stability of performance of simulated annealing when the threshold reaches 200. Augmenting the threshold does not mean improving the performance of queries. Therefore, the threshold should be

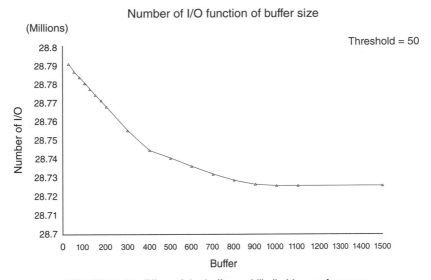

FIGURE 25.17. *Effect of the buffer on hill climbing performance.*

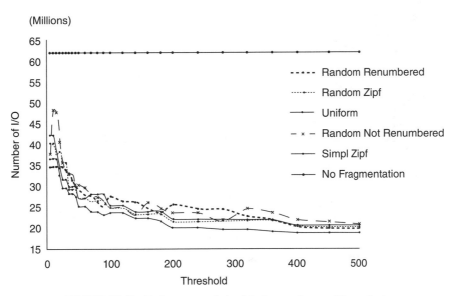

FIGURE 25.18. *Performance of simulated annealing and its variants.*

chosen carefully by the DBA. Even for small thresholds, simulated annealing gives interesting results compared to the no-fragmentation case.

Figure 25.19 gives the running time required by simulated annealing. Note that hill climbing execution is very fast (a most 3 seconds). In this experiment, the threshold value is set from 10 and 200. Simulating annealing is time-consuming compared to hill climbing. When the threshold is very large, the execution time increases rapidly. Based on these experiments, we issue some recommendations that could be

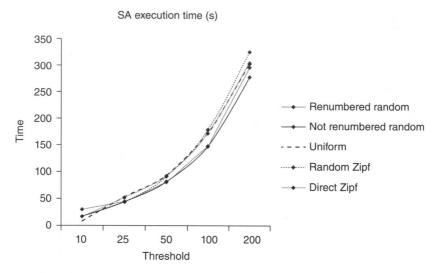

FIGURE 25.19. *Execution time required for simulated annealing and its variants.*

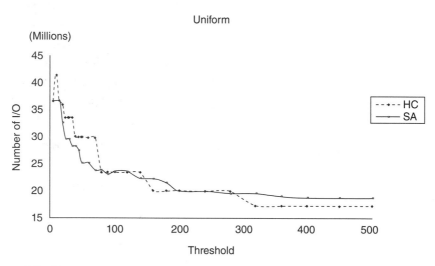

FIGURE 25.20. *Simulated annealing versus hill climbing (for uniform distribution).*

exploited by DBA: If the execution time of the partitioning algorithm is the most important criteria, she or he may choose hill climbing.

25.7.3 Simulated Annealing Algorithm versus Hill Climbing Algorithm

In Figure 25.20, we compare the performance of hill climbing and simulated annealing using uniform distribution. An interesting result is obtained from this experimentation: Simulated annealing outperforms hill climbing for small threshold (when it varies from 5 to 160), whereas hill climbing gives better performance for a large number of threshold (when it varies from 300 to 500). For small thresholds, hill

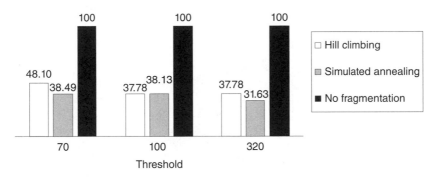

Cost of hill climbing, simulated annealing, no fragmentation (%)

FIGURE 25.21. *Gain in percent obtained by simulated annealing and hill climbing algorithms.*

climbing performs more merge operations in initial solution, which usually increase the sizes of generated fragments. Consequently, HP does not perform well in this situation. For a large number of thresholds, hill climbing performs split operations in initial solution, where the number of generated fragments increases the HP, which is usually the best scenario for HP, especially when their sizes are uniform. Simulated annealing is doing the same task, but split and merge operations are done randomly. Based on this result, the DBA may choose the selection algorithm based on her or his threshold. For large threshold, hill climbing is used with a shorter execution time and high-quality solution. For fewer thresholds, simulated annealing may be used with short execution time.

Figure 25.21 shows the percentage of reduction of our algorithms (using a uniform distribution as an initial solution) computed against the nonfragmentation case. The results show the benefit of partitioning in reducing query processing cost. This reduction is almost stable when varying the maintenance cost (threshold). That is why commercial DBMSs advocated massively HP.

25.7.4 Evaluation of Combined Selection of HP and BJI

To evaluate our combined approach against the isolated selection approach, we conduct the following experiment. We use a genetic algorithm with threshold $B = 100$ and $\lambda = 0.6$ (used to identify the profitable queries from HP). After the execution of this algorithm, we identify that 25% of queries are nonprofitable and eight attributes are used to partition the data warehouse. The BJI selection module uses two candidate attributes, the set of no profitable queries Q' and a space bound equal 20 Mo. Two BJIs have been selected. The performance of our approach is shown in Figure 25.22 It reduces the cost obtained by only HP by 12% and without adding extra space cost.

25.8 PHYSICAL DESIGN SIMULATOR TOOL

During our experiments for evaluating the quality of our partitioning and BJI algorithms, we identify the need for development of a tool facilitating the setup of

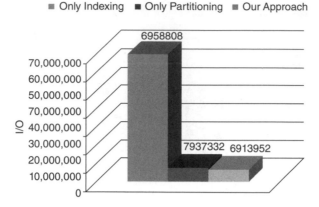

FIGURE 25.22. *Performance of our approach.*

different parameters of the used algorithms during the physical design. By exploring the literature, we identify the existence of such tools owned by the most important commercial DBMS editors: Server Database Tuning Advisor (DTA), Oracle SQL Access Advisor, and DB2 Index Advisor. Their main role is to assist the DWA during their tasks. They allow *what-if* design exploration and propose DWA useful user interfaces. Other academic tools have been proposed such as *PARINDA* [36]. The main characteristic of these tools is that they are used when the data warehouse is under exploitation. Also, they suppose the knowledge of the target DBMS. Since physical design could be done without having a precise idea on the target DBMS, the use of simulation may contribute in getting efficient database applications. The main contributions of the use of simulators during the physical design are (1) aiding in guaranteeing an efficient physical design, since the database designer (DBD) can test/evaluate several optimization scenarios and (2) helping the DBD in choosing the target DBMS based on the proposed recommendations (for instance, if the simulator recommends the use of referential HP, which is only supported by Oracle, and if the DBD is convinced by this solution, he or she may adopt Oracle DBMS for his or her application). Based on the discussion, we propose a simulator tool, called SimulPh.D [37], offering DWAs the possibility to choose their favorite optimization technique(s), to evaluate their benefits, and to measure the used resources (e.g., storage). Once these choices are done, SimulPh.D proposes DWA recommendations summarizing different information regarding optimization techniques. If the DWA is satisfied with this recommendation, he or she by a simple click generates appropriate scripts that will execute on the target DBMS (if it is available).

25.8.1 SimulPh.D Overview

We develop our simulator tool under C++ as a modular application. SimulPh.D consists of a set of seven modules (see Fig. 25.23): (1) metabase querying module, (2) managing queries module, (3) horizontal partitioning selection module (HPSM), (4) HP module, (5) query rewriting module, (6) BJI selection module, and (7) indexing module. The metabase querying module is a very important module that allows the tool to work with any type of DBMS. From a type of DBMS, user name, and

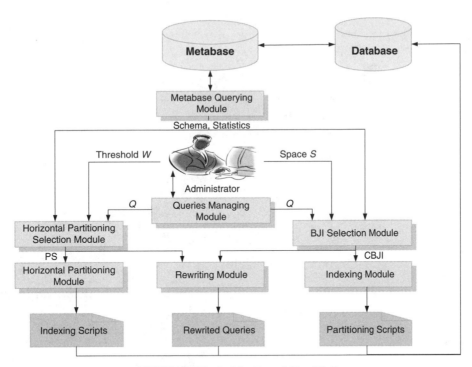

FIGURE 25.23. Architecture of SimulPh.D.

password, the module allows connection to that account and collection of some information from the metabase. This information concerns logical and physical levels of the data warehouse. Information of the logical level includes tables and attributes in these tables. Information of the physical level includes optimization techniques used and a set of statistics on tables and attributes of the data warehouse (number of tuples, cardinality, etc.). The managing queries module helps the administrator to define the workload of queries (W) on which the selection is based. The module allows manual editing of a query or import from external files. It may also manage the workload, giving the possibility to add, delete, or update queries. This module integrates a parser that identifies syntax errors as well as tables and attributes used by each query. HPSM requires as inputs a schema of data warehouse, a workload, and a threshold B. Using these data, HPSM selects a partitioning schema (PS) to minimize the cost of the workload and to generate a number of fragments not exceeding B. Our tool supports three selection algorithms: genetic algorithm [38, 39], simulated annealing algorithm, and hill climbing algorithm (see previous sections). The HP module fragments physically the data warehouse using partitioning schema obtained from HPSM. From the partitioning schema, this module determines the dimension table(s) to partition by horizontal primary partitioning and the attributes used to perform this fragmentation. The module is also used to partition the fact table by horizontal derived partitioning mode using fragments of dimension tables. The query rewriting module rewrites queries on a fragmented and/or indexed schema. It starts with identifying valid fragments for each query, rewriting the query on each of these fragments, and finally performing union of the obtained results. The BJI selection module selects a configuration of BJI under constraint storage.

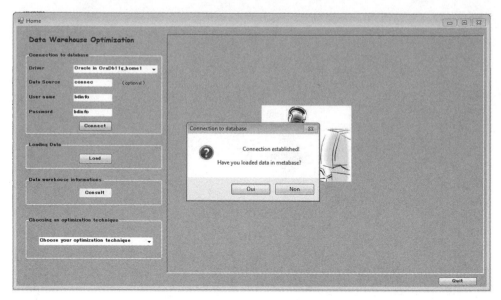

FIGURE 25.24. *Connection with target DBMS.*

This selection can be made on a partitioned or unpartitioned data warehouse. The indexing module generates scripts to create the selected BJI on the data warehouse.

25.8.2 SimulPh.D Features

The main features of SimulPh.D are

1. Displaying the current state of the database (the schema, attributes, size of each table, definition of each attribute, etc.) and the workload (description of queries, number of selection operations, selection predicates, etc.). Figures 25.24 and 25.25 show the connection of SimulPh.D with the target DBMS and the displaying information interface, respectively.

2. Offering personalized or nonpersonalized partitioning of the data warehouse. If the administrator chooses nonpersonalized partitioning (zero administration), SimulPh.D selects a partitioning schema in a transparent manner without designer intervention (this mode is well adapted when the administrator wants an autoadministration of his or her database). In the personalized partitioning, the administrator chooses candidate dimension tables, candidate attributes, and selection algorithms and sets different parameters that he or she considers important. In Figure 25.26, the administrator chooses a personalized administration, where three dimension tables participate in the partitioning process (ChanLevel, ProdLevel, and TimeLevel) and only table Custlevel is not a candidate for partitioning. Among the 10 attributes, the administrator has chosen two attributes of the table ProdLevel, two attributes of the table TimeLevel, and one attribute of the table ChanLevel. Figure 25.27 shows the partitioned dimension tables and the fragmentation attributes.

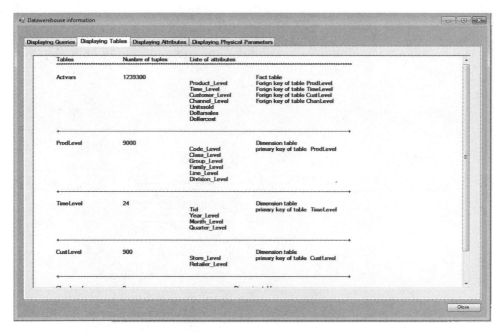

FIGURE 25.25. *Visualization of data warehouse state.*

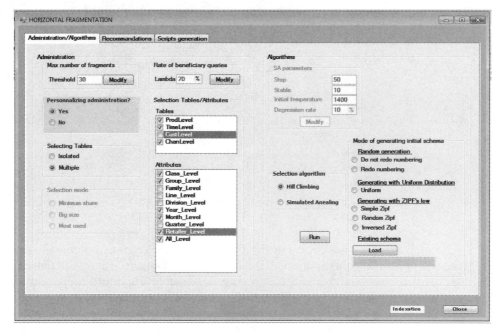

FIGURE 25.26. *Personnalized administration.*

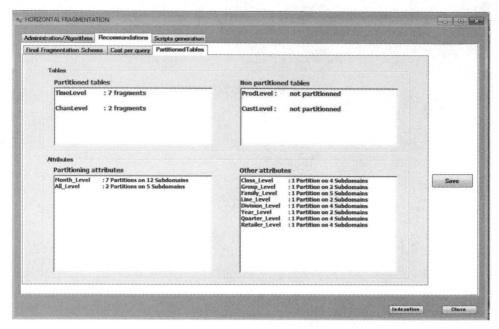

FIGURE 25.27. Partitioning recommendations.

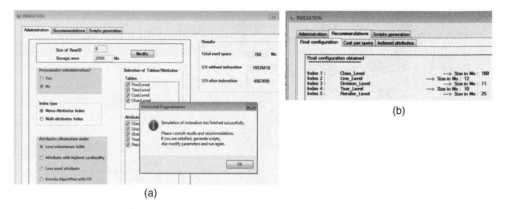

(a)

(b)

FIGURE 25.28. (a) Combined selection (HP&BJI) and (b) indexing recommendations.

3. Indexing the data warehouse using two modes: isolated and combined with HP (HP&BJI). In the first mode, the DWA must choose the candidate indexable attributes and storage space S. The BJI selection module supports two selection algorithms, a greedy algorithm, and a data mining-based algorithm. SimulPh.D generates a recommendation that provides some information: BJI selected, cost reduction, indexed tables and attributes, storage cost, and so on (see Fig. 25.28b). In the second mode, the SimulPh.D tool automatically chooses the candidate indexed attributes among the selection attributes with low cardinality not used to partition the data warehouse and that are referenced in no profitable queries. Figure 25.28a shows the HP&BJI interface. For

example, attributes Month_level and All_level are not used in BJI selection because they are used to partition the data warehouse.

4. Improving iteratively the selected partitioning and/or indexing schema based on the proposed recommendation based on feedback. SimulPh.D displays the quality of the final partitioning or indexing schema. This quality is based on a cost model estimating the number of inputs outputs required for executing each query [14]. Therefore, if some queries do not benefit from the suggested partitioning schema, the administrator can refine some parameters in order to satisfy them. Figure 25.27 shows an example of recommendations concerning partitioned dimension tables. For example, the tables Custlevel and ProdLevel should not be fragmented, when table TimeLevel is fragmented on seven fragments using the attribute Month_level. Attributes Class_level, Line_level, Division_level, Year_level, and Rctailer_level are not used to partition the data warehouse. Therefore, they can be used to index the fragmented data warehouse using HP&BJI approach (see Fig. 25.28a).

5. Generating scripts for primary and derived HP and BJI. They can be directly executed on the data warehouse to partition and/or index it physically, in the case where the administrator is satisfied with the suggested recommendations.

25.9 CONCLUSION AND PERSPECTIVES

Horizontal data partitioning is considered as a precondition for distributed and parallel database design. It has been largely studied by the academic community in the last decades and has recently been massively advocated by most commercial database systems (Oracle, SQL Server, IBM DB2, MySQL, and PostgreSQL), where they offer native DDL support for defining horizontal partitions of a table using several modes. This adoption has been motivated by business intelligence applications. In this chapter, we showed the spectacular evolution of HP on commercial systems, especially in Oracle, which proposes a large variety of partitioning modes of fragmenting a single table using either primary partitioning or referential partitioning. A complete state of the art concerning the different fragmentation algorithms in classical database systems is presented. A classification of these algorithms is presented with a criticism of each approach. Based on this study, a formalization of the referential HP problem in relational data warehouses is presented. We derive the complexity of the problem of selecting an optimal partitioning schema and we study its hardness. To the best of our knowledge, we are the first to study in detail this complexity. In order to select a near-optimal solution, we proposed two algorithms: hill climbing and simulated annealing with various variants. The main characteristic of these algorithms is that they partition simultaneously dimension and fact tables. We presented in this chapter a new interest of HP in physical design. It can be used to prune the search space of BJI. We presented a combined selection approach of HP and BJI (HP&BJI) exploiting the similarities we have identified between these two techniques. Intensive experimental studies have been presented using data sets of the APB 1 benchmark and Oracle11g. The different results show the important role of HP in reducing query processing cost and in pruning the search space of the BJI selection problem. Based on the obtained results, some recommendations are given to help administrators in choosing their favorite algorithm.

We identify the need for the development of simulators during the physical design and then we propose a simulator tool, called SimulPh.D, to assist administrators during physical design. It gives recommendations for each workload and the quality of the generated partitioning and/or indexing schemes. Administrators have the possibility to tune algorithms and their parameters to get the best solutions. We are currently working on the deployment of our algorithms on data partitioning Teradata. The initial results are encouraging [40].

REFERENCES

[1] S. Papadomanolakis and A. Ailamaki, "Autopart: Automating schema design for large scientific databases using data partitioning," in *Proceedings of the 16th International Conference on Scientific and Statistical Database Management (SSDBM 2004)*, pp. 383–392, June 2004.

[2] H. Lei and K.A. Ross, "Faster joins using join indices," *VLDB Journal*, 8(1):1–24, 1999.

[3] L. Bellatreche, R. Missaoui, H. Necir, and H. Drias, "A data mining approach for selecting bitmap join indices," *Journal of Computing Science and Engineering*, 2(1):206–223, 2008.

[4] M.T. Özsu and P. Valduriez, *Principles of Distributed Database Systems: Second Edition*. Prentice Hall, 1999.

[5] D. Saccà and G. Wiederhold, "Database partitioning in a cluster of processors," *ACM Transactions on Database Systems*, 10(1):29–56, 1985.

[6] L. Bellatreche, A. Cuzzocrea, and S. Benkrid, "Query optimization over parallel relational data warehouses in distributed environments by simultaneous fragmentation and allocation," in *The 10th International Conference on Algorithms and Architectures for Parallel Processing (ICA3PP)*, pp. 124–135, Busan Korea, May 2010.

[7] G. Eadon, E.I. Chong, S. Shankar, A. Raghavan, J. Srinivasan, and S. Das, "Supporting table partitioning by reference in Oracle," in *Proceedings of the ACM SIGMOD International Conference on Management of Data*, pp. 1111–1122, 2008.

[8] A. Sanjay, V.R. Narasayya, and B. Yang, "Integrating vertical and horizontal partitioning into automated physical database design," in *Proceedings of the ACM SIGMOD International Conference on Management of Data*, pp. 359–370, June 2004.

[9] K. Tzoumas, A. Deshpande, and C.S. Jensen, "Sharing-aware horizontal partitioning for exploiting correlations during query processing," *PVLDB*, 3(1):542–553, 2010.

[10] A. Sanjay, C. Surajit, and V.R. Narasayya, "Automated selection of materialized views and indexes in Microsoft SQL Server," in *Proceedings of the International Conference on Very Large Databases*, pp. 496–505, September 2000.

[11] T. Stöhr, H. Märtens, and E. Rahm, "Multi-dimensional database allocation for parallel data warehouses," in *Proceedings of the International Conference on Very Large Databases*, pp. 273–284, 2000.

[12] S. Ceri, M. Negri, and G. Pelagatti, "Horizontal data partitioning in database design," in *Proceedings of the ACM SIGMOD International Conference on Management of Data. SIGPLAN Notices*, pp. 128–136, 1982.

[13] Oracle Corporation, "Partitioning with Oracle Database 11g Release 2," *An Oracle White Paper*, 2010. Available at http://www.oracle.com/technetwork/database/bi-datawarehousing/twp-partitioning-11gr2-2010-10-189137.pdf.

[14] L. Bellatreche, K. Boukhalfa, and P. Richard, "Horizontal partitioning in data warehouses: Hardness study, heuristics and Oracle validation," in *International Conference on Data Warehousing and Knowledge Discovery (DaWaK 2008)*, pp. 87–96, 2008.

[15] S.B. Navathe and M. Ra, "Vertical partitioning for database design: A graphical algorithm," in *Proceedings of the ACM SIGMOD International Conference on Management of Data*, pp. 440–450, 1989.

[16] K. Karlapalem, S.B. Navathe, and M. Ammar, "Optimal redesign policies to support dynamic processing of applications on a distributed database system," *Information Systems*, 21(4):353–367, 1996.

[17] H. Mahboubi and J. Darmont, "Enhancing XML data warehouse query performance by fragmentation," in *Proceedings of the 2009 ACM Symposium on Applied Computing (SAC)*, pp. 1555–1562, 2009.

[18] S. Dimov, D. Pham, and C. Nguyen, "An incremental *K*-means algorithm," *Journal of Mechanical Engineering Science*, 218(7):783–795, 2004.

[19] L. Bellatreche, K. Karlapalem, and A. Simonet, "Algorithms and support for horizontal class partitioning in object-oriented databases," *Distributed and Parallel Databases Journal*, 8(2):155–179, 2000.

[20] L. Bellatreche, K. Boukhalfa, and M.K. Mohania, "Pruning search space of physical database design," in *International Conference on Database and Expert Systems Applications (DEXA '07)*, pp. 479–488, 2007.

[21] International Business Machines Corporation, "DB2 partitioning features, an overview for data warehouses," 2006. Available at http://www.ibm.com/developerworks/data/library/techarticle/dm-0608mcinerney/.

[22] Microsoft Corporation, "Partitioned tables and indexes in SQL server 2005," 2005. Available at http://msdn.microsoft.com/en-us/library/ms345146.aspx.

[23] PostgresSQL, "Partitioning," Available at http://www.postgresql.org/docs/8.1/static/ddl-partitioning.html.

[24] MySQL, "Partition types," Available at http://dev.mysql.com/doc/refman/5.1/en/partitioning-types.htm.

[25] M.C. Er, "A fast algorithm for generating set partitions," *The Computer Journal*, 31(3):283–284, 1988.

[26] M.R. Garey and D.S. Johnson, *Computers and Intractability: A Guide to the Theory of NP-Completeness*. New York: W. H. Freeman & Co., 1990.

[27] Y. Ioannidis and Y. Kang, "Randomized algorithms for optimizing large join queries," in *Proceedings of the ACM SIGMOD International Conference on Management of Data*, pp. 9–22, 1990.

[28] G. Das, D. Gunopulos, N. Koudas, and D. Tsirogiannis, "Answering top-k queries using views," in *Proceedings of the International Conference on Very Large Databases*, pp. 451–462, 2006.

[29] L. Breslau, P. Cue, P. Cao, L. Fan, G. Phillips, and S. Shenker, "Web caching and Zipf-like distributions: Evidence and implications," in *In INFOCOM*, pp. 126–134, 1999.

[30] S. Kirkpatrick, C.D. Gelatt, and M.P. Vecchi, "Optimization by simulated annealing," *Science*, 220(4598):671–680, 1983.

[31] L. Bellatreche and K. Boukhalfa, "Yet another algorithms for selecting bitmap join indexes," in *12th International Conference on Data Warehousing and Knowledge Discovery (DaWaK)*, pp. 105–116, 2010.

[32] K. Aouiche, O. Boussaid, and F. Bentayeb, "Automatic selection of bitmap join indexes in data warehouses," *7th International Conference on Data Warehousing and Knowledge Discovery (DAWAK '05)*, pp. 64–73, August 2005.

[33] R. Bouchakri and L. Bellatreche, "On simplifying integrated physical database design," in *15th East European Conference on Advances in Databases and Information Systems (ADBIS'2011)*, pp. 333–346, September 2011.

[34] K. Boukhalfa, L. Bellatreche, and Z. Alimazighi, "HP&BJI: A combined selection of data partitioning and join indexes for improving olap performance," *Annals of Information Systems, Special Issue on New Trends in Data Warehousing and Data Analysis, Springer*, 3:179–2001, 2008.

[35] OLAP Council, *Apb-1 OLAP Benchmark, Release II.* 1998. Available at http://www.olapcouncil.org/research/bmarkly.htm.

[36] M. Cristina, D. Debabrata, A. Ioannis, A. Anastasia, and H. Thomas, "PARINDA: An interactive physical designer for PostgreSQL," in *Proceedings of the 13th International Conference on Extending Database Technology (EDBT)*, pp. 701–704, New York: ACM, 2010.

[37] L. Bellatreche, K. Boukhalfa, and Z. Alimazighi, "SimulPh.D.: A physical design simulator tool," in *20th International Conference on Database and Expert Systems Applications (DEXA '09)*, pp. 263–270, 2009.

[38] L. Bellatreche and K. Boukhalfa, "An evolutionary approach to schema partitioning selection in a data warehouse environment," in *Proceedings of the International Conference on Data Warehousing and Knowledge Discovery (DAWAK 2005)*, pp. 115–125, August 2005.

[39] J.H. Holland, *Adaptation in Natural and Artificial Systems.* Ann Arbor, MI: University of Michigan Press, 1975.

[40] L. Bellatreche, S. Benkrid, A. Ghazal, A. Crolotte, and A. Cuzzocrea, "Verification of partitioning & allocation techniques on teradata dbms," in *The 11th International Conference on Algorithms and Architectures for Parallel Processing (ICA3PP 2011)*, pp. 158–169, Melbourne, Australia, October 2011.

26

Scalable Runtime Environments for Large-Scale Parallel Applications

Camille Coti and Franck Cappello

26.1 INTRODUCTION

Parallel programming techniques define the sequence of instructions that each process must execute on some data and how these data are provided to each process. Parallel programming environments take this parallelism into account and support a parallel application by putting its components in touch with one another and managing the distributed execution.

Parallel programming environments are made of three distinct components [1]:

- a job scheduler, deciding which machines will be used by a given parallel application
- a runtime environment, in charge of making interprocess communications possible, I/O and signal forwarding, monitoring the processes, and ensuring the finalization of the application
- a communication library, in charge of data movements between the processes.

This chapter presents the support provided to the application by the runtime environment in the context of large-scale systems. First, we define what a runtime environment is and how it interacts with the other components of the parallel

Scalable Computing and Communications: Theory and Practice, First Edition. Edited by
Samee U. Khan, Albert Y. Zomaya, and Lizhe Wang.
© 2013 John Wiley & Sons, Inc. Published 2013 by John Wiley & Sons, Inc.

programming and execution environment in Section 26.2. Then we present how it can deploy the application in a scalable way in Section 26.4 and how the communication infrastructure that supports the application is important in Section 26.3. We present its role in fault tolerance in Section 26.5 and we finish by two case studies in Section 26.6.

26.1.1 Parallel Programming Models and Runtime Environments

Parallel programming paradigms can be classified into two main categories: those that follow the *shared-memory model* and those that follow the *distributed-memory model*. These two models are similar to those commonly used to describe distributed systems [2].

The *message-passing interface* (MPI [3,4]) follows the distributed-memory model. Each process can access its own memory space, and only its own one. Accesses to data held by other processes are made by *explicit* communications through messages sent between processes.

On the other hand, in the shared-memory model, all the processes or execution threads have access to a common area of memory and can read and write data in. For instance, OpenMP [5] is a programming paradigm for shared-memory, multiprocessor machines. Unified Parallel C (UPC [6]), Co-Array Fortran [7], and Titanium [8] are among the implementations of this model for distributed-memory architectures.

Using shared-memory programming techniques over a distributed-memory architecture requires some support from the compiler and from the runtime system. The compiler translates accesses to shared-memory areas into remote memory accesses. The runtime system performs the data movements. This concept is called *partitioned global address space* (PGAS), and languages that rely on it are called *PGAS languages*.

As a consequence, applications programmed using a PGAS language require more support from the runtime system than applications using MPI. However, it has been seen that in terms of features, the MPI-2 standard can be used as a low-level target for PGAS languages [9]. Hence, we can see the runtime system required to run PGAS languages as an extension of a runtime system designed for distributed-memory applications that communicate using explicit message passing. Henceforth, we will focus on runtime environments for distributed parallel applications.

26.1.2 Large-Scale Parallel Computing

With performance beyond a petaflop per second, large-scale systems provide never-reached computational power that allow performance of simulations for science and engineering to help break barriers in many domains. However, although these systems provide extremely high performance, managing and using them efficiently remains a challenge for hardware and software designers.

One of these challenges is how such a large number of resources can be orchestrated to run parallel applications in an efficient way. The resulting challenge is how this orchestration can be achieved efficiently.

In this chapter, we examine the various roles of the runtime environment of a parallel application, which is meant to support the application and to provide some services to this application. More specifically, we will look in further detail at how large scale systems affect these services and how the runtime environment can be designed to face the scalability challenge.

26.2 GOALS OF A RUNTIME ENVIRONMENT

In this section, we present runtime environments in general: their purpose, their goals, and how they serve parallel applications. We first present the software stack that is necessary to run a parallel application on a set of distributed machines and how the runtime environment interacts with the other components of this stack (Section 26.2.1). Then, we define how it ensures the portability of parallel applications (Scction 26.2.2). Finally, we present how it supports the application itself and the communication library (Section 26.2.3).

26.2.1 What Is a Runtime Environment?

The execution of a parallel application must be supported by *middleware* placed between the application and the hardware it is executed on. This runtime system is meant to support the application in order to allow it to make the best and most efficient possible use of the hardware that is available for it [10].

26.2.1.1 Runtime System A runtime system provides portability to the application, between machines and between systems (cluster, massively parallel processing system, etc.). For instance, applications programmed using MPI use a naming system for its processes using integers called ranks. Processes are assigned ranks in a deterministic way ranging between 0 and $(N - 1)$, if N is the number of processes of the application. This abstraction is a key concept for the portability of interprocess communications. On the hardware level, processes communicate with one another using connection information, for transmission control protocol (TCP) communications, a tuple $(IP\ address, port)$. The port used by a given process can be different between executions. Moreover, if the set of machines used by the application is not exactly the same between two executions, the IP address will be different.

Figure 26.1 depicts the stack of components that are necessary for the execution of a parallel application over a set of distributed resources. The set of machines are

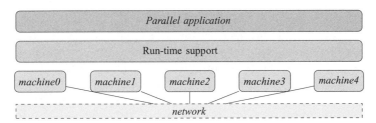

FIGURE 26.1. *Run-time support for executing a parallel application on several machines: the run-time support provides services to the parallel application to help it use distributed resources.*

interconnected by a network. The runtime system orchestrates this set of resources and provides some services to allow the application to be executed in parallel on these resources.

26.2.1.2 Runtime Environment The runtime environment focuses on allowing the *execution* of the application. In the context of parallel applications, it must provide the following services:

- start-up, launching, and finalization of the parallel application as a whole while considering each process individually
- putting the processes in relationship with each other so that they are able to communicate with each other
- monitoring: failure detection, behavior to be followed upon process failures. Monitoring can be extended to a finer-grain watch on the state of the machines, such as supervision of data on the hardware state of the machines like CPU load or temperature. The runtime environment then chooses whether or not to start processes on a given machine or to migrate them on a healthier machine at runtime.

The runtime environment is generally composed of a set of (daemon) processes executed on the machines that are used by the application. Each process of the application is managed by a daemon of the runtime, with which it can communicate. In general, the daemon is executed on the same compute node as the process(es) it is managing. Some supercomputers such as BlueGene/L are exceptions, since BlueGene/L supports only one process, and the notion of "compute node" on this machine cannot be defined as "an instance of the operating system." The runtime environment can be executed in a persistent fashion and used by several parallel applications or dedicated to a single application.

These daemons are interconnected together, forming a *connected topology*. This topology is used for communications within the runtime environment. Hence, it forms a *communication infrastructure*, used by the daemons of the runtime environment to communicate and circulate messages. These messages are called *out-of-band (OOB) messages* because they are strictly internal to the runtime environment and are not used by the parallel application itself.

The software stack executed on each machine involved in a parallel computation is depicted in Figure 26.2. The runtime environment provides services to the parallel application and to the communication library.

26.2.2 Portability

The runtime system also provides hardware portability. If we keep the example of interprocess communications, the networks available for communications can be different between executions if the machines used are not the same. For instance, the application can be executed on a cluster that features a high-speed network that requires specific libraries to be used and then on another cluster that uses only an Ethernet network. The interconnection network technology is hidden from the application by the abstraction provided by communication primitives provided by the runtime system.

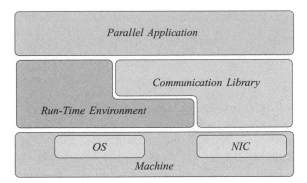

FIGURE 26.2. *Software stack running on a machine that is part of the execution of a parallel application. The run-time support (made of the run-time environment and the communication library) is placed between the hardware and the application.*

Hence, the runtime system provides an abstraction layer that provides the application with high-level communication routines and hides the communication media by taking care of low-level management. The application can focus on communications themselves rather than on how they are performed.

26.2.3 Support Provided to the Application and Communication Library

The runtime environment is meant to support the *life cycle* of the parallel application and to support it during its execution.

It supports the life cycle of the application by *deploying* it on the available resources. During the execution, it *monitors* the state of the application and it *takes the appropriate actions upon failures*. At the end of the execution, it makes sure the parallel application is *terminated*.

During the execution, it is in charge of *forwarding I/Os and signals* from and to the processes of the parallel application. It also supports the communication library by *permitting interprocess communications*.

26.3 COMMUNICATION INFRASTRUCTURE

The daemons of the runtime environment are interconnected by a given topology. This set of links forms a communication infrastructure used by the runtime environment to transmit OOB messages, that is, messages used internally (information circulation, I/O and signal forwarding, transmission of commands). The performance of this communication infrastructure is crucial for the scalability of the runtime environment and the features provided to the application.

This section takes a closer look at the communications that are transmitted within the runtime environment in Section 26.3.1. The performance criteria that are taken into account for scalability are examined in Section 26.3.2. Finally, in Section 26.3.3, we propose a scalable communication infrastructure for runtime environments.

26.3.1 Communications within the Runtime Environment

The runtime environment is meant to support the execution of parallel application. The first aspect of this support is to provide features for the life cycle of the application.

26.3.1.1 Application Start-Up

At first, the application must be *started* on each one of the compute nodes that are available for it. A list of nodes is provided to the runtime environment by the job scheduler. Starting an application consists in launching remotely a command on each of these nodes. This command can be different for each process, as required, for example, by the MPI specification [3]. The command to be started on each node circulates on the communication infrastructure of the runtime environment.

26.3.1.2 Connecting Processes with Each Other

During the course of the application's execution, the runtime environment must provide an *information service on the contact information* of the processes. If a process needs to communicate with another process, it will need to find out how the remote process can be contacted. This information is provided through circulation of the contact information of the processes of the application.

The runtime environment collects this information from each process during the initialization phase of the communication library. There exist two approaches to return this information to the processes.

The first approach can be called the *prefetching* approach. At the end of the initialization phase of the library, each process of the application has in its memory all the contact information of all the other processes. At runtime, when it needs to communicate with another process, it just has to look in its local memory and find this information. A variant of this approach consists in keeping all the contact information in the local daemon's memory. An application process that needs the contact information of another process asks its local daemon, which is a local, inexpensive communication.

In this approach, the information is fully replicated in all the compute nodes used by the application. This can be considered at first glance as expensive in terms of memory consumption. However, if we are considering TCP/IPv4 networks, the contact information for one network interface card (NIC) is made of $4 + 1$ bytes. If each process uses two NICs, the contact information for each process uses 10 bytes. For an execution involving 2^20 processes (about a million), the total size for this information is 10 MB, which is totally reasonable considering the available memory on current machines.

The second drawback of this approach is the fact that it requires a synchronization between all the processes of the application. This circulation of information is actually a collective operation. All the processes put together their contact information and the result of this operation is distributed among all the processes (*allgather* operation, in MPI terminology).

This approach is the most common approach for current implementations of the MPI standard, such as Open MPI and MPICH2. The two aforementioned drawbacks have been so far considered as reasonable.

The second approach can be called the *on-demand* approach. The application processes declare their contact information to the runtime environment at startup time, just like in the prefetching approach. The difference is on how this information is distributed to the application processes. Unlike the previous approach, the information is not distributed among the approach processes at the beginning of the execution but only when a process needs it.

During the initialization phase of the library, the runtime environment only gathers the contact information of all the processes. At runtime, when a process needs to communicate with another process, it has to query it from the runtime environment. If the information is not available in the local daemon's memory, the query circulates within the runtime environment until this information is found and transmitted to the process that needs it.

This approach leverages a more lightweight initialization of the application since it does not require any synchronization between the processes. Whether or not paying the cost of this synchronization is a reasonable option will probably be crucial for very-large-scale systems.

Moreover, it can be useful on systems that have dynamic properties. For example, the MPI implementation targeting institutional grids QCG-OMPI [11] provides features such as NAT and firewall bypassing. Depending on the configuration of the administrative domains of the sites used by the computation, these features can rely on dynamic properties such as changing ports or use advanced connectivity techniques to establish interprocess communications. Hence, QCG-OMPI provides the contact information of remote processes when they are required.

The second purpose of communications within the runtime environment is I/O and signal forwarding. This service is provided by the runtime environment. For example, if the user wants to send a signal to each process of the parallel application, this signal must be transmitted by the runtime environment to each one of the processes of the application. In a similar manner, if a process of the parallel application performs an output on its standard output, `stdout`, it must be forwarded to the user's `stdout` (in general, the standard output of the process that initiated the parallel application, such as `mpiexec` in the context of MPI applications).

26.3.1.3 *Forwarding I/Os and Signals*

The runtime environment forwards these signals and I/Os through its communication infrastructure. Hence, it can be used as a *concentration network* (many-to-one communication) and as a *distribution network* (one-to-many communication).

To summarize, the communication infrastructure of a runtime environment for parallel application must support the following communications:

- *Collective Communications.* One-to-many and many-to-one communications, data gathering, data gathering with or without redistribution of the result, synchronization barrier.
- *Point-to-Point Communications.* One-to-one communication between two daemons of the runtime environment.

26.3.2 Performance Criteria for Scalability

The topology of the communication infrastructure must allow it to scale and to communicate in a scalable way. From a performance point of view, two criteria on this topology must be examined carefully to determine whether a topology is scalable or not.

The first one is the *diameter* of the graph formed by this topology. The diameter is the longest distance between two nodes of a graph. In other words, if a process sends a message to another process, the diameter is the maximal number of hops that this message will have to do to reach its destination.

If the diameter of the graph of the topology used by a runtime environment is large, it will perform poorly on both point-to-point and collective communications since the latency of the communications will be high.

The second criteria is the *degree* of the vertices of this graph. The degree of a vertex of a graph is the number of edges that are connected to this vertex. In the context of runtime environment, it is represented by the number of daemons that are connected to a given daemon.

If the degree of a node of the communication infrastructure is high, the daemon will have to manage a large number of other daemons. In terms of system implementation, it means that the daemon will have to poll over a large number of sockets. At a lower level, the network buffers will have to handle a large number of communications and, in case of a connection storm or of an intense concentration of incoming communications (many-to-one communication), some of these buffers may be overflown and some packets may be lost.

Hence, a scalable topology for the communication infrastructure of a runtime environment must have a good trade-off between these two criteria.

26.3.3   Scalable Communication Infrastructure

A *star topology* (all the daemons are connected to a master daemon, also called *seed*) is the most basic topology there is. It has a diameter of 2: A message can reach any daemon in two hops, except if the sender or the receiver is the master daemon, in which case it is sent directly to the receiver. However, if N denotes the total number of daemons, the master daemon has a degree that is equal to $(N - 1)$. The seed daemon has to manage connections from all the other daemons and to forward all the messages sent between them, which makes it a central point of congestion. Hence, and for the reasons listed above, this topology is not suitable for large-scale systems.

An opposite topology would be an undirected *ring topology*. Each node is connected with two other nodes, considered as its *neighbors*. The degree of each node is equal to 2. The diameter, however, is too large to be reasonable since it is equal to $\lceil N/2 \rceil$. Each daemon has to manage only two other daemons, and there is no central point in this topology. However, message latency is too high and grow linearly with the number of daemons. This topology is therefore not suitable for large-scale systems either.

Tree-based topologies are often used for collective communications because they allow a good parallelism between the communications. Fibonacci trees (also called k-ary trees) and binomial trees are among the trees that are commonly used for one-to-many and many-to-one communications. On a one-port model, that is, a model in which a process can only send or receive one message from or to one other process, the binomial tree algorithm has been proven to be optimal in number of messages for a power-of-two number of processes and quasi-optimal if the number of processes is not a power of two.

In most cases, messages are sent on the communication infrastructure of a runtime environment from or to the seed daemon, and the one-to-many and many-to-one communications are rooted by the seed daemon. Hence, regarding this property of the communication patterns, a tree topology is a reasonable choice for the topology of a communication infrastructure. The degree of all the nodes (except the leaves) of a Fibonacci tree is the parameter k of the tree. In a binomial tree, it is at most $\log_2(N)$. The depth of a Fibonacci tree is $\log_k(N)$, and that of a binomial tree is $\log_2(N)$. Hence, if messages can be rooted up and down the tree, the diameter of a binomial tree is $\mathcal{O}(\log_2(N))$ and the diameter of a Fibonacci tree is $\mathcal{O}(\log_k(N))$.

This seed-based tree topology sets a central role for the seed daemon. If we consider a topology where each daemon is the root of a binomial tree, we obtain a topology where a message can be sent by any daemon and reach any other daemon in, at most, $\log(N)$ hops without any routing up and down the tree while maintaining a degree in $\mathcal{O}(\log_2(N))$. This topology is called a *binomial graph* [12].

Like tree-based topologies, binomial graphs have good properties for one-to-many and many-to-one collective operations. They are also well suited for data gathering with redistribution of the result (allgather in the MPI terminology) since specific algorithms can take direct advantage of the topology [13]. Tree-based topologies, on the other hand, have to perform this operation in two steps: They first gather the data and then broadcast the result.

For these reasons, binomial graph topologies present good properties for large-scale systems. They take tree-based topologies' good communication performance abilities and add more flexibility while keeping a logarithmic degree. Besides, we will see other properties of binomial graphs in Section 26.5.

26.4 APPLICATION DEPLOYMENT

In this section, we present the first role of a runtime environment: how it starts a parallel application on a set of available computing resources. First, we present how an application is deployed in Section 26.4.1. Then we explain why the deployment topology is of major importance at a large scale in Section 26.4.2. Last, we present an approach for scalable application deployment in Section 26.4.3.

26.4.1 Steps in the Deployment of an Application

A parallel application is deployed by the runtime environment on a set of remote resources provided by the job scheduler. At first, the runtime environment must be deployed on these resources. Then it proceeds with launching the processes of the parallel application on the computing nodes.

When a daemon is started, it must join the communication infrastructure. Most of the time, this infrastructure uses a TCP network. It does not use the high-speed network, if any is available, in order to keep it free for the communications of the parallel application. Hence, each daemon of the runtime environment starts with the contact information (IP address and port) of another daemon, which is waiting for incoming connections as a parameter.

As a consequence, before starting other daemons, the very first step of the deployment process consists in opening a socket and starting to listen on it. How the port this socket is listening on is chosen can be discussed. It can be a fixed port, in which case the port is already known by all the daemons of the runtime environment. However, this is a limitation for the system since the chosen port may not be free on all the resources. A direct consequence is that two instances of the runtime environment cannot run on the same machine (in the case, e.g., of a multicore machine that is shared by several applications).

If the port is not fixed and known in advance, it has to be discovered when the socket is opened and transmitted to the daemons that are further started. For portability reasons, the IP address of the machine that runs the daemon that will accept incoming connections cannot be known in advance and must also be provided when a daemon is started.

Once the runtime environment is running on the computing nodes, the parallel application can be started. The command to launch on each node is communicated to the daemons of the runtime environment by a communication on its communication infrastructure and, upon reception of this command, daemons spawn their local processes.

The last step is related to the support of the communication library. At the beginning of the execution of the parallel application, the communication library must be initialized. At this moment, it discovers the available communication interfaces it can use to communicate and declares it and how it can be contacted on these interfaces (its contact information) to the runtime environment. This information is kept in the runtime environment, as discussed in Section 26.3.1.

Therefore, the command that starts a parallel application proceeds as follows:

- Get the list of resources to be used for the computation.
- Open a socket; discover which port it is listening on.
- Spawn daemons on remote resources.
- Build the communication infrastructure.
- Broadcast the command to be launched on the remote resources.
- Initialize the communication library.

The daemons of the runtime environment can simply join the communication infrastructure by connecting to the daemon whose contact information has been passed to it as a parameter (the communication infrastructure's point of contact), but it can also be part of it as an active node of the infrastructure and can accept incoming connections. Various topologies for the communication infrastructure are presented in Section 26.3.3.

Each daemon of the runtime environment takes part in the application start-up as follows:

- Start on a given compute node.
- Connect to the communication infrastructure's point of contact.
- If the daemon has to be connected to by other daemons, open a socket and then discover which port it is listening on.

- If the daemon has children in the deployment process, spawn child daemons.
- Receive the command corresponding to the parallel application.
- Spawn the local processes of the parallel application.
- Initialize the communication library.

26.4.2 Importance of the Deployment Topology

Deploying a runtime environment consists in spawning a daemon on remote resources. Hence, a fast deployment relies on a fast spawning algorithm, that is, an algorithm that can propagate commands in the smallest possible number of steps.

The most naive deployment topology is *a star*. The initial daemon is called seed.[1] The seed daemon spawns all the other daemons one by one. In a one-port model, where a daemon can spawn one daemon at a time, such a deployment on N daemons (plus the seed daemon) takes N steps.

Inspired by one-to-all broadcast algorithms, a *k-ary tree* allows several remote spawns to be performed in parallel. The height of a k-ary tree containing N nodes is equal to $\log_k N$. Each node spawns at most k remote daemons that will, if they are not leaves of the tree, spawn at most other k daemons. Hence, in a one-port model, the total time required to spawn N daemons is equal to $N \log_k N$.

A binomial tree topology extracts a high parallelism between spawns. In a one-port model, it is the optimal deployment topology if the number of daemons that must be spawned is a power of two, and quasi-optimal if the number of daemons is not a power of two. Each daemon of rank r spawns the daemons of ranks $r_k = r + 2^k$, k being integers strictly larger than $\lfloor \log_2 r \rfloor$ and such that r_k is smaller than N (i.e., $\lfloor \log_2 r \rfloor < k \le \lfloor \log_2 (N - r) \rfloor$). In a one-port model, the total time required to spawn N daemons using a binomial tree is equal to $\lceil \log_2 N \rceil$.

As a consequence, the deployment time depends strongly on the topology used to deploy the runtime environment. At a large scale, the binomial tree requires the smaller number of steps among the three topologies presented here. The three topologies described above are depicted in Figure 26.3.

Figure 26.3a shows a star topology with six daemons in total. The seed daemon spawns five daemons.

Figure 26.3b shows a binary tree topology with seven daemons in total. Each daemon spawns two nodes, except the leave nodes. The daemon of rank 6 is spawned last. It is the second daemon spawned by its parent daemon, daemon 2. Daemon 2 is the second daemon spawned by the seed daemon. In total, the last daemon is spawned after four steps.

Figure 26.3c shows a binomial tree topology with eight daemons in total. During the first time step, the seed daemon (called daemon 0) spawns daemon 1. During the second time step, daemon 0 and daemon 1 spawn one daemon each: daemon 2 and daemon 3. During the third time step, the four daemons spawn one daemon each. Hence, spawning these seven daemons using a binomial tree requires three time steps (see Fig. 26.4).

---

[1]In general, the seed daemon is the same for the deployment topology and the communication infrastructure (see Section 26.3.3).

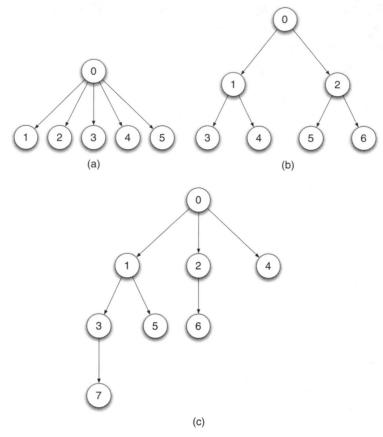

FIGURE 26.3. Some possible deployment topologies: (a) star, (b) binary tree, and (c) binomial tree.

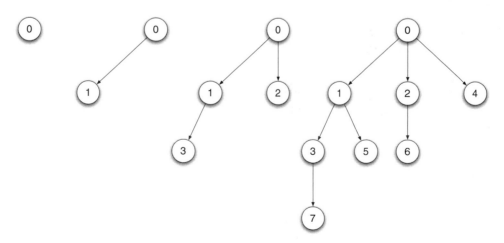

FIGURE 26.4. Steps in a binomial tree-based deployment.

26.4.3   Scalable Application Deployment

If the communication infrastructure (described in Section 26.3) is built independently from the deployment of the runtime environment and in a centralized manner, all the daemons join the communication infrastructure by connecting to the daemon they know, that is, the seed daemon. This can cause a connection storm on the seed daemon.

One can notice that tree-based topologies are suitable for both the deployment and the communication infrastructure[2] of the runtime environment. As a consequence, the construction of the communication infrastructure can be done in a distributed way, while the deployment progresses along the deployment tree.

Distributing the construction of the communication infrastructure eliminates the central point of congestion that exists on the seed daemon with centralized approaches. Moreover, the tree of the communication infrastructure is therefore built directly and does not require execution of any specific algorithm to construct the tree after the deployment.

We have seen in Section 26.4.1 that daemons join the communication infrastructure by connecting themselves to another daemon whose contact information is passed at spawn time. In the centralized approach, all the daemons are given the contact information of the seed daemon. A distributed approach consists in giving the contact information of several daemons instead of only one. As a consequence, the connections are distributed between several daemons.

In a tree-based deployment, each daemon can connect to its parent in the deployment tree. Therefore, the communication infrastructure is built along the deployment tree with a matching topology. The number of incoming connections that must be handled by each node is equal to its degree in the topology graph: There is no central point of congestion that needs to handle a connection storm, such as the one induced by a centralized approach.

The performance of these approaches has been compared and analyzed in Reference 15. We have measured the time required to deploy a trivial application (`/bin/true`) on the GdX cluster of the Grid'5000 testbed [16]. This cluster is made of 342 nodes that feature two AMD Opteron CPUs (two frequencies are available: 2.0 and 2.4 GHz), 2 GB of RAM, 2-Gb Ethernet NICs and a Myri10g NIC. The Myrinet switch features 512 ports. In order to have a flat network topology, we used the TCPoMX driver. These two approaches have been implemented in Open MPI version 1.4a1. Daemons were spawned on remote resources using the Secure Shell (SSH) client.

The deployment time of this trivial application is represented in Figure 26.5. We ran each experiment 10 times, and the values plotted on this figure are the mean and the standard deviation. We can see that at a small scale (less than about 40 nodes), the star topology performs better: It is more simple and, at this scale, congestion issues do not really matter.

The deployment time of the tree-based approach increases quasi-logarithmically, with a step when the number of nodes is a power of two.

On the other hand, the deployment time with a star-based topology increased almost linearly, with a 3-second step around 140 nodes and a high standard deviation

[2]A binomial graph can be built from any tree, as shown in Reference 14.

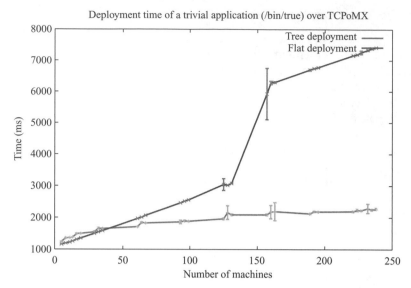

FIGURE 26.5. *Deployment time of a trivial application using a tree-based topology and a star topology.*

around this number of nodes. We used the traffic monitoring tool `tcpdum`[3] to count the incoming TCP SYN packets on the machines on which we spawned remote daemons. We noticed that beyond about 140 nodes, some packets were sent twice. They had probably been lost because of an overflowing backlog buffer, which had a size of 128 on this machine. The number of nodes beyond which packets were lost changed a bit between executions, ranging from about 135 to 145, which explains the variations between measurements and, therefore, the high standard deviation. If a SYN packet is lost, the client machine does not receive any SYN/ACK packet. It retries to send this SYN packet after 3 seconds for the first time. As a consequence, the TCP connection itself takes at least 3 seconds. This can explain the 3-second delay in the star-based, centralized deployment.

The distributed approach presented here presents promising results by constructing the communication infrastructure as the deployment of the daemons of the runtime environment progresses, and, since it is distributed, it eliminates central points of convergence.

However, it requires a tight integration of the communication infrastructure with the spawning system. A custom, integrated launching system with SSH was used in the implementation presented here, which allowed us to interleave the launching system with the construction of the communication infrastructure. This cannot be achieved if a third-party launching system is used, such as, for instance, OAR [17], SLURM [18], or Platform LSF.[4] In this case, all the daemons are spawned with similar command-line arguments and environment variables: They all get the same

[3]http://www.tcpdump.org.
[4]http://www.platform.com.

contact information. Moreover, the distributed approach requires that each daemon opens a socket in listen mode and then proceeds with its participation to the spawning tree. Third-party launching systems spawn all the daemons at once and do not allow interleaving of the deployment itself and local actions on the daemons.

26.5 FAULT TOLERANCE AND ROBUSTNESS

In this section, we describe the role of the runtime environment when failures occur. Failures are inherent to large-scale systems and cannot be ignored for large-scale applications [19]. The runtime environment has a major role to play in the robustness and fault tolerance of the application.

The most basic task it must fulfill for fault tolerance is failure detection. We describe in Section 26.5.1 how this can be achieved.

To be able to support robust parallel applications, the runtime environment must be robust itself. Section 26.5.2 describes some possible topologies for the communication infrastructure and examines their properties in terms of robustness.

Last, in Section 26.5.3, we describe how this support for fault tolerance can be carried out, in function of what is expected from the runtime environment. We see that the features that must be provided by the runtime environment depend on the type of fault-tolerance mechanisms that are implemented and which features are required by different categories of fault-tolerance mechanisms.

26.5.1 Error Detection

Monitoring the state of the processes of the parallel application is part of the role of the runtime environment. The most basic monitoring service consists in detecting failures. When a machine on which processes of the parallel application are running fails, the runtime environment must detect it and take appropriate actions.

The most common failure model is the *fail-stop model* [20]: Upon failures, the processes stop doing anything. Such failures are considered definitive: A failed process will not work again later with no intervention.

Besides, it is often considered that machines fail as a whole: If a failure occurs on a machine, all the processes running on this machine are crashed. In general, a daemon of the runtime environment is running on each machine involved in a parallel application. Hence, if the runtime environment detects that one of its daemons is dead, it considers that the processes running on this machine are dead as well.

Failure detection is not a trivial problem. If a daemon stops answering requests, is it dead or is it just slow? This problem is equivalent to a distributed system problem called *group membership service* (GMS). The set of daemons of the runtime forms a group, and when a daemon dies, it is considered as leaving the group. Yet, it has been proven to be impossible for asynchronous systems with failures in Reference 21.

Heartbeat [22] is a failure detector that is *unreliable* and *eventually perfect*. It is unreliable because at a given moment, daemons or processes are suspected to be dead, but for the aforementioned reasons, the failure detector cannot say if it is dead or not. It is eventually perfect because if a daemon dies, it is eventually detected as dead and, conversely, if a daemon is alive, there is a time after which it is not suspected to have crashed.

Each daemon of the runtime environment maintains a list of other daemons it is watching. Daemons periodically send messages to their neighbors: These messages are called *heartbeats*. Each daemon maintains a vector of counters corresponding to the heartbeats it has received from the other daemons. If it suspects the failure of a daemon, it puts it into a local list of suspected daemons. Some processes may be wrongfully put in this list, for example, if their heartbeat has been received late. If the heartbeat is received later, it is considered as alive and removed from this list.

Heartbeat circulates on the communication infrastructure of the runtime environment: Heartbeats are a specific kind of point-to-point OOB messages.

26.5.2 Robust Topologies

A runtime environment for parallel applications must be robust. The minimal criteria for this robustness is that the topology must remain connected upon failures. For example, the MPI standard versions 1.X, 2.0, and 2.1 specify that if a process of the parallel application fails, the whole application must be finalized. Hence, the surviving processes of the application must be terminated by a specific message that circulates on the communication infrastructure of the runtime environment.

The second level of robustness is when the runtime environment is able to *heal* itself. It can be done in two ways: Either the topology is reknit and the communication infrastructure keeps the same topology (but the number of daemons may or may not be different), or it is healed but the topology is *degraded*; that is, its properties and its structure are different from what they were before the failure.

A star topology is, in that sense, very robust. All the daemons are connected to only one central daemon. Under the assumption that the central daemon does not fail, it cannot be disconnected. However, we have seen in Section 26.3.3 that this topology is not scalable.

A ring topology is robust if no more than two nonconsecutive daemons fail at the same time. If only one daemon fails, the topology is not disconnected and its two neighbors can connect with each other to reknit the ring. It is used in *multipurpose daemon* (MPD) [1]. More details about MPD are given in Section 26.6.1. However, and like the star topology, we have seen in Section 26.3.3 that the ring topology is not scalable.

Tree topologies have, as seen in Section 26.3.3, good scalability properties. However, they are not robust: If a node fails, all the processes in its subtree are disconnected from the rest of the system. Fibonacci trees (*k*-ary trees) can be modified by adding a ring that interconnects together the nodes placed at the same level of the tree. This topology is called a *k-ary sibling tree* [23]. They have the same advantages and the same drawbacks as regular trees in terms of performance. They are robust, except in some situations described in Reference 23. They were designed mostly to be able to keep working in spite of failures, without replacing the failed nodes.

Binomial graphs [24], described in Section 26.3.3, also have good scalability properties. They also have good robustness properties, as shown in Reference 12. If N denotes the number of nodes in the system, they can tolerate the failure of $\mathcal{O}(\log_2(N))$ nodes and $\mathcal{O}(\log_2(N))$ communication links. Hence, they can keep working in spite of failures, but they can also rebuild their topology, as seen in Reference 14.

26.5.3 The Runtime Environment as a Support for Fault Tolerance

Fault tolerance for parallel applications can be achieved in two ways: Either the application can tolerate failures itself or the execution support provides a fault-tolerance layer that makes failures transparent from the application's point of view.

In general, the runtime environment must be robust and able to heal itself upon failures. It must be robust in a sense that it must be able to keep serving the other nodes while recovering the failed processes. Depending on the fault-tolerance approach that is followed, it must also provide additional features to support the fault-tolerance mechanism.

Automatic fault tolerance does not require any modification in the parallel application. The runtime system (the runtime environment and the communication library) are in charge of tolerating failures from the underlying system. It often relies on rollback recovery: Processes are checkpointed by the runtime system on a regular basis and checkpoints are stored by a specific component of the runtime environment called a *checkpoint server*. Upon failures, failed processes can be restarted from their latest checkpoint on a new machine.

A large number of protocols for automatic, transparent fault tolerance exist. They can be coordinated (such as the well-known Chandy and Lamport algorithm [25], implemented in MPICH-*Vcl* [26] and MPICH-*Pcl* [27]) or uncoordinated, using message logging (sender-based message logging [28], causal message logging [29]) or deterministic properties of the application's communications [30]. Message-logging protocols require an additional component from the runtime environment to store causality information on the messages in order to be able to replay them in the same order if a re-execution is required: This component is called a *message logger*. Some protocols log the messages in *channel memories* [31], which are also provided by the runtime environment.

In the particular case of coordinated checkpoint–restart protocols, upon failures, the whole application is restarted from a previous checkpoint. In this case, the runtime environment needs to terminate the application and restart it from a checkpoint. For other protocols, it must not only recover the failed processes (and in some cases help the communication library to replay logged messages) but must also keep serving the rest of the application that has not been hit by the failure.

Algorithm-based fault tolerance (ABFT) [32] requires the parallel application to handle fault tolerance itself. The application is responsible for recovering the state of the application and the data lost with the failed process. It also requires that the runtime environment provides features for the application to implement such mechanisms.

The fault-tolerant linear algebra (FTLA) package [33] implements this approach for linear algebra computations. It relies on a specific MPI middleware called fault-tolerant message-passing interface (FT-MPI) [34] that provides such features to the application. The programmer of the parallel application can choose the general behavior of the application upon failures between four possibilities: shrink, where the failed process is replaced and the naming of the surviving processes is modified so that the names form a continuous set of numbers; blank, where the failed processes are not replaced and the naming of the surviving processes is not modified; rebuild, where new processes are spawned to replace the failed processes and are given the same names as the failed ones; abort, where the application is terminated.

FT-MPI relies for these features on its runtime environment, HARNESS [35]. HARNESS uses a k-ary sibling tree, as described in Section 26.5.2, which allows it to maintain a connected communication infrastructure and, indeed, be able to serve the surviving processes while implementing the behavior specified by the programmer of the parallel application. It also provides some additional information to the processes of the parallel application so that they know if they are running for the first time or if they have been restarted.

The time taken by this healing protocol has been evaluated in Reference 15. Using the same platform as the one used in Section 26.4.3, we have injected failures on a parallel system and have measured the time spent between the failure injection and the end of the recovery protocol (i.e., the end of the initialization of the new MPI processes). For the sake of simplicity and symmetry, we have used a *star* topology: All the daemons are connected to a central daemon, as described in Section 26.5.2. We implemented a self-healing protocol in ORTE, which is Open MPI's runtime environment. We used intermediate time measurements to evaluate the time taken by each step of the recovery protocol:

- *Failure Detection.* When the failure of the remote daemon has been detected by the runtime environment.
- *Before SSH.* When the system has decided what actions must be taken and it is ready to launch a new daemon.
- *Begin ORTE's Initialization.* When the new remote daemon has been spawned and it is about to start its initialization.
- *End ORTE's Initialization.* When the remote daemon is done with its initialization and it is about to spawn the local processes of the application.
- *Application Restart.* When the new application processes are done with their reinitialization.

Figure 26.6a shows the scalability of the healing of the communication infrastructure and restart of processes located on the *first* machine of the system, with respect to the size of the overall system. Figure 26.6b shows the time taken by the healing protocol on a fixed-size system (250 machines), with respect to the rank of the killed daemon.

The time spent before the system starts spawning the new daemon looks constant. Actually, it involves going through lists of machines and local operations. These operations are computing operations, which take a negligible time compared to the time taken by operations over the network (operations involving communications). We can see that the time taken by the initialization of the new daemon of the runtime environment is constant when the first machine is killed, but it increases linearly with the rank of the killed machine. This is due to the linearity of the topology of the communication infrastructure of the runtime environment. When the communication infrastructure heals itself and integrates the daemon that has just been restarted, communications are involved within the runtime system. These communications are therefore performed in linear time.

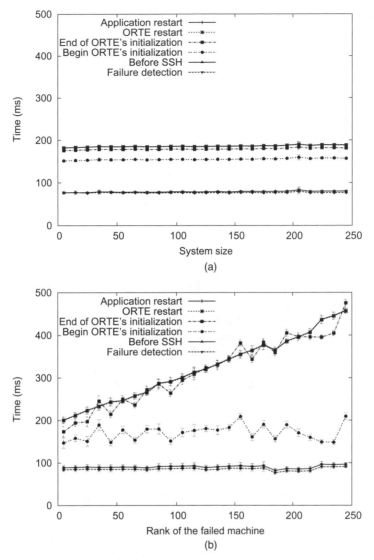

FIGURE 26.6. *Scalability of the healing protocol. (a) First machine killed. (b) Fixed size (250 machines), varying the rank of the killed machine.*

The reinitialization of the application processes involve a pseudoglobal communication: The new process declares its contact information to all the other processes, and it receives all the other processes' contact information. Since there exists at least one process that knows the contact information of all the processes, the latter is done with only one communication. The former requires a global communication, which is executed in a time that increases with the size of the system.

We notice that even in the worst case (restarting the processes of the last machine of a large system), healing the runtime environment and restarting application processes is faster than restarting the whole application (see deployment performance measured in Section 26.4.3).

26.6 CASE STUDIES

This section presents two runtime environments used by popular open-source MPI implementations: MPD, used by MPICH2, and ORTE, used by Open MPI. These two runtime environments were designed following two different approaches, and we think they both should be described here.

26.6.1 MPICH2/MPD

MPICH2 [36] is a well-known MPI implementation and successor of MPICH [37]. The first runtime environment used by MPICH2 was the MPD [1]. It now also features a new runtime environment called *Hydra*. We are focusing here on MPD because of its interesting design and features.

MPD uses a set of daemons that are running on a set of machines and are interconnected together. They must be started *before* the MPI application and by a *separate command* (`mpdboot`). MPD does not finalize itself at the end of an MPI implementation: Indeed, it is not bound to the life cycle of a particular MPI implementation. It can be even used by several MPI applications at the same time.

MPD was originally meant to run *persistently* on a set of machines. The daemons can be started as the machines boot up, and potentially run forever. It was also designed in a matter of security since it was expected to be runnable with superuser privileges.

The MPD daemons are interconnected according to a ring topology. This topology is described in Section 26.3.3. It was chosen for several reasons. First, it is a very simple topology. Being connected with only two neighbors reduces the potential for connections from malicious programs. Moreover, it makes it easier to review by system administrators who want to audit the code of the daemons before they allow them to run with superuser privileges on the nodes.

Besides, one goal of the design of MPD was to avoid having any central manager or master component. Hence, and unlike treelike topologies, a ring topology fulfills this requirement.

A ring is also a robust topology. If a daemon dies, its neighbors detect the ring has been broken and connect themselves together in order to reknit the ring. If no simultaneous failures occur, the topology is not disconnected.

The properties in terms of scalability obtained by this choice are questionable and are worth a discussion. A ring is scalable in terms of numbers of connections: Each daemon has to handle only two connections. However, as described in Section 26.3.3, it is not scalable in terms of diameter and, therefore, in the number of hops in the communications.

The trade-off between the degree and the diameter of the communication infrastructure's topology, described in Section 26.3.2, was chosen regarding the machines that were commonly used and foreseen for future machines at the time when MPD was designed.

The structure of MPD and how it supports MPI applications is depicted in Figure 26.7. The MPD daemons are running on the machines of the cluster and are interconnected by a ring topology. When an MPI application is started on a given set of nodes, the application connects itself to the MPD ring and communicates the

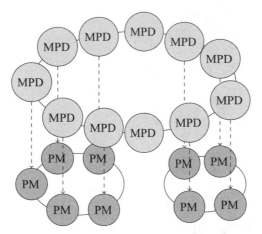

FIGURE 26.7. *MPICH2's run-time environment MPD and two applications spawned over part of the available resources.*

command. The MPD daemons on the nodes that will be used are cloned, and each of them starts a specific daemon called *process manager* (PM). The PMs of a particular MPI application are interconnected by a ring topology and control the MPI application. Hence, the set of PMs is an instance of the runtime environment dedicated to a given MPI application.

The PMs are forked to execute the application's processes on the nodes. The basic operations required to support the life cycle of a parallel application are defined by the *process management interface* (PMI [38]) and are implemented by MPD.

For example, if a process of the MPI application needs to connect to another process to perform a communication, it first asks its runtime environment how the remote process can be contacted. This operation is defined by the PMI and implemented by MPD to provide this information service to the parallel application.

26.6.2 Open MPI/Open RTE

Open MPI [39] is another well-known open-source MPI implementation. It relies on a modular architecture [40] that makes it flexible and portable. It is composed of three sections:

- a low-level layer that ensures portability (open portability abstraction layer)
- the runtime environment (open runtime environment)
- the implementation of the MPI application programming interface (API) (OMPI).

These three sections are not actually *layers*, but they interact with one another and with the local operating system as depicted in Figure 26.8.

Each internal functionality is provided by a *framework* that provides an API implemented in the *components*. A component implements a way to fulfill the functionality featured by the framework; for example, high-level communication routines can be implemented for different kinds of networks. Concretely, a component

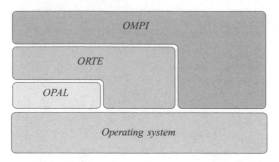

FIGURE 26.8. *General view of the architecture of Open MPI.*

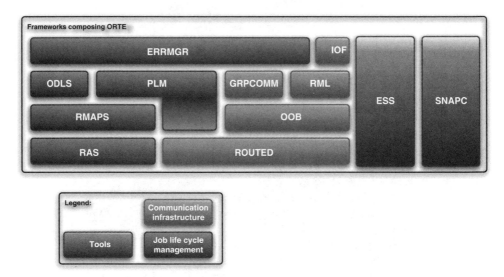

FIGURE 26.9. *Architecture of ORTE: organization of the frameworks.*

is implemented in a dynamic-linked library. With some frameworks, several instances of components (and even several instances of the same component) can be used at the same time, for example, if the system provides several kinds of networks and we want to be able to use them all. At runtime, one or several instances of a component that is linked by the system and used by Open MPI is called a *module*.

Each framework provides a given feature. However, they do not all depend on one another like in a layered architecture. For instance, there is no relationship between the framework that is in charge of spawning the remote daemons and the one in charge of OOB communications.

The organization of the frameworks of ORTE is depicted in Figure 26.9. They can be sorted into three categories:

- the frameworks that manage ORTE's and the application's life cycles, that is, deployment of the runtime environment, spawning of the application, and error management
- the frameworks that compose the communication infrastructure
- the tools that interfere with all the runtime environment itself.

Since we are focusing here on ORTE [41], we will describe the various frameworks it is composed of and see how the features described in this chapter are provided by it.

26.6.2.1 Job's Life Cycle

Resource Allocation System (RAS)   The RAS is in charge of getting the resources the application will be executed on. It can read a file profided by the user of by a resource reservation system. The various components available allow support of several methods to obtain this resource list, depending on the reservation system that is used.

Resource Mapping System (RMAPS)   The RMAPS is in charge of matching the processes of the MPI application, the daemons of the runtime environment, and the list of available machines obtained by the RAS. The various components available implement several policies to schedule the processes over the available resources such as, for instance, round-robin.

Process Life Cycle Management (PLM)   The PLM is in charge of the deployment of the runtime environment according to the map determined by the RMAPS. It spawns daemons on remote machines and makes sure they join the communication infrastructure. Once the daemons are ready, it propagates the command that spawns the application processes from the daemons.

Open RTE Daemon's Local Launch Subsystem (ODLS)   The ODLS is in charge of spawning the local application's processes that will be attached to the local daemon. For this purpose, it uses the map determined by the RMAPS and clones the daemon process to spawn the application's processes.

Error Manager (ERRMGR)   The ERRMGR frameworks implements error detection mechanisms and the behavior that ORTE follows upon node failures. For instance, one component implements clean termination of the application and folding of the runtime environment if a daemon is detected as dead. Fault-tolerance policies can be implemented as components of this framework, such as spawning of a new daemon to replace the failed one (as described in Reference 15).

26.6.2.2 Communication Infrastructure

ROUTED   The ROUTED framework computes the routing tables of the communication infrastructure. Messages are routed through a communication infrastructure by intermediate daemons that forward them toward their destination; the ROUTED framework computes these routes for each message sent and, more precisely, the identifiers of the daemons it will be sent to. The various components available implement several routing algorithms.

OOB   Low-level communications are implemented by the OOB framework. In order to keep the communications of the application free of any disturbance if they are performed on a high-speed network, the only component implemented uses TCP communications.

Runtime Messaging Layer (RML)   The high-level communication routines used by the runtime environment are implemented by the RML framework. The RML calls the OOB and follows the active-message model.

Group Communications (GRPCOMM)   Collective communications are an essential part of the features required by a runtime environment. They are implemented in ORTE in the GRPCOMM framework, which calls the ROUTED framework to choose where messages are routed and therefore send fewer messages. This framework uses the RML for point-to-point communications.

Input/Output Forwarding Service (IOF)   I/Os from the application's processes are forwarded to the `mpiexec` process, which acts like a gateway between the application and the user, by the IOF framework.

26.6.2.3 Tools

Environment-Specific Service (ESS)   During the initialization phase of the daemons of the runtime environment and the MPI processes, the ESS is in charge of the initialization of the ORTE part depending on the role of the process.

Snapshot Coordination Interface (SNAPC)   This framework is used only by the rollback-recovery fault-tolerance system. It is in charge of initiating a checkpoint wave and of copying and storing the checkpoints on the machine that executes the `mpiexec` process.

26.7 CONCLUSION

In this chapter, we have examined some of the challenges faced by parallel, distributed runtime environments on large-scale systems. We have listed the services provided by runtime environments to support parallel applications running on a set of distributed resources and how their large scale makes them highly critical for the performance of the application.

We have emphasized the importance of the topology used by the runtime environment for several of the services it provides. We have seen that using matching topologies or compatible topologies (a binomial tree can be extracted from a binomial graph) leverages good performance and reduces the effects of communication concentration (e.g., connection storms or all-to-one collective communication patterns).

Fault tolerance is a critical issue for large-scale systems. Hence, we have examined it as an additional feature that must be provided by runtime environments. We have seen how the runtime environment can support various types of fault tolerance and how it must be handled internally by the runtime environment.

Finally, we have analyzed carefully how the runtime environments of two well-known, open-source parallel programming environments (MPICH2 and Open MPI) are implemented, which design choices have been made, and what the consequences of these choices are.

REFERENCES

[1] R.M. Butler, W.D. Gropp, and E.L. Lusk, "A scalable process-management environment for parallel programs," in *Recent Advances in Parallel Virtual Machine and Message Passing Interface, 7th European PVM/MPI Users' Group Meeting (EuroPVM/MPI'02)* (J. Dongarra, P. Kacsuk, and N. Podhorszki, eds.), Vol. 1908, pp. 168–175, Springer, 2000.

[2] G. Tel, *Introduction to Distributed Algorithms*. Cambridge University Press, 1994.

[3] Message Passing Interface Forum, "MPI: A message-passing interface standard." Technical Report UT-CS-94-230, Department of Computer Science, University of Tennessee, April 1994, May 22 101 17:44:55 GMT.

[4] A. Geist, W.D. Gropp, S. Huss-Lederman, A. Lumsdaine, E.L. Lusk, W. Saphir, A. Skjellum, and M. Snir, "MPI-2: Extending the message-passing interface," in *1st European Conference on Parallel and Distributed Computing (EuroPar'96)*, (L. Bougé, P. Fraigniaud, A. Mignotte, and Y. Robert, eds.), Vol. 1123 of *Lecture Notes in Computer Science*, pp. 128–135, Springer, 1996.

[5] L. Dagum and R. Menon, "OpenMP: An industry standard API for shared-memory programming," *IEEE Computational Science and Engineering*, 5:46–55, 1998.

[6] UPC Consortium, "UPC Language Specifications, v1.2." Technical Report LBNL-59208, Lawrence Berkeley National, 2005.

[7] C.C. Coarfa, Y. Dotsenko, J. Mellor-Crummey, D. Chavarria-Miranda, F. Cantonnet, T. El-Ghazawi, A. Mohanti, and Y. Yao, An evaluation of global address space languages: Co-array Fortran and unified parallel, June 2005.

[8] P. Hilfinger, D. Bonachea, K. Datta, D. Gay, S. Graham, B. Liblit, G. Pike, J. Su, and K. Yelick, "Titanium language reference manual." Technical Report UCB/CSD-2005-15, UC Berkeley, 2005.

[9] D. Bonachea and J. Duell, "Problems with using MPI 1.1 and 2.0 as compilation targets for parallel language implementations," *International Journal of High Performance Computing and Networking (IJHPCN)*, 1(1/2/3):91–99, 2004.

[10] R. Namyst, *Contribution á la conception de supports exécutifs multithreads performants*. Habilitation á diriger des recherches, Université Claude Bernard de Lyon, pour des travaux effectués á l'école normale supérieure de Lyon, DEC 2001.

[11] C. Coti, T. Herault, S. Peyronnet, A. Rezmerita, and F. Cappello, "Grid services for MPI," in *Proceedings of the 8th IEEE International Symposium on Cluster Computing and the Grid (CCGrid'08)* (T. Priol et al., ed.), pp. 417–424, Lyon, France: ACM/IEEE, May 2008.

[12] T. Angskun, G. Bosilca, and J. Dongarra, "Binomial graph: A scalable and fault-tolerant logical network topology," in *Proceedings of the 5th International Symposium on Parallel and Distributed Processing and Applications (ISPA 2007)* (I. Stojmenovic, R.K. Thulasiram, L. Tianruo Yang, W. Jia, M. Guo, and R. Fernandes de Mello, eds.), Vol. 4742 of *Lecture Notes in Computer Science*, pp. 471–482, Springer, 2007.

[13] J. Bruck, C.-T. Ho, S. Kipnis, E. Upfal, and D. Weathersby, "Efficient algorithms for all-to-all communications in multiport message-passing systems," *IEEE Transactions on Parallel and Distributed Systems*, 8(11):1143–1156, 1997.

[14] G. Bosilca, C. Coti, T. Herault, P. Lemarinier, and J. Dongarra, "Constructing resiliant communication infrastructure for runtime environments," *Advances in Parallel Computing*, 19:441–451, 2010. Available at http://dx.doi.org/10.1016/j.future.2007.02.002.

[15] C. Coti, "Environnements d'exécution pour applications parallèles communiquant par passage de messages pour les systèmes à grande échelle et les grilles calcul." PhD Thesis, Université Paris Sud-XI, November 2009.

[16] F. Cappello, E. Caron, M. Dayde, F. Desprez, Y. Jegou, P. Vicat-Blanc Primet, E. Jeannot, S. Lanteri, J. Leduc, N. Melab, G. Mornet, B. Quetier, and O. Richard, "Grid'5000: A large scale and highly reconfigurable grid experimental testbed," in *Proceedings of the 6th IEEE/ACM International Workshop on Grid Computing CD (SC\05)*, pp. 99–106, Seattle, WA: IEEE/ACM, November 2005.

[17] N. Capit, G. Da Costa, Y. Georgiou, G. Huard, C. Martin, G. Mounié, P. Neyron, and O. Richard, "A batch scheduler with high level components," in *Proceedings of the 5th International Symposium on Cluster Computing and the Grid (CCGRID '05)*, pp. 776–783, Cardiff, UK: IEEE Computer Society, May 2005.

[18] M.A. Jette, A.B. Yoo, and M. Grondona, "SLURM: Simple linux utility for resource management," in *Proceedings of the 9th International Workshop on Job Scheduling Strategies for Parallel Processing (JSSPP'03)* (D.G. Feitelson, L. Rudolph, and U. Schwiegelshohn, eds.), Vol. 2862, pp. 44–60, Springer-Verlag, 2003.

[19] D.A. Reed, C. da Lu, and C.L. Mendes, "Reliability challenges in large systems," *Future Generation Computer Systems*, 22(3):293–302, 2006.

[20] R.D. Schlichting and F.B. Schneider, "Fail stop processors: An approach to designing fault-tolerant computing systems," *ACM Transactions on Computer Systems*, 1:222–238, 1983.

[21] T.D. Chandra, V. Hadzilacos, S. Toueg, and B. Charron-Bost, "Impossibility of group membership in asynchronous systems," in *Proceedings of the 15th ACM SIGACT-SIGOPS Symposium on Principles of Distributed Computing*, pp. 322–330, May 1996.

[22] M.K. Aguilera, W. Chen, and S. Toueg, "Heartbeat: A timeout-free failure detector for quiescent reliable communication," in *Proceedings of the 11th Workshop on Distributed Algorithms (WDAG'97)* (M. Mavronicolas and P. Tsigas, eds.), Vol. 1320 of *Lecture Notes in Computer Science*, pp. 126–140, Springer, 1997.

[23] T. Angskun, G.E. Fagg, G. Bosilca, J. Pjesivac-Grbovic, and J. Dongarra, "Self-healing network for scalable fault-tolerant runtime environments," *Future Generation Computer Systems*, 26(3):479–485, 2010.

[24] T. Angskun, G. Bosilca, and J. Dongarra, "Self-healing in binomial graph networks," in *OTM Workshops (2)* (R. Meersman, Z. Tari, and P. Herrero, eds.), Vol. 4806 of *Lecture Notes in Computer Science*, pp. 1032–1041, Springer, 2007.

[25] K.M. Chandy and L. Lamport, "Distributed snapshots: Determining global states of distributed systems," *ACM Transactions on Computer Systems*, 3(1):63–75, 1985.

[26] P. Lemarinier, A. Bouteiller, T. Herault, G. Krawezik, and F. Cappello, "Improved message logging versus improved coordinated checkpointing for fault tolerant MPI," in *IEEE International Conference on Cluster Computing (Cluster 2004)*, IEEE CS Press, 2004.

[27] D. Buntinas, C. Coti, T. Herault, P. Lemarinier, L. Pilard, A. Rezmerita, E. Rodriguez, and F. Cappello, "Blocking versus non-blocking coordinated checkpointing for large-scale fault tolerant MPI," *Future Generation Computer Systems*, 24(1):73–84, 2008. Available at http://dx.doi.org/10.1016/j.future.2007.02.002.

[28] A. Bouteiller, F. Cappello, T. Hérault, G. Krawezik, P. Lemarinier, and F. Magniette, "MPICH-V2: A fault tolerant MPI for volatile nodes based on pessimistic sender based message logging," in *High Performance Networking and Computing (SC2003)*, Phoenix, AZ, IEEE/ACM, November 2003.

[29] A. Bouteiller, B. Collin, T. Herault, P. Lemarinier, and F. Cappello, "Impact of event logger on causal message logging protocols for fault tolerant MPI," in *Proceedings of*

the 19th IEEE International Parallel and Distributed Processing Symposium (IPDPS'05), p. 97, Washington, DC: IEEE Computer Society, 2005.

[30] A. Guermouche, T. Ropars, E. Brunet, M. Snir, and F. Cappello, Uncoordinated check-pointing without domino effect for send-deterministic message passing applications, May 2011.

[31] G. Bosilca, A. Bouteiller, F. Cappello, S. Djilali, G. Fédak, C. Germain, T. Hérault, P. Lemarinier, O. Lodygensky, F. Magniette, V. Néri, and A. Selikhov, "MPICH-V: Toward a scalable fault tolerant MPI for volatile nodes," in *High Performance Networking and Computing (SC2002)*, Baltimore, MD: IEEE/ACM, November 2002.

[32] Z. Chen, G.E. Fagg, E. Gabriel, J. Langou, T. Angskun, G. Bosilca, and J. Dongarra, "Fault tolerant high performance computing by a coding approach," in *Proceedings of the ACM SIGPLAN Symposium on Principles and Practice of Parallel Programming, PPOPP 2005, June 15–17, 2005, Chicago, IL* (K. Pingali, K.A. Yelick, and A.S. Grimshaw, eds.), pp. 213–223, ACM, 2005.

[33] G. Bosilca, R. Delmas, J. Dongarra, and J. Langou, "Algorithm-based fault tolerance applied to high performance computing," *Journal of Parallel and Distributed Computing*, 69(4):410–416, 2009.

[34] G.E. Fagg and J. Dongarra, FT-MPI: Fault tolerant MPI, supporting dynamic applications in a dynamic world, 2000.

[35] G.E. Fagg and J.J. Dongarra, "HARNESS fault tolerant MPI design, usage and performance issues," *Future Generation Computer Systems*, 18(8):1127–1142, 2002.

[36] W. Gropp, "Mpich2: A new start for mpi implementations," in *Recent Advances in Parallel Virtual Machine and Message Passing Interface* (D. Kranzlmller, J. Volkert, P. Kacsuk, and J. Dongarra, eds.), Vol. 2474 of *Lecture Notes in Computer Science*, pp. 37–42, Berlin/Heidelberg: Springer, 2002.

[37] W.D. Gropp and E.L. Lusk, "A high-performance MPI implementation on a shared-memory vector supercomputer," *Parallel Computing*, 22(11):1513–1526, 1997.

[38] P. Balaji, D. Buntinas, D. Goodell, W. Gropp, J. Krishna, E. Lusk, and R. Thakur, "PMI: A scalable parallel process-management interface for extreme-scale systems," in *Recent Advances in the Message Passing Interface* (R. Keller, E. Gabriel, M. Resch, and J. Dongarra, eds), Vol. 6305 of *Lecture Notes in Computer Science*, pp. 31–41. Berlin/Heidelberg: Springer, 2010.

[39] E. Gabriel, G.E. Fagg, G. Bosilca, T. Angskun, J.J. Dongarra, J.M. Squyres, V. Sahay, P. Kambadur, B. Barrett, A. Lumsdaine, R.H. Castain, D.J. Daniel, R.L. Graham, and T.S. Woodall, "Open MPI: Goals, concept, and design of a next generation MPI implementation," in *Recent Advances in Parallel Virtual Machine and Message Passing Interface, 11th European PVM/MPI Users' Group Meeting (EuroPVM/MPI '04)*, pp. 97–104, Budapest, Hungary, September 2004.

[40] B. Barrett, J. Squyres, A. Lumsdaine, R. Graham, and G. Bosilca, "Analysis of the component architecture overhead in Open MPI," in *Recent Advances in Parallel Virtual Machine and Message Passing Interface* (B. Di Martino, D. Kranzlmüller, and J. Dongarra, eds.), Vol. 3666 of *Lecture Notes in Computer Science*, pp. 175–182, Berlin/Heidelberg: Springer, 2005.

[41] R.H. Castain, T.S. Woodall, D.J. Daniel, J.M. Squyres, B. Barrett, and G.E. Fagg, "The open run-time environment (openRTE): A transparent multi-cluster environment for high-performance computing," in *Recent Advances in Parallel Virtual Machine and Message Passing Interface, 12th European PVM/MPI Users' Group Meeting* (B. Di Martino, D. Kranzlmüller, and J. Dongarra, eds.), Vol. 3666 of *Lecture Notes in Computer Science*, pp. 225–232, Sorrento, Italy: Springer, September 2005.

27

Increasing Performance through Optimization on APU

Matthew Doerksen, Parimala Thulasiraman, and Ruppa Thulasiram

27.1 INTRODUCTION

As we move into the exascale era of computing, heterogeneous architectures have become an integral component of high-performance systems (HPSs) and high-performance computing (HPC). Over time, we have transitioned from homogeneous central processing unit (CPU)-centric HPSs such as Jaguar [1] to heterogeneous HPSs such as Roadrunner [2], which uses a modified Cell processor and the graphics processing unit (GPU)-based Tianhe-1A [3]. The use of these HPSs has been vital for research applications but, until recently, has not been a factor in the consumer-level experience. However, with new technologies such as AMD's accelerated processing unit (APU) architecture, which fuses the CPU and the GPU onto a single chip, consumers now have an affordable HPS at their disposal.

27.2 HETEROGENEOUS ARCHITECTURES

To begin, we will provide a basic overview of the different types of heterogeneous architectures currently available. A short list includes the Cell Broadband Engine (Cell BE) [4], GPUs from AMD [5] and NVIDIA, and lastly, AMD's Fusion APU [6]. Each of these architectures has its own advantages and disadvantages that, in part, determine how well it will perform in a particular situation or algorithm.

Scalable Computing and Communications: Theory and Practice, First Edition. Edited by
Samee U. Khan, Albert Y. Zomaya, and Lizhe Wang.
© 2013 John Wiley & Sons, Inc. Published 2013 by John Wiley & Sons, Inc.

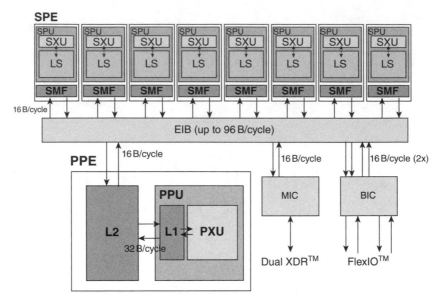

FIGURE 27.1. *Cell Broadband Engine processor composed of the power processing element, multiple synergistic processing units and communication enabled via the element interconnect bus [18]. MIC, memory interface controller; SPE, Synergistic Processing Element. BIC, bus interface controller; SXU, synergistic execution unit; PXU, power execution unit; LS, local store.*

We now look at the Cell BE, based on the Power Architecture and a collaborative work by Sony, Toshiba, and IBM for HPC for a variety of applications including the most visible, video games. From a high-level perspective, the Cell BE is laid out in a hierarchical structure with the power processing unit at the top and the synergistic processing units (SPU) underneath for computational support.

27.2.1 Cell BE

27.2.1.1 Power Processing Element (PPE) At the top of the hierarchy lies the "master" PowerPC core known as the PPE, which uses a 64-bit Power Architecture with two-way hardware multithreading. The PPE also contains a 32-kB L1 instruction cache and a 32-kB L1 data cache to reduce access times, speeding up computation. Above this is a 512-kB L2 cache to store any data that may be needed during computation. Given that the PPE is the master, it is designed for control-intensive tasks and is able to task switch quickly, making it perfect for running the operating system. Due to this design, however, the PPE is not suited to data-intensive computations, which is why it is supported by up to eight SPUs, which perform the majority of computations. Even so, the PPE is able to execute up to eight single-precision operations per cycle, giving it a theoretical peak performance of 25.6 gigafloating-point operations per second (Gflops) when running at 3.2 GHz (Fig. 27.1).

27.2.1.2 SPUs Each SPU beneath the PPE is a core built for data-intensive applications such as graphics. The SPU uses dual-issue, 128-bit single-instruction multiple-data (SIMD) architecture, which gives it a large amount of computational power for parallel workloads. Each SPU has 128 register files, each of which is 128 bits wide and a 256-kB local data store that holds all instructions and data used by the SPU. Since the SPUs use a SIMD architecture, many features such as out-of-order execution, hardware-managed caches and dynamic branch prediction are absent in an attempt to reduce complexity and die size and to increase performance. These simplifications give the SPU amazing processing power, reaching a single-precision theoretical peak of 25.6 Gflops. Multiplying this value over the eight SPUs, we see that, in total, the Cell BE can provide up to 204.8 Gflops of single-precision performance, greatly outperforming your standard CPU. However, because of the SIMD architecture, SPUs have the disadvantage of large latency times if they do not have data to work on. To reduce this factor of performance, the SPUs connect to the main memory through direct memory access (DMA) commands. DMA allows the SPUs to asynchronously overlap data transfer and computation without going through the PPE in order to hide memory latency. This data transfer occurs over the element interconnect bus (EIB) and is the key to the Cell BE's performance.

27.2.1.3 EIB   The PPE and SPUs communicate with each other and the main memory through the EIB. The EIB is a high-bandwidth, low-latency four-ring structure with two rings running clockwise and two counterclockwise with an internal bandwidth of 96 bytes/cycle. This gives the EIB a maximum 25.6 GB/s in each direction for each port with a sustainable peak throughput of 204.8 GB/s and a 307.2-GB/s maximum throughput between bus units. Additionally, the EIB has support for up to 100 outstanding DMA requests at any given time to ensure the SPUs do not run out of data.

27.2.2   GPUs

After examining the Cell BE, we see it is a very powerful architecture when properly utilized. However, the same implementation that makes it so powerful means that the SPU building blocks are too large to replicate more than a few times. The GPU takes this "slimmed down" approach one step further and uses hundreds of miniature cores (depending on architecture and model) to take advantage of data-parallel work such as graphics. Before we dig any deeper into the GPU architecture and how we will exploit its advantages, we will first examine the GPU's two main components: the core itself and the off-chip memory. To do so, we turn to AMD's "Evergreen" architecture, used in their Radeon 5xxx series GPUs [7].

27.2.2.1 GPU Core   AMD's GPUs are composed of many cores that utilize a very long instruction word (VLIW) architecture. We will define each of these miniature cores as stream processors (SPs), which are the smallest block of computational resources. Due to the VLIW design choice, SPs are able to execute up to five (dependent on architecture; from here on we will focus on VLIW5, which is the basis of the Evergreen architecture) operations on the available arithmetic and logic units (ALUs) simultaneously given there are no dependencies. Abstracting these small blocks, we have what are known as SIMD Engines (SEs); these groupings are built out of many SPs (16 in the case of AMD's current GPU architectures) and are the smallest building block used for each GPU. Before we continue, it should be

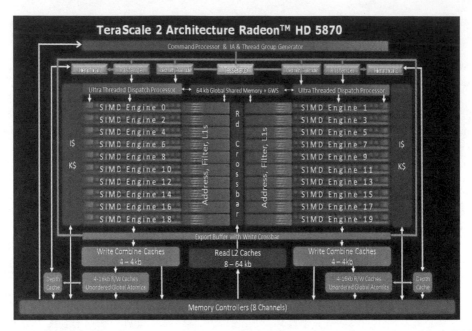

FIGURE 27.2. *The TeraScale 2 architecture used in the Radeon 5870 showing the multiple SIMD Engines that comprise the GPU. Upon closer inspection, we can see the 16 SPs that make up a single SIMD Engine [5].*

noted that the number of SEs is often determined by the model of GPU. For example, Figure 27.2 details an AMD Radeon 5870, which contains 20 SEs, while an AMD Radeon 5450 only contains a single SE. Thus, to obtain the shader count for any given GPU for AMD's Evergreen architecture, we simply multiply the number of SEs by 80 (16 SPs multiplied by 5 because it is a VLIW5 architecture). This vast number of shaders provides the AMD GPU with immense processing power, a single-precision theoretical peak of 2.72 Tflops; even outpacing the Cell by a factor of 10. We also should note that each SE can support 1587 concurrent threads. This allows the Radeon 5870 to support up to 31,744 concurrent threads, providing a large base for extracting performance out of parallel workloads.

27.2.2.2   VLIW   Though the VLIW architecture is very powerful when ALU utilization is high, VLIW architectures are not without flaws. For instance, in cases where very complex operations are used (or instructions are dependent on one another), as few as a single ALU in the SP may be utilized. This leads to a worst-case scenario where theoretical peak performance is limited to one-fifth of the peak performance. It should now be noted that, for simplicity, we assume all instructions take the same amount of time and the four simple ALUs are equal in speed to the single complex ALU (though their supported operations may vary) used in the Evergreen architecture. VLIW also relies heavily on the compiler to properly pack the instructions in order to utilize the ALUs (as opposed to the SIMD approach, which uses hardware to pack instructions dynamically at runtime to improve utilization). It is important to note these drawbacks since the application or algorithm will determine on which type of hardware it will run the best.

27.2.2.3 GPU Off-Chip Memory As important as the GPU core is, the memory subsystem is critical in extracting performance. A GPU core cannot run to the best of its abilities if it is always starved for data (just like the SPUs of the Cell BE); this is where the advanced memory subsystem of AMD's Evergreen architecture comes into play. The memory subsystem enables high-speed communication between individual shaders and SEs (in general). The first advancement made in the Evergreen architecture was the redesigned memory controller to support error detection code (EDC) for use with higher speed (compared to their previous architectures) Graphics Double Data Rate version 5 (GDDR5) memory. Moving to the shaders, the L2 cache was doubled to 128 kB per memory controller. Additionally, cache bandwidth was also increased from the previous generation to 1 TB/s for L1 texture fetch and 435 GB/s between the L1 and L2 caches. At the highest level, we have a large memory with massive bandwidth for the GPU (for the Radeon 5870, 1–2 GB of GDDR5 memory with 153.6 GB/s of bandwidth). These advances enable the memory system to keep the SEs fed with data in order to maximize the performance of the architecture. However, even with these increases at the GPU level, GPUs are still limited by the additional latency and slow data transfer rate of the PCI Express bus of 16 GB/s in each direction.

27.2.3 APUs

The APU was built in order to combat the memory wall, which is particularly important in systems with discrete GPUs. In a typical system, there is a CPU and a GPU, which must communicate via the PCI Express bus. In an APU-based system, however, the CPU and GPU are on the same chip, meaning there is no need for communication to occur over the PCI Express bus. Each implementation has both advantages and disadvantages, which we will cover as we look at each implementation.

27.2.3.1 Typical Separate CPU/GPU System First, we have Figure 27.3, which shows a traditional system with a separate CPU and GPU [6]. As we already covered, communication between the CPU and GPU must occur over the PCI Express bus. This causes a large performance penalty in both latency and bandwidth, even with the latest PCI Express 3.0 specification. The first advantage of these discrete GPU systems is that multi-GPU support is simplified since we can worry less about differing latencies and bandwidth between dedicated GPUs. Next, these systems are typically built with a larger focus on modularity, enabling performance upgrades much easier than an APU-based system (which would require the replacement of the APU chip, even if we only want a faster CPU or integrated GPU). This modularity comes at its own cost, however, as these types of systems cost more than an APU system due to the increased number of chips being used (CPU and GPU vs. APU) and the increased complexity required during system design. This, however, is not a major factor in the HPC sector, but for the average consumer, price is one of the key factors in purchasing a system.

27.2.3.2 Fused CPU/GPU System Moving to the APU in Figure 27.4, we have covered that the APU has both the CPU and GPU (in this case, a member of the 5xxx series) on a single chip. This enables the CPU to communicate with the GPU

FIGURE 27.3. *A typical system with the CPU located at the top of the figure, which must communicate with the GPU at the bottom of the figure via the PCI Express bus located in the Northbridge [6].*

FIGURE 27.4. *An APU-based system with a combined CPU and GPU. Note the use of the high-performance on-chip bus that enables communication between the CPU and the GPU at much higher speeds and lower latency than the PCI Express bus [6].*

using an on-chip interconnection network rather than the PCI Express bus, reducing latency and increasing bandwidth. While good, this can lead to issues for some types of algorithms.

One problem is the potential lack of compute resources as the integrated GPU is a fairly low-end GPU compared to available dedicated GPUs. A second potential problem is the lack of on-chip memory bandwidth. With the APU, the GPU portion only has as much bandwidth as system memory (17 GB/s for a system with dual-channel DDR3 memory running at 1066 MHz), which pales in comparison to the dedicated GPU's 153.6 GB/s of on-chip bandwidth we noted earlier. From this, it should be simple to see that the APU has corner cases (just like the GPU) where it performs extremely well, such as where data must be moved explicitly back and forth from the CPU to the GPU and vice versa due to algorithmic constraints.

For the large majority of consumers, this is not an issue as few have GPUs above the level of those found in the "standard" APU. It does, however, have the benefit of less expensive systems because fewer hardware components are needed, enabling better performance at lower prices. Looking at things from a programming point of view, an APU system with an additional dedicated GPU is much more difficult to program as we now have to examine the algorithms and determine which ones should execute on which piece of hardware based on the hardware's characteristics.

27.3 RELATED WORK

27.3.1 The History of Heterogeneous Computing

Heterogeneous computing is not exactly an untouched area; a number of years ago, a few extremely intelligent developers recognized the GPU's strengths and how it could be used for purposes other than graphics. The problem, however, was that no application programming interface (API) existed to use the GPU for computation. These pioneers began GPU computing by tricking the device into executing code (specified in terms of vertices, vectors, etc.) through the use of the Open Graphics Library (OpenGL). This meant that code was complex and writing it this way was not a viable solution for quick, efficient programs. Eventually, NVIDIA realized the need for a language to abstract the programming issues associated with OpenGL when used for general-purpose computation. We also note that NVIDIA was not the only one with this idea as ATI (which was acquired by AMD in 2006) also worked on two similar projects, namely, Close to Metal and Brook, but has now moved entirely to Open Computing Language (OpenCL). In this section, we will only cover NVIDIA's solution as it has become the leading GPU compute solution compared to today's newcomers, OpenCL and DirectCompute.

27.3.2 Compute Unified Device Architecture (CUDA)

Released in 2007, the CUDA framework provided a way to abstract the complication out of using a GPU for general-purpose computation. To do so, NVIDIA started with a C-based language and added specific functionality both in the software development kit (SDK) and driver to handle the difficulties of GPU computing including device setup, memory transfers, and the computation of kernel code. Due to CUDA being the first simple GPU computing language, it gained a large following and became the standard for GPU compute. It has been such a success that both producers and a small number of consumers have taken it to the next level because of the advantages it brings.

To provide a few examples, we look at HPC researchers that have taken NVIDIA GPUs and integrated them into three of the top four supercomputers in the world (as of November 2010). With these supercomputers (and, in general, smaller GPU-based workstations), researchers have built and run CUDA programs in the following areas:

- medical imaging [8]
- N-body simulations [9]
- earthquake modeling [10].

Looking at general results obtained from these applications, researchers were able to speed up computation anywhere from 1.63 times to more than 250 times given the problem type and level of optimization (device specific or general). In all, we see that GPU computing has become an important aspect of the research community because it allows us to run simulations at speeds we never would have thought were possible only a few years ago.

"Regular" consumers, however, have had limited exposure to the advantages of GPU computing. This is due to a few reasons, first being that most consumers will not have a GPU with performance great enough to make GPU computing worthwhile. Second is the price of high-performance GPUs and the associated low market share. For those select few (with high-performance GPUs) that are able to utilize CUDA's advantages, we see developers integrate GPU computing into programs such as

- Maya's Shatter plug-in [11]
- Cyberlink's PowerDVD 10 (and newer) [12]
- enhanced physics calculations in games such as Mafia II [13].

For consumer applications, we will not look at the effect of CUDA in terms of "program X takes Y time units so we can run bigger instances in the same amount of time." Though this is important for "regular old" computation influencing a user's experience in terms of wait time, we will instead look at how general-purpose computation using CUDA is able to enhance the user's experience. To do so, we turn to one of the most visible uses of CUDA in the consumer workspace, gaming. Mafia II, developed by 2K Czech and published by 2K Games, uses CUDA and NVIDIA's proprietary physics engine, PhysX, for a number of gameplay enhancements including (more) destructible environments, advanced cloth simulations, and more realistic particle-based effects such as smoke and explosions.

Using images taken from Mafia II, we can see the impact that the added GPU computation has on the user experience. When an explosion takes place (see Fig. 27.5), instead of just a few flashy effects, we are able to do much more, such as making the environment destructible or enabling dynamic smoke effects (see Fig.

FIGURE 27.5. *A screen capture of Mafia II running with PhysX disabled. Note the lack of particles and effects such as smoke and debris [13].*

FIGURE 27.6. *A second screen capture from Mafia II but with PhysX enabled. Here we see many more particles such as debris and smoke being added to the user experience [13].*

27.6), allowing many additional bodies in the world with which the player can interact, improving the overall experience. The drawback, however, is that all this extra computation takes time away from the GPU to render the graphical portion of the game. This can be seen in the drop in both current and average frame rates moving from one PhysX setting (off) to another (high), resulting in the game just being playable. Moving back to the user experience, this type of system would only be possessed by a researcher/enthusiast (as the GPU and CPU used in this system cost hundreds of dollars each), pushing this type of user experience out of the regular user's domain.

27.4 OpenCL, CUDA OF THE FUTURE

The problem with CUDA is that it will only work with an NVIDIA GPU and, more often than not, requires a powerful GPU as was shown by the framerate change in Mafia II in the previous section. Although NVIDIA recently enabled CUDA to run on the CPU, it still requires running proprietary CUDA code. OpenCL steps in with respect to this and allows a single piece of code to run on any supported platform such as CPUs, GPUs, and most importantly, accelerators (excellent at performing one very specific task) from any supporting vendor including Intel, AMD, and NVIDIA. ARM has also announced its plan to support OpenCL with their next devices, enabling OpenCL to become one of the most pervasive "for consumer use" as well as "for HPC" APIs in the world [14]. In terms of actual developers/companies, Corel (creator of graphic design and video/audio editing software), Blender (a free, open-source 3-D content creation suite), and Bullet (an open-source physics engine) have taken a shine to OpenCL, reinforcing the belief that OpenCL will become the heterogeneous computing API of the future.

27.4.1 OpenCL

Now that we have covered the Cell BE, a discrete GPU system and APU systems as well as the history of GPU computing, we can begin to look at the future of GPU computing, the OpenCL, originally developed by Apple and, in 2008, passed to the Khronos group. From the Khronos website, we have a thorough explanation of OpenCL, after which we will explain its relevance to our applications.

> OpenCL is an open, royalty free-standard for cross-platform, parallel programming of modern processors found in personal computer computers, servers and handheld/embedded devices. OpenCL (Open Computing Language) greatly improves speed and responsiveness for a wide spectrum of applications in numerous market categories from gaming and entertainment to scientific and medical software [15].

OpenCL provides a flexible way to program for a heterogeneous architecture usable on almost any combination of operating system and hardware, making it an important starting point for our own applications. We begin with Table 27.1, which provides a quick comparison of OpenCL and CUDA and why we view OpenCL as the computing language of the future.

27.4.2 OpenCL Threading Model

Now that we have a basic understanding of OpenCL, we will look at the threading model OpenCL has in place to help us extract the maximum performance out of our GPUs. In OpenCL, each item or element we wish to compute is known as a work item. From these we have two groupings, one known as the local workgroup, the other being the global workgroup. To simplify the idea, we use Figure 27.7, which

TABLE 27.1. OpenCL versus CUDA, Hardware and Software Support

OpenCL	CUDA
Operating system agnostic	Operating system agnostic
Hardware agnostic	NVIDIA GPUs only
Open standards API	Proprietary, closed-source API
Gaining support (ARM) [14]	NVIDIA development only
Future proof (APU ready)	Not future ready (APU, ARM)

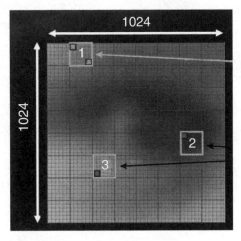

FIGURE 27.7. *OpenCL group dimensions are shown: 1, 2, and 3 are local workgroups composed of 128 × 128 elements, while the global workgroup includes 64 workgroups (128 × 128 elements), which total to 1024 × 1024 elements [19].*

shows a square with dimensions of 1024 × 1024. This large square represents our global workgroup composed of 1,048,576 (1024 × 1024) individual work items. From there, we must determine how our work will be split up on an OpenCL device (to create our local workgroups). It is important to note that this value (the maximum local workgroup size) is determined by the OpenCL device itself and is available through documentation or by performing a query of the OpenCL device's capabilities during runtime. From Figure 27.7 we can see the chosen local workgroup size is 128 × 128 given by 1024 items (width or height) divided into eight groups. This creates a total of 64 local workgroups (that make up the global workgroup) that our OpenCL device will run.

27.4.2.1 Data Partitioning Workgroup size becomes very important with respect to how we must partition our data for a number of reasons, first, being that all local workgroups are executed in parallel, which means they can be executed in any order. For example, workgroup 3 could be executed before workgroup 1 even though workgroup 1 comes "first" based on numbering. This leads into our next point being that only work items within a local workgroup can be synchronized in order to ensure the correct ordering of operations, such as in group 1. For some tasks, this is not important as all work items may be calculated in parallel if there are no data dependencies. If we are dealing with a situation similar to where group

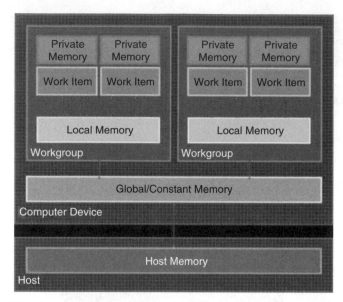

FIGURE 27.8. *The OpenCL memory model involves a few different types of memory provided by the GPU. These include the global memory, constant memory, local memory, and private memory. Each of these has a particular purpose, which will be explained in "GPU Memory Types," Section 27.4.4 [19].*

3 requires some data from group 2, we will have issues. This will mainly consist of the necessity of passing data from one local workgroup to another through global memory (which will be explained momentarily), incurring a large performance penalty in addition to the time required for synchronization.

27.4.3 OpenCL Memory Model

OpenCL provides a simple abstraction of device memory, though not to the level given by most modern programming languages. This has the disadvantage of forcing you as the programmer to manage memory, leading to slightly more complex programs. The upside of this manual memory management is that the algorithm can be tuned to take advantage of the incredibly fast memory architecture some devices such as GPUs provide. Before we show the differences between CPU and GPU memories, we will look at the different types of memory OpenCL provides with regard to GPUs as they include more varied and accessible memory than CPUs (Fig. 27.8).

27.4.4 GPU Memory Types

27.4.4.1 *Private Memory* At the lowest level, we have private memory, which is allocated by the runtime and is given to each thread (recall that each thread is a single work item) in the same manner as memory that is allocated to a CPU [7]. Private memory is not managed by the user other than through simply declaring variables within the OpenCL kernel. Due to this, we will not discuss private memory

TABLE 27.2. GPU Memory Types and Bandwidth for AMD Radeon 5870 [20]

Memory Type	Size per SE	Total Size on GPU	Peak Bandwidth
Private (registers)	256 kB	5120 kB	10 TB/s
Local	32 kB	640 kB	2 TB/s
Constant	–	48 kB	4 TB/s
Global	–	1 GB	153 GB/s
PCI Express v3.0	–	–	16 GB/s

any further other than its relevance to the other memory types with regard to memory bandwidth.

27.4.4.2 Local Memory   Next, we have the local memory, which is a block of at least 32 kB that is both read and write accessible to all threads in a local workgroup. We should also make the distinction that local memory is not a single block split over all workgroups, but rather, each local workgroup has its own 32 kB of local memory for its threads to share. This local memory is essentially a user-managed cache to speed access of items that are used within a workgroup. Another feature of local memory that is key to performance is the lack of mandatory memory coalescing. In layman's terms, without coalesced memory, out-of-order memory requests are performed sequentially instead of in parallel; local memory solves this problem for us. Local memory is an incredibly powerful tool when extracting performance since it is able to provide each SE with more than 100 GB/s of bandwidth, totaling over 2 TB/s for the entire GPU in the case of the AMD Radeon 5870.

27.4.4.3 Constant Memory   Constant memory (in the Radeon 5870) provides the second fastest method to access data with registers being the only faster type of storage. To give some hard numbers, we look at Table 27.2 to analyze the memory resources of a Radeon 5870. Note that some of the numbers will need to be changed based on the model of GPU as some hardware may be fused off, reducing the total amount of memory and aggregate bandwidth.

As we can see, registers obviously provide the most bandwidth at 10 TB/s, while constant memory can transfer 4 TB/s and local memory being limited to a "paltry" 2 TB/s. Due to constant memory's high bandwidth, we should attempt to use constant memory wherever possible. The drawback of constant memory is, obviously, that it is read only and is limited to 48 kB for the entire GPU as opposed to the 640 kB of local memory. The idea we are pushing is that the PCI Express bus should be avoided at all costs due to its increased latency and low bandwidth compared to any on-chip GPU memory. This includes global memory, which operates at a factor of roughly 1/13th the speed of local memory.

27.4.4.4 Global Memory   Up next is the global memory on the GPU device. It is a slow type of memory compared to the caches, constant and local memories, but it is accessible from all workgroups. This property enables global synchronization at the cost of increased latency and reduced bandwidth. Global memory also serves as the access point between the host (the CPU) and a compute device (a CPU [which can be the same as the host], GPU, or other accelerator). This means that

TABLE 27.3. CPU Memory Types and Bandwidth for Intel Xeon X5570 [21]

Memory Type	Memory Size	Bandwidth (GB/s)
L1 cache	32 kB (per core)	45.6
L2 cache	256 kB (per core)	31.1
L3 cache	8 MB	26.2
System RAM	–	10.1

you as the programmer must explicitly move data from the host to the device (and into local, constant, etc., memory) and back.

27.4.5 CPU Memory Types

There is a large difference in the memory available to CPUs as opposed to GPUs. CPUs typically have the caches abstracted out of the programming model and thus do not allow the programmer to choose a particular memory type to use. This abstraction causes problems with OpenCL code written for a GPU device when it is run on the CPU as local and global/constant memory are emulated in host/main memory (as the CPU does not have user accessible caches like the GPU). This leads to situations where local memory appears to have no benefit on the CPU but is quite beneficial on the GPU. This is an important difference to note as it goes to show that with OpenCL, no single algorithm can extract maximum performance from an architecture without being properly tuned. Additionally, we provide the following table just to show the difference in memory speed between CPUs and GPUs (see Table 27.3).

27.5 SIMPLE INTRODUCTION TO OpenCL PROGRAMMING

To give you a basic idea of what OpenCL code consists of, we will now look at a very simple, unoptimized algorithm after which we will implement a few optimization techniques to improve performance. Before we begin, if you have not read Section 27.2, "Heterogeneous Architectures," earlier, please go back and do so to gain a better understanding of the GPU architecture. This will provide the background regarding why the code looks like it does and should enable a basic understanding of how and why the optimization techniques work. You should also read over the OpenCL section once more to become familiar with the terminology used here and to begin to understand, from a high level, the OpenCL model of programming. Lastly, in an effort to abstract the complexity out of the host code, we will simply provide a pseudocode as this is not as important as the kernel code itself.

First, we look at the pseudocode for the host that is required to set up an OpenCL device, set parameters, enqueue a kernel for execution, and retrieve results with respect to a simple program. This program will take three values from an array of size 256 (to eliminate the complexities of scaling the algorithm for beginners), sum them together, and store them in a separate array.

Listing 27.1: OpenCL Host Program

```
// Retrieve a list of all devices in the system.
// Choose the device (CPU, GPU or accelerator).
// Create a device context; it controls device functions
// such as the command queue, memory and the kernel
// itself. These will be explained shortly.
// Create a command queue. This will enable you to tell
// the device what to do, such as writing to memory
// on the device or executing a kernel.
// Build the OpenCL program.
// Create input and output buffers on the device (two
// buffers are used so we don't write to the same
// memory location).
// Set the kernel arguments.
// Enqueue the kernel for execution.
// Retrieve results from the output buffer.
```

Next, for the sake of readability, please see the Appendix to view the OpenCL kernel codes, which, while very simple, show how an OpenCL program is very similar to a standard C program.

There are a few things to mention when looking at the code, which may be different from a similar code in C. We begin with the function declaration, which has two main points that differ from a function header in C. In OpenCL, every kernel is prefixed with "__kernel" to differentiate it from a standard function (even though OpenCL kernels can be called from the CPU). Next is that we have "__global" prefixed to certain variables in the header. The purpose of this is to show where these variables (or arrays in our case) will be stored on the device. In this example, we have chosen to store the arrays in the large, slow global memory, although local, constant, and texture memories are also options.

Now inside the kernel, we retrieve the thread ID, which is unique to each thread (using the get_global_id() function, as a sidenote, a get_local_id() function also exists) so that it knows which piece of data it should be working on. If we were to implement this same algorithm on a CPU, we would see one major difference: the use of a loop to go through each position of the new array and calculate its value. With OpenCL, we must change our thinking from "single thread executing all elements" to "hundreds or thousands of threads executing simultaneously." When thinking in these terms, we see that by executing the code on the OpenCL device, we define the outer loop in terms of parameters when setting up the kernel, such as creating a global workgroup of, say, 256 items. This way, we will have 256 threads executing one item in the OpenCL version, while the same sequential CPU code would have a loop so that one thread calculates all 256 items. This concludes the introduction to OpenCL programming section of this chapter, but continue reading to see how we can make some changes to the algorithm to speed it up.

27.5.1 A Few Optimization Techniques

Now that we have a basic algorithm that works correctly, we would like to improve performance. If we were designing an algorithm for the CPU, there would not be much more additional optimization that could be performed because CPU compilers are already very good at making optimizations for a particular device architecture. Since we are using a heterogeneous device, compilers are not yet as advanced as we would like them to be. This forces us to manually perform optimizations that eventually will be done by the compiler to maximize performance for the particular device architecture. In this section, we will cover a few techniques at a high level and explain why we try to use this optimization technique.

27.5.1.1 *Local Memory*

The first optimization we will look at is local memory, which can, depending on the nature of memory access in the algorithm (e.g., random and sequential), speed up the algorithm by a large factor due to the difference in speed, roughly 10 times if the algorithm is limited by memory speed. To begin, we can reuse almost the entire source code from earlier, but we must now add another buffer in the host code for the local memory (not shown). Additionally, because local memory is not directly accessible, we must move data from the host's memory to global memory to local memory (and back if necessary).

In the source code itself (see Appendix), we now have the additional buffer "loc_input." We prefix the name with "__local" to show that we would like this array to be created in the device's local memory as opposed to the device's global memory. Next, we copy over the data from global memory into local memory. Then, we have a new command, "barrier," which forces a synchronization step to occur. Synchronization is used to ensure all threads executing the code stop and wait until all other threads have also reached the synchronization point. This is necessary because, if we look at the code, we are reading from locations –1 to +1 of our ID. These values must be loaded into local memory before we execute the code; otherwise, we may retrieve incorrect (or uninitialized) values from local memory. The final change to our source code includes changing the read location from "input" to "loc_input" since we are now using local memory.

27.5.1.2 *Vectorization*

Another technique for improving performance is vectorization. From the earlier section on VLIW architectures, vectorization packs multiple small instructions into a single large instruction that the hardware can execute at one time. The simple example we provide performs two computes and stores per thread, which do not have any dependencies. Under a traditional model, there would be two individual instructions, which would be executed sequentially. Using vectorization, however, we have two instructions, each of which can be executed in parallel, potentially speeding up execution by two times. We will also note that vectorization support by current AMD GPUs is up to 16 items in parallel (though the hardware only supports a maximum of 4).

While vectorization does have the potential to speed up many of our computations, it also does complicate the code. First is that the host code must be changed to work with vectorized OpenCL data types such as the "cl_int2" type used here, rather than the simple "int" type used previously. We must also change the kernel header to note this new data type. This was done by changing the input data type to "int2" from "int." Finally, we have the calculations themselves as we must now manually determine how to map the work so that we get good device utilization. This can be seen in the kernel code (see the Appendix), which now has three extra calculations (one per "if" statement) in order to be able to execute two elements simultaneously.

27.6 PERFORMANCE AND OPTIMIZATION SUMMARY

If we were to use these algorithms and scale up the input to a large value such as 30,000 elements, we would see that even a simple GPU can provide extraordinary computational power if the algorithm has a large amount of data parallelism. What we have not covered here is that GPU solutions do not do well when data sizes are small. This is to be expected because we are more limited by the time it takes to transfer data back and forth from the GPU than the actual computation does (compared to the CPU). Providing a short summary of the advantages and disadvantages of each algorithm, we begin with the basic kernels that use global and local memory.

Overall, this is a very basic kernel that would work well as the array size increases, particularly since global memory is very large, enabling us to hold the entire array in just one memory location. The downside to this simple algorithm is that global memory is very slow compared to the other types of memory, and thus, we lose out on a large amount of performance. To somewhat alleviate this problem, we brought in the use of local memory, which can be many times faster than global memory. This has its own downsides, though, as local memory is not only small but is also subject to bank conflicts (two or more threads accessing the same memory location), which cause memory requests to be done sequentially, degrading performance. We will also note that bank conflicts may be introduced because of our next technique, as we are storing multiple subelements into a data type.

Next, in an effort to increase device utilization, we introduced vectorization, a method of packing independent instructions so that they may be executed in parallel. Vectorization also has its own problems, namely, it requires (at times) manually coding which work can be done in parallel, and vectorization may cause branching, which, on GPUs can drastically hurt performance as each branch must be executed sequentially. Lastly, vectorization is only beneficial on AMD GPUs due to their VLIW architecture (NVIDIA GPUs support vectorization but, because they use scalar ALUs, vectorized instructions are still executed sequentially). This concludes the optimization section of the chapter where we introduced a few techniques to improve GPU performance, though other techniques such as loop unrolling also exist.

27.7 APPLICATION

Now that we have covered some of the basics of OpenCL programming and a few of the optimization techniques that can be applied, we will look at the 0-1 knapsack problem to show how GPU computing performs. We begin with Figure 27.9 [16], which shows the execution times of the 0-1 knapsack problem for various sizes when run sequentially, in parallel, and on the GPU. As we can see, this naive algorithm does not perform well on the GPU simply because we are forcing synchronization to occur after each iteration. We also are limited to just 256 items for this initial GPU implementation as that is the largest size allowable for a single local workgroup.

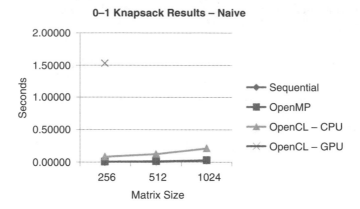

FIGURE 27.9. *The execution times from running a naive 0-1 knapsack algorithm on both a CPU and a GPU [16].*

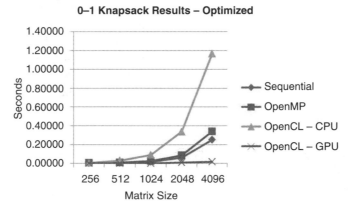

FIGURE 27.10. *The execution times from running an optimized 0-1 knapsack algorithm on both a CPU and a GPU [16].*

Next, Figure 27.10 shows the execution times for the algorithm optimized to take advantage of local memory and to avoid returning to the CPU for synchronization after every iteration. In this case, the algorithm has also been scaled up so that it supports input sizes greater than 256 items, enabling the parallel nature of the GPU to shine. Here, we see a drastic increase in performance compared to the previous algorithm for the GPU. However, upon closer examination, the OpenCL algorithm running on the CPU has actually become slower. This is due to the optimizations for the GPU, which add synchronization, something the CPU performs very poorly at compared with the GPU.

We now end with Figure 27.11 to show the speedup of the algorithm compared to the sequential algorithm. From the graph, we see that even with a relatively small input size of 512, the GPU is much faster than the CPU with the difference only becoming greater at larger input sizes. However, we should note that this algorithm was not fully optimized to take advantage of all the compute units within the GPU, leaving a large amount of performance untapped. It did, however, use a few of the

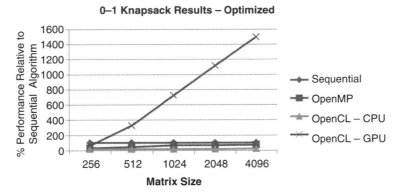

FIGURE 27.11. *The speedup of the GPU algorithm compared to the sequential CPU algorithm [16].*

optimization techniques we talked about in the previous section such as local memory and loop unrolling.

27.8 SUMMARY

This has been a very simple introduction to heterogeneous architectures and OpenCL's programming model and performance. We hope you have enjoyed this intoduction to OpenCL enough to take a serious look at its use for HPC. If you wish to learn more about OpenCL, please visit the Khronos website [15]. If you want to learn more about existing applications using AMD's Accelerated Parallel Processing SDK with examples using OpenCL, you can visit AMD's developer web page [17]. We will now spend a little time recapping everything we have learned about OpenCL and HPC. We have learned that there are various architectures, each of which has its own strengths and weaknesses. GPUs are of particular interest to us as they provide a great deal of computational power when used with algorithms that have a large amount of data parallelism. APUs, on the other hand, are somewhat weaker in terms of execution units but have the benefit of increased bandwidth and reduced latency between the CPU and GPU, enabling many more algorithms to be accelerated. We have seen that OpenCL can be used to extract the performance of the GPU in a simple example, and in the future, we will study more advanced OpenCL features to enable APU computing in situations where standard GPU computing is not possible.

Appendix

LISTING A.2: OPENCL KERNEL

```
__kernel void sum_values( __global int* input,
  __global int* output,
  int size)
{
```

```
// get the thread's global id, we use dimension 0 as
// the input because our arrays are 1 dimensional.
int id = get_global_id(0);
// handle the corner cases for the first and
// last threads so we don't go out of bounds.
if ( id == 0 )
{
output[id] = input[id] + input[id + 1];
}
else if ( id == size - 1 )
{
output[id] = input[id - 1] + input[id];
}
else
{
// split over two lines for formatting
output[id] = input[id - 1] + input[id]
+ input[id + 1];
}
}
```

LISTING A.3: OPENCL KERNEL OPTIMIZATION 1: LOCAL MEMORY

```
__kernel void sum_values( __global int* input,
__global int* output,
int size,
__local int* loc_input)
{
int id = get_global_id(0);
// load into local memory. Local memory is used
// because we will be re-using the data in multiple
// threads and local memory is much faster to access.
loc_input[id] = input[id];
// synchronize to ensure all threads have copied
// their data into loc_input before continuing.
barrier(CLK_LOCAL_MEM_FENCE);
if ( id == 0 )
{
output[id] = loc_input[id] + loc_input[id + 1];
}
else if ( id == size - 1 )
{
output[id] = loc_input[id - 1] + loc_input[id];
}
else
{
// split over two lines for formatting
output[id] = loc_input[id - 1] + loc_input[id]
```

```
+ loc_input[id + 1];
 }
 }
```

LISTING A.4: OPENCL KERNEL OPTIMIZATION 2: VECTORIZATION

```
__kernel void sum_values( __global int2* input,
 __global int2* output,
 int size,
 __local int2* loc_input)
{
 int id = get_global_id(0);
 loc_input[id].s0 = input[id].s0;
 loc_input[id].s1 = input[id].s1;
 barrier(CLK_LOCAL_MEM_FENCE);
 // The number of active threads will be cut by 1/2
 // since each thread will compute 2 values.
 if ( id < size )
 {
 if ( id == 0 )
 {
 // there is no input[-1]
 output[id].s0 = local_input[id].s0 +
 local_input[id].s1;
 output[id].s1 = local_input[id].s0 +
 local_input[id].s1 +
 local_input[id + 1].s0;
 }
 else if ( id == size - 1 )
 {
 // there is no input[id + 1]
 output[id].s0 = local_input[id - 1].s1 +
 local_input[id].s0 +
 local_input[id].s1;
 output[id].s1 = local_input[id].s0 +
 local_input[id].s1;
 }
 else
 {
 output[id].s0 = local_input[id - 1].s1 +
 local_input[id].s0 +
 local_input[id].s1;
 output[id].s1 = local_input[id].s0 +
 local_input[id].s1 +
 local_input[id + 1].s0;
 }
 }
 }
```

REFERENCES

[1] No author listed, *Top500—Jaguar*. Available at http://top500.org/system/10184.

[2] No author listed, *Top500—Roadrunner*. Available at http://top500.org/system/10377.

[3] No author listed, *Top500—TianHe-1A*. Available at http://top500.org/system/10587.

[4] J.A. Kahle, M.N. Day, H. Hofstee, C.R. Johns, T.R. Maeurer, and D. Shippy, "Introduction to the Cell multiprocessor," *IBM Journal of Research and Development*, 49(4.5):589–604, 2005.

[5] Advanced Micro Devices, *Heterogeneous Computing OpenCL™ and the ATI Radeon™ HD 5870 ("Evergreen") Architecture*. Available at http://developer.amd.com/gpu_assets/ Heterogeneous_Computing_OpenCL_and_the_ATI_Radeon_HD_5870_Architecture _201003.pdf.

[6] N. Brookwood, *AMD Fusion™ Family of APUs: Enabling a Superior, Immersive PC Experience*. March 2010.

[7] B. Gaster, L. Howes, D.R. Kaeli, P. Mistry, and D. Schaa, *Heterogeneous Computing with OpenCL*. Waltham, MA: Morgan Kaufmann, 2011.

[8] L. Pan, L. Gu, and J. Xu, "Implementation of medical image segmentation in CUDA," in *International Conference on Information Technology and Applications in Biomedicine, 2008*. Shenzhen, China, pp. 82–85, May 2008.

[9] L. Nyland and J. Prins, "Fast N-body simulation with CUDA," *Simulation*, 3:677–696, 2007.

[10] D. Komatitsch, D. Michéa, and G. Erlebacher, "Porting a high-order finite-element earthquake modeling application to NVIDIA graphics cards using CUDA," *Journal of Parallel and Distributed Computing*, 69(5):451–460, 2009.

[11] "Maya Shatter." Available at http://www.nshatter.com/index.html.

[12] *Video Editing Software, Multimedia Software and Blu-ray Playback Software by CyberLink*. Available at http://www.cyberlink.com/.

[13] *Guides: Mafia II Tweak Guide—GeForce*. Available at http://www.geforce.com/#/ Optimize/Guides/mafia-2-tweak-guide.

[14] A. Lokhmotov, *Mobile and Embedded Computing on Mali™ GPUs*. December 2010. Available at http://www.many-core.group.cam.ac.uk/ukgpucc2/talks/Lokhmotov.pdf.

[15] *OpenCL—The Open Standard for Parallel Programming of Heterogeneous Systems*. Available at http://www.khronos.org/opencl/.

[16] M. Doerksen, S. Solomon, P. Thulasiraman, and R.K. Thulasiram, "Designing APU oriented scientific computing applications in OpenCL," IEEE 13th International Conference on High Performance Computing and Communications (HPCC), Banff, Canada, pp. 587–592, September 2011.

[17] "AMD APP Developer Showcase," Available at http://developer.amd.com/sdks/ AMDAPPSDK/samples/showcase/Pages/default.aspx.

[18] M. Gschwind, "Chip multiprocessing and the cell broadband engine," in *Proceedings of the 3rd Conference on Computing frontiers*, CF '06, pp. 1–8, ACM, 2006.

[19] B.R. Gaster and L. Howes, *OpenCL™—Parallel Computing for CPUs and GPUs*. July 2010. Available at http://developer.amd.com/zones/OpenCLZone/courses/Documents/ AMD_OpenCL_Tutorial_SAAHPC2010.pdf.

[20] Advanced Micro Devices, *Ati Stream SDK OpenCL Programming Guide*. June 2010. Available at http://developer.amd.com/gpu_assets/ATI_Stream_SDK_OpenCL_ Programming_Guide.pdf.

[21] D. Molka, D. Hackenberg, R. Schone, and M.S. Muller, "Memory performance and cache coherency effects on an intel nehalem multiprocessor system," in *18th International Conference on Parallel Architectures and Compilation Techniques*, Raleigh, NC, pp. 261–270, September 2009.

28

Toward Optimizing Cloud Computing: An Example of Optimization under Uncertainty

Vladik Kreinovich

28.1 CLOUD COMPUTING: WHY WE NEED IT AND HOW WE CAN MAKE IT MOST EFFICIENT

In many application areas (bioinformatics, geosciences, etc.), we need to process large amounts of data, which require fast computers and fast communication. Historically, there have been limits to the amount of the information that can be transmitted at high speed, and these limits have affected information processing.

A few decades ago, computer connections were relatively slow, so electronically transmitting a large portion of a database required a lot of time. It was, however, possible to transmit the results of the computations quite rapidly. As a result, the best strategy to get fast answers to users' requests was to move all the data into a central location, close to the high-performance computers for processing this data.

In the last decades, it became equally fast to move big portions of databases needed to answer a certain query. This enabled the users to switch to a *cyberinfrastructure* paradigm, when there is no longer a need for time-consuming moving of data to a central location: The data are stored where they were generated, and when needed, the corresponding data are moved to processing computers; see, for example, References 1–5 and references therein.

Scalable Computing and Communications: Theory and Practice, First Edition. Edited by Samee U. Khan, Albert Y. Zomaya, and Lizhe Wang.
© 2013 John Wiley & Sons, Inc. Published 2013 by John Wiley & Sons, Inc.

Nowadays, moving whole databases has become almost as fast as moving their portions, so there is no longer a need to store the data where they were produced—it is possible to store the data where they will be best for future data processing. This idea underlies the paradigm of *cloud computing*.

The main advantage of cloud computing is that, in comparison with the centralized computing and with the cyberinfrastructure-type computing, we can get answers to queries faster—by finding optimal placement of the servers that store and/or process the corresponding databases. So, in developing cloud computing schemes, it is important to be able to solve the corresponding optimization problems.

We have started solving these problems in Reference 6. In this chapter, we expand our previous results and provide a solution to the problem of the optimal server placement—and to the related optimization problems.

28.2 OPTIMAL SERVER PLACEMENT PROBLEM: FIRST APPROXIMATION

For each database (e.g., a database containing geophysical data), we usually know how many requests (queries) for data from this database come from different geographic locations x. These numbers of requests can be described by the *geographic (request) density* function $\rho_r(x)$ describing the number of requests per unit time and per unit area around the location x. We also usually know the number of duplicates D of this database that we can afford to store.

Our objective is to find the optimal locations of D servers storing these duplicates—to be more precise, locations that minimize the average response time. The desired locations can also be characterized by a density function, namely, by the *storage density* function $\rho_s(x)$ describing the number of copies per geographic region (i.e., per unit area in the vicinity of the location x).

Once a user issues a request, this request is communicated to one of the servers storing a copy of the database. This server performs the necessary computations, after which the result is communicated back to the user. The necessary computations are usually relatively fast—and the corresponding computation time does not depend on where the database is actually stored. So, to get the answers to the users as soon as possible, we need to minimize the communication time delay.

Thus, we *need to determine* the storage density functio $\rho_s(x)$ that minimizes the average communication delay.

28.2.1 First Approximation Model: Main Assumption

In the first approximation, we can measure the travel delay by the average travel distance. Under this approximation, minimizing the travel delay is equivalent to minimizing the average travel distance.

28.2.2 Derivation of the Corresponding Model

How can we describe this distance in terms of the density $\rho_s(x)$? When the density is constant, we want to place the servers in such a way that the largest distance r to a server is as small as possible. (Alternatively, if r is fixed, we want to minimize the number of servers for which every point is at a distance $\leq r$ from one of the servers.)

In geometric terms, this means that every point on a plane belongs to a circle of radius r centered on one of the servers—and thus, the whole plane is covered by such circles. Out of all such coverings, we want to find the covering with the smallest possible number of servers.

It is known that the smallest such number is provided by an equilateral triangle grid, that is, a grid formed by equilateral triangles; see, for example, References 7 and 8.

Let us assume that we have already selected the server density function $\rho_s(x)$. Within a small region of area A, we have $A \cdot \rho_s(x)$ servers. Thus, if we, for example, place these servers on a grid with distance h between the two neighboring ones in each direction, we have:

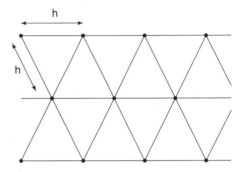

For this placement, the set of all the points that are closest to a given server forms a hexagonal area:

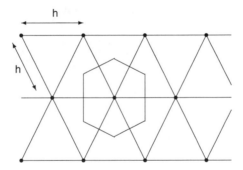

This hexagonal area consists of six equilateral triangles with height $h/2$:

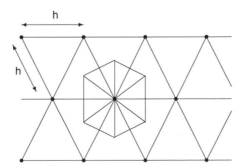

In each triangle, the height $h/2$ is related to the size s by the formula

$$\frac{h}{2} = s \cdot \sin(60°) = s \cdot \frac{\sqrt{3}}{2};$$

hence,

$$s = \frac{h}{\sqrt{3}} = h \cdot \frac{\sqrt{3}}{3}.$$

Thus, the area A_t of each triangle is equal to

$$A_t = \frac{1}{2} \cdot s \cdot \frac{h}{2} = \frac{1}{2} \cdot \frac{\sqrt{3}}{3} \cdot \frac{1}{2} \cdot h^2 = \frac{\sqrt{3}}{12} \cdot h^2.$$

So, the area A_s of the whole set is equal to six times the triangle area:

$$A_s = 6 \cdot A_t = \frac{\sqrt{3}}{2} \cdot h^2.$$

Each point from the region is the closest to one of the points from the server grid, so the region of area A is thus divided into $A \cdot \rho_s(x)$ (practically) disjoint sets of area $\sqrt{3}/2 \cdot h^2$. So, the area of the region is equal to the sum of the areas of these sets:

$$A = (A \cdot \rho_s(x)) \cdot \frac{\sqrt{3}}{2} \cdot h^2.$$

Dividing both sides of this equality by A, we conclude that

$$1 = \rho_s(x) \cdot \frac{\sqrt{3}}{2} \cdot h^2,$$

and hence, that

$$h = \frac{c_0}{\sqrt{\rho_s(x)}},$$

where we denote

$$c_0 \overset{\text{def}}{=} \sqrt{\frac{2}{\sqrt{3}}}.$$

The largest distance r to a server is thus equal to

$$r = \frac{h}{2} = \frac{c_0}{2 \cdot \sqrt{\rho_s(x)}}.$$

The average distance $\bar{d}$ is proportional to r, since when we rescale the picture, all the distances, including the average distance, increase proportionally. Since the distance r is proportional to $(\rho_s(x))^{-1/2}$, the average distance near the location

x is thus also proportional to this same value: $\bar{d}(x) = \text{const} \cdot (\rho_s(x))^{-1/2}$ for some constant.

At each location x, we have $\sim \rho_r(x)$ requests. Thus, the total average distance—the value that we would like to minimize—is equal to $\int \bar{\rho}(x) \cdot \rho_r(x) dx$ and is therefore proportional to

$$\int (\rho_s(x))^{-1/2} \cdot \rho_r(x) dx.$$

So, minimizing the average distance is equivalent to minimizing the value of the above integral.

We want to find the server placement $\rho_s(x)$ that minimizes this integral under the constraint that the total number of server is D, that is, that $\int \rho_s(x) dx = D$.

28.2.3   Resulting Constraint Optimization Problem

Thus, we arrive at the following optimization problem:

- We know the density $\rho_r(x)$ and an integer D.
- Under all possible functions $\rho_s(x)$ for which $\int \rho_s(x) dx = D$, we must find a function that minimizes the integral $\int (\rho_s(x))^{-1/2} \cdot \rho_r(x) dx$.

28.2.4   Solving the Resulting Constraint Optimization Problem

A standard way to solve a constraint optimization problem of optimizing a function $f(X)$ under the constraint $g(X) = 0$ is to use the Lagrange multiplier method, that is, to apply unconstrained optimization to an auxiliary function $f(X) + \lambda \cdot g(X)$, where the parameter λ (called *Lagrange multiplier*) is selected in such a way so as to satisfy the constraint $g(X) = 0$.

With respect to our constraint optimization problem, this means that we need to select a density $\rho_s(x)$ that optimizes the following auxiliary expression:

$$\int (\rho_s(x))^{-1/2} \cdot \rho_r(x) dx + \lambda \cdot \left(\int \rho_s(x) dx - D \right).$$

Having an unknown function $\rho_s(x)$ means, in effect, that we have infinitely many unknown values $\rho(x)$ corresponding to different locations, x. Optimum is attained when the derivative with respect to each variable is equal to 0. Differentiating the above expression with respect to each variable $\rho_s(x)$, and equating the result to 0, we get the equation

$$-\frac{1}{2} \cdot (\rho_s(x))^{-3/2} \cdot \rho_r(x) + \lambda = 0;$$

hence $\rho_s(x) = c \cdot (\rho_r(x))^{2/3}$ for some constant c.

The constant c can be determined from the constraint $\int \rho_s(x) dx = D$; that is,

$$\int c \cdot (\rho_r(x))^{2/3} dx = c \cdot \int (\rho_r(x))^{2/3} dx = D.$$

Thus,

$$c = \frac{D}{\int (\rho_r(x))^{2/3} dx},$$

and we arrive at the following solution.

28.2.5 Solution to the Problem

Once we know the request density $\rho_r(x)$ and the total number of servers D that we can afford, the optimal server density $\rho_s(x)$ is equal to

$$\rho_s(x) = D \cdot \frac{(\rho_r(x))^{2/3}}{\int (\rho_r(y))^{2/3} dy}.$$

28.2.6 Discussion

In line with common sense, the optimal server density increases when the request density increases, that is,

- in locations that generate more requests, we place more servers, and
- in locations that generate fewer requests, we place fewer servers.

However, when the request density decreases, the server density decreases slower because, otherwise, if we took the server density simply proportional to the request density, the delays in areas with few users would have been huge.

It is worth mentioning that similar conclusions come from the analysis of a different—security-related—optimization problem in which, instead of placing servers, we need to place sensors; see Reference 8.

28.3 SERVER PLACEMENT IN CLOUD COMPUTING: TOWARD A MORE REALISTIC MODEL

28.3.1 First Idea

In the above first approximation, we took into account only the time that it takes to move the data to the user. This would be all if the database was not changing. In real life, databases need to be periodically updated. Updating also takes time. Thus, when we find the optimal placement of servers, we need to take into account not only expenses on moving the data to the users but also the expenses of updating the information.

How do we estimate these expenses? In a small area, where the user distribution is approximately uniform, the servers are also uniformly distributed; that is, they form a grid with distance $h = 2r$ between the two neighboring servers [7, 8]. Within a unit area, there are $\sim 1/r^2$ servers, and reaching each of them from one of its neighbors requires time proportional to the distance $\sim r$. The overall effort of updating all the servers can be obtained by multiplying the number of servers by an effort needed to update each server and is thus proportional to $1/r^2 \cdot r \sim 1/r$. We already know that $r \sim (\rho_s(x))^{-1/2}$; thus, the cost of updating all the servers in the vicinity of a location x is proportional to $(\rho_s(x))^{1/2}$. The overall update cost can thus be obtained by integrating this value over the whole area. Thus, we arrive at the following problem.

28.3.2 Resulting Optimization Problem

- We know the density $\rho_r(x)$, an integer D, and a constant C that is determined by the relative frequency of updates in comparison with frequency of normal use of the database.
- Under all possible functions $\rho_s(x)$ for which $\int \rho_s(x)dx = D$, we must find a function that minimizes the expression

$$\int (\rho_s(x))^{-1/2} \cdot \rho_r(x)dx + \int C \cdot (\rho_s(x))^{1/2} dx.$$

28.3.3 Solving the Problem

To solve the new optimization problem, we can similarly form the Lagrange multiplier expression

$$\int (\rho_s(x))^{-1/2} \cdot \rho_r(x)dx + \int C \cdot (\rho_s(x))^{1/2} dx + \lambda \cdot \left(\int \rho_s(x)dx - D \right),$$

differentiate it with respect to each unknown $\rho_s(x)$, and equate the resulting derivative to 0. As a result, we get an equation,

$$-\frac{1}{2} \cdot (\rho_s(x))^{-3/2} \cdot \rho_r(x) + \frac{1}{2} \cdot C \cdot (\rho_s(x))^{-1/2} + \lambda = 0.$$

This is a cubic equation in terms of $(\rho_s(x))^{-1/2}$, so while it is easy to solve numerically, there is no simple analytical expression as in the first approximation case.

The resulting solution $\rho_s(x)$ depends on the choice of the Lagrange multiplier λ; that is, in effect, we have $\rho_s(x) = \rho_s(x, \lambda)$. The value λ can be determined from the condition that $\int \rho_s(x, \lambda)dx = D$.

28.3.4 Second Idea

The second idea is that, usually, a service provides a time guarantee, so we should require that, no matter where a user is located, the time for this user to get the desired information from the database should not exceed a certain value. In our model, this means that a distance r from the user to the nearest server should not exceed a certain given value r_0. Since $r \sim (\rho_s(x))^{-1/2}$, this means, in turn, that the server density should not decrease below a certain threshold, ρ_0.

This is an additional constraint that we impose on $\rho_s(x)$. In the first approximation model, it means that instead of the formula $\rho_s(x) = c \cdot (\rho_r(x))^{2/3}$, which could potentially lead to server densities below ρ_0, we should have $\rho_s(x) = \max c \cdot (\rho_r(x))^{2/3}, \rho_0)$.

The parameter c can be determined from the constraint

$$\int \rho_s(x)dx = \int \max(c \cdot (\rho_r(x))^{2/3}, \rho_0)dx = D.$$

Since the integral is an increasing function of c, we can easily find the solution c of this equation by bisection (see, e.g., Reference 9).

28.3.5   Combining Both Ideas

If we take both ideas into account, then we need to consider only those roots of the above cubic equation that are larger than or equal to ρ_0; if all the roots are $<\rho_0$, we take $\rho_s(x) = \rho$.

The resulting solution $\rho_s(x)$ depends on the choice of the Lagrange multiplier λ; that is, in effect, we have $\rho_s(x) = \rho_s(x, \lambda)$. The corresponding value λ can also be similarly determined from the equation $\int \rho_s(x, \lambda)dx = D$.

28.4   PREDICTING CLOUD GROWTH: FORMULATION OF THE PROBLEM AND OUR APPROACH TO SOLVING THIS PROBLEM

28.4.1   Why It is Important to Predict the Cloud Growth

In the previous sections, when selecting the optimal placement of servers, we assumed that we know the distribution of users' requests; that is, we know the density $\rho_r(x)$. In principle, the information about the users' locations and requests can be determined by recording the users' requests to the cloud.

However, cloud computing is a growing enterprise, so when we plan to select the server's location, we need to take into account not only the current users' locations and requests but also their future requests and locations. In other words, we need to be able to predict the growth of the cloud—both of the cloud in general and of the part corresponding to each specific user location. In other words, we need to predict, for each location x, how the corresponding request density $\rho_r(x)$ changes with time. This density characterizes the size $s(t)$ of the part of the cloud that serves the population located around x.

In the following text, we will refer to this value $s(t)$ as simply "cloud size," but what we will mean is the size of the part of the cloud that serves a certain geographic location (e.g., the United States as whole or the Southwest part of the United States). Similarly, for brevity, we will refer to the increase in $s(t)$ as simply "cloud growth."

28.4.2   How We Can Predict the Cloud Growth

To predict the cloud growth, we can use the observed cloud size $s(t)$ at different past moments of time t. Based on these observed values, we need to predict how the rate ds/dt with which the size changes depends on the actual size, that is, to come up with a dependence $ds/dt = f(s)$ for an appropriate function $f(s)$, and then use the resulting differential equation to predict the cloud size at future moments of time.

28.4.3 Why This Prediction is Difficult: The Problem of Uncertainty

The use of differential equations to predict the future behavior of a system is a usual thing in physics: This is how Newton's equations work; this is how many other physical equations work. However, in physics, we usually have a good understanding of the underlying processes, an understanding that allows us to write down reasonable differential equations—so that often, all that remains to be done is to find the parameters of these equations based on the observations. In contrast, we do not have a good understanding of factors leading to the cloud growth. Because of this uncertainty, we do not have a good understanding of which functions should be used to predict the cloud growth.

28.4.4 Main Idea of Our Solution: Uncertainty Itself Can Help

The proposed solution to this problem is based on the very uncertainty that is the source of the problem.

Specifically, we take into account that the numerical value of each quantity—in particular, the cloud size—depends on the selection of the measuring unit. If, to measure the cloud size, we select a unit that is λ times smaller, then instead of the original numerical value s, we get a new numerical value, $s' = \lambda \cdot s$. The choice of a measuring unit is rather arbitrary. We do not have any information that would enable us to select one measuring unit and not the other one. Thus, it makes sense to require that the dependence $f(s)$ look the same no matter what measuring unit we choose.

28.5 PREDICTING CLOUD GROWTH: FIRST APPROXIMATION

28.5.1 How to Formalize This Idea: First Approximation

How can we formalize the above requirement? The fact that the dependence has the same form irrespective of the measuring unit means that when we use the new units, the growth rate takes the form $f(s') = f(\lambda \cdot s)$. Thus, in the new units, we get a differential equation $ds'/dt = f(s')$. Substituting $s' = \lambda \cdot s$ into both sides of this equation, we get $\lambda \cdot ds/dt = f(\lambda \cdot s)$. We know that $ds/dt = f(s)$, so we get $f(\lambda \cdot s) = \lambda \cdot f(s)$.

28.5.2 Solution to the Corresponding Problem

From the above equation, for $s = 1$, we conclude that $f(\lambda) = \lambda \cdot \text{const}$, that is, that $f(s) = c \cdot s$ for some constant c.

As a result, we get a differential equation: $ds/dt = f(s) = c \cdot s$. If we move all the terms containing the unknown function s to one side of this equation and all the other terms to the other side, we conclude that $ds/s = c \cdot dt$. Integrating both sides of this equation, we get $\ln(s) = c \cdot t + A$ for some integration constant A. Exponentiating both sides, we get a formula, $s(t) = a \cdot \exp(c \cdot t)$ (with $a = \exp(A)$), which describes exponential growth.

28.5.3   Limitations of the First Approximation Model

Exponential growth is a good description for a certain growth stage, but in practice, the exponential function grows too fast to be a realistic description on all the growth stages. It is therefore necessary to select more accurate models.

28.6   PREDICTING CLOUD GROWTH: SECOND APPROXIMATION

28.6.1   Second Approximation: Main Idea

While it makes sense to assume that the equations remain the same if we change the measuring unit for cloud size, this does not mean that other related units do not have to change accordingly if we change the cloud size unit. In particular, it is possible that if we change a unit for measuring the cloud size, then to get the same differential equation, we need to select a different unit of time, a unit in which the numerical value of time takes the new form $t' = \mu \cdot t$ for some value μ, which, in general, depends on λ. Thus, in the new units, we have a differential equation, $ds'/dt' = f(s')$. Substituting $s' = \lambda \cdot s$ and $t' = \mu(\lambda) \cdot t$ into both sides of this equation, we get $\lambda/\mu(\lambda) \cdot ds/dt = f(\lambda \cdot s)$. We know that $ds/dt = f(s)$, so we get $f(\lambda \cdot s) = g(\lambda) \cdot f(s)$, where we denoted $g(\lambda) \overset{\text{def}}{=} \lambda/\mu(\lambda)$.

28.6.2   Solving the Corresponding Problem

If we first apply the transformation with λ_2 and then with λ_1, we get

$$f(\lambda_1 \cdot \lambda_2 \cdot s) = g(\lambda_1) \cdot f(\lambda_2 \cdot s) = g(\lambda_1) \cdot g(\lambda_2) \cdot f(s).$$

On the other hand, if we apply the above formula directly to $\lambda = \lambda_1 \cdot \lambda_2$, we get

$$f(\lambda_1 \cdot \lambda_2 \cdot s) = g(\lambda_1 \cdot \lambda_2) \cdot f(s).$$

By comparing these two formulas, we conclude that $g(\lambda_1 \lambda_2) = g(\lambda_1) \cdot g(\lambda_2)$. It is well known that every continuous solution to this functional equation has the form $g(\lambda) = \lambda^q$ for some real number q; see, for example, Reference 10. Thus, the equation $f(\lambda \cdot s) = g(\lambda) \cdot f(s)$ takes the form $f(\lambda \cdot s) = \lambda^q \cdot f(s)$.

From this equation, for $s = 1$, we conclude that $f(\lambda) = \lambda^q \cdot \text{const}$, that is, that $f(s) = c \cdot s^q$ for some constants c and q. As a result, we get a differential equation, $ds/dt = f(s) = c \cdot s^q$. If we move all the terms containing the unknown function s to one side of this equation and all the other terms to the other side, we conclude that

$$\frac{ds}{s^q} = c \cdot dt.$$

We have already considered the case $q = 1$. For $q \neq 1$, integrating both sides of this equation, we conclude that $s^{1-q} = c \cdot t + A$ for some integration constant A. Thus, we get $s = C \cdot (t + t_0)^b$ for some constants C and b (with $b = 1/(q - 1)$). In particular, if we start the time with the moment when there was no cloud, when we had $s(t) = 0$, then this formula takes the simpler form $s(t) = C \cdot t^b$.

This growth model is known as the *power function model*; see, for example, References 11–13.

28.6.3 Discussion

The power function model is a better description of growth than the exponential model, for example, because it contains an additional parameter that enables us to get a better fit with the observed values $s(t)$. However, as mentioned in References 12 and 13, this model is relatively rarely used to describe the growth rate, since it is viewed as a empirical model, a model that lacks theoretical foundations, and is therefore less reliable: We tend to trust more those models that are not only empirically valid, but also follow from some reasonable assumptions.

In the above text, we have just provided a theoretical foundation for the power function model, namely, we have shown that this model naturally follows from the reasonable assumption of unit independence. We therefore hope that with such a theoretical explanation, the empirically successful power function model will be perceived as more reliable—and thus, it will be used more frequently.

28.6.4 Limitations of the Power Function Model

While the power function model provides a reasonable description for the actual growth rate—usually a much more accurate description than the exponential model—this description is still not perfect. For example, in this model, the growth continues indefinitely, while in real life, the growth often slows down and starts asymptotically reaching a certain threshold level.

28.7 PREDICTING CLOUD GROWTH: THIRD APPROXIMATION

28.7.1 Third Approximation: Main Idea

To achieve a more accurate description of the actual growth, we need to have growth models with a larger number of parameters that can be adjusted to observations. A reasonable idea is to consider, instead of a single growth function $f(s)$, a linear space of such functions, that is, to consider functions of the type $f(s) = c_1 \cdot f_1(s) + c_2 \cdot f_2(s) + \ldots + c_n \cdot f_n(s)$, where $f_1(s), \ldots, f_n(s)$ are given functions and $c_1, \ldots, c_n$ are parameters that can be adjusted based on the observations.

Which functions $f_i(s)$ should be chosen? Our idea is the same as before: Let us use the functions $f_i(s)$ for which the change in the measuring unit does not change the class of the corresponding functions. In other words, if we have a function $f(s)$ from the original class, then, for every λ, the function $f(\lambda \cdot s)$ also belongs to the same class. Since the functions $f(s)$ are linear combinations of the basic functions $f_i(s)$, it is sufficient to require that this property be satisfied for the functions $f_i(s)$, that is, that we have

$$f_i(\lambda \cdot s) = c_{i1}(\lambda) \cdot f_1(s) + \ldots + c_{in}(\lambda) \cdot f_n(s)$$

for appropriate values $c_{ij}(\lambda)$ depending on λ.

28.7.2   Solving the Corresponding Problem

It is reasonable to require that the functions $f_i(s)$ be smooth (differentiable). In this case, for each i, if we select n different values $s_1, \ldots, s_n$, then for n unknowns $c_{i1}(\lambda), \ldots, c_{in}(\lambda)$, we get a system of n linear equations:

$$f_i(\lambda \cdot s_1) = c_{i1}(\lambda) \cdot f_1(s_1) + \ldots + c_{in}(\lambda) \cdot f_n(s_1);$$

$$\ldots$$

$$f_i(\lambda \cdot s_n) = c_{i1}(\lambda) \cdot f_1(s_n) + \ldots + c_{in}(\lambda) \cdot f_n(s_n).$$

By using Cramer's rule, we can describe the solutions $c_{ij}(\lambda)$ of this system of equations as a differentiable function in terms of $f_i(\lambda \cdot s_j)$ and $f_i(s_j)$. Since the functions f_i are differentiable, we conclude that the functions $c_{ij}(\lambda)$ are differentiable as well. Differentiating both sides of the equation

$$f_i(\lambda \cdot s) = c_{i1}(\lambda) \cdot f_1(s) + \ldots + c_{in}(\lambda) \cdot f_n(s)$$

with respect to λ, we get

$$s \cdot f_i'(\lambda \cdot s) = c_{i1}'(\lambda) \cdot f_1(s) + \ldots + c_{in}'(\lambda) \cdot f_n(s),$$

where g' denotes the derivative of the function g. In particular, for $\lambda = 1$, we get

$$s \cdot \frac{df_i}{ds} = c_{i1}' \cdot f_1(s) + \ldots + c_{in}' \cdot f_n(s),$$

where we denoted $c_{ij}' \overset{\text{def}}{=} c_{ij}'(1)$. This system of differential equations can be further simplified if we take into account that $ds/s = dS$, where $S \overset{\text{def}}{=} \ln(s)$. Thus, if we take a new variable $S = \ln(s)$ for which $s = \exp(S)$ and new unknowns $F_i(S) \overset{\text{def}}{=} f_i(\exp(S))$, the above equations take a simplified form:

$$\frac{dF_i}{dS} = c_{i1}' \cdot F_1(S) + \ldots + c_{in}' \cdot F_n(S).$$

This is a system of linear differential equations with constant coefficients. A general solution of such a system is well known: It is a linear combination of functions of the type $\exp(a \cdot S)$, $S^k \cdot \exp(a \cdot S)$, $\exp(a \cdot S) \cdot \cos(b \cdot S + \varphi)$, and $S^k \cdot \exp(a \cdot S) \cdot \cos(b \cdot S + \varphi)$.

To represent these expressions in terms of s, we need to substitute $S = \ln(s)$ into the above formulas. Here,

$$\exp(a \cdot S) = \exp(a \cdot \ln(s)) = (\exp(\ln(s))^a = s^a.$$

Thus, we conclude that the basic functions $f_i(s)$ have the form s^a, $s^a \cdot (\ln(s))^k$, $s^a \cdot \cos(b \cdot \ln(s) + \varphi)$, and $s^a \cdot \cos(b \cdot \ln(s) + \varphi) \cdot (\ln(s))^k$.

28.7.3   Discussion

Models corresponding to $f_i(s) = s^{a_i}$ have indeed been used to describe the growth; see, for example, References 12 and 13. In particular, if we require that the functions $f_i(s)$ be not only differentiable but also analytical, we then conclude that the only remaining functions are monomials $f_i(s) = s^i$. In particular, if we restrict ourselves to monomials of second order, we thus get growth functions $f(s) = c_0 + c_1 \cdot s + c_2 \cdot s^2$. Such a growth model is known as the *Bass model* [12–14]. This model describes both the almost-exponential initial growth stage and the following saturation stage.

Oscillatory terms $s^a \cdot \cos(b \cdot \ln(s) + \varphi)$ and $s^a \cdot \cos(b \cdot \ln(s) + \varphi) \cdot (\ln(s))^k$ can then be used to describe the fact that, in practice, growth is not always persistent; periods of faster growth can be followed by periods of slower growth and vice versa.

In the above description, we assumed that at each moment of time t and for each location x, the state of the part of the cloud that serves requests from this location can be described by a single parameter—its size, $s(t)$. In practice, we may need several related parameters, $s^{(1)}(t), \ldots, s^{(k)}(t)$, to describe the size of the cloud: the number of nodes, the number of users, the amount of data processing, and so on. Similar models can be used to describe the growth of two or more dependent growth parameters:

$$\frac{ds^{(i)}(t)}{dt} = f^{(i)}(s^{(1)}(t), \ldots, s^{(k)}(t)).$$

For example, in the analytical case, the rate of change of each of these parameters is a quadratic function of the current values of these parameters:

$$\frac{ds^{(i)}(t)}{dt} = a^{(i)} + \sum_{j=1}^{k} a_j^{(i)} \cdot s^{(j)}(t) + \sum_{j=1}^{k} \sum_{\ell=1}^{k} a_{j\ell}^{(i)} \cdot s^{(j)}(t) \cdot s^{(\ell)}(t).$$

For $k = 2$, such a model was proposed by Givon et al. [13, 15].

Similar models can be used to describe *expenses* related to cloud computing; see the Appendix.

28.8 CONCLUSIONS AND FUTURE WORK

28.8.1 Conclusions

This chapter presents the mathematical solutions for two related cloud computing issues: server placement and cloud growth prediction. For each of these two problems, we first list the simplifying assumptions then give the derivation of the corresponding model and the solutions. Then, we relax the assumptions and give the solution to the resulting more realistic models.

28.8.2 Future Work

The server placement problem is very similar to the type of problems faced by Akamai and other companies that do web acceleration via caching; we therefore hope that our solution can be of help in web acceleration as well.

ACKNOWLEDGMENTS

This work was supported in part by the National Center for Border Security and Immigration, by the National Science Foundation grants HRD-0734825 and DUE-0926721, and by Grant 1 T36 GM078000-01 from the National Institutes of Health. The author is thankful to the anonymous referees for useful advice.

Appendix
Description of Expenses Related to Cloud Computing

ANALYSIS OF THE PROBLEM

The chapter [16] analyzes how the price per core C_{core} depends on the per-core throughput T_{core} and on the number of cores N_{core}.

Some expenses are needed simply to maintain the system, when no computations are performed and $T_{\mathrm{core}} = 0$. In other words, in general, $C_{\mathrm{core}}(0) \neq 0$. It is therefore desirable to describe the additional expenses $\Delta C_{\mathrm{core}}(T_{\mathrm{core}}) \overset{\mathrm{def}}{=} C_{\mathrm{core}}(T_{\mathrm{core}}) - C_{\mathrm{core}}(0)$ caused by computations as a function of these computations' intensity. Thus, we would like to find a function $f(s)$ for which $\Delta C_{\mathrm{core}} \approx f(T_{\mathrm{core}})$.

MAIN IDEA

Similar to the growth case, we can use the uncertainty to require that the shape of this dependence $f(s)$ does not depend on the choice of a unit for measuring the throughput—provided that we correspondingly change the unit for measuring expenses.

RESULTING FORMULA

As a result, we get a power law, $\Delta C_{\mathrm{core}} \approx c_T \cdot (T_{\mathrm{core}})^b$; in other words, $C_{\mathrm{core}} \approx a + c_T \cdot (T_{\mathrm{core}})^b$, where we denoted $a \overset{\mathrm{def}}{=} C_{\mathrm{core}}(0)$.

DISCUSSION

Empirically, the above formula turned out to be the best approximation for the observed expenses [16]. Our analysis provides a theoretical justification for this empirical success.

DEPENDENCE ON THE NUMBER OF CORES IN A MULTICORE COMPUTER

A similar formula, $C_{\mathrm{core}} \approx a + c_N \cdot (N_{\mathrm{core}})^d$ can be derived for describing how the cost per core depends on the number of cores N_{core}. This dependence is also empirically the best [16]. Thus, our uncertainty-based analysis provides a justification for this empirical dependence as well.

REFERENCES

[1] A. Gates, V. Kreinovich, L. Longpré, P. Pinheiro da Silva, and G.R. Keller, "Towards secure cyberinfrastructure for sharing border information," in *Proceedings of the Lineae*

Terrarum: International Border Conference, pp. 27–30, El Paso, Las Cruces, and Cd. Juarez, March 2006.

[2] G.R. Keller, T.G. Hildenbrand, R. Kucks, M. Webring, A. Briesacher, K. Rujawitz, A.M. Hittleman, D.J. Roman, D. Winester, R. Aldouri, J. Seeley, J. Rasillo, T. Torres, W.J. Hinze, A. Gates, V. Kreinovich, and L. Salayandia, "A community effort to construct a gravity database for the United States and an associated Web portal," in *Geoinformatics: Data to Knowledge* (A.K. Sinha, ed.), pp. 21–34. Boulder, CO: Geological Society of America Publications, 2006.

[3] L. Longpré and V. Kreinovich, "How to efficiently process uncertainty within a cyber-infrastructure without sacrificing privacy and confidentiality," in *Computational Intelligence in Information Assurance and Security* (N. Nedjah, A. Abraham, and L. de Macedo Mourelle, eds), pp. 155–173. Berlin: Springer-Verlag, 2007.

[4] P. Pinheiro da Silva, A. Velasco, M. Ceberio, C. Servin, M.G. Averill, N. Del Rio, L. Longpré, and V. Kreinovich, "Propagation and provenance of probabilistic and interval uncertainty in cyberinfrastructure-related data processing and data fusion," in *Proceedings of the International Workshop on Reliable Engineering Computing REC'08* (R.L. Muhanna and R.L. Mullen, eds.), pp. 199–234, Savannah, GA, February 20–22, 2008.

[5] A.K. Sinha, ed., *Geoinformatics: Data to Knowledge*. Boulder, CO: Geological Society of America Publications, 2006.

[6] O. Lerma, E. Gutierrez, C. Kiekintveld, and V. Kreinovich, "Towards optimal knowledge processing: From centralization through cyberinsfrastructure to cloud computing," *International Journal of Innovative Management, Information & Production (IJIMIP)*, 2(2):67–72, 2011.

[7] R. Kershner, "The number of circles covering a set," *American Journal of Mathematics*, 61(3):665–671, 1939.

[8] C. Kiekintveld and O. Lerma, "Towards optimal placement of bio-weapon detectors," in *Proceedings of the 30th Annual Conference of the North American Fuzzy Information Processing Society NAFIPS'2011*, pp. 18–20, El Paso, Texas, March 2011.

[9] T.H. Cormen, C.E. Leiserson, R.L. Rivest, and C. Stein, *Introduction to Algorithms*. Cambridge, MA: MIT Press, 2009.

[10] J. Aczel, *Lectures on Functional Differential Equations and their Applications*. New York: Dover, 2006.

[11] G. Kenny, "Estimating defects in commerical software during operational use," *IEEE Transactions on Reliability*, 42(1):107–115, 1993.

[12] H. Pham, *Handbook of Engineering Statistics*. London: Springer-Verlag, 2006.

[13] G. Zhao, J. Liu, Y. Tang, W. Sun, F. Zhang, X. Ye, and N. Tang, "Cloud computing: A statistics aspect of users," in *CloudComp 2009*, Springer Lecture Notes in Computer Science (M.G. Jattun, G. Zhao, and C. Rong, eds), Vol. 5931, pp. 347–358. Berlin: Springer-Verlag, 2009.

[14] F.M. Bass, "A new product growth for model consumer durables," *Management Science*, 50(Suppl. 12):1825–1832, 2004.

[15] M. Givon, V. Mahajan, and E. Muller, "Software piracy: Estimation of lost sales and the impact of software diffusion," *Journal of Marketing*, 59(1):29–37, 1995.

[16] H. Li and D. Scheibli, "On cost modeling for hosetd enterprise applications," in *CloudComp 2009*, Lecture Notes of the Institute of Computer Sciences, Social-Informatics, and Telecommunications Engineering (D.R. Avresky, ed.), Vol. 34, pp. 261–269. Heidelberg: Springer-Verlag, 2010.

29

Modeling of Scalable Embedded Systems

Arslan Munir, Sanjay Ranka, and Ann Gordon-Ross

29.1 INTRODUCTION

The word "embedded" literally means "within," so embedded systems are information processing systems *within* (embedded into) other systems. In other words, an embedded system is a system that uses a computer to perform a specific task but is neither used nor perceived as a computer. Essentially, an embedded system is virtually any computing system other than a desktop computer. Embedded systems have links to physics and physical components, which distinguishes them from traditional desktop computing [1]. Embedded systems possess a large number of common characteristics such as real-time constraints, dependability, and power/energy efficiency.

Embedded systems can be classified based on their functionality as transformational, reactive, or interactive [2]. *Transformational* embedded systems take input data and transform the data into output data. *Reactive* embedded systems react continuously to their environment at the speed of the environment, whereas *interactive* embedded systems react with their environment at their own speed.

Embedded systems can be classified based on their orchestration/architecture as *single-unit* or *multiunit* embedded systems. Single-unit embedded systems refer to embedded systems that possess computational capabilities and interact with the physical world via sensors and actuators but are fabricated on a single chip and are enclosed in a single package. Multiunit embedded systems, also referred to as *networked embedded systems*, consist of a large number of physically distributed nodes

Scalable Computing and Communications: Theory and Practice, First Edition. Edited by
Samee U. Khan, Albert Y. Zomaya, and Lizhe Wang.
© 2013 John Wiley & Sons, Inc. Published 2013 by John Wiley & Sons, Inc.

that possess computation capabilities, interact with the physical world via a set of sensors and actuators, and communicate with each other via a wired or wireless network (since networked embedded systems are synonymous with multiunit embedded systems, we use the term multiunit embedded systems to describe these systems). Cyberphysical systems (CPSs) and wireless sensor networks (WSNs) are typical examples of multiunit embedded systems.

Interaction with the environment, timing of the operations, communication network, short time to market, and increasing customer expectations/demands for embedded system functionality have led to an exponential increase in design complexity (e.g., current automotive embedded systems contain more than 100 million lines of code). While industry focuses on increasing the number of on-chip processor cores and leveraging multiunit embedded systems to meet various application requirements, designers face an additional challenge of design scalability.

Scalability refers to the ability of a system or subsystem to be modified or adapted under varying load conditions. In other words, a system is scalable if the system's reliability and availability are within acceptable thresholds as the load or subsystems in the system increases. The scalability of a system can be classified based on geography and load [3]. A system is *geographically scalable* if the availability and reliability of the system are within acceptable thresholds no matter how far away the system's subsystems are located from each other. A *load-scalable* system exhibits acceptable availability and reliability as the load or subsystems in the system increases.

Scalability is of immense significance to embedded systems, in particular those that require several complex subsystems to work in synergy in order to accomplish a common goal (e.g., WSNs, CPSs). These systems often require adding more subsystems to the system without reengineering the existing system architecture. There are two main strategies for scaling embedded systems: scale-out and scale-up. In *scale-out*, which is commonly employed in multiunit embedded systems, more nodes or subsystems are added to the system (e.g., adding more sensor nodes in a WSN normally increases the sensor coverage in the sensor field as well as increases the availability and mean time to failure (MTTF) of the entire WSN due to an increase in the sensor node density). In *scale-up*, which is equally applicable to single- and multiunit embedded systems, more resources (e.g., computing power, memory) are added to the existing subsystems (e.g., sensor nodes can be equipped with more powerful transceivers to increase coverage).

Scalability should be distinguished from performance because these terms are related but are not synonymous (i.e., a system that scales well does not necessarily perform well). Ideally, the performance of a scalable system increases (or remains the same) and the availability increases as the system load or the number of subsystems in the system increases. The performance of an embedded system may or may not increase with scale-out or scale-in strategies. *Throughput* and *latency* are two important performance metrics for an embedded system. The throughput is the amount of work processed by a system in a given unit of time, whereas the latency is the amount of time required to complete a given task. In our WSN example, increasing the number of sensor nodes to increase situational awareness may actually decrease performance because of increased network congestion, which may increase the latency of the data delivered to a base-station node (sink node) and therefore may also delay the data processing at the sink node.

The scalability of embedded systems benefits from structured, distributed, and autonomous design. In particular, autonomous embedded systems that are able to perform data processing and decision making *in situ* are generally more scalable than nonautonomous embedded systems. In many applications, sensors in an embedded system generate an enormous amount of data, and limited communication bandwidth restrains the transmission of all the raw data to a central control unit. Scalability requires embedded systems/subsystems to process the information gathered from the sensors *in situ* and to make decisions based on the processed information. These autonomous embedded systems can scale to a very large number of nodes networked together while also reducing the need for human intervention/input by sending only concise, processed information to the network manager. To facilitate the design of scalable embedded systems with a complex design space and stringent design constraints, embedded system designers rely on various modeling paradigms.

Modeling of embedded systems helps to reduce the time to market by enabling fast application-to-device mapping, early proof of concept, and system verification. Original equipment manufacturers (OEMs) increasingly adopt model-based design methodologies for improving the quality and reuse of hardware/software (HW/SW) components. A model-based design allows development of control and dataflow applications in a graphical language familiar to control engineers and domain experts. Moreover, a model-based design enables the components' definition at a higher level of abstraction, which permits modularity and reusability. Furthermore, a model-based design allows verification of system behavior using simulation. However, different models provide different levels of abstraction for the system under design (SUD). To ensure timely completion of embedded system design with sufficient confidence in the product's market release, design engineers must make trade-offs between the abstraction level of a model and the accuracy a model can attain.

This chapter focuses on the modeling of scalable embedded systems. Section 29.2 elaborates on several embedded system application domains. Section 29.3 discusses the main components of a typical embedded system's hardware and software. Section 29.4 gives an overview of modeling, modeling objectives, and various modeling paradigms. We discuss scalability and modeling issues in single- and multiunit embedded systems along with the presentation of our work on reliability and MTTF modeling of WSNs as a modeling example in Section 29.5. Section 29.6 concludes this chapter and discusses future research directions related to the modeling of scalable embedded systems.

29.2 EMBEDDED SYSTEM APPLICATIONS

Embedded systems have applications in virtually all computing domains (except desktop computing), such as automobiles, medical, industry automation, home appliances (e.g., microwave ovens, toasters, washers/dryers), offices (e.g., printers, scanners), aircraft, space, military, and consumer electronics (e.g., smartphones, feature phones, portable media players, video games). In this section, we discuss some of these applications in detail.

29.2.1 CPSs

A CPS is an emerging application domain of multiunit embedded systems. The CPS term emphasizes the link to physical quantities, such as time, energy, and space. Although CPSs are embedded systems, this new terminology has been proposed by researchers to distinguish CPSs from simple microcontroller-based embedded systems. CPSs enable monitoring and control of physical systems via a network (e.g., Internet, Intranet, or wireless cellular network). CPSs are hybrid systems that include both continuous and discrete dynamics. Modeling of CPSs must use hybrid models that represent both continuous and discrete dynamics and should incorporate timing and concurrency. Communication between single-unit embedded devices/subsystems performing distributed computation in CPSs presents challenges due to uncertainty in temporal behavior (e.g., jitter in latency), message ordering because of dynamic routing of data, and data error rates. CPS applications include process control, networked building control systems (e.g., lighting, air-conditioning), telemedicine, and smart structures.

29.2.2 Space

Embedded systems are prevalent in space and aerospace systems where safety, reliability, and real-time requirements are critical. For example, a fly-by-wire aircraft with a 50-year production cycle requires an aircraft manufacturer to purchase, all at once, a 50-year supply of the microprocessors that will run the embedded software. All of these microprocessors must be manufactured from the same production line using the same mask to ensure that the validated, real-time performance is maintained. Consequently, aerospace systems are unable to benefit from the technological improvements in this 50-year period without repeating the software validation and certification, which is very expensive. Hence, for aerospace applications, efficiency is of less relative importance as compared to predictability and safety, which is difficult to ensure without freezing the design at the physical level [4].

Embedded systems are used in satellites and space shuttles. For example, small-scale satellites in low Earth orbit (LEO) use embedded systems for earth imaging and detection of ionospheric phenomenon that influences radio wave propagation (the ionosphere is produced by the ionization of atmospheric neutrals by ultraviolet radiation from the Sun and resides above the surface of the earth stretching from a height of 50 km to more than 1000 km) [5]. Embedded systems enable unmanned and autonomous satellite platforms for space missions. For example, the dependable multiprocessor (DM), commissioned by NASA's New Millennium Program for future space missions, is an embedded system leveraging multicore processors and field-programmable gate array (FPGA)-based coprocessors [6].

29.2.3 Medical

Embedded systems are widely used in medical equipment where a product life cycle of 7 years is a prerequisite (i.e., processors used in medical equipment must be available for at least 7 years of operation) [7]. High-performance embedded systems are used in medical imaging devices (e.g., magnetic resonance imaging (MRI), computed tomography (CT), digital X-ray, and ultrasound) to provide high-quality images, which can accurately diagnose and determine treatment for a variety of patients' conditions. Filtering noisy input data and producing high-resolution images at high data processing rates require tremendous computing power (e.g., video imaging applications often require data processing at rates of 30 images per second or more). Using multicore embedded systems helps in efficient processing of these high-resolution medical images, whereas hardware coprocessors, such as graphics processing units (GPUs) and FPGAs, take parallel computing on these images to the next step. These coprocessors off-load and accelerate some of the processing tasks that the processor would normally handle.

Some medical applications require real-time imaging to provide feedback while performing procedures, such as positioning a stent or other devices inside a patient's heart. Some imaging applications require multiple modalities (e.g., CT, MRI, ultrasound) to provide optimal images since no single technique is optimal for imaging all types of tissues. In these applications, embedded systems combine images from each modality into a composite image that provides more information than images from each individual modality separately [8].

Embedded systems are used in cardiovascular monitoring applications to treat high-risk patients while undergoing major surgery or cardiology procedures. Hemodynamic monitors in cardiovascular embedded systems measure a range of data related to a patient's heart and blood circulation on a beat-by-beat basis. These systems monitor the arterial blood pressure waveform along with the corresponding beat durations, which determines the amount of blood pumped out with each individual beat and heart rate.

Embedded systems have made telemedicine a reality, enabling remote patient examination. Telemedicine virtually eliminates the distance between remote patients and urban practitioners by using real-time audio and video with one camera at the patient's location and another with the treatment specialist. Telemedicine requires standards-based platforms capable of integrating a myriad of medical devices via a standard I/O connection, such as Ethernet, Universal Serial Bus (USB), or video port. Vendors (e.g., Intel) supply embedded equipment for telemedicine that supports real-time transmission of high-definition audio and video while simultaneously gathering data from the attached peripheral devices (e.g., heart monitor, CT scanner, thermometer, X-ray, ultrasound machine) [9].

29.2.4 Automotive

Embedded systems are heavily used in the automotive industry for measurement and control. Since these embedded systems are commonly known as electronic control units (ECUs), we use the term ECU to refer to any automotive embedded system. A state-of-the-art luxury car contains more than 70 ECUs for safety and comfort functions [10]. Typically, ECUs in automotive systems communicate with each other over controller area network (CAN) buses.

ECUs in automotive systems are partitioned into two major categories: (1) ECUs for controlling mechanical parts and (2) ECUs for handling information systems and entertainment. The first category includes chassis control, automotive body control (interior air-conditioning, dashboard, power windows, etc.), powertrain control (engine, transmission, emissions, etc.), and active safety control. The second category includes office computing, information management, navigation, external communication, and entertainment [11]. Each category has unique requirements for computation speed, scalability, and reliability.

ECUs responsible for powertrain control, motor management, gear control, suspension control, airbag release, and antilock brakes implement closed-loop control functions as well as reactive functions with hard real-time constraints and communicate over a class C CAN bus typically operating at 1 Mbps. ECUs responsible for the powertrain have stringent real-time and computing power constraints requiring an activation period of a few milliseconds at high engine speeds. Typical powertrain ECUs use 32-bit microcontrollers running at a few hundred megahertz, whereas the remainder of the real-time subsystems use 16-bit microcontrollers running at less than 1 MHz. Multicore ECUs are envisioned as the next-generation solution for automotive applications with intense computing and high reliability requirements.

The body electronics ECUs, which serve the comfort functions (e.g., air-conditioning, power window, seat control, and parking assistance), are mainly reactive systems with only a few closed-loop control functions and have soft real-time requirements. For example, the driver and passengers issue supervisory commands to initiate power window movement by pressing the appropriate buttons. These buttons are connected to a microprocessor that translates the voltages corresponding to button up and down actions into messages that traverse over a network to the power window controller. The body electronics ECUs communicate via a class B CAN bus typically operating at 100 Kbps.

ECUs responsible for entertainment and office applications (e.g., video, sound, phone, and global positioning system [GPS]) are software intensive with millions of lines of code and communicate via an optical data bus typically operating at 100 Mbps, which is the fastest bus in automotive applications. Various CAN buses and optical buses that connect different types of ECUs in automotive applications are, in turn, connected through a central gateway, which enables the communication of all ECUs.

For high-speed communication of large volumes of data traffic generated by 360° sensors positioned around the vehicle, the automotive industry is moving toward the FlexRay communication standard (a consortium that includes BMW, DaimlerChrysler, General Motors, Freescale, NXP, Bosch, and Volkswagen/Audi as core members) [11]. The current CAN standard limits the communication speed to 500 Kbps and imposes a protocol overhead of more than 40%, whereas FlexRay defines the communication speed at 10 Mbps with comparatively less overhead than the CAN. FlexRay offers enhanced reliability using a dual-channel bus specification. The dual-channel bus configuration can exploit physical redundancy and can replicate safety-critical messages on both bus channels. The FlexRay standard affords better scalability for distributed ECUs as compared with CAN because of a time-triggered communication channel specification such that each node only needs to know the time slots for its outgoing and incoming communications. To promote high scalability, the node-assigned time slot schedule is distributed across the ECU nodes where each node stores its own time slot schedule in a local scheduling table.

29.3 EMBEDDED SYSTEMS: HARDWARE AND SOFTWARE

An interesting characteristic of embedded system design is *HW/SW codesign*, wherein both hardware and software must be considered together to find the

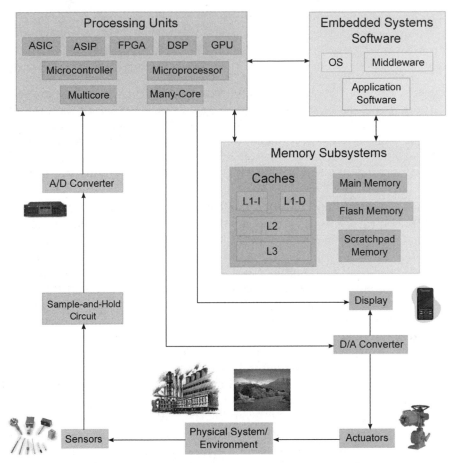

FIGURE 29.1. *Embedded system hardware and software overview. A/D converter, analog-to-digital converter; D/A converter, digital-to-analog converter; ASIC, application-specific integrated circuit; ASIP, application-specific instruction set processor; FPGA, field-programmable gate array; DSP, digital signal processor; GPU, graphics processing unit; OS, operating system; L1-I, level one instruction cache; L1-D, level one data cache; L2, level two unified cache; L3, level three unified cache.*

appropriate combination of hardware and software that would result in the most efficient product meeting the requirement specifications. The mapping of application software to hardware must adhere to the design constraints (e.g., real-time deadlines) and objective functions (e.g., cost, energy consumption) (objective functions are discussed in detail in Section 29.4). In this section, we give an overview of embedded system hardware and software as depicted in Figure 29.1.

29.3.1 Embedded System Hardware

Embedded system hardware is less standardized as compared to desktop computers. However, in many embedded systems, hardware is used within a loop where sensors gather information about the physical environment and generate continuous sequences of analog signals/values. Sample-and-hold circuits and analog-to-digital (A/D) converters digitize the analog signals. The digital signals are processed and the results are displayed and/or used to control the physical environment via actuators. At the output, a digital-to-analog (D/A) conversion is generally required because many actuators are analog. In the following sections, we briefly describe the hardware components of a typical embedded system [1]:

Sensors: Embedded systems contain a variety of sensors since there are sensors for virtually every physical quantity (e.g., weight, electric current, voltage, temperature, velocity, acceleration). A sensor's construction can exploit a variety of physical effects including the law of induction (voltage generation in an electric field) and photoelectric effects. Recent advances in smart embedded system design (e.g., WSNs, CPSs) can be attributed to the large variety of available sensors.

Sample-and-Hold Circuits and A/D Converters: Sample-and-hold circuits and A/D converters work in tandem to convert incoming analog signals from sensors into digital signals. Sample-and-hold circuits convert an analog signal from the continuous time domain to the discrete time domain. The circuit consists of a clocked transistor and a capacitor. The transistor functions like a switch, where each time the switch is closed by the clocked signal, the capacitor is charged to the voltage $v(t)$ of the incoming voltage $e(t)$. The voltage $v(t)$ essentially remains the same even after opening the switch because of the charge stored in the capacitor until the switch closes again. Each of the voltage values stored in the capacitor are considered as an element of a discrete sequence of values generated from the continuous signal $e(t)$. The A/D converters map these voltage values to a discrete set of possible values afforded by the quantization process that converts these values to digits. There exists a variety of A/D converters with varying speed and precision characteristics.

Processing Units: The processing units in embedded systems process the digital signal output from the A/D converters. Energy efficiency is an important factor in the selection of processing units for embedded systems. We categorize processing units as three main types:

1. *Application-Specific Integrated Circuits (ASICs).* ASICs implement an embedded application's algorithm in hardware. For a fixed process technology, ASICs provide the highest energy efficiency among available processing units at the cost of no flexibility (Fig. 29.1).

2. *Processors.* Many embedded systems contain a general-purpose microprocessor and/or a microcontroller. These processors enable flexible programming but are much less energy efficient than ASICs. High-performance embedded applications leverage multicore/many-core processors, application domain-specific processors (e.g., digital signal processors [DSPs]), and application-specific instruction set processors (ASIPs) that can provide the required energy efficiency. GPUs are often used as coprocessors in imaging applications to accelerate and off-load work from the general-purpose processors (Fig. 29.1).

3. *FPGAs.* Since ASICs are too expensive for low-volume applications and software-based processors can be too slow or energy inefficient, reconfigurable logic (of which FPGAs are the most prominent) can provide an energy-efficient solution. FPGAs can potentially deliver performance com-

parable to ASICs but offer reconfigurability using different specialized configuration data that can be used to reconfigure the device's hardware functionality. FPGAs are mainly used for hardware acceleration for low-volume applications and rapid prototyping. FPGAs can be used for rapid system prototyping that emulates the same behavior as the final system and thus can be used for experimentation purposes.

Memory Subsystems: Embedded systems require memory subsystems to store code and data. Memory subsystems in embedded systems typically consist of on-chip caches and an off-chip main memory. Caches in embedded systems are organized hierarchically: the level one instruction cache (L1-I) stores instructions; the level one data cache (L1-D) stores data; the level two unified cache (L2) stores both instructions and data; and recently, the level three unified cache (L3). Caches provide much faster access to code and data as compared to the main memory. However, caches are not suitable for real-time embedded systems because of limited predictability of hit rates and therefore access time. To offer better timing predictability for memory subsystems, many embedded systems, especially real-time embedded systems, use scratchpad memories. Scratchpad memories enable software-based control for temporary storage of calculations, data, and other work in progress instead of hardware-based control as in caches. For nonvolatile storage of code and data, embedded systems use flash memory that can be electrically erased and reprogrammed. Examples of embedded systems using flash memory include personal digital assistants (PDAs), digital audio and media players, digital cameras, mobile phones, video games, and medical equipment.

D/A Converters: Since many of the output devices are analog, embedded systems leverage D/A converters to convert digital signals to analog signals. D/A converters typically use weighted resistors to generate a current proportional to the digital number. This current is transformed into a proportional voltage by using an operational amplifier.

Output Devices: Embedded system output devices include displays and electro-mechanical devices known as actuators. Actuators can directly impact the environment based on the processed and/or control information from the embedded system. Actuators are key elements in reactive and interactive embedded systems, especially CPSs.

29.3.2 Embedded System Software

Embedded system software consists of an operating system (OS), middleware, and application software (Fig. 29.1). Embedded software has more stringent resource constraints (e.g., smaller memory footprint, smaller data word sizes) than traditional desktop software. In the following sections, we describe an embedded system's main software components:

OS: Except for very simple embedded systems, most embedded systems require an OS for scheduling, task switching, and I/O. Embedded operating systems (EOSs) differ from traditional desktop OSs because EOSs provide limited functionality but a high level of configurability in order to accommodate a wide variety of application requirements and hardware platform features. Many embedded system applications (e.g., CPSs) are real time and require support from a real-time operating system (RTOS). An RTOS leverages deterministic scheduling policies and provides predictable timing behavior with guarantees on the upper bound of a task's execution time.

Middleware: Middleware is a software layer between the application software and the EOS. Middleware typically includes communication libraries (e.g., message-passing interface (MPI), iLib application programming interface (API) for TILERA [12]). Some real-time embedded systems require a real-time middleware.

Application Software: Embedded systems contain application software specific to the embedded application (e.g., portable media player, phone framework, health-care application, and ambient conditions monitoring application). Embedded applications leverage communication libraries provided by the middleware as well as EOS features. Application software development for embedded systems requires knowledge of the target hardware architecture because assembly language fragments are often embedded within the software code for hardware control or performance purposes. The software code is typically written in a high-level language, such as C, which promotes application software conformity to stringent resource constraints (e.g., limited memory footprint and small data word sizes).

Application software development for real-time applications must consider real-time issues, especially the worst-case execution time (WCET). The WCET is defined as the largest execution time of a program for any input and any initial execution state. We point out that the exact WCET can only be computed for certain programs and tasks such as those without recursion, without while loops, and whose loops have statically known numbers of iterations [1]. Modern pipelined processor architectures with different types of hazards (e.g., data and control hazards) and modern memory subsystems composed of different cache hierarchies with limited hit rate predictability makes WCET determination further challenging. Since exact WCET determination is extremely difficult, designers typically specify upper bounds on the WCET.

29.4 MODELING: AN INTEGRAL PART OF THE EMBEDDED SYSTEM DESIGN FLOW

Modeling stems from the concept of abstraction (i.e., defining a real-world object in a simplified form). Marwedel [1] formally defines a model as: "A model is a simplification of another entity, which can be a physical thing or another model. The model contains exactly those characteristics and properties of the modeled entity that are relevant for a given task. A model is minimal with respect to a task if it does not contain any other characteristics than those relevant for the task."

The key phases in the embedded system design flow are requirement specifications, HW/SW partitioning, preliminary design, detailed design, component implementation, component test/validation, code generation, system integration, system verification/evaluation, and production [10]. The first phase, requirement specifications, outlines the expected/desired behavior of the SUD, and *use cases* describe potential applications of the SUD. Young et al. [13] commented on the importance of requirement specifications: "A design without specifications cannot be right or wrong, it can only be surprising!" HW/SW partitioning partitions an application's functionality into a combination of interacting hardware and software. Efficient and effective HW/SW partitioning can enable a product to more closely meet the requirement specifications. The preliminary design is a high-level design with minimum functionality that enables designers to analyze the key characteristics/functionality of an SUD. The detailed design specifies the details that are absent from the preliminary design, such as detailed models or drivers for a component. Since embedded systems are complex and are composed of many components/subsystems, many embedded systems are designed and implemented component-wise, which adds component implementation and component testing/validation phases to the design flow. Component validation may involve simulation followed by a code generation phase that generates the appropriate code for the component. System integration is the process of integrating the design of the individual components/subsystems into the complete, functioning embedded system. Verification/evaluation is the process of verifying quantitative information of key objective functions/characteristics (e.g., execution time, reliability) of a certain (possibly partial) design. Once an embedded system design has been verified, the SUD enters the production phase that produces/fabricates the SUD according to market requirements dictated by a supply-and-demand economic model. Modeling is an integral part of the embedded system design flow, which abstracts the SUD and is used throughout the design flow, from the requirement specifications phase to the formal verification/evaluation phase.

Most of the errors encountered during embedded system design are directly or indirectly related to incomplete, inconsistent, or even incorrect requirement specifications. Currently, the requirement specifications are mostly given in sentences of a natural language (e.g., English), which can be interpreted differently by the OEMs and the suppliers (e.g., Bosch or Siemens that provide embedded subsystems). To minimize the design errors, the embedded industry prefers to receive the requirement specifications in a modeling tool (e.g., graphical- or language-based). Modeling facilitates designers in deducing errors and quantitative aspects (e.g., reliability, lifetime) early in the design flow.

Once the SUD modeling is complete, the next phase is validation through simulation followed by code generation. Validation is the process of checking whether a design meets all of the constraints and performs as expected. Simulating embedded systems may require modeling the SUD, the operating environment, or both. Three terminologies are used in the literature depending on whether the SUD or the real environment or both are modeled: "Software-in-the-loop" refers to simulation where both the SUD and the real environment are modeled for early system validation; "rapid prototyping" refers to simulation where the SUD is modeled and the real environment exists for early proof of concept; and "hardware-in-the-loop" refers to simulation where the physical SUD exists and the real environment is modeled for exhaustive characterization of the SUD.

Scalability in modeling/verification means that if a modeling/verification technique can be used to abstract/verify a specific small system/subsystem, the same technique can be used to abstract/verify large systems. In some scenarios, modeling/ verification is scalable if the correctness of a large system can be inferred from a small verifiable modeled system. Reduction techniques, such as partial order reduction and symmetry reduction, address this scalability problem; however, this area requires further research.

29.4.1 Modeling Objectives

Embedded system design requires characterization of several objectives, or design metrics, such as the average-case execution time and WCETs, code size, energy/ power consumption, safety, reliability, temperature/thermal behavior, electromagnetic compatibility, cost, and weight. We point out that some of these objectives can be taken as design constraints since in many optimization problems, objectives can be replaced by constraints and vice versa. Considering multiple objectives is a unique characteristic of many embedded systems and can be accurately captured using mathematical models. A system or subsystem's mathematical model is a mathematical structure consisting of sets, definitions, functions, relations, logical predicates (true or false statements), formulas, and/or graphs. Many mathematical models for embedded systems use objective function(s) to characterize some or all of these objectives, which aids in early evaluation of embedded system design by quantifying information for key objectives.

The objectives for an embedded system can be captured mathematically using linear, piecewise linear, or nonlinear functions. For example, a linear objective function for the reliability of an embedded system operating in state s (Fig. 29.2) can be given as [14]

$$f_r(s) = \begin{cases} 1, & r \geq U_R \\ (r - L_R)/(U_R - L_R), & L_R < r < U_R \\ 0, & r \leq L_R, \end{cases} \tag{29.1}$$

where r denotes the reliability offered in the current state s (denoted as s_r in Fig. 29.2), and the constant parameters L_R and U_R denote the minimum and maximum allowed/tolerated reliability, respectively. The reliability may be represented as a multiple of a base reliability unit equal to 0.1, which represents a 10% packet reception rate [15].

Embedded systems with multiple objectives can be characterized by using either multiple objective functions, each representing a particular design metric/objective, or a single objective function that uses a weighted average of multiple objectives. A single overall objective function can be formulated as

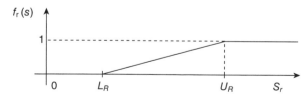

FIGURE 29.2. A linear objective function for reliability.

$$f(s) = \sum_{k=1}^{m} \omega_k f_k(s)$$

$$s.t. \quad s \in S$$

$$\omega_k \geq 0, \quad k = 1, 2, \ldots, m \tag{29.2}$$

$$\omega_k \leq 1, \quad k = 1, 2, \ldots, m$$

$$\sum_{k=1}^{m} \omega_k = 1,$$

where $f_k(s)$ and ω_k denote the objective function and weight factor for the kth objective/design metric (weight factors signify the weightage/importance of objectives with respect to each other), respectively, given that there are m objectives. Individual objectives are characterized by their respective objective functions $f_k(s)$ (e.g., a linear objective function for reliability is given in Equation 29.1 and is depicted in Fig. 29.2).

A single objective function allows selection of a single design from the design space; however, the assignment of weights for different objectives in a single objective function can be challenging using informal requirement specifications. Alternatively, the use of multiple, separate objective functions returns a set of designs from which a designer can select an appropriate design that meets the most critical objectives optimally/suboptimally. Often, embedded system modeling focuses on optimization of an objective function (e.g., power, throughput, reliability) subject to design constraints. Typical design constraints for embedded systems include safety, hard real-time requirements, and tough operating conditions in a harsh environment (e.g., aerospace), though some or all of these constraints can be added as objectives to the objective function in many optimization problems as described above.

29.4.2 Modeling Paradigms

Since embedded systems contain a large variety of abstraction levels, components, and aspects (e.g., hardware, software, functional, verification) that cannot be supported by one language or tool, designers rely on various modeling paradigms, each of which targets a partial aspect of the complete design flow from requirement specifications to production. Each modeling paradigm describes the system from a different point of view, but none of the paradigms covers all aspects. We discuss some of the modeling paradigms used in embedded system design in the following sections, each of which may use different tools to assist with modeling:

Differential Equations: Differential equation-based modeling can either use ordinary differential equations (ODEs) or partial differential equations (PDEs). ODEs (linear and nonlinear) are used to model systems or components characterized by quantities that are continuous in value and time, such as voltage and current in electrical systems, speed and force in mechanical systems, or temperature and heat flow in thermal systems [10]. ODE-based models typically describe analog electrical networks or the mechanical behavior of the complete system or component. ODEs are especially useful for studying feedback control systems that can make an unstable system stable (feedback systems measure the error [i.e., difference between the actual and desired behavior] and use this error information to correct the behavior). We emphasize that ODEs work for smooth motion where linearity, time invariance, and continuity properties hold. Nonsmooth motion involving collisions requires hybrid models that are a mixture of continuous- and discrete-time models [16].

PDEs are used for modeling behavior in space and time, such as moving electrodes in electromagnetic fields and thermal behavior. Numerical solutions for PDEs are calculated by finite element methods (FEMs) [16].

State Machines: State machines are used for modeling discrete dynamics and are especially suitable for reactive systems. Finite-state machines (FSMs) and statecharts are some of the popular examples of state machines. Communicating finite-state machines (CFSMs) represent several FSMs communicating with each other. Statecharts extend FSMs with a mechanism for describing hierarchy and concurrency. Hierarchy is incorporated using *superstates* and *substates*, where superstates are states that comprise other substates [1]. Concurrency in statecharts is modeled using *AND-states*. If a system containing a superstate S is always in all of the substates of S whenever the system is in S, then the superstate S is an *AND-superstate*.

Dataflow: Dataflow modeling identifies and models data movement in an information system. Dataflow modeling represents processes that transform data from one form to another, external entities that receive data from a system or send data into the system, data stores that hold data, and dataflow that indicates the routes over which the data can flow. A dataflow model is represented by a directed graph where the nodes/vertices, *actors*, represent computation (computation maps input data streams into output data streams) and the arcs represent communication channels. Synchronous dataflow (SDF) and Kahn process networks (KPNs) are common examples of dataflow models. The key characteristics of these dataflow models is that SDFs assume that all actors execute in a single clock cycle, whereas KPNs permit actors to execute with any finite delay [1].

Discrete Event-Based Modeling: Discrete event-based modeling is based on the notion of firing or executing a sequence of discrete events, which are stored in a queue and are sorted by the time at which these events should be processed. An event corresponding to the current time is removed from the queue, processed by performing the necessary actions, and new events may be enqueued based on the action's results [1]. If there is no event in the queue for the current time, the time advances. Hardware description languages (e.g., VHDL, Verilog) are typically based on discrete event modeling. SystemC, which is a system-level modeling language, is also based on the discrete event modeling paradigm.

Stochastic Models: Numerous stochastic models exist, which mainly differ in the assumed distributions of the state residence times, to describe and analyze system performance and dependability. Analyzing an embedded system's performance in an early design phase can significantly reduce late-detected, and therefore cost-intensive, problems. Markov chains and queueing models are popular examples of stochastic models. The state residence times in Markov chains are typically assumed to have exponential distributions because exponential distributions lead to efficient numerical analysis, although other generalizations are also possible. Performance measures are obtained from Markov chains by determining steady-state and transient-state probabilities. Queueing models are used to model systems that can be associated with some notion of queues. Queueing models are stochastic models since these models represent the probability of finding a queueing system in a particular configuration or state.

Stochastic models can capture the complex interactions between an embedded system and the embedded system's environment. Timeliness, concurrency, and interaction with the environment are primary characteristics of many embedded systems, and *nondeterminism* enables stochastic models to incorporate these characteristics. Specifically, nondeterminism is used for modeling unknown aspects of the environment or system. Markov decision processes (MDPs) are discrete stochastic dynamic programs, an extension of discrete-time Markov chains, that exhibit nondeterminism. MDPs associate a reward with each state in the Markov chain.

Petri Nets: A Petri net is a mathematical language for describing distributed systems and is represented by a directed, bipartite graph. The key elements of Petri nets are conditions, events, and a flow relation. Conditions are either satisfied or not satisfied. The flow relation describes the conditions that must be met before an event can fire as well as prescribes the conditions that become true after an event fires. Activity charts in unified modeling language (UML) are based on Petri nets [1].

29.4.3 Strategies for Integration of Modeling Paradigms

Describing different aspects and views of an entire embedded system, subsystem, or component over different development phases requires different modeling paradigms. However, sometimes, partial descriptions of a system need to be integrated for simulation and code generation. Multiparadigm languages integrate different modeling paradigms. There are two types of multiparadigm modeling [10]:

1. One model describing a system complements another model, resulting in a model of the complete system.
2. Two models give different views of the same system.

UML is an example of multiparadigm modeling, which is often used to describe software-intensive system components. UML enables the designer to verify a design before any HW/SW code is written/generated [17] and allows generation of the appropriate code for the embedded system using a set of rules. UML offers a structured and repeatable design: If there is a problem with the behavior of the application, then the model is changed accordingly, and if the problem lies in the performance of the code, then the rules are adjusted. Similarly, MATLAB's Simulink modeling environment integrates continuous-time and discrete-time models of computation based on equation solvers, a discrete event model, and an FSM model.

Two strategies for the integration of heterogeneous modeling paradigms are [10]:

1. integration of operations (analysis, synthesis) on models
2. integration of models themselves via model translation.

We briefly describe several different integration approaches that leverage these strategies in the following sections.

Cosimulation: Cosimulation permits simulation of partial models of a system in different tools and integrates the simulation process. Cosimulation depends on a central cosimulation engine, called a *simulation backplane*, that mediates between the distributed simulations run by the simulation engines of the participating computer-aided software engineering (CASE) tools. Cosimulation is useful and sufficient for model validation when simulation is the only purpose of model integration. In general, cosimulation is useful for the combination of a system model with a model of the system's environment since the system model is constructed completely in one tool and enters into the code generation phase, whereas the environment model is only used for simulation. Alternatively, cosimulation is insufficient if both of the models (the system and the system's environment) are intended for code generation.

Code Integration: Many modeling tools have associated code generators, and code integration is the process of integrating the generated code from multiple modeling tools. Code integration tools expedite the design process because in the absence of a code integration tool, subsystem code generated by different tools have to be integrated manually.

Code Encapsulation: Code encapsulation is a feature offered by many CASE tools that permits code encapsulation of a subsystem model as a black box in the overall system model. Code encapsulation facilitates automated code integration as well as overall system simulation.

Model Encapsulation: In model encapsulation, an original subsystem model is encapsulated as an equivalent subsystem model in the modeling language of the enclosing system. Model encapsulation permits *coordinated code generation*, in which the code generation for the enclosing system drives the code generator for the subsystem. The enclosing system tool can be regarded as a master tool and the encapsulated subsystem tool as a slave tool; therefore, model encapsulation requires the master tool to have knowledge of the slave tool.

Model Translation: In model translation, a subsystem model is translated syntactically and semantically to the language of the enclosing system. This translation results in a homogeneous overall system model so that one tool chain can be used for further processing of the complete system.

29.5 SINGLE- AND MULTIUNIT EMBEDDED SYSTEM MODELING

In this section, we discuss the scalability and modeling issues in single- and multiunit embedded systems. We elaborate on the modeling of scalable embedded systems using our work on reliability and MTTF modeling of WSNs [18].

29.5.1 Single-Unit Embedded Systems

A single-unit embedded system is an embedded system that contains various components (e.g., processor, memory, sensors, A/D converter) typically integrated onto a single chip and enclosed in a single package. Based on the specific application requirements, a single-unit embedded system can leverage any processor architecture, such as single-, multi-, or many-core.

As the number of cores in a single-unit multicore embedded system increases, scalability becomes a key design concern. To enhance scalability, particularly for many-core embedded systems, designers favor a distributed and structured design. Hence, cores in many-core embedded systems are typically arranged in a gridlike pattern and possess a distributed private memory and a common shared memory, similarly to TILERA's TILEPro64 [19]. The interconnection network has a significant affect on the scalability of many-core embedded systems. The interconnection network for a single-unit embedded system can contain buses, point-to-point connections, or a network-on-chip (NoC).

Buses and point-to-point connections are commonly used for single-unit embedded systems that consist of a small number of processor cores. Point-to-point and bus connections do not scale well as the number of processor cores increases because point-to-point connections suffer from an exponential increase in the number of connections between the processor cores due to the following two reasons [20]:

1. A single bus cannot provide concurrent transactions since, depending on the arbitration algorithm, access is granted to the device/component with the highest priority. Hence, bus-based interconnection networks block transactions that could potentially execute in parallel.
2. Large bus wire lengths can lead to unmanageable clock skews for large system-on-chips (SoCs) at high clock frequencies.

NoCs provide a scalable interconnection network solution for many-core embedded systems. NoCs provide higher bandwidths, higher flexibility, and solve the clock skew problems inherent in large SoCs. Inspired from the success and scalability of the Internet, NoCs use switch-based routers and packet-based communication. The following summarizes some of NoC's features that enable the NoC to scale well for many-core embedded systems [20]:

1. NoCs do not require dedicated address lines (like in bus-based interconnection networks) because NoCs use packet-based communication where the destination address is embedded in the packet header.
2. NoCs enable concurrent transactions if the network provides more than one transmission channel between a sender and a receiver.
3. NoCs eliminate clock skew issues in large SoCs because routers provide the necessary decoupling.
4. NoCs facilitate routing of wires since cores are arranged on a chip in a regular manner connected by routers and wires.

29.5.2 Multiunit Embedded Systems

Multiunit embedded systems are composed of two or more single-unit embedded systems interconnected by a wired or a wireless link. Since multiunit embedded systems consist of single-unit embedded systems, the modeling and scalability issues for single-unit embedded systems are also applicable to each constituting unit in multiunit embedded systems. Therefore, for brevity, we do not discuss the modeling and scalability issues of the single units within a multiunit embedded system. Additional scalability issues arise in multiunit embedded systems as the number of single-unit embedded systems increases. Furthermore, multiunit embedded systems present additional challenges in the design flow, particularly in modeling and verification.

Verification of multiunit embedded systems is a two-level process: single-unit verification and multiunit verification. Single-unit verification ensures that the individual embedded units work properly with well-defined interfaces that interact with the environment. Single-unit verification requires a model for the single-unit embedded system and specifications for the desired behavior. Multiunit verification ensures the correctness of the integrated system given a correct single-unit behavior. Multiunit verification requires an integrated model for the complete system, which is composed of single-unit models and the underlying communication network model.

Meeting real-time constraints in multiunit embedded systems introduces further challenges. Any real-time, multiunit embedded system requires the underlying interconnection/communication network to provide real-time guarantees for message transmissions, which is challenging given current networking technologies.

29.5.3 Reliability and MTTF Modeling of WSNs

This section presents our work on MTTF and reliability modeling of WSNs to elaborate on the modeling of scalable embedded systems with a practical modeling example. WSNs consist of spatially distributed autonomous sensor nodes that collaborate with each other to perform an application task. Figure 29.3 shows a typical WSN architecture. The sensor nodes distributed in the *sensor field* gather information (sensed data or statistics) about an observed phenomenon (e.g., environment, target) using attached sensors. A group of sensor nodes is called a *WSN cluster*. Each WSN cluster has one *cluster head*. Sensed data within a WSN cluster is collected by the cluster head and is relayed to a *sink node* (or base station) via the sensor nodes' ad hoc network. The sink node transmits the received information back to the *WSN designer* and/or the *WSN manager* via a gateway node connected to a computer network. The WSN designer is responsible for designing the WSN for a particular application to meet application requirements, such as lifetime, reliability, and throughput. After WSN design and deployment, the WSN manager manages WSN operations, such as data analysis, monitoring alive and dead sensor nodes, and alarm conditions (e.g., forest fire, volcano eruption, enemy troops).

WSN sensor nodes are typically mass produced and are often deployed in unattended and hostile environments, making them more susceptible to failures than other systems [21]. Additionally, manual inspection of faulty sensor nodes after deployment is typically impractical. Nevertheless, many WSN applications are

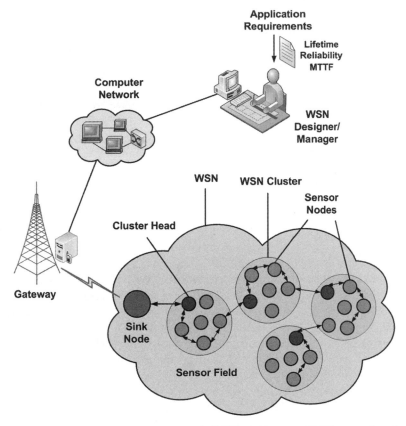

FIGURE 29.3. *A typical wireless sensor network (WSN) architecture. MTTF, mean time to failure.*

mission critical, requiring continuous operation. Thus, in order to meet application requirements reliably, WSNs require fault detection and fault-tolerance (FT) mechanisms.

Fault detection encompasses distributed fault detection (DFD) algorithms that identify faulty sensor readings that indicate faulty sensors. DFD algorithms typically use existing network traffic to identify sensor failures and therefore do not incur any additional transmission cost. A fault detection algorithm's *accuracy* signifies the algorithm's ability to accurately identify faults. Though fault detection helps in isolating faulty sensors, WSNs require FT to reliably accomplish application tasks.

One of the most prominent FT techniques is to add hardware and/or software redundancy to the system [22]. However, WSNs are different from other systems as they have stringent constraints, and the added redundancy for FT must justify the additional cost. Studies indicate that sensors (e.g., temperature, humidity) in a sensor node have comparatively higher fault rates than other components (e.g., processors, transceivers) [23, 24]. Fortunately, sensors are cheap and adding spare sensors contributes little to the individual sensor node's cost.

29.5.3.1 *FT Parameters* The FT parameters leveraged in our Markov model are *coverage factor* and *sensor failure probability*. The coverage factor c is defined

as the probability that the faulty active sensor is correctly diagnosed, disconnected, and replaced by a good inactive spare sensor. The c estimation is critical in an FT WSN model and can be determined by

$$c = c_k - c_c, \tag{29.3}$$

where c_k denotes the accuracy of the fault detection algorithm in diagnosing faulty sensors and c_c denotes the probability of an unsuccessful replacement of the identified faulty sensor with a good spare sensor. c_c depends upon the sensor switching circuitry and is usually a constant, and c_k depends upon the average number of sensor node neighbors k and the probability of sensor failure p [25, 26].

The sensor failure probability p can be represented using an exponential distribution with failure rate λ_s over the period t_s (the period t_s signifies the time over which the sensor failure probability p is specified) [27]. Thus, we can write

$$p = 1 - \exp(-\lambda_s t_s). \tag{29.4}$$

29.5.3.2 *Fault-Tolerant Sensor Node Model*

We propose an FT duplex sensor node model consisting of one active sensor (such as a temperature sensor) and one inactive spare sensor. The inactive sensor becomes active only once the active sensor is declared faulty by the fault detection algorithm. Figure 29.4 shows the Markov model for our proposed FT sensor node. The states in the Markov model represent the number of good sensors. The differential equations describing the sensor node duplex Markov model are

$$
\begin{aligned}
P_2'(t) &= -\lambda_t P_2(t) \\
P_1'(t) &= \lambda_t c P_2(t) - \lambda_t P_1(t) \\
P_0'(t) &= \lambda_t (1-c) P_2(t) + \lambda_t P_1(t),
\end{aligned}
\tag{29.5}
$$

where $P_i(t)$ denotes the probability that the sensor node will be in state i at time t and $P_i'(t)$ represents the first-order derivative of $P_i(t)$. λ_t represents the failure rate of an active temperature sensor and the rate at which recoverable failure occurs is $c\lambda_t$. The probability that the sensor failure cannot be recovered is $(1 - c)$, and the rate at which an unrecoverable failure occurs is $(1 - c)\lambda_t$.

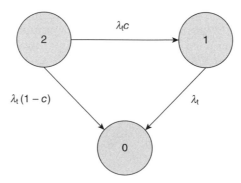

FIGURE 29.4. *Sensor node Markov model.*

Solving Equation (29.5) with the initial conditions $P_2(0) = 1$, $P_1(0) = 0$, and $P_0(0) = 0$, the reliability of the duplex sensor node is given by

$$R_{s_d}(t) = 1 - P_0(t)$$
$$= e^{-\lambda_t t} + c\lambda_t t e^{-\lambda_t t}. \qquad (29.6)$$

The MTTF of the duplex sensor system is

$$\text{MTTF}_{s_d} = \int_0^\infty R_{s_d}(t)dt$$
$$= \frac{1}{\lambda_t} + \frac{c}{\lambda_t}. \qquad (29.7)$$

The average failure rate of the duplex sensor system depends on k (since the fault detection algorithm's accuracy depends on k [Section 29.5.3.1]) and is given by

$$\lambda_{s_d(k)} = \frac{1}{\text{MTTF}_{s_d(k)}}. \qquad (29.8)$$

29.5.3.3 Fault-Tolerant WSN Cluster Model

A typical WSN consists of many clusters, and we assume for our model that all nodes in a cluster are neighbors to each other. If the average number of nodes in a cluster is n, then the average number of neighbor nodes per sensor node is $k = n - 1$. Figure 29.5 depicts our Markov model for a WSN cluster. We assume that a cluster fails (i.e., fails to perform its assigned application task) if the number of alive (nonfaulty) sensor nodes in the cluster reduces to k_{min}. The differential equations describing the WSN cluster Markov model are

$$P_n'(t) = -n\lambda_{s_d(n-1)}P_n(t)$$
$$P_{n-1}'(t) = n\lambda_{s_d(n-1)}P_n(t) - (n-1)\lambda_{s_d(n-2)}P_{n-1}(t)$$
$$\vdots \qquad (29.9)$$
$$P_{k_{min}}'(t) = (k_{min} + 1)\lambda_{s_d(k_{min})}P_{k_{min}+1}(t),$$

where $\lambda_{s_d(n-1)}$, $\lambda_{s_d(n-2)}$, and $\lambda_{s_d(k_{min})}$ represent the duplex sensor node failure rates (Equation 29.8) when the average number of neighbor sensor nodes are $n - 1, n - 2$, and k_{min}, respectively. For mathematical tractability and closed-form solution, we analyze a special (simple) case of the above WSN cluster Markov model where $n = k_{min} + 2$, which reduces the Markov model to three states, as shown in Figure 29.6.

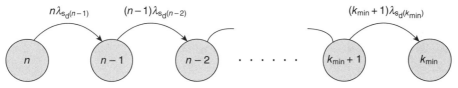

FIGURE 29.5. *WSN cluster Markov model.*

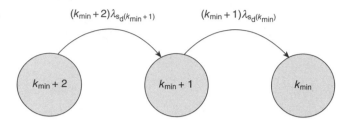

FIGURE 29.6. WSN cluster Markov model with three states.

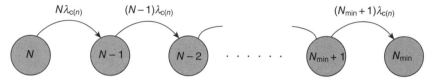

FIGURE 29.7. WSN Markov model.

Solving Equation (29.9) for $n = k_{min} + 2$ with the initial conditions $P_{k_{min}+2}(0) = 1$, $P_{k_{min}+1}(0) = 0$, and $P_{k_{min}}(0) = 0$, the WSN cluster reliability is given as

$$R_c(t) = 1 - P_{k_{min}}(t)$$

$$= e^{-(k_{min}+2)\lambda_{sd(k_{min}+1)}t} + \frac{(k_{min}+2)\lambda_{sd(k_{min}+1)}e^{-(k_{min}+2)\lambda_{sd(k_{min}+1)}t}}{(k_{min}+1)\lambda_{sd(k_{min})} - (k_{min}+2)\lambda_{sd(k_{min}+1)}} \quad (29.10)$$

$$+ \frac{(k_{min}+2)\lambda_{sd(k_{min}+1)}e^{-(k_{min}+1)\lambda_{sd(k_{min})}t}}{(k_{min}+2)\lambda_{sd(k_{min}+1)} - (k_{min}+1)\lambda_{sd(k_{min})}}.$$

The MTTF of the WSN cluster is

$$\mathrm{MTTF_c} = \int_0^\infty R_c(t)dt = \frac{1}{(k_m+2)\lambda_{sd(k_m+1)}} + \frac{1}{(k_m+1)\lambda_{sd(k_m)} - (k_m+2)\lambda_{sd(k_m+1)}} \quad (29.11)$$

$$+ \frac{(k_m+2)\lambda_{sd(k_m+1)}}{(k_m+2)(k_m+2)\lambda_{sd(k_m)}\lambda_{sd(k_m+1)} - (k_m+1)^2\lambda_{sd(k_m)}^2},$$

where we denote k_{min} by k_m in Equation (29.11) for conciseness. The average failure rate of the cluster $\lambda_c(n)$ depends on the average number of nodes in cluster n at deployment time and is given by

$$\lambda_{c(n)} = \frac{1}{\mathrm{MTTF}_{c(n)}}. \quad (29.12)$$

29.5.3.4 Fault-Tolerant WSN Model A typical WSN consists of $N = n_s/n$ clusters, where n_s denotes the total number of sensor nodes in the WSN and n denotes the average number of nodes in a cluster. Figure 29.7 depicts our WSN Markov model. We assume that the WSN fails to perform its assigned task when the number of alive clusters reduces to N_{min}. The differential equations describing the WSN Markov model are

$$P'_N(t) = -N\lambda_{c(n)}$$
$$P'_{N-1}(t) = N\lambda_{c(n)}P_N(t) - (N-1)\lambda_{c(n)}P_{N-1}(t)$$
$$\vdots$$
$$P'_{N_{\min}}(t) = (N_{\min}+1)\lambda_{c(n)}P_{N_{\min}+1}(t),$$

(29.13)

where $\lambda_{c(n)}$ represents the average cluster failure rate (Equation 29.12) when the cluster contains n sensor nodes at deployment time.

Solving Equation (29.13) for $N = N_{\min} + 2$ with the initial conditions $P_{N_{\min}+2}(0) = 1$, $P_{N_{\min}+1}(0) = 0$, and $P_{N_{\min}}(0) = 0$, the WSN reliability is given as

$$R_{wsn}(t) = 1 - P_{N_{\min}}(t)$$
$$= e^{-(N_{\min}+2)\lambda_{c(n)}t} + (N_{\min}+2)\lambda_{c(n)} \times \left[e^{-(N_{\min}+1)\lambda_{c(n)}t} - e^{-(N_{\min}+2)\lambda_{c(n)}t} \right],$$

(29.14)

where $\lambda_{c(n)}$ represents the average cluster failure rate (Equation 29.12) when the cluster contains n sensor nodes at deployment time. The WSN MTTF when $N = N_{\min} + 2$ is

$$\text{MTTF}_{wsn} = \int_0^\infty R_{wsn}(t)dt = \frac{1}{(N_{\min}+2)\lambda_{c(n)}} + \frac{N_{\min}+2}{N_{\min}+1} - 1.$$

(29.15)

29.5.3.5 Results and Analysis We use the SHARPE Software Package [28] to obtain our FT sensor node, WSN cluster, and WSN model results. We assume $c_c = 0$ in (Equation 29.3) (i.e., once a faulty sensor is identified, the faulty sensor is replaced by a good spare sensor perfectly, and thus, $c = c_k$ in Equation 29.3). We use typical c_k values for our analysis that represent c_k for different fault detection algorithms [25, 26]. We compare the MTTF for FT and non-fault-tolerant (NFT) sensor node, WSN cluster, and WSN models. The MTTF also reflects the system reliability (i.e., a greater MTTF implies a more reliable system).

Figure 29.8 depicts the MTTF for an NFT and FT sensor node (based on our sensor node duplex model; see Section 29.5.3.2) for k values of 5, 10, and 15 versus

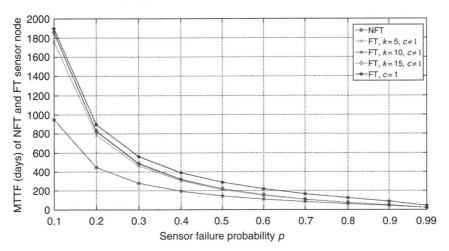

FIGURE 29.8. *MTTF (days) for an FT and an NFT sensor node.*

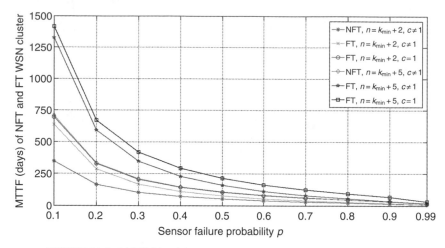

FIGURE 29.9. *MTTF (days) for the FT and NFT WSN clusters with* $k_{min} = 4$.

the sensor failure probability p when t_s in Equation (29.4) is 100 days [26]. The FT results are obtained for different k because a fault detection algorithm's accuracy, and thus c, depends upon k. The results show that the MTTF for an FT sensor node improves with increasing k. However, the MTTF shows negligible improvement when $k = 15$ over $k = 10$ as the fault detection algorithm's accuracy improvement gradient (slope) decreases between large k values. Figure 29.8 also compares the MTTF for an FT sensor node when $c = 1 \ \forall \ k, p$ representing the ideal case (i.e., the fault detection algorithm is perfect and the faulty sensor is identified and replaced perfectly for any number of neighbors and sensor failure probabilities). Whereas $c \neq 1$ for existing fault detection algorithms, however, comparison with $c = 1$ provides insight into how the fault detection algorithm's accuracy affects the sensor node's MTTF. Figure 29.8 shows that the MTTF for the FT sensor node with $c = 1$ is always greater than the FT sensor node with $c \neq 1$. We observe that the MTTF for both the NFT and FT sensor nodes decreases as p increases; however, the FT sensor node maintains better MTTF than the NFT sensor node for all p-values.

Figure 29.9 depicts the MTTF for NFT and FT WSN clusters versus p when $k_{min} = 4$ (we observed similar trends for other k_{min} values). The FT WSN cluster consists of sensor nodes with duplex sensors (Section 29.5.3.2), and the NFT WSN cluster consists of NFT nonduplex sensor nodes. The figure shows the results for two WSN clusters that contain on average $n = k_{min} + 2$ and $n = k_{min} + 5$ sensor nodes at deployment time. The figure reveals that the FT WSN cluster's MTTF is considerably greater than the NFT WSN cluster's MTTF for both cluster systems ($n = k_{min} + 2$ and $n = k_{min} + 5$). Figure 29.9 also compares the MTTF for FT WSN clusters when $c = 1$ with $c \neq 1$ and shows that the MTTF for FT WSN clusters with $c = 1$ is always better than the FT WSN clusters with $c \neq 1$. We point out that both the NFT and FT WSN clusters with $n > k_{min}$ have redundant sensor nodes and can inherently tolerate $n - k_{min}$ sensor node failures. The WSN cluster with $n = k_{min} + 5$ has more redundant sensor nodes than the WSN cluster with $n = k_{min} + 2$ and thus has a comparatively greater MTTF.

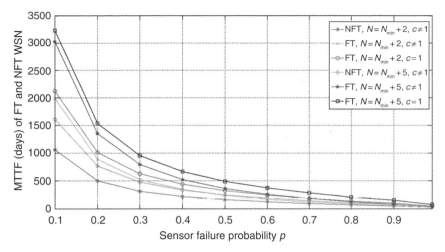

FIGURE 29.10. *MTTF (days) for the FT and NFT WSNs with* N*min* = 0.

Figure 29.10 depicts the MTTF for two WSNs containing, on average, $N = N_{\min} + 2$ and $N = N_{\min} + 5$ clusters at deployment time, and each WSN fails when there are no more active clusters (i.e., $N = N_{\min} = 0$). The FT WSN contains sensor nodes with duplex sensors (Section 29.5.3.2) and the NFT WSN contains NFT nonduplex sensor nodes. We assume that both WSNs contain clusters with $n = k_{\min} + 5$, where $k_{\min} = 4$ (Section 29.5.3.3). The figure reveals that the FT WSN improves the MTTF considerably over the NFT WSN for both cases ($N = N_{\min} + 2$ and $N = N_{\min} + 5$). Figure 29.10 also shows that the MTTF for FT WSNs when $c = 1$ is always greater than the MTTF for FT WSNs when $c \neq 1$. We observe that as $p \rightarrow 1$, the MTTF for the FT WSN drops close to the NFT WSN, thus leading to an important observation that, to build a more reliable FT WSN, it is crucial to have low failure probability sensors. We observe that the MTTF for WSNs with $N = N_{\min} + 5$ is always greater than the MTTF for WSNs with $N = N_{\min} + 2$. This observation is intuitive because WSNs with $N = N_{\min} + 5$ have more redundant WSN clusters (and sensor nodes) and can survive more cluster failures before reaching the failed state ($N = 0$) as compared with WSNs with $N = N_{\min} + 2$.

We present example reliability calculations using our Markov models for an NFT sensor node with a sensor failure rate $\lambda_t = (-1/100)\ln(1 - 0.05) = 5.13 \times 10^{-4}$ failures/day. SHARPE gives $P_1(t) = e^{-5.13 \times 10^{-4} t}$ and sensor node reliability $R_s(t) = P_1(t)$. Evaluating $R_s(t)$ at $t = 100$ gives $R_s(t)|_{t=100} = e^{-5.13 \times 10^{-4} \times 100} = 0.94999$.

Using our Markov models for an FT sensor node reliability calculation when $c \neq 1$, different reliability results are obtained for different k because the fault detection algorithm's accuracy and coverage factor c depends on k. For $k = 5, c = 0.979$, SHARPE gives $P_2(t) = e^{-5.13 \times 10^{-4} t}$ and $P_1(t) = 5.0223 \times 10^{-4}\, te^{-5.13 \times 10^{-4} t}$. The reliability $R_s(t) = P_2(t) + P_1(t) = e^{-5.13 \times 10^{-4} t} + 5.0223 \times 10^{-4}\, te^{-5.13 \times 10^{-4} t}$ and $R_s(t)|_{t=100} = e^{-5.13 \times 10^{-4} \times 100} + 5.0223 \times 10^{-4} \times 100 \times e^{-5.13 \times 10^{-4} \times 100} = 0.94999 + 0.04771 = 0.99770$.

Similarly, we performed reliability calculations for an NFT and an FT WSN cluster and a complete WSN. Based on these reliability calculations, Table 29.1 shows the reliability for an NFT WSN and an FT WSN evaluated at $t = 100$ days when

TABLE 29.1. Reliability for an NFT WSN and an FT When $N = N_{min} + 2$ ($N_{min} = 0$)

p	NFT	FT ($c \neq 1$)	FT ($c = 1$)
0.05	0.99557	0.99883	0.99885
0.1	0.98261	0.99474	0.99534
0.2	0.93321	0.97583	0.98084
0.3	0.85557	0.93775	0.95482
0.4	0.75408	0.87466	0.91611
0.5	0.63536	0.78202	0.86218
0.6	0.51166	0.65121	0.78948
0.7	0.36303	0.49093	0.69527
0.8	0.20933	0.30328	0.55494
0.9	0.08807	0.11792	0.39647
0.99	4.054×10^{-3}	4.952×10^{-3}	0.08807

$N = N_{min} + 2$ ($N_{min} = 0$) for clusters with nine sensor nodes on average (though similar calculations can be performed for WSN clusters containing a different number of sensor nodes on average). We observe similar trends as with sensor node reliability and WSN cluster reliability, where reliability for both an NFT WSN and an FT WSN decreases as p increases (i.e., reliability $R_{wsn} \to 0 \Leftrightarrow p \to 1$) because a WSN contains clusters of sensor nodes, and decreased individual sensor node reliability with increasing p decreases both WSN cluster and WSN reliability. Table 29.1 shows that an FT WSN with $c = 1$ outperforms an FT WSN with $c \neq 1$ and an NFT WSN for all p-values. For example, the percentage improvement in reliability for an FT WSN with $c = 1$ over an NFT WSN and an FT WSN with $c \neq 1$ is 5% and 0.5% for $p = 0.2$ and 350% and 236% for $p = 0.9$, respectively. These results show that the percentage improvement in reliability attained by an FT WSN increases as p increases because the fault detection algorithm's accuracy and c decreases as p increases.

29.6 CONCLUSIONS

In this chapter, we discussed scalability issues in single- and multiunit embedded systems. We provided an overview of an embedded system's hardware and software components and elaborated on different applications for embedded systems with an emphasis on CPSs, space, medicine, and automotive. We discussed different approaches for modeling single- and multiunit embedded systems and the associated modeling challenges. To demonstrate the modeling of a scalable embedded system, we presented our work on reliability and MTTF modeling for WSNs. We conclude this chapter by giving future research directions related to the modeling of embedded systems.

Novel methods and tools for system-level analysis and modeling are required for embedded system design, particularly modeling tools for architecture evaluation and selection, which can profoundly impact the embedded systems' cost, performance, and quality. Further work is required in the design of modeling tools that integrate models for wireless links, which capture radio range and interference effects, in addition to the currently modeled bus-based/wired interconnection networks. Many current sensor models typically assume a circular sensing model, and there is a need to incorporate sensing irregularities in sensor models for embedded systems.

Modeling of real-time, multiunit embedded systems (e.g., CPSs) is an interesting research avenue, which requires incorporation of timing semantics in programming languages and nondeterminism in models. Memory subsystems for embedded systems, which have a profound impact on computing performance scalability, require further research to improve the timing predictability. Although scratchpad memories enable software-based control, further work is needed in this area to ensure timing guarantees. Additional research is required in networking techniques that can provide timing guarantees since current transmission control protocol/Internet protocols (TCP/IPs) are best-effort techniques over which it is extremely challenging to achieve timing predictability for real-time, multiunit embedded systems. Furthermore, network time synchronization techniques require improvement to offer better timing coherence among distributed computations.

Energy modeling for embedded systems, particularly for multiunit and many-core embedded systems, is an important research avenue. Specifically, modeling techniques to determine energy consumption for sampling sensors, packet reception, computation, and network services (e.g., routing and time synchronization) require further investigation.

ACKNOWLEDGMENTS

This work was supported by the Natural Sciences and Engineering Research Council of Canada (NSERC) and the National Science Foundation (NSF) (CNS-0905308 and CNS-0953447). Any opinions, findings, and conclusions or recommendations expressed in this material are those of the author(s) and do not necessarily reflect the views of the NSERC or NSF.

REFERENCES

[1] P. Marwedel, "Embedded and cyber-physical systems in a nutshell," *Design Automation Conference (DAC) Knowledge Center Article*, November 2010.

[2] S. Edwards, L. Lavagno, E. Lee, and A. Sangiovanni-Vincentelli, "Design of embedded systems: Formal models, validation, and synthesis," *Proceedings of the IEEE*, 85(3):366–390, 1997.

[3] P. Sridhar, "Scalability and performance issues in deeply embedded sensor systems," *International Journal on Smart Sensing and Intelligent Systems*, 2(1):1–14, 2009.

[4] L. Edward, "Cyber-physical systems—Are computing foundations adequate?" NSF Workshop on Cyber-Physical Systems: Research Motivations, Techniques and Roadmap (Position Paper), Austin, TX, October 2006.

[5] G. Starr, J.M. Wersinger, R. Chapman, L. Riggs, V. Nelson, J. Klingelhoeffer, and C. Stroud, "Application of embedded systems in low Earth orbit for measurement of ionospheric anomalies," *Proceedings of the International Conference on Embedded Systems & Applications (ESA '09)*, Las Vegas, NV, July 2009.

[6] J. Samson, J. Ramos, A. George, M. Patel, and R. Some, "Technology validation: NMP ST8 dependable multiprocessor project," *Proceedings of the IEEE Aerospace Conference*, Big Sky, MT, March 2006,

[7] Intel, "Advantech puts Intel architecture at the heart of LiDCO's advanced cardiovascular monitoring system," in *White Paper*, 2010.

[8] M. Reunert, "High performance embedded systems for medical imaging," in *Intel's White Paper*, October 2007.

[9] Intel, "Intel technology helps medical specialists more quickly reach—And treat—Patients in remote Areas," in *White Paper*, 2011.

[10] K. Muller-Glaser, G. Frick, E. Sax, and M. Kuhl, "Multiparadigm modeling in embedded systems design," *IEEE Transactions on Control Systems Technology*, 12(2):279–292, 2004.

[11] A. Sangiovanni-Vincentelli and M. Natale, "Embedded system design for automotive applications," *IEEE Computer*, 40(10):42–51, 2007.

[12] TILERA, "TILERA multicore development environment: iLib API reference manual," in *TILERA Official Documentation*, April 2009.

[13] W. Young, W. Boebert, and R. Kain, "Proving a computer system secure," *Scientific Honeyweller*, 6(2):18–27, 1985.

[14] A. Munir and A. Gordon-Ross, "An MDP-based dynamic optimization methodology for wireless sensor networks," *IEEE Transactions on Parallel and Distributed Systems*, 23(4):616–625, April 2012.

[15] J. Zhao and R. Govindan, "Understanding packet delivery performance in dense wireless sensor networks," *Proceedings of ACM SenSys*, Los Angeles, CA, November 2003.

[16] C. Myers, "Modeling and verification of cyber-physical systems," in *Design Automation Summer School*, University of Utah, June 2011.

[17] OMG, "Unified modeling language," in *Object Management Group Standard*, 2011.

[18] A. Munir and A. Gordon-Ross, "Markov modeling of fault-tolerant wireless sensor networks," *Proceedings of the IEEE International Conference on Computer Communication Networks (ICCCN)*, Maui, HI, August 2011.

[19] TILERA, "Manycore without boundaries: TILEPro64 processor," July 2011.

[20] J. Henkel, W. Wolf, and S. Chakradhar, "On-chip networks: A scalable, communication-centric embedded system design paradigm," *Proceedings of the International Conference on VLSI Design (VLSID '04)*, Mumbai, India, January 2004.

[21] G. Werner-Allen, K. Lorincz, M. Welsh, O. Marcillo, J. Johnson, M. Ruiz, and J. Lees, "Deploying a wireless sensor network on an active volcano," *IEEE Internet Computing*, 10(2):18–25, 2006.

[22] I. Koren and M. Krishna, *Fault-Tolerant Systems*. San Francisco, CA: Morgan Kaufmann Publishers, 2007.

[23] F. Koushanfar, M. Potkonjak, and A. Sangiovanni-Vincentelli, "Fault tolerance techniques for wireless ad hoc sensor networks," *Proceedings of IEEE Sensors*, Orlando, FL, June 2002.

[24] A. Sharma, L. Golubchik, and R. Govindan, "On the prevalence of sensor faults in real-world deployments," *Proceedings of the IEEE Communications Society Conference on Sensor, Mesh and Ad Hoc Communications and Networks (SECON)*, San Diego, CA, June 2007.

[25] P. Jiang, "A new method for node fault detection in wireless sensor networks," *Sensors*, 9(2):1282–1294, 2009.

[26] B. Krishnamachari and S. Iyengar, "Distributed bayesian algorithms for fault-tolerant event region detection in wireless sensor networks," *IEEE Transactions on Computers*, 53(3):241–250, 2004.

[27] N. Johnson, S. Kotz, and N. Balakrishnan, *Continuous Univariate Distributions*. New York: John Wiley and Sons, Inc., 1994.

[28] R. Sahner, K. Trivedi, and A. Puliafito, *Performance and Reliability Analysis of Computer Systems: An Example-Based Approach Using the SHARPE Software Package*. Dordrecht: Kluwer Academic Publishers, 1996.

30

Scalable Service Composition in Pervasive Computing

Joanna Siebert and Jiannong Cao

30.1 INTRODUCTION

Nowadays, a majority of the appliances in physical environments around us are embedded with computing capabilities. Also, devices with communicating capabilities are growing in numbers and becoming more powerful. How to coordinate these smart devices and make them serve people in a less obtrusive manner has become one of the main research concerns in pervasive computing. In the vision of pervasive computing [34], the environment built on the physical world with embedded computing devices is a medium that provides a user with all the functionality he or she needs. Such a functionality of a computational entity whose execution satisfies the requestor's requirement is called a service.

This chapter is concerned with scalable service composition in pervasive computing environments (PvCEs). Service composition refers to the process of finding the best suited service providers in the environment, identifying and combining component functionalities to compose a higher-level functionality. It also provides the means to perform the requested functionality and to make services better suited by adapting to changes in the request and in the environment. The motivation behind the research on service composition in PvCEs derives from the huge gap between the high-level requirements from pervasive computing applications and the complexity of the PvCEs. In order to allow the massive deployment of service providers

Scalable Computing and Communications: Theory and Practice, First Edition. Edited by Samee U. Khan, Albert Y. Zomaya, and Lizhe Wang.
© 2013 John Wiley & Sons, Inc. Published 2013 by John Wiley & Sons, Inc.

in PvCEs and its efficient composition, we need new architectures and techniques. Scalability of the service composition indicates the ability of the mechanisms to maintain the performance even if more service providers are present in the environment and when composed requests become more complex.

In this chapter, we present a review of recent research on scalable service composition in pervasive computing. The chapter is organized as follows. In Section 30.2, we analyze the functionalities of a service composition framework and present the background on scalable service composition in PvCE. In Section 30.3, we present the principles and the corresponding techniques for achieving scalable service composition with the evaluation of their advantages and disadvantages. Finally, in Section 30.4, we conclude the chapter with a discussion of the future directions of scalable service composition in PvCE research.

30.2   SERVICE COMPOSITION FRAMEWORK

Service composition in pervasive computing fills in the gap between users and service providers embedded in PvCEs. Service composition mechanisms facilitate interaction between entities in PvCEs and free users from tedious and redundant administrative and configuration works. Therefore, service composition research is critical to the success of pervasive computing. Scalability is a primary consideration in the design of mechanisms for service composition in pervasive computing systems. Mechanisms that work well in a small and relatively static system are not suitable for growing and dynamic systems.

30.2.1   Service Composition Mechanisms

In this section, we shall discuss the framework and the major components of a service composition system. As described in Figure 30.1, the service composition framework has two operational modules—the functional module and the execution module. Basic functions include means to specify the requirement by users and service descriptions by service providers, specifying the composition plan, and selecting the best suited service providers. The execution functionalities include service monitoring and adaptation policies to suit the user need under dynamic environment changes. The lowest layer of a service composition framework consists of the PvCE. Selection of service providers is facilitated by the use of various protocols designed for different composition models. Users, human or devices alike, can specify the composition plan and access services using different primitives. Service composition systems require scalability supports as well as measures to deal with dynamicity of the environments. We consider all the horizontal boxes as core components of a generic service composition system and the vertical boxes as essential system support service components. Different protocols may choose to implement the system support modules depending on the application and user requirements. Below, we describe the issues associated with different parts of the framework.

30.2.1.1   PvCE   We define PvCE as a medium that provides users with all the functionality they need to satisfy their requirements. It is built on objects in the physical world with embedded computing devices interconnected according to

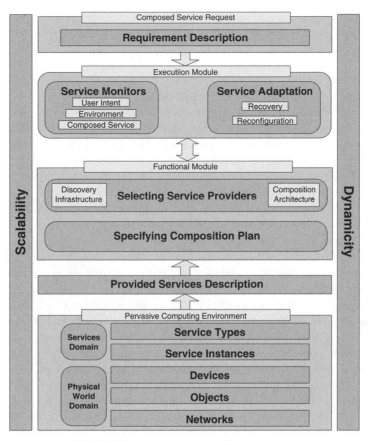

FIGURE 30.1. Service composition framework.

the underlying communication network. Functionalities provided by devices embedded in PvCE are exposed as services. A service instance is software deployed on the device. It exists to be invoked or to be interacted with. Abstract descriptions of service instances are classified into service types. In PvCE, many service providers can provide the same functionality. Also, there may be no atomic service provider that can meet the requirement. Moreover, service providers can enter and leave the environment dynamically.

30.2.1.2 Provided Services Description Smart objects may deliver functionalities for other objects and become service providers. Therefore, the service providers will provide description of their atomic services. Sometimes [1], they also specify composition plans in which they can take part. Existing service composition approaches are characterized by different expressiveness of the language used to describe the provided services.

30.2.1.3 Requirement Description In the meantime, the service requester can also express the requirement in a service specification language. Regarding the way that requested services are defined, we observe two approaches: low-level description and high-level description. In low-level description [1–13], requested service is specified as a workflow, given the set of atomic services to be composed. In high-level description, the requested service is specified as a goal to be achieved [3, 12, 13].

30.2.1.4 *Specifying the Composition Plan*   Next, the service composition system tries to provide the needed functionalities by composing the available functionalities that are exposed by service providers. It tries to generate one or several composition plans with the service providers available in the environment. Since PvCEs are saturated with service providers, often there can be several ways to satisfy the same requirement. In order to create the composition plan, diverse techniques can be used. In the most common approach [1–5, 9–11, 13–15], a composite service is broken down into a sequence of interactions between atomic services. The system generates a customized composition plan that describes how various services should interact with one another as well as with the requestor.

30.2.1.5 *Selecting Service Providers*   While many similar service providers are available to a requestor, it is important to determine which service provider should be used. It is challenging to find service providers for requestors efficiently and accurately. Service provider selection is a process of choosing a service provider among discovered candidates. Many service providers can expose the same or similar functionalities. In that case, the services can be ranked based on the information provided from the nonfunctional attributes. In pervasive environments, this evaluation depends strongly on many criteria like the application context, the ability to interact with other service providers chosen to satisfy the requirement, the quality of the network, and the nonfunctional service quality of service (QoS) properties. In the majority of the solutions, selection is done by the service requestor [16–19]. After receiving a full or partial list of available services, a user chooses a service based on service information and additional information, such as context. However, too much user involvement causes inconvenience. It may be distracting for a user to examine many candidates for service providers and to compare them. The second group of approaches is protocol-based selection, in which protocols may select services for a user [20]. The advantage of protocol-based selection is that it decreases user distraction. However, it is difficult to design a protocol selection that will reflect the actual user's will since predefined selection criteria may not apply to all cases. A balance between protocol selection and user selection is needed. One way to achieve this is to enhance protocol-based service selection with context information [1–3, 5–15, 20–23]. In addition to that, more desirable service providers can be identified and proposed to the user by considering the QoS of service providers [1, 4, 9–11].

30.2.1.6 *Service Adaptation*   Service providers may leave environments due to mobility, unexpected power off, or failures. In a PvCE, even when once the initial composition is identified and a service provisioning is established, the dynamicity of the environment may require change of the composed solution, which is called service recovery. In addition to dynamicity of the environment, the context in which composed services are deployed changes dynamically. For example, user intent may change during execution of the service. Moreover, the requirement may be changed

according to new environment conditions. Composed service must adapt to such changes. Reconfiguration of composed service refers to the capability of a service to adapt to changing user needs and environment conditions.

30.2.1.7 Service Monitors In order to successfully perform recovery or reconfiguration of the composed service, first, the system needs to decide when it is necessary to invoke such functions. In general, recovery and reconfiguration should be invoked upon detected changes regarding user intent (new needs), environment (new opportunities), or currently executed composed service (failure handling). This function is provided by service monitors.

30.2.2 Scalability in PvCEs

When designing mechanisms for service composition in PvCE, issues of scalability and dynamicity must be taken into consideration. Both environment and users are impacted by the scale and dynamicity of PvCE. Due to increased interactions, users experience the problem of distraction. Also, in saturated PvCE, the response time becomes an issue. Increased interactions are also a problem to be tackled from the point of view of environments, where service providers must handle messages generated by different composed service requests. Moreover, with the increase of service providers, heterogeneity is more likely. Because computing resources are embedded in a physical environment, the distance between service providers and users becomes an issue.

This implies that algorithms and techniques should be different for PvCEs than they are for small-scale and static computing systems. There is a need for efficient mechanisms to perform service composition that will scale well and manage well dynamic and large-scale PvCE.

30.2.2.1 Dynamicity Support Dynamicity of the environments is one of the major challenges in pervasive computing, and to handle it efficiently, service recovery mechanisms are necessary. For example, users with their mobile phones may walk out of a room while their mobile phones were providing a service in collaboration with other devices in this room, or the users' mobile phones may no longer be available due to power limitations. In scenarios of one of atomic services in a composed service becoming suddenly unavailable, the challenge is to recompose the service as quickly as possible considering the new state of the environment. The majority of the proposed solutions to the service composition problem assume static service composition. In this approach, if one of the services fails, service composition needs to start over again. Dynamic service composition approaches [9–13, 25] support replanning of the composed service during the execution of the composition. Services can be replaced, added, or removed without starting the service composition processes over. Dynamic service composition is more difficult to implement than static service composition since every service provider of the composed service is being monitored and should be replaced immediately in case of failure.

30.2.2.2 Scalability Support Scalable service composition is the main consideration when designing PvCE. We measure scale of the environment along several dimensions—scale of services and service providers, scale of service requests, and scale of interactions in the environment. First, we are concerned with the number of service providers as well as the number and granularity of service types. Scale of environments varies, from small personal networks, through smart spaces and smart cities to all Earth connected into the Internet of Things. Within each environment, the number of embedded services grows. Moreover, the scale of the request, such as the size of the request, the number of requests, and the number of users is important as well. An additional consideration is the distance between collaborating services, as well as distance between users and services. There are more and more interactions between users and computing environments.

In fact, all the mechanisms in service composition frameworks should be designed with a goal to achieve scalability. However, it is most critical in the case of mechanisms that depend on the knowledge of the environment state, such as service selection. Since in large-scale, dynamic PvCE we assume that service requestors do not know what services are available in the environment and service providers may join and leave the environment at runtime, collecting knowledge about the environment state is very expensive. Therefore, in the next section, we will mostly focus on selecting service providers in service composition.

30.3   APPROACHES AND TECHNIQUES FOR SCALABLE SERVICE COMPOSITION IN PvCE

In the previous section, we have presented mechanisms in the service composition framework followed by issues introduced by scalability considerations. In this section, we focus on techniques to achieve scalability to address these issues. We will show how to build scalable service composition mechanisms for PvCE.

30.3.1   Approaches to Achieve Scalability

An important part of the service composition framework presented in the previous section is identifying appropriate service providers to contribute to the composed service. Depending on the environment characteristics, different approaches can be chosen when designing techniques for selecting service providers. Service composition mechanisms in this respect adopt either a centralized, decentralized, or hybrid architecture. They are presented in Figures 30.2–30.4. These approaches detail how the knowledge about the environment (such as knowledge about service providers) is managed. Specifically, they differ from each other with respect to if global knowledge is necessary and how many entities collect any knowledge about the environment. In addition to three approaches presented in Figures 30.2–30.4, we will also discuss a localized version of the decentralized approach to service composition.

30.3.1.1   Centralized Approach   Many works [1, 2, 5, 14, 15] for PvCE propose centralized solutions to service composition. This category of works depends on the existence of a centralized directory of services, namely, they rely on one or more central entities to maintain the global service information in order to make composition decisions. Service requestors submit requirements to the directory and the directory makes a decision on the list of services that should be returned to the requestors. This approach works well for environments that are well managed and

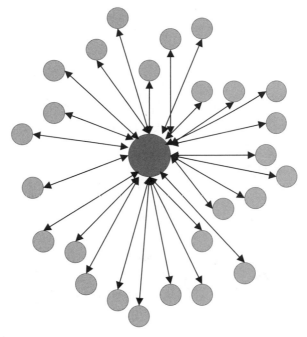

FIGURE 30.2. Centralized approach.

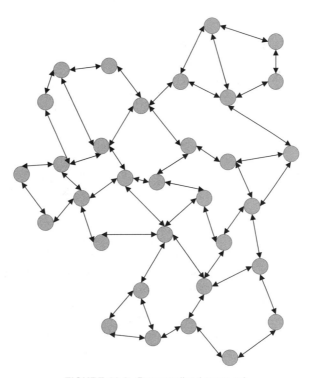

FIGURE 30.3. Decentralized approach.

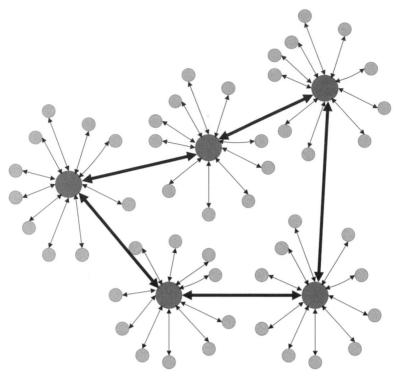

FIGURE 30.4. Hybrid approach.

are relatively stable. However, the assumption on centralized control becomes impractical in scenarios with dynamic arrivals and departures of service providers, which requires frequent updates of the central entities, resulting in large system overhead. Moreover, relying on central entities to maintain global knowledge leads to inability of the system to serve the request when the central manager is compromised.

30.3.1.2 Decentralized Approach The next category of distributed service composition approaches removes the need for a service directory and provides a fully distributed search for needed services. In Reference 24, a hierarchical task graph-based approach to do service composition in ad hoc environments has been proposed. A composite service is represented as a task graph and subtrees of the graph are computed in a distributed manner. This approach assumes that the service requestor is one of the services and relies on this node to coordinate service composition. The coordinator uses global search across the whole network to do composition. The same domain of the problem was studied in Reference 25. It is different from Reference 24 in terms of the way of electing the coordinator. For each composite request, a coordinator is selected from within a set of nodes. The service requestor delegates the responsibility of composition to the elected coordinator. The elected coordinator utilizes distributed service discovery architecture and subsequently integrates and executes services needed for a composite request. However, many decentralized approaches still rely on global information. Even if there is no central directory, there is still need for a coordinator to collect global information. One category of decentralized approaches that do not rely on global information is localized algorithms.

Localized scalability is an important issue in service composition. It is often better to identify service providers that are closer to the user and there is no need to know the environment status in other parts of the PvCE. Therefore, localized algorithms can benefit from the scalable service composition in PvCE. They can significantly decrease the communication cost as well as response delay.

In general, a localized algorithm is a distributed algorithm where each node decides on its own behavior based on the information received from only nodes in its immediate neighborhood.

We have proposed a localized approach to the service composition process in Reference 26. Our work is based on the analysis of the requirements of the fully decentralized service composition: (1) There should be no special entity to manage the service composition process; (2) service providers can communicate only with their local neighbors, not all other service providers; and (3) no service provider knows the full global information or gathers it.

Our approach starts at lower levels of hierarchy and decisions arise from joint involvement of entities. Service providers distributed in the physical environment utilize localized interactions to satisfy the given requested composite service. In this approach, it is necessary for service providers to collaborate with their neighbors. We assume that all service providers in the environment can access a whiteboard showing the user-specified service description, which is a set of component functionalities together with composition relationships. Our problem is to construct the composite service in a distributed manner, through localized interactions between service providers. We transform this problem to a subgraph isomorphism problem, which is proven to be NP-complete.

Unlike previous algorithms that rely on global knowledge, in our algorithm, each device only maintains local state information about its physical neighbors. As a result, service providers will build an overlay network graph that satisfies the requirement with the QoS comparable to the centralized approach. We propose an algorithm for the devices to cooperatively construct the requested services through localized interactions. Device candidates decide with whom to cooperate based only on the information of the devices within its physical neighborhood. Our idea is to grow sections of composed service from available services. First, the service provider identifies what service type it needs to interlock with through his or her output and then searches for an appropriate service provider with matching input type. It is possible that service provider forms a section with another section. By merging pieces with each other, eventually, a global solution emerges.

30.3.1.3 Hybrid Approach In order to address deficiencies of centralized approaches, some works exploiting the hybrid approach have already been proposed. As the first step toward decentralization of service composition, they introduce a distributed directory of services. For example, in Reference 27, a hierarchical directory has been proposed. The resource-poor devices depend on resource-rich devices to support service discovery and composition.

In the rest of this section, we compare the approaches discussed above in terms of their scalability. We further characterize them by the knowledge that algorithms rely on. In the centralized approach, an algorithm relies on global information to make composition decisions, while the decentralized and hybrid approaches can be designed either based on global or local information. The localized approach is an example of a decentralized algorithm with local information. In this section, we only compare the centralized approach as an example of an algorithm requiring global information against the localized approach, which requires local information only.

Our comparison is in two dimensions, network size and request complexity. They describe the ability of the service composition mechanism to manage an increasing number of service providers and of atomic services in the request, with minimal effort given in number of messages and response delay [26].

30.3.1.4 *Network Size*
Network size in the service composition in PvCE is bounded by the number of service providers as well as their distribution in the physical environment. To discuss the impact of the network size on the scalability of service composition approaches, we consider the number of messages necessary to find the first response and the time necessary to find the first answer.

Localized service composition mechanisms require fewer messages than centralized approaches for finding the first result. This is because the centralized directory needs to pull the request from the network, which includes generating and forwarding messages for sending the request and receiving the response, while the localized approach takes advantage of localized interactions: does not collect global information and considers only some limited neighborhood. Moreover, the localized approach scales very well with the growing size of the network, while centralized mechanisms impose larger cost when the network grows.

Similar observations can be made for the time necessary to find the first answer, according to the size of the network. The localized mechanism performs better than the centralized mechanism. Since in the centralized approach messages are flooded in the network, the collision effect causes increase in delay. The localized approach experiences a lower rate of collisions due to forwarding node selection. Similar to message cost, the localized approach scales better than the centralized approach due to considering only the local neighborhood.

30.3.1.5 *Request Complexity*
The size of the request influences scalability of the service composition mechanisms as well. We discuss the influence of the request complexity on the number of messages generated and the time necessary to find the first answer by the service composition protocol.

Although the localized mechanism avoids flooding the network with messages, the number of messages generated increases with the complexity of the request. In this respect, the centralized approach is more scalable. Since the centralized mechanism collects global information, it collects the same amount of information for a different request complexity and incurs only a little additional cost for computing the result, while the cost of the localized mechanism depends on the complexity result.

With respect to the time necessary to find the first answer, according to the size of the request, the localized approach performs better than centralized for finding the first result. This is possible due to the localized nature of discovery of services to be composed. If service providers are close to each other, they can compose service faster than it takes for the central entity to collect information from the environment. With respect to scalability, the performance of localized and decentralized approaches is similar. The centralized approach requires longer time for more complex requests. Although the time for collecting the information from the environment is similar for different requests, however, the centralized mechanism will need additional time for evaluating the information and for making a decision.

30.3.2 Techniques for Achieving Scalability

We discuss further three main techniques for achieving scalability in service composition. We show not only how to select service providers for the composed service but also how to recover from the failed composed service. The service replication objective is to provide several copies of services that are kept consistent. In case of service failure, copies can be used. In accordance with the service locality principle, a service provider that is nearer should be used. Environment partitioning is a principle in which PvCE is split into parts that can operate independently to a large extent, such as smart houses and smart classrooms.

30.3.2.1 Service Replication Service composition mechanisms must provide a consistent view of service providers available in the network. They must be scalable and resilient to changes in the network's status. Service redundancy allows fast recovery of service composition. Service redundancy can apply to redundant service providers or redundant composition plans. Redundant service providers act as duplicates to failed services. Redundant composition plans allow choosing a completely different solution to the user request.

There are two main categories of methods in redundancy-based service recovery. The persistence-based method [28] assumes that the failure causes no further problems in the composed service. The failing service provider is ignored and has to provide its own recovery actions if it wants to join the composition again. The relocation-based method [29] migrates service from a failing service provider to a different one.

Repair and reconfiguration are also objectives of composition plan adaptation works, which focus on action that modifies the composition plan in a way that changes composition plan behavior in response to the change of context considered relevant to that composition plan. Reconfiguration is an adaptation that is triggered by the change of context related to the user's need, such as the need for new services or the replacement of an original service. Repair is triggered by changes in the environment during execution of the composed service. A service that is bound to a task might become unavailable and the composition plan needs to adapt to compensate the failure.

The composition plan adaptations can be done in many methods. One of them is specifying all the possible adaptations in the composition plan itself [21]. However, this method is not flexible since the composition plan must be changed every time a new adaptation is needed. It is only suitable for a composition plan that does not change often.

Another method is utilizing the abstract composition plan concept [30]. The abstract composition plan allows for adaptation in the abstract composition plan by determining the actual implementation of services in the abstract composition plan at execution time based on the context. In this method, the abstract composition plan contains one or more abstract activities that are replaced by one of the concrete implementations, which are predefined, to customize the service for the user. A variability point defines a part of the composition plan to which the service is selected and bound during execution. Flexibility of utilizing the abstract composition plan is limited, but it ensures that the adapted composition plan gives the expected result and is suitable for a rigid composition plan such as the hospital workflow presented as their scenario. Taking into account the resource context, this method may require the executing task to restart if the resource becomes unavailable.

Adapting the composition plan instance [31] is yet another method. Each service in the functional model is attached to a set of service versions that can be added at runtime. During execution, either the original service is executed or is replaced by one of the available versions based on various types of sensed context and the predefined adaptation rules. Therefore, the adaptation in this method takes place at the instance level and the service is bound during execution. This is the more flexible method but requires runtime service discovery and that the list of available services be maintained.

These adaptation levels imply a different composition plan management. Composition plan instance adaptation can be handled easier, while the adaptation in the concrete definition requires the handling of the running composition plan instances. Late binding, in which the services in the composition plan are bound to the services as the execution proceeds to each service in the composition plan instance, provides more flexibility but requires runtime service discovery and that the list of available services be maintained.

30.3.2.2 Service Locality

In service composition for PvCE, service locality refers to the distance between the services used in composition, and it is required that it should be as small as possible. Composition locality is an important factor when the tasks include services that need to interact with each other and if they are embedded on different service providers in the network. To minimize such cost of composition, all atomic services in the composed service need to be located as close to each other as possible. Localized approaches naturally tend to select compositions with a high degree of composition locality. Service locality can also be achieved by caching of service descriptions.

30.3.2.3 Environment Partitioning

Works in traditional areas of identifying service providers as well as service recovery share a common feature, which is the globalized nature of algorithms. As mentioned earlier, in a globalized algorithm, at least one node needs to maintain global network information. This is unsuitable for highly dynamic and large-scale environments. Gathering such global information creates huge communication overhead, especially with frequent changes of topology. Moreover, global knowledge is not always necessary. Splitting service environment into parts that operate independently increases scalability of the service composition mechanisms. This can be achieved by deployment of cooperating directories within the network. A distributed set of directories is deployed over base stations, and the directories are responsible for a spatial region. The traffic generated by the service discovery process is kept to a minimum, and consumption of resources, in particular energy, is minimized.

30.4 CONCLUSIONS

As discussed in this chapter, service composition concerns several functionalities for bridging the gap between users and services embedded in PvCE. In particular, scalable service composition is concerned with the ability of the service composition mechanism to manage an increasing scale of service providers and service requests with minimal effort given in the number of messages and response delay. The growing scale of the environments as well as their dynamicity make it more difficult to manage information about available service providers. Traditional centralized approaches that rely on a special node collecting global information become unsuitable for such environments. Techniques that adopt decentralized and more specifically localized architectures are proposed to address scalability issues. Further, service replication, service locality, and environment partitioning are important principles to achieve scalability of the service composition mechanism.

Several issues are still worth investigating. One core challenge that remains more or less unexplored is how we can further utilize localized algorithms for service composition in PvCEs. Developing localized algorithms can be the key to address the challenges posed by the dynamic and ad hoc nature of pervasive systems. Pervasive devices must coordinate locally with peer devices to achieve some global objective with respect to service composition.

REFERENCES

[1] S.B. Mokhtar, N. Georgantas, and V. Issarny, "Cocoa: Conversation-based service composition in pervasive computing environments," *Proceedings of the IEEE International Conference on Pervasive Services*, 2006.

[2] Z. Song, Y. Labrou, and R. Masuoka, "Dynamic service discovery and management in task computing," in *Mobiquitous*, pp. 310–318, 2004.

[3] C. Hesselman, A. Tokmakoff, P. Pawar, and S. Iacob, "Discovery and composition of services for context-aware systems," *Proceedings of the 1st European Conference on Smart Sensing and Context*, 2006.

[4] A. Mingkhwan, P. Fergus, O. Abuelma'Atti, M. Merabti, B. Askwith, and M.B. Hanneghan, "Dynamic service composition in home appliance networks," *Multimedia Tools and Applications*, 29:257–284, 2006.

[5] H. Pourreza and P. Graham, "On the fly service composition for local interaction environments," in *IEEE International Conference on Pervasive Computing and Communications Workshops*, p. 393, IEEE Computer Society, 2006.

[6] A. Qasem, J. Hein, and H. Munoz-Avila, "Efficient source discovery and service composition for ubiquitous computing environments," *Workshop on Semantic Web Technology for Mobile and Ubiquitous Applications*, 2004.

[7] M. Sheshagiri, N.M. Sadeh, and F. Gandon, "Using semantic web services for context-aware mobile applications," *Second International Conference on Mobile Systems (MobiSys 2004), Applications, and Services—Workshop on Context Awareness*, 2004.

[8] T. Cottenier and T. Elrad, "Adaptive embedded services for pervasive computing," *Workshop on Building Software for Pervasive Computing—ACM SIGPLAN conf. on Object-Oriented Programming, Systems, Languages, and Applications*, 2005.

[9] W.L.C. Lee, S. Ko, S. Lee, and A. Helal, "Context-aware service composition for mobile network environments," *International Conference on Ubiquitous Intelligence and Computing*, 2007.

[10] G. Kaefer, R. Schmid, G. Prochart, and R. Weiss, "Framework for dynamic resource-constrained service composition for mobile ad hoc networks," *UBICOMP, Workshop on System Support for Ubiquitous Computing*, 2006.

[11] U. Bellur and N.C. Narendra, "Towards service orientation in pervasive computing systems," in *Proceedings of the International Conference on Information Technology: Coding and Computing*, pp. 289–295, 2005.

[12] A. Ranganathan and R.H. Campbell, "Autonomic pervasive computing based on planning," in *International Conference on Autonomic Computing*, pp. 80–87, 2004.

[13] A. Ranganathan and S. McFaddin, "Using workflows to coordinate web services in pervasive computing environments," in *Proceedings of the IEEE International Conference on Web Services*, pp. 288–295, 2004.

[14] M. Vallee, F. Ramparany, and L. Vercouter, "Flexible composition of smart device services," in *International Conference on Pervasive Systems and Computing*, pp 165–171, CSREA Press, 2005.

[15] A. Bottaro, J. Bourcier, C. Escoffier, and P. Lalanda, "Autonomic context-aware service composition," *2nd IEEE International Conference on Pervasive Services*, 2007.

[16] E. Guttman and C. Perkins, "Service location protocol," version 2, 1999.

[17] S. Helal, N. Desai, V. Verma, and C. Lee, "Konark—A service discovery and delivery protocol for ad hoc networks," *Proceedings of the 3rd IEEE Conference on Wireless Communication Networks*, 2003.

[18] Sun Microsystems, Jini Technology Core Platform Specification, v. 2.1.2. 2003. Available at http://river.apache.org/doc/spec-index.html.

[19] UPnP Forum, UPnP Device Architecture 1.0. 2008. Available at http://upnp.org/specs/arch/UPnP-arch-DeviceArchitecture-v1.0.pdf.

[20] M. Nidd, "Service discovery in DEAPspace," *IEEE Personal Communications*, 8:39–45, 2001.

[21] M. Wieland, P. Kaczmarczyk, and D. Nicklas, "Context integration for smart workflows," *Proceedings of the 6th Annual IEEE International Conference on Pervasive Computing and Communications*, IEEE Computer Society, 2008.

[22] S.Y. Lee, J.Y. Lee, and B.I. Lee, "Service composition techniques using data mining for ubiquitous computing environments," *International Journal of Computer Science and Network Security*, 6(9):110–117, 2006.

[23] Q. Ni, "Service composition in ontology enabled service oriented architecture for pervasive computing," *Workshop on Ubiquitous Computing and e-Research*, 2005.

[24] T.D.C. Little, B. Prithwish, and K. Wang, "A novel approach for execution of distributed tasks on mobile ad hoc networks," *IEEE WCNC*, 2002.

[25] D. Chakraborty, A. Joshi, T. Finin, and Y. Yesha, "Service composition for mobile environments," *Mobile Networks and Applications*, Special Issue on Mobile Services, 10:435–451, 2005.

[26] J. Siebert, J.N. Cao, L. Cheng, E. Wei, C. Chen, and J. Ma, "Decentralized service composition in pervasive computing environments," *International Wireless Communications and Mobile Computing Conference*, 2010.

[27] S. Kalasapur, M. Kumar, and B.Z. Shirazi, "Dynamic service composition in pervasive computing," *IEEE Transactions on Parallel and Distributed Systems*, 18:907–918, 2007.

[28] C. Dabrowski and K. Mills, "Understanding self-healing in service-discovery systems," in *WOSS '02: Proceedings of the 1st Workshop on Self-Healing Systems*, pp. 15–20, ACM, 2002.

[29] J. Albrecht, D. Oppenheimer, A. Vahdat, and D.A. Patterson, "Design and implementation trade-offs for wide-area resource discovery," *ACM Transactions on Internet Technology*, 8:1–44, 2008.

[30] N.C. Narendra, B. Umesh, S.K. Nandy, and K. Kalapriya, "Functional and architectural adaptation in pervasive computing environments," in *Proceedings of the 3rd International Workshop on Middleware for Pervasive and Ad-Hoc Computing*, ACM, 2005.

[31] T. Chaari, D. Ejigu, F. Laforest, and V.M. Scuturici, "A comprehensive approach to model and use context for adapting applications in pervasive environments'," *Journal of Systems and Software*, 80:1973–1992, 2007.

[32] M. Satyanarayanan, "Pervasive computing vision and challenges," *IEEE Personal Communications*, 8:10–17, 2001.

31

Virtualization Techniques for Graphics Processing Units

Pavan Balaji, Qian Zhu, and Wu-Chun Feng

31.1 INTRODUCTION

General-purpose graphics processing units (GPGPUs or GPUs) are becoming increasingly popular as accelerator devices for core computational kernels in scientific and enterprise computing applications. The advent of programming models such as NVIDIA's CUDA [1], AMD/ATI's Brook+ [2], and Open Computing Language (OpenCL) [3] has further accelerated the adoption of GPUs by allowing many applications and high-level libraries to be ported to them [4–7]. While GPUs have heavily proliferated into high-end computing systems, current programming models require each computational node to be equipped with one or more local GPUs, and application executions are tightly coupled to the physical GPU hardware. Thus, any changes to the hardware (e.g., if it needs to be taken down for maintenance) require the application to stall.

Recent developments in virtualization techniques, on the other hand, have advocated decoupling the application view of "local hardware resources" (such as processors and storage) from the physical hardware itself; that is, each application (or user) gets a "virtual independent view" of a potentially shared set of physical resources. Such decoupling has many advantages, including ease of management, ability to hot-swap the available physical resources on demand, improved resource utilization, and fault tolerance.

Scalable Computing and Communications: Theory and Practice, First Edition. Edited by Samee U. Khan, Albert Y. Zomaya, and Lizhe Wang.

For GPUs, virtualization technologies offer several benefits. GPU virtualization can enable computers without physical GPUs to enjoy *virtualized* GPU acceleration ability provided by other computers in the same system. Even in a system where all computers are configured with GPUs, virtualization allows allocating more GPU resources to applications that can be better accelerated on GPUs, thus improving the overall resource utilization.

However, with the current implementations of GPU programming models, such virtualization is not possible. To address this situation, we have investigated the role of accelerators, such as GPUs, in heterogeneous computing environments. Specifically, our goal is to understand the feasibility of virtualizing GPUs in such environments, allowing for compute nodes to *transparently* view remote GPUs as *local virtual GPUs*. To achieve this goal, we describe a new implementation of the OpenCL programming model, called virtual OpenCL (VOCL). The VOCL framework provides the OpenCL-1.1 API but with the primary difference that it allows an application to view all GPUs available in the system (including remote GPUs) as local virtual GPUs. VOCL internally uses the message-passing interface (MPI) [8] for data management associated with remote GPUs and utilizes several techniques, including argument caching and data pipelining, to improve performance.

We note that VOCL does not deal with using GPUs on virtual machines, which essentially provide operating system (OS)-level or even lower-level virtualization techniques (i.e., full or paravirtualization). Instead, it deals with user-level virtualization of the GPU devices themselves. Unlike full or paravirtualization using virtual machines, VOCL does not handle security and OS-level access isolation. However, it does provide similar usage and management benefits and the added benefit of being able to transparently utilize remote GPUs. As shown in Figure 31.1, VOCL allows a user to construct a virtual system that has, for example, 17 virtual GPUs even though no physical machine in the entire system might have 17 colocated physical GPUs.

We describe here the VOCL framework and the optimizations used to improve its performance. Next, we present a detailed evaluation of the framework, including a microbenchmark evaluation that measures data transfer overheads to and from GPUs associated with such virtualization and a detailed profiling of overheads for many OpenCL functions. We also evaluate the VOCL framework with real application kernels, including SGEMM/DGEMM, *N*-body computations, matrix transpose

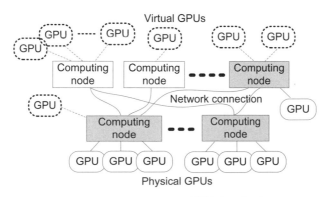

FIGURE 31.1. *Transparent GPU virtualization.*

kernels, and the Smith–Waterman application from biology. We observe that for compute-intensive kernels (high ratio of computation required to data movement between host and GPU), VOCL's performance differs from native OpenCL performance by only a small percentage. However, for kernels that are not as compute intensive (low ratio of computation required to data movement between host and GPU) and where the PCI-Express bus connecting the host processor to the GPU is already a bottleneck, such virtualization does have some impact on performance, as expected.

The rest of the chapter is organized as follows. Section 31.2 provides an overview of the GPU architecture and the OpenCL programming model. Sections 31.3 and 31.4 describe the VOCL framework, its implementation, and the various performance optimization techniques we used. Section 31.5 presents the performance evaluation. Section 31.6 describes related work, and Section 31.7 presents our conclusions.

31.2 BACKGROUND

In this section, we provide a brief overview of the NVIDIA GPU architecture and the OpenCL programming model.

An NVIDIA GPU consists of single-instruction multiple-data (SIMD) streaming multiprocessors (SMs), and each SM contains a few scalar processors. A GPU has a multilevel memory hierarchy, which includes on-chip memory and off-chip memory. On-chip memory contains private local memory, shared memory, texture memory, and constant memory. Off-chip memory includes local memory and global memory. On-chip memory has low access latency, but its size is small. In contrast, off-chip memory is large, but the access latency is high. In addition, on the latest generation of NVIDIA Fermi architecture, L1 and L2 caches are provided to access the off-chip memory more efficiently, particularly for irregular access.

OpenCL [3] is a framework for programming heterogeneous computing systems. It provides functions to define and control the programming context for different platforms. It also includes a C-based programming language for writing *kernels* to be executed on different platforms such as the GPU, CPU, and Cell Broadband Engine (Cell BE) [9]. A kernel is a special function called on the host and executed on the device in heterogeneous systems. Usually, the data-parallel and compute-intensive parts of applications are implemented as kernels to take advantage of the computational power of the GPU. A kernel consists of a few workgroups, with each workgroup consisting of work items. Work items in a workgroup are organized as groups (called *warps*), and the same instructions are executed across them if there are no divergent branches. However, if different threads execute different instructions, they are serialized, thus losing performance.

The current implementations of the OpenCL programming model only provide capabilities to utilize accelerators installed locally on a compute node.

31.3 VOCL FRAMEWORK

The VOCL framework consists of the VOCL library on the local node and a VOCL proxy process on each remote node, as shown in Figure 31.2. The VOCL library

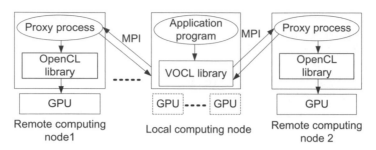

FIGURE 31.2. *Virtual OpenCL framework.*

exposes the OpenCL API to applications and is responsible for sending information about the OpenCL calls made by the application to the VOCL proxy using MPI and for returning the proxy responses to the application. The VOCL proxy is essentially a service provider for applications, allowing them to utilize GPUs remotely. The proxies are expected to be set up initially (e.g., by the system administrator) on all nodes that would be providing virtual GPUs to potential applications. The proxy is responsible for handling messages from the VOCL library, executing the actual kernel on physical GPUs, and sending results back to the VOCL library. When an application wants to use a virtual GPU, its corresponding VOCL library would connect to the appropriate proxy, utilize the physical GPUs associated with the proxy, and disconnect when it is done.

We chose OpenCL as the programming model for two reasons. First, OpenCL provides general support for multiple accelerators (including AMD/ATI GPUs, NVIDIA GPUs, Intel accelerators, and the Cell BE), as well as for general-purpose multicore processors. By supporting OpenCL, our VOCL framework can support transparent utilization of varieties of remote accelerators and multicore processors. Second, OpenCL is primarily based on a library-based interface rather than a compiler-supported user interface such as CUDA. Thus, a runtime library can easily implement the OpenCL interface without requiring the design of a new compiler.

31.3.1 VOCL Library

VOCL is compatible with the native OpenCL implementation available on the system with respect to its abstract programming interface (API) as well as its abstract binary interface (ABI). Specifically, since the VOCL library presents the OpenCL API to the user, all OpenCL applications can use it without any source code modification. At the same time, VOCL is built on top of the native OpenCL library available on the system and utilizes the same OpenCL headers on the system. Thus, applications that have been compiled with the native OpenCL infrastructure need only to be relinked with VOCL and do not have to be recompiled. Furthermore, if the native OpenCL library is a shared library and the application has opted to do dynamic linking of the library (which is the common usage mode for most libraries and default linker mode for most compilers), such linking can be performed at runtime just by preloading the VOCL library through the environment variable LD_PRELOAD.

The VOCL library is responsible for managing all virtual GPUs exposed to the application. Thus, if the system has multiple nodes, each equipped with GPUs, the

VOCL library is responsible for coordinating with the VOCL proxy processes on all these nodes. Moreover, the library should be aware of the locally installed physical GPUs and call the native OpenCL functions on them if they are available.

31.3.1.1 VOCL Function Operations When an OpenCL function is called, VOCL performs the following operations:

- Check whether the physical GPU to which a virtual GPU is mapped is local or remote.
- If the virtual GPU is mapped to a local physical GPU, call the native OpenCL function and return.
- If the virtual GPU is mapped to a remote physical GPU, check whether the communication channels between applications and proxy processes have been connected. If not, call the MPI_Comm_connect() function to establish the communication channel.
- Pack the input parameters of the OpenCL functions into a structure and call MPI_Isend() to send the message (referred to as *control message*) to the VOCL proxy. Here, a different MPI message tag is used for each OpenCL function to differentiate them.
- Call MPI_Irecv() to receive output and error information from the proxy process, if necessary.
- Call MPI_Wait() when the application requires completion of pending OpenCL operations (e.g., in blocking OpenCL calls or flush calls).

This functionality is illustrated in Figure 31.3.

```
1   clSetKernelArg(kernel, argIndex, argValue, argSize)
2   {
3       //check whether the proxy process is created,
4       checkProxyProcess();
5
6       //message to be sent to the proxy process
7       struct strSetKernelArg setKernelArg;
8
9       //initialize the message according to inputs
10      setKernelArg = kernel,argIndex,argValue,argSize
11
12      //send parameters to remote node
13      MPI_Isend(&setKernelArg, sizeof(setKernelArg),
14          MPI_BYTE, 0, SET_KERNEL_ARG, conMsgComm, ...);
15      //send argument value to the remote node
16      MPI_Isend((void *)arg_value, arg_size, MPI_BYTE,
17          0, SET_KERNEL_ARG1, dataComm, ...);
18
19      //wait for return code from the real OpenCL func
20      MPI_Irecv(&setKernelArg, sizeof(setKernelArg),
21          MPI_BYTE, 0, SET_KERNEL_ARG, conMsgComm, ...);
22      //Guarantee return code is received
23      MPI_Waitall(requests, status);
24      return setKernelArg.res;
25  }
```

FIGURE 31.3. Pseudocode for the function clSetKernelArg().

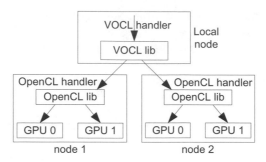

FIGURE 31.4. *Multiple-level handler translation.*

31.3.1.2 *Multiple-Level Handle Translation* In OpenCL, kernel execution is performed within a host-defined context, which includes several objects such as devices, program objects, memory objects, and kernels. A context can contain multiple devices; therefore, objects such as programs and memory buffers within the context need to be mapped onto a specific device before computation can be performed. In environments where a node is equipped with multiple physical GPUs, to do this mapping, the OpenCL library includes additional information in each object that lets it identify which physical GPU the object belongs to. For example, when OpenCL returns a memory object (i.e., `cl_mem`), this object internally has enough information to distinguish which physical GPU the memory resides on.

With VOCL, since the physical GPUs might be located on multiple physical nodes, the VOCL library might internally be coordinating with the native OpenCL library on multiple nodes (through the VOCL proxy). Thus, VOCL needs to add an additional level of virtualization for these objects to identify which native OpenCL library to pass each object to. We show this in Figure 31.4. Specifically, within VOCL, we define an equivalent object for each OpenCL object. Together with the native OpenCL handler, the VOCL object contains additional information to identify which physical node (and thus, which native OpenCL library instance) the object corresponds to.

31.3.2 VOCL Proxy

The VOCL proxy is responsible for (1) receiving connection requests from the VOCL library to establish communication channels with each application process, (2) receiving inputs from the VOCL library and executing them on its local GPUs, (3) sending output and error codes to the VOCL library, and (4) destroying the communication channels after the program execution has completed.

31.3.2.1 *Managing Communication Channels* Communication channels between the VOCL library and VOCL proxy are established and destroyed dynamically. Each proxy calls `MPI_Comm_accept()` to wait for connection requests from the VOCL library. When such a request is received, a channel is established between them, which is referred to as the *control message channel*. Once the application has completed utilizing the virtual GPU, the VOCL library sends a termination message to the proxy. Then `MPI_Comm_disconnect()` is called by both the VOCL library and the VOCL proxy to terminate the communication channel.

In the VOCL framework, each application can utilize GPUs on multiple remote nodes. Similarly, GPUs on a remote node can be used by multiple applications simultaneously. In addition, applications may start their execution at different times. Thus, the proxy should be able to accept connection requests from application processes at any arbitrary time. To achieve this, we used an additional thread at the proxy that continuously waits for new incoming connection requests. When a connection request is received, this thread updates the communication channels such that messages sent by the VOCL library can be handled by the main proxy process, and the thread waits for the next connection request.

31.3.2.2 *Handling Native OpenCL Function Calls* Once a control message channel is established between the VOCL proxy and the VOCL library, the proxy preposts buffers to receive control messages from the VOCL library (using nonblocking MPI receive operations). Each VOCL control message is only a few bytes large, so the buffers are preposted with a fixed maximum buffer size that is large enough for any control message. When a control message is received, it contains information on what OpenCL function needs to be executed as well as information about any additional input data that needs to be sent to the physical GPU. At this point, if any data needs to be transferred to the GPU, the proxy posts additional receive buffers to receive this data from the VOCL library. It is worth noting that the actual data communication happens on a separate communicator to avoid conflicts with control messages; this communicator will be referred to as the *data channel*.

Specifically, for each control message, the proxy process performs the following steps:

- When a control message is received, the corresponding OpenCL function is determined based on the message tag. Then the proxy process decodes the received message according to the OpenCL function. Depending on the specific OpenCL function, other messages may be received as inputs for the function execution in the data channel.

- Once all of the input data are available, the native OpenCL function is executed.

- Once the native OpenCL function completes, the proxy packs the output and sends it back to the VOCL library.

- If dependencies exist across different functions or if the current function is a blocking operation, the proxy waits for the current operation to finish and the result is sent back to the VOCL library before the next OpenCL function is processed. On the other hand, if the OpenCL function is nonblocking, the proxy will send out the return code and continue processing other functions.

- Another nonblocking receive will be issued to replace the processed control message.

Since the number of messages received is not known beforehand, the proxy process uses a continuous loop waiting to receive messages. It is terminated by a message with a specific tag. Once the termination message is received, the loop is ended and the MPI communicator released.

This functionality is illustrated in Figure 31.5.

```
1    MPI initialize
2
3    //prepost buffers to receive control messages
4    for i = 1 to BUFFER_NUM
5       MPI_Irecv(buff+i, size, MPI_BYTE, MPI_ANY_SOURCE,
6          MPI_ANY_TAG, conMsgComm, funcRequest+i);
7    end for
8
9    while loop
10      MPI_Waitany(numOpenCLFunc, funcRequest, &index,
11         &status);
12      if status.MPI_TAG is SET_KERNEL_ARG
13         //receive messages
14         MPI_Irecv(argValue, argSize, MPI_BYTE, rank,
15            SET_KERNEL_ARG1, dataComm, &setArgRequest)
16         MPI_Wait(&setArgRequest, &setArgStatus);
17         //call real opencl function
18         errcode_ret = clSetKernelArg(kernel,
19            argIndex, argSize, argValue);
20
21         MPI_Isend(&errcode_ret, 1, MPI_INT, tag,
22            rank, conMsgComm, &setArgRequest);
23         MPI_Wait(&setArgRequest, &setArgStatus);
24
25      end if
26
27      if status.MPI_TAG is proxyTermination
28         break;
29
30      //Issue another nonblocking receive to replace
31      //the processed control message
32      MPI_Irecv(buff+index, size, MPI_BYTE, MPI_ANY_SOURCE,
33         MPI_ANY_TAG, conMsgComm, funcRequest+index);
34   end while
35
36   MPI finalize
```

FIGURE 31.5. *Pseudocode of the proxy process.*

31.4 VOCL OPTIMIZATIONS

For each OpenCL function, the input data and the kernel program must be transferred to the proxy on the remote node, and the output sent back to the local node once the remote processing has completed. The data that need to be transferred for various OpenCL functions can vary from a single variable with only a few bytes to a data chunk of hundreds of megabytes. Furthermore, depending on the function, data may be transferred to the CPU memory of the remote node (e.g., inputs to the OpenCL API functions) or to the GPU memory (e.g., inputs to the kernel). Data transfer time depends on the data size and the network bandwidth between the local and remote nodes. Such overhead varies significantly and can be smaller than, equal to, or even larger than the actual OpenCL function execution time. The number of times that an OpenCL function is called also affects the overhead of the total program execution time.

Table 31.1 shows the OpenCL functions and their invocation counts in the Smith–Waterman application for aligning a pair of 6K-letter genome sequences. The functions in Table 31.1a,c are essentially used for initializing and finalizing the OpenCL environment, and the number of times they occur is independent of the number of

TABLE 31.1. OpenCL API Functions Used in Smith–Waterman

(a) Functions for Setting Up Environment

Function Name	Number of Calls
clGetPlatform	2
clGetDeviceID	2
clCreateContext	1
clCreateCommandQueue	1
clCreateProgramWithSource	1
clBuildProgram	1
clCreateBuffer	12
clCreateKernel	2

(b) Functions Related to Kernel Execution

Function Name	Number of Calls
clEnqueueWriteBuffer	10
clSetKernelArg	86,028
clEnqueueNDRangeKernel	12,288
clEnqueueReadBuffer	3

(c) Functions for Releasing Environment

Function Name	Number of Calls
clReleaseKernel	2
clReleaseMemObj	12
clReleaseProgram	1
clReleaseCmdQueue	1
clReleaseContext	1

TABLE 31.2. Overhead (in ms) of API Functions Related to Kernel Execution

Function Name	Runtime Local	Runtime Remote	Overhead	Overhead Percentage (%)
clEnqueueWriteBuffer	191.64	537.50	345.85	39.84
clSetKernelArg	4.33	420.45	416.12	47.93
clEnqueueNDRangeKernel	1210.85	1316.92	106.07	12.22
clEnqueueReadBuffer	0.57	0.65	0.08	0.01
TotalTime	1407.39	2275.52	868.13	100.00

problem instances that are executed. Therefore, from an optimization perspective, these are less critical and thus are of little interest (their overhead is amortized for reasonably long-running applications—e.g., anything more than few tens of seconds). Functions in Table 31.1b, on the other hand, are core functions whose performance directly impacts the overall application performance.

In Table 31.2, we compare the OpenCL function call overheads for VOCL (using a remote GPU) versus the native OpenCL library for aligning 6K base-pair sequences on an NVIDIA Tesla M2070 GPUs with the QDR InfiniBand as the network connection between different nodes. In general, such overhead is caused mainly by the data transfer between the local host memory and the GPU memory. For instance, in clEnqueueWriteBuffer, data transfer from the host memory to the GPU memory accounts for about 39.84% of the total overhead. Since the size of the data transferred in the reverse direction from the GPU memory to the local host memory is

TABLE 31.3. Overhead (in ms) of API Functions Related to Kernel Execution with Kernel Argument Caching Optimization

Function Name	Native OpenCL	VOCL (Remote)	Overhead	Overhead Percentage (%)
clEnqueueWriteBuffer	191.64	536.74	345.10	72.20
clSetKernelArg	4.33	4.03	−0.30	−0.06
clEnqueueNDRangeKernel	1210.85	1344.01	133.17	27.86
clEnqueueReadBuffer	0.57	0.61	0.04	0.01
TotalTime	1407.39	1885.40	478.01	100.00

small, it accounts for less than 1% of the total overhead. The number of function invocations also affects the overhead. In this example, clSetKernelArg() has an overhead of 416.12 ms, which accounts for 47.93% of the total overhead for the Smith–Waterman execution. The reason is that, although the overhead of each call is small, the function is called more than 86,000 times (the kernel is called 12,288 times, and seven parameters have to be set for each call).

To reduce these overheads, we have implemented three optimizations: (1) kernel argument caching, (2) improvement to the bandwidth by pipelining data transfer between the local host memory and the GPU memory, and (3) modifications to error handling.

31.4.1 Kernel Argument Caching

The basic idea of kernel argument caching is to combine the message transfers for multiple clSetKernelArg() calls. Instead of sending one message for each call of clSetKernelArg(), we send kernel arguments to the remote node only once for every kernel launch, irrespective of how many arguments the kernel has. Since all arguments should be set before the kernel is launched, we just cache all the arguments locally at the VOCL library. When the kernel launch function is called, the arguments are sent to the proxy. The proxy performs two steps on being notified of the kernel launch: (1) It receives the argument message and sets the individual kernel arguments, and (2) it launches the kernel.

Table 31.3 shows the execution time of Smith–Waterman for aligning 6K base-pair sequences using our kernel argument caching approach. As we can see in the table, the execution time of clSetKernelArg() is reduced from 420.45 ms (Table 31.2) to 4.03 ms (Table 31.3). We notice a slight speedup compared with native OpenCL; the reason is that, with VOCL, the arguments are cached in host memory and are not passed to the GPU immediately. We also notice a slightly higher overhead for the kernel execution time (increase from 1344.01 to 1316.92 ms), which is due to the additional kernel argument data passed to the proxy within this call. On the whole, the total execution time of the four kernel execution-related functions decreases from 2275 to 1885 ms, or by 17.1%.

31.4.2 Data Transfer Pipelining

Two types of data need to be transferred between the VOCL library and the VOCL proxy. The first type is the input arguments to the OpenCL functions; this type of data is transferred from the local host memory to the remote host memory. The size

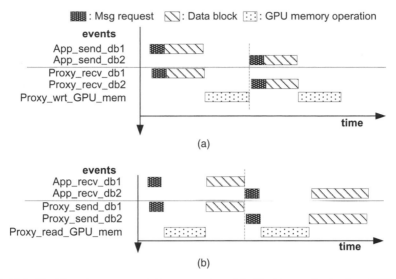

FIGURE 31.6. *Blocking data transmission scenarios. (a) Blocking write to the GPU memory. (b) Blocking read from the GPU memory.*

of such input arguments is at most a few hundred bytes. For the proxy, once the input data are received, the corresponding OpenCL functions are executed, and the output (if any) is returned to the VOCL library. Such data transfers cause negligible overhead.

The second type is the input data used by the compute kernel, which are transferred from the local host memory to the remote GPU memory. Such data transfer has two stages: (1) between the VOCL library and the VOCL proxy, and (2) between the VOCL proxy and the GPU. In a naive implementation of VOCL, these two stages would be serialized. Such an implementation, though simple, has three primary problems. First, the size of the data transferred to the GPU memory can be several gigabytes. So, for each data transfer, an appropriate sized memory region needs to be allocated at the VOCL proxy before the data can be transmitted. Second, there is no pipelining of the data transfer between the two stages, thus causing loss of performance. Third, since the temporary buffer used for storing data at the VOCL proxy is dynamically allocated and freed, this buffer is not statically registered with the local GPU device and has to be registered for each data transfer[1]; this causes additional loss of performance. This nonpipelined model is illustrated in Figure 31.6.

In order to optimize the data transfer overhead within VOCL, we designed a data pipelining mechanism (Fig. 31.7). In this approach, the VOCL proxy maintains a buffer pool, where each buffer in this buffer pool is of size B bytes. This buffer pool is statically allocated and maintained at the VOCL proxy; thus, it does not encounter the buffer allocation or buffer registration overheads that we face in the nonpipelined approach. When the VOCL library needs to write some user data to

---

[1]All hardware devices require the host memory to be registered, which includes pinning virtual address pages from swapping out, as well as caching virtual-to-physical address translations on the device.

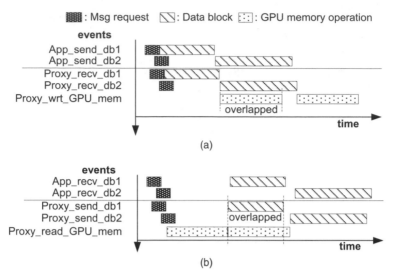

FIGURE 31.7. *Nonblocking data transmission scenarios. (a) Nonblocking write to the GPU memory. (b) Nonblocking read to the GPU memory.*

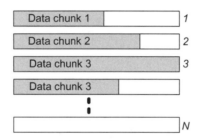

FIGURE 31.8. *Buffer pool on proxy processes.*

the GPU, it segments this data into blocks of size at most B bytes and transfers them to the VOCL proxy as a series of nonblocking sends. The VOCL proxy, on receiving each block, initiates the transfer of that data block to the GPU. The read operation is similar but in the opposite direction. Figure 31.8 illustrates this buffer pool model utilized in VOCL. In the example shown, data segments 1 and 2 are smaller than the maximum size of each buffer in the buffer pool. Thus, they are transmitted as contiguous blocks. Data segment 3, however, is larger than the maximum size and hence is segmented into smaller blocks. Since the number of buffers in the pool is limited, we reuse buffers in a circular fashion. Note that before we reuse a buffer, we have to ensure that the previous data transfers (both from the network transfer as well as the GPU transfer) have been completed. The number of buffers available in the pool dictates how often we need to wait for such completion and thus has to be carefully configured.

We also note that, at the VOCL proxy, the tasks of sending/receiving data from the VOCL library and of writing/reading data from the GPU are performed by two different threads. This allows each thread to perform data movement in a dedicated manner without having to switch between the network communication and GPU communication. This approach allowed us to further improve the data transfer performance by a few percent.

31.4.3 Error Return Handling

Most OpenCL functions provide a return code to the user: either `CL_SUCCESS` or an appropriate error code. Such return values, however, are tricky for VOCL to handle, especially for nonblocking operations. The OpenCL specification does not define how error codes are handled for nonblocking operations; that is, if the GPU device is not functional, is a nonblocking operation that tries to move data to the GPU expected to return an error?

While the OpenCL specification does not describe the return value in such cases, current OpenCL implementations do return an error. For VOCL, however, since every OpenCL operation translates into a network operation, significant overhead can occur for nonblocking operations if the VOCL library has to wait until the OpenCL request is transferred over the network, a local GPU operation is initiated by the VOCL proxy, and the return code sent back.

We believe this is an oversight in the OpenCL specification since all other specifications or user documents that we are aware of (including MPI, CUDA, and InfiniBand) do not require nonblocking operations to return such errors—the corresponding *wait-for-completion* operation can return these errors at a later time. In our implementation, therefore, we assume this behavior and return such errors during the corresponding *wait* operation.

31.5 EXPERIMENTAL EVALUATION

In this section, we evaluate the efficiency of the proposed VOCL framework. First, we analyze the overhead of individual OpenCL operations with VOCL. Then, we quantitatively evaluate the VOCL framework with several application kernels: SGEMM/DGEMM, matrix transpose, *N*-body [10], and Smith–Waterman [11, 12], of which SGEMM/DGEMM and *N*-body are compute intensive, while the others are data-transfer bound.

The compute nodes used for our experiments are connected with QDR InfiniBand. Each node is installed with two Magny-core AMD CPUs with host memory of 64 GB and two NVIDIA Tesla M2070 GPU cards, each with 6-GB global memory. The two GPU cards are installed on two different PCIe slots, one of which shares the PCIe bandwidth with the InfiniBand adapter as shown in Figure 31.9. The computing nodes are installed with the Centos Linux OS and the CUDA 3.2 toolkit. We

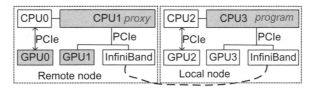

FIGURE 31.9. *GPU configuration and the scenario for the bandwidth rest.*

TABLE 31.4. Overhead of OpenCL API Functions for Resource Initialization/Release (Unit: ms)

Function Name	Native OpenCL	VOCL (Remote)	Overhead
clGetPlatformIDs	50.84	453.52	402.68
clGetDeviceIDs	0.002	0.173	0.171
clCreateContext	253.28	254.11	0.83
clCreateCommandQueue	0.018	0.044	0.026
clCreateProgramWithSource	0.009	0.042	0.033
clBuildProgram	488.82	480.90	−7.92
clCreateBuffer	0.025	0.051	0.026
clCreateKernel	0.019	0.030	0.011
clReleaseKernel	0.003	0.012	0.009
clReleaseMemObj	0.004	0.011	0.007
clReleaseProgram	0.375	0.291	−0.084
clReleaseCmdQueue	0.051	0.059	0.008
clReleaseContext	177.47	178.43	0.96

use the MVAPICH2 [13] MPI implementation. Each of our experiments was conducted three times and the average reported.

31.5.1 Microbenchmark Evaluation

In this section, we study the overhead of various individual OpenCL operations using the SHOC benchmark suite [14] and a benchmark suite developed within our group.

31.5.1.1 Initialization/Finalization Overheads   In this section, we study the performance of initializing and finalizing OpenCL objects within the VOCL framework. These functions are listed in Table 31.4. As we can notice in the table, for most functions, the overhead caused by VOCL is minimal. The one exception to this is the clGetPlatform() function, which has an overhead of 402.68 ms. The reason for this overhead is that clGetPlatform is typically the first OpenCL function executed by the application in order to query the platform. Therefore, the VOCL framework performs most of its initialization during this function, including setting up the MPI communication channels, as described in Section 31.3.

The overall overhead caused by all the initialization and finalization functions together is a few hundred milliseconds. However, this overhead is a one-time overhead unrelated to the total program execution time. Thus, in practice, for any program that executes for a reasonably long time (e.g., a few tens of seconds), these overheads play a little role in the noticeable performance of VOCL.

31.5.1.2 Performance of Kernel Execution on the GPU   Kernel execution on the GPU would be the same no matter which host processor launches the kernel. Thus, utilizing remote GPUs via VOCL should not affect the kernel execution on the GPU card. By evaluating the SHOC microbenchmark [14] with VOCL, we verified that the maximum flops, on-chip memory bandwidth, and off-chip memory bandwidth are the same as native OpenCL. These results are not provided here because they show no useful difference in performance.

31.5.1.3 Data Transfer between Local Host Memory and GPU Memory In this section, we measure the data transfer bandwidth achieved for GPU write and read operations using VOCL. The experiment is performed with different message sizes. For each message size, a window of 32 messages is issued in a nonblocking manner, followed by a flush operation to wait for their completion. This is repeated for a large number of iterations, and the bandwidth is calculated as the total data transferred per second. A few initial "warm-up" iterations are skipped from the timing loop.

Figure 31.10 shows the performance of native OpenCL, VOCL when using a local GPU (legend "VOCL (local)"), and VOCL when using a remote GPU (legend "VOCL (remote)"). Native OpenCL only uses the local GPU. Two scenarios are shown—bandwidth between CPU3 and GPU0 (Fig. 31.10c,d) and between CPU3 and GPU1 (Fig. 31.10a,b); see Figure 31.9. In our experiments, the VOCL proxy is bound to CPU1. For native OpenCL, the application process is bound to CPU1.

As shown in the figures, VOCL-local has no degradation in performance as compared to native OpenCL, as expected. VOCL-remote, however, has some degradation in performance because of the additional overhead of transmitting data over the network. As the message size increases, the bandwidth increases for native OpenCL as well as VOCL (both local and remote). However, VOCL-remote saturates at a bandwidth of around 10–25% lesser than that of native OpenCL. Comparing the bandwidth between GPU0 and GPU1, we notice that the absolute bandwidth of native OpenCL as well as VOCL (local and remote) is lesser when using GPU0 as compared to GPU1. The reason for this behavior is that data transmission between CPU1 and GPU0 requires additional hops compared to transmission between CPU1 and GPU1, causing some drop in performance. This lower absolute performance also results in lesser difference between VOCL-remote and native OpenCL (10% performance difference, as compared to the 25% difference when transmitting from CPU1 to GPU1). The results for reading data from the GPU are similar.

We also note that the shared PCIe between the network adapter and GPU1 does not degrade performance because, for most communications, the direction of data transfer to/from the network and to/from the GPU does not conflict. Specifically, when the application is writing data to the GPU, the proxy reads the data from the network and writes it to the GPU. Similarly, when the application is reading data from the GPU, the proxy reads the data from the GPU and writes it to the network. Since PCIe is a bidirectional interconnect, data transfers in opposite directions do not share the bandwidth. This allows transfers to/from GPU1 to achieve a higher bandwidth as compared with GPU0. Consequently, the performance difference for VOCL is higher for GPU1 than for GPU0.

For the remaining results, we use GPU1 because of the higher absolute performance it can achieve.

31.5.2 Evaluation with Application Kernels

In this section, we evaluate the efficiency of the VOCL framework using four application kernels: SGEMM/DGEMM, N-body, matrix transpose, and Smith–Waterman. Table 31.5 shows the computation to memory access ratios for these four kernels. The first two kernels, SGEMM/DGEMM and N-body, can be classified as compute

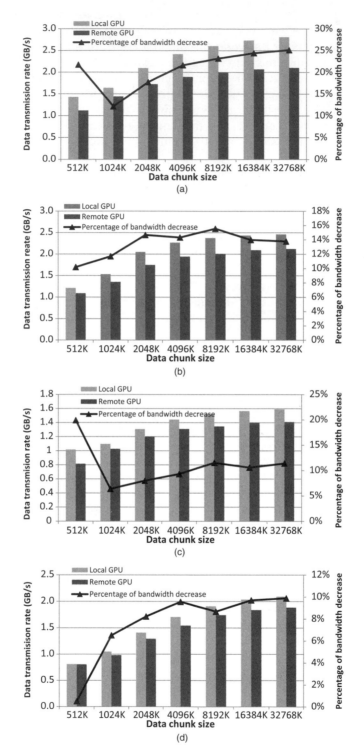

FIGURE 31.10. *Bandwidth between host memory and device memory for nonblocking data transmission. (a) Bandwidth from host memory to device memory (local transmission is from CPU1 to GPU1, and remote transmission is from CPU3 to GPU1). (b) Bandwidth from device memory to host memory (local transmission is from GPU1 to CPU1, and remote is from GPU1 to CPU3). (c) Bandwidth from host memory to device memory (local transmission is from CPU1 to GPU0, and remote transmission is from CPU3 to GPU0). (d) Bandwidth from device memory to host memory (local transmission is from GPU0 to CPU1, and remote transmission is from GPU0 to CPU3).*

TABLE 31.5. Computation and Memory Access Complexities of the Four Applications

Application Kernels	Computation	Memory Access
SGEMM/DGEMM	$O(n^3)$	$O(n^2)$
N-body	$O(n^2)$	$O(n)$
Matrix transpose	$O(n^2)$	$O(n^2)$
Smith–Waterman	$O(n^2)$	$O(n^2)$

In matrix multiplication and matrix transpose, n is the number of rows and columns of the matrix; in N-body, n is the number of bodies; in Smith–Waterman, n is the number of letters in the input sequences.

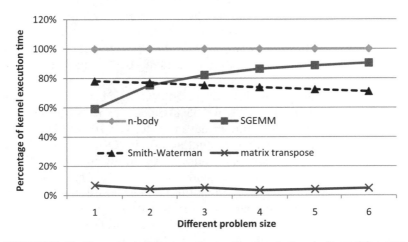

FIGURE 31.11. *Percentage of the kernel execution time in the single-precision case.*

intensive based on their computational requirements, while the other two require more data movement.

This difference in the computational intensity of these four kernels is further illustrated in Figure 31.11, where the percentage of time spent on computation for each of these kernels is shown. As we can see in the figure, the N-body kernel spends almost 100% of its time computing. SGEMM/DGEMM spend a large fraction of time computing, and this fraction increases with increasing problem size. Matrix transpose spends a very small fraction of time computing. While Smith–Waterman spends a reasonable amount of time computing (70–80%), most of the computational kernels it launches are very small kernels that, as we will discuss later, are harder to optimize because of the large number of small message transfers they trigger.

Next, we evaluate the overhead of program execution time with different problem sizes. Recall that the program execution time in this experiment includes the data transfer time, kernel argument setting, and kernel execution. We ran both the single-precision and double-precision implementations of all application kernels except Smith–Waterman since sequence alignment scores are usually stored as integers or single-precision floats in practice. We ran multiple problem instances in a nonblocking manner to pipeline data transfer and kernel execution. After we issue all nonblocking function calls, the OpenCL function `clFinish()` is called to ensure that all computations and data transfers have been completed before measuring the overall execution time. We also profile the percentage of the kernel execution in the total execution time to show the relationship between the percentage of kernel execution time and overall overhead caused by using remote GPUs.

Figure 31.12 shows the performance and the overhead of the application kernels for single-precision computations. We notice that the performance of native OpenCL is identical to that of VOCL-local; this is expected as VOCL does not do any additional processing in this case. For VOCL-remote, however, the performance depends on the application. For compute-intensive algorithms, the overhead of VOCL is very small, 1–4% for SGEMM and nearly 0% for *N*-body. This is because, for these applications, the total execution time is dominated by the kernel execution. For SGEMM, we further notice that the overhead decreases with increasing problem size. This is because the computation time for SGEMM increases as $O(N^3)$, while the amount of data that needs to be transferred only increases as $O(N^2)$; thus, the computation time accounts for a larger percentage of the overall execution for larger problem sizes.

For data-intensive algorithms, the overhead of VOCL is higher. For matrix transpose, for example, this is between 20% and 55%, which is expected because it spends a large fraction of its execution time in data transfer (based on Fig. 31.11, matrix transpose spends only 7% of its time computing). With VOCL-remote, this data has to be transmitted over the network, causing significant overhead. For Smith–Waterman, the overhead is much higher and closer to 150%. This is because of two reasons. First, since the VOCL proxy is a multithreaded process, the MPI implementation has to be initialized to support multiple threads. It is well known in the MPI literature that multithreaded MPI implementations can add significant overhead in performance, especially for small messages [15–18]. Second, Smith–Waterman relies on a large number of kernel launches for a given amount of data [12]. For a 1K sequence alignment, for example, more than 2000 kernels are launched, causing a large number of small messages to be issued, which, as mentioned above, cause a lot of performance overhead. We verified this by artificially initializing the MPI library in single-threaded mode and noticed that the overhead with VOCL comes down to around 35% by doing so.[2]

Figure 31.13 shows the performance and the overhead of the application kernels for double-precision computations. The observed trends for double precision are nearly identical to the single-precision cases. This is because the amount of data transferred for double-precision computations is double that of single-precision computations; and on the NVIDIA Tesla M2070 GPUs, the double-precision computations are about twice as slow as single-precision computations. Thus, both the computation time and the data transfer time double, resulting in no relative difference. On other architectures, such as the older NVIDIA adapters where the double-precision computations were much slower than the single-precision computations, we expect this balance to change and the relative overhead of VOCL to reduce.

---

[2]Note that, in this case, the VOCL proxy can accept only one connection request each time it is started. After an application finishes its execution and disconnects the communication channel, we would need to restart the proxy process for the next run, a process that is unusable in practice. We only tried this approach to understand the overhead of using a multithreaded versus a single-threaded MPI implementation.

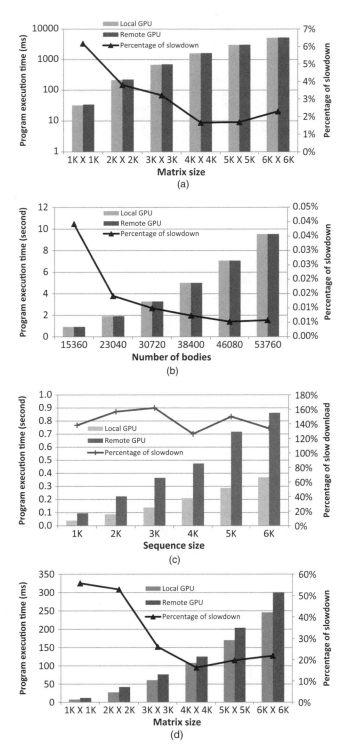

FIGURE 31.12. *Overhead in total execution time for single-precision computations. (a) SGEMM.* *(b) N-body. (c) Smith–Waterman. (d) Matrix transpose.*

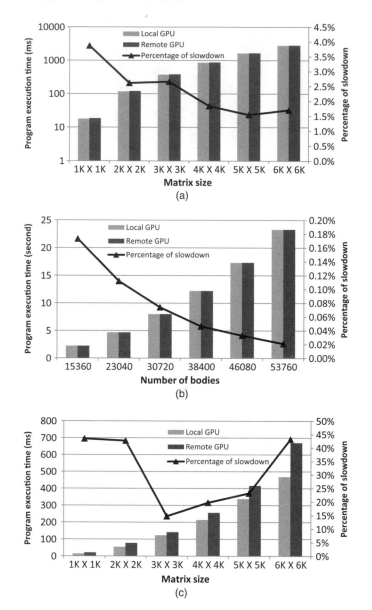

FIGURE 31.13. *Overhead in total execution time for double-precision computations.*

31.5.3 Multiple Virtual GPUs

OpenCL allows applications to query for the available GPUs and to distribute their problem instances on them. Thus, with native OpenCL, an application can query for all the local GPUs and utilize them. With VOCL, on the other hand, the application would have access to all the GPUs in the entire system; thus, when the application executes the resource query function, it would look like it has a very large number of GPUs.

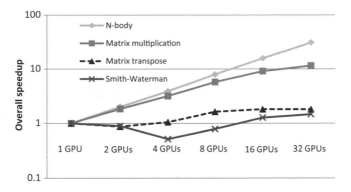

FIGURE 31.14. *Performance improvement with multiple virtual GPUs utilized (single precision).*

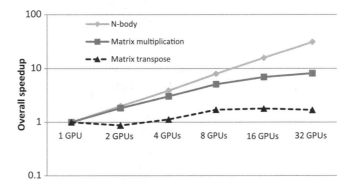

FIGURE 31.15. *Performance improvement with multiple virtual GPUs utilized (double precision).*

In this section, we perform experiments with a setup that has 16 compute nodes, each with two local GPUs; thus, with VOCL, it would appear that the applications running in this environment have 32 local (virtual) GPUs. Thus, the application can distribute its work on 32 GPUs instead of the 2 GPUs that it would use with native OpenCL. Figure 31.14 shows the total speedup achieved with 1, 2, 4, 8, 16, and 32 virtual GPUs utilized. With one and two GPUs, only local GPUs are used. In the other cases, two of the GPUs are local, and the remaining are remote.

As shown in the figure, for compute-intensive applications such as SGEMM and *N*-body, the speedup can be significant; for instance, with 32 GPUs, the overall speedup of *N*-body is about 31-fold. For SGEMM, the overall speedup is 11.5 (some scalability is lost because of the serialization of the data transfer through a single network link). For data-intensive applications such as matrix transpose and Smith–Waterman, on the other hand, there is almost no performance improvement; in fact, the performance degrades in some cases. The reason for this behavior is that most of the program execution time is for data transfer between the host memory and the device memory. As data transfer is serialized to different GPUs, program execution still takes approximately the same amount of time as with the single GPU case.

Figure 31.15 illustrates a similar experiment, but for double-precision computations. Again, we notice almost identical trends as single-precision computations because there is no relative difference in data transfer time and computation time, as explained in Section 31.5.2.

31.6 RELATED WORK

Several researchers have studied GPU virtualization and data transfer between computing nodes and GPUs.

Lawlor proposed the cudaMPI library, which provides an MPI-like message passing interface for data communication across different GPUs [19]. They compared the performance of different approaches for inter-GPU data communication and suggested various data transfer strategies. Their work is complementary to VOCL and can be adopted in our framework for efficient data transfer.

Athalye et al. designed and implemented a preliminary version of GPU-aware MPI (GAMPI) for CUDA-enabled device-based clusters. It is a C library with an interface similar to MPI, allowing application developers to visualize an MPI-style consistent view of all GPUs within a system. With such API functions, all GPUs, local or remote, in a cluster can be used in the same way. This work provides a general approach for using both local and remote GPUs. However, their solution requires invoking GPUs in a way different from the CUDA or OpenCL programming models, and thus is *nontransparent*. In comparison, our framework supports both local and remote GPUs without any source code modification. To the best of our knowledge, ours is the first research effort that proposes a *transparent* virtualization mechanism for utilization of remote GPUs.

Duato et al. [21] presented a GPU virtualization middleware that makes remote CUDA-compatible GPUs available to all compute nodes in a cluster. They implemented the software on top of TCP sockets to ensure portability over commodity networks. Similar to the work by Athalye et al., API functions have to be called explicitly for data transfer between the local node and the remote node. Thus, additional efforts are needed to modify the GPU programs to use their virtualization middleware. Further, this work requires all CUDA kernels to be separated into a different file, so this file can be shipped to the remote node and executed. This is a fundamental limitation of trying to utilize remote GPUs with the CUDA programming model because of its dependency on a compiler. With OpenCL, on the other hand, the compilation of the computational kernel is embedded into the runtime library, thus allowing such virtualization to be done transparently.

Shi et al. [22] proposed a framework that allows high-performance computing applications in virtual machines to benefit from GPU acceleration, where a prototype system was developed on top of KVM and CUDA. This work considers OS-level virtualization of GPUs installed locally, and the overhead comes from the usage of virtual machines. Therefore, GPUs that can be used in vCUDA are restricted by local GPUs. In contrast, our VOCL framework provides the transparent utilization of both local and remote GPUs. Overhead in VOCL applies only to remote GPUs, which comes from data transfer between the local and remote nodes.

In summary, the proposed VOCL framework provides a unique and interesting enhancement to the state of art in GPU virtualization.

31.7 CONCLUDING REMARKS

GPUs have been widely adopted to accelerate general-purpose applications. However, the current programming models, such as CUDA and OpenCL, can support usage of GPUs only on local computing nodes. In this chapter, we described the VOCL framework to support the transparent utilization of GPUs allowing applications to use local or remote GPUs. Performance measurements demonstrate that, for compute-intensive kernels, VOCL has no performance overheads compared to native OpenCL.

REFERENCES

[1] NVIDIA, NVIDIA CUDA Programming Guide-3.2. November 2010. Available at http://developer.download.nvidia.com/compute/cuda/3_2_prod/toolkit/docs/CUDA_C_Programming_Guide.pdf.

[2] AMD/ATI, Stream Computing User Guide. April 2009. Available at http://developer.amd.com/gpu_assets/Stream_Computing_User_Guide.pdf.

[3] Khronos OpenCL Working Group, The OpenCL Specification. June 2011. Available at http://www.khronos.org/registry/cl/specs/opencl-1.1.pdf.

[4] S.A. Manavski and G. Valle, "CUDA compatible GPU cards as efficient hardware accelerators for Smith–Waterman sequence alignment," *BMC Bioinformatics*, 9, 2008.

[5] Y. Munekawa, F. Ino, and K. Hagihara, "Design and implementation of the Smith–Waterman algorithm on the CUDA-compatible GPU," in *Proceedings of the 8th IEEE International Conference on BioInformatics and BioEngineering*, pp. 1–6, October 2008.

[6] C.I. Rodrigues, D.J. Hardy, J.E. Stone, K. Schulten, and W.W. Hwu, "GPU acceleration of cutoff pair potentials for molecular modeling applications," in *Proceedings of the Conference on Computing Frontiers*, pp. 273–282, May 2008.

[7] M.G. Striemer and A. Akoglu, "Sequence alignment with GPU: Performance and design challenges," in *IPDPS*, May 2009.

[8] Message Passing Interface Forum, The Message Passing Interface (MPI) Standard. Available at http://www.mcs.anl.gov/research/projects/mpi.

[9] T. Chen, R. Raghavan, J. Dale, and E. Iwata, "Cell Broadband Engine architecture and its first implementation," in *IBM developerWorks*, November 2005.

[10] L. Nyland, M. Harris, and J. Prins, "Fast *N*-body simulation with CUDA," in *GPU Gems*, Vol. 3. 677–695. 2007.

[11] T. Smith and M. Waterman, "Identification of common molecular subsequences," *Journal of Molecular Biology*, 147(1):195–197, 1981.

[12] S. Xiao, A. Aji, and W. Feng, "On the robust mapping of dynamic programming onto a graphics processing unit," *Proceedings of the International Conference of Parallel and Distributed System*, December 2009.

[13] Network-Based Computing Laboratory, MVAPICH2 (MPI-2 over OpenFabrics-IB, OpenFabrics-iWARP, PSM, uDAPL and TCP/IP). Available at http://mvapich.cse.ohio-state.edu/overview/mvapich2.

[14] A. Danaliszy, G. Mariny, C. McCurdyy, J.S. Meredithy, P.C. Rothy, K. Spaffordy, V. Tipparajuy, and J.S. Vetter, The Scalable Heterogeneous Computing (SHOC) Benchmark Suite. March 2010. Proceedings of the 3rd Workshop on General-Purpose Computation on Graphics Processing Units, pp. 63–74, 2010.

[15] P. Balaji, D. Buntinas, D. Goodell, W. Gropp, and R. Thakur, "Toward efficient support for multithreaded MPI communication," in *Proceedings of the 15th EuroPVM/MPI*, pp. 120–129, September 2008.

[16] P. Balaji, D. Buntinas, D. Goodell, W. Gropp, and R. Thakur, "Fine-grained multithreading support for hybrid threaded MPI programming," *International Journal of High Performance Computing Applications (IJHPCA)*, 24(1):49–57, 2009.

[17] G. Dozsa, S. Kumar, P. Balaji, D. Buntinas, D. Goodell, W. Gropp, J. Ratterman, and R. Thakur, "Enabling concurrent multithreaded MPI communication on multicore petascale systems," in *Proceedings of the 15th EuroMPI*, pp. 11–20, September 2010.

[18] D. Goodell, P. Balaji, D. Buntinas, G. Dozsa, W. Gropp, S. Kumar, B.R. de Supinski, and R. Thakur, "Minimizing MPI resource contention in multithreaded multicore environments," in *Proceedings of the IEEE International Conference on Cluster Computing*, pp. 1–8, September 2010.

[19] O.S. Lawlor, "Message passing for GPGPU clusters: cudaMPI," in *IEEE Cluster PPAC Workshop*, 1–8, August 2009.

[20] A. Athalye, N. Baliga, P. Bhandarkar, and V. Venkataraman, GAMPI is GPU Aware MPI—A CUDA Based Approach. May 2010.

[21] J. Duato, F.D. Igual, R. Mayo, A.J. Pena, E.S. Quintana-Orti, and F. Silla, "An efficient implementation of GPU virtualization in high performance clusters," *Lecture Notes in Computer Science*, 6043:385–394, 2010.

[22] L. Shi, H. Chen, and J. Sun, "vCUDA: GPU accelerated high performance computing in virtual machines," *IEEE Transactions on Computers*, 99:804–816, 2011.

32

Dense Linear Algebra on Distributed Heterogeneous Hardware with a Symbolic DAG Approach

George Bosilca, Aurelien Bouteiller, Anthony Danalis, Thomas Herault, Piotr Luszczek, and Jack J. Dongara

32.1 INTRODUCTION AND MOTIVATION

Among the various factors that drive the momentous changes occurring in the design of microprocessors and high-end systems [1], three stand out as especially notable:

1. The number of transistors per chip will continue the current trend, that is, double roughly every 18 months, while the speed of processor clocks will cease to increase.
2. The physical limit on the number and bandwidth of the CPUs pins is becoming a near-term reality.
3. A strong drift toward hybrid/heterogeneous systems for petascale (and larger) systems is taking place.

While the first two involve fundamental physical limitations that current technology trends are unlikely to overcome in the near term, the third is an obvious

Scalable Computing and Communications: Theory and Practice, First Edition. Edited by
Samee U. Khan, Albert Y. Zomaya, and Lizhe Wang.
© 2013 John Wiley & Sons, Inc. Published 2013 by John Wiley & Sons, Inc.

consequence of the first two, combined with the economic necessity of using many thousands of computational units to scale up to petascale and larger systems.

More transistors and slower clocks require multicore designs and an increased parallelism. The fundamental laws of traditional processor design—increasing transistor density, speeding up clock rate, lowering voltage—have now been stopped by a set of physical barriers: excess heat produced, too much power consumed, too much energy leaked, and useful signal overcome by noise. Multicore designs are a natural evolutionary response to this situation. By putting multiple processor cores on a single die, architects can overcome the previous limitations and continue to increase the number of gates per chip without increasing the power densities. However, since excess heat production means that frequencies cannot be further increased, deep-and-narrow pipeline models will tend to recede as shallow-and-wide pipeline designs become the norm. Moreover, despite obvious similarities, multicore processors are not equivalent to multiple-CPUs or to symmetric multi-processors (SMPs). Multiple cores on the same chip can share various caches (including translation look-aside buffer [TLB]) while competing for memory band-width. Extracting performance from such configurations of resources means that programmers must exploit increased thread-level parallelism (TLP) and efficient mechanisms for interprocessor communication and synchronization to manage resources effectively. The complexity of fine-grain parallel processing will no longer be hidden in hardware by a combination of increased instruction-level parallelism (ILP) and pipeline techniques, as it was with superscalar designs. It will have to be addressed at an upper level, in software, either directly in the context of the applications or in the programming environment. As code and performance portability remain essential, the programming environment has to drastically change.

A thicker memory wall means that communication efficiency becomes crucial. The pins that connect the processor to the main memory have become a strangle point, which, with both the rate of pin growth and the bandwidth per pin slowing down, is not flattening out. Thus, the processor-to-memory performance gap, which is already approaching a thousand cycles, is expected to grow by 50% per year according to some estimates. At the same time, the number of cores on a single chip is expected to continue to double every 18 months, and since limitations on space will keep the cache resources from growing as quickly, the cache per core ratio will continue to diminish. Problems with memory bandwidth and latency, and cache fragmentation will, therefore, tend to become more severe, and that means that communication costs will present an especially notable problem. To quantify the growing cost of communication, we can note that time per flop, network bandwidth (between parallel processors), and network latency are all improving, but at significantly different rates: 59% per year, 26% per year and 15% per year, respectively [2]. Therefore, it is expected to see a shift in algorithms' properties, from computation bound, that is, running close to peak today, toward communication bound in the near future. The same holds for communication between levels of the memory hierarchy: Memory bandwidth is improving 23% per year, and memory latency only 5.5% per year. Many familiar and widely used algorithms and libraries will become obsolete, especially dense linear algebra algorithms, which try to fully exploit all these architecture parameters. They will need to be reengineered and rewritten in order to fully exploit the power of the new architectures.

In this context, the PLASMA project [3] has developed new algorithms for dense linear algebra on shared-memory systems based on tile algorithms. Widening the scope of these algorithms from shared to distributed memory, and from homogeneous architectures to heterogeneous ones, has been the focus of a follow-up project, DPLASMA. DPLASMA introduces a novel approach to schedule dynamically dense linear algebra algorithms on distributed systems. Similar to PLASMA, to whom it shares most of the mathematical algorithms, it is based on tile algorithms and takes advantage of DAGuE [4], a new generic distributed direct acyclic graph (DAG) engine for high-performance computing (HPC). The DAGuE engine features a DAG representation independent of the problem size, overlaps communications with computation, prioritizes tasks, schedules in an architecture-aware manner, and manages microtasks on distributed architectures featuring heterogeneous many-core nodes. The originality of this engine resides in its capability to translate a sequential nested-loop code into a concise and synthetic format, which it can interpret and then execute in a distributed environment. We consider three common dense linear algebra algorithms, namely, Cholesky, LU, and QR factorizations, part of the DPLASMA library, to investigate through the DAGuE framework their data-driven expression and execution in a distributed system. It has been demonstrated, through performance results at scale, that this approach has the potential to bridge the gap between the peak and the achieved performance that is characteristic in the state-of-the-art distributed numerical software on current and emerging architectures. However, one of the most essential contributions, in our view, is the simplicity with which new algorithmic variants may be developed and how they can be ported to a massively parallel heterogeneous architecture without much consideration, at the algorithmic level, of the underlying hardware structure or capabilities. Due to the flexibility of the underlying DAG scheduling engine and the powerful expression of parallel algorithms and data distributions, the DAGuE environment is able to deliver a significant percentage of the peak performance, providing a high level of performance portability.

32.2 DISTRIBUTED DATAFLOW BY SYMBOLIC EVALUATION

Early in the history of computing, DAGs have been used to express the dependencies between the inputs and outputs of a program's tasks [5]. By following these dependencies, tasks whose data sets are independent (i.e., respect the Bernstein conditions [6]) can be discovered, hence enabling parallel execution. The dataflow execution model [7] is iconic of DAG-based approaches; although it has proved very successful for grid and peer-to-peer systems [8, 9], in the last two decades, it generally suffered on other HPC system types, generally because the hardware trends favored the single-program, multiple-data (SPMD) programming style with massive but uniform architectures.

Recently, the advent of multicore processors has been undermining the dominance of the SPMD programming style, reviving interest in the flexibility of dataflow approaches. Indeed, several projects [10–14], mostly in the field of linear algebra, have proposed to revive the general use of DAGs, as an approach to tackle the challenges of harnessing the power of multicore and hybrid platforms. However, these recent projects have not considered the context of distributed-memory environments, with a massive number of many-core compute nodes clustered in a single system. In Reference 15, an implementation of a tiled algorithm based on dynamic scheduling for the LU factorization on top of Unified Parallel C (UPC) is proposed. Gustavson et al. [16] uses a static scheduling of the Cholesky factorization on top of message-passing interface (MPI) to evaluate the impact of data representation structures. All of these projects address a single problem and propose ad hoc solutions; there is clearly a need for a more ambitious framework to enable expressing a larger variety of algorithms as dataflow and to execute them on distributed systems.

Scheduling DAGs on clusters of multicores introduces new challenges: The scheduler should be dynamic to address the nondeterminism introduced by communications, and in addition to the dependencies themselves, data movements must be tracked between nodes. Evaluation of dependencies must be carried in a distributed, problem size- and system size-independent manner: The complexity of the scheduling has to be divided by the number of nodes to retain scalability at a large scale, which is not the case in many previous works that unroll the entire DAG on every compute node. Although dynamic and flexible scheduling is necessary to harness the full power of many-core nodes, network capacity is the scarcest resource, meaning that the programmer should retain control of the communication volume and pattern.

32.2.1 Symbolic Evaluation

There are three general approaches to building and managing the DAG during the execution. The first approach is to describe the DAG itself, as a potentially cyclic graph, whose set of vertices represents the tasks whose edges represent the data access dependencies. Each vertex and edge of the graph are parameterized and represent many possible tasks. At runtime, that concise representation is completely unrolled in memory, in order for the scheduling algorithm to select an ordering of the tasks that does not violate causality. The tasks are then submitted in order on the resources, according to the resulting scheduling [9]. The main drawback of this approach lies in the memory consumption associated with the complete unrolling of the DAG. Many algorithms are represented by DAGs that hold a huge number of tasks: the dense linear algebra factorizations that we use in this chapter to illustrate the DAGuE engine have a number of tasks in $\mathcal{O}(n^3)$, when the problem is of size n.

The second approach is to explore the DAG according to the control flow dependency ordering given by a sequential solution to the problem [12, 14, 17, 18]. The sequential code is modified with pragmas to isolate tasks that will be run as atomic entities. Every compute node then executes the sequential code in order to discover the DAG by following the sequential control flow and adding dynamic detection of the data dependency, allowing for the scheduling of tasks in parallel. Optionally, these engines use bounded buffers of tasks to limit the impact of the unrolling operation in memory. The depth of the unrolling decides the number of potential pending tasks and has a direct impact on the degree of freedom of the scheduler to find the best matched task to be scheduled. One of the central drawbacks of this approach is that a bounded buffer of tasks limits the exploration of potential parallelism according to the control flow ordering of the sequential code. Hence, it is a mixed control/dataflow approach, which is not as flexible as a true dataflow approach.

The third approach consists of using a concise, symbolic representation of the DAG at runtime. Using structures such as a parameterized task graph (PTG) proposed in Reference 19, the memory used for DAG representation is linear in the number of task types and is totally independent of the total number of tasks. At runtime, there is no a need to unroll the complete DAG, which can be explored in any order, in any direction (following a task successor or finding a task predecessor), independent of the control flow. Such a structure has been considered in References 20 and 21, where the authors propose a centralized approach to schedule computational linear algebra tasks on clusters of SMPs using a PTG representation and remote procedure calls (RPCs).

In contrast, our approach, in DAGuE, leverages the PTG representation to evaluate the successors of a given task in a completely decentralized, distributed fashion. The IN and OUT dependencies are accessible between any pair of tasks that have a dependent relation, in the successor or predecessor direction. If task A modifies a data, d_A, and passes it to task B, task A can compute that task B is part of its successors simply by instantiating the parameters in the symbolic expression representing the dependencies of A; task B can compute that task A is part of its predecessors in the same way; and both tasks know what access type (read-write, read-only) the other tasks use on the data on this edge. Indeed, the knowledge of the IN and OUT dependencies, accessible anywhere in the DAG execution, thanks to the symbolic representation of edges, is sufficient to implement a fully distributed scheduling engine. Each node of the distributed system evaluates the successors of tasks that it has executed, only when that task completed. Hence, it never evaluates parts of the DAG pertaining to tasks executing on other resources, sparing memory and compute cycles. Not only does the symbolic representation allow the internal dependence management mechanism to efficiently compute the flow of data between tasks without having to unroll the whole DAG, but it also enables discovery of the communications required to satisfy remote dependencies, on the fly, without a centralized coordination.

As the evaluation does not rely on the control flow, the concept of algorithmic looking variants, as seen in many factorization algorithms of LAPACK and ScaLAPACK, becomes irrelevant: Instead of hard coding a particular variant of tasks ordering, such as right-looking, left-looking, or top-looking [22], the execution is now data driven; the tasks to be executed are dynamically chosen based on the resource availabilities. The issue of which "looking" variant to choose is avoided because the execution of a task is scheduled when the data are available, rather than relying on the unfolding of the sequential loops, which enables a more dynamic and flexible scheduling. However, most programmers are not used to think about the algorithm as a DAG. It is oftentimes difficult for the programmer to infer the appropriate symbolic expressions that depict the intended algorithm. We will describe in Section 32.4 how, in most cases, the symbolic representation can be simply and automatically extracted from decorated sequential code, akin to the more usual input used in code flow-based DAG engines, such as StarPU [14] and SMPSS [17]. We will then illustrate, by using the example of the QR factorization, the exact steps required from a linear algebra programmer to achieve outstanding performance on clusters of distributed heterogeneous resources, using DAGuE.

32.2.2   Task Distribution and Dynamic Scheduling

Beyond the evaluation of the DAG itself, there are a number of major principles that pertain to scheduling tasks on a distributed system. A major consideration is toward data transfers across distributed resources, in other terms, distribution of tasks across nodes and the fulfillment of remote dependencies. In many, previously cited, related projects, messaging is still explicit; the programmer has to either insert communication tasks in the DAG or insert sends and receives in the tasks themselves. As each computing node is working in its own DAG, this is equivalent to coordinating with the other DAGs using messages. This approach limits the degree of asynchrony that can be achieved by the DAG scheduling, as sends and receives have to be posted at similar time periods to avoid messaging layer resource exhaustion. Another issue is that the code tightly couples the data distribution and the algorithm. Should one decide for a new data distribution, many parts of the algorithm pertaining to communication tasks have to be modified to fit that new communication pattern.

In DAGuE, the application programmer is relieved from the low-level management: Data movements are implicit, and it is not necessary to specify how to implement the communications; they automatically overlap with computations; all computing resources (cores, accelerators, communications) of the computing nodes are handled by the DAGuE scheduler. The application developer has only to specify the data distribution as a set of immutable computable conditions. The task mapping across nodes is then mapped to the data distribution, resulting in a static distribution of tasks across nodes. This greatly alleviates the burden of the programmer who faces the complex and concurrent programming environments required for massively parallel distributed-memory machines while leaving the programmer the flexibility to address complex issues, like load balancing and communication avoidance, that are best addressed by understanding the algorithms.

This static task distribution across nodes does not mean that the overall scheduling is static. In a static scheduling, an ordering of tasks is decided offline (usually by considering the control flow of the sequential code), and resources execute tasks by strictly following that order. On the contrary, a dynamic scheduling is decided at runtime, based on the current occupation of local resources. Besides the static mapping of tasks on nodes, the order in which tasks are executed is completely dynamic. Because the symbolic evaluation of the DAG enables implicit remote dependency resolution, nodes do not need to make assumptions about the ordering of tasks on remote resources to satisfy the tight coupling of explicit send–receive programs. As a consequence, the ordering of tasks, even those whose dependencies cross node boundaries, is completely dynamic and depends only on reactive scheduling decisions based on current network congestion and the resources available at the execution location.

When considering the additional complexity introduced by nonuniform memory hierarchies of many-core nodes and the heterogeneity from accelerators, and the desire for performance portability, it becomes clear that the scheduling must feature asynchrony and flexibility deep at its core. One of the key principles in DAGuE is the dynamic scheduling and placement of tasks within node boundaries. As soon as a resource is idling, it tries to retrieve work from other neighboring local resources in a job-stealing manner. Scheduling decisions pertaining not only to task ordering but also to resource mapping are hence completely dynamic. The programmer is relieved from the intricacies of the hardware hierarchies; his or her major role is to describe an efficient algorithm capable of expressing a high level of parallelism, and to let the DAGᴜE runtime take advantage of the computing capabilities of the machine and solve load imbalances that appear within nodes, automatically.

32.3 THE DAGᴜE DATAFLOW RUNTIME

The DAGᴜE engine has been designed for efficient distributed computing and has many appealing features when considering distributed-memory platforms with heterogeneous multicore nodes:

1. a symbolic dataflow representation that is independent of the problem size
2. automatic extraction of the communication from the dependencies
3. overlapping of communication and computation
4. task prioritization
5. and architecture-aware scheduling and management of tasks.

32.3.1 Intranode Dynamic Scheduling

From a technical point of view, the scheduling engine is distributively executed by all the computing resources (nodes). Its main goal is to select a local ready task for which all the IN dependencies are satisfied, that is, the data are available locally, and then to execute the body of the task on the core currently running the scheduling algorithm or on the accelerator serving this core, in the case of an accelerated-enabled kernel. Once executed, the core returns in the scheduler and releases all the OUT dependencies of this task, thus potentially making more tasks available to be scheduled, locally or remotely. It is noteworthy to mention that the scheduling mechanism is architecture aware, taking into account not only the physical layout of the cores but also the way different cache levels and memory nodes are shared between the cores. This allows the runtime to determine the best local task, that is, the one that minimizes the number of cache misses and data movements over the memory bus.

Task selection (from a list of ready to be executed tasks) is guided by a general heuristic, data locality, and a user-level controlled parameter, soft priority. The data locality policy allows the runtime to decrease the pressure on the memory bus by taking advantage of the cache locality. In Figure 32.1, two different policies of ready task management are analyzed in order to identify their impact on the task duration. The global dequeue approach manages all ready tasks in a global dequeue, shared by all threads, while the local hierarchical queue manages the ready tasks using queues shared among threads based on their distance to particular levels of memory. One can see the slight increase in the duration of the GEMM tasks when the global dequeue is used, partially due to the increased level of cache sharing between ready

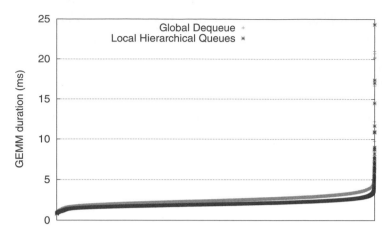

FIGURE 32.1. *Duration of each individual GEMM operation in a dpotrf 10,000 × 10,000 run on 48 cores (sorted by duration of the operation).*

tasks temporarily close to each other that get executed on cores without far-apart memory sharing. At the same time, the user-defined priority is a critical component for driving the DAG execution as close as possible to the critical path, ensuring a constant high degree of parallelism while minimizing the possible starvations.

32.3.2 Communication and Data Distribution in DAGuE

The DAGuE engine is responsible for moving data from one node to another when necessary. These data movements are necessary to release dependencies of remote tasks.

The communication engine uses a type qualifier, called *modifier*, to define the memory layout touched by a specific data movement. Such a modifier can be expressed as MPI data types or other types of memory layout descriptors. It informs the communication engine of the shape of the data to be transferred from one memory location to another, potentially remote, memory location. The application developer is responsible for describing the type of data (by providing the above-mentioned modifier for each dataflow). At runtime, based on the data distribution, the communication engine will move the data transparently using the modifiers. The data tracking engine (described below) is capable of understanding if the different data types overlap and behaves appropriately when tracking the dependencies.

The communication engine exhibits a strong level of asynchrony in the progression of network transfers to achieve communication/computation overlap and asynchronous progress of tasks on different nodes. For that purpose, in DAGuE, communications are handled by a separate dedicated thread, which takes commands from all the other threads and issues the corresponding network operations. This thread is usually not bound on a specific core; the operating system schedules this oversubscribed thread by preempting computation-intensive threads when necessary. However, on some specific environments, due to operating system or architectural discrepancies, dedicating a hardware thread to the communication engine has been proven to be beneficial.

Upon completion of a task, the dependence resolution is executed. Local task activations are handled locally, while a *task completion* message is sent to processes corresponding to remote dependencies. Due to the asynchrony of the communication engine, the network congestion status does not influence the local scheduling. Thus, compute threads are able to focus on the next available compute task as soon as possible in order to maximize communication/computation overlap.

A task completion message contains information about the task that has been completed, to uniquely identify which task was completed and, consequently, to determine which data became available. Task completion messages targeting the same remote process can be coalesced, and then a single command is sent to each destination process. The successor relationship is used to build the list of processes that run tasks depending on the completed task, and these processes are then notified. The communication topology is adapted to limit the outgoing degree of one-to-all dependencies and to establish proper collective communication techniques, such as pipelining or spanning three approaches.

Upon the arrival of a task completion message, the destination process schedules the reception of the relevant output data from the parent task by evaluating, in its communication thread, the dependencies of the remote completed task. A control message is sent to the originating process to initiate the data transfers; all output data needed by the destination are received by different rendezvous messages. When one of the data transfers completes, the receiver invokes locally the dependence resolution function associated with the parent task, inside the communication thread, to release the dependencies related to this particular transfer. Remote dependency resolutions are data specific, not task specific, in order to maximize asynchrony. Tasks enabled during this process are added to the queue of the first compute thread as there are no cache constraints involved.

In the current version, the communications are performed using MPI. To increase asynchrony, data messages are nonblocking, point-to-point operations allowing tasks to concurrently release remote dependencies while keeping the maximum number of concurrent messages limited. The collaboration between the MPI processes is realized using *control messages*, short messages containing only the information about completed tasks. The MPI process preposts persistent receives to handle the control messages for the maximum number of concurrent task completions. Unlike data messages, there is no limit to the number of control messages that can be sent, to avoid deadlocks. This can generate unexpected messages but only for small size messages. Due to the rendezvous protocol described in the previous paragraph, the data payloads are never unexpected, thus reducing memory consumption from the network engine and ensuring flow control.

32.3.3 Accelerator Support

Accelerator computing units feature tremendous computing power, but at the expense of supplementary complexity. In large multicore nodes, load balance between the host CPU cores and the accelerators is paramount to reach a significant portion of the peak capacity of the entire node. Although accelerators usually require explicit movements of data to off-load computation to the device, considering them as mere "remote" units would not yield satisfactory results. The large discrepancy between the performance of the accelerators and the host cores renders

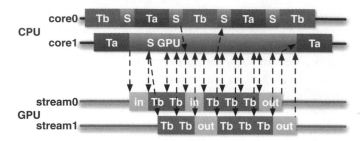

FIGURE 32.2. Schematic (not to scale) DAGuE execution on a GPU-enabled system; kernels Ta and Tb alternate with scheduling actions (S) and in/out GPU asynchronous memory accesses.

any attempt at defining an efficient static load balance difficult. One could tune the distribution for a particular platform, but unlike data distribution among nodes, which is a generic approach to balance the load between homogeneous nodes (with potential intranode heterogeneity), static load balance for what is inherently a source of heterogeneity threatens performance portability, meaning that the code needs to be tuned, eventually significantly rewritten, for different target hardware.

In order to avoid these pitfalls, accelerator handling in DAGuE is dynamic and deeply integrated within the scheduler. Data movements are handled in a different manner as data movement between processes, while tasks local to the node are shared between the cores and the accelerators. In the DAGuE runtime, each thread alternates between the execution of kernels and running the lightweight scheduler (see Fig. 32.2). When an accelerator is idling and some tasks can be executed on this resource (due to the availability of an equivalent accelerator-aware kernel), the scheduler for this particular thread switches into graphics processing unit (GPU) support mode. From this point on, this thread orchestrates the data movement and submission of tasks for this GPU and remains in this mode until either the GPU queues are full or no more tasks for the GPU are available. During this period, other threads continue to operate as usual, except if additional accelerators are available. As a consequence, each GPU effectively subtracts a CPU core from the available computing power as soon as (and only if) it is processing. This cannot be avoided because the typical compute time of a GPU kernel is 10-fold smaller than a CPU one; should all CPU cores be processing, the GPU controls would be delayed to the point that would, on average, make the GPU run at the CPU speed. However, as GPU tasks are submitted asynchronously, a single CPU thread can fill all the streams of hardware supporting concurrent executions (such as NVIDIA Fermi); similarly, we investigated using a single CPU thread to manage all available accelerators, but that solution proved experimentally less scalable as the CPU processing power is overwhelmed and cannot treat the requests reactively enough to maintain all the GPUs occupied.

A significant problem introduced by GPU accelerators is data movement back and forth from the accelerator memory, which is not a shared-memory space. The thread working in GPU scheduler mode multiplexes the different memory movement operations asynchronously, using multiple streams and alternating data movement orders and computation orders, to enable overlapping of I/O and GPU computation. The regular scheduling strategy of DAGuE is to favor data reuse by selecting when possible a task that reuses most of the data touched by prior tasks. The same approach is extended for the accelerator management to prioritize on the device tasks whose data have already been uploaded. Similarly, the scheduler avoids running tasks on the CPU if they depend on data that have been modified on the device (to reduce CPU/GPU data movements). A *modified owned exclusive shared invalid* (MOESI) [23] coherency protocol is implemented to invalidate cached data in the accelerator memory that have been updated by CPU cores. The flexibility of the symbolic representation described in Section 32.2.1 allows the scheduler to take advantage of the data proximity, a critically important feature for minimizing the data transfers to and from the accelerators. A quick look to the future tasks using a specific data provides not a prediction but a precise estimation of the interest of moving the data on the GPU.

32.4 DATAFLOW REPRESENTATION

The depiction of the data dependencies, of the task execution space, as well as the flow of data from one task to another is realized in DAGuE through an intermediary-level language named Job Data Flow (JDF). This is the representation that is at the heart of the symbolic representation of folded DAGs, allowing DAGuE to limit its memory consumption while retaining the capability of quickly finding the successors and predecessors of any given task. Figure 32.3 shows a snippet from the JDF of the linear algebra one-sided factorization QR. More details about the QR factorization and how it is fully integrated into DAGuE will be given in Section 32.5.

Figure 32.3 shows the part of the JDF that corresponds to the task class unmqr(k, n). We use the term *task class* to refer to a parameterized representation of a collection of tasks that all perform the same operation but on different data. Any two tasks contained in a task class are differing in their values of the parameters. In the case of unmqr(k, n), the two variables, k and n, are the parameters of this task class and, along with the ranges provided in the following two lines, define the

```
1   unmqr(k,n)
2     k = 0..inline_c %{ return MIN((A.nt-2),(A.mt-1)); %}
3     n = (k+1)..(A.nt-1)
4
5     : A.mat(k,n)
6
7     READ  E <- C geqrt(k)    [type = LOWER_TILE]
8     READ  F <- D geqrt(k)    [type = LITTLE_T]
9     RW    G <- (k==0) ? B DAGUE_IN_A(0, n) : M tsmqr(k-1, k, n)
10            -> (k<=A.mt-2) ? L tsmqr(k, k+1, n) : P DAGUE_OUT_A(k, n)
11
12  BODY
13    ...
14  END
```

FIGURE 32.3. *Sample Job Data Flow (JDF) representation.*

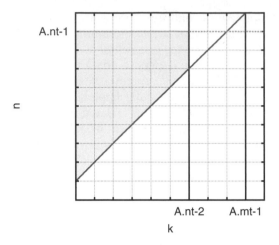

FIGURE 32.4. *2-D Execution space of unmqr(k, n).*

two-dimensional (2-D) polygon that constitutes the execution space of this task class. A graphic representation of this polygon is provided by the shaded area in Figure 32.4.[1] Each lattice point included in this polygon (i.e., each point with integer coordinates) corresponds to a unique task of this task class. As implied by the term "inline_c" in the first range, the ranges of values that the parameters can take do not have to be bound by constants but can be the return value of the arbitrary C code that will be executed at runtime.

Below the definition of the execution space, the line

```
: A.mat(k,n)
```

defines the affinity of each task to a particular block of the data. The meaning of this notation is that the runtime must schedule task $unmqr(k_i, n_i)$ on the node where the matrix tile $A[k_i][n_i]$ is located, for any given values k_i and n_i. Following the affinity, there are the definitions of the dependence edges. Each line specifies an incoming or an outgoing edge. The general pattern of a line specifying a dependence edge is

```
(READ|WRITE|RW) IDa (<-|->) [(condition) ?] IDb peer(params)
                            [: IBc peer(params)] [type]
```

The keywords READ, WRITE, and RW specify if the corresponding data will be read, written, or both by the tasks of this task class. The direction of the arrow specifies whether a given edge is input or output. A right-pointing arrow specifies an output edge, which, for this example, means that each task, $unmqr(k_i, n_i)$, of the task class $unmqr(k, n)$ will modify the given data, and the task (or tasks) specified on the right-hand side of the arrow will need to receive the data from task $unmqr(k_i, n_i)$ once this task has been completed. Conversely, a left pointing arrow specifies that

---

[1]For this depiction, A.nt-2 was arbitrarily chosen to be smaller than A.mt-1, but in the general case, they can have any relation between them.

the corresponding data needs to be received from the task specified on the right-hand side of the arrow. The input and output identifiers (`IDa` and `IDb`) are used, in conjunction with the tasks on the two ends of an edge, to uniquely identify an edge. On the right-hand side of each arrow, there is (1) an optional, conditional ternary operator "?:"; (2) a unique identifier and an expression that specifies the peer task (or tasks) for this edge; and (3) an optional type specification. When a ternary operator is present, there can be one or two identifier–task pairs as the operands of the operator. When there are two operands, the condition specifies which operand should be used as the peer task (or tasks). Otherwise, the condition specifies the values of the parameters for which the edge exists. For example, the line

```
RW  G  <-  (k==0)  ?  B  DAGUE_IN_A(0,n)  :  M  tsmqr(k-1,k,n)
```

specifies that, given specific numbers k_i and n_i, task unmqr(k_i, n_i) will receive data from task `DAGUE_IN_A(0,` n_i) if and only if k_i has the value zero. Otherwise, unmqr(k_i, n_i) will receive data from task tsmqr($k_i - 1, k_i, n_i$). Symmetrically, the JDF of task class `DAGUE_IN_A(i,j)` contains the following edge:

```
RW  B  ->  (0==i)  &  (j>=1)  ?  G  unmqr(0,j)
```

that uniquely matches the aforementioned incoming edge of unmqr(k, n) and specifies that, for given numbers I and J, task `DAGUE_IN_A`(I, J) will send data to unmqr($0, J$) if and only if I is equal to zero and J is greater or equal to one.

The next component of an edge specification is the task or tasks that constitute this task's peer for this dependence edge. All the edges shown in the example of Figure 32.3 specify a single task as the peer of each task of the class unmqr(k, n) (i.e., for each specific pair of numbers k_i and n_i). The JDF syntax also allows for expressions that specify a range of tasks as the receivers of the data. Clearly, since unmqr(k, n) receives from geqrt(k) (as is specified by the first edge line in Fig. 32.3), for each value k_i, task geqrt(k_i) must send data to multiple tasks from the task class unmqr(k, n) (one for each value of n, within n's valid range). Therefore, one of the edges of task class geqrt(k) will be as follows:

```
RW  C  ->  (k<=A.nt-2)  ?  E  unmqr(k,  (k+1)..(A.nt-1))
```

In this notation, the expression `(k+1)..(A.nt-1)` specifies a range that guides the DAGuE runtime to broadcast the corresponding data to several receiving tasks. At first glance, it might seem that the condition "`k<=A.nt-2`" limiting the possible values for the parameter k in the outgoing edge of geqrt(k) (shown above) is not sufficient since it only bounds k by `A.nt-2`, while in the execution space of unmqr(k, n), k is also upper bound by `A.mt-1`. However, this additional restriction is guaranteed since the execution space of geqrt(k) (not shown here) bounds k by `A.mt-1`. In other words, in an effort to minimize wasted cycles at runtime, we limit the conditions that precede each edge to those that are not already covered by the conditions imposed by the execution space.

Finally, the last component of an edge specification is the type of the data exchanged during possible communications generated by this edge. This is an optional argument and it corresponds to an MPI data type, specified by the developer. The type is used to optimize the communication by avoiding the transfer of data that will not be used by the task (the data type does not have to point to a contiguous block of memory). This feature is particularly useful in cases where the operations, instead of being performed on rectangular data blocks, are applied on a part of the block, such as the upper or lower triangle in the case of QR.

Following the dependence edges, there is the body of the task class. The body specifies how the runtime can invoke the corresponding codelet that will perform the computation associated with this task class. The specifics of the body are not related to the dataflow of the problem, so they are omitted from Figure 32.3 and are discussed in Section 32.5.

32.4.1   Starting from Sequential Source Code

Given the challenge that writing the dataflow representation can be to a nonexpert developer, a compiler tool has been developed to automatically convert an annotated C code into JDF. The analysis methodology used by our compiler is designed to only handle programs that call pure functions (no side effects) and have structured control flow. The current implementation focuses on codes written in C, with affine loop nests with array accesses and optional "if" statements. To simplify the implementation of our code analysis, we currently rely on annotations provided by the user to identify purity of functions and whether function arguments are either read or modified, or both read and modified by the function body.

Figure 32.5 shows an example code that implements the tile QR factorization (from the PLASMA math library [12]), with minor preprocessing and simplifications performed on the code for improving readability. The code consists of four imperfectly nested loops with a maximum nesting depth of three. In the body of each loop, there are calls to the kernels that implement the four mathematical operations that constitute the QR factorization: *geqrt, unmqr, tsqrt*, and *tsmqr* (more details will be given in Section 32.5.1). The data matrices "A" and "T" are organized in tiles, and notations such as "A[m][k]" refer to a block of data (a tile) and not a single element of the matrix. We chose to use PLASMA code as our input for several reasons. First, the linear algebra operations that are implemented in PLASMA are important to the scientific community. Second, the application programming interface (API) of PLASMA includes hints that function as annotations that can help compiler analysis. In particular, for every parameter passed to a kernel, which corresponds to a matrix tile, the parameter that follows it specifies whether this tile is read, modified, or both, using the special values `INPUT`, `OUTPUT`, and `INOUT`, or if it is temporary, locally allocated `SCRATCH` memory. Further keywords specify if only a part of a tile is read, or modified, which can reduce unnecessary dependencies between kernels and increase available parallelism. Finally, all PLASMA kernels are side-effect free. This means that they operate on, and potentially change, only memory pointed to by their arguments. Also, this memory does not contain overlapping regions; that is, the arguments are not aliased.

These facts are important because they eliminate the need for interprocedural analysis or additional annotations. In other words, DAGuE's compiler can process PLASMA code without requiring human intervention. However, the analysis performed by the compiler is not limited in any way to PLASMA codes and can accept any code for which some form of annotations (or interprocedural analysis) has

```
1   void geqrf(tiled_matrix_t A, tiled_matrix_t T) {
2       int k, m, n;
3
4       for (k = 0; (k < A.mt && k < A.nt); k++) {
5           Task( geqrt,
6                   A.mat[k][k], INOUT,
7                   T.mat[k][k], OUTPUT,
8                   phony,   SCRATCH,
9                   phony,   SCRATCH);
10
11          for (n = k+1; n < A.nt; n++) {
12              Task( unmqr,
13                      A.mat[k][k], INPUT|REGION_LOWER,
14                      T.mat[k][k], INPUT,
15                      A.mat[k][n], INOUT,
16                      phony,   SCRATCH);
17          }
18          for (m = k+1; m < A.mt; m++) {
19              Task( tsqrt,
20                      A.mat[k][k], INOUT|REGION_UPPER|REGION_DIAGONAL,
21                      A.mat[m][k], INOUT,
22                      T.mat[m][k], OUTPUT,
23                      phony,   SCRATCH,
24                      phony,   SCRATCH);
25
26              for (n1 = k+1; n1 < A.nt; n1++) {
27                  Task( tsmqr,
28                          A.mat[k][n1], INOUT,
29                          A.mat[m][n1], INOUT,
30                          A.mat[m][k],  INPUT,
31                          T.mat[m][k],  INPUT,
32                          phony,    SCRATCH);
33              }
34          }
35      }
36  }
```

FIGURE 32.5. Tile QR factorization in PLASMA.

provided the behavior of the functions with respect to their arguments as well as a guarantee that the functions are side-effect free.

32.4.2 Conditional Dataflow

As stated previously, the compiler tool provided with DAGuE derives the JDF in Figure 32.3 from the code shown in Figure 32.5. The first information that needs to be derived is which parts of the code constitute tasks. This is done via the user-provided annotation "Task."[2] Then, for each task, we need to derive the parameters

---

[2]The actual term used in PLASMA is "QUARK_Insert_Task," but we abbreviate it here to "Task" for readability reasons.

and their bounds in order to determine the execution space of the task. As can be seen in Figure 32.5, the kernel "unmqr" is marked as a task and is enclosed by two loops, with induction variables k and n, respectively. Therefore, k and n will be the two parameters of the task class unmqr(k, n). Regarding the bounds, we can see that k is bound by zero below and by the minimum of $A.mt - 1$ and $A.nt - 1$ above. Note that for this analysis, the bounds are inclusive. The second loop provides the bounds for n. Additionally, this second loop provides a tighter bound for the parameter k. In particular, the condition of the second loop can be written as $k + 1 \leq n < A.nt \Rightarrow k < A.nt - 1 \Rightarrow k \leq A.nt - 2$. Thus, from the bounds of these two loops, we derive the parameters and the execution space of the task class unmqr(k, n).

The affinity of each task class is set by the compiler to the first tile that is written by the corresponding kernel (in this case, A.mat[k][n]). However, this decision is related to the data distribution and is often better to be overwritten by the developer, who is expected to understand the overall execution of the algorithm better than the compiler. The original code can be annotated with specific pragmas to overwrite this association of a task with a block of data.

Deriving the dependence edges is the most important and difficult problem that the compiler solves. The first edge, "READ E <- C geqrt(k)" is a very simple one. It states that data are coming into unmqr(k, n) from geqrt(k) unconditionally. By looking at the serial code, we can easily determine that for each execution of the kernel unmqr, the tile A.mat[k][k] comes from the kernel geqrt that executed in the same iteration of the outer loop (i.e., with the same value of k). The following edge is a little less obvious:

```
RW G -> (k<=A.mt-2) ? L tsmqr(k,k+1,n)
```

First, let us note that the kernel tsmqr is enclosed by the loops with induction variables k, m, and $n1$ (abbreviated as for-k, for-m and for-$n1$ hereafter). Therefore, the task class is tsmqr($k, m, n1$), and it only shares the outermost loop, for-k, with unmqr(k, n). For every unique pair of numbers k_i, n_i (within valid ranges), there is a task unmqr(k_i, n_i). When this task executes, it modifies the tile A.mat[k_i][n_i] (since this tile is declared as INOUT). At the same time, for every triplet of numbers k_j, m_j, and $n1_j$, there is task tsmqr($k_j, m_j, n1_j$) that reads (and modifies) the tile A.mat[k_j][$n1_j$] (since this tile is declared as INOUT). Therefore, when "$k_i == k_j \wedge n_i == n1_j$" is true, unmqr($k_i, n_i$) will write into the same memory region that tsmqr($k_j, m_j, n1_j$) will read (for every valid value of m_j). This means that there is a dataflow between these tasks (unless some other task modifies the same memory in between). The conjunction of conditions so formed includes all the conditions imposed by the loop bounds and by the demand that the two memory locations match. Thus, we use the following notation to express this potential dataflow:

```
{[k,n]  ->  [k',m,n1]  :  0<=k<=A.mt-1 &&
                          k<=A.nt-1 && k+1<=n<=A.nt-1
&&
                          0<=k'<=A.mt-1 && k'<=A.nt-1
&&
                          k'+1<=m<=A.mt-1 && k=k' &&
                          k'+1<=n1<=A.nt-1 && n=n1}
```

This is the notation of the Omega test [24], which is the polyhedral analysis framework our compiler uses internally to handle these conditions. In Omega parlance, this mapping from one execution space to another followed by a conjunction of conditions is called a *relation*. Simplifying this relation, with the help of the Omega library, results in the relation from unmqr to tsmqr, R_{ut}:

```
R_ut := { [k,n]  ->  [k,m,n]  :  0<=k<n<=A.nt-1 && k<m<=A.mt-1}
```

However, examining the code in Figure 32.5 reveals that the kernel tsmqr has a dataflow to itself. This is true because the location of the tile A.mat[k][n1] is loop invariant with respect to the for-*m* loop and is read and modified by the kernel. In other words, every task tsmqr(k_i, m_i, $n1_i$) will read the same memory A.mat[k_i][$n1_i$] that some other task tsmqr(k_i, m_j, $n1_i$) modified (for $m_j < m_i$). This edge, in simplified form, is expressed by the relation

```
R_tt := { [k,m,n1]  ->  [k,m',n1]  :  0<=k<m<m'<A.mt && k<n1 <A.nt}
```

The important question that our compiler (or a human developer) must answer is "Which was the last task to modify the tile, when a given task started its execution?" To explain how our analysis answers this question, we need to introduce some terminology.

In compiler parlance, every location in the code where a memory location is read is called a *use*, and every location where a memory location is modified is called a *definition*. Also, a path from a use to a definition is called a *flow* dependency, and the path from a definition to another definition (of the same memory location) is called an *output* dependency. Consider a code segment such that A is a definition of a given memory location, B is another definition of the same memory location, and C is a use of the same memory location. Consider also that B follows A in the code but precedes C. We then say that B kills A, so there is no flow dependency from A to C. However, if A, B, and C are enclosed in loops with conditions that define different iteration spaces, then B might kill A only some of the time, depending on those conditions. To find exactly when there is a flow dependency from A to C, we need to perform the following operations. Form the relation that describes the flow edge from A to C (R_{ac}). Then, form the relation that describes the flow edge from B to C (R_{bc}). Then, form the relation that describes the output edge from A to B (R_{ab}). If we compose R_{bc} with R_{ab}, we will find all the conditions that need to hold for the code in location B to overwrite the memory that was defined in A and then make it all the way to C. In other words, $R^{kill} = R_{bc} \circ R_{ab}$ tells us exactly when the definition in B kills the definition in A with respect to C. If we now subtract the two relations $R_0 = R_{ac} - R^{kill}$, we are left with the conditions that need to hold for a flow dependency to exist from A to C.

In the example of the unmqr(k, n) and tsmqr(k, m, $n1$) given above, the code locations A, B, and C are the call sites of unmqr, tsmqr, and tsmqr (again), respectively. Therefore, we have $R_{ab} \equiv R_{ut}$, $R_{ac} \equiv R_{ut}$, and $R_{bc} \equiv R_{tt}$, which leads to $R_0 = R_{ut} - (R_{tt} \circ R_{ut})$. Performing this operation results in

```
R_0 := { [k,n]  ->  [k,k+1,n]  :  0<=k<n<=A.nt-1 && k<=A.mt-2}
```

which is exactly the dataflow edge we have been trying to explain in this example.

Converting the resulting relation, R_0, into the edge

```
RW  G  -> (k<=A.mt-2)  ?  L  tsmqr(k,k+1,n)
```

that we will store into the JDF segment that describes unmqr(k, n) is a straightforward process. The symbol `RW` signifies that the data are read/write, which we infer from the annotation `INOUT` that follows the tile `A.mat[k][n]` in the source code. The identifiers `G` and `L` are assigned by the compiler to the corresponding parameters `A.mat[k][n]` and `A.mat[k][n1]` of the kernels unmqr and tsmqr, respectively. These identifiers, along with the two task classes unmqr(k, n) and tsmqr$(k, m, n1)$, uniquely identify a single dataflow edge. The condition (`k<=A.mt-2`) is the only condition in the conjunction of R_0 that is more restrictive than the execution space of unmqr(k, n), so it is the only condition that needs to appear in the edge. Finally, the parameters of the peer task come from the destination execution space of the relation R_0 (remember that a relation defines the mapping of one execution space to another, given a set of conditions). Since we store this edge information in the JDF for the runtime to be able to find the successors of unmqr(k, n) given a pair of numbers (k_i, n_i), it follows that the destination execution space can only contain expressions of the parameters k and n or constants. When, during our compiler analysis, Omega produces a relation with a destination execution space that contains parameters that do not exist in the source execution space, our compiler traverses the equalities that appear in the conditions of the relation in an effort to substitute acceptable expressions for each additional parameter. When this is impossible, due to lack of such equalities, the compiler traverses the inequalities in order to infer the bounds of each unknown parameter. Consecutively, it replaces each unknown parameter with a range defined by its bounds. As an example, if the relation R_{ut}, shown above, had to be converted to a JDF edge, then the parameter m would be replaced by the range "`(k)..(A.mt-1)`," which is defined by the inequalities that involve m.

32.5   PROGRAMMING LINEAR ALGEBRA WITH DAGuE

In this section, we present in detail how some linear algebra operations have been programmed with the DAGuE framework in the context of the DPLASMA library. We use one of the most common one-sided factorizations as a walkthrough example, QR. We first present the algorithm and its properties, then, we walk through all the steps a programmer must perform to get a fully functional QR factorization. We present how this operation is integrated in a parallel MPI application, how some kernels are ported to enable acceleration using GPUs, and some tools provided by the DAGuE framework to evaluate the performance and to tune the resulting operation.

32.5.1   Background: Factorization Algorithms

Dense systems of linear equations are critical cornerstones for some of the most compute-intensive applications. Any improvement in the time to solution for these dense linear systems has a direct impact on the execution time of numerous applications. A short list of domains directly using dense linear equations to solve some of the most challenging problems our society faces includes airplane wing design, radar cross-section studies, flow around ships and other off-shore constructions, diffusion of solid bodies in a liquid, noise reduction, and diffusion of light by small particles.

The electromagnetic community is a major user of dense linear system solvers. Of particular interest to this community is the solution of the so-called radar cross-section problem—a signal of fixed frequency bounces off an object; the goal is to determine the intensity of the reflected signal in all possible directions. The underlying differential equation may vary, depending on the specific problem. In the design of stealth aircraft, the principal equation is the Helmholtz equation. To solve this equation, researchers use the method of moments [25, 26]. In the case of fluid flow, the problem often involves solving the Laplace or Poisson equation. Here, the boundary integral solution is known as the panel methods [27, 28], so named from the quadrilaterals that discretize and approximate a structure such as an airplane. Generally, these methods are called boundary element methods. The use of these methods produces a dense linear system of size $\mathcal{O}(N)$ by $\mathcal{O}(N)$, where N is the number of boundary points (or panels) being used. It is not unusual to see size $3N$ by $3N$ because of three physical quantities of interest at every boundary element. A typical approach to solving such systems is to use LU factorization. Each entry of the matrix is computed as an interaction of two boundary elements. Often, many integrals must be computed. In many instances, the time required to compute the matrix is considerably larger than the time for solution. The builders of stealth technology who are interested in radar cross sections are using direct Gaussian elimination methods for solving dense linear systems. These systems are always symmetric and complex, but not Hermitian. Another major source of large dense linear systems is problems involving the solution of boundary integral equations [29]. These are integral equations defined on the boundary of a region of interest. All examples of practical interest compute some intermediate quantity on a 2-D boundary and then use this information to compute the final desired quantity in three-dimensional (3-D) space. The price one pays for replacing three dimensions with two is that what started as a sparse problem in $\mathcal{O}(n^3)$ variables is replaced by a dense problem in $\mathcal{O}(n^2)$. A recent example of the use of dense linear algebra at a very large scale is physics plasma calculation in double-precision complex arithmetic based on Helmholtz equations [30].

Most dense linear system solvers rely on a decompositional approach [31]. The general idea is the following: Given a problem involving a matrix A, one factors or decomposes A into a product of simpler matrices from which the problem can easily be solved. This divides the computational problem into two parts: First determine an appropriate decomposition, and then use it in solving the problem at hand. Consider the problem of solving the linear system

$$Ax = b, \tag{32.1}$$

where A is a nonsingular matrix of order n. The decompositional approach begins with the observation that it is possible to factor A in the form

$$A = LU, \tag{32.2}$$

where L is a lower triangular matrix (a matrix that has only zeros above the diagonal) with ones on the diagonal, and U is upper triangular (with only zeros below the diagonal). During the decomposition process, diagonal elements of A (called pivots) are used to divide the elements below the diagonal. If matrix A has a zero pivot, the process will break with division-by-zero error. Also, small values of the pivots excessively amplify the numerical errors of the process. So for numerical stability, the method needs to interchange rows of the matrix or to make sure pivots are as large (in absolute value) as possible. This observation leads to a row permutation matrix P and modifies the factored form to

$$PA = LU. \tag{32.3}$$

The solution can then be written in the form

$$x = A^{-1}Pb, \tag{32.4}$$

which then suggests the following algorithm for solving the system of equations:

- Factor A according to Equation (32.3).
- Solve the system $Ly = Pb$.
- Solve the system $Ux = y$.

This approach to matrix computations through decomposition has proven very useful for several reasons. First, the approach separates the computation into two stages: the computation of a decomposition followed by the use of the decomposition to solve the problem at hand. This can be important, for example, if different right-hand sides are present and need to be solved at different points in the process. The matrix needs to be factored only once and reused for the different right-hand sides. This is particularly important because the factorization of A, step 1, requires $O(n^3)$ operations, whereas the solutions, steps 2 and 3, require only $O(n^2)$ operations. Another aspect of the algorithm's strength is in storage: The L and U factors do not require extra storage but can take over the space occupied initially by A. For the discussion of coding this algorithm, we present only the computationally intensive part of the process, which is step 1, the factorization of the matrix.

The decompositional technique can be applied to many different matrix types:

$$A_1 = LL^T \quad A_2 = LDL^T \quad PA_3 = LU \quad A_4 = QR, \tag{32.5}$$

such as symmetric positive definite (A_1), symmetric indefinite (A_2), square nonsingular (A_3), and general rectangular matrices (A_4). Each matrix type will require a different algorithm: Cholesky factorization, Cholesky factorization with pivoting, LU factorization, and QR factorization, respectively.

32.5.1.1 *Tile Linear Algebra: PLASMA, DPLASMA* The PLASMA project has been designed to target shared-memory multicore machines. Although the idea of tile algorithm does not specifically resonate with the typical specificities of a distributed-memory machine (where cache locality and reuse are of little significance when compared to communication volume), a typical supercomputer tends to be structured as a cluster of commodity nodes, which means many cores and sometimes accelerators. Hence, a tile-based algorithm can execute more efficiently on each node, often translating into a general improvement for the whole system. The core idea of the DPLASMA project is to reuse the tile algorithms developed for PLASMA, but using the DAGuE framework to express them as parametrized DAGs that can be scheduled on large-scale distributed systems of such form.

32.5.1.2   *Tile QR Algorithm*   The QR factorization (or QR decomposition) offers a numerically stable way of solving full rank underdetermined, overdetermined, and regular square linear systems of equations. The QR factorization of an $m \times n$ real matrix A has the form $A = QR$, where Q is an $m \times m$ real orthogonal matrix and R is an $m \times n$ real upper triangular matrix.

A detailed tile QR algorithm description can be found in Reference 32. Figure 32.5 shows the pseudocode of the tile QR factorization. It relies on four basic operations implemented by four computational kernels for which reference implementations are freely available as part of either the BLAS, LAPACK, or PLASMA [12].

- *DGEQRT.* The kernel performs the QR factorization of a diagonal tile and produces an upper triangular matrix R and a unit lower triangular matrix V containing the Householder reflectors. The kernel also produces the upper triangular matrix T as defined by the compact WY technique for accumulating Householder reflectors [33]. The R factor overrides the upper triangular portion of the input and the reflectors override the lower triangular portion of the input. The T matrix is stored separately.

- *DTSQRT.* The kernel performs the QR factorization of a matrix built by coupling the R factor, produced by DGEQRT or a previous call to DTSQRT, with a tile below the diagonal tile. The kernel produces an updated R factor, a square matrix V containing the Householder reflectors, and the matrix T resulting from accumulating the reflectors V. The new R factor overrides the old R factor. The block of reflectors overrides the corresponding tile of the input matrix. The T matrix is stored separately.

- *DORMQR.* The kernel applies the reflectors calculated by DGEQRT to a tile to the right of the diagonal tile using the reflectors V along with the matrix T.

- *DSSMQR.* The kernel applies the reflectors calculated by DTSQRT to the tile two tiles to the right of the tiles factorized by DTSQRT, using the reflectors V and the matrix T produced by DTSQRT.

32.5.2 Walkthrough QR Implementation

The first step to write the QR algorithm of DPLASMA is to take the sequential code presented in Figure 32.5 and process it through the DAGuE compiler (as described in Section 32.4). This produces a JDF file that then needs to be completed by the programmer.

The first part of the JDF file contains a user-defined prologue (presented in Fig. 32.6). This prologue is copied directly in the generated C code produced by the JDF compiler so the programmer can add suitable definitions and includes necessary for the body of tasks. An interesting feature is automatic generation of a variety of numerical precisions from a single source file, thanks to a small helper translator

```
1    /* Prologue, dumped "as is" in the generated file */
2    extern "C" %{
3      /**
4       * TILE QR FACTORIZATION
5       * @precisions normal z -> s d c
6       */
7    #include <plasma.h>
8    #include <core_blas.h>
9
10   #include "dague.h"
11   [...] /* more includes */
12   #include "dplasma/cores/cuda_stsmqr.h"
13   %}
14
15   /* Input variables used when creating the
16    * algorithm object instance */
17   descA  [type = "tiled_matrix_desc_t"]
18   A      [type = "dague_ddesc_t *"]
19   descT  [type = "tiled_matrix_desc_t"]
20   T      [type = "dague_ddesc_t *" aligned=A]
21   ib     [type = "int"]
22   p_work [type = "dague_memory_pool_t *"
23           size = "(sizeof(PLASMA_Complex64_t)*ib*(descT.nb))"]
24   p_tau  [type = "dague_memory_pool_t *"
25           size = "(sizeof(PLASMA_Complex64_t)   *(descT.nb))"]
26
27   /* Tasks descriptions follow */
```

FIGURE 32.6. Samples from the JDF of the QR algorithm: prologue.

that does source-to-source pattern matching to adapt numerical operations to the target precision. The next section of the JDF file declares the inputs of the algorithm and their types. From these declarations, the JDF compiler creates automatically all the interface functions used by the main program (or the library interface) to create, manipulate, and dispose of the DAGuE object representing a particular instance of the algorithm.

Then, the JDF file contains the description of all the task classes, usually generated automatically from the decorated sequential code. For each task class, the programmer needs to define (1) the data affinity of the tasks (: A.mat(k, n) in Fig. 32.3) and (2) user-provided bodies, which are, in the case of linear algebra, usually as simple as calling a BLAS or PLASMA kernel. Sometimes, algorithmic technicalities result in additional work for the programmer: Many kernels of the QR algorithm use a temporary scratchpad memory (the *phony* arguments in Figure 32.5). This memory is purely local to the kernel itself; hence, it does not need to appear in the dataflow. However, to preserve Fortran compatibility, scratchpad memory needs to be allocated outside the kernels themselves and passed as an argument. As a consequence, the bodies have to allocate and release these temporary arrays. We have designed a set of helper functions while designing DPLASMA, whose purpose is to ease the writing of linear algebra bodies; the code presented in Figure 32.7 illustrates how the programmer can push and pop scratchpad memory

```
1    /* Prologue precedes, other tasks */
2
3    ztsmqr(k,m,n)
4      [...] /* Execution space (autogenerated) */
5
6      /* Variable names translation table (autogenerated) */
7      /* J == A(k,n) */
8      [...] /* more translations */
9
10     /* dependencies (autogenerated)
11     RW  J <- (m==k+1) ? E zunmqr(m-1,n) : J ztsmqr(k,m-1,n)
12            -> (m==descA.mt-1) ? J ztsmqr_out_A(k,n) : J ztsmqr(k,m+1,n)
13     [...] /* more dependencies */
14
15     /* Task affinity with data (edited by programmer) */
16     : A(m, n)
17
18   BODY  /* edited by programmer */
19     /* computing tight tile dimensions
20      * (tiles on matrix edges contain padding) */
21     int tempnn = (n==descA.nt-1) ? descA.n-n*descA.nb : descA.nb;
22     int tempmm = (m==descA.mt-1) ? descA.m-m*descA.mb : descA.mb;
23     int ldak = BLKLDD( descA, k );
24     int ldam = BLKLDD( descA, m );
25
26     /* Obtain a scratchpad allocation */
27     void* p_elem_A = dague_private_memory_pop( p_work );
28     /* Call to the actual kernel */
29     CODELET_ztsmqr(PlasmaLeft, PlasmaConjTrans, descA.mb,
30                    tempnn, tempmm, tempnn, descA.nb, ib,
31                    J /* A(k,n) */, ldak,
32                    K /* A(m,n) */, ldam,
33                    L /* A(m,k) */,  ldam,
34                    M /* T(m,k) */,  descT.mb,
35                    p_elem_A, ldwork );
36     /* Release the scratchpad allocation */
37     dague_private_memory_push( p_work, p_elem_A );
38   END
```

FIGURE 32.7. Samples from the JDF of the QR algorithm: task body.

from a generic system call free memory pool. The variable name translation table, dumped automatically by the sequential code dependency extractor, helps the programmer navigate the generated dependencies and select the appropriate variable as a parameter of the actual computing kernel.

32.5.2.1 Accelerator Port
The only action required from the linear algebra package to enable GPU acceleration is to provide the appropriate codelets in the body part of the JDF file. A codelet is a piece of code that encapsulates a variety of implementations of an operation for a variety of hardware. Just like CPU core kernels, GPU kernels are sequential and pure; hence, a codelet is an abstraction of

a computing function suitable for a variety of processing units, either a single core or a single GPU stream (even though they can still contain some internal parallelism, such as vector single-instruction multiple-data [SIMD] instructions). Practically, that means that the application developer is in charge of providing multiple versions of the computing bodies. The relevant codelets, optimized for the current hardware, are loaded automatically during the algorithm initialization (one for the GPU hardware, one for the CPU cores, etc.). Today, the DAGuE runtime supports only CUDA and CPU codelets, but the infrastructure can easily accommodate other accelerator types (Intel Many Integrated Core [MIC or Xeon Phi], Open Computing Language [OpenCL], field-programmable gate arrays [FPGAs], Cell, etc.). If a task features multiple codelets, the runtime scheduler chooses dynamically (during the invocation of the automatically generated scheduling hook CODELET_kernelname) between all these versions in order to execute the operation on the most relevant hardware. Because multiple versions of the same codelet kernel can be in use at the same time, the workload of this type of operations, on different input data, can be distributed on both CPU cores and GPUs simultaneously.

In the case of the QR factorization, we selected to add a GPU version of the STSMQR kernel, which is the matrix–matrix multiplication kernel used to update the remainder of the matrix, after a particular panel has been factorized (hence representing 80% or more of the overall compute time). We have extended a handmade GPU kernel [34], originally obtained from MAGMA [12]. This kernel is provided in a separate source file and is developed separately as a regular CUDA function. Should future versions of CuBLAS enable running concurrent GPU kernels on several hardware streams, these vendor functions could be used directly.

32.5.2.2 Wrapper As previously stated, scratchpad memory needs to be allocated outside of the bodies. Similarly, because we wanted the JDF format to be oblivious of the transport technology, data types, which are inherently dependent on the description used in the message-passing system, need to be declared outside the generated code. In order for the generated library to be more convenient to use for end users, we consider it good practice to provide a wrapper around the generated code that takes care of allocating and defining these required elements. In the case of linear algebra, we provide a variety of helper functions to allocate scratchpads (line 9 in Fig. 32.8), and to create most useful data types (like triangular matrices) (lines 13 and 18 in the same figure), like band matrices and square or rectangular matrices. Again, the framework-provided tool can create all floating-point precisions from a single source.

32.5.2.3 Main Program A skeleton program that initializes and schedules a QR factorization using the DAGuE framework is presented in Figure 32.9. Since DAGuE uses MPI as an underlaying communication mechanism, the test program is an MPI program. It thus needs to initialize and finalize MPI (lines 8 and 33) and the programmer is free to use any MPI functionality, around DAGuE calls (line 9, where arguments should also be parsed). A subset of the DAGuE calls is to be considered as a collective operation from an MPI perspective: All MPI processes must call them in the same order, with a communication scheme that allows these operations to match. These operations are the initialization function (`dague_init`), the progress function (`dague_progress`), and the finalization function (`dague_`

```
1    dague_object_t* dplasma_sgeqrf_New( tiled_matrix_desc_t *A,
2                                        tiled_matrix_desc_t *T )
3    {
4      dague_sgeqrf_object_t* d = dague_sgeqrf_new(*A, (dague_ddesc_t*)A,
5                                                  *T, (dague_ddesc_t*)T,
6                                                  ib, NULL, NULL);
7
8      d->p_tau = malloc(sizeof(dague_memory_pool_t));
9      dague_private_memory_init(d->p_tau, T->nb * sizeof(float));
10     [...] /* similar code for p_work scratchpad */
11
12     /* Datatypes declarations, from MPI datatypes */
13     dplasma_add2arena_tile(d->arenas[DAGUE_sgeqrf_DEFAULT_ARENA],
14                            A->mb*A->nb*sizeof(float),
15                            DAGUE_ARENA_ALIGNMENT_SSE,
16                            MPI_FLOAT, A->mb);
17     /* Lower triangular part of tile without diagonal */
18     dplasma_add2arena_lower(d->arenas[DAGUE_sgeqrf_LOWER_TILE_ARENA],
19                             A->mb*A->nb*sizeof(float),
20                             DAGUE_ARENA_ALIGNMENT_SSE,
21                             MPI_FLOAT, A->mb, 0);
22     [...] /* similarly, U upper triangle and T (IB*MB rectangle)*/
23
24     return (dague_object_t*)d;
25   }
```

FIGURE 32.8. *User-provided wrapper around the DAGuE generated QR factorization function.*

fini). dague_init will create a specified number of threads on the local process, plus the communication thread. Threads are bound on separate cores when possible. Once the DAGuE system is initialized on all MPI processes, each must choose a local scheduler. DAGuE provides four scheduling heuristics, but the one preferred is the Local Hierarchical Scheduler, developed specifically for DAGuE on NUMA many-core heterogeneous machines. The function dague_set_scheduler of line 12 sets this scheduler.

The next step consists of creating a data distribution descriptor. This code holds two data distribution descriptors: ddescA and ddescT. DAGuE provides three built-in data distributions for tiled matrices: an arbitrary index-based distribution, a symmetric 2-D block-cyclic distribution, and a 2-D block-cyclic distribution. In the case of QR, the latter is used to describe the input matrix *A* to be factorized and the workspace array T. Once the data distribution is created, the local memory to store this data should be allocated in the fields mat of the descriptor. To enable DAGuE to pin memory, and allow for direct DMA transfers (to and from the GPUs or some high-performance networks), the helper function dague_data_allo-cate of line 15 is used. The workspace array T should be described and allocated in a similar way on line 16.

Then, this test program uses DPLASMA functions to initialize the matrix *A* with random values (line 18), and the workspace array T with 0 (line 19). These functions are coded in DAGuE: They create a DAG representation of a map operation that

```
1   int main(int argc, char **argv)
2   {
3       dague_context_t *dague;
4       two_dim_block_cyclic_t ddescA;
5       two_dim_block_cyclic_t ddescT;
6       dague_object_t* zgeqrf_object;
7
8       MPI_Init(&argc, &argv);
9       [...]
10
11      dague = dague_init(NBCORES, &argc, &argv);
12      dague_set_scheduler(dague, &dague_sched_LHQ);
13
14          /* Matrix allocation and random filling */
15      two_dim_block_cyclic_init(&ddescA, matrix_ComplexDouble, [...]);
16      ddescA.mat = dague_data_allocate([...]);
17      dplasma_zplrnt(dague, &ddescA, 3872);
18      dplasma_zlaset(dague, PlasmaUpperLower, 0., 0., &ddescT);
19      [...] /* Same for other matrices */
20
21      zgeqrf_object = dplasma_zgeqrf_New(&ddescA, &ddescT);
22      dague_enqueue(dague, zgeqrf_object);
23
24          /* Computation happens here */
25      dague_progress(dague);
26
27      dplasma_zgeqrf_Destruct(zgeqrf_object);
28
29      [...]
30
31      dague_data_free(ddescA.mat);
32      dague_ddesc_destroy((dague_ddesc_t*)&ddescA);
33      [...]
34
35      dague_fini(&dague);
36      MPI_Finalize();
37
38      return 0;
39  }
```

FIGURE 32.9. *Skeleton of a DAGuE main program driving the QR factorization.*

will initialize each tile in parallel with the desired values, making the engine progress on these DAGs.

Once the data are initialized, a `zgeqrf` DAGuE object is created with the wrapper that was described above. This object holds the symbolic representation of the local DAG, initialized with the desired parameters and bound to the allocated and described data. It is (locally) enqueued in the DAGuE engine on line 22.

To compute the QR operation described by this object, all MPI processes call to `dague_progress` on line 24. This enables all threads created on line 8 to work on the QR operation enqueued before in collaboration with all the other MPI

```
1    int dplasma_sgeqrf( dague_context_t *dague, tiled_matrix_desc_t *A,
2                                        tiled_matrix_desc_t *T )
3    {
4        dague_object_t *dague_sgeqrf = dplasma_sgeqrf_New(A, T);
5
6        dague_enqueue(dague, dague_sgeqrf);
7        dplasma_progress(dague);
8
9        dplasma_sgeqrf_Destruct(dague_sgeqrf);
10       return 0;
11   }
```

FIGURE 32.10. DPLASMA SPMD interface for the DAGuE generated QR factorization function.

processes. This call returns when all enqueued objects are completed, thus, when the factorization is done. At this point, the `zgeqrd` DAGuE object is consumed and can be freed by the programmer at line 26. The result of the factorization should be used on line 28, before the data are freed (line 30), and the descriptors destroyed (line 31). Line 32 should hold a similar code to free the data and destroy the descriptor of T. Then, the DAGuE engine can release all resources (line 34) before MPI is finalized and the application terminates.

32.5.2.4 *SPMD Library Interface*   It is possible for the library to encapsulate all dataflow-related calls inside a regular (ScaLAPACK like) interface function. This function creates an algorithm instance, enqueues it in the dataflow runtime, and enables progress (lines 6, 7, and 9 in Fig. 32.10). From the main program point of view, the code is similar to a SPMD call to a parallel BLAS function; the main program does not need to consider the fact that dataflow is used within the linear algebra library. While this approach can simplify the porting of legacy applications, it prevents the program from composing DAG-based algorithms. If the main program takes full control of the algorithm objects, it can enqueue multiple algorithms and then progress all of them simultaneously, enabling optimal overlap between separate algorithms (such as a factorization and the associated solve); if it simply calls the SPMD interface, it still benefits from complete parallelism within individual functions, but it falls back to a synchronous SPMD model between different algorithms.

32.5.3 Correctness and Performance Analysis Tools

The first correctness tool of the DAGuE framework sits within the code generator tool, which converts the JDF representation into C functions. A number of conditions on the dependencies and execution spaces are checked during this stage and can detect many instances of mismatching dependencies (where the input of task A comes from task B, but task B has no outputs to task A). Similarly, conditions that are not satisfiable according to the execution space raise warnings, as is the case for pure input data (operations that read the input matrix directly, not as an output of another task) that do not respect the task–data affinity. These warnings help the programmer detect the most common errors when writing the JDF.

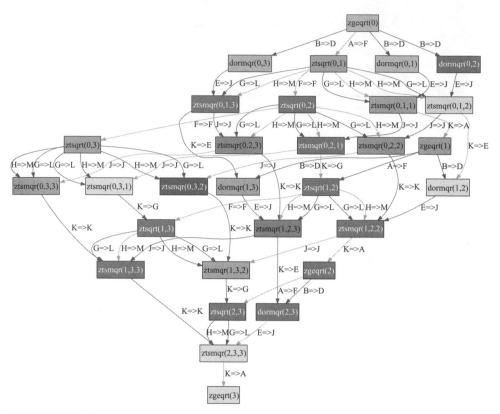

FIGURE 32.11. *The runtime can output a graphical version of the DAG for validation purposes. In this example, the output shows the execution of the QR operation on a 4 × 4 tiled matrix, on two nodes with eight cores per node.*

At runtime, algorithm programmers can generate the complete unrolled DAG for offline analysis purposes. The DAGuE engine can output a representation of the DAG, as it is executed, in the `dot` input format of the GraphViz graph plotting tool. The programmer can use the resulting graphic representation (see Fig. 32.11) to analyze which kernel ran on what resource, and which dependence released which tasks into their ready state. Using such information has proven critical when debugging the JDF representation (for an advanced user who wants to write his or her own JDF directly without using the DAGuE compiler), or to understand contentions and improve the data distribution and the priorities assigned to tasks.

The DAGuE framework also features performance analysis tools to help programmers fine-tune the performance of their application. At the heart of these tools, the profiling collection mechanism optionally records the duration of each individual task, communication, and scheduling decision. These measurements are saved in thread-specific memory, without any locking or other forms of atomic operations, and are then output at termination time in an XML file for offline analysis.

This XML file can then be converted by tools provided in the framework to portable trace formats (like open trace format [OTF] [35]), or simple spreadsheets, representing the start date and duration of each critical operation. Figure 32.12 presents two Gantt chart representations of the beginning of a QR DAGuE execution on a single node, eight cores using two different scheduling heuristics: the

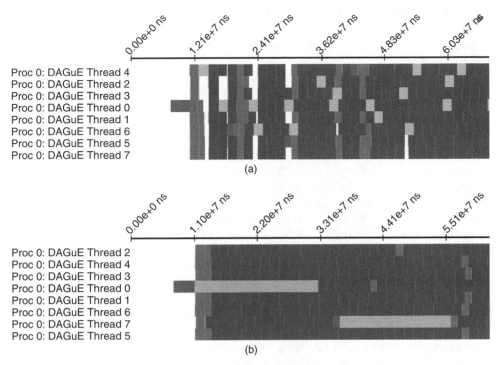

FIGURE 32.12. Gantt representation of a shared-memory run of the QR factorization on 8 threads.

simple first in, first out (FIFO) scheduling and the scheduler of DAGuE (local hierarchical queues, described in Section 32.3.1). The ability of the local hierarchical queues scheduler to increase the data locality, allow for maximal parallelism, and avoid starvations is highlighted in these graphs. Potential starvations are easily spotted, as they appear as large stripes where multiple threads do not execute any kernel. Similar charts can be generated for distributed runs (not presented here), with a clear depiction of the underlying communications in the MPI thread, annotated by the data they carry and tasks they connect. Using these results, a programmer can assess the efficiency, on real runs, of the proposed data distribution, task affinity, and priority. Data distribution and task affinity will both influence the amount and duration of communications, as well as the amount of starvation, while priority will mostly influence the amount of starvation.

In the case of the QR factorization, these profiling outputs have been used to evaluate the priority hints given to tasks, used by the scheduler when ordering tasks (refer to Section 32.3.1). The folklore knowledge about scheduling DAG of dense factorizations is that the priorities should always favor the tasks that are closer to the critical path. We have implemented such a strategy and discovered that it is easily outperformed by a completely dynamic scheduling that does not respect any priorities. There is indeed a fine balance between following the absolute priorities along the critical path, which enables maximum parallelism, and favoring cache reuse even if it progresses a branch that is far from the critical path. We have found a set of beneficial priority rules (which are symbolic expressions similar to the dependencies) that favor progressing iterations along the k direction first, but favor only a couple iterations of the critical path over update kernels.

32.6   PERFORMANCE EVALUATION

The performance of the DAGuE runtime has been extensively studied in related publications [4, 34, 36]. The goal here is to illustrate the performance results that can be achieved by the porting of linear algebra code to the DAGuE framework. Therefore, we present a summary of these results to demonstrate that the tool chain achieves its main goals of overall performance, performance portability, and capability to process different nontrivial algorithms.

The experiments we summarize here have been conducted on three different platforms. The Griffon platform is one of the clusters of Grid'5000 [37]. We used 81 dual socket Intel Xeon L5420 quad core processors at 2.5 GHz to gather 648 cores. Each node has 16 GB of memory and is interconnected to the others by a 20-Gb Infiniband network. Linux 2.6.24 (Debian Sid) is deployed on these nodes. The Kraken system of the University of Tennessee and National Institute for Computational Science (NICS) is hosted at the Oak Ridge National Laboratory. It is a Cray XT5 with 8256 compute nodes connected on a 3-D torus with SeaStar. Each node has a dual six-core AMD Opteron cadenced at 2.6 GHz. We used up to 3072 cores in the experiments we present here. All nodes have 16 GB of memory and run the Cray Linux Environment (CLE) 2.2.

The benchmark consists of three popular dense matrix factorizations: Cholesky, LU, and QR. The Cholesky factorization solves the problem $Ax = b$, where A is symmetric and positive definite. It computes the real lower triangular matrix with positive diagonal elements L such that $A = LL^T$. The QR factorization has been presented in previous sections, to explain the functionality and behavior of DAGuE. It offers a numerically stable way of solving full rank underdetermined, overdetermined, and regular square linear systems of equations. It computes Q and R such that $A = QR$, Q is a real orthogonal matrix, and R is a real upper triangular matrix. The LU factorization with partial pivoting of a real matrix A has the form $PA = LU$, where L is a real unit lower triangular matrix, U is a real upper triangular matrix, and P is a permutation matrix.

All three of these operations are implemented in the ScaLAPACK numerical library [38]. In addition, some of these factorizations have more optimized versions; we used the state-of-the-art version for each of the existing factorizations to measure against. The Cholesky factorization has been implemented in a more optimized way in the DSBP software [16] using static scheduling of tasks and a specific, more efficient data distribution. The LU factorization with partial pivoting is also solved by the well-known high-performance LINPACK (HPL) benchmark [39], used to measure the performance of high-performance computers. We have distributed the initial data following a classical 2-D block-cyclic distribution used by ScaLAPACK and have used the DAGuE runtime engine to schedule the operations on the distributed data. The kernels consist of the BLAS operations referenced by the sequential codes, and their implementation was the most efficient, available on each of the machine.

Figure 32.13 presents the performance measured for DAGuE and ScaLAPACK, and when applicable, DSBP and HPL, as a function of the problem size. Six hundred forty-eight cores on 81 multicore nodes have been used for the distributed run, and the data were distributed according to a 9×9 2-D block-cyclic grid for DAGuE. A similar distribution was used for ScaLAPACK, and the other benchmarks when

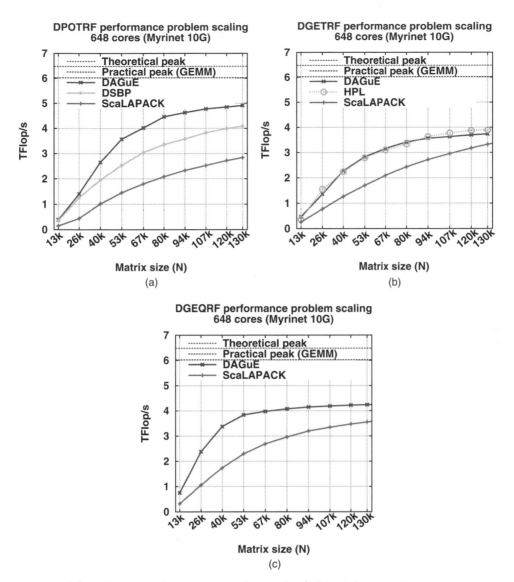

FIGURE 32.13. *Performance comparison on the Griffon platform with 648 cores.*

appropriate, and the block size was tuned to provide the best performance on each setup. As the figures illustrate, on all benchmarks, and for all problem sizes, the DAGuE framework was able to outperform ScaLAPACK and to perform as well as the state-of-the-art, hand-tuned codes for specific problems. The DAGuE approach, that is, completely automatic conversion from sequential code to the corresponding parallel version, is able to outperform DSBP and compete favorably with the HPL implementation on this machine.

Figure 32.14a presents the performance of the DAGuE Cholesky algorithm on a GPU cluster, featuring 12 Fermi C2070 accelerators (one per node). Without GPU accelerators, the DAGuE runtime extracts the entire available performance; asymptotic performance matches the performance of the GEMM kernel on this processor,

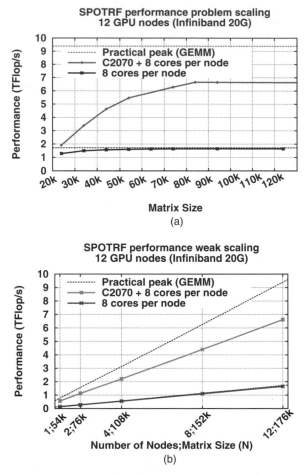

FIGURE 32.14. *Performance of DAGuE Cholesky on the Dancer GPU accelerated cluster.*

which is an upper bound to the effective peak performance. When using one GPU accelerator per node, the total efficiency reaches as much as 73% of the GEMM peak, which is a 54% efficiency of the theoretical peak (typical GPU efficiency is lower than CPU efficiency; the HPL benchmark on the TianHe-1A GPU system reaches a similar 51% efficiency, which compares with 78% on the CPU-based Kraken machine). Scalability is a concern with GPU accelerators as they provoke a massive imbalance between computing power and network capacity. Figure 32.14b presents the Cholesky factorization weak scalability (the number of nodes varies; problem size grows accordingly to keep memory load per node constant) on the GPU enabled machine. The figure outlines the perfect weak scalability up to 12 GPU nodes.

Last, Figure 32.15 compares the performance of the DAGuE implementation of these three operations with the libSCI implementation, specifically tuned by Cray for this machine. The value represented is the relative time overhead of DAGuE compared to libSCI for different matrix sizes and the number of nodes on the QR factorization (similar weak scaling as in the previous experiment, $N = 454,000$ on

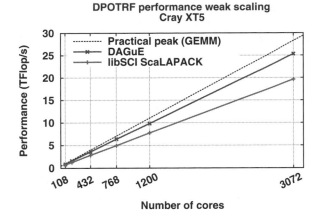

FIGURE 32.15. *Scalability on the Kraken platform.*

3072 cores). On this machine, the DAGuE runtime can effectively use only 11 of 12 cores per node for compute tasks; due to kernel scheduler parameters (long, non-preemptive time quantum), the MPI thread must be exclusively pinned to a physical core to avoid massive and detrimental message jitter. Even considering that limitation, which is only technical and could be overcome by a native port of the runtime to the portal messaging library instead of MPI, the DAGuE implementation competes favorably with the extremely efficient libSCI QR factorization. The DAGuE approach demonstrates an excellent scalability, up to a massive number of nodes, thanks to the distributed evaluation of the DAG not requiring centralized control nor complete unrolling of the DAG on each node.

On different machines, the DAGuE compiler coupled with the DAGuE runtime significantly outperformed standard algorithms and competed closely, usually favorably, with state-of-the-art optimized versions of similar algorithms, without any further tuning process involved when porting the code between radically different platform types. Another significant fact to be highlighted is the sizes of the problem where DAGuE achieves peak performance. In all graphs in Figure 32.13, one can notice that while ScaLAPACK asymptotically reaches peak performance, for some of the algorithms, DAGuE achieves the same level of performance on data four times smaller (in the case of Cholesky, ScaLAPACK achieves 3 Tflop/s on Griffon when $N = 130,000$, while DAGuE reaches the same level for $N = 44,000$).

32.7   CONCLUSION

Although hardware architectural paradigm shifts are threatening the scientific productivity of dense linear algebra codes, we have demonstrated that by slightly changing the execution paradigm and using a dataflow representation extracted from a decorated sequential code, dense matrix factorization can reach excellent performance. The DPLASMA package aims at providing the same functionalities as the ScaLAPACK legacy package, but using a more modern approach, based on tile algorithm and dataflow representation, that enables better cache reuse and asynchrony, which are paramount features to perform on multicore nodes. Furthermore, the DAG dataflow representation enables the algorithm to adapt easily to a variety of differing and heterogeneous hardware, without involving a major code refactoring for each target platform. We describe how the DPLASMA project uses the DAGuE framework to convert a decorated sequential code (which can be executed efficiently on multicore machines but not on distributed-memory systems) into a concise DAG dataflow representation. This representation is then altered by the programmer to add data distribution and task affinity on distributed memory. The resulting intermediate format is then compiled into a series of runtime hooks incorporating a DAG scheduler that automatically orchestrates the resolution of remote dependencies, orchestrates the execution to favor cache locality and other scheduling heuristics, and accounts for the presence of heterogeneous resources such as GPU accelerators. This description gives insight to linear algebra programmers as to the methods, challenges, and solutions involved in porting their code to a dataflow representation. The performance analysis section demonstrates the vast superiority of the DAG-based code over legacy programming paradigms on newer multicore hardware.

32.8 SUMMARY

The tumultuous changes occurring in the computer hardware space, such as flatlining of processor clock speeds after more than 15 years of exponential increases, mark the end of the era of routine and near-automatic performance improvements that the research community had previously enjoyed [40]. Two main factors converged to force processor architects to turn to multicore and heterogeneous designs and, consequently, to bring an end to the "free ride." First, system builders have encountered intractable physical barriers—too much heat, too much power consumption, and too much leaking voltage—to further increases in clock speeds. Second, physical limits on the number of pins and bandwidth on a single chip mean that the gap between processor performance and memory performance, which was already bad, has gotten increasingly worse. Consequently, the design trade-offs made to address the previous two factors rendered commodity processors, absent any further augmentation, inadequate for the purposes of extreme-scale systems for advanced applications. This daunting combination of obstacles forced the designers of new multicore and hybrid systems to explore architectures that software built on the old model are unable to effectively exploit without radical modification.

To develop software that will perform well on extreme-scale systems with thousands of nodes and millions of cores, the list of major challenges that must now be confronted is intimidating:

- Automatic adaptation to the dramatic escalation in the costs of intrasystem communication between processors and/or levels of memory hierarchy
- Acclimatization to the increased hybridization of processor architectures (mixing CPUs, GPUs, etc.), in varying and unexpected design combinations
- Cooperating processes must be dynamically and unpredictably scheduled for asynchronous execution due to high levels of parallelism and more complex constraints.

- Software will not run at scale without much better resilience to faults and increased robustness.
- New levels of self-adaptivity will be required to enable software to modulate process speed in order to satisfy limited energy budgets.

The software project presented above meets the aforementioned challenges and allows the users to run their computationally intensive codes at scale and to achieve a significant percentage of peak performance on the contemporary hardware systems that may soon break the barrier of 100 Pflop/s. This is achieved by finding and integrating solutions to problems in two critical areas: novel algorithm design as well as management of parallelism and hybridization.

REFERENCES

[1] P. Kogge, K. Bergman, S. Borkar, D. Campbell, W. Carlson, W. Dally, M. Denneau, P. Franzon, W. Harrod, K. Hill, J. Hiller, S. Karp, S. Keckler, D. Klein, R. Lucas, M. Richards, A. Scarpelli, S. Scott, A. Snavely, T. Sterling, R.S. Williams, and K. Yelick, "Exascale computing study: Technology challenges in achieving exascale systems," Technical Report TR-2008-13, Department of Computer Science and Engineering, University of Notre Dame, September 28 2008.

[2] National Research Council Committee on the Potential Impact of High-End Computing on Illustrative Fields of Science and Engineering, *The Potential Impact of High-End Capability Computing on Four Illustrative Fields of Science and Engineering*. Washington, DC: National Academies Press, 2008.

[3] University of Tennessee, PLASMA Users' Guide, Parallel Linear Algebra Software for Multicore Architectures, Version 2.2, November 2009.

[4] G. Bosilca, A. Bouteiller, A. Danalis, T. Herault, P. Lemarinier, and J.J. Dongarra, "DAGuE: A generic distributed DAG engine for high performance computing," *Parallel Computing*, 38:37–51, 2011.

[5] E.G. Coffman, Jr. and P.J. Denning, *Operating Systems Theory*. Upper Saddle River, NJ: Prentice Hall Professional Technical Reference. 1973.

[6] A.J. Bernstein, "Analysis of programs for parallel processing," *IEEE Transactions on Electronic Computers*, EC-15:757–763, 1966.

[7] J.A. Sharp ed., *Data Flow Computing: Theory and Practice*. Norwood, NJ: Ablex Publishing Corp., 1992.

[8] J. Yu and R. Buyya, "A taxonomy of workflow management systems for grid computing," Technical Report, *Journal of Grid Computing*, 3:171–200, 2005.

[9] O. Delannoy, N. Emad, and S. Petiton, "Workflow global computing with YML," *7th IEEE/ACM International Conference on Grid Computing*, September 2006.

[10] A. Buttari, J.J. Dongarra, J. Kurzak, J. Langou, P. Luszczek, and S. Tomov, "The impact of multicore on math software," in *Applied Parallel Computing, State of the Art in Scientific Computing, 8th International Workshop, PARA*, Vol. 4699 of *Lecture Notes in Computer Science*, pp. 1–10, Springer, 2006.

[11] E. Chan, F.G. Van Zee, P. Bientinesi, E.S. Quintana-Ortí, G. Quintana-Ortí, and R. van de Geijn, "Supermatrix: A multithreaded runtime scheduling system for algorithms-by-blocks," in *PPoPP '08: Proceedings of the 13th ACM SIGPLAN Symposium on Principles and Practice of Parallel Programming*, pp. 123–132, ACM, 2008.

[12] E. Agullo, J. Demmel, J.J. Dongarra, B. Hadri, J. Kurzak, J. Langou, H. Ltaief, P. Luszczek, and S. Tomov, "Numerical linear algebra on emerging architectures: The PLASMA and MAGMA projects," *Journal of Physics: Conference Series*, 180:12–37, 2009.

[13] R. Dolbeau, S. Bihan, and F. Bodin, "HMPP: A hybrid multi-core parallel programming environment," in *Workshop on General Purpose Processing on Graphics Processing Units (GPGPU 2007)*, 2007.

[14] C. Augonnet, S. Thibault, R. Namyst, and P.-A. Wacrenier, "StarPU: A unified platform for task scheduling on heterogeneous multicore architectures," *Concurrency and Computation: Practice and Experience*, 23(2):187–198, 2011.

[15] P. Husbands and K.A. Yelick, "Multi-threading and one-sided communication in parallel LU factorization," in *Proceedings of the ACM/IEEE Conference on High Performance Networking and Computing, SC 2007*, November 10–16, 2007 (B. Verastegui, ed.), Reno, NV: ACM Press, 2007.

[16] F.G. Gustavson, L. Karlsson, and B. Kågström, "Distributed SBP Cholesky factorization algorithms with near-optimal scheduling," *ACM Transactions on Mathematical Software*, 36(2):1–25, 2009.

[17] J. Perez, R. Badia, and J. Labarta, "A dependency-aware task-based programming environment for multi-core architectures," *2008 IEEE International Conference on Cluster Computing*, pp. 142–151, October 1–29, 2008.

[18] F. Song, A. YarKhan, and J.J. Dongarra, "Dynamic task scheduling for linear algebra algorithms on distributed-memory multicore systems," in *SC '09: Proceedings of the Conference on High Performance Computing Networking, Storage and Analysis*, pp. 1–11, New York: ACM, 2009.

[19] M. Cosnard and E. Jeannot, "Automatic parallelization techniques based on compact DAG extraction and symbolic scheduling," *Parallel Processing Letters*, 11:151–168, 2001.

[20] M. Cosnard, E. Jeannot, and T. Yang, "Compact dag representation and its symbolic scheduling," *Journal of Parallel and Distributed Computing*, 64:921–935, 2004.

[21] E. Jeannot, "Automatic multithreaded parallel program generation for message passing multiprocessors using parameterized task graphs," *International Conference "Parallel Computing 2001" (ParCo2001)*, September 2001.

[22] A. Haidar, H. Ltaief, A. YarKhan, and J.J. Dongarra, "Analysis of dynamically scheduled tile algorithms for dense linear algebra on multicore architectures," *Concurrency and Computation: Practice and Experience*, 24:305–321, 2011.

[23] AMD, "Amd64 architecture programmer's manual volume 2: System programming," Technical Report, AMD64 Technology, 2011.

[24] W. Pugh, "The omega test: A fast and practical integer programming algorithm for depend ence analysis," in *Supercomputing '91: Proceedings of the 1991 ACM/IEEE Conference on Supercomputing*, pp. 4–13, New York, 1991.

[25] R. Harrington, "Origin and development of the method of moments for field computation," *IEEE Antennas and Propagation Magazine*, 32:31–35, 1990.

[26] J.J.H. Wang, *Generalized Moment Methods in Electromagnetics*. New York: John Wiley & Sons, 1991.

[27] J.L. Hess, "Panel methods in computational fluid dynamics," *Annual Review of Fluid Mechanics*, 22:255–274, 1990.

[28] L. Hess and M.O. Smith, "Calculation of potential flows about arbitrary bodies," in *Progress in Aeronautical Sciences* (D. Kuchemann, ed.), Vol. 8. Pergamon Press, 1967.

[29] A. Edelman, "Large dense numerical linear algebra in 1993: The parallel computing influence," *International Journal of High Performance Computing Applications*, 7(2):113–128, 1993.

[30] R.F. Barrett, T.H.F. Chan, E.F. D'Azevedo, E.F. Jaeger, K. Wong, and R.Y. Wong, "Complex version of high performance computing LINPACK benchmark (HPL)," *Concurrency and Computation: Practice and Experience*, 22(5):573–587, 2010.

[31] G.W. Stewart, "The decompositional approach to matrix computation," *Computing in Science & Engineering*, 2:50–59, 2000.

[32] A. Buttari, J. Langou, J. Kurzak, and J.J. Dongarra, "Parallel tiled QR factorization for multicore architectures," *Concurrency and Computation: Practice and Experience*, 20(13):1573–1590, 2008.

[33] R. Schreiber and C. van Loan, "A storage-efficient WY representation for products of Householder transformations," *SIAM Journal on Scientific and Statistical Computing*, 10:53–57, 1991.

[34] G. Bosilca, A. Bouteiller, T. Herault, P. Lemarinier, N. Saengpatsa, S. Tomov, and J.J. Dongarra, "Performance portability of a GPU enabled factorization with the DAGuE framework," in *Proceedings of the IEEE Cluster 2011 Conference (PPAC Workshop)*, pp. 395–402, IEEE, September 2011.

[35] A.D. Malony and W.E. Nagel, "The open trace format (OTF) and open tracing for HPC," *Proceedings of the 2006 ACM/IEEE Conference on Supercomputing, SC '06*, New York: ACM, 2006.

[36] G. Bosilca, A. Bouteiller, A. Danalis, M. Faverge, A. Haidar, T. Herault, J. Kurzak, J. Langou, P. Lemarinier, H. Ltaief, P. Luszczek, A. YarKhan, and J.J. Dongarra, "Flexible development of dense linear algebra algorithms on massively parallel architectures with DPLASMA," in *IEEE International Symposium on Parallel and Distributed Processing, 12th IEEE International Workshop on Parallel and Distributed Scientific and Engineering Computing (PDSEC-11)*, pp. 1432–1441, May 2011, Anchorage, AK.

[37] R. Bolze, F. Cappello, E. Caron, M. Daydé, F. Desprez, E. Jeannot, Y. Jégou, S. Lanteri, J. Leduc, N. Melab, G. Mornet, R. Namyst, P. Primet, B. Quetier, O. Richard, E.-G. Talbi, and I. Touche, "Grid'5000: A large scale and highly reconfigurable experimental grid testbed," *International Journal of High Performance Computing Applications*, 20(4):481–494, 2006.

[38] L.S. Blackford, J. Choi, A. Cleary, E. D'Azevedo, J. Demmel, I. Dhillon, J.J. Dongarra, S. Hammarling, G. Henry, A. Petitet, K. Stanley, D. Walker, and R.C. Whaley, *ScaLAPACK Users' Guide*. Philadelphia, PA: Society for Industrial and Applied Mathematics, 1997.

[39] J.J. Dongarra, P. Luszczek, and A. Petitet, "The LINPACK benchmark: Past, present and future," *Concurrency and Computation: Practice and Experience*, 15(9):803–820, 2003.

[40] H. Sutter, "The free lunch is over: A fundamental turn toward concurrency in software," *Dr. Dobb's Journal*, 30(3), 2005.

33

Fault-Tolerance Techniques for Scalable Computing

Pavan Balaji, Darius Buntinas, and Dries Kimpe

33.1 INTRODUCTION AND TRENDS IN LARGE-SCALE COMPUTING SYSTEMS

The largest systems in the world already use close to a million cores. With upcoming systems expected to use tens to hundreds of millions of cores, and exascale systems going up to a billion cores, the number of hardware components these systems would comprise would be staggering. Unfortunately, the reliability of each hardware component is not improving at the same rate as the number of components in the system is growing. Consequently, faults are increasingly becoming common. For the largest supercomputers that will be available over the next decade, faults will become a norm rather than an exception.

Faults are common even today. Memory bit flips and network packet drops, for example, are common on the largest systems today. However, these faults are typically hidden from the user in that the hardware automatically corrects these errors by error correction techniques such as error correction codes (ECCs) and hardware redundancy. While convenient, unfortunately, such techniques are sometimes expensive with respect to cost as well as to performance and power usage. Consequently, researchers are looking at various approaches to alleviate this issue.

Broadly speaking, modern fault-resilience techniques can be classified into three categories:

1. *Hardware Resilience.* This category includes techniques such as memory error correction techniques and network reliability that are transparently handled

Scalable Computing and Communications: Theory and Practice, First Edition. Edited by
Samee U. Khan, Albert Y. Zomaya, and Lizhe Wang.
© 2013 John Wiley & Sons, Inc. Published 2013 by John Wiley & Sons, Inc.

by the hardware unit, typically by utilizing some form of redundancy in either the data stored or the data communicated.

2. *Resilient Systems Software.* This category includes software-based resilience techniques that are handled within systems software and programming infrastructure. While this method does involve human intervention, it is usually assumed that such infrastructure is written by expert "power users" who are willing to deal with the architectural complexities with respect to fault management. This category of fault resilience is mostly transparent to end domain scientists writing computational science applications.

3. *Application-Based Resilience.* The third category involves domain scientists and other high-level domain-specific languages and libraries. This class typically deals with faults using information about the domain or application, allowing developers to make intelligent choices on how to deal with the faults.

In this chapter, we describe each of these three categories with examples of recent research. In Section 33.2, we describe various techniques used today for hardware fault resilience in memory, network, and storage units. In Section 33.3, we discuss fault-resilience techniques used in various systems software libraries, including communication libraries, task-based models, and large data models. In Section 33.4, we present techniques used by application and domain-specific languages in dealing with system faults. In Section 33.5, we summarize these different techniques.

33.2   HARDWARE FEATURES FOR RESILIENCE

This section discusses some of the resilience techniques implemented in processor, memory, storage, and network hardware. In these devices, a failure occurs when the hardware is unable to accurately store, retrieve, or transmit data. Therefore, most resilience techniques focus on detection and reconstruction of corrupted data.

33.2.1   Processor Resilience

Detecting errors in the execution of processor instructions can be accomplished by redundant execution, where a computation is performed multiple times and the results are compared. In Reference 1 , Qureshi et al. identify two classes of redundant execution: space redundant and time redundant. In space-redundant execution, the computation is executed on distinct hardware components in parallel, while in time-redundant execution, the computation is executed more than once on the same hardware components. The technique presented in Reference 1 is a time-redundant technique that uses the time spent waiting for cache misses to perform the redundant execution. Oh et al. describe a space-redundant technique in Reference 2 using superscalar processors. In this technique, separate registers are used to store the results for each of the duplicated instructions. Periodically, the values in the registers are compared in order to detect errors.

33.2.2   Memory Resilience

A memory error can be defined as reading the logical state of one or more bits differently from how they were written. Memory errors are classified as either *soft* or *hard*. Soft errors are transient; in other words, they typically do not occur repeatedly when reading the same memory location and are caused mainly by electric or magnetic interference. Hard errors are persistent. For example, a faulty electrical contact causing a specific bit in a data word to be always set is a hard memory error. Hard errors are often caused by physical problems. Note that memory errors do not necessarily originate from the memory cell itself. For example, while the memory contents can be accurate, an error can occur on the path from the memory to the processor.

The failure rate (and trend) of memory strongly depends on the memory technology [3]. DRAM stores individual bits as a charge in a small capacitor. Because of leaking from the capacitor, DRAM requires periodic refreshing. DRAM memory cells can be implemented by using a single transistor and capacitor, making them relatively inexpensive to implement, so most of the memory found in contemporary computer systems consists of DRAM. Unfortunately, like other memory technologies, DRAM is susceptible to soft errors. For example, neutrons originating from cosmic rays can change the contents of a memory cell [4].

It is often assumed that when decreasing chip voltages in order to reduce the energy required to flip a memory bit and increasing memory densities, the per-bit soft error rate will increase significantly [5, 6]. A number of studies, however, indicate that this is not the case [7–9].

The DRAM error rate, depending on the source, ranges from 10^{-10} to 10^{-17} errors/bit/h. Schroeder and Gibson show that memory failures are the second leading cause of system downtime [10, 11] in production sites running large-scale systems.

Memory resilience is achieved by using *error detection* and *error correction* techniques. In both cases, extra information is stored along with the data. On retrieval, this extra information is used to check data consistency. In the case of an ECC, certain errors can be corrected to recover the original data.

For error detection, the extra information is typically computed by using a hash function. One of the earliest hash functions used for detecting memory errors is the parity function. For a given word of d bits, a single bit is added so that the number of 1 bits occurring in the data word extended by the parity bit is either odd (odd parity) or even (even parity). A single parity bit will detect only those errors modifying an *odd* number of bits. Therefore, this technique can reliably detect only those failures resulting in the modification of a single data bit.

Parity checking has become rare for the main memory (DRAM), where it has been replaced by error-correcting codes. However, parity checking and other error detection codes still have a place in situations where detection of the error is sufficient and correction is not needed. For example, instruction caches (typically implemented by using SRAM) often employ error detection since the cache line can simply be reloaded from the main memory if an error is detected. On the Blue Gene/L and Blue Gene/P machines, both L1 and L2 caches are parity protected [12].

Since on these systems memory writes are always write-through to the L3 cache, which uses ECC for protection, error detection is sufficient in this case even for the data cache.

When an error-correcting code is used instead of a hash function, certain errors can be corrected in addition to error detection.

For protecting computer memory, hamming codes [13] are the most common. While pure hamming codes can detect up to 2-bit errors in a word and can correct a single-bit error, a double-bit error from a given data word, and a single-bit error from another data word can result in the same bit pattern. Therefore, in order to reliably distinguish single-bit errors (which can be corrected) from double-bit errors (which cannot be corrected), an extra parity bit is added. Since the parity bit will detect whether the number of error bits is odd or even, a failed data word that fails both the ECC and the parity check indicates a single-bit error, whereas a failed ECC check but correct parity indicates an uncorrectable dual-bit error. Combining a hamming code with an extra parity bit results in a code that is referred to as single-error correction, double-error detection (SECDED).

Unfortunately, memory errors are not always independent. For example, highly energetic particles might corrupt multiple adjacent cells or a hard error might invalidate a complete memory chip. In order to reduce the risk of a single error affecting multiple bits of the same logical memory word, a number of techniques have been developed to protect against these failures. These techniques are, depending on the vendor, referred to as *chip-kill*, *chipspare*, or *extended ECC*. They work by spreading the bits (including ECC) of a logical memory word over multiple memory chips, so that each memory chip contains only a single bit of each logical word. Therefore, the failure of a complete memory chip will affect only a single bit of each word as opposed to four or eight (depending on the width of the memory chip) consecutive bits.

Another technique is to use a different ECC. Such ECC codes become relatively more space-efficient as the width of the data word increases. For example, a SECDED hamming code for correcting a single bit in a 64-bit word takes 8 ECC bits. However, correcting a single bit in a 128-bit word requires only 9 ECC bits. By combining data into larger words, one can use the extra space to correct more errors. With 128-bit data words and 16 ECC bits, it is possible to construct an ECC that can correct random single-error bits but up to 4 (consecutive) error bits.

Since ECC memory can tolerate only a limited number of bit errors and since errors are detected and corrected only when memory is accessed, it is beneficial to periodically verify all memory words in an attempt to reduce the chances of a second error occurring for the same memory word. When an error is detected, the containing memory word can be rewritten and corrected before a second error in the same word can occur. This is called *memory scrubbing* [14]. Memory scrubbing is especially important for servers since these typically have large amounts of memory and very large uptimes, thus increasing the probability of a double error.

The use of ECC memory is almost universally adopted for supercomputers and servers. This is the case for the IBM Blue Gene/P [12] and the Cray XT5 [15]. Note that the IBM Blue Gene/L did not employ error correction or detection for its main memory. Personal computing systems such as laptops and home computers typically do not employ ECC memory.

33.2.3   Network Resilience

Network fault tolerance has been a topic of continued research for many years. Several fault-tolerance techniques have been proposed for networks. In this section, we discuss three techniques: reliability, data corruption, and automatic path migration (APM).

33.2.3.1   *Reliability* Most networks used on large-scale systems today provide reliable communication capabilities. Traditionally, reliability was achieved by using kernel-based protocol stacks such as TCP/IP. In the more recent past, however, networks such as InfiniBand [16] and Myrinet [17] have provided reliability capabilities directly in hardware on the network adapter. Reliability is fundamentally handled by using some form of a handshake between the sender and receiver processes, where the receiver has to acknowledge that a piece of data has been received before the sender is allowed to discard it.

33.2.3.2   *Data Corruption* Most networks today automatically handle data corruption that might occur during communication. Traditional TCP communication relied on a 16-bit checksum for data content validation. Such low-bit checksums, however, have proved to be prone to errors when used with high-speed networks or networks on which a lot of data content is expected to be communicated [18]. Modern networks such as InfiniBand, Myrinet, and Converged Ethernet[1] provide 32-bit cyclic-redundancy checks (CRCs) that allow the sender to hash the data content into a 32-bit segment and the receiver to verify the validity of the content by recalculating the CRC once the data are received. Some networks, such as InfiniBand, even provide dual CRC checks (both 16 and 32 bits) to allow for both end-to-end and per-network-hop error corrections.

One of the concerns of hardware-managed data corruption detection is that it is not truly end to end. Specifically, since the CRC checks are performed on the network hardware, they cannot account for errors while moving the data from the main memory to the network adapter. However, several memory connector interconnects, such as PCI Express and HyperTransport, also provide similar CRC checks to ensure data validity. Nevertheless, the data have no protection all the way from the main memory of the source node to the main memory of the destination node. For example, if an error occurs after data validity is verified by the PCI Express link, but before the network calculates its CRC, such an error will go undetected. Consequently, researchers have investigated software techniques to provide truly end-to-end data reliability, for example, by adding software CRC checks within the message-passing interface (MPI) library.[2]

33.2.3.3   *APM* APM is a fairly recent technique for fault tolerance provided by networks such as InfiniBand. The basic idea of APM is that each connection uses a primary path but also has a passive secondary path assigned to it. If any error occurs on the primary path (e.g., a network link fails), the network hardware automatically moves the connection to the secondary fallback path. Such reliability allows only one failure instance since only one secondary path can be specified. Further, APM protects communication only in cases where an intermediate link in the network fails. If an end-link connecting the actual client machine fails, APM will not be helpful.

---

[1]Converged Ethernet is also sometimes referred to as Converged Enhanced Ethernet, Data Center Ethernet, or lossless Ethernet.

[2]The MVAPICH project is an example of such an MPI implementation: http://mvapich.cse.ohio-state .edu.

A secondary concern that researchers have raised with APM is the performance implication of such migration. While migrating an existing connection to a secondary path would allow the communication to continue, it might result in the migrated communication flow interfering with other communication operations, thus causing performance loss. Unfortunately, currently no techniques have been shown to work around this issue specifically, although the recently introduced adaptive routing capabilities in InfiniBand work around this problem.

33.2.4 Storage Resilience

Two types of storage devices can be found in modern large installation sites: electromechanical devices, which contain spinning disks (i.e., traditional magnetic hard drives), and solid-state drives (SSDs), which use a form of solid-state memory.

Spinning disks partition data into sectors. For each sector, an ECC is applied (typically a Reed–Solomon code [19]).

The most common type of SSD uses flash memory internally to hold the data. There are two common types of flash, differentiated by how many bits are stored in each cell of the flash memory. In single-level cell (SLC) flash, a cell is in either a low or high state, encoding a single bit. In multilevel cell (MLC) flash, there are four possible states, making it possible to store two bits in a single cell.

For SLC devices, hamming codes are often used to detect and correct errors. A common configuration is to organize data in 512-byte blocks, resulting in 24 ECC bits. For MLC devices, however, where a failure of a single cell results in the failure of two consecutive bits, a different ECC has to be used. For these devices, Reed–Solomon codes offer a good alternative. Because of the computational complexity of the Reed–Solomon code, the Bose–Chaudhuri–Hocquenghem (BCH) algorithm is becoming more popular since it can be implemented in hardware [20].

However, while resilience techniques within each physical device can protect against small amounts of data corruption, uncorrectable errors do still occur [10, 21]. In addition, it is possible for the storage device as a whole to fail. For example, in rotating disks, mechanical failure cannot be excluded. Moreover, storage devices are commonly grouped into a larger, logical device to obtain higher capacities and higher bandwidth, increasing the probability that the combined device will suffer data loss due to the failure of one of its components.

Because of the nature of persistent storage, persistent data loss typically has a higher cost. In order to reduce the probability of persistent data loss, storage devices can be grouped into a redundant array of independent disks (RAID) [22].

A number of RAID levels, differing in how the logical device is divided and replicated among the physical devices, have become standardized. A few examples are described below:

RAID0. Data are spread over multiple disks without adding any redundancy. A single failure results in data loss.

RAID1. Data are replicated on one (or more) additional drives. Up to $n - 1$ (assuming n devices) can fail without resulting in data loss.

RAID2. Data are protected by using an ECC. For RAID2, each byte is spread over different devices, and a hamming code is applied to corresponding bits. The resulting ECC bits are stored on a dedicated device.

RAID3 and RAID4. These are like RAID2, but instead of on a bit level, RAID3 and RAID4 use byte granularity for error correction. XOR is used as ECC. RAID3 and RAID4 differ in how the data are partitioned (block vs. stripe).

RAID5. This is like RAID4, but the parity data are spread over multiple devices.

RAID6. This is like RAID5 but with two parity blocks. Therefore, RAID6 can tolerate two failed physical devices.

When a failure is detected, the failed device needs to be replaced, after which the array will regenerate the data of the failed device and store it on the new device. This is referred to as rebuilding the array. Because of the difference in increases in bandwidth and capacity for storage devices, a rebuild can take a fairly long time (hours). During this time, all RAID levels except for RAID6 are vulnerable as they offer no protection against further failures. As is the case with memory, many RAID arrays employ a form of scrubbing to detect failure before errors can accumulate.

33.3 SYSTEMS SOFTWARE FEATURES FOR RESILIENCE

In this section, we discuss fault-resilience techniques used in various systems software libraries, including communication libraries, task-based models, and large data models. We start by describing checkpointing, which is used in many programming models, then describe techniques used for specific programming models.

33.3.1 Checkpointing

Checkpointing is a fault-tolerance mechanism where the state of a system running an application is recorded in a global *checkpoint* so that, in the event of a fault, the system state can be rolled back to the checkpoint and allowed to continue from that point, rather restarting the application from the beginning. System-level checkpointing is popular because it provides fault tolerance to an application without requiring the application to be modified.

A global checkpoint of a distributed application consists of a set of checkpoints of individual processes. Figure 33.1 shows three processes (represented by horizontal lines) and two global checkpoints (represented as dotted lines) consisting of individual checkpoints (represented as rectangles). The global checkpoint on the

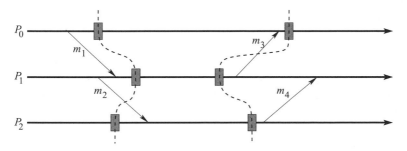

FIGURE 33.1. *Consistent versus inconsistent checkpoints.*

left is *consistent* because it captures a global state that may have occurred during the computation. Note that while the global state records message m_2 being sent but not received, this could have occurred during the computation if the message was sent and was still in transit over the network. The second global checkpoint is *inconsistent* because it captures message m_3 as being received but not sent, which could never have occurred during the computation. Messages such as m_3 are known as *orphan* messages.

Checkpointing protocols use various methods either to find a consistent global checkpoint or to allow applications to roll back to inconsistent global checkpoints by logging messages.

33.3.1.1 *System-Level Checkpointing*   In Reference 23, Elnozahy et al. classify checkpoint recovery protocols into *uncoordinated, coordinated, communication-induced*, and *log-based* protocols.

In uncoordinated checkpoint protocols, processes independently take checkpoints without coordinating with other processes. By not requiring processes to coordinate before taking checkpoints, a process can decide to take checkpoints when the size of its state is small, thereby reducing the size of the checkpoint [24]. Also because processes are not forced to take checkpoints at the same time, checkpoints taken by different processes can be spread out over time, thereby spreading out the load on the file system [25]. When a failure occurs, a consistent global checkpoint is found by analyzing the dependency information recorded with individual checkpoints [26]. Note, however, that because checkpoints are taken in an uncoordinated manner, orphan messages are possible and may result in checkpoints taken at some individual process that are not part of any consistent global checkpoint, in which case that process will need to roll back to a previous checkpoint. Rolling back that process can produce more orphan messages requiring other processes to roll back further. This is known as cascading rollbacks or the domino effect [27] and can result in the application rolling back to the its initial state because no consistent global checkpoint exists.

Coordinated checkpoint protocols [28, 29] do not suffer from cascading rollbacks because the protocol guarantees that *every* individual checkpoint taken is part of a consistent global checkpoint. Because of this feature, only the last global checkpoint needs to be stored. Once a global checkpoint has been committed to stable storage, the previous checkpoint can be deleted. This also eliminates the need to search for a consistent checkpoint during the restart protocol. Coordinated checkpoints can be *blocking* or *nonblocking*. In a blocking protocol, all communication is halted, and communication channels are flushed while the checkpointing protocol executes [30]. This ensures that there are no orphan messages. In a nonblocking protocol, the application is allowed to continue communicating concurrently with the checkpointing protocol. Nonblocking protocols use markers sent either as separate messages or by piggybacking them on application messages. When a process takes a checkpoint, it sends a marker to every other process. Upon receiving a marker, the receiver takes a checkpoint if it has not already. If the markers are sent before any application messages or if the marker is piggybacked and therefore processed before the application message is processed, then orphan messages are avoided.

In communication-induced checkpointing [31–33], processes independently decide when to take a checkpoint, similar to uncoordinated checkpoints, but also take *forced* checkpoints. Processes keep track of dependency information of messages by using Lamport's *happened-before* relation. This information is piggybacked on all application messages. When a process receives a message, if, based on its dependency information and the information in the received message, it determines that processing the application message would result in an orphan message, then the process takes a checkpoint before processing the application message.

Log-based protocols [34–37] require that processes be *piecewise deterministic*, meaning that given the same input, the process will behave exactly the same every time it is executed. Furthermore, information on any nondeterministic events, such as the contents and order of incoming messages, can be recorded and used to replay the event. In *pessimistic* logging, event information is stored to stable storage immediately. While this can be expensive during failure-free execution, only the failed process needs to be rolled back because all the messages it has received since its last checkpoint are recorded and can be played back. In *optimistic* logging, event information is saved to stable storage periodically, thus reducing the overhead during failure-free execution. However, the recovery protocol is complicated because the protocol needs to use dependency information from the event logs to determine which checkpoints form a consistent global state and which processes need to be rolled back.

33.3.1.2 *Complete versus Incremental Checkpoints* A complete system-level checkpoint saves the entire address space of a process. One way to reduce the size of a checkpoint is to use incremental checkpointing. In incremental checkpointing, unmodified portions of a process's address space are not included in the checkpoint image. In order to determine which parts of the address space have been modified, some methods use a hash over blocks of memory [38]; other approaches use a virtual memory system [39, 40].

Page-based methods use two approaches. In one approach, the checkpointing system creates an interrupt handler for page faults. After a checkpoint is taken, all of the process's pages are set to read-only. When the application tries to modify a page, a page fault is raised and the checkpointing system will mark that page as having been modified. This approach has the advantage of not requiring modification of the operating system kernel; however, it does have the overhead of a page fault the first time the process writes to a page after a checkpoint. Another approach is to patch the kernel and to keep track of the dirty bit in each page table entry in a way that allows the checkpointing system to clear the bits on a checkpoint without interfering with the kernel. This has the benefit of not forcing page faults, but it does require kernel modification.

Incremental checkpoints are typically used with periodic complete checkpoints. The higher the ratio of incremental to complete checkpoints, the higher the restart overhead because the current state of the process must be reconstructed from the last complete checkpoint and every subsequent incremental checkpoint.

33.3.2 Fault Management Enhancements to Parallel Programming Models

While checkpointing has been the traditional method of providing fault tolerance and is transparent to the application, nontransparent mechanisms are becoming popular. Nontransparent mechanisms allow the application to control how faults should be handled. Programming models must provide features that allow the application to become aware of failures and to isolate or mitigate the effects of failures. We describe various fault-tolerance techniques appropriate to different programming models.

33.3.2.1 Process-Driven Techniques   In Reference 41, Fagg and Dongarra proposed modifications to the MPI-2 application programming interface (API) to allow processes to handle process failures. They implemented the standard with their modification in fault-tolerant message-passing interface (FT-MPI). An important issue to address when adding fault-tolerance features to the MPI standard is how to handle communicators that contain failed processes. A communication operation will return an error if a process tries to communicate with a failed process. The process must then repair the communicator before it can proceed. FT-MPI provides four modes in which a communicator can be repaired: SHRINK, BLANK, REBUILD, and ABORT. In the SHRINK mode, the failed processes are removed from the communicator. When the communicator is repaired in this way, the size of the communicator changes and possibly the ranks of some processes. In the BLANK mode, the repaired communicator essentially contains holes where the failed processes had been, so that the size of the communicator and the ranks of the processes do not change, but sending to or receiving from a failed process results in an invalid-rank error. In the REBUILD mode, new processes are created and replace the failed processes. A special return value from MPI_Init tells a process whether it is an original process or it has been started to replace a failed process. In the ABORT mode, the job is aborted when a process fails.

Another important issue is the behavior of collective communication operations when processes fail. In FT-MPI, collective communication operations are guaranteed to either succeed at every process or to fail at every process. In FT-MPI, information about failed processes is stored on an attribute attached to a communicator, which a process can query. It is not clear from the literature how FT-MPI supports MPI one-sided or file operations.

The MPI Forum is working on defining new semantics and API functions for MPI-3 to allow applications to handle the failure of processes. The current proposal (when this chapter was written) is similar to the BLANK mode of FT-MPI in that the failure of a process does not change the size of a communicator or the ranks of any processes. While FT-MPI requires a process to repair a communicator as soon as a failure is detected, the MPI-3 proposal does not have this requirement. The failure of some process will not affect the ability of live processes to communicate.

Because of this approach, wildcard receives (i.e., receive operations that specify MPI_ANY_SOURCE as the sender) must be addressed differently. If a process posts a wildcard receive and some process fails, the MPI library does not know whether the user intended the wildcard receive to match a message from the failed process. If the receive was intended to match a message from the failed process, then the process might hang waiting for a message that will never come, in which case the library should raise an error for that receive and cancel it. However, if a message sent from another process can match the wildcard receive, then raising an error for that receive would not be appropriate. In the current proposal, a process must *recognize* all failed processes in a communicator before it can wait on a wild-card receive. So, if a communicator contains an unrecognized failed process, the MPI library will return an error whenever a process waits on a wildcard receive, for example, through a blocking receive or an MPI_Wait call, but the receive will not be canceled. This approach will allow an application to check whether the failed processes were the intended senders for the wildcard receive.

The proposal requires that collective communication operations not hang because of failed processes, but it does not require that the operation uniformly complete either successfully or with an error. Hence, the operation may return successfully at one process while returning with an error at another. The MPI_Comm_validate function is provided to allow the MPI implementation to restructure the communication pattern of collective operations to bypass failed processes. This function also returns a group containing the failed processes that can be used by the process to determine whether any processes have failed since the last time the function was called. If no failures occurred since the last time the function was called, then the process can be sure that all collective operations performed during that time succeeded everywhere. Similar validation functions are provided for MPI window objects for one-sided operations and MPI file objects to allow an application to determine whether the preceding operations completed successfully.

Process failures can be queried for communicator, window, and file objects. The query functions return MPI group objects containing the failed processes. Group objects provide a scalable abstraction for describing failed processes (compared to, e.g., an array of integers).

Another problem for exascale computing is silent data corruption (SDC). As the number of components increases, the probability of bit flips that cannot be corrected with ECC or even detected with CRC increases. SDC can result in an application returning invalid results without being detected. To address this problem, RedMPI [42] replicates processes and compares results to detect SDC. When the application sends a message, each replica sends a message to its corresponding receiver replica. In addition, a hash of the message is sent to the other receiver replicas so that each receiver can verify that it received the message correctly and that if SDC occurred at the sender, it did not affect the contents of the message. Using replicas also provides tolerance to process failure. If a process fails, a replica can take over for the failed process.

33.3.2.2 Data-Driven Techniques

33.3.2.2 *Data-Driven Techniques* Global Arrays [43] is a parallel programming model that provides indexed array-like global access to data distributed across the machine using *put*, *get*, and *accumulate* operations. In Reference 44, Ali et al. reduce the overhead of recovering from a failure by using redundant data. The idea is to maintain two copies of the distributed array structure but to distribute them differently so that both copies of a chunk of the array are not located on the same node. In this way, if a process fails, there is a copy of every chunk that was stored on that process on one of the remaining processes. The recovery process consists of starting a new process to replace the failed one and restoring the copies of the array stored at that process. Furthermore, because the state of the array is preserved, the nonfailed processes can continue running during the recovery process. This approach significantly reduces the recovery time compared with that of checkpointing and rollback.

33.3.2.3 Task-Driven Techniques Charm++ [45] is a C++-based object-oriented parallel programming system. In this system, work is performed by tasks, or *chares*, which can be migrated by the Charm++ runtime to other nodes for load balancing. Charm++ provides fault tolerance through checkpointing and allows the application to mark which data in the chare to include in the checkpoint image, thus reducing the amount of data to be checkpointed. There are two modes for checkpointing [46]. In the first mode, all threads collectively call a checkpointing function periodically. In this mode, if a node fails, the entire application is started from the last checkpoint. In order to reduce the overhead of restarting the entire application, checkpoints can be saved to memory or local disk as well as to the parallel file system. Thus, nonfailed processes can restart from local images, greatly reducing the load on the parallel file system.

The other checkpointing mode uses message logging so that, if a process fails, only that process needs to be restarted. When a process fails, it is restarted from its last checkpoint on a new node. Then, the process will replay the logged messages in the original order. When a node fails, the restarted processes need not be restarted on the same node but can be distributed among other nodes to balance the load of the restart protocol.

CiLK [47] is a thread-based parallel programming system using C. CiLK-NOW [48] is an implementation of CiLK over a network of workstations. The CiLK-NOW implementation provides checkpointing of the entire application if critical processes fail but also is able to restart individual threads if they crash or the nodes they are running on fail.

33.4 APPLICATION OR DOMAIN-SPECIFIC FAULT-TOLERANCE TECHNIQUES

While hardware and systems software techniques for transparent fault tolerance are convenient for users, such techniques often impact the overall performance, system cost, or both. Several computational science domains have been investigating techniques for application or domain-specific models for fault tolerance that utilize information about the characteristics of the application (or the domain) to design specific algorithms that try to minimize such performance loss or system cost. These techniques, however, are not completely transparent to the domain scientists.

In this section, we discuss two forms of fault-tolerance techniques. The first form is specific to numerical libraries, where researchers have investigated approaches in which characteristics of the mathematical computations can be used to achieve reliability in the case of node failures (discussed in Section 33.4.1). The second form is fault-resilience techniques utilized directly in end applications (discussed in Section 33.4.2); we describe techniques used in two applications: mpiBLAST (computational biology) and Green's function Monte Carlo (GFMC) (nuclear physics).

33.4.1 Algorithmic Resilience in Math Libraries

The fundamental idea of algorithm-based fault tolerance (ABFT) is to utilize domain knowledge of the computation to deal with some errors. While the concept is generic, a large amount of work has been done for algorithmic resilience in matrix computations. For instance, Huang and Abraham [49] and Anfinson and Luk [50] showed that it is possible to encode a hash of the matrix data being computed on, such that if a process fails, data corresponding to this process can be recomputed based on this hash without having to restart the entire application. This technique is applicable to a large number of matrix operations including addition, multiplication, scalar product, LU decomposition, and transposition.

This technique was further developed by Chen and Dongarra to tolerate fail-stop failures that occurred during the execution of high-performance computing (HPC) applications [51, 52] (discussed in Section 33.4.1.1). The idea of ABFT is to encode the original matrices by using real number codes to establish a checksum type of relationship between data, and then to redesign algorithms to operate on the encoded matrices in order to maintain the checksum relationship during the execution. Wang et al. [53] enhanced Chen and Dongarra's work to allow for nonstop hot-replacement-based fault recovery techniques (discussed in Section 33.4.1.2).

33.4.1.1 Fail-Stop Fault Recovery
Assume there will be a single process failure. Since it is hard to locate which process will fail before the failure actually occurs, a fault-tolerant scheme should be able to recover the data on any process. In the conventional ABFT method, it is assumed that at any time during the computation, the data D_i on the ith process P_i satisfies

$$D_1 + D_2 + \cdots + D_n = E, \tag{33.1}$$

where n is the total number of processes and E is data on the encoding process. Thus, the lost data on any failed process can be recovered from Equation (33.1). Suppose P_i fails. Then, the lost data D_i on P_i can be reconstructed by

$$D_i = E - (D_1 + \cdots + D_{i-1} + D_{i+1} + \cdots + D_n). \tag{33.2}$$

In practice, this kind of special relationship is by no means natural. However, one can design applications to maintain such a special checksum relationship throughout the computation, and this is one purpose of ABFT research.

33.4.1.2 Nonstop Hot-Replacement-Based Fault Recovery
For the simplicity of presentation, we assume there will be only one process failure. However, it is straightforward to extend the results here to multiple failures by using multilevel redundancy or by regenerating the encoded data. Suppose that, at any time during the computation, the data D_i on process P_i satisfies

$$D_1 + D_2 + \cdots + D_n = E. \tag{33.3}$$

If the ith process fails during the execution, we replace it with the encoding process E and continue the execution instead of stopping all the processes to recover the lost data D_i. Note that this kind of transformation can be effective only when there is an encoding relationship among the data.

From a global view, the original data are

$$D = (D_1 \cdots D_{i-1} D_i D_{i+1} \cdots D_n), \tag{33.4}$$

and the transformed data (after replacement) are

$$D' = (D_1 \cdots D_{i-1} E D_{i+1} \cdots D_n). \tag{33.5}$$

We can establish a relationship between the transformed data and the original data as

$$D' = D \times T, \tag{33.6}$$

and T can be represented as an $n \times n$ matrix in the form

$$T = \begin{pmatrix} 1 & & & 1 & & & \\ & \ddots & & \vdots & & & \\ & & 1 & 1 & & & \\ & & & 1 & & & \\ & & & 1 & 1 & & \\ & & & \vdots & & \ddots & \\ & & & 1 & & & 1 \end{pmatrix}, \tag{33.7}$$

where the elements omitted in the diagonal and the ith column are all 1 and the other elements omitted are 0. We can see that T is a nonsingular matrix. If operations on the data are linear transformations (e.g., matrix operations such as decomposition), the relationship $D' = D \times T$ will always be kept. At the end of computation, the original correct solution based on D can be recomputed through the intermediate solution based on D'. And this recomputation is actually a transformation related to T.

One can see that the encoding relationship $D' = D \times T$ cannot be maintained under all HPC applications. However, for a class of them, including matrix computations involving linear transformations (e.g., matrix decomposition, matrix–matrix multiplication, and scalar product), the encoding relationship can be maintained.

33.4.2 Application-Level Checkpointing

In this section, we present case studies for two application-specific fault-tolerance techniques: sequence alignment with mpiBLAST and GFMC.

33.4.2.1 Fault-Tolerance Techniques and Sequence Alignment with mpi-BLAST   With the advent of rapid DNA sequencing, the amount of genetic sequence data available to researchers has increased exponentially [54]. The GenBank database, a comprehensive database that contains genetic sequence data for more than 260,000 named organisms, has exhibited exponential growth since its inception over 25 years ago [55]. This information is available for researchers to search new

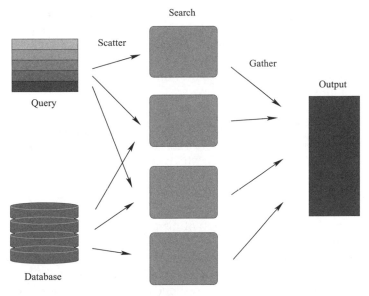

FIGURE 33.2. *High-level algorithm of mpiBLAST.*

sequences against and infer homologous relationships between sequences or organisms. This helps in a wide range of projects, from assembling the tree of life [56] to pathogen detection [57] and metagenomics [58].

Unfortunately, the exponential growth of sequence databases necessitates faster search algorithms to sustain reasonable search times. The Basic Local Alignment Search Tool (BLAST), which is the de facto standard for sequence searching, uses heuristics to prune the search space and to decrease search time with an accepted loss in accuracy [59, 60]. BLAST is parallelized by mpiBLAST using several techniques, including database fragmentation, query segmentation [61], parallel I/O [62], and advanced scheduling [63]. As shown in Figure 33.2, mpiBLAST uses a *master–worker* model and performs a *scatter–search–gather–output* execution flow. During the scatter, the master splits the database and query into multiple pieces and distributes them among worker nodes. Each worker then searches the query segment against the database fragment that it was assigned. The results are gathered by the master, formatted, and output to the user. Depending on the size of the query and the database, such output can be large. Thus, for environments with limited I/O capabilities, such as distributed systems, the output step can cause significant overheads.

One of the characteristics of sequence alignment with mpiBLAST is that the computation and output associated with each query sequence are independent. Thus, splitting the query sequences into multiple independent executions and combining the output in a postprocessing step would not affect the overall outcome of the application. This behavior is true even with the database itself; that is, for each query sequence, mpiBLAST searches for the "best matching" sequence in the database. Thus, as long as these best matching sequences are available, even deleting some of the other sequences in the database does not affect the overall outcome. In order to take advantage of such application characteristics, the ParaMEDIC framework was developed [64–68]. Though initially designed for optimizing the I/O requirements of mpiBLAST, the ParaMEDIC framework allows the application to work through system faults. Specifically, if a part of the computation fails because of a system fault, that part of the computation is discarded and recomputed. This approach allows the overall final output of the application to not change based on intermediate faults.

33.4.2.2 *Green's Function Monte Carlo*

The quantum Monte Carlo code developed by Steven C. Pieper and coworkers at Argonne National Laboratory [69, 70] uses the GFMC method. The GFMC code is part of the SciDAC Universal Nuclear Energy Density Functional (UNEDF) effort to understand the physics of light nuclei. The fundamental computation involved in quantum Monte Carlo is a $3N$-dimensional integral—where N is the number of nucleons—evaluated by using Monte Carlo methods. In the first step of the calculation, variational Monte Carlo, a single integration is performed to get an approximation to the ground-state eigenvector. In the second step, GFMC uses imaginary-time propagation to refine the ground-state solution. Each step in the propagation involves a new $3N$-dimensional integral, and the entire calculation corresponds to an integral of more than 10,000 dimensions. GFMC is parallelized by using a master–worker programming model called ADLB [69].

GFMC initially relied on system-level checkpointing, as discussed in Section 33.3.1, for fault tolerance. However, given that GFMC is memory intensive, the amount of I/O required for each checkpointing operation was tremendous and was growing rapidly with the problem size. To address this concern, GFMC developed its own application-specific checkpointing approach that utilizes application knowledge to write only a small part of critical data to the disk instead of the entire memory space of the application.

To explain this approach, we first describe the overall parallelism structure of GFMC. Specifically, in GFMC, the application processes are distributed into three segments:

1. *Master.* This process reads input, makes initial distribution of work, receives results (energy packets), averages them, and writes averaged results to disk and stdout.
2. *Walker Nodes.* These each manage a group of GFMC configurations. They control the propagation of these configurations, but the actual work is done on worker nodes by using ADLB. The walker nodes do branching, which kills or replicates configurations, and do load balancing, which redistributes configurations to other walker nodes to keep the number of configurations equal on the walkers.
3. *Worker Nodes.* These accept work packages from ADLB and return results. They have no long-term data.

Most of the checkpointing in GFMC is handled by the walker nodes. The walker nodes receive all the starting configurations from the master. They then go into a loop doing propagation time steps. Each configuration is put into ADLB as a propagation work package. The walker processes loops, getting propagation answers and possibly accepting propagation work packages. If the time step is not the next branching step, the work package is put back into ADLB for another time step. Every few time steps, branching is done that can increase or decrease the total number of configurations.

The walker nodes have the current status of all the configurations. This is the only information needed to resume the calculation in case of a failure. Thus, every few time steps, the walker nodes coordinate and dump the current status of the configurations to a checkpoint file. In order to avoid failures while the checkpoint is ongoing, multiple checkpoint files are maintained.

33.5 SUMMARY

With system sizes growing rapidly, faults are increasingly becoming the norm rather than the exception. To handle such faults, researchers are working on various techniques, some of which are transparent to the end users, while others are not. But each class of fault-tolerance techniques has its own pros and cons.

In this chapter, we described various fault-tolerance techniques, broadly classified into three categories. The first category deals with hardware fault tolerance, which is fully transparent to the user. These are handled by hardware redundancy and other related techniques. The second category deals with resilient systems software, which is not transparent to the software stack on the machine but is handled mostly by expert users developing systems software stacks such as MPI or operating systems. Therefore, in some sense, it is still hidden from computational domain scientists developing end applications. The third category deals with application or domain-specific fault-tolerance techniques that utilize application-specific knowledge to achieve fault tolerance. This category requires changes to the applications and thus is, obviously, not transparent to the end user.

REFERENCES

[1] M.K. Qureshi, O. Mutlu, and Y.N. Patt, "Microarchitecture-based introspection: A technique for transient-fault tolerance in microprocessors," in *International Conference on Dependable Systems and Networks*, pp. 434–443, 2005.

[2] N. Oh, P. Shirvani, and E.J. McCluskey, "Error detection by duplicated instructions in super-scalar processors," *IEEE Transactions on Reliability*, 51(1):63–75, 2002.

[3] C. Slayman, "Whitepaper on soft errors in modern memory technology," Technical Report, OPS A La Carte, 2010.

[4] T.J. Dell, "A white paper on the benefits of Chipkill-correct ECC for PC server main memory," Technical Report, IBM Microelectronics Division, November 1997.

[5] D. Milojicic, A. Messer, J. Shau, G. Fu, and A. Munoz, "Increasing relevance of memory hardware errors: A case for recoverable programming models," in *Proceedings of the 9th Workshop on ACM SIGOPS European Workshop: Beyond the PC: New Challenges for the Operating System*, pp. 97–102, ACM, 2000.

[6] B. Schroeder, E. Pinheiro, and W.D. Weber, "DRAM errors in the wild: A large-scale field study," in *Proceedings of the 11th International Joint Conference on Measurement and Modeling of Computer Systems*, pp. 193–204, ACM, 2009.

[7] J.L. Autran, P. Roche, S. Sauze, G. Gasiot, D. Munteanu, P. Loaiza, M. Zampaolo, and J. Borel, "Altitude and underground real-time ser characterization of CMOS 65 nm SRAM," *IEEE Transactions on Nuclear Science*, 56(4):2258–2266, 2009.

[8] L. Borucki, G. Schindlbeck, and C. Slayman, "Comparison of accelerated DRAM soft error rates measured at component and system level," in *Proceedings of the International Reliability Physics Symposium, 2008*, pp. 482–487, IEEE, 2008.

[9] P. Hazucha and C. Svensson, "Impact of cmos technology scaling on the atmospheric neutron soft error rate," *IEEE Transactions on Nuclear Science*, 47(6):2586–2594, 2000.

[10] B. Schroeder and G.A. Gibson, "Disk failures in the real world: What does an MTTF of 1,000,000 hours mean to you?" in *Proceedings of the 5th USENIX Conference on File and Storage Technologies*, p. 1, USENIX Association, 2007.

[11] B. Schroeder and G.A. Gibson, "A large-scale study of failures in high-performance computing systems," *IEEE Transactions on Dependable and Secure Computing*, 7(4):337–351, 2010.

[12] IBM Blue Gene Team, "Overview of the IBM Blue Gene/P project," *IBM Journal of Research and Development*, 52(1/2):199–220, 2008.

[13] R.W. Hamming, "Error detecting and error correcting codes," *Bell System Technical Journal*, 29(2):147–160, 1950.

[14] A.M. Saleh, J.J. Serrano, and J.H. Patel, "Reliability of scrubbing recovery-techniques for memory systems," *IEEE Transactions on Reliability*, 39(1):114–122, 1990.

[15] Cray, Inc., *Cray XT5 Compute Blade*. 2008. Available at http://wwwjp.cray.com/downloads/CrayXT5Blade.pdf. Accessed November 20, 2011.

[16] Mellanox Technologies, *InfiniBand and TCP in the Data-Center*. Available at http://www.mellanox.com/pdf/whitepapers/IB_TCP_in_the_datacenter_WP_110.pdf.

[17] N.J. Boden, D. Cohen, R.E. Felderman, A.E. Kulawik, C.L. Seitz, J.N. Seizovic, and W.K. Su, "Myrinet: A gigabit-per-second local area network," *IEEE Micro*, 15:29–36, 1995.

[18] J. Stone and C. Partridge, "When the CRC and TCP checksum disagree," *ACM SIGCOMM Computer Communication Review*, 30(4):309–319, 2000.

[19] S.B. Wicker and V.K. Bhargava, *Reed–Solomon Codes and Their Applications*. Hoboken, NJ: Wiley-IEEE Press, 1999.

[20] S.W. Wei and C.H. Wei, "A high-speed real-time binary bch decoder," *IEEE Transactions on Circuits and Systems for Video Technology*, 3(2):138–147, 1993.

[21] E. Pinheiro, W.D. Weber, and L.A. Barroso, "Failure trends in a large disk drive population," in *Proceedings of the 5th USENIX Conference on File and Storage Technologies*, pp. 2–2, 2007.

[22] D.A. Patterson, G. Gibson, and R.H. Katz, "A case for redundant arrays of inexpensive disks (RAID)," *ACM SIGMOD Record*, 17(3):109–116, 1988.

[23] E.N. Mootaz Elnozahy, L. Alvisi, Y.-M. Wang, and D.B. Johnson, "A survey of rollback-recovery protocols in message-passing systems," *ACM Computing Surveys*, 34:375–408, 2002.

[24] Y.-M. Wang, "Space reclamation for uncoordinated checkpointing in message-passing systems." PhD Thesis, University of Illinois at Urbana-Champaign, Champaign, IL, 1993. UMI Order No. GAX94-11816.

[25] R.A. Oldfield, S. Arunagiri, P.J. Teller, S. Seelam, M.R. Varela, R. Riesen, and P.C. Roth, "Modeling the impact of checkpoints on next-generation systems," in *Proceedings of the 24th IEEE Conference on Mass Storage Systems and Technologies*, pp. 30–46, Washington, DC: IEEE Computer Society, 2007.

[26] B. Bhargava and S.-R. Lian, "Independent checkpointing and concurrent rollback for recovery in distributed systems-an optimistic approach," in *Proceedings of the Seventh Symposium on Reliable Distributed Systems.*, pp. 3–12, October 1988.

[27] B. Randell, "System structure for software fault tolerance," *IEEE Transactions on Software Engineering*, 1:220–232, 1975.

[28] K.M. Chandy and L. Lamport, "Distributed snapshots: Determining global states of distributed systems," *ACM Transactions on Computer Systems*, 3:63–75, 1985.

[29] T.H. Lai and T.H. Yang, "On distributed snapshots," *Information Processing Letters*, 25:153–158, 1987.

[30] Y. Tamir and C.H. Séquin, "Error recovery in multicomputers using global checkpoints," in *Proceedings of the International Conference on Parallel Processing*, pp. 32–41, 1984.

[31] J.-M. Hélary, A. Mostefaoui, and M. Raynal, "Preventing useless checkpoints in distributed computations," in *Proceedings of the 16th Symposium on Reliable Distributed Systems, SRDS '97*, pp. 183–190, Washington, DC: IEEE Computer Society, 1997.

[32] R.H.B. Netzer and J. Xu, "Necessary and sufficient conditions for consistent global snapshots," *IEEE Transactions on Parallel and Distributed Systems*, 6:165–169, 1995.

[33] D.L. Russell, "State restoration in systems of communicating processes," *IEEE Transactions on Software Engineering*, SE-6(2):183–194, 1980.

[34] A. Guermouche, T. Ropars, E. Brunet, M. Snir, and F. Cappello, "Uncoordinated checkpointing without domino effect for send-deterministic message passing applications," in *Proceedings of the International Parallel and Distributed Processing Symposium*, pp. 989–1000, 2011.

[35] D.B. Johnson, "Distributed system fault tolerance using message logging and checkpointing." PhD Thesis, Rice University, Department of Computer Science, 1989.

[36] D.B. Johnson and W. Zwaenepoel, "Sender-based message logging," in *Digest of Papers, FTCS-17, 17th Annual International Symposium on Fault-Tolerant Computing*, pp. 14–19, 1987.

[37] R. Strom and S. Yemini, "Optimistic recovery in distributed systems," *ACM Transactions on Computer Systems*, 3:204–226, 1985.

[38] S. Agarwal, R. Garg, M.S. Gupta, and J.E. Moreira, "Adaptive incremental checkpointing for massively parallel systems," in *Proceedings of the 18th annual International Conference on Supercomputing, ICS '04*, pp. 277–286, New York: ACM, 2004.

[39] J. Heo, S. Yi, Y. Cho, J. Hong, and S.Y. Shin, "Space-efficient page-level incremental checkpointing," in *Proceedings of the 2005 ACM Symposium on Applied computing, SAC '05*, pp. 1558–1562, New York: ACM, 2005.

[40] C. Wang, F. Mueller, C. Engelmann, and S.L. Scott, "Hybrid full/incremental checkpoint/restart for MPI jobs in HPC environments," in *Proceedings of the International Conference on Parallel and Distributed Systems*, December 2011.

[41] G.E. Fagg and J. Dongarra, "FT-MPI: Fault tolerant MPI, supporting dynamic applications in a dynamic world," in *Proceedings of the 7th European PVM/MPI Users' Group Meeting on Recent Advances in Parallel Virtual Machine and Message Passing Interface*, pp. 346–353, London: Springer-Verlag, 2000.

[42] D. Fiala, "Detection and correction of silent data corruption for large-scale high-performance computing," in *International Symposium on Parallel and Distributed Processing Workshops and Ph.D. Forum (IPDPSW), 2011*, pp. 2069–2072, May 2011.

[43] J. Nieplocha, B. Palmer, V. Tipparaju, M. Krishnan, H. Trease, and E. Aprà, "Advances, applications and performance of the Global Arrays shared memory programming toolkit," *International Journal of High Performance Computing Applications*, 20:203–231, 2006.

[44] N. Ali, S. Krishnamoorthy, N. Govind, and B. Palmer, "A redundant communication approach to scalable fault tolerance in PGAS programming models," in *19th Euromicro International Conference on Parallel, Distributed and Network-Based Processing (PDP), 2011*, pp. 24–31, February 2011.

[45] L.V. Kalé and S. Krishnan, "Charm++: A portable concurrent object oriented system based on C++," *SIGPLAN Notices*, 28:91–108, 1993.

[46] L.V. Kalé and G. Zheng, "Charm++ and AMPI: Adaptive runtime strategies via migratable objects," in *Advanced Computational Infrastructures for Parallel and Distributed Applications* (M. Parashar, ed.), pp. 265–282. Hoboken, NJ: Wiley-Interscience, 2009.

[47] R.D. Blumofe, C.F. Joerg, B.C. Kuszmaul, C.E. Leiserson, K.H. Randall, and Y. Zhou, "CiLK: An efficient multithreaded runtime system," *SIGPLAN Notices*, 30:207–216, 1995.

[48] R.D. Blumofe and P.A. Lisiecki, "Adaptive and reliable parallel computing on networks of workstations," in *Proceedings of the Annual Conference on USENIX Annual Technical Conference*, pp. 10–10, Berkeley, CA: USENIX Association, 1997.

[49] K.H. Huang and J.A. Abraham, "Algorithm-based fault tolerance for matrix operations," *IEEE Transactions on Computers*, C-33(6):518–528, 1984.

[50] J. Anfinson and F.T. Luk, "A linear algebraic model of algorithm-based fault tolerance," *IEEE Transactions on Computers*, 37:1599–1604, 1988.

[51] Z. Chen and J. Dongarra, "Algorithm-based checkpoint-free fault tolerance for parallel matrix computations on volatile resources," in *Proceedings of the 20st IEEE International Parallel and Distributed Processing Symposium*, p. 76, 2006.

[52] Z. Chen and J. Dongarra, "Algorithm-based fault tolerance for fail-stop failures," *IEEE Transactions on Parallel and Distributed Systems*, 19(12):1628–1641, 2008.

[53] R. Wang, E. Yao, P. Balaji, D. Buntinas, M. Chen, and G. Tan, "Building algorithmically nonstop fault tolerant MPI programs," *IEEE International Conference on High Performance Computing (HiPC)*, Bangalore, India, December 2011.

[54] S.F. Altshul, M.S. Boguski, W. Gish, and J.C. Wootton, "Issues in searching molecular sequence databases," *Nature Genetics*, 6(2):119–129, 1994.

[55] D.A. Benson, I. Karsch-Mizrachi, D.J. Lipman, J. Ostell, and D.L. Wheeler, "GenBank," *Nucleic Acids Research*, 36(Database issue):25–30, 2008.

[56] A.C. Driskell, C. Ané, J.G. Burleigh, M.M. McMahon, B.C. O'Meara, and M.J. Sanderson, "Prospects for building the tree of life from large sequence databases," *Science*, 306(5699):1172–1174, 2004.

[57] J.D. Gans, W. Feng, and M. Wolinsky, "Whole genome, physics-based sequence alignment for pathogen signature design," *12th SIAM Conference on Parallel Processing for Scientific Computing*, San Francisco, CA (electronic version unavailable), February 2006.

[58] S.L. Havre, B.-J. Webb-Robertson, A. Shah, C. Posse, B. Gopalan, and F.J. Brockma, "Bioinformatic insights from metagenomics through visualization," in *Proceedings of the Computational Systems Bioinformatics Conference, 2005*, pp. 341–350, August 8–11, 2005.

[59] S.F. Altschul, W. Gish, W. Miller, E.W. Myers, and D.J. Lipman, "Basic Local Alignment Search Tool," *Journal of Molecular Biology*, 215(3):403–410, 1990.

[60] S.F. Altschul, T.L. Madden, A.A. Schaffer, J. Zhang, Z. Zhang, W. Miller, and D.J. Lipman, "Gapped BLAST and PSI–BLAST: A new generation of protein database search programs," *Nucleic Acids Research*, 25:3389–3402, 1997.

[61] A.E. Darling, L. Carey, and W. Feng, "The design, implementation, and evaluation of mpiBLAST," *ClusterWorld Conference & Expo and the 4th International Conference on Linux Cluster: The HPC Revolution*, 2003.

[62] H. Lin, X. Ma, P. Chandramohan, A. Geist, and N. Samatova, "Efficient data access for parallel BLAST," in *IPDPS*, 2005.

[63] O. Thorsen, B. Smith, C. Sosa, K. Jiang, H. Lin, A. Peters, and W. Feng, "Parallel genomic sequence-search on a massively parallel system," *ACM International Conference on Computing Frontiers*, May 2007, Ischia, Italy.

[64] P. Balaji, W. Feng, J. Archuleta, and H. Lin, "ParaMEDIC: Parallel metadata environment for distributed I/O and computing," *Proceedings of the IEEE/ACM International Conference for High Performance Computing, Networking, Storage and Analysis (SC)*, Reno, NV, November 2007.

[65] P. Balaji, W. Feng, J. Archuleta, H. Lin, R. Kettimuttu, R. Thakur, and X. Ma, "Semantics-based distributed I/O for mpiBLAST," in *Proceedings of the ACM SIGPLAN Symposium on Principles and Practice of Parallel Programming (PPoPP)*, Salt Lake City, UT, February 2008.

[66] P. Balaji, W. Feng, and H. Lin, "Semantics-based distributed I/O with the ParaMEDIC framework," in *Proceedings of the ACM/IEEE International Symposium on High Performance Distributed Computing (HPDC)*, Boston, MA, June 2008.

[67] P. Balaji, W. Feng, H. Lin, J. Archuleta, S. Matsuoka, A. Warren, J. Setubal, E. Lusk, R. Thakur, I. Foster, D.S. Katz, S. Jha, K. Shinpaugh, S. Coghlan, and D. Reed, "Distributed I/O with ParaMEDIC: Experiences with a worldwide supercomputer," *Proceedings of the International Supercomputing Conference (ISC)*, Dresden, Germany, June 2008.

[68] P. Balaji, W. Feng, H. Lin, J. Archuleta, S. Matsuoka, A. Warren, J. Setubal, E. Lusk, R. Thakur, I. Foster, D.S. Katz, S. Jha, K. Shinpaugh, S. Coghlan, and D. Reed, "Global-scale distributed I/O with ParaMEDIC," *Concurrency and Computation: Practice and Experience*, 22(16):2266–2281, 2010.

[69] E. Lusk, S. Pieper, and R. Butler, "More scalability, less pain," *SciDAC Review*, 17:30–37, 2010.

[70] S.C. Pieper and R.B. Wiringa, "Quantum Monte Carlo calculations of light nuclei," *Annual Review of Nuclear and Particle Science*, 51(1):53–90, 2001.

34

Parallel Programming Models for Scalable Computing

James Dinan and Pavan Balaji

34.1 INTRODUCTION TO PARALLEL PROGRAMMING MODELS

A *programming model* can be thought of as the abstract machine that a programmer is writing instructions for. Such models form a rich topic for computer science research since programmers prefer them to be (1) expressive (capable of expressing any abstract algorithm), (2) portable (capable of being used on any computer architecture), (3) efficient (capable of delivering performance commensurate with that of the underlying hardware), and (4) easy to use. Often, simultaneously meeting all four of these requirements is hard, so different programming models make different trade-offs. This is one of the primary reasons several dozen scientific programming models exist today.

At the core of parallel computing is the broad space of languages and libraries used to craft parallel programs. Recent changes in system architecture have led to renewed interest in programming models as a means for mapping computation to complex hardware architectures and for enhancing the productivity of parallel programming on these platforms. Deepening memory hierarchies and nonuniformity in both the communication and the memory subsystems has led to an increased interest in models that can effectively incorporate the cost of data access, allowing programmers to exploit data locality in their application.

Scalable Computing and Communications: Theory and Practice, First Edition. Edited by
Samee U. Khan, Albert Y. Zomaya, and Lizhe Wang.
© 2013 John Wiley & Sons, Inc. Published 2013 by John Wiley & Sons, Inc.

A *parallel programming model* defines the methods and mechanisms used to express and manage parallelism within an application. Parallel programming models encapsulate many diverse concepts. At their core, such models must define two components: a data model and a computation model. The data model defines data visibility boundaries and methods of data exchange. The computation model specifies the control and execution models, defining the characteristics of the computational entities in a parallel application. In addition to these core properties, parallel programming models define methods by which parallelism can be expressed as well as models and methods for reasoning about and tuning the performance of a parallel program.

Trends in system architecture are driving rapid increases in the number of processing elements (cores and threads) per chip. Such trends have resulted in application programmers looking at what are referred to as *hybrid programming models*, in which more than one programming model is used in the same application. Using different programming models within the node and across nodes is a common example of a hybrid programming model.

34.1.1   Data Model

The data model defines the visibility of data across computational entities as well as how these entities exchange information. The two most common data visibility models are shared memory and private memory. In the shared-memory model, multiple computational entities (e.g., threads) share a common region of memory that can be used to exchange information using load and store instructions. In the private-memory model, the memory belonging to a computational entity (e.g., a process) is accessible only by that entity. Data exchange in this model is often accomplished by using explicit send and receive operations.

A third data model, remotely accessible memory, lies in between conventional shared and private models. In this model, an entity's memory is divided into private regions and remotely accessible regions. Data within shared regions is exchanged by using asynchronous, one-sided get and put operations that copy data between the data spaces of the origin and target entities. Data within private regions is exchanged by copying information into the shared space or through send and receive operations.

34.1.2   Computation Model

The computational model defines the control and execution mechanisms of the programming model. Many control and execution models are possible; common control models define computational entities as processes, persistent threads, lightweight threads, or tasks. Often, the control model implies a data visibility model; however, the relationship between control and data visibility models is not strict since some models utilize both shared memory and processes (e.g., distributed shared memory or interprocess communication systems), whereas others provide private memory when using threads (e.g., Threaded MPI [1]).

34.1.3   Expression of Parallelism

Many diverse methods of expressing parallelism have been proposed in the parallel computing literature. Each method captures different classes of parallelism, affecting the programmability of a particular computational task under that method. Examples of these methods are loop-level data parallelism and fork–join task parallelism.

Often the method of expressing parallelism also defines a model for how work will be mapped to the underlying computational entities. A common mechanism is static assignment of work to computational entities; this method provides very low overhead and is effective when the optimal mapping can be computed a priori. When a fixed work assignment is not possible, the work mapping is dynamic. The dynamic mapping can be achieved through collective rebalancing steps (e.g., graph partitioning, space-filling curve) or through noncollective redistribution of work. Noncollective work distribution can be achieved through centralized and distributed schemes. A common centralized scheme is master–worker, and a commonly used distributed strategy is work stealing.

34.1.4 Performance Model

In the high-performance computing space, parallelism is a means for increasing the performance of a given computation. Therefore, most parallel programming models also define a performance model that is used by programmers to reason about the execution time of their algorithm. The performance model defines the relative cost of operations for a particular programming model. In addition, it may define ways to utilize low-level operations to increase performance.

34.2 THE MESSAGE-PASSING INTERFACE (MPI)

Traditionally, supercomputing vendors each provided different system-specific techniques for computation and data movement. While this approach allowed each vendor to provide an interface best suited for the platforms supported by the vendor, it created a portability hassle for applications; that is, applications written on one system could not easily be ported to other systems. This situation was cumbersome and counterproductive for large applications because they were either locked in to specific platforms or had to be rewritten for every new machine acquired.

In an attempt to mitigate these portability problems, several researchers designed portability interfaces, such as p4 [2], Chameleon [3], and PVM [4], that were intended to allow applications to execute on any platform without any modifications. However, it was hard for such interfaces to keep up with the rapidly evolving landscape of supercomputing architectures without support from vendors developing these architectures. In November 1992, a group of computer science researchers, application developers, and vendors gathered together to standardize the best practices in distributed-memory parallel programming into a common interface. The idea of such standardization was to provide a portable interface that is rich with respect to features and is expressive enough to allow different platforms to optimize their implementations. This standardized interface came to be known as MPI [5] and the standardization body as the MPI Forum.

In May 1994, the MPI Forum released the first version of the MPI standard: MPI-1.0. This provided a large set of functionality, including two-sided point-to-point communication, and group/collective communication operations, that allowed applications to express their algorithms easily and to achieve high performance on every platform. MPI quickly gained popularity among application developers because of its standardized interface, which would portably work on all platforms. Consequently, many applications migrated to using MPI.

In May 1995, the MPI Forum reconvened to correct minor errors within the MPI-1.0 standard (the versions were referred to as MPI-1.1, MPI-1.2, etc.) and to form the MPI-2.0 standard. This new standard consisted of major new feature additions to MPI, including one-sided communication operations, file I/O capabilities, interoperability with threading models, and dynamically spawned processes. The MPI-2.0 standard was released in July 1997.

Over the past two decades, several MPI implementations have emerged for various supercomputing platforms, allowing users to portably take advantage of the performance provided by those platforms. Today, MPI is considered the de facto standard of parallel programming and is available on virtually every supercomputing system in the world.

The rest of the section describes various capabilities in MPI. Section 34.2.1 discusses some of the core concepts in MPI, including its execution model semantics. Next, we discuss two fundamental communication methodologies within MPI: two-sided communication (Section 34.2.2) and group/collective communication (Section 34.2.3).

34.2.1   Core Concepts in MPI

MPI utilizes a process-centric model in which the user launches a number of processes and explicitly partitions work on these processes. In order to understand MPI, four concepts need to be clarified: communicators, ranks, tags, and data types.

34.2.1.1 Communicators   A communicator is a combination of a group (which lists a set of processes) and a context identifier (which, in some sense, is a name alias to the group of processes). Multiple communicators can be created on the same group of processes. A communicator provides a conduit for communication; use of separate communicators allows multiple libraries linked into a single executable to safely communicate without interfering with the communication of other libraries within the same executable.

34.2.1.2 Ranks   Every process in MPI has an identifier, known as the process rank, for every communicator that it is a part of. The end points of all communication in MPI are identified by using process ranks.

34.2.1.3 Tags   Every point-to-point message in MPI has an associated tag. The tag is user defined and can be used to distinguish messages from one process rank to another over the same communicator.

34.2.1.4 Data Types   MPI defines data types that describe the data being communicated. Most C, Fortran, and C++ data types have predefined equivalents in MPI. Further, MPI also allows users to create user-defined data types such as vectors, structures, and multidimensional subarrays.

34.2.2 Two-Sided Communication

Two-sided communication in MPI involves two process ranks: a sender and a receiver. Every message sent by a process rank has to be explicitly received by the destination process rank.

34.2.2.1 *Communication Operations*

A process rank can send a point-to-point message to another process rank using four types of send operations: regular send, buffered send, ready send, and synchronous send. A regular send operation is the most commonly used variant whereby the completion of the send operation guarantees only that the user buffer is free to be reused. The MPI implementation might choose to internally copy the data to a temporary buffer if available or to perform some form of zero-copy communication. Depending on how much memory the MPI implementation is willing to expend, it might or might not have temporary buffer space available to perform a copy—this implementation detail is completely hidden from the user. To provide better control over this to the user, MPI also provides a buffered send operation through which the user can provide this temporary intermediate buffer to the MPI implementation, thus potentially optimizing communication performance.

When a process performs a regular or buffered send, the receiver is not required to have called a corresponding receive operation yet. Thus, the MPI implementation has to perform the necessary synchronization between the processes in such cases. A ready send allows the user to specify to the MPI implementation that the receiver process is "ready" and has already called a corresponding receive operation.

Completion of a regular, buffered, or ready send operation does not guarantee that the message has been received by the receiver, just that the sender buffer is free to be reused. A synchronous send operation, on the other hand, allows the user to wait until the message has been received by the destination process.

For all four forms of communication, three variants are allowed: blocking, nonblocking, and persistent. With blocking communication, when a send call returns, the send operation has completed. With nonblocking communication, when a send call returns, it means only that the send operation has been initiated and can be tested or waited on for completion at a later time. This allows the MPI implementation to perform communication in the background while the application computes between the nonblocking send and wait calls. With persistent communication, the user can "initiate" a send operation prior to actually issuing it. This allows the MPI implementation to perform some optimizations before the actual send operation, such as registering the communication buffer with the network interface.

For receive operations, only a regular receive is provided, which can receive data sent using any form of send operation. All three variants of receive—blocking, nonblocking, and persistent—are provided as well.

34.2.2.2 *Matching Semantics*

MPI matches point-to-point communication based on three elements: the communicator, the source, and the tag. Two messages sent over the same communicator from the same source using the same tag are always ordered with respect to matching, though not necessarily with respect to completion; that is, if the receiver process posts two nonblocking receive operations on a communicator to receive data from the same source using the same tag, the first message sent by the sender will be deposited into the buffer pointed to by the first nonblocking receive, and the second message into the buffer pointed to by the second nonblocking receive.

However, no guarantees are made about the completion of the two send or receive operations for nonblocking communication; that is, the second send can finish before the first send; similarly, the second receive can finish before the first receive.

34.2.2.3 Wildcard Receives For receive operations, MPI allows users to specify a wildcard source or tag, which matches all values of source ranks or tags. Such wildcards are useful when the destination process cannot deterministically decide which source rank might send it a message or which message tag it might receive next. Once the receive is complete, the user can query for which source sent the message and what tag the message contained.

34.2.3 Collective or Group Communication

Collective or group communication is "collective" over all process ranks in a communicator; that is, they need to be called by all process ranks in the communicator. There are three major types of collective communication operations: synchronization, communication-only, and communication and computation. Other types of collective operations, such as communicator creation operations and process spawning operations, also exist, but we do not discuss them in this chapter.

34.2.3.1 Synchronization MPI provides one operation for synchronizing processes within a communicator—MPI_Barrier. This operation performs a logical barrier between all processes, so no process can exit a barrier before all other processes have arrived at the barrier. It does not guarantee any global synchronization with respect to the clock timing.

34.2.3.2 Communication-Only MPI provides several operations, such as MPI_Bcast, MPI_Gather, MPI_Allgather and MPI_Alltoall, which are communication-only operations in that their only purpose is to move data between a group of processes. The MPI_Bcast operation broadcasts data from one process to all other processes in the communicator. The MPI_Gather operation gathers data provided by all processes in the communicator into a single process's buffer. The MPI_Allgather operation is similar to the MPI_Gather operation except that the data collected from all the processes are deposited at all processes, instead of a single process. The MPI_Alltoall operation allows each process to send a unique message to every other process in the communicator. Several other communication-only collective operations are also provided by MPI.

34.2.3.3 Communication and Computation MPI provides a few combined communication–computation operations, such as MPI_Reduce and MPI_Allreduce. The MPI_Reduce operation is similar to a gather operation except that, instead of simply accumulating the data, it performs a reduction operation on the data. Several reduction operations are defined in MPI, such as a sum, product, and bitwise AND/OR operations. The MPI_Allreduce operation is similar to an MPI_Reduce operation except that the resulting data are deposited at all processes instead of a single process.

34.3 PARTITIONED GLOBAL ADDRESS SPACE (PGAS) MODELS

The family of PGAS programming models shares a common data model that allows for global access to distributed, shared data. In this model, computational entities make a portion of their memory accessible to others in the computation. The aggregation of these shared-memory regions forms a global space (shown in Fig. 34.1) that can be accessed throughout the computation by using portable global addresses. The global address space itself is partitioned in both performance and capability through the locality of a given piece of data; if data are local, they can be quickly accessed, frequently through load and store operations.

Both language and library implementations of PGAS models have been proposed in the literature. In this section, we describe three of the most popular models: Unified Parallel C (UPC), Co-Array Fortran (CAF), and Global Arrays (GA). UPC and CAF are general-purpose language extensions that add a global address space to C and Fortran, respectively. GA takes a library approach that can be used with a variety of languages and focuses specifically on distributed shared arrays.

34.3.1 UPC

UPC [6] is an extension to the C programming language that adds support for a PGAS. UPC presents the programmer with a single-program, multiple-data (SPMD) execution model in which multiple instances of the same program are executed concurrently and each execution is parameterized by an integer identity. In the UPC terminology, an instance is referred to as a thread, the identity of the current instance is the constant MYTHREAD, and the number of instances is THREADS. The threads of execution in UPC can be implemented either as processes or as persistent threads; both are supported by some UPC environments.

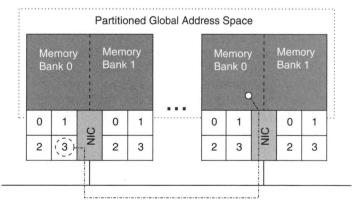

FIGURE 34.1. *Low-level implementation of a partitioned global address space model showing a one-sided access operation. NIC, network interface controller.*

In a UPC execution, the standard C stack and heap are private; a shared heap is added that contains a given thread's partition of the global address space. A shared type qualifier is added to the C language that can be used to specify that a particular heap variable should be placed in the global address space or that a pointer points to a location on the shared heap. Shared pointers are portable and can be transmitted from one thread to another, making it possible to build distributed, shared, linked data structures (e.g., linked lists and trees) in UPC. A thread affinity is associated with the location targeted by a shared pointer. The affinity specifies on which thread the data resides and can be queried, allowing the programmer to leverage locality for improved performance. When a given piece of data has affinity to the local thread, the sharedness of the pointer can be type cast away, allowing for more efficient direct local access to the data.

Shared arrays in UPC have an associated data distribution. This data distribution determines the mapping between elements of the array and their thread affinity in the global address space. UPC supports a block-cyclic distribution method and a layout qualifier can be provided in the array declaration that specifies the block size of an array:

```
shared [B] double data[N];
```

In this example, the array data will contain N elements distributed with a block size of B. Data distribution in UPC is block-cyclic in the linearized representation of the array. When the layout qualifier is omitted, the default block size of 1 is used. An empty block size or a block size of 0 is referred to as an *indefinite* block size and results in all elements being allocated on thread 0. A block size of * tells UPC to create equal-sized blocks and to assign one block per thread.

UPC also adds a parallel for loop to the C language. This loop has the following form:

```
for (initialization-expr; conditional-expr; update-expr;
     affinity-expr) { . . . }
```

The affinity expression in the loop statement is an integer or shared expression that identifies the thread that should execute the given iteration. If a shared pointer or shared array reference is given, the thread with affinity to the given element executes the iteration. When an integer expression (e.g., i% THREADS) is given, the thread with the given identity executes the iteration.

A notable feature of UPC is its trade-off between programmability and performance. It is possible to quickly port a shared-memory or sequential application to UPC by adding the shared qualifier or by using UPC's shared-memory allocator for shared data structures and utilizing UPC's parallel loops. The programmer then can specify a data distribution and leverage locality to improve performance. In addition to these tools, the programmer can relax the consistency model on a per-object basis. The default *strict* consistency model provides strong, but costly, data consistency. The *relaxed* consistency model offers better performance but requires the programmer to perform explicit consistency-management operations. In addition, UPC provides one-sided data movement operations that can be used to further tune accesses to shared data.

34.3.2 CAF

CAF [7] is a PGAS extension to the Fortran programming language that adds support for distributed, shared array data structures. CAF was originally created as an extension to Fortran 95 and has recently been incorporated into the Fortran 2008 language standard [8]. The designers of CAF strove to create the smallest possible extension to Fortran that can enable its use as an effective and efficient parallel programming language. To this end, CAF extends Fortran with a PGAS data model and an SPMD execution model. In the CAF terminology, each SPMD execution instance is referred to as an *image*, and array data structures that are accessible from all images are referred to as *coarrays*.

Many PGAS models, such as UPC and GA, take a top-down approach to creating shared arrays, specifying the dimensions of the full array and how its elements should be distributed. In contrast, CAF takes a bottom-up approach, in which individual pieces located on different images are assembled to form the full array. This is accomplished through the addition of array codimensions that are used to create a logical array of the given corank, in which each element in the coarray is an array of the given rank.

Several examples of coarray specifications and their data layouts are shown in Figure 34.2. The dimensions of the array portion of a coarray are given in the standard parenthesized Fortran notation; the *codimension* is given in brackets. The *corank*, or number of codimensions, is one in Figure 34.2a and two in Figure 34.2b,c. The codimensions specify a logical organization of the constituent parts of the coarray, and the corank can be chosen independently of the array rank. A codimension of * indicates that CAF should calculate the given cobound to include as many

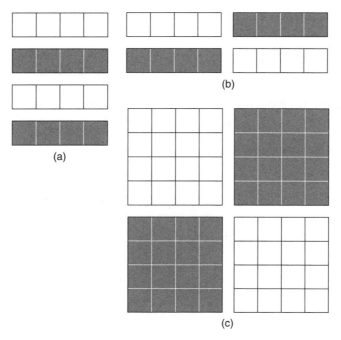

FIGURE 34.2. *Several coarrays and their associated shapes for a four-image execution.*

images as possible. The *coshape* is the name used to describe the exact codimensions at runtime. In Figure 34.2 the coshape is shown for an execution with four images. For example, in Figure 34.2b, the coshape will be [2, N], where $N = \lceil num\_images/2 \rceil$. An explicit corange can also be specified as the codimension (e.g., -1 : *).

When accessing a coarray, programmers must specify the coindex that they wish to access. For the coarray given in Figure 34.2c, this could be performed as follows.

```
y = X(1,1)
y = X(1,1) [1,1]
Z(:,:) = X(:,:) [2,1]
```

In the first example, the coindex is omitted, resulting in an access to the image's local piece of the coarray. This type of array reference provides the fastest access to local data in the coarray. In the second example, an element of X is copied into the local variable y, potentially resulting in communication to fetch the value from the image that holds the given coindex. In the third example, the entire X array at coindex [2,1] is copied into the local array Z.

Locality plays an important role in the performance of PGAS programs. CAF provides several mechanisms for querying locality with respect to a given image index. These mechanisms can be used to reduce communication overheads. Split-phase barriers and teamwise synchronization are also provided to localize synchronization and to reduce overheads. In addition, several synchronization and data consistency mechanisms are available to ensure that data are available for access by other images. CAF also provides several collective functions for operating on coarrays. These can be used to perform Boolean evaluation of coarrays, to locate minimum or maximum values, or to find the sum or product of elements in the coarray.

34.3.3 Global Arrays

Global Arrays (GA) [9, 10] is a library-based PGAS programming model that provides support for large, distributed, shared-array data structures. This model is especially appropriate when an array data structure that is larger than the memory of a single node is needed, and asynchronous or irregular accesses will be performed. This type of array is common to several important computational chemistry and physics methods that make extensive use of GA [11].

At present, GA provides C, C++, Fortran, and Python language interfaces. GA is built on top of the low-level aggregate remote memory copy interface (ARMCI) [12], which provides support for mapping remotely accessible memory regions and for performing one-sided data movement operations. GA and ARMCI are designed to be interoperable with MPI, and many GA programs use both GA and MPI.

In the GA model, an array is allocated on a group of processes, and the elements of the array are distributed across the processes according to a specified data distribution. The programmer can choose from several standard distribution patterns or specify an arbitrary, customized data layout. Once an array has been allocated, it is accessed using get, put, and accumulate operations that perform one-sided data transfer from the array into a local buffer. The data to be transferred are specified as a rectangular patch in the index space of the array. The local buffer may also be a rectangular patch of a larger local buffer, and a *leading dimensions* argument is provided to GA to specify the local buffer layout. The location of an element in a global array and its distribution can be queried, enabling the programmer to leverage locality to reduce communication overheads. When the desired data are available locally, the programmer can call a local access routine that returns a pointer to the data and allows for direct load/store access.

Because of its one-sided communication model, GA and other PGAS models are frequently said to provide a get-compute-put model of computation. This name arises because, in contrast with shared-memory systems, data in the global address space is not operated on in-place; data must be copied into a local buffer before it can be processed. Once processing has completed, the global address space is updated with the results.

In addition to these features, GA provides a library of high-level mathematical routines that operate on arrays in parallel. Routines include matrix multiplication, diagonalization, and solvers. GA also supports several specialized features for different types of computations, such as ghost cells, mirrored (i.e., replicated) arrays, and disk-resident arrays for out-of-core array processing.

34.4 TASK-PARALLEL PROGRAMMING MODELS

Many applications pose significant challenges to the efficient management of parallelism. In dynamic parallel computations, additional work is uncovered as the computation progresses. This new work must be distributed to workers, and any dependence and data flow must be handled. Irregular workloads arise when the domain of the computation is sparse or irregular in computational intensity. These types of computations can result in load imbalance at runtime, leading to inefficient use of compute resources.

Many parallel programming models have been developed to address the needs of dynamic, irregular, and unbalanced parallel computations. In this section, we describe three models that take a task-parallel approach to expressing parallelism. *Task parallelism* is generic parallelism that is expressed in terms of individual chunks of work. Tasks from different programs can have a variety of properties: divisible, idempotent, strict dependence, persistence, and so forth. Most task-parallel programming models assume a task model in which tasks have particular properties that are leveraged to enhance performance, expressivity, or fitness to a particular class of application.

34.4.1 Charm++

Charm++ is an object-oriented parallel programming model that extends the C++ programming language with concurrent objects stored in a global object space. Parallelism in Charm++ is expressed through concurrently executing objects called *chares*. A Charm++ program begins execution with one or more (typically one) *main chares*, which expose parallelism by creating additional chares. Once created, chares can communicate with each other by using remote method invocation. Unlike conventional models for parallel programming, Charm++ programs are expressed in terms of object-level concurrency rather than the number of processors or cores executing the computation.

Charm++ uses inheritance and other language features to extend C++ with parallelism. Because it works within the C++ standard, it does not require a special compiler and is compatible with existing C++ compilers. To create a Charm++ program, programmers must add a Charm++ interface file to their project specifying which C++ classes will be chares and indicating any *entry methods*, or methods that can be invoked by other chares. A Charm++ tool is then used to process the interface files and to generate additional source files that must be included in the project.

Invoking an entry method on a chare sends a message to the given object; the method is invoked asynchronously, and the call returns at the callsite as soon as the send has completed. Because of this asynchronous model, entry methods are not permitted to return a value; a return message can be generated by the callee by invoking an entry method on its caller. The Charm++ runtime system, referred to as the *charm kernel*, maintains a queue of incoming messages. Message forwarding is performed to route messages to the location of the desired object, and messages are processed from the queue as resources become available.

Parallelism in Charm++ can be structured through the use of chare collections. Collections can be used to influence the mapping of chares to processor cores and nodes as well as to express a structure in the set of chares used to define the computation. In addition, chare collections allow the programmer to act on many chares concurrently. The most commonly used chare collection is the chare array, which defines a multidimensional grid of chares that can be constructed to follow the structure of the computation. When a chare array is used, any chare can identify itself and others in the grid by index and perform, for example, neighborhood data exchange.

The charm kernel is also responsible for distributing chares across available resources and for balancing the workload by migrating chares from highly to lightly loaded nodes. Many load balancing strategies have been incorporated into Charm++, including asynchronous and synchronous methods. For many of its load balancing methods, Charm++ collects runtime information about the workload to inform the mapping of chares to computational resources. Because the runtime has control over the mapping of computation to resources, the Charm++ runtime system is also able to provide automated fault tolerance by migrating chares away from faulty nodes and recovering individual chares when they are lost because of failures.

34.4.2 Scioto

Scioto (scalable collections of task objects) [13] is a library extension to programming models with PGAS data spaces that adds support for task parallelism. Currently, Scioto supports the GA PGAS model; however, its task-based programming model was designed to be compatible with any global address space system.

In the Scioto model, the programmer expresses the computation as a collection of tasks that can be executed concurrently. Scioto tasks operate on data that are stored in a global address space (e.g., a global array); task inputs are fetched from and outputs written to globally accessible locations. This approach enables Scioto tasks to be executed by any process in the computation and gives the runtime system the flexibility to perform automatic load balancing. A Scioto task is defined by a callback function that operates on a *task descriptor* that contains a header with task metadata, and a user-defined body that contains the task's arguments.

A typical Scioto program begins in the SPMD execution model of the programming model that provides the global address space. The programmer creates a task collection and *seeds* it with an initial set of tasks. The programmer can select which process each task is assigned to, providing an initial work distribution. Once the task pool has been seeded, all processes participating in the task-parallel computation enter a task-processing phase by collectively calling the Scioto *process* function. During this phase, processes effectively give up their SPMD ranks and execute global address space tasks. Tasks can be dynamically created and added to the current task collection or to a new task collection that will be processed in a separate phase. The Scioto runtime system automatically detects quiescence of the task-parallel phase when all tasks have completed and returns the program to SPMD mode.

Scioto uses a strict task dependence model. In this model, tasks can create new subtasks, enabling the expression of dynamic parallelism. However, this type of ancestor–descendant control flow is the only type of task–task dependence allowed. If a task is not a descendant of another task, then it should not depend on its execution in order to complete. This restriction allows Scioto to achieve high efficiency in the scheduling and execution of tasks by avoiding overheads associated with time-sharing resources and task migration.

Scioto's runtime system performs automatic, dynamic load balancing of tasks across available computational resources using work stealing [14]. In the Scioto performance model, the computation is made up of work-stealing end points (e.g., GA processes) that contain a local work queue. When a task is created, the programmer can select the work queue in which it should be placed. This approach allows the programmer to make an initial placement of tasks that can be fine-tuned by the Scioto runtime system. In addition, it allows the programmer to push tasks to specific locations where they should be executed. If the programmer would like to explicitly map tasks to end points, work stealing can be disabled while still providing support for dynamic parallelism.

34.4.3 ADLB

ADLB, the asynchronous dynamic load balancing library [15], is a library extension to MPI that adds support for task-parallel execution. ADLB provides a Linda [16]-like shared task space where the application *put*s work into the logically shared task space and *get*s work for execution. ADLB tasks contain user-defined data that provides the task's input. Tasks can produce output in the memory of the process that executes the task as well as spawn child tasks. In addition to their input buffer, tasks are tagged with a *work type* that is used to select matching tasks when a process performs a task get operation. A process can specify multiple work types when requesting work, and it can provide a wildcard if any work type is acceptable.

An ADLB work request is composed of two steps: reservation and retrieval. Work is first reserved, and work metadata are received by the requesting process. This approach allows the worker to allocate space in local memory for the task's input buffer before retrieving it. Once the worker is ready, it performs a get operation that transfers task inputs to the process's local memory. ADLB utilizes a strict task execution model in which tasks are not permitted to communicate with each other. Hence, the input buffer is the primary means for passing input to ADLB tasks. This design choice relaxes the load balancing problem and enables ADLB to achieve better performance.

The ADLB architecture utilizes a master–worker execution model in which a user-defined subset of processes act as masters by calling the ADLB server function. The remaining processes act as workers, and each associates itself with a particular master that serves as its work manager. Masters communicate with one another to distribute work and assign tasks to workers. When a new task is created, the input data are stored on the originating worker to avoid resource exhaustion on the master. MPI one-sided communication is then used to retrieve input data when the get operation is performed for that task.

34.5   HIGH-PRODUCTIVITY PARALLEL PROGRAMMING MODELS

X10, Chapel, and Fortress are new parallel programming languages that have been developed as a part of the Defense Advanced Research Projects Agency (DARPA) High Productivity Computing Systems (HPCS) program. The goal of HPCS was to develop new high-performance computing systems, including both hardware and software components, that radically increase both performance and productivity. Thus, X10, Chapel, and Fortress take new and holistic approaches to parallel programming with the goals of greatly improving the ease of expressing parallelism and achieving high performance.

34.5.1   X10

X10 [17] is an object-oriented parallel programming language whose development has been led by IBM Research in conjunction with academic partners. The X10 language derives from popular imperative programming languages, especially Java, and focuses on distributed-memory fork–join parallelism. An X10 execution is composed of multiple *places*, represented by the places array, each of which encapsulates a data locality domain (e.g., processor or compute node). When aggregated, X10 places form a PGAS for storing data such as distributed arrays.

An X10 program is composed of multiple activities. Execution begins with the *main activity*, which executes on the *first place*. Additional parallelism is expressed by spawning concurrent computations as *async* activities. Activities can be synchronized with a parent or other ancestor activity through a corresponding *finish* statement. Thus, X10 activities naturally form a tree with the main activity at the root. When a finish statement is encountered in an activity, the activity is suspended, and the next statement is not executed until the corresponding asynchronous activities and any descendant activities have completed. This model of joining activities is referred to as a terminally strict fork–join model, which encapsulates and extends the fully strict model used by Cilk [18].

X10 provides support for exceptions using Java-like try-catch and throw constructs. Exceptions thrown by asynchronous activities are handled by using a *rooted exception model*. At any moment in time, every activity is said to have a root in the activity tree, which corresponds to the nearest ancestor that is awaiting termination of the activity. The path from an activity to its root is referred to as the *activation path* of the activity. When an exception occurs, X10 forwards the exception along the activation path until it is caught, possibly all the way to the main activity at the root of the tree.

An activity executes in the context of a particular place and can access data objects located at that place. When the programmer wishes to migrate the activity or access data in a different place, an at expression is used. A statement such as at(p) { fcn( ); } executes the given statements (in this case, the function, fcn) at place p. Asynchronous activities can also be spawned at different places by combining async and at expressions, for example, async at(p) { ... }.

Activities can be synchronized through several mechanisms: atomic blocks, when clauses, and clocks. Atomic blocks guarantee that the given statement or block of statements executes atomically. A *when clause* is used to suspend an activity until a particular condition becomes true, for example, when $(x > 5)$ { ... }. Clocks can be used to synchronize execution phases across a set of activities. Activities can be registered with one or more clocks when they are created; when an activity completes its phase of the computation, it *advances* the corresponding clocks to indicate that it is ready to advance to the next stage of the computation. The activity then waits for all other activities registered on the clock to arrive before continuing.

34.5.2 Chapel

Chapel [19] is a multithreaded, object-oriented parallel programming language whose development has been led by Cray Inc. Chapel inherits features and concepts from many existing programming languages and models. One of the most significant relatives of Chapel is the ZPL programming language [20], which has influenced Chapel's array-based parallelism. As a language, Chapel is imperative and block structured, similar to many familiar languages such as C, C++, and Java. Like X10, Chapel also incorporates many popular, modern programming language features, including object; generic programming; and a strong, static type system. Chapel also provides several novel features, including intents that are used to specify how function arguments will be used (as inputs, outputs, or both); type inference, which allows the programmer to omit type information when it can be inferred statically; and first-class domains, which incorporate index sets for aggregate data structures (e.g., arrays) as language-level entities.

A Chapel program begins execution as a single thread. Additional parallelism is exposed through a variety of task-parallel and data-parallel constructs. A Chapel execution is composed of a set of locales, which is exposed to the programmer through the locales array. A *locale* is an abstract unit of the system on which the program is running, most commonly a compute node or a processor. Chapel utilizes a global address space, where every data element is associated with the locale on which it resides.

Asynchronous tasks in a Chapel program can be spawned through begin statements, for example, begin { f( ); g( ); }. If the parent thread wishes to wait for the completion of a task, it synchronizes on begun tasks and their children by wrapping one or more such tasks in a sync block. Chapel also provides another mechanism for spawning tasks: cobegin { f( ); g( ); }. In a cobegin, each statement in the block is executed concurrently, and execution does not proceed past the cobegin until all tasks have completed.

Threads synchronize with each other using atomic sections or through *synchronized variables* in Chapel's global address space. An atomic block can be used to execute a block of statements as an indivisible update to memory that executes atomically with respect to the operations of other threads. Similar to the programming model of the Tera MTA [21] computer system, Chapel's synchronized variables are logically full or empty. Full variables become empty when read, and empty variables become full when written to. Reading from an empty location or writing to a full location causes the thread initiating the operation to block until the corresponding location becomes full or empty, respectively. Additional data access operations are provided that can be used to influence whether the initial state of a location is ignored and to set a specific state for a location after data access operation has completed.

Chapel also provides several data-parallel operations, including forall and coforall loops and parallel reduction and scan operations. The forall construct defines a loop where each iteration of the loop can be executed in parallel; the coforall variation synchronizes completion of all iterations before proceeding to the next statement in the parent thread. Chapel domains play an important role in data-parallel expressions. Because the domain of an array or other aggregated data objects is a first-class object in Chapel, *sliced* and *zippered* subsets of the domain can be readily specified to provide the set of data elements that will be operated on by data-parallel operations.

34.5.3 Fortress

Fortress [22] is a new, high-productivity programming language whose development was initiated by Sun Microsystems and has been continued by Oracle. Fortress aims to duplicate the success of Fortran by providing a modern, robust language for expressing the mathematical formulation of technical computing problems. To this end, Fortress programs are encoded in Unicode, which makes it possible to use standard mathematical characters and notations when writing a program. In addition, Fortress incorporates many modern language features, such as objects; exceptions; generic programming; type inference; and built-in aggregate data structures, including sets, arrays, maps, and lists. Object traits, similar to interfaces in Java, are used to extend the functionality supported by a particular object. In contrast to Java's abstract interfaces, however, traits define code for their associated methods.

Both task and data parallelism are provided by Fortress. Many operations, such as whole-array operations, evaluation of function arguments, and for loops, are implicitly parallel and can be executed concurrently by the Fortress runtime system. Iterative and reductive parallelism in Fortress is controlled by a *generator*, or domain expression, that defines the iteration space. Asynchronous threads can also be created by using a spawn statement.

Fortress provides the programmer with a logical global view of data and allows the user to define the distribution of aggregate data structures, for example, arrays. When an aggregate data structure is used as the generator for iteration, it also defines the locality of each iteration. When synchronized access to shared data is needed, the programmer performs the access within a transactional atomic block.

34.6 SUMMARY AND CONCLUDING REMARKS

With the dramatic increase in the concurrency of large-scale systems, a broad spectrum of parallel programming models has been created. Parallel programming models are distinguished by unique approaches to managing and exchanging data and mechanisms for expressing the units of work that comprise the computation. This chapter has discussed some of the popular parallel programming models used on supercomputers today, including MPI; various PGAS models such as GA, UPC, and CAF; some of the HPCS models such as X10 and Chapel; and task-parallel programming and work-stealing models such as Scioto, Charm++, and ADLB.

ACKNOWLEDGMENT

This work was supported by the Office of Advanced Scientific Computing Research, Office of Science, U.S. Department of Energy, under contract DE-AC02-06CH11357.

REFERENCES

[1] H. Tang and T. Yang, "Optimizing threaded MPI execution on smp clusters," *Proceedings of the 15th International Conference on Supercomputing, ICS '01*, pp. 381–392, New York: ACM, 2001.

[2] R. Butler and E. Lusk, "Monitors, messages, and clusters: The p4 parallel programming system," *Parallel Computing*, 20(4):547–564, 1994.

[3] W. Gropp and B. Smith, "Users manual for the chameleon parallel programming tools," Technical Report ANL-93/23, Argonne National Laboratory, 1993.

[4] A. Geist, A. Beguelin, J. Dongarra, W. Jiang, R. Manchek, and V. Sunderam, *PVM: Parallel Virtual Machine—A Users' Guide and Tutorial for Networked Parallel Computing*. Scientific and Engineering Computation Series. Cambridge, MA: MIT Press, 1994.

[5] MPI Forum, "MPI-2: Extensions to the message-passing interface," Technical Report, University of Tennessee, Knoxville, 1996.

[6] UPC Consortium, "UPC language specifications, v1.2," Technical Report LBNL-59208, Lawrence Berkeley National Lab, 2005.

[7] R.W. Numrich and J. Reid, "Co-Array Fortran for parallel programming," *ACM SIGPLAN Fortran Forum*, 17(2):1–31, 1998.

[8] R.W. Numrich and J. Reid, "Co-arrays in the next Fortran standard," *ACM SIGPLAN Fortran Forum*, 24:4–17, 2005.

[9] J. Nieplocha, R.J. Harrison, and R.J. Littlefield, "Global Arrays: A portable 'shared-memory' programming model for distributed memory computers," in *Proceedings of the ACM/IEEE Conference on Supercomputing (SC '94)*, pp. 340–349, 1994.

[10] J. Nieplocha, B. Palmer, V. Tipparaju, M. Krishnan, H. Trease, and E. Aprà, "Advances, applications and performance of the Global Arrays shared memory programming toolkit," *International Journal of High Performance Computing Applications*, 20(2):203–231, 2006.

[11] M. Valiev, E.J. Bylaska, N. Govind, K. Kowalski, T.P. Straatsma, H.J.J. Van Dam, D. Wang, J. Nieplocha, E. Apra, T.L. Windus, and W.A. de Jong, "NWChem: A comprehensive and

scalable open-source solution for large scale molecular simulations," *Computer Physics Communications*, 181(9):1477–1489, 2010.

[12] J. Nieplocha and B. Carpenter, "ARMCI: A portable remote memory copy library for distributed array libraries and compiler run-time systems," *Lecture Notes in Computer Science*, 1586:533–546, 1999.

[13] J. Dinan, S. Krishnamoorthy, D.B. Larkins, J. Nieplocha, and P. Sadayappan, "Scioto: A framework for global-view task parallelism," *Proceedings of the 2008 37th International Conference on Parallel Processing, ICPP '08*, 2008.

[14] J. Dinan, D.B. Larkins, P. Sadayappan, S. Krishnamoorthy, and J. Nieplocha, "Scalable work stealing," *Proceedings of the Conference on High Performance Computing Networking, Storage and Analysis, SC '09*, 2009.

[15] E.L. Lusk, S.C. Pieper, and R.M. Butler, "More scalability, less pain: A simple programming model and its implementation for extreme computing," *SciDAC Review*, 17:30–37, 2010.

[16] N. Carriero and D. Gelernter, "Applications experience with Linda," in *Proceedings of the ACM/SIGPLAN Conference on Parallel Programming: Experience with Applications, Languages and Systems, PPEALS '88*, pp. 173–187, New York: ACM, 1988.

[17] P. Charles, C. Grothoff, V. Saraswat, C. Donawa, A. Kielstra, K. Ebcioglu, C. von Praun, and V. Sarkar, "X10: An object-oriented approach to non-uniform cluster computing," in *Proceedings of the Conference on Object Oriented Programming Systems, Languages, and Applications (OOPSLA '05)*, pp. 519–538, 2005.

[18] M. Frigo, C.E. Leiserson, and K.H. Randall, "The implementation of the Cilk-5 multi-threaded language," in *Proceedings of the Conference on Programming Language Design and Implementation (PLDI)*, pp. 212–223, ACM SIGPLAN, 1998.

[19] B.L. Chamberlain, D. Callahan, and H.P. Zima, "Parallel programmability and the Chapel language," *International Journal of High Performance Computing Applications*, 21(3):291–312, 2007.

[20] B.L. Chamberlain, S.-E. Choi, C. Lewis, C. Lin, L. Snyder, and W.D. Weathersby, "ZPL: A machine independent programming language for parallel computers," *IEEE Transactions on Software Engineering*, 26(3):197–211, 2000.

[21] R. Alverson, D. Callahan, D. Cummings, B. Koblenz, A. Porterfield, and B. Smith, "The Tera computer system," in *Proceedings of the 4th International Conference on Supercomputing, ICS '90*, pp. 1–6, New York: ACM, 1990.

[22] G.L. Steele, Jr., "Parallel programming and parallel abstractions in Fortress," in *Proceedings of the 14th International Conference on Parallel Architecture and Compilation Techniques (PACT '05)*, p. 157, 2005.

35

Grid Simulation Tools for Job Scheduling and Data File Replication

Javid Taheri, Albert Y. Zomaya, and Samee U. Khan

35.1 INTRODUCTION

In recent years, grid computing has emerged as one of the main computational platforms to perform many extremely difficult and/or time-consuming tasks. The amount of data generated every second is in fact sometimes much more than what can be processed even by dedicated grids. This makes the design of optimum solutions to efficiently balance and deploy existing systems one of the main objectives/bottleneck in grids. These computational platforms are, however, too complicated to estimate/gauge efficiency of any algorithm without actually testing it. Thus, because accessing real systems is almost impossible for many reasons, including cost and trust, simulation becomes one of the inevitable stages before actual deployment of any algorithm in this field. In this chapter, first several simulation tools are listed, and then the problem statement behind all these grids is mathematically modeled and presented.

Simulation is one major step in modeling many real-world processes before their actual deployments. Proper simulations can provide an extensive study of a system and reveal its many unknown aspects before actual deployment, including, but not limited to, feasibility, behavioral, and performance analysis. Industrial processes, parallel and distributed systems, and environmental resources are among many that receive direct benefits from such simulations. Although simulations mean to represent the operations of one system through using another, they are always designed for very specific purposes. For example, simulation of the heating process of a gas is quite different from its volume expansion, although they are related.

Research in grids can be divided into two major categories: analytical and experimental. In analytical studies, the overall goal is to develop purely analytical/mathematical models for different aspects of computing in grids. Analytical studies are particularly very useful to discover the tractability of many grid-related problems, for example, NP-completeness of routing, partitioning, and scheduling. Therefore, although through such simulators fundamental theorems might be found, their models and assumptions are usually too simple to encompass all parameters of real systems and consequently to convince engineers to deploy them in reality. Thus, these analytical results are always followed by proper experiments to validate. Experimental research in grids aims to investigate, design, or implement real-world applications. Although such experiments are eminently believable and demonstrate feasibility of the proposed algorithms to be implemented in practice, they are usually very time and/or labor intensive: An experimental study may take hours, days, or even months of preparation. Furthermore, for such studies, the entire application should be designed and built to be fully functional; for example, it must include all design/algorithm alternatives as well as all hooks of deployments. Thus, it is usually considered as an acceptable engineering practice provided it is equipped with many full-fledged solutions so that the best algorithm could be found.

To this end, two different test beds are used to facilitate studies in this category of research: owned test beds and real grids. Owned test beds are usually small, well behaved, controlled, and stable; thus, they cannot be counted as true substitutes for real grids in most cases. Using real test beds, on the other hand, is not very practical, either. For example, having privileged access to real grids is still very challenging for many researchers. Also, real grids are not made as scientists' playpens where different experiments may disrupt each other and result in infidelity of the whole grid. Such experiments can also easily be affected by platform failures and configuration changes. As a result, because experiments in real grids are assumed uncontrollable and unrepeatable, they cannot disclose true analysis of novel algorithms in many cases. Furthermore, regardless of what type of test bed (owned or real) is used, experiments are always limited to the test bed itself. Thus, it is always difficult (1) to detect what part of the experiment were due to idiosyncrasies of the test bed, (2) to convince extrapolation of results, and (3) to justify viability of a solution in many untested situations (e.g., different network capacities). These issues result in the lack of interest in using test beds for testing novel algorithms in many studies.

Simulation of real grids, on the other hand, can solve many, if not all, of the aforementioned difficulties. In such simulations, (1) there is no need to build a real system; (2) it is easy to conduct controlled and repeatable experiments; (3) there is no limit to experimental scenarios; and (4) it is possible for others to repeat the experiment and reproduce the results. However, the key issue of validation as a correspondence between the simulated environment and the real world still remains challenging and questionable if not dealt with properly. Although simulation of distributed computing platforms (as the ancestor of grids) has decades of history, most of these works cannot be generalized into this fairly new discipline. Simplistic platform models, simplistic application models, and too-straightforward simulation are major reasons for such inapplicability.

To solve these issues, grid simulation has gone through many phases to migrate from such simplistic models with hardly justifiable environments to encompass real systems. To achieve this, grid simulators are usually built using synthetic data of the following three components: (1) network topology, (2) computer resources, and (3) applications. Network topology is modeled as graphs with individual bandwidth and latency characteristics for each link. Computer resources are to model all aspects of computing or storing elements of a grid, for example, heterogeneous computer resources or storage capacities. Applications are to model/represent attributes of many well-known grid applications, for example, bioinformatics or astronomy. The level of simulation in any of the aforementioned sections can significantly affect the performance and reliability of a simulator. For example, to model networks, two extreme approaches are (1) to model connections as unlimited links or (2) to scrutinize every single packet in the network. The first approach is very simple and fast; however, it is questionable for large grids with petabytes of data to transfer. The second approach, on the other hand, is very precise; however, it is unnecessarily complicated. Therefore, a trade-off is usually chosen in simulating many aspects of grids. Here, for example, extensive studies showed that assuming network links with only two attributes of bandwidth and latency is sufficiently precise in many cases [1–3].

35.2 SIMULATION PLATFORMS

Based on different levels of abstraction in the aforementioned components, several simulators are already designed and implemented to test/verify algorithms. A few of these simulators are designed to simulate specific characteristics, while others are designed to model general-purpose platforms.

35.2.1 SimJava

SimJava [4, 5] is a Java-based toolkit designed by the University of Edinburgh (United Kingdom) to simulate complex event-based systems. SimJava uses a discrete event simulation kernel and provides visual animation of its simulated objects during its simulation process. SimJava uses Java technology to ensure easy incorporation of its live diagrams into web pages as well as easier portability across different platforms. SimJava provides a set of foundation classes to enable easy creation and animation of discrete event simulation models and comprises the following three packages: (1) eduni.simjava, (2) eduni.simanim, and (3) eduni.simdiag. eduni.simjava builds text-based java simulation and produces an output trace file to reflect the results of a simulation; eduni.simanim is equipped with easy applet templates to provide easy visualization of eduin.simjava output files; and eduni.simdiag is a collection of JavaBeans-based classes to provide high-level presentation of simulation results.

SimJava is designed to simulate static networks with active entities that communicate with each other through sending/receiving passive event objects. As a result, SimJava is able to provide efficient lightweight packages to simulate and model hardware and distributed software systems, including communication protocols, parallel software modeling, and computer architectures [4, 5]. In fact, although

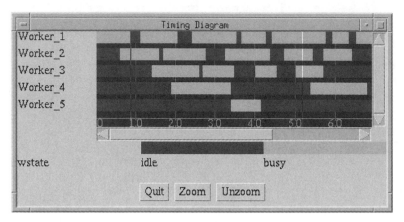

FIGURE 35.1. *A sample SimJava's snapshot.*

SimJava is not specifically designed to simulate grid environments, it has been used as a medium platform by many exclusively designed simulators in this area. Figure 35.1 shows a sample snapshot of SimJava during its simulation.

35.2.2 Bricks

Bricks [5,6] is a performance evaluation system developed in Java by Tokyo Institute of Technology (Japan) to analyze and compare the performance of various scheduling schemes in high-performance global computing environments. Bricks provides (1) simulation of various behaviors of resource scheduling algorithms, (2) programming modules for scheduling, (3) network topology of clients and servers in global computing systems, and (4) processing schemes for networks and servers. Bricks also gathers information on global computing resources to analyze resource scheduling algorithms as well as to systematically monitor and predict resources in global computing environments. Using its foreign interfaces, this component-based architecture also enables exploiting of different system components to simulate different system algorithms.

Bricks operates as a discrete event simulator of a queuing system in virtual time and consists of following two components to coordinate the simulation behavior of global computing systems: (1) a global computing environment and (2) a scheduling unit. The global computing environment module in Bricks consists of clients, networks, and servers. Clients represent users who submit specifically described computing jobs; networks represent interconnection of clients and servers; and servers represent computing resources that are executing submitted jobs. The scheduling unit of Bricks consists of NetworkMonitor, ServerMonitor, ResourceDB, Predictor, and Scheduler. NetworkMonitor measures network characteristics (e.g., bandwidth and latency) of every link in the network and stored in ResourceDB for later use; ServerMonitor measures the performance (e.g., load and availability) of different servers in a system and stores its results in ResourceDB; ResourceDB works as a scheduling database and stores all types of information about different parts of a system; Predictor uses stored information in ResourceDB and predicts resource availability and network conditions; and Scheduler uses Predictor's suggestions and

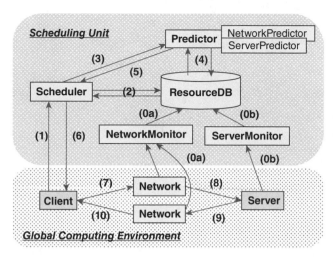

FIGURE 35.2. Bricks' architecture.

schedules new submitted jobs to computing resources of a system. Figure 35.2 shows the overall architecture of this simulator [6].

35.2.3 MicroGrid

MicroGrid [5, 7] is developed by the University of California at San Diego (United States) to provide platforms for developing/implementing virtual grid infrastructures. MicroGrid platforms can be used to analyze grid resource management issues of Globus applications. Virtual grid infrastructures allow analysis of dynamic resource management techniques with a minimum amount of effort to increase transparency of many repeatable/controllable experiments. Using different control algorithms, MicroGrid provides full-scale evaluation of middleware, applications, and network services for computational grids. MicroGrid aims to achieve the following goals: (1) to support scalable simulations of grid applications using a wide variety of scalable clustered resources, (2) to support realistic grid software environments so that simulated applications can be executed with identical application programming interfaces (APIs) and achieve accurate results, (3) to support configuring grid resource performance attributes, and (4) to be based on an open software environment so that other researchers can easily extend and improve its capabilities.

MicroGrid comprises two separate parts: (1) a local resource simulator to simulate and (2) a network simulator (NS) to simulate interactions among local resources. Figure 35.3 shows the overall diagram of this simulator [7].

35.2.4 SimGrid

SimGrid [5, 8, 9] is also developed by University of California at San Diego (United States) to evaluate scheduling algorithms for distributed applications in heterogeneous computational grids. SimGrid aims to provide fundamental/abstract functions so that domain-specific simulations can be built upon it. SimGrid specifically tried

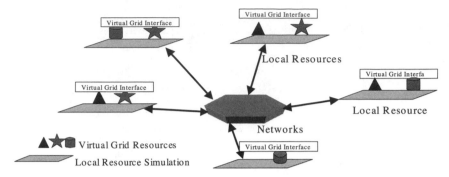

FIGURE 35.3. MicroGrid's diagram.

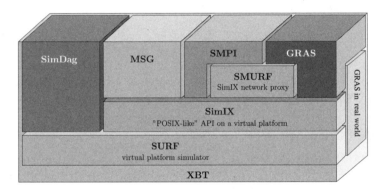

FIGURE 35.4. SimGrid's component overview.

to (1) provide the right model and level of abstraction for its intended purposes, (2) rapidly prototype and evaluate scheduling algorithms, (3) enable more realistic simulations, and (4) generate more accurate simulation results.

SimGrid includes many features such as (1) resource models for CPUs and network links; (2) arbitrary, dynamic, trace-based resource performance metrics; (3) resource time sharing and time slicing; (4) task dependencies; (5) performance prediction of simulation errors; (6) flexible simulation termination conditions; and (7) simple APIs.

Because resources (such as CPUs and network links) are assumed independent in SimGrid, no interconnection topology exists in this simulator. As a result, users can deploy this flexible computing environment to simulate their application-specific environments with arbitrary requirements. Here, because SimGrid cannot differentiate between computations and data transfers (both are seen as tasks), users must pay extra attention to ensure that computations and file transfers are properly scheduled on processors and network links, respectively. PSTSim [5] and DAGSim [5, 10] are among many applications that benefit from the flexible characteristic of SimGrid. PSTSim is to simulate scheduling of parameter sweep applications, and DAGSim is to evaluate scheduling algorithms for DAG-structured applications. Figure 35.4 shows the overall component overview of this simulator [9].

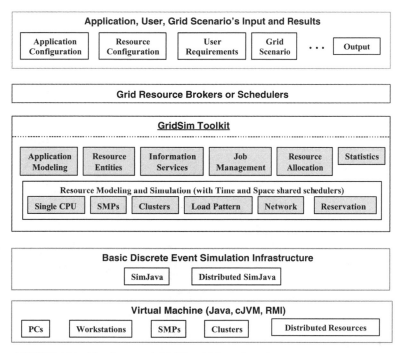

FIGURE 35.5. *Five layers of GridSim. SMPs, shared memory multiprocessors.*

35.2.5 GridSim

GridSim [5, 11] is developed by Monash University (Australia) to simulate application schedulers for distributed computing systems such as clusters and grids. GridSim is Java based and allows simulation of different classes of heterogeneous resources, users, applications, resource brokers (RBs), and schedulers in a distributed computing environment.

GridSim's architecture has five layers (Fig. 35.5). The first layer is to provide a portable/scalable Java interface and runtime environment. This layer is implemented using Java Virtual Machine (JVM) and can be executed in both single and multiprocessor (including clusters) systems. The second layer is to provide basic discrete event infrastructures. SimJava [4] is used to build this layer on top of interfaces provided by the first layer. The third layer is to model and simulate core grid entities such as resources and information services. This layer is based on discrete event services defined in the second layer. The fourth layer is to simulate resource aggregators called grid RBs or schedulers. The fifth/final layer is to evaluate scheduling and resource management policies, heuristics, and algorithms. This layer uses its lower two layers and focuses on application and resource modeling with different scenarios.

GridSim entities are users, brokers, resources, grid information services, and input/outputs. Users represent grid customers with individual attributes (jobs types, scheduling optimization policies, activity rates, time zones, job deadlines, and budget affordability); brokers schedule jobs to resources based on users' requirements; resources represent individual computing resources with individual characteristics

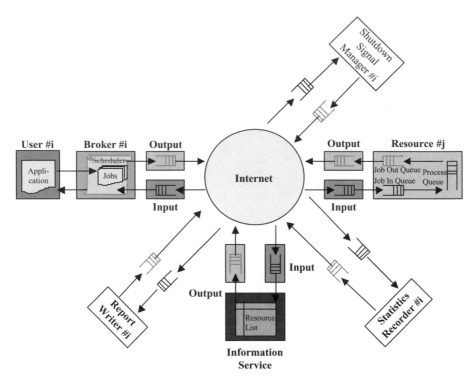

FIGURE 35.6. *A sample GridSim flow diagram.*

(number of processors, cost of processing, processors' speed, internal scheduling policy, local load factors, and time zone); grid information services provide resource registration services and monitor the list of available resources in a grid; and input/ outputs define input/output information flow links among different entities of a grid. The Nimrod-G [12] RB and Libra [13] are among many products that use GridSim as their intermedium simulation framework. Figure 35.6 show a sample flow diagram of a GridSim-based simulation [11].

35.2.6 GangSim

GangSim [14] is developed by The University of Chicago (United States) to support studies of scheduling strategies in grid environments with a particular focus on investigating interactions among local and community resource allocation policies. GangSim is based on the Ganglia distributed monitoring framework in which mixing of simulated and real grids is allowed. GangSim models comprise the following real grid elements: a job submission infrastructure, a monitoring infrastructure, and a usage policy infrastructure. As shown in Figure 35.7, the principal components of GridSim are external schedulers (ESs), local schedulers (LSs), data schedulers (DSs), monitoring distribution points (MDPs), site policy enforcement points (S-PEPs), and virtual organization policy enforcement points (V-PEPs). In GangSim, sites aggregate computing nodes and VOs aggregate users, who may be further organized into groups. Here, each site is characterized by its capacity, number of CPUs, disk space, and its connecting networks. A VO is composed of a set of user

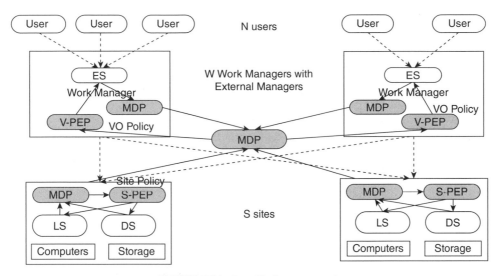

FIGURE 35.7. *GangSim's components.*

groups. Users submit jobs and/or workloads. ESs, LSs, and DSs are decision-making points for different purposes. An ES queues submitted jobs and selects the best site candidate to execute each job. Upon this assignment, corresponding LSs receive jobs and schedule them to actual CPUs inside sites, while DSs provide data files needed to execute these jobs. GridSim assumes that data files are distributed once among sites prior to job scheduling and are not moved afterward. Pegasus and Euryale are examples of ES policies; Condor, PBS, and LSF are examples of LS policies [14]. In GangSim, MDPs represent monitoring infrastructure equipped with various metrics to evaluate performance of different components of a grid environment. Policy enforcement points (PEPs) enforce policies to steer resource allocation units so that users' required policies are always met. S-PEPs and V-PEPs perform this task in sites and VO levels, respectively.

35.2.7 MONARC

MONARC [15] is developed in Java through the collaboration of Politechnica University of Bucharest (Romania), CERN and Caltech (United States). MONARC is a multithreaded process oriented simulation framework to model large-scale distributed systems. It is designed to provide realistic simulation of a wide-range of distributed system technologies with respect to their specific components and characteristics. MONARC particularly aims to (1) extend and optimize grid modules to provide better simulation of processing nodes, (2) design and run simulation experiments for data processing activities, job scheduling, and minimum spanning tree computation in overlay networks, and (3) make multithreading performance tests on multiprocessor platforms (Sun Enterprise 10,000, multicore PCs).

The two fundamental components of MONARC are computing and monitoring. The computing component aims to provide realistic simulations of all grid modules and their interactions through abstraction, while monitoring aims to provide measurement metrics for better analysis of a system. Computing components are further

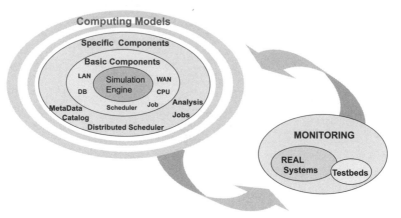

FIGURE 35.8. MONARC's components and layers. DB, database.

categorized into three layers: simulation engine, basic components, and specific components. The simulation engine layer is the core of this event-driven simulator; basic components aim to model jobs, CPUs, WANs, data files, LANs, as well as other fundamental modules of a system. Specific components use basic components to simulate the behavior of different types of jobs, for example, job schedulers with specific scheduling algorithms or database servers that support data replication. Using this structure, a wide range of models, from centralized to distributed systems, with arbitrary levels of complexity can be developed. Multiple regional centers with different hardware configurations and possibly different sets of replicated data are examples of models that can be created/simulated by MONARC. Figure 35.8 shows MONARC's components and their comprising layers [15].

35.2.8 OptorSim

OptorSim [16] is a time-based simulation package also written in Java to investigate the performance of different job scheduling and data replication schemes. OptorSim is designed based on the structure of the European DataGrid and has tried to simulate all its necessary components with an emphasis on its replication infrastructure. OptorSim is composed of computing elements (CEs), storage elements (SEs), an RB, and a replica manager (RM).

CEs accept file-dependent jobs; SEs host data files required to execute jobs; RBs control scheduling of jobs in grid sites (CEs/SEs); and RMs inside SEs deploy their replica optimizers (ROs) to automatically create, delete, or replicate data files for each SE. OptorSim also incorporates a simulated peer-to-peer messaging system to implement auction-based replica algorithms. OptorSim can also be used to test new dynamic replication strategies to optimize data access efficiency in data grids. To launch OptorSim, it is provided with a grid configuration and a tailor-made RO algorithm as input, and in turn, it simulates execution of the provided file-dependent jobs in a grid environment. OptorSim also provides facilities to visualize simulation results for better performance analysis of replication algorithms.

OptorSim provided tools to define arbitrary data grid topologies, job creation patterns, jobs' file access patterns, jobs' processing time scheduling algorithms for

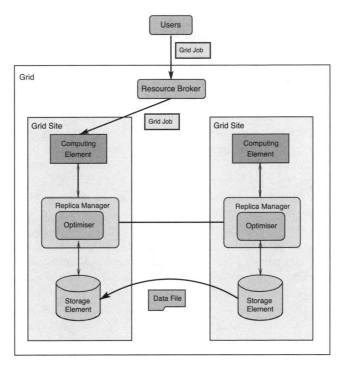

FIGURE 35.9. OptorSim's architecture.

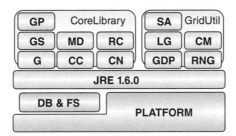

FIGURE 35.10. EcoGrid's components.

RBs, replication algorithms for ROs, traffic patterns in network, and many more. Figure 35.9 shows the overall architecture of this simulator [16].

35.2.9 EcoGrid

EcoGrid [17] is another Java-based simulator to evaluate the performance of scheduling algorithms in grids. EcoGrid is dynamically configurable and supports resource modeling, advance reservation of resources, and integration of new scheduling policies. Although EcoGrid is primarily designed to evaluate economy-based scheduling algorithms, it can also be used for non-economy-based scheduling algorithms by setting only one of its parameters. EcoGrid uses the following components to model its grid environment (Fig. 35.10): configuration manager (CM), random number generator (RNG), load generator (LG), resource calendar (rc), computer node

(CN), computer cluster (CC), media directory (MD), grid process (GP), grid (G), grid scheduler (GS), statistical analyzer (SA), and grid data provider (GDP). CM is to dynamically configure the grid simulator; RNG provides random numbers based on different statistical distributions; RC determines load, price, booking status, holidays, time zone, and many other attributes of CNs; LG produces various work processing loads for simulation; SA provides computational components to analyze generated statistics of different component of a system; GDP facilitates data access from various sources and separates the data access functionality from the core grid functionality of a system; CCs are collections of CNs to present processing units of a grid; MD (1) stores details of service providing clusters to be later accessed by resource consumers and (2) provides a resource matching algorithm to determine the most suitable cluster and the most suitable node; GP represents a task with specific characteristics (e.g., execution time, input data file size, starting date, and deadline date) to be executed on a grid; GS represents a set of algorithms to schedule processes on clusters and nodes; the grid (G) represents a set of clusters to perform jobs; CNs consist of hard disks, memories, and processors to represent actual CEs of a grid.

35.2.10 GridNet

GridNet [18] is a modular NS-based simulator, written in C++, to model different data grid configurations and resource specifications. GridNet modules are composed of objects (nodes, links, and messages) that are mapped into the NS's application level object classes. Different network configurations, different types of nodes, different node resources, replication strategies, and cost functions can be built using these NS-based objects. Here NS's packets are used to simulate all actions inside a grid, for example, data exchange among nodes, user requests, and start/end of data transmission. To make a replication decision in GridNet performed by NS's data transfer control unit, nodes generate new NS traffic to forward requests to other nodes or send requested data to a client. In fact, GridNet only added grid-specific elements such as grid nodes and replication strategies into the NS and uses NS's event-driven capability to simulate a data grid environment.

GridNet adopts CERN's data grid architecture (the European Organization for Nuclear Research) and Grid Physics Network (GriPhyN) [19] and assumes that a grid consists of several sites with different computational and data-storage resources. Here, each node can specify its relative computing capacity, specify its storage capacity, organize its local data files, and maintain a list of its peer replica neighbors. GridNet uses the following three node types to define its components: servers, caches, and clients. Server nodes represent main storage sites where grid data are stored (each node may host the whole or just some parts of a data file); cache nodes represent intermediate storage sites (e.g., a regional storage site) to replicate parts of data stored in main storage sites/servers; and client nodes represent sites where data access is requested. Figure 35.11 shows the simulation architecture of this simulator.

35.2.11 Opportunistic Grid Simulation Tools

Opportunistic Grid Simulation Tool (OGST) [20] was developed in Java as an extension to the GridSim toolkit. OGST's main objectives are (1) to assist developers of

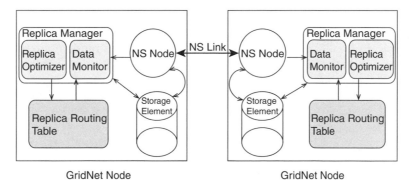

FIGURE 35.11. *GridNet's architecture.*

opportunistic grid middlewares on validating their new concepts and implementations under different execution conditions and scenarios, as well as (2) to simulate large-scale applications and resource scenarios involving several users in a repetitive and controlled way. OGST, which was developed based on the InteGrade project, also allows automatic creation of simulated grid environments composed of a large number of highly heterogeneous nodes. OGST explicitly implements two application execution models: regular and bag-of-tasks. OGST provides a library of scheduling algorithms composed of four scheduling heuristics: InteGrade, OLB, MCT, and Min-Min; and also provides the support for implementing other algorithms. OGST uses the following components to simulate its environments: (1) feature generators (FG) to define simulated grid environments (nodes and network links) and applications with their arrival rate; (2) application submission and control tool (ASCT) to handle grid users for their application submissions and receive notification upon their jobs' conclusions; (3) global resource manager (GRM) to receive application submissions; (4) scheduling strategy (SS) to schedule application tasks for execution on grid nodes; (5) trader manager (TM) to provide data availability of grid resources including node failure and recovery; (6) local resource manager (LRM) to execute scheduled application tasks scheduled to a node, maintain a list of waiting tasks for execution, and handle local resource loads; (7) simulation data record manager (SDRM) to store and collect simulation data such as conclusion time stamps and to generate performance graphs such as the average application completion time; and (8) application replication manager (ARM) to replicate resources in case of accidental node failures. Figure 35.12 shows how the main components of this simulator are connected to each other [20].

35.2.12   SchMng

Schelling Manager (SchMng) is a Visual Net C++-based software package developed at The University of Sydney (Australia) to gauge the combined performance of different job scheduling and data replication techniques. Because different approaches made different assumptions to capture the complexity of solving grid-related job scheduling and data replication problems, SchMng was designed to encompass as many features as possible from all approaches [1, 21–31] previously designed to solve grid-related optimization problems. SchMng's framework (shown

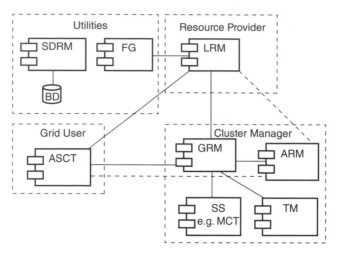

FIGURE 35.12. *OGST's components.*

in Fig. 35.13) consists of heterogeneous (1) computational nodes, (2) storage nodes (SNs), (3) interconnecting networks, (4) schedulers, (5) users, (6) jobs, and (7) data files.

In SchMng, computer centers with heterogeneous CEs are modeled as a collection of computational nodes (CNs); each CN (1) consists of several homogeneous CEs with identical characteristics and (2) is equipped with a local storage capability. Figure 35.14 shows a sample computer center consisting of four CNs with such storage capability. CNs are characterized by (1) their processing speed and (2) their number of processors. The processing speed for each CN is a relative number to reflect the processing speed of a CN as compared to other CNs in the system. The number of processors for each CN determines its capability to execute jobs with certain degrees of parallelism in a nonpreemptive fashion; that is, jobs cannot interrupt execution of each other during their runtimes. SNs are SEs in the system that host data files required by jobs. Two types of SNs exist in SchMng: isolated and attached. Isolated SNs are individual entities that only host data files and deliver them to requesting CNs; attached SNs, on the other hand, are local storage capacities of CNs to host their local data files as well as to provide them to other CNs if requested. Although from the optimization point of view there is no difference between the two and they are treated equally in a grid system, isolated SNs usually have more capacity than the attached ones, whereas attached SNs can upload data files to their associated CNs almost instantly.

CNs and SNs are connected through an interconnection network that is composed of individual links. Each link has its own characteristics and is modeled using two parameters: delay and bandwidth. Delay is set based on the average waiting time for a data file to start flowing from one side of the link to the other; bandwidth is set based on the average bandwidth between two sides of the link. Although the above formulation differs from reality in which delay and bandwidth among nodes significantly vary based on a system's traffic, extensive simulation showed that this difference is negligible when the number of jobs and data files increases in a system [1–3]. Schedulers are independent entities in the system that accept jobs and data

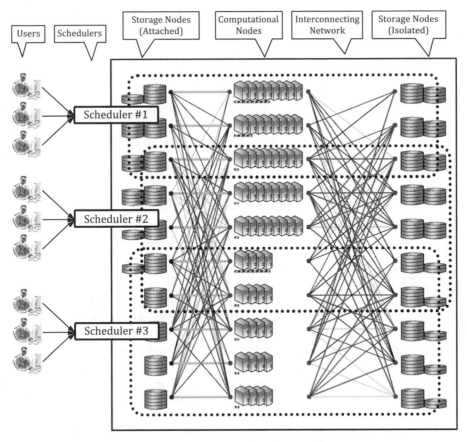

FIGURE 35.13. *SchMng's framework.*

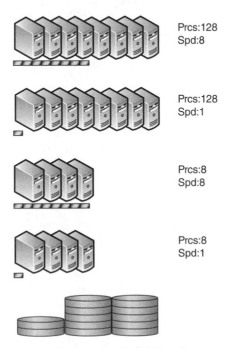

Prcs:128
Spd:8

Prcs:128
Spd:1

Prcs:8
Spd:8

Prcs:8
Spd:1

FIGURE 35.14. *A sample computer center in SchMng. Prcs, processors; spd, speed.*

files from users and schedule/assign/replicate them to relevant CNs and SNs. Schedulers, which can be connected to all CNs/SNs or only to a subset of them, are in fact the decision makers of the whole system that decide where each job and/or data file should be executed or stored/replicated, respectively. Schedulers can be either subentities of CNs/SNs or individual job/data file brokers that accept jobs and data files from users. In SchMng, the more general case in which schedulers are treated as individual job/data file brokers is assumed.

Users generate jobs with specific characteristics. Each user is only connected to one scheduler to submit his or her jobs. Here, although the majority of users only use preexisting data files in a system, they can also generate their own data files should they want to. Jobs are generated by users and are submitted to schedulers to be executed by CNs. Each job consists of several dependent tasks described by a DAG with specific characteristics, that is, (1) execution time and (2) number of processors. The execution time determines the number of seconds a particular task needs to be executed/finalized in the slowest CN in the system; the actual execution time of a task can be significantly reduced if it is assigned to a faster CN instead; the number of processors determines a task's degree of parallelism. Using this factor, schedulers eliminate CNs whose processors are not enough to execute specific jobs/tasks. Jobs are generated with different shapes to reflect different classes of operations as outlined by Task Graphs for Free (TGFF) [32] and have the following characteristics: (1) width, (2) height, (3) number of processors, (4) time to execute, (5) shape, and (6) a list of required data files. Width is the maximum number of tasks that can run concurrently inside a job; height is the number of levels/stages a job has; the number of processors is the maximum number of processors its containing tasks need to be run; the time to execute determines the minimum time a job can be run on the slowest CN in a system; and the list of required data files determines a list of data files a CN must download before executing a job. Jobs' shapes are (1) serious–parallel, (2) homogeneous–parallel, (3) heterogeneous–parallel, and (4) single task. Figure 35.15 and Table 35.1 show sample jobs and their characteristics. Data files are assumed to be owned by SNs and are allowed to have up to a predefined number of replicas in a system. Schedulers can only delete or move replicas; that is, the original data files are always kept untouched.

35.3   PROBLEM STATEMENT: DATA-AWARE JOB SCHEDULING (DAJS)

This section describes the underlying problem all GSs are trying to solve. Regardless of the type of applications submitted to grids, GSs are always trying to (1) minimize the execution of the submitted jobs, (2) minimize the transfer time of all data files to their requested jobs, or (3) both. Therefore, in this section, the DAJS problem is formally defined to cover both cases [2, 3].

DAJS is a bi-objective optimization problem and is defined as assigning jobs to CNs and replicating data files on SNs to concurrently minimize (1) the overall execution time of a batch of jobs as well as (2) the transfer time of all data files to their dependent jobs. As can be seen, DAJS can be easily converted to solely either optimize the execution time or the transfer time of a system. In its general formulation, because these two objectives are usually interdependent, and in many cases even conflicting, minimizing one objective usually results in compromising the other.

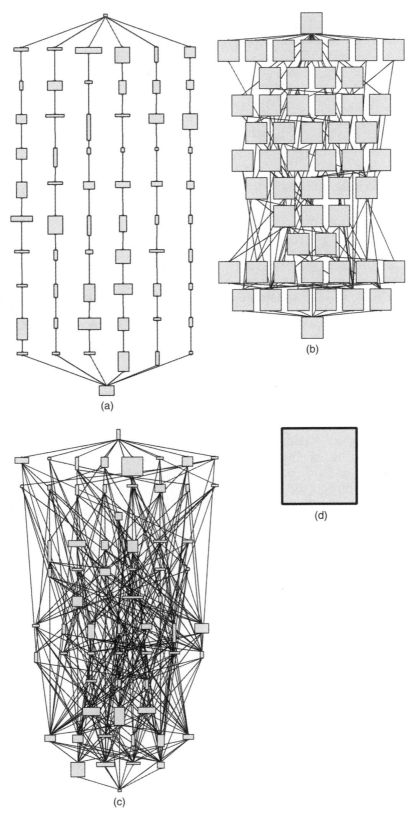

FIGURE 35.15. Job's shape: (a) serious–parallel, (b) homogeneous–parallel, (c) heterogeneous–parallel, and (d) single task.

TABLE 35.1. Tasks' Characteristics for Jobs (see Fig. 35.15)

Shape	Width	Height	Number of Tasks	Number of Processors	Time to Execute
Serious–parallel	6	12	62	7	491
Homogeneous–parallel	7	12	53	8	260
Heterogeneous–parallel	9	14	65	6	470
Single task	1	1	1	4	20

TABLE 35.2. Notation Summary

Symbol	Description
N_{CN}, N_{SN}, N_J, ND	Total number of CNs, SNs, jobs, and data files in the system
CN_i^{prcs}	Total number of processors for the CN #i
SN_i^{size}	Size of the SN #i
J_i^{ST}, J_i^{EX}, J_i^{TT}	Start, execution time, and transfer time for all data files after executing job #i
$JSet_i^{EX}$, $JSet_i^{TT}$	Execution time and total transfer time of all data files addressed by a collection of jobs described in $JSet_i$ to be executed by CN_i
$DSet_i^{size}$	Total size of a collection of data files addressed by $DSet_i$ to be hosted by SN_i

For example, achieving lower execution time requires scheduling jobs to powerful CNs; whereas, achieving lower transfer times requires using powerful links with higher bandwidths in a system. Table 35.2 summarizes symbols we use to mathematically formulate the DAJS problem.

To formulate this problem, assume jobs are partitioned into several job sets, $JobSets = \{JSet_1, JSet_2, \ldots, JSet_{N_J}\}$ to be executed by CNs, and data files are partitioned into several data file sets, $DataSets = \{DSet_1, DSet_2, \ldots, DSet_{N_D}\}$, to be replicated on SNs; a partition of a set is defined as the decomposition of a set into disjoint subsets whose union is the original set. For example, if $N_J = 9$ and $N_{CN} = 3$; then, $JobSets = \{\{1, 5, 7\}, \{2, 4, 8, 9\}, \{3, 6\}\}$ means jobs $\{J_1, J_5, J_7\}$, $\{J_2, J_4, J_8, J_9\}$, and $\{J_3, J_6\}$ are assigned/scheduled to CN_1, CN_2, and CN_3, respectively.

Based on this model, DAJS is defined as finding elements of job sets and data file sets to minimize the following two objective functions:

$$
\begin{cases}
1.\ MinMax_{i=1}^{N_{CN}} JSet_i^{EX} \\
2.\ Min \sum_{i=1}^{N_{CN}} JSet_i^{TT} \\
s.t. \\
1.\ JSet_i^{prcs} \leq CN_i^{prcs} \qquad i = 1, \ldots, N_{CN} \\
2.\ DSet_i^{size} \leq SN_i^{size} \qquad i = 1, \ldots, N_{SN}
\end{cases}
$$

Here, if $JSet_i = \{J_1, J_2, J_K\}$ contains K jobs scheduled to be executed by CN_i, then the execution time and the total transfer time of this job set can be calculated as follows:

$$
JSet_i^{EX} = Max_{k=1}^{K}(J_k^{ST} + J_k^{EX})
$$

and

$$\mathrm{JSet}_i^{\mathrm{TT}} = \sum_{k=1}^{K} J_k^{\mathrm{TT}}.$$

In the stated bi-objective formulation, the first constraint is to guarantee that all CNs are capable of executing their assigned jobs, while the second constraint is to guarantee that the total size of all data files each SN hosts is less than its total capacity. It is also worth mentioning that the overall execution time of a set of jobs greatly depends on each CN's local scheduling policy; thus, such scheduling policies must be carefully set for each case to achieve the best performance. Extensive research, however, showed that the local scheduling policy of first come, first served with backfilling usually results in optimal deployment of CNs' resources when large numbers of jobs are submitted [33]. Based on extensive studies, SchMng also assumes that if several jobs in a CN require the same data file, the requested data file will be downloaded only once and then stored in a local repository (cache) for further local requests [1, 21–29, 34, 35].

REFERENCES

[1] R. McClatchey, A. Anjum, H. Stockinger, A. Ali, I. Willers, and M. Thomas, "Data intensive and network aware (DIANA) grid scheduling," *Journal of Grid Computing*, 5(1):43–64, 2007.

[2] J. Taheri, Y.C. Lee, A.Y. Zomaya, H.J. Siegel, "A bee colony based optimization approach for simultaneous job scheduling and data replication in grid environments," *Computers & Operations Research*, available online 25 November 2011, ISSN 0305-0548, 10.1016/j.cor.2011.11.012.

[3] J. Taheri, Y.C. Lee, and A.Y. Zomaya, "Bestmap: Network aware job and data allocation in grid environments," Technical Report TR671, The University of Sydney, 2011.

[4] F. Howell and R. McNab, "SimJava: A discrete event simulation package for java with applications in computer systems modelling," *First International Conference on Web-Based Modelling and Simulation*, 1998, San Diego, CA.

[5] A. Sulistio, C.S. Yeo, and R. Buyya, "Simulation of parallel and distributed systems: A taxonomy and survey of tools," Available at http://ww2.cs.mu.oz.au/~raj/papers/simtools.pdf.

[6] A. Takefusa, S. Matsuoka, and H. Nakada, "Overview of a performance evaluation system for global computing scheduling algorithms," in *8th IEEE International Symposium on High Performance Distributing Computing (HPDC8)*, pp. 97–104, 1999.

[7] H.J. Song, X. Liu, D. Jakobsen, R. Bhagwan, X. Zhang, K. Taura, and A. Chien, "The MicroGrid: A scientific tool for modeling computational grids," *Scientific Programming*, 8(3):127–141, 2000.

[8] H. Casanova, "SimGrid: A toolkit for the simulation of application scheduling," in *First IEEE/ACM International Symposium on Cluster Computing and the Grid*, pp. 430–437, 2001.

[9] H. Casanova, A. Legrand, and M. Quinson, "SimGrid: A generic framework for large-scale distributed experiments," in *10th International Conference on Computer Modeling and Simulation*, pp. 126–131, 2008.

[10] A. Jarry, H. Casanova, and F. Berman, "DAGSim: A simulator for dag scheduling algorithms," Technical Report RR2000-46, LIP, 2000.

[11] R. Buyya and M. Murshed, "GridSim: A toolkit for the modeling and simulation of distributed resource management and scheduling for grid computing," *Concurrency and Computation: Practice and Experience*, 14(13):1175–1220, 2002.

[12] R. Buyya, D. Abramson, and J. Giddy, "Nimrod/G: An architecture for a resource management and scheduling system in a global computational grid," in *The 4th International Conference/Exhibition on High Performance Computing in the Asia-Pacific Region (HPC-ASIA)*, Vol. 1, pp. 283–289, 2000.

[13] J. Sherwan, N. Ali, N. Lotia, Z. Hayat, and R. Buyya, "Libra: An economy driven job scheduling system for clusters," in *6th International Conference on High Performance Computing in Asia Pacific Region (HPC-Asia)*, pp. 16–19, 2002.

[14] C.L. Dumitrescu and I. Foster, "GangSim: A simulator for grid scheduling studies," in *IEEE International Symposium on Cluster Computing and the Grid (CCGrid)*, Vol. 2, pp. 1151–1158, 2005.

[15] C. Dobre and C. Stratan, "MONARC simulation framework," *Transactions on Automatic Control and Computer Science*, 49(63):35–42, 2004.

[16] D.G. Cameron, A.P. Millar, C. Nicholson, R. Carvajal-schiaffino, F. Zini, and K. Stockinger, "OptorSim: A simulation tool for scheduling and replica optimisation in data grids," in *Computing in High Energy Physics (CHEP 2004)*, Interlaken, Switzerland, 2004.

[17] H. Mehta, P. Kanungo, and M. Chandwani, "EcoGrid: A dynamically configurable object oriented simulation environment for economy-based grid scheduling algorithms," in *The 4th Annual ACM Bangalore Conference*, pp. 1–8, Bangalore, India: ACM, 2011.

[18] H. Lamehamedi, Z. Shentu, B. Szymanski, and E. Deelman, "Simulation of dynamic data replication strategies in data grids," 2003.

[19] GriPhyN, "Grid physics network in atlas." Available at http://www.usatlas.bnl.gov/computing/grid/griphyn/.

[20] G.C. Filho and F.J. da Silva e Silva, "OGST: An opportunistic grid simulation tool," in *2nd International Workshop Latin American Grid (LAGrid 2008)*, Campo Grande, Mato Grosso do Sul, 2008.

[21] K. Ranganathan and I. Foster, "Decoupling computation and data scheduling in distributed data-intensive applications," in *Proceedings of 11th IEEE International Symposium on High Performance Distributed Computing (HPDC '02)*, pp. 352–358, 2002.

[22] W. Hoschek, J. Jaen-Martinez, A. Samar, H. Stockinger, and K. Stockinger, "Data management in an international data grid project," in *Grid Computing*, Vol. 1971 of *Lecture Notes in Computer Science* (R. Buyya and M. Baker, eds), pp. 77–90. New York: Springer-Verlag, 2000.

[23] W.H. Bell, D.G. Cameron, L. Capozza, A.P. Millar, K. Stockinger, and F. Zini, "OptorSim: A grid simulator for studying dynamic data replication strategies," *International Journal of High Performance Computing Applications*, 17(4):403–416, 2003.

[24] A. Chakrabarti and S. Sengupta, "Scalable and distributed mechanisms for integrated scheduling and replication in data grids," in *Distributed Computing and Networking*, Vol. 4904 of *Lecture Notes in Computer Science* (S. Rao, M. Chatterjee, P. Jayanti, C. Murthy, and S. Saha, eds), pp. 227–238. Berlin/Heidelberg: Springer, 2008.

[25] M. Tang, B.-S. Lee, X. Tang, and C.-K. Yeo, "The impact of data replication on job scheduling performance in the data grid," *Future Generation Computer Systems*, 22(3):254–268, 2006.

[26] R.-S. Chang, J.-S. Chang, and S.-Y. Lin, "Job scheduling and data replication on data grids," *Future Generation Computer Systems*, 23(7):846–860, 2007.

[27] N.N. Dang and S.B. Lim, "Combination of replication and scheduling in data grids," *International Journal of Computer Science and Network Security*, 7(3):304–308, 2007.

[28] S. Abdi and S. Mohamadi, "Two level job scheduling and data replication in data grid," *International Journal of Grid Computing & Applications*, 1(1):23–37, 2010.

[29] A. Anjum, R. McClatchey, A. Ali, and I. Willers, "Bulk scheduling with the diana scheduler," *IEEE Transactions on Nuclear Science*, 53(6):3818–3829, 2006.

[30] F. Berman, G. Fox, and A.J.G. Hey, *Grid Computing: Making the Global Infrastructure a Reality. Wiley Series in Communication Networking & Distributed Systems*. New York: John Wiley & Sons, 2003.

[31] R. Subrata, A.Y. Zomaya, and B. Landfeldt, "A cooperative game framework for qos guided job allocation schemes in grids," *IEEE Transactions on Computers*, 57(10):1413–1422, 2008.

[32] R.P. Dick, D.L. Rhodes, and W. Wolf, "TGFF: Task Graphs for Free," in *Proceedings of the 6th International Workshop on Hardware/Software Codesign*, pp. 97–101, 1998.

[33] H. Shan, L. Oliker, and R. Biswas, "Job superscheduler architecture and performance in computational grid environments," in *Proceedings of the ACM/IEEE SC2003 Conference (SC '03)* (L. Oliker and R. Biswas, eds), pp. 44–58, 2003.

[34] S.-M. Park and J.-H. Kim, "Chameleon: A resource scheduler in a data grid environment," in *Proceedings of the 3rd IEEE International Symposium on Cluster Computing and the Grid (CCGRID '03)*, pp. 258–265, 2003.

[35] A. Chakrabarti, R. Dheepak, and S. Sengupta, "Integration of scheduling and replication in data grids," in *High Performance Computing—HiPC 2004*, Vol. 3296 of *Lecture Notes in Computer Science* (L. Bougé and V. Prasanna, eds), pp. 85–101. Berlin/Heidelberg: Springer, 2005.

Index

Note: Page numbers in **bold** indicate tables; those in *italics* indicate figures.

Scalable Computing and Communications: Theory and Practice, First Edition. Edited by Samee U. Khan, Albert Y. Zomaya, and Lizhe Wang.
© 2013 John Wiley & Sons, Inc. Published 2013 by John Wiley & Sons, Inc.

WILEY SERIES ON PARALLEL AND DISTRIBUTED COMPUTING
Series Editor: Albert Y. Zomaya

Parallel and Distributed Simulation Systems / Richard Fujimoto

Mobile Processing in Distributed and Open Environments / Peter Sapaty

Introduction to Parallel Algorithms / C. Xavier and S.S. Iyengar

Solutions to Parallel and Distributed Computing Problems: Lessons from Biological Sciences / Albert Y. Zomaya, Fikret Ercal, and Stephan Olariu (Editors)

Parallel and Distributed Computing: A Survey of Models, Paradigms, and Approaches / Claudia Leopold

Fundamentals of Distributed Object Systems: A CORBA Perspective / Zahir Tari and Omran Bukhres

Pipelined Processor Farms: Structured Design for Embedded Parallel Systems / Martin Fleury and Andrew Downton

Handbook of Wireless Networks and Mobile Computing / Ivan Stojmenovic (Editor)

Internet-Based Workflow Management: Toward a Semantic Web / Dan C. Marinescu

Parallel Computing on Heterogeneous Networks / Alexey L. Lastovetsky

Performance Evaluation and Characterization of Parallel and Distributed Computing Tools / Salim Hariri and Manish Parashar

Distributed Computing: Fundamentals, Simulations, and Advanced Topics, 2nd Edition / Hagit Attiya and Jennifer Welch

Smart Environments: Technology, Protocols, and Applications / Diane Cook and Sajal Das

Fundamentals of Computer Organization and Architecture / Mostafa Abd-El-Barr and Hesham El-Rewini

Advanced Computer Architecture and Parallel Processing / Hesham El-Rewini and Mostafa Abd-El-Barr

UPC: Distributed Shared Memory Programming / Tarek El-Ghazawi

Ruling Distributed Dynamic Worlds / Peter Sapaty

Parallel Metaheuristics: A New Class of Algorithms / Enrique Alba (Editor)

Handbook of Sensor Networks: Algorithms and Architectures / Ivan Stojmenovic (Editor)

Dependable Computing: Paradigms, Performance Issues, and Applications / Hassan B. Diab and Albert Y. Zomaya (Editors)

High Performance Computing: Paradigm and Infrastructure / Laurence T. Yang and Minyi Guo (Editors)

Parallel Computing for Bioinformatics and Computational Biology / Albert Y. Zomaya (Editor)

Parallel Combinatorial Optimization / El-Ghazali Talbi (Editor)

Design and Analysis of Distributed Algorithms / Nicola Santoro

Task Scheduling for Parallel Systems / Oliver Sinnen

Lotos and Petri-Net Based Verification of Systems and Circuits / Michael Yoeli and Rakefet Kol

Architecture-Independent Programming and Synthesis / Amol B. Bakshi and Viktor K. Prasanna

High Performance Parallel Databases and Grid Databases / David Taniar, Clement H.C. Leung, Wenny Rahayu, and Sushant Goel

Algorithms and Protocols for Wireless, Ad Hoc Networks / Azzedine Boukerche

Algorithms and Protocols for Wireless Sensor Networks / Azzedine Boukerche

Emerging Wireless LANs, Wireless PANs, and Wireless MANs / Yang Xiao and Yi Pan

Optimization Techniques for Solving Complex Problems / Enrique Alba, Christian Blum, Pedro Asasi, Coromoto Leon, Juan Antonio Gomez

High Performance Heterogeneous Computing / Jack Dongarra and Alexey Lastovestsky

Market-Oriented Grid and Utility Computing / Rajkumar Buyya and Kris Bubendorfer (Editors)

Advanced Computational Infrastructures for Parallel and Distributed Applications / Manish Parashar, Xiaolin Li

Mobile Intelligence / Laurence Yang

Cloud Computing Principles and Paradigms / Rajkumar Buyya, James Broberg and Andrzej Goscinski (Editors)

Large-Scale Computing Techniques for Complex System Simulations / Werner Dubitzky, Krzysztof Kurowski and Bernhard Schott (Editors)

Energy-Efficient Distributed Computing Systems / Albert Y. Zomaya and Young-Choon Lee (Editors)

Scalable Computing and Communications: Theory and Practice / Samee U. Khan, Albert Y. Zomaya, Lizhe Wang (Editors)